W9-CCY-646

UNIVERSITY CASEBOOK SERIES®

PENSION AND EMPLOYEE BENEFIT LAW

SIXTH EDITION

by

JOHN H. LANGBEIN
Sterling Professor of Law and Legal History
Yale University

DAVID A. PRATT
Professor of Law
Albany Law School

SUSAN J. STABILE
Professor of Law
St. Thomas University School of Law

ANDREW W. STUMPFF
Lecturer
University of Michigan Law School
Adjunct Professor
University of Alabama Law School

FOUNDATION
PRESS

University Casebook Series is a trademark registered in the U.S. Patent and Trademark Office.

© 1990, 1995, 2000 FOUNDATION PRESS
© 2006, 2010 THOMSON REUTERS/FOUNDATION PRESS
© 2015 LEG, Inc. d/b/a West Academic
    444 Cedar Street, Suite 700
    St. Paul, MN 55101
    1-877-888-1330

Printed in the United States of America

ISBN: 978-1-62810-021-1

PREFACE

The Fourth Edition saw an extensive revision in the organization of the book. This Sixth Edition generally retains the structure put in place in that edition, but collects the material relating to employer-sponsored health plans into a new Part 5. This Sixth Edition reflects all significant statutory and regulatory changes, including the Affordable Care Act of 2010, and many new regulations under ERISA and the Internal Revenue Code. The book also adds coverage of several Supreme Court decisions on issues relating to the constitutionality of the Affordable Care Act, same-sex marriage, fiduciary responsibility, remedies, and retiree health benefits. Many recent lower court decisions are also examined.

This Sixth Edition makes significant changes in the authorship of this text. Professor John H. Langbein, who co-edited the first five editions, and Professor Susan J. Stabile, who co-edited the Fourth and Fifth Editions, took no part in the preparation of this edition. However, their contributions pervade the entire work. Each of them is, in his or her own way, irreplaceable, but we are fortunate that Professor Andrew Stumpff, a prominent scholar and practitioner in the employee benefits field, joins us on this edition. Professor Pratt has been primarily responsible for updating the first eleven chapters. Professor Stumpff has been primarily responsible for Chapters 12–19.

Coverage. Pension and employee benefits law is a vast field, full of minutiae that matter in practical settings but that do not invite curricular treatment in an introductory law school course. Our challenge in each edition has been to identify and present the topics of greatest importance and intellectual interest. We try to provide a solid grounding in the main areas of regulatory law, fiduciary law, and pension taxation, with an emphasis on structure and policy. We omit or provide only minimal coverage of the specialized law of multiemployer plans and the associated withdrawal liability scheme. We also do not explore the financial machinations that pass under the name of employee stock ownership plans (ESOPs).

It continues to be a challenge to make room for coverage of the extensive developments that have occurred in this field while keeping the book to a tolerable length. We continue to trim incessantly and hope that we have struck a sound balance between comprehensiveness and teachability.

Editing practices. In preparing these materials we continue in this edition to adhere to a set of editing conventions that we employed in past editions, which depart from customary legal scholarly practice in disclosing deletions from cases or other sources extracted in the book. Bluebook form requires ellipses for any omission. For teaching materials, however, the clutter of dots outweighs the gain in fidelity to the source. Accordingly, we have adhered to the casebook editing conventions developed by Geoffrey R. Stone et al. for their book Constitutional Law (6th ed. 2009, 1st ed. 1986). Thus, in editing judicial decisions (and other sources), we delete many citations of cases and other authorities and almost all footnotes, and we do so without disclosure tags like citations omitted. We do, of course, disclose when substantive material has been deleted from a case or other source. We use ellipses when a deletion occurs at the end of a paragraph, but otherwise, deletions are disclosed mostly by bracketing the word before or after the omission.

We believe that these practices, which largely suppress ellipses, make a coursebook easier for students to read. The standards of scholarly accuracy for identifying omissions are unnecessarily cumbersome for teaching materials. Brackets suffice to warn that there has been alteration. Obviously, users wishing to adhere to scholarly standards will need to return to the original texts.

Another editorial practice that should be noticed concerns the handling of citations to ERISA. As explained in Chapter 3, ERISA was enacted with its own section numbers, beginning with § 1. When codified in title 29 of the U.S. Code, ERISA's sections were renumbered, beginning with § 1001. ERISA lawyers use ERISA numbers, for example, in the widely used published editions of ERISA, in the practitioner services, and in commentary and scholarly writing. However, law clerks who polish up judicial opinions often use U.S. Code numbers. In this coursebook, we use only the ERISA numbers. When the original source gives only U.S. Code numbers, we substitute the ERISA numbers. When the original source employs parallel citations, we delete the U.S. Code reference.

Statute book and supplement. Selected Sections: Pension and Employee Benefit Statutes and Regulations supplements this casebook. The 2011 through 2015 editions have been prepared by Professor Pratt. Commencing with the 2016 edition, Professor Stumpff will participate in preparing the volume.

As in past years, we expect that when later developments require, we will provide an annual supplement, to be published by Foundation Press.

Acknowledgements. We thank the many authors, journals, publishers, and other copyright holders who have granted us permission to reproduce excerpts from their work. We supply full citations to such material where it appears in this book. We carry forward from the previous edition the following acknowledgements to copyright holders who prefer particular forms of acknowledgement: for Nancy J. Altman, Rethinking Retirement Income Policies: Nondiscrimination, Integration, and the Quest for Worker Security, 42 Tax Law Review 435, copyright 1987 by New York University School of Law, all rights reserved; for Kingsley Davis, Our Idle Retirees Drag Down the Economy, copyright 1987 by The New York Times Company, reprinted by permission; and for William C. Greenough & Francis P. King, Pension Plans and Public Policy, copyright 1976 Columbia University Press, used by permission.

We wish to record our gratitude for research assistance on this edition to Davinder Sahota of Albany Law School.

DAVID A. PRATT

ANDREW W. STUMPFF

April 2015

SUMMARY OF CONTENTS

PART 2. PENSION TAXATION

PART 3. ERISA FIDUCIARY LAW

PART 4. ERISA LITIGATION

PART 5. EMPLOYER-SPONSORED HEALTH PLANS

TABLE OF CONTENTS

PART 2. PENSION TAXATION

PART 3. ERISA FIDUCIARY LAW

PART 5. EMPLOYER-SPONSORED HEALTH PLANS

TABLE OF CASES

The principal cases are in bold type.

TABLE OF STATUTES

PENSION AND EMPLOYEE BENEFIT LAW

SIXTH EDITION

PART 1

PURPOSES AND BASIC PRINCIPLES

CHAPTER 1

ORIGINS AND FUNDAMENTALS OF THE PENSION SYSTEM

Analysis

Introduction

This book is devoted to the study of the legal regulation of employer-provided pension and benefit plans. Pension funds are hugely important institutions. Data canvassed later in this chapter indicate that private and public pension assets reached 24 trillion dollars at June 30, 2014. Investment Company Institute, Retirement Assets Total $24.0 Trillion in Second Quarter 2014, http://www.limra.com/Secure_Retirement_Institute/News_Center/Retirement_Industry_Report/Retirement_Plans_-_Investment_Company_Institute__Retirement_Assets_on_the_Rise_in_2014.aspx. Attention will be centered on two large federal statutory regimes, the Employee Retirement Income Security Act (ERISA) of 1974 as amended, and the pension tax provisions of the Internal Revenue Code (IRC).

The American private pension system as it has evolved has three defining characteristics. Private plans are employer-sponsored, voluntary, and tax-favored.

    1.   *Employment-based*. Private pension plans are employer-sponsored. Although saving for retirement involves a tradeoff between a worker's current and future consumption, and thus would seem to belong to the realm of personal decision-making about the employee's personal finances, the employer makes large decisions about the type and amount of pension that will be offered to that firm's employees. Those decisions are constrained by whatever competitive considerations the employer faces in the relevant labor market. In unionized firms, the collective

bargaining process also affects the employer's decisions, since pensions and other benefit plans are characteristic subjects of negotiation.

2. *Voluntary.* The private pension system is voluntary. Even though the system is centered in the workplace, no employer is required to offer pension coverage, and many do not. The voluntary character of private pension plans contrasts strongly with the Social Security system, in which both the employer and the employee are required to participate; and with the workers' compensation and unemployment insurance programs, which are obligatory.

3. *Tax deferred.* The private pension system is tax favored. Both the contributions to a plan and the plan's investment returns are generally untaxed until benefits are paid, typically across the retirement years of the worker and his or her spouse. In effect, the pension plan or pension account receives a tax free loan from the government in the amount of the deferred taxes. These "borrowed" proceeds compound tax deferred until distribution. The subsidy for retirement plans is one of the largest components of the federal tax expenditure budget, estimated at more than $147 billion for fiscal year 2015. Office of Management and Budget, Analytical Perspectives, Budget of the U.S. Government, Fiscal Year 2015, table 14–1. Pension funds scarcely existed until the end of the nineteenth century, and they were relatively unimportant until World War II. The materials in this chapter are designed to help put the rise of the pension fund in some perspective. Section A, on the origins of pension funds, addresses the question of why the private pension system is such a comparatively recent phenomenon. Section B, on the purposes of the private pension system, supplies data on the magnitudes (pension assets, pension coverage in the workforce), and directs attention to the question of why pension saving is organized through the employment relationship. Section C deals with the connections between the private and public systems—how private pension plans relate to Social Security, and what combined levels of retirement income the two systems should aim to achieve. (So-called welfare benefit plans, that is, employee benefit plans that provide benefits other than retirement income, such as health care and occupational disability insurance, are introduced in Chapter 3, infra.)

A. ORIGINS OF THE PENSION FUND

1. THE EMERGENCE OF RETIREMENT

1. *Life cycle effects.* People in the workforce are both producers and consumers. The income stream from employment supports consumption. But across a lifetime, the consumption function does not correlate very neatly with the production function. When we are very young, we are supported by our parents before we can become productive. Toward the other end of life, most people retire, hence cease to produce before they cease consuming. Retirement income is needed to fill the gap when employment earnings cease.

Earnings over the life cycle

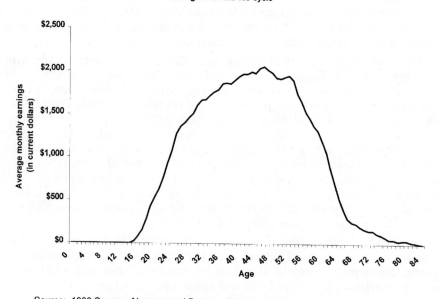

Source: 1993 Survey of Income and Program Participation. Reprinted from Michael J. Graetz and Jerry L. Mashaw, *True Security — Rethinking American Social Insurance* (New Haven, CT: Yale University Press, 1999), p. 95. Reprinted with permission.

Much retirement income is supplied through the public transfer programs, in particular, Social Security, but the benefit ceilings on Social Security are below what many people need to maintain their lifestyles in retirement. The private pension fund has become a characteristic modern device for generating additional retirement income.

The pension fund serves during the years of employment as a means of conducting a savings program for retirement. Workers who participate in pension plans consume during their years of employment less of what they earn. The foregone earnings, together with investment income, are saved for distribution during retirement. In a conventional pension plan (the so-called defined benefit plan which promises a monthly payment in retirement), distribution typically takes the form of an annuity for the worker and his or her spouse, though other forms of distribution (including lump sums) have recently become more common. The annuity provides a lifetime income stream from the onset of retirement until their deaths. In the other main type of pension plan, the defined contribution plan, the employee (and usually the employer) contribute to an investment account, whose proceeds will be available to fund retirement income. Thus, either type of pension plan shifts income from the years of employment to the years of retirement.

2. *The novelty of retirement.* Retirement is a remarkably recent social phenomenon, only about a century old. Well into the nineteenth century, life expectancies were low enough that most people died while still in the workforce or shortly thereafter. The expectation of a regular and substantial period of superannuation constitutes one of the largest changes in social structure in the advanced countries. See generally Dora L. Costa, The Evolution of Retirement: An American Economic History,

1880–1990 (1998); Leslie Hannah, Inventing Retirement: The Development of Occupational Pensions in Britain (1986); William Graebner, A History of Retirement: The Meaning and Function of an American Institution 1885–1978 (1980).

In 1850, 76.6 percent of males aged 65 and over were in the labor force. By 1990 the figure was 18.4 percent. Costa, supra, at 29–30. (In France the figure for 1990 was 5 percent. Id. at 30.) However, "Census Bureau data show that the percentage of men and women aged 62 and older who work in paid employment has risen over the past several years. . . . Of men aged 65 to 69, 33% were employed in March 2009, compared with 26% in 1990 and 30% in 2000. . . . Among women 65 to 69 years old, 25% were working in March 2009, compared with 17% in 1990 and 20% in 2000. There also has been a trend toward more full-time employment among older Americans who work." Patrick Purcell, Older Workers: Employment and Retirement Trends, Congressional Research Service Report for Congress, Sept. 16, 2009.

3. *The demographic revolution.* "One of the most impressive achievements of mankind is the control of mortality and the extension of human life through improved public health measures and advances in modern medicine. Between 1900 and 1984, life expectancy at birth in the United States increased a full 28 years, from 47 to 75 years. [Since] the late 1960s, death rates for persons 65 and over have been reduced by 20 percent. [In] 1984 a typical 65-year-old could expect to live an additional 16.8 years, up from 13.9 extra years in 1950." Thomas Espenshade & Tracy Ann Goodis, "Demographic Trends Shaping the American Family and Workforce," in America in Transition: Benefits for the Future 5, 17–18 (Employee Benefit Research Institute) (1987). By 2030, life expectancy at age 65 is expected to be 17.5 years for men (82.5 years of age) and 21.1 years (86.1 years of age) for women. Alicia H. Munnell, The Financial Crisis and Restoring Retirement Security, Testimony before the Committee on Education and Labor, U.S. House of Representatives, February 24, 2009 (citing the 2008 Annual Report of the Board of Trustees of the Federal Old-Age and Survivors Insurance and Federal Disability Insurance Trust Funds).

"The 45-year life expectancy that prevailed a century ago is a composite figure, greatly distorted by infant mortality. As late as 1907, '1 of 7 newborns died in their first year of life, whereas in 1977, 1 of 67 died then; between the ages of one and four, 1 in about 17 of those born in 1907 died, whereas 1 in about 360 died among those born in 1977— representing a 21-fold reduction.' [But] even after we correct for infant mortality, the diminished life expectancy of the last century was marked enough to explain why contemporaries so seldom had occasion to talk about what we call the retirement income problem. If you chanced to outlive your productive years, you did not in general do it for very long." John H. Langbein, The Twentieth-Century Revolution in Family Wealth Transmission and the Future of the Probate Bar, 14 Probate Lawyer 1, 28–29 (1988).

4. *Overcoming infectious disease.* The main cause of the increase in life expectancy has been a precipitous decline in mortality from infectious disease. In 1840, tuberculosis was the leading cause of death in the United States. As late as the year 1900, one American in 500 died

from TB each year. TB mortality declined more than 99 percent in the twentieth century. Antibiotics delivered the final blow, but changes in public health were mainly responsible for the eradication of TB: pasteurization of milk, inspection of cattle, improved nutrition, quarantining of infected persons, and so forth. Similar declines have been recorded in mortality rates from smallpox, polio, diphtheria, tetanus, typhoid fever, whooping cough, and syphilis. The main modern causes of death are cardiovascular disease and cancer. What has made these diseases so prominent "is not an epidemic; rather, it is a result of the success in virtually eliminating infectious diseases. Survival from the illnesses that used to kill early in life allowed the diseases that occur later in life to increase in frequency as a cause of death." James F. Fries & Lawrence M. Crapo, The Elimination of Premature Disease, in Wellness and Health Promotion for the Elderly 19, 19–22 (K. Dychtwald, ed.) (1986).

5. *Retirement age.* Bismarck popularized the notion of age 65 as the appropriate retirement age when he set that age for benefits to commence in the state pension program he introduced in Germany in 1889. Notice, however, that age 65 was well beyond the then-normal life expectancy. Translated to modern life expectancies, Bismarck's plan was roughly equivalent to a pension program whose benefits would commence when the participants reached their mid-80s. Age 65 has remained the "normal retirement age" for private pension plans, see infra Chapter 18, despite the changed circumstances that allow so many people to live to those ages. Indeed, many plans allow so-called early retirement at younger ages—a subject whose mechanics and demographics are also discussed in Chapter 18.

6. *Wealth.* The growing affluence of the elderly in advanced countries, evidenced both in privately owned assets and in government transfer payments such as Social Security and Medicare, has had an important bearing on the growth of retirement. "Among the most popular explanations for the rise of retirement is that individuals can afford it." Costa, supra, at 14.

A notable indicator of the growth in the wealth of the elderly is found in the data on their rates of separate home ownership. In 1880, 46 percent of retired males lived with their children. The figure declined to 22 percent by 1940 and to 5 percent in 1990. Id. at 110. As of 1991, 77 percent of householders aged 65 and over owned a home or had equity in it. "The amount of mortgage debt on those homes is usually very low; in fact, about four-fifths of elderly homeowners own their homes free of any mortgage." James H. Schulz, The Economics of Aging 24 & tbl. 1–11 (7th ed. 2001) (citing Census Bureau data). The official poverty rate among the elderly has declined from 30 percent in 1967 to about 9.5 percent in 2013. U.S. Census Bureau, Income, Poverty and Health Insurance Coverage in the United States: 2013, available through http://www.census.gov/newsroom/press-releases/2014/cb14-169.html. Poverty among the elderly "is concentrated among ethnic minorities and women." Schulz at 39. Rates of poverty among the elderly are affected by changing work patterns and life expectancies (see the data cited in notes 2 and 3 supra) and, more recently, by the current economic crisis.

7. *Phased retirement.* Despite the spread of retirement, many of the elderly, including those who are retired for purposes of receiving Social Security or private pension income, continue to have some employment income, often from part-time work. This pattern of so-called phased retirement is discussed further in this chapter in the note on sources of retirement income.

2. HISTORY OF PRIVATE PENSION FUNDS

William C. Greenough & Francis P. King,
Pension Plans and Public Policy
27–47 (1976).

Pension historians generally cite 1875 as the year in which the first formal pension plan was established, that of the American Express Company, then closely associated with the business of railroad transportation. Murray Latimer, in his monumental two-volume study of American pension plans [*Industrial Pension Systems in the United States and Canada*] published in 1932, describes the American Express plan as the first noncontributory private plan in North America, following by one year the start of the contributory plan of the Grand Trunk Railway of Canada.

Unlike the retirement benefits provided by present-day plans, the benefits of the early American Express plan applied only to "permanently incapacitated" workers, i.e., disabled elderly employees. To be eligible for the benefits the disabled worker had to have served the company for at least 20 years and to have reached age 60. Also, there had to be a recommendation for retirement by the general manager and approval by the executive committee of the board of directors. . . .

During the new American nation's first century, economic and social conditions made it natural for the family to serve as the principal institution of old-age support. The economic life of the nation, largely rural and based mainly on agriculture, emphasized the family and indeed depended on it. A relatively independent producing unit in an agricultural economy, the family tended to retain most or all of its members, of whatever generation, as a part of that functioning unit. One generation would provide its children with livelihood on the land, gradually decreasing activity as age advanced and as the children grew old enough to assume ownership responsibilities. The cycle continued and at any one time two or three generations might exist in a relationship of mutual support. Although the physical labor of older family members decreased, the aged still played an important supervisory role in the family structure, participating in the productive enterprise of the farm or artisanship, and sharing in the working and supportive processes.

In the more populated trade or business centers the pattern was much the same. An individual would continue in business as long as health permitted. Members of the younger generation would follow the occupational footsteps of their parents, providing economic security for the parents who had earlier provided children with their opportunities for training and work.

For workers not self-employed in agriculture or trade—the people in the employ of others for wages or salary—old-age support was perhaps less certain, depending on continuation of employment in old age (there were no mandatory retirement ages), on the fruits of frugality and savings, or on support of family members. The very poor aged were the objects of public or private charity or, if infirm and without other means of support, the poorhouse. . . .

However, in the late 19th century far-reaching changes began to take place in virtually every aspect of American life, including the economic and social situation of the elderly. Industrialization, the dramatic impact of the railways, and the accelerating movement of America to urban centers created vast changes and posed new and unfamiliar problems.

The Twentieth Century. The first organized pension plans were a tiny aspect of various attempts to respond to conditions in a society that was changing from rural to urban, from agricultural to industrial, from multigenerational family self-sufficiency to a cash-exchange base. Compared with such issues as hours of work, working conditions, pay scales, and the right of employees to organize, pensions occupied a low priority. The recognition due pension plans as a means of meeting needs of employees in their old age was slow in coming; by 1900 only about a dozen plans had been started.

The lead was taken by the railroads, which employed large numbers of workers in hazardous jobs. . . . Other industry groups pioneering in the establishment of formal pension arrangements before 1900 included municipal utility companies, street railways, banking institutions, and a handful of manufacturing companies whose plans did not last long. The first enduring pension plan in a manufacturing firm was established in 1901 as part of the relief fund for employees of the Carnegie Steel Company. . . . The period of greatest early growth in pension plans was between 1900 and 1920. By 1920, most of the major railroads, utility companies, banks, mining companies, and petroleum companies had set up formal pension plans, and parallel pension plan growth was recorded for manufacturers of machinery, agricultural implements, chemicals, paints and varnishes, food products, rubber, paper and printing products, and electrical apparatus. After 1920 the pension plan growth rate declined. . . . By the end of 1929, [a] total of 421 industrial pension plans had been established since 1875, [and] employees of corporations with pension plans numbered 3,745,000, about 10 percent of the nonagricultural labor force, although not all were eligible for plan membership. Because of the eligibility rules, perhaps less than 10 percent of plan members would ever qualify for benefits.

Retirement Age. Among the plans operating in 1929, the retirement age at which members became eligible for benefits was sometimes set at 65, sometimes 70. . . . In addition, a continuous service of at least 20 years was required, and for disability benefits, 20 or 25 years. . . . The uniformity of provisions among various plans is ascribed by Latimer's 1932 study to a tendency for new plans to copy older plans. . . .

Except for a small number of contributory plans, none of the plans in effect in 1929 provided for the vesting of benefits for employees who terminated employment before reaching the prescribed retirement age, nor did the pension literature of the time find the absence of such vesting worthy of comment. . . .

Financing. Benefits of the majority of plans operating in the late 1920s were financed from the current income of the employing companies. Latimer reported that 60 percent of noncontributory plans in 1929 were paying their pensions from the employer's current income, 25 percent had set up an in-company balance sheet reserve, and the remaining 15 percent had set up trust funds or were using insured arrangements. Among contributory plans, the use of trust fund reserves was more common than among noncontributory plans. . . .

Employee Rights. Employers were presumably aware that the pay-as-you-go financing methods generally in use and the level of reserves in funded plans could not be depended upon to assure or guarantee benefits under all possible future circumstances. Consequently, they were hesitant to commit themselves or their successors to the unalterable maintenance of an obligation the full burden of which was not foreseeable. In no case, therefore, did any of the 400 or so industrial pension plans in operation in the late 1920s contain any contractual obligation for the future maintenance of benefit promises or payments. . . .

Most of the plans contained a clause similar to the following:

> The right to change from time to time any of the foregoing provisions and substitute others in their stead and the right to revise or alter from time to time the plan under which this pension system has been established or to abandon said system is hereby reserved.

In addition to prudent guardianship of the employer's rights of plan discontinuance or alteration, employers pursued clarification of the position of the employee in language which became virtual boilerplate in every industrial plan. The following [is] typical: . . .

> The allowances are voluntary gifts from the company and constitute no contract and confer no legal rights upon any employee. The continuance of the retirement allowance depends upon the earnings of the company and the allowances may at any time be reduced, suspended, or discontinued on that, or any other account, at the option of the Board of Directors. . . .

[One author] described industrial pension systems as "if and maybe" propositions. In effect, he stated, such a system says to the worker:

> *If* you remain with this company throughout your productive lifetime,
>
> *If* you do not die before the retirement age,
>
> *If* you are not discharged or laid off for an extended period,
>
> *If* you are not refused a benefit as a matter of discipline (i.e., because of joining a union, asking for a raise, or, in some cases, for "immoral" conduct),
>
> *If* the company continues in business, and
>
> *If* the company does not decide to abandon this plan, you will receive a pension at the age of _____, subject to the

contingency of its discontinuance or reduction, after it has been entered upon. . . .

Decline of the Railroad Plans. . . . By 1934 about 90 percent of all employees of Class I railroads were covered by noncontributory private pension plans. The last Class I railroad retirement plan was established in 1929. . . .

Beginning with the Great Depression, railroad revenues declined sharply and at the same time the number of railroad workers expecting to be retired because of age or years of service was increasing. Had the railroads been able to continue as profitable business enterprises, they would probably have had less difficulty in meeting their heavy pension promises. But the plans had not accumulated sufficient reserves to meet their obligations, and current revenues were insufficient to support these underfunded plans. Of the 82 pension plans operated by the Class I roads in 1929, only one had followed the policy of fully funding the accumulating service credits. . . .

Without sufficient pension reserves, with a declining capacity to sustain a pay-as-you-go retirement system amidst the economic shambles of the Great Depression, and with growing competition from the trucking industry, the railroads' benevolent and optimistic pension promises were turning into a financial monster. . . . There was little prospect that the troubled railroads could make good on their pension promises for the quarter-million older employees due to retire within three or four years. Strong pressure developed for some kind of legislative action to bail the railroads out. . . . The federal government responded with a plan to take over and administer the pension promises of the railroads. . . . An initial attempt at legislation was declared unconstitutional. Subsequent legislation resulted in the Railroad Retirement Act of 1935, amended in 1937, and the Carriers' Taxing Act of 1937. These acts covered all employees of the railroads, employees of related transportation companies and associations, and railroad labor union employees. The system now operates something along the lines of Social Security and functions as a substitute Social Security system for railroad employees.

The present-day Railroad Retirement System thus grew out of a set of pension plans that failed, were rescued with public funds, and were transformed into a quasi-public system for the employees of the industry. This hybrid arrangement, under which general public revenues are added to employee and employer contributions, is unique among American pension plans. It embodies an acknowledgment that private pension plan failures are, at times at least, matters of public policy requiring corrective public action. . . .

Pension Plans and Labor. While the larger industrial employers were establishing their pension plans in the early years of the 20th century, the trade unions, independently of employers, were attempting their own programs of member benefits. . . . The earliest mutual aid activities of the trade unions concentrated not on old-age pensions, but on the much more immediate needs of both the workers and their unions: death benefits, sickness benefits, disability benefits, and whatever arrangements the union might be able to make for some kind of wage replacement during strikes or unemployment. Pensions, to the extent that unions were able to manage some kind of pension program, were initially related to the need for a continuing benefit during permanent disability, and somewhat later, to the movement for the establishment of homes for aged union members who could no longer work. The lack of emphasis on provisions for the aged is perhaps explained by the fact that in the early years of the trade union movement the intensity of the struggle to gain members, raise wages, and shorten hours left little energy for items of longer-term priority. Also, the militancy of the movement made it attractive primarily to young men, so that concern for old-age dependency was rarely voiced.

Old-Age Plans. The first union plan to provide for periodic old-age payments, as distinct from lump-sum or periodic benefits for permanent disability, was established by the Patternmakers in 1900. . . . The first large union to adopt its own pension program was the Typographical Union in 1906–7. . . . None of these plans provided benefits as a matter of right, and the payments depended largely upon the state of the union treasury.

The first union plan offering old-age benefits as a matter of right rather than as gratuities was established by the Brotherhood of Locomotive Engineers in 1912. . . .

Weakness of Union Plans. By 1928, it was estimated that about 40 percent of trade union membership belonged to national unions offering one form or another of old age and permanent and total disability benefits. But the funds for the benefits necessarily had to be derived from assessments on union members . . . within a few years after the Great Depression began almost all of the union welfare plans had collapsed. . . . After the adoption of Social Security in 1935 only a handful of national unions continued to offer old-age homes or old-age pensions. . . .

Attitude Toward Employer Plans. Labor had largely failed in its attempts to maintain its own welfare plans. While the large employers had made considerable strides in the development of their own pension plans, labor did not view these plans with much warmth. In the mid 1930s it appeared that there had been little change in the labor attitude phrased in 1914 by James Lynch of the International Typographical Union that "wage earners look askance at these company-instituted and company-controlled funds, as they give the impression that they are instituted in order that the worker may be more firmly bound to the industry and less liable to form industrial organizations for the regulation of hours, wages, and working conditions. . . ."

The wage stabilization policy of the National War Labor Board during World War II maintained wage stability at the price of "greater flexibility on secondary lines," specifically on fringe benefits. This wartime focus on fringe benefits popularized the idea and helped create in the minds of labor leaders and workers the notion that they were entitled to such benefits as a matter of right.

The Mine Workers' Plan. The first struggle of a large union for a negotiated pension plan was that of John L. Lewis and the United Mine Workers of America. . . . [After a 7 week strike in 1946] Secretary of the Interior J.A. Krug, acting for the U.S. government, seized the mines. Krug and Lewis entered into an agreement on May 29, 1946, which established a welfare and retirement fund, to be financed by a contribution of five cents a ton from employers. . . .

The Steel Plans. In 1949 pensions became an issue in the steel industry negotiations. The union presented pension demands under a 1949 wage reopening provision in a contract due to expire in 1950. With the exception of Inland Steel, the companies took the position that pensions were not bargainable under the reopening clause because pensions were not wage rates within the meaning of the applicable contract provision. . . . President Truman, in the face of a threatened national steel strike, appointed a fact-finding board to make recommendations. . . . The board accepted the union's "human depreciation" theory and also found that the cost of the pensions could be met without "unduly narrowing the profit margin of the industry or its ability to hold or even lower its prices." The steel industry objected to the cost conclusions and to the noncontributory principle. After three postponements, a nationwide steel strike went into effect, lasting for 42 days.

Bethlehem Steel settled first for a noncontributory plan, partly because the firm had had a noncontributory pension plan in effect since 1923. Others followed. . . .

The Automobile Industry. At about the same time, pension negotiations were going on in the automobile industry. In 1947, Ford workers had rejected pensions in favor of a direct wage increase, but by 1949 Walter Reuther of the United Automobile Workers was ready to say: "Slackening of the rise in the cost of living enables us to turn our attention to other [matters], pension plans and social security." . . . The resulting settlement provided for a joint board to oversee the pension benefits structure, within the single-employer plan. . . .

The concluding phase of the inauguration of pension negotiations in the automobile industry was marked by a United Automobile Workers strike against Chrysler in 1950 that lasted 104 days. As Reuther said some years later:

> It was not about the size of the pension. It was about whether the pension would be based on pay-as-you-go or whether it would be a funded plan. And the Chrysler workers, about 90,000 of them, walked the bricks for 104 days on that principle alone, because we felt that we should not start down the road of a pension program except as we funded the pension and backed up the benefits with an actuarially sound fund. . . .

That union negotiators would emphasize financial soundness of pension plans, however defined, and the avoidance of pay-as-you-go plans, suggests that labor organizations had learned a good deal from their own earlier experiences with benefit plans, most of which had failed because of funding inadequacies.

3.   GROWTH OF THE PRIVATE PENSION SYSTEM

1.   *Wage stabilization.* As Greenough and King mention, wage and price controls during World War II and the Korean War tended to deflect compensation demands into nonwage forms, and this was an important factor in the explosive postwar growth of the private pension system.

"Employers competing for labor could not offer the inducement of higher wages. Under these conditions, union leaders found it difficult to prove to their membership the merits of unionism. Therefore, the War Labor Board attempted to relieve the pressure on management and labor for higher wage rates by permitting the establishment of fringe benefit programs, including pensions." Everett T. Allen, et al., Pension Planning: Pension, Profit Sharing, and Other Deferred Compensation Plans 11 (9th ed. 2003).

2. *The value of tax deferral.* It will be seen in the tax materials, infra Chapters 8–11, that federal tax policy encourages private pension plans in two main ways. The employer is allowed to deduct contributions to a pension plan at once, even though the employee is not taxed on those sums at that time. Second, the investment yield on the plan's assets also escapes current taxation. Taxation is deferred until the period of distribution, typically after the employee retires.

Not until the eve of World War II did the federal income tax affect most workers in a significant way. As late as 1935, only 4.1 percent of income earners paid income taxes, and the median taxpayer had a marginal income tax rate of only 4 percent of income. In 1945, 65.3 percent of earners paid taxes, and the median marginal tax rate was 23 percent. The marginal corporate tax rate paid by large firms was 13.7 percent in 1935, 40 percent in 1945, and 52 percent in 1955. Richard A. Ippolito, Pensions, Economics and Public Policy 25 & tbl. 2–4 (1986) [hereafter cited as Ippolito, Pension Economics].

How does the burgeoning importance of the federal income tax in the period leading into and during World War II bear on the timing of the rise of the private pension system?

3. *Public and eleemosynary employers.* In portions of their account of the history of the pension system that are not reproduced in the extract above, Greenough and King recount the growth of pension plans sponsored by state and local government units. They also describe the origins of Teachers Insurance and Annuity Association/College Retirement Equity Fund (TIAA-CREF), the peculiar industry-wide pension system for college teachers and for employees of certain other nonprofits. Greenough & King, supra, at 49–57.

4. *Vesting and funding.* Greenough and King explain that the pre-Depression private pension system exhibited weaknesses in funding. Both the railroad plans and the union plans were pay-as-you-go plans that paid pensions out of current income. Greenough and King also point out that under the terms of many plans, promised benefits were forfeitable for long periods, sometimes until or even after retirement. Bear these facts in mind in considering the path that pension regulation took under ERISA in 1974.

ERISA's Title 4, which creates the termination insurance program for underfunded pension plans, is examined in Chapter 6, infra. In studying Title 4, keep in mind Greenough and King's account of the first major federal intervention in the private pension system: the bailout of the failed plans of the railroad industry in the 1930s through the Railroad Retirement Act.

5. *Historical dimensions.* The federal government operated an extensive pension system in the nineteenth century for veterans and their survivors, especially after the Civil War. In the 1890s an astonishing portion of federal revenue, over 40 percent, was being spent on these pensions. Theda Skocpol, Protecting Soldiers and Mothers: The Political Origins of Social Policy in the United States 114 & fig. 3 (1992); see also Robert L. Clark et al., A History of Public Sector Pensions in the United States (2003). State and local governments also ran fragmentary pension programs for various classes of workers and others (police and firefighters, civil servants, soldiers, the elderly). See Susan M. Sterett, Public Pensions: Gender and Civic Service in the States, 1850–1937 (2003).

Steven Sass has directed attention to the role played by the major life insurance companies, who were already experienced in underwriting annuities for individual customers, in developing employment-based pension plans in the first half of the twentieth century. In the years after World War II the trend set in for large employers to operate pension plans on their own, rather than to buy insurance company products for their workers. This trend brought about the rise of a new class of pension professionals, the consulting actuaries. See Steven A. Sass, The Promise of Private Pensions: The First Hundred Years (1997). The regulation of insurance companies has been a preserve of state law in the United States. ERISA, which mostly regulates employer-operated plans, can be seen in part as a federal regulatory response to the relative decline of insurance-industry pension products.

6. *Theories of the pension promise.* Greenough and King emphasize that early corporate pension plans contained terms characterizing plan benefits as "voluntary gifts" and authorizing the employer to revoke the plan at will. The main import of this so-called *gratuity theory* of pensions was to prevent the worker from vesting in the plan benefits, at least until retirement. The gratuity theory is further discussed in Chapter 4, infra, treating the anti-forfeiture policy of modern pension regulatory law.

One attempt to overcome the gratuity theory of pensions was the *human depreciation theory,* which, as Greenough and King mention, was advanced by the United Mine Workers in the 1940s. A UMW broadside argued that "the cost of caring for the human equity in the coal industry is inherently as valid as the cost of the replacement of mining machinery [or] any other factor incident to the production of a ton of [coal]." Allen et al., Pension Planning, supra, at 15. The human depreciation theory has not won much acceptance as an account of the rationale for pensions. Why?

The commonly accepted modern account of pension obligations is the *deferred wage theory,* which treats pensions as compensation earned during employment but paid during retirement. Id. at 16.

B. PURPOSES AND EXTENT OF THE PRIVATE PENSION SYSTEM

1. "PENSION FUND SOCIALISM"

Peter Drucker, Pension Fund "Socialism"
The Public Interest 3–6, 44–46 (Win.1976).

If "socialism" is defined as "ownership of the means of production by the workers"—and this is the orthodox definition—then the United States is the most "socialist" country in the world. . . .

[The] large employee pension funds—those of the 1000 to 1300 largest companies plus the 35 [collectively bargained multiemployer] funds (e.g., that of the Teamsters)—own a controlling interest in practically every single one of the "command positions" in the economy. These include the 1000 largest industrial corporations [and] the 50 largest companies in each of the "non-industrial" groups—that is, in banking, insurance, retail, communications, and transportation. Indeed, a larger sector of the American economy (outside of farming) today is owned by the American worker—through his investment agent, the pension fund—than Allende in Chile proposed to bring under government ownership to make Chile a "socialist country," than Castro's Cuba has actually nationalized, or than is nationalized in Yugoslavia or even Poland. . . .

"Socialism" came to America through the efforts of the most unlikely revolutionary of them all, the chief executive officer of America's largest manufacturing company, General Motors (GM). Charles Wilson, then GM's chairman, proposed to the United Auto Workers (UAW) [in] April 1950, the establishment of a pension fund for GM workers. By that time pensions had become a priority demand of the American labor-union movement. Yet the UAW was at first far from enthusiastic. It realized clearly that Wilson's proposal aimed at "privatizing" the pension system; and the UAW—in common with most American unions—in those years was deeply committed to a governmental pension system through social security. Moreover, Wilson's proposal gave the union no role whatever in administering the GM pension fund. Instead, the company was to be responsible for the fund, which would be entrusted to professional "asset managers." And the union feared—with good reason, as subsequent events have demonstrated—that the pension fund would thus strengthen management and make the union members more dependent on management. Wilson had in mind a pension fund investing in the "American economy"—that is, in the private-enterprise system; and while this made financial sense to the union leaders, their strong preference until then had been for pension funds invested in government securities—that is, in the "public sector." The union leadership was also greatly concerned lest a company-financed and company-managed pension plan—negotiated with the union and incorporated into the collective bargaining agreement—would open up a conflict within the union membership between older workers, interested in the largest possible pension payments, and younger workers, interested primarily in the amount of cash in the weekly pay envelope. Above all, the union suspected that one of the main reasons behind Wilson's proposal was a desire to blunt union militancy by making visible the workers' stake in company profits and company success. One of the stalwarts in the GM department of the UAW proposed at that time, in all seriousness, that the union should lodge an unfair-labor-practices complaint against Wilson, since his pension proposal could have no purpose except to undermine the union.

But the offer was too tempting, especially to the then rapidly growing number of older workers within the UAW. And so in October 1950, the GM pension fund began to operate. . . .

[The] GM plan had an unprecedented impact. Within one year after its inception, 8000 new plans were written—four times as many as had been set up in the hundred years before. And the one innovation of the GM plan was adopted by every single one of the new plans and has since been written into most of the older company plans as well. The GM plan was to be an "investment trust"—that is, it was to invest in the capital market, including equities. Practically all earlier plans had been "annuity" plans, to be invested in standard life-insurance investments, such as mortgages and other fixed-interest-bearing instruments. . . .

For the reality, and the great lesson of the American experiment, is that the alternatives today are not those of the 19th century—i.e., "capitalism" or "socialism," or even "individualism" and "collectivism." If the American experience proves anything, it is that the fundamental conflict in the developed countries—for all that it invokes the old battle cries and waves the old banners—is not about "capitalism" and "socialism." *It is about power.* It is a conflict between those who want a decentralization of power, a society in which a substantial number of pluralist power centers make decisions, thus leaving a meaningful sphere of freedom for the individual, and those who wish for a monopoly of power by a small élite, one which keeps itself in power either by brute force, or by buying, through "transfer payments," the support of the less productive or non-productive groups. Marx would have called this élite, a cabal of the "lumpen intellectuals" and the "lumpen proletariat."

2. Assets and Investments

1. *Pension fund capitalism?* One critic takes a hostile view of Drucker's "pension fund socialism":

> In fact, pension-fund socialism is a gloss for the real truth that Drucker has uncovered in Wilson's April 1950 offer. Aware of the enormous sums that were and would be generated in pension funds, Wilson sought to insure that this growing pool of capital would be responsibly invested—that is, as capitalists like him would invest it. . . . The "prudent man" concept of fiduciary responsibility, written into the 1974 Employee Retirement Income Security Act (ERISA), only defined what had been the standard investment practice for decades; the banks and insurance companies that control most of the funds have used these pools of capital to support a sagging market in the equity of the largest American corporations. As Drucker

demonstrates, a "revolution" in the sense of a radical reshaping of the pension system did take place in the postwar years. Its consequence, however, was not pension-fund socialism but pension-fund capitalism; neither, as Charles Wilson's actions demonstrate, was it "unseen." Business had found still another use for retirement.

William Graebner, A History of Retirement: The Meaning and Function of an American Institution: 1885–1978, at 220–21 (1980). For similarly hostile views of so-called welfare capitalism, see Jennifer Klein, For All These Rights: Business, Labor, and the Shaping of America's Public-Private Welfare State (2003); Teresa Ghilarducci, Labor's Capital: The Economics and Politics of Private Pensions (1992).

2.   *Magnitudes.* As of June 30, 2014, private and public pension assets in the U.S. totaled $24 trillion. Individual retirement accounts (IRAs) represented 30 percent of this total, followed by defined contribution plans (27.5 percent), government defined benefit plans (21 percent), private defined benefit plans (13 percent), private insured plans (12 percent), and annuity reserves (8 percent). Investment Company Institute, www.ici.org. "IRAs became the dominant source of U.S. retirement assets in 1998, fueled primarily by rollovers from other types of retirement plans (such as defined benefit pensions and defined contribution 401(k)-type plans). . . . In 1985, private trusteed defined benefit plans accounted for 34.0 percent of all retirement plan assets, but by 2005 that percentage had declined to 15.1 percent." Employee Benefit Research Institute [hereafter EBRI], Assets in Qualified Retirement Plans, 1985–2005: Updated, EBRI Notes, vol. 28, no. 8, available at www.ebri.org (August, 2007). "Pension assets have been growing rapidly compared to the economy as a whole: in 1950, pensions held 3 percent of all financial assets; in 1984 they held 16.7 percent." Richard A. Ippolito, Pension Economics, supra, at 123–24. As of year-end 1998 pension funds held 27.3 percent of all equities, and 11.9 percent of all corporate and other nominally taxable bonds. EBRI, Pension Investment Report: 4th Quarter 1998, at 37 (Table 19) (1999).

Recall as well the dimensions of the tax subsidy, previously noticed: for fiscal year 2015, above $147 billion. This number is clearly overstated, as it is calculated on a cash flow basis rather than a present value basis, but the true number is still very substantial.

3.   *Financial intermediation.* Drucker's essential insight is that workers are coming to own the means of production, not through the medium of the state, as Marx foresaw, but through the process of financial intermediation. Drucker elaborated his article as a book: The Unseen Revolution: How Pension Fund Socialism Came to America (1976).

Pension funds are financial intermediaries, comparable in a sense to the earlier forms of financial intermediation (banking, insurance, the securities markets, mutual funds) in whose instruments pension funds often invest. On the importance of the rise of financial intermediation, see generally Robert C. Clark, The Four Stages of Capitalism, 94 Harvard L.Rev. 561 (1981). A financial intermediary is positioned between the suppliers of capital (savers, investors) and the users (borrowers, enterprises). The intermediary pools wealth for investment, monitors investments, and distributes investment returns.

Pension funds invite contrast not only with state socialism, but also with the workers' cooperative, the regime under which workers own their own firms. A main difference between the modern pension fund and the worker-owned coop is that when a firm funds a pension plan to save and invest for the employees' retirement, the pension investment is spread across many industries and firms. A workers' cooperative, by contrast, concentrates savings and investment in a single firm, indeed, just that firm to whose fortunes the employees are already at risk through the employment relationship. The workers' cooperative exaggerates the intrinsic underdiversification that results from the workers having to tie so much of their "human capital" to the firm. Emphasis on diversification of investments is a main tenet of modern finance. ERISA mandates diversification for most pension fund investments (subject to an exception for certain plans that invest in employer stock), see infra Chapters 13–14.

Worker ownership is further discussed in connection with employee stock ownership plans (ESOPs) in Chapter 2, infra. On the extent of employee ownership and the difficulties associated with it, see Henry Hansmann, The Ownership of Enterprise 66ff (1996).

4.   *Measuring success.* Drucker describes private pension funds as "an outstanding example of the efficacy [of] private, non-governmental institutions [for] the formulation and achievement of social goals and the satisfaction of social needs." Hold open your answers to the questions (1) how private are private pension plans, and (2) how successful are they? Chapters 8–11 of this book develop the theme that the private pension system is tax-driven, in the sense that tax concessions ("tax subsidies") provide the motivation for much of the "voluntary" plan formation. Throughout the study of pension law, be alert to the question: How much of the private system would survive if the tax preferences did not exist?

In deciding whether an institution is successful, one needs to know what it is meant to achieve. That requires some attention to the purposes of the pension system, discussed infra in this chapter. We shall see that the current private pension system leaves major portions of the workforce with no coverage. In assessing the system, it is important to develop a view of how serious that shortcoming is, and whether it can be remedied.

5.   *Corporate governance implications of pension investing.* The growth of pension funds has "exacerbated the growth of institutional holdings of corporate securities. [Thus], pension plans can be implicated in issues surrounding the emergence of institutional control of corporate America." Ippolito, Pension Economics, supra, at 157. Pension funds are the largest holders of American financial assets. As of year-end 2006 institutional investors held 21 percent of American financial assets and 66.3 percent of total equity; pension funds owned nearly two-fifths of institutional assets. Conference Board, Institutional Investment Report: Trends in Institutional Assets and Equity Ownership of U.S. Corporations 9, 11, 20 & tbls. 1, 3, 10 (2008) [hereafter 2008 Conference Board Report]. By contrast, in 1950, pension funds held less than 1 percent of all equities. Richard A. Ippolito, Pensions, Economics and

Public Policy 123 (Pension Research Council) (1986). Institutional investors held 76.4 percent of the equity in the largest 1,000 American companies in 2007, up from 46.6 percent in 1987. 2008 Conference Board Report, at 6, 26 & tbl. 18.

ERISA's fiduciary rules regulate the conduct of pension trustees in their investment functions, see infra Chapters 13 and 14.

In a portion of Drucker's article that is not reproduced above, he argues that pension funds worsen the problem of the divorce of ownership and control in the modern corporation. Pension trustees are passive investors, not active managers of the corporations in which they hold securities. "Yet this leaves management without anyone to be accountable to." Drucker, "Pension Fund Socialism," supra, at 20. Might the ownership by pension trustees of large blocks of shares in publicly traded companies actually increase management accountability?

3. SOURCES OF RETIREMENT INCOME

Until recent times, the most characteristic pattern of support for the elderly was reverse transfer from adult children to aged parents. This pattern fit more easily into a world in which it was still common for the elderly to live with or near adult children. Some propertied persons lived from investment income, or by liquidating capital. For property-less and childless persons, charity (especially through the church) provided a backstop.

1. *Income of the elderly.* In modern circumstances, the patterns of support for the elderly are quite different. "Today fewer than 3 percent of elderly households receive income from their children. These contributions represent less than 1 percent of the income of the elderly." Lawrence J. Kotlikoff & Daniel E. Smith, Pensions in the American Economy § 1.1, at 1 (1983).

Important sources of income for today's elderly include Social Security, pension income, private savings, and employment income (often from part-time employment in a calling less demanding than one's pre-retirement career). The needy receive some welfare and charitable support. In the year 2007, the income of Americans aged 65 and older was derived 38.6 percent from Social Security payments, 18.6 percent from pensions and retirement plans, 25.3 percent from employment earnings, 15.6 percent from assets, and 1.8 percent from other sources. Ken McDonnell, Income of the Elderly Population Age 65 and Over, 2007, EBRI Notes, May 2009, at 9–12 & fig. 1. Within these aggregate figures there were large differences across income cohorts. The least affluent quintile drew 89 percent of its income from Social Security, three percent from pensions, two percent from earnings, and four percent from assets. In the most affluent quintile, Social Security supplied only 17 percent of income; the rest came 38 percent from earnings, 21 percent from pensions, and 22 percent from assets. Id. at 9 & fig. 4. See also Congressional Research Service, Income of Americans Aged 65 And Older: 1968 to 2008, Nov. 4, 2009, RL 33387.

2. *Social Security.* The Social Security system was founded in the 1930s and extended to embrace Medicare (medical care for the elderly) in

the 1960s. Social Security is now the core of American retirement income policy.

Social Security is in an important sense the successor to the older reverse transfer system, in which children supported their elderly parents. Today's adult children support their parents through the federal transfer system of Social Security rather than individually within the family. "Intrafamilial wealth transfer now plays virtually no role in the retirement income of the elderly. [The replacement system] has many advantages. Because the old system of reverse wealth transfer was limited to the family, persons who were childless, or whose children did not survive, or whose children were unable or unwilling to support them, could be left destitute. By making Social Security mandatory, the government harnessed the earning power of substantially the entire workforce to support the core retirement income needs of the nation's elderly. This attribute of Social Security, universal coverage, is why the program is understood as social insurance. Social Security funds a risk pool that covers persons who, in the days when old-age support was family-based, would not have had assistance. Social Security has also facilitated the growth of our ever more mobile national labor market, freeing workers to locate at great remove from their elderly parents." John H. Langbein, Social Security and the Private Pension System, in In Search of Retirement Security: The Changing Mix of Social Insurance, Employee Benefits and Individual Responsibility 109, 110–11 (T. Ghilarducci et al. eds. 2004).

Section C of this chapter, infra, discusses the relations between Social Security and the private pension system.

3. *Income from private pensions.* In 2007 the mean annual private pension income for persons aged 65–67 was $18,364. There were large gender differences ($19,787 for all males, $13,573 for all females), reflecting the lesser workforce experience and lower compensation levels for women. Ken McDonnell, Retirement Annuity and Employment-Based Pension Income Among Individuals Age 50 and Over: 2007, EBRI Notes, Nov. 2008, at 3–4 & fig. 5. Benefit levels varied greatly. The median pension income figure for persons in the highest quintile in 2007 was $31,320 per year; for those in the lowest quintile, $2,628. Id., fig. 4.

4. *Employment earnings; phased retirement.* "The job stopping process is generally initiated by the termination of career employment and frequently includes periods of post career employment, part-time work, partial retirement, and temporary retirement. [Accordingly,] the transition out of the labor force is a gradual process rather than an abrupt event." The Work and Retirement Patterns of Older Americans, EBRI Issue Brief, Dec. 1991, at 1, 3. This phenomenon of gradual withdrawal from the workforce has come to be known as phased retirement.

"Many older Americans leave the labor force gradually, utilizing 'bridge jobs' between employment on a full-time career job and complete labor force withdrawal. These bridge jobs are often part-time, often in a new line of work, and sometimes involve a switch from wage and salary work to self-employment. Estimates suggest that between one-third and one-half of older Americans will work on a bridge job before retiring completely, and for these workers retirement is best viewed as a process, not as a single event." EBRI, Issue Brief No. 206: Retirement Patterns and Bridge Jobs in the 1990s, at 1 (Feb. 1999); see also Kevin E. Cahill, Michael D. Giandrea and Joseph F. Quinn, U.S. Department of Labor, Bureau of Labor Statistics, Are Traditional Retirements a Thing of the Past? New Evidence on Retirement Patterns and Bridge Jobs (2005, http://www.bls.gov/ore/abstract/ec/ec050100.htm).

Among employed males in 2009, 90 percent of those aged 55 to 61 worked full time as against only ten percent who worked part time. With age, the proportion of the employed who worked part time increased to 20.2 percent for those 62 to 64, 31.4 percent for those 65 to 69, and 45.6 percent for those 70 and older. Patrick Purcell, Older Workers: Employment and Retirement Trends: Congressional Research Service Report for Congress tbl. 3 (2009). For employed women, the percentages in part time employment rose from 21.8 percent for those aged 55 to 61 in 2009, to 61.4 percent of those 70 and over. Id., tbl. 4.

Earnings of the elderly from employment decline steeply with age, providing "nearly 40 percent of income for those aged 65 to 69, to only 10 percent for those aged 75 to 79, down to five percent for those 80 or older." Robert L. Clark et al., The Economics of an Aging Society 40 (2004) (data for 2000). Regarding tax and ERISA complexities to phased retirement, see Pamela Perun, Phased Retirement Programs for the Twenty-First Century Workplace, 35 J. Marshall L. Rev. 623 (2002); Patricia L. Scahill & Jonathan Barry Forman, Protecting Participants and Beneficiaries in a Phased Retirement World, 2002 N.Y.U. Rev. Employee Benefits & Compensation 5–1 (2002); ERISA Advisory Council Report on Phased Retirement, http://www.dol.gov/ebsa/publications/2008ACreport2.html (2008). On November 10, 2004, the Treasury Department and Internal Revenue Service published proposed regulations (69 Fed. Reg. 65108) relating to phased retirement, but they have not finalized the regulations as of the date of publication of this book.

4. PENSION COVERAGE

As an easy generalization that will need to be modified slightly, it is fair to say that only about half the American workforce has pension coverage, and that the half that has pension coverage is the top or better-paid half.

Recall the three defining characteristics of the American private pension system: Pension plans are employer-sponsored, voluntary, and tax-favored. These attributes strongly influence the patterns of pension coverage and participation. Because the system is driven by tax benefits, employers whose workers are less well-paid, hence less tax-sensitive, tend not to offer pension plans; and less well-paid employees are less likely to participate, or participate fully, in pension saving opportunities offered to them. Because the pension system is voluntary, employers may elect not to offer pension plans, and thus, many workers are not offered pension coverage. Even when the employer does sponsor a pension plan, the employer may design it in a fashion that excludes some employees, or causes pension interests to forfeit when employment terminates before satisfying the plan's vesting criteria. The voluntary nature of the system also acts as a constraint on regulation: the more intrusive the regulation, the greater the danger that it will discourage plan formation.

Aggregates. As of 2012, 48.6 percent of the workforce worked for an employer or as a member of a union that sponsored a pension or retirement plan; the so-called "take up" rate, the number of these persons actually participating, was 39.4 percent. For the subset of the workforce consisting of wage and salary workers aged 21 to 64, the sponsorship rate increases to 53.4 percent and the portion participating increases to 44.2 percent. Craig Copeland, Employment-Based Retirement Plan Participation; Geographic Differences and Trends, 2012 EBRI Issue Brief No. 392, Nov. 2013 [hereafter, Copeland, Plan Participation]. The gap between sponsorship and take up is largely a consequence of the growth of defined contribution plans over the past quarter century, a subject discussed in Chapter 2, infra. Unlike defined benefit plans, which automatically cover eligible employees, most defined contribution plans leave to each eligible employee the decision of whether or not to participate.

2. *Income.* Coverage is not randomly distributed. How much a worker earns is a factor that correlates strongly with private pension coverage. "Less than one-fifth (16.2 percent) of wage and salary workers ages 21–64 who had annual earnings of $10,000–$19,999 participated in a plan, compared with 69.8 percent of those earning $75,000 or more." [Copeland, Plan Participation, at 10].

3. *Industry characteristics.* There are marked differences in coverage from one industry to another. "Workers in the manufacturing industry and the transportation, utilities, information, and financial industry had the highest probability of participating, while those in the other-services industry had the lowest probability. Public-sector workers were significantly more likely to participate than private-sector workers." Id. What accounts for these differences? Why is coverage notably high in the public sector and among utilities (telephone, power and light, natural gas, water works)? Why is coverage so much lower in retailing and in the service industries?

4. *Firm size.* Firm size is a powerful predictor of pension coverage. "For wage and salary workers ages 21–64 who worked for employers with fewer than 10 employees, 13.5 percent participated in a plan, compared with 54.8 percent of those working for employers with 1,000 or more employees." Id.

"Most employers in the United States are *small* employers with fewer than 20 employees," and "[m]ost small employers *do not* sponsor a retirement plan for their workers. . . ." Patrick J. Purcell, Social Security Individual Accounts and Employer Sponsored Pensions, 31 J. Pension Planning & Compliance 15, 16 (Sum. 2005).

According to the 2002 Small Employer Retirement Survey (SERS) (involving employers with 5 to 100 full-time workers), the most commonly cited "most important" reasons for not having a plan were: employees prefer wages and/or other benefits; revenue is too uncertain to commit to a plan; a large portion of workers are seasonal, part time or high turnover; required company contributions are too expensive; and it costs too much to set up and administer a plan. 2002 Small Employer Retirement Survey, Summary of Findings, www.ebri.org. According to a 2001 U.S. Department of Labor Working Group Report, "Significant reasons why more employers do not sponsor pension plans for any or some of their employees include: concerns over the business realities of revenues and profit; the nature of the employer's workforce; employee preferences for cash and health insurance; the decline in unionization; the cost of setting-up and administering a plan; concerns about government regulation and liability; and a lack of information or knowledge among employers and employees." U.S. Department of Labor, Report of the Working Group on Increasing Pension Coverage, Participation and Benefits, November 13, 2001.

5.   *Unionization.* Pension coverage also correlates strongly with unionization. As of the mid-1980s, "private-sector [e]mployees in collective bargaining units, although making up only 21 percent of all full-time workers, accounted for over one-third of all pension plan participants. [Union] representation was a particularly important factor related to coverage for workers in establishments with fewer than 100 employees. Seventy percent of bargaining unit members employed in small establishments were covered by a plan compared to only 26 percent of non-bargaining unit employees." The Handbook of Pension Statistics: 1985, at 90 (R. Ippolito & W. Kolodrubetz eds., 1986). Union membership has declined steadily in recent years. According to Bureau of Labor Statistics data, unionized workers comprised 12.5 percent of the total workforce and 7.9 percent of the private-sector workforce in 2004. Very Old Labor, Wall St. J., Jul. 26, 2005, at A24.

Union membership also correlates strongly with coverage in other types of employee benefit plans. "In September 2007, 82.7 percent of union workers were covered by health benefits through their own job, compared with 58.2 percent of nonunion workers." P. Fronstin, The Relationship Between Union Status and Employment-Based Health Benefits, EBRI Notes, October 2009.

Health care plans are discussed in Chapters 3, 4 and 19, infra.

What factors might account for the high correlation between unionization and coverage?

6.   *Service characteristics.* Pension coverage correlates positively with other traits of job tenure, including hours worked and length of service. EBRI Databook, available at www.ebri.org.

7.   *Age.* Older workers are much more likely to have pension coverage. Data for 2012 show that 16.4 percent of workers aged 21 to 24 participated in retirement plans, compared to 52.4 percent of workers aged 55 to 64. Copeland, Plan Participation, at 9–10.

8.   *Gender.* In 2012, "Female wage and salary workers ages 21–64 were found to participate in a retirement plan at a lower level than males. However, among full-time, full-year workers of these same ages, females had a higher rate of participation in a plan (55.0 percent for women, compared with 52.3 percent for men). In fact, across all work-status categories, females were more likely to participate in a retirement plan than males (Figure 3). This result has persisted since 2001, when the full-time, full-year participation level was slightly higher for females than for males at 58.5 percent to 58.1 percent (Figure 4). Furthermore, when examining participation by earnings level, the proportion of females participating in a plan was significantly higher than males at each earnings level, except the lowest category where it was only slightly

higher (Figure 5). Consequently, it appears that female workers' lower probability of participation in the aggregate was a result of their overall lower average earnings and lower rates of full-time work in comparison with males—characteristics often associated with lower participation levels." Copeland, Plan Participation, at 10.

The outlook for women is, however, less favorable when attention shifts from coverage rates to benefit levels. Recently, the gap has narrowed: "A woman age 65 or over in 2006 was almost two thirds as likely to receive an annuity and/or pension payment as her male counterpart; if she did receive one, her mean benefit was likely to be about 65 percent of that received by a man in the same age group. However, as other EBRI research has shown, women's participation in retirement plans has risen significantly relative to men in recent years, closing the 'gender gap' in retirement plan participation—even though retirement plan participation has been declining for both men and women. Hence, the aggregate pension and annuity recipiency for women and the amounts they receive are likely to increase over time as these younger generations retire." Retirement Annuity and Employment-Based Pension Income, Among Individuals Age 50 and Over: 2006, EBRI Notes, January, 2008, at 2.

In 2006, men with graduate degrees received nearly three times the median annuity and/or pension income of men without a high school diploma. Retirement Annuity and Employment-Based Pension Income, Among Individuals Age 50 and Over: 2006, EBRI Notes, January, 2008, at 2.

9.   *Race and Ethnicity.* Hispanic wage and salary workers were significantly less likely than both white and black workers to participate in a retirement plan. The overall gap between the percentages of black and white plan participants narrowed when compared across earnings levels, with blacks surpassing whites at the income level of $50,000–$74,999 (Figure 6). In contrast, the gap between Hispanics and whites persisted in all earnings groups, although it showed some narrowing in the higher-earnings groups." Copeland, Plan Participation, at 10.

10.   *Coverage and pension policy.* Consider again the point raised at the outset of this note, that the private pension system covers only about half the workforce, and in general the top half. Why is coverage so limited? Why does coverage tend to benefit the better off? Does a pension system whose coverage is so partial and so skewed deserve a tax subsidy of more than $100 billion per year?

5.   WHY ARE PENSION PLANS EMPLOYMENT-BASED?

Why do employers sponsor pension plans? Why are employers not content to allow employees to save for retirement on their own?

1.   *Cash and fringes as substitutes.* Employees pay for pensions and other fringe benefits in reduced cash compensation. "In general, a worker will prefer a dollar of after-tax earnings to a dollar of employee benefits tied to the provision of a particular commodity or service." Daniel S. Hamermesh & Albert Rees, The Economics of Work and Pay 341 (4th ed. 1988). Participation in some pension and benefit plans is optional with the employee, if the plan has optional features, but participation in many

defined benefit pension plans is obligatory, and many other benefits (e.g., health care, child care) are offered on a take it or lose it basis. Participation in such plans may not align with the preferences of those employees who wish not to engage in pension saving, or who have little or no interest in other benefit plans.

"The great advantage of current cash compensation is that it maximizes workers' freedom to spend their income how and when they like and to make such provision for contingencies and risks as they think proper. In contrast, other forms of compensation determine part of [workers'] consumption pattern for them and, at worst, may be entirely useless. For example, group life insurance may have little value to single workers without dependents." Id. An employer who imposes pension saving on a worker who does not want it will be at a competitive disadvantage if the worker can find another employer who will pay the full wage in cash.

A significant factor in the movement toward defined contribution plans since the 1980s (which is discussed infra in Chapter 2) is the argument that defined contribution plans, by leaving to the employee the decision about whether and how much to participate, do a better job of tailoring pensions to employees who will value them fully. Pension economist Richard Ippolito has argued that pension-preferring employees have a more general sensitivity to long-term considerations, which makes such persons more desirable employees. Richard A. Ippolito, Pension Plans and Employee Performance: Evidence, Analysis, and Policy 107–28 (1997).

2. *The trend toward pensions and other fringes.* Over the past generation, employee benefits have burgeoned as a percentage of compensation. Nonmonetary compensation rose from 1.3 percent of total compensation in 1929 to 17.0 percent in 1986. Hamermesh & Rees, supra, at 340 & tbl. 12.8. Including legally required benefits (Social Security, federal and state unemployment and workers' compensation), benefits costs constituted 28.6 percent of compensation costs in September 2004, or 19.9 percent if legally required benefits are excluded. Compensation Costs in the Private and State/Local Sectors, Facts from EBRI, Mar. 2005, at 1. For employees of state and local governments, benefits as a percentage of total compensation were slightly higher, reaching 31.4 percent. Id. at 2.

Many employers direct significant proportions of compensation into fringe benefits despite the risk that some employees will disprefer fringe benefits and view the dispreferred benefits at least in part as reductions in compensation. There must be offsetting advantages that explain why employers direct so much compensation into fringe benefits, especially private pensions.

3. *Tax benefits.* A central explanation for the trend toward fringe benefits is that many forms of fringe benefits are tax advantaged. The extensive tax preferences for pension plans are discussed infra in Chapter 8. At least for the employee who wants to engage in pension saving (or to buy health insurance or to take advantage of any other tax-deferred or tax-exempt fringe benefit), saving or purchasing with pretax dollars is superior to doing it with after-tax dollars.

The private pension system is organized so that only the employer can deliver the pension tax benefit. (An employee whose employer does not offer pension coverage can set up an individual retirement account (IRA), but the IRA has a relatively low annual contribution ceiling.)

To the question, how much of the private pension system would survive if it were tax-neutral, the answer would surely be, "Much less." But the answer would not be "None," because a variety of nontax incentives also dispose firms to offer pension plans.

4. *Bonding to the firm.* If the employee's pension entitlement can be made contingent upon continuing employment with the firm, it can serve a hostage function. The employee would have an incentive to remain with the firm and to perform well, thereby sparing the employer the costs of recruitment and training that result from employee turnover, as well as lowering the costs of monitoring and supervising the employee. The employer, in turn, is more likely to invest in training an employee who has a greater incentive to remain with the firm; and as the employee's skills increase, the employer will need to pay more to retain that employee. Thus, paying some compensation in a contingent form is value-enhancing both to the firm and to the employee. See generally Hamermesh & Rees, supra, at 203–07; Dennis E. Logue, Legislative Influence on Corporate Pension Plans 25–26 (American Enterprise Institute) (1979).

It will be seen in Chapter 4 that a major theme of federal pension regulation under ERISA has been to circumscribe the former freedom of employee and employer to agree to make the employee's pension entitlements contingent. ERISA and the IRC now impose vesting rules that restrict, but do not eliminate, pension forfeitability. As originally enacted, ERISA allowed a plan to impose total forfeiture upon an employee who quit or was discharged in less than ten years. The 1986 amendments to ERISA reduced the permitted period to five years. Thus, although the scope of pension forfeitability has been reduced, it remains significant.

"Pension coverage matters [on the question of length of employment]. Among manufacturing jobs, we estimate the average completed job to last 6.48 years, with a median tenure of 2.56 years. If the current pension system were to be abolished and all jobs to be uncovered, we estimate the mean tenure in manufacturing would drop from 6.48 to 4.09 years with a drop in median tenure from 2.56 to 2.26 years." Douglas A. Wolf & Frank Levy, Pension Coverage, Pension Vesting, and the Distribution of Job Tenures, in Retirement and Economic Behavior 23, 25 (Brookings Institution) (H.J. Aaron & G. Burtless eds., 1984).

The median job tenure in the American economy in January, 2014 was 4.6 years, which is less than the number of years of service needed for full vesting under 3 of the 4 statutory vesting schedules (5 year cliff, 3 to 7 year graded and 2 to 6 year graded). 21% of all workers had been with their current employer for 12 months or less. U.S. Department of Labor, Bureau of Labor Statistics, News Release, Employee Tenure in 2014, available at *www.bls.gov/news.release/pdf/tenure.pdf*. The median tenure in the private sector was 4.1 years (7.8 years in the public sector). Pension plans are not the only device that, by making a portion of the employee's compensation contingent, promotes bonding to the firm. The year-end bonus has that effect. So does a scheme, such as the associate-to-partner promotion system in law firms, which defers and makes contingent some compensation.

See, e.g., Ronald J. Gilson & Robert H. Mnookin, Coming of Age in a Corporate Law Firm: The Economics of Associate Career Patterns, 41 Stanford L.Rev. 567, 572–73 (1989).

If partnership systems serve some of the functions of pensions, should partnership denials be subject to ERISA-style regulatory standards, which are discussed infra Chapter 4?

5. *Superannuation policy.* Having helped the employer retain employees, the pension plan may also serve an opposite objective for the employer: facilitating employees' departure. "[A]n employee's productivity begins to decline at some point in his career, but because of the customs of the internal labor market, a firm cannot reduce a long-term employee's wages. For this reason, a firm has an interest in encouraging employees to retire at certain ages. The retirement income provided by a pension facilitates such induced retirement." Wolf & Levy, supra, at 27.

The Age Discrimination in Employment Act (ADEA), discussed infra Chapter 18, now largely prohibits the employer from imposing age-specific mandatory retirement rules. Although ADEA forbids the stick, it does not much interfere with the carrot. ERISA § 3(24) continues to set a benchmark normal retirement age (NRA) of 65. Despite ADEA, most workers have been retiring earlier than NRA. To the extent that the employer wants to encourage employees to retire before their productivity declines, the practice of imposing a retirement savings program upon those employees who might not voluntarily save enough may help the employer achieve an ADEA-compatible superannuation policy.

6. *Comparative advantage in financial matters.* Saving for retirement entails investment, and investing is a highly specialized activity. As between the typical worker and the typical employer, the employer is the more likely to be able to select and monitor financial intermediaries and investment programs.

A large employer is likely to realize economies of scale not only in investing plan funds but also in distributing benefits. Many defined benefit plans offer only annuities, not lump sums. "[A]nnuities purchased at older ages are costly because of classic selectivity problems. People who prefer annuities tend to be those who have private information suggesting that they will live to be relatively old; those expecting relatively early death will take the lump sum. Retirees with average life expectancies therefore are faced with relatively low annuities because the pool is over-represented by people with long life expectancies. If, however, a group of individuals can commit itself early in life and penalize early-outs, the selectivity problem can be overcome and, further, group rates can be obtained." Ippolito, Pension Economics, supra, at 30–31. By annuitizing benefits for the entire workforce, a defined benefit plan can obtain materially more favorable rates than those available to individual annuity purchasers.

Similar economies of scale have been an important factor in the spread of employment-based group insurance products for health, accident, and life. When a plan covers an entire workforce, it narrows or eliminates the risk of adverse selection that inheres in the market for individual coverage, and it spares the costs of investigation at the application stage that characterize the market for individual coverage.

The employee's relative disadvantage in the conduct of investment matters is a central concern in the decline of defined benefit plans and the growth of defined contribution plans, discussed infra in Chapters 2 and 14.

7. *Forced savings.* "[E]mployees may be concerned about their own myopia and the way in which current financial pressures may undermine their plans to save for retirement out of current income. Enforced pension contributions shield current income from these pressures." Wolf & Levy, supra, at 28.

8. *Welfare benefit plans.* Some but not all of the analysis of the question of why employers offer pension plans applies to the question of why employers offer non-pension plans, that is, welfare benefit plans such as health care, life insurance, disability, severance pay, and others. Welfare benefit plans are discussed infra in Chapters 3 and 19 of this book, and they figure importantly in the materials on ERISA preemption (infra Chapter 17) and judicial review of benefit denials (infra Chapter 15).

"Of course, with the position that has the benefits—medical, dental, et cetera—there is no salary."

Welfare benefit plans are mostly current expense plans that do not entail a significant savings component, and accordingly, aspects of the analysis that center on the employer's role in investing and helping workers save will not pertain. On the other hand, the role of competitive labor markets in pressuring employers to offer benefit plans is as evident in non-pension plans as in pension plans. In 1999, for example, the *Wall Street Journal* published an account of how tightness in the Kansas City labor market forced a variety of small and low-wage employers, including child care centers, fast food franchises, and motels, to begin offering health care benefits. A precipitating factor, according to the report, was competition for these workers from other employers, especially the nascent gambling industry, which offered health benefits to workers in staffing riverboat casinos. Lucette Lagnado, Small Employers Offer Health Benefits to Lure Workers in Kansas City, Wall St. J., Apr. 15, 1999, at A1.

C. SOCIAL SECURITY AND PRIVATE PENSIONS

1. SUBSTITUTION, INTEGRATION, AND REPLACEMENT

Alicia H. Munnell, The Economics of Private Pensions
7, 13–19 (Brookings Institution) (1982).

The development of the social security program and private pension system, in the wake of the Great Depression, reflected a shift in the nation's preference away from individual saving for retirement and toward organized savings plans. The two systems developed simultaneously, since neither program provided adequate retirement income. Yet they clearly are alternative ways to accomplish the same goal—namely, providing an adequate retirement income. In fact, many private plans are explicitly integrated with social security and so reduce private pension benefits as social security benefits are increased. Because of the substitutability of the two programs, as the gap between desired and actual retirement assets narrows, an expansion in either social security or private pensions will lead to a decline in the relative role of the other.

The recent expansion of social security, therefore, has profound implications for the development of private plans. In the 1970s social security benefits grew particularly fast as a result of ad hoc increases and automatic cost-of-living adjustments. Despite this growth, a substantial gap still exists—especially for workers with above-average earnings—between retirees' income needs and social security benefits. Whether the gap is filled by private pensions or a larger social security program will depend on the relative ability of the two programs to provide good retirement protection. . . .

The Interaction of Social Security and Private Pensions. . . . At first glance, the simultaneous expansion of public and private programs during the last thirty years seems to imply that social security has not infringed on the development of private pension plans. For instance, despite a major increase in social security benefits in 1950, private pension plans continued to grow rapidly. Many argue that social security has actually encouraged the growth of private pensions by establishing sixty-five as an acceptable retirement age and by providing a basic retirement benefit that permits workers to plan for an independent future. However, the simultaneous expansion of social security and private plans can also be explained as society's attempt to close the large gap between actual and desired retirement assets. Social security and private pensions are alternative vehicles to achieve a targeted level of guaranteed retirement benefits. That these two mechanisms are substitutes is suggested not only by anecdotal evidence from union leaders that employer contributions to private plans are implicitly considered in contract negotiations but also by the existence of integrated private pension plans under which the worker's social security benefit is explicitly factored into the calculation of his private pension benefit.

Integration. The concept of integration is based on the notion that public and private retirement programs should function as a unified system. Congress incorporated this reasoning into the tax code in the Revenue Act of 1942 by including the proviso that public and private retirement benefits would be considered together in determining whether or not a plan discriminates against low-wage workers. Since the social security program is weighted in favor of low-income workers, integrated private plans favor high-income workers, so that all workers receive about the same ratio of their preretirement earnings when they retire. . . .

The Role for Private Pensions. In view of the relative substitutability of the two programs, the potential role for private pensions is determined by the gap between the income requirements of the elderly and the benefits provided by social security. Although social security benefits as a percentage of preretirement earnings are projected to decline slightly, they will remain higher than they were at the beginning of the 1970s. Therefore, given the substitutability of the two benefit systems, private pensions will have a relatively smaller role than they would have had without the expansion of social security. Nevertheless, as the following discussion reveals, ample room still exists for supplementary private pension benefits—especially for workers with above-average earnings.

The Expansion of Social Security. After three decades of relatively minor changes in the OASI program, the 1970s brought a significant expansion in retirement benefits . . . social security benefits will continue to replace a considerably higher proportion of preretirement earnings than during the 1960s.

As social security benefits have grown, the taxable wage base has also risen sharply. In 1969 taxes and benefits were calculated on earnings up to a maximum of $7,800. . . . In 2015 the figure is $118,500, with no cap on the Medicare contribution base, which is taxed at 1.45 percent for both the employer and the employee for sums above the wage base.—Eds.] Because of the increase in replacement rates and the expansion of the earnings base, social security is now a substantial source of retirement income for a large part of the population.

2. REPLACEMENT RATES AND GOALS

For a concise introduction to the main attributes of Social Security, see C. Eugene Steuerle & Jon M. Bakija, Basic Features of the Social Security System, 62 Tax Notes 1457 (1994); see also David A. Pratt, The Social Security and Medicare Answer Book, 5th ed. (Wolters Kluwer, 2014). Regarding the relationship between Social Security and the private pension system in the formative period of each, see Jacob S. Hacker, The Divided Welfare State: The Battle over Public and Private Social Benefits in the United States 71–175 (2002).

The average monthly Social Security benefit for a retired worker in December, 2014 was $1,329, and for a spouse, $673. Social Security Administration, Monthly Statistical Snapshot, Dec., 2014, http://www. ssa.gov/policy/docs/quickfacts/stat_snapshot/. Total benefit payments to retirees in that month were $53.8 billion; a further $11.1 billion was paid in disability benefits. Id. For detail on benefit levels and taxes see Jonathan Barry Forman, Making Social Security Work, 65 Ohio St. L. J. 148 (2004).

1. *Social Security replacement rates.* The following shows estimated Social Security benefits for workers reaching retirement age (age 66) in 2015 at different earnings levels and illustrates the downward gradation in Social Security replacement levels that occurs as earnings levels increase. Low earnings 44.5%; medium earnings 32.9%; high earnings 27.3%. Source: Social Security Administration Office of the Chief Actuary, Actuarial Note Number 2014.9, July 2014, http://www. socialsecurity.gov/OACT/NOTES/ran9/an2014-9.pdf.

These replacement ratios will decline over the next 20 to 30 years. Reasons for this decline include the legislated increase in the "full-benefit age" for receiving Social Security benefits, increased income taxation of Social Security benefits, and rising Medicare premiums that are deducted directly from Social Security benefits.

2. *Redistributive effects.* Social Security benefits are sometimes said to be *bottom-weighted,* meaning (as the above table shows) that Social Security replaces larger proportions of the pre-retirement earnings of the less well paid. See generally C. Eugene Steuerle & Jon M. Bakija, How Social Security Redistributes Income, 62 Tax Notes 1763 (1994).

Even though Social Security benefit schedules are bottom-weighted, however, the aggregate redistributive effects are complex. "Government retirement programs involve massive income redistribution from the young to the old. Increasingly, this is also a transfer from a poorer and less economically secure population to a richer and more secure one," because in terms of wealth (although not income) the young are poorer than the old. Robert J. Samuelson, Reinventing Retirement, The New Republic, Apr. 12, 1999, at 36, 41 (citing median 1996 household wealth of $107,000 for the age group 65–74 compared to $51,000 for the age group 35–44). For discussion and data, see GAO, Social Security: Distribution of Benefits and Taxes Relative to Earnings Level (GAO–04–747) (2004).

3. *Private pension plan replacement rates.* Private pension plan replacement rates are difficult to calculate because so many employers

do not have plans, defined benefit plans have largely been replaced by defined contribution plans, and replacement rates under defined contribution plans are heavily dependent on the individual's savings history and plan design. For average replacement rates under defined benefit plans as of 1993, see the EBRI, Databook, www.ebri.org. See also Social Security Administration, Comparing Replacement Rates Under Private and Federal Retirement Systems, Social Security Bulletin, Vol. 65 No. 1, 2003/2004, available at http://www.ssa.gov/policy/docs/ssb/v65n1/v65n1p17.html.

Unlike Social Security, the private plans do not replace materially higher fractions of pre-retirement income for the less well paid workers. However, because Social Security is so strongly bottom-weighted, the replacement rates achieved under the combined systems are lower for higher paid employees, even allowing for the effects of integration.

4. *Replacement goals.* How much income do people need in retirement? The Carter Administration's Commission on Pension Policy hinted at relatively high levels of replacement. "The Commission believes that the replacement of pre-retirement disposable income from all sources is a desirable retirement income goal." President's Commission on Pension Policy, Coming of Age: Toward a National Retirement Income Policy 42 (1981). One commissioner scoffed at this recommendation. "A pleasant goal to contemplate—yes; a realistic one—no. If accomplished, it would mean that a large number of people would live in retirement better than they ever had before except just prior to retirement. Fairness in our society means balancing fairness to young families at lower early earnings who are buying homes and educating their children while paying for Social Security, as well as fairness to the retired." Id. at 63 (statement of William C. Greenough).

There are a variety of reasons why 100 percent replacement may not be necessary in retirement to sustain pre-retirement living standards. Taxes are lower for the elderly—persons over 65 have additional standard deductions, and some or all of their Social Security income is untaxed. Various states and localities apply lower income and real estate tax rates to the elderly. Retirees no longer incur work-related expenses—commuting, work clothes, and so forth. Retirees ordinarily have lower consumption profiles than younger families with growing children. The main category of expenditure that increases with old age is medical care: see Chapter 19, infra, for treatment of retiree health issues. Moreover, the elderly also have lower aggregate housing costs, on account of their high levels of home ownership discussed supra.

For reasons such as these, the tendency among employee benefits specialists has been to consider replacement rates of about 60 to 70 percent as adequate to sustain pre-retirement living standards. See, e.g., Emily S. Andrews, The Changing Profile of Pensions in America 129–30 (1985). However, some recent studies have suggested that far higher replacement rates may be necessary. According to two 2008 studies, the average projected postretirement income replacement need among employees of large U.S. employers is 126% of final pay, a level only about 19% of employees are expected to satisfy, and most middle income Americans earning between $50,000 and $100,000 a year are at risk of being unable to maintain their standard of living in retirement. Hewitt

Associates, Total Retirement Income at Large Companies: The Real Deal 2008, July 1, 2008; Ernst & Young, Retirement Vulnerability of New Retirees: The Likelihood of Outliving Their Assets, July 2008.

"Given the huge variation of individual circumstances (such as age, health, and income) and the complexity of retirement risks that need to be dealt with—such as longevity (addressed through annuitization of assets), old-age infirmity (addressed through long-term care insurance), and asset preservation (addressed through investment allocation)—a simple one-size-fits-all replacement rate will not work for most Americans. The results of this model reveal, in many cases, the sobering (if not staggering) amounts of money needed to provide a reasonable high chance of being able to afford retirement. However, they also show the positive results that can be obtained by annuitizing assets in retirement to protect against the risk of longevity. In this regard, the model points not only to a more realistic size of the retirement income problem but also ways that individuals can begin to deal with it." EBRI Issue Brief No. 297, Sept. 2006, Measuring Retirement Income Adequacy: Calculating Realistic Income Replacement Rates, By Jack VanDerhei. See also Peter J. Brady, Measuring Retirement Resource Adequacy, Investment Company Institute, pbrady@ici.org, February 2008; Center for Retirement Research at Boston College, August 2007, Brief Number 7–11, Is There Really a Retirement Savings Crisis? An NRRI Analysis.

5.   *The future of Social Security.* Social Security is largely financed through payroll taxes on current workers and their employers, which fund transfer payments to current retirees. Because of declining birth rates, the number of active workers relative to retirees is declining and will continue to decline across the twenty-first century. See Laurence J. Kotlikoff & Scott Burns, The Coming Generational Storm 6–7 (2004). These demographic trends have made the financing of the Social Security system unstable. See C. Eugene Steuerle & Jon M. Bakija, Social Security: The Inevitable Reform of an Imbalanced System, 62 Tax Notes 1597 (1994); C. Eugene Steuerle & Jon M. Bakija, Options for Reforming the Social Security Payroll Tax, 63 Tax Notes 109 (1994).

Not surprisingly, the recent economic crisis has adversely affected the solvency of Social Security. The 2014 Social Security Trustees' Report (available at www.ssa.gov) states that under the Trustees' intermediate assumptions, annual costs exceed tax income, starting in 2010: in the 2010 report, this was projected to occur in 2016. The 2014 report projects that the Social Security trust funds will be exhausted in 2033, three years earlier than projected in 2011 and eight years earlier than projected in 2008. At that time, tax income to the funds is projected to cover 77 percent of the cost of benefit payments. The OASI Trust Fund is projected to be able to pay full benefits on time until 2034 (one year earlier than projected in 2013), but the Disability Insurance (DI) Trust Fund is projected to be able to pay full benefits only until 2016 (as was projected in 2013).

The government's accounting practices for Social Security disguise the extent of the financial problems confronting the system. "Social Security reports its financial performance on a cash-flow basis: it compares annual revenues to annual costs," disregarding the liabilities it accrues in that year for future benefits. Howell E. Jackson, It's Even

Worse Than You Think, N.Y. Times, Oct. 9, 2003, at A35. According to Jackson, on an accrual accounting basis such as that required of private pension plans, Social Security had (in 2003) an accumulated deficit of $10.5 trillion (liabilities for future benefits of $14 trillion less current reserves and projected future taxes of $3.5 trillion). As of 2003, "[t]his implicit debt of the Social Security System [was] more than two and a half times larger than the government's public debt." Id. See also Howell E. Jackson, Accounting for Social Security and Its Reform, 41 Harvard J. Legislation 59 (2004), and related symposium papers. According to the 2014 Trustees' report, the unfunded obligation over the next 75 years is $ 10.6 trillion in discounted present value, an increase of $1 billion from the amount shown in the 2013 report.

A 2007 monograph from the American Academy of Actuaries concluded that: "The problems facing Social Security, when placed in the context of the enormous U.S. economy, are not nearly as daunting as they might seem when presented in stark dollar terms. In the 70-year history of Social Security, the tax rate has increased from 2 to 12.4 percent of taxable payroll; the estimated increase required to fund the current system over the next 75 years is far less. Further, the need for such tax increases can be reduced, or even eliminated, by changes in benefits and other features; and any required changes can be phased in gradually. Does this mean we can do nothing and just wait to see what develops? While waiting will not destroy the system, there are advantages to acting now." [American Academy of Actuaries, Public Policy Monograph, Social Security Reform Options. Jan. 2007, available at www.actuary.org]

Adjustments are likely to occur in order to increase revenues and restrain benefits. Among the policy options are reducing or eliminating the cap on earnings subject to Social Security (FICA) taxes, which is $118,500 in 2015; increasing Social Security tax rates; subjecting more of Social Security benefits to income taxation; funding some of Social Security from general revenue; reducing the automatic cost-of-living adjustment, probably by redesigning the components of the adjustment formula; and extending normal retirement age (hence shortening the period of benefit recipiency). See Bruce D. Schobel, Sooner Than You Think: The Coming Bankruptcy of Social Security, Policy Review 41 (Fall 1992). On potential avenues for reform, see Maureen B. Cavanaugh, Social Security: Can the Promise Be Kept? An Introduction, 58 Washington & Lee L. Rev. 1197 (2001), and related symposium papers; Thomas N. Bethell, What's the Big Idea? There's More than One Solution for Social Security (Apr. 2005), www.aarp.org; Peter A. Diamond and Peter R. Orszag, Saving Social Security: The Diamond-Orszag Plan, The Economists' Voice, Vol. 2, Issue 1, 2005, Article 8.

The Bush Administration made proposals in 2005 to supplement or partially to replace Social Security with a system of individual investment accounts resembling defined contribution plans in the private system. For a review of the daunting complexities that would arise if such a program were attempted, see the National Academy of Social Insurance Report, Uncharted Waters.

Two final comments are in order. First, despite near-universal agreement among politicians that entitlement reform is an urgent priority, nothing concrete has been attempted since the Bush proposal, let alone enacted. Second, the problems of Social Security are far less severe and urgent than the problems facing Medicare.

CHAPTER 2

DEFINED BENEFIT AND DEFINED CONTRIBUTION PLANS

Analysis

Introduction

The central divide in the pension landscape is between defined benefit and defined contribution plans, although, as discussed later in this chapter, there has also been a growth in plans that are a hybrid of the two types. In considering the differences between defined benefit and defined contribution plans, bear in mind the question of why an employer or an employee might prefer one or the other.

Edward A. Zelinsky, The Defined Contribution Paradigm
114 Yale L.J. 451, 455–58 (2004).

[T]he distinction between defined benefit and defined contribution plans is surprisingly clear. A defined benefit pension, as its name implies, specifies an output for the participant. Traditionally, such plans defined benefits for particular employees based on the employees' respective salary histories and their periods of employment. Thus, for example, a prototypical defined benefit formula specifies that a participant is entitled at retirement to an annual income equal to a percentage of her average salary times the number of years of her employment with the sponsoring employer.

In contrast, a defined contribution arrangement, as its equally apt moniker indicates, specifies an input for the participant. Commonly, the plan defines the employer's contribution for each participant as a percentage of the participant's salary for that year. Having made that contribution, the employer's obligation to fund is over because the employee is not guaranteed a particular benefit, just a specified input. In a defined contribution context, the participant's ultimate economic entitlement is the amount to which the defined contributions for her, plus earnings, grow or shrink.

Defined contribution plans classically took the form of employer-sponsored pensions (often denoted "money purchase pensions") and of employment-based profit-sharing arrangements. In the pension incarnation, the employer sponsoring a defined contribution arrangement has a fixed annual obligation to contribute, typically a percentage of the participant's salary. The profit-sharing alternative, on the other hand, gives the employer flexibility in determining its contribution. Most obviously, the sponsoring employer need not contribute anything in a year without profits, unlike a pension obligation, which is a fixed cost unrelated to profitability. Profit-sharing plans can also be designed to permit the employer to decide annually how much of its profits it wants to contribute. The great flexibility of profit-sharing plans explains their increasing popularity in recent years, particularly when that flexibility is contrasted with the regulatory rigidities surrounding defined benefit pensions.

Traditionally, defined benefit arrangements have promised participants benefits at retirement in the form of periodic (typically monthly) payments for the duration of the retired participant's life. Amounts to fund these benefits (paid by the employer, sometimes augmented by employee contributions) are invested in a trust fund supervised by trustees. At retirement, the fund pays the now-retired employee her defined benefit or purchases an annuity contract for her to provide such periodic benefit.

Thus, for purposes of this discussion, traditional defined benefit pensions have four major characteristics as a matter of plan design. First, they provide income on a deferred basis at retirement and not before then. Second, traditional defined benefit plans provide such retirement income as periodic, annuity-type payments rather than as single lump sums. Third, traditional defined benefit plans are funded collectively, the employer's contributions being pooled in a common trust fund from which all participants receive their benefits. Finally, the defined benefit format places on the employer rather than the employee the obligation to fund the benefit promised to the participating employee. If the funds in the trust are inadequate to pay promised benefits, the employer is obligated to make up the shortfall. Thus, [the] risks associated with funding a defined benefit pension fall principally on the employer.

In all four respects, today's prototypical defined contribution plan differs. The contemporary defined contribution arrangement distributes to an employee when she leaves employment, even if she is well short of retirement age. Typically the distribution from a defined contribution plan today takes the form of a single lump sum payout of the employee's account balance rather than an annuity or other periodic distribution spread over time. By its nature, a defined contribution plan does not pool resources like a defined benefit pension but rather establishes for each participant his own individual account. Allocated to that account are the employer's contributions for the employee, the employee's own contributions (if any), and the earnings or losses generated by the investment of all those contributions. For this reason, defined contribution plans are synonymously known as individual account plans.

Since the employee's entitlement under the plan is the balance of her individual account, good investment performance redounds to the employee's benefit (because her account balance is larger), while, symmetrically, poor investment performance hurts the employee (because her account balance is smaller and the employer has no obligation to fund a defined benefit). Thus, defined contribution plans, in contradistinction to defined benefit arrangements, shift investment risk and reward from the employer to the employee.

Increasingly, defined contribution assets, while formally held in trust funds, are invested by each employee herself. Under such self-directed arrangements, the employee chooses the investments for the amounts in her individual account.

In short, the label "defined benefit," standing by itself, is in important ways incomplete. The traditional defined benefit plan specified a quite particular kind of benefit: a deferred annuity, starting at retirement, typically measured by the employee's work and salary history. Similarly, today the moniker "defined contribution" predominantly refers to a profit-sharing plan with a salary reduction (401(k)) arrangement and participant-directed investing, a plan that distributes to a participant as a lump sum upon the severance of employment (which, in a world of employee mobility, often takes place before retirement age). The shift from the defined benefit modality to the defined contribution one has altered in a fundamental manner the way in which Americans experience and think about retirement savings; simultaneously it has transformed our approach to other areas of tax and social policy.

NOTE

Many legal consequences turn upon the question of whether a plan is a defined benefit (hereafter DB) or defined contribution (hereafter DC) plan. Yet, despite its importance, the distinction is not well articulated in ERISA's definitional provisions.

ERISA § 3(34) equates the terms "individual account plan" and "defined contribution plan." ERISA mostly uses the former term, whereas in common parlance the latter is normal. Section 3(34) defines either of these terms to mean "a pension plan which provides for an individual account for each participant and for benefits based *solely* upon the [contributions, forfeitures and investment experience allocated to the] participant's account." (Emphasis added) The parallel IRC provision is § 414(i).

The statute is especially unhelpful in defining DB plans. ERISA § 3(35) says that a DB plan is "a pension plan other than an individual account plan," that is, anything but a DC plan. The parallel IRC definition is § 414(j). In ordinary usage, a DB plan is one that promises a benefit, and hence, shifts to the plan and its sponsor the responsibility for paying the benefit. However, it also includes a plan that looks like a DC plan but does not meet the statutory definition, such as a plan that maintains individual accounts (actual or notional) and credits each account with a minimum annual rate of return. This includes cash balance plans, the most common type of hybrid plan, discussed infra in section D.1. of this chapter: it would also include a plan to which actual employer contributions are credited to a real separate account for the employee, but the amount of investment earnings credited to the account is at a fixed rate, or subject to a minimum that could exceed the actual rate of return.

In addition to the defined benefit or defined contribution plans described in this chapter, which carry favorable tax treatment, a number of employers also offer nonqualified plans to certain of their highly compensated or other key employees. Nonqualified plans are discussed in Chapter 8, infra.

A. DEFINED BENEFIT PLANS

1. *Defined benefit formulas.* "Although [defined benefit plan] formulas vary considerably, they may be classified into two broad categories: unit benefit formulas and flat benefit formulas. [When] a unit benefit formula is used, the employee is credited with some specified unit of benefit for each year of service with the employer. Sometimes this benefit unit is expressed as a specific dollar amount, particularly in plans where the range of hourly wage rates among participants is relatively narrow. A more common procedure, used particularly for salaried workers, is to credit the employee with a specified percentage of compensation for each year of service. For example, the employee may earn 1.5 percentage points a year and after thirty years of service receive a benefit equal to 45 percent of preretirement compensation. Flat benefit formulas assume a variety of forms. One commonly used formula pays retirees a specified flat percentage of their earnings, usually 20 to 40 percent, regardless of their length of service. Another formula pays a flat dollar amount for each year of service. Under this type of formula a worker might accrue $150 for each year of service and after thirty years of service be entitled to an annual pension of $4,500. Finally, a small number of plans use a flat amount formula that pays the same benefit to all eligible retirees, regardless of age, service, or compensation." Alicia H. Munnell, The Economics of Private Pensions 214 (Brookings 1982).

2. *Investment risk.* DB and DC plans allocate investment risk oppositely. In a DB plan, the employer or other plan sponsor bears the risk. If the funds are invested poorly, the employer has to make up the shortfall. If the investment experience is exceptionally good, the employer's pension contributions will be reduced. Because defined benefit plans have (until recently) been the prevalent form of pension plan among large employers, it can be inferred that such employers have been willing to shoulder this risk. Why? Are there reasons why employees might also prefer to have the employer shoulder this risk?

3. *Complexity.* DB plans require actuarial calculation of future liabilities and assets, a subject discussed in Chapter 6, infra. A DC plan,

by contrast, is much simpler to administer. A DC account resembles a bank, brokerage, or mutual fund account. The participant's pension will be based on whatever happens to be in this account when he or she retires.

4. *Regulation.* ERISA's regulatory regime is centered on DB plans, which were dominant at the time the statute was enacted. It is unlikely that ERISA would have been enacted if all plans had been DC plans. Money purchase pension plans are subject to the funding rules of ERISA Title 1, Part 3; otherwise neither the funding rules nor the plan insurance scheme of Title 4 apply to DC plans. Why?

5. *The strengths of DB plans.* What factors explain the historical prevalence of DB plans among large employers? Consider the following account, from Everett Allen et al., Pension Planning: Pension, Profit Sharing, and Other Deferred Compensation Plans 48–50 (9th ed. 2003):

> This historical preference for defined benefit plans over defined contribution plans is based on many factors:
>
> 1. If an employer has specific income-replacement objectives in mind, these can be accommodated with a defined benefit plan. The defined contribution approach, on the other hand, may produce plan benefits that fail to meet or that exceed such objectives as they affect individual employees. This depends on a number of factors such as length of participation, age at retirement, inflation, investment results, and the like.
>
> 2. By the same token, most employers wish to take Social Security benefits into account so that the combined level of benefits from both sources will produce desired results. Although defined contribution plans can be integrated with social security benefits by adjusting contribution levels, integration of benefits cannot be accomplished as efficiently as under defined benefit plans.
>
> 3. The typical defined contribution plan provides that the employee's account balance is payable in the event of death and, frequently, in case of disability. This, of course, produces additional plan costs or, alternatively, lower retirement benefits if overall costs are held constant. An employer who is interested primarily in providing retirement benefits can use available funds more efficiently for this purpose under a defined benefit plan.
>
> 4. Some think a more equitable allocation of employer contributions occurs under a defined benefit plan, since the employee's age, past service, and pay may all be taken into account. Others think just the opposite, that allocations on the basis of pay only produce fairer results. This characteristic of defined contribution plans is one of the reasons they do not lend themselves to achieving consistent income-replacement objectives. It should be noted, however, that defined contribution plans can be structured with allocations weighted by age and service, thus achieving allocation patterns more consistent with those of defined benefit plans.

5. A defined benefit plan can be (and often is) structured to provide a benefit that is related to an employee's final pay, thus protecting the employee against the effects of preretirement inflation. Equivalent protection cannot be provided under a defined contribution plan. Thus, in a defined contribution plan, the risk of inflation is assumed by employees, who must rely primarily on investment results to increase the value of their benefits during inflationary periods.

6. *Superannuation policy.* As between DB and DC plans, DB plans have an advantage in facilitating the departure of workers, discussed infra in Chapter 18.

7. *Backloading.* It will be seen in Chapter 4 that a major theme of ERISA's regulation of pension plans is to restrict so-called "backloading," which is the practice of designing a plan in such a fashion that benefits accrue disproportionately toward the end of the employee's service. Notwithstanding ERISA's restrictions, for reasons discussed in Chapter 4, DB plans are intrinsically backloaded, on account of the final career average benefit formulas commonly used. Backloading promotes retention of long service employees, hence is an advantage in circumstances in which that is an objective of the employer.

8. *Eliminating moral hazard in the distribution phase.* Richard A. Ippolito, Pensions, Economics and Public Policy 30–31 (Pension Research Council 1986), observes that "annuities purchased at older ages are costly because of classic selectivity problems. People who prefer annuities tend to be those who have private information suggesting they will live to be relatively old; those expecting relatively early death will take the lump sum. Retirees with average life expectancies therefore are faced with relatively low annuities because the pool is overrepresented by people with long life expectancies. If, however, a group of individuals can commit itself early in life and penalize early-outs, the selectivity problem can be overcome and, further, group rates can be obtained."

B. DEFINED CONTRIBUTION PLANS (DC Plans)

Defined contribution (DC) plans come in greater variety than defined benefit (DB) plans, bespeaking the more varied functions of DC plans. Following are capsule accounts of the main types of DC plans. Further description will be found in various portions of this coursebook, especially in the tax materials in Part II. Useful descriptive accounts may be found elsewhere, e.g., Allen et al., Pension Planning, supra; Dan M. McGill et at, Fundamentals of Private Pensions (8th ed. 2005); Employee Benefit Research Institute, Fundamentals of Employee Benefit Programs (5th ed. 1997); and Jeffrey D. Mamorsky, Employee Benefits Handbook (6d ed. 1998). This section will introduce different types of defined contribution plans. Section C then discusses the shifting balance between defined benefit and defined contribution plans.

1. **MONEY PURCHASE PLANS** — has funding requirements based on the wages (Annuity-payout Provision) contributed

1. *Traditional money purchase plans.* The plain vanilla of DC plans is the money purchase plan. The employer or other sponsor creates the plan. The plan maintains a separate account to receive employer

— Has to offer Annuity options

contributions for each employee. The benefits to which each employee will ultimately be entitled depend exclusively upon the contribution and investment experience of his or her individual account. A money purchase plan is distinguished from a profit sharing plan in that contributions must be fixed or determinable and cannot depend upon the profits of the employer or other sponsor. Treas. Reg. § 1.401–1(b)(1)(i). Typically, the contribution formula is based on a fixed percentage of an employee's compensation, e.g., 10 percent of compensation, each year.

Unlike other DC plans, which typically make distributions in the form of a lump-sum, a money purchase plan is generally required to provide for an annuity option. Because the plan is an individual account plan, however, it typically provides for the purchase of an annuity contract from a third party provider. See McGill et al., supra, at 283.

2. *Target benefit plans.* A target benefit plan is a money purchase plan with a wrinkle in the contribution formula designed to mimic a DB plan. Contributions are made at levels meant to fund a benefit level specified in the plan (the "target"). Unlike a DB plan, however, the target benefit plan does not promise that benefit. The plan only calculates its contributions in the expectation of achieving that benefit level. As with any DC plan, the participant and not the sponsor bears the risk that the investment experience of the plan will turn out to be disappointing—in this instance, below the target.

handwritten margin note: — No Funding Requirement (dissimilar to Def. Benefit) Plan in this regard

handwritten margin note: EER calculates how much money it has to contribute to meet the Target

BUT EER does NOT have obligation to Fund if the Investment falls short

"Target benefit plans are a relatively rare type of plan design that has gained little favor among either large employers or small employers. A large employer who desires to provide a specified retirement income benefit for employees is more likely to adopt a defined benefit plan, while a small employer is more likely to opt for the simplicity of a standard defined contribution plan. A target benefit plan does make a larger annual contribution for older employees than for younger employees, a feature often coveted by small business owners, but the annual contributions to each employee's account are still [subject to the Code's limitations]." McGill, et al., supra, at 283–84.

2. PROFIT-SHARING PLANS *— handwritten:* Discretionary by Employer ??

1. *Cash vs. deferred profit-sharing plans.* A profit-sharing plan, as the name implies, is a plan that calls for contributions based on the employer's profits. A central distinction is between "cash" and "deferred" plans. A cash plan is not a retirement plan, but simply a program for basing some compensation on profits. Once profits for the relevant period (typically, the firm's fiscal year) are determined, the employees receive whatever fraction the plan provides in the form of cash (or less commonly, in the form of company shares). Such distributions are, of course, taxable income to the employees who receive them.

handwritten margin note: — Cash Plan
- CASH PROFIT SHARING (take money immediately) TAXED IMMEDIATELY
V.

A deferred profit-sharing plan, by contrast, is part of the retirement plan universe. It is a DC plan whose contributions depend upon profits, but whose other attributes resemble a money purchase plan: Individual accounts are maintained, taxation is deferred, and distribution typically occurs upon retirement. Almost always, the plan provides for lump sum distribution upon such events as disability or termination of employment. Treas. Reg. § 1.401–1(b)(1)(ii) explains: "A profit-sharing

handwritten margin note: — Deferred profit-sharing plan (do NOT take money immediately BUT instead upon Retirement

plan is a plan established and maintained by an employer to provide for the participation in his profits by his employees or their beneficiaries. The plan must provide a definite predetermined formula for allocating the contributions made to the plan among the participants and for distributing the funds accumulated under the plan after a fixed number of years, the attainment of a stated age, or upon the prior occurrence of some event such as layoff, illness, disability, retirement, death, or severance of employment. A formula for allocating the contributions among the participants is definite if, for example, it provides for an allocation in proportion to the basic compensation of each participant."

The requirement that contributions to profit-sharing plans must be made from profits was eliminated by the Tax Reform Act of 1986. Not only can contributions now be made without regard to current or accumulated profits, but also tax-exempt organizations, that is, non-profit-making entities, may sponsor profit-sharing plans. IRC § 401(a)(27). Unlike a money purchase plan, which requires a fixed or determinable formula, a profit-sharing plan is not required to have any formula at all. Many plans merely specify that the contribution will be determined annually by the board of directors. Other plans base contributions upon specific formulas, for example, "15 percent of total employee compensation, but not to exceed 5 percent of the employer's net profits" or "5 percent of net profits, but not in excess of the maximum deductible amount."

Profit-sharing plans were typically used as secondary or supplementary plans for workers already covered by basic DB plans. However, over the last 30 years, with the decline of DB plans and the emergence of 401(k) plans as the new paradigm, it has become the norm for workers to be covered only by a 401(k) plan.

Why might a firm want to tie a portion of its employees' retirement saving to the profitability of the firm? Why might employees prefer or disprefer such a plan?

2. *Stock bonus plans.* Treas.Reg. § 1.401–1(b)(1)(iii) defines a stock bonus plan as "a plan established and maintained by an employer to provide benefits similar to those of a profit-sharing plan, except that the contributions by the employer are not necessarily dependent upon profits and the benefits are distributable in stock of the employer company." Typically, contributions under a stock bonus plan are expressed as a percentage of compensation, or as a percentage of profits but not less than a certain dollar amount. Most stock bonus plans are also designated as ESOPs (see 4, below).

Employer contributions to a stock bonus plan may be made in stock or in cash; if in cash, the plan ordinarily provides for company stock to be purchased on the market for allocation to plan accounts. The Code provides that in general participants must have the right to receive plan distributions in the form of employer securities, although a cash option may be offered. However, employees may be required to take a cash distribution if the employer's "charter or bylaws restrict the ownership of substantially all outstanding employer securities to employees or to a [qualified plan]" or if the employer is an S corporation. IRC § 409(h)(2)(B)(ii).

3. 401(k) and Cash-or-Deferred Arrangements

1. *Growth in 401(k) plans.* So-called 401(k) plans have mushroomed in importance over the past three decades. The distinctive trait of the 401(k) plan is that the employee voluntarily elects to make contributions (on either a pre-tax or a Roth basis) to his or her account in the plan. Most employers devise plans in which the employer matches the employee's contributions, commonly with a match rate of 50 percent, usually up to a ceiling such as five or six percent of compensation.

"A qualified cash or deferred arrangement [CODA], under section 401(k) of the Internal Revenue Code (IRC), allows an employee to elect to have a portion of his or her compensation (otherwise payable in cash) contributed to a qualified retirement plan. The employee contribution is treated not as current income, but most commonly as a pretax reduction in salary, which is then paid into the plan by the employer on behalf of the employee. [The] employee defers income tax on the 401(k) plan contribution until the time of withdrawal." EBRI, Fundamentals of Employee Benefit Programs, supra, at 93. The tax treatment of 401(k) plans is discussed in Chapters 8–11, infra.

Although there were some cash or deferred profit-sharing plans in effect before ERISA, for practical purposes these plans entered the DC plan universe in the early 1980s, after the Revenue Act of 1978 added IRC § 401(k) and proposed regulations issued in November 1981 effected the present regime of tax deferral. The use of 401(k) plans has since burgeoned. Census Bureau data indicate that 47 percent of fulltime private wage and salary workers participated in 401(k) plans in 1993, compared to 3 percent in 1983. "401(k) Participation Balloons Since '83," Pensions & Investments, Jun. 13, 1994, at 16. Between 1984 and 1998, "all dimensions of 401(k) plans increased dramatically, rising from 25–35 percent of the defined contribution totals to 70–80%." Alicia H. Munnell and Annika Sunden, Coming Up Short: The Challenge of 401(k) Plans 18 (2004). "In 2008, 49.8 million American workers were active 401(k) plan participants. By year-end 2008, 401(k) plan assets had grown to represent 16 percent of all retirement assets, amounting to $2.3 trillion." Jack VanDerHei et al., 401(k) Plan Asset Allocation, Account Balances, and Loan Activity in 2008, EBRI Issue Brief No. 335, at 5 (Oct. 2009). See also EBRI, History of 401(k) Plans: An Update, Facts from EBRI (2005), at 3 (at the end of 2003, 438,000 401(k) plans were in effect).

Several factors appear to have driven the popularity of 401(k) plans:

(1) The transparency of the employer match feature is attractive to the employer, because it permits participating employees to see and to value the employer's contributions on a current basis.

(2) Because employee participation is voluntary, employees who do not wish to engage in pension saving will not participate, hence will not receive the employer match. Accordingly, the employer may be able to lower its aggregate pension costs while still offering pension coverage to the workforce. Because higher earning employees are more likely to elect to participate in a 401(k) plan, this feature of voluntary employee participation puts such plans in tension with the

antidiscrimination norm of pension taxation, discussed in Chapter 9, infra.

(3) Workers whose employment patterns are more episodic or mobile may prefer 401(k) plans, because such workers do not stay with an employer long enough to get the big payoff from the final career average benefit formulas characteristic of defined benefit plans. This topic is discussed in Section E of Chapter 4, infra, treating portability.

(4) 401(k) plans, like all DC plans, allocate investment experience to the account, hence to the employee rather than to the employer. Accordingly, these plans have allowed employees to reap some of the rewards of the great bull market in the securities markets that lasted from 1982 to 2000. Because 401(k) plans developed late, participants have until lately had little experience with the corollary, that in falling markets investment losses incide on the employee. "Looking at consistent participants in the EBRI/ICI 401(k) database over the five-year period from 2003 to 2008 (which included one of the worst bear markets for stocks since the Great Depression), [an EBRI] study found:

- After rising in 2003 and for the next four consecutive years, the average 401(k) retirement account fell 24.3 percent in 2008.

- The average 401(k) account balance moved up and down with stock market performance, but over the entire five-year time period increased at an average annual growth rate of 7.2 percent, attaining $86,513 at year-end 2008.

- The median (mid-point) 401(k) account balance increased at an average annual growth rate of 11.4 percent over the 2003–2008 period to $43,700 at year-end 2008." VanDerHei et al., supra.

A more recent study found that the average account balance of consistent 401(k) participants increased at a compound annual average growth rate of 6.8 percent from 2007 to 2012, to $107,053 at year-end 2012. The median 401(k) account balance increased at a compound annual average growth rate of 11.9 percent over the period, to $49,814 at year-end 2012. VanDerhei, Holden, Alonso & Bass, What Does Consistent Participation in 401(k) Plans Generate? Changes in 401(k) Account Balances, 2007–2012, EBRI Issue Brief No. 402, July, 2014.

(5) Again in common with all DC plans, 401(k) plans escape the administrative and regulatory costs associated with DB plans. DC plans are excluded from the plan termination insurance system of ERISA Title IV, discussed infra in Chapter 6, hence they escape the annual premium, a minimum of $57 (for 2015) per plan participant per year. ERISA § 4006(a)(3)(A)(i). The administrative and regulatory compliance costs of DB plans make such plans uneconomic for most small employers, the sector that has been responsible for much of the employment growth since the 1990s.

(6) Because the employee is the owner of his or her own pension account under a 401(k) or other DC plan, the employer has less interest in how benefits are distributed, whereas under a DB plan the employer can lower its costs by mandating annuitization. Thus, DC plans do not have the same insistence as DB plans on annuitization as the only or the predominant mode of distribution and 401(k) plans are much more likely to allow plan loans and lump sum distributions. These features allow the employee to treat his or her interest in the plan, at least in part, as a mere tax-favored savings account, as opposed to a pure retirement plan, and lead to two concerns: that the employee will use the funds to meet current needs, rather than preserving them for retirement, and that the funds remaining at retirement will be insufficient to last for the employee's lifetime.

(7) Recent stock market volatility and very low interest rates have increased the funding requirements of many defined benefit plans. For many employers, the unpredictability of future funding requirements is unacceptable. In addition, many employers today, even very large employers, are unwilling to make the long term commitments associated with a defined benefit plan.

Initially 401(k) plans were regarded as supplementary plans, that is, tax-deferred savings vehicles for employees who wished to do additional saving for retirement. In recent years, however, especially among smaller employers, there has been a tendency to offer the 401(k) plan as the only retirement plan. The 401(k) plan thus displaces traditional DB plans, both by encouraging the termination of DB plans (especially smaller ones), and by attracting into the 401(k) mode some new plan formation that would have taken DB form. See Leslie E. Papke, Are 401(k) Plans Replacing Other Employer-Provided Pensions? Evidence from Panel Data, National Bureau of Economic Research Working Paper 5736 (Aug. 1996).

2. *Participation and savings rates.* The 401(k) plan puts the decision whether to participate in the plan in the hands of the employee. In 2001, 26% of employees eligible to participate in 401(k) plans did not participate. Munnell & Sunden, supra, at 56. Both earnings and age affect an employee's decision to participate. Not surprisingly, lower income employees are less likely to participate in a 401(k) plan. "Among workers with earnings between $20,000 and $40,000, only about half are eligible to join the plan; among those eligible, 70% participate. Among workers earning more than $40,000, two out of three are eligible and 80% or more participate." Munnell & Sunken, supra, at 56–57.

Although accumulating sufficient retirement assets in a 401(k) plan is much easier the earlier an employee begins contributing, younger employees are less likely to participate. "Fewer than half of workers aged twenty to forty with earnings below $20,000 choose to participate in a 401(k) plan. Even for workers with salaries close to average ($20,000–$40,000), participation rates are low. It is not until workers approach age 50 that participation rates are similar to those for high-income workers. [A] worker who postpones participation until age fifty will have only 26 percent of the retirement wealth of a similar worker who participated since age thirty." Munnell & Sunden, supra, at 57.

Workers who do participate in 401(k) plans don't always contribute enough to accumulate sufficient retirement savings. Only about five percent of participants contribute the maximum amount permitted under the Code. See Joseph A. Pechman, Hearing Testimony before the House Education and the Workforce Committee, Strengthening Defined Benefit Pension Plans, Feb. 25, 2004; John C. Goodman & Peter Orszag, Retirement Savings Reforms on Which the Left and Right Can Agree, National Center for Policy Analysis Brief No. 495 (Dec. 1, 2004) at 1. Thus, 95 percent of the 401(k) workforce does not maximize the income tax deferral that such plans allow. The maximum deferral for 2015 is $18,000 ($24,000 for an employee aged 50 or older): many employees simply cannot afford to forego this much current income, despite the associated reduction in income taxes.

In an effort to increase employee participation, a number of employers have shifted to automatic enrollment (sometimes called "autopilot") plans, placing an affirmative burden on the employee to opt out in order to escape participating rather than requiring the employee to enroll in order to participate. As further discussed in Chapter 9, automatic enrollment plans do increase plan participation, although they do not materially increase aggregate plan savings, because participants who are automatically enrolled tend to retain the low default contribution rate and the conservative default asset allocation established by the plan sponsor. However, "[g]iven that the lowest income workers have the lowest participation rates prior to automatic enrollment, they appear to have the most to gain and indeed the median replacement rate is 61 percent higher at retirement for the lowest-income quartile after the introduction of automatic enrollment." Retirement Income Security: A Look at Social Security, Employment-Based Retirement Plans, and Health Savings Accounts, EBRI Notes, Aug. 2005, at 5.

Some employers have attempted further to increase savings by including a contribution escalation provision, which allows workers automatically to increase plan contributions over time. According to a 2005 Hewitt Associates survey of large employers, the number of employers offering such plans increased from three to 20 percent between 2003 and 2005. Hewitt Associates, Hewitt Study Shows More Companies Putting 401(k) Plans on Autopilot, Hewitt News & Information, Jun. 14, 2005 (also reporting a substantial increase in the number of plans providing for automatic enrollment). The Pension Protection Act of 2006 encourages automatic enrollment and contribution escalation provisions by exempting "qualified automatic contribution arrangements" from the normal 401(k) nondiscrimination requirements. PPA § 920, enacting IRC §§ 401(k)(13), 401(m)(12). These provisions are discussed infra, in Section E.7 of Chapter 9.

3. *Investment risk and investment decisions.* As with all DC plans, 401(k) plans place investment risk on the employee, since the employer makes no promise to pay any particular level of benefits. The employer or other plan sponsor arranges for investment alternatives to be offered to the plan participants; the fiduciary rules of ERISA § 404(c) and

associated DoL regulations (discussed in Chapter 14, infra) structure this process. Thereafter, the plan participant makes his or her own investment selections. A typical 401(k) plan offers a range of stock and bond portfolios from one or more investment providers, such as mutual fund companies, banks, and insurance companies. The plan may also offer employer stock, an option that has generated a significant amount of litigation of late, as discussed infra in Chapter 14.

Whereas the responsibility for investment policy in a DB plan rests with the employer's financial officers and their expert advisers, in a 401(k) plan workers who often have no financial sophistication make important elections about the investment of their individual accounts among an increasingly large number of investment options. "The fear of making the wrong decision increases with the number of choices and often paralyzes people. Many workers also lack knowledge to make complicated financial decisions. The result appears to be that participants in general follow simple investment strategies and end up with either too much or too little stock in their portfolios. And once they have made a decision on how to allocate their funds they rarely change. [This] means that many participants are at risk for ending up with unacceptably low retirement income." Munnell & Sunden, supra at 94. Not surprisingly, DC plans experience inferior investment returns compared to DB plans. Id. at 75. The problems with participant direction of investments are discussed in more detail infra in Section C of Chapter 14.

The presence of an employer stock fund as a 401(k) plan investment option creates a particular risk, magnifying the underdiversification that inheres in having one's human capital tied to the employer. As discussed in Chapter 14, infra, although ERISA generally requires diversification in pension plans, participant-directed 401(k) plans are expressly exempted from the diversification requirement.

EBRI data drawn from a large sample of 401(k) plans indicate that at year-end 2012, on average, 61 percent of 401(k) participants' assets were invested in equity securities through equity funds, the equity portion of balanced funds, and company stock. Thirty-three percent was in fixed-income securities such as stable-value investments and bond and money funds. Among individual participants, the allocation of account balances to equities varies widely. VanDerHei et al., 401(k) Plan Asset Allocation, Account Balances, and Loan Activity in 2012, EBRI Issue Brief, Dec. 2013. Thirty-six percent of the participants were in plans that offered company stock as an investment option. Among these participants, 76 percent held 20 percent or less of their account balances in company stock, including 54 percent who held none. 7 percent had more than 80 percent of their account balances invested in company stock. Id.

The danger of excessive holdings of company stock was dramatically demonstrated in the Enron debacle in 2001. At the end of 2000, 62% of Enron's 401(k) plan assets were invested in Enron common stock. Patrick Purcell, The Enron Bankruptcy and Employer Stock Retirement Plans, CRS Report for Congress, Jan. 22, 2002, at p.3. Employees saw their account balances fall 98.8% in value during 2001, thus depriving them of their retirement security at the same time that they were losing their jobs. Notwithstanding the publicity surrounding the fall of Enron, employees at many companies still have large percentages of their 401(k) assets in company stock. Litigation arising over 401(k) plan investments in company stock is discussed in Chapter 14, section D, infra. For discussions of the problems of excessive 401(k) plan holdings of company stock, see Susan J. Stabile, Another Look at 401(k) Plan Investments in Employer Securities, 35 J. Marshall L. Rev. 815 (2002); Colleen E. Medill, The Individual Responsibility Model of Retirement Plans Today: Conforming ERISA Policy to Reality, 49 Emory L.J. 1 (2000); Susan J. Stabile, Pension Plan Investments in Employer Securities: More is Not Always Better, 15 Yale J. Regulation 61 (1998).

Other ramifications of having individual employees serve as their own investment managers are also discussed infra in Chapter 14. Is ERISA wise to excuse 401(k) plans, ESOPs, and certain other DC plans from the diversification and the anti-self-dealing norms of ERISA fiduciary law, which would otherwise prevent excessive holdings of employer stock?

4. ESOPs — *good wealth preservation tool*

Section 4975(e)(7) of the IRC defines an employee stock ownership plan (ESOP) as a stock bonus plan, or a combination of a stock bonus plan and a money purchase plan, "designed to invest primarily in qualifying employer securities," which are defined in IRC § 409(l). See also ERISA 407(d)(6). An ESOP is ordinarily "leveraged," meaning that it borrows from the employer (or from another lender, usually on the employer's credit by means of a guarantee) to buy employer securities. ESOP assets are held in trust and managed by a trustee, who is usually selected by the employer.

- Favorable tax consequences to owner

- Good Dividends for owner + employees
- EER would make contributions to it each year
(+ this pays down the security note)

ESOPs are exempt from some of the rules of pension fiduciary law that are discussed in Part III of this book. An ESOP need not diversify investments. ERISA § 404(a)(2). An ESOP can purchase securities from the employer or other parties in interest such as major shareholders, or borrow money from such persons for those purposes, without offending the prohibited transaction rules. ERISA § 408(e), (b)(3); IRC § 4975(d)(3), (13).

McGill et al. explain how ESOPs function:

A simple ESOP (not leveraged) functions very much like a profit sharing plan. The amount of contributions may be based on a formula or determined at the employer's discretion. A formula may be based on profits or the compensation of participants. The contribution commitment is often expressed as a flat percentage of covered compensation. . . .

Contributions to an ESOP may be made in cash or in employer securities. If contributions are made in cash, part or all of the cash is used to purchase stock, either from the employer or in the market. Stock and any contributions not applied to purchase stock are allocated to employee accounts. Any dividends on the stock may be paid in cash to participants or may be used as additional contributions to buy more shares to be added to employee accounts. . . .

[Under] a leveraged ESOP, the trustee of the trust created under the plan arranges for a loan from a lending institution and uses the loan to purchase employer stock. The employer stock acquired is held by the trustee and gradually allocated to participants as cash contributions are made on their behalf under the plan. The stock is pledged as collateral for the loan, which is customarily also guaranteed by the employer or some other party. Since the trust cannot generate income on its own other than dividends on the stock, the employer corporation or other outside party is usually required to guarantee the loan.

The loan, including interest, is repaid by the trustee from the cash contributions of the employer, and the plan generally requires the employer to contribute an amount sufficient to repay the loan. As loan payments reduce the principal of the loan, part of the stock is released as collateral for the loan. The plan commonly provides for allocations of the stock to employees as the stock is released as collateral.

McGill, et al., supra, at 299–300.

Why would the employer want to engage in a leveraged ESOP such as that just described? The answer is found in the tax treatment of leveraged ESOPs. "The ESOP can borrow money to purchase employer stock on the market, but more typically from the firm or from firm insiders (due to an exception from the prohibited transaction rules). The loan is secured by the stock, which is allocated to participant accounts as the loan is repaid. The loan is generally repaid with employer contributions to the ESOP, which are deductible." Norman P. Stein, An Alphabet Soup Agenda for Reform of the Internal Revenue Code and ERISA Provisions Applicable to Qualified Deferred Compensation Plans, 56 S.M.U. L. Rev. 627, 646–47 (2003). Another tax benefit associated with the ESOP is that the employer "gets an immediate tax deduction for stock contributions to the ESOP, even though the stock is treasury stock and has no immediate cash cost to the employer." Id. at 647.

On the other hand, "[w]hile there are many business reasons for establishing an ESOP, there are also business reasons for not establishing one. In particular, [the] applicable ERISA fiduciary responsibility rules can cause a privately owned company to become subject to the type of scrutiny which is ordinarily reserved for publicly held companies." Roger C. Siske, "Employee Stock Ownership Plans," in ALI-ABA Pension Policy Invitational Conference Materials 171, 178 (1991).

Can you reconcile the ESOP with the predominant purposes of the private pension system? In answering the question, consider the fate of the employees of United Airlines. When United went bankrupt, its employees owned 55% of the company's equity through an ESOP. See Jeffrey N. Gordon, Proceedings: Employee Stock Ownership after Enron, 7 Empl. Rts. & Employ. Pol'y J 213, 227 (2003). Because of the risks they impose, ESOPs should not be viewed as a sole or primary source of retirement income. Indeed, ESOPs are best understood as a medium of corporate finance, somewhat quixotically entangled with the world of pension plans.

The present coursebook gives only passing attention to ESOPs. However, be aware that ESOPs have been trenchantly criticized on a variety of policy grounds. See, e.g., Michael W. Melton, Demythologizing ESOPs, 45 Tax L. Rev. 363 (1990); Richard L. Doernberg & Jonathan R. Macey, ESOPs and Economic Distortion, 23 Harvard J. Legislation 103 (1986); D. Bret Carlson, ESOPs and Universal Capitalism, 31 Tax L. Rev. 289 (1976); Andrew Stumpff Morrison and Norman P. Stein, Repeal Tax Incentives for ESOPs, Tax Notes, Vol. 125, No. 3, pp. 337–340, October 19, 2009.

ESOPs are connected to a deeper set of issues about the rationale for employee ownership of enterprise. Why do employees tend to own law firms but not, say, companies that manufacture automobiles or operate supermarket chains? See especially Henry Hansmann, The Ownership of Enterprise 66ff (1996); Henry Hansmann, When Does Worker Ownership Work? ESOPs, Law Firms, Codetermination, and Economic Democracy, 99 Yale L.J. 1749 (1990); compare Alan Hyde, In Defense of Employee Ownership, 67 Chicago-Kent L. Rev. 159 (1991); see generally Understanding Employee Ownership (C. Rosen & K.M. Young, eds.) (1991); The Expanding Role of ESOPs in Public Companies (K.M. Young, ed.) (1990).

5. 403(b) PLANS

Under IRC § 403(b), certain tax-exempt organizations and educational institutions are allowed to offer plans which, like 401(k) plans, generally include a salary reduction feature. The employer and the participant contribute to the participant's DC account, which is invested. At retirement, the proceeds are used to purchase annuities for the account owner and his or her spouse, unless another form of distribution is elected. The distribution options are discussed in Chapter 11, infra. Many such employers use TIAA-CREF, the college teachers' pension fund, as the annuity provider and many also offer employees the option, authorized under IRC § 403(b)(7), to invest their accounts wholly or partially in mutual funds. A 403(b) plan resembles a 401(k) plan in that the employer commonly matches employee contributions up to a ceiling. Some 403(b) plans make the employee's participation in the plan a condition of employment. The tax treatment of 403(b) plans, which are not qualified plans but are taxed in the same fashion, is discussed in Chapter 8, infra.

6. HEALTH ACCOUNTS

So prevalent has the defined contribution concept become that it has begun to spill over from pension plans to welfare benefit plans, in the form of the health savings account (HSA). HSAs are discussed further in Chapter 19.

7. INDIVIDUAL RETIREMENT ACCOUNTS (IRA)

Individual retirement accounts (IRAs) resemble DC plans, but fall outside the qualified plan regime of IRC § 401(a). Most IRAs are established and maintained by individuals, not by employers and so are not covered by ERISA. ERISA § 3(2). Those IRAs that are employer-sponsored (under IRC § 408(c), 408(k) (simplified employee pensions) or 408(p) (SIMPLE IRAs)) are exempt from many of ERISA's substantive rules. The IRC regulates IRAs under § 408. Congress created IRAs in 1974, as part of the ERISA package. IRAs were originally limited to persons who were not covered under employer-sponsored qualified plans. IRA participants were allowed to contribute on a tax-deductible basis the lesser of $1,500 or 15 percent of earnings. See Russell K. Osgood, Qualified Pension and Profit-Sharing Plan Vesting: Revolution Not Reform, 59 Boston U.L.Rev. 452, 465–69 (1979).

In 1981 the Economic Recovery Tax Act (ERTA) raised the contribution ceiling to $2,000 and allowed all workers to make tax-deductible contributions up to that amount, even if the worker was also covered under an employer-sponsored plan. "The Tax Reform Act of 1986 (TRA) retained tax-deductible IRAs for those families in which neither spouse was covered by an employment-based pension but restricted the tax deduction among those with pension coverage to families with incomes below specified levels. IRC § 219(g). In addition, TRA '86 added two new categories of IRA contributions: nondeductible contributions, which accumulate tax free until distributed; and partially deductible contributions, which are deductible up to a maximum amount less than the maximum contribution otherwise allowable." EBRI, Fundamentals of Employee Benefit Programs, *supra*, at 163.

"Twenty-three percent of workers ages 21–64 owned an IRA at the end of 2005, an increase from 15.9 percent in 1996. We know IRA ownership increases with family income and age: Among workers with annual family income of $10,000–$19,999, 8.3 percent owned an IRA, compared to 35.1 percent of those with family income above $75,000. We also know education is a more striking indicator: 2.7 percent of those without a high school diploma have an IRA, compared to 46.5 percent of those with a graduate degree." Dallas Salisbury, Employee Benefit Research Institute, Statement for the House Ways and Means Committee, Select Revenue Measures Subcommittee, The Role of Individual Retirement Accounts (IRAs) in the U.S. Retirement System, June 26, 2008.

IRAs and qualified plans overlap in the area of the "rollover IRA." **Rollover IRA** The participant in a qualified plan who takes an eligible rollover distribution for any reason (commonly, on termination of employment with the plan sponsor) may receive a direct rollover of the account balance from the qualified plan to the rollover IRA, or may receive the distribution and then make a rollover within 60 days of the date of the distribution. A direct rollover avoids taxation of the account balance— the rolled over sum remains tax deferred in the rollover IRA. An indirect rollover requires the plan to withhold 20% of the distribution for federal income tax [IRC § 3405(c)], so complete tax deferral is possible only if the participant can make up the withheld funds from other sources.

Assets held in IRAs "more than quadrupled" in the decade 1990 to 2000, from $640 billion in 1990 to $2.65 trillion in 2000. Vinette Anand, IRAs Now Nation's Top Source of Private Retirement Assets, Pensions & Investments, Apr. 1, 2002, at p.1. Total IRA assets at June 30, 2014 were $7.2 trillion, up from $4.75 trillion at the end of 2007. By contrast, defined contribution (401(k)-type) plans held $6.6 trillion, and private-sector defined benefit plans held $3.2 trillion. IRA growth continues to be fueled by rollovers from other types of retirement plans, not new contributions. Investment Company Institute, Retirement Assets Total $24.0 Trillion in Second Quarter 2014, http://www.limra.com/Secure_Retirement_ Institute/News_Center/Retirement_Industry_Report/Retirement_Plans_- _Investment_Company_Institute__Retirement_Assets_on_the_Rise_in_ 2014.aspx.

The Taxpayer Relief Act of 1997 created a new type of IRA, the "Roth IRA." There are a number of differences between traditional IRAs and Roth IRAs; most importantly, contributions to Roth IRAs are nondeductible, and distributions are generally untaxed. Roth IRAs are governed by IRC § 408A. Contribution limits and other aspects of IRAs and Roth IRAs are discussed in Chapter 8, infra.

[Handwritten margin note: Roth IRA — Contributions to Roth IRA are NonDeductible — Distributions are Untaxed]

C. THE CHANGING BALANCE BETWEEN DEFINED BENEFIT AND DEFINED CONTRIBUTION PLANS

Into the mid 1980s the DB plan was the norm of American pension practice. Outside the world of educational and eleemosynary employment, where § 403(b) plans have long been the prevalent type of retirement plan, DB plans were the prototype. Over the past quarter century the use of 401(k) plans has burgeoned. As of 2001, "[f]orty-seven percent of families with a worker between the ages of 21 and 64 included someone who participated in a defined contribution plan [whereas] only 25% of families included at least one worker who was covered by a defined benefit [plan]." Patrick J. Purcell, Retirement Savings and Household Wealth: A Summary of Recent Data, CRS Report for Congress, Dec. 11, 2003, at p.3. Between 1992 and 2001, "the share of households with pension coverage that relies solely on a defined contribution plan increased from 37 percent to 58 percent. At the same time, the share of households with only a defined benefit plan dropped from about 40 percent to 19 percent. About 23 percent of households had dual coverage." Munnell and Sunden, supra, at 21. By 2007, "approximately 21 million workers in the private sector participated in defined benefit plans, while more than 40 million workers participated in defined contribution plans." Patrick J. Purcell, Retirement Savings and Household Wealth in 2007, CRS Report for Congress, Apr. 8, 2009, Summary.

The number of DB plans declined from 114,000 in 1985 to 31,200 in 2004. Gregory Crawford & Vineeta Anand, The Looming Retirement Disaster, Pensions & Investments, Apr. 18, 2005, at p.1. The Pension Benefit Guaranty Corporation (PBGC), which insures DB plans, covered more than 110,000 single-employer plans in 1985. Id. "By the beginning of 2006, PBGC insured only 28,923 single-employer plans, just a quarter of the number it insured in 1985. (See Figure 1.) More than 85 percent of this decline was among small plans, plans with fewer than 100 participants. PBGC, Pension Insurance Data Book, 2008, at 2–3. Very few employers are creating new DB plans, and many existing plans have either been terminated or have been closed to new employees. Vineeta Anand, 1 in 5 Corporations Freeze DB Plans, Pensions & Investments, Apr. 5, 2004, at p.3 (citing Aon Consulting survey finding that 21% of

1000 large pension plans were frozen to newcomers between 2001 and 2003).

At June 30, 2014, of $24 trillion in total retirement plan assets, only 13% was in private sector DB plans, compared to 30% in IRAs and 27.5% in DC plans. Investment Company Institute, Retirement Assets Total $24.0 Trillion in Second Quarter 2014, http://www.limra.com/Secure_Retirement_Institute/News_Center/Retirement_Industry_Report/Retire ment_Plans_-_Investment_Company_Institute__Retirement_Assets_ on_the_Rise_in_2014.aspx.

What are the causes and what will be the consequences of the trend towards DC plans? Consider the following evaluations:

1. THE EMPLOYMENT RELATIONSHIP

Steven Sass, Crisis in Pensions
Regional Review 13, 14–16 (Federal Reserve Bank of Boston) (Spr. 1993).

[In the essay extracted here, the author uses the terms "pension plan," "employer pension," or "pension" for what is technically the defined benefit plan, and he uses the term "retirement savings plan" for the defined contribution plan.—Eds.]

Pension plans are creatures of large, long-lived organizations. The bulk of those enrolled in pension programs thus work for governments or giant corporations, or belong to similarly large and long-lived unions. Such organizations use pensions as a performance bond to define a long-term employment relation. They hold back a piece of the compensation stream, invest it through a pension fund, and pay out an old-age annuity upon final receipt of a proper career.

Pensions are especially adept at keeping middle-aged employees in harness. Such workers are old enough to appreciate the benefit, but young enough to have viable options in the labor market. [In] the 1980s, however, [powerful] economic shocks created an environment distinctly hostile to traditional pension sponsors. Global competition undercut the position of U.S. mass production industries, like steel, autos, and rubber, which were bastions of pension provision. Continuous technological jolts likewise destabilized old-line corporation businesses. They obsolesced tiers of career middle managers and drove the mercurial rise and fall of small and mid-sized firms. Employment in firms with more than 10,000 workers fell from roughly 29 to 25 percent of the work force between 1979 and 1988; government employment went from 19 percent to 17 percent; and partly because of declines in these sectors, union membership plummeted from 27 to 17 percent of the work force. [As of 2004, union membership had declined further to 12.5 percent of the total work force, and to 7.9 percent of the private sector work force. See Very Old Labor, Wall St. J., Jul. 26, 2005, at A24.—Eds.]

Smaller firms are much less likely to promise lifetime tenures. To compensate workers with a distant pension, commencing long after the employment relationship ends, would strike employers and their employees as odd. Nor can small firms generally bear the risks. [As] large, long-lived organizations lost their labor market grip, so did participation in the pension system. An estimated 43 percent of all nonagricultural employees were earning credits toward an employer pension in 1979. By 1988, the figure had fallen to 33 percent. Retirement savings plans meanwhile grew rapidly and compensated, in part, for the pension fall-off. These plans enjoy tax advantages much like pensions: contributions to worker accounts escape taxation, investment income accumulates tax-free, and taxes are levied only when funds are paid out. For many workers and employers, these savings plans are elbowing out pensions as their primary retirement program.

Even the largest firms are shifting their focus from pensions to retirement savings plans. The reason is the collapse of the career employment model. The nation's giant corporations, having gone through wrenching layoffs, project uncertain and volatile long-term demands for labor. They want flexibility in layoffs and hires. [Pensions], as instruments of long-term stability, run counter to this objective. Pension plans penalize leavers (only those who stay see their benefits rise with inflation and real salary gains). And they deter firms from hiring middle-aged workers (old-age allowances are far more costly as the time-to-retirement shrinks and funds have fewer years to accumulate investment income).

Some large employers are actually coming to view the savings plan as their primary retirement [program]. This setup suits the emerging model of corporate employment—one of abbreviated careers and tenures. . . .

The ebb of large enterprise and career employment has undermined management's interest in pensioning off its work force. Most of the money in the popular 401(k)s, for example, thus comes from participants themselves. . . . The reshaped system serves employers reasonably well. . . . Retirement savings plans are in many ways quite serviceable for workers. [They] are far better suited than pensions to today's high rate of job mobility. When workers leave a firm, the dollar amount of their future pension is calculated based on their current salary. Under even moderate rates of inflation, the value of a string of pensions, from a string of former employers, will shrivel up quite quickly. The value of a savings account balance, by contrast, is unaffected by a change of employers. Assuming all firms offer comparable plans, a worker's final accumulation will be the same whether employed by one firm or ten.

Savings schemes, however, have problems of their own. Unlike accumulations in a pension fund, the assets in these plans are allocated to individual accounts, and workers tend to view them much like a balance in a bank. They try periodically to tap the money—perhaps to buy a boat, perhaps to send the kids to college. Employers have little reason to bar the door; indeed, flexibility makes the plan more attractive. So some experts fear workers will spend these funds well before retirement.

To get an adequate old-age income out of these programs, workers must also save early, vigorously, and well. . . . to capture the exponential magic of compound interest, the long campaign needs to start more quickly and capture heftier rates of return. The young are noticeably absent and set aside far less than their elders. . . .

A more difficult problem . . . is that workers, individually, bear all the risk. They absorb the hit should financial markets crumble or inflation surge—both of which happened in the 1970s. They also run the risk of living too long and exhausting their savings. [In] pension plans, these financial and mortality risks are pooled, thereby reduced, and borne by parties better able to absorb such shocks—employers and the PBGC.

In retirement savings plans, reducing these risks will not be easy. Workers can protect themselves from outliving their assets by buying annuities—insurance company contracts paying a fixed sum of money for the rest of their lives. But annuities tend to be expensive. Marketing costs are high and insurers (rightly) assume "adverse selection"—that the long-lived among us are the primary buyers. Annuities, moreover, generally are fixed-dollar payments exposed to inflation. (Employers often make ad hoc improvements to pension allowances that partially keep pace with price-level changes.)

2.   INTERGENERATIONAL WEALTH TRANSFER

John H. Langbein, Social Security and the Pension System

In Search of Retirement Security (Teresa Ghilarducci et al. eds.) (2004).

The private pension system is only incidentally about retirement income. To be sure, private pension plans do and will deliver retirement income to many participants, but in its larger dimension the system is best understood as part of a group of tax shelters that are designed to abate the progressivity of the income tax for the affluent. . . .

More and more of the wealth that is channeled through private pension accounts is being accumulated not for the purpose of providing retirement income but for discretionary savings and for intergenerational wealth transfer to children and grandchildren. The use of pension accounts as tax-favored savings, investment, and wealth transmission devices is possible only in a defined contribution system, in which the participant builds an individual account whose unexpended proceeds can be accessed for nonretirement purposes or left to transferees. In a 401(k) or 403(b) plan or an IRA, the participant can cash out in whole or in part at any time (free of penalty after age fifty-nine and a half). If the participant or spouse leaves unexpended proceeds at death, the minimum distribution rules allow heirs or other transferees to perpetuate the tax shelter for many years as they draw down the account. These attributes of individual account plans have been a major attraction in the notable shift from defined benefit to defined contribution plans that has been going on in the private system over the past two decades. Defined benefit plans typically pay retirement income only, and only for the participant and spouse. If they die early, the shortening of the payment obligation benefits the plan sponsor, not the heirs.

The very term "pension plan" is increasingly a misnomer for defined contribution plans. They are in truth multipurpose savings, investment, and wealth transmission vehicles for the tax-sensitive classes.

D. HYBRID PLANS

[handwritten: –have hypothetical "account balances" –combination of Defined Benefit + Defined Contribution.]

Hybrid retirement plans contain features of both DB and DC plans. Sometimes a DC plan mimics features of a DB plan, sometimes a DB plan takes on attributes of a DC plan.

1. CASH BALANCE PLANS AND PENSION EQUITY PLANS

The decline of the career employment model and the increasing preference for defined contribution plans has induced many firms with longstanding conventional defined benefit plans to amend their plans in order to convert them to so-called "cash balance" plans. As the executive director of PBGC wrote in 1999, "Non-traditional plans, such as cash balance plans, are the only defined benefit plans that are selling in today's market. They're selling because-by combining some of the best features of both defined benefit and defined contribution plans-they better meet the needs of many of today's employers and workers. . . . Hybrid plans, such as cash balance plans, are key to strengthening and expanding the current defined benefit pension system." David M. Strauss in the September/October, 1999, issue of Contingencies.

[handwritten left margin: Cash Benefit Plans] A cash balance plan is a defined benefit plan that provides a benefit that largely mimics the account balance of a defined contribution plan. The recent trend toward cash balance plans began in 1985, when the Bank of America replaced its traditional defined benefit plan with a cash balance plan. Regarding that event and the surrounding circumstances, see "How a Single Sentence By IRS Paved the Way to Cash-Balance Plans," Wall St. J., Dec. 28, 1999, at A1, A6. Despite legal uncertainties, the number of cash balance plans has continued to increase. 9,648 new cash balance plans were created from 2001 through 2012. Cash balance plans now make up 25% of all defined benefit plans, up from 2.9% in 2001. Kravitz National Cash Balance Research Report, www.cashbalancedesign.com. In May, 2009, Watson Wyatt reported that, for the first time, more Fortune 100 companies offered hybrid pension plans rather than traditional defined benefit plans and this trend has continued. See Towers Watson, Defined Contribution Plans of Fortune 100 Companies in 2013. http://www.towers watson.com/en/Insights/Newsletters/Americas/Insider/2015/02/defined-contribution-plans-of-fortune-100-companies-in-2013.

[handwritten left margin: –hypothetical account balance for each account balance] Under a cash balance plan, each participant has a hypothetical account balance. Amounts are credited to the account on a monthly or annual basis according to a formula specified in the plan. The formula has two components. First, a contribution is treated as having been made, calculated on the participant's compensation. For example, each month the plan might credit each participant's account with an amount equal to 8 percent of the participant's compensation for that month. Second, each account is credited with interest, typically on a monthly basis. The interest rate is specified by the plan. It can be a fixed rate, but more often it is tied to a market rate, such as that of 30-year Treasury bonds.

The retirement benefit of a cash balance plan is simply the amount of this hypothetical account balance at normal retirement age, payable in a lump sum if the participant (and spouse) elect, otherwise in the form of an actuarially equivalent annuity. An employee who terminates prior to retirement age may elect to leave his or her balance in the plan and continue to accrue the specified interest rate until distribution. From the employee's perspective, the cash balance plan seems much like a money purchase defined contribution plan. But in reality the account is merely a bookkeeping device, unrelated to the underlying plan assets. The interest rate specified in the plan might be 6 percent in a given year, but the underlying assets (invested in a diversified portfolio of equities, bonds, real estate, and the like) might be earning far more (or less). Since a cash-balance plan is a defined benefit plan, the employer bears the risk and reward of investment returns. When the investment return on plan assets exceeds the interest rate assumption, the employer's cost under a cash balance plan will be lower than an equivalent money purchase plan with the same formula for additions to the participant's accounts.

Virtually all cash balance plans have been created by converting prior traditional defined benefit plans. These conversions have frequently been controversial, on account of their effect on older workers. It will be seen in Chapter 4, infra, that the traditional defined benefit plan, because it links its benefits to final pay, is inherently "backloaded." The present value of the benefits accrued in the years close to retirement is greater than the value of the benefits that younger workers accrue, even when earning identical salaries. When a plan shifts to a cash balance plan, older workers find that the value of their expected future accruals declines dramatically. No benefits that have already accrued are reduced; as discussed infra in Chapter 5, ERISA forbids that. But future benefits will accrue on a less generous basis for older workers. This attribute of cash balance plans has led to claims that such plans might violate the laws forbidding age discrimination, an issue discussed in Chapter 18, infra. Concern about the effect of conversions on older employees has led some employers to provide more favorable transitional treatment for employees nearing retirement. For a detailed discussion of the operation of cash balance plans and of the problems they potentially create for older workers, see Barry Kozak, The Cash Balance Plan: An Integral Component of the Defined Benefit Plan Renaissance, 37 J. Marshall L. Rev. 753 (2004); Regina T. Jefferson, Striking a Balance in the Cash Balance Debate, 49 Buffalo L. Rev. 513 (2001).

Cash balance plans have usually resulted from conversions of existing DB plans, rather than as new plan adoptions. Although such a conversion responds to the decline in the career employment model in a way beneficial for mobile younger employees, the conversion also commonly allows the employer to use surplus plan assets (to fund the ongoing cash balance plan) without the negative tax consequences (discussed in Chapter 6, infra) associated with plan termination and replacement by a DC plan. See Richard A. Ippolito, Replicating Default Risk in a Defined-Benefit Plan, Financial Analysts J., Nov./Dec. 2002, at 31, 32–34.

Pension equity plans first became widely known when RJR Nabisco *Pension Equity Plans* implemented one in 1993. Both cash balance and pension equity plans define benefits in terms of a current lump-sum value rather than a deferred annuity, but a pension equity plan is a final-average lump-sum plan, whereas a cash balance plan is a career-average lump-sum plan. Furthermore, a pension equity plan does not have the individual accounts and interest credits associated with cash balance plans. For each year worked under a pension equity plan, employees are credited with a percentage that will be applied to their final average earnings. As an employee ages or as an employee's years of service increase, the percentage earned increases. Organizations may also choose to apply additional percentages to earnings above a threshold amount to provide an additional benefit for the portion of pay not eligible for Social Security benefits. On termination of employment or retirement, most employers allow employees to receive a lump-sum benefit that is equal to final average earnings multiplied by the sum of the percentages earned during a career (since lump-sum distributions do not guarantee that retirees will have continuing retirement benefits, some employers offer only annuities). Employees can take the lump sum as cash, convert it to an annuity under the plan, or roll it over into either an IRA or another employer's retirement plan. EBRI Fundamentals of Employee Benefits, chapter 10.

2. AGE-WEIGHTED DC PLANS

Age-weighted plans (sometimes called "new comparability plans") are profit-sharing plans that base allocations, at least in part, on the age of the participant, rather than entirely on compensation. Whereas a traditional profit-sharing plan allocates the same dollar amount to employees of different ages who receive the same compensation, an age-weighted plan applies an age factor that results in giving a larger allocation to older employees, who are closer to retirement and who, therefore, have less time to accumulate retirement funds. Age-weighted plans have tended to be adopted by smaller employers.

Why would an employer adopt an age-weighted DC plan rather than a DB plan? "Those who decide about plan design are generally older and better-paid employees, typically the owners or managers of the firm. New comparability and age-weighted formulas give these decisionmakers the advantages of defined benefit funding patterns weighted in their favor while sparing the firm the inflexibility and the costs of the minimum funding rules and PBGC premiums." Edward A. Zelinsky, The Defined Contribution Paradigm, 114 Yale L.J. 451, 503–04 (2004).

As will be discussed in Chapter 9, infra, the Code contains rules designed to ensure that plans do not discriminate in favor of highly compensated employees. The issue of whether age-weighted plans, which give larger allocations to older employees, who tend to have higher compensation, create a nondiscrimination problem is addressed in Stein, 56 S.M.U. L. Rev. at 645–46. Regulations issued in 2001 now address this issue: Treas. Reg. § 1.401(a)(4)–8(b).

3. MULTIEMPLOYER PLANS

Most pension plans are single-employer plans. The firm (or a group of related firms) sponsors one or more plans for its employees only. In some industries, however, especially those in which employment patterns are episodic, or in which most employers are small, individual companies do not sponsor pension plans. Rather, groups of unrelated firms within an industry contribute to a common plan. Virtually all such plans take the form known as "multiemployer" plans ("multi's" for short). ERISA § 3(37) defines a multiemployer plan as a plan "maintained pursuant to one or more collective bargaining agreements" between a union or unions and employers, "to which more than one employer is required to contribute."

Section 302(c)(5) of the Taft-Hartley Act of 1947, 29 U.S.C. § 186(c)(5), governs the structure of multiemployer plans. This provision is reproduced and discussed in Chapter 15, infra. The main requirement is that equal numbers of union and employer representatives serve as plan trustees.

"By 1950, multiemployer pension plans covered 1 million workers. Participation under these plans rose to 3.3 million workers in 1960 and to 10.1 million active workers and retirees in 1991." EBRI, Fundamentals of Employee Benefit Programs, supra, at 149. As of 1999 there were 13,617 multiemployer pension plans covering 11.2 million participants, almost 9 million of whom were in defined benefit plans and the remainder in defined contribution plans. DoL, Abstract of 1999 Form 5500 Annual Reports.

The following discussion of multiemployer plans is extracted from EBRI, Fundamentals of Employee Benefit Programs, 6th ed., 2009, at 122–126.

Plan Characteristics

In a multiemployer plan, there must be at least two companies and at least two employees, but there is no maximum limit. Most participants in multiemployer pension plans are in large defined benefit plans. DOL reports that in 2005, the latest year for which data are available, 96 percent of the 13.3 million participants and retirees were in plans with 1,000 or more participants per plan, and 72 percent of participants were in defined benefit plans (U.S. Department of Labor, 2008).

Multiemployer plans are concentrated in certain industries, in which there are many small companies, each too small to justify an individual plan. They are also found in industries in which, because of seasonal or irregular employment and high labor mobility, few workers would qualify under an individual company's plan if one were established. For example, construction workers are commonly hired by a given contractor for only a few weeks or months. When the job is completed, the worker may be unemployed until another contractor needs his or her particular skills or talent.

There is frequently more than one multiemployer plan within each large industry. Multiemployer plans may cover industry employees on a national, regional, or local basis, and some cut across several related industries (e.g., crafts or trades in one geographic area). . . .

Qualified Plan Rules

ERISA and the IRC set out rules that multiemployer plans, like single employer plans, must follow to qualify for preferential tax treatment. The rules govern fiduciary responsibility, disclosure and reporting, eligibility, vesting, benefit accrual, funding, coverage and participation, integration, and plan termination.

Some of the requirements—such as those for fiduciary responsibility and disclosure and reporting—are essentially the same for both types of plans, while other requirements differ. Benefits of the union-represented participants in multiemployer pension plans are generally deemed to meet the tax code's nondiscrimination standards automatically, but the coverage for any other employees (e.g., the staff of the sponsoring union or of the fund itself) will have to meet the generally applicable nondiscrimination tests.

Establishing the Plan

Once a union and various companies agree to set up a multiemployer plan, the first step is usually to negotiate how much each employer will contribute to the plan. Employer and union representatives then adopt a trust agreement that establishes a board of trustees, defines the board's powers and duties, and covers the affairs of both the trustees and the pension or welfare plan. . . . Benefit and actuarial consultants assist the trustees in working out plan details and determining a supportable benefit level. The trustees probably will retain a professional investment advisor or portfolio manager to ensure competent asset management. The trustees will also hire a salaried plan administrator and staff or retain an outside administration firm to manage the plan and handle day-to-day details such as the collection of employer contributions and employee claims, payments, recordkeeping, and inquiries. Finally, the trustees must adopt a formal plan document and publish a booklet in lay language informing employees of plan benefits, eligibility rules, and procedures for filing benefit claims. . . .

Contributions and Benefits

Plan contributions are normally made by the employers that are signatory to the collective bargaining agreement. However, an increasing number of multiemployer 401(k) plans have been adopted to permit participants to defer a portion of their wages for retirement. Occasionally, employees are required or permitted to make additional contributions to welfare plans (e.g., during short unemployment periods). The employer's contribution amount is determined through negotiations and fixed in the bargaining agreement. It is usually based on some measure of the covered employee's work (e.g., $1 for each hour worked by each employee). All the contributions are pooled in a common fund that pays for the plan benefits. Investment earnings augment the fund.

Portability

By their nature, multiemployer plans provide portability by enabling participants to shift from employer to employer under the plan without interrupting their benefit coverage. Normally, pension credits cannot be transferred from one multiemployer plan to another unless the trustees of the various plans have negotiated reciprocity agreements. Under such agreements, a worker can move among employers contributing to different plans that are signatory to the agreements without impairing his or her pension credits. About 60 percent of the workers covered by multiemployer health, welfare, and pension programs in the construction industry were covered by reciprocity agreements in 1995. A number of multiemployer plans in other industries, such as trucking, also have industrywide reciprocity agreements. Still other multiemployer plans are merging or joining larger funds, thus expanding the reach of their internal portability, as international unions continue to encourage plan consolidation for greater efficiencies.

Benefits

Benefit formulas under multiemployer defined benefit pension plans vary widely: they may be a flat-dollar amount for each year of service, a percentage of contributions required on the individuals' covered service, or a service-related percentage of the participants' covered earnings. Most multiemployer plans base benefits on length of service and not on earnings level. This is partly because the range of earnings for workers covered by multiemployer plans tends to be narrower than that for workers covered by single-employer plans. Under multiemployer plans that do not base benefits on pay, the need to collect and keep individual earnings records is eliminated; the contribution rate for all employees at a given benefit level is usually identical.

Most multiemployer plans suspend pension benefit payments to retirees in their jurisdictions who work in the same trade or industry while receiving pensions. The restriction is intended to prevent retirees from competing for jobs with active workers or practicing their skills in the nonunion sector of the industry. Under rules issued by DOL, a multiemployer plan may suspend benefits for a retiree who completes 40 or more hours of service in one month under certain circumstances, such as: in an industry in which other employees covered by the plan were employed and accrued benefits under the plan at the time benefit payments commenced or would have commenced if the retired employee had not returned to employment; in a trade or craft in which the retiree was employed at any time under the plan; and, in the geographic area covered by the plan at the time benefit payments commenced or would have commenced if the retired employee had not returned to employment.

Advantages of Multiemployer Plans

Multiemployer plans offer attractive portability features. Employees may carry pension credits with them as they move from employer to employer. Thus, they can earn pensions based on all accumulated credits, even if some of their former employers have gone out of business or stopped making plan contributions. Similarly, continuity of coverage can be assured for other benefits, such as medical insurance, when the worker switches jobs within the same industry. Multiemployer plans may also provide an incalculable advantage to employees of small companies, who might not receive benefits if multiemployer plans did not make benefit programs more affordable for their employers.

There are several advantages for employers who participate in multiemployer plans. First, economies can be achieved through group purchasing and in effect outsourcing all plan administration to be handled by the trustees. Second, benefit and labor costs throughout a region or even an industry may be stabilized. This can help reduce employee turnover, because workers will not be attracted to other jobs by the promise of better benefits elsewhere. As with all benefit plans qualified under the IRC, company contributions to a multiemployer plan are generally tax deductible.

Multiemployer plans proved to be especially problematic under ERISA's plan termination insurance system and required special legislation, the Multiemployer Pension Plan Amendments Act of 1980 (MPPAA). The following capsule account of the changes wrought by MPPAA is from Russell K. Osgood, The Law of Pensions and Profit-Sharing § 9.3.3, at 300–02 (1984).

Multiemployer plans have over the years been the least adequately funded of all classes of qualified plans. This has probably been caused by the separation in identity and interest of the sponsor, frequently a union, and the contributing employers. The sponsor's plan sets a benefit, usually a defined benefit, but then after negotiations the employers promise to contribute some fixed amount, typically determined on a cents per hour basis, without regard to whether the contribution is actuarially sound. Another cause of the problem has been that a number of multiemployer plans have been established in highly volatile industries and the benefits have been out of line with respect to the ability of the employers to pay.

At the time ERISA was passed Congress was aware that multiemployer plans were significantly underfunded and it provided that the plan termination insurance provisions would not apply to such plans until after December 31, 1977 except that the Pension Benefit Guaranty Corporation (PBGC) could exercise discretion to cover certain plans. This deadline was later extended to August 1, 1980. Shortly after that date, Congress passed the Multiemployer Act. Its primary goal was to save the PBGC from the enormous and perhaps unmanageable burden of insuring benefits in multiemployer plans.

Three provisions are at the heart of the Multiemployer Act. The liability of an employer who withdraws from a multiemployer plan is established. Multiemployer plans are brought into the plan termination insurance provisions, although on a segregated basis with more limited benefit guarantees. Plans that are in financial straits may attain either reorganization or insolvency status, which confers special powers to limit benefits in ways that would otherwise be prohibited under the Code rules.

Withdrawal liability. Prior to the enactment of ERISA an employer's liability to a multiemployer plan was defined in terms of the collective bargaining agreement. Such agreements typically provide for a flat contribution without any contingent liability. Thus, upon the expiration without a breach of such an agreement the employer's liability was at an end. This could be so even if an employer's contributions had not funded the full current costs of the benefits provided for its employees during the period of the agreement.

The plan termination insurance title of ERISA imposed for the first time liability on the withdrawal of a substantial employer from any plan under which more than one employer made contributions. . . .

The Multiemployer Act created more stringent rules for withdrawals from multiemployer plans. They apply to all employers who contribute to a multiemployer plan covered by the plan termination insurance title. [In] the event of a complete or partial withdrawal the Multiemployer Act requires the withdrawing employer, in effect, to fund certain benefits. Special rules apply in the case of the construction, entertainment, trucking, and certain other industries. . . . A withdrawing employer must pay withdrawal liability, computed under a complex series of statutory alternatives. Payment can be made all at once or in installments in an amount equal to the withdrawing employer's highest contribution, i.e., cents per hour times the highest average annual contribution base units, i.e., hours worked over any three year period within the ten year period ending with the withdrawal. The annual payments received may not exceed the total withdrawal liability computed. In the case of a complete withdrawal an employer is only obligated to make a maximum of 20 annual payments even if the 20 payments do not completely amortize his computed withdrawal liability. In the case of a complete termination by virtue of a withdrawal of all employers the 20 year cap does not apply.

The constitutionality of MPPAA's withdrawal liability scheme was sustained in Connolly v. PBGC, 475 U.S. 211 (1986). MPPAA has bred a large but specialized set of litigation issues that fall outside the coverage of this book. For a discussion of such issues, see Israel Goldowitz and Ralph L. Landy, Special Rules for Multiemployer Plans, in Jayne E. Zanglein, Lawrence A. Frolik & Susan J. Stabile, ERISA Litigation, Chapter 40 (BNA) (4th ed. 2011).

NOTES AND QUESTIONS

1.   *Plan trustees.* Section 302(c)(5) of the Taft-Hartley Act requires equal numbers of trustees from union and employer ranks. Does this structure result in equal influence for union and management trustees? See infra Chapter 15.

2. *Portability.* A major unfulfilled goal of the designers of the pension reform legislation that became ERISA was to promote the portability of pension plan credits when a worker moved from one employer to another. As enacted, ERISA makes almost no provision for portability among single employer plans, apart from the plan-to-plan rollover option that is discussed in Chapter 11, infra.

By contrast, as discussed in the EBRI excerpt, supra, multiemployer plans achieve routine portability, since a worker who moves from one employer to another within the group of participating employers will have continuous coverage under the plan. According to Bureau of Labor Statistics for 1994–95, only 3% of employees in single-employer defined benefit plans were covered by portability provisions. Harriet Weinstein & Wm. J. Wiatrowski, Multiemployer Plans, Compensation and Working Conditions, Spring 1999, at 19, 22. As a result, many employees face "job lock," a compulsion to stay in a job because of non-portability of benefits. See Katherine Elizabeth Ulrich, You Can't Take it With You: An Examination of Employee Benefit Portability and its Relationship to Job Lock and the New Psychological Contract, 19 Hofstra Labor & Employment L.J. 173, 177–179 (2001) (discussing problems created by job lock).

Why has it been so difficult to achieve portability within the single-employer defined benefit plan universe? See Chapter 4, infra. Why is portability a routine incident of multiemployer plans, when it is virtually unobtainable in the single-employer plan system?

CHAPTER 3

ORIGINS AND STRUCTURE OF ERISA

Analysis

A. THE STUDEBAKER INCIDENT

Michael Allen, The Studebaker Incident and Its Influence on the Private Pension Plan Reform Movement
(research memorandum prepared for this coursebook) (1985).

The closing of the Studebaker automobile plant in South Bend, Indiana, in December of 1963 is widely regarded as a pivotal event in the history of the movement toward comprehensive federal regulation of private pension plans. The closing of the plant and the accompanying termination of a pension plan that covered 11,000 autoworkers has been called the most important event leading to the enactment of the Employee Retirement Income Security Act of 1974 (ERISA). See, e.g., 19C Sheldon M. Young, Business Organizations: Pension and Profit Sharing Plans § 23.11[4] (1981); Paul H. Jackson, Symposium Remarks, in Private Pensions and the Public Interest 57–58 (American Enterprise Institute) (1969). The funding and vesting rules that constitute the centerpiece of Title 1 of ERISA and the pension insurance program created under Title 4 can be traced to the Studebaker incident.

1. *The plant closing.* On December 9, 1963, Studebaker Corporation announced that it was closing its automotive manufacturing plant in South Bend, Indiana, and consolidating its remaining automaking activity at its Hamilton, Ontario, plant. U.S. News & World Report, Dec. 23, 1963, at 76. This announcement followed a long period in which the American plant had been losing money. As a result of the plant closing, some 5,000 workers were dismissed (2,000 of them had already been laid off in the hard times before the closing). A further 1,800 workers in South Bend eventually lost their jobs.

The dismissed workers were members of the United Automobile Workers (UAW) and were covered under a single-employer pension plan negotiated between the UAW and Studebaker. The plan is summarized in testimony in Private Pension Plans: Hearings Before the Subcomm. on Fiscal Policy of the Joint Economic Comm., 89th Cong., 2nd Sess. 104–05 (1966) (statement of Clifford M. MacMillan, Studebaker vice president) [hereafter 1966 JEC Hearings].

2. *The termination agreement.* When the plant closed, the UAW and the company entered into an agreement dated October 15, 1965, settling the terms for terminating the plan. The termination of the pension plan did not produce litigation. The termination agreement implemented default priorities contained in the plan. The agreement divided the plan participants into three groups: (1) 3,600 retirees and active workers who had already reached the permitted retirement age of 60; (2) approximately 4,000 employees, aged 40 to 59, who had at least ten years of service with the company and whose pension benefits had therefore vested; and (3) a residual group of 2,900 workers who had no vested rights. American Enterprise Institute, The Debate on Private Pensions 41 (1968) [hereafter AEI, Debate]; see also 1966 JEC Hearings at 105 (statement of Clifford M. MacMillan, Studebaker vice president); id. at 127–29 (statement of Willard Solenberger, UAW officer).

Persons in the first group had the first claim on the assets of the pension fund; they received full lifetime annuities. The cost of the annuities purchased for this group was about $21.5 million. Once the annuities had been purchased, only $2.5 million remained in the pension fund. This sum was far from adequate to cover the vested claims of employees in the second group. These workers received lump-sum payments equal to about 15 percent of the actuarial value of their accrued pension benefits. The nonvested employees in the third group received nothing. 1966 JEC Hearings 128.

3. *Why the underfunding?* The original Studebaker-UAW pension plan went into effect on November 11, 1950. It granted prior service credits, creating an immediate unfunded liability of $18 million that was supposed to be funded over a thirty-year period. Benefits were increased in 1953, 1955, 1959, and 1961. 1966 JEC Hearings 104. Each time, additional unfunded liabilities for past service credits were created. Each increase was to be amortized over a new thirty year period. See AEI, Debate at 42. These unfunded past service liabilities were the reason that the pension fund assets were inadequate to provide for the vested claims of all employees when the plan terminated.

4. *"Studebaker" as a battle cry.* Although there had been some interest in regulating the private pension system prior to the Studebaker incident, the events in South Bend gave the movement considerable momentum. . . .

The human side of the Studebaker situation was brought out in [1966] Senate hearings by the testimony of Nolan Miller, a 59-year-old former Studebaker employee, who had worked at Studebaker for 38 years, but barely missed qualifying for full retirement benefits under the termination scheme because he had not reached the age of 60 by November 1, 1964. Mr. Miller testified:

I had depended on my Studebaker pension along with social security for a living when I reached retirement age because my savings from income from Studebaker were far too little to provide for retirement income.

I and the other employees at the plant looked forward to our Studebaker pension in the same way as we did to our social security and had the opinion that we were just as sure to get it. There was never any serious thought that we might lose it because of the plant closing. . . . When we finally came to realize that only those already retired, or who would reach age 60 by November 1, 1964, could get a pension because the plan wasn't sufficiently funded to do more, it was probably the most bitter news we ever received.

1966 Reinsurance Hearings at 57.

In the early 1970s, advocates of federal pension regulation emphasized the frustrated expectations of long-service employees who were caught in pension plan terminations. . . .

The average age and length-of-service of the workers who received only a small percentage of their expected pension benefits made them a very appealing group of victims. The 4,000 or so workers in the age 40–59 group, who got only fifteen cents for every expected dollar of vested pension benefits, had an average age of 52 and an average period of service with the company of just under 23 years. 1966 Reinsurance Hearings at 59. There were numerous hardship cases like Nolan Miller's. One 59-year-old man in the fifteen-cents-on-the-dollar group was just a few months short of 60, and he had 43 years of service with Studebaker. 1966 JEC Hearings at 127.

5.   *Questioning the legend.* The Studebaker incident had persuasive force in the movement for federal insurance of private pension plans because, as Walter Reuther put the matter, such a termination was the kind of problem "[t]hat is beyond the economic capability of finding a rational answer at the bargaining [table]." 1966 Reinsurance Hearings at 50. This perspective on the Studebaker incident is not without its critics. See Young, supra, § 23.11[4] (1981). Speaking in 1966, shortly after the events, Robert Royes, a pension plan official with AT & T, made the following observations about the expectations of the parties who negotiated the Studebaker pension plan:

the parties entered into an arrangement which would work well if Studebaker prospered, and which would not yield all of the hoped-for results if Studebaker could not afford to continue it. . . .

Was there anything anti-social or against sound public policy in an agreement between Studebaker and the U.A.W. to run the risks which were inherent in their bargain?

Should the parties who assume the risk of establishing a pension plan with large unfunded liabilities expect others to bail them out if things go wrong?

Robert Royes, Statement, in AEI, at Debate 42–43.

A decade later another author questioned the reliance of the Studebaker employees:

> The frequency with which the Studebaker Corporation case of the early 1960's is cited is evidence of the rarity of similar cases, and to offer this as proof of reneging [by companies on their pension plan promises] is tantamount to arguing that most automobiles are commercial failures by pointing to the Edsel [an unsuccessful Ford product of the late 1950s]. Moreover, at the time of its last pension contract, Studebaker was not particularly creditworthy. It was in no position to offer a "defined benefit" plan, and it would be hard, in my judgment, to argue that the employees did not sense this.

Dennis Logue, Legislative Influence on Corporate Pension Plans 21 n.12 (American Enterprise Institute) (1979).

NOTES AND QUESTIONS

1.   Under the funding schedule of the Studebaker plan, current service liabilities were funded as they accrued, and liabilities for past service credits were being amortized over thirty-year periods. Why did these practices result in such serious underfunding? Would you expect ERISA, the pension regulatory measure that in some sense resulted from the Studebaker case, to prevent a recurrence of such underfunding? Does it? See ERISA § 302(b)(2)(B)(ii)–(iii). After many years of debate, the minimum funding requirements were tightened by the Pension Protection Act of 2006: see Chapter 6, infra.

2.   Did the termination of the Studebaker plan frustrate the expectations of the workers? Were those expectations justified? In the light of hindsight, what might the employer have done better to have avoided frustrating employee expectations (apart from building more successful cars, thereby remaining in business and perpetuating the plan)? What might the UAW have done better?

3.   The pension plan that Studebaker and the union negotiated provided an abatement formula in the event that the plan had insufficient assets. The formula gave 100 cents on the dollar to retirees and to vested workers aged over 60 before younger vested workers received anything. Thus, when the plan terminated, workers under 60 received only 15 cents on the dollar. See Steven A. Sass, The Promise of Private Pensions 183–86 (1997). Students familiar with labor law might ask how the union's conduct in negotiating such a pact squared with its duty of fair representation. Legal rubrics apart, what aspects of internal union dynamics might explain why the union seemed to overbalance the interests of older versus younger workers?

4.   Notice that the event that precipitated the pension defaults in the Studebaker plan was not the sponsoring company's bankruptcy, but rather its termination of the plan in connection with the closing of the South Bend manufacturing plant and the termination of the employees. Although the company was still solvent, the plan participants who suffered the default had no recourse against the company. The reason is that *the pension promise was expressed to run from the plan, not from the plan sponsor*. Studebaker's promise, reinforced in its collective bargaining agreements with the UAW,

was to make contractually agreed contributions to the plan, which it did. See James A. Wooten, The Employee Retirement Income Security Act of 1974: A Political History 53 (2005) [hereafter cited as Wooten, ERISA History]. Designing a pension plan in this way, which was common before ERISA, see id. at 95, effectively placed the risk of underfunding on the plan participants. As discussed infra in Chapter 6, ERISA now forbids such a "fund-specific" defined benefit plan, that is, a plan that limits the sponsor's liability to the assets in the fund. For further detail about the Studebaker plan and its termination, see James A. Wooten, "The Most Glorious Story of Failure in the Business": The Studebaker-Packard Corporation and the Origins of ERISA, 49 Buffalo L. Rev. 683 (2001), substantially republished in Wooten, ERISA History, at 51–79.

B. LEGISLATIVE HISTORY OF ERISA

Michael S. Gordon, Overview: Why Was ERISA Enacted?
U.S. Senate, Special Comm. on Aging, The Employee Retirement Income Security Act of 1974: The First Decade 6–25 (Information Paper) (1984).

[The author of this account of the legislative history of ERISA, Michael Gordon, worked for the Department of Labor in the 1960s, and during the period 1970–75 he served under an appointment from Senator Javits as minority counsel on pensions to the Senate Committee on Labor and Public Welfare.—Eds.]

Congressional interest in the problems of improper practices in connection with employee benefit plans goes back to the early 1950's. . . . Both House and Senate committees concentrated on abuses in the administration of these funds although in the Senate some concern was also expressed with respect to the adequacy of funding for pension plans. The Senate committee investigations found that the extremely rapid growth of private pension plans had led to all manner of abuses, ranging from ineptness and lack of know-how to outright looting of benefit funds and corrupt administration. In addition to embezzlements, kickbacks, unjustifiably high administrative costs, and excessive investment of funds in employer securities, serious examples of improper insurance practices were also found, including exorbitantly high commission and administrative charges, fictitious fees, retention by some insurance carriers of an unduly large share of the premiums, unequal treatment of policyholders, switching carriers to obtain high first-year commissions and collusion between insurance representatives, union officials and management.

These abuses led to the Douglas-Ives bill which became the basis for the Welfare and Pension Plans Disclosure Act (the WPPDA) enacted in 1958. The theory of the law was that full disclosure to participants and beneficiaries of the provisions of their plan and its financial operations would deter abuse ("sunlight being the best disinfectant") and would enable them to police the plans themselves without requiring greater Government regulations or interference.

In fact, the WPPDA was a greatly diluted version of the bill that had passed the Senate and deprived the Secretary of Labor of investigatory and enforcement powers, leading President Eisenhower to remark that it was signed only because it created a precedent of Federal responsibility and that it would have to be improved. . . .

Nonetheless, the precedent of broad regulatory coverage for all types of plans was significant as was the selection of the Department of Labor as the administering agency. The latter was intended to validate the labor interest in benefit fund regulation although at the time the competition came not from the IRS but rather the SEC, where the Douglas-Ives bill had originally placed administration of the disclosure provisions. . . . Amendments to the WPPDA were enacted in 1962 to restore most of the enforcement provisions that had been eliminated by the House in 1958. These amendments provided the Department of Labor limited investigatory authority and power to issue regulations. . . .

[On] March 28, 1962, President Kennedy established a cabinet-level committee known as the Committee on Corporate Pension Funds and other Private Retirement and Welfare Programs. . . .

[T]he passage of the WPPDA in 1958 had unleashed a nonstop torrent of mail from employees all over the country complaining over their failure to qualify for private pension benefits and mistakenly assuming that the WPPDA provided some remedy in this respect. This was a phenomenon which did not cease until ERISA was enacted and was the basis for the enduring grassroots constituency in support of broad pension reforms.

The second was the Studebaker case. [The] incident burst like a bombshell on the private pension scene and contributed greatly to the sense that serious problems affected the plans that needed addressing. . . .

When finally issued in 1965, the Cabinet committee's report . . . made as its principal recommendations:

(1) The imposition of mandatory minimum vesting standards, suggesting that employees be vested 50 percent after 15 years of service and 100 percent after 20 years of service.

(2) The imposition of mandatory minimum funding standards.

(3) That a voluntary portability system (referring to the transferability of pension credits among plans) and a system of plan termination insurance (called "reinsurance"), to protect against loss of vested pension benefits when a plan was terminated prior to full funding (as in the Studebaker case), be studied further to determine their feasibility.

(4) That in the fiduciary area, no steps be taken to impose Federal statutory standards until the effectiveness of the disclosure provisions were further tested, but that pension funds should be subject to something like a 10-percent limitation on the amount of plan funds that could be invested in employer securities; and

(5) Amendments to the tax code should be made to cure serious inequities in the tax treatment of pension benefits, the most important of which was the recommendation to place a

dollar limitation on contributions to a plan for any employee or an equivalent limitation on benefits in order for a plan to maintain tax qualified status.

The President's committee report excited wide discussion and controversy in the pension community. . . .

Except for restrictions on plan investments in a plan sponsor's securities, the President's committee report had virtually dismissed out-of-hand the need for Federal fiduciary standards for private plans. In the same year that the report was released, however, the Senate Permanent Subcommittee on Investigations . . . discovered was that one George Barasch, the founder of the two New Jersey unions involved, had managed to manipulate and divert the funds of the employee benefit plans connected with the unions in such a way as to make himself a prospective multimillionaire. . . .

Senator McClellan . . . introduce[d] a bill in October 1965, that amended the WPPDA to set fiduciary standards for trustees of all types of plans. This bill became the forerunner of the fiduciary provisions that ultimately were enacted in ERISA. . . . [T]he UAW, concerned that the President's committee report had not made a clear cut recommendation in favor of a termination insurance program ("reinsurance") to handle Studebaker problems, prevailed on Senator Vance Hartke of Indiana to introduce a reinsurance bill and the Senate Finance Committee held a 1-day hearing on the matter in 1966.

[O]n February 20 [1967] the administration unveiled its Welfare and Pension Plan Protection Act, a bill providing fiduciary and added disclosure requirements and modeled after the McClellan bill, but with important refinements added by the interagency task force. . . .

[O]n February 28, 1967, [Senator Javits] introduced the first broad-scaled pension reform bill, S. 1103. In addition to a section on fiduciary responsibility, the bill contained provisions for vesting and funding standards, a program of plan termination insurance and a voluntary central portability fund. . . .

The bill also established an independent SEC-type commission to administer the new regulatory provisions. . . .

[T]he [inter-agency] task force decided that the recommendations of the President's committee report were too conservative, not up-to-par with the more progressive private plans, and, if translated without change into a legislative proposal, would not compete successfully with the Javits initiative. Accordingly, faster vesting requirements (10 years after reaching age 25), faster funding (funding of vested liabilities within 25 years) and establishment of a corporation within the Department of Labor to administer a termination insurance program were all adopted. The only matter left to further study was the portability issue.

A bill incorporating these decisions was not introduced, however, until May 1968. . . .

The key happening was the release in March of 1971 of a controversial segment of [a] study dealing with historical forfeiture rates in a small sample of specific pension plans which had been surveyed by the staff of the Labor Subcommittee. . . . The study found that in the sample of plans studied, which had lengthy service requirements, only 5 percent of the millions of employees covered since 1950 had ever received benefits, only 8 percent had qualified for benefits, and while most of these employees had only worked a very short period of time (less than 5 years), there were substantial numbers of workers who had longer periods of service and failed to qualify for benefits.

These findings created an overnight sensation and caused a furor among pension experts. . . . Throughout 1971, the Labor Subcommittee held hearings on the principal areas of purported plan deficiencies. . . .

The new [Nixon] administration initiative endorsed a federally mandated vesting standard, albeit one considerably weaker than the one proposed by Javits, but the administration continued to stoutly oppose funding and plan termination insurance requirements.

But, the big news was a major new proposal in the tax area, one that was clearly conceived as the centerpiece of the initiative and destined to become the administration's one truly popular proposal. In addition to raising the tax deductible limits allowed to self-employed persons for funding their retirement benefits under so-called Keogh or H.R. 10 plans, the administration recommended the establishment of counterpart plans for employed individuals who lacked coverage under an employer or union sponsored pension program. Although the tax deductible limits for these individual retirement account plans (IRA's) were considerably lower than those provided under Keogh plans, the administration reasoned that the self-employed were entitled to a greater deduction because their plans were required to cover their employees in order to obtain tax qualification. . . .

Thus, by 1972, battle was joined between the administration and the Senate Labor Subcommittee on the substance and scope of the reforms that should be legislated, including the jurisdictional basis for legislating the reforms, but the administration had made an important concession by offering vesting proposals. What was left was funding, termination insurance, and portability, and the prospects of the administration bending on the latter two subjects did not appear very bright. . . .

In May of 1972, Williams and Javits, after months of staff negotiations, introduced a joint bill which henceforth replaced the original Javits proposal. . . . The Labor Subcommittee now determined to probe the depth of support for the new Williams-Javits bill and in June held legislative hearings on both that bill and the administration's proposal, even though, technically, the latter was not before the subcommittee. In general, industry representatives gave their support to the administration's proposals and labor to the Williams-Javits bill. . . .

[The] Williams-Javits bill was reported unanimously by the full Senate Committee on Labor and Public Welfare in mid-September 1972, the first congressional committee to report a comprehensive pension reform bill. . . .

[T]he Senate Finance Committee requested a referral of the bill on grounds that it affected tax jurisdiction. Within 10 days, thereafter, spurred on by a coalition of business groups and the administration, the Finance Committee had gutted the bill of all its significant reforms, stating that it believed that coverage, vesting, funding and related provisions should continue to be dealt with by the tax committees of Congress. . . .

The action of the Finance Committee killed chances of passing pension reforms later that session but [a] Javits' speech ignited a firestorm of criticism against the Finance Committee, and their rejection of the Williams-Javits bill became a blessing in disguise. Within weeks, letters of protest poured into Congress from all over the country and editorial writers had a field day. When Congress recessed to campaign during the Presidential election year, many Congressmen and Senators, who had never heard of the pension bill, discovered a great many disturbed and resentful constituents on their hands for whom they had no ready answers.

It was apparent that the enemies of the Williams-Javits bill had made a serious miscalculation, and that the issue of private pension reform had truly captured the public imagination. Now there was little room for doubt that a broad consensus had formed behind the comprehensive reforms adopted by the Committee on Labor and Public Welfare. . . .

Many hurdles remained to be overcome before ERISA became a reality. The fate of termination insurance still hung in the balance. The resolution of the labor-tax jurisdictional issue remained the most delicate of many delicate problems. The fiduciary provisions, long taken for granted as settled, came under searching scrutiny and turned out to be far from settled. New provisions emerged, such as joint and survivor benefits, and stirred new debates. Entire sections of the Internal Revenue Code pertaining to pension plans were to undergo extensive revision and arouse even more heated controversy than some of the original Williams-Javits proposals. . . .

NOTES AND QUESTIONS

1. *Sources.* The various draft bills, floor proceedings, and committee reports from the period 1973–74 that culminated in ERISA were reprinted in a three-volume work: Legislative History of the Employee Retirement Income Security Act of 1974: Public Law 93–406, Senate Subcomm. on Labor of the Comm. on Labor and Public Welfare, 94th Cong., 2d Sess. (1976). The most important of these documents, the Joint Explanatory Statement of the Committee of Conference, generally known as the Conference Committee Report, appears 3 id. at 4518–4654, and is widely reprinted elsewhere.

2. *Multiemployer plans.* Gordon reports that the multiemployer plans sought without success to be exempted from ERISA's vesting requirements. What would have been the arguments for and against such an exemption?

3. *Interests.* Fisk reads Gordon's account to support the view that ERISA "was an interest-group deal [among] large employers, pension consultants, organized labor, insurers, and financial advisors of all sorts." Catherine L. Fisk, *Lochner* Redux: The Renaissance of Laissez-Faire Contract in the Federal Common Law of Employee Benefits, 56 Ohio St. L.J. 153, 163 n. 23 (1995). Is that analysis sound? Consider in particular labor unions: If ERISA was a union victory, how did it happen that the movement to enact ERISA came to fruition under the Republican Nixon and Ford administrations?

Bear in mind Gordon's account of the central role played by organized labor, especially the UAW, in drafting and promoting ERISA's Title 4, the plan termination insurance system administered by an ERISA-created federal entity, the Pension Benefit Guaranty Corporation (PBGC). PBGC and the insurance system are discussed infra in Chapter 6.

4.   *Preemption.* The legislative history of ERISA's preemption clause, § 514, is discussed in Chapter 17, infra, in the detailed account by Daniel M. Fox & Daniel C. Schaffer.

5.   *The trust law model for plan administration.* In Firestone Tire & Rubber Co. v. Bruch, 489 U.S. 101, 110 (1989), the Supreme Court remarked that "ERISA's legislative history confirms that the Act's fiduciary responsibility provisions 'codif[y] and make[ ] applicable to [ERISA] fiduciaries certain principles developed in the evolution of the law of trusts.'" It follows from this language and history, the Court said, that in reviewing plan decisionmaking, "we are guided by principles of trust law." Id. at 111. What aspects of the legislative history recounted by Michael Gordon might explain why Congress turned to the juridical form of the trust, which is prototypically a branch of the law of gratuitous transfers, for deriving the standards appropriate to the administration of pension and benefit plans?

6.   *ERISA's compliance industry.* One unmistakable group of ERISA winners has been the corps of pension-law professionals that the legislation called forth—regulators, consulting actuaries, pension and benefits lawyers, and others. Data on the magnitude of the expenditures for ERISA compliance and ERISA enforcement have not been found.

The cost of regulatory compliance has been repeatedly cited as a factor in the decline of defined benefit pension plans, especially small plans. The former director of the PBGC, Kathleen Utgoff, presented figures in 1991 indicating that "[a] large employer's plan administration expenses generally run at about 4 percent of average contributions, but administrative costs for a plan with fewer than 15 participants will eat up 30 percent to 50 percent of contributions." 18 BNA Pension Reporter 826 (1991). In addition, a defined benefit plan that is covered by the PBGC insurance program must pay a basic annual premium of $57 per participant for 2015. The plan must pay an additional premium if it is underfunded. ERISA section 4006(a)(3).

Speaking of the shortcomings of ERISA's prohibited transaction regime (discussed in Chapter 13, infra), Utgoff and a coauthor wrote that "over the last few years our tiny law firm—charging modest rates—has received several million dollars in fees for advising clients on [prohibited transactions issues arising in connection with proposed plan investments]." Kathleen P. Utgoff & Theodore R. Groom, The Regulation of Pensions: Twenty Questions After Twenty Years, 21 J. Pension Planning & Compliance 1, 13 (1995). The authors say, id. at 4:

> Billions of dollars are spent on compliance every year. For some types of regulation, it can be difficult to tell whether compliance costs are a waste because the cost/benefit analysis is not always straightforward. But for many pension rules the analysis is easy. The compliance costs are very high and the rules achieve *no* useful objective. Most of the money squandered on compliance would be better spent on almost anything else: bigger

pensions or a lower [federal government budget] deficit are excellent alternatives.

C. THE STRUCTURE OF ERISA — *enacted in 1974 — Plans that fall under ERISA must comply w/ it*

1. *The statutory outline.* ERISA's main headings are organized as follows:

What matters:
① *What is a Plan*
② *What is an Employee*
③ *What is an Employer*

Title 1.		Protection of Employee Benefit Rights
		Definitions
	Part 1.	Reporting and Disclosure
	Part 2.	Participation and Vesting
	Part 3.	Funding
	Part 4.	Fiduciary Responsibility
	Part 5.	Administration and Enforcement
	Part 6.	Continuation Coverage Under Group Health Plans
	Part 7.	Group Health Plan Requirements
Title 2.		Amendments to the Internal Revenue Code
Title 3.		Miscellanea
Title 4.		Plan Termination Insurance

Title 1 of ERISA is commonly called "the labor title." Title 2 was recodified in the IRC and is not separately cited.

Part 6 of Title 1 was added by Title 10 of the Consolidated Omnibus Budget Reconciliation Act (COBRA) of 1985. Part 7 of Title 1 was added by the Health Insurance Portability and Accountability Act of 1996 (HIPAA). Parts 6 and 7 are discussed in section C of chapter 19.

2. Nonpension plans. ERISA's fiduciary rules, certain of its reporting and disclosure requirements, and much of its enforcement system (Title 1, Parts 1, 4, and 5) apply not only to pension plans, but also to arrangements called "employee welfare benefit plans." See ERISA § 3(1) (definition). Welfare benefit plans are maintained for employees either by an employer or by a union (or jointly). Included are plans providing health care benefits; benefits upon accident, death, or disability; unemployment benefits; vacation benefits; training programs; and a variety of others. There are major differences between pension plans and these nonpension plans. A pension plan envisions a decades-long program of saving for retirement and dissaving during retirement; the potential for forfeitures and for underfunding—practices that ERISA was meant to restrict—arise on account of the long-term character of a pension plan. The typical single-employer welfare benefit plan, by contrast, is handled on the sponsor's books on a current or pay-as-you-go basis. Thus, the drafters of ERISA carefully avoided extending the vesting and funding rules to welfare benefit plans.

It will be seen repeatedly in this book (especially in Chapters 12–17, infra, treating fiduciary law, remedies, and preemption) that Congress' decision to lump both pension and nonpension plans under ERISA has created considerable difficulty. ERISA regulates the content of pension plans in considerable detail, but provides almost no such regulation of welfare benefit plans. Nevertheless, ERISA's broad preemption provision applies to both types of plan, and most preemption litigation involves welfare plans rather than pension plans. Bear in mind as you study the

Welfare Benefit Plans (Non-Pension Plans)
- *handled on a current or pay-as-you-go basis (the vesting + funding rules that apply to Pension Plans do NOT apply to welfare Benefit Plans)*

ERISA provides almost No regulation to content of Welfare Benefit Plans (opposite of Pension Plans)

- *Broad Preemption Provision of ERISA applies to both Pension and Welfare Plans* later chapters of this book the question of whether Congress made a misjudgment in extending ERISA to nonpension plans.

What light does the legislative history throw on the rationale for subjecting such disparate plans to a common scheme of regulation in the areas of reporting and disclosure, fiduciary responsibility, enforcement and remedies, and preemption?

3. *The ERISA agencies* Gordon's essay explains that the original Javits bill of 1967 envisaged a single pension regulatory agency, on the model of the Securities and Exchange Commission. Instead, ERISA dispersed primary responsibility for pension matters among three bodies, sometimes called "the ERISA agencies." They are the Department of Labor (DoL), the Internal Revenue Service (IRS), and (for the insurance scheme of Title 4) the Pension Benefit Guaranty Corporation (PBGC). Why did that happen? As you study the law that has developed around ERISA, keep in mind the question of whether it has been disadvantageous to scatter the regulatory authority as ERISA did. DoL and IRS have different priorities, and this sometimes results in their taking inconsistent policy positions. In the United Kingdom, by contrast, pension jurisdiction is consolidated in the Ministry of Work and Pensions.

4. *The Department of Labor* DoL administers the reporting and disclosure provisions of ERISA's Title 1, Part 1. ERISA's enforcement section (Title 1, Part 5) contains a variety of provisions empowering the Secretary of Labor to investigate and to take legal action on behalf of participants and beneficiaries of ERISA-covered plans. Various provisions of Titles 1 and 4 of ERISA grant rule-making authority to the Secretary of Labor. In order to discharge its responsibilities in the field, DoL created a specialized office, formerly the Office of Pension and Welfare Benefits Administration (PWBA), renamed in 2003 as the Employee Benefits Security Administration (EBSA), which is headed by an Assistant Secretary of Labor for Employee Benefits Security.

A pension plan is a device of financial intermediation, an arrangement for saving and investment. Pension plans are akin to other modes of financial intermediation—the securities and mutual fund industries; the insurance industry; and the banking industry. Pension plans are part of the world of investment. Does the Department of Labor seem an apt place to locate regulatory authority over financial intermediation? What factors explain the decision to lodge this authority there?

5. *Congressional committees.* ERISA's legislative history of contending jurisdiction between the Congressional tax-writing and labor committees continues to influence legislation in the pension and employee benefits field. Thus, in both House and Senate, the labor committees and the finance (or ways and means) committees deal with pension and benefits matters; they have been joined by the committees on aging.

6. *Statutory overlap.* The labor/finance struggle also helps explain the curious duplicate structure of ERISA. The Internal Revenue Code (IRC) (Title 2 of ERISA) tends to duplicate the substantive regulation of ERISA's labor title (Title 1) on such matters as funding and vesting. IRC

regulation takes the form of conditions for tax qualification. For example, the vesting rules of ERISA § 203 reappear as IRC § 411. This book does not in general supply parallel citations to IRC sections when discussing the main regulatory sections of ERISA Title 1.

(2)(3)   7. *DoL/IRS jurisdiction; 1978 reorganization.* "In the face of this statutory overlapping, the Labor Department and the Internal Revenue [Service] have de facto sorted out their responsibilities in accordance with the following two rules: (1) in areas where there is single agency jurisdiction that agency will have sole jurisdiction; (2) in areas where there is concurrent jurisdiction, the [IRS] has effective jurisdiction unless it involves a matter within the traditional sphere of Labor Department regulation, such as defining an hour of service. [Reorganization] Plan No. 4, 43 Fed.Reg. 47,713 (1978), explicitly [authorizes] this informal sorting out of [responsibilities]." Russell Osgood, Qualified Pension and Profit-Sharing Plan Vesting: Revolution Not Reform, 59 Boston U.L.Rev. 452 n.2 (1979).

The IRS has jurisdiction over *funding, participation, benefit accrual,* and *vesting.* DoL has primary *jurisdiction* over *fiduciary responsibility* — *deals w/ Hours-worked* and *prohibited transactions.* Section 103 of the Reorganization Plan gives DoL an effective veto over IRS enforcement of the exclusive benefit rule of IRC § 401(a), which overlaps ERISA § 404(a)(1)(A). The ERISA agencies observe these lines of responsibility in issuing regulations.

     8. *Confusing numbering.* ERISA is not only clumsily organized, it is also poorly numbered. The several levels of subheadings can produce a citation like ERISA § 205(e)(1)(A)(ii)(IV). Moreover, some of the section numbering invites confusion. The fiduciary law of ERISA's Title 1 is numbered in the 400s; e.g., the rule of mandatory trusteeship appears as ERISA § 403(a), and the rule exempting insurance company plans from this requirement is ERISA § 403(b). Meanwhile, most pension tax law is contained in the 400s of the Internal Revenue Code. Thus, IRC § 403(a) governs the taxation of beneficiaries under a qualified annuity plan, and IRC § 403(b) deals with a particular type of retirement program for employees of educational institutions and certain other nonprofit organizations. Needless to say, the potential for confusion between two sets of 400 numbers is ample. Get in the habit, therefore, of writing "ERISA § 403(b)" or "IRC § 403(b)" rather than a section number alone.

     9. *ERISA and United States Code numbering.* A further source of confusion in statutory section numbering results from the recodification of the nontax provisions of ERISA (Titles 1, 3 and 4) as part of the labor title of the United States Code, Title 29. ERISA appears as 29 U.S.C. § 1000 et seq. The ERISA number is not easily recognizable when rendered as a U.S.C. number. For example, ERISA § 514(a), the preemption provision examined infra in Chapter 17, becomes 29 U.S.C. § 1144(a).

     Courts are in the habit of using U.S.C. numbers, sometimes instead of ERISA numbers, sometimes as parallel citations. ERISA lawyers, by contrast, tend to use ERISA numbers. *Throughout this book we use ERISA numbers only.* In this book cases or other sources that used U.S.C. numbers, either instead of or in addition to ERISA numbers, have been edited to show ERISA numbers only. The statutory supplement prepared for use with this book supplies parallel USC cites for each ERISA section.

10. *Defined benefit and defined contribution.* Did Ralph Nader get pension policy right? Would the purposes of ERISA have been better served by abolishing defined benefit plans, hence by limiting private pension plans to defined contribution plans that would have been required to be 100 percent vested and portable? (The difficulties in achieving portability within the defined benefit system are discussed in Chapter 4, infra.)

1. POST-1974 AMENDMENTS AND ENACTMENTS

ERISA has been considerably modified since the statute came into force in 1974, both by amendments to the statute, and by enactment of other bodies of federal law that have affected ERISA's scope. Pension taxation has also undergone fundamental revisions, as well as annual congressional tinkering. There has been a spate of recent legislation in response to the economic crisis and its effects on defined benefit plan funding and defined contribution plan balances. In addition to these statutory changes, there are extensive regulations and other guidance under ERISA and the Code. The frequency and scope of these developments mean that, more so than in most areas of federal law, close attention must be paid to the rules that were in effect when a particular transaction or event took place.

2. GOVERNMENTAL AND CHURCH PLANS — *Not governed by ERISA*

ERISA § 4(b) excludes from coverage the plans of certain types of sponsor, especially "governmental" and "church" plans as defined in ERISA §§ 3(32)–(33). When a plan falls within the exclusion, the federal courts lack subject matter jurisdiction over benefit claims or other grievances. Shirley v. Maxicare Texas, Inc., 921 F.2d 565 (5th Cir.1991).

Whether a plan falls within these exclusions can sometimes be problematic. See, e.g., Lown v. Continental Casualty Co., 238 F.3d 543 (4th Cir.2001) (holding Baptist hospital's plan to be ERISA-covered because hospital was not church controlled within meaning of ERISA § 3(33)(C)(i)); Rose v. Long Island Railroad Pension Plan, 828 F.2d 910 (2d Cir.1987) (plan maintained by railroad that was governmental agency was ERISA-exempt). Cases are collected in Annotation, Construction and Application of § 4(b) of [ERISA], 135 A.L.R. Fed. 533 (1996 & Supp. 2005).

1. *Magnitudes.* Governmental plans include not only those maintained by the federal government, but those of state and local governments as well. As of 1999, "state and local plans held about 11 percent of the U.S. equity market." Mark A. Sarney, State and Local Pension Plans' Equity Holdings and Returns, 63 Social Security Bulletin 12 (No. 2, 2000). As of June 30, 2014, government defined benefit plans held $5.1 trillion in assets. Investment Company Institute, Retirement Assets Total $24.0 Trillion in Second Quarter 2014, http://www.limra.com/ Secure_Retirement_Institute/News_Center/Retirement_Industry_Report/ Retirement_Plans_-_Investment_Company_Institute__Retirement_ Assets_on_the_Rise_in_2014.aspx.

See also Public Fund Survey, Summary of Findings, FY 2012 at 1, available at www.publicfundsurvey.org.

As of 2007 state and local plans covered over 18 million participants and paid out $62 billion in benefits. EBRI, Databook on Employee Benefits, ch. 19, tbl. 19.1a (online ed., Jan. 2009).

2. *Underfunding.* Do not confuse assets with financial health. Many of the state and local plans that ERISA exempts have historically been quite poorly funded. The Public Fund Survey found that the aggregate actuarial funding level of its members (state and local governmental plans) declined from 91.1% in 2003 to 73.5% in 2012. Public Fund Survey, Summary of Findings, FY 2012, available at www. publicfundsurvey.org.

Most of the states are in very poor financial condition, so it is not surprising that there is intense focus on the level of benefits under, and funded status of, public employee plans. Many of the allegations are highly partisan, but the respected Pew Center on the States reported in February, 2010 that there was a $1 trillion gap at the end of fiscal year 2008 between the $2.35 trillion states had set aside to pay for employees' retirement and retiree health benefits and the $3.35 trillion cost of those promises. [The Trillion Dollar Gap: Underfunded State Retirement Systems and the Road to Reform, http://www.pewcenteronthestates.org/report_detail.aspx?id=56695] New accounting rules approved by the Governmental Accounting Standards Board (GASB) in June, 2012 (GASB 67 and 68) are likely to put additional pressure on governmental pension sponsors.

The bankruptcy filings by Detroit and several California cities have recently focused attention on underfunded public sector plans. See, generally, David Pratt, The Detroit Bankruptcy and Its Implications for Public Employee Retirement Plans, 21 J of Pension Benefits No. 2 at 3 (2014); Amy Monahan, Understanding the Legal Limits on Public Pension Reform, American Enterprise Institute (2013); Christine S. Chung, Government Budgets As The Hunger Games: The Brutal Competition For State and Local Government Resources Given Municipal Securities Debt, Pension and OBEP Obligations, And Taxpayer Needs, 33 Review of Banking and Financial Law 663 (2014); Christine S. Chung, Zombieland/the Detroit Bankruptcy: Why Debts Associated with Pensions, Benefits, and Municipal Securities Never Die . . . and How They Are Killing Cities Like Detroit, 41 Fordham Urban Law Journal 771 (2014).

3. *Maldesign.* Scandals arising from municipal plans in Houston, Milwaukee, and San Diego, and from the enormous New York State Common Retirement Fund, in recent years have highlighted the danger of conflict of interest on the part of the officials who negotiate with unions and otherwise set benefit levels and determine other aspects of plan design on behalf of the public entity that is the plan sponsor. When these officials are covered under the plan as participants, they often benefit from agreeing to generous plan terms, such as the practice called "spiking," which entails various means of inflating participants' compensation in the final year or years of employment, in order to drive up pension benefits under a final compensation formula. See Revell, supra, at 140.

According to the SEC, "Investment advisers are often selected by one or more trustees who are appointed by elected officials. While such a selection process is common, fairness can be undermined if advisers seeking to do business with state and local governments make political contributions to elected officials or candidates, hoping to influence the selection process. The selection process also can be undermined if elected officials or their associates ask advisers for political contributions or otherwise make it understood that only advisers who make contributions will be considered for selection. Hence the term "pay to play." Advisers and government officials who engage in pay to play practices may try to hide the true purpose of contributions or payments." SEC Proposes Measures to Curtail "Pay to Play" Practices, July 22, 2009, www.sec.gov/news/press/2009/2009-168.htm.

"The average public sector employee now collects an annual pension benefit of 60% after 30 years on the job" in addition to Social Security, compared to an average 45% in private sector defined benefit plans. Revell, supra, at 137–38. "In Pembroke Pines, Fla., police officers and firefighters can retire after 20 years with 80 percent of their pay." James Dao, "55 and Out" Comes Home to Roost, N.Y. Times, May 1, 2005. Benefit levels for plans covering elective officeholders can be lavish. In 1992 it was reported that the senior member of the Texas state senate could retire with a pension that would exceed final salary by 660 percent. The senior Oklahoma senator was entitled to a pension benefit of 172 percent of final salary. Louisiana's senior senator was entitled to a pension of 116 percent of final salary. Legislators' Benefits Can Exceed Pay, Pensions & Investments, Aug. 3, 1992, at 3.

What might account for these dramatic replacement ratios?

Retirement plans for federal employees are also significantly underfunded. As of 2007 these plans had 12.6 million participants. EBRI, Databook on Employee Benefits, ch. 18 (online ed., Jan. 2009). Until recently, most governmental plans have been defined benefit plans. The growing financial pressures associated with these plans have caused some movement away from defined benefit and toward defined contribution plans. "According to the U.S. Bureau of Labor Statistics, roughly ninety percent of state and local government employees participate in a [DB] plan as their primary retirement benefit; [DC] plans serve as the primary retirement benefit for most others. Some workers have a hybrid plan as their primary benefit." National Association of State Retirement Administrators, Overview of plan types and their use among statewide retirement systems, Nov. 2008, www.nasra.org/. See generally Jonathan Barry Forman, Public Pensions: Choosing Between Defined Benefit and Defined Contribution Plans, 1999 L. Rev. Michigan St. Univ.-Detroit Col. L. 187. In New York, the state constitution has been held to preclude any reduction in the rate of future benefit accruals. "The rights of public employees are thus fixed as of the time the employee becomes a member of the [retirement] system." Civil Service Employees Ass'n v. Regan, 525 N.E.2d 1 (N.Y. 1988) (interpreting N.Y. Const., Art. 5, § 7, which forbids reducing or diminishing public employee retirement benefits).

4. *An ERISA for public plans?* There has been discontent that public plans are not subject to ERISA's funding, vesting, disclosure, and fiduciary rules. Proposals to impose federal standards have not succeeded. The last serious effort was the proposed Public Employee

Pension Plan Reporting and Accountability Act (PEPPRA) of 1984, which foundered. See H.R. Comm. on Education and Labor, H.R. Rep. No. 98–1138 (1984). What accounts for the reluctance of Congress to extend ERISA-type regulation to state and local plans?

In 1997 the Uniform Law Commission promulgated the Uniform Management of Public Employee Retirement Systems Act (UMPERS) for state and local pension plans. 7A Uniform Laws Annotated 336 (Supp. 1998). The act prescribes ERISA-like fiduciary standards and reporting and disclosure rules. See generally Steven L. Willborn, Public Pensions and the Uniform Management of Public Employee Retirement Systems Act, 51 Rutgers L. Rev. 141 (1998). UMPERS omits to cover a number of major topics regulated in ERISA, including funding, vesting, the prohibited transactions rules, and the plan termination insurance program. Why the omissions? UMPERS has not been widely enacted. Why not?

Recently, governmental plans have been subjected to greater scrutiny by both IRS and the SEC. On April 22, 2008, the IRS held a governmental plans roundtable in Washington, DC, as part of its new effort to "assist" governmental plans. The stated goal was to raise awareness in the governmental plan sector of the need to comply with Federal tax qualification requirements, and to begin a dialogue on how to ensure that governmental plans succeed. In February, 2009, IRS surveyed a group of 25 governmental plans as part of a new "compliance" initiative, to be followed by a larger survey. The IRS initiative coincides with a push to encourage public plans to seek determination letters. This initiative has raised concerns.

In addition, on July 22, 2009, the Securities and Exchange Commission voted unanimously to propose measures to curtail "pay to play" practices by investment advisers seeking to manage money for state and local governments. "The measures are designed to prevent an adviser from making political contributions or hidden payments to influence their selection by government officials." SEC Proposes Measures to Curtail "Pay to Play" Practices, SEC Press Release 2009–168, July 22, 2009, www.sec.gov/news/press/2009/2009–168.htm.

In November, 2011, the IRS and Treasury solicited comments on possible standards for determining if a retirement plan is a governmental plan under Code § 414(d). The request for comment is contained in two advance notices of proposed rulemaking published in the Federal Register on November 8, 2011. (Determination of Governmental Plan Status, 76 FR 69172, and Indian Tribal Governmental Plans, 76 FR 69188). It is important to note that the draft regulations have not yet been formally proposed. Although the anticipated proposed regulations would only be applicable for purposes of Code § 414(d), the DoL and PBGC were consulted in drafting the proposal. Copies of the comments on the regulations will be forwarded to the DoL and the PBGC.

5.   _State constitutional and public law._ In the absence of ERISA-type vesting and funding requirements, the state courts have on occasion found other ways to enforce state and local pension promises. See, e.g., Dadisman v. Moore, 384 S.E.2d 816 (W.Va.1988) (mandamusing the governor to include pension funding in the budget and voiding legislative appropriations of pension trust funds, on the authority of state

constitutional law and common law trust concepts). Compare Claypool v. Wilson, 4 Cal.App.4th 646, 6 Cal.Rptr.2d 77 (1992) (refusing to prevent legislative appropriations from the California public employees fund).

6.   *The Church Plan Litigation.* There has been a recent flurry of lawsuits involving defined benefit plans claimed by their sponsors, large healthcare organizations, to be church plans and thus exempt from the funding and other requirements of ERISA. In most of these cases the plan sponsors have claimed, with a dexterity worthy of Humpty Dumpty, that their 401(k) plans and health and welfare plans *are* subject to ERISA. See, e.g., Norman Stein, An Article of Faith: The Gratuity Theory of Pensions and Faux Church Plans, ABA Section of Labor and Employment Law, Employee Benefits Committee Newsletter, Summer 2014; G. Daniel Miller, The Church Plan Definition—A Reply to Norm Stein, ABA Section of Labor and Employment Law, Employee Benefits Committee Newsletter, Fall 2014; Emily Hootkins and Elizabeth Wilson Vaughan Living on a Prayer? Recent Challenges to the Church Plan Exemption, Benefits Law journal, vol. 27, no. 2 (2014).

3.   THE MEANING OF "PLAN"

Massachusetts v. Morash
490 U.S. 107 (1989).

■ JUSTICE STEVENS delivered the opinion of the Court.

Issue —
This case requires us to determine whether a company's policy of paying its discharged employees for their unused vacation time constitutes an "employee welfare benefit plan" within the meaning of § 3(1) of [ERISA], and whether a criminal action to enforce that policy is foreclosed by the Act's broad preemption provision.

In May 1986, petitioner, the Commonwealth of Massachusetts, issued two complaints in the Boston Municipal Court against respondent, Richard N. Morash, president of the Yankee Bank for Finance and Savings (Bank). The complaints charged Morash with criminal violations of the Massachusetts Payment of Wages Statute, Mass.Gen.Laws c. 149 § 148 (1987).

Under the Massachusetts law, an employer is required to pay a discharged employee his full wages, including holiday or vacation payments, on the date of discharge. Similar wage payment statutes have been enacted by 47 other States, the District of Columbia, and the United States, and over half of these include vacation pay. The complaints filed in Boston Municipal Court alleged that respondent had failed to compensate two discharged bank vice presidents for vacation time they accrued but did not use.

Respondent moved to dismiss the criminal complaints on the ground that the Massachusetts statute, insofar as it applied to these complaints, had been pre-empted by ERISA. He argued that the Bank's vacation policy constituted an "employee welfare benefit plan" under the Act, and that the State's prosecution of him for failure to comply with the policy therefore ran afoul of § 514(a) of the Act, which pre-empts "any and all State laws insofar as they . . . relate to any employee benefit plan."

Without ruling on the motion, the trial judge reported the preemption question to the Massachusetts Appeals Court for decision; the Supreme Judicial Court then transferred the case to its docket on its own initiative. For the purpose of answering the reported question, the parties stipulated that the Bank had made oral or written agreements stemming from handbooks, manuals, memoranda, and practices to pay employees in lieu of unused vacation time, and that "such payments are made out of the Bank's general assets" in lump sums upon termination of employment.

The Supreme Judicial Court held that the policy constituted an employee welfare benefit plan and that the prosecution was preempted by ERISA. 402 Mass. 287, 522 N.E.2d 409 (1988). The court found that under the plain language of the statute and its earlier decision in *Barry v. Dymo Graphic Systems, Inc.*, 394 Mass. 830, 478 N.E.2d 707 (1985), the Bank's policy constituted a plan, fund, or program for the purpose of providing its participants vacation benefits. It rejected the Commonwealth's argument that a regulation promulgated by the Secretary of Labor (the Secretary),[6] had excepted payments out of an employer's general assets for unused vacation time from the definition of a welfare plan because even if regular vacation pay was not included in ERISA, the lump-sum payment for unused vacation time upon discharge was akin to severance pay covered by ERISA. The fact that it would be necessary for an employer to maintain records relating to its employees' unused vacation time, plus the need to accumulate funds to pay the benefits, made it appropriate to treat the employer's promise to its employees as a "plan." The court concluded that the Massachusetts statute related to the plan within the meaning of § 514, and was not excluded from its coverage by the provision saving from pre-emption a "generally applicable criminal law." ERISA § 514(b)(4).

Because the federal question decided by the Supreme Judicial Court is an important one over which the courts have disagreed, we granted [certiorari]. We now reverse. . . .

The precise coverage of ERISA is not clearly set forth in the Act. ERISA covers "employee benefit plans" which it defines as plans that are either "an employee welfare benefit plan," or "an employee pension benefit plan," or both. ERISA § 3(3). An employee welfare benefit plan, in turn, is defined as:

Ruling (*No to #1*)

> "[A]ny plan, fund, or program which was heretofore or is hereafter established or maintained by an employer or by an employee organization, or by both, to the extent that such plan,

---

[6]   The Secretary's payroll practice regulation provides, in part:

"(b) *Payroll practices.* For purposes of Title I of the Act and this chapter, the terms 'employee welfare benefit plan' and 'welfare plan' shall not include—

. . .

"(3) Payment of compensation, out of the employer's general assets, on account of periods of time during which the employee, although physically and mentally able to perform his or her duties and not absent for medical reasons (such as pregnancy, a physical examination or psychiatric treatment) performs no duties; for example—

"(i) Payment of compensation while an employee is on vacation or absent on a holiday, including payment of premiums to induce employees to take vacations at a time favorable to the employer for business reasons." 29 CFR § 2510.3–1(b)(3) (1987).

fund, or program was established or is maintained for the purpose of providing for its participants or their beneficiaries, through the purchase of insurance or otherwise, (A) medical, surgical, or hospital care or benefits, or benefits in the event of sickness, accident, disability, death or unemployment, or vacation benefits, apprenticeship or other training programs, or day care centers, scholarship funds, or prepaid legal services, or (B) any benefit described in section 186(c) of this title (other than pensions on retirement or death, and insurance to provide such pensions)." ERISA § 3(1).

The Act does not further define "plan, fund, or program" or "vacation benefits" and does not specify whether every policy to provide vacation benefits falls within its ambit.

The words "any plan, fund, or program . . . maintained for the purpose of providing . . . vacation benefits," may surely be read to encompass any form of regular vacation payments to an employee. A multiemployer fund created to provide vacation benefits for union members who typically work for several employers during the course of a year, see, *e.g., Franchise Tax Bd. v. Construction Laborers Vacation Trust for Southern California,* 463 U.S. 1, 4, n. 2 (1983), undoubtedly falls within the scope of the Act. In addition, the creation of a separate fund to pay employees vacation benefits would subject a single employer to the regulatory provisions of ERISA. We do not believe, however, that the policy here to pay employees for unused vacation time constitutes an employee welfare benefit plan. *So not subject to ERISA (bc not an Employee welfare Benefit Plan)*

The interpretation of § 3(1) is governed by the familiar principles that " 'words grouped in a list should be given related meaning,' " and that "in expounding a statute, we [are] not . . . guided by a single sentence or member of a sentence, but look to the provisions of the whole law, and to its object and policy." In enacting ERISA, Congress' primary concern was with the mismanagement of funds accumulated to finance employee *bc* benefits and the failure to pay employees benefits from accumulated *Not* funds. To that end, it established extensive reporting, disclosure, and *Pre-fun* fiduciary duty requirements to insure against the possibility that the *but in* employee's expectation of the benefit would be defeated through poor *contin* management by the plan administrator. Because ordinary vacation *upon so* payments are typically fixed, due at known times, and do not depend on *future* contingencies outside the employee's control, they present none of the *occur* risks that ERISA is intended to address. If there is a danger of defeated expectations, it is no different from the danger of defeated expectations of wages for services performed—a danger Congress chose not to regulate in ERISA.

This conclusion is supported by viewing the reference to vacation benefits not in isolation but in light of the words that accompany it and give the provision meaning. Section 3(1) subjects to ERISA regulation plans to provide medical, sickness, accident, disability and death benefits, training programs, day care centers, scholarship funds, and legal services. The distinguishing feature of most of these benefits is that they accumulate over a period of time and are payable only upon the occurrence of a contingency outside of the control of the employee. Thus, for example, plans to pay employees severance benefits, which are payable *only* upon termination of employment, are employee welfare benefit plans within the meaning of the Act. The reference to vacation payments in § 3(1) should be understood to include within the scope of ERISA those vacation benefit funds, analogous to other welfare benefits, in which either the employee's right to a benefit is contingent upon some future occurrence or the employee bears a risk different from his ordinary employment risk. It is unlikely that Congress intended to subject to ERISA's reporting and disclosure requirements those vacation benefits which by their nature are payable on a regular basis from the general assets of the employer and are accumulated over time only at the election of the employee.

The Secretary, who is specifically authorized to define ERISA's "accounting, technical, and trade terms," ERISA § 505, and to whose reasonable views we give deference, has also so understood the statute. In a Notice of Proposed Rulemaking published shortly after the effective date of the Act, the Secretary identified a basic distinction between the benefit programs covered by the Act and the types of regular compensation, including vacation pay, that are not covered:

> "The Secretary also anticipates issuance of regulations that will make it clear that other programs, including certain employer practices (whether pursuant to a collective bargaining agreement or not) under which employees are paid as a part of their regular compensation directly by the employer and under which no separate fund is established will not subject the employer to any filing or disclosure duties under Title I of the Act. Examples of the employer practices that may receive this treatment are payment of overtime pay, *vacation pay,* shift premiums, Sunday premiums, holiday premiums, jury duty or military duty, make-up pay, and pay while absent on account of illness or excused absences." 39 Fed.Reg. 42236 (1974) (emphasis added).

The Secretary subsequently proposed regulations excluding payment of compensation for work performed at night or during holidays and paid sick leave and vacation leave from the definition of an employee benefit. 40 Fed.Reg. 24642–24643 (1975). He explained:

> "[P]aid vacations . . . are not treated as employee benefit plans because they are associated with regular wages or salary, rather than benefits triggered by contingencies such as hospitalization. Moreover, the abuses which created the impetus for the reforms in Title I were not in this area, and there is no indication that Congress intended to subject these practices to Title I coverage."

The proposed regulations promulgated by the Secretary were adopted without significant modification. They provide that numerous "payroll practices," including the payment of vacation benefits "out of [an] employer's general assets" rather than from a trust fund, are not employee welfare benefit plans within the meaning of ERISA. In addition, under the regulations, the term employee welfare benefit plan does not include the payment by an employer of premium rates for work performed during special periods such as holidays and weekends. The Secretary has consistently adhered to this position even when the premium pay is accumulated and carried over to later years.

A contrary interpretation, including routine vacation pay policies within ERISA, would have profound consequences. Most employers in the United States provide some type of vacation benefit to their employees.[15] ERISA coverage would put all these employers to the choice of complying with the statute's detailed requirements for reporting and disclosure or discontinuing the practice of compensating employees for unused vacation time. In addition, the extension of ERISA to claims for vacation benefits would vastly expand the jurisdiction of the federal courts, providing a federal forum for any employee with a vacation grievance.[16] Finally, such an interpretation would also displace the extensive state regulation of the vesting, funding and participation rights of vacation benefits; because ERISA's vesting and funding requirements do not apply to welfare benefit plans, employees would actually receive less protection if ERISA were applied to ordinary vacation wages paid from the employer's general assets. See Note, 87 Colum.L.Rev. 1702, 1718 (1987).[17] The States have traditionally regulated the payment of wages, including vacation pay. Absent any indication that Congress intended such far-reaching consequences, we are reluctant to so significantly interfere with "the separate spheres of governmental authority preserved in our federalist system." *Fort Halifax Packing Co. v. Coyne*, 482 U.S. [1, 19 (1987)]. . . .

The fact that the payments in this case were due at the time of the employee's termination does not affect their character as a part of regular compensation. Unlike normal severance pay, the employees' right to compensation for accrued vacation time is not contingent upon the termination of their employment.

In reaching this conclusion, we emphasize that the case before us—and the Secretary's regulations on which we rely—concern payments by a single employer out of its general assets. An entirely different situation would be presented if a separate fund had been created by a group of employers to guarantee the payment of vacation benefits to laborers who regularly shift their jobs from one employer to another. Employees who are beneficiaries of such a trust face far different risks and have far greater need for the reporting and disclosure requirements that the federal law imposes than those whose vacation benefits come from the same fund from which they receive their paychecks. It is sufficient for this case that the Secretary's determination that a single employer's administration of a vacation pay policy from its general assets does not possess the characteristics of a welfare benefit plan constitutes a reasonable construction of the statute.[18]

---

[15] A 1988 survey reflects that paid vacations are provided to 98 percent of the 31,000,000 employees in medium and large establishments.

[16] A 1983 survey found that state agencies each year resolve more than 19,000 vacation pay claims, involving more than $7.5 million. Note, 16 Loyola U.Chi.L.J. 387, 422 (1985).

[17] Many States have provisions for the vesting of vacation benefits, see Note, 87 Colum.L.Rev. 1702, 1714 (1987), and for the administrative resolution of vacation pay claims, Note, 16 Loyola U.Chi.L.Rev., at 421–422. An interpretation of ERISA to include ordinary vacation pay would imperil these mechanisms designed for the benefit of employees.

[18] We therefore have no occasion to address the Commonwealth's alternative argument that Mass.Gen.Laws c. 149 § 148 (1987) is a "generally applicable criminal law of a State" within the meaning of ERISA § 514(b)(4).

The judgment of the Massachusetts Supreme Judicial Court is reversed and the case is remanded for further proceedings not inconsistent with this opinion.

4. WHAT IS A PLAN UNDER ERISA?

ERISA regulates plans, both pension plans and nonpension (i.e., welfare benefit) plans. If a court concludes that the arrangement in controversy is not a plan, none of ERISA will apply. Accordingly, for litigants wishing to escape ERISA claims, the contention that no plan is involved is an attractive position, and it has generated a large case law.

ERISA regulates Pension + Non Pension plans

1. *ERISA's definitions* The definitions in ERISA §§ 3(1), 3(2), and 3(3) are each circular; "plan" is defined as "plan," with the result that "plan" is effectively an undefined term. Nevertheless, § 3(1) expressly envisions that an ERISA-covered plan may be one that provides "vacation benefits." In reasoning that ERISA's "reference to vacation payments in § 3(1)" really meant vacation benefit funds that differ materially from ordinary wages, the Court in *Morash* was engaging in purposive as opposed to literal interpretation.

✓ Yes ERISA (bc NOT current compensation)

Applying *Morash*, and aided once again by a supportive DoL regulation, the courts have also concluded that an employer who pays for sick leave is engaging in a payroll practice rather than operating an ERISA-covered plan. See, e.g., Stern v. IBM Corp., 326 F.3d 1367 (11th Cir.2003); Funkhouser v. Wells Fargo Bank, N.A., 289 F.3d 1137 (9th Cir.2002). Compare McMahon v. Digital Equipment Corp., 162 F.3d 28, 37 (1st Cir.1998), finding that an employer's "Salary Continuation Plan" for disabled employees, which was partially funded by insurance contracts and supported by a fidelity bond, was a welfare benefit plan and not a mere payroll practice funded by the employer's general assets.

✗ Not ERISA (because Payroll practice current compensation)

Is a labor union's "death benefit fund," which pays $300 on the death of a member or retiree, an ERISA plan? See Devlin v. Transportation Communications Int'l Union, 175 F.3d 121 (2d Cir.1999), invoking 29 C.F.R. § 2510.3–1(g).

2. *Factors that test for a plan.* Donovan v. Dillingham, 688 F.2d 1367, 1372 (11th Cir.1982), is prominently cited in opinions that wrestle with the question of what is a plan. Judge Godbold wrote: "Commentators and courts define 'plan, fund or program' by synonym—arrangement, scheme, unitary scheme, program of action, method of putting into effect an intention or proposal, design—but do not specify the prerequisites of a 'plan, fund, or program.' At a minimum, however, a 'plan, fund, or program' under ERISA implies the existence of intended benefits, intended beneficiaries, a source of financing, and a procedure to apply for and collect benefits."

"ERISA Plan" definition under ERISA

What makes these so-called *Dillingham* factors relevant to the issue of whether something is or is not a plan? Is the list exhaustive? Why did the drafters of ERISA leave so fundamental a term undefined?

The *Dillingham* test has been criticized. "If a source of financing cannot be identified for an employer program relating to payment of benefits, then *either* the program is not a plan *or* it is a plan in violation of ERISA. The *Dillingham* test, without any attempt at justification, simply assumes the former. [Whether] a plan exists—whether ERISA

— Providing current compensation NOT an ERISA Plan (because not retirement) — must be a promise for the future (but Not a contract)
— Must be in writing

regulation is necessary and appropriate—must be made to depend on employer representations and employee expectations, not on the benefits that may or may not be provided." Jay Conison, Foundations of the Common Law of Plans, 41 DePaul L. Rev. 575, 648–49 (1992). Also critical of the case law is Peter J. Wiedenbeck, Implementing ERISA: Of Policies and "Plans," 72 Washington U.L.Q. 559, 576–96 (1994). See also Daft v. Advest, Inc., 658 F. 3d 583 (6th Cir. 2011), holding that the existence of a plan is a nonjurisdictional element of an ERISA claim, so the fact that a plan did not meet the ERISA definition of a plan did not deprive the court of jurisdiction.

3.   *Retirement income.* ERISA § 3(2)(A)(i) defines an "employee pension benefit plan" as one that provides "retirement income to employees." The courts have consistently held that conventional stock option plans, widely used in executive compensation, fall outside the definition, because such plans provide current compensation rather than retirement income. See, e.g., Oatway v. American Int'l Group, 325 F.3d 184 (3d Cir.2003); Murphy v. Inexco Oil Co., 611 F.2d 570 (5th Cir.1980). Should the case be decided differently if the employee shows that he or she intended to use the asset to help fund his or her retirement? See Houston v. Aramark Corp., 112 Fed.Appx. 132 (3d Cir.2004).

Do noncash benefits qualify as "retirement income to employees"? Consider the well known case, Musmeci v. Schwegmann Giant Super Markets, Inc., 332 F.3d 339 (5th Cir.2003). A grocery store company terminated unilaterally in 1997 a program that it had begun in 1985, which promised to award a monthly voucher worth $216 in store merchandise, valid only for 30 days, and not redeemable for cash, to each employee who retired at 60 or older after having served for at least 20 years. The Fifth Circuit held that the program was an ERISA pension plan that paid "retirement income" in kind rather than in cash. The court gave weight to the company's having deducted the total face value of the vouchers on its tax returns as a business expense under the category of retirement plans. 332 F.3d at 343. The court also concluded that an award of money damages in place of the terminated in-kind benefit constituted an award of "benefits due" under ERISA § 502(a)(1)(B), the remedial provision discussed in Chapter 16, infra. For commentary, see Note, When Is a Snickers Bar a Pension Plan?—The 5th Circuit's View, 11 ERISA Litigation Rptr. 4 (Aug. 2003); No Good Deed Goes Unpunished—District Court Holds Former Grocery Chain Owner Personally Liable for Unfunded Grocery Voucher "Pension," 29 Tax Management Compensation Planning J. 294 (2001) (discussing the district court opinion, 159 F.Supp.2d 329 (E.D.La. 2001)).

In Stoffels v. SBC Communications, Inc., 677 F. 3d. 720 (5th Cir. 2012), the plaintiffs alleged that the defendants' practice of offering reimbursements for telephone services to retirees who lived outside defendants' service region constituted a "pension plan" under ERISA. The district court judge entered an interlocutory order in which he found that the program was a pension plan covered by ERISA, but he recused himself before entering final judgment. The second judge assigned to the case reconsidered the interlocutory order. He concluded that the program was not a pension plan, and entered final judgment. The appeals court concluded that he did not abuse his discretion by revising the interlocutory order, and affirmed his judgment. See also Boos v. AT&T, Inc., 643 F. 3d 127 (5th Cir. 2011), cert. den. 132 S. Ct. 816 (2011) (affirming district court decision that a similar program was not a pension plan).

4. *Pressure from ERISA preemption: Fort Halifax.* ERISA § 514(a) preempts state laws that "relate to any employee benefit plan." It will be seen, infra in Chapter 17, that the breadth of this language, coupled with an initial tendency on the part of the Supreme Court to construe it expansively, has produced a huge and complex case law. Because the courts initially found the "relate to" language hard to limit, attention came to be focused on restricting the concept of "plan" as used in the same phrase. Much of the case law construing the term "plan" arises in preemption cases.

In Fort Halifax Packing Co. v. Coyne, 482 U.S. 1 (1987), discussed in *Morash*, the Court relied upon the definition of "plan" in order to prevent preemption. ERISA § 3(1), it has been seen, defines which "plan, fund or program" qualifies as an "employee welfare benefit plan." Subsection (B) incorporates by reference from § 302 of the Taft-Hartley Act any "plan, fund, or program" that provides "severance or similar benefits." Maine enacted a statute requiring that when an employer closes a plant within the state, the employer must pay the terminated workers one week's severance pay for each year of service with the firm. Fort Halifax closed a poultry processing plant, dismissing over a hundred workers, many of them long-service employees. Fort Halifax contended that the Maine statute was preempted under ERISA. In a 5–4 decision, the Supreme Court held for the workers. Justice Brennan rested the majority opinion upon the distinction between "benefits" and a benefit "plan":

> The purposes of ERISA's pre-emption provision make clear that the Maine statute in no way raises the types of concerns that prompted pre-emption. Congress intended pre-emption to afford employers the advantages of a uniform set of administrative procedures governed by a single set of regulations. This concern only arises, however, with respect to benefits whose provision by nature requires an ongoing administrative program to meet the employer's obligation. It is for this reason that Congress pre-empted state laws relating to *plans*, rather than simply to *benefits*. Only a plan embodies a set of administrative practices vulnerable to the burden that would be imposed by a patchwork scheme of regulation.

> The Maine statute neither establishes, nor requires an employer to maintain, an employee benefit *plan*. The requirement of a one-time lump-sum payment triggered by a single event requires no administrative scheme whatsoever to meet the employer's obligation. . . . To do little more than write a check hardly constitutes the operation of a benefit plan. Once this single event is over, the employer has no further responsibility. The theoretical possibility of a one-time obligation in the future simply creates no need for an ongoing administrative program for processing claims and paying benefits. . . .

The Maine statute therefore creates no impediment to an employer's adoption of a uniform benefit administrative scheme. Neither the possibility of a one-time payment in the future, nor the act of making such a payment, in any way creates the potential for the type of conflicting regulation of benefit plans that ERISA pre-emption was intended to prevent. As a result, pre-emption of the Maine law would not serve the purpose for which ERISA's pre-emption provision was enacted.

482 U.S. at 11–12, 14–15.

Justice White's dissent faults the majority for creating "a loophole in ERISA's preemption statute which will undermine Congress' decision to make employee-benefit plans a matter of exclusive federal regulation." Id. at 23. "I dissent because it is incredible to believe that Congress intended that the broad preemption provision contained in ERISA would depend upon the extent to which an employer exercised administrative foresight in preparing for the eventual payment of employee benefits." Id.

Does the majority's emphasis on the single-contingent-payment feature of the Maine statute imply that employer-provided life insurance arrangements are not ERISA-covered welfare benefit plans, since the death benefit afforded through life insurance takes the form of a single, contingent payment? See id. at 14 n.9.

Later cases have wrestled with the scope of *Fort Halifax*. In James v. Fleet/Norstar Financial Group, 992 F.2d 463 (2d Cir.1993), the employer announced that it would provide certain employees being terminated 60 days of pay following their last day of work if they would remain on the job until a future termination date. The employer then cancelled the offer. Applying *Fort Halifax*, the court held that the offer did not create an ERISA plan, hence that state law litigation arising from the cancellation was not preempted by ERISA.

Wells v. General Motors Corp., 881 F.2d 166 (5th Cir.1989), involved a collectively bargained "voluntary termination of employment plan" under which terminating employees exchanged seniority and rehire rights for a severance payment. The Fifth Circuit held the plan not an ERISA plan and refused to preempt state law litigation alleging fraudulent inducement to accept. "The operative facts in *Fort Halifax* are remarkably similar to those in the instant case. GM established a procedure by which employees could elect to receive a one-time lump payment if they ceased working at the plant. The plan was not ongoing, nor was there any need for continuing [administration]." Id. at 176.

Contrast Akau v. Tel-A-Com Hawaii, 12 E.B.C. 1378 (D.Haw.1990). A statute of Hawaii required that an employer provide terminated workers with a dislocation allowance. The court held the statute preempted despite *Fort Halifax*. The statute required employers to provide this benefit "not only upon a closing or relocation, as in the Maine statute, but also upon a partial closing. Thus, as defendants argue, the allowance may be triggered by a wide range of possible business interest transactions," making the statute more burdensome, as in this case, in which the transfer of a 1.68% unit of the company's business triggered the benefit entitlement. Further, whereas the Maine statute called for a single lump sum payment, the Hawaii statute required the employer to cut four weekly checks, according to a formula that was more complex than the Maine scheme. Because the statute "places significant administrative burdens on Hawaii employers, and it is quite distinguishable from the Maine [statute,] it is an 'employee benefit plan' for purposes of ERISA and is thereby pre-empted." Are you persuaded? Should the need for four checks rather than one decide the question of ERISA preemption?

On which side of the *Fort Halifax* line—and why—would you place Massachusetts' "tin parachute" law? The statute requires that when an employee's termination occurs incident to a change in corporate control, the employee is entitled to a lump-sum severance payment equal to twice the employee's weekly compensation multiplied by the employee's total years of service. See Simas v. Quaker Fabric Corp. of Fall River, 6 F.3d 849 (1st Cir.1993), noted in 2 ERISA Litigation Reporter 23 (Dec. 1993).

Velarde v. PACE Membership Warehouse, Inc., 105 F.3d 1313 (9th Cir.1997), involved the employer's offer of a "stay-on bonus" to workers who agreed to remain employed until an announced shutdown of the workplace. Should the court analogize the bonus to an ERISA-covered severance pay plan? Held, the bonus was not an ERISA plan "because it necessitates no 'ongoing administrative scheme.'" Id. at 1347.

Fort Halifax emphasized the single lump sum payment feature of the Maine statute as an attribute that pointed away from treating the mandated scheme as an ERISA plan. In Collins v. Ralston Purina Co., 147 F.3d 592 (7th Cir.1998), which involved the claim that an employer reneged on its promise to make payments to an executive under a change-of-control retention agreement, the court distinguished *Fort Halifax* and found an ERISA plan, citing this employer's "prospect of multiple payments to various managers, at different times and under different circumstances. [The employer] could not satisfy its obligation by cutting a single check and making a 'single set of payments' to all of its managers at once. The individual retention agreement required the company to budget for the prospect of paying out disbursements of varying amounts to its managers and at various times." Id. at 595–96. Has the court effectively distinguished *Fort Halifax*? Is the decision reconcilable with *Velarde*, described supra in the previous paragraph?

In New England Mutual Life Ins. Co. v. Baig, 166 F.3d 1 (1st Cir.1999), the employee purchased a disability insurance policy from the insurer. The employer reimbursed the premium payments to the employee. The First Circuit, sustaining the district court's finding that there was no ERISA plan, quoted a portion of the district court's opinion that the case might have been decided differently if the employer had purchased the policy directly: " 'When an employer deals directly with the insurer and actually purchases an insurance policy for an employee, there may be sufficient participation to meet the "established or maintained" requirement under ERISA [§ 3(1)(A)].'" Id. at 4, quoting the district court opinion, 985 F.Supp. at 14. Since reimbursement was a means of having the employer pay for the policy, why should it make a difference whether employer or employee actually cut the checks that went to the insurer?

DoL regulations clarify that an employer who facilitates the purchase of group life insurance through an outside insurer does not operate an ERISA plan if the employer makes no contributions and employees' participation is completely voluntary. The employer may, however, remit premiums to the insurer through payroll deduction. 29 C.F.R. § 2510.3–1(j), followed in Thompson v. American Home Assurance Co., 95 F.3d 429 (6th Cir.1996). In July, 2009, a federal appeals court held that an insured benefit program under which an employer pays the premiums for at least one employee is subject to ERISA with respect to all employees. Helfman v. GE Group Life Assurance Company, 573 F.3d 383 (6th Cir.2009). The plaintiff argued that a hybrid approach was appropriate under the DoL safe harbor: because he met the four criteria of the safe harbor, his plan was exempt from ERISA and subject to state law, whereas the remaining employees participating in the plan, on whose behalf the company contributed to premiums, remained subject to ERISA. The court held that allowing a single plan to be at once subject to state and federal law, depending on the employee, would frustrate the purposes of ERISA and would be inconsistent with the Supreme Court's decision in Yates v. Hendon, 541 U.S. 1 (2004).

5. *Plain meaning*? Justice White's dissent in *Fort Halifax* treats the question of statutory interpretation with disdain. Since ERISA § 3(1) defines an "employee welfare benefit plan" as "any plan, fund, or program" by which the employer or other sponsor provides any of the statutorily enumerated benefits, and since severance benefits are among those benefits, Justice White reasoned that the Maine statute "clearly 'relate[s] to' benefit plans as contemplated by ERISA's pre-emption provision." 482 U.S. at 24.

Nobody could doubt that the Maine statute relates to the provision of benefits; the question is whether it relates to benefit plans. ERISA § 3(3) purports to define the term "plan" or "employee benefit plan," but only for the purpose of establishing that these terms cover both pension plans and welfare benefit plans. Otherwise, ERISA § 3(3) is content to say that a plan is a plan. That throws the analysis back on ERISA §§ 3(1) and 3(2) which define, respectively, welfare benefit and pension plans. Each commences by saying that the defined terms "mean any plan, fund, or program" providing the enumerated benefits. Once again, therefore, ERISA says that a plan is a plan.

6. *Single participant plans.* Does a plan presuppose numerosity, that is, more than one employee, or may an arrangement tailored to a single employee qualify?

The *Dillingham* factors speak in the plural, of "intended beneficiaries." In Williams v. Wright, 927 F.2d 1540 (11th Cir.1991), however, a single-participant plan was upheld. The employer, attempting to encourage the employee to retire, had written the employee a letter promising to pay him $500 per month, to pay his country club dues, and to provide him a car and office space. When the employer, in dissolution, later reneged on most of the promised benefits, the employee sued. The Eleventh Circuit, reversing the district court, held that some of the promised retirement benefits fell within the scope of an ERISA plan. "[We] find nothing in the ERISA legislation pointing to the exclusion of plans covering only a single employee." Id. at 1545. The court framed the question as whether the arrangement set forth in the letter "was designed primarily for the purpose of providing retirement income or whether [it] contemplated the payment of post-retirement income only incidentally to a contract for current employment." Id. at 1547. The court found that the payment of retirement income was the prevailing purpose. For discussion, see Note, Pension Payments to One Former Employee, 1 ERISA Litigation Reporter 7 (Jul.–Aug. 1991).

In Dakota, Minnesota and Eastern Railroad Corp. v. Schieffer, 648 F. 3d 935 (8th Cir. 2011), the court took the position that the language of ERISA suggests that a plan must provide benefits to more than one person. "Although severance benefits are clearly among those described in [the statute], the words "plan" and "program" in § 1002(1) strongly imply benefits that an employer provides to a class of employees. Even more significantly, the plain language of this statute—the reference to "participants or *their* beneficiaries"—reflects the congressional intent that a covered "plan" is one that provides welfare benefits to more than one person. Although 1 U.S.C. § 1 provides that "unless the context indicates otherwise . . . words importing the plural include the singular," that statute is only applied where "necessary to carry out the evident intent of the statute." Here, Congress's use of the plural is evidence of its intent."

[handwritten margin note: A plan must provide benefits to more than one person to be considered an ERISA plan]

In ruling that a plan must provide benefits to more than one person, the Eighth Circuit consciously rejected the contrary position taken by the Eleventh, Fourth and Seventh Circuits. "We recognize that several circuit court decisions have concluded that a contract with a single employee to provide post-termination benefits *may* be a "one-person" ERISA plan if it satisfies the "administrative scheme" criteria of Fort Halifax. But the reasoning in these opinions was quite perfunctory, and none considered the plain language of § 1002(1). Moreover, none considered the broader context of this preemption issue. Congress in the National Labor Relations Act broadly preempted state laws that interfere with multi-employee collective bargaining, and in ERISA broadly preempted state laws that interfere with multi-employee benefit plans. But Congress has never preempted state laws that regulate and enforce individual employment contracts between employers and their executives. That remains an important prerogative of the States, no matter how complex a contract may be to administer. Neither the administrative nor the remedial purposes of ERISA preemption apply to the resolution of contractual disputes between an employer and a single, salaried employee. Considering ERISA's statutory language, purpose, and historical context, we conclude that an individual contract providing severance benefits to a single executive employee is not an ERISA employee welfare benefit plan within the meaning of 29 U.S.C. § 1002(1)."

A motel chain contracted with its general counsel to pay three times annual salary should the counsel be terminated within three years of employment. If the counsel were terminated after three years, the severance payment would be reduced by one-third for each year of employment greater than three. The Department of Labor, in an advisory opinion letter (DoL 91–20A) determined that the arrangement was not a pension plan, but was a severance plan covered under the definition of employee welfare benefit plan in ERISA § 3(1). 18 BNA Pension Reporter 1423 (1991).

7.   *Fringe fringes.* Employee benefits that have been held not to be ERISA plans include airline programs allowing employees to travel free or at reduced rates, Constantine v. American Airlines Pension Benefit Plan, 162 F.Supp.2d 552, 554–56 (N.D.Tex.2001); a golden parachute severance pay agreement for executives, Kulinski v. Medtronic Bio-Medicus, Inc., 21 F.3d 254 (8th Cir.1994); an indemnity agreement, Floerchinger v. Intellicall, Inc., 802 F.Supp. 1480 (N.D.Tex.1992); and an agreement to provide rent-free housing to the employee, Jervis v. Elerding, 504 F.Supp. 606 (C.D.Cal.1980).

In Brady v. General Dynamics Corp., 915 F.Supp. 1103 (S.D.Cal.1996), the court found that a program under which employees were given access to a fitness center and recreational park was not an ERISA plan. The court said it was unable to fit the program within any of the categories of welfare benefit plan contained in ERISA's definition in § 3(1). The DoL gave a similar rationale in an advisory opinion that an airline's free or reduced cost travel pass program for former employees was not an ERISA plan. See 26 BNA Pension & Benefits Rptr. 1060 (1999).

Contrast Madonia v. Blue Cross & Blue Shield of Virginia, 11 F.3d 444 (4th Cir.1993), finding that a closely held corporation that subsidized health insurance for several of its employees had established an ERISA-covered welfare benefit plan.

Is an employer's promise to pay relocation expenses following termination of employment a welfare benefit plan? See Riofrio Anda v. Ralston Purina Co., 772 F.Supp. 46 (D.P.R.1991).

In Fraver v. North Carolina Farm Bureau Mutual Ins. Co., 801 F.2d 675 (4th Cir.1986), reversing 643 F.Supp. 633 (E.D.N.C.1985), the employer was a firm that marketed insurance through a force of sales agents, whom it treated as independent contractors. The salespeople received commission income, and the company reported their income to the IRS on Form 1099 (for independent contractors) rather than under Form W-2 (withholding for employees). The contract between the company and the agents specified, under the heading "Retirement, Death, and Disability Benefits," that agents reaching 65 who then retired would be entitled to receive, over a five year period, an amount equal to the agent's renewal commission for the year immediately preceding retirement. A condition of receiving the benefit was that the agent "not be licensed to sell any kind of insurance in North Carolina during the payment period." The company maintained no fund or trust for the payment of such benefits. The plaintiffs in the litigation were former agents who became licensed to sell insurance in North Carolina and went to work for competitors. The plaintiffs alleged that their retirement benefit was vested under ERISA § 203, and that the forfeiture clause was void. The district court so held. The Fourth Circuit reversed on the ground that the arrangement was not a plan. The court focused on ERISA § 3(2), which defines a pension plan as a "plan, fund or program [that] provides retirement income to employees," and it saw the question in the case as "whether [the disputed provisions] provide retirement income." It reasoned:

The post-termination benefits are calculated on the basis of the agent's commissions for the prior year and, in that respect, are like a final commission, paid over an extended term.

Further, the nature of the payments is not indicative of a pension or retirement plan. The provisions in question are entitled "Retirement, Death and Disability Benefits." Of course, the nature of the benefits cannot be determined from the title alone. The terms make it clear that the benefits were not limited to termination for death, disability, or retirement. The agent could terminate his contract at any age, and the payments were to be made regardless of the reason for termination except when the agent was terminated for reasons of fraud or criminal act. The amount of the payment is tied to only one factor, the amount of business in the last year prior to termination. Finally, the payments are recouped from the individual's successor. In sum, the benefits are in the nature of a buy-out in which the departing agent receives payments based on what he leaves behind in the way of business for his successor. If the departing agent goes into competition with his successor, he is destroying the resource that would be used to pay him.

Under these specific circumstances, we find that the agreements were simply employment or agency contracts, that the terms in question simply established a final form of compensation for the business created by the agent, and that these payments do not constitute retirement income. Therefore, we find that these benefits are not pension plans and do not come within the scope of ERISA.

801 F.2d at 678. Could you write a persuasive dissent to the court's opinion? (Insurance agent relationships figure prominently in another set of ERISA definitional cases, e.g., Nationwide Mutual Ins. Co. v. Darden, 503 U.S. 318, 321 (1992), discussed infra, involving the question of whether such agents are "employees" within the meaning of ERISA.)

8. *Informal or unwritten plans.* ERISA § 402(a)(1) requires that ERISA plans be "established and maintained pursuant to a written instrument." Courts have been reluctant to allow plan participants to prove oral modifications to written plans. See infra, Chapter 15. Nevertheless, in cases in which the question is whether some arrangement amounts to a plan, courts have sometimes been willing to infer the existence of a plan despite the failure of the employer to reduce it to writing as required by ERISA. E.g., Scott v. Gulf Oil Corp., 754 F.2d 1499 (9th Cir.1985). Why is it easier for a plaintiff to avoid ERISA's writing requirement when the entire plan is unwritten than when the unwritten provision modifies a prior written plan?

Informal plans have also been found to have been evidenced in correspondence, e.g., Deboard v. Sunshine Mining & Refining Co., 208 F.3d 1228 (10th Cir.2000); and in corporate minutes, see Hollingshead v. Burford Equipment Co., 747 F.Supp. 1421 (M.D.Ala.1990) (discussing company's "guidelines for employee retirement"). For cases resisting asserted informal or oral plans, see Mattie v. Evans Industries, Inc., 21 F.Supp.2d 746 (E.D.Mich.1998); Barker v. Ceridian Corp., 918 F.Supp. 1298 (D.Minn.1996) ("disability program" to pay premiums related to disabled employees' other benefit plans), reversed on another ground, 122 F.3d 628 (8th Cir.1997).

Even a formal document can fail as a plan if its terms are too vague. In Brines v. XTRA Corp., 304 F.3d 699 (7th Cir.2002), a severance plan contained a term promising that the firm "will develop and implement an appropriate separation program if business and economic conditions necessitate a reduction in force." The court rejected the claim that this provision was an informal plan that replaced the severance provision in the prior plan, saying: "A court will not enforce a contract that is so vague that the court rather than the parties would have to formulate essential terms." 304 F.3d at 701.

Needless to say, it is perilous for an employee to rely upon an unwritten plan. Consider the fate of Wilford Harris:

> [Arkansas Book Company (ABC)] discharged warehouse manager Wilford Harris, without warning or a hearing. Harris was sixty-six years old and had been with the company forty-nine years. Over the years, Harris had been told by supervisors that he could expect to be employed by ABC until the age of seventy, and that he could expect a substantial pension upon retiring. After a formal demand, Harris learned that ABC had no intention of providing him with a pension. Earl Kruse, an ABC employee for twenty-five years, received monthly checks from ABC after his retirement. Kruse's checks were discontinued after Harris demanded a pension.

> Harris filed this action in federal court for civil enforcement of his pension benefits under [ERISA].

> The [question] is whether ABC's promise to pay retirement benefits to Harris, together with its monthly pension payments to Kruse, constitute an employee benefit plan, fund or program covered under ERISA. The existence of a plan is a prerequisite to jurisdiction under ERISA. . . .

> Neither the payments to Kruse nor the promise of payments to Harris create such a plan. Kruse testified that the money he received after retirement came as a surprise and that he had not been told that the company had a pension program. He was told that the money was a gift for staying with the company so long. Additionally, the promise to Harris can not constitute a plan. Thus, the district court was without jurisdiction on the ERISA claim, and properly granted summary judgment on this issue.

Harris v. Arkansas Book Co., 794 F.2d 358 (8th Cir.1986). How might you resist the court's argument? Further, if the court is correct that Harris was not the beneficiary of a pension plan, does it follow that he is without remedy against the company?

9. *Literature.* See Ethan Lipsig, Downsizing: Law and Practice 277–306 (1996 & Supp. 1998); Peter J. Wiedenbeck, ERISA's Curious Coverage, 76 Washington U.L.Q. 311 (1998); Marty Denis, ERISA "Plans"—How Informal Can They Be?, 18 Employee Relations L.J. 603 (1993).

5.   WHO IS AN "EMPLOYEE" OR "EMPLOYER"? *Must be EEE + EER to have an ERISA plan*

The question of whether someone qualifies as an employee is another threshold issue that, if decided adversely to the claimant, will defeat any cause of action based on ERISA. ERISA plans are for employees— "employee welfare benefit plan" under ERISA § 3(1), "employee pension benefit plan" under § 3(2)(A), "employee benefit plan" under § 3(3). Alas, when defining who qualifies as an employee, § 3(6) says in its entirety: "The term 'employee' means any individual employed by an employer." *— "Employee" definition (not an Independent Contractor)*

1.   *Employee or independent contractor: Darden.* In Nationwide Mutual Ins. Co. v. Darden, 503 U.S. 318, 323 (1992), the Supreme Court complained that the ERISA § 3(6) definition of employee "is completely circular and explains nothing." *Darden* involved the question of whether to treat an insurance agent as an employee or an independent contractor. Darden sold insurance for Nationwide from 1962 until Nationwide terminated its relationship with him in 1980. During those years Nationwide contracted with Darden to pay him commissions on sales, and also to "enroll him in a company retirement scheme called the 'Agent's Security Compensation Plan' (Plan) [under] which Nationwide annually credited an agent's retirement account with a sum based upon his [sales]." The Plan contained a noncompetition clause providing that Darden would forfeit his retirement benefits if he sold insurance for Nationwide's competitors within one year of his termination and within 25 miles of his former business location. When Nationwide terminated Darden, Darden immediately began selling insurance for Nationwide's competitors, doing business from his old office. Nationwide disqualified him from Plan benefits.

Prove you're an Employee by showing:
① .
②
③

Darden sued, claiming that his benefits were protected against forfeiture under the vesting protection of ERISA § 203(a). Nationwide replied that the vesting rules did not pertain to the Plan, because the Plan was not an ERISA-covered employee benefit plan. Rather, the Plan was a business deal between independent contractors, and ERISA did not apply.

The Supreme Court reasoned that Darden's enforcement action, which he brought in his asserted capacity as an ERISA plan "participant" under ERISA § 502(a), could pertain only if Darden satisfied the definition of "participant" under ERISA § 3(7). 503 U.S. at 320. That section defines "participant" as "any employee or former employee of an employer [who] is or may become eligible to receive a benefit of any type from an employee benefit [plan]." Accordingly, the Court said, "Darden's ERISA claim can succeed only if he was Nationwide's 'employee,' " the term that is so unhelpfully defined in ERISA § 3(6).

Was Darden employed by Nationwide, or was he an independent contractor not employed within the meaning of the statute? The Fourth Circuit had found for Darden, although conceding that "Darden most probably would not qualify as an employee" under conventional notions of agency law. Darden v. Nationwide Mutual Ins. Co., 796 F.2d 701, 705 (4th Cir.1986). The Fourth Circuit applied a standard purportedly derived from the broader purposes of ERISA as manifested in ERISA's preamble, § 2(a). The court decided that a person can become an employee in the ERISA sense by showing "(1) that he had a reasonable expectation *①* that he would receive benefits, (2) that he relied on this expectation, and (3) that he lacked the economic power to contract out of [the plan's] forfeiture provisions." Darden v. Nationwide Mutual Ins. Co., 922 F.2d 203, 205 (4th Cir.1991).

The Supreme Court reversed the Fourth Circuit and dealt harshly with its rationale. Since the contract between Darden and Nationwide called for the forfeiture that Nationwide enforced, the Fourth Circuit was wrong to rest its result on the ground of enforcing Darden's expectations. The contract gave him no expectations if he disobeyed the noncompetition clause. "Thus, the Fourth Circuit's test would turn not on a claimant's actual 'expectations,' [but] on his statutory entitlement to relief, which itself depends upon his very status as an 'employee.' This begs the question." 503 U.S. at 327.

In a unanimous opinion, the Supreme Court resolved to "adopt a common-law test for determining who qualifies as an 'employee' under [ERISA]." The Court borrowed its account of the relevant principles of common law from its earlier opinion in Community for Creative Non-Violence v. Reid, 490 U.S. 730 (1989), a case interpreting the term "employee" as used in the Copyright Act of 1976. Reid identifies "the hiring party's right to control the manner and means by which the product is accomplished" as the proper test, and it lists a variety of factors that bear on the question whether the purported employer exercised sufficient control to make the other party an employee. The Supreme Court remanded Darden to the Fourth Circuit for application of this test, pointedly reminding the Fourth Circuit of its earlier admission that " 'Darden most probably would not qualify as an employee' under traditional agency [law.]" 503 U.S. at 328.

For the view that the Fourth Circuit's approach to the issue in Darden should have prevailed as against the Supreme Court's rationale, see Note, Insurance Agents Slip Through the "Good Hands" of ERISA, 28 Wake Forest L. Rev. 1099 (1993). Cases applying Darden to deny employee status include Trustees of Resilient Floor Decorators Insurance Fund v. A & M Installations, Inc., 395 F.3d 244 (6th Cir.2005) (carpet installers); Capital Cities/ABC, Inc. v. Ratcliff, 141 F.3d 1405 (10th Cir.1998) (newspaper carriers); Trombetta v. Cragin Federal Bank for Sav. ESOP, 102 F.3d 1435 (7th Cir.1996) (loan originators). Contract terms in a collective bargaining agreement can provide plan-specific criteria for determining employee status. See, e.g., Central States, Southeast & Southwest Areas Pension Fund v. Kroger Corp., 226 F.3d 903 (7th Cir.2000).

The distinction between employees and independent contractors was also at issue in the prominent case of Vizcaino v. Microsoft Corp., 120 F.3d 1006 (9th Cir.1997) (en banc), vacating 97 F.3d 1187. A group of workers engaged by Microsoft in the late 1980s signed contracts reciting that they were independent contractors and not in an "employer-employee relationship" with Microsoft. However, they worked on teams with regular employees, performing sometimes identical functions, on Microsoft premises. Microsoft did not withhold income taxes for them nor did it pay employer's employment taxes (Social Security and unemployment taxes). It also excluded the workers from participation in an ERISA-covered defined contribution plan and in a non-ERISA employee stock purchase program that allowed employees to buy Microsoft stock at a discount from the market price. Microsoft stock subsequently increased in value many fold. In 1989 and 1990 the IRS determined that the workers were employees and should have been subject to income tax withholding and employment taxes. The employees then sued for retrospective inclusion in the two plans. The Ninth Circuit panel opinion construed the language of the plans to include the workers, once it was determined that they were employees. The en banc opinion agreed that the Microsoft plans erred in excluding the workers, but remanded on constructional and remedial issues.

The question of who is an employee for ERISA purposes arises in a different setting under the leased employee provisions of IRC § 414(n), discussed infra Chapter 9. Although a worker is treated as a leased employee under IRC § 414(n), he or she may still be excluded from coverage as a matter of plan design under ERISA, provided that the plan otherwise satisfies the various minimum coverage criteria of the tax law. Burrey v. Pacific Gas & Electric Co., 159 F.3d 388 (9th Cir.1998); Abraham v. Exxon Corp., 85 F.3d 1126 (5th Cir.1996). Issues somewhat similar to those concerning who qualifies as an employee under ERISA arise in Chapter 16, infra, treating questions about whether certain kinds of persons qualify as participants or beneficiaries eligible to bring suit under ERISA.

It will be seen in Chapter 15, infra, that the Supreme Court has held that courts should apply a deferential standard of review, effectively presuming the correctness of plan decisionmaking about questions of benefit entitlement, if the plan terms so provide. Boilerplate grants of such discretion are routine. In some cases, the courts have read these grants of discretion as justifying deferential review of the plan decisionmaker's determination about whether the claimant was an employee for ERISA purposes. For example, in Collins v. Central States, Southeast and Southwest Areas Health and Welfare Fund, 18 F.3d 556 (8th Cir.1994), the question was whether a legislative lobbyist for a labor union was an employee of the union or an independent contractor. The plan terms reserved discretion to the plan trustees to determine eligibility issues. The court deferred to the trustees' determination that the lobbyist was not an employee. Accord, Montesano v. Xerox Corp. Retirement Income Guarantee Plan, 256 F.3d 86 (2d Cir.2001).

2. *Can an employer also be an employee?* In Clackamas Gastroenterology Associates, P.C. v. Wells, 538 U.S. 440 (2003), the Supreme Court supplied further detail on the "common law" factors that help identify whether a person qualifies as an employee. *Clackamas* dealt with the meaning of the term under the Americans with Disabilities Act (ADA), but the Court relied upon *Darden*, and it would be hard to find a ground of functional distinction that would prevent applying *Clackamas* to ERISA. *Clackamas* involved not the employee/independent contractor distinction, but rather the employee/employer line. The question was whether the physicians who were shareholders and directors of the employing clinic were employees or employers. Among the factors that inclined the Court to think that they were employers and not employees: "they apparently control the operation of their clinic, they share the

They are Employers not Employees, so 'can't participate in the Plan

profits, and they are personally liable for malpractice claims." 538 U.S. at 451.

DoL has taken the view that "the term employee benefit plan shall not include any plan fund or program [under] which no employees are participants covered under the [plan]." 29 C.F.R. § 2510.3–3. In Meredith v. Time Insurance Co., 980 F.2d 352 (5th Cir.1993), a sole proprietor bought a health insurance policy covering herself and her spouse. State court litigation arose when the insurer denied her coverage on the ground that she had allegedly concealed a preexisting condition. The insurer removed the case to federal court on the ground of ERISA preemption. The Fifth Circuit determined that the insurance policy was not issued under an ERISA plan. Following 29 C.F.R. § 2510.3–3, the court said that the sole proprietor could not be "simultaneously an employer and an employee."

In 2004 the Supreme Court held that a working owner of a business could qualify as an employee, provided that "the plan covers one or more employees other than the business owner and his or her spouse." Yates v. Hendon, 541 U.S. 1, 2 (2004).

Persons who have the nominal status of partner but whose rights under the partnership agreement are severely limited may lack sufficient rights of ownership and control to qualify as employers, and may instead be treated as employees of the partnership for ERISA purposes. Simpson v. Ernst & Young, 100 F.3d 436 (6th Cir.1996) (accounting firm with more than 2,100 partners).

3. *Who is an "employer"?* ERISA § 3(5) defines "employer" with circularity comparable to the definition of "employee" that the Supreme Court disparaged in *Darden*. An employer is "any person directly acting as an employer, or indirectly in the interest of an employer, in relation to an employee benefit plan; and includes a group or association of employers acting for an employer in such capacity." ERISA § 3(5). An employer is an employer.

If some person or entity fails to qualify as an employer (or as an "employee organization"), that entity cannot sponsor an ERISA plan, because ERISA defines both welfare benefit plans and pension plans as "maintained by an employer or by an employee organization." (An "employee organization" is defined as a labor union or other employee association, § 3(4)).

4. *Association-arranged plans.* In Cross v. Bankers Multiple Line Ins. Co., 810 F.Supp. 748 (N.D.Tex.1992), a self-employed electrician bought health insurance through a plan administered by a nonprofit professional association. The court held that because the association was not the electrician's employer, the plan was not an ERISA-covered welfare benefit plan under § 3(1). Accord, McCaslin v. Blue Cross & Blue Shield of Alabama, 779 F.Supp. 1312 (N.D.Ala.1991), construing 29 C.F.R. § 2510.3–1(j).

In Cooley v. Protective Life Ins. Co., 815 F.Supp. 189 (S.D.Miss.1993), the court refused to apply ERISA preemption to a health insurance policy that the defendant issued to the Mississippi Association of Educators (MAE). The insurer argued that MAE was an "employee organization," a type of entity that can establish a plan under ERISA

§ 3(1). The court found that MAE had not purchased group insurance for its members, but rather, had merely endorsed the policy and advertised it to the MAE membership. Accord, du Mortier v. Massachusetts General Life Ins. Co., 805 F.Supp. 816 (C.D.Cal.1992). See also MDPhysicians & Associates v. State Board of Insurance, 957 F.2d 178 (5th Cir.1992), holding that an insurance plan marketed through an organization of physicians was not issued to an employer or group of employers, hence was not an ERISA-covered employee welfare benefit plan.

Contrast Allmendinger v. Aetna Life Ins. Co., 804 F.Supp. 432 (D.Conn.1992), finding sufficient involvement by an employer to create an ERISA welfare benefit plan. Aetna issued the health insurance policy to the Connecticut Business and Industry Service Corporation (CBIA), which in turn marketed it to member employers too small to qualify for a group policy of their own. Hartford Thoracic & Cardiovascular Group, Allmendinger's employer, a CBIA member, subscribed to the policy and executed a participation agreement under the policy. Hartford Thoracic paid for the coverage, maintained eligibility records, and processed claims for employees. The court found that "Hartford Thoracic's direct participation in certain administrative and maintenance aspects of the policy, its processing of claims for its employees, and its contributions to the Plan on behalf of its employees constitutes sufficient involvement to qualify the policy as an employee benefit plan under ERISA."

D. WELFARE BENEFIT PLANS: WHY REGULATE NONPENSION PLANS?

— ERISA still regulates

This unit concerns ERISA's regulation of plans that provide benefits other than retirement income. ERISA calls these plans "welfare benefit" plans. In modern employment practice the most important type of welfare benefit plan is the health care plan, which is discussed in detail in chapter 19. Other common types of welfare benefit plans provide life, accident, and occupational disability benefits; and severance or termination pay. Welfare benefit plans have given rise to an extensive case law regarding the standards of judicial review of benefit denials, discussed in Chapter 15, infra.

ERISA is centered on pension plans, a preoccupation reflected in the very title of the Act, which addresses "retirement income security." The statute is widely called the "pension reform law." The decision to include nonpension plans within ERISA has given rise to major difficulties, especially in regard to judicial review of benefit denials (discussed in Chapter 15, infra) and preemption of state law (discussed in Chapter 17, infra). Accordingly, it is important to ask why the drafters determined to reach beyond pension plans. First, we begin with a look at just how ERISA covers welfare benefit plans.

1. *Structure of the statute.* ERISA § 3(1) defines the term "employee welfare benefit plan" to include any "plan, fund, or program" within its subsections (A) or (B). Subsection (A) enumerates "medical, surgical, or hospital care or benefits, or benefits in the event of sickness, accident, disability, death or unemployment, or vacation benefits, apprenticeship or other training programs, or day care centers, scholarship funds, or prepaid legal services." Subsection (B) incorporates

by reference benefits identified in § 302(c) of the Taft-Hartley Act of 1947, 29 U.S.C. § 186(c). Section 302(c)(5)(A) of the Taft-Hartley Act, which is reproduced and discussed in Chapter 15, infra, enumerates most of the ERISA § 3(1)(A) benefits. Taft-Hartley § 302(c)(6) enumerates "vacation, holiday, severance or similar benefits. . . ."

ERISA § 4(a) provides, with some exclusions not presently important, that Title 1 applies to "any employee benefit plan." Section 3(3) defines "employee benefit plan" to include both pension and welfare benefit plans. Consequently, the provisions of ERISA will pertain to welfare benefit plans except as excluded. The main exclusions, which are cross-referenced in § 4(a), are §§ 201 and 301. Section 201 excludes welfare benefit plans from ERISA's vesting rules and related participation rules. Section 301 excludes welfare benefit plans from the funding rules. Title 4, ERISA's plan termination insurance system, also excludes welfare benefit plans; the insurance system affects defined benefit pension plans only.

The result of this statutory latticework is that the only portions of ERISA as originally enacted that applied to welfare benefit plans were three parts of Title 1: the reporting and disclosure requirements of Part 1, the fiduciary rules of Part 4, and the enforcement and remedial measures of Part 5. Title 1 of ERISA was subsequently amended to add Parts 6 and 7, which regulate various aspects of health care plans and are discussed in chapter 19. These parts of ERISA apply exclusively to such welfare benefit plans.

2.   *ERISA's exclusions: vesting, funding, termination insurance.* Pension plans are prototypically arrangements of long duration. Benefits accrue across decades of employment and are distributed across further decades of retirement. Welfare benefit plans, by contrast, provide services or other benefits on a "current account" or "pay as you go" basis. With the important exception of retiree health care, which is discussed in chapter 19, welfare benefit plans do not ordinarily entail long-term promises. The covered employee either uses or declines the child care, health care, job training, life insurance, or whatever, but these entitlements do not cumulate over time. Unlike pension benefits, welfare benefit entitlements are too short-term in character to have attracted much in the way of long-term service conditions. Thus, vesting protections have not been thought necessary.

Likewise, the framers of ERISA saw no need to impose funding requirements for transitory benefits. Funding rules guard against default by the plan sponsor in the conduct of its long-term saving program for distantly payable benefits. By contrast, in the parlance of accounting, the sponsor of a welfare benefit plan "expenses" the plan's costs on a current basis as they arise; the sponsor carries the plan on a "pay-as-you-go" basis.

ERISA's funding rules also function derivatively to protect the Pension Benefit Guaranty Corporation (PBGC). PBGC operates the plan termination insurance system of ERISA's Title IV, which insures against the consequences of sponsor default on pension promises. Title 4 does not apply to welfare benefit plans.

3.   *Rationale for inclusion.* Perhaps more difficult to understand than the exclusion of welfare benefit plans from ERISA's vesting, funding, and termination insurance requirements is Congress' decision to subject welfare benefit plans to ERISA at all. Why regulate under a common scheme such fundamentally different things as a long-duration pension plan and a short-duration welfare benefit plan?

The legislative history provides a straightforward explanation for ERISA's entanglement of pension and welfare benefit plans. The reporting-and-disclosure, fiduciary, and enforcement measures that ERISA imposes upon both pension and welfare benefit plans were directed at abuses that affected both types of plans. The animating concern behind these parts of ERISA was to prevent the looting, self-dealing, and other forms of corruption that had been discovered in union-dominated multiemployer plans. (See Michael Gordon's account, extracted supra in this chapter.) Moreover, before ERISA forced the separation of the two types of plan, it was common for one multiemployer plan to offer both pension and nonpension benefits. See, e.g., UMWA Health & Retirement Funds v. Robinson, 455 U.S. 562, 563 (1982) (collectively bargained plan established in 1950 provided both pension and health benefits, until separated in 1974 to comply with ERISA).

From the standpoint of the victim, it does not much matter whether money is stolen from your pension plan or from your health or accident insurance plan. Thus, in the movement to interpose fiduciary restraints against self-dealing and other mismanagement in multiemployer plans, the drafters of ERISA chose (in Title 1, Part 4) to impose a common scheme of fiduciary regulation on both pension plans and welfare benefit plans. The reporting rules (Title 1, Part 1) that were also made applicable to welfare benefit plans reinforce the fiduciary law through disclosure (and through the deterrence that the threat of disclosure is meant to promote). Likewise, ERISA's remedial provisions (Title 1, Part 5) were extended to welfare benefit plans, in order to facilitate enforcement of the substantive fiduciary standards.

Assuming that the drafters were on sound policy grounds in applying ERISA fiduciary law and its ancillary disclosure and enforcement provisions to some welfare benefit plans, was it a mistake to include all such plans? If the problem was multiemployer plans, why should the statute have applied to single-employer plans, in which the plan sponsor's incentives and powers under corporate law to prevent waste and thievery were so much stronger?

4.   *Preemption.* In hindsight, the decision to lump pension and welfare benefit plans in a single regulatory endeavor has revealed two major flaws. First, as discussed in chapter 19, so-called retiree health plans (plans that promise health care for retired workers) do not fit easily where the statute puts them, on the welfare benefit side of the pension/welfare benefit line.

The other great sore point has been the application of ERISA's immensely broad preemption clause to welfare benefit plans. Section 514 effectively federalizes the law of welfare benefit plans, except in a few preserves, notably under the insurance savings clause. Yet ERISA supplies standards for these plans only in the spheres of fiduciary responsibility, reporting and disclosure and the specific group health plan requirements later enacted as Parts 6 and 7 of Title 1. As a result, federal courts have displaced state courts in areas in which state law was often adequate, sometimes denying all remedy, or else intruding patchy federal common law in place of comprehensive state law. *Most preemption litigation concerns welfare benefit plans.* There is little reason to think that Congress understood how ERISA preemption would magnify the decision Congress made to impose federal fiduciary standards to prevent looting and other abuse of these non-pension plans. (The legislative history of ERISA's preemption provision is discussed in Chapter 17, infra.)

CHAPTER 4

PREVENTING FORFEITURE

Analysis

Introduction

ERISA embodies three distinct programs of protection for plan participants and their beneficiaries, responding to three distinct sorts of risk. ERISA's fiduciary rules (and the related reporting and disclosure requirements) are addressed to what has been called *administrative* or *agency risk* that is, the danger that the persons who administer a plan and invest plan funds will misappropriate or mismanage the funds, or will misapply the standards for determining entitlement to plan benefits. ERISA's system of funding and plan termination insurance, discussed in Chapter 6, infra, is addressed to the *default risk* the danger that a defined benefit pension plan will renege on paying promised benefits, typically because too little was contributed or because of adverse investment experience. The present chapter addresses ERISA's regulation of *forfeiture risk* meaning plan terms that cause promised benefits to be lost if the employee does not remain employed long enough or otherwise fails to fulfill some condition specified in the plan.

Plan benefits arise from the contract of employment between employer and employee (which, in a unionized workforce, will be largely determined by the collective bargaining agreement between employer and union). ERISA's vesting and related anti-forfeiture rules restrict the freedom of the contracting parties to agree upon the forfeiture of pension benefits, either upon termination of employment or for alleged misconduct during employment.

Section A of this chapter examines the logic of forfeiture terms and of anti-forfeiture restrictions, notably vesting. Section B examines the vesting rules, ERISA § 203, a centerpiece of the statute. Section C, "Protecting Against Employer Misconduct," covers provisions of ERISA and the IRC that are meant in large measure to secure the vesting rules against evasion. Section D treats the benefit accrual rules of ERISA § 204. It will be seen that benefit accrual rules, although doctrinally distinct from vesting, are a necessary corollary of the decision to impose vesting rules. Section E discusses an oft-proposed measure for reducing forfeitures, requiring portability of pension credits from one plan to another, which ERISA's drafters considered but did not enact.

A. VESTING POLICY

1. THE GRATUITY THEORY OF PENSIONS

In the early days of employer-provided pension plans, it was common for the plan to recite that the promised pension was a gift from the employer, hence that the employee had no right to a pension until paid. Pension credits accrued could be unilaterally denied. In the celebrated case of McNevin v. Solvay Process Co., 53 N.Y.S. 98 (App. Div. 1898), the court summarized some of the terms of such a plan:

> By the 3d article [of the plan] the sums set apart are expressly declared to be gifts, and that the sums allotted to the employees remain the property of the defendant until they are actually paid over to the employees, and by the 4th article it is provided that the fund is to remain under the sole control of the defendant's trustees, who are authorized to decide all questions concerning the rights of employees in the fund without appeal.

53 N.Y.S. at 99. Other plan terms stipulated that the employer had no duty to contribute particular sums to the plan, and that an employee dismissed for cause could be denied any pension. The court concluded that "this pension fund [is] a gift by the [employer.]" Accordingly, the court held that "none of the employees has a vested interest in any part of this fund, even though credited upon their pass books, until the gift is completed by actual payment." Id.

The Solvay Process case exemplifies the so-called gratuity theory of pension rights. Because the plan authorized the employer to revoke promised pension benefits at will, those promises were treated like a promise to make a gift in the future, which is unenforceable until the gift is actually completed.

The gratuity theory appeared in the case law into the 1950s. See Annot., Rights and Liabilities as Between Employer and Employee with Respect to General Pension or Retirement Plan, 42 A.L.R.2d 461, 464–67 (1955); see also Annot., Private Pension Plan: Construction of Provision Authorizing Employer to Terminate or Modify Plan, 46 A.L.R.3d 464 (1972). However, courts attempted to construe the terms of such a plan strictly against the drafter. See, e.g., Cantor v. Berkshire Life Ins. Co., 171 Ohio St. 405, 171 N.E.2d 518 (1960); Tilbert v. Eagle Lock Co., 116 Conn. 357, 165 A. 205 (1933); Comment, Consideration for the Employer's Promise of a Voluntary Pension Plan, 23 U. Chicago L.Rev. 96 (1955).

ERISA's vesting rules effectively abrogate the gratuity theory, by severely limiting the forfeitability of pension rights. There was already a trend away from unilateral revocability of pension promises in the decades before ERISA. Pension plans increasingly tended to contain vesting schedules protecting employees against forfeiture. A 1969 study by the Bureau of Labor Statistics found that 77 percent of workers covered by private plans were working under plans that provided some vesting protection, although the requirements for vesting were in general less liberal than those that ERISA came to require. Harry E. Davis & Arnold Strasser, Private Pension Plans: 1960 to 1969—An Overview, 93 Monthly Labor Rev. 45, 49 (Table 2) (Jul. 1970). For a review of data on the extent of vesting before ERISA, see William C. Greenough & Francis P. King, Pension Plans and Public Policy 164–69 (1976).

QUESTIONS

1. The court in *Solvay Process* called a pension a gift by the employer. Does an employer make gifts to its employees in the sense that parents make gifts to their children? Suppose after making some pension payments to retirees, the directors of Solvay Process had been sued in a shareholder action alleging dissipation of corporate funds, on the ground that since the *Solvay Process* decision had determined that the pension payments were gifts rather than wages, the expenditures were necessarily ultra vires. How would that suit have been decided?

2. In the years before ERISA imposed vesting requirements, why did so many employers not take full advantage of their ability to make pension rights forfeitable? Might it not have been in the employer's interest to insist on making pension rights forfeitable indefinitely, or for very long periods?

[handwritten margin note: whole point of ERISA is to protect what regular EE's pay into the Pension Plan]

2. PERMITTING FORFEITURES under ERISA

[handwritten margin note: — applies only to Pension Plans, NOT welfare Benefit + NonQualified Plans]

ERISA's vesting rules, which are reviewed below in Section B of this chapter, restrict but do not forbid forfeitures. ERISA therefore reflects a policy balance that permits some forfeiture. Why?

1. *Restraining turnover* The rationale for allowing forfeiture is to give employers a tool that helps promote employee retention. Wolf and Levy write:

[handwritten margin note: Justifies Forfeiture abilities]

> [A] number of authors have advanced the proposition that employers provide private pensions to increase employee tenure and reduce the costs of turnover. *(saves Employer Money)*

[handwritten margin note: reduces cost of turnover (saves EER money) + promotes EEE Retention]

> [Empirical study shows that having a] vesting rule matters. The probability of leaving a job with a ten-year vesting rule is about four times larger in the year after vesting than in the year before vesting. Thus the length of the vesting rule exerts an impact on the ability of a pension to reduce turnovers. . . .

> The typical career will involve a modest number of short-term jobs (when the young worker is job shopping) followed by one or two jobs of long duration. Thus if we ask the average duration of all [jobs], the answer is fairly short—perhaps as brief as three or four years. But if we define the significance of long-term jobs (for example, those jobs lasting fifteen years or more) in the context of a worker's career, we find them quite important in the sense that the typical worker will spend most of his working life in one or two such jobs. (Note, however, that

these long-term jobs will not be an important fraction of the number of jobs the worker holds.) . . .

Existing data sets have permitted analysts to examine the effect of pensions on [the] probability that an employee will leave a job in the near future. The findings of these studies are generally consistent with the consensus theory of the impact of pensions on tenure.

There are two main elements in the consensus theory. The first is the idea that employees build up firm-specific human capital with increased tenure on the job. Because a firm must expend resources to invest in a new employee, employee turnover can generate substantial costs to an employer. For this reason, a firm has an interest in designing compensation schemes that discourage such turnover. One such scheme is to pay rising wage rates with advances in an employee's tenure. Another is to offer pension plans that require minimum service requirements before the employer's contribution to that plan is vested in the employee.

A second element in the theory is that an employee's productivity begins to decline at some point in his career, but because of the customs of the internal labor market, a firm cannot reduce a long-term employee's wages. For this reason, a firm has an interest in encouraging employees to retire at certain ages. The retirement income provided by a pension facilitates such induced retirement.

In summary, this theory holds that a firm has an interest in keeping employees both from leaving too soon and from staying too long. The provision of a pension plan has the potential to promote both objectives. The plan's vesting rule—the minimum time that an employee must work on the job before he becomes eligible for any benefits at retirement age—creates an incentive to complete job tenures in excess of some desired minimum. Other features of pension plans, such as the pension benefit formula, credit for work past the "normal" retirement age, early retirement provisions, and integration of benefits with social security, may be manipulated to encourage job exit among older workers. . . .

Douglas A. Wolf & Frank Levy, Pension Coverage, Pension Vesting, and the Distribution of Job Tenures, in Retirement and Economic Behavior (H.J. Aaron & G. Burtless, eds.) (Brookings Institution) 23, 25–28, 54–55 (1984).

2. *Promoting mobility of labor.* A recurrent theme in critiques of pension plan terms that permit forfeitures is that such terms interfere with the mobility of labor. Greenough and King set forth that theme:

Mobility of the American labor force is an essential factor in the efficient allocation of human and physical resources. It has permitted shifts from buggy-making to bicycles to railways to autos to airplanes and back to bicycles; from war production to peace endeavors; from production of goods to production of services; from old, dying industries to dynamic new endeavors.

Companies and jobs disappear; other companies and jobs take their place.

Some workers stay with one employer from graduation from high school or college until retirement, but most change jobs several times during their careers. This mobility is an essential part of a dynamic society. It helps each individual develop his own career to the fullest and it adds strength and flexibility to the economy.

Pension forfeitures resulting from an employee's changing jobs where vesting has been delayed have been described as a form of industrial feudalism. Delayed vesting has also been called a kind of indenturing system, a golden chain that fastens a person to his employer. Long delays in vesting of pensions tend to result in misallocation of human resources. Attracting experienced personnel for a new or growing company or industry becomes more difficult, for it requires the breaking loose of workers' golden pension chains.

Vesting delays are especially harmful to middle-aged employees. The golden chain becomes stronger and stronger; an individual cannot afford to change jobs and at the same time give up his or her accrued pension rights. A potential new employer may not be willing to take on the triple expense of a salary high enough to counteract the job change risk, costs of current service pensions, and possible compensation to the new employee for forfeiting an unvested pension with the previous employer. Delay in the vesting of pensions is often a real factor in age discrimination.

A pension plan that vests benefits early allows the individual to stay with his present employer, attracted by good pension arrangements, job satisfaction, opportunity, even climate or location. Or it allows him to seek without loss a new employer where his individual capacities, skills, or preferences may be better met.

William C. Greenough & Francis P. King, Pension Plans and Public Policy, 155–57 (1976).

QUESTIONS

1.   ERISA's vesting protection is so often described as a triumph of "reform" that one can forget to ask whether vesting rules are justifiable. Forfeiture sounds like a bad thing, so protection against forfeiture sounds like a good thing. But another way to understand ERISA's vesting requirement (or indeed any other regulatory requirement) is as an interference with private autonomy. ERISA forbids employer and employee to contract for that particular term in the compensation package. ERISA allows the parties to contract for no pension plan at all, but ERISA forbids them to contract for a pension plan whose benefits are made contingent beyond ERISA's permitted forfeiture periods. Why forbid private parties to contract as they please?

2.   Greenough and King believe that public policy should favor vesting rules that promote labor mobility. On what grounds might that view be resisted?

3.   Greenough and King report, id. at 157, that job tenures were averaging 3.9 years in 1973. As enacted in 1974, ERISA § 203(a)(2)(A) permitted a pension plan to impose total forfeiture of pension rights on employees who departed with less than ten years service. (Congress has revised this so-called "ten-year cliff" vesting schedule several times, shortening the permitted period of forfeiture from ten years to the current five for defined benefit plans and three for defined contribution plans.) As a matter of regulatory policy, why did Congress prescribe vesting standards that permit forfeiture for periods so much longer than average job tenures?

Despite the changes in ERISA's vesting schedules over the years, the situation is no different today. As already noted in Chapter 1, supra, the median job tenure in the U.S. is shorter than the number of years needed for full vesting under three of the four statutory vesting schedules in effect today.

4.   Wolf and Levy suggest that protecting the employee against pension forfeiture could actually disadvantage the employee. Suppose the employer is willing to invest in training the employee for a higher paying job only if the employer can use the sanction of pension forfeiture to increase the period over which the employer can retain the employee and thereby recoup the firm's investment in training. In such a case, an employment arrangement that stipulates forfeitures of pension benefits might actually maximize the joint advantage of the parties. (On the use of forfeiture periods to facilitate the employer's recovering the costs of employee training, see Ronald G. Ehrenberg & Robert S. Smith, Modern Labor Economics 146, 152–57 (10th ed. 2009).) Why should the federal government restrict the liberty of the parties to agree to such a mutually beneficial contract?

5.   In 1986, the year ERISA was amended to reduce ten-year cliff vesting to five-year cliff, ten-year cliff vesting was in force in plans affecting 89 percent of full-time participants in a sample of plans of medium and large size firms. See DoL, Bureau of Labor Statistics, Employee Benefits in Medium and Large Firms: 1986, at 74 (Table 68) (June 1987). Thus, most pension plans featured the longest period of forfeiture the law allowed. Why? Employer power? Mutual advantage of the sort implied by the Wolf and Levy article?

6.   ERISA § 201(2) excludes from its vesting and related requirements "a plan which is unfunded and is maintained by an employer primarily for the purpose of providing deferred compensation for a select group of management or highly compensated employees." Why does the policy that supports interfering with the autonomy of plan participants in conventional pension plans not extend to plans that benefit highly compensated workers?

B. ERISA'S VESTING REQUIREMENTS

1. HOW A VESTING SCHEDULE WORKS

1.   *Immediate vesting.* The simplest vesting regime is immediate vesting. The defined contribution plans operated by TIAA-CREF for university teachers using IRC § 403(b) annuities exemplify immediate

- simplest type (EEE's fully vested at all times)
     - No Forfeiture can occur be always vested
     - Allows mobility for EEE to move jobs + reta
               benefi

vesting. Participating institutions and their employees make contributions, usually monthly, that are credited to the account of each individual employee. The employee's account is fully vested at all times, and thus no forfeiture occurs if the employee leaves the institution. The TIAA-CREF system is unusual. TIAA originated as a noncontributory charitable undertaking of the Carnegie Foundation. See William C. Greenough & Francis P. King, Pension Plans and Public Policy 53–57 (1976). Notice that the TIAA-CREF system achieves portability among participating employers. A professor who moves from one school to another keeps the same TIAA-CREF account; the new employer replaces the old in making the matching contributions that typify IRC § 403(b) plans.

high turn over jobs + lower educated EEES. + good for expensive training of EEES + ease of administration for EER

2. *Cliff vesting.* The most common type of vesting provision is cliff vesting. After a specified waiting period, during which the employee's pension is wholly forfeitable the pension becomes fully vested. As originally enacted in 1974, ERISA allowed ten-year cliff vesting. A plan could provide that an employee who departed after nine years and eleven months forfeited all benefits. See, e.g., Coleman v. Interco Inc. Divs.' Plans, 933 F.2d 550 (7th Cir.1991); Swaida v. IBM Retirement Plan, 570 F.Supp. 482 (S.D.N.Y.1983), aff'd per curiam 728 F.2d 159 (2d Cir.1984). The maximum period for cliff vesting under the present law is five years for a defined benefit plan and (as a result of changes effected by the Pension Protection Act of 2006) three years for a defined contribution plan. ERISA § 203(a)(2)(A)(ii), (B)(ii).

– most common type
– wholly forfeitable for a specified waiting period until the pension becomes Fully Vested
max. waiting periods

3. *Graduated vesting.* Under a graduated vesting schedule, the employee's protection against forfeiture increases incrementally across time. Consider the following examples, adapted from Russell K. Osgood, Qualified Pension and Profit-Sharing Plan Vesting: Revolution Not Reform, 59 Boston U.L.Rev. 452, 456–57 (1979).

– is better for higher-paid EEE's (compared to cliff) vesting – this is best for low-paid employees

4. *Example No. 1: defined contribution.* Able is an employee at Acme. Able is covered under Acme's defined contribution plan. Able quits Acme after completing five years of service, when $1,000 has been credited to Able's account. The plan features the following vesting schedule, which tracks ERISA § 203(a)(2)(B)(iii):

Years of Service	Vested Percentage
less than 2	0%
2 to 3	20%
3 to 4	40%
4 to 5	60%
5 to 6	80%
6 or more	100%

Since Able has completed five years of credited service, he is entitled to 80 percent of the account balance, or $800.

5. *Example No. 2: defined benefit.* Vesting in a defined benefit plan operates in a similar fashion, but because the participant in a defined benefit plan has no separate "account," the plan must provide a means of calculating the rate at which the participant earns the projected benefit. To illustrate, assume the facts in Example No. 1, except that Able is now participating in a defined benefit plan that promises a retirement benefit

of 50 percent of the employee's average annual compensation; and assume further that Able's compensation is and has been at all times a constant $30,000 per year. Able's projected retirement benefit is $15,000 (50% of $30,000). Able is 55 years old and the plan has a normal retirement age of 65. The plan has adopted the "fractional benefit accrual rule" of ERISA § 204(b)(1)(C). Under the formula contained in that rule, the participant's accrued benefit is computed by multiplying the projected benefit of $15,000 per year by a fraction whose numerator is the number of years of plan participation at the time of severance (5) and whose denominator is the number of years of service that the participant would have had until normal retirement age (here 15, which is the difference between age at employment, 50, and normal retirement age, 65), ergo ⅓. Multiplying $15,000 by ⅓ yields an accrued benefit of $5,000 per year, payable at age 65. To determine the percentage of Able's accrued benefit that is nonforfeitable at the time of Able's severance, the plan's vesting schedule is then applied. Under the schedule reproduced in Example No. 1, supra, Able's five years of completed service results in 80 percent vesting. Eighty percent of the $5,000 accrued benefit is $4,000, which is the amount of the annual pension that the Acme pension plan will pay Able when Able attains age 65.

6. *Defined benefit vs. defined contribution plans.* The trend toward defined contribution plans and away from defined benefit plans has already been remarked in Chapter 2, supra. Cliff vesting schedules predominate in defined benefit plans. In 2005, 89% percent of employees covered by defined benefit plans were subject to cliff vesting, compared with only two percent benefiting from immediate vesting and seven percent subject to graduated vesting. See DoL, Bureau of Labor Statistics, National Compensation Survey: Employee Benefits in Private Industry in the United States, 2005, at 70 (Table 57) (May 2007). By contrast only 22 percent of employees covered under defined contribution plans were subject to cliff vesting, while 47 percent were subject to graduated vesting and 22 percent enjoyed immediate vesting. See id. at 83 (Table 75).

2. STRUCTURE OF THE STATUTE

1. *ERISA's original rules.* As enacted in 1974, ERISA § 203(a)(2) authorized three vesting schedules. Subsection (A) authorized ten-year cliff vesting; subsection (B) authorized 15-year graded vesting; and subsection (C) provided for a seldom used standard called "the rule of 45" that combined five-year cliff with the further requirement that "the sum of [the participant's] age and years of service equals or exceeds 45."

2. *The current schedules.* ERISA § 203(a)(2) now permits either five-year cliff or seven-year graded vesting for defined benefit plans (§ 203(a)(2)(A)) and either three-year cliff or six-year graded vesting for defined contribution plans (§ 203(a)(2)(B)). The plan schedule used in Example No. 1 in the previous section ("How a Vesting Schedule Works") reproduces the six-year graded schedule of ERISA § 203(a)(2)(B). The former rule-of-45 standard, being less stringent than the five-year cliff vesting instituted in 1986, was repealed.

Originally, defined contribution and defined benefit plans were subject to the same vesting schedule. However, ERISA was amended in

2001 to shorten the permitted vesting periods in the case of matching contributions to defined contribution plans, to 3 years for cliff vesting and 6 years for graded. The PPA subsequently extended application of this shorter vesting period to all employer contributions to defined contribution plans, not just to matching contributions. ERISA § 203(a)(2)(B). IRC § 411(a)(13)(B) provides a special three-year vesting rule for hybrid pension plans such as cash balance plans. Such plans must provide 100% vesting after three years of service.

3. *Alternative vesting regimes.* In addition to the main vesting rules of ERISA § 203(a)(2), there are some special-purpose vesting schedules. IRC 416(b) applies the vesting period for defined contribution plans to so-called top-heavy plans, under IRC § 416(b). The rules governing plan termination also operate as a substitute vesting schedule, requiring immediate vesting of all accrued benefits before any reversion to the sponsor. See IRC § 411(d)(3), discussed following *Boruta v. Commissioner,* infra in this chapter; see also ERISA § 4044(d)(1). Plan termination is treated in Chapter 6, infra.

4. *Other vesting requirements.* ERISA prefaces the vesting schedules with two other requirements. First, ERISA § 203(a) says: "Each pension plan shall provide that an employee's right to his normal retirement benefit is nonforfeitable upon the attainment of normal retirement [age]." The concept of normal retirement age is further discussed in Section D of this chapter, treating benefit accrual, and in Chapter 18 (age discrimination). Second, ERISA § 203(a)(1) requires that the portion of an employee's "accrued benefit derived from his own contributions" must in all events be nonforfeitable. Furthermore, ERISA § 203(c)(1) prevents amendments to a vesting schedule that reduce the vested portion of a participant's benefit.

5. *Impact of ERISA's vesting rules.* ERISA appears to have made a difference in vesting rates. "In 1972—prior to ERISA—only 32 percent of the full-time private sector employees who were covered by pension plans reported that they were entitled to eventual retirement benefits; by 1979 the comparable rate had increased 16 percentage points, to 48 percent. [By] 1988 the rate had increased by another 16 points, to 64 percent." John R. Woods, Pension Vesting and Preretirement Lump Sums Among Full-Time Private Sector Employees, 56 Social Security Bull. 3, 4 (Fall 1993). By 2003, the vesting rate for private sector employees covered by pension plans increased to 93%. Employee Benefit Research Institute, EBRI Data Book on Employee Benefits, Table 10.5 (online; updated January 2006).

6. *Forfeiture on death.* ERISA's vesting rules *do not protect the participant against forfeiture on death.* The plan may provide that a participant who dies before retiring receives no benefits. ERISA § 203(a)(3)(A). The rationale for such a rule is that a decedent does not need retirement income. Dependents, however, often do. REAct amended ERISA in 1984 to require that "in the case of a vested participant who dies before the annuity starting date and who has a surviving spouse, a qualified preretirement survivor annuity shall be provided to the [spouse]." ERISA § 205(a)(2). The spousal annuity rules are discussed infra in Chapter 7.

7. *Vesting rules and the antidiscrimination norm.* Well before ERISA, the IRS had developed some criteria for vesting. "Even though the Treasury Department was without explicit statutory authority in the vesting area, it did successfully require certain plans to adopt a vesting schedule on the grounds that without such a schedule these plans had violated, or might violate, the antidiscrimination norm established by [IRC §] 401(a)(4). [If the IRS] discovered that a disproportionate number of the employees who remained until retirement—and therefore received the plan's benefits—were highly compensated, it would find that there was de facto discrimination in the awarding of benefits." Osgood, supra, at 459. The antidiscrimination norm is extensively discussed infra in Chapter 9.

When ERISA imposed the minimum vesting schedules of ERISA § 203(a), discussed above, which are duplicated as IRC 411(a), the question was presented whether compliance with the ERISA vesting scheme also satisfied the antidiscrimination norm. IRC § 411(d) coordinates the vesting rules with the antidiscrimination requirement of IRC § 401(a)(4). Section 411(d)(1) treats compliance with the vesting rules as presumptive compliance with any vesting requirements resulting from the application of IRC § 401(a)(4) "unless (A) there has been a pattern of abuse under the plan (such as dismissal of employees before their accrued benefits become nonforfeitable) tending to discriminate in favor of employees who are highly compensated [or] (B) there have been, or there is reason to believe there will be, an accrual of benefits or forfeitures tending to discriminate in favor of employees who are highly compensated. . . ."

For further discussion of the pattern-of-abuse standard of IRC § 411(d)(1), see Section C of this chapter, "Protecting Against Employer Misconduct."

8. *Minimum participation standards.* ERISA § 202(a) allows a pension plan to establish waiting periods before allowing the employee to commence participation. ERISA permits the plan to refuse participation to persons under the age of 21 (reduced by REAct in 1985 from ERISA's original age 25). Further, the plan may require that the employee complete one year of service before being eligible to participate. These waiting periods do not affect the time it takes an employee to vest, since for vesting purposes all years of service with the employer after age 18, including pre-participation service, are generally to be taken into account. ERISA § 203(b)(1).

Section 202(a)(1)(B)(i) allows a plan that provides for 100 percent vesting after two years of service to have a two-year waiting period for participation as opposed to the normal one-year minimum participation rule. This option conveniently illustrates the point that, unless regulated, a plan's minimum participation requirement can do the work of a forfeiture rule.

9. *Measuring service.* Vesting protection leads to further regulatory steps. Since the permitted forfeiture periods are measured in time, time needs to be defined, hence the rules of ERISA § 203(b), which regulate the measurement of years of service and breaks in service. ERISA §§ 202(a)(3) and 202(b) contain similar provisions for the minimum participation rules. These matters receive little attention in

this coursebook, but they loom large in the practical administration of pension plans. For example, a number of cases have turned on the correct computation of a year of service for ERISA vesting purposes. ERISA § 203(b)(2)(A) defines the term "year of service" to mean a 12-month period in which the employee serves not less than 1000 hours. However, Treas.Reg. § 1.410(a)–7 permits an "elapsed time" alternative, which permits calculation "with reference to the total period of time which elapses while the employee is employed." Numerous decisions have sustained the use of the prevalent "elapsed time" method of measuring service. See, e.g., Johnson v. Buckley, 356 F.3d 1067 (9th Cir.2004); Jefferson v. Vickers, Inc., 102 F.3d 960 (8th Cir.1996); Coleman v. Interco Inc. Divs.' Plans, 933 F.2d 550 (7th Cir.1991), Swaida v. IBM Retirement Plan, 570 F.Supp. 482 (S.D.N.Y.1983), aff'd per curiam, 728 F.2d 159 (2d Cir.1984). Those cases are followed in Montgomery v. PBGC, 601 F.Supp.2d 139 (D.D.C.2009) (citing *Johnson* and *Swaida* with approval) and Apitz v. Teledyne Monarch Rubber Hourly Pension Plan, 800 F.Supp. 1526, 1542 (N.D.Ohio 1992) (employees who had worked 1,000 hours but had not satisfied the plan's elapsed time requirement in their thirtieth year of service did not qualify for plan's early retirement benefit).

The rules regarding breaks in service have also given rise to litigation. See, e.g., DiGiacomo v. Teamsters Pension Trust Fund of Phila. & Vicinity, 420 F.3d 220 (3d Cir.2005) (finding violation where plan failed to include years of service prior to break in service in calculating plan benefits).

— Plan must include prior years of service prior to a break in service [handwritten annotation]

Perhaps the most important consequence of the 1,000-hour rule for defining a year of service is that it permits plans to exclude many part-time employees. An employee who does not work more than 1,000 hours in any 12-month period never satisfies the minimum service requirement, even if the part-time employment endures for decades. Of course, a plan could by its terms elect to cover such employees, even though ERISA does not require it.

Although Congress has tinkered with ERISA's vesting rules several times, surprisingly, in view of changes in work patterns since 1974, it has never changed the 1,000-hour rule for defining a year of service. Does its failure to do so undermine the effect of accelerating ERISA's vesting schedules?

10. *Cash-outs and buy-backs.* Suppose Able in Example No. 1, supra, receives the $800, but three years later returns to work for Acme. Is the $200 that he forfeited gone forever? The answer is no. He can, in effect, buy it back by repaying the $800 to the plan. ERISA § 204(d)–(e), IRC § 411(a)(7)(B)–(C). This raises the question of where the $200 comes from if the plan has reallocated the forfeiture to the other participants. See Treas.Reg. § 1.411(a)–7(d)(6)(iii)(C) (permissible sources for restoration of accrued benefit are income or capital gain to the plan, forfeitures, or employer contributions).

11. *IRS jurisdiction.* Under the 1978 executive order allocating responsibility for ERISA between DoL and IRS, IRS interprets the vesting and related participation and benefit accrual rules. IRC § 411, Treas.Regs. § 1.411(a) et seq.

12. *Nonpension plans.* ERISA's vesting rules do not apply to welfare benefit plans. ERISA § 201(1). See supra Chapter 3, regarding ERISA's inclusion of welfare benefit plans; and infra Chapter 5, regarding amending such plans.

3. EMPLOYEE MISCONDUCT: BAD BOY CLAUSES

[handwritten: Doing away with special-purpose forfeiture clauses in pension plans (not welfare benefits or non-qualified]

"Prior to ERISA, pension plans commonly included clauses under which, for a variety of what the employer felt were improper activities, an employee could forfeit part or all of the pension benefits which he or she had in some cases worked many years to build up. One of the major reasons for the enactment of ERISA was to do away with this practice and thus to help workers claim the benefits they had earned." Nedrow v. MacFarlane & Hays Co. Employees' Profit Sharing Plan & Trust, 476 F.Supp. 934, 935 (E.D.Mich.1979).

In *Nedrow*, for example, the plan contained a forfeiture-for-cause provision that purported to undercut the plan's regular vesting schedule under certain circumstances. It read in part:

> FORFEITURE OF BENEFITS FOR CERTAIN CAUSES.
> Notwithstanding any other provisions of this Agreement to the contrary, the right of any Participant or former Participant to receive or to have paid to any other person and the right of any such other person to receive any benefits hereunder shall terminate and shall be forever forfeited if such Participant's employment with the Employer is terminated because of his fraud, embezzlement or dishonesty or if the Participant or former Participant, within a period of one year after the termination of his employment, engages in any occupation or in a business which, in the Administrator's opinion, is in competition with the Employer, or becomes associated in any manner with such a competitor.

The quoted language exemplifies what has been known in pension argot as a "bad boy" clause, a provision terminating pension benefits for employee wrongdoing. It is typical of the genre in prohibiting two very different classes of conduct: (1) fraud, embezzlement, or dishonesty; and (2) subsequent competition with the employer.

Prior to ERISA's vesting requirements, there were no statutory restrictions on the reach of a bad boy clause. A bad boy clause is best understood as a special-purpose forfeiture rule, forfeiture for cause. ERISA's vesting rules make no exception for forfeiture for cause, and hence forbid bad boy clauses that impose forfeiture beyond the periods permitted under ERISA's regular vesting schedules.

A common variety of bad boy clause, restraining a departing employee from competing with the former employer, is consistent with the idea that a main rationale for pension plan forfeitures is to facilitate employer investment in recruitment and training by deterring employees from quitting. For an indication of the range of issues that can arise under this type of bad boy clause, see Lojek v. Thomas, 716 F.2d 675 (9th Cir.1983) (involving an associate and his former law firm).

Does ERISA's vesting (antiforfeiture) rule trump the equitable maxim that a wrongdoer should not profit from his own wrong? For example, may the plan sponsor recover from the vested pension account of an employee who has stolen from the firm? See Chapter 7, infra, reproducing Guidry v. Sheet Metal Workers National Pension Fund, 493 U.S. 365 (1990), on the interrelationship of vesting protections and the so-called antialienation rule, ERISA § 206(d)(1), IRC § 401(a)(13).

Because ERISA's vesting protections apply only to pension plans and not to welfare benefit plans, bad boy clauses in welfare benefit plans continue to be enforced. Severance plans, for example, typically provide that benefits will not be paid in the event a participant is terminated for cause. For example, in Moos v. Square D Co., 72 F.3d 39 (6th Cir.1995), the firm's "Change of Control Separation Plan for Salaried Employees," effectively a supplemental unemployment compensation or severance-type plan, provided benefits for management employees who lost their jobs within two years of a change in management. The plan excluded benefits for an employee who was terminated for good cause, defined to include "willful engaging by the Employee [in] gross misconduct which is materially and demonstrably injurious to the Company." Moos, an accounting employee of the firm for 21 years, was found to have falsified his degree in accounting. The plan administrator cited Moos' obligation to enforce the company's honesty rules in determining that his own dishonesty constituted "gross misconduct" under the plan. The Sixth Circuit affirmed the district court's grant of summary judgment in favor of the plan. Courts have sustained denial of severance benefits on the basis of for cause termination where termination resulted from misuse of confidential information, Anderson v. U.S. Bancorp, 484 F.3d 1027 (8th Cir.2007), violation of an employer's rules against sexual harassment, Chalmers v. Quaker Oats Co., 61 F.3d 1340 (7th Cir.1995), and the improper use of workplace internet to access pornography, Thygeson v. U.S. Bancorp, 34 E.B.C. 2097 (D.Or.2004).

Certain pension plans are exempted from ERISA's vesting protections, especially unfunded deferred compensation plans for a "select group of management or highly compensated employees," so-called "top hat" plans. ERISA § 201(2). Such plans commonly contain bad boy clauses.

C. PROTECTING AGAINST EMPLOYER MISCONDUCT

The protections of a vesting schedule may not suffice to guarantee pension benefits if the employer or other plan sponsor is allowed to manipulate the circumstances of the employment relationship to defeat pension entitlement. IRC § 411(d) and ERISA § 510 are directed against such behavior.

1. BORUTA V. COMMISSIONER

9 E.B.C. 2013 (Tax Ct.1988).

■ STERRETT, CHIEF JUDGE. [Petitioner] Peter M. Boruta, M.D., P.C., a professional corporation, had its principal place of business in Rochester, Michigan, when it filed its petition in this case. Beginning on or about May 1, 1979, petitioner established and maintained the Peter M. Boruta, M.D., P.C. Pension Plan and Trust, a money purchase plan that initially constituted a qualified trust under [IRC §] 401(a). In the Plan, petitioner

[handwritten margin notes: Welfare Benefit Plans; Exceptions to ERISA's limitation on Forfeiture Clauses; (Non-Qualified Plan) —ERISA doesn't apply here bc these "higher-ups" have more bargaining power]

included a provision that upon a full or partial termination of the Plan, the interests of the participants would be nonforfeitable.

At the beginning of the Plan year commencing on May 1, 1982, petitioner's three employees, including Dr. Boruta, an orthopedic surgeon, all participated in the Plan. However, during that Plan year, petitioner closed its medical office, terminated its employment relationship with the other two employees,[3] and treated their retirement account balances as forfeitable to the trust.[4]

In a final adverse determination letter dated February 10, 1987, respondent determined that petitioner had partially terminated the Plan in 1982 because petitioner terminated a "significant number" (2 out of 3) of the Plan participants. Respondent further determined that petitioner, by failing to treat the terminated employees' Trust account balances as nonforfeitable after the partial termination, thereby violated the nonforfeiture provisions of the Plan and also of section 411(d)(3), as referenced through section 401(a)(7). Consequently, respondent determined that the Trust did not constitute a qualified trust under section 401(a) for years beginning on or after May 1, 1982.

We consider whether the Trust constituted a qualified trust under section 401(a) for Plan years beginning on or after May 1, 1982. Respondent determined that petitioner partially terminated the Plan in 1982 and, by failing to treat the Trust account balances of the two employees as nonforfeitable, thereby violated the nonforfeiture provisions of the Plan and also of section 411(d)(3), as referenced through section 401(a)(7). Petitioner, however, asserts that factually no partial termination occurred in the present case. For the reasons discussed below, we hold for respondent.

In order for the Trust to constitute a qualified trust under the provisions of section 401(a), petitioner must include provisions in the Plan that satisfy the requirements of section 411, relating to certain minimum vesting standards. Section 401(a)(7). Specifically, and as relevant to this case, petitioner must provide in the Plan that the rights of certain employees to funded benefits will be nonforfeitable upon the Plan's termination or partial termination. Section 411(d)(3). In the present case, respondent does not dispute that petitioner included a provision in the Plan that facially satisfies the requirements of section 411(d)(3). However, respondent asserts that petitioner, during the 1982 Plan year, partially terminated the Plan because it reduced its workforce in 1982 by a significant percentage. Accordingly, respondent determined that petitioner, by failing to treat the terminated employees' Trust account balances as nonforfeitable upon the partial termination, violated the nonforfeiture provisions of the Plan and also of section 411(d)(3), for Plan years commencing on and after May 1, 1982.

---

[3] At this time, Dr. Boruta was planning to join another medical practice. Accordingly, the other two employees were terminated on October 25, 1982, and December 17, 1982, respectively, because their services were considered unnecessary and duplicative of the services of the employees in Dr. Boruta's new practice.

[4] Subsequently, at the time of petitioner's own corporate dissolution on May 1, 1983, petitioner completely terminated the Plan and treated the Trust account balance of the remaining participant, Dr. Boruta, as fully vested and nonforfeitable.

On the other hand, petitioner asserts that respondent failed to consider, as required by applicable regulations, certain facts and circumstances including, as discussed in *Kreis v. Charles O. Townley, M.D. & Associates, P.C.*, 833 F.2d 74, 79–80 (6th Cir.1987), a purported lack of a bad faith or predatory efforts to profit from forfeitures to the Trust. Petitioner contends, therefore, that in accordance with the factual inquiry discussed by the Sixth Circuit in *Kreis v. Townley, supra,* no partial termination occurred during its 1982 Plan year.

In *Kreis,* the Sixth Circuit, applying the facts and circumstances test under the regulations, examined whether a partial termination occurred by inquiring, among other factors, into the bad faith or predatory efforts to profit from the plan forfeitures. The Sixth Circuit, however, applied that test in connection with its finding that the percentages of terminated participants in the plans in question were too low (13.6 and 15 percent), standing alone, to warrant findings of partial plan terminations. In contrast, petitioner, which concedes on brief that it terminated 66⅔ percent of its workforce, terminated a percentage of participants that, standing alone, generally is sufficient to warrant a finding of a partial termination.

Notwithstanding this significant percentage reduction, however, petitioner argues that its alleged lack of bad faith or predatory efforts in the present case precludes a finding of a partial termination. Indeed, in *Kreis,* the Sixth Circuit stated that "as a general matter we must look beyond the mere percentages unless and until Congress or the Treasury Department provide otherwise."

In our view, however, petitioner is attempting to use a sword as a shield. Under *Kreis,* the inquiry into bad faith or predatory efforts assisted the Sixth Circuit in examining whether a partial termination occurred after the percentage of terminated employees was insufficient, standing alone, to support such a finding. However, standing alone, the absence of bad faith or predatory efforts does not, as petitioner contends, preclude a finding of a partial termination when, as in the present case, the employer terminated a significant percentage of plan participants.

Even if we were to accept petitioner's argument, we are not persuaded that petitioner lacked bad faith or predatory efforts in the present case considering that, by closing its office and determining that it no longer desired or needed the services of the two employees, petitioner initiated their departures and, by failing to treat their Trust account balances as nonforfeitable, petitioner created a potential for a windfall to the remaining participant. We can only conclude, therefore, that the inquiry under *Kreis* regarding bad faith or predatory efforts is not helpful to petitioner in the present case.

On this record, petitioner simply presents no facts and circumstances indicating anything contrary to a partial termination during the 1982 Plan year as a result of a significant percentage reduction in Plan participants. Accordingly, we find that petitioner, by failing to treat the balances of the two employees' Trust accounts as nonforfeitable after a partial termination, violated the nonforfeiture provisions of section 411(d)(3).

Finding

— Horrible taxes for EER's + EEE's

* (count plan as fully vested – protects the EEE's) *
because EER terminated certain % of EEE's

Petitioner presents no further arguments of merit. Accordingly, we hold that the Trust does not constitute a qualified trust under section 401(a) for the Plan years beginning on or after May 1, 1982.

2. IRC § 411(d)

1. *Forfeiture as discrimination.* IRC § 411(d), which protects against employer misconduct associated with the administration of pension forfeiture rules, is expressed as a subprinciple of IRC § 401(a)(4), the antidiscrimination norm. Most explicitly, IRC § 411(d)(1) proscribes "pattern of abuse" cases, such as sacking employees to keep their pension rights from vesting, when that pattern would "[tend] to discriminate" in favor of the highly compensated. Regarding the antidiscrimination norm, see Chapter 9 infra.

IRC § 411(d) has no explicit counterpart in the vesting rules of ERISA § 203, although the antidiscrimination provision of ERISA § 510, discussed next in this chapter, serves much the same purpose.

2. *Termination as discrimination.* It is fairly easy to see why sacking workers to keep them from vesting in a plan that otherwise favors highly compensated employees can be characterized as discrimination. But IRC § 411(d)(3), the provision involved in the *Boruta* case, links *termination of the plan* to the antidiscrimination norm. Section 411(d)(3) requires as a condition of tax qualification that a plan provide that, upon termination or partial termination of the plan, accrued benefits must vest. IRC § 411(d)(3) is, therefore, another substituted special-purpose vesting schedule, 100 percent vesting on termination or partial termination.

Why should termination or partial termination of a plan be viewed as a likely occasion for discrimination, justifying the imposition of a no-forfeiture rule?

3. *Vertical partial termination.* *Boruta* involves the question of when a reduction in the number of participants results in a partial termination for purposes of IRC § 411(d)(3). Excluding previously covered plan participants, whether by dismissing them or by amending the plan, has come to be known as "vertical" partial termination. The statute does not provide close guidance about how to determine whether such a partial termination has occurred. The Regulations instruct the IRS to apply a facts and circumstances test:

> Whether or not a partial termination of a qualified plan occurs (and the time of such event) shall be determined by the Commissioner with regard to all the facts and circumstances in a particular case. Such facts and circumstances include: the exclusion, by reason of a plan amendment or severance by the employer, of a group of employees who have previously been covered by the plan; and plan amendments which adversely affect the rights of employees to vest in benefits under the plan.

Treas.Reg. § 1.411(d)–2(b)(1). Such a test works ex post; the employer finds out only after acting that the plan violates the facts and circumstances test. Would not a flat-fraction rule be preferable?

Generally, a vertical partial termination will occur when a significant percentage of participants is excluded from the plan. See, e.g., Halliburton Co. v. Commissioner, 100 T.C. 216, 234 (1993). For many years the IRS applied a 50/20 bright line test. Auditors were supposed to question whether a partial termination had occurred if the percentage of participants excluded exceeded 20 percent, and were supposed to assert that a partial termination had occurred if the percentage exceeded 50. In 1990 these numerical guidelines were removed from the Internal Revenue Manual, which now states: "There is no fixed turnover rate which determines whether a partial termination occurred, but the rate must be substantial." Internal Revenue Manual 7.12.1.2.7.1.

While declining to accord "talismanic significance to the 20 percent rule," the Tax Court has held that a percentage of less than 20 percent is not significant unless there are egregious circumstances:

> A rule of thumb has developed that a percentage drop of at least 20 percent is sufficient, if coupled with other circumstances, e.g., the closing of a plant or division, to suggest that a partial termination has occurred. A drop of less than 20 percent has been considered significant only if accompanied by egregious abuse on the part of the employer, such as discrimination in favor of the highly compensated, manipulation of the pension rules to obtain tax benefits, creation of a reversion of plan assets to the employer, or an attempt to prevent employees from becoming vested in accrued benefits.

Halliburton, 100 T.C. at 237. The court held in that case that a 19.85 percent reduction was not sufficiently large to be significant.

A drop of more than 20 percent does not automatically result in a partial termination. In Administrative Comm. of the Sea Ray Employees' Stock Ownership and Profit Sharing Plan v. Robinson, 164 F.3d 981 (6th Cir.1999), a pleasure boat manufacturer experiencing declining orders laid off 15.9 percent of the worker-participants in 1989–90 and 27.9 percent in 1990–91. The court refused to find partial termination, because "both years were below 30 percent [and because there was no] damage to the Plan or improper motive for profit. . . ." Id. at 989.

In a 2004 opinion, the Seventh Circuit presented a chart of the prior partial termination cases and rulings, which in Judge Posner's view "reveals the surprising robustness of the 20 percent benchmark." Matz v. Household International Tax Reduction Investment Plan, 388 F.3d 570, 576–77 (7th Cir.2004). Judge Posner, id. at 577–78, formulated the following partial termination standard:

> In an effort to make the law as certain as possible without opening up gaping loopholes, we shall generalize from the cases and the rulings a rebuttable presumption that a 20 percent or greater reduction in plan participants is a partial termination and that a smaller reduction is not. How rebuttable? One can imagine cases in which a somewhat smaller reduction in the percentage of plan participants would be tax-driven and might on that account be thought a "partial" termination, and other cases, like *Sea Ray*, in which the reduction is perhaps not so far above 20 percent that further inquiry is inappropriate. We

assume in other words that there is a band around 20 percent in which consideration of tax motives or consequences can be used to rebut the presumption created by that percentage. A generous band would run from 10 percent to 40 percent. Below 10 percent, the reduction in coverage should be conclusively presumed not to be a partial termination; above 40 percent, it should be conclusively presumed to be a partial termination.

In *Boruta* the percentage was 67 percent, which under this standard would have been conclusively presumed to be a partial termination. Why should Dr. Boruta be precluded from rebutting the presumption by arguing that he had a legitimate business purpose in closing his firm and firing his two employees (he was going to join another medical practice, which made the employees' service "unnecessary")?

4. *Mechanics of computation.* How to compute the percentage has given rise to dispute. Is the proper ratio terminated nonvested participants divided by total nonvested participants, or is it total terminated participants (vested and nonvested) divided by total participants? In Weil v. Retirement Plan Administrative Committee of the Terson Co., 933 F.2d 106, 110 (2d Cir.1991), the court concluded that the IRS' choice of the latter ratio was a "reasonable construction." After toying with a different approach in an earlier case, the Seventh Circuit in *Matz* also determined that the percentage should be computed using both vested and nonvested participants.

There seems to be general agreement that terminations on account of death, normal retirement, termination for cause, and normal turnover, should be excluded. See *Halliburton*, 100 T.C. at 230, 238; Internal Revenue Manual 7.12.1.2.7.1–2. Why? Although Halliburton and other courts treat it as a matter of black letter law that employees who terminate voluntarily should not be counted for purposes of determining whether a partial termination occurred, there is often dispute over whether, in fact, certain employees have terminated voluntarily. E.g., Jeffries v. Pension Trust Fund of the Pension, Hospitalization and Benefit Plan of the Electrical Industry, 2007 WL 2454111 (S.D.N.Y.2007) (involving disagreement over whether defendants' special programs and break in service rules rendered some terminations voluntary). *Jeffries* also illustrates that there may be questions of fact concerning the percentage of employees who have been terminated. Id.

What is the relevant time period within which terminations should be treated as a single termination? One can imagine an employer cutting its work force 10 percent each year for four years. Can one consider the entire 4-year period? In In re Gulf Pension Litigation, 764 F.Supp. 1149, 1167–68 (S.D.Tex.1991), the court held that a partial termination could "occur from a significant corporate event that manifests itself in employer-initiated terminations occurring over [a 30 month] period." However, in *Sea Ray*, discussed supra, drops of 15.9 percent in one year and 27.9 percent in the succeeding year were not combined because the causes were unrelated.

5. *Participant claims.* The requirement of vesting upon full or partial termination is a requirement for qualifying a plan under the IRC, and not a requirement found in ERISA. *Boruta* and *Halliburton* involved attempts by the IRS to disqualify a plan, but *Weil, Sage, Sea Ray,* and

Matz were brought by participants seeking benefits based on the partial termination rule. How were the participants able to bring such claims if ERISA does not require full vesting upon partial termination? Note that in *Sea Ray* the Sixth Circuit also held that the plan administrator's decision that certain layoffs did not amount to a partial termination was subject to review under an arbitrary and capricious standard, rather than *de novo* review. The scope of judicial review of fiduciary decisionmaking is discussed in Chapter 15, infra.

6. *Horizontal partial terminations.* Under a special rule in the regulations, a partial termination will be deemed to occur if a defined benefit plan ceases or decreases "future benefit accruals," and as a result a potential reversion to the employer maintaining the plan is created or increased. Treas.Reg. § 1.411(d)–2(b)(2). Such partial terminations have been dubbed "horizontal" partial terminations. Unlike a vertical partial termination, when participants cease to be covered by the plan, a horizontal partial termination entails a cutback in future benefits for employees who continue to participate in the plan. The effect of a vertical termination is to vest those who are no longer covered; the effect of a horizontal termination is to vest those whose future benefits are cut back. Why is a reduction in future benefit accruals treated as a partial termination?

Horizontal partial termination cases are rare. In In re Gulf Pension Litigation, 764 F.Supp. 1149 (S.D.Tex.1991), aff'd sub nom., Borst v. Chevron Corp., 36 F.3d 1308 (5th Cir.1994), the court concluded that a horizontal partial termination had occurred when Gulf's pension plan was amended to cut back certain accruals of future benefits. The benefits reduced or eliminated were largely so-called "ancillary benefits," such as disability benefits, incidental death benefits, and Social Security supplements, rather than "accrued benefits." The court rejected arguments that only cutbacks of future "accrued benefits" should trigger a horizontal termination. It noted that although IRC § 411 is full of references to "accrued benefits," IRC § 411(d)(3) uses the term "rights [to] benefits accrued." Id. at 1176. The court also found it irrelevant that the bulk of the ancillary benefits were replaced by new life insurance and long-term disability insurance outside the plan.

What magnitude of reduction in future accruals is sufficient to cause a horizontal partial termination? Is the 20 percent rule-of-thumb for vertical partial terminations relevant? In *In re Gulf Pension Litigation*, the court deemed a 10 percent reduction in future projected accruals to be sufficient. See 764 F.Supp. at 1178 n.36.

3. ERISA'S ANTIDISCRIMINATION RULE: § 510

ERISA § 510 protects against interference with rights protected under ERISA, including vesting rights. Section 510 echoes the prohibition on abuse in IRC § 411(d)(1). Rights under § 510 are individually actionable, whereas only the IRS enforces the IRC.

Be aware that the concept of antidiscrimination figures in a quite distinct realm of pension law, in the provisions of the tax law that are designed to encourage pension plans to provide coverage to less-well-paid workers. See infra Chapter 9.

1. *Scope.* ERISA § 510 makes it unlawful "to discharge, fine, suspend, expel, discipline, or discriminate against a participant or beneficiary for exercising any right to which he is entitled under the provisions of an employee benefit plan [or under Title I of ERISA] or for the purpose of *interfering with the attainment of any right to which such participant may become entitled* under the plan [or under Title I]" (emphasis supplied). Section 510 has been invoked in cases in which employees claim that they were laid off to save pension costs, hence to prevent them from attaining pension rights. Section 510 can, therefore, remedy interference with ERISA's protections of vesting and benefit accrual.

Section 510 also makes it unlawful to discharge or otherwise penalize "any person because he has given information or has testified or is about to testify in any inquiry or proceeding relating to [ERISA]." Courts remain split on whether § 510 protects employees who participate in internal inquiries as well as those involved in external proceedings. The Second, Third and Fourth Circuits have held that internal complaints to management are not protected because they are not part of an "inquiry or proceeding." Edwards v. A.H. Cornell and Son, Inc., 610 F.3d 217 (3d Cir.2010); Nicolaou v. Horizon Media, Inc., 402 F.3d 325 (2d Cir.2005); King v. Marriott Int'l Inc., 337 F.3d 421 (4th Cir.2003). In contrast, the Fifth and Ninth Circuits have held that complaining to management about alleged ERISA violations is protected by § 510. Anderson v. Elec. Data Sys. Corp., 11 F.3d 1311 (5th Cir.1994); Hashimoto v. Bank of Haw., 999 F.2d 408 (9th Cir.1993).

The Seventh Circuit recently expressed its understanding of § 510 as "divid[ing] the world into the informal sphere of giving information in or in response to inquiries and the formal sphere of testifying in proceedings. This means that an employee's grievance is within § 510's scope whether or not the employer solicited information. It does not mean that § 510 covers trivial bellyaches—the statute requires retaliation to be "because" of a protected activity. . . . Someone must ask a question, and the adverse action must be caused by the question or the response. What's more, the grievance must be a plausible one, though not necessarily one on which the employee is correct." George v. Junior Achievement of Cent. Indiana, Inc., 694 F.3d 812, 817 (7th Cir.2012), as amended on denial of reh'g (Sept. 24, 2012).

The Sixth Circuit emphasized in Sexton v. Panel Processing, Inc., 2014 U.S. App. LEXIS 8752 (6th Cir. May 9, 2014) that an actual "inquiry" is a precondition to a claim under § 510. The court rejected a claim of violation of § 510 that was based on an e-mail from plaintiff suggesting that he believed the act of removing him as plan trustee violated ERISA and that he planned to bring the violation to the attention of the DoL. There was no response to the e-mail and the plaintiff took no further action after sending it. Six months after sending the e-mail, the plaintiff was fired as General Manager of the company. The fact that the e-mail was not sent in connection with an official investigation or in response to a request for information, and that it neither asked nor answered any questions, meant that the e-mail could not be characterized as giving information in an inquiry. The court observed that ERISA's statutory language does not provide protection for people who merely report or complain about unlawful practices outside of an inquiry or proceeding.

2. *Welfare benefit plans.* Although ERISA § 510 is centrally concerned with protecting pension benefits, thus reinforcing the vesting protections against subterfuge, § 510 is part of the remedial system of Title 1, Part 5, which extends to all ERISA-covered plans. In Inter-Modal Rail Employees Ass'n v. Atchison, Topeka & Santa Fe Railway Co., 520 U.S. 510 (1997), the Supreme Court reversed a Ninth Circuit decision that read § 510 to be applicable only to pension benefits, hence not to welfare benefits. One issue now under wide discussion is the possibility of § 510 attacks on employers' staffing decisions in response to the Affordable Care Act: see, e.g., James R. Napoli and Brian S. Neulander, The View From Proskauer: Health Care Reform Litigation Risks—The Intersection of ERISA Section 510 and the Affordable Care Act's Whistleblower Provisions, ERISA Litigation Newsletter, June 2013, available at www.proskauer.com; Law360, Trying To Avoid ACA Mandate? ERISA 510 May Catch You, August 22, 2013, available at www.law360.com.

3. *The Gavalik/McLendon litigation.* For pension plans, the leading § 510 action has been the group of cases arising from Gavalik v. Continental Can Co., 812 F.2d 834 (3d Cir.1987). In the mid-1970s, Continental, a maker of steel cans, began experiencing a steady decline in business, owing to competition from aluminum and other sorts of containers. In deciding which plants to close and which employees to lay off, Continental developed a "liability avoidance program" that turned out to be a misnomer. The program aimed "to avoid triggering future vesting by placing employees who had not yet become eligible [on] layoff, and to retain those employees whose benefits had already vested." Id. at 840. In the class action brought on behalf of affected employees under § 510, the district court found for Continental, on the ground that Continental "was also motivated by legitimate business considerations." Id. at 858. The Third Circuit reversed. Drawing upon Supreme Court cases treating employment discrimination under Title VII of the Civil Rights Act, the court reasoned that when the plaintiff proves discriminatory intent on the part of the employer, the burden shifts to the employer to prove "that it would have reached the same decision or engaged in the same conduct in any [event]." Id. at 863. "[W]e are convinced that the desire to defeat pension eligibility was a 'determinative' factor in each of Continental's challenged actions." Id. at 864. "We emphasize our holding that Continental's liability avoidance scheme constituted a violation of ERISA when, pursuant to that scheme, [employees] were designated as permanently laid off for the purpose of defeating their pension eligibility." Id. at 865. Subsequent proceedings in the *Gavalik/McLendon* litigation are reported in McLendon v. Continental Can Co., 908 F.2d 1171 (3d Cir.1990). The liability phase of the litigation was settled at year-end 1990, when the plaintiffs accepted $415 million from the parent corporation of Continental Can in satisfaction of their ERISA § 510 and related claims. 18 BNA Pension Rptr. 8 (1991). For an extensive account of the facts surrounding the litigation, see Gordon L. Clark, Pensions and Corporate Restructuring in American Industry: A Crisis of Regulation 48–98 (1993).

[handwritten margin notes:] §510 claims: TT must show, prove, discrimination + 1 then burden shifts to Δ to show no But-For causation b/tun discrimination + decision (show motivation was something else besides liability costs)

For another instance in which the court determined that dismissals were motivated by the desire to save on employee benefit costs and hence in violation of ERISA § 510, see Pickering v. USX Corp., 809 F.Supp. 1501, 1546–49 (D.Utah 1992). The case is discussed in Dana M. Muir, Plant Closings and ERISA's Noninterference Provision, 36 Boston Col. L. Rev. 201, 210–12 (1995). She reads the case to stand for the proposition "that an employer violates section 510 when it makes a plant closing decision based exclusively on benefit costs." Id. at 212.

4.   *Defending against § 510.* With *Gavalik/McLendon* and *Pickering,* contrast Nemeth v. Clark Equipment Co., 677 F.Supp. 899 (W.D.Mich.1987). Clark had three manufacturing plants. It resolved on account of declining business to close its plant at Benton Harbor, Michigan. One of the factors known to management when it decided to close the Benton Harbor plant rather than an Asheville, North Carolina, plant was that pension costs at Benton Harbor would have run about $6 million more than at Asheville. The Benton Harbor employees sued under ERISA § 510. The district court distinguished *Gavalik* and found for Clark. "At most, pension costs amounted to 20% of the total difference in cost between the two plants. Although this is a substantial amount, the Court finds that Clark would have made the decision to close Benton Harbor even if it had ignored the cost of the pension plan altogether." Id. at 909.

In Apsley v. The Boeing Company, 691 F.3d 1184 (10th Cir.2012), the Tenth Circuit held that the mere fact that an employer enters into an asset sale agreement with the hope of achieving cost savings by operating a division with a smaller workforce is not sufficient to make out a claim of a § 510 violation. Evidence suggested that Boeing did not look at pension costs specific to the division it planned to divest until after the decision to divest had been made. Boeing and Spirit, the buying company, expected that buyer would achieve savings by paying its workers less and employing fewer of them.

5.   *Why protect fringes but not wages?* The opinion in *Nemeth* distinguishes wage costs and pension costs. "While termination of employees in order to reduce labor costs is not always illegal, ERISA prohibits such actions if the primary reason for high labor costs is pension liability." 677 F.Supp. at 907. Why should ERISA § 510 distinguish between cash wages and pension benefits? Why permit the employer to sack the worker to save the pay packet but not the fringes?

Do you think that employers make plant closure or other large scale layoff decisions in ignorance of fringe benefit costs? In Unida v. Levi Strauss & Co., 986 F.2d 970, 980 (5th Cir.1993), the company officer who made the decision to close the plant in question testified that his "decision to close the San Antonio plant was made without regard to costs associated with pension, workers' compensation, or other employee benefits." Do you think good managers make such decisions ignorant of such fundamentally relevant information? From the standpoint of corporate law, would the business judgment rule protect managers who had behaved in such a fashion?

From an ex ante perspective, how would you expect employers in sick firms to respond to the existence of liability in a case like *Gavalik?* Does the risk of such liability promote or retard the adoption and the sweetening of pension and employee benefit plans?

6. *Deception.* Section 510 is not by its terms an antifraud measure, but in practice nondisclosure is often a central factor in establishing that conduct amounts to prohibited discrimination or interference. Consider Pippin v. RCA Global Communications, 756 F.Supp. 446 (N.D.Cal.1991), involving the sale of an RCA unit to MCI. Before completing the transaction, MCI determined that the plaintiffs, RCA employees, would be terminated. RCA's severance pay plan provided 52 weeks of benefits, MCI's provided 30 weeks. The plaintiffs were not told of their impending termination while covered under the RCA plan. The day after being transferred to MCI, they were notified of their dismissal. The court reasoned that "[t]his timing defeats any argument by defendants that the transfer was in good faith," and the court inferred that "plaintiffs' momentary employment with MCI was a sham, designed to deprive plaintiffs of [the larger RCA] severance benefits to which they were otherwise entitled." Id. at 448. The Ninth Circuit reversed, Pippin v. RCA Global Communications, 979 F.2d 855 (9th Cir.1992), saying that "[t]he plaintiffs acknowledged at oral argument that there was no § [510] violation." Did the plaintiffs give up too soon?

In Healy v. Axelrod Construction Company Defined Benefit Pension Plan & Trust, 787 F.Supp. 838 (N.D.Ill.1992), the plaintiff alleged that the employer persistently deceived him about the character of the firm's pension plan, for the purpose of encouraging him not to participate. The court held the claim stated a cause of action. "An act of fraud directed at preventing an employee's pension benefits from accruing is analogous to threatening or harassing an employee in order to prevent the accrual of benefits." Id. at 845.

Suppose in the facts at stake in the *Gavalik/McLendon* litigation, supra, management had publicized its "Liability Avoidance Program," announcing it to the employees' union and on plant bulletin boards, as the planned response to declining employment. Would disclosure have defeated the § 510 action? If so, aren't § 510 cases really just fraud cases?

7. *Overlap with ADEA.* In Reichman v. Bonsignore, Brignati & Mazzotta P.C., 818 F.2d 278 (2d Cir.1987), the employer fired Marjorie Reichman ten months before her interest in the firm's pension plan became fully vested, causing her to forfeit almost $60,000 in unvested benefits. Reichman contended that she was fired to prevent her pension benefits from vesting fully; she also alleged age discrimination under the Age Discrimination in Employment Act (ADEA). The employer contended that Reichman was discharged for inadequate job performance. The lower court found to the contrary. She recovered under ADEA rather than ERISA, as ADEA allowed her a larger sum: $85,280 for lost wages and benefits, and a further $85,280 under ADEA's double recovery rule for cases of "willful violation" under 29 U.S.C. § 626(b). The relation between ERISA and ADEA is discussed in Chapter 18, infra.

8. *Burden of proof.* The courts have extended the burden allocating standards developed under Title VII of the Civil Rights Act and under the ADEA to actions under ERISA § 510 as well. "The allocation of burdens and imposition of presumptions in Title VII and ADEA cases recognizes the reality that direct evidence of discrimination is difficult to

find precisely because its practitioners deliberately try to hide it. Employers of a mind to act contrary to law seldom note such a motive in their employee's personnel dossier. . . ." Dister v. Continental Group, Inc., 859 F.2d 1108 (2d Cir.1988), applying McDonnell Douglas Corp. v. Green, 411 U.S. 792, 802–05 (1973). Under *McDonnell Douglas*, there is a three-step burden allocating sequence:

> First, the plaintiff has the burden of proving by the preponderance of the evidence a prima facie case of discrimination. Second, if the plaintiff succeeds in proving the prima facie case, the burden shifts to the defendant "to articulate some legitimate, nondiscriminatory reason for the employee's [rejection]" Third, should the defendant carry this burden, the plaintiff must then have an opportunity to prove by a preponderance of the evidence that the legitimate reasons offered by the defendant were not its true reasons, but were a pretext for discrimination.

Dister, 859 F.2d at 1111.

In Parker v. Cooper Tire and Rubber Co., 2014 U.S. App. LEXIS 3318 (5th Cir. Feb. 21, 2014), the Fifth Circuit held that a plaintiff must demonstrate his qualification to do a job as part of making out a prima facie case of retaliatory termination. Parker, who had worked for Cooper Tire for ten years, was terminated the day after he delivered the company a letter from his treating physician that he had severe and possibly end-stage liver disease. The company's defense to his retaliation claim related to his loss of benefits was that his firing was based on a legitimate nondiscriminatory reason: several unreported absences from work. Although the Fifth Circuit had earlier issued an unpublished ruling that Parker met his burden by showing that Cooper Tire's articulated reason was a mere pretext for discrimination due to the "close timing between Cooper Tire's discovery of Parker's severe disability requiring serious medical treatment and his subsequent termination" (2013 U.S. App. LEXIS 24730), it subsequently withdrew that opinion. The court said that "[b]ecause the qualification requirement is part of an employee's prima facie claim, our case law dictates that a disabled employee who is unable to perform his job will not be able to establish a prima facie claim of ERISA retaliation, even if it is otherwise undisputed that the employer terminated him solely to avoid paying ERISA benefits. The court acknowledged that its position conflicted with several other circuits, explaining that in those circuits "the plaintiff's ability to do the job may be a factor in assessing whether the employer had a legitimate, nondiscriminatory reason for the allegedly discriminatory conduct."

Loss of the opportunity to accrue additional pension benefits does not make a prima facie case. "This kind of deprivation occurs whenever an ERISA employer discharges an employee and is not alone probative of an intent to interfere with pension rights. Where this is the only deprivation, a prima facie case requires some additional evidence suggesting that pension interference might have been a motivating factor." Turner v. Schering-Plough Corp., 901 F.2d 335, 348 (3d Cir.1990), following Clark v. Resistoflex, 854 F.2d 762, 771 (5th Cir.1988). Accord Libel v. Adventure Lands of America, Inc., 482 F.3d 1028 (8th Cir.2007).

Likewise, failure to rehire terminated former employees is not actionable under § 510. "Unlike a discharge or other workplace harassment, a failure to hire does not amount to a circumvention of promised benefits because job applicants who have yet to be hired have not been promised any benefits." Becker v. Mack Trucks, Inc., 281 F.3d 372, 382 (3d Cir.2002).

Where there is direct evidence of discriminatory motivation, the *McDonnell Douglas* burden-shifting framework does not apply. See, e.g., Lessard v. Applied Risk Management, 307 F.3d 1020 (9th Cir.2002). Nonetheless, even if a plaintiff can provide direct evidence of discriminatory motivation, an employer may avoid liability if it can demonstrate that the termination or other interference would have occurred even in the absence of the unlawful motivation. In *Gavalik*, discussed supra, the Third Circuit instructed the district court to which it remanded the case that if defendant could prove that individual class members would have been terminated for lawful reasons, there would be no damages owed to them. 812 F.2d at 840–42.

9. *Remedy.* The narrowing of relief for consequential injury under ERISA as a result of the Supreme Court decisions in Mertens v. Hewitt Associates, 508 U.S. 248 (1993), and Great-West Life & Annuity Insurance Co. v. Knudson, 534 U.S. 204 (2002), is a major theme of Chapter 16, infra. That development has affected the scope of remedy in § 510 actions. In contrast to some decisions that had taken an expansive view of the relief available in a § 510 action, in Millsap v. McDonnell Douglas Corp., 368 F.3d 1246 (10th Cir.2004), discussed infra Chapter 16, the court concluded that the compensation for backpay that plaintiffs sought was "legal" rather than "equitable," hence not available under the grant of "appropriate equitable relief" under ERISA § 502(a)(3).

D. BENEFIT ACCRUAL — ERISA regulates the rate at which benefits accrue (doesn't regulate the amount of benefits)

ERISA does not stipulate any required *amount* of benefits that a pension plan must pay, but ERISA's benefit accrual rules do regulate the *rate* at which benefits accrue.

1. *Backloading.* The decision to regulate vesting necessarily entails regulating the formulas by which benefits accrue under a defined benefit plan. Consider what might happen if the statute prescribed vesting but did not regulate accrual rates. A plan could be designed that would vest employees in 100 percent of accrued benefits after five years, thereby complying fully with ERISA's five-year cliff vesting schedule; yet the formula for accruing benefits under the plan could provide that employees accrue no benefits (or very skimpy benefits) over, say, the first twenty years of employment. Thereafter benefits would accrue very rapidly. Under such a plan, an employee would be 100 percent vested after the fifth year in a pension plan with a benefit of nothing.

Understand that 100 percent of nothing is nothing and you understand the rationale for ERISA's benefit accrual rules. The idea is that unless vesting rules are reinforced by accrual rules that smooth out the accretion of benefits, vesting protection could be evaded by what is called *backloading,* that is, by a plan's use of a benefit accrual formula that postpones to the later years of service most or all of the employee's accrual.

2. *ERISA's accrual formulas.* ERISA § 204(b)(1) propounds three alternative formulas for accruing benefits in a defined benefit plan and requires that a plan satisfy at least one of them. Each is designed to prevent backloading, by requiring that benefits accrue relatively evenly across the period of the worker's active service. Subsection (A), the *3 percent rule,* prescribes that percentage of the ultimate retirement benefit as a minimum of the maximum benefit available under a plan that must accrue each year. Subsection (B), the *133⅓ percent rule,* permits the use of a formula under which the accrual rate for any one year does not vary from that for any other year beyond the indicated percentage. Subsection (C), the *fractional rule,* prorates the benefit accruing in any one year to the number of years of service until normal retirement age. For analysis of the three formulas, see Dan M. McGill, Kyle N. Brown, John J. Haley, & Sylvester J. Scheiber, Fundamentals of Private Pensions (Pension Research Council) 262–63 (8th ed. 2005).

3. *Normal retirement age.* The three formulas of ERISA § 204(b)(1) calculate the benefit at "normal retirement age," commonly abbreviated NRA. Subject to exceptions, NRA is age 65 unless the plan provides for a lower age. ERISA § 3(24), IRC § 411(a)(8). Most plans do use age 65. In Chapter 18, infra, treating age discrimination, the point is emphasized that NRA is definitely not a mandatory or even an expected retirement age. Many employees retire earlier, some later than NRA. As a result of 1986 amendments to ERISA, the plan may no longer cease accruals to an employee's benefit on account of age. ERISA § 204(b)(1)(H) (defined benefit); § 204(b)(2)(A) (defined contribution). Accruals must continue beyond NRA for an employee who remains employed after NRA.

"[N]ormal retirement age should be viewed more as an element in the definition of the retirement benefit than as a statement of when the participants are expected to retire. In actuality, the participants may retire over a wide range of ages, with appropriate adjustments in their benefits." McGill et al., supra, at 247–48. Plans commonly contain early retirement options, typically offering actuarially reduced benefits, discussed in Chapter 18, infra.

4. *Relation of accrual to funding.* Accruals are liabilities; in order for the liabilities to be discharged, assets must be put in place to fund the accruals. For discussion of key actuarial principles involved in funding pension plans, especially actuarial assumptions (including the interest rate assumption), see Chapter 6, infra.

5. *Inflation.* The largest factor affecting the interest rate assumption is the assumed rate of inflation. Inflation bears on both sides of the pension funding equation. It pushes salaries (hence liabilities) up, but it also erodes the value of accrued benefits. Speaking of the period of high inflation in the 1970s and early 1980s, the pension economist Jeremy Bulow (Stanford Business School) told a Senate Committee in 1985: "I estimate that an increase in long term [interest] rates from 7 to 11 percent reduced the present value of pension obligations by about a third." Bulow, The Termination of Overfunded Pension Plans, in Overfunded Pension Plans, Joint Hearing before the House Select Comm. on Aging and the Subcomm. on Labor-Management Relations of the

Comm. on Education and Labor, 99th Cong., 1st Sess. 256, at 257 (1985). Elsewhere Bulow has pointed out that even in times when inflation was moderate, "defined benefit plans provided a distribution of benefits which gave younger workers a somewhat lower fraction of their compensation in the form of pension benefits than older workers received. With current high inflation rates [of the early 1980s] this effect has been greatly exaggerated." Jeremy I. Bulow, The Effect of Inflation on the Private Pension System, in Inflation: Causes and Effects 123, 135 (R. Hall, ed.) (Nat'l Bureau of Economic Research) (1982).

Bulow's observation has important implications for the policy against backloading. *A defined benefit plan is intrinsically backloaded,* notwithstanding the effort of ERISA's accrual rules to overcome backloading. This point is further illustrated in connection with the discussion of portability in Section E of this chapter, infra. Because defined benefit formulas are commonly expressed as a fraction of final average salary, and because salary increases across time, even a flat benefit accrual schedule is worth more in the final years of employment. Inflation magnifies this effect.

Inflation affects the value of accrued benefits not only during the years of active employment when the employee is building pension credits, but also across the years of retirement. The table reproduced below, from President's Commission on Pension Policy, Coming of Age: Toward a National Retirement Income Policy 32 (1981), illustrates the depreciation in pension purchasing power at different rates of inflation. The table shows the real value of retirement income based on an initial replacement rate of 100 percent.

Years in Retirement	No Inflation	3% Annual Inflation	5% Annual Inflation	10% Annual Inflation
0	100	100	100	100
5	100	86	78	62
10	100	74	61	39
15	100	64	48	24
20	100	55	38	15
25	100	48	30	9

6. *Retrospective enhancement of benefits: past service credits.* Defined benefit pension plans are sometimes lauded by comparison with defined contribution plans on the ground that they are more inflation-resistant. One reason is that a final average pay formula will partially "index" the pension benefit to an inflation-sensitive factor, namely, salary, during the period of accrual. Preretirement compensation growth is a crude proxy for inflation.

Another reason why defined benefit plans have proven inflation-resistant is that employers sometimes make retrospective improvements in their defined benefit plans. Such enhancements have benefitted both current workers and retirees, that is, employees whose pensions are already in pay status. Unions often bargain for such improvements in collectively bargained plans, and nonunion employers also grant improvements. A survey conducted by DoL indicates that during the inflation-scarred years 1973 to 1979, "post-retirement adjustments represented approximately 40 percent of the [increase in the consumer price index]. Virtually all of the post-retirement adjustments [were] not required by law or contract." Handbook of Pension Statistics: 1985, at 177–78 (R. Ippolito & W. Kolodrubetz, eds.) (1986). See also Alicia H. Munnell, The Economics of Private Pensions 184–85 (Brookings Institution) (1982).

Very few plans have automatic cost-of-living adjustments. Those that do (covering three percent of covered employees in 1995) usually call for annual adjustments linked to the Consumer Price Index. See DoL, Bureau of Labor Statistics, Employee Benefits in Medium and Large Private Establishments: 1995, at 104, 117 & tbl. 132 (Apr. 1998). During the period 1990–1994, plans that made discretionary adjustments to the benefits of those already in pay status covered four percent of covered employees. Contrast this figure for the low-inflation 1990s with the practice in the high-inflation times of the late 1970s and early 1980s. Plans representing 47 percent of covered employees made at least one post-retirement adjustment during the period 1979–1983. See DoL, Bureau of Labor Statistics, Employee Benefits in Medium and Large Firms: 1984, at 14, 54–55 & tbl. 1.52 (June 1985). General Electric is reported to have made six increases between 1980 and 2000 in a defined benefit plan covering 134,000 retirees. Wall St. J., Apr. 18, 2000, at A3. For further discussion of post-retirement experience see Harriet Weinstein, Post-Retirement Pension Increases, Compensation and Working Conditions (Bureau of Labor Statistics) (Fall 1997). The issue of whether plan amendments to eliminate cost-of-living adjustments constitute a prohibited cutback of benefits is addressed in Chapter 5.

In Lightfoot v. Arkema, Inc., 2013 U.S. Dist. LEXIS 90415 (D.N.J., June 27, 2013), a federal judge in New Jersey ruled that that a plan that provided cost-of-living adjustments to distributions in the form of monthly annuity payments but not the equivalent value of the COLAs to one-time lump-sum payments violated ERISA. Because ERISA requires that lump-sum payments be the actuarial equivalent of the accrued benefit, and the COLA was part of the plan's definition of accrued benefit, the actuarial equivalent of the COLAs had to be included in the lump sum payment.

Retrospective improvements in a plan, whether for active workers or for retirees, are called past service credits (or past service benefits). It will be recalled from the discussion in Chapter 3, supra, that the granting of past service benefits figured largely in the underfunding of the Studebaker plan.

How sound is the assumption that a defined benefit plan is more inflation-resistant than a defined contribution plan? In a defined contribution plan, during the accumulation phase the assets in the participant's account are invested. Pension investments usually produce a real rate of return in excess of the inflation rate, although there have been periods—for example, during the stagflation of the 1970s, when neither equities nor bonds kept up with inflation. Even when a defined contribution account is in pay status, the undistributed assets remain invested, unless the account has been annuitized. From the standpoint of protection against inflation, which type of pension plan would you rather have? Would your answer vary depending on whether the inflation you feared was moderate and gradual as opposed to sudden and steep?

7. *Union influences.* Data canvassed in the note on "Pension Coverage" in Chapter 1, supra, shows that pension coverage strongly correlates with unionization. Unions have a tendency to prefer older workers over younger, a tendency that is manifested most prominently in unions' propensity to negotiate compensation and job security terms on a seniority basis. "Seniority" is a euphemism for a policy of discriminating in favor of older workers, that is, basing compensation on time served rather than on performance, and laying off younger workers before older. Defined benefit pension plans fit this profile of arrangements that favor older workers over younger. Because defined benefit pension plans are intrinsically backloaded, they favor older workers. Freeman and Medoff undertook to measure this effect:

> For a worker in his twenties, we estimate that the value of pensions rises annually by the equivalent of a 3 percent wage increase; for a worker in his forties, the value rises annually by the equivalent of a five percent wage increase; for a worker in his early sixties, the value rises annually by the equivalent of 10 percent wage increase. If we translate the pension into annual wages we see that it improves the position of older relative to younger workers by as much as a 7 percent wage increase for older workers (10 percent less 3 percent). Once again the tilt toward the senior worker is greater under unionism, because [the authors' data shows that] union workers [are] 20 to 25 percent more likely to have a pension plan than otherwise comparable nonunion workers, and because the union plans are more likely to be of the defined benefit type.

Richard B. Freedman & James L. Medoff, What Do Unions Do? 130 (1984).

8. *Drafting benefit formulas.* A defined benefit plan typically promises a benefit as a formula that multiplies an accrual unit (e.g., 2 percent) *times* years of service (usually subject to a cap such as 30 years) *times* final average compensation (i.e., the average pay that the worker receives over some period such as the last three years of employment). Under such a formula, a long-service employee would expect a pension benefit of 60 percent (2×30) of final average pay. For empirical data on benefit formulas, see U.S. Dept. of Labor, Bureau of Labor Statistics, Employee Benefits in Medium and Large Private Establishments: 1995, at 100–01, 106–08 & tbls. 114, 188 (Apr. 1998).

As a matter of ERISA fiduciary law, provisions specifying plan benefit levels are matters within the discretion of the sponsor (unless it has contracted away this autonomy, which sometimes occurs in collectively bargained plans). Setting benefit formulas is a matter of "plan design," a so-called "settlor" function. These concepts are developed in chapters 12–13, infra.

Drafting benefit formulas requires extreme care. Consider Eckersley v. WGAL TV, Inc., 831 F.2d 1204 (3d Cir.1987). The plan formula promised a pension benefit based on the employee's final average earnings, defined as "the average of [total] nondeferred annual earnings from the Employer during the final five consecutive [years of the employee's service]." Id. at 1206. A bonus clause in Eckersley's compensation agreement expressed his annual salary as a base plus three percent of the after-tax profits of the TV station he managed. The station was sold, then Eckersley retired. Under his bonus compensation clause, Eckersley demanded a three percent share of the profits from the sale of the station for the year of the sale. Litigation ensued, which was settled by a $200,000 payment to Eckersley. Thereafter, Eckersley sued to force the inclusion of the $200,000 in the calculation of his pension benefit as a part of his "final average earnings." Held, the $200,000 was to be included. For a contrary case, construing different plan terms, see Licciardi v. Kropp Forge Division Employees' Retirement Plan, 990 F.2d 979 (7th Cir.1993).

Are an employee's stock options included as earnings for purposes of determining the pension benefit? See Soule v. Retirement Income Plan for Salaried Employees of Rexham Corp., 723 F.Supp. 1138 (W.D.N.C.1989). See also Gilliam v. Nevada Power Co., 488 F.3d 1189 (9th Cir.2007) (upholding determination that "earnings" does not include severance pay for purposes of calculating pension benefit); Wolberg v. AT & T Broadband Pension Plan, 123 Fed.Appx. 840 (10th Cir.2005) (upholding exclusion of retention bonus amounts in calculating pension benefits).

In 1991 Polaroid recovered $925 million from Eastman Kodak pursuant to litigation alleging patent infringement over the years from 1976 through 1986. The plaintiff, a former employee of Polaroid, sued Polaroid, alleging that Polaroid's contributions to its profit sharing plan for those years had been undersubscribed. Polaroid recognized the entire $925 million as 1991 income for tax purposes. Polaroid defended the suit by pointing to the language of the plan, which provided that Polaroid's determination of "net profits shall be conclusive for all purposes under the Plan." What result? See Pizzuti v. Polaroid Corp., 985 F.2d 13 (1st Cir.1993).

When issues of benefit calculation become litigious, they are filtered through the standard of judicial review of plan decisionmaking, the subject of Chapter 15 of this coursebook, infra. Application of the arbitrary and capricious standard will typically lead to a conclusion that the plan administrator's determination was reasonable. See, e.g., Wagener v. SBC Pension Benefit Plan-Non Bargained Program, 407 F.3d 395 (D.C.Cir.2005) (committee interpretation of average annual compensation held reasonable); Wolberg v. AT & T Broadband Pension Plan, 123 Fed.Appx. 840 (10th Cir.2005) (decision to exclude retention bonus from formula for calculating pension benefits not arbitrary and capricious); O'Neil v. Retirement Plan for Salaried Employees of RKO General, Inc., 37 F.3d 55 (2d Cir.1994) (decision to exclude payments under stock incentive compensation plan from definition of "earnings" in retirement plans held not arbitrary and capricious). However, courts will occasionally come to the opposite conclusion. See Kennedy v. Electricians Pension Plan, IBEW No. 995, 954 F.2d 1116 (5th Cir.1992) (plan interpretation excluding past service credit for apprentices held an abuse of discretion).

E. PORTABILITY

Michael Gordon's account of the history of ERISA extracted in Chapter 3, supra, emphasizes that much of ERISA's ultimate regulatory agenda originated with the proposals contained in the Cabinet Committee report of 1965, including minimum vesting schedules, funding requirements, termination insurance, disclosure rules, and fiduciary standards. See President's Committee on Corporate Pension Funds and Other Retirement and Welfare Programs, Public Policy and Private Pension Programs: A Report to the President on Private Employee Retirement Plans vi–xvi (1965).

The Cabinet Committee made a further policy recommendation that ERISA did not follow: to devise a system for making pension credits portable from one employer to another when a participant changed jobs. The Cabinet Committee urged "serious study" of "[t]he possibility of some institutional arrangement for transferring and accumulating private pension credits." Id. at xii, see also id. at 55–57. Portability has continued to be discussed in pension policy circles ever since.

Although ERISA permits a terminating participant's pension credits to be carried over to the new employer's plan, few plans accept such credits, for the reasons discussed in Michael Falivena's account of the impediments to portability, referred to infra in this unit. See also Steven L. Willborn, The Problem with Pension Portability, 77 Nebraska L. Rev. 344 (1998). What is the case for portability? Why might plan sponsors not care for it? What difficulties might arise in implementing a system of transfers from one pension plan to another, or from various plans to a central portability fund? Would a central portability fund have to take the form of a defined contribution plan as opposed to a defined benefit plan? For discussion of these issues, see Joint Comm. on Taxation, Proposals and Issues Relating to the Portability of Pension Plan Benefits (JCS 11–88) (1988); Donald S. Grubbs, Jr., Vesting and a Federal Portable Pension System, 9 J. Pension Planning & Compliance 381 (1983).

Portability is importantly connected to the topic of pension forfeitures, especially in defined benefit plans, because a portability program would (1) perpetuate *nonvested* accruals, enabling them to survive and to vest during subsequent employment; and (2) cause *vested* benefits to obtain the multiplier effect of subsequent years of accruals, a point illustrated in the table from Falivena, infra.

1. *Rollover IRAs.* Although ERISA did not devise a portability system of this character, ERISA did in fact create an immensely important portability device, the *rollover IRA*. A rollover IRA is an IRA that is funded not with annual contributions based on current earnings, but rather by means of one or more distributions from a qualified plan, an IRC 403(b) plan, a governmental 457(b) plan or another IRA. Under IRC § 402(c), the proceeds transferred in such a rollover remain tax deferred. Although most rollovers are from lump sum distributions (LSDs), many non-LSD distributions are also eligible for rollover. The rollover rules are addressed in Chapter 11, infra.

Zelinsky observes that the rollover IRA "was destined to play a more critical role" than the drafters of ERISA had envisaged, because "in a world of employee mobility, the rollover process stimulated a long-term shift of retirement savings from employer plans to IRAs." Edward A. Zelinsky, The Defined Contribution Paradigm, 114 Yale L.J. 451, 474 (2004). Many IRC 401(k) plans offer no annuity option on distribution, but only LSDs. "The availability of the IRA as a rollover device encouraged plans to eschew annuity-style payouts and instead to distribute lump sums, transferable tax free to departing participants' IRAs." Id.

The largest share of IRA assets comes from rollover contributions. "Rollovers to IRAs overwhelmingly outweighed new IRA contributions in dollar terms. While almost 2.4 million accounts received contributions, compared with the 1.3 million accounts that received rollovers in 2012, 10 times the amount of dollars were added to IRAs through rollovers than from contributions (Figure 17). This is not surprising, considering the annual contribution limit of $5,000 ($6,000 for those ages 50 or older) for IRAs in 2012, relative to the theoretically unlimited amount that could be added via a rollover. The average and median rollover amounts were $71,447 and $15,580, respectively, compared with the average contribution of $3,904." Craig Copeland, Individual Retirement Account Balances, Contributions, and Rollovers, 2012, EBRI Issue Brief, May 2014, at 10.

The taxation of distributions from rollover IRAs is discussed in Chapter 11, infra. For a participant who is subject to federal estate and gift taxation, and who wishes to transfer retirement assets to descendants or others, there are notable tax advantages to the use of the rollover IRA, discussed there.

2. *Lump sum distributions.* When a participant terminates employment, nonvested benefit accruals forfeit. Vested accruals may be left in the plan as pension credits and distributed in the ordinary course as an annuity (or, if the plan permits, in one or more LSDs) when the worker reaches retirement age (or early retirement age). In the alternative, almost all pension plans permit a terminating worker, including one who is nowhere near retirement, to cash out his or her pension accumulation in whole or in part as an LSD. If the terminating participant is taking an LSD from a defined benefit plan, the plan will discount the accrued benefit to present value. Under a defined contribution plan, the vested account balance is available for LSD.

A Congressional Research Service (Library of Congress) study published in 2003 but based on 1998 Census Bureau data reported that 82 percent of workers covered under occupational pension plans were in plans that offered LSDs. Patrick J. Purcell, Pension Issues: Lump-Sum Distributions and Retirement Income Security 6–7 (2003). The study noted that virtually all defined contribution plans offer LSDs, and that "the conversion of several hundred large defined benefit pension plans to 'cash balance plans' " in recent years had increased the trend to LSDs. Id. at 6. It has been estimated that only two percent of the defined benefit plans of large and medium sized sponsors offered LSDs in 1989, but that by 1997 23 percent of such plans offered LSDs. James H. Moore, Jr., & Leslie A. Muller, An Analysis of Lump-Sum Pension Distribution Recipients, 125 Monthly Labor Rev. 29, 30 (May 2002). By 2005, this had increased to 52 percent. U.S. Department of Labor, National

Compensation Survey: Employee Benefits in Private Industry in the United States, 2005, Bulletin 2589, May 2007.

3. *Optional forms of benefit payment.* Although the accrued benefit payable under a defined benefit plan is expressed as an annuity commencing at normal retirement age, a plan can offer a participant the option of receiving the benefit in some other form, such as a lump sum. However, the IRS takes the position that the present value of any optional form of benefit cannot be less than the present value of the normal retirement benefit using an IRS specified mortality table and the interest rate on 30-year Treasury securities. Treas.Reg. § 1.417(e)–1(d)(1); Treas.Reg. § 1.411(a)–11(a)(1). Although the statute is hardly clear on the matter, two circuits have concluded that the regulations imposing these valuation requirements on optional distributions reflect a reasonable executive branch interpretation of an ambiguous statute entitled to deference. See Esden v. Bank of Boston, 229 F.3d 154, 175 (2d Cir.2000); Lyons v. Georgia-Pacific Corp. Salaried Employees Retirement Plan, 221 F.3d 1235, 1249 (11th Cir.2000). Both *Esden* and *Lyons* addressed the application of the regulations to distributions under cash balance plans. As noted in Chapter 18, infra, the PPA permits a cash balance or other hybrid plan to pay lump sums equal to the balance of a recipient's hypothetical account balance, without engaging in the analysis the IRS had suggested was required by the application of its regulations.

The PPA adopts a new (and generally higher) interest rate for use in computing the present value of lump sums and other nonannuity forms of distribution. Instead of the 30-year Treasury rate, the new rate is based on the same three-segment yield curve for investment grade corporate securities used for minimum funding purposes (see Chapter 6, infra), but without 24-month averaging. IRC § 417(e)(3). The new rate is phased in over five years beginning in 2008. The higher interest rate means that lump sum distributions will be smaller (in some cases dramatically so) than under the prior rules, which probably in part explains the five-year phase-in.

If the lump sum distribution is optional, why not allow a plan to use any reasonable interest rate? If the participant finds the resulting lump sum inadequate, the participant can choose another option or simply take the benefit in its standard annuity form. Would you expect most participants to be able to make their own determination of the relative value of various payment options? From a policy perspective, what benefits do you see from mandating a higher interest rate?

Suppose a defined benefit plan provides for a cost-of-living adjustment to its annuity payments. If a participant elects a lump sum distribution, must the plan take account of expected cost-of-living adjustments in computing the value of the lump sum distribution? See Williams v. Rohm and Haas Pension Plan, 497 F.3d 710 (7th Cir.2007) (plan must provide COLA's actuarial equivalent).

4. *Involuntary LSDs.* Although most preretirement LSDs are participant-initiated, in one circumstance the plan can require that the participant take an LSD: when the participant terminates employment and his or her account balance is less than $5,000. Congress has made the judgment that the employer should not be required to bear the

administrative burden of carrying such small accounts for former employees across the years. Accordingly, IRC § 411(a)(11) and ERISA § 203(e) permit the plan to provide for immediate distribution of the account without the participant's consent.

In 2001, Congress reversed the default rule for the handling of such involuntary distributions, requiring in new IRC § 401(a)(31) that when the sum distributed is above $1,000, the distribution must be made to a rollover IRA unless the participant elects to the contrary. Selecting the investment vehicle for the IRA in such circumstances is fiduciary conduct. DoL has issued safe harbor regulations to ease the burden on the plan sponsor. See 29 C.F.R. § 2550.404a–2, discussed in Joni L. Andrioff, Fiduciary Responsibility under ERISA: Automatic Rollover Safe Harbor, 33 Tax Management Compensation Planning J. 3 (2005).

5. *Promoting preservation.* Although the rollover IRA is now widely available as a portability mechanism to plan participants who receive LSDs either before or during retirement, many neglect to take advantage of it. According to the 2006 Census Bureau data, 55 percent of those who took an LSD cashed out at least part of it rather than rolling it over. Patrick J. Purcell, Pension Issues: Lump-Sum Distributions and Retirement Income Security (2009), at 5. Those who spent as opposed to saved part or all of the LSD tended to be the poorest and the least well-paid, that is, those whose retirement income needs are likely to be the most acute. Id.

Congress has taken some action across the years to try to deter preretirement consumption of retirement savings. The Tax Reform Act of 1986 imposed a 10-percent additional income tax (in addition to ordinary income tax) on an LSD taken before the age of 59 1/2 that is not rolled over to another qualified plan or to a rollover IRA. See IRC § 72(t), discussed infra in Chapter 11. The 2001 legislation discussed supra, reversing the default rule to presume rollover treatment for involuntary distribution of account balances above $1,000, is another indication of concern to try to limit leakage of LSD proceeds away from retirement savings.

Regarding the impact of the 10-percent additional income tax, according to a recent GAO report, the penalty has reduced the overall incidence and amount of leakage from plans. Nonetheless, the GAO found that leakage from cashouts has remained reasonably steady in recent years and still has a significant impact on a participant's preparedness for retirement. General Accounting Office, Report to the Chairman, Special Committee on Aging, U.S. Senate, 401(k) Plans: Policy Changes Could Reduce the Long-Term Effect of Leakage on Workers' Retirement Savings (Aug. 2009).

6. *Multiemployer plans.* "In the private sector, 21 percent of employees of small establishments—mostly those covered by multiemployer plans—had partially portable benefits. Among employees of medium-sized and large establishments, fewer than 10 percent had such benefits." Congressional Budget Office, CBO's Online Guide to Tax Incentives for Retirement Savings (Updated June 2006).

Recall from the discussion in Chapter 2, supra, that portability is an intrinsic feature of a multiemployer plan, because the benefit accrual formula consolidates the credits arising from an employee's service with all employers who contribute to the plan.

7. *Effects of Lack of Portability.* The effects of the lack of portability of defined benefit plan is illustrated by this chart extracted from Michael Falivena, Pension Portability: No Easy Solution, Pensions & Investments 15 (February 5, 1990), which compares the benefits of four workers with identical pay histories (6% pay increases each year for 30 years, with a starting salary of $20,000 and an ending salary of $108,370) and identical final pay pension plans (1.5% times final year's pay times years of service). Worker 1 spends his entire career with the same employer; Worker 2 works half his career with one employer and half with a second employer; Worker 3 works for three employers, each for 10 years; Worker 4 works six years for each of five employers. Compare their final pensions:

Pension non-portability

Worker	Employer no.	Yearly accrual rate	Years of service	Final year's pay	Total pension
1	1	1.5%	30	$108,370	**$49,000**
2	1	1.5	15	45,219	10,174
	2	1.5	15	108,370	24,383
					35,000
3	1	1.5	10	33,791	5,069
	2	1.5	10	60,513	9,077
	3	1.5	10	108,370	16,256
					30,000
4	1	1.5	6	26,765	2,409
	2	1.5	6	37,967	3,417
	3	1.5	6	53,856	4,847
	4	1.5	6	76,396	6,876
	5	1.5	6	108,370	9,753
					27,000

8. *The difficulties involved in addressing lack of portability.* Falivena's article, supra, discusses the difficulties inherent in trying to introduce portability into the U.S. pension system. Since it is unrealistic to expect employers to voluntarily agree on a uniform pension formula, the cost of any single employer offering portability would be excessive. Falivena, supra. See also Steven L. Wilborn, The Problem with Pension Portability, 77 Neb. L. Rev. 344 (1998). Wilborn suggests that resolving the concern about limited portability of defined benefit plans will be difficult both because it will be difficult to resolve questions about the "cost and distributional effects of changes in the rules relating to portability" and because "any changes affect, not only the ability of employees to transfer benefits, but also the calculus employers make when they decide whether to offer pension as an employee benefit." Id. at 345.

CHAPTER 5

PLAN AMENDMENT

Analysis

Introduction

ERISA requires that every employee benefit plan be amendable. ERISA § 402(b)(3). Because the tax and regulatory law changes across time, plans need to be amended to be brought into compliance. For example, when the Retirement Equity Act of 1984 mandated spousal survivor annuities (discussed in Chapter 7, infra), or when the Tax Reform Act of 1986 revised the integration standards, plans had to be revised to incorporate the new requirements.

Procedures for amending. ERISA requires the plan documents of every plan to "provide a procedure for amending such plan, and for identifying the persons who have authority to amend the [plan]." ERISA § 402(b)(3). The Supreme Court construed this provision in Curtiss-Wright Corp. v. Schoonejongen, 514 U.S. 73 (1995), which involved a welfare benefit plan whose terms provided: "The Company reserves the right at any time and from time to time to modify or amend, in whole or in part, any or all of the provisions of the plan." The employer maintained that its reservation of power to amend effectively specified itself as having the power to amend. The Third Circuit disagreed, reasoning that "[a] simple reservation of a right to amend is not the same as a 'procedure for amending [the] plan'; nor does it provide a procedure 'identifying the persons who have the authority to amend the plan.' " Schoonejongen v. Curtiss-Wright Corp., 18 F.3d 1034, 1038 (3d Cir.1994). The Supreme Court unanimously reversed. The Court said that the plan's designation of "[t]he Company" in the reservation clause was adequate to identify the persons authorized to amend. By clarifying that a "unilateral company decision to amend" suffices, the reservation clause "states an amendment procedure" within the meaning of ERISA § 402(b)(3). 514 U.S. at 79. Plans typically contain language similar to the language in the Curtiss-Wright plan, reserving to the employer the ability to adopt plan amendments.

The Supreme Court also observed in its decision in *Schoonejongen* that "[w]hatever level of specificity a company ultimately chooses in an amendment procedure or elsewhere, it is bound to that level." 514 U.S. at 85. Once set forth in a plan, amendment procedures "constrain the employer from amending the plan by other means." Winterrowd v.

American General Annuity Ins. Co., 321 F.3d 933, 937 (9th Cir.2003). Thus, for example, in Depenbrock v. CIGNA Corp., 389 F.3d 78 (3d Cir.2004), involving an amendment converting a defined benefit plan to a cash balance plan, the court held that the amendment was effective not when announced, but only much later, when the CEO executed a formal written amendment as required under the plan terms.

ERISA § 402(a)(1) requires every plan to be "established and maintained pursuant to a written instrument." This means that plan amendments must be in writing. Kalda v. Sioux Valley Physician Partners, Inc., 481 F.3d 639 (8th Cir.2007). The requirement of written terms has caused considerable difficulty in cases in which a participant relies upon an oral misrepresentation, see infra Chapter 15.

Just as a document need not be labeled a plan to satisfy the requirement that a plan be in writing, a plan amendment may be found in a document that is not labeled a plan amendment. In Evans v. Sterling Chem. Inc., 660 F.3d 862, 871 (5th Cir.2011), the Fifth Circuit held that a retiree benefits-related provision included in an asset purchase agreement was a valid plan amendment. The court found that the "plan amendment formalities" were satisfied by "a written corporate agreement" directing "the maintenance of benefits and premiums."

Fiduciary law. In Part III of this book, treating ERISA fiduciary law, it will be seen that the law distinguishes between the fiduciary and nonfiduciary roles of an employer or other plan sponsor. The Supreme Court has said that "an employer's decision to amend a pension plan concerns the composition or design of the plan itself and does not implicate the employer's fiduciary duties, which consist of such actions as the administration of the plan's assets." Hughes Aircraft Co. v. Jacobson, 525 U.S. 432, 444 (1999). Regarding this dimension of plan amendment, see Dana M. Muir, The Plan Amendment Trilogy: Settling the Scope of the Settlor Doctrine, 15 Labor Lawyer 205 (1999).

Although some earlier decisions treated multiemployer plans differently, holding that multiemployer plan trustees act as fiduciaries when they amend multiemployer plans, the Second Circuit recently ruled to the contrary. In Janese v. Fay, 692 F.3d 221, 227 (2d Cir.2012), the court viewed the Supreme Court's decisions in Curtiss-Wright Corp. v. Schoonejongen, 514 U.S. 73 (1995), Lockheed Corp. v. Spink, 517 U.S. 992 (1996) and Hughes Aircraft v. Jacobson, 525 U.S. 432 (1999) as abrogating those earlier decisions. It found that the Court's language analyzing fiduciary duties in those cases is equally applicable to multiemployer plans.

Although an employer's decision to amend (or terminate) a plan is a settlor act, a participant may bring a fiduciary claim challenging the implementation of the decision to amend or terminate. E.g., Tatum v. R.J. Reynolds Tobacco Co., 392 F.3d 636 (4th Cir.2004) (liquidation of funds in plan account incident to a plan amendment was a discretionary act subject to ERISA's fiduciary standards).

A. THE ANTI-REDUCTION RULE FOR PENSION PLANS

One of the things that a pension plan may not do by amendment is to reduce benefits that have already been accrued. The so-called anti-reduction or anti-cutback rule of ERISA § 204(g) is an essential component of ERISA's design to restrain pension forfeitures, discussed supra in Chapter 4. Without § 204(g), a retroactive plan amendment could subvert the plan's vesting regime. Notice as well the rule of ERISA § 203(c)(1)(A), which reinforces the anti-reduction rule by forbidding any retroactive alteration of a vesting schedule that would be unfavorable to the plan participant.

IRC § 411(d)(6) echoes ERISA § 204(g) as a condition for tax qualification; there are extensive regulations interpreting the statutory protection. Treas.Reg. § 1.411(d)–4.

ERISA's vesting and benefit accrual rules, including the anti-reduction rule of § 204(g), apply to pension plans, but not to welfare benefit plans. The sponsor is "generally free under ERISA, for any reason at any time, to adopt, modify, or terminate welfare plans." Curtiss-Wright Corp. v. Schoonejongen, 514 U.S. 73, 78 (1995). Accordingly, as a matter of ERISA regulatory law, the sponsor may unilaterally amend a welfare benefit plan to reduce benefits. However, as a matter of contract law, the sponsor may bind itself not to reduce plan benefits even though ERISA would permit such a reduction. A considerable case law has developed on the question of whether particular plan terms or other documents evidence such a contract. This is an issue that arises with some frequency in the context of retiree medical benefits, discussed in Chapter 19 infra.

1. SHAW V. INTERNATIONAL ASS'N OF MACHINISTS

563 F.Supp. 653 (C.D.Cal.1983), aff'd, 750 F.2d 1458 (9th Cir.1985).

■ HAUK, SENIOR DISTRICT JUDGE. These cross motions for summary judgment came on regularly for hearing on April 4, 1983. Plaintiff, by his motion, is seeking to reverse action taken by the defendants in "phasing out" the cost-of-living feature in his pension plan. Defendants seek affirmance of their having amended this cost-of-living feature out of the plan. Stipulated facts form the basis of these motions and both parties concede that the case may be disposed of as a matter of law. . . .

Plaintiff, Edward Shaw, retired as a District Lodge Business Representative of the International Association of Machinists and Aerospace Workers (hereafter IAM) on January 1, 1975, following 10 years of service. At the time of plaintiff's retirement his pension plan included a cost-of-living feature referred to as a "living pension." Under the living pension feature, increases in the retiree's pension were indexed to salary increases in the position the retiree held immediately prior to retirement.

In September, 1976, the delegates to the quadrennial IAM convention voted to amend the pension plan provisions of the constitution so as to phase out the living pension feature. This phase-out provided that the full percentage adjustment would be paid to retirees in 1977 and 1978, but thereafter, the living pensions adjustments would be as follows:

1979 and 1980—75% of full adjustments

1981 and 1982—50% of full adjustments

1983 and 1984—25% of full adjustments

After December 31, 1984—no further adjustments. The decision to phase the living pension feature out of the plan came after the IAM's actuaries had advised it that, if the pre-phase-out course should continue, the plan would suffer serious financial instability. . . .

[The] plaintiff alleges that the 1976 amendment violates [ERISA] § 204(g), which provides: "The accrued benefit of a participant under a plan may not be decreased by an amendment of the [plan]." Defendants initially argue that their action does not run afoul of ERISA because the living pension feature of plaintiff's plan does not amount to an "accrued benefit" within the definition of that term in [ERISA § 3(23)]:

The term "accrued benefit" means

(A) In the case of a defined benefit plan, the individual's accrued benefit determined under the plan [and] expressed in the form of an annual benefit commencing at normal retirement age.

Defendants argue that this language embraces only benefits promised upon retirement and does not include post-retirement benefits such as the living pension feature. Plaintiff, on the other hand, contends that an accrued benefit may be expressed in the form of a *formula*. While relevant authority on this issue is sparse, plaintiff's argument appears to be the more meritorious. For example, section 411(a)(7)(A)(i) of the Internal Revenue Code defines the term "accrued benefit" in precisely the same words as section [3(23)] of ERISA. The Internal Revenue Service through a Technical Information Release has stated:

IRC section 411(a)(7)(A)(i) provides, in part, that in the case of a defined benefit plan, the "accrued benefit" must be expressed in the form of an annual benefit commencing at normal retirement age. *The plan must provide a formula under which each participant's actual accrued benefit under the plan can be determined in each plan year.*

Internal Revenue Service T.I.R. No. 1403 (Sept. 17, 1975) (emphasis added). In addition, there is case law suggesting that an accrued benefit may be expressed by a formula as opposed to a sum certain that the pensioner will receive upon retirement. In *Pompano v. Michael Schiavone & Sons, Inc.,* 680 F.2d 911, at 914 (2d Cir.1982), the Second Circuit held:

the plan must specify the basis on which payments are to be made to participants and beneficiaries so as to meet the legislative purpose of having each participant know exactly where he stands with respect to the plan.

The IAM's own pension plan booklet states:

ADJUSTMENT OF PENSION AMOUNT AFTER RETIREMENT

If, after your retirement, the salary for the position you held immediately prior to your retirement is changed, the amount of your pension will be adjusted accordingly. The change in pension amounts, however, will not be retroactive.

In addition, Article XIV, section 7 of the Constitution of the International Association of Machinists and Aerospace Workers provides in pertinent part:

Computation of Pension

Pensions being paid to previously retired officers and employees shall be adjusted by applying the appropriate foregoing percentage to the straight-time compensation for the classifications or positions corresponding to those in which they were employed immediately prior to their retirement, provided, however, that in no case shall any such adjustment be made on a retroactive basis, nor increase any benefit to a survivor or beneficiary then being paid. Effective January 1, 1973, neither shall any such adjustment result in a pension payment which is less than the amount paid to the retiree at the time of retirement.

Applying the above language against the various authorities which permit accrued benefits to be expressed through a formula, the conclusion is inescapable that the living pension feature was an integral part of the formula through which the plaintiff's accrued benefits were expressed. Defendants' attempts to distinguish the living pension from other components of the retirement compensation formula are, accordingly, void of merit.

2. APPLYING THE ANTI-REDUCTION RULE

1. *Cost of living.* The Seventh Circuit followed *Shaw* in Hickey v. Chicago Truck Drivers, Helpers and Warehouse Workers Union, 980 F.2d 465 (7th Cir.1992), holding that a plan-prescribed cost of living adjustment clause is an "accrued benefit" protected under the anti-reduction rule of ERISA § 204(g)(1). See also Laurenzano v. Blue Cross & Blue Shield, 134 F.Supp.2d 189 (D.Mass.2001) (where plan provided for COLAs for participants who elected annuity payments, COLA was protected as an accrued benefit).

Shaw involved an employee who had already retired before the cost of living feature was amended. What about employees who have accrued benefits but have not yet retired? Can the amendment eliminating the cost of living feature be applied to them?

Suppose an employer amends a plan to add a cost of living adjustment to a plan for participants who retired before the plan was amended. Can the employer later eliminate the cost of living adjustment for such participants? The Fourth Circuit in Board of Trustees of the Sheet Metal Workers' National Pension Fund v. Commissioner, 318 F.3d 599 (4th Cir.2003), held that such a cost of living adjustment was not a protected benefit under the anti-reduction rule of IRC § 411(d)(6). The Treasury has disagreed with the Fourth Circuit by regulation: "The protection of section 411(d)(6) applies to a participant's entire accrued benefit under the plan as of the applicable amendment date, without regard to whether the entire accrued benefit was accrued before a participant's severance from employment or whether any portion was the result of an increase in the accrued benefit of the participant pursuant to a plan amendment adopted after the participant's severance from employment." Treas.Reg. § 1.411(d)–3(a)(1). In Thornton v. Graphic Communications Conference of the International Brotherhood of Teamsters Supplemental Retirement and Disability Fund, 566 F.3d 597

(6th Cir.2009), the Sixth Circuit declined to determine whether the Treasury's regulations were entitled to deference. The post-retirement benefit increase in question in that case was adopted in 1999 and rescinded in 2002. As the Treasury's regulations apply only to amendments of benefit plans adopted on or after Aug. 12, 2005, they were not applicable in the case before it. Citing *Sheet Metal Workers'* extensively, the Sixth Circuit concluded that

> "the Fourth Circuit's thorough analysis of the text and context of IRC § 411(a)(7)(A)(i) demonstrates that Congress did not consider a post-retirement increase in pension benefits to be an 'accrued' benefit. Section 411's repeated emphasis on the accrual of benefits during 'service' makes plain that the terms of pension plan document(s) in effect while a participant worked for a covered employer dictate his or her 'accrued benefits.'"

Id. at 606.

Is there merit in the Treasury's position? What is the harm in allowing an employer to grant a temporary benefit increase to an already retired participant, with the understanding that the increase could be rescinded thereafter? The anti-reduction rule is usually justified on the basis that it protects the employee's reliance interest. Does a retiree have a reliance interest?

2. *Ancillary benefits.* Benefits protected by ERISA § 204(g) and IRC § 411(d)(6) are usually referred to as "section 411(d)(6) protected benefits." Treas.Reg. § 1.411(d)–4, Q & A–1(d) provides examples of benefits that are not protected, including ancillary life, accident, or health insurance benefits; and the right to a particular form of investment in a defined contribution plan. Social Security supplements are generally ancillary benefits that are not protected. Treas. Reg. § 1.411(d)–4, Q & A–1(d)(3); Meehan v. Atlantic Mutual Ins. Co., 2008 WL 268805 (E.D.N.Y.2008). See Robinson v. Sheet Metal Workers' National Pension Fund, 441 F.Supp.2d 405 (D.Conn.2006), aff'd in relevant part, 515 F.3d 93 (2d Cir.2008) (industry-related disability benefits were unprotected ancillary benefits despite being described as a pension benefit).

Likewise, an early retirement supplement that is included in a plan's benefit formula as an "applicable supplement" is an accrued benefit. Savani v. Washington Safety Mgmt. Solutions, 474 Fed. Appx. 310 (4th Cir. Mar. 20, 2012) (plan defined "accrued benefit" as the normal retirement benefit ". . . plus any applicable supplement"). Subsequent to the Fourth Circuit's ruling in *Savani*, a class was certified. In a subsequent proceeding involving class members who did not meet the eligibility for the supplemental benefits as of Dec. 31, 2005 (the date as of which the plan had been amended), a federal district court held that those class members should have the opportunity to "grow into" eligibility for the supplemental benefits. Savani v. Washington Safety Mgmt. Solutions, LLC, 2013 U.S. Dist. LEXIS 45233 (D.S.C. Mar. 29, 2013).

In Bonneau v. Plumbers and Pipefitters Local Union 51 Pension Trust Fund, 736 F.3d 33 (1st Cir.2013), the First Circuit addressed a claim made to an amendment of benefit conferred during the merger of several plans. Each of the plans had provided that members who accrued hours of service in excess of the hours required to earn a full year of service could bank those hours for a variety of uses. Because the banked provisions were different in each of the premerger plans, the post-merger plan gave everyone the benefit of the most generous term from the premerger plans in calculating banked-hour benefits. Subsequently the trustees amended the plan to reduce the retrospective banked-hour benefits to the original lower levels earned under the pre-merger plans. The First Circuit held that the benefit in question constituted a "benefit attributable to service" and thus was an accrued benefit that could not be reduced. In so doing, it rejected the argument that because the retrospective benefits were a gratuity resulting from the plan merger, they had not been "earned" and thus should not be viewed to be part of participants' accrued benefits. "The term 'earned' appears nowhere in the statute, although it does in some case law as a shorthand term, and we do not adopt it as a substitute term for the statutory language."

3. *Altering valuations.* Kay v. Thrift & Profit Sharing Plan for Employees of Boyertown Casket Co., 780 F.Supp. 1447 (E.D.Pa.1991), concerned a profit sharing plan whose terms provided for the calculation and distribution of benefits for terminated employees using plan values as of the last day of the quarter in which the employee was terminated. In the plaintiffs' case, that date would have been September 30, 1987. A few weeks later occurred the October 19, 1987, stock market plunge ("Black Monday"), which caused the value of plan assets to decline severely. Employer-dominated plan fiduciaries amended the plan retroactively to allow an October 30, 1987, valuation date, with the result that $128,820 in plan losses were shifted from the plan to the withdrawing plaintiffs. The court found the retroactive amendment in violation of ERISA § 204(g)(1). Astonishingly, the court imposed the liability not on the plan, which had incurred the loss, but on the fiduciaries "for damages incurred as a result of breaches of their fiduciary [duty.]" 780 F.Supp. at 1465. Since the loss arose from Black Monday, and would have occurred had the fiduciaries not undertaken to shift the loss to the plaintiffs, can the court's decision to impose the liability on the fiduciaries rather than on the plan be defended?

Laying aside the handling of damages in *Kay*, the court's decision to prevent the retroactive alteration of the valuation date was a straightforward application of the anti-reduction rule. Accord, Pratt v. Petroleum Prod. Management Inc. Employee Savings Plan & Trust, 920 F.2d 651 (10th Cir.1990). Can *Pratt* and *Kay* be reconciled with Treas. Reg. § 1.411(d)–4, which states that "valuation dates for account balances" are not section 411(d)(6) protected benefits? The court in *Pratt* stated that "for those plan members not yet separated, [plan] valuation dates may be changed by amendment because they are not protected benefits." Id. at 663.

The Seventh Circuit recently held that a plan does not violate ERISA by retroactively modifying the discount rate used to calculate lump-sum distributions under the plan. Dennison v. MONY Retirement Income Security Plan, 710 F.3d 741 (7th Cir.2013). The plan in question was amended in 2009 to raise the applicable discount rate to the maximum permitted by the 2006 PPA. Because the effect of the PPA was to allow the change to be made without creating an ERISA problem, the question was whether the amendment violated the terms of the plan.

The Seventh Circuit found that the plan permitted amendments to change the discount rate retroactively so long as the amendment did not reduce participants' "Accrued Benefit," a term defined in the plan as "the value of a Participant's Retirement Benefit expressed as a Straight-Life Annuity determined in accordance with the terms of the Plan." The court interpreted the plan's definition "to mean that the Accrued Benefit—that which cannot be reduced retroactively by amendment—is the annuity, and that the lump sum, while a Retirement Benefit, is not the Accrued Benefit and therefore can be reduced retroactively. . . . Nothing in the plan forbids retroactively amending the discount rate used to calculate the lump sum benefit if the participant chooses the lump sum in preference to the annuity." Id. at 744.

Imposing retrospective conditions on plan benefits can also violate the anti-reduction rule. See, e.g., Central Laborers' Pension Fund v. Heinz, 541 U.S. 739 (2004), holding that a plan amendment adding further grounds for which early retirement benefits could be suspended violated ERISA § 204(g).

4. *Early retirement benefits.* ERISA § 204(g) and IRC § 411(d)(6) as originally enacted did not expressly prevent the reduction of a plan's alternative schedule of benefits for workers who retired early, although some courts had implied such a prohibition. In 1984 Congress undertook to clarify the matter, adding the present ERISA § 204(g)(2)(A) and IRC § 411(d)(6)(B)(i). Thus, a plan may not be amended to eliminate or reduce an early retirement benefit or a "retirement-type" subsidy "with respect to benefits attributable to service before the amendment."

The Senate Report on the legislation illustrates how ERISA § 204(g)(2)(A) operates:

> For example, consider a plan that provides an annual benefit of 1 percent of average pay per year of service at normal retirement age [age 65]. The plan provides an early retirement benefit to a participant who has attained age 55. This early retirement benefit is actuarially reduced to 50 percent of the benefit payable [at] age 65. In the case of a participant who attains age 55 and who has completed 30 years of service, the amount of the annual benefit payable at age 55 is not actuarially reduced under the plan.

> [The] plan is amended on January 1, 1985 [to] require a full actuarial reduction of early retirement benefits in all cases. [If] as of January 1, 1985, employee B was age 50, had completed 25 years of service, and had average pay of $10,000, then the plan amendment could not reduce B's benefit below $2,500 ($10,000 × 1 percent × 25 years). If B's average pay increased at 6 percent annually until age 55, then B's accrued benefit at age 55 under the plan as amended would be $4,016 ($13,382 × 1 percent × 30 years). But for the bill, [the] actuarial reduction would reduce B's annual benefit to $2,008. Under the bill, the amendment could not reduce B's benefit payable at age 55 below $2,500.

S. Rep. No. 575, 98th Cong., 2d Sess. 28–29 (1984).

The statute provides that in the case of a retirement-type subsidy, the anti-cutback rule does not apply unless the participant "satisfies (either before or after the amendment) the preamendment conditions for the subsidy." Thus, if a plan is amended to eliminate a subsidized early retirement benefit for employees who have completed 30 years of service, the plan would not be required to provide the benefit to an employee who does not complete 30 years of service.

This limitation can be extremely important in corporate reorganization settings. Suppose employee A works for a division of employer X and would be eligible for a subsidized early retirement benefit from X's plan if he completed 30 years of service with X. The division is sold to Y prior to A's completing 30 years of service. A continues to work at his same desk. Does A's service with Y count toward the needed 30 years of service to qualify for the early retirement subsidy? In Hunger v. AB, 12 F.3d 118 (8th Cir.1993), cert. denied, 512 U.S. 1206 (1994), the court said no. The plan requires service with X, and Y is simply not X. *Hunger* distinguished Gillis v. Hoechst Celanese Corp., 4 F.3d 1137 (3d Cir.1993), cert. denied, 511 U.S. 1004 (1994), a case that seemed to reach a contrary conclusion, by noting that in *Gillis* "[t]he sale of the division [was] made pursuant to an agreement that [the purchaser] would provide substantially the same employee benefits as those [the seller] had provided. Thus, the employee/plaintiffs were subsequently employed by the plan sponsor that had assumed both the obligations and assets of the retirement plan." 12 F.3d at 121–22. The D.C. Circuit came to the same conclusion as the Eighth Circuit in Andes v. Ford Motor Co., 70 F.3d 1332 (D.C.Cir.1995).

To make A's case seem more appealing, assume that A had planned to retire on June 1, the date he would have completed 30 years of service. Assume that with the early retirement subsidy, his pension is $3,000 per month, but without it his pension would be $1,500. On May 31, A's employer sells his division. In one day his pension drops in half. Does A have a reliance interest that should be protected? What would have happened to A if instead of his division being sold on May 31, A had simply been fired?

5. *Optional form of benefits.* The 1984 amendment also added ERISA § 204(g)(2)(B) and IRC § 411(d)(6)(B)(ii), enlarging the anti-reduction rule to prohibit "eliminating an optional form of benefit" contained within an accrued benefit. For example, a plan that provides benefits in the form of an annuity, but also provides a lump sum option, cannot be amended to eliminate the lump sum option as to benefits already accrued. The lump sum option can, however, be eliminated as regards benefits attributable to service after the amendment. Other optional forms of benefits might include the right to select among annuities with different terms and survivor options and even the right to receive distributions from a profit-sharing plan upon demand.

May a plan condition a benefit option on employer discretion? According to Treas.Reg. § 1.411(d), Q & A–4, a plan that permits employer discretion to deny the availability of an IRC § 411(d)(6) protected benefit violates IRC § 411(d)(6) and the definitely determinable requirement of IRC § 401(a) (see Treas.Reg. § 1.401–1(b)(1)(i)). Some courts disagree, holding that the exercise of employer discretion pursuant to the terms of a plan is not an "amendment" and the anti-reduction rule applies only to amendments. See, e.g., Collignon v. Reporting Services Co., 796 F.Supp. 1136 (C.D.Ill.1992). The regulations do permit "limited discretion with respect to the ministerial or mechanical administration of the plan, including the application of objective plan criteria specifically set forth in the plan." Treas.Reg. § 1.411(d)–4, Q & A–4(b). Could a plan condition the availability of lump sum distribution on the execution of a covenant not to compete? See Treas.Reg. § 1.411(d)–4, Q & A–6(a)(2).

6. *Plant shutdown and other contingent benefits.* Suppose a plan provides that if a participant's service ceases by reason of a permanent shutdown of a plant, and if the participant meets certain age and service requirements at the time of the shutdown, the participant is entitled to the benefit that would be payable at normal retirement age. Can this form of benefit be removed from the plan? Compare Ross v. Pension Plan for Hourly Employees of SKF Industries, 847 F.2d 329 (6th Cir.1988) (unprotected), with Bellas v. CBS, 221 F.3d 517, 532 (3d Cir.2000) (protected). Although for a time the IRS aligned itself with the holding in *Ross*, the current view of the IRS, as expressed in Treas.Reg. § 1.411(d)–3(b)(1)(ii), is that benefits contingent on an unpredictable event, such as a plant shutdown, are 411(d)(6)—protected benefits, even prior to the occurrence of the contingency.

[handwritten margin note: Protected benefits]

Is an employee's reliance interest in connection with a plant shutdown benefit the same as the employee's reliance interest in a subsidized early retirement benefit? Suppose an employer has a pension plan without any plant shutdown benefit, but in addition maintains a separate unfunded severance pay plan that provides a substantial lump sum payment to employees with 30 years or more service if their termination occurs as part of plant shutdown. Since a severance pay plan is a welfare benefit plan, it is not subject to ERISA's vesting and anti-reduction rules. The employer is free to terminate the plan at any time. Is the employee's reliance interest less strong because the benefit is paid in a lump sum, instead of an enhancement to his monthly pension check?

7. *Limited relief from the anti-reduction rules.* Administering the anti-reduction rule has proved to be burdensome to many plan sponsors. Optional forms of benefit that prove to be difficult to administer or no longer desirable cannot be eliminated, at least with respect to accrued benefits. These restrictions can be particularly troublesome in the event that a merger or other corporate reorganization occurs. If plans are merged, the various optional forms must be preserved, creating extraordinary complexity. The plan administrator of the combined plan must keep track of which employees are entitled to which options with respect to what portions of their accrued benefits. Moreover, these steps have to be explained in the summary plan description.

In 2001 Congress provided several statutory exceptions to the anti-reduction rules. Under IRC § 411(d)(6)(E) and ERISA § 204(g)(5), as amended, except to the extent provided in regulations, a defined contribution plan may be amended to eliminate a previously available form of distribution, provided that (1) a single sum payment is available at the same time or times as the form of distribution being eliminated, and (2) such single sum payment is based on the same or greater portion of the participant's account as the form of distribution being eliminated. A second, more limited exception, embodied in IRC § 411(d)(6)(D) and ERISA § 204(g)(4), applies to certain transfers between defined contribution plans.

For example, a profit-sharing plan that permitted distributions to be made in installments over the life expectancy of a participant or a beneficiary could be amended to eliminate this form of distribution as long as the plan permitted a single sum distribution of the entire account at the time such installment distributions would have begun. This exception is eminently sensible due to the ability of the participant to roll over the single sum distribution into an IRA (see Chapter 11, infra). Investments by and distributions from IRAs are completely flexible, permitting a participant to replicate any form of distribution that was available under the plan.

Additionally, the regulations under IRC § 411 provide a number of situations in which the elimination or reduction of certain accrued benefits does not violate § 411(d)(6). One of those is the elimination of provisions for transfers between and among defined contribution plans and defined benefit plans. See Tasker v. DHL Ret. Sav. Plan, 621 F.3d 34 (1st Cir. 2010) (amendment of plan to eliminate the right of participants to transfer savings plan balance into the company's retirement plan, eliminating their ability to take advantage of the retirement plan's more favorable actuarial assumptions, does not violate ERISA).

The 2001 Act also directed the Treasury to issue regulations that would permit the reduction or elimination of benefits or subsidies "which create significant burdens or complexities for the plan and plan participants, unless such amendment adversely affects the rights of any participant in a more than de minimis manner." IRC § 411(d)(6)(B)(third sentence); ERISA § 204(g)(2)(third sentence). The Conference Report provides the following example:

> Employer A acquires employer B and merges B's defined benefit plan into A's defined benefit plan. The defined benefit plan maintained by B before the merger provides an early retirement subsidy for individuals age 55 with a specified number of years of service. E1 and E2 are employees of B and who transfer to A in connection with the merger. E1 is 25 years old and has compensation of $40,000. The present value of E1's early retirement subsidy under B's plan is $75. E2 is 50 years old and also has compensation of $40,000. The present value of E2's early retirement subsidy under B's plan is $10,000. Assume that A's plan has an early retirement subsidy for individuals who have attained age 50 with a specified number of years of service, but the subsidy is not the same as under B's plan. Under A's plan, the present value of E2's early retirement subsidy is $9,850. Maintenance of both subsidies after the plan merger would create burdens for the plan and complexities for the plan and its participants.

> Treasury regulations could permit E1's early retirement subsidy under B's plan to be eliminated entirely (i.e., even if A's plan did not have an early retirement subsidy). Taking into account all relevant factors, including the value of the benefit,

E1's compensation, and the number of years until E1 would be eligible to receive the subsidy, the subsidy is de minimis. Treasury regulations could permit E2's early retirement subsidy under B's plan to be eliminated as [sic] to be replaced by the subsidy under A's plan, because the difference in the subsidies is de minimis. However, A's subsidy could not be entirely eliminated.

147 Cong. Rec. H2726–05 (daily ed., May 25, 2001).

In 2006, the Treasury issued final regulations to implement Congress' directive. Treas.Reg. § 1.411(d)–3. The rules are quite technical and offer plan sponsors only limited relief. Moreover, much will depend on one's view of the meaning of "de minimis."

8. *Repeat amendments.* If an employer repeatedly amends a plan to provide "one-time-only" benefits, such as an ad hoc cost-of-living adjustment or an early retirement window benefit, can it be argued that at some point such benefits become section 411(d)(6) protected benefits that are permanent parts of the plan? The Treasury takes the position that when "an employer establishes a pattern of repeated plan amendments providing for similar benefits in similar situations for substantially consecutive, limited periods of time, such benefits will be treated as provided under the terms of the plan, without regard to the limited periods of time." Treas.Reg. § 1.411(d)–4, Q & A–1(c)(1).

[margin handwriting: Repetitive — 'one-time-only' benefits can become Protected Benefits]

Because successive early retirement window benefits had become an important tool in downsizing corporate workforces, practitioners breathed a sigh of relief when the IRS ruled in Rev. Rul. 92–66, 1992–2 C.B. 92, that an employer who experienced a significant economic downturn did not violate IRC § 411(d)(6) when it offered substantially similar early retirement window benefits in four successive years. "Although no one particular fact is determinative, relevant factors include: (i) whether the amendments are made on account of a specific business event or condition; (ii) the degree to which the amendment relates to the event or condition; and (iii) whether the event or condition is temporary or discrete or whether it is a permanent aspect of the employer's business." Id. at 94. See also DeCarlo v. Rochester Carpenters Pension, Annuity, Welfare and S.U.B. Funds, 823 F.Supp. 115 (W.D.N.Y.1993), holding that the decision of multiemployer plan trustees to pay extra benefits (a "thirteenth check") in five out of six years on account of a plan surplus did not confer a permanent benefit within the meaning of IRC § 411.

9. *Reduction of future accruals; wear-away formulas.* Although a plan amendment may not reduce accrued benefits, ERISA and the IRC do permit the plan to reduce future accruals. For example, suppose a plan provides an annual benefit at normal retirement age equal to two percent of highest three-year average compensation multiplied by the participant's years of service. If employee X has 10 years of service, X's accrued benefit is equal to 20 percent of X's highest three-year average compensation. A plan amendment cannot reduce this accrued benefit. However, the plan could be amended to provide, for example, that for all future years the accrual rate would be one percent.

[margin handwriting: can reduce Future accrued benefits]

[bottom handwriting: but must give Notice (within a "reasonable time" before the effective date of amendment)]

Is it sensible that ERISA protects benefits that have already been earned, but may be payable in the future, but does not protect benefits that have not yet been earned? Might employees have expectations about their eventual pension benefits that include the effect of future years of service? Why are these expectations not protected?

In the above example, the plan was amended to reduce future accruals to one percent for each year of service. But the plan sponsor could have done something quite different. The plan could instead have been amended to provide a benefit equal to the greater of (1) one percent of compensation multiplied by all years of service (both pre-and post-amendment), or (2) the participant's accrued benefit as of the date of the amendment. Under this formula, X would initially have an accrued benefit of 20 percent of compensation, but this benefit would remain frozen for as many as ten years, depending on how quickly X's compensation increased. A formula of this sort is known as a "wear-away" formula.

Plaintiffs continue to bring lawsuits alleging that cash balance plans result in the cut-back of an already accrued benefit. E.g., Walker v. Monsanto Co. Pension Plan, 614 F.3d 415, 422 (7th Cir.2010), cert. denied, 131 S. Ct. 1678 (2011) (interest credits deposited monthly into participant's cash balance accounts are not benefit accruals where the "discounting of the opening cash balance of employees under age 55 and then crediting back that discount until the employee reaches age 55 functions like an early retirement discount").

Employees are never happy about reductions in prospective pension benefits, but wear-away formulas are particularly controversial because they can cause existing employees not to accrue new benefits for years. Note that the longer the employee has participated in the plan, the longer it takes to begin accruing additional benefits. Because long-term employees often tend to be older, wear-away formulas raise a potential issue of age discrimination, which is discussed as regards conversions to cash balance plans in Chapter 18, infra.

Since there will be years of zero accrual, followed by years of positive accrual, why doesn't a wear-away formula violate the anti-backloading rules? See Treas.Reg. § 1.411(b)–1(b)(2).

See also Tomlinson v. El Paso Corp., 653 F.3d 1281 (10th Cir. 2011) (not deferring to Treasury Department interpretation of its regulations and concluding that a plan did not illegally backload benefits where a period of zero accrual was followed by accrual in later years); Engers v. AT&T, 466 Fed. Appx. 75 (3d Cir. June 22, 2011), cert. denied, 132 S. Ct. 1101 (2012).

Several employers have recently adopted adjustable pension plans, in which employers and employees share investment risk. Such plans provide a floor benefit and an adjustable benefit tied to the pension fund's investment performance. To the extent that employers merely freeze their existing defined benefit plans and begin future accruals under an adjustable pension plan, some of the issues raised in cash balance plan conversions will be avoided.

10. *Notice of amendment to reduce future benefit accrual.* Although employers are free to reduce future benefit accruals, such reductions can

be quite upsetting to employees. Their pensions will be less then they had anticipated, often considerably less, given the inherent backloading of typical defined benefit plans. Beginning in 1984, and later expanded in 2001 largely in response to the controversy over cash balance plans, Congress imposed special notice requirements with respect to any plan amendment that works "a significant reduction in the rate of future benefit accrual." IRC § 4980F; ERISA § 204(h). A reduction in an early retirement benefit or a retirement-type subsidy is treated as a reduction in the rate of future benefit accrual.

A key feature of this so-called "Section 204(h) notice" is its timing. It must be furnished to participants within a "reasonable" time *before* the effective date of the amendment, which has been interpreted in the Regulations generally to mean a minimum of 45 days (15 days in connection with an acquisition or disposition). See Treas.Reg. § 54.4980F–1, Q & A–9. Normally ERISA does not require a notification of a plan amendment until well after the close of the plan year. See ERISA § 104(b).

Plan administrators are required to provide the notice "in a manner calculated to be understood by the average plan participant" and must provide sufficient information to allow participants to understand the effect of the amendment. ERISA § 204(h)(2). The Regulations interpret this to mean that the notice "must include sufficient information for each [individual] to determine the approximate magnitude of the expected reduction for that individual." Treas.Reg. § 54.4980F–1, Q & A–11(a)(4). Since the effect on each employee can vary dramatically and depends on a variety of assumptions including expected years of future service, expected future compensation, and interest rates, preparing these notices can be a costly and burdensome undertaking.

The notice requirement is given teeth in two ways. First, there is a $100 per day per omitted participant excise tax imposed on an employer who fails to comply with the notice requirement, subject to certain "reasonable diligence" exceptions and the possibility of waiver by the IRS in the case of a failure due to reasonable cause and not willful neglect. IRC § 4980F. Second, if the failure to comply with the notice requirement is "egregious," the participants are entitled to the greater of their preamendment benefits or their benefits under the amendment. ERISA § 204(h)(6)(A). An "egregious" failure is defined as either an intentional failure or a failure, whether or not intentional, to provide most of the individuals with most of the information they are entitled to receive. ERISA § 204(h)(6)(B); Treas.Reg. § 54.4980F–1, Q & A–14(a)(2). How does receiving such a notice benefit the plan participant?

Lawsuits alleging noncompliance with the notice requirements of § 204(h) continue to arise in connection with cash balance conversion, with mixed results for plaintiffs. Compare Charles v. Pepco Holdings, Inc., 314 Fed. Appx. 450 (3d Cir. Sept. 22, 2008) and Hurlic v. S. Cal. Gas Op. Co., 539 F.3d 1024 (9th Cir. 2008) (both finding violations); with Tomlinson v. El Paso Corp., 653 F.3d 1281 (10th Cir. 2011) (finding no violation). See also Jensen v. Solvay Chemicals, Inc., 721 F.3d 1180 (10th Cir.2013)(participants not entitled to restoration of their benefits where inadequate notice of changes effected by conversion of plan to cash balance plan did not constitute an "intentional failure").

11. *Exceptions.* ERISA § 302(c)(8) provides a partial exception from the anti-reduction rule of § 204(g) for certain troubled plans, and a separate regime for terminated multiemployer plans, § 4281.

12. *Amendment vs. Interpretation.* ERISA § 204(g) prohibits plan amendments that reduce benefits that have already accrued. What about a plan administrator's interpretation of a plan that has the effect of reducing benefits? As a general matter, courts have held that Section 204(g) "applies only to formal plan amendments [and] does not apply to interpretations of ambiguous plan language." McDaniel v. Chevron Corp., 203 F.3d 1099 (9th Cir.2000). Accord Adams v. Louisiana-Pacific Corp., 177 Fed.Appx. 335 (4th Cir.2006). However, in Hein v. Federal Deposit Insurance Corp., 88 F.3d 210 (3d Cir.1996), the Third Circuit held that "[a]n erroneous interpretation of a plan provision that results in the improper denial of benefits to a plan participant may be construed as an 'amendment' for purposes of ERISA 204(g)."

13. *Constructive Amendment of Pension Plan.* Although welfare benefit plans are not subject to ERISA § 204(g) and can be freely amended, an amendment to a welfare benefit plan that has the effect of amending a pension plan in a manner that reduces benefits that have already accrued violates ERISA. In Battoni v. IBEW Local Union No. 102 Emp. Pension Plan, 594 F.3d 230 (3d Cir. 2010), the Third Circuit addressed a situation where a pension plan had permitted participants to take retirement benefits in the form of either a lump sum or a monthly pension. Following a union merger, the newly merged welfare plan was amended to eliminate welfare plan benefits for any participant who had made an election to receive a lump-sum benefit from the pension plan. The Third Circuit rejected the plan's argument that the amendment was exempt from the anti-cutback rule, concluding that "by conditioning the receipt of welfare benefits on a retiree not exercising her right to receive a lump sum pension benefit under the Local 102 Pension Plan, [the welfare plan amendment] constituted an amendment to the Local 102 Pension Plan", Id. at 234, in that it "constructively amended the right to receive a lump sum pension benefit." Id. The welfare benefit plan thus violated ERISA because the new condition it imposed decreased the value of the lump sum pension benefit.

14. *Amendment of Social Security Offset Formula.* The formula for determining benefits in some defined benefit plans contains an offset for Social Security benefits. When a plan amends its offset calculation, is it cutting back on an accrued benefit? In Cinotto v. Delta Air Lines, Inc., 674 F.3d 1285 (11th Cir. 2012), the Eleventh Circuit held that a plan amendment that changed the Social Security offset calculation for participants age 52 and older was a separate benefit that did not accrue until a plan participant reached age 52. It thus rejected the claim that the plan amendment violated ERISA's anti-cutback rule, finding that the amendment affected only a future benefit expectation based on future service. The court found that "[w]hile the Plan arguably gave a participant a right to a certain offset formula upon reaching age 52 and becoming entitled to a retirement benefit, that right was dependent upon future service." Id. at 1296.

B. DEFINED BENEFIT PENSION PLANS IN CORPORATE TRANSACTIONS

Plan amendment issues loom large in any business merger or acquisition. An underfunded defined benefit plan may present serious funding or termination liabilities. On the other hand, an overfunded plan may be a valuable asset. ERISA's funding requirements are discussed in Chapter 6, infra. Investigating potential ERISA liabilities is an important part of the due diligence responsibilities of counsel assisting the buyer in acquiring a firm that sponsors a plan. Counsel in turn will rely upon actuarial reports from consulting actuaries and valuations prepared by investment bankers and others.

The nondiscrimination rules of pension tax law also present serious issues. As discussed in Chapter 9, infra, the acquisition or disposition of a business requires new testing to ensure compliance with the minimum coverage rules of IRC § 410(b) and the minimum participation rules of IRC § 401(a)(26), which depend on the number of employees and their compensation. Special rules in IRC §§ 410(b)(6)(C) and 401(a)(26)(E) provide for a transition period after an acquisition or disposition, but eventually a plan may need to be restructured in some fashion.

1. THE BUYER'S OPTIONS

1. *Plan continuation.* When a company acquires the assets of a selling business or acquires a subsidiary, the acquiror will typically take over the operation of the seller's pension plan. The acquiror has a number of options respecting the plan, the most obvious of which is simply to continue it.

IRC § 414(a) provides rather cryptically that "in any case in which the employer maintains a plan of a predecessor employer, service for such predecessor shall be treated as service for the employer." There is very little authority on what this provision means. Presumably, an employee who was covered under the seller's plan would have any prior service with the seller counted toward the plan's eligibility and vesting requirements.

2. *Plan termination.* If the parties to the sale of a firm do not agree for the buyer to assume the seller's plan, they may choose to terminate the plan. In that event, all accrued benefits vest at once, regardless of the otherwise applicable vesting schedule. IRC § 411(d)(3). The issues arising in plan terminations are discussed in Chapter 6, infra.

3. *Plan freezes.* A plan can simply be "frozen," meaning that participants do not accrue further benefits under the plan, and no new participants are allowed. If the buyer has a plan, the participants under the old plan will usually accrue future benefits under the buyer's plan. Notice of a freeze must be given to participants at least 15 days prior to its effective date. Treas.Reg. § 54.4980F–1, Q & A–9(d)(1).

Note that a frozen plan is not a terminated plan. The buyer must continue to ensure that the plan remains qualified, and to make any further minimum funding contributions that may be needed. The IRC nondiscrimination rules (see Chapter 9, infra) continue to apply, requiring careful attention to the plan's demographics to avoid impermissibly favoring highly compensated employees. Changes in the law may necessitate amendments to a frozen plan to avoid disqualification.

4. *Plan mergers.* Frequently in a corporate acquisition, the acquiring firm wishes to consolidate the acquired firm's pension plan into the acquiror's plan, in order to simplify administration and to unify benefit schedules for both sets of employees. When integrating plan benefit formulas, care must be taken to obey the anti-reduction rules of ERISA § 204(g) and IRC § 411(d)(6), which require that the merged plan protect the benefits that the participants in the acquired firm's plan have accrued, including early retirement subsidies and optional forms of benefit.

Care must also be taken to avoid violating the nondiscrimination rules under IRC § 401(a)(4), discussed in Chapter 9, infra. In order to avoid the need for complex and costly testing, and a possible failure under the general nondiscrimination test, it is important to preserve the plan's "safe-harbor" status as a plan with a uniform benefit formula. Under Treas.Reg. § 1.401(a)(4)–3(b)(6)(vii) and IRS Notice 92–31, 1992–2 C.B. 359, a plan can make a "fresh start" with regard to the employees affected by the merger, i.e., apply a benefit formula and accrual rate after a fresh-start date that differs from the one used before the fresh-start date, without jeopardizing the plan's safe harbor status.

The regulations provide the buyer with three permissible fresh-start formula options. See Treas.Reg. § 1.401(a)(4)–13(c)(4). First, there is the fresh-start formula "without wear-away." This provides the employee with a benefit equal to the sum of (A) the employee's transferred frozen accrued benefit under the seller's plan, plus (B) the benefit accrued under the buyer's plan for years of service after the fresh-start date. Second, there is the fresh-start formula "with wear-away." This provides a benefit equal to the greater of (A) the employee's transferred frozen accrued benefit under the seller's plan, or (B) the benefit accrued under the buyer's plan for all years of service including the prior service with the seller. Third, there is the fresh-start formula "with extended wear-away." This provides a benefit equal to the greater of (A) the fresh-start formula without wear-away, or (B) the benefit accrued under the buyer's plan for all years of service including the prior service with the seller.

2.   THE HOLD-HARMLESS STANDARD FOR MERGERS AND SPIN-OFFS

When two plans are merged, the assets and liabilities (benefits owed to the participants) are combined, and the assets in the merged plan are available to pay the benefits of all the participants. A "spin-off," by contrast, occurs when assets and liabilities are separated from one plan and transferred to another. In that case, the assets of each plan are available to pay the benefits only of the participants covered under that plan. ERISA § 208 and IRC § 414(*l*) require that in any merger or spin-off, each participant must be entitled to a benefit such that if the plan were to terminate immediately after the merger or spin-off, the participant's benefit would be equal to or greater than the benefit to which the participant would have been entitled if the plan had terminated immediately before the merger or spin-off. These provisions do not apply to multiemployer plans (which have their own merger and spin-off rules under ERISA §§ 4231–4235), governmental plans, church plans and certain other plans.

1.   *Mergers.* The purpose of ERISA § 208 and IRC § 414(*l*) is to see to it that the participants in one plan not have their accrued benefits placed in jeopardy by a merger with another, underfunded plan. See also Treas.Reg. § 1.414(*l*)–1 (specifying procedures for allocating assets when a plan is terminated within 5 years of a merger).

If an underfunded plan is merged with an overfunded plan, and the resulting combined plan is overfunded, then ERISA § 208 and IRC § 414(*l*) are automatically satisfied, "because all the accrued benefits of the plan as merged are provided on a termination basis by the plan as merged." Treas.Reg. § 1.414(*l*)–1(e)(1). The effect of such a merger is to allow the employer to use the surplus in one plan to eliminate a deficit in another. As is discussed in Chapter 6, infra, the nondeductible 50 percent excise tax under IRC § 4980 makes it uneconomic for an employer to terminate a plan and recover the surplus. A plan merger is one of the few ways for a plan sponsor to make economic use of a plan surplus. Moreover, by wiping out a plan deficit, the employer may reduce a minimum funding obligation and save on that portion of the PBGC premium that is based on the amount of underfunding.

2.   *Spin-offs.* Suppose Employer X has two divisions, A and B. X maintains a single pension plan covering the employees of both divisions. If X negotiates a sale of division B to Y, there are basically two options with respect to the plan. First, X and Y can leave the plan out of the sale entirely. The employees of division B will be covered by whatever plan Y provides, and they will simply cease accruing benefits under X's plan, just as would any employee who ceases working for X. Second, X can spin off the assets and liabilities of the plan relating to the employees of division B and transfer them to a new plan or to an existing plan of Y's. The spin-off option is the more common one.

A spin-off raises essentially the same issues as a merger under ERISA § 208 and IRC § 414(*l*). Neither the division B employees nor the division A employees are to be worse off after the spin-off. Under Treas.Reg. § 1.414(*l*)–1(n), IRC § 414(*l*) is satisfied if "the value of the assets allocated to each of the spun-off plans is not less than the sum of the present value of the benefits on a termination basis in the plan before the spin-off for all participants in that spun-off plan."

The computation of a participant's benefits on a termination basis can be quite complex. The IRS has ruled that the benefits must include protected benefits under IRC § 411(d)(6), such as early retirement benefits, retirement type subsidies, and optional forms of benefits, as well as qualified preretirement survivor annuity benefits, "without regard to whether the participant has satisfied all of the conditions for such benefits as of the spin-off." Rev. Rul. 86–48, 1986–1 C.B. 216. The regulations also require "reasonable actuarial assumptions"; the assumptions used by the PBGC are deemed reasonable. Treas.Reg. § 1.414(*l*)–1(b)(5). The reasonableness standard leaves room for some manipulation. Under one set of assumptions the benefits in the spun-off plan might be worth $100 million, but under another just $80 million.

Thus, ascertaining the value of the benefits can be a crucial part of a corporate transaction.

3. *Allocation of the surplus.* In the case of an overfunded plan that is spinning off part of its assets and liabilities, how is the surplus to be allocated? IRC § 414(*l*)(2), added in 1988, provided the first guidance on this issue. IRC § 414(*l*)(2) is a very limited provision. It applies to a plan involved in a spin-off only if the employer maintaining the plan is a member of the same controlled group as the employer maintaining the original plan, and if the plan is not terminated pursuant to the transaction involving the spin-off. If a plan is covered by IRC § 414(*l*)(2), it must receive a proportionate share of the surplus. Without the impediment of IRC § 414(*l*)(2), the sponsor of an overfunded plan could split the plan in two, allocate the surplus to one, and thus enable itself to make larger deductible contributions to the other.

IRC § 414(*l*)(2) does not provide the rule for dividing up the surplus when the spin-off is in connection with a sale to an employer outside the controlled group. Although participants have brought suits alleging that ERISA § 404 requires a proportional division of surplus assets when a plan is spun off, the courts have generally rejected this theory. See Bigger v. American Commercial Lines, 862 F.2d 1341 (8th Cir.1988); Foster Medical Corp. Employees' Pension Plan v. Healthco, Inc., 753 F.2d 194 (1st Cir.1985). The judicial view is that the extent of the participants' rights is governed by ERISA § 208 and that the allocation of any surplus assets is an employer prerogative.

4. *Selling the surplus.* ERISA provides that plan assets shall "never inure to the benefit of any employer and shall be held for the exclusive purpose of providing benefits to the participants in the plan"; ERISA also prohibits various forms of self-dealing between plans and employers. See ERISA §§ 403(c)(1), 404(a)(1)(A), 406(a)–(b). See Chapter 13, infra. Suppose a seller transfers its entire business operation including an overfunded pension plan. An overfunded plan is presumably worth more than one that is not. Does ERISA permit the seller to receive a premium for the value of the overfunding, or is this a form of prohibited self-dealing with the assets of the plan?

One case, In re Gulf Pension Litigation, 764 F.Supp. 1149 (S.D.Tex.1991), aff'd, 36 F.3d 1308 (5th Cir.1994), suggests that such a transaction would violate ERISA. Most courts have found oppositely, that ERISA permits the receipt of such a premium. See, e.g., United Steelworkers, Local 2116 v. Cyclops Corp., 860 F.2d 189, 203 (6th Cir.1988) (adjustment to the purchase price of a facility to reflect the buyer's assumption of pension liabilities and assets is not a violation of ERISA § 406). In Flanigan v. General Electric Co., 242 F.3d 78, 88 (2d Cir.2001), the court noted that the transaction in question did not "result in an unlawful inurement to GE, [the seller]. Although GE might have received some benefit, such as a higher sale price, because it was able to transfer some of the surplus to [the buyer, ERISA § 403] focuses exclusively on whether fund assets were used to pay pension benefits to plan participants. In this case, all of the pension surplus that GE transferred [was] used to fund pension benefits. Any benefit received by GE was, at most, indirect."

CHAPTER 6

FUNDING AND TERMINATING DEFINED BENEFIT PLANS

Analysis

Introduction

A defined benefit (DB) pension plan commonly promises to pay pension benefits decades after the participant begins accruing credits. Such a plan envisages that the sponsor will conduct a program of contributing and investing funds across those decades in order to fund the ultimate payments. The danger of *default risk*, that is, that the plan will not have enough assets to be able to honor its pension promises, inheres in the structure of a DB plan.

ERISA and the IRC respond to the danger of default risk in three ways. First, the *funding rules*, discussed in Section A of this chapter, have as their ostensible purpose requiring the plan sponsor to make contributions to the fund that, when appropriately invested, will produce returns sufficient to pay the promised benefits. Second, ERISA's *rules of fiduciary investing*, discussed in Chapters 12–14, are meant to protect plan assets against misappropriation or mismanagement. Third, ERISA's Title 4 institutes a system of *plan termination insurance* under which an agency of the federal government—the Pension Benefit Guaranty Corporation (PBGC)—will pay most DB promises if the plan defaults. Section B of this chapter examines the PBGC termination insurance program.

We saw in Chapter 3, treating the origins of ERISA, that much of the political movement that led to the enactment of ERISA traces to the termination and resulting default on promised benefits under the Studebaker plan in 1963. At that time, a defined benefit plan could be (and typically was) designed to leave upon the plan participants and beneficiaries the risk of insufficiency. We will see in this chapter that ERISA largely transfers that risk to the employer and, secondarily, to the PBGC.

The issues that arise when a DB plan is terminated differ radically, depending on whether the plan is or is not adequately funded. If the plan is underfunded, the question is who bears the loss. If the plan is overfunded, the question is how to allocate the surplus. Section C of this chapter raises the question of who is entitled to the surplus when a well funded plan terminates with assets in excess of liabilities. This so-called "asset reversion" issue was the subject of litigation and intense political controversy in the 1980s, but has now been largely resolved by legislation. Procedurally, terminating either sort of DB plan— sufficiently or insufficiently funded—requires compliance with Title 4's rules for filing with the PBGC and for giving notice to affected persons. ERISA § 4041.

Defined contribution (DC) plans do not figure in this chapter. Because DC plans define the contribution to be made each year by the employer, there is no need for the type of funding requirements imposed on DB plans. ERISA § 4021(b)(1) explicitly excludes DC plans from coverage under the plan insurance system of Title 4. Title 4 insures pension benefit promises, and by definition a defined contribution plan makes no benefit promise, other than to pay the account balance. There is no promised benefit amount to insure. Likewise, asset reversion is a phenomenon of defined benefit plans; the surplus in question is whatever is left when the plan has distributed accrued benefits. In a defined contribution plan, the participant or beneficiary is entitled to the entire balance in that individual account, hence no surplus can arise.

A. MINIMUM FUNDING

Prior to ERISA, retirement plans generally were not required to be funded. Out of concern that underfunded plans were more likely to default and thus to deprive employees of expected benefits, ERISA established a complex minimum funding requirement for pension plans, now found both in ERISA §§ 301–306 and in IRC § 412.

1. FUNDING POLICY

Before the enactment of ERISA in 1974, the only pension funding requirement was found in a Treasury regulation, which permitted the IRS to treat a plan as having terminated unless the plan funded the cost of the benefits accruing during the current year and any interest on unfunded costs. Treas.Reg. § 1.401–6(a)(2) (1963). The level of contributions was largely within the sponsor's discretion, subject to limits on the maximum amount of deductible contributions, hence limits on overfunding, designed to protect against tax manipulation. ERISA's minimum funding rules (ERISA §§ 301–306, IRC § 412) now require that money be set aside to pay for the benefits that are promised under defined benefit plans. The funding rules encourage orderly saving and protect against underfunding.

It is important to bear in mind the relationship between the funding rules and the plan termination insurance system of ERISA Title 4. Before ERISA, the risk of plan default incided entirely upon the plan participants, as exemplified in the Studebaker incident. The termination insurance system transfers most of that risk to the employer and the PBGC. Since underfunding today often arises in situations that result in employer insolvency, the PBGC absorbs the main expense when a plan terminates with insufficient funds. However, some plan participants continue to bear a portion of the default risk, because plan termination insurance is limited to protecting a statutory maximum annual benefit, inflation adjusted to $60,136 for 2015. Concerns about the solvency of the PBGC following a number of significant plan terminations led Congress to tighten the funding requirements in 1987 and again in 1994. These changes helped the PBGC generate a surplus for a while, but severe plan underfunding in a number of industries, particularly in the steel, auto, and airline industries, has created a huge deficit and threatens to undermine the PBGC's long-term solvency. As a result, Congress acted again to amend the funding rules in 2006. The economic crisis caused Congress to provide some relief from the provisions of the 2006 Act via statutes enacted between 2008 and 2014: see section A.3 below. . The fiscal plight of the PBGC and the plan termination insurance program are discussed later in this chapter. We begin by examining the plan funding requirements.

The funding standards of ERISA and the IRC are identical, but they are applied differently. IRC § 412 applies only to plans that are (or were) qualified plans. Accordingly, the IRC § 4971 excise tax on underfunding applies only to plans subject to IRC § 412. ERISA, on the other hand, applies to plans whether or not they are qualified, although a properly designed nonqualified plan is excepted. Many types of plans are not subject to either provision. These include profit-sharing and stock bonus plans, certain fully insured plans, governmental and church plans, and plans providing only for employee contributions. For convenience, citations to the minimum funding requirements in this chapter will generally be made only to IRC § 412, since under the ERISA Reorganization Plan the Treasury has responsibility for issuing minimum funding regulations and rulings.

2. ACTUARIAL ASSUMPTIONS

A defined benefit plan envisions pension promises that may extend across four or five decades. The pension promise is expressed as a formula rather than an amount. An employee may begin to accrue benefits thirty or more years before benefit payments begin, which can be fifty or sixty years before the final benefit check is written. The plan sponsor's challenge is to devise a savings program appropriate to liabilities that are so distant and contingent.

The people who calculate the funding needs are actuaries. Large national actuarial and pension consulting firms purvey actuarial services, and there are also local practitioners. The major provision of ERISA's skimpy Title 3 is the requirement of what amounts to licensing of pension actuaries through a body that ERISA created, the Joint Board for the Enrollment of Actuaries. ERISA § 3041. For details see 20 CFR § 901.0 et seq. Only ERISA-enrolled actuaries can sign the funding reports required pursuant to ERISA's reporting and disclosure rules. See, e.g., ERISA § 103(a)(4)(A). ERISA's federal standard-setting for actuaries in the 1970s echoes the movement toward rudimentary federal regulation of accounting standards under the Securities Acts in the 1930s.

Actuaries undertake to estimate plan liabilities and to value plan assets, discounting to present values in order to reckon current and future funding needs. In making these projections for a defined benefit plan, the actuary works with an array of variables, many requiring assumptions about future facts. Among the factors that must be projected into the future are the interest rate; work force experience (terminations, deaths, disabilities, forfeitures, salary progression, length of service, age of retirement); and investment experience (because the more the fund earns the less the employer has to contribute). Because human foresight is in short supply, actuarial projections must be revised from time to time to adjust for experience.

Actuaries are not completely free to choose the assumptions that underlie their calculations. Both ERISA and the IRC require the use of actuarial assumptions "each of which is reasonable (taking into account the experience of the plan and reasonable expectations)" and "which, in combination, offer the actuary's best estimate of anticipated experience under the plan." IRC § 430(h)(1); ERISA § 303(h)(1).

The courts have interpreted the "best estimate" requirement (previously contained in IRC § 412(c)(3)) in a fashion that gives actuaries tremendous leeway in selecting assumptions. For example, in Citrus Valley Estates, Inc. v. Commissioner, 49 F.3d 1410 (9th Cir.1995), the court stated:

> Congress consciously left the specifics of [plan] funding in the able hands of professional actuaries. Although Congress initially toyed with the idea of legislating mandatory funding assumptions and methods for [plans], it quickly rejected the notion as excessively inflexible, even though it understood that giving actuaries room in which to exercise their professional judgment would result in a broad range of funding assumptions. We will not disturb this legislative choice to delegate to actuaries an important role in plan funding decisions. . . .

> [The] "best estimate" provision of [IRC §] 412(c)(3), properly construed, is essentially procedural in nature. The "best estimate" language is "principally designed to insure that the chosen assumptions actually represent the actuary's own judgment rather than the dictates of plan administrators or sponsors." . . .

> Despite what the Commissioner asserts, our decision, faithful to the statutory scheme, does not give actuaries "unfettered liberty" to produce desirable tax results rather than prudent plan funding. First and foremost, plan funding decisions and methods must be [reasonable]. In addition, they

must represent the actuary's professional judgment, not the tax-motivated wishes of plan sponsors or administrators. Finally, plan actuaries must live up to national professional, ethical, and technical standards which help to minimize the risk of untoward advice.

49 F.3d at 1414–15.

The most important factor among the many that actuaries must consider is the interest rate.

> The present value of a series of future contingent payments is a function of the rate of investment return, or of interest at which the payments are discounted—the higher the interest assumption, the smaller the present value. Pension plan costs and liabilities are extremely sensitive to the interest assumption in the valuation formula because of the long time-lapse between the accrual of a benefit credit and its payment. [It] is a fairly sound generalization that, for a typical plan, a change (upward or downward) of 1 percent in the interest assumption (e.g., an increase from 6 to 7 percent) alters the long-run cost estimate by about 25 percent. This relationship seems to hold within any reasonable range of interest assumptions.

Dan M. McGill, Kyle N. Brown, John J. Haley, & Sylvester J. Scheiber, Fundamentals of Private Pensions 611–12 (8th ed. 2005). Because the choice of the interest rate can have such a dramatic effect on plan funding, plan sponsors have tested the limits of the term "reasonable" in both directions: Plan sponsors seeking to keep their current contributions as low as possible have assumed high interest rates, while plan sponsors seeking the tax benefit of large upfront deductions have assumed low interest rates. As discussed below, concern about such manipulation has led Congress to constrain the choice of the interest rate in certain situations. Note that the actuarial assumptions for plan funding purposes must be the same as those used to determine the maximum federal income tax deduction. See IRC § 404(o)(6).

3.   FUNDING REQUIREMENTS

1.   *Background to the Pension Protection Act of 2006 minimum funding amendments.* Problems with ERISA's minimum funding system first began to surface in the 1980's. A number of large plans became seriously underfunded, in many cases because ERISA allowed the cost of past service credits to be funded over 30 years. Employers were raising the pension benefits of current employees, thereby creating huge liabilities. A few years later the employer would fail, leaving the plan woefully underfunded. This scenario should hardly have come as a surprise, since the Studebaker plan, whose failure is widely regarded as a major impetus for ERISA, had itself been funding past service on a 30-year basis and would have been in compliance with ERISA's minimum funding rules had they applied. See Chapter 3, supra. Due to concerns about the solvency of the defined benefit pension plan insurance system, the Pension Protection Act of 1987 imposed additional funding requirements on underfunded single employer plans with more than 100

participants. These rules were further tightened in the Retirement Protection Act (RPA) of 1994.

Despite these reform efforts, weaknesses in the funding rules remained. It was still possible for there to be a significant time lag between the development of a funding deficiency and the contributions needed to cover it. If each year plan assets keep declining while at the same time liabilities keep rising due to interest rate declines, the unfunded liability can rapidly outpace the required contributions. In fact, according to a GAO study of the 100 largest defined benefit plans, just such a "perfect storm" occurred beginning in 2000:

> As a group, funding levels among the 100 largest plans were reasonably stable and strong from 1996 to 2000. Except for 1999, in no year did more than 39 plans have liabilities exceeding assets, and no more than 9 plans each year were below 90 percent funded. In 2001 there were signs of increased underfunding, and by 2002, more than half of the largest plans were less than 100 percent funded, with 23 plans less than 90 percent funded. Two factors in the deterioration of many plans' finances were the decline in stock prices and in interest rates. From 2000 to 2002, the Standard & Poor's (S & P) 500 stock index declined sharply each year. Given that DB plans on average held approximately half of their assets in stocks from 1995 to 2000, the decline in stock prices meant a sharp decline in the value of many plans' pension assets. In addition, over the sample period, 30-year Treasury bond rates, which served as the benchmark for the rate used by plans to calculate pension liabilities, generally fell steadily, raising liabilities. The combination of lower asset values and higher pension liabilities had a serious adverse effect on overall defined benefit funding levels.

GAO, Private Pensions: Recent Experiences of Large Defined Benefit Plans Illustrate Weaknesses in Funding Rules 13–14 (GAO–05–294) (2005). According to another GAO report, Bethlehem Steel's plan went from 97 percent funded in 1999 to 45 percent in December 2002. GAO, Pension Benefit Guaranty Corporation: Long-Term Financing Risks to Single Employer Insurance Program Highlight Need for Comprehensive Reform 16–17 (GAO–04–150T) (2003).

Generous plan terms can worsen a troubled plan's situation. A classic example is a plan that provides enhanced retirement benefits, such as lump sum distributions or highly subsidized early retirement benefits, in the event of a plant shutdown. A plant shutdown triggers increased mandatory contributions at a time when the employer can least afford it and may well be headed for, or even in the process of, bankruptcy. Worse, the employer generally cannot fund the shutdown benefits until the event occurs.

2. *Minimum required contribution.* The Pension Protection Act of 2006 (PPA) established a new set of funding rules that generally require a plan sponsor to fund 100 percent of the plan's liability (up from 90 percent under prior law). Because the Act significantly increased the minimum contribution for many employers, Congress decided to make the new rules effective in 2008 and provided a four-year phase-in of the

100 percent funding target. However, new plans and severely underfunded plans are not eligible for the four-year phase-in. See IRC § 430(c)(5)(B)(iii).

Under IRC § 412(a)(2)(A), an employer sponsoring a single-employer plan must contribute at least the "minimum required contribution" determined under IRC § 430. The first step in computing the minimum required contribution is to determine two "targets": the "funding target" of the plan and the "target normal cost" of the plan. The funding target is "the present value of all benefits accrued or earned under the plan as of the beginning of the plan year." IRC § 430(d)(1). The target normal cost is basically the present value of all benefits which are expected to accrue or be earned under the plan during the plan year. IRC § 430(b). It is increased by the amount of plan-related expenses expected to be paid from plan assets and reduced by the amount of any mandatory employee contributions expected to be made during the plan year. If any benefit attributable to services performed in a preceding plan year is increased by reason of an increase in compensation during the current plan year, the present value of such increase is included in the target normal cost. Id.

For example, assume a plan provides a benefit of 2 percent of final average compensation for each year of service, payable at age 65. At the beginning of the plan year employee X is age 40 and has 10 years of service and an average compensation of $40,000. The funding target attributable to employee X is the present value of an annuity of $8,000 (i.e., 20 percent of $40,000) commencing in 25 years. Now suppose we expect employee X to accrue another year of service during the current year and that his average compensation at the end of the year will be $42,000. The target normal cost attributable to employee X is the present value of an annuity of $840 (i.e., 2 percent of $42,000) commencing in 25 years plus the present value of an annuity of $400 (i.e., 20 percent of $2,000) commencing in 25 years.

The next step is to compare the funding target with the value of plan assets. If the funding target exceeds the value of plan assets, there is a "funding shortfall" equal to such excess. IRC § 430(c)(4). If there is a funding shortfall, the minimum required contribution is equal to the plan's target normal cost plus the "shortfall amortization charge" for the current year. IRC § 430(a)(1). The shortfall amortization charge for a plan year is the "aggregate total (not less than zero) of the shortfall amortization installments for such plan year with respect to the shortfall amortization bases for such plan year and each of the 6 preceding plan years." IRC § 430(c)(1). The "shortfall annual installments" are the amounts necessary to amortize the "shortfall amortization base" for any plan year in level annual installments over a seven-year period. IRC § 430(c)(2).

The technical terms seem to be spiraling out of control, so before proceeding any further let us consider a simple example. Assume that on the first day of plan Year One the plan's funding target is $10,000,000 and the value of the plan assets is $9,000,000. There is a funding shortfall of $1,000,000. Assume further that this is the first year the plan had a funding shortfall. The plan has a shortfall amortization base of $1,000,000 for Year One. This must be amortized over a seven-year period using statutory "segment" interest rates, which are discussed below. Think of the installments as the payments on a seven-year mortgage with a principal amount of $1,000,000. Assume that this results in a level annual installment of $180,000. The minimum required contribution for Year One is $180,000 plus the target normal cost.

Now assume that on the first day of plan Year Two there is still a funding shortfall, but it has grown to $1,200,000 mainly due to a decline in the value of plan assets. The shortfall amortization base for Year Two is this funding shortfall minus the present value of shortfall amortization installments remaining to be paid from preceding years. In our example this would be the present value of the six remaining $180,000 installments. If we assume that this present value would be $885,000, the shortfall amortization base for Year Two would be $315,000 (i.e., $1,200,000 minus $885,000). Amortizing this amount over a seven-year period yields, let us assume, an annual installment of $56,000. The minimum required contribution for Year Two is then $56,000 plus the $180,000 installment attributable to Year One plus the target normal cost for Year Two.

Each year a similar computation is made. Note that it is possible for the shortfall amortization base for a given year to be negative, which has the effect of reducing future minimum required contributions. For example, suppose in Year Three the value of the plan assets increases dramatically so that the funding shortfall is just $300,000. Assuming the total present value of the five remaining $180,000 and six remaining $56,000 shortfall amortization installments is $1,030,000, the shortfall amortization base for Year Three would then be negative $730,000 (i.e., $300,000 minus $1,030,000). This too must be amortized over seven years, yielding, let us assume, an annual shortfall amortization installment of negative $130,000. The minimum required contribution for Year Three would then be $106,000 (i.e., $56,000 plus $180,000 minus $130,000) plus the target normal cost.

Although a given shortfall amortization installment can be negative, the shortfall amortization charge, which is the total of all the installments (both positive and negative) due for the year, cannot be negative. This is due to the "not less than zero" language in IRC § 430(c)(1). This means that in any year in which there is a funding shortfall the plan sponsor must always contribute at least the target normal cost.

If in any year there is no funding shortfall (i.e., the plan's assets exceed its funding target) the computation changes radically. The shortfall amortization bases for that year and all preceding years, as well as all shortfall amortization installments attributable to such years, are reduced to zero, not only for the current year but all future years as well. IRC §§ 430(c)(5)(A) & (6). The minimum required contribution for such a year is simply the target normal cost, reduced by the excess of the plan's assets over the funding target. IRC § 430(a)(2). Thus, in the example above, if in Year Four the funding target is $10,200,000 and the value of the plan assets is $10,300,000, the minimum required contribution is the target normal cost minus the $100,000 excess. The logic here is that the target is 100 percent funding and employers should not be forced to contribute anything more. Why not require a "cushion" in excess of full funding? We shall see in Chapter 10, infra, that plan sponsors are permitted to create or maintain a limited cushion.

Note that under prior law there were special rules to take account of changes in actuarial assumptions as well as discrepancies between what the actuaries predicted would happen and what actually did happen. The new rules dispense with all that. A change in actuarial assumptions will simply change the funding target. If assets earn only 2 percent, instead of the projected 6 percent, the value of the plan's assets will simply be lower. Basically all we need to know is the present value of the future promises and compare that with what is in the plan. If the assets are insufficient, the plan has seven years to make up the current year's deficiency. Also under prior law, actuaries had discretion to select among a number of actuarial cost methods, i.e., methods that would determine what costs were properly allocable to the current year. The new system takes away that discretion.

Why did Congress choose seven years instead of a shorter time period? Why not require immediate funding of deficits, so that liabilities and assets are never out of balance? In particular, if the mismatch occurs due to an increase in benefits, why not require that increase be immediately funded? One justification for a substantial amortization period is that it reduces volatility in plan funding:

> Amortization rules require the sponsor to smooth certain events that affect plan finances over several years, and accumulated credit balances act as a buffer against swings in future funding requirements. These features often allow sponsors to better regulate their annual level of contributions. In contrast, contributions and funding levels might fluctuate greatly from year to year if funding were based strictly on yearly differences between the market value of plan assets and current liabilities. Thus, a contribution system with an [amortization] feature may make funding requirements less volatile and contributions more predictable than one in which funding was based entirely on current assets and liabilities. Similarly, current-law measurement and funding rules provide a plan with some ability to dampen volatility in required funding caused by economic events that may sharply change a plan's liabilities or assets. Pension experts told us that this predictability and flexibility make DB sponsorship more attractive to employers.

GAO, Recent Experiences, supra, at 21.

Responding to the severity of the economic crisis and its impact on plan sponsors' ability to meet their funding requirements, in December 2008, Congress enacted the Worker, Retiree, and Employer Recovery Act of 2008 (Recovery Act). The Recovery Act provide temporary relief for plans that fall below their funding target. Under the PPA, the effect of a plan's failing to meet its funding target would be to cause the plan to lose the benefit of the PPA's transition rule and become subject to 100% funding for the following year. The Recovery Act allows plans that fall below their funding target for a year to fund up to the specified funding percentage required for each transition year.

Further relief is provided by the Moving Ahead for Progress in the 21st Century Act of 2012 (MAP-21) and the Highway and Transportation Funding Act of 2014 (HATFA). These statutes temporarily reduce minimum required contributions to DB plans. HATFA also made related changes to the annual funding notice and the restrictions on certain benefits for underfunded plans. The statutes reduce the effect of short-term changes in interest rates.

3.   *Valuing assets and liabilities.* The values of a plan's assets and liabilities play a crucial role in determining a plan's minimum required contribution. The value of plan assets may simply be the fair market value of such assets, but plans have the option of averaging fair market values over any period up to 24 months. IRC § 430(g)(3)(B). However, the average value is not permitted to vary from the actual fair market value by more than 10 percent. This "smoothing" of asset values serves to reduce volatility of contributions, but may delay somewhat a needed response to a developing funding problem. Under the prior law the risk from such delay was far greater, since the smoothing period was four years instead of two, and the maximum deviation from actual fair market value was 20 percent, not 10 percent. MAP-21 and HATFA have relaxed the interest rates that may be used under this smoothing process.

Assets are fairly easy to value, but liabilities require the use of numerous actuarial assumptions. As noted above, each of these assumptions must be reasonable. The choice of the appropriate interest rate has been a frequent source of controversy. Recall that a 1 percent decline in the interest rate can increase the present value of plan liabilities by 25 percent. For a number of years Congress required plans in some cases to use a weighted average of long-term Treasury bonds, but employers favored a significantly higher rate based on long-term corporate bonds. Employers argued that the corporate bond rate was more realistic, because it reflected the rate of return on a type of prudent plan investment. Do you agree with the employer argument? If the purpose of the minimum contribution requirement is to provide some measure of security to participants (and the PBGC) in the face of potential asset declines, why isn't a risk-free rate of return appropriate? On the other hand if concerns about security would have plans use a risk-free rate of return to value liabilities, why do we not otherwise require plans to invest solely in risk-free investments?

The Pension Protection Act of 2006 requires the use of a three-segment yield curve to determine a plan's funding target and target normal cost. IRC § 430(h)(2). Different interest rates apply depending on when the future benefit is payable. The first segment rate applies to benefits payable during the first 5 years, the second to benefits payable during the next 15 years, the third to benefits payable thereafter. The rate for each segment is determined monthly by the Treasury based on a 24-month average of the yield on investment-grade corporate bonds maturing during the segment period. Rather than using the three segment rates, a plan sponsor may make a one-time election to use the full corporate bond yield curve, without 24-month averaging. IRC § 430(h)(2)(D)(ii). For example, if a liability were expected to be payable in 23 years, the interest rate used to compute the present value of that liability would be the current corporate bond rate on bonds maturing in 23 years.

In addition to specifying an interest rate, the PPA directs the Treasury to prescribe mortality tables to be used in making any computation under the minimum contribution rules. IRC § 430(h)(3). Large employers can request approval from the Treasury to use a plan-specific mortality table, provided certain requirements are met.

On October 15, 2009, the IRS and Treasury issued final regulations reflecting various provisions added by the PPA and the Recovery Act. 74 F.R.53004. The regulations provide guidance regarding the determination of the value of plan assets and benefits liabilities for purposes of the funding requirements, as well as rules regarding benefit restrictions for certain underfunded ("at-risk") plans. The regulations are generally effective for the 2010 plan year, but employers may use them for 2008 and 2009. The regulations are highly technical, and an explanation of their detailed provisions is beyond the scope of this book. For a summary see, e.g., IRS Issues Final Regs on Benefit Restrictions for Underfunded Plans, Measurement of Plan Assets and Liabilities, CCH® Pension, Oct. 20, 2009, http://hr.cch.com/news/pension/102 209a.asp.

4. *At-risk plans.* Certain severely underfunded plans are deemed to be "at-risk" and must make higher minimum required contributions than the rules described above would normally require. IRC § 430(i). The increase can arise in two ways. First, at-risk plans must use more conservative actuarial assumptions in computing the funding target and target normal cost. Participants eligible to retire within 10 years are assumed to retire at the earliest possible date (but not before the end of the current plan year) and to elect the form of benefit with the highest present value. Second, a plan that has also been in at-risk status for at least 2 of the preceding 4 years must (1) increase its funding target by a "loading factor" of $700 per participant plus 4 percent of the standard funding target and (2) increase its target normal cost by a loading factor of 4 percent of the standard target normal cost.

A plan is considered "at-risk" if the value of plan assets is (1) less than 80 percent of the funding target (without the at-risk actuarial adjustments) *and* (2) less than 70 percent of the funding target (with the at-risk actuarial assumptions). IRC § 430(i)(4). The added plan funding required by the at-risk rules phases in at 20 percent per year for each consecutive year beginning after 2007 that the plan is at-risk. Thus, only plans that have been at-risk for five or more consecutive years will be subject to the full at-risk funding requirements. Plans with 500 or fewer participants during the preceding plan year are exempt from the at-risk rules. IRC § 430(i)(6). Why would Congress exempt small plans?

5. *Credit balances.* The minimum funding standard requires a minimum level of funding as a protection against default, but suppose a plan sponsor wishes to contribute more. In Chapter 10, infra, we explore both the tax advantages of accelerating contributions and the limitations on the amount of such contributions. For now let us assume that a plan sponsor is able to contribute an amount in excess of the minimum required contribution. The question is what effect such

"overcontributing" in one year should have on the minimum required contributions in future years.

One possible approach would be to accord such contributions no special treatment. Putting more money in one year has the effect of increasing plan assets, which automatically serves to reduce future contributions under the current minimum funding scheme outlined above. But prior law was much more generous to such contributions. Simplifying somewhat, a plan sponsor who put an extra dollar into a plan was permitted to add the dollar to a "credit balance," which could be used to satisfy a dollar of required funding in any future year. If the credit balance were not so used in a given year it was credited with interest at a presumed interest rate. One problem with this approach is that in a declining market, allowing the use of the credit balance can mask the need for additional funding. For example, an extra dollar contributed in Year One and used to purchase plan assets that are worth only 50 cents in Year Two could nevertheless be used to satisfy a full dollar of minimum funding in Year Two.

Although many reformers sought to eliminate any special treatment for credit balances, the PPA reflects a compromise. A plan sponsor may elect to maintain a "prefunding balance" to reflect the amount of contributions in excess of the minimum required contribution. IRC § 430(f). This balance is credited with interest each year at a rate determined by the actual rate of return on plan investments during the year. Each year a plan sponsor can elect to use all or part of the prefunding balance toward the minimum required contribution for the year, provided the value of plan assets is at least 80 percent of the plan's funding target. IRC § 430(f)(3).

The compromise the PPA struck is that the election to maintain a prefunding balance comes with a potentially significant cost. The amount of the prefunding balance must be subtracted from the value of plan assets for purposes of determining: (1) the plan's funding shortfall; (2) whether the plan is at-risk; and (3) whether certain benefit restrictions (discussed below) apply. IRC § 430(f)(4)(B)(i). Recognizing that because of these rules a credit balance may actually work to the disadvantage of a plan sponsor, the PPA permits a plan sponsor to elect to make a permanent reduction in the prefunding balance. IRC § 430(f)(5). Initial reports from practitioners indicated that such elections to "burn" all or a portion of the sponsor's credit balance were quite common.

There is also a transitional rule for plans that had existing credit balances in 2007 under the old rules. Such "funding standard carryover balances" are treated much the same as prefunding balances.

6. *Restrictions on underfunded plans.* As a plan's underfunding worsens, the PPA not only imposes increases in minimum required contributions, but also places significant restrictions on benefit increases and accelerated benefit payments that would make the underfunding even worse. These limitations depend on a plan's "adjusted funding target attainment percentage," which is basically the ratio (expressed as a percentage) of the value of the plan assets (reduced by any credit balances) to the funding target of the plan. See IRC §§ 430(d)(2) & 436(j)(2). If annuities were purchased by the plan for nonhighly compensated employees during the preceding two years, the amount of

such purchases is added to both the numerator and the denominator in determining the ratio, which has the effect of increasing the percentage and helping such plans avoid the various restrictions.

A plan sponsor may not amend a plan to increase benefits if the adjusted funding target attainment percentage is less than 80 percent or would be less than 80 percent taking into account the amendment. IRC § 436(c)(1). A plan sponsor can avoid this restriction if it makes a contribution (in addition to any minimum required contribution) equal to: (1) the amount of increase in the plan's funding target attributable to the amendment, if the plan's adjusted funding target attainment percentage is less than 80 percent; or (2) the amount sufficient to result in an adjusted funding target attainment percentage of 80 percent, if plan's adjusted funding target attainment percentage would be less than 80 percent taking into account the amendment. IRC § 436(c)(2). The restriction does not apply to an amendment to a benefit formula not based on compensation as long as the rate of benefit increase does not exceed the contemporaneous rate of increase in the average wages of the participants covered by the amendment. IRC § 436(c)(3).

A nearly identical restriction applies to the payment of shutdown benefits or other unpredictable contingent event benefits, except that the threshold is 60 percent instead of 80 percent. IRC § 436(b). But even more significantly, a plan with an adjusted funding target attainment percentage less than 60 percent must cease all benefit accruals, unless the plan sponsor makes a contribution (in addition to any minimum required contribution) equal to the amount sufficient to result in an adjusted funding target attainment percentage of 60 percent. IRC § 436(e).

Once a plan drops below the 60 percent threshold it cannot pay benefits in any form other than a life annuity. IRC § 436(d)(1). The same restriction on payments applies to any plan whose sponsor is in bankruptcy, unless the adjusted funding target attainment percentage is 100 percent or greater. IRC § 436(d)(2). If a plan is between the 60 and 80 percent threshold, a single partial lump sum payment is permitted, provided it does not exceed the lesser of (1) one-half of the lump sum otherwise payable, or (2) the present value of the participant's PGBC guaranteed benefits. IRC § 436(d)(3). Any remaining benefit must be paid in the form of an annuity. These lump sum limitations are designed to prevent a raid on the plan assets, which could dramatically increase the PBGC's liability to the remaining participants. There is an exception for lump sum payments that are immediately distributable without the participant's consent, i.e., when the participant's vested benefit does not exceed $5,000. See IRC §§ 411(a)(11); 436(d)(5).

New plans are exempt from all of the above restrictions (except the limit on accelerated payments) during their first five plan years. IRC § 436(g). The five-year exemption for new plans can be justified on the basis that (1) new plans have not had a chance to generate sufficient benefits to create a significant potential PBGC liability and (2) the PBGC liability for new benefits phases in over a five-year period. Also, in computing the adjusted funding target attainment percentage a plan can count as an asset of the plan any proper security provided by the plan sponsor. IRC § 436(f)(1). Generally, in computing the funding target attainment percentage, any credit balance is subtracted from the value of plan assets, which can be a significant drawback to maintaining such balances. However, if the funding target attainment percentage is 100 percent or more before such subtraction, the percentage is determined without regard to such reduction. IRC § 436(j)(3)(A). The PPA also imposes significant actuarial certification requirements, which if not met result in presumed underfunding for purposes of the various benefit limitations. IRC § 436(h).

All of these restrictions depend on a determination of the adjusted funding target attainment percentage, which for most plans is based on actuarial valuations as of the first day of the plan year. See IRC § 430(g)(2)(A). Obviously it will take the plan's actuary some time after that date to determine the plan's funding level. How are the benefit limitations to be applied during the period when it is uncertain whether they apply? The 2006 PPA provides a number of presumptions. See IRC § 436(h). If any of the benefit limitations applied to the plan during the preceding plan year, the plan's adjusted funding target attainment percentage is presumed to be equal to the prior year's percentage until the actuary certifies the percentage for the current year. If the actuary fails to certify the percentage by the first day of the tenth month (October 1 for plans with a calendar plan year), the percentage is presumed to be less than 60 percent. If a plan in the preceding plan year was within ten percentage points of being subject to a benefit limitation or restriction and the plan's actuary does not certify the plan's adjusted funding target attainment percentage by the first day of the fourth month of the current year (April 1 for plans with a calendar plan year), the adjusted funding target attainment percentage is presumed to be ten percentage points lower than in the previous year, thereby triggering the respective benefit limitation or restriction.

For example, suppose the funding percentage in the preceding year were 69 percent. This triggered the lump sum payment restriction applicable to plans funded between 60 and 80 percent. This restriction is presumed to apply to the current year, so lump sum distributions would be limited to one-half of what the participant would otherwise be entitled to. But if the actuary fails to certify the current year's percentage by April 1, all lump sum distributions would be prohibited, because the plan would be presumed to have a funding percentage of 59 percent.

7.   *Timing and sanctions.* An employer is required to make the minimum required contribution to the plan within 8½ months following the close of the plan year. IRC § 430(j)(1). Any payment must be adjusted for interest accruing at the plan's effective interest rate for the plan year for the period between the valuation date and the payment date. IRC § 430(j)(2). Since the valuation date, except for small plans, is the first day of the plan year, an employer that waited until the last possible moment to make the contribution would need to contribute 20½ months of interest.

Plans that had a funding shortfall for the preceding plan year must make quarterly contributions. IRC § 430(j)(3). Interest is payable on any underpayment of a quarterly installment at the plan's effective interest rate plus 5 percentage points. Each member of a controlled group is jointly and severally liable for the minimum required contribution, as well as any required quarterly installments. IRC § 412(b)(2). If the unpaid amounts exceed $1,000,000 and the funding target attainment percentage is less than 100 percent, a lien in the amount of the excess over $1,000,000 arises in favor of the plan (but enforceable by the PBGC) upon the assets of the employer owing the amounts and all of the members of the controlled group. IRC § 430(k).

Although plan participants and fiduciaries may bring suit under ERISA to enforce the minimum funding requirement, the main enforcement device for encouraging compliance with the minimum funding rules is the nondeductible IRC § 4971 excise tax, imposed on the employer. First, there is an initial 10 percent tax on any unpaid minimum required contributions for any plan year ending within the employer's taxable year. This is levied each year until the deficiency is corrected and cannot be waived by the IRS, even for unintentional or inadvertent deficiencies. D.J. Lee, M.D., Inc. v. Commissioner, 931 F.2d 418 (6th Cir.1991). Second, there is a 100 percent tax on the unpaid minimum required contribution to the extent it is not paid within a specified time period, which extends at least to the earlier of the time the 10 percent tax is assessed or when a deficiency notice is issued with respect to the 10 percent tax, but may extend even longer. IRC §§ 4971(b), (c)(3), 4961, 4963(e). Each member of a controlled group is jointly and severally liable for the tax. IRC § 4971(e).

As a practical matter, by the time sanctions arise, the employer is often in bankruptcy. At that point collecting the sanctions becomes difficult. See United States v. Reorganized CF & I Fabricators of Utah, 518 U.S. 213 (1996)(the "tax" under IRC § 4971 is a penalty and therefore has the priority of an ordinary unsecured claim, rather than the higher priority given to an excise tax).

8. *Waivers.* A commitment made to fund a pension during good business times may prove difficult to keep during hard times. Forcing the employer to keep its funding promise, no matter what the circumstances, might disrupt the employer's business or even push the employer into bankruptcy, results which might be harmful to the future funding and continued existence of the plan. The PPA continues to provide the IRS limited authority to waive all or a portion of a minimum required contribution for a plan year. IRC § 412(c).

Waivers may be granted if an employer is unable to satisfy the minimum funding standard without "temporary substantial business hardship" and if enforcing the minimum funding standard would be "adverse to the interest of the plan participants in the aggregate." No more than 3 waivers may be made in any 15 year period. The requirement that the hardship be "temporary" was added in 1987, following reports that indicated that a significant portion of the large claims made against the PBGC under plan terminations arose from plans in which contributions were overdue or had been waived. Note that the request for a waiver must be submitted within 2 1/2 months of the close of the plan year. IRC § 412(c)(5)(A).

The factors to be used by the IRS in determining whether there is a temporary substantial business hardship include, but are not limited to, whether (A) the employer is operating at an economic loss, (B) there is substantial unemployment or underemployment in the trade or business and the industry concerned, (C) the sales and profits of the industry concerned are depressed or declining, and (D) it is reasonable to expect that the plan will be continued only if the waiver is granted. IRC § 412(c)(2). If an employer is a member of a controlled group, the hardship requirement must be met both by the employer and the entire controlled group. IRC § 412(c)(5)(B).

Mechanically, the waived funding deficiency is amortized in equal annual installments over 5 plan years using the appropriate segment interest rates. This gives rise to a "waiver amortization installment" that is added to the minimum required contribution for the five succeeding years. IRC § 430(e). If a plan's funding shortfall for a plan year is zero (i.e., the value of the plan's assets reduced by any credit balances is at least equal to the plan's funding target), all waiver amortization installments for the current and future years attributable to any preceding year are reduced to zero. IRC § 430(e)(5). The purpose of this rule is the same as the parallel rule for shortfall amortization installments: once a plan becomes fully funded, there is no reason to force additional contributions based on a prior year's underfunding.

Plan benefits, including rates of accrual and vesting rules, may not be increased during any period in which a waiver is in effect. IRC § 412(c)(7)(A). An amendment violating this provision will cause the waiver to terminate with respect to any plan year ending on or after the date the amendment is adopted.

A funding waiver is of obvious interest to participants, beneficiaries, and employee organizations. The employer must notify these parties of the waiver request. IRC § 412(c)(6). A waiver is also of profound interest to the PBGC, which may become financially responsible if the assets of the plan are inadequate to pay the promised benefits. For this reason the IRS is required to consult with the PBGC before granting any waiver if the requested waiver plus the present value of all waiver amortization installments for the current and succeeding plan years equals or exceeds $1,000,000. IRC § 412(c)(4)(B) & (C). In such cases the IRS may also require the employer to provide security to the plan as a condition for the waiver. IRC § 412(c)(4)(A).

4. FINANCIAL ACCOUNTING

Separate from the issue of how pension plans should be funded is the issue of how they should be reported in financial statements. No matter what funding requirements are imposed, accountants need a method of allocating the cost of the pension promise to each accounting period in order to determine properly a firm's income and expenses. Accountants must also decide whether a plan's surplus or deficit should be reflected on the firm's balance sheet. In 1985, after many years of deliberation, the accounting profession, through the Financial Accounting Standards Board, adopted Statement of Financial Accounting Standards No. 87 (SFAS 87), "Employers' Accounting for Pensions." A related Statement, SFAS 88, was adopted at the same time to deal with the special accounting issues of plans that terminate or are significantly curtailed.

SFAS 87 places significant limitations on the flexibility that accountants once enjoyed in accounting for pensions. It gives specific guidance on the selection of appropriate interest rates for determining the present value of benefit obligations and rates of return on plan investments. These rates may differ from those used for minimum funding purposes. SFAS 87 requires that final pay and career average pay plans use the projected unit credit cost method, and that flat benefit plans use the unit credit cost method, for attributing the cost of pension benefits to an accounting period. Although employers may continue to use the entry age normal cost method for funding purposes, they may not use it for accounting purposes. In order to avoid the burden of accounting under two different standards, many plan sponsors have switched to the projected unit credit method for both purposes.

SFAS 87 provides a number of smoothing rules. For example, the cost of a pension benefit increase attributable to prior service must generally be amortized over the future period of service of the employees active at the date of the amendment giving rise to the cost. SFAS 87 also provides methods for dealing with "gains and losses," which can arise out of changes in either the projected benefit obligation or the value of plan assets that may result from experience different from that assumed or from changes in actuarial assumptions. Firms may use any systematic method of amortization as long as it produces an amount greater than the so-called "corridor approach." Under the corridor approach, only the portion of the net gain or loss exceeding 10 percent of the greater of the projected benefit obligation or the value of the plan assets must be amortized. If amortization is required, this excess is amortized over the average remaining service period of active employees expected to receive benefits. Instead of amortizing, the sponsor has the option of immediately recognizing such gains and losses as they occur, provided it does so consistently.

Because the plan's assets are invested, the investment results need to be reflected in the firm's earnings. SFAS 87 does not use the plan's actual earnings, but uses the expected rate of return on the actuarial value of the assets. On the other hand, there is an offsetting interest cost due to the fact that the projected benefit obligation at the beginning of the year is one year closer to being paid at the end of the year. If the assumed discount rate for future obligations is the same as the expected rate of return on plan assets (they can be different), the two components together result in a cost equal to interest on the unfunded portion of the projected obligation, or a credit equal to the interest on any surplus.

A notable and somewhat controversial result of these rules is that if a plan has a surplus, the deemed rate of return on the surplus is added to earnings. Although the press today is filled with reports of underfunded plans, "in the late 1990's, pension funds produced big enough investment gains to offset the reported cost of providing the benefits. So companies were able to add some of those gains to their earnings as pension income." Mary W. Walsh, Most Big Corporate Pension Funds Showed Gains in 2004, N.Y. Times, April 13, 2005, at C12. Since the pension plan assets are in a separate trust and investment gains cannot be withdrawn for use in the plan sponsor's business, is it sensible to treat such gains as part of the business income?

What SFAS 87 did not do was require that the assets and liabilities of a pension plan be included in the plan sponsor's balance sheet. Thus, suppose a plan had been fully funded until the current year, when a dramatic stock market decline left it with assets of $8 billion and liabilities of $10 billion. Although ERISA imposes full liability on employers for plan underfunding, this $2 billion shortfall was not shown on the plan sponsor's balance sheet. It appeared only in the footnotes to the financial statements.

In response to concerns that information regarding pension obligations and assets should be more useful and transparent for investors, FASB has now changed the balance sheet rules. Under SFAS 158, "Employers' Accounting for Defined Benefit Pension and Other Postretirement Plans," adopted in 2006, plan sponsors must now recognize plan assets and obligations in their balance sheets. SFAS 158 made no change in the way net pension expense is included in the plan sponsor's income statement, but FASB has an ongoing project reviewing those rules as well.

SFAS 158 will make balance sheets much more volatile. Recall that the minimum funding standard still permits a limited amount of smoothing (e.g., asset values can be averaged over a two-year period) and even SFAS 87 continues to allow smoothing for reporting net income. Should FASB have provided for some kind of balance sheet smoothing?

B. TERMINATION WITH INSUFFICIENT ASSETS

In the drafting of ERISA, Congress' decision to create the plan termination insurance system embodied a judgment that the funding rules being put in place to protect against plan default would not fully succeed. Because some plans would continue to terminate with insufficient assets to pay promised benefits, Congress created a government program designed to insure against such defaults.

Multiemployer plans. Title 4 is ERISA's largest title, in part because it contains the complex rules for underfunded multiemployer plans, especially Part E (§§ 4201–4303). The Multiemployer Pension Plan Amendments Act of 1980 (MPPAA) extensively revised and elaborated the system for insuring multiemployer plan benefits. Although the detail of the multiemployer system lies beyond the scope of this coursebook, this chapter supplies an overview of the difficulties that beset the separate PBGC insurance program for those plans infra in Section B.7. Otherwise, when speaking of Title 4, this book refers to the regime for single-employer plans, ERISA §§ 4001–4071.

This unit is necessarily introductory in character and omits many qualifications and subtopics. For further treatment of Title 4, see E. Thomas Veal & Edward R. Mackiewicz, Pension Plan Terminations (2d ed. 1998) [hereafter Veal & Mackiewicz].

Unionization. Wooten's history of the enactment of ERISA establishes that Title 4 was devised and initially drafted by the United Auto Workers (UAW), the union whose members suffered the pension default in the Studebaker termination. James A. Wooten, The Employee Retirement Security Act of 1974: A Political History 67–79, 94, 160–61 (2005).

According to a study of the PBGC's claims experience through 1986, 63 percent of all claims paid to that date came from steel and auto industry plans. Another 31.6 percent came from other collectively bargained plans. Only 5.4 cents on the PBGC claims dollar went to nonunion workers. Richard A. Ippolito, The Economics of Pension Insurance 43, 45 & tbl. 3–5 (1989). More recent evidence suggests that the skew to unionized industries continues, but with changes in the mix of unions, especially as a result of airline industry terminations. PBGC reported that as of 2010, 26.8 percent of all claims paid since inception of the single-employer plan termination insurance program have come from plans classified as being in the "primary metals" industry (steel), 31.5 percent from air transportation, and 31.9 percent from machinery, fabricated metals, and other manufacturing. The residual category, industries in which unions are somewhat less well represented, comprised 9.8 percent. See the data tables available on PBGC's website at http://www.pbgc.gov/documents/pension-insurance-data-tables-2010.pdf, table S–19. These figures are for plans in the single-employer program, hence they exclude claims experience in the multiemployer plan program, which is by definition 100 percent unionized.

Do these figures imply an interest-group account of the political economy of the pension plan termination insurance system under Title 4 of ERISA? The analysis would be that the PBGC system taxes healthy plans that present little or no risk of default, in order to finance transfers to sick plans that promised more benefits than they could afford to pay. Overwhelmingly, the sick plans have been designed by unions and unionized employers in the collective bargaining process. Because such a small fraction of the private sector workforce is unionized (under 8 percent in 2005), much of PBGC's premium income is paid by nonunion firms. Thus, the insurance system functions in part to tax employment at nonunion firms, for the benefit of union workers. The program encourages unions and employers in sick companies to agree to lavish pension demands, secure in the knowledge that these claims can be largely transferred to an agency that is a loose proxy for the federal treasury, and mostly paid for by the nonunion sector. As you study the operation of the plan termination insurance system, ask yourself whether this interest-group account is sound, and if so, what policy implications it presents.

1. THE PENSION BENEFIT GUARANTY CORPORATION

Title 4 creates the Pension Benefit Guaranty Corporation (PBGC), establishes procedures for terminating pension plans, prescribes the coverage and characteristics of the plan termination insurance program, and specifies PBGC's rights against a plan sponsor whose termination of an insufficiently funded plan results in the PBGC becoming liable to the plan's participants and beneficiaries.

1. *PBGC.* ERISA §§ 4002–4003 establish the PBGC, grant it juridical capacity, and bestow upon it extensive investigatory and enforcement powers.

2. *Covered plans.* Section 4022 establishes the insurance program. Section 4001 contains particular definitions for Title 4. Section 4001(a)(15) defines "single-employer plan" opaquely—"any defined

benefit plan (as defined in section 3(35)) which is not a multiemployer plan." The basic coverage rule of § 4022(a) is that the PBGC "shall guarantee [the] payment of all nonforfeitable benefits [under] a single employer plan"; the net effect of these circumlocutions is to limit termination insurance to defined benefit plans. Section 4021(b)(1) confirms that any "individual account plan, as defined in [ERISA § 3(34)]" is not covered.

Section 4021(b) excludes a variety of plans from Title 4 coverage: federal, state and local plans, church plans, foreign plans, unfunded plans for the highly compensated, nonqualified excess benefit plans, and others. Perhaps the most surprising is § 4021(b)(13), excluding any plan "established and maintained by a professional service employer which does not [have] more than 25 active participants in the plan." For the meaning of the term "professional service employer," see § 4021(c)(2).

3. *Premiums.* The plan termination program is financed through premium charges imposed on all covered defined benefit plans. When enacted in 1974, the figure was $1. In addition, in 1987 PPA introduced a supplemental or second-tier premium for plans with unfunded vested benefits, in the amount of $6 for each $1,000 of unfunded vested benefits, divided by the number of participants, subject to a cap of $50 ($16 basic + $34 supplemental) per participant. For plan years beginning in 2014, the per-participant premium rate was $49 for single-employer plans. This increases to $57 in 2015 and $64 in 2016. The 2014 supplemental premium for plans with unfunded vested benefits was $14 per $1000 of unfunded vested benefits, capped at $412 times the number of participants in the plan. These rates and caps increase to $24 and $412 in 2015 and $29 and $500 in 2016. [See Premium Rates, http://www.pbgc.gov/prac/prem/premium-rates.html]

For employers with 25 or fewer employees on the first day of the plan year the 2006 PPA caps the supplemental premium for *each participant* at $5 times the number of participants. ERISA § 4006(a)(3)(H). PPA's imposition of supplemental premiums responded to a longstanding criticism of the previous flat-rate PBGC premium structure. The criticism was that under ordinary insurance principles, premiums should be risk-related. In the life insurance business, for example, the 60-year-old pays a higher premium for term life insurance than the 20-year-old, because the 60-year-old poses the greater mortality risk. So with plan termination insurance, the risk of a plan default on which the PBGC will have to make good increases with the level of the plan's underfunding. The PPA amendment moved in the direction of a risk-related premium structure.

ERISA's plan termination insurance system differs from private insurance in many respects, notably that coverage is involuntary. All covered DB plans must participate, no matter how healthy, and PBGC must cover all such plans, no matter how risky. In that setting, wouldn't it be more honest to label payments to PBGC as taxes rather than insurance premiums? On the contrasts between the PBGC system and private insurance markets, see Steven Boyce & Richard A. Ippolito, The Cost of Pension Insurance, 69 J. Risk & Ins. 121 (2002) (estimating that PBGC insurance understates true cost by half); Richard A. Ippolito, The Economics of Pension Insurance (1989).

In goading Congress over the years to raise PBGC's premium income, PBGC has been attempting to develop reserves on a reasonably current basis, reserves that are adequate to offset PBGC's accrued liabilities for future benefit payments under terminated insufficient plans. The premium could be much lower if PBGC were to operate as a transfer system like Social Security, satisfied in the main to take in just enough current-year premium income to defray current-year benefit payments. Why is it better to require today's healthy companies to subsidize certain of tomorrow's retirees, as opposed to requiring tomorrow's healthy companies (or other taxpayers) to pay the subsidy?

4. *Covered benefits.* Subject to important limitations, § 4022(a) announces the principle that the PBGC will guarantee "the payment of all nonforfeitable benefits." Thus, only vested benefits are insured. Benefits accrued but not yet vested are not covered.

Also excluded are "benefits becoming nonforfeitable solely on account of the termination of a plan." As discussed more fully in Chapter 4, supra, a qualified plan must provide that upon its termination all affected employees must vest in their accrued but unvested benefits to the extent funded. See IRC § 411(d)(3). This accelerated vesting will not occur for purposes of the PBGC guarantee.

5. *Benefits cap.* As enacted in 1974, the maximum pension benefit that was insurable was $750 per month. ERISA § 4022(b)(3)(B). The $750 figure was inflation-indexed (by reference to the Social Security contribution and benefit formula). For plans terminating in 2015, the maximum benefit for a covered participant retiring at age 65 is $5,011 per month or $60,136 per year. If the payment of benefits commences before age 65, the maximum monthly benefit is actuarially reduced, in accordance with the principles discussed in the unit on early retirement (see Chapter 18, infra). For 2015 the maximum monthly guaranteed benefit is s $3,959 at age 62, $3,257 at age 60, and $2,255 at age 55.

The plan participant whose monthly benefit exceeds the cap remains at risk for the excess when the plan defaults, if the plan sponsor is insolvent. On the other hand, relatively few participants are so exposed. The average monthly pension benefit paid by PBGC in 2010 was $594. See the data tables available on PBGC's website at http://www.pbgc.gov/documents/pension-insurance-data-tables-2010.pdf, table S–20. The vast majority of participants are not affected by the cap, although in some of the recent situations in the airline and auto industries the cap has had, or might have, a big effect on some retirees, particularly those who took early retirement. Where the cap applies, it can affect individuals who have been retired for many years.

6. *The phase-in.* Under § 4022(b)(7), the PBGC guarantee is phased in over a five year period. Thus, benefits created shortly before plan termination (an acute moral hazard problem) will not be covered, or will not be covered fully. Benefits for "majority owners" (generally those owning more than a 50 percent interest in the plan sponsor) phase in over a 10-year period. ERISA § 4022(b)(5).

2. THE INSURABLE EVENT AND ITS CONSEQUENCES

Dan M. McGill, Kyle N. Brown, John J. Haley, & Sylvester J. Scheiber, Fundamentals of Private Pensions
803–10, 819–20 (8th ed. 2005).

[ERISA §§ 4041 and 4062 originally] provided that a plan termination would activate the insurance mechanism, even though the sponsor continued in business and perhaps established another plan. This meant that the insured event was plan termination. The sponsor and all members of its control group were liable to the PBGC for any unfunded insured benefits up to 30 percent of its net worth at the time of plan termination. If the unfunded insured liability exceeded 30 percent of the sponsor's net worth, the PBGC had to absorb the excess and spread the loss over all insured plans.

Prior to enactment of [the Single-Employer Pension Plan Amendments Act of 1986 (SEPPA)], plan sponsors generally had an unrestricted right to terminate a pension plan at any time, on the condition that they provide 10 days advance notice to the PBGC. An exception to this applied (and still applies) to plans subject to collective bargaining, which generally may not be terminated or modified during the period of the collective bargaining agreement without the union's consent.

This was a flawed concept. Contrary to sound insurance principles, the insured event was largely under the control of the plan sponsor, an interested party. Coupled with this, the law created an incentive for a plan sponsor to terminate the plan at any time the unfunded insured liability exceeded 30 percent of its net worth. It also created a disincentive to fund at the maximum tax-deductible level, since there was always the potential of terminating the plan at some future date under circumstances that would relieve the sponsor of some of its unfunded insured liabilities. Many such plan terminations occurred, and they created large liabilities for the PBGC. Some of the firms that terminated their plans were ongoing employers, and some of these immediately set up other pension or profit-sharing plans.

SEPPA substantially restricted the ability of plan sponsors to terminate plans with unfunded guaranteed [benefits]. While plan termination is still the insured event, an employer is no longer free to terminate a plan with unfunded accrued benefits except in a "distress" [situation. ERISA § 4041(c)]. If an employer that is not in a distress situation desires to terminate a plan with unfunded accrued benefits, it may need first to freeze the accrual of benefits and continue funding the plan until all accrued benefits are funded, at which time it could terminate the plan. Thus plan terminations with unfunded accrued benefits are now limited to distress situations. [In 1987 the OBRA amendments eliminated the 30 percent limit on the plan sponsor's liability.] . . .

[*PBGC's Claim against the Assets of the Plan Sponsor.* The PBGC must have recourse against the assets of a plan sponsor if it is to enforce its claim for reimbursement in respect of benefits paid by the PBGC on behalf of a terminated plan.] . . .

If a plan sponsor [does] not make acceptable arrangements to pay its liability to the PBGC, [the] PBGC automatically acquires a lien against all the assets and property rights of the [sponsor. ERISA § 4068]. The lien remains in effect for six years after termination of the plan, or for the duration of any collection agreement entered into between the plan sponsor (or members of its controlled group) and the PBGC. In the event that the plan sponsor becomes insolvent or bankrupt before settling its obligation to the PBGC, the latter's claim is treated as a judgment lien, that is, it has the same priority as a judgment lien of the federal government for unpaid taxes. The only claims with higher priority are those of secured creditors (only with respect to the collateral), mechanics' liens, and a few other special claims. . . .

Allocation of Single Employer Plan Assets. Since not all benefits under a pension plan are insured, it was necessary for ERISA to provide a procedure for allocating the assets of a single-employer plan that has become subject to an insured event between the benefits that are insured and those that are not insured. The allocation procedure is important to plan participants, since it can affect the amount of benefits they receive. It also is important to both the PBGC and the employer, and they both profit from maximizing the proportion of assets going to insured benefits. The more assets that are assigned to insured benefits, the smaller the amount of PBGC resources that must be applied to the payment of insured benefits. On the other hand, the more plan assets that are allocated to insured benefits, the smaller the amount of noninsured benefits that will be paid from plan assets.

PBGC Priority Classes. It might have been assumed that the law would give first priority against the plan assets to insured benefits. However, Congress decided that the benefits payable to participants who had been retired for at least three years on the date of the insured event, or who could have been retired for three years, should be given priority over employer-financed benefits of other insured participants, even for amounts in excess of the insurance limit. This meant that some uninsured benefits were to have a higher priority than other insured benefits, making it necessary to establish priority classes even among the insured benefits.

The statutory allocation formula establishes six classes of benefits, in descending order of priority, with the assets for the first four classes being allocated on a pro rata basis, if necessary, within each successive class. [ERISA § 4044.] . . .

Plan Termination Initiated by the Plan Sponsor. As first enacted, ERISA provided a virtually unlimited right for plan sponsors to terminate their plans, which contributed to very large liabilities being placed upon the PBGC, thereby creating substantial deficits in the benefits insurance program. [SEPPA] was enacted to ameliorate the situation, by amending ERISA to limit the sponsor's right to terminate a defined benefit plan. Now, a defined benefit plan may not be terminated voluntarily unless it meets the condition of a standard termination or a distress termination. ERISA § 4041(a).

Standard Termination. A standard termination is a plan termination in which the plan assets are sufficient to cover all liabilities for benefits earned to date, and to protect participants from the loss of such benefits without imposing any liability on the PBGC. Benefit liabilities include all accrued benefits. [ERISA § 4001(a)(16), IRC § 401(a)(2), Rev.Rul. 85–6.] Benefit liabilities also include early retirement supplements and subsidies such as early retirement reduction factors which are more liberal than actuarial equivalent factors, as well as special benefits that become payable only upon plant shutdown or certain other special events. . . .

Distress Terminations. If plan assets are less than the benefit liabilities, a plan may not be terminated voluntarily unless each contributing employer (and each member of a controlled group with such employers) satisfies the requirements for a distress termination. [ERISA § 4041(c)]. An employer is in distress if it satisfies any one of four criteria:

1. A petition for liquidation of the employer has been filed under bankruptcy laws.

2. The employer is in the process of reorganization under bankruptcy laws, the bankruptcy court determines that the employer will be unable to pay its debts under reorganization and to continue in business outside reorganization, and the court approves the termination.

3. The employer demonstrates to the PBGC that it will be unable to pay its debts when they come due and will be unable to continue in business unless the distress termination occurs.

4. The employer demonstrates to the PBGC that its pension costs have become unreasonably burdensome solely as a result of a decline in the employer's workforce.

To initiate a distress termination, the plan administrator must provide notice of intent to terminate to plan participants and beneficiaries and union representatives as for a standard termination except that for a distress termination the notice of intent must also be sent to the PBGC.

The plan administrator must provide the PBGC with the information it needs to determine whether the criteria for a distress termination have been satisfied. In addition, the information must include a certification by the enrolled actuary including, as of the proposed termination date, the projected value of plan assets, the present value of all benefit liabilities, and the present value of the portion of benefits guaranteed under the plan benefits insurance program. The certification must state whether the plan assets are sufficient for benefit liabilities or for guaranteed benefits, or for neither. The information must also include the name and address of each participant and beneficiary and the information the PBGC or the trustee needs to pay future benefits to them. . . .

Amendment to Reduce or Freeze Plan Benefits. At times a plan sponsor may desire to make a plan amendment to reduce or discontinue all future benefit accruals, but without terminating the plan. Such a step may be taken for many of the same reasons that a plan termination is undertaken, generally in order to reduce plan costs or to make changes where reduction or elimination of accruals is appropriate, as in a change to a different type of plan for future service or in a plant closing.

The least disruptive of such courses of action would be a plan amendment (effective only with respect to service after the effective date of the amendment) to reduce the rate at which pension benefits accrue, to decrease or eliminate ancillary benefits (such as those payable upon death or disability), or to cut back on other attractive but costly plan features. This type of action is called a plan curtailment and does not involve any official response (other than IRS approval) or penalty.

A more drastic form of action would be a plan amendment to discontinue all future benefit accruals, but with the recognition of future service for vesting and phase-in purposes and with the continuation of contributions for the funding of benefits already accrued. With no further change of policy, all accrued benefits of continuing employees would eventually become fully vested and fully funded. This type of action is referred to as freezing of the plan or, in the terminology of the IRS, as a suspension of the plan. In some circumstances—for example, when it creates or increases a potential reversion of assets to the employer—the IRS may regard a suspension as a partial termination requiring all accrued benefits to vest to the extent then funded. [IRC § 411(d)(3).]

3. FORBIDDING THE FUND-SPECIFIC DEFINED BENEFIT PROMISE

Before the enactment of ERISA, the sponsor of a DB plan could contract in the plan to limit its responsibility for benefit levels to whatever assets were contained in the fund. The Studebaker plan, discussed supra in Chapter 3, contained such a term. Here is the language of such a provision, taken from a plan that was involved in an early ERISA case, Matter of Defoe Shipbuilding Co., 639 F.2d 311 (6th Cir.1981):

> In the event of termination of the Plan, [accrued] benefits shall be non-forfeitable to the extent funded. [Payments] by the Company [computed] in accordance with [the plan's contribution schedule] shall be in complete discharge of the Company's financial obligation under this Plan. The Company shall have no liability in respect to payments under the Plan except to pay over to the Trustee such contributions. [Each] employee or retired employee [shall] look solely to the Trust Fund for any payments or benefits under the Plan.

ERISA outlaws this sort of fund-specific defined benefit promise, as a result of the vesting rules of § 203 and the insurance system of Title 4. Section 203 makes pension promises nonforfeitable; § 4022(a) requires that PBGC guarantee nonforfeitable benefits; and § 4062 gives the PBGC recourse against the employer to recoup any such benefits that the PBGC has to pay.

The effect of these interrelated provisions is to say to the employer: "If you promise a benefit, it must vest within the statutory period; and once it vests, you must pay it. ERISA denies you and your employees your preexisting freedom of contract. Not only may you no longer contract for forfeitures beyond the vesting periods permitted under § 203, you are also forbidden from contracting to limit the employer's liability for its defined benefit promises to whatever assets are in the fund." However, such a provision would be permitted in a plan not subject to Title IV, for example, a small professional employer's plan.

Why should Congress want to prohibit this fund-specific defined benefit promise? Bear in mind that defined contribution plans are supremely fund-specific. Each participant's benefit will be based solely on whatever happens to be in that participant's individual account upon retirement or termination. Since ERISA allows defined contribution plans, why should ERISA forbid such a mechanism under a defined benefit plan?

4.   PBGC v. OUIMET CORP.

630 F.2d 4 (1st Cir.1980).

■ BOWNES, CIRCUIT JUDGE. Jurisdiction in this interlocutory appeal from the United States District Court for the District of Massachusetts is predicated upon 28 U.S.C. § 1292(b). The issue is one of first impression involving the interpretation of [ERISA].

The case began with the bankruptcy of a corporation, Avon, and its wholly owned subsidiary, Tenn-ERO, which were part of a larger group of corporations, the Ouimet Group. A brief prefatory explanation of ERISA, and the role in it of the Pension Benefits Guaranty Corporation (PBGC), is necessary to appreciate the issues. Under ERISA, PBGC assumes the administration and payment of benefits of a terminated pension plan whose assets are insufficient to cover all guaranteed benefits. PBGC may recover from the employer 30% of its net worth determined as of a date within one hundred twenty days of the plan termination, or the deficit, whichever is less. The bankrupts, here, had no positive net worth as of the valuation date. This means that, if the term "employer" is limited to the bankrupts, PBGC recovers nothing and a dividend will be paid to the creditors. If, on the other hand, "employer" is construed to mean the Ouimet Group of corporations, including the bankrupts, it is probable that PBGC will receive all of the bankrupts' assets with the creditors receiving nothing.

The Ouimet Group of Corporations.

Emil Ouimet owns 100% of Trust; 80% of Ouimet; and 80% of Stay. He owned all stock in Avon which, in turn, held 100% of Tenn-ERO's stock. Stay has a 100% interest in Ouimet Welting; and a 50% interest in Brockton. At all times pertinent to this litigation, Emil Ouimet was president of all Ouimet Group corporations except Ouimet and Stay, of which Richard was president.

The Plan. Pursuant to a collective bargaining agreement with the Rubber Workers Union and the International Brotherhood of Firemen and Oilers, Avon instituted a pension plan for its hourly workers in 1959. The plan provided for full vesting after ten years of service, if certain age criteria were satisfied. It gave the company the right to "amend, modify, suspend or terminate the Plan" and limited the benefits payable upon termination of the plan to "the assets then remaining in the Trust Fund." Avon made all actuarially mandated contributions, but at all times the plan was underfunded. There were three reasons for this. (1) Initial underfunding occurred because credit was given for past years of service while no immediate contribution to the plan for this credit was required. Rather, the deficit was expected to be amortized over thirty years. (2) Ouimet negotiated several benefit increases which were not met by current contributions. (3) A decrease in the value of certain fund investments in 1974 and 1975 led to a devaluation of the plan assets. When Ouimet purchased Avon, the underfunding amounted to $92,000. By March 25, 1975, the day Avon closed its doors, it was $552,339.64.

Prior Proceedings. On June 18, 1975, Avon and Tenn-ERO filed Chapter XI bankruptcy petitions; on March 22, 1976, they were adjudicated bankrupts. . . .

On March 31, 1976, PBGC filed suit against the Ouimet Group in the United States District Court for the District of Massachusetts. After filing suit against Ouimet, Stay, Welting, Avon, and Tenn-ERO, PBGC determined that Trust should be treated as an employer as well and it was joined as an additional defendant.

The district court named PBGC trustee of the Avon plan. It appointed the bankruptcy judge sitting on the Avon/Tenn-ERO proceedings to serve as master. Following a twelve-day trial in December, 1976, the bankruptcy judge recommended that no liability attach to the Group and that Avon/Tenn-ERO's negative net worth relieved them of liability to PBGC. After release of the bankruptcy judge's memorandum, Union moved to intervene to protect the interests of former Avon employees and the district court granted the motion. The court held a hearing on March 13, 1979. In its opinion, it ruled that ERISA imposes joint and several liability on all members of a controlled group of corporations. After a careful analysis of the statutory and constitutional issues, it granted PBGC's motions for partial summary judgment and for relief from the automatic stay in bankruptcy and remanded the case to the bankruptcy court for a determination of the net worth of the Ouimet Group of corporations. *Pension Benefit Guaranty Corp. v. Ouimet Corp.,* 470 F.Supp. 945, 954, 958 (D.Mass.1979). We affirm, but on somewhat different grounds. . . .

We start with the definition section of [ERISA Title 4—Plan] Termination Insurance. [ERISA § 4001(b)] provides in part:

> For purposes of this subchapter, under regulations prescribed by the corporation, *all employees of trades or businesses (whether or not incorporated) which are under common control shall be treated as employed by a single employer and all such trades and businesses as a single employer.* The regulations prescribed under the preceding sentence shall be consistent and co-extensive with regulations prescribed for similar purposes by the Secretary of the Treasury under [IRC] § 414(c) (emphasis added).

Section [4001(b)] applies, by its terms, only to groups "under common control" as that term is defined in regulations coextensive with the regulations under [IRC] § 414(c). Those regulations define a group "under common control" as a parent-subsidiary group, brother-sister group, or combined group. The regulations go on to define these terms according to the degree and nature of common stock ownership. The Ouimet Group, with the exception of Brockton, which was excluded by stipulation, clearly meets the test of stock ownership in the regulations. The group is, therefore, under common control for purposes of section [4001(b)].

The apparent meaning of section [4001(b)] is that a group under common control is to be treated as a single employer for purposes of subchapter III, which is entitled Plan Termination Insurance. It appears, then, that the term "employer," as used in section [4062(b)], refers, in the case of a group under common control, to all the "trades or businesses" which are members of the group. Under this reading of the statute, all members of the Ouimet Group would be jointly and severally liable to PBGC.

Ouimet argues, however, that section [4001(b)] does not mean what it appears to mean. Rather, in Ouimet's view, this language was intended only to prevent employers from avoiding application of ERISA by shifting employees around among various corporate entities. . . .

If Congress had intended to limit the application of section [4001(b)] to certain purposes, such as computing the number of employees for application of section [4021(b)(13)], or the length of an employee's service for application of section [4022(b)(3)(A)], it could have done so by referring specifically to the affected sections. Instead, Congress referred to "this subchapter." We must assume that Congress meant, by that phrase, the whole subchapter, including section [4062(b)]. . . .

We are not persuaded that, because only one of a group of corporations under common control contributes to a plan, it is unjust to make the group responsible for the plan's deficit. The facts of this case illustrate why such a group should be treated as an integrated whole. Ouimet purchased Avon with full knowledge of the plan and its funding requirements. Ouimet participated in the labor negotiations resulting in greater pension benefits that contributed to the deficit. The Ouimet Group filed a consolidated tax return on which the Avon contributions were deducted. We see nothing unfair in treating the Ouimet Group as a single employer.

We agree with the district court that the group under common control consists of Ouimet, Trust, Stay, Welting, and Avon/Tenn-ERO.

5.   PROTECTING THE PBGC

Underfunding a PBGC-insured pension plan is classic moral hazard behavior. See Daniel Keating, Pension Insurance, Bankruptcy and Moral Hazard, 1991 Wisconsin L. Rev. 65. Because the plan termination insurance system confronts the PBGC with so much risk of moral hazard, a large part of Title 4 is devoted to protecting the PBGC. The system of required notices to PBGC and the early warning program (PBGC Technical Update 00–3) are also designed to protect PBGC.

1.   *PBGC's finances.* PBGC ran a persistent deficit from its inception until 1996, then went into surplus. The surplus peaked at $9.7 billion in 2000, as the strong economy of the 1990s both reduced terminations and increased the value of financial assets and investment income. Legislative changes in 1987 and 1994 that required accelerated funding for underfunded plans, discussed supra, also played a role.

Subsequently, the stock market declines, interest rate declines, and major plan terminations (especially those in the airline industry) in the 2000s again sent the program into deficits, which reached $23.3 billion in 2004 before declining to $13.1 billion in 2007. PBGC, 2007 Data Book, at 18 & fig. 1.

The PBGC's financial statements reflect only plan terminations that have already taken place, not those which may occur in the future. Although estimates of plan funding levels vary, the PBGC estimated that the total underfunding in PBGC-insured single-employer plans was $225.1 billion in 2007, down from a high of $452.1 billion in 2004. 2007 Data Book, at 86 & Table S–47.

In its most recent report, the PBGC reports that "The financial position remains in deficit for both single-employer and multiemployer programs. The net financial position of our larger single-employer program is projected to likely improve over the next decade. As explained further in the Management's Discussion and Analysis section, the multiemployer program's net position has dramatically worsened." During that year, the multiemployer plan deficit increased by $34 billion, but the single employer deficit fell by $ 8 billion. PBGC Annual Report (2014). The Consolidated and Further Continuing Appropriations Act of 2014, enacted in December, 2014, made major changes that affect multiemployer plans in the Multiemployer Pension Reform Act which is part of the new law.

2. *Underfunding.* The court in *Ouimet* remarked that "Avon made all actuarially mandated contributions, but at all times the plan was underfunded." The case exemplifies several of the common causes of underfunding previously discussed.

(a) *Prior and past service credits.* When created in 1959, the Avon plan was immediately underfunded, because it gave credit for years of service before the inception of the plan (called prior service credits). Following accepted actuarial practice, the employer was allowed 30 years to amortize the resulting deficit. In addition, "Ouimet negotiated several benefit increases which were not met by current contributions."

As mentioned earlier in this chapter, ERISA's past allowance of a 30-year amortization period for past service credits allowed for the creation of substantial liabilities. Professor Keating has written that "the biggest single cause of the PBGC's present financial crisis is the decision of Congress at the PBGC's inception to guarantee what is known as 'past service liability.' [In consequence, a] firm may properly fund a plan on an ongoing basis but still severely underfund it on a termination basis. TWA [Trans World Airlines, which ultimately terminated its plan], for example, properly funded its pension plan on an ongoing basis, but nevertheless underfunded the plan on a termination basis by $900 million." Daniel Keating, Chapter 11's New Ten-Ton Monster: The PBGC and Bankruptcy, 77 Minnesota L. Rev. 803, 811–12 (1993).

As discussed earlier, the changes to the funding rules wrought by the Pension Protection Act of 2006 change substantially the amortization rules.

(b) *Unfavorable investment experience.* According to the court in *Ouimet*, "[a] decrease in the value of certain fund investments in 1974 and 1975" (a period of generally poor returns on financial assets) further impaired the funding of the Avon plan.

If a pension fund experiences substandard investment returns, PBGC's exposure in the event of plan termination is correspondingly magnified. Should PBGC have a voice in determining the investment practices, especially the level of portfolio risk, of an underfunded pension plan? If so, is the force of that insight limited to the investment of pension assets? Should PBGC have a say in (or a veto over) other decisions of a firm that might impair the firm's net worth when that firm is the sponsor of an underfunded defined benefit pension plan? Should PBGC have the power to forbid a firm like Allis-Chalmers from paying dividends to its stockholders? Should PBGC be able to forbid such a firm from launching (or continuing) particular business ventures? In short, should severe underfunding be treated as a species of potential bankruptcy, justifying a receivership-type regime in favor of PBGC?

3.   *PBGC recourse.* The *Ouimet* case predates both SEPPA (1986) and PPA (1987). As originally enacted in 1974, ERISA limited PBGC to recourse against the employer in the amount of 30 percent of the employer's net worth, the figure used in the *Ouimet* case. The 1986 and 1987 changes expand § 4062 by creating a liability of the employer to the PBGC for 100 percent of the plan's unfunded benefit liabilities. However, although the employer is now liable to the PBGC for the full amount of unfunded benefit liabilities, the changes in the statute limit the lien in § 4068 to 30 percent of the employer's net worth. As a result, the PBGC has a secured interest against the employer of up to 30 percent of net worth of the employer and an unsecured interest for any remaining liability under § 4062, up to the full amount of the unfunded benefit liabilities.

If the employer is insolvent, whether PBGC can recover 30 percent or 100 percent of the employer's net worth of zero ordinarily will not matter. Bankrupt employers figure commonly enough in PBGC cases. What made *Ouimet* worth fighting about was that only Avon and its subsidiary Tenn-ERO were bankrupt. Other associated persons were solvent. For more on the *Ouimet* litigation, see PBGC v. Ouimet Corp., 711 F.2d 1085 (1st Cir.1983); Comment, Extending ERISA Liability for Pension Plan Terminations to Controlled Group Members, 61 Boston U.L. Rev. 477 (1981). PBGC's standing in bankruptcy is discussed later in this chapter.

4.   *Common control regulations.* The common control rule instanced in *Ouimet* is also oriented to protecting the PBGC. Not only is each contributing sponsor of a plan liable for any underfunding upon plan termination, but so is each member of a contributing sponsor's "controlled group." ERISA § 4062(a). The controlled group is defined as the sponsor and "all other persons under common control" with the sponsor. ERISA § 4001(a)(14)(A). ERISA § 4001(a)(14)(B) arranges to borrow the IRS common control regulations under IRC §§ 414(b)–(c) for this purpose. These regulations are discussed more fully in Chapter 9, infra.

The notion that employers under common control should be aggregated for some purposes is a way of piercing the corporate veil. "In order to make the antidiscrimination, participation, vesting, and benefit [limits] of the [IRC] operate effectively, [Title 2 of] ERISA added [in 1974

IRC] § 414, which requires the aggregation of employees of commonly controlled enterprises, whether incorporated or [not. IRC] § 414 is meant to apply, in a sophisticated manner, to the commonly subdivided modern business entity." Russell K. Osgood, The Law of Pensions and Profit-Sharing § 9.1, at 276 (1984). ERISA § 4001(b) applies the same common control principles to all provisions of Title 4. Common control issues frequently arise with respect to the withdrawal liability provisions of the multiemployer plan system, discussed infra. E.g., PBGC v. East Dayton Tool & Die Co., 14 F.3d 1122 (6th Cir.1994); Central States, Southeast & Southwest Areas Pension Fund v. Ditello, 974 F.2d 887 (7th Cir.1992).

Although a shareholder of a corporation is not directly liable for any plan termination or withdrawal liability of the corporation, *Ditello* illustrates how personal liability can arise as a result of the common control regulations. The Ditellos were the sole shareholders of a trucking company that incurred withdrawal liability to a plan. They also owned commercial real estate that they leased to the trucking company. The court concluded that leasing property to a withdrawing employer is a trade or business. Since the Ditellos owned 100 percent of the two businesses, the two businesses formed a brother-sister group under Treas.Reg. § 1.414(c)–2(c) and were therefore under common control. Because the real estate was directly owned by the Ditellos, they became personally liable for the withdrawal liability. The Seventh Circuit reached a similar conclusion more recently in Cent. Ill. Carpenters Health & Welfare Trust Fund v. Olson, 467 Fed. Appx. 513 (7th Cir. Mar. 15, 2012), holding the owner of two sole proprietorships jointly liable as a single employer for unpaid contributions to multiemployer plans.

"[I]t is altogether irrelevant" under ERISA § 4001(b) whether one trade or business has an "economic nexus" with another owned by the same persons. Connors v. Incoal, Inc., 995 F.2d 245, 249 (D.C.Cir.1993). *Connors* involved the withdrawal liability of a coal mining corporation owned by four individuals who also owned a partnership that owned land used for hunting and some tobacco growing and cattle raising. The court of appeals remanded the case to the district court for a determination whether the partnership's activities constituted a trade or business.

5. *Transactions to evade liability.* "Another way a firm can evade the control test is to sell an about-to-fail division or subsidiary before the division or subsidiary terminates an insufficient plan." Ippolito, Pension Insurance, supra, at 74.

The transaction involved in the protracted *Harvester/Wisconsin Steel* litigation allegedly followed that script. International Harvester sold Wisconsin Steel, a Harvester subsidiary, to a buyer, Envirodyne, in 1977 for $65 million. The buyer had no meaningful capital of its own; Harvester lent the buyer $50 million of the purchase price; the other $15 million came from a bank loan secured by Wisconsin Steel's inventory and receivables. As part of the transaction, Envirodyne contracted to take over the pension obligations of Wisconsin Steel, which included unfunded obligations variously calculated at $45 to $86 million. In 1980, Envirodyne went bankrupt and PBGC assumed the insufficiently funded terminated pension plan. ERISA § 4062(a) as it then read made the "employer who maintained a single employer plan at the time it was terminated" liable to PBGC for the shortfall. (SEPPA, the 1986 revision of Title 4, revised the language but not the principle.) Harvester took the position that since Envirodyne was the employer at the time the plan was terminated, PBGC had no recourse against Harvester under § 4062(a). PBGC claimed that the employer was Harvester, not Envirodyne, on account of Harvester's "domination" of Envirodyne.

In 1988 the district court denied Harvester's motion to dismiss PBGC's claim. In re Consolidated Litigation Concerning International Harvester's Disposition of Wisconsin Steel, 681 F.Supp. 512 (N.D.Ill.1988). The court characterized Harvester's position on the reach of § 4062 thus: "[A]ll that [an] employer needs to do to [escape liability for pension promises] is to convey his business to an insolvent nominee." 681 F.Supp. at 520. Rejecting that view, the court held "that when an employer sells his business under circumstances which would constitute abuse of the insurance program he is liable under [§ 4062]." Id. at 524. The decision led to a settlement by which Harvester's successor, Navistar International Corp., agreed to pay PBGC some $65 million in cash and securities. 19 BNA Pension Rptr. 1514 (1992). For further detail on the *Harvester/Wisconsin Steel* case, see Gordon L. Clark, Pensions and Corporate Restructuring in American Industry: A Crisis of Regulation 101–22 (1993).

ERISA § 4069(a), added by SEPPA in 1986, allows a five-year lookback period on a transaction "[i]f a principal purpose of any person in entering into [it] is to evade liability to which such person would be subject under this [subtitle]." The Third Circuit has said of § 4069 that "Congress codified the *Harvester* predecessor liability rule with one change. [Whereas *Harvester*] required the plaintiff to prove that the new employer had no reasonable chance of fulfilling the pension obligations it assumed, [ERISA § 4069] substituted the requirement that the plan terminate within five years of the date the transaction became effective." PBGC v. White Consolidated Industries, 998 F.2d 1192, 1199 (3d Cir.1993), cert. denied, 510 U.S. 1042 (1994). In that case the court held that the five-year clock does not begin to run "until the company that transferred a pension plan no longer makes substantial pension contributions." Id. Thus, a seller who continues to fund its former plan to keep it from terminating cannot escape liability. The Third Circuit remanded the case to the district court, which determined that the sale transaction should be regarded as a sham and that, thus, White Consolidated was liable under § 4069. PBGC v. White Consolidated Industries, Inc., 1999 WL 680185 (1999), aff'd, 215 F.3d 407 (3d Cir.2000).

6. *The actuarial component in underfunding.* As discussed supra in the note on "Actuarial Assumptions," funding entails projections that are inherently subjective. It has been argued that ERISA's funding rules leave "too much discretion to employers to determine precisely what their minimum funding obligations will be in a given year. [Among] the actuarial assumptions that affect the minimum funding figure are mortality, interest earned on plan assets, employee turnover, and salary projections. Although these assumptions must be 'reasonable,' there is nevertheless a significant range within which employers can accommodate their own funding preferences." Keating, supra, 77 Minnesota L. Rev. at 810.

Because actuarial estimation of a company's pension assets and liabilities affects the value of residual share prices, the Securities and Exchange Commission (SEC) is also involved in overseeing the work of actuaries. In 1993 the SEC was reported to be pressing firms to lower assumed interest rates to reflect the decline in interest rates that occurred in the later 1980s and early 1990s. In question was both the discount rate used to estimate future pension obligations and the rate-of-return assumptions used in projecting the growth of plan assets. The SEC wanted firms to use a discount rate of 7 percent, roughly the then-current yield on long-term high-grade corporate bonds. "According to a Goldman, Sachs & Co. study, 307 companies out of 366 surveyed assume a discount rate of 8% or more to calculate pension obligations. These companies will show a higher pension liability if they assume a 7% discount rate." SEC Is Challenging Funding for Plans, Wall St. J., Nov. 17, 1993, at C1. Goldman Sachs concluded, for example, that General Electric Company, by using a 9 percent discount rate, reported 1992 net income that was $494 million, or 12 percent higher, than would have resulted had GE used a 7 percent discount rate. Id. General Motors was using an 11 percent rate of return assumption in 1992, when its actual rate of return on plan assets was 6.4 percent. Hopeful Assumptions Let Firms Minimize Pension Contributions, Wall St. J., Sept. 2, 1993, at A1. GM agreed with DoL in May 1994 to contribute $10 billion in cash and securities to reduce its accumulated underfunding. 21 BNA Pension & Benefits Rptr. 949 (1994).

7.   *Shutdown benefits: confusing pensions with unemployment compensation?* The PBGC by regulation (29 C.F.R. § 2621.4) has determined that guaranteed benefits "include the payment of pretermination *shutdown benefits.* This means that if a plan has a provision to pay, for example, full unreduced benefits to all workers with 30 years' service on plant shutdown, a worker age 48 would be guaranteed full benefits at the PBGC (subject to the maximum benefits limit). In comparison to a rule that could have been consistent with the social security system (full benefits at age 65), the PBGC agreement to pay shutdown benefits to a 48-year-old worker is equivalent to paying unemployment benefits for 17 years and retirement benefits thereafter." Ippolito, supra, at 38 (emphasis in original).

Shutdown benefits loom surprisingly large in the PBGC claims experience. The GAO reported to Congress in 1992:

> PBGC estimates than more than 25 percent of its deficit may be attributable to shutdown benefits from steel industry [plans]. Shutdown benefits continue to pose a threat to PBGC because a large portion of its current exposure is from plans with shutdown-type benefit provisions in the steel, automobile, and tire and rubber industries.

General Accounting Office, Pension Plans: Hidden Liabilities Increase Claims Against Government Insurance Program 4–5 (1992). In 2003, the PBGC estimated that it had a potential exposure of over $15 billion in shutdown benefits in PBGC-insured plans. Letter of Executive Director Steven A. Kandarian to Senate Committee on Finance, April 1, 2003.

The 2006 PPA provides significant new protection to the PBGC by treating benefit increases attributable to plant shutdowns or other contingent events as plan amendments. ERISA § 4022(b)(8). As discussed earlier in the Chapter, this has the effect of phasing in the PBGC guarantee for these increased benefits over a five-year period. See ERISA § 4022(b)(7).

8. *Funding waivers.* As discussed above in Section A treating funding (and in Chapter 10, infra), under ERISA § 303 and IRC § 412, the IRS can allow temporary waivers of the ordinarily applicable funding rules for struggling firms in circumstances of "temporary substantial business hardship." ERISA § 303(b) lists the factors to be taken into account, which include whether the employer is operating at a loss, whether there is substantial unemployment in the industry, whether the industry is depressed, and whether "it is reasonable to expect that the plan will be continued only if the waiver is granted."

Is there a tension between the purposes of this section and the interests of the PBGC insurance system?

If PBGC becomes liable for a terminated insufficient plan, the employer is liable to the PBGC for the outstanding balance of any accumulated funding deficiency, including deficiencies resulting from funding waivers under ERISA § 303 and IRC § 412. See ERISA § 4062(c). Should that protection cause the PBGC to be unconcerned about funding waivers?

For empirical evidence that funding waivers have contributed materially to the size of the PBGC's losses on plans that were subsequently terminated, see Ippolito, Pension Insurance, at 114–17.

9. *Preventing long-run loss.* ERISA § 4042 allows the PBGC to terminate a plan involuntarily to prevent "long-run loss" that would "increase unreasonably if the plan is not terminated." Such a termination may proceed without regard to the usual automatic stay imposed in bankruptcy proceedings. ERISA § 4042(e). When the PBGC invokes its authority under this section, further vested accrual of PBGC-insured benefits ceases. For cases in which the courts have sustained the PBGC's exercise of its power under this section, see PBGC v. FEL Corp., 798 F.Supp. 239 (D.N.J.1992); and In re Pan American World Airways, Inc., 777 F.Supp. 1179 (S.D.N.Y.1991), aff'd, 970 F.2d 896 (2d Cir.1992).

Many employers who enter bankruptcy proceedings continue to operate their underfunded plans during the reorganization and then terminate the plans right before exiting bankruptcy or before liquidating. While the plans continue, the PBGC's potential liability for guaranteed benefits continues to grow. Under the 2006 PPA this will no longer occur. If a plan terminates during bankruptcy or insolvency proceedings, the PBGC's liability for guaranteed benefits is determined as of the bankruptcy filing date, not the date of actual termination. ERISA § 4022(g).

10. *Termination premiums.* If after terminating a plan in a distress termination the employer manages to avoid liquidation, a nasty surprise awaits. The Deficit Reduction Act of 2005 imposes a special termination premium of $1,250 per participant per year for three years following the plan termination. ERISA § 4006(a)(7). Typically employers in distress termination situations are also in bankruptcy reorganization. In that case the three-year period for paying the premiums does not begin until

the reorganized employer emerges from bankruptcy. ERISA § 4006(a)(7)(C)(ii). The intent seems to be to try and recoup from the reorganized employer some of the PBGC's losses in connection with the plan termination, but it may make reorganizing the employer that much more difficult and increase the likelihood of liquidation as opposed to reorganization.

11. *LTV: restoring a terminated plan.* ERISA § 4047 authorizes the PBGC to restore a terminated plan to the sponsor, thus restoring its liabilities. The prominent case of PBGC v. LTV Corp., 496 U.S. 633 (1990), arose from PBGC's decision to restore the terminated plan of LTV, a troubled steel manufacturer. PBGC had terminated the plan to prevent the accrual of further vested benefits, thereby assuming LTV's massively underfunded plan. Thereafter, LTV and the Steelworkers Union negotiated a new "follow on" pension plan, free of the burden of underfunding in the old plan. The new plan effectively promised the participants what they had lost in the termination. The Supreme Court sustained PBGC's action in restoring the plan:

> The PBGC's anti-follow-on policy is premised on the belief, which we find eminently reasonable, that employees will object more strenuously to a company's original decision to terminate a plan (or to take financial steps that make termination likely) if the company cannot use a follow-on plan to put the employees in the same (or a similar) position after termination as they were in before. The availability of a follow-on plan thus would remove a significant check—employee resistance—against termination of a pension plan.

> Consequently, follow-on plans may tend to frustrate one of the objectives of ERISA that the PBGC is supposed to accomplish—the "continuation and maintenance of voluntary private pension plans." [ERISA § 4002(a)(1)]. In addition, follow-on plans have a tendency to increase the PBGC's deficit and increase the insurance premiums all employers must pay, thereby frustrating another related statutory objective—the maintenance of low premiums.

496 U.S. at 650.

Keating links the danger of follow-on plans to the moral hazard problem inherent in insurance contracts:

> The primary cost of follow-on plans is that they destroy the co-insurance feature of the current PBGC system. . . .

> If follow-on plans such as LTV's were allowed as a matter of course, then employers could underfund, have their plans terminated, and still keep their employees and retirees happy by paying the relatively small cost of the uninsured pension benefits. With the *LTV* decision, the employer's choice following a plan termination and assumption by the PBGC will be: (1) to fail to create a follow-on plan (and contend with employee discontent), or (2) to create a follow-on plan but then contend with the cost of restoring the plan originally terminated. Faced with these choices, most employers would simply opt not to create a follow-on plan.

Daniel Keating, Pension Insurance, Bankruptcy and Moral Hazard, 1991 Wisconsin L. Rev. 65, 81–82.

12. *Policy: questioning termination insurance.* For years, there have been suggestions that improving ERISA's funding rules were a better alternative to the plan termination insurance scheme. E.g. D. Don Ezra, The Struggle for Pension Fund Wealth 76 (1983). As early as 1994, the Joint Committee explored the question of whether ERISA should eliminate or limit the ability of underfunded plans to increase benefits. Joint Committee on Taxation, Description and Analysis of S. 1780 ("Retirement Protection Act of 1993") (JCS–4–94), Jun. 14, 1994, reprinted in 21 BNA Pension & Benefits Reporter 1224, 1243 (1994).

If ERISA's new funding rules are successful in prevent underfunding, would termination insurance be needed?

6. PBGC CLAIMS IN BANKRUPTCY

The PBGC's main claims in bankruptcy are the somewhat overlapping claims against the plan sponsor and its controlled group for (1) the amount of the unfunded benefit liability, and (2) the unpaid minimum funding contributions. ERISA § 4062(b), (c). The PBGC will also have claims for any unpaid premiums payable, including the "termination premium" implemented as part of the Deficit Reduction Act of 2005. ERISA § 4006(a)(7). The main issues in bankruptcy have involved the priority of the PBGC's claims and the proper method to value them.

1. *Claim priority and possible liens.* The PBGC has a number of possible liens at its disposal to enhance its priority in bankruptcy, but these have not proved very advantageous in practice.

Under ERISA § 4068, if the plan sponsor fails, upon notice and demand, to pay the unfunded benefit liability, the PBGC has a lien in an amount up to 30 percent of the collective net worth of the plan sponsor and the members of its controlled group. The lien is entitled to the same priority in bankruptcy as a tax due and owing to the United States. There are two problems with this lien. First, if there is no collective net worth the lien is worthless. Second, most distress terminations occur during bankruptcy and the PBGC is unable to perfect the lien because of the automatic stay provision of the Bankruptcy Code, 11 U.S.C. § 362(a)(4), which stays "any act to create, perfect, or enforce any lien against property of the estate."

Whenever the total unpaid minimum funding contributions exceed $1 million, the PBGC receives a lien for the excess against all controlled group property. ERISA § 303(k). If the PBGC perfects the lien prior to bankruptcy, it has a secured claim with the status of a tax lien. The perfection and priority of the lien are determined under IRC § 6323. Also, if funding waivers have been granted conditioned on adequate security, the PBGC has a security interest in the collateral.

The PBGC has argued that the minimum funding obligations accruing after the bankruptcy petition is filed constitute administrative expenses, which are the highest priority unsecured property claim. However, the courts have been willing to treat as administrative expense only the portion of the minimum funding obligation directly attributable to the post-petition labor of the participants, excluding that part of the obligation representing the past service cost for such participants. See In re Bayly Corp., 163 F.3d 1205 (10th Cir.1998); In re Sunarhauserman, 126 F.3d 811, 816–20 (6th Cir.1997).

2. *Valuation of the PBGC's claims.* The PBGC has consistently argued that the actuarial assumptions, especially the interest rate, used in valuing its claim should be those specified in Title 4 of ERISA. The PBGC points to ERISA § 4062, which defines the employer's liability based on the "amount of unfunded benefit liabilities," and ERISA § 4001(a)(18), which specifies that the computation of the amount of unfunded benefit liabilities is to be "based on assumptions prescribed by the [PBGC]." Debtors and their creditors have argued that the valuation method is an issue for the bankruptcy court to decide.

In In re Chateaugay Corp., 126 Bankr. 165, 172 (S.D.N.Y.1991), the court selected an interest rate four percentage points higher than the one proposed by the PBGC. "In a large case, the choice of a discount rate for the PBGC's claims has major implications. In the *LTV* case, for example, each single percentage point difference in the chosen discount rate would affect the PBGC's claim by $250 million. The lower the discount rate, the higher would be the present value of any claim for a future payment from the debtor." Daniel Keating, Chapter 11's New Ten-Ton Monster: The PBGC and Bankruptcy, 77 Minn. L. Rev. 803, 820 (1993) (discussing PBGC v. LTV Corp., 496 U.S. 633 (1990)).

A number of courts have held that a "prudent investor rate" should be used, on the theory that the claims of unsecured creditors in the same class should be valued in the same way. See In re CSC Industries, 232 F.3d 505 (6th Cir.2000); PBGC v. CF & I Fabricators of Utah, 150 F.3d 1293 (10th Cir.1998). Use of a "prudent investor rate" was expressly rejected in In re U.S. Airways Group, 303 B.R. 784, 798 (Bankr.E.D.Va. 2003):

> [The] PBGC's claim for unfunded benefit liabilities should be determined using the PBGC valuation regulation, since Congress has chosen to define the claim by reference to that regulation. . . . Because the PBGC's valuation regulation— which seeks to replicate the cost of a private-sector annuity paying the promised benefits—gives proper weight to Congress's goal of protecting the health of the nation's private pension system, it is to be preferred over the use of discount rate premised on uncertain projections of future stock market returns.

The PBGC has sought legislation that would give it a high priority in bankruptcy. "This approach, however, ignores a number of realities. First, bankruptcy is not the place to solve the problems of underfunding, since it was outside of bankruptcy that the PBGC allowed the underfunding to occur. Second, creating a bankruptcy priority for retirees will likely accelerate the financial demise of companies most guilty of underfunding by restricting their access to credit both before and after a bankruptcy filing. Finally, giving a special priority to retiree benefits necessarily reduces the bankruptcy recovery of other claimants, many of whom are arguably in groups as worthy of sympathy as are the retirees." Keating, supra, at 842.

3. *Termination Premiums*. As noted supra, the Deficit Reduction Act of 2005 imposed a special termination premium in situations where a plan is terminated involuntarily or in a distress termination. In the first published decision on this issue, the Second Circuit held in 2009 that the obligation to pay the termination premium is not a prepetition claim, and thus survives a Chapter 11 bankruptcy proceeding. PBGC v. Oneida Ltd., 562 F.3d 154 (2d Cir.2009). In the view of the court, treating the termination premium as a prepetition claim would "directly thwart Congress's aim in establishing the Special Rule." Id. at 158.

4. *PBGC's Proactive Approach.* As the text above emphasizes, once a bankruptcy has occurred, PBGC's remedies are limited. In view of that, the agency is highly proactive, monitoring news reports and transactions and sponsor financial health. It is aided in this activity by the "reportable event" requirements of ERISA § 4043. Under this provision the sponsor of a PBGC-insured plan must notify the agency of certain enumerated events of the sort that might raise the possibility of increased financial vulnerability, including, among others: transactions or extraordinary dividends undertaken by the sponsor; precipitous drops in the number of plan participants; or the plan's becoming "unable to pay benefits thereunder when due." In the case of a significantly underfunded plan, the PBGC must be notified by the sponsor *before* the reportable event takes place.

When the PBGC sees risk developing, it often steps in, contacts the plan sponsor and requires that it post some form of security or make a special contribution to the plan. The agency's leverage to make such demands is supplied by the threat of its triggering an "involuntary" plan termination, as it is authorized to do under ERISA § 4042(a)(4) when "the possible long-run loss of the [PBGC] with respect to the plan may reasonably be expected to increase unreasonably if the plan is not terminated." Even the PBGC's making known that it is considering such action is typically enough to disrupt, for example, a planned corporate transaction

It is now common for sponsors of underfunded plans to be approached by PBGC in this proactive, anticipatory, creditor-protection manner. Often, the outcome is that the plan sponsor reaches a settlement, providing security to PBGC or the plan.

The Consolidated and Further Continuing Appropriations Act of 2014 enacted a new section 4062(e) of ERISA, applicable to cessations of operations on or after the date of enactment, December 18, 2014. Employers that had substantial cessations under the old law, but have not yet arranged with the PBGC to satisfy their 4062(e) liability, are allowed to elect a new additional contribution option. See, e.g., Steptoe and Johnson, Congress Revises PBGC's Controversial Substantial Cessation Liability (§ 4062(e)) Rules, available at www.steptoe.com; Groom Law Group, Major Changes in "Shutdown" Liability under ERISA Section 4062(e), available at www.groom.com.

7. MULTIEMPLOYER PLANS

Alicia H. Munnell, Guaranteeing Private Pension Benefits: A Potentially Expensive Business

New England Economic Rev. 24, 28–33 (Mar.–Apr. 1982).

The PBGC and Multiemployer Plans. [When enacting ERISA in 1974,] Congress delayed extending full coverage of termination insurance to multiemployer plans because of uncertainty about the incidence of multiemployer plan terminations and about the potential impact of Title 4 provisions on such plans. Some experts told Congress that because multiemployer plans rely on a large number of employers, they would rarely terminate. Others were concerned that because many multiemployer plans were experiencing rapidly rising costs in the face of large unfunded liabilities and declining industry employment, the PBGC insurance provisions might actually encourage their termination. The postponement of coverage was designed to allow the PBGC to gain experience with multiemployer plans and to determine the potential financial burden associated with full termination insurance coverage.

Because early studies prepared by the PBGC concluded that the insurance provisions would have a detrimental impact on multiemployer plans forcing the PBGC to assume large scale liabilities, Congress postponed mandatory coverage four times to allow substantial revision of the insurance rules for multiemployer plans. Since a revised multiemployer termination insurance program was not passed nor another deferral date approved, Title 4 of ERISA as originally enacted became effective in August 1980. Shortly thereafter, however, legislation was passed that made major changes in the insurance program for multiemployer plans. This legislation was signed into law on September 26, 1980. . . .

Multiemployer plans usually cover employees working within an industry or craft in a specified geographic area. The plans are created and maintained under collective bargaining agreements negotiated between a union and employers. The plans are governed by a board of trustees comprised of equal representation by labor and management. The trustees, however, have no control over the annual contributions to the plan, since the amount is usually determined in the collective bargaining process with the employers who agree to contribute so many cents per hour of covered employment. The trustees merely accept the agreed-on contributions and establish benefit levels based on assumptions about future employment trends, investment return, retirement patterns and turnover of the workforce. Traditionally, the trustees, operating within specific revenue constraints, have sought to maximize benefit levels at the expense of funding the plan, leaving most multiemployer plans with large unfunded liabilities. With multiemployer plans functioning somewhat on a pay-as-you-go basis, fiscal soundness depends on a stable or growing number of employees in an industry. Financial problems occur when an industry experiences a protracted decline in employment, since a smaller base of employers must support the pension costs of an increasing number of retired workers.

In recent years, technological obsolescence in certain industries such as printing, foreign competition in industries such as millinery, and changing consumption patterns in industries such as milk delivery have resulted in a significant decline in the number of employers contributing to some multiemployer pension plans. This decline in employment has led to a higher ratio of retirees to active workers, thus imposing a larger funding burden on the remaining employers.

The Multiemployer Pension Plan Amendments Act of 1980. This legislation contains six major provisions that are designed to foster continuation of multiemployer plans by strengthening their ongoing operations and by providing PBGC assistance for plans that experience severe financial hardship.

(1) Strengthened Funding Standards. Revised minimum funding standards were introduced to ensure that financially healthy plans remain sound and troubled plans do not run out of money. . . .

(2) Strengthened Withdrawal Rules. To discourage withdrawals of individual employers, which increase the cost to remaining employers and the likelihood of eventual plan insolvency, the legislation institutes an absolute rather than a contingent liability. Regardless of whether the plan terminates within five years, withdrawing employers must continue making contributions to the plan in order to complete funding their share of the plan's vested liabilities. Their liability is calculated on the basis of their highest contribution rate and highest three-year average contribution base in the 10 years prior to withdrawal. Unlike the provisions for single employer plans, [that were in effect until SEPPA in 1986] the liability of sponsors of multiemployer plans is not limited to 30 percent of their net worth.

(3) Reorganization. Even with revised funding and employer withdrawal rules, reduced employment in declining industries will create serious financial problems for severely underfunded multiemployer plans. In order to allow these plans to work their way out and avoid financial failure, the legislation introduced the possibility of plan reorganization to alleviate financial pressures. . . .

(4) Insured Event Changed. The legislation revised the event insured by the PBGC, from voluntary plan termination to plan insolvency, in order to assure that premium funds are available only for unavoidable financial hardship. . . .

(5) Scaled Back Guarantees. In order to keep insurance costs at reasonable levels and to discourage both parties from allowing the plan to fall into insolvency, the level of guaranteed benefits was reduced substantially for participants in multiemployer plans. The PBGC now insures 100 percent of the first $5 of monthly benefits per year of service. The next $15 per year of service is insured at 75 percent for strong plans and 65 percent for weak plans. At most, this guarantee amounts to slightly less than half of the maximum [per] month guaranteed to employees in single employer plans. An exception is made in the case of pensioners on the rolls as of July 1980 or those who were within three years of retirement at that time. These workers are guaranteed benefits up to the limit provided for participants in single employer plans.

(6) Increased Premiums. To cover the cost of future terminations the premium for multiemployer plans was increased from the existing rate of 50 cents per participant to $1.40 per participant, [and for 2015, $13.00].

The net impact of the Multiemployer Act of 1980 has been to shift the risks associated with financially troubled multiemployer plans away from the PBGC and back to plan participants and the sponsoring employers. The level of benefits guaranteed by the PBGC has been dramatically reduced while the premiums required to pay for the guarantee have been substantially increased.

Allocating the risks associated with multiemployer plans among the PBGC, withdrawing employers and continuing employers is a delicate and difficult exercise. Many multiemployer plans have huge unfunded liabilities and are sponsored by employers in declining industries. Under the first version of ERISA, a company could withdraw from a multiemployer plan without any penalty if the plan did not terminate within five years. This provision was clearly unfair to the surviving employers who were left with millions of dollars of liabilities incurred by other firms. The sponsors of the weakened plan often then had a strong incentive to terminate the plan, thereby shifting the burden to the PBGC.

[MPPAA], however, in attempting to make it more difficult for companies to withdraw, has created a situation where liabilities on the withdrawing employer can be excessively burdensome. A company in a multiemployer plan is now inescapably saddled with large unfunded liabilities many of which can be attributed to benefits credited for service prior to the inception of the plan, often with employers who are no longer with the plan or even in existence. Moreover, a firm's pension liability is not related to its resources. [In] the trucking industry, hard hit by deregulation, the prospect of substantial withdrawal liabilities has prevented many marginal firms from liquidating.

The severe penalties seem certain to discourage employers from withdrawing from multiemployer plans, but critics charge that the bill also discourages companies from joining these plans. Without an inflow of new employers and with the traditional high attrition among sponsoring firms, multiemployer plans will decline in importance. Congress, in trying to structure a more equitable system, may have shifted too much of the burden to withdrawing employers.

NOTES

1. *Constitutionality of MPPAA.* The Supreme Court sustained the constitutionality of the 1980 legislation against Takings Clause objections in Connolly v. PBGC, 475 U.S. 211 (1986), and PBGC v. R.A. Gray & Co., 467 U.S. 717 (1984). MPPAA's retroactive imposition of enhanced liability on participating employers was deeply resented on grounds of unfairness. To see why, notice the distinctive feature of multiemployer plan finance:

> Multiemployer pension plans straddle the line between defined contribution and defined benefit plans. From the standpoint of the employee the plan looks like a defined benefit plan, since the plan sets benefit levels that are not tied to individual accounts. From the employer's standpoint, however, the multiemployer plan looks like

a defined contribution plan. The collective bargaining agreement fixes the amount the employer must contribute (for example, so-many-dollars-per-covered-employee-per-month), typically without explicit connection to the plan's benefit levels. It is the [plan] trustees' job to align the benefit levels that the plan promises with the expected contribution levels.

Daniel Fischel & John H. Langbein, ERISA's Fundamental Contradiction: The Exclusive Benefit Rule, 55 U. Chicago L. Rev. 1105, 1113 (1988).

Accordingly, in the period before MPPAA, the employer's thinking was: "We pay an outside supplier so-much-per-cubic-foot for natural gas; we pay another outside entity so-much-per-employee-hour to provide pension benefits for employees. A bill is a bill. We pay it. We are not responsible for what the gas company promises its customers, nor for what the multiemployer plan trustees promise the employees."

MPPAA effectively decided that after plan trustees had paid overgenerous benefits, they could send participating employers a second bill for the shortfall. Notice further that most such employers are small firms, especially in the construction trades and the trucking industry.

2. *Underfunding.* As of 2004, about a quarter century after the MPPAA amendments to ERISA, PBGC estimated that multiemployer plans as a group were underfunded by $150 billion. Most participants were in underfunded plans; only 11 percent were in fully funded plans. Hearing Before the Subcomm. on Select Revenue Measures of the H. Comm. on Ways and Means, 109th Cong. 1, 4 (2005) (statement of Douglas Holtz-Eakin, Director, Congressional Budget Office). Other estimates suggest that multiemployer plans were underfunded by more than $200 billion in 2008. PBGC data tables, supra, at tbl. M–10.

3. *Multiemployer Pension Reform.* Further pension changes were enacted in December, 2014, by the Consolidated and Further Continuing Appropriations Act of 2014. The most important changes affect multiemployer plans and appear in the Multiemployer Pension Reform Act which is part of the new law. The Act:

Authorizes multiemployer plans to suspend benefits for active and retired participants where a plan in "critical and declining status" meets certain requirements. This change is highly controversial;

Doubles PBGC premiums for multiemployer plans;

Permanently extends the PPA critical and endangered status funding rules that were scheduled to sunset at the end of 2014;

Repeals the reorganization rules and amends the insolvency rules;

Disregards PPA surcharges and certain other contributions when calculating withdrawal liability;

Expands PBGC authority to approve plan partitions and facilitate plan mergers; and

Clarifies PPA and IRC rules impacting multiemployer plans.

C. TERMINATION WITH SUFFICIENT ASSETS

When a well-funded plan terminates with assets in excess of liabilities, the question arises of who is entitled to the surplus.

In the 1980s the practice of terminating a pension plan for the purpose of capturing the surplus ("asset reversion") became highly controversial. In 1981 two prominent firms—the publishing house of Harper & Row and the A&P grocery store chain—terminated their plans as part of major corporate restructurings. The two terminations provoked lawsuits and Congressional hearings. Walsh v. Great Atlantic & Pacific Tea Co., 726 F.2d 956 (3d Cir.1983); District 65, United Auto. Workers v. Harper & Row, Publishers, Inc., 576 F.Supp. 1468 (S.D.N.Y.1983), Hearings Before the Senate Comm. on Labor and Human Resources on Francis Xavier Lilly to Be Solicitor, U.S. Department of Labor, 98th Cong., 2d Sess. (1984); Pension Asset Raids, Hearing before the House Select Comm. on Aging, 98th Cong., 1st Sess. (1983).

The sustained runup in the stock and bond markets that began in 1982 caused pension plan assets to experience large increases in values. "Many plans had assets and liabilities approximately in balance at the time of the passage of [ERISA in] 1974. Since that time the stock market went up, increasing the value of plan assets. Also, [in the high inflation years of the late 1970s and early 1980s] long term interest rates went up. This reduced the value of bonds held as pension assets, but mainly it reduced the value of pension benefit promises. The reason is that pension obligations are very long-term in nature: A 50 year old worker may have a pension benefit that involves payments only starting 15 years hence. This long term nature makes pension benefits super-sensitive to interest rates. I estimate that an increase in long term rates from 7 to 11 percent reduced the present value of pension obligations by about a third." Jeremy Bulow, The Termination of Overfunded Pension Plans, in Overfunded Pension Plans, Joint Hearing Before the Select Comm. on Aging and the Subcomm. on Labor-Management Relations of the Comm. on Education and Labor, House of Representatives, 99th Cong. 1st Sess., 89, at 256–57 (Jun. 12, 1985) [hereafter, Overfunded Pension Plans].

As the number of overfunded plans burgeoned, so did the number of terminations whose purpose was to recapture the reversion for the employer. A recurrent script in the early/mid 1980s was for outside investors to conduct a successful takeover contest for a company with an overfunded plan, then terminate the plan and use the surplus to help recoup what the investors had paid for the company. As will be seen below, the matter has now been largely resolved by legislation.

1. THE LAW AND PRACTICE OF ASSET REVERSION

1.   *The statutory regime governing reversion.* The principal texts governing asset reversion are IRC § 411(d)(3) and ERISA § 4044(d)(1).

IRC § 411(d)(3), previously studied in Chapter 4, supra, regarding partial termination, denies tax qualification under IRC § 401(a) unless a plan provides that upon termination all accrued benefits shall become nonforfeitable to the extent funded. Thus, *all benefits accrued but not yet vested become vested upon plan termination.*

ERISA § 4044(d)(1)(A) authorizes the return of residual assets to the employer when "all liabilities of the plan to participants and their beneficiaries have been satisfied." The liabilities of a terminating plan are ordinarily satisfied in two ways. The plan purchases annuities from an insurance company to fund the accrued benefits of longer service employees; or employees may in certain situations receive lump sum distributions. The 1984 ERISA Agencies Guidelines restate these requirements. ERISA Agencies Guidelines, CCH Pension Plan Guide, ¶ 10,185L, at 13,599.

Thus, the reversion is the residue left after all accrued benefits are made nonforfeitable and are discharged by means of annuities or lump sum distributions.

ERISA § 402(b)(3) requires that every plan "provide a procedure for amending such plan, and for identifying the persons who have authority to amend the plan." The employer typically retains the power. A number of asset reversion cases arose in circumstances in which the plan did not initially authorize the reversion; the employer then amended the plan to authorize the reversion and terminated the plan. E.g., Washington-Baltimore Newspaper Guild Local 35 v. Washington Star Co., 555 F.Supp. 257 (D.D.C.1983); In re C.D. Moyer Co. Trust Fund, 441 F.Supp. 1128 (E.D.Pa.1977).

The Omnibus Budget Reconciliation Act (OBRA) of 1987 amended ERISA § 4044 to add § 4044(d)(2)(A), which provides that any amendment authorizing or increasing the employer's reversion must have been in effect for five years before the amended power is exercised.

2. *Recovering the surplus.* From the employer's standpoint, the purpose of a DB plan pension fund is to pay off the employer's pension promises. The distinctive trait of a defined benefit pension plan, by comparison with a defined contribution plan, is that the employer bears the investment risk. Since the employer is responsible for paying the promised benefits and is responsible for any shortfall, the employer reasons that it should be able to recover the gain if the plan becomes overfunded. Indeed, the technique of ceasing contributions while creating new liabilities against an overfunded plan is an indirect way for the employer to spend the surplus. ERISA, however, provides no direct mechanism for the employer to withdraw surplus assets from a continuing pension plan.

Because ERISA does not expressly authorize the employer to withdraw surplus assets from an ongoing plan, the exclusive benefit rule would forbid such a withdrawal. Section 403(c)(1), the "noninurement" version of the exclusive benefit principle, seems particularly telling. It says that "the assets of a plan shall never inure to the benefit of any employer and shall be held for the exclusive purposes of providing benefits to participants in the plan and their [beneficiaries]." Even though this language may have been meant to prevent a pension plan from becoming underfunded, and hence insufficient to discharge its obligations, the statute does not speak in those terms. Thus, if the employing firm tried to write itself a check from the assets of its overfunded pension plan on the ground that the plan no longer needed all the money, the exclusive benefit rule would surely be violated.

ERISA expressly authorizes the employer to recover surplus pension assets by another avenue—as an incident to the termination of the plan, when all accrued benefits and other liabilities have been paid. ERISA § 4044(d)(1) provides for distributing to the employer "[any] residual assets of a single-employer plan" once "all liabilities of the plan to participants and their beneficiaries have been [satisfied]." ERISA carefully reconciles this authorization for reversion on termination with the exclusive benefit rule. Both the exclusive benefit rule of ERISA § 404(a)(1)(A) and the noninurement rule of ERISA § 403(c)(1) are made subject to the provisions of ERISA § 4044. As the Third Circuit observed in Malia v. General Electric Co., 23 F.3d 828 (3d Cir.1994), a defined benefit plan "gives current and former employees property interests in their pension benefits but not in the assets held by the trust." Id. at 832.

3. *Implicit contract not to terminate?* Although ERISA § 4044(d)(1) authorizes reversion, the argument has been made that plan participants have or should have a larger claim than ERISA § 4044(d)(1) recognizes. Employees expect over the course of employment that the plan will improve the benefits, both to offset future expected inflation, and to reward future long-term service. Because present law recognizes no interest beyond the nominal value of presently accrued benefits, it does not adequately reflect the employees' expectations in the fund. "The crux of the matter is [that] participants and beneficiaries have a reasonable expectation that a defined benefit plan will be continued unless some legitimate business necessity compels the employer to abandon it." Michael S. Gordon, Testimony, in Overfunded Pension Plans, supra, at 76. This expectation has been called an implied term of the pension contract, and the argument has been made that asset reversion violates that term. E.g., Richard A. Ippolito, Pensions, Economics and Public Policy 239, 250 (Pension Research Council) (1986); Richard A. Ippolito, Issues Surrounding Pension Terminations for Reversion, 5 American J. Tax Policy 81, 83–87, 96–97 (1986). Under this implied contract theory,

> the timing of compensation is back loaded. The firm implicitly promises to pay workers above their marginal product in their later years of work in exchange for paying them less than their marginal product in their early years. The worker becomes a bondholder of the firm. The firm owes the worker the foregone wages. This is an implicit obligation, however, not a legal one. The firm is legally obligated to pay only accrued benefits, not implicitly promised future benefits. The cumulative amount of foregone benefits is what I shall refer to as the pension bond. This is the amount the firm can take from workers by breaking the implicit contract and ending the pension plan.

Mitchell A. Petersen, Pension Reversions and Worker-Stockholder Wealth Transfers, 107 Quarterly J. Economics 1033, 1038 (1992).

Fischel and Langbein take the contrary view. "The great difficulty with this argument is that it begs the question of why so important a term would be left implicit rather than made explicit. The employees, who are often represented in pension negotiations by capable labor unions [would] seem to have every incentive to see to it that so important a term of the pension contract be spelled out. The persistent failure to spell out the term suggests that it does not exist." Fischel & Langbein, supra, at 1152 n. 164.

Another strand of the argument for inferring an implied contract to maintain the plan is that such a term is needed to offset the effects of inflation on the future value of pension benefits that are expressed in nominal current values. Ippolito writes that workers do "not anticipate termination, but expect the firm to keep the plan intact and pay an indexed pension, regardless of the firm's legal right to terminate." Ippolito, 5 American J. of Tax Policy, at 83. Why is it that private pension plans virtually never promise expressly to pay an inflation-indexed benefit?

Do workers also expect inflation adjustments to benefit levels after they retire? If so, most are disappointed. "For those receiving a pension, the median replacement rate was 27 percent in the first year of retirement (meaning the percentage of income earned just prior to retirement) that is replaced by the pension income. While these rates vary, the replacement rate can be expected to fall for private-sector retirees, since most private-sector pensions are not indexed to inflation. The older the retiree, the lower the replacement rate was." EBRI, Pension Income of the Elderly and Characteristics of their Former Employers, EBRI Notes, March 2007, at p.1.

Stein has suggested that ERISA be changed to require that a terminating plan provide benefits indexed for inflation before the surplus could revert to the employer. Norman P. Stein, Raiders of the Corporate Pension Plan: The Reversion of Excess Plan Assets to the Employer, 5 American J. Tax Policy 117, 174 (1986). What are the merits and demerits of this proposal?

In the United Kingdom pension plans are required to index pension benefits to inflation, up to 5 percent per year. 21 BNA Pension & Benefits Rptr. 1531 (1994).

4. *Express contracting about reversions.* Even though ERISA § 4044(d)(1) authorizes the employer to recover the surplus, the employer who is entitled to the reversion is free to contract away that entitlement. E.g., Delgrosso v. Spang & Co., 769 F.2d 928 (3d Cir.1985).

It is not unknown for management to renounce the right to the reversion without explicit contractual quid pro quo, as part of a scorched earth anti-takeover defense (a so-called "pension parachute"). For example, during its (ultimately unsuccessful) effort to defeat an unfriendly takeover by the Bank of New York, Irving Bank Corp. amended its plans to provide that surplus pension assets could only be used to provide benefits for retirees and persons retiring within five years of any change of control. Irving Protecting Its Pension Fund, N.Y. Times, Jan. 28, 1988, at D6. Another instance: Great Northern Nekoosa Corp., attempting (ultimately unsuccessfully) to resist a takeover bid from Georgia-Pacific, amended its pension plan to provide that, in the event of a change of corporate control, the surplus would be awarded to the plan participants, including those who had not yet met the plan's ordinary time-of-service requirements. Johnson v. Georgia-Pacific Corp., 19 F.3d 1184 (7th Cir.1994).

5. *De facto withdrawal.* A firm that terminates an overfunded defined benefit plan frequently replaces the terminated plan with a new plan. Such a transaction has the effect of manipulating ERISA's termination provisions to achieve a result that resembles withdrawal by the employer of funds from an ongoing plan—just the power that ERISA does not grant to the employer, and that the exclusive benefit rule by terms would forbid. A set of guidelines promulgated in 1984 by the so-called "ERISA Agencies" (IRS, DoL, PBGC) facilitates termination transactions that are designed to offer substitute or continuing pension coverage for the employees. May 23, 1984, Guidelines (PBGC News Release 84–23), reprinted in CCH Pension Plan Guide, ¶ 10,185L, at 13,599–601 (hereafter cited as ERISA Agencies Guidelines). The rationale for the guidelines is that since the employer has the undoubted power to terminate the plan and recapture the surplus without providing for replacement pension arrangements, the employer should be encouraged to exercise the power to terminate the plan in a manner that results in substitute pension coverage for the employees.

6. *The excise taxes.* The boom in terminating plans for asset reversion triggered a political struggle in the mid-1980s. Opponents of asset reversion, often allied with organized labor, would prohibit the employer from recapturing plan assets. The Reagan Administration defended asset reversion but supported a 10 percent nondeductible excise tax on asset reversions received from qualified plans after December 31, 1985; this excise tax was enacted as part of the Tax Reform Act of 1986. IRC § 4980. See generally Norman P. Stein, Taxing Reversions from Pension Plans, 35 Tax Notes 1131 (1987).

In 1988, the 10 percent tax on reversions was temporarily raised to 15 percent. Technical and Miscellaneous Revenue Act (TAMRA) of 1988, §§ 5072 & 6069, amending IRC §§ 4980(a) and (c). The Omnibus Budget Reconciliation Act of 1990 (OBRA 1990) amended IRC § 4980(a) to increase the tax on reversions from 15% to 20%.

OBRA 1990 also added new IRC § 4980(d), further increasing the tax on employer reversions to 50% unless the employer either (A) establishes a "qualified replacement plan," or (B) increases benefits under the terminating plan pro rata for each participant by a minimum of 20% of the expected reversion. The qualified replacement plan must, under § 4980(d)(2), receive at least 25% of the assets otherwise available for reversion, and the plan must cover "[a]t least 95% of the active participants in the terminated plan who remain as employees of the employer after the [termination]." See Yale D. Tauber & William A. Bader, Surplus Pension Assets: History and Opportunity, 18 J. Pension Planning & Compliance 19, 24–26 (1992).

7. *Reversion magnitudes before and after the 1986 excise tax.* The 1986 excise tax was meant to discourage terminations for reversion. The before-and-after data imply that the measure was quite successful. The Employee Benefit Research Institute (EBRI) gathered data on pension plan terminations that have yielded asset reversions in excess of $1 million. For the two years 1985–86, 848 such terminations affecting 956,000 participants occurred, yielding reversions in excess of $10.9 billion. By contrast, in 1988 after the excise tax was in effect, there were 7 such reversions affecting three thousand participants and amounting

to $36.8 million. EBRI, Questions and Answers about Employee Benefits, EBRI Issue Brief 10 (Table 12) (May 1988).

The reversions that now occur mostly arise in connection with the dissolution of the plan sponsor. The type of transaction that drove the 1980s boom in asset reversion, that is, terminating the plan of a continuing firm in order to capture the reversion, has largely ceased.

8. *Using the surplus without terminating the plan.* There are many ways for a plan sponsor to take advantage of a surplus without terminating the plan. The most obvious strategy is simply to maintain the plan and use the surplus to reduce the level of future contributions. For many plans with large surpluses, the minimum funding requirement is zero and will be zero for many years into the future. Thus, pension benefits can continue to accrue to participants at no out-of-pocket cost to the plan sponsor.

The surplus can also be used to fund an increase in the level of benefits by means of a plan amendment. The increase can be targeted at certain classes of participants and former participants. For example, a cost-of-living adjustment can be provided to retirees without changing the benefit formula for active participants. Many employers have also used surpluses to fund special early retirement benefits for older employees as a means of downsizing their work forces or reducing payroll costs by replacing older, higher-paid workers with younger lower-paid ones. The coverage of a plan can also be expanded to additional employees. In Hughes Aircraft Co. v. Jacobson, 525 U.S. 432 (1999), the employer used part of a billion dollar surplus to fund expanded coverage and an early retirement incentive. The Supreme Court rejected the contention that the surplus could not be so used because it was in some sense attributable to employee contributions. Does it make sense to prohibit the employer from obtaining the surplus by means of termination and asset reversion if the employer may still reach the proceeds by another technique?

Another way to reach a plan surplus is to merge the plan with an underfunded plan. As discussed in Section A, supra, by reducing or eliminating a plan deficit, the plan sponsor can shrink its minimum funding obligation and cut back its PBGC insurance premiums, which are based in part on the amount of plan underfunding. This technique can also be used when the underfunded plan is a multi-employer plan. In an IRS Private Letter Ruling, an employer that sponsored a pension plan for its non-union employees also contributed to a multi-employer plan for its union employees. IRS, PLR 1999–35–076 (1999). The union plan was underfunded and the non-union plan had a surplus. The employer decided to withdraw from the multi-employer plan, but faced a large withdrawal liability because the plan was underfunded. The employer reached an agreement with the multi-employer plan and the PBGC under which the employer could withdraw from the multi-employer plan, but have the liability for the pensions of the employer's union employees transferred from the multi-employer plan to the employer's overfunded plan. In return, the employer was relieved of its withdrawal liability. The IRS ruled that the transaction did not constitute a reversion subject to the IRC § 4980 excise tax. In effect, the surplus was used to pay the employer's withdrawal liability, but without being subject to any taxes or penalties.

Perhaps the most aggressive use of a plan surplus is to "monetize" it by selling part of the business, including the plan, to another company that has an underfunded plan. Even if the surplus could return only 60 percent of its value when sold, this produces a far greater after-tax return than a reversion would. The savings are so attractive that there are some companies that make their living brokering such transactions. Typically, the plans involved are those of sole-proprietorships or closely held corporations where the bulk of the plan liability is for benefits to the owners. Benefits have likely already been raised to the maximum permitted under IRC § 415 and there are no underfunded plans in the same controlled group with which to merge.

The usual technique is to create a (or use an existing) sister company and then transfer the sponsorship of the plan to the new company. To give the transaction the aura of a business purpose, other assets may be transferred, usually assets that are of little use to the business, especially those with a high basis that would reduce the taxable gain from the sale. The new business is then sold to the buyer seeking the surplus. The plan benefits are usually paid out in a lump sum to the participants, who then roll them over to a new retirement plan or an IRA.

The "monetization" of a plan surplus is viewed as a risky transaction. The relevant IRS rulings to date have dealt only with mergers of overfunded and underfunded plans within the same controlled group and not with buy/sell transactions. The IRS may well challenge such transactions under the tax benefit rule and even argue that the substance of the transaction is in fact a taxable reversion subject to IRC § 4980. See Vince Amoroso, Transferring Pension Assets: IRS is Watching, 25 BNA Pension Rptr. 2064 (1998).

The Revenue Act of 1990 added to the IRC a provision that echoes the idea of de jure withdrawal, but for a limited purpose. Subject to a number of requirements, IRC § 420 allows the transfer of surplus pension assets to an IRC § 401(h) account for the payment of retiree health expenses. "The chief benefit [for the employer of the IRC § 420 mechanism] is that it allows the employer to pay current health care expenses for retirees, their spouses, and dependents under the pension plan of which the Section 401(h) account is a part from excess pension assets, rather than from the general assets of the employer." Michael S. Melbinger & Marianne W. Culver, Excess Plan Assets Can Pay Retiree Benefits, Taxation for Lawyers 4, 7 (Jul.–Aug. 1991). See also Tauber & Bader, supra, at 27–29. IRC §§ 401(h) and 420 are discussed in Chapter 9, infra.

9. *Conversions to cash balance plans.* Although a plan surplus can be transferred tax-free from one defined benefit plan to another via a merger of the plans, it is well established that the transfer of a plan surplus from a defined benefit plan to a defined contribution plan is a taxable reversion. See Lee Engineering Supply Co. v. Commissioner, 101 T.C. 189 (1993); IRS Notice 88–58, 1988–1 C.B. 546. This creates a difficulty for a plan sponsor who has an existing defined benefit plan with a surplus, but who wishes to terminate the plan and switch over to a defined contribution plan.

One solution used by a significant number of large companies is to convert the plan to a cash balance plan. As discussed in Chapter 2, supra, a cash balance plan is a defined benefit plan whose benefit formula mimics the benefits of a defined contribution plan. Benefits under the old formula no longer accrue, so that the plan surplus ends up funding the new cash balance benefits. Because the plan amendment simply changes the benefit formula and no assets are removed from the plan, there is no taxable reversion. Yet the plan sponsor can achieve many of the benefits of a defined contribution plan, such as increased portability and elimination of the structural backloading that skews benefits towards older employees in conventional defined benefit plan formulas.

10. *Fiduciary law: settlor functions.* When an employer who is otherwise a fiduciary terminates a plan in order to capture the reversion, the employer is under no fiduciary duty to abstain from this manifestly self-interested act. DoL, relying upon supporting case law, has stated that "in light of the voluntary nature of the private pension system, [DoL] has concluded that there is a class of discretionary activities which relate to the formation, rather than the management, of plans. These so-called 'settlor' functions include decisions relating to the establishment, termination and design of plans and are not fiduciary activities subject to Title 1 of ERISA." Labor Department Letter on Fiduciary Responsibility and Plan Terminations, reprinted in 13 BNA Pension Reporter 472 (1986) (Mar. 13, 1986, letter from Dennis M. Kass, Ass't Sec'y) [hereafter cited as Kass Letter]. (The concept of the employer's "settlor" or "business" functions is explored in Chapters 13–15, infra.)

The noninurement rule of ERISA § 403(c)(1), the exclusive benefit rule of § 404(a)(1)(A), and the prohibited transaction rule of § 408(b)(9) all contain provisos cross-referring to the reversion authority in § 4044.

The Kass Letter of 1986 takes the position that while the decision to terminate is a settlor function not subject to ERISA fiduciary law, certain "activities undertaken to implement the termination decision are generally fiduciary in nature." Thus, the exercise of discretion in determining whether the preconditions for reversions contained in § 4044(d)(1) have been satisfied falls within the scope of fiduciary discretion envisioned in ERISA § 3(21)(A). Likewise, the "choice of an insurer would appear to involve the type of discretionary authority over the disposition of plan assets covered in section 3(21)(A)."

The plan sponsor's fiduciary responsibilities in selecting an insurer from whom to purchase annuities for the participants in a terminated plan became a central concern in the early 1990s when Executive Life Insurance Co., an insurer that had been prominent in writing annuity contracts for terminating plans, failed. The Executive Life saga is recounted below.

In Beck v. PACE International Union, 551 U.S. 96 (2007), an employer (Crown) in bankruptcy proceedings sought to terminate its overfunded plan by purchasing annuities for the participants, leaving the employer a $5 million reversion. An employee union (PACE), conceding that the decision to terminate or merge a plan is a settlor function, nevertheless argued that in deciding how to terminate the plan, the employer had a fiduciary obligation to consider merging the plan's assets and liabilities with the union's multiemployer plan. The Supreme Court unanimously rejected the union's claim, holding that merger is not a permissible method of terminating a single-employer defined-benefit pension plan.

11. *Tax policy.* It has been argued that the asset reversion excise tax under IRC § 4980 may not adequately recover the tax benefit that is impounded in the surplus. Ippolito contends that "[t]he essence of the tax advantage is that in contrast to profits generated from an investment in the corporation, earnings of the pension fund are not subject to taxation." Ippolito, 5 American J. Tax Policy, supra, at 88. He calculates that, depending upon the interest rate and the number of years at which taxation of pension plan investment assets has been foregone, the portion of an asset reversion attributable to pension tax preferences can exceed 30 percent. Id. at 90 (Table 2).

"The major problem involved in creating an appropriate recovery tax is that no single rate is appropriate in all situations." EBRI, Pension Plan "Surplus": Revert, Transfer, or Hold?, EBRI Issue Brief, Mar. 1989, at 1, 19–20. The GAO reported in 1990 on a study of 55 terminated plans. The study concluded that the then-current 15-percent excise tax on reversion surplus was ineffective to recover the tax benefit impounded in the pension surplus. An average tax rate of 37 percent would have been needed. General Accounting Office, Pension Plan Terminations: Effectiveness of Excise Tax in Recovering Tax Benefits in Asset Reversions (1990).

2.   INSURER DEFAULT: THE FAILURE OF EXECUTIVE LIFE

ERISA allows a terminating plan to discharge its obligations to plan participants by "purchas[ing] irrevocable commitments from an insurer to provide all liabilities under the [plan]." ERISA § 4041(b)(3)(A)(i). Such commitments from an insurer take the form of annuity contracts. The insurance company that issues the annuity contracts replaces the plan as the obligor responsible for paying the participants their retirement benefits. This substitution of insurer for plan is what allows the plan to terminate without defaulting on its pension liabilities.

But what if the insurer defaults? In 1991 the failure of a large insurer active in the pension annuity markets, Executive Life Insurance Co. of California, resulted in defaults that imposed losses on pension plan participants. During the reversion boom of the late 1980s, Executive Life had been particularly aggressive in soliciting annuity business from terminating defined benefit plans. Executive Life attracted this business by undercharging its competitors. Executive Life obtained its price advantage by pursuing a higher risk investment policy, investing heavily in so-called junk bonds. When the junk bond market collapsed, Executive Life became insolvent. In receivership Executive Life was able to pay its pension annuitants about 70 cents on their promised dollars.

Another major insurer, Mutual Benefit Life Insurance Company of New Jersey, also became insolvent in 1991, also as a result of bad investments—in real estate rather than junk bonds. The insolvency was not as severe, and pension annuity defaults, although feared, did not occur.

For background on these events, see Veal & Mackiewicz, supra, at 77–78, 332–35; Harry DeAngelo et al., The Collapse of First Executive Corporation: Junk Bonds, Adverse Publicity, and the "Run on the Bank" Phenomenon, 36 J. Financial Economics 287 (1994); Pension Annuity Protection in Light of the Executive Life Insurance Company Failure: Hearings Before the Subcomm. on Retirement Income and Employment, House Comm. on Aging, 102d Cong., 1st Sess. (1991) (Parts I & II) [hereafter, Pension Annuity Hearings]; General Accounting Office, Private Pensions: Millions of Workers Lose Federal Protection at Retirement (1991) [hereafter, 1991 GAO Report]; Michael S. Melbinger, Insurance Company Insolvency and Retirement Plans, 19 Tax Management Compensation Planning J. 311 (1991); and reports in 18 BNA Pension Rptr. 783, 1081, 1241, 1246, 1524 (1991); 19 id. 200 (1992).

1. *PBGC insurance.* An early question that arose as the Executive Life debacle unfolded was whether the annuitants who had been former participants in PBGC-insured defined benefit plans had any claim to PBGC insurance to restore the value of their Executive Life pension annuities.

PBGC insures single employer and multiemployer defined benefit plans, plans whose assets are held in trust. Insurance company plans, which do not take the trust form, are not PBGC-insured, and they do not pay PBGC premiums. In 1991 as the Executive Life defaults loomed, PBGC insisted that PBGC had no responsibility to guaranty insurance company annuity contracts that had been issued to discharge the accrued liabilities of a terminated defined benefit plan—a plan that had, during the life of the plan, been PBGC-insured.

When, therefore, a terminating DB plan bought Executive Life annuities on which the insurer subsequently defaulted, the transaction extinguished two systems of protection for the plan participants. PBGC insurance ceased when the DB plan terminated, as did the employer's former responsibility as plan sponsor. See "PBGC Letter on PBGC Liability for Payment of Benefits in Case of Annuity Contract Failure," (Jan. 14, 1991) [hereafter, PBGC Liability Letter], reprinted in 18 BNA Pension Rptr. 850 (1991), discussed infra, explaining why PBGC disclaimed responsibility; and "PBGC Letter on Plan Sponsor Liability After Purchase of Group Annuity Contract," (May 3, 1991), reprinted in 18 BNA Pension Rptr. 850 (1991), concluding that the former plan sponsors of terminated plans have "no liability for plan benefits that have been satisfied through the purchase of" now-defaulted annuity contracts.

PBGC reasoned that plan termination is the insurable event in the PBGC insurance system, citing ERISA §§ 4022(a) and 4061. "Nowhere in the statute is PBGC authorized to pay benefits upon the occurrence of any other event, such as the failure of an insurance company." PBGC Liability Letter, supra, 18 BNA Pension Rptr. at 851. "The 'insurable event' is plan termination which, in the case of a sufficient plan, is completed upon final distribution of assets in payment of all benefits under the plan through the purchase of annuity contracts or the distribution of lump sum amounts. The distribution of plan assets in the correct amount and proper form extinguishes the PBGC's guarantee obligation." Id.

In testimony to a committee of Congress, pension law scholar Norman Stein took issue with the PBGC's reading of the statute, and with the argument that "the purchase of an annuity contract is itself the payment of all guaranteed benefits." He said:

> The purchase of an annuity contract from a company without the ability to pay the plan's liabilities is simply not the payment of all plan benefits, no matter how one looks at it. Certainly, the PBGC would not take the position that its guarantees would be extinguished by a plan that satisfied its liabilities by cashing out benefits with counterfeit dollars. Purchasing annuity contracts from insurance companies on the verge of financial collapse may be different from paying benefits with counterfeit money, but only as a matter of degree.

> Moreover, the language of ERISA does not support this position. ERISA has never provided that the purchase of an annuity contract automatically satisfies plan benefits, regardless of whether the insurance company issuing the annuity contract has the ability to make benefit payments over the relevant time horizon. This is a regulatory position invented by the PBGC. . . .

Statement of Norman P. Stein, Pension Annuity Hearings, supra, pt. II, at 70–71.

In reaching the conclusion that it would not protect annuitants against pension default in these circumstances, PBGC was embarrassed to have to disaffirm a contrary position that it had announced in 1981. Responding to a comment on a notice of proposed rulemaking, the agency had said in the preamble to final regulations on termination procedures for sufficient plans that "in the unlikely event that an insurance company should fail and its obligations cannot be satisfied (e.g., through a [state] reinsurance system), the PBGC would provide the necessary benefits." 46 Fed. Reg. 9532, at 9534 (Jan. 28, 1981). A decade later, PBGC backed off. "We have searched PBGC records and found no legal memoranda or other document to support this statement. And, after a detailed and extensive legal analysis of the statutory provisions, we have reached a contrary conclusion. Thus, the statement in the preamble was made without legal analysis, and was simply incorrect." PBGC Liability Letter, supra, at 851–52.

Regarding PBGC's argument that PBGC should not owe benefits to Executive Life annuitants because Executive Life did not pay PBGC insurance premiums, Norman Stein replied that "[t]he PBGC's policy argument is basically that it is an insurance company, and its premiums do not reflect the risk of insurance company failure. [But] PBGC was not conceived primarily as an insurance agency." Stein pointed to ERISA § 4002(a)(2), which describes among the purposes of the PBGC, "to provide for the timely and uninterrupted payment of pension benefits to participants and beneficiaries under plans to which this title [applies]." Stein contended that "[t]he PBGC's position contradicts the principal goal of Title 4, i.e., providing for the timely and uninterrupted payment of pension benefits. The centrality of the Studebaker case to ERISA's passage underscores just how important this goal actually is. It is inconceivable that Congress in enacting ERISA thought it would be okay for benefit payments to disappear whenever a plan decided to transfer liabilities on the cheap to a low-quality insurer." Statement of Norman P. Stein, Pension Annuity Hearings, supra, pt. II, at 71–72.

Does Stein's argument prove too much? Does he not challenge the fundamental architecture of ERISA Title 4 in two respects—(1) Congress' decision to limit the PBGC plan insurance system to trusteed plans, excluding insurance company plans; and (2) Congress' decision to finance the PBGC insurance system through premium income? Why should PBGC honor defaulted annuity contracts from Executive Life for retirees who once were participants of terminated defined benefit plans, while continuing not to help retirees whose employers did business with Executive Life from the beginning, by sponsoring an insurance company plan?

2. *Federalism issues.* An important factor in the initial decision to limit the PBGC system to trusteed defined benefit plans, hence to exclude insurance company plans from PBGC reinsurance, was the concern not to disturb the allocation of regulatory authority over the insurance industry to the states under the McCarran-Ferguson Act of 1945, 15 U.S.C. §§ 1011–1015. Suppose PBGC were to assume responsibility for reinsuring annuity contracts for retirees, at least for annuity contracts arising from terminated defined benefit plans. How would the system work? Could those assets be separated from the insurer's general account? If not, would PBGC have to displace state insurance regulation, partially abrogating the McCarran-Ferguson Act?

In Kayes v. Pacific Lumber Co., 51 F.3d 1449, 1455–57 (9th Cir.1995), one of the cases involving a terminated plan that purchased Executive Life annuities, the Ninth Circuit held that the McCarran-Ferguson Act did not bar ERISA fiduciary claims brought by the former plan participants. On remand the sponsor paid $7 million to settle the case. 23 BNA Pension & Benefits Rptr. 1881 (1996).

Under existing law, most states operate state guaranty funds for the victims of insurance company default. Many of these funds are thinly capitalized, and coverage and conditions vary from state to state. Some states have no such funds, some do not cover pension annuities, most have relatively low caps on amounts covered, and some restrict coverage to state residents, excluding out-of-state victims of an insurer domiciled or operating from within the state. See Honeywell, Inc. v. Minnesota Life & Health Ins. Guaranty Ass'n, 110 F.3d 547 (8th Cir.1997), sustaining the constitutionality of Minnesota legislation retroactively narrowing that state guaranty fund's exposure to claims arising from the Executive Life collapse. For discussion of the state funds and their shortcomings, see Pamela Perun, Putting Annuities Back Into Savings Plans, in Employee Pensions: Policies, Problems and Possibilities 143, 151–52 (2007); GAO, Private Pensions: Protections for Retirees Insurance Annuities Can Be Strengthened (HRD–93–29) (1993); GAO, Private Pensions: Risks to Retirees Posed by Insurance Company Failures (T–HRD–91–23) (1991).

Another possibility is to federalize all termination annuities, having PBGC serve as the annuity provider. The terminating plan would pay the cost of providing the annuities directly to the PBGC at the time of plan termination.

3. *Restore the plan?* Stein's testimony to Congress, supra, contains the suggestion that, on analogy to *PBGC v. LTV Corp.*, supra, the PBGC "could use its authority under [ERISA §] 4047 to restore responsibility for benefit payment to the employer who selected an impaired insurer to assume a plan's pension liabilities." Statement of Norman P. Stein, Pension Annuity Hearings, supra, pt. II, at 78–79 n.12.

Should such a restoration remedy be applied whenever the insurer defaults, regardless of how prudent the sponsor has been in selecting the insurer? Or should the restoration remedy be limited to cases in which the sponsor was imprudent in selecting the particular insurer? In other words, should the terminating sponsor be strictly liable for the subsequent behavior and commercial misfortunes of the insurer? If so, for how long? Would there be tracing problems in applying such a remedy to cases in which the former sponsor was itself dissolved?

4. *Fiduciary law.* DoL has insisted that although the decision to terminate a pension plan is a settlor function that is not subject to ERISA fiduciary standards, certain "activities undertaken to implement the termination decision are generally fiduciary in nature." Labor Department Letter on Fiduciary Responsibility and Plan Terminations, Mar. 13, 1986 (Kass Letter), supra. Among those implementing activities, the "choice of an insurer would appear to involve the type of discretionary authority over the disposition of plan assets covered in [ERISA §] 3(21)(A)."

When the Executive Life defaults occurred, DoL rapidly invoked ERISA fiduciary law in litigation and threatened litigation against the sponsors of terminated plans that had bought Executive Life annuity contracts. Prominent among these cases were Martin v. Pacific Lumber Co., 1993 WL 832744 (N.D.Cal.1993); Martin v. Geosource, Inc., No. H–91–3196 (S.D. Tex); and Martin v. Smith Int'l Inc., No. CV–92–1196 (C.D. Cal.), e.g., Martin v. Pacific Lumber Co., No.CA–91–1812–SBA (N.D. Cal.); Martin v. Magnatek, Inc., No. 91–C–613 (E.D. Wis.). Plan participants and retirees also brought claims for breach of fiduciary duty against sponsors of ongoing plans that had selected Executive Life investment products, mostly so-called guaranteed investment contracts (GICs), as plan investments or investment options. E.g., In re Unisys Savings Plan Litigation, 74 F.3d 420 (3d Cir.1996) (Unisys I) (holding that employer's selection of Executive Life annuities was subject to fiduciary review for prudence under ERISA § 404(a)); In re Unisys Savings Plan Litigation, 173 F.3d 145 (3d Cir.1999) (Unisys II) (sustaining trial court's finding that employer acted prudently).

In some cases plan sponsors assumed the losses on Executive Life GICs, in order to preclude litigation. Revlon, for example, agreed with DoL to guarantee an $88.7 million Executive Life contract. Pensions & Investments, Feb. 21, 1994, at 7. The former owner of Cannon Mills forestalled litigation by personally paying for the shortfall on Executive Life annuities that Cannon Mills had bought to terminate its pension plan. 18 BNA Pension Rptr. 1420 (1991). Several plan sponsors obtained DoL exemptions from ERISA's prohibited transaction rules to allow them (as ERISA parties in interest) to purchase the troubled GICs from their plans, or to advance proceeds to the plan on condition that repayment to the sponsor would be limited to any amounts recovered from the insurer.

See, e.g., PT Exemption No. 92–36, 57 Fed. Reg. 24828 (Jun. 11, 1992) (Campbell Soup Co.; Executive Life); PT Exemption No. 92–34, 57 Fed. Reg. 24828 (Jun. 11, 1992) (Vital Signs, Inc.; Mutual Benefit); PT Exemption No. 92–54, 57 Fed. Reg. 32814 (Jul. 23, 1992) (Miles Inc.; Executive Life).

These conditional restorative payments would in most cases have violated numerous IRC provisions, adversely affecting the qualified status of the plans and resulting in additional income and excise taxes. The IRS resolved this problem by providing a temporary closing agreement program under which a plan sponsor could, if it agreed to certain reasonable conditions, avoid any adverse tax consequences. See Rev. Proc. 92–16, 1992–1 C.B. 673.

The question arose whether former participants or beneficiaries in a terminated plan for whom Executive Life annuities were substituted had standing to sue the plan fiduciaries for breach of fiduciary duty in selecting Executive Life as the provider. Some cases held that such persons fell outside ERISA's definitions of participants and beneficiaries, e.g., Kayes v. Pacific Lumber Co., 1993 WL 187730 (N.D.Cal.1993), aff'd and reversed in part, 51 F.3d 1449 (1995); Maher v. Strachan Shipping Co., 17 E.B.C. 1700 (E.D.La.1993). The Ninth Circuit decided oppositely, in Waller v. Blue Cross of California, 32 F.3d 1337 (9th Cir.1994). Congress intervened to settle the point with the grandly named "Pension Annuitants Protection Act," enacted in the fall of 1994 but retroactive to 1993, which amends ERISA to add § 502(a)(9). The new provision authorizes suit by a former plan participant or beneficiary, as well as by the Secretary of Labor or by a plan fiduciary, in cases alleging breach of fiduciary duty arising from the purchase of insurance contracts in plan termination settings. The Fifth Circuit upheld the constitutionality of the legislation in Maher v. Strachan Shipping Co., 68 F.3d 951, 957 (5th Cir.1995), reversing the 1993 district court opinion.

The fiduciary cases often allege imprudent procedures as well as breach of the duty of loyalty, that is the duty under ERISA § 404(a)(1)(A) to act "solely in the interest of the participants and beneficiaries" and "for the exclusive purpose [of] providing benefits to participants and their beneficiaries." Thus, in the *Pacific Lumber* case, DoL contended that the fiduciaries disregarded the recommendations of their own insurance expert, who cautioned them about the level of junk bonds in Executive Life's portfolio and pointed to the superior claims-paying ability of several of the other insurers who bid for the annuity contract. 18 BNA Pension Rptr. 991 (1991). In the *Smith International* case, DoL contended that the terminating sponsor hired Hewitt Associates, the consulting actuaries, to solicit bids from insurers. Hewitt obtained bids from five leading insurers. Smith disregarded the bids, contacted Executive Life on its own, and placed the contract there, because Executive Life's lower bid increased the amount of the reversion. DoL alleged that Smith acted without investigating Executive Life's financial stability, credit-worthiness, or claims-paying ability. 19 BNA Pension Rptr. 435 (1992). In *Geosource*, the firm bought Executive Life annuities without soliciting other bids. 18 BNA Pension Rptr. 2012 (1991). DoL's *Magnatek* suit alleged that MagnaTek bought Executive Life annuities even though Executive Life was a 10 percent shareholder of Magnatek and thus a party in interest, in violation of ERISA's prohibited transactions rules. 18 BNA Pension Rptr. 991 (1991), 17 BNA Pension Rptr. 587–88 (1990). In both *Geosource* and *Magnatek,* the former plan sponsors settled the cases by making good on the amount of the Executive Life defaults. 19 BNA Pension Rptr. 805 (1992).

What does ERISA fiduciary law require of a terminating sponsor? There is an inherent conflict of interest in the purchase of plan termination annuity contracts. The risk/return curve lowers the price to the sponsor as it increases the risk to the annuitant. In Congressional testimony in 1991, DoL's Assistant Secretary for PWBA, David G. Ball, said that terminating employers have been continuously under a fiduciary obligation to "attempt to obtain the safest annuity available to the plan." Statement of David G. Ball, Pension Annuity Hearings, supra, pt. II, at 19, a position reiterated when the DoL issued Interpretive Bulletin 95–1, codified as 29 C.F.R. § 2509.95–1. As originally issued, the interpretive bulletin said that "a fiduciary's decision to purchase more risky, lower-priced annuities in order to ensure or maximize a reversion of excess assets that will be paid solely to the employer-sponsor [would] violate the fiduciary's duties under ERISA to act solely in the interest of the plan participants and beneficiaries."

However, the PPA included a "clarification" provision, Section 625, which gave the Secretary of Labor one year to "issue final regulations clarifying that the selection of an annuity contract as an optional form of distribution from an individual account plan to a participant or beneficiary . . . is not subject to the safest available annuity standard under Interpretive Bulletin 95–1," but is otherwise subject to all applicable fiduciary standards. 29 C.F.R. § 2509.95–1 has been so revised. Thus, plan sponsors must still select annuity contracts in accordance with prudent procedures of risk and cost analysis.

Executive Life enjoyed top ratings from the leading rating agencies, A.M. Best and Standard & Poor's, until January 1990. "Don't Blame Ratings Agencies," Business Insurance, Mar. 9, 1992, at 8. If the experts are unable to spot trouble in an insurer's portfolio until the eve of collapse, can plan fiduciaries be expected to do it, even with expert guidance? If not, is fiduciary law simply inadequate to the problem? What would be the policy implications of such a conclusion?

The most prominent fiduciary litigation arising from the Executive Life debacle has been the series of opinions that culminated in *Unisys II,* supra. The case did not arise in the setting of plan termination, but as the result of a loss incurred by an ongoing plan when it selected Executive Life GICs as plan investments. The Third Circuit held that the employer did not breach its fiduciary obligation of prudent investing when it caused the plan to make the investments. The court emphasized that the employer consulted investment experts, had sound reasons for preferring various features of the Executive Life GICs, and reasonably relied upon Executive Life's superior ratings. For a contrary result, see Bussian v. RJR Nabisco, Inc., 223 F.3d 286 (5th Cir.2000), disparaging "blind reliance" on experts and credit ratings, and finding that "a reasonable factfinder could conclude that RJR placed its interests in the reversion ahead of the beneficiaries' interests in full and timely payment of their benefits." Id. at 306.

5. *Discouraging annuities?* The Executive Life saga has shaped a principle of ERISA fiduciary law with ramifications well beyond plan termination practice. The cases have established that selecting an annuity provider is a fiduciary function, requiring compliance with ERISA's fiduciary duties of prudence and loyalty. The question has arisen of whether this liability has played a role in deterring the sponsors of defined contribution plans from offering annuity-type alternatives to lump sum distributions. Annuitization is often a highly desirable way for a plan participant to draw down accumulated pension wealth. Annuitization protects against outliving one's pension wealth, and by transferring responsibility for investing the funds from the participant to the annuity company, it substitutes professional for amateur investment management. Yet only about a quarter to a third of defined contribution plans offer annuity options; in one sample, the percentage of plans offering annuities fell from 31 percent in 1999 to 17 percent in 2003. Perun, supra, at 148 (citing Hewitt, GAO, BLS, and Profit Sharing Council data).

Perun writes that "the real reason why plan sponsors don't offer annuities" is that legal advisers strongly advise against them, because offering annuity options "expose[s] plan sponsors to a significant and long-term risk of fiduciary liability." Id. at 149. She points to the known weaknesses of the state guaranty funds as bearing on this liability, id. at 151–52, because they increase the riskiness of annuity products. The danger of hindsight bias in the courts when an annuity provider fails is large, as evidenced, perhaps, in *Bussian*, supra.

It is doubtful that the change effected by Section 625 of the PPA, discussed in note 4, supra, has had any effect on the failure of plan sponsors to offer annuities in defined contribution plans.

CHAPTER 7

SPOUSAL AND OTHER THIRD-PARTY INTERESTS

Analysis

Introduction

The central relationship in a pension plan is that of employer and employee. In the prototypical single-employer plan, the employer sponsors a savings scheme for the employee's retirement. The employee, however, wears other hats. He or she has relationships outside the workplace that may give rise to claims on the pension savings. Pension law must deal with these third-party claims. The most important of third-party claimants is the employee's spouse, and much of this chapter concerns the rights of the nonemployee spouse. A much less common but legally quite troublesome type of third-party interest is the claim founded on the employee's wrongdoing, that is, the claim made by the employee's victim. The chapter concludes with a unit on the rights of the employee's creditors in bankruptcy against the employee's pension assets.

A. THE ANTIALIENATION RULE

The bedrock principle that underlies ERISA's treatment of third-party claims is the antialienation or antiassignment rule, also called the spendthrift rule. ERISA § 206(d)(1) requires: "Each pension plan shall provide that benefits provided under the plan may not be assigned or alienated." IRC § 401(a)(13) imposes a similar rule as a condition of tax qualification. Note well that the antialienation rule applies to pension plans only, not to welfare benefit plans. The Seventh Circuit has said of this language that "the addition of 'alienation' to 'assignment' makes crystal clear that the anti-assignment provision bars involuntary as well as voluntary assignments of pension-plan benefits." Morlan v. Universal Guaranty Life Ins. Co., 298 F.3d 609, 614 (7th Cir.2002).

1. *The protective or spendthrift policy.* The congressional conference report on ERISA ascribes no stated purpose to the antialienation rule, doubtless on the ground that the purpose is too obvious for words. The antialienation rule is protective. It prevents the participant from doing indirectly what most plans forbid directly, namely, spending retirement savings before retirement. It would scarcely make sense to stop the participant from drawing down his or her pension account for current consumption if the participant's creditor could present the bills arising from the participant's consumption spree to the pension plan by way of assignment or in the form of a judgment debt.

The American law of trusts has for a century permitted the settlor of a private trust to impose spendthrift terms, terms that protect the trust beneficiaries against their own improvidence by preventing them from alienating the corpus of the trust. Here is a fairly typical spendthrift clause, from the trust instrument that was litigated in Shelley v. Shelley, 354 P.2d 282, 284 (Or.1960): "Each beneficiary hereunder is hereby restrained from alienating, anticipating, encumbering, or in any manner assigning his or her interest or estate, either in principal or income, and is without power so to do, nor shall such interest or estate be subject to his or her liabilities or obligations nor to judgment or other legal process, bankruptcy proceedings or claims of creditors or others."

Despite the similarity to conventional spendthrift trust law, ERISA's antialienation rule differs in important respects. In a private trust, the drafter needs to insert the spendthrift clause in the trust instrument. ERISA's antialienation rule, by contrast, is a mandatory term that the statute requires every pension trust to contain. Until recent decades it was relatively uncommon to see a spendthrift clause in a private trust. The trust settlor imposed such a term only when there was some particular reason to doubt the ability of the beneficiary ("the spendthrift") to manage his or her finances. Spendthrift clauses have now become more common in private trusts; some drafters routinely include such a clause in every trust.

Trust law has developed certain exceptions that limit the scope of the spendthrift immunity against certain privileged creditors. One of these exceptions—allowing the spendthrift beneficiary's domestic relations creditors to attach the trust funds—has, with the enactment of REAct in 1984, acquired an important ERISA analogue, discussed in Section B of this chapter, infra. For the trust rule, see Restatement (Third) of Trusts § 59(a) (2003). Another important trust-law exception, which favors creditors who have supplied necessaries (e.g., food, shelter, medical care), id., § 59(b), has no counterpart in ERISA.

ERISA's antialienation rule thus weighs more heavily on the pension trust than spendthrift law does on the private gratuitous trust. The ERISA rule is mandatory, hence universal, whereas spendthrift trusts arise only under the terms of the instrument; and the ERISA rule does not replicate all the common law exceptions. The stringency of ERISA's antialienation rule can be seen to bespeak a pension law protective policy of special intensity: Retirement funds shall remain inviolate until retirement.

2. *Questioning the protective policy.* Reflection should raise some doubts about whether this protective policy is consistently pursued, and about whether its purposes can be achieved. Lump sum distributions can occur before retirement, especially when the participant's employment is terminated, but also in various other circumstances. The option to elect lump sum distribution (LSD) has been rare in defined benefit plans, apart from the provision for cashing out small plan balances of departing workers, although the spread of cash balance plans has made LSDs more common within the defined benefit world. By contrast, LSD options are prevalent in many defined contribution plans, especially profit sharing and 401(k) plans. In such cases, the participant or beneficiary has the option to use the proceeds for consumption whenever he or she chooses (subject to the 10 percent penalty for early withdrawal when plan proceeds are distributed before the participant turns 59 1/2). Since in these circumstances participants are not effectively prevented from reaching pension money before retirement, should creditors be disadvantaged on the false premise that pension assets are inviolate until retirement?

Furthermore, as mentioned in Chapter 1, there is reason to doubt how effective pension policy can hope to be in inducing a pension plan participant to save for retirement if the participant is determined to prefer current consumption. Even if pension law were to succeed in preventing the participant from obtaining access to the pension proceeds during the years of active employment, the participant remains free to engage in compensating consumption activity outside the pension accounts. Whether or not articulated, the worker's inclination may be to say: "Force me to save more than I want to save in my pension accounts and I'll dissave in my other accounts, for example, in my nonpension savings or in my home mortgage." Bear in mind the coverage data from Chapter 1, which indicates that pension coverage affects mostly the best paid half of the workforce, precisely the people most likely to have other assets.

The issue, in other words, is: How effective can the protective policy be when it is limited to a single type of asset, the pension account? For the suggestion that pension plans achieve only 35 cents of increased retirement savings for each dollar in the fund, see Alicia H. Munnell, The Economics of Private Pensions 77 (1982).

Leaving aside the question of effectiveness, does Congress have any business interfering with individual liberty in attempting to pressure people to alter the patterns of consumption and saving they would achieve voluntarily? Is it fair to prefer that policy over the interests of innocent creditors or tort victims?

A curious departure from the protective policy has grown up in cases in which the plan participant waives pension benefits in order to settle pending or threatened litigation. See, e.g., Rhoades v. Casey, 196 F.3d 592, 599 (5th Cir.1999), in which the former CEO of a failed bank waived his pension entitlement, as part of a deal to settle regulatory charges. The Fifth Circuit held that it would be "an unreasonable interpretation" of ERISA's antialienation provision to treat that measure as "frustrat[ing] knowing and voluntary settlements, such as [this one]." If the purpose of the antialienation rule is to preserve pension assets for retirement, why would it have been unreasonable to prevent the participant from applying these assets to this preretirement use? For a discussion of *Rhoades* and related cases see Albert Feuer, When are Releases of Claims for ERISA Plan Benefits Effective?, 38 J. Marshall L. Rev. 773 (2005).

3. *Compare the self-settled spendthrift trust.* Restatement (Second) of Trusts § 156(1) (1959) provides that spendthrift protections are ineffective when the settlor creates the trust "for his own benefit." Accord, Restatement (Third) of Trusts § 58(2) (2003). Scott, the original Restatement reporter, stated the rationale for the rule in his treatise: "It is plainly against public policy to permit the owner of property to create for his or her own benefit an interest in the property that is beyond the reach of creditors." 3 Austin W. Scott, William F. Fratcher & Mark L. Archer, Scott and Archer on Trusts § 15.4, at 954–55 (5th ed. 2007).

This prohibition upon the self-settled spendthrift trust was universal in American trust law until the mid-1990s, when two states, Alaska and Delaware, began to depart from it, permitting so-called "asset protection trusts." The movement to validate asset protection trusts, which permit the trustee to distribute trust proceeds to the settlor, is discussed in Adam J. Hirsch, Fear Not the Asset Protection Trust, 27 Cardozo L. Rev. 2685 (2006); Stewart E. Sterk, Asset Protection Trusts: Trust Law's Race to the Bottom?, 85 Cornell L. Rev. 1035, 1043–44 (2000); John E. Sullivan III, Gutting the Rule Against Self-Settled Trusts: How the New Delaware Trust Law Competes with Offshore Trusts, 23 Delaware. J. Corp. L. 423 (1998).

Contrast the rule against self-settled spendthrift trusts with the reality of the pension trust. Because pensions are deferred wages, regardless of whether the pension plan is contributory or noncontributory, each plan participant is in an important sense the settlor of his or her own pension account. Does the respect for creditors' rights that has led trust law to refuse to enforce self-settled spendthrift trusts undercut the rationale of ERISA's antialienation rule?

4. *Debt of a plan vs. debt of a participant.* In Milgram v. The Orthopedic Assocs. Defined Contribution Pension Plan v. Orthopedic Assoc. of 65 Penn Ave, 666 F.3d 68 (2d Cir. 2011), the Second Circuit addressed the question whether a federal court order requiring a defined contribution plan to return funds that were erroneously transferred out of a plan participant's account before the plan recouped those funds violated ERISA's antialienation provision. A divorce settlement between the participant and his wife entitled the ex-wife to half the balance of the participant's profit-sharing plan and a fixed amount from his defined contribution plan. As a result of a clerical error, half of both plan accounts were transferred to the wife, giving her $663,848 more than she was entitled to receive. In the participant's suit against the plan, the district court entered judgment against the plan in the amount of $1.57 million, representing the principal amount, accumulated earnings and prejudgment interest, as well as ordering the ex-wife to pay restitution to the plan. The Second Circuit rejected the plan's argument that requiring payment of the award before the plan recovered from the ex-

wife would violate ERISA's antialienation provision. In the view of the court, Section 206(d)(1) of ERISA "does not prevent pension plan assets from being used to satisfy a judicial judgment that has been entered against the plan itself." Id. at 73.

B. SPOUSAL ANNUITIES

1. RETIREMENT EQUITY ACT OF 1984

Prior to the enactment of the Retirement Equity Act (REAct) in 1984, the spouse of a pension plan participant, the so-called nonemployee spouse, had rather limited rights to share in the participant's pension. REAct vastly augments the nonemployee spouse's interests. These interests arise upon dissolution of the marriage. Marriages can terminate in either of two ways, divorce or death.

1. *Dissolution on divorce.* REAct's solution to the problem of pension rights in marriages ending in divorce was foreshadowed in pre-REAct case law, noted in Chapter 17, infra, in which the federal courts refused to apply ERISA's preemption clause to state domestic relations orders dealing with pension assets. REAct prescribes conditions for enforcing state-court decrees that divide or transfer pension property, so-called "qualified domestic relations orders" (QDROs), discussed infra in Section C of this chapter. A QDRO may include provisions for support of a child or other dependent, as well as the spousal share.

REAct's provisions for enforcing QDROs effectively cured a statutory oversight, ratifying the judicial consensus that neither antialienation nor preemption should insulate pension wealth from the reach of state domestic relations jurisdiction.

2. *Dissolution on death: survivor shares.* For marriages ending on death REAct requires that pension plans create contingent survivorship interests for the nonemployee spouse in the participant's pension. ERISA § 205(a). These spousal interests arise if the nonemployee spouse survives the participant, but not when the nonemployee spouse predeceases the participant. These entitlements were previously unknown in state or federal law.

The guiding purpose of the 1984 legislation was to enhance the retirement income security of the homemaker, characteristically the wife, in traditional support marriages, in which only the employed spouse has significant earnings opportunities outside the home. If both spouses could be predicted to have substantially equal earnings and pension-saving opportunities, neither spouse would be particularly likely to need pension support from the other. In conventional marriage patterns, however, childrearing and homemaking have been women's work, and the homebound wife has been cut off from opportunities for doing her own pension saving. In seven out of ten marriages that end on death, the wife is the survivor. If the husband's pension income stream terminates on his death, the widow is left without support. REAct, which is expressed in gender-neutral terms, creates a survivorship interest in the nonemployee spouse. Said Congresswoman Geraldine Ferraro in introducing the bill that became REAct: "Women are shortchanged by private pension plans because the system does not truly recognize the contribution that women make to the economy or take into account women's unique work patterns, patterns which revolve around childrearing and other family responsibilities. [The homemaker] is dependent on her husband and his earnings and at the mercy of death or divorce." Pension Equity for Women, Hearings before the Subcomm. on Labor Management Relations of the House Comm. on Education and Labor, 98th Cong., 1st Sess. 26 (1983). Given the purpose of REAct, one of us (Pratt) always found it ironic that the participants in his clients' plans who most strongly objected to the REAct were women, many of whom did not want their husbands to receive an interest in their plan benefits.

REAct requires that pension plans adopt two distinct systems for protecting the nonemployee spouse from the financial consequences of dissolution on death, although the nonemployee spouse can waive either entitlement. First, if the participant survives to retirement age, REAct requires that the plan provide that the participant's annuity be a "qualified joint and survivor annuity" (QJSA), under which payments continue for the lives both of the participant and of the nonemployee spouse. Second, for the case in which a vested plan participant dies before retirement, REAct requires that the plan recognize the nonemployee spouse as a plan beneficiary, with an interest that survives the participant's death, called a "qualified preretirement survivor annuity" (QPSA).

The REAct rules governing spousal survivorship benefits appear as ERISA § 205 and again in the tax law as IRC §§ 401(a)(11), 417. Under the 1978 reorganization plan between the departments of Treasury and Labor, Treasury has the interpretive authority over benefit accrual issues. Accordingly, the regulations governing the QJSA and QPSA, which appear in question and answer format, are found at Treas.Reg. § 1.401(a)–20.

3. *Impact.* According to a General Accounting Office study, REAct has materially increased the level of spousal survivorship coverage. Before REAct, the employee unilaterally decided whether to take the pension distribution in survivorship form. The GAO reports that the "survivor benefit coverage rate," defined as the rate at which married men chose the joint and survivor annuity after the spousal consent requirement took effect, increased by 15 percent, from 65 percent before REAct to 80 percent in 1988–89. General Accounting Office, Pension Plans: Survivor Benefit Coverage for Wives Increased after 1984 Pension Law 7 (1992).

4. *Definition of Spouse.* This is discussed in section C.1.9 of this chapter.

5. *Literature.* For a detailed account of the historical background to REAct's survivorship interests, including Congress' failure to include them in ERISA in 1974 and the developments of the intervening decade, see Camilla E. Watson, Broken Promises Revisited: The Window of Vulnerability for Surviving Spouses under ERISA, 76 Iowa L. Rev. 431, 449–91 (1991). For literature on QDRO practice, see Jayne E. Zanglein, Lawrence A. Frolik & Susan J. Stabile, ERISA Litigation, ch. 27 (4th ed. 2011); David Clayton Carrad, The Complete QDRO Handbook: Dividing ERISA, Military and Civil Service Pensions and Collecting Child Support from Employee Benefit Plans (3d ed. 2010); John H. Williamson, The

Attorney's Handbook on Qualified Domestic Relations Orders (3d ed. 2000); Michael B. Snyder, Qualified Domestic Relations Orders (1998 ed.).

QUESTIONS

1.   If the feminization of poverty was the concern that motivated REAct, was ERISA a sensible place for Congress to attempt to deal with the problem, since, as explained in Chapter 1, supra, the private pension system covers mainly the wealthier half of the workforce?

2.   REAct has been called the largest wealth transfer in American history, because the survivorship rights were imposed retroactively in 1984 upon pension accumulations from previous years. Why was the retroactivity of REAct not thought to be unfair? Why, that is, did Congress not impose the new survivorship regime only prospectively?

3.   Wife abandoned Husband, and Husband sued for divorce but died before divorce was granted. In accordance with plan terms, Husband designated Daughter to receive the $2-plus million in his plan account. Wife claimed her survivor's QPSA share. Should her abandonment of Husband affect her interest? See In re Lefkowitz, 767 F.Supp. 501, 507 n.11 (S.D.N.Y.1991), aff'd sub nom. Lefkowitz v. Arcadia Trading Co. Ltd. Benefit Pension Plan, 996 F.2d 600 (2d Cir.1993). Wife died before the litigation was resolved. Should her estate be allowed to receive the QPSA survivorship interest in preference to Daughter? See id.

4.   Kentucky has a statute that a spouse who abandons the other and lives in adultery forfeits his or her right to property in the estate of the nonadulterous spouse. Does the Kentucky statute defeat the adulterous spouse's QPSA claim? See Moore v. Philip Morris Cos., 8 F.3d 335 (6th Cir.1993).

5.   When a plan neglects to comply with REAct's requirement that the plan adopt terms implementing the QJSA/QPSA system, what is the remedy? In Lefkowitz v. Arcadia Trading Co. Ltd. Benefit Pension Plan, 996 F.2d 600 (2d Cir.1993), the court held that the plan should be treated as though it had been properly amended to adopt the QJSA/QPSA survivorship interests. In Gallagher v. Park West Bank & Trust Co., 921 F.Supp. 867 (D.Mass.1996), a district court following this principle held that it would not treat the plan as having adopted a merely optional feature of the QJSA/QPSA system—in the particular case, the plan's power under ERISA § 205(f)(1) to impose a minimum one-year duration rule on the marriage before the QPSA entitlement attaches.

2.   QUALIFIED JOINT AND SURVIVOR ANNUITIES

1.   *Pre-REAct QJSA.* As originally enacted, ERISA § 205(a) (and IRC § 401(a)(11)(A)) required that if a plan made any provision for the payment of benefits in the form of an annuity (the common form of distribution for defined benefit plans and for money purchase defined contribution plans) the plan had to offer as one annuity option a "qualified joint and survivor annuity" (QJSA). Pre-REAct, the participant decided whether to elect the QJSA or the higher paying single life annuity that expired on the participant's death. The participant had the

unilateral power to choose a single life annuity and thereby to impose on the nonemployee spouse the consequence that pension income would cease completely upon the participant's death.

ERISA § 205(d) (as revised by REAct, previously § 205(g)(3)) defines a QJSA as an annuity for the life of the participant with a survivor annuity for the life of the participant's spouse, which survivor annuity is not less than half nor more than 100 percent of the annuity that is payable during their joint lives; and which is the actuarial equivalent of a single life annuity for the life of the participant. The most common form is the 50 percent survivor annuity, under which, if the nonemployee spouse survives the participant, he or she is entitled to an annuity at least half as large as that paid during their joint lives.

The 2006 PPA requires plans to offer an additional survivor annuity option, called a qualified optional survivor annuity (QOSA). ERISA § 205(c)(1)(A)(ii). If the plan's QJSA has a survivor annuity less than 75 percent of the annuity payable during the joint lives of the participant and spouse, the plan must offer a 75 percent survivor annuity option. If the QJSA has a survivor percentage greater than or equal to 75 percent, the plan must offer a 50 percent survivor annuity option. ERISA § 205(d)(2)(b)(i).   .

2. *Transferring the election to the nonemployee spouse.* REAct's major reform was to transfer, in effect, from the participant to the nonemployee spouse the power to choose joint and survivor annuitization. ERISA now provides that the participant may elect to waive the QJSA only if "the spouse of the participant consents in writing." ERISA § 205(c)(2)(A)(i).

REAct makes the QJSA the default option. Unless the participant's spouse elects to decline the QJSA, the pension must be paid in that form.

3. *Marital duration.* Section 205(b)(3) carries forward the pre-REAct rule that the plan may contain a term requiring that a marriage have endured for a minimum of one year before the nonemployee spouse qualifies for the QJSA. In Cajun Indus., L.L.C., 401(k) Plan v. Kidder, 454 Fed. Appx. 294 (5th Cir. Dec. 8, 2011), the Fifth Circuit underscored that a plan may, but need not contain such a term, holding that if a plan does not contain a term requiring that the marriage have endured for a minimum of one year, a spouse will be treated as a surviving spouse regardless of the duration of the marriage.

4. *Procedures for waiver.* The election to waive the QJSA must be in writing and either notarized or else witnessed by a plan representative. ERISA § 205(c)(2)(A)(iii). Noncompliance with this requirement has been held to render the spousal waiver ineffective. Lasche v. George W. Lasche Basic Profit Sharing Plan, 111 F.3d 863 (11th Cir.1997). In Butler v. Encyclopedia Britannica, Inc., 41 F.3d 285, 294 (7th Cir.1994), dealing with a claim of ineffective notarization for a QPSA waiver, the court said that "we cannot adopt a substantial compliance doctrine as a matter of federal common law in this case if it would conflict with ERISA's literal requirement that a spousal consent be 'witnessed.'"

ERISA § 205(c)(2)(A)(i) also requires that a spousal waiver designate another beneficiary, "which may not be changed without" the waiving spouse's further consent. In Hagwood v. Newton, 282 F.3d 285, 291 (4th Cir.2002), a premarital agreement that did not satisfy this requirement was found ineffective. The court said that this requirement "gives the surviving spouse control over who would receive the benefits in lieu of the surviving spouse." It follows that a spousal waiver may be conditioned, for example, on the condition that the account proceeds be distributed in a lump sum to a rollover IRA irrevocably naming the spouse as the primary death beneficiary.

Once made, the election can be altered only with spousal consent, § 205(c)(2)(A)(ii). Each plan is required to provide a written explanation of the QJSA and of the election procedures, § 205(c)(3)(A). Although ERISA previously required that an election be made within 90 days of the annuity starting date, the PPA extended the period to 180 days, § 205(c)(7). The idea is to have an election made shortly before the participant retires, when the spouses can judge their respective needs for retirement income in the light of their other resources. The statute somberly declares that no spousal waiver is required of an unmarried participant, § 205(c)(2)(B).

Consent to waiver of surviving spouse benefits pretty obviously requires that the surviving spouse have the mental capacity to consent at the time the waiver is executed. In Ponsetti v. GE Pension Plan, 614 F.3d 684 (7th Cir. 2010), an employee originally designated his wife as the primary beneficiary under GE's pension plan. Ten years later he signed a declaration of trust that would divide his pension assets among his wife, children, siblings and parents. He completed a signed beneficiary designation form designating the trustee as primary beneficiary of his plan benefits. The form contained a signature purportedly that of his wife, although the employee who notarized the form did not watch the wife sign it. The Seventh Circuit upheld the plan's denial of the trust's claim for benefits, finding that the plan's determination was based on "voluminous evidence of [the spouse's] incapacity at the time she supposedly signed the document." Id. at 694.

The Small Business Job Protection Act of 1996 required the Secretary of the Treasury to develop sample language, written to be understood by the average person, that could be incorporated in a form used for a spouse to consent to a QJSA or QPSA waiver. The IRS responded by developing form language found at Notice 97–10, 1997–1 C.B. 370.

Negligence by the plan administrator in notifying participants of the pre-REAct QJSA election rules has been held to be a breach of fiduciary duty, justifying the award of a survivor's annuity as remedy. Kaszuk v. Bakery and Confectionery Union and Industry Intern. Pension Fund, 791 F.2d 548 (7th Cir.1986). Consider in the light of your study of the Supreme Court's restrictive treatment of ERISA remedy law, infra Chapter 16, whether *Kaszuk* would be decided similarly today. Should similar liability pertain when a plan administrator bungles the REAct notice rules governing waiver of the survivor's annuity?

Although the Seventh Circuit continues to reject applicability of the doctrine of substantial compliance to the issue of validity of a waiver, it has decided, based on ERISA's failure to define the term "witnessed," that a participant may validly witness his wife's consent to waive a survivor annuity without being physically present when his wife signed the consent form. The court said that "[w]hen a plan participant, who is also the plan representative, signs a beneficiary-designation form requiring spousal consent, gives the form to his consenting wife, who in turn signs it in multiple places acknowledging her consent and returns it to her husband," invalidating the consent "would produce an absurd result." Burns v. Orthotek, Inc. Employees' Pension Plan and Trust, 657 F.3d 571, 576–577 (7th Cir. 2012).

    5. *Premarital waiver: Who is a spouse, and when?* In spousal property planning, persons intending to marry may enter into an antenuptial agreement to govern their property relations in advance of the marriage. See, e.g., the Uniform Premarital Agreement Act (1983), encouraging such contracts under conditions of thorough disclosure and fairness; and Uniform Probate Code § 2–213 (1993 rev.), providing for waiver of forced share rights "before or after marriage, by a written contract" duly signed. The Uniform Premarital Agreement Act envisions that a premarital agreement "may include rights [in] employee benefit plans [and] pension and retirement [accounts]." Id. § 1 (official comment). Estate planners especially recommend the use of such premarital agreements in the case of remarriage later in life, when one or both spouses have children by a former marriage, in order to mesh the support undertakings of the new marriage with the succession interests of the children.

    To the dismay of the estate planning bar, REAct has had the effect of preventing effective premarital agreements about ERISA-covered pension wealth. ERISA § 205(c)(2)(A) requires the written consent of the spouse, and the governing Treasury regulation takes the position that someone who is not yet the spouse cannot so consent. Treas.Reg. § 1.401(a)–20, A–28, endorsed in *Hagwood*, supra, 282 F.3d at 290; Manning v. Hayes, 212 F.3d 866 (5th Cir.2000); Pedro Enterprises, Inc. v. Perdue, 998 F.2d 491, 494 (7th Cir.1993); Hurwitz v. Sher, 982 F.2d 778 (2d Cir.1992). See generally, Lynn Wintriss, Waiver of REA Rights in Premarital Agreements, Probate & Property 16 (May/Jun. 1993); Michael D. Rose, Why Antenuptial Agreements Cannot Relinquish Survivor Benefits, 43 Florida L. Rev. 723 (1991).

    Should federal law facilitate deceit and fraud? If Mary insists that she will marry John only on condition that John will not on Mary's death advance any claim to Mary's pension wealth, which Mary has designated under the pension plan to pass to her children of a former marriage, and John so promises in writing, should John be allowed to claim Mary's pension wealth anyhow under ERISA § 205(c)(2)(A)? Or should John be estopped to plead his own fraud?

    Mattei v. Mattei, 126 F.3d 794 (6th Cir.1997), concerned the usual parties to litigation about antenuptial waivers, spouse of the second marriage against children of the first. Louis married Maria late in life. Their antenuptial agreement provided that Louis' estate would pay her a lifetime support of $300 per week and allow her to occupy the marital home for life. In return, Maria waived all claims to Louis' other assets, including his ERISA-covered pension plan. The agreement did not comply with the REAct standards for waiving the QJSA. After Louis' death, Maria demanded her QJSA share and the plan complied. Louis' estate responded by ceasing to pay her the $300 weekly allowance due under the antenuptial agreement. Maria sued under ERISA § 510, the antidiscrimination measure discussed in Chapter 4, supra, which forbids "interfering with the attainment of any right" under the plan. The Sixth Circuit, in a 2–1 opinion by Judge Boggs, held that her complaint stated a cause of action. Judge Merritt dissented, arguing that the estate's decision to withhold non-ERISA-covered assets was not an ERISA violation. He would have remitted the case to state law. "If it was [Louis'] intention to allow his wife to choose the trust assets or the nontrust ERISA assets, but not both, then the [estate's] action should be upheld, but if not, then it should be set aside by the state court." Id. at 810. Judge Merritt does not explain how he would reconcile that result with ERISA preemption. Can you? Consider this question in the light of *Boggs v. Boggs*, discussed in Section D, infra. For commentary on *Mattei*, see "Boggs Bobbles *Mattei* by Blowing *Boggs*," 6 ERISA Litigation Rptr. 16 (No. 5, Dec. 1997).

6. *Marital waiver: the 180-day rule.* Estate planning is also frustrated by REAct's requirement that a spousal waiver of the QJSA entitlement not be made more than 180 days in advance of the annuity starting date. ERISA § 205(c)(7)(A). Although an improvement over the 90-day rule previously imposed, the 180-day rule still impedes long term estate planning, and has the potential to create "creates serious, and sad, difficulties if the employee's spouse is unable to consent to the desired estate plan due to mental disability. In that case, the consent must be provided by the spouse's legal guardian." Natalie B. Choate, Love, Marriage and the Retirement Plan, 142 Trusts & Estates 58, 62 (Nov. 2003), citing Treas.Reg. § 1.401(a)–20, A–27.

7. *Plans affected.* When REAct's QJSA provisions were enacted in 1984, the defined benefit plan paying annuitized benefits was still the prevalent type of pension plan. REAct's QJSA rules simply impose conditions on the statutorily permitted form for such annuities. REAct requires all defined benefit plans and all money purchase defined contribution plans to offer QJSA coverage (and hence to offer annuity coverage). ERISA § 205(b)(1)(A) and (B), cross-referencing § 302, regarding which see § 301(a)(8).

Extending spousal protection to defined contribution plans such as 401(k) plans that commonly pay benefits in lump sums rather than as annuities was harder for the REAct drafters. Instead of requiring QJSAs, REAct requires such plans to provide that the participant's entire vested account balance be "payable in full, on the death of the participant, to the participant's surviving spouse." ERISA § 205(b)(1)(C)(i). In such a case, unless the spouse executes a valid waiver of the QJSA, a married participant cannot name a nonspouse to receive the account balance upon the participant's death. See, e.g., Donohue v. Shell Provident Fund, 656 F.Supp. 905 (S.D.Tex.1987) (beneficiary designations leaving most of three plan accounts to participant's children and grandchildren held ineffective; spouse awarded 100 percent under REAct-mandated plan term). See also MidAmerican Pension and Employee Benefits Plans Administrative Committee v. Michael G. Cox, 720 F.3d 715 (8th Cir.2013) (waiver of 401(k) plan benefits by spouse ineffective because it did not reflect spouse's acknowledgement of the effect of waiving the survivor annuity).

By comparison with the 50 percent minimum spousal annuity required under the QJSA regime for defined benefit plans and for money purchase defined contribution plans, the REAct rules for other defined contribution plans can be either more or less protective of the nonemployee spouse. If the participant dies before drawing down much of the account balance, the surviving spouse's 100 percent survivorship interest can be worth considerably more than the 50 percent minimum QJSA. But if the participant empties the account during his or her lifetime, the surviving spouse is not protected at all, having an entitlement to a 100 percent interest in an account that may be worth nothing.

In contrast to the reality when REAct's QJSA provisions were enacted, the predominant form of plan is now a 401(k) plan, which typically requires no spousal consent for distribution. Moreover, there is now more money in IRAs than in private sector DB or DC plans. Yet spouses have no survivor rights in an IRA. This seems anomalous.

Does it make sense that spouses have no survivor rights in an IRA even where some of the funds in the IRA originated from an ERISA pension plan? See Charles Schwab & Co., Inc. v. Debickero, 593 F. 3d 916 (9th Cir. 2010) (no spousal rights even though plan money was rolled over into an IRA).

8. *Protecting the plan against multiple claims.* When a plan fiduciary has relied upon a spousal waiver or upon a determination that the participant is unmarried, § 205(c)(6) protects "the plan from liability to the extent of payments made" even if the plan's determination was in error.

James retired in 1991 and began drawing retirement benefits from the Western Conference of Teamsters Pension Trust Fund. He "got a single life annuity by falsely informing the Plan's administrator [that] he was single. Relying on this representation and on its own records (which disclosed no contrary evidence), the Trust Fund paid benefits under a single life annuity" to James until he died nine months later. In truth James had been married to Brenda since 1982. Brenda applied to the Plan for the QJSA benefit. "The Trust Fund nonetheless denied her benefits on the ground that [James'] election had become final when his annuity payments began." Brenda conceded that the Plan reasonably relied on James' misrepresentation and upon its own records in allowing James to take a single life annuity. The Ninth Circuit held that Brenda took a QJSA, but that the Plan would be allowed to suspend payments to her until it completely recovered the amount by which its payments to James calculated on a single life annuity rate exceeded what the Plan would have paid him had the annuity been calculated as a dual life QJSA. Hearn v. Western Conference of Teamsters Pension Trust Fund, 68 F.3d 301 (9th Cir.1995). Thus, as between the defrauded plan and the victimized spouse, it was the spouse and not the plan that bore the loss.

Discussing *Hearn*, a commentator noted: "Multiemployer pension plans are particularly susceptible to participants' lies about their marital status, as these plans are commonly administered some distance from the workplace in an office which serves no other personnel functions." Peter O. Shinevar, The Case of the Perfidious Participant, 4 ERISA Litigation Rptr. 10, 15 n.2 (No.5, 1995).

9. *Comparing forced-share regimes.* REAct's QJSA resembles the forced-share statutes that operate in state decedents' estate law. Such a statute protects a decedent's surviving spouse against disinheritance by granting the spouse a fixed fraction (usually one third) of the decedent's property. Older statutes applied the fraction to the decedent's probate estate; newer statutes, such as the Uniform Probate Code (UPC), extend the forced share to certain nonprobate property as well. UPC § 2–205 (1993 rev.). The forced share assures that the survivor who depended upon the decedent's property during the marriage will not be wholly stripped of it when death dissolves the marriage. For discussion of the purposes and mechanisms of modern forced-share law, see UPC Article II, Part 2, General Comment (1990 rev.), discussed in Lawrence Waggoner, Spousal Rights in Our Multiple-Marriage Society: The Revised Uniform Probate Code, 26 Real Property, Probate & Trust J. 683 (1992).

In thinking about a system such as the forced share or REAct's QJSA, it is important to keep in mind that most spouses do not want to disinherit or otherwise to pauperize each other. A marriage that endures into retirement years is ordinarily one of mutual devotion. Several empirical studies show that, unless their property is large enough to entail tax planning, spouses overwhelmingly strain to leave everything to the surviving spouse, commonly disinheriting children in the process. The empirical literature is summarized in Restatement (Third) of Property: Wills and Other Donative Transfers § 2.2, Reporter's Note 1, at 71–72 (1999); UPC § 2–102, Comment (1993 rev.). Like REAct's QJSA, the forced share is waivable under all state statutes. REAct, however, by reversing the default rule and making its forced-share analogue apply unless the spouses manifest the contrary intention, protects against accidental nonprovision for the surviving spouse. The intestacy laws serve that function for probate property.

Both in purpose and effect, REAct's QJSA system may be described as a federal-law, asset-specific forced-share system, a forced share for pensions. The same is true of REAct's "qualified preretirement survivor annuity" (QPSA) discussed infra.

10. *Issues of policy in REAct's forced share.* The comparison between QJSA and forced share suggests many questions.

(a) *What federal interest?* The forced share is supremely a sphere of state law—it combines marital property law and succession, hence domestic relations and probate, two of the most fundamental state-law enclaves. Is it an appropriate exercise of federal power for Congress to intervene in this domain of state law, prescribing a separate federal forced-share system for pension wealth?

(b) *Why pension wealth alone?* Laying aside the tensions of federalism and focusing on the merits of the QJSA, what is the rationale for constructing a forced-share system that is limited to a single type of property, pension wealth? Why, for example, is there no comparable provision imposing an asset-specific forced-share regime on, say, FDIC-insured bank accounts and certificates of deposit?

(c) *Community property.* Community property states create in each spouse a present half interest in the earnings of the other. Accordingly, these states have no forced-share systems (except in California and Idaho, where so-called quasi-community property applies a forced-share-like solution to the property of migratory spouses who acquired property in non-community-property states). Why is it more accurate to liken REAct's QJSA to the forced share than to community property?

Although the QJSA resembles community property, it sometimes conflicts with state community property and succession law. Regarding the reach of ERISA preemption in such circumstances, see infra Section D of this chapter.

QUESTIONS

1.   Alice was 64 when she married Andrew, who was then 68. Andrew had retired at 65, taking his pension in the form of a single-life annuity. Alice is now 65 and about to retire. What rights has each spouse in the pension of the other?

2.   Suppose Alice had three children by a former marriage, Andrew had none. Would those facts alter any outcome under the previous question? As a matter of policy, should any outcome be altered?

3.   If a participant elects early retirement, does the spouse's QJSA attach at that time?

4.   Frank is 60, married to Lucy, and has a $1 million account balance in his employer's profit sharing plan. Can Frank withdraw his account balance without Lucy's consent? Why does ERISA guarantee survivor benefits to the spouse of a participant in a pension plan but not to the spouse of a participant in a profit sharing plan?

3.   QUALIFIED PRERETIREMENT SURVIVOR ANNUITIES

1.   *Pre-REAct.* ERISA's vesting rule, it will be recalled, permits the plan to provide that the pension "is not payable if the participant dies. . . ." ERISA § 203(a)(3)(A). A plan can provide that an unmarried participant forfeits his or her otherwise vested accumulation. The justification is that pensions are meant to provide retirement income; decedents do not need retirement income. Allowing the plan rather than the participant's death beneficiaries to capture the participant's accrued benefit lowers the cost to the sponsor of providing pension benefits, thus encouraging plan sponsors to establish plans and to sweeten plan benefits.

Although the deceased participant does not need retirement income, his dependent spouse may well need such support. Before the REAct amendments, however, ERISA did not require that a plan offer joint-and-survivor-annuity coverage for the spouse of a participant who died before retiring. Thus, in Hernandez v. Southern Nevada Culinary and Bartenders Pension Trust, 662 F.2d 617 (9th Cir.1981), the participant died three months short of reaching the plan's normal retirement age of 62. Although his interest was fully vested, and although he had elected the plan's joint and survivor annuity option, his widow received no survivor annuity because he had not satisfied the plan's requirement that participants live to age 62 before benefits became payable. This result effectively extended to the survivor the forfeiture-on-death exception to ERISA's vesting scheme.

2. *QPSA.* REAct mandates that "in the case of a vested participant who dies before the annuity starting date and who has a surviving spouse, a qualified preretirement survivor annuity [QPSA] shall be provided to the surviving spouse of such participant." ERISA § 205(a)(2). Thus, a QPSA must now be provided whenever the participant had any vested benefits.

Many of the rules governing the QPSA are consolidated with those for the QJSA. The same types of plans are affected. There is a provision for spousal waiver of the QPSA, but most plans fully subsidize the cost of the QPSA and do not provide for a waiver, which ERISA § 205(c)(5) permits.

As with the QJSA, a plan can require that the participant and spouse be married for at least one year as of the date of the participant's death. ERISA § 205(f)(1). Can you see the moral hazard danger to the plan that does not impose the one-year rule?

3. *Amount.* The QPSA intends to provide the spouse with a survivor's annuity that is calculated from the date of the participant's death. For the statutory minima, see § 205(e). The common survivor's annuity is half what the participant would have received.

Typically, profit-sharing plans avoid the QJSA requirements by making the vested account balance automatically payable to a surviving spouse. There is no QPSA requirement for such plans, but none is needed, since the surviving spouse gets everything. In the case of money purchase defined contribution plans, which are subject to the QJSA requirements, the QPSA is a life annuity for the surviving spouse that is actuarially equivalent to at least 50 percent of the participant's vested account balance. The remainder of the account can be distributed to other beneficiaries as the plan provides.

4. *Distribution.* The plan must authorize the spouse's annuity to commence "not later than the month in which the participant would have attained the earliest retirement age under the plan." ERISA § 205(e)(1)(B). This is the plan's early retirement age rather than its normal retirement age.

5. *Example.* The following example, illustrating the operation of the QPSA, is adapted from Thomas D. Terry & Carolyn E. Smith, Guide to the Retirement Equity Act of 1984, 24 Tax Notes 1195, 1196 (1984). Employee A begins work at age 24 and enters the plan at age 25. The plan has 5-year cliff vesting and an early retirement age of 55. A pre-retirement survivor annuity will be required if A dies any time after attaining age 29. Suppose A dies at age 29. Assume that based on A's accrued benefit on the date of death, had A survived until age 55, A would be entitled to a benefit in the form of a joint and survivor annuity of $100 per month. A's spouse is therefore entitled to a survivor benefit of $50 per month. Unless A's spouse elects otherwise, payments must begin no later than the month in which A would have had his 55th birthday.

6. *Life insurance?* The QPSA can be understood as nothing more than a clumsy way of mandating that employers supply life insurance for the surviving spouse of a worker who dies during his or her period of employment. Were such coverage to be required, it would probably be larger than the typical QPSA annuity, especially for the widow of a younger worker whose pension accumulation was still modest at the time of death. Was the QPSA a triumph of ideology over common sense—insisting on allocating to the surviving spouse a portion of what the decedent "earned," as opposed to asking how best to protect the interests of the surviving spouse?

7. *Who is the spouse?* John married Susie. The couple separated but never divorced. John subsequently married Gwendolyn, who thought he was divorced. Susie also remarried. John was a vested participant in a multiemployer pension plan. John died. Both Susie and Gwendolyn claimed the plan's QPSA benefit; the plan interpleaded in federal district court. Susie contended that she was entitled because her marriage to John had never terminated; she contended that Gwendolyn did not qualify as John's spouse because Gwendolyn's marriage to John was bigamous and hence void. The court held for Gwendolyn, applying the marriage law of Texas, John's domicile at death. Gwendolyn was a "putative spouse," the court held, because she married John in good faith, and under Texas law, a putative spouse has the same property rights as a lawful spouse. Susie, on the other hand, was estopped to claim as John's wife on account of her subsequent marriage. Central States, Southeast & Southwest Areas Pension Fund v. Gray, 31 E.B.C. 1748, 1750 (N.D.Ill.2003). Suppose Susie had never remarried?

See also the discussion of same sex marriage in section C.1.9 of this chapter, infra.

C. SPOUSAL INTERESTS ON DIVORCE

1. QUALIFIED DOMESTIC RELATIONS ORDERS (QDRO)

REAct's other great initiative, beyond the QJSA and QPSA for the marriage that dissolves on death, is to protect the interests of the nonemployee spouse (and other dependents) when the marriage terminates on divorce. In the QJSA and QPSA, REAct imposes new substantive entitlements for the nonemployee spouse as a matter of federal law. By contrast, in dealing with the pension consequences of dissolution on divorce, REAct defers strongly to state law.

1. *Curing antialienation and preemption.* In 1984 REAct amended ERISA to ratify a judicially developed exception that abridged the antialienation rule. REAct facilitates enforcement of state domestic relations decrees that "qualify" as so-called qualified domestic relations orders (QDROs). "Each pension plan shall provide for the payment of benefits in accordance with the applicable requirements of any [QDRO]." ERISA § 206(d)(3); cf. IRC § 414(p).

A conforming amendment, ERISA § 514(b)(7), exempts QDROs from ERISA's preemption section.

The QDRO rules undertake to subject pension wealth to state domestic relations jurisdiction as fully as possible, while nevertheless minimizing the burden on plans.

2. *The "alternate payee."* Section 206(d)(3)(K) of the amended ERISA identifies a person called the "alternate payee," who is "any spouse, former spouse, child, or other dependent of a participant who is recognized by a domestic relations order as having a right to receive all, or a portion of, the benefits payable under a plan with respect to such participant." Resign yourself to this statutory newspeak and do not try to substitute the familiar language of family law for "alternate payee." Section 206(d)(3)(B)(ii) defines a "domestic relations order" as "any judgment, decree, or order (including approval of a property settlement agreement) [relating] to the provision of child support, alimony payments, or marital property [rights, which order] is made pursuant to a State domestic relations law (including a community property law)."

Alternate Payee ←

Because a QDRO assigns plan benefits to the domestic relations judgment holder, it materially eases the enforcement problems that can otherwise arise in attempting to collect alimony, child support, or other awards.

It has been held that it is appropriate for a federal court to defer to a prior state court determination that a state decree is a QDRO, without independent review of the merits of that determination. Board of Trustees of the Laborers Pension Trust Fund v. Levingston, 816 F.Supp. 1496 (N.D.Cal.1993). See also DoL Advisory Opinion 92–17A (1992) (plan administrator may rely on state court determination that someone is an alternate payee). State courts have subject matter jurisdiction to decide that a domestic relations order issued by a state court is a QDRO. The Ninth Circuit explained that it follows from the fact that a state court has concurrent jurisdiction over § 502(a)(1)(B) claims "that it has jurisdiction to decide the intermediate question of whether or not the DRO is a QDRO." Mack v. Kuckenmeister, 619 F.3d 1010, 1018 (9th Cir. 2010).

Daughter was awarded a $2,000,000 state-court judgment against Father for physical and sexual abuse. Daughter sought to collect against Father's pension account by treating the judgment as a QDRO. What result? Mills v. Mills, 790 F.Supp. 172 (S.D.Ohio 1992). Regarding efforts to reach the pension assets of wrongdoers apart from the QDRO setting, see infra, Section E of this chapter ("Victims of the Participant's Wrongdoing").

3. *Procedural Requirements* for QDROs. What transforms a state court's domestic relations order into a QDRO is compliance with a set of requirements designed to protect the plan from administrative expense or increased liability. Section 206(d)(3)(C) requires that the QDRO clearly specify "(i) the name and the last known mailing address (if any) of the participant and the name and mailing address of each alternate payee covered by the order, (ii) the amount or percentage of the participant's benefits to be paid by the plan to each such alternate payee, or the manner in which such amount or percentage is to be determined, (iii) the number of payments or period to which such order applies, and (iv) each plan to which such order applies."

(✓) *also* talk about survivorship issue/rights under a QDRO

These procedural requirements throw upon the attorney for the alternate payee the burden of drafting and obtaining a state court decree that specifies with precision the relief that the payee is entitled to have from the plan. Noncompliance can defeat QDRO status. For example, in Von Haden v. Supervised Estate of Von Haden, 699 N.E.2d 301, 304 (Ind. App. 1998), it was held that a decree embodying a marital property agreement was not a QDRO, because although the agreement awarded half the husband's pension to the wife, the agreement did not contain language specifying the number of payments or the time period during which the wife could enforce the order. However, some courts have been willing to approve QDROs that have satisfied the QDRO requirements less than perfectly. E.g., Unicare Life & Health Ins. Co. v. Phanor, 472 F.Supp.2d 8 (D.Mass.2007) (holding probate court order sufficient to satisfy requirements as a QDRO even though "read literally" it failed to meet all of the statutory requirements).

The REAct amendments did impose new procedural responsibilities upon the plan for administering the QDRO rules. Each plan must establish written procedures for determining whether a decree is a QDRO and for administering QDROs. The form books and specialist plan administration firms have now developed standardized language for these purposes. Other sources of authoritative models are the PBGC publication, "Divorce Orders & PBGC" (Dec. 2008) and IRS Notice 97–11, Sample Language for a Qualified Domestic Relations Order (Jan. 13, 1997). Another source of useful guidance is DOL, The Division of Pensions Through Qualified Domestic Relations Orders (1997). The procedures required under REAct emphasize the plan's duties to supply affected persons with written notice of the receipt of any purported QDRO, and to notify them of the plan's determination that an order is a QDRO. ERISA § 206(d)(3)(G).

In Blue v. UAL Corp., 160 F.3d 383 (7th Cir.1998), the divorced husband against whom a QDRO was entered contended that the plan administrator should refuse to honor it on the ground that the issuing Illinois court erred in its application of certain matters of domestic relations law. In rejecting the husband's claim, Judge Easterbrook said, id. at 385–86:

> ERISA does not require, or even permit, a pension fund to look beneath the surface of the order. Compliance with a QDRO is obligatory. "Each pension plan *shall* provide for the payment of benefits in accordance with the applicable requirements of any qualified domestic relations order." [ERISA § 206(d)(3)(A)] (emphasis added). . . .

Mandatory

ERISA's allocation of functions—in which state courts apply state law to the facts, and pension plans determine whether the resulting orders adequately identify the payee and fall within the limits of benefits available under the plan—is eminently sensible. Pension plan administrators are not lawyers, let alone judges, and the spectacle of administrators second-guessing state judges' decisions under state law would be repellent. Unsuccessful litigants would refile their briefs from the state litigation with pension administrators, in the hope that lightning may strike as laymen review the work of judges. It is far better to let the states' appellate courts take care of legal errors by trial judges. Pension plans are high-volume operations that rely heavily on forms, such as designations of beneficiaries. Administrators are entitled to implement what the forms say, rather than what the signatories may have sought to convey. So, too, may plans mechanically implement orders from state courts.

4. *Substantive Protection for the plan.* Section 206(d)(3)(D) spells out REAct's great substantive protection for the plan, the prohibition against any decree purporting to enlarge the entitlement of the alternative payee beyond that of the participant. In order to qualify as a QDRO, the state decree may not require the plan "to provide any type or form of benefit, or any option, not otherwise provided under the [plan]." So, for example, a QDRO may not require a plan that does not provide for lump sum distributions to pay a lump sum to an alternate payee. Likewise, a QDRO may not "require the plan to provide increased [benefits]."

Nor will the plan be disadvantaged if the participant is twice divorced or otherwise has multiple domestic relations creditors. A QDRO may "not require the payment of benefits to an alternate payee which are required to be paid to another alternate payee under another order previously determined to be a [QDRO]." From the plan's standpoint, whichever QDRO-holder wins the race to the plan's door (usually the first ex-spouse) will be the appropriate alternate payee if the participant's account or benefit is not large enough to satisfy both.

5. *Permitted types of benefits.* As a result of REAct, ERISA now invites the state domestic relations court to fashion a decree that assimilates the alternate payee to the status of a beneficiary under the plan. Section 206(d)(3)(E)(i)(III) approves a decree that requires the alternate payee to be awarded benefits "in any form in which such benefits may be paid under the plan *to the participant*" (emphasis supplied). The effect is to substitute the alternate payee as a plan beneficiary. Section 206(d)(3)(J) declares the alternate payee to be a beneficiary "for purposes of any provision of [ERISA]," including, therefore, the enforcement measures of Title 1, part 5.

A QDRO can't impose a duty on a plan that does NOT exist

Notwithstanding the general prohibition against a domestic relations order that would require a plan to provide a benefit "not otherwise provided under the plan," § 206(d)(3)(D)(i), the statute does authorize as a QDRO (and hence does require a plan to honor) a type of decree that vexed pre-REAct law. Under § 206(d)(3)(E)(i)(I) a QDRO may now require the plan to commence payments to an alternate payee when the participant reaches the plan's early retirement age, even though the participant remains in the plan sponsor's active employment. Thus, early retirement age prevails over normal retirement age for the commencement of benefits if a QDRO so orders. In such a case, when the participant eventually retires, his or her benefit will be reduced by the value of the alternate payee's benefit.

6. *Taxation of QDROs.* Under IRC § 402(e)(1), a spouse or former spouse who is an alternate payee under a QDRO is treated as the distributee and is therefore taxable under the usual rules of IRC §§ 72 & 402(a). Such a distribution to a spouse or former spouse may also qualify

as a lump sum distribution, provided the balance to the account of the spouse or former spouse is distributed and the distribution would have been a lump sum distribution had it been a payment of the balance to the credit of the employee. IRC § 402(e)(4)(D). Payments to other alternate payees, such as support paid to a child under a QDRO, are taxable to the participant. An alternate payee who is a spouse or former spouse can also roll over distributions in the same manner as if the alternate payee were the employee. IRC § 402(e)(1)(B).

7. *The 18-month respite period.* The plan is given a fairly easy escape from entanglement in domestic relations litigation. Section 206(d)(3)(H) authorizes the plan administrator to suspend payment for up to 18 months while determining or awaiting determination of a dispute about whether a state court decree is or is not a QDRO. If the litigation lasts more than 18 months, the administrator must commence payments to the party thought to be entitled, but even if another party ultimately wins, the plan's payments up to that time satisfy the plan's liability.

Suppose the participant dies during that interval, before the QDRO has been finalized and been accepted by the plan? Gregory Price, who had children from a former marriage, married Lucille in 1989. They were divorced on January 21, 2003. The divorce decree awarded Lucille half the value of Gregory's 401(k) plan account with his former employer, IBM, for whom Gregory had worked for 25 years from 1977 to 2002. The plan required that a proposed QDRO be approved by the plan administrator before being submitted to the court. Lucille submitted a proposed QDRO to the plan office on January 16, 2003. Her proposed QDRO had not been processed by February 5, 2003, when Gregory died. Accordingly, the QDRO had not been presented to the divorce court by the time of his death. In September 2003 Lucille petitioned the divorce court for a retroactive decree, which the court granted, *nunc pro tunc* (now for then), awarding half Gregory's account balance to Lucille, effective as of January 2003. Gregory's children filed an opposing claim with the plan; the plan interpleaded in federal court. The court sustained the state court decree, emphasizing that its "Order was filed during the eighteen-month period permitted under ERISA to secure a QDRO." IBM Savings Plan v. Price, 349 F.Supp.2d 854, 858–59 (D.Vt.2004). There is a split of circuit court authority on whether, as in this case, a post-mortem QDRO is effective. Compare Files v. ExxonMobil Pension Plan, 428 F.3d 478 (3d Cir.2005) and Patton v. Denver Post Corp., 326 F.3d 1148 (10th Cir.2003) (pro), with Samaroo v. Samaroo, 193 F.3d 185 (3d Cir.1999) (con); see also Aaron Klein, Divorce, Death, and Posthumous QDROs: When Is It Too Late to Claim Pension Benefits under ERISA, 26 Cardozo L. Rev. 1651 (2005); Note, When Is It Too Late to Get a QDRO?, 8 ERISA Litigation Rptr. (Feb. 2001), at 24.

Section 1001 of the 2006 PPA requires the Department of Labor to issue regulations within one year clarifying that

(1) a domestic relations order otherwise meeting the requirements to be a qualified domestic relations order, including the requirements of [ERISA § 206(d)(3)(D)] and [IRC § 414(p)(3)], shall not fail to be treated as a qualified domestic relations order solely because—

(A) the order is issued after, or revises, another domestic relations order or qualified domestic relations order; or

(B) of the time at which it is issued; and

(2) any order described in paragraph (1) shall be subject to the same requirements and protections which apply to qualified domestic relations orders, including the provisions of [ERISA § 206(d)(3)(H)] and [IRC § 414(p)(7)].

The DOL has issued a final regulation with a number of interpretive examples. DOL Reg. § 2530.206. In one example, an initial defective order was issued while the participant was employed, but a corrected order was issued after the participant died. The regulation holds that the second order will not fail to be a QDRO merely because it was issued after the participant's death. The regulations also make clear that a subsequent domestic relations order cannot assign benefits to an alternate payee that were previously assigned to another alternate payee under a prior QDRO.

8. *Extending the QDRO regime to nonpension benefits?* (Welfare Benefit plans) The antialienation rule applies only to pension benefits, and the QDRO regime is expressed as an exception to antialienation. Thus, some courts have treated the QDRO regime as limited to pension plans. E.g., Anweiler v. American Elec. Power Serv. Corp., 3 F.3d 986, 994 (7th Cir.1993); United States v. International Brotherhood of Teamsters, 941 F.2d 1292, 1298 (2d Cir.1991).

In Metropolitan Life Ins. Co. v. Wheaton, 42 F.3d 1080 (7th Cir.1994), a Seventh Circuit panel expressed its willingness to extend QDRO enforcement to a welfare benefit plan. The divorce decree obligated the decedent to maintain his employer-provided life insurance for his ex-spouse and their two sons. The decedent remarried, changed the beneficiary designation to name the new wife, and died. The divorce decree satisfied the formal requirements for a QDRO. In finding that the QDRO regime applied to protect the decedent's former spouse and sons, Judge Posner said, id. at 1083:

> We cannot understand why, if a qualified domestic relations order can override the designation of beneficiary in a pension plan, as Congress in the Retirement Equity Act decided that it can, Congress would not have allowed such an order to override the designation of beneficiary in a welfare plan. The draftsmen of the Retirement Equity Act were concerned with the financial security of the spouses and other survivors of employees who died enrolled in ERISA plans. . . . [To] distinguish between pension benefits and life insurance proceeds so far as the validity of domestic relations orders is concerned would be arbitrary. The employee's life insurance will often be as important to the survivors as his pension benefits.

Do you agree that the omission of welfare benefit plans from the QDRO regime was a Congressional oversight that the courts can and should cure? Should judicial extension of QDRO enforcement be limited to life insurance plans, on the ground that, as mentioned in *Wheaton*, life insurance often serves the same income replacement function as pensions?

In Carland v. Metropolitan Life Ins. Co., 935 F.2d 1114 (10th Cir.1991), the Tenth Circuit applied the QDRO regime to a welfare benefit plan providing life insurance, refusing to treat the QDRO regime as limited to pension plans. The court pointed out that ERISA § 514(b)(7), the conforming amendment to ERISA's preemption regime, which cross-references to the QDRO regime of § 206(d)(3)(B)(i), does not explicitly restrict QDROs to pension plans. The Sixth Circuit followed *Carland* in Metropolitan Life Ins. Co. v. Marsh, 119 F.3d 415 (6th Cir.1997). The First Circuit came to the same conclusion in Barrs v. Lockheed Martin Corp., 287 F.3d 202, 209 n.7 (1st Cir.2002) (also applying the reasoning that ERISA 514(b)(7) is part of ERISA's preemption regime, which applies to welfare plans as well as pension plans). A federal district court recently reached the same conclusion. Metropolitan Life Insurance Co. v. Hanson, 2009 WL 3268640 (D.N.H.2009).

If the antialienation rule does not apply to a welfare benefit plans such as one providing life insurance, does a creditor need a QDRO to attach the participant's interest in the plan? Mackey v. Lanier Collection Agency & Service, Inc., 486 U.S. 825 (1988), allows a creditor to reach welfare benefits under generally applicable state law. *Mackey* is discussed in Guidry v. Sheet Metal Workers National Pension Fund, 493 U.S. 365 (1990), reproduced infra in this chapter

9. *Who is a spouse?* Same-sex marriage is now legal in a number of states. In addition to those states that have addressed the issue by statute, over the last year or so courts in at least a dozen states have declared bans against same-sex marriage to be unconstitutional.

The Federal Defense of Marriage Act of 1966 (DOMA) defined "marriage" to mean the union of one man and one woman only, and defined "spouse" to mean a different-sex husband or wife only, for purposes of interpreting any federal law or regulation. 1 U.S.C. § 7. The effect of DOMA had been that plans have not been required to recognize a same-sex spouse or same-sex domestic partner as a "spouse" for purposes of the spousal benefits provided by ERISA. However, on June 26, 2013, the Supreme Court, in a 5–4 decision, held that the above provision of DOMA is unconstitutional as a deprivation of the equal liberty of persons protected by the Fifth Amendment. U.S. v. Windsor, 133 S.Ct. 2675 (2013). In the view of the Court, it represents a departure from the history and tradition of reliance on state law to define marriage.

Although it will take time before the full ramifications of the Court's decision are clear, in states that recognize same-sex marriages, employers will be required to treat employees' same-sex and opposite-sex spouses equally for purposes of benefits provided to spouses. Among other things, employers will need to provide QJSAs and QPSAs to same-sex spouses and a domestic relations order with respect to a same-sex spouse could qualify as a QDRO. See, e.g., Cozen O'Connor P.C. v. Tobits, 2013 U.S. Dist. LEXIS 105507 (E.D. Pa. July 29, 2013) (Illinois, which recognizes same-sex marriages, is required to recognize a valid Canadian same-sex marriage for purposes of determining proper distribution of survivor benefits under profit-sharing plan governed by ERISA).

Section 2 of DOMA, which provides that states that do not allow same-sex marriage need not recognize such marriages performed in other states, was not before the Court. Thus, absent further legal action, same-sex couples living and working in states that do not recognize same-sex marriage might not be entitled to ERISA's spousal protections even if they have been legally married in another state. Whether that provision survives further challenge is an open question.

Many large employers, of course, have some employees in states that recognize same-sex marriages and other employees in states that do not recognize such marriages. Recognizing the difficulties this creates, the DoL issued a Technical Release providing that for purpose of ERISA the term spouse "will be read to refer to any individuals who are lawfully married under any state law, including individuals married to a person of the same sex who were legally married in a state that recognizes such marriages, but who are domiciled in a state that does not recognize such marriages." It further provided that the term marriage "will be read to include a same-sex marriage that is legally recognized as a marriage under any state law." The DoL's Release explained that its interpretation was justified because

> [a] rule for employee benefit plans based on state of domicile would raise significant challenges for employers that operate or have employees (or former employees) in more than one state or whose employees move to another state while entitled to benefits. Furthermore, substantial financial and administrative burdens would be placed on those employers, as well as the administrators of employee benefit plans. For example, the need for and validity of spousal elections, consents, and notices could change each time an employee, former employee, or spouse moved to a state with different marriage recognition rules. To administer employee benefit plans, employers (or plan administrators) would need to inquire whether each employee receiving plan benefits was married and, if so, whether the employee's spouse was the same sex or opposite sex from the employee. In addition, the employers or plan administrators would need to continually track the state of domicile of all same-sex married employees and former employees and their spouses. For all of these reasons, plan administration would grow increasingly complex, administrators of employee benefit plans would have to be retrained, and systems reworked, to comply with an unprecedented and complex system that divided married employees according to their sexual orientation. In many cases, the tracking of employee and spouse domiciles would be less than perfectly accurate or timely and would result in errors or delays.

> Such a system would be burdensome for employers and would likely result in errors, confusion, and inconsistency for employers, individual employees, and the government. In addition, given the interconnectedness of statutory provisions affecting employer benefit plans, recognition of marriage based on domicile could prevent qualification for tax exemption, lead to loss of vested rights if spouses move, and complicate benefits determinations if spouses live in different states. All of these problems are avoided by the adoption of a rule that recognizes marriages that are valid in the state in which they were

celebrated. That approach is consistent with the core intent underlying ERISA of promoting uniform requirements for employee benefit plans.

DOL Technical Release 2013–14. IRS has taken the same position: see Rev. Rul. 2013–17, 2013–38 IRB 201, and the answers to frequently asked questions posted at http://www.irs.gov/uac/Answers-to-Frequently-Asked-Questions-for-Same-Sex-Married-Couples.

May an employer define "spouse" in its plan in a manner that excludes same-sex couples from beneficiary status? See Roe v. Empire Blue Cross Blue Shield, 2014 U.S. Dist. LEXIS 61345 (S.D.N.Y. May 1, 2014) (yes).

For further discussion of DOMA and the employee benefit issues raised by same-sex unions, see Chapter 18.

Neither DOMA nor state law prevents an employer from offering benefits for domestic partners, whether of the same or opposite sex. "According to a 2007 survey by Hewitt Associates, 54 percent of surveyed firms offered coverage for domestic partners. Seventeen percent of firms offered domestic partner coverage to same-sex couples only; 1 percent of firms offered coverage to opposite-sex couples only; 32 percent of surveyed firms offered coverage for same or opposite-sex couples. According to a 2005 Hewitt Associates study, of those employers that offered domestic partner benefits, 83 percent offered the coverage to dependents of domestic partners. These numbers represent a significant increase since 2002, when 19 percent of surveyed firms offered domestic partner benefits." EBRI, Domestic Partner Benefits: Facts and Background, Facts from EBRI, at 1 (Feb. 2009). Regarding the challenges employers face in designing and implementing domestic partner plans, see Joseph S. Adams & Todd A. Solomon, Domestic Partner Benefits: An Employer's Guide (2d ed. 2003).

Does ERISA preempt a local ordinance from requiring private employers to extend domestic partner benefits to employees? See Air Transport Ass'n v. City and County of San Francisco, 992 F.Supp. 1149, 1180 (N.D.Cal.1998), aff'd 266 F.3d 1064 (9th Cir.2001) (ordinance held preempted). For contrary views, see Jeffrey G. Sherman, Domestic Partnership and ERISA Preemption, 76 Tulane L.Rev. 373, 403–27 (2001).

10. *IRAs and divorce.* IRAs are not governed by ERISA and are therefore not subject to the rules regarding antialienation or preemption. State courts may order the division or transfer of an IRA account upon divorce; no QDRO is necessary. Nevertheless, the IRC governs how such transfers are taxed. As long as the transfer of an individual's interest in an IRA is made to a spouse or former spouse "under a divorce or separation instrument," the transfer is not considered a taxable event and the interest of the spouse is treated as an IRA of the spouse, not the individual. IRC § 408(d)(6). Any other assignment of an IRA is a deemed distribution of the amount assigned. Treas.Reg. § 1.408–4(a)(2). Thus, if H owns an IRA that is community property and pursuant to a marital property agreement between H and W not made in connection with a divorce or separation, one half of the IRA is transferred into an IRA for W, each IRA to be the separate property of the owner, the transfer of W's

interest in the original IRA to W's IRA is a taxable distribution. IRS, Private Letter Ruling 1999–37–055. Divorce lawyers don't always understand the difference between the QDRO rules and the IRA rules, making the rules something of a trap for the unwary.

11. *QMCSO: QDRO-like health care benefits for children.* OBRA '93 amended ERISA Title 1, Part 6, which contains the COBRA rules for continuation of health care benefits. The amendment added new ERISA § 609, which requires ERISA-covered health plans to comply with a court-ordered "Qualified Medical Child Support Order" (QMCSO). For further details, see chapter 19.

12. *Survivorship.* The REAct provisions coordinate the QDRO regime for divorcing spouses with the QJSA and QPSA rules for surviving spouses in one respect. Section 206(d)(3)(F) permits a QDRO to be drafted to provide that "the former spouse of a participant shall be treated as a surviving spouse of such participant for purposes of section 205," with the result that any subsequent "spouse of the participant shall not be treated as a spouse of the participant for such purposes."

Note well that the former spouse obtains this survivorship protection as alternate payee only if the QDRO expressly provides it. Unlike the regular QJSA or QPSA, under ERISA's QDRO rules survivorship is not the default option. Counsel for the nonemployee spouse has to draft the proposed QDRO to contain the provision (and counsel has to fight for it if necessary in the dissolution proceedings).

Consider Dugan v. Clinton, 8 E.B.C. 2065 (N.D.Ill.1987). James and Lillian were divorced in 1982. The 1982 marital property decree awarded Lillian a 25 percent share in James' pension with the Midwest Operating Engineers Pension Fund. Understandably, since the decree was drafted two years before Congress enacted REAct, the decree did not make express provision for Lillian to have survivorship rights if James predeceased her, as ERISA § 206(d)(3)(F) now allows. James died in 1986, at age 52, survived by his second wife, Lois. Held, Lois takes a QPSA and Lillian takes nothing. Even deeming the 1982 decree to constitute a QDRO, it neglected to stipulate survivorship rights for Lillian as § 206(d)(3)(F) requires. Was Lillian's suit so hopeless that she should be made to pay Lois' counsel fees under Rule 11 of the Federal Rules of Civil Procedure? See Dugan v. Clinton, No. 86–C8492, 1987 WL 28405, at 7–8 (N.D.Ill.1987).

This issue does not arise if a participant has already begun receiving benefits in the form of a joint and survivor annuity at the time of divorce. "Because the retirement of a plan participant ordinarily creates a vested interest in the surviving spouse at the time of the participant's retirement, we conclude that a [QDRO] issued after the participant's retirement may not alter or assign the surviving spouse's interest to a subsequent spouse." Carmona v. Carmona, 544 F.3d 988 (9th Cir.2008). In 2010 the Ninth Circuit amended, and denied rehearing of, its earlier decision in *Carmona*, affirming its view that "a state DRO may not create an enforceable interest in surviving spouse benefits to an alternate payee after a participant's retirement, because ordinarily at retirement the surviving spouse's interest irrevocably vests." Carmona v. Carmona, 603 F.3d 1041, 1060 (9th Cir. 2010), cert. denied, 131 S. Ct. 1492 (2011).

13. *Expensing the costs of QDRO and QMCSO administration.* DoL has changed its mind about whether to allow the costs arising in connection with a plan's processing of a QDRO or QMCSO to be charged to the account of the affected participant, as opposed to being absorbed by the plan. Attorney fees incurred in examining and accepting a draft QDRO "can run from hundreds to thousands of [dollars]." Jennifer Saranow, Cost of Divorce Just Went Up—in Your 401(k), Wall St. J., Nov. 9, 2004, at D4. In an advisory opinion issued in 1994, DoL took the position that "nothing in Title 1 of ERISA requires or permits a plan to impose any separate fees or costs" for determining the status of a QDRO. DoL Opinion 94–32 A, 1994 ERISA Lexis 33, Aug. 4, 1994. A decade later, DoL repudiated that position. ERISA's silence on the matter means that the plan sponsor "has considerable discretion in determining the method of expense allocation." Thus, "ERISA does not, in our view, preclude the allocation of reasonable expenses attendant to QDRO or QMSCO determinations to the account of the participant or beneficiary seeking the determination," provided that the plan and the SPD disclose the practice of making such charges. DoL, EBSA Field Assistance Bulletin 2003–3, May 19, 2003.

14. *No QDRO default regime.* For a marriage that dissolves upon death, both the QJSA rules and the QPSA rules impose a survivor's annuity as the default regime—that is, as the regime that applies if the parties (participant and nonemployee spouse) do not elect against it. The QDRO rules impose no default regime for the marriage that ends in divorce, no presumptive division of the pension into shares. Rather, REAct defers to the state domestic relations decree, which in turn commonly embodies a negotiated settlement.

Parties to a divorce are ordinarily represented by counsel. In a marital property settlement the parties will consider the pension fund in relation to the entirety of both spouses' property. In a contested divorce, the court's decree will do likewise. The circumstances of divorcing couples vary so greatly that it would be difficult to devise a broadly satisfying default regime for pension wealth alone. In divorce, therefore, federal law stops at the water's edge, leaving to state law and to state courts the tricky decisions about whether, how, and when to divide a pension. The difficulty in fashioning such decrees is evident in pre-QDRO cases such as *Robert C.S. v. Barbara J.S.*, 434 A. 2d 383 (Del. 1981) and is further discussed in section 3.

15. *Government plans.* The QDRO rules aren't needed for government plans, but most do accept DROs. Section 414(p)(11) of the Code provides that such orders are treated as QDROs if they satisfy certain minimal requirements.

2. KENNEDY V. PLAN ADMINISTRATOR FOR DUPONT SAVINGS AND INVESTMENT PLAN

129 S.Ct. 865 (2009).

■ JUSTICE SOUTER delivered the opinion of the Court.

The Employee Retirement Income Security Act of 1974 (ERISA) generally obligates administrators to manage ERISA plans "in accordance with the documents and instruments governing" them.

[ERISA § 404(a)(1)(D)]. At a more specific level, the Act requires covered pension benefit plans to "provide that benefits . . . under the plan may not be assigned or alienated," [ERISA § 206(d)(1)], but this bar does not apply to qualified domestic relations orders (QDROs), [ERISA § 206(d)(3)]. The question here is whether the terms of the limitation on assignment or alienation invalidated the act of a divorced spouse, the designated beneficiary under her ex-husband's ERISA pension plan, who purported to waive her entitlement by a federal common law waiver embodied in a divorce decree that was not a QDRO. We hold that such a waiver is not rendered invalid by the text of the antialienation provision, but that the plan administrator properly disregarded the waiver owing to its conflict with the designation made by the former husband in accordance with plan documents.

I

The decedent, William Kennedy, worked for E.I. DuPont de Nemours & Company and was a participant in its savings and investment plan (SIP), with power both to "designate any beneficiary or beneficiaries . . . to receive all or part" of the funds upon his death, and to "replace or revoke such designation." The plan requires "[a]ll authorizations, designations and requests concerning the Plan [to] be made by employees in the manner prescribed by the [plan administrator]," and provides forms for designating or changing a beneficiary. If at the time the participant dies "no surviving spouse exists and no beneficiary designation is in effect, distribution shall be made to, or in accordance with the directions of, the executor or administrator of the decedent's estate."

[T]he parties do not dispute that the plan satisfies ERISA's antialienation provision, [ERISA § 206(d)(1)], which requires it to "provide that benefits provided under the plan may not be assigned or alienated." The plan does, however, permit a beneficiary to submit a "qualified disclaimer" of benefits as defined under the Tax Code, see [IRC § 2518], which has the effect of switching the beneficiary to an "alternate . . . determined according to a valid beneficiary designation made by the deceased."

In 1971, William married Liv Kennedy, and, in 1974, he signed a form designating her to take benefits under the SIP, but naming no contingent beneficiary to take if she disclaimed her interest. William and Liv divorced in 1994, subject to a decree that Liv "is . . . divested of all right, title, interest, and claim in and to . . . [a]ny and all sums . . . the proceeds [from], and any other rights related to any . . . retirement plan, pension plan, or like benefit program existing by reason of [William's] past or present or future employment." William did not, however, execute any documents removing Liv as the SIP beneficiary, even though he did execute a new beneficiary-designation form naming his daughter, Kari Kennedy, as the beneficiary under DuPont's Pension and Retirement Plan, also governed by ERISA.

On William's death in 2001, petitioner Kari Kennedy was named executrix and asked DuPont to distribute the SIP funds to William's Estate. DuPont, instead, relied on William's designation form and paid the balance of some $400,000 to Liv. The Estate then sued respondents DuPont and the SIP plan administrator (together, DuPont), claiming that the divorce decree amounted to a waiver of the SIP benefits on Liv's part, and that DuPont had violated ERISA by paying the benefits to William's designee.

[T]he District Court entered summary judgment for the Estate. . . .

The Fifth Circuit [reversed and] held that Liv's waiver constituted an assignment or alienation of her interest in the SIP benefits to the Estate, and so could not be honored. . . .

We granted certiorari to resolve a split among the Courts of Appeals and State Supreme Courts over a divorced spouse's ability to waive pension plan benefits through a divorce decree not amounting to a QDRO. We subsequently realized that this case implicates the further split over whether a beneficiary's federal common law waiver of plan benefits is effective where that waiver is inconsistent with plan documents, and after oral argument we invited supplemental briefing on that latter issue, upon which the disposition of this case ultimately turns. We now affirm, albeit on reasoning different from the Fifth Circuit's rationale.

II

A

By its terms, the antialienation provision, [ERISA § 206(d)(1)], requires a plan to provide expressly that benefits be neither "assigned" nor "alienated," the operative verbs having histories of legal meaning: to "assign" is "[t]o transfer; as to assign property, or some interest therein," Black's Law Dictionary 152 (4th rev. ed.1968), and to "alienate" is "[t]o convey; to transfer the title to property," *id.*, at 96. We think it fair to say that Liv did not assign or alienate anything to William or to the Estate later standing in his shoes.

The Fifth Circuit saw the waiver as an assignment or alienation to the Estate, thinking that Liv's waiver transferred the SIP benefits to whoever would be next in line; without a designated contingent beneficiary, the Estate would take them. The court found support in the applicable Treasury Department regulation that defines "assignment" and "alienation" to include

"[a]ny direct or indirect arrangement (whether revocable or irrevocable) whereby a party acquires from a participant or beneficiary a right or interest enforceable against the plan in, or to, all or any part of a plan benefit payment which is, or may become, payable to the participant or beneficiary." [Treas.Reg. § 1.401(a)–13(c)(1)(ii) (2008)].

Casting the alienation net this far, though, raises questions that leave one in doubt. Although it is possible to speak of the waiver as an "arrangement" having the indirect effect of a transfer to the next possible beneficiary, it would be odd usage to speak of an estate as the transferee of its own decedent's property, just as it would be to speak of the decedent in his lifetime as his own transferee. And treating the estate or even the ultimate estate beneficiary as the assignee or transferee would be strange under the terms of the regulation: it would be hard to say the estate or future beneficiary "acquires" a right or interest when at the time of the waiver there was no estate and the beneficiary of a future estate might be anyone's guess. If there were a contingent beneficiary (or the participant made a subsequent designation) the estate would get no interest; as for an estate beneficiary, the identity could ultimately turn on the law of intestacy applied to facts as yet unknown, or on the contents of the participant's subsequent will, or simply on the participant's future exercise of (or failure to invoke) the power to designate a new beneficiary directly under the terms of the plan. Thus, if such a waiver created an "arrangement" assigning or transferring anything under the statute, the assignor would be blindfolded, operating, at best, on the fringe of what "assignment" or "alienation" normally suggests.

The questionability of this broad reading is confirmed by exceptions to it that are apparent right off the bat. Take the case of a surviving spouse's interest in pension benefits, for example. Depending on the circumstances, a surviving spouse has a right to a survivor's annuity or to a lump-sum payment on the death of the participant, unless the spouse has waived the right and the participant has eliminated the survivor annuity benefit or designated a different beneficiary. See [ERISA §§ 205(a), (b)(1)(C), (c)(2)]. This waiver by a spouse is plainly not barred by the antialienation provision. Likewise, DuPont concedes that a qualified disclaimer under the Tax Code, which allows a party to refuse an interest in property and thereby eliminate federal tax, would not violate the antialienation provision. See [IRC § 2518]. In each example, though, we fail to see how these waivers would be permissible under the Fifth Circuit's reading of the statute and regulation.

Our doubts, and the exceptions that call the Fifth Circuit's reading into question, point us toward authority we have drawn on before, the law of trusts that "serves as ERISA's backdrop." *Beck v. PACE Int'l Union,* 551 U.S. 96, 101 (2007). We explained before that [ERISA § 206(d)(1)] is much like a spendthrift trust provision barring assignment or alienation of a benefit, and the cognate trust law is highly suggestive here. Although the beneficiary of a spendthrift trust traditionally lacked the means to transfer his beneficial interest to anyone else, he did have the power to disclaim prior to accepting it, so long as the disclaimer made no attempt to direct the interest to a beneficiary in his stead. See 2 Restatement (Third) of Trusts § 58(1), Comment *c,* p. 359 (2001) ("A designated beneficiary of a spendthrift trust is not required to accept or retain an interest prescribed by the terms of the trust. . . . On the other hand, a purported disclaimer by which the beneficiary attempts to direct who is to receive the interest is a precluded transfer").

We do not mean that the whole law of spendthrift trusts and disclaimers turns up in [ERISA § 206(d)(1)], but the general principle that a designated spendthrift can disclaim his trust interest magnifies the improbability that a statute written with an eye on the old law would effectively force a beneficiary to take an interest willy-nilly. . . .

The Fifth Circuit found "significant support" for its contrary holding in the QDRO subsections, reasoning that "[i]n the marital-dissolution context, the QDRO provisions supply the *sole* exception to the anti-alienation provision," a point that echoes in DuPont's argument here. But the negative implication of the QDRO language is not that simple. If a QDRO provided a way for a former spouse like Liv merely to waive benefits, this would be powerful evidence that the antialienation provision was meant to deny any effect to a waiver within a divorce decree but not a QDRO, else there would have been no need for the QDRO exception. But this is not so, and DuPont's argument rests on a false premise. In fact, a beneficiary seeking only to relinquish her right to benefits cannot do this by a QDRO, for a QDRO by definition requires that it be the "creat[ion] or recogni[tion of] the existence of an alternate payee's right to, or assign[ment] to an alternate payee [of] the right to, receive all or a portion of the benefits payable with respect to a participant under a plan." [ERISA § 206(d)(3)(B)(i)(I)]. There is no QDRO for a simple waiver; there must be some succeeding designation of an alternate payee. Not being a mechanism for simply renouncing a claim to benefits, then, the QDRO provisions shed no light on whether a beneficiary may waive by a non-QDRO.

In sum, Liv did not attempt to direct her interest in the SIP benefits to the Estate or any other potential beneficiary, and accordingly we think that the better view is that her waiver did not constitute an assignment or alienation rendered void under the terms of [ERISA § 206(d)(1)]. . . .

III

The waiver's escape from inevitable nullity under the express terms of the antialienation clause does not, however, control the decision of this case, and the question remains whether the plan administrator was required to honor Liv's waiver with the consequence of distributing the SIP balance to the Estate.[10] We hold that it was not, and that the plan administrator did its statutory ERISA duty by paying the benefits to Liv in conformity with the plan documents.

ERISA requires "[e]very employee benefit plan [to] be established and maintained pursuant to a written instrument," [ERISA § 402(a)(1)], "specify[ing] the basis on which payments are made to and from the plan," [ERISA § 402(b)(4)]. The plan administrator is obliged to act "in accordance with the documents and instruments governing the plan insofar as such documents and instruments are consistent with the provisions of [Title I] and [Title IV] of [ERISA]," [ERISA § 404(a)(1)(D)], and the Act provides no exemption from this duty when it comes time to pay benefits. On the contrary, [ERISA § 502(a)(1)(B)] (which the Estate happens to invoke against DuPont here) reinforces the directive, with its provision that a participant or beneficiary may bring a cause of action "to recover benefits due to him under the terms of his plan, to enforce his

---

[10] Despite our following answer to the question here, our conclusion that [ERISA § 206(d)(1)] does not make a nullity of a waiver leaves open any questions about a waiver's effect in circumstances in which it is consistent with plan documents. Nor do we express any view as to whether the Estate could have brought an action in state or federal court against Liv to obtain the benefits after they were distributed. Compare *Boggs v. Boggs,* 520 U.S. 833, 853 (1997) ("If state law is not preempted, the diversion of retirement benefits will occur regardless of whether the interest in the pension plan is enforced against the plan or the recipient of the pension benefit"), with *Sweebe v. Sweebe,* 474 Mich. 151, 156–159, 712 N.W.2d 708, 712–713 (2006) (distinguishing *Boggs* and holding that "while a plan administrator must pay benefits to the named beneficiary as required by ERISA," after the benefits are distributed "the consensual terms of a prior contractual agreement may prevent the named beneficiary from retaining those proceeds"); *Pardee v. Personal Representative for Estate of Pardee,* 2005 OK CIV APP. 27, ¶¶ 20, 27, 112 P.3d 308, 313–314, 315–316 (2004) (distinguishing *Boggs* and holding that ERISA did not preempt enforcement of allocation of ERISA benefits in state-court divorce decree as "the pension plan funds were no longer entitled to ERISA protection once the plan funds were distributed").

rights under the terms of the plan, or to clarify his rights to future benefits under the terms of the plan."

The Estate's claim therefore stands or falls by "the terms of the plan," a straightforward rule of hewing to the directives of the plan documents that lets employers " 'establish a uniform administrative scheme, [with] a set of standard procedures to guide processing of claims and disbursement of benefits.' " *Egelhoff v. Egelhoff,* 532 U.S. 141, 148 (2001). The point is that by giving a plan participant a clear set of instructions for making his own instructions clear, ERISA forecloses any justification for enquiries into nice expressions of intent, in favor of the virtues of adhering to an uncomplicated rule: "simple administration, avoid[ing] double liability, and ensur[ing] that beneficiaries get what's coming quickly, without the folderol essential under less-certain rules." *Fox Valley & Vicinity Const. Workers Pension Fund v. Brown,* 897 F.2d 275, 283 (C.A.7 1990) (Easterbrook, J., dissenting).

And the cost of less certain rules would be too plain. Plan administrators would be forced "to examine a multitude of external documents that might purport to affect the dispensation of benefits," *Altobelli v. IBM Corp.,* 77 F.3d 78, 82–83 (C.A.4 1996) (Wilkinson, C. J., dissenting), and be drawn into litigation like this over the meaning and enforceability of purported waivers. The Estate's suggestion that a plan administrator could resolve these sorts of disputes through interpleader actions merely restates the problem with the Estate's position: it would destroy a plan administrator's ability to look at the plan documents and records conforming to them to get clear distribution instructions, without going into court.

The Estate of course is right that this guarantee of simplicity is not absolute. The very enforceability of QDROs means that sometimes a plan administrator must look for the beneficiaries outside plan documents notwithstanding [ERISA § 404(a)(1)(D)]; [ERISA § 206(d)(3)(J)] provides that a "person who is an alternate payee under a [QDRO] shall be considered for purposes of any provision of [ERISA] a beneficiary under the plan." But this in effect means that a plan administrator who enforces a QDRO must be said to enforce plan documents, not ignore them. In any case, a QDRO enquiry is relatively discrete, given the specific and objective criteria for a domestic relations order that qualifies as a QDRO, requirements that amount to a statutory checklist working to "spare [an administrator] from litigation-fomenting ambiguities," *Metropolitan Life Ins. Co. v. Wheaton,* 42 F.3d 1080, 1084 (C.A.7 1994). This is a far cry from asking a plan administrator to figure out whether a claimed federal common law waiver was knowing and voluntary, whether its language addressed the particular benefits at issue, and so forth, on into factually complex and subjective determinations.

These are good and sufficient reasons for holding the line, just as we have done in cases of state laws that might blur the bright-line requirement to follow plan documents in distributing benefits. Two recent preemption cases are instructive here. *Boggs v. Boggs,* 520 U.S. 833, held that ERISA preempted a state law permitting the testamentary transfer of a nonparticipant spouse's community property interest in undistributed pension plan benefits. We rejected the entreaty to create "through case law . . . a new class of persons for whom plan assets are to be held and administered," explaining that "[t]he statute is not amenable to this sweeping extratextual extension." And in *Egelhoff* we held that ERISA preempted a state law providing that the designation of a spouse as the beneficiary of a nonprobate asset is revoked automatically upon divorce. We said the law was at fault for standing in the way of making payments "simply by identifying the beneficiary specified by the plan documents," and thus for purporting to "undermine the congressional goal of 'minimiz[ing] the administrative and financial burden[s]' on plan administrators."

What goes for inconsistent state law goes for a federal common law of waiver that might obscure a plan administrator's duty to act "in accordance with the documents and instruments." See *Mertens v. Hewitt Associates,* 508 U.S. 248, 259 (1993) ("The authority of courts to develop a 'federal common law' under ERISA . . . is not the authority to revise the text of the statute"). And this case does as well as any other in pointing out the wisdom of protecting the plan documents rule. Under the terms of the SIP Liv was William's designated beneficiary. The plan provided an easy way for William to change the designation, but for whatever reason he did not. The plan provided a way to disclaim an interest in the SIP account, but Liv did not purport to follow it.[13] The plan administrator therefore did exactly what [ERISA § 404(a)(1)(D)] required: "the documents control, and those name [the ex-wife]." *McMillan v. Parrott,* 913 F.2d 310, 312 (C.A.6 1990).

[The SIP and the summary plan description] provide that the plan administrator will pay benefits to a participant's designated beneficiary, with designations and changes to be made in a particular way. William's designation of Liv as his beneficiary was made in the way required; Liv's waiver was not.[14]

IV

Although Liv's waiver was not rendered a nullity by the terms of [ERISA § 206], the plan administrator properly distributed the SIP benefits to Liv in accordance with the plan documents.

The judgment of the Court of Appeals is affirmed on the latter ground.

NOTE

The Supreme Court's decision in *Kennedy* resolved a split among lower courts regarding whether a former spouse designated as a beneficiary can waive her rights to a pension benefit pursuant to a divorce or settlement agreement. Compare Fox Valley & Vicinity Construction Workers Pension Fund v. Brown, 897 F.2d 275 (7th Cir.1990) with McMillan v. Parrott, 913

---

[13] The Estate does not contend that Liv's waiver was a valid disclaimer under the terms of the plan. We do not address a situation in which the plan documents provide no means for a beneficiary to renounce an interest in benefits.

[14] The Estate also contends that requiring a plan administrator to distribute benefits in conformity with plan documents will allow a beneficiary who murders a participant to obtain benefits under the terms of the plan. The "slayer" case is not before us, and we do not address it. See *Egelhoff v. Egelhoff,* 532 U.S. 141, 152 (2001) (declining to decide whether ERISA preempts state statutes forbidding a murdering heir from receiving property as a result of the killing).

F.2d 310 (6th Cir. 1990). Although the Court held that ERISA's antialienation provision does not bar such a waiver, it also held that the plan administrator had no duty to honor the waiver. The Court purported to establish a bright-line rule that allows plan administrators to pay benefits in accordance with plan terms, thus making the life of plan administrators easier. Does that make it a good result?

In the wake of the Supreme Court's decision in *Kennedy*, courts have predictably found that a divorce decree is insufficient to waive a right to plan benefits. Metropolitan Life Ins. Co. v. Gulino, 2009 WL 1564232, at *5 (W.D.Wash.2009) ("following *Kennedy*, this Court must conclude that under ERISA, the Plan documents control, and those documents name [the ex-spouse] as beneficiary"). More troubling, several decisions have concluded, based on *Kennedy*, that a plan administrator could rely on a plan beneficiary designation even in circumstances that suggest the designation was the result of undue influence. E.g., Dunlap v. Ormet Corp., 2009 WL 763382 (N.D.W.Va.2009) (upholding payment under a life insurance policy in accordance with beneficiary designation notwithstanding claim that decedent changed the beneficiary designation while in a confused and disoriented state under the influence of his step-son and daughter). Accord, Young v. Anderson, 2009 WL 1133492 (E.D.Mich.2009). Such cases lend credence to the claim of some that Kennedy represents a triumph of convenience over equity. See Attorneys Discuss Effect Kennedy Decision Might Have on Drafting Plan Documents, Daily Labor Report, Mar. 9, 2009.

In a footnote in *Kennedy* (footnote 13 supra), the Court states that it does not "address a situation in which the plan documents provide no means for a beneficiary to renounce an interest in benefits." In Boyd v. Metro. Life Ins. Co., 636 F.3d 138 (4th Cir. 2011), the Fourth Circuit held that the fact that the plan at issue contained no formal means for a beneficiary to renounce an interest in benefits did not prevent the plan document rule from applying. In Matschiner v. Hartford Life and Accident Ins. Co., 622 F.3d 885 (8th Cir. 2010), the Eighth Circuit came to the same conclusion, also observing that the rule established in *Kennedy* applies to welfare benefit plans as well as to pension benefit plans.

After a plan pays benefits in accordance with the plan documents to a former spouse who has executed a waiver, may the estate of a participant sue the former spouse to enforce the waiver and recover the plan proceeds? In Estate of Kensinger v. URL Pharm. Inc., 674 F.3d 131 (3d Cir. 2012), the Third Circuit held that it may, in an action filed by a 401(k) plan participant's estate against the former wife and the employer. The court began by noting that, in light of *Kennedy*, the plan administrator is obligated to pay the 401(k) plan proceeds to the former spouse notwithstanding her waiver, because the participant had never replaced her as the designated beneficiary. It then ruled that the estate may sue to recover the funds distributed to the former spouse, finding that neither of the policy considerations underlying the Supreme Court's decision in *Kennedy*—simple administration and avoidance of double liability—are implicated in such a suit. Such a suit, suggested the court, "will be litigated as an ordinary contracts dispute." Id. at 136. Accord., Andochick v. Ronald and June Byrd, 709 F.3d 296, 299 (4th Cir. 2013) (post-distribution suits to enforce state law waivers do "nothing to interfere with" ERISA's objectives of simple administration, avoiding double liability and ensuring beneficiaries quickly receive what is due to them). The Supreme Court declined to review the decision of the Fourth Circuit. 134 S. Ct. 235 (2013).

Kensinger and Andochick have both been implicitly overruled in a non-ERISA case, Hillman v. Maretta, 133 S. Ct. 1943 (2013). For a critique of Hillman, see John H. Langbein, Destructive Federal Preemption of State Wealth Transfer Law in Beneficiary Designation Cases: Hillman Doubles Down on Egelhoff, 67 Vanderbilt L. Rev. 1665 (2014).

In a case involving a governmental plan that was exempt from ERISA, the Maryland Court of Appeals held that the trial court did not abuse its discretion in issuing a posthumous order requiring the plan to allocate a portion of a deceased participant's death benefits to his ex-wife pursuant to their dissolution agreement and in imposing a constructive trust on a share of such benefits already paid to his widow, Robinette v. Hunsecker, 96 A.3d 94 (2014).

3. DIVIDING AND VALUING PENSIONS

1. *The strategic framework.* The division of pension rights incident to divorce usually results from a bargain about the division of the entirety of the spouses' marital property. The bargain is usually negotiated by counsel and is strongly influenced by perceptions about what the court would award if the result were left to adjudication. See generally Robert H. Mnookin & Lewis Kornhauser, Bargaining in the Shadow of the Law: The Case of Divorce, 88 Yale L.J. 950 (1979). In community-property states, bargaining commences on the basis of the half interest that each spouse acquires in the earnings of the other during the marriage. In non-community-property states (called separate-property states), the starting point is the more discretionary system of equitable distribution.

Negotiating marital property settlements is the basic work of domestic relations counsel. A host of considerations having little to do with pension law affects these compacts. The settlement is reported to the divorce court and embodied in the judicial decree, which should be drafted to satisfy the QDRO rules if it touches pension wealth. The court all but invariably ratifies the parties' deal. Only when the parties cannot agree must the court take responsibility for dividing the marital property.

2. *Standards for adjudicated division: present value versus reserved jurisdiction.* The law regarding the division of pension assets in contested cases developed (before REAct) two distinct solutions, ascertaining the present value or postponing it by reserving jurisdiction. "[Under] the 'present cash value method,' [the] court determines the community [or marital] interest in the pension, figures the present cash value of that interest, and awards half of that amount to the non-employee spouse in a lump sum, usually in the form of equivalent property; the employee thus receives the entire pension right free of community [or marital] ties. Under the 'reserved jurisdiction method,' the court determines the formula for division at the time of the decree but delays the actual division until payments are received, retaining jurisdiction to award the appropriate percentage of each pension payment if, as, and when, it is paid out." Johnson v. Johnson, 638 P.2d 705, 708 (Ariz.1981).

The reserved jurisdiction method, which avoids present division in favor of a formula for the future, has the advantage of avoiding valuation problems. Nevertheless, courts have mostly preferred the present value method, especially when enough other property has been available for division so that the participant can be awarded the entirety of the pension while the nonemployee spouse is compensated with an equivalent allocation from the nonpension property. The preference for present value over reserved jurisdiction has rested mainly on two grounds: (1) reserved jurisdiction entangles hostile ex-spouses in unwelcome, continuing financial interdependence; and (2) present division, by disposing of the pension issue at the time of the divorce, promotes finality for parties and court.

Consider In re Marriage of Keedy, 813 P.2d 442 (Mont.1991), involving the division of the divorcing husband's future pension from his job as a district judge. The lower court determined that the pension account if currently distributed was worth $28,115, but that the account had a "present value" of $91,364 if the husband remained on the bench and retired at age 65. The lower court awarded the wife half the larger amount. The Montana Supreme Court reversed, pointing to the contingent nature of the larger figure. If the husband "dies, resigns from the bench, is defeated in a re-election campaign, or for any other reason is not a judge at age sixty-five," the larger value would not materialize. "If [the divorcing wife] wishes to receive a present lump-sum distribution as her share of the retirement benefits, it should be based upon the $28,115 accrued contributions," but if she is willing "to share in the risk of future contingencies [she] is entitled to her proportionate share of the future benefits at such time as [the husband] actually receives the retirement benefits."

On the special difficulties associated with valuing and dividing the community interest in pension wealth in a community property state, see Katherine Shaw Spaht, To Divide or Not to Divide the Community Interest in an Unmatured Pension: Present Cash Value Versus Fixed Percentage, 53 Louisiana L. Rev. 753 (1993).

3. *Use of the QDRO.* In many circumstances the QDRO will be superior either to present division or to reserved jurisdiction. The QDRO can achieve the advantages of reserved jurisdiction without the drawbacks. Recall that ERISA § 206(d)(3)(C)(ii) allows a QDRO to award a "percentage of the participant's benefits to be paid by the plan to each such alternate payee"; and that under § 206(d)(3)(J) the alternate payee becomes a beneficiary of the plan. Thus, future dealings are with the plan, not with the participant/ex-spouse, and further court proceedings are unnecessary. Yet the QDRO, like the decree of reserved jurisdiction, avoids the valuation problems that inhere in the present value approach.

The QDRO has a variety of other advantages over pre-REAct practice. The QDRO formula can be shaped to allow the alternate payee to share in post-divorce growth in the participant's account (for example, by awarding a percentage of the participant's final benefit at retirement, as opposed to using the account value at the time of the divorce). And under § 206(d)(3)(F), the alternate payee can be given the survivorship protections of the QJSA/QPSA scheme.

In some states, and for some plans (particularly ERISA-exempt governmental plans), additional procedural steps must be taken before a DRO can be enforced.

4. *Valuing the defined benefit pension.* It is seldom difficult to value the participant's interest in a defined contribution plan; such a pension is worth today's account balance. By contrast, an interest in a defined benefit plan usually requires actuarial calculation: What, for example, is the present discounted value of a pension that promises the participant, who is now 50 years old, a pension at age 65 in the amount of one-and-one-half percent per year of service times his average salary over his final three years? Because actuaries have considerable discretion in selecting assumptions that greatly affect valuation, it is common in a contested divorce involving substantial pension wealth for each side to engage an actuarial expert. In such circumstances the experts' assumptions not infrequently conflict.

The term "unmatured benefits," which appears frequently in domestic relations cases dealing with pension benefits, should be avoided. It sometimes refers to pension benefits that have not vested, sometimes to benefits vested but not yet payable because the participant has not reached normal (or early) retirement age, and sometimes to the possibility that further benefits will accrue.

Literature: David L. Baumer & J.C. Poindexter, Women and Divorce: The Perils of Pension Division, 57 Ohio St. L.J. 203 (1996); Willard J. Lassers, Pension Evaluation and Distribution Following Divorce Made Simple, 10 J. Pension Planning & Compliance 383 (1984).

5. *Vesting.* The issue of whether to treat an unvested account as divisible marital property was controversial into the 1970s. The decision of the California Supreme Court in the *Brown* case, 15 Cal. 3d 838 (1976), was influential in establishing the modern view. The point is now generally understood that forfeitability is a contingency that lowers, but does not eliminate, expected value. At root, therefore, the vesting status of a pension is simply another factor affecting valuation.

Courts remain loath to order the transfer of an unvested pension benefit, not because it cannot be valued, but because such an order raises a moral hazard problem. The participant can beggar the ex-spouse by quitting employment or otherwise behaving so as to trigger the forfeiture. When, therefore, the pension is not fully vested, the inclination is especially strong to compensate the nonemployee spouse with other property and to leave the pension property (and its attendant risk of forfeiture) on the participant.

6. *Quantum.* Easily confused with valuation problems are much deeper issues of domestic relations principle: not what the pension is worth, but what the spouse is worth—how, that is, to "value" the equity of the nonemployee spouse in the participant's pension and other wealth.

Is the spouse only entitled to a share of pension benefits earned during the marriage? Should the participant's financial responsibility to the spouse be limited to the division of plan participant's present wealth? Or does the logic of the marriage imply that the spouse should receive lifetime support in compensation for, say, the permanent reduction in her human capital and her prospects that she incurred as a result of shouldering the childrearing and homemaking responsibilities for many years? See generally Lloyd Cohen, Marriage, Divorce, and Quasi Rents; or, "I Gave Him the Best Years of My Life," 16 J. Legal Studies 267 (1987).

When, as is often the case, the spouses' nonpension wealth is meager, the court's attitude toward the proper division of the pension wealth—in particular, whether to employ a present value standard, or whether to use an inflation-sensitive QDRO formula that tries to capture more of the plan participant's future earnings stream—is likely to reflect a judgment about the underlying equities in the dissolved marriage.

7. *Federal pensions.* In McCarty v. McCarty, 453 U.S. 210 (1981), the Supreme Court held that a state court could not apply state community property law to divide a military pension between the veteran and his spouse. Congress responded with the Former Spouses Protection Act, 10 U.S.C. § 1408 (1982), authorizing state courts to treat the pay of military retirees as community property, and creating a QDRO-like mechanism for direct payment of state court awards to a former spouse in both community property and separate property states. In Mansell v. Mansell, 490 U.S. 581 (1989), a divided Court held that under the 1982 act, state court marital property decrees do not reach military disability benefits, even when disability benefits are paid under the statutory condition that the recipient waive an equivalent amount of military retirement pay.

In a similar cycle of Supreme Court decision and Congressional revision, the Court held in Hisquierdo v. Hisquierdo, 439 U.S. 572 (1979), that a California divorce decree could not divide a Railroad Retirement Act (RRA) pension. The RRA was then amended to conform to the spousal eligibility rules under the Social Security Act. 45 U.S.C. § 231a(c)(4). A divorced spouse is now entitled to Social Security benefits if he or she was married to the Social Security insured for at least ten years when the divorce became final, is unmarried, is at least 62 years old, and is not entitled to a larger benefit in his or her own capacity as a Social Security insured. Social Security Act, §§ 202(b)(1), 202(c)(1), 216(d), 42 U.S.C. §§ 402(b)(1), 402(c)(1), 416(d). Federal foreign service retirement benefits were held divisible in Matter of Rogers, 609 P.2d 877 (Or.App.1980), modified, 615 P.2d 412 (Or.App.1980), 623 P.2d 1108 (Or.App.1981).

An excellent resource on dividing different types of governmental plans is David Clayton Carrad, The Complete QDRO Handbook: Dividing ERISA, Military and Civil Service Pensions and Collecting Child Support from Employee Benefit Plans (3d ed. 2010).

D. TENSIONS WITH COMMUNITY PROPERTY: *BOGGS*

In common law states, spouses do not have shares in each other's earnings and property during the marriage. Each is the sole owner of his or her earnings. The spouses do owe each other duties of support; and as we have just seen in Section C of this chapter, in the event of divorce the property of each is subject to division and allocation to the other, pursuant to the state equitable distribution statutes. In the community property states, by contrast, each spouse is treated as having a present half interest in the other's earnings.

When Congress amended ERISA in 1984 to create the REAct spousal interests (that is, both the QJSA/QPSA survivorship interests and the QDRO interests arising on divorce), Congress gave scant attention to the relation between these new entitlements and the marital property regime in the community property jurisdictions. Since ERISA § 514(a) preempts any state law that "relate[s] to" an ERISA-covered plan, the question arose: Do the QJSA/QPSA and QDRO provisions defeat inconsistent marital property law in the community property states? In 1997 in *Boggs v. Boggs*, reproduced here, a divided Supreme Court held for preemption. For simplicity, the opinions and the complex facts in *Boggs* have been extensively edited to delete the Court's references to an IRA account and an ESOP account that the decedent owned, in addition to the defined benefit pension plan annuity that was the main subject of dispute.

Boggs v. Boggs

520 U.S. 833 (1997).

■ KENNEDY, J., delivered the opinion of the Court. . . .

We consider whether the Employee Retirement Income Security Act of 1974 (ERISA) pre-empts a state law allowing a nonparticipant spouse to transfer by testamentary instrument an interest in undistributed pension plan benefits. Given the pervasive significance of pension plans in the national economy, the congressional mandate for their uniform and comprehensive regulation, and the fundamental importance of community property law in defining the marital partnership in a number of States, the question is of undoubted importance. We hold that ERISA pre-empts the state law. . . .

Isaac Boggs worked for South Central Bell from 1949 until his retirement in 1985. Isaac and Dorothy, his first wife, were married when he began working for the company, and they remained husband and wife until Dorothy's death in 1979. They had three sons. Within a year of Dorothy's death, Isaac married Sandra, and they remained married until his death in 1989.

Upon retirement, Isaac [received] a monthly annuity payment during his retirement of $1,777.67 from the Bell South Service Retirement Program.

The instant dispute over ownership of the benefits is between Sandra (the surviving wife) and the sons of the first marriage. The sons' claim to a portion of the benefits is based on Dorothy's will. Dorothy bequeathed to Isaac one-third of her estate, and a lifetime usufruct in the remaining two-thirds. A lifetime usufruct is the rough equivalent of a common-law life estate. She bequeathed to her sons the naked ownership in the remaining two-thirds, subject to Isaac's usufruct. All agree that, absent pre-emption, Louisiana law controls and that under it Dorothy's will would dispose of her community property interest in Isaac's undistributed pension plan [benefits].

Sandra contests the validity of Dorothy's 1980 testamentary transfer, basing her claim to those benefits on her interest under Isaac's will and [ERISA § 205]. Isaac bequeathed to Sandra outright certain real property including the family home. His will also gave Sandra a lifetime usufruct in the remainder of his estate, with the naked ownership interest being held by the sons. Sandra argues that the sons' competing claim, since it is based on Dorothy's 1980 purported testamentary transfer of her community property interest in undistributed pension plan benefits, is pre-empted by ERISA. The Bell South Service Retirement Program monthly annuity is now paid to Sandra as the surviving spouse.

After Isaac's death, two of the sons filed an action in state court requesting the appointment of an expert to compute the percentage of the retirement benefits they would be entitled to as a result of Dorothy's attempted testamentary transfer. They further sought a judgment awarding them a portion [of] Sandra's survivor annuity payments, both received and payable.

In response, Sandra Boggs filed a complaint in the United States District Court for the Eastern District of Louisiana, seeking a declaratory judgment that ERISA pre-empts the application of Louisiana's community property and succession laws to the extent they recognize the sons' claim to an interest in the disputed retirement benefits. The District Court granted summary judgment against Sandra Boggs. [A] divided panel of the Fifth Circuit affirmed. [We] now reverse. . . .

ERISA is an intricate, comprehensive statute. Its federal regulatory scheme governs employee benefit plans, which include both pension and welfare plans. All employee benefit plans must conform to various reporting, disclosure and fiduciary requirements, while pension plans must also comply with participation, vesting, and funding requirements. The surviving spouse annuity and QDRO provisions, central to the dispute here, are part of the statute's mandatory participation and vesting requirements. These provisions provide detailed protections to spouses of plan participants which, in some cases, exceed what their rights would be were community property law the sole measure.

ERISA's express pre-emption clause states that the Act "shall supersede any and all State laws insofar as they may now or hereafter relate to any employee benefit plan. . . ." [ERISA § 514(a)]. We can begin, and in this case end, the analysis by simply asking if state law conflicts with the provisions of ERISA or operates to frustrate its objects. We hold that there is a conflict, which suffices to resolve the case. . . .

The annuity at issue is a qualified joint and survivor annuity mandated by ERISA. [ERISA] requires that every qualified joint and survivor annuity include an annuity payable to a nonparticipant surviving spouse. The survivor's annuity may not be less than 50% of the amount of the annuity which is payable during the joint lives of the participant and spouse. Provision of the survivor's annuity may not be waived by the participant, absent certain limited circumstances, unless the spouse consents in writing to the designation of another beneficiary, which designation also cannot be changed without further spousal consent, witnessed by a plan representative or notary public. Sandra Boggs, as the surviving spouse, is entitled to a survivor's annuity under these provisions. She has not waived her right to the survivor's annuity, let alone consented to having the sons designated as the beneficiaries. . . .

ERISA's solicitude for the economic security of surviving spouses would be undermined by allowing a predeceasing spouse's heirs and legatees to have a community property interest in the survivor's annuity. Even a plan participant cannot defeat a nonparticipant surviving spouse's statutory entitlement to an annuity. It would be odd, to say the least, if Congress permitted a predeceasing nonparticipant spouse to do so. . . .

In the face of this direct clash between state law and the provisions and objectives of ERISA, the state law cannot stand. [It] would undermine the purpose of ERISA's mandated survivor's annuity to allow Dorothy, the predeceasing spouse, by her testamentary transfer to defeat in part Sandra's entitlement to the annuity [ERISA § 205] guarantees her as the surviving spouse. This cannot be. States are not free to change ERISA's structure and balance. . . .

[The] principal object of the statute is to protect plan participants and beneficiaries. [ERISA] confers beneficiary status on a nonparticipant spouse or dependent in only narrow circumstances delineated by its provisions. For example, as we have discussed, [ERISA § 205] requires provision of a surviving spouse annuity in covered pension plans, and, as a consequence the spouse is a beneficiary to this extent. [ERISA § 206's] QDRO provisions likewise recognize certain pension plan community property interests of nonparticipant spouses and dependents. [In] creating the QDRO mechanism Congress was careful to provide that the alternate payee, the "spouse, former spouse, child, or other dependent of a participant," is to be considered a plan beneficiary. [ERISA § 206(d)(3)(K), (J).] These provisions are essential to one of [REAct's] central purposes, which is to give enhanced protection to the spouse and dependent children in the event of divorce or separation, and in the event of death the surviving spouse. Apart from these detailed provisions, ERISA does not confer beneficiary status on nonparticipants by reason of their marital or dependent status. . . .

The surviving spouse annuity and QDRO provisions, which acknowledge and protect specific pension plan community property interests, give rise to the strong implication that other community property claims are not consistent with the statutory scheme. ERISA's silence with respect to the right of a nonparticipant spouse to control pension plan benefits by testamentary transfer provides powerful support for the conclusion that the right does not exist. . . .

We conclude the sons have no claim under ERISA to a share of the retirement benefits. To begin with, the sons are neither participants nor beneficiaries. A "participant" is defined as an "employee or former employee of an employer, or any member or former member of an employee organization, who is or may become eligible to receive a benefit." [ERISA § 3(7).] A "beneficiary" is a "person designated by a participant, or by the terms of an employee benefit plan, who is or may become entitled to a benefit thereunder." [ERISA § 3(8).] Respondents' claims are based on Dorothy Boggs' attempted testamentary transfer, not on a designation by Isaac Boggs or under the terms of the retirement plans. They do not even attempt to argue that they are beneficiaries by virtue of the judgment of possession qualifying as a QDRO. . . .

Respondents and their *amicus* in effect ask us to ignore [ERISA § 3(8)'s] definition of "beneficiary" and, through case law, create a new class of persons for whom plan assets are to be held and administered. The statute is not amenable to this sweeping extratextual extension. It is unpersuasive to suggest that third parties could assert their claims without being counted as "beneficiaries." A plan fiduciary's responsibilities run only to participants and beneficiaries. [ERISA § 404(a)(1).] Assets of a plan are held for the exclusive purposes of providing benefits to participants and beneficiaries and defraying reasonable expenses of administration. [ERISA § 403(c)(1).] Reading ERISA to permit nonbeneficiary interests, even if not enforced against the plan, would result in troubling anomalies. Either pension plans would be run for the benefit of only a subset of those who have a stake in the plan or state law would have to move in to fill the apparent gaps between plan administration responsibilities and ownership rights, resulting in a complex set of requirements varying from State to State. Neither result accords with the statutory scheme.

The conclusion that Congress intended to pre-empt respondents' nonbeneficiary, nonparticipant interests in the retirement plans is given specific and powerful reinforcement by the pension plan anti-alienation provision. [ERISA § 206(d)(1)] provides that "each pension plan shall provide that benefits provided under the plan may not be assigned or alienated." Statutory anti-alienation provisions are potent mechanisms to prevent the dissipation of funds. [The] anti-alienation provision can "be seen to bespeak a pension law protective policy of special intensity: Retirement funds shall remain inviolate until retirement." J. Langbein & B. Wolk, Pension and Employee Benefit Law 547 (2d ed. 1995).

Dorothy's 1980 testamentary transfer, which is the source of respondents' claimed ownership interest, is a prohibited "assignment or alienation." An "assignment or alienation" has been defined by regulation, with certain exceptions not at issue here, as "any direct or indirect arrangement whereby a party acquires from a participant or beneficiary" an interest enforceable against a plan to "all or any part of a plan benefit payment which is, or may become, payable to the participant or beneficiary." 26 C.F.R. § 1.401(a)–13(c)(1)(ii). Those requirements are met. Under Louisiana law community property interests are enforceable against a plan. If respondents' claims were allowed to succeed they would have acquired, as of 1980, an interest in Isaac's pension plan at the expense of plan participants and beneficiaries. . . .

Community property laws have, in the past, been pre-empted in order to ensure the implementation of a federal statutory scheme. *Free* v. *Bland*, [369 U.S. 663 (1962)], is of particular relevance here. A husband had purchased United States savings bonds with community funds in the name of both spouses. Under Treasury regulations then in effect, when a co-owner of the bonds died, the surviving co-owner received the entire interest in the bonds. After the wife died, her son—the principal beneficiary of her will—demanded either one-half of the bonds or reimbursement for loss of the community property interest. The Court held that the regulations pre-empted the community property claim, explaining:

One of the inducements selected by the Treasury is the survivorship provision, a convenient method of avoiding complicated probate proceedings. Notwithstanding this provision, the State awarded full title to the co-owner but required him to account for half of the value of the bonds to the decedent's estate. Viewed realistically, the State has rendered the award of title meaningless. Id., at 669.

The same reasoning applies here. If state law is not pre-empted, the diversion of retirement benefits will occur regardless of whether the interest in the pension plan is enforced against the plan or the recipient of the pension benefit. The obligation to provide an accounting, moreover, as with the probate proceedings referred to in *Free*, is itself a burden of significant proportions. Under respondents' view, a pension plan participant could be forced to make an accounting of a deceased spouse's community property interest years after the date of death. If the couple had lived in several States, the accounting could entail complex, expensive, and time-consuming litigation. Congress could not have intended that pension benefits from pension plans would be given to accountants and attorneys for this purpose. . . .

■ JUSTICE BREYER, with whom JUSTICE O'CONNOR joins, and with whom THE CHIEF JUSTICE and JUSTICE GINSBURG join except as to Part II–B–3, dissenting.

Louisiana community property law "relates to" an ERISA plan within the meaning of [ERISA § 514(a)] if it expressly "refers" to such a plan, or if it has an impermissible "connection with" a plan. Neither of these grounds for pre-emption is present here.

The relevant Louisiana statute does not refer to ERISA or to pensions at all. It simply says that "property acquired during the existence of the legal regime through the effort, skill, or industry of either spouse" is "community property." Nor does the statute act exclusively on, or rely on the existence of, ERISA plans. . . .

The state law in question concerns the ownership of benefits. I concede that a primary concern of ERISA is the proper financial management of pension and welfare benefit funds themselves, and that payment of benefits (which amounts to the writing of checks from those funds) is closely "connected with" that management. I also concede that state laws that affect those payments lie closer to ERISA's federal heart than do state laws that, say, affect those goods and services that ERISA benefit plans purchase, such as apprenticeship training programs, or medical benefits. But, even so, I cannot say that the state law at issue here concerns a subject that Congress wished to place outside the State's legal reach.

My reason in part lies in the fact that the state law in question involves family, property, and probate—all areas of traditional, and important, state concern. When this Court considers pre-emption, it works "on the 'assumption that the historic police powers of the States were not to be superseded by the Federal Act unless that was the clear and manifest purpose of Congress.'" . . .

The lawsuit before us concerns benefits that the fund has already distributed; it asks not the fund, but others, for a subsequent accounting.

And, as I discuss in Part II–B–3 below, this lawsuit will not interfere with the payment of a survivor annuity to Sandra. Under these circumstances, I do not see how allowing the respondents' suit to go forward could interfere with the administration of the BellSouth pension plan according to ERISA's requirements. Whether or not the children are allowed to seek an accounting, the plan fiduciaries will continue to owe a duty only to plan participants and beneficiaries. Contrary to the majority's suggestion, Dorothy's children are not the equivalent of plan "participants" or "beneficiaries" any more than would be a grocery store, a bank, an IRA account, or any other recipient of funds that have emerged from a pension plan in the form of a distributed benefit, and no one here claims the contrary. Moreover, the children here are seeking an accounting only after the plan participant has died. But even were that not so, any threat the children's lawsuit could pose to plan administration is far less than that posed by the division of plan assets upon separation or divorce, which is allowed under [ERISA § 206(d)].

Sandra Boggs, supported by the Solicitor General, points [to] statutory provisions with which, she believes, Louisiana law conflicts. . . .

ERISA's "anti-alienation" provision, [ERISA § 206(d)(1)], says that "benefits provided under the [qualified ERISA plan] may not be assigned or alienated." We have stated that this provision reflects "a decision to safeguard a stream of income for pensioners (and their dependents . . .)." *Guidry v. Sheet Metal Workers Nat. Pension Fund.* Sandra Boggs and the Solicitor General claim that Louisiana law interferes with a significant "anti-alienation" objective, both (1) by permitting Dorothy, the nonparticipant spouse, to obtain an undivided interest in the pension of Isaac, the participant spouse; and (2) by permitting Dorothy to transfer that interest on her death to her children, who, as far as ERISA is concerned, are third parties.

The first claim—simply attacking Dorothy's possession of an undivided one-half interest in that portion of retirement benefits that accrued during her marriage to Isaac—does not attack any "assignment" of an interest nor any "alienation" of an interest, for Dorothy's interest arose not through assignment or alienation, but through the operation of Louisiana's community property law itself. Thus, Sandra's claim must be that community property law's grant of an undivided one-half interest in retirement benefits to a nonparticipant wife or husband itself violates some congressional purpose. But what purpose could that be? Congress has recognized that community property law, like any other kind of property law, can create various property interests for nonparticipant spouses. See [ERISA § 206(d)(3)(B)(ii)(II)]. Community property law, like other property law, can provide an appropriate legal framework for resolving disputes about who owns what. The anti-alienation provision is designed to prevent plan beneficiaries from prematurely divesting themselves of the funds they will need for retirement, not to prevent application of the property laws that define the legal interest in those funds. One cannot find frustration of an "anti-alienation" purpose simply in the state law's definition of property.

The second claim—attacking Dorothy's testamentary transfer to her children—is more plausible. Nonetheless, [ERISA] does not concern itself with what a pension fund beneficiary, such as Isaac, does with his pension money at his death. That is not surprising, for after the death of a beneficiary the money is no longer needed for that beneficiary's support. And if ERISA does not embody a congressional purpose to restrict what Isaac can do with his pension funds after his death, there is no reason to believe it embodies some similar general purpose with respect to Dorothy. Insofar as the pension is community property, it belongs to both Dorothy and Isaac equally; it is just as much hers as his. Why, then, should ERISA restrict her testamentary power in respect to her property any more than it restricts his? . . .

[II.B.3]

Sandra Boggs and the Solicitor General rely on [ERISA § 205], which sets forth specific provisions concerning the payment of annuities to a plan participant's surviving spouse. . . .

The $1,800 monthly annuity payments [were] paid from the BellSouth Management Pension Plan, a "defined benefit" pension plan, initially to Isaac during his lifetime, and then to his second wife, Sandra, for her life. [I] agree with the majority that Louisiana cannot give Dorothy's children a share of the pension annuity that Sandra is receiving without frustrating the purpose of [ERISA § 205]. . . .

In this case, Isaac apparently retained possession of other, nonpension assets from the Dorothy-Isaac community after Dorothy's death because her will gave him a lifetime usufruct in the portion of her estate that she did not bequeath to him outright. [In] such a circumstance, Louisiana law might provide an accounting to allow Dorothy's estate, or her heirs, to recover Dorothy's community property share of those nonpension assets, from Isaac's estate, or from his heirs, after his death. In applying such a law, a Louisiana court might allocate property so that federally granted property rights, such as Sandra's right to a survivor annuity, are fully protected.

I cannot understand why Congress would want to pre-empt Louisiana law if (or insofar as) that law provides for an accounting and collection from other property—i.e., property other than the annuity that [ERISA § 205] requires the BellSouth plans to pay to Sandra. The survivor annuity provision assures Sandra that she will receive an annuity for the rest of her life. Louisiana law (on my assumption) would not take from her either that annuity or any other asset that belongs to her. The most one could say is that Sandra will not receive certain other assets—assets which belonged to the Dorothy-Isaac community and which Isaac had no right to give to anyone in the first place.

Nothing in ERISA suggests that it cares about what happens to those other assets. The survivor annuity provision says nothing about them. . . .

In sum, an annuity goes to Sandra, a surviving spouse; but otherwise Dorothy would remain free not only to have, but to bequeath, her share of the marital estate to her children. This reading of the relevant statutory provisions and purposes protects Sandra, limits ERISA's interference with basic state property and family law, and minimizes the extent to which ERISA would interfere with Dorothy's pre-existing property.

NOTES AND QUESTIONS

1. Justice Kennedy's opinion in *Boggs* drew the unqualified support of four other justices (Stevens, Scalia, Souter, Thomas). Two others (Ginsburg, Rehnquist) joined in some but not all of the opinion. Only Justice O'Connor joined the portion of Justice Breyer's dissent in which he argues that although Louisiana's community property law could not deprive Sandra of her right to her QJSA under the terms of Isaac's pension plan, Louisiana could, consistent with ERISA, deprive Sandra of other assets stemming from the Dorothy-Isaac community that rightfully belong to Dorothy's heirs. Breyer would allow Louisiana to take account of the *value* of Dorothy's community property interest in Isaac's pension at the time of her death in determining Dorothy's proper share.

The rejection of this part of Breyer's dissent by seven justices has implications beyond community property. As discussed supra in Section B of this chapter, the Uniform Probate Code directs state probate courts to set off a surviving spouse's pension benefits derived from the decedent against the surviving spouse's forced-share entitlement. Does *Boggs* signal that the UPC system will be preempted?

2. The commentary on *Boggs* has been critical. See Tony Vecino, *Boggs v. Boggs*: State Community Property and Succession Rights Wallow in ERISA's Mire, 28 Golden Gate U.L. Rev. 571 (1998); Alvin J. Golden, A Preliminary Analysis of *Boggs v. Boggs*—and the Problems It Does Not Answer, 23 ACTEC Notes 139 (1997); Note, *Boggs v. Boggs* Holds that a Predeceasing Nonparticipant Spouse Has No Property Interest in an ERISA Pension Plan, 6 ERISA Litigation Rptr. 4 (Aug. 1997); Comment, ERISA Preemption, Community Property, and the Nonemployee Spouse: A Study in Confused Equities, 30 Houston L. Rev. 1695 (1993). Nonetheless, Boggs is controlling and courts continue to preempt community property laws. See, e.g., Orr v. Orr, 542 Fed. Appx. 574 (9th Cir. Oct. 15, 2013).

3. The QJSA/QPSA regime of ERISA § 205 applies only to pension benefits. In Emard v. Hughes Aircraft Co., 153 F.3d 949 (9th Cir.1998), involving life insurance benefits, the Ninth Circuit purported to distinguish *Boggs,* holding that California community property law prevails over the beneficiary designation in the disposition of ERISA-plan life insurance. The court said that "[n]o ERISA provision expressly governs disputes between claimants to insurance proceeds." Id. at 957. Further, "[b]ecause California's community property law does not regulate ERISA plans as such, its application is not barred by field preemption." Id. at 961. Does *Emard* successfully escape the rationale of *Boggs*?

4. *Boggs* interferes with transfer tax planning for married persons subject to the estate tax. For discussion, and for planning responses, see Marjorie A. Rogers et al., Overcoming the *Boggs* Dilemma in Community Property States (pts. 1 & 2), Tax Adviser 584, 664 (Aug., Sept. 1999).

5. Since *Boggs* is a statutory interpretation case, Congress could alter the outcome by amending ERISA to subordinate preemption to community property. Should it? See Cynthia A. Samuel & Katherine S. Spaht, Fixing What's Broke: Amending ERISA to Allow Community Property to Apply upon the Death of a Participant's Spouse, 35 Family L.Q. 425 (2001).

E. VICTIMS OF THE PARTICIPANT'S WRONGDOING

When the plan participant steals from the employer or the plan, can the plan recover against the wrongdoer's pension assets? Such "employee wrongdoing" cases direct attention to the core purposes of the antialienation rule, ERISA § 206(d)(1), IRC § 401(a)(13). For the various spousal interests reviewed supra in Sections B and C of this chapter, the REAct amendments to ERISA in 1984 abridged the antialienation rule. In the employee wrongdoing cases, by contrast, the legislation did not address the question of whether criminal or tortious behavior by the participant justifies an exception to the protective policy of the antialienation rule. The courts were more divided about whether to create such an exception than they had been for domestic relations decrees pre-REAct. In 1990 the issue reached the Supreme Court in *Guidry*, reproduced infra.

1. *Should ERISA's protective policy extend to wrongdoers?* In a variety of ordinary private-law circumstances, the courts apply a fundamental maxim of equity, that the wrongdoer should not profit from his wrong. ERISA's antialienation rule is protective. Its purpose is to preserve pension assets for retirement by preventing the participant or his creditors (including judgment creditors) from obtaining preretirement access to those assets. (That goal is better achieved in defined benefit plans and in those money purchase defined contribution plans whose only mode of distribution is annuitization than in types of defined contribution plans that permit the participant to take lump sum distributions.) The issue in *Guidry* and other employee wrongdoing cases is whether the pension assets should also be immunized when the participant's conduct entails not simply preretirement spending, but rather a crime or tort that has brought loss to the plan, to the plan sponsor, to other plan participants, or to an outsider.

2. *Background in spendthrift trust law.* The Restatement of Trusts provides that "tortious conduct by a beneficiary [may] on policy grounds justify a court's refusal to allow spendthrift immunity to protect the trust interest and the lifestyle of that beneficiary, especially one whose willful or fraudulent conduct or persistently reckless behavior causes serious harm to others." Restatement (Third) of Trusts § 59, comment a(2) (2003). Scott's influential treatise on trust law observes that in spendthrift trust cases involving trade creditors the courts justify the hardship on the creditor by saying that the creditor had the opportunity to investigate the spendthrift beneficiary's finances before extending credit. That reasoning does not apply to an involuntary creditor, such as a tort victim, "who is about to be hit by an automobile. [There] is something plainly wrong with the notion that a [spendthrift beneficiary] should be able to continue to enjoy an interest in trust without satisfying the claims of those he or she injures." 3 Austin W. Scott, William F. Fratcher & Mark L. Archer, Scott and Archer on Trusts § 15.5.5, at 1008 (5th ed. 2007).

Is that conduct any less shocking when the victim seeks to recover from the wrongdoer's pension account rather than from the wrongdoers's spendthrift trust?

1. GUIDRY V. SHEET METAL WORKERS NATIONAL PENSION FUND

493 U.S. 365 (1990).

■ JUSTICE BLACKMUN delivered the opinion of the Court.

Petitioner Curtis Guidry pleaded guilty to embezzling funds from his union. The union obtained a judgment against him for $275,000. The District Court imposed a constructive trust on Guidry's pension benefits, and the United States Court of Appeals for the Tenth Circuit affirmed that judgment. Petitioner contends that the constructive trust violates the statutory prohibition on assignment or alienation of pension benefits imposed by [ERISA].

From 1964 to 1981, petitioner Guidry was the chief executive officer of respondent Sheet Metal Workers International Association, Local 9 (Union). From 1977 to 1981 he was also a trustee of respondent Sheet Metal Workers Local No. 9 Pension Fund. Petitioner's employment made him eligible to receive benefits from three union pension funds.

In 1981, the Department of Labor reviewed the Union's internal accounting procedures. That review demonstrated that Guidry had embezzled substantial sums of money from the Union. This led to petitioner's resignation. A subsequent audit indicated that over $998,000 was missing. In 1982, petitioner pleaded guilty to embezzling more than $377,000 from the Union, in violation of § 501(c) of the Labor-Management Reporting and Disclosure Act of 1959 (LMRDA), 29 U.S.C. § 501(c). Petitioner began serving a prison sentence. In April 1984, while still incarcerated, petitioner filed a complaint against two of the plans in the United States District Court for the District of Colorado, alleging that the plans had wrongfully refused to pay him the benefits [of about $1,200 per month] to which he was entitled.

The Union intervened, [seeking to have a constructive trust imposed on Guidry's pension benefits from the two plans].

Petitioner previously had negotiated a settlement with the Local No. 9 Pension Fund. The other two plans, however, contended that petitioner had forfeited his right to receive benefits as a result of his criminal misconduct. In the alternative those plans contended that, if petitioner were found to have a right to benefits, those benefits should be paid to the Union rather than to Guidry.

The District Court therefore was confronted with three different views regarding the disbursement of petitioner's pension benefits. Petitioner contended that the benefits should be paid to him. The two funds argued that the benefits had been forfeited. The Union asserted that the benefits had not been forfeited, but that a constructive trust should be imposed so that the benefits would be paid to the Union rather than to petitioner.

The District Court first rejected the funds' claim that petitioner had forfeited his right to benefits. The court relied on § 203(a) of ERISA, which declares that "[e]ach pension plan shall provide that an employee's right to his normal retirement benefit is nonforfeitable" if the employee meets the statutory age and years of service requirements. The court noted other district court and court of appeals decisions holding that pension benefits were not forfeitable even upon a showing of the covered employee's misconduct.

The court concluded, however, that the prohibition on assignment or alienation of pension benefits contained in ERISA's § 206(d)(1) did not preclude the imposition of a constructive trust in favor of the Union. The court appeared to recognize that the anti-alienation provision generally prohibits the garnishment of pension benefits as a means of collecting a judgment. The court, nevertheless, stated: "ERISA must be read in pari materia with other important federal labor legislation." In the Labor Management Relations Act, 1947, as amended, 29 U.S.C. § 141 et seq., and in the LMRDA, Congress sought to combat corruption on the part of union officials and to protect the interests of the membership. Viewing these statutes together with ERISA, the District Court concluded: "In circumstances where the viability of a union and the members' pension plans was damaged by the knavery of a union official, a narrow exception to ERISA's anti-alienation provision is appropriate." The court therefore ordered that benefits payable to petitioner from all three funds should be held in constructive trust until the Union's judgment and interest thereon were satisfied.

[The] Tenth Circuit affirmed. The court concluded that ERISA's anti-alienation provision could not be invoked to protect a dishonest pension-plan fiduciary whose breach of duty injured the beneficiaries of the plan. The court deemed it "extremely unlikely that Congress intended to ignore equitable principles by protecting individuals such as [petitioner] from the consequences of their misconduct." The court concluded that "the district court's imposition of a constructive trust on [petitioner's] pension benefits both accorded [with] principles of trust law and was well within its discretionary power as defined by the common law and ERISA."

Because Courts of Appeals have expressed divergent views concerning the availability of exceptions to ERISA's anti-alienation provision, we granted certiorari.

Both the District Court and the Court of Appeals presumed that § 206(d)(1) of ERISA erects a general bar to the garnishment of pension benefits from plans covered by the Act. This Court, also, indicated as much, although in dictum, in *Mackey v. Lanier Collection Agency & Service, Inc.*, 486 U.S. 825 (1988). [We] see no meaningful distinction between a writ of garnishment and the constructive trust remedy imposed in this case. That remedy is therefore prohibited by § 206(d)(1) unless some exception to the general statutory ban is applicable.

The Court of Appeals, in holding that "the district court's use of a constructive trust to redress breaches of ERISA was proper," indicated that an exception to the anti-alienation provision can be made when a pension plan fiduciary breaches a duty owed to the plan itself. The court relied on § 409(a) of ERISA, which provides that a faithless pension plan fiduciary "shall be personally liable to make good to such plan any losses to the plan resulting from each such breach [and] shall be subject to such other equitable or remedial relief as the court may deem appropriate." We need not decide whether the remedial provisions contained in § 409(a) supersede the bar on alienation in § 206(d)(1), since petitioner has not been found to have breached any fiduciary duty *to the pension plans*. [It] is clear, however, that petitioner was convicted of stealing money only from the Union. [Respondents'] argument plays on the natural tendency to blur the distinctions between a fund and its related union (since an injury to either will hurt the union's membership). Respondents, however, cannot avoid the fact that the funds here and the Union are distinct legal entities. (Indeed, at an earlier stage of the litigation these parties took inconsistent positions: the funds argued that petitioner's benefits were subject to forfeiture, while the Union contended that petitioner retained his right to benefits but that the benefits should be placed in constructive trust). Although petitioner's actions may have harmed the Union's members who are the beneficiaries of the funds, petitioner has not been found to have breached any duty to the plans themselves. In our view, therefore, the Court of Appeals erred in invoking § 409(a)'s remedial provisions. . . .

Nor do we think it appropriate to approve any generalized equitable exception—either for employee malfeasance or for criminal misconduct— to ERISA's prohibition on the assignment or alienation of pension benefits. Section 206(d) reflects a considered congressional policy choice, a decision to safeguard a stream of income for pensioners (and their dependents, who may be, and perhaps usually are, blameless), even if that decision prevents others from securing relief for the wrongs done them. If exceptions to this policy are to be made, it is for Congress to undertake that task.

As a general matter, courts should be loath to announce equitable exceptions to legislative requirements or prohibitions that are unqualified by the statutory text. The creation of such exceptions, in our view, would be especially problematic in the context of an antigarnishment provision. Such a provision acts, by definition, to hinder the collection of a lawful debt. A restriction on garnishment therefore can be defended *only* on the view that the effectuation of certain broad social policies sometimes takes precedence over the desire to do equity between particular parties. It makes little sense to adopt such a policy and then to refuse enforcement whenever enforcement appears inequitable. A court attempting to carve out an exception that would not swallow the rule would be forced to determine whether application of the rule in particular circumstances would be "especially" inequitable. The impracticability of defining such a standard reinforces our conclusion that the identification of any exception should be left to Congress.

Understandably, there may be a natural distaste for the result we reach here. The statute, however, is clear. In addition, as has been noted above, the malefactor often is not the only beneficiary of the pension.

The judgment of the Court of Appeals is reversed, and the case is remanded for further proceedings consistent with this opinion.

2. AN EXCEPTION FOR WRONGDOING?

1. *Deference to Congress?* The opinion in *Guidry* places the responsibility for the outcome on the "considered congressional policy choice" of ERISA § 206(d). Did Congress really consider outcomes such as that in *Guidry* when enacting ERISA § 206(d)?

In a prominent pre-*Guidry* case, United Metal Products Corp. v. National Bank of Detroit, 811 F.2d 297 (6th Cir.1987), the court explained why it thought that only Congress should decide whether to create exceptions to ERISA's antialienation rule for cases of wrongdoing. The case involved a bookkeeper who embezzled $441,000 from her employer, then fled to Brazil as a fugitive. The employer obtained a civil judgment for the $441,000 and attempted to garnish the employee's $35,000 profit-sharing account.

> [W]hether an exception should be created is a question for legislative rather than judicial judgment. Only when a literal construction of a statute yields results so manifestly unreasonable that they could not fairly be attributed to congressional design will an exception to statutory language be judicially implied. We believe Congress could have reasonably concluded that stability and certainty of pension and profit sharing plans, as well as the avoidance of delay or non-receipt of promised benefits, are important and legitimate goals of ERISA.

811 F.2d at 300. Is this a garden-variety slippery slope argument, or is there legitimate concern that the need to balance competing interests in wrongdoing cases would interfere with the value of routinized administration of pension plans that Congress emphasized when enacting ERISA's preemption clause?

In Ellis National Bank of Jacksonville v. Irving Trust Co., 786 F.2d 466 (2d Cir.1986), the wrongdoer, a stockbroker, was convicted of theft and fraud and was jailed. His unauthorized transactions resulted in increased commission income, a portion of which he contributed to two employer-sponsored defined contribution plans. *Ellis* instances a particularly compelling case for intervention, because the fruits of the wrong were, in part, directly deposited in the wrongdoer's pension accounts. The employer, which had to make good on the three-million-dollar loss to the firm's customers, sought to recoup a portion of the loss by having a constructive trust imposed on the wrongdoer's pension accounts. The Second Circuit refused the employer's claim to set aside the antialienation rule, saying that "even a narrow judicially created 'criminal misconduct' exception would undermine, rather than promote, the stability of the pension plan and its employee members by creating uncertainty and potentially delayed receipt or non-receipt of benefits." Id. at 471.

Are you persuaded by these courts' expressions of concern that they would have difficulty discerning whether particular instances of wrongdoing were serious enough to justify invoking the equitable maxim against allowing the wrongdoer to profit from his own wrong?

2. *The wrongdoer's family. Guidry* echoes a theme found in some of the earlier employee wrongdoing cases, that ERISA's antialienation rule means to protect not only the employee, but his or her dependents, "who may be, and perhaps usually are, blameless."

This strand of reasoning became prominent in Vink v. SHV North America Holding Corp., 549 F.Supp. 268 (S.D.N.Y.1982). The court said that even if an exception to the antialienation rule could be justified for the wrongdoer, ERISA also means to protect the retirement income of the families of pension plan participants, and an exception for wrongdoers would "in no [way] promote the well-being of the dependents of faithless employees whose pension benefits are taken away." Id. at 271.

Do you think Congress meant to promote a right of family members to enjoy stolen property? Compare Restatement of Restitution § 123 (1937).

3. *The relation of antialienation and vesting.* In *Vink*, the employee, Vink, was convicted of mail fraud and other offenses arising out of schemes to accept kickbacks and to divert more than three million dollars in revenue from the employer. The employer sued Vink for damages and refused to pay him his vested profit-sharing account. The court said it was uncertain whether the employer "has employed a species of forfeiture or of involuntary assignment of Vink's benefits back to the pension fund. Whichever the case may be, ERISA's nonforfeitability and nonassignability provisions clearly cover it." *Vink*, 549 F.Supp. at 270. Treating the case as one of vesting, the court reasoned that when Vink stole from his employer, he was among those whom Congress meant to protect by forbidding "bad boy" clauses that forfeit vested pension benefits.

It will be recalled from the discussion in Chapter 4, supra, that the typical bad boy clause imposed a pension forfeiture when the former employee engaged in competition with the employer, or when the employee engaged in acts of disloyalty or dishonesty. ERISA now subjects bad boy clauses to the vesting rules; such forfeitures are only allowed within the periods permitted under § 203(a).

How might the employee wrongdoing cases such as *Guidry* differ from the circumstances entailed in the application of the ordinary bad boy clause? One factor underlying the prohibition of bad boy clauses was concern about the potential for abuse by the employer (or, in multiemployer plans, by the union). If an employment relationship soured, a vengeful employer could allege (or threaten to allege) disloyalty or dishonesty as a pretext for stripping the employee of his pension. Does it matter in *Guidry* and other wrongdoer cases that there has been an indictment, a criminal conviction, or a tort judgment—in other words, that an independent determination has been made that the plan participant indeed committed a serious misdeed?

In *Guidry* the Supreme Court refused to impose a constructive trust on Guidry's pension assets for fear of conflict with the antialienation rule of ERISA § 206(d). Could the opinion also have been rested on the ground that such a remedy would impair the vesting rules of ERISA § 203, working a forfeiture of vested pension benefits? Are the plaintiffs in the employee wrongdoing cases asking the courts to devise and impose retroactive bad boy clauses in the form of judicial remedies?

In Woolsey v. Marion Laboratories, 934 F.2d 1452 (10th Cir.1991), an employee who resigned under accusations of unethical conduct received his profit sharing account as a lump sum distribution. He asked to take half his account balance in company stock, an optional mode of distribution that lay in the discretion of the plan fiduciaries. They refused to grant him stock, on account of his unethical conduct. Subsequently, the shares increased materially in value and the former employee sued for the lost gains. Among his contentions was the claim, citing *Guidry*, that "ERISA prohibits the denial of benefits because of alleged wrongdoing during employment." Id. at 1458. May the plan fiduciaries take his misconduct into consideration in deciding the form of the distribution?

4. *When the wrongdoing beneficiary is also a plan fiduciary.* In Crawford v. La Boucherie Bernard Ltd., 815 F.2d 117 (D.C.Cir.1987), the court dealt with a pair of businessmen who, as trustees of a profit-sharing plan, looted and otherwise shortchanged the plan for nearly a million dollars. The court held that the wrongdoers' account balances could be offset against their liability to the plan. Citing the treatises of Scott and Bogert, the court invoked the rule of trust law that when a trustee who is also a beneficiary commits a breach of trust, the other beneficiaries are entitled to a charge upon the wrongdoing trustee's beneficial interest in the trust. Restatement (Second) of Trusts § 257 (1959). The court reasoned that ERISA's antialienation rule does not alter the application of that rule. "A contrary interpretation would permit trustee wrongdoers to benefit from their misdeeds at the expense of those whom ERISA was designed to protect." 815 F.2d at 121. Does that argument fairly respond to the wrongdoers' claim that the antialienation rule intends to protect the retirement savings even of wrongdoers?

In cases such as *Guidry, United Metal Products, Vink,* and *Ellis National Bank,* wrongdoers who committed serious crimes were held not to have lost the protection of the antialienation rule. Is there any argument for treating breach of trust as more serious than felony? It turns out that the answer to that question is "yes," not on account of the underlying merits, but because ERISA § 409(a) supplies a superior linguistic basis for reaching the assets of the wrongdoing fiduciary.

ERISA § 409(a) provides that a fiduciary who breaches ERISA's fiduciary responsibilities "shall be personally liable to make good to such plan any losses to the plan resulting from each such breach, and to restore to such plan any profits of such fiduciary which have been made through use of assets of the plan by the fiduciary, and shall be subject to such other equitable or remedial relief as the court may deem appropriate. . . ."

In *Guidry*, it will be recalled, the Supreme Court was careful to sidestep the question of the relation between ERISA § 409(a) and § 206(d)(1). The Court observed that the victim in *Guidry* was the union, not the pension plans, which were "distinct legal entities." Accordingly, the Court said that it "need not decide whether the remedial provisions contained in § 409(a) supersede the bar on alienation in § 206(d)(1) since [Guidry] has not been found to have breached any fiduciary duty *to the pension plans*" (emphasis in original).

In *Coar v. Kazimir*, 990 F.2d 1413 (3d Cir.1993), cert. denied, 510 U.S. 862 (1993), the Third Circuit accepted the opening that the Supreme Court had left in *Guidry* to set off civil damages against the pension accounts of a wrongdoing fiduciary under ERISA § 409(a). Coar was both a fiduciary of and a participant in the Pension Fund of the Mid-Jersey Trucking Local 701 (the Fund). He was convicted of conspiring to receive kickbacks for investing Fund assets. In companion civil litigation, Coar was assessed $25 million in damages to the Fund under ERISA §§ 409(a) and 502(a)(3), and a further $96 million in RICO damages to the Fund.

The judgments were unsatisfied, and the Fund notified Coar that it would offset his pension benefits under § 409(a). The Third Circuit, reversing the district court, sustained the setoff.

The Third Circuit panel offered two reasons for its result. Judge Becker dissented from both but concurred in the result. The majority asserted that "the more specific language of section 409(a) serves as a better indicator of congressional intent than the general language of section 206(d)(1)." 990 F.2d at 1420. Judge Becker replied that "the statutory language dealing with alienation in § 206(d)(1) is more specific in that content than the language dealing with equitable remedies under § 409(a)." Id. at 1425. The majority further reasoned that "when the Pension Fund, without Coar's consent, set off the benefits due to him against his debt to it there was simply not an alienation within section 206(d)(1)." Id. at 1422. Judge Becker also resisted this distinction between prohibited alienation and setoff, which he characterized as a distinction between third-party and second-party creditors, the Fund being a second-party creditor. Judge Becker thought that "the plain meaning of § 206(d)(1) seems to encompass both the involuntary alienation arising by reason of Coar's criminal fiduciary breach in the context of a claim by the Fund and a claim by a third party." Id. at 1425. Judge Becker joined the majority, however, on the ground that offsetting Coar's pension serves "the broad purpose of [ERISA,] which is to protect and ensure the availability of pension funds for retirees. [To] allow Coar to collect his pension from the very Fund he defrauded would detract from this overriding purpose of ERISA." Id. at 1425–26.

Suppose the participant's wrongdoing consists of bringing a frivolous lawsuit against the plan. May the plan offset its attorney fees against the participant's pension benefits? See Martorana v. Board of Trustees of Steamfitters Local Union 420 Health, Welfare & Pension Fund, 404 F.3d 797 (3d Cir.2005). See also Kickham Hanley v. Kodak Retirement Income Plan, 558 F.3d 204 (2d Cir.2009) (anti-alienation provision barred law firm's claim for attorney's fees from undistributed pension benefits).

5. *Congress intervenes: ERISA § 206(d)(4).* Congress effectively codified the result in *Coar v. Kazimir* in the Taxpayer Relief Act of 1997, enacting new ERISA § 206(d)(4) and IRC § 401(a)(13)(C), which create limited exceptions to the antialienation rule. These provisions permit a participant's benefits to be reduced to satisfy liabilities of the participant to the plan in circumstances in which (1) the participant has been convicted of committing a crime involving the plan, (2) a court has entered a civil judgment (or consent order or decree) against the participant in an action brought to redress a violation of the fiduciary provisions of ERISA, or (3) the participant has entered into a settlement agreement with the Secretary of Labor or with the PBGC in connection with a violation of the fiduciary provisions of ERISA. The court order establishing such liability must decree that the participant's benefit in the plan be applied to satisfy the liability. Spousal consent is required unless the judgment, order, decree, or settlement also requires the spouse to pay an amount to the plan or provides a 50-percent survivor annuity for the spouse.

Note that the 1997 legislation would not alter the result in *Guidry*. Section 206(d)(4) and its IRC analogue apply solely when the liability is to the plan. The provision is broader than the holding in *Coar v. Kazimir*, in that it applies not only to fiduciary wrongdoers, but also to nonfiduciaries who commit a crime involving the plan, such as an employee who steals from the plan.

Is it a fair criticism of *Coar v. Kazimir* and the 1997 legislation to say that this solution makes the availability of a remedy turn on the character of the victim, as opposed to the character of the wrongdoer's conduct? Suppose, for example, that the same wrongdoer injures two victims—the pension fund of which he is a fiduciary, and a neighborhood child whom he ran down while driving drunk. Suppose further that the pension fund is overfunded by $1 billion, and that the child's family is destitute. What is the case for waiving ERISA's antialienation rule to allow the pension fund to recover against the wrongdoer, but not waiving the rule for the maimed child whom the wrongdoer mowed down in a drunken stupor?

6. *Temporal limits to ERISA's antialienation protection.* The *Guidry* litigation returned to the Tenth Circuit on appeal from remand proceedings in Guidry v. Sheet Metal Workers Int'l Association, Local No. 9, 10 F.3d 700 (10th Cir.1993) [hereafter, *Guidry Remand Appeal I*]. The question was whether the union, as judgment creditor for the damages caused to it by Guidry's embezzlement, could garnish Guidry's pension income after he received it. Guidry arranged to have his pension payments paid into a separate bank account, in order to preserve their character as pension receipts. The district court, on remand from the Supreme Court proceedings, held that ERISA's immunity from garnishment endured, " 'so long as the [pension] proceeds are clearly identified as such and have not been commingled with other [funds].' " *Guidry Remand Appeal I*, 10 F.3d at 704, quoting district court decree.

The Tenth Circuit reversed in a 2–1 panel opinion, which subjected Guidry's bank account to garnishment. The court treated the main issue as one of statutory construction of § 206(d)(1), which requires "that benefits provided under the plan may not be assigned or alienated." Id. at 708. The court pointed to Treasury regulations interpreting § 206(d)(1), which define "assignment" and "alienation" as an arrangement "whereby a party acquires from a participant or beneficiary *a right or interest enforceable against the plan* in, or to, all or any part of a plan benefit payment which is or may become payable to the participant or beneficiary." Treas.Reg. 1.401(a)–13(c)(1)(ii), quoted with the emphasis added by the court. The court reasoned that the union "seeks only to enforce a judgment against Mr. Guidry by garnishing his bank account containing pension benefits paid and received; [the union] does not seek to enforce an interest or right against the plan. Because garnishment of Mr. Guidry's received retirement income is not an action against the plan, we conclude it is not prohibited by ERISA § 206(d)(1) as implemented by the ERISA Regulations." Id. at 710.

The Tenth Circuit en banc affirmed the panel opinion. Guidry v. Sheet Metal Workers Nat'l Pension Fund, 39 F.3d 1078 (10th Cir.1994) [hereafter, *Guidry Remand Appeal II.*] The en banc opinion offered an additional justification for the interpretation that ERISA's antialienation provision does not protect pension proceeds once paid. The court observed that provisions of the Social Security and Veterans Benefits Acts protect proceeds paid under those regimes from creditors even after the beneficiary receives payment. "Congress knew how to draft a statute protecting benefits that had left the pension plan, and it did not use similar language with ERISA section 206(d)(1)."

The Tenth Circuit in *Guidry Remand Appeal II* split 7–3 on the further question of whether ERISA preempted a Colorado act that exempts from garnishment 75 percent of "disposable earnings," a term that is defined to include pension benefits. The majority refused to apply ERISA preemption, treating the Colorado garnishment statute as a state law of general application similar to the Georgia garnishment law that was sustained in Mackey v. Lanier Collection Agency & Service, Inc., 486 U.S. 825 (1988). Accordingly, the Tenth Circuit allowed Guidry to shield three quarters of the pension payments under Colorado law. As a matter of ERISA antialienation law under § 206(d)(1), however, the Tenth Circuit en banc persists in the view that ERISA's protection ceases when pension proceeds are paid.

Several other circuits have followed the Tenth Circuit in holding that ERISA § 206(d)(1) ceases to protect retirement funds after the plan pays the beneficiary. Hoult v. Hoult, 373 F.3d 47, 54–55 (1st Cir.2004); Central States, Southeast & Southwest Areas Pension Fund v. Howell, 227 F.3d 672 (6th Cir.2000). The Fourth Circuit took a different position in U.S. v. Smith, 47 F.3d 681 (4th Cir.1995). In a 2–1 decision, the court distinguished lump sum distributions from retirement annuities, reasoning that creditors should be allowed to reach "funds disbursed from an ERISA plan before an employee retire[s]," but that when "the funds are paid pursuant to the terms of the plan as income during retirement years, ERISA prohibits their alienation." Id. at 683.

If the analysis in *Guidry Remand Appeals I & II* prevails, as it now has in several circuits, how much of ERISA's antialienation protection survives? As modified by *Guidry Remand Appeals I & II*, does *Guidry* now stand for the proposition that the victim can recover from the wrongdoer, but only on a postponed basis, when the wrongdoer reaches retirement age or otherwise takes a distribution of pension assets? If so, the victim's remedy is delayed, but the wrongdoer is denied the retirement income stream that is the supposed purpose of the antialienation rule. What is the logic of such a result? The seeming answer in *Guidry Remand Appeals I & II* is that garnishing the pension in Guidry's account rather than in the Pension Fund spares interference with plan administration, but that answer is unresponsive to the policy supposedly being implemented in the antialienation rule, which has nothing to do with sparing the plan the burden of honoring the garnishment. From the standpoint of plan administration, it matters little whether the plan cuts the check to the participant or to his or her judgment creditor, which is why, for example, Congress was willing to order plans to accept substituted payees in the REAct amendments for spousal interests. The policy of the antialienation rule is to protect the retirement income stream of the plan participant.

If the Supreme Court in *Guidry* was correct to protect that stream even when the participant was a wrongdoer, is the Tenth Circuit in *Guidry Remand Appeals I & II* wrong in withdrawing the protection when the participant tries to live off the pension income stream? Do the

Guidry Remand Appeals I & II err by misunderstanding the purpose of the antialienation rule? If, on the other hand, the Supreme Court in *Guidry* was in error, is the Tenth Circuit achieving a desirable evasion of a mistaken Supreme Court precedent?

7. *Ancillary effect on criminal sanctions.* Should ERISA's antialienation provision prevent criminal courts from imposing restitution orders other than those authorized under ERISA § 206(d)(4)? In U.S. v. Novak, 476 F.3d 1041 (9th Cir.2007), the Ninth Circuit held that the 1996 Mandatory Victims Restitution Act authorized the enforcement of restitution orders against ERISA pension plan benefits, notwithstanding ERISA's antialienation provision, overruling an earlier Ninth Circuit decision to the contrary. See U.S. v. Jackson, 229 F.3d 1223 (9th Cir.2000). Prior to the passage of the 1996 federal restitution statute, another circuit had held that ERISA prevents criminal courts from imposing restitution orders other than those authorized by ERISA. U.S. v. Smith, supra, 47 F.3d at 684. In the years following passage of the Mandatory Victims Restitution Act, other courts have come to the same conclusion as the Ninth Circuit, that the statute "constitutes a Congressional exception to ERISA's antialienation provision when it comes to the enforcement of a restitution order against a criminal defendant." U.S. v. Miller, 588 F.Supp.2d 789 (W.D.Mich.2008).

8. *ERISA-exempt plans.* State and local government pension plans that are exempt from ERISA under § 4(b) often contain forfeiture provisions as a sanction against corruption. In California, for example, a public official convicted of a felony directly connected with his or her office forfeits the taxpayer-funded portion of his pension benefit. Cal. Gov. Code § 1243. Public employees in Florida forfeit the taxpayer-funded portions of their pensions if they commit crimes including theft and any felony involving misuse of public office. Fla. Stat. Ann. § 112.3173(3). For discussion see James B. Jacobs et al., Pension Forfeiture: A Problematic Sanction for Public Corruption, 35 American Criminal L. Rev. 57 (1997).

3. THE SLAYER CASES

Perhaps the best known example of the principle that a wrongdoer should not profit from his or her wrong is the slayer rule, now codified in most states, but originally developed in case law. The rule prevents an heir or devisee from succeeding to the property of a decedent whom the heir or devisee has feloniously slain, by treating the slayer as though he or she predeceased the victim. See Restatement (Third) of Property: Wills and Other Donative Transfers § 8.4 (2003) [hereafter Wills Restatement]; Restatement of Restitution § 187(2) (1937) (to be revised as Restatement (Third) of Restitution § 45 (forthcoming)); 4 George E. Palmer, The Law of Restitution § 20.10(a), at 243–45 (1978). Most states now have comprehensive legislation dealing with these situations. The statutes extend the slayer rule to cases in which the victim had named the slayer in a beneficiary designation to receive life insurance or other death benefits that pass outside of probate. See, e.g., Uniform Probate Code § 2–803 (1990 rev.). Before the modern statutes, the courts commonly reached that result by applying a constructive trust to the slayer's share, for the benefit of those persons who would have received the death benefit under the beneficiary designation or by intestate distribution had the slayer predeceased the victim. The various state statutes are summarized and the case law reviewed in the Reporter's Note to Wills Restatement § 8.4, supra, at 172–94.

What the slayer cases share with *Guidry* is that they involve the question of how wrongdoing should affect the interest of a person otherwise entitled to ERISA-plan proceeds. The main difference between the slayer cases and cases such as *Guidry* is that in *Guidry* the plan participant has been the wrongdoer and is seeking to shield his or her pension account from the resulting claims. In the slayer cases, by contrast, the participant has been the victim of the wrong, slain by a person whom he or she had designated to receive death benefits. ERISA's antialienation rule does not apply to such cases, nor does ERISA otherwise address the problem. The question arises of whether the state slayer statute governs, or whether ERISA's broad preemption measure, § 514(a), which supersedes state laws that "relate to" an ERISA plan, defeats the application of the state law. If the state slayer statute is preempted, the question then arises of whether to apply a comparable rule as federal common law, or to allow the slayer to benefit.

ERISA § 514(b)(4), which provides that the preemption clause of § 514(a) "shall not apply to any generally applicable criminal law of a State," might seem to bear on the question of whether the slayer takes, but in fact it does not. Most crimes are also torts, civil wrongs. The issue in a slayer case is civil, not criminal: Which civil party succeeds to the assets?

The first prominent ERISA slayer case was Mendez-Bellido v. Board of Trustees of Division 1181, A.T.U. New York Employees Pension Fund & Plan, 709 F.Supp. 329 (E.D.N.Y.1989). Carlos Mendez, the participant, had been slain by his second wife, who had pleaded guilty to first degree manslaughter. The plan trustees ruled that she was entitled to the qualified preretirement survivor annuity (QPSA) under ERISA. The guardian of Mendez' children by his first marriage asked the federal district court to apply the rule of New York law that forbids a slayer to share in the victim's estate. It did: "[T]he Court must conclude that a state law prohibiting a killer from profiting from her crime is not preempted by ERISA. This common law rule is rooted in public policy and has broad application to insurance policies, wills and intestacy." Id. at 331. Is this rationale persuasive? Why does the antiquity or the wisdom of the state law spare it from preemption if the law "relates to" the distribution of ERISA plan proceeds? The New York slayer rule is state law that determines who takes plan proceeds, the slayer whom the participant named in compliance with the plan-specified procedure; or somebody else, who is substituted according to a provision of state law.

In a General Counsel Memorandum interpreting IRC § 401(a)(13), the Code's version of the antialienation rule, the IRS anticipated the result and rationale in *Mendez-Bellido*. G.C.M. 39000 (1983) found "an implied exception to section 401(a)(13) for purposes of applying the common law principle that an individual who has killed another individual cannot inherit or otherwise benefit in any manner from that person's death, as reflected in a particular state's 'killer statute.' " *Mendez-Bellido* has been followed in numerous decisions. See Mack v.

Mack, 206 P.3d 98 (Nev. 2009) (listing cases determining that ERISA does not preempt slayer statutes).

If the court in *Mendez-Bellido* had decided that ERISA preempted the New York slayer law, could the court have applied the identical rule as federal common law? See Ahmed v. Ahmed, 817 N.E.2d 424 (Ohio App. 7 Dist.2004), in which the ERISA-plan insured was murdered by her husband, the primary beneficiary. The court held that ERISA preempted Ohio's slayer statute, but that federal common law should be applied to prevent the slayer from taking; the slayer was to be treated as though he had predeceased his victim. In Connecticut General Life Ins. Co. v. Riner, 351 F.Supp.2d 492, 497 (W.D.Va.2005), aff'd, 142 Fed.Appx. 690 (4th Cir.2005), the court said that it did not have to choose between the two theories: "Neither Virginia's slayer statute nor federal common law allow" the slayer to benefit. See also Estate of Burkland v. Burkland, 2012 U.S. Dist. LEXIS 419 (E.D. Pa. Jan. 3, 2012) (holding that insurance proceeds should not be distributed under either ERISA or the state slayer statue); Mitchell v. Robinson, 2011 U.S. Dist. LEXIS 147226 (E.D. Mo. Dec. 22, 2011) (preempting state slayer statute but applying it as a matter of federal common law).

Guidry was decided after *Mendez-Bellido*. Should *Guidry* alter either the outcome or the reasoning in *Mendez-Bellido*? In New Orleans Electrical Pension Fund v. Newman, 784 F.Supp. 1233, 1237 (E.D.La.1992), a slayer case decided after *Guidry*, the court asserted that "the congressional policy choice articulated in *Guidry* of safeguarding the stream of income for pensioners and their blameless dependents is not offended by this Court's decision that the policy considerations that underlie the 'killer statutes' provide an implied exception to the anti-alienation rule." Recall that in *Guidry* the Supreme Court expressed its concern that the "impracticability" of asking the courts to decide "particular circumstances would be 'especially' inequitable"; The Court said that this concern reinforced the Court its "conclusion that the identification of any exception should be left to Congress." Does this reasoning render *New Orleans Electrical Pension Fund v. Newman* irreconcilable with *Guidry*?

The Supreme Court refused to confront the slayer problem although urged to do so in Egelhoff v. Egelhoff, 532 U.S. 141 (2001), reproduced infra in Chapter 17. In that case the Court found that ERISA preempted a state statute that treats a divorced spouse named in a prior beneficiary designation as though he or she has predeceased the decedent. Because the slayer statutes employ the same mechanism, the dissenters argued that the rationale in *Egelhoff* would require preempting state slayer statutes as well. The Court said: "These statutes are not before us, so we do not decide the issue." Id. at 152. However, the Court hinted that slayer statutes might not be preempted, because they "are more or less uniform nationally," hence less likely to "interfere[ ] with the aims of [ERISA]."

Thus far, therefore, what has been in doubt in the slayer cases has not been the outcome but the rationale: Slayers do not take, usually because the federal courts apply the state slayer statute despite the language of ERISA preemption, or else as a matter of federal common law.

F. CREDITORS IN BANKRUPTCY

ERISA's anti-alienation requirement shields a debtor's pension benefits from normal creditors, but not necessarily in bankruptcy. ERISA provides that nothing in ERISA "shall be construed to alter, amend, modify, invalidate, impair, or supersede any law of the United States." ERISA § 514(d). Since bankruptcy law is federal, it could presumably override any protection that ERISA might provide.

The reach of the bankruptcy statute is extremely broad. The bankruptcy estate of a debtor includes "all legal or equitable interests of the debtor in property." 11 U.S.C. § 541(a). Furthermore, such interests become the property of the estate notwithstanding "any provision in an agreement, transfer instrument, or applicable nonbankruptcy law [that] restricts or conditions transfer of such interest by the debtor." 11 U.S.C. § 541(c)(1). However, this general rule has an important exception: "A restriction on the transfer of a beneficial interest of the debtor in a trust that is enforceable under applicable nonbankruptcy law is enforceable in a case under this title." 11 U.S.C. § 541(c)(2).

Spendthrift trusts fall within this exception, because state spendthrift trust law qualifies as applicable nonbankruptcy law. For a time the courts were divided about whether the anti-alienation provision in a pension plan subject to ERISA constituted a restriction on transfer enforceable under "applicable nonbankruptcy law." The issue eventually reached the United States Supreme Court, which held that "applicable nonbankruptcy law" can include federal law as well as state law, and that ERISA's anti-alienation provision "constitutes an enforceable transfer restriction for purposes of § 541(c)'s exclusion of property from the bankruptcy estate." Patterson v. Shumate, 504 U.S. 753 (1992).

The holding in *Shumate* meant that any interest of a debtor in a pension plan subject to ERISA's anti-alienation requirement was excluded from the bankruptcy estate and therefore beyond the reach of creditors. However, the ERISA provision does not apply to many types of retirement plans, including governmental plans, church plans, IRAs, and plans for the self-employed under which only partners or only a sole-proprietor are participants.

1. *BAPCPA.* The Bankruptcy Abuse Prevention and Consumer Protection Act of 2005 (BAPCPA) places these non-ERISA plans largely beyond the reach of creditors as well. BAPCPA adds a new federal bankruptcy exemption for "retirement funds to the extent those funds are in a fund or account that is exempt from taxation under section 401, 403, 408, 408A, 414, 457, or 501(a) of the Internal Revenue Code of 1986." 11 U.S.C. § 522(d)(12). This covers the whole range of tax-favored retirement savings including qualified plans, tax-sheltered annuities, IRAs and Roth IRAs, governmental and church plans, and 457(b) plans of nonprofits and state and local governments. Prior to BAPCPA there was a much more limited provision that exempted these types of plans only "to the extent reasonably necessary for the support of the debtor and any dependent of the debtor." 11 U.S.C. § 522(d)(10)(E).

States may normally choose to opt out of the federal exemption scheme and create their own exemptions, which might be more or less generous to debtors. 11 U.S.C. § 522(b)(2). Because *Shumate* created an *exclusion*, not a federal exemption, states could not give creditors access to ERISA plans by opting out of the federal exemption scheme. BAPCPA creates the same protection for non-ERISA plans by providing that the exemption for tax-exempt retirement funds will continue to apply even if a state opts out of the federal exemptions. 11 U.S.C. § 522(b)(3)(C).

The BAPCPA exemption for tax-exempt retirement funds is unlimited in amount, with one important exception. There is a cap of $1,000,000 on the aggregate amount of traditional and Roth IRA accounts that can be exempted. 11 U.S.C. § 522(n). The cap does not apply to amounts attributable to rollovers from qualified plans or 403(b) plans, nor does it apply to SEP-IRAs or SIMPLE-IRAs. Given the historically low annual limit on IRA contributions, few IRAs today are likely to exceed the cap when rollovers are excluded, but even then bankruptcy courts have the power to increase the cap "if the interests of justice so require." It is not at all clear how this discretion will be exercised. Note that many of the states that have opted out of the federal exemption scheme provide a complete exemption for IRAs under their state exemption scheme. See, e.g., Tex. Prop. Code Ann. § 42.0021 (Vernon 2004). The $1,000,000 is adjusted every three years to reflect changes in the Consumer Price Index and, as of the most recent revision in 2013, stands at $1,245,475. Judicial Conference of the United States, Revision of Certain Dollar Amounts in the Bankruptcy Code Prescribed Under Section 104(b) of the Code, 78 Fed. Reg. 12089 (Feb. 21, 2013).

Why should pension plans receive an unlimited bankruptcy exemption? Why should a negligent driver whose only major asset is $2 million in a profit-sharing plan be allowed to retain his plan balance and avoid paying a $2 million judgment against him obtained by a paralyzed victim of his negligence? Why should a debtor who accumulates $200,000 in a profit-sharing plan be treated differently from a debtor whose employer has no plan and who accumulates $200,000 in a bank account to fund his retirement? Would it make more sense to provide a general age-related exemption, such as an amount of assets equal to the present value of an annuity of $X per month commencing at the Social Security retirement age, multiplied by some type of age factor to reflect the fact that the exemption is accrued over a working lifetime?

On June 12, 2014, the U.S. Supreme Court unanimously held in Clark v. Rameker, 134 S. Ct. 2242, that an inherited IRA does not qualify for the "retirement funds" exemption in the Bankruptcy Code and is not excluded from a bankruptcy estate on that basis.

2. *Nonexempt plans.* In enacting the new exemption for tax-exempt retirement funds, Congress did not amend 11 U.S.C. § 541(c)(2) and thus *Shumate* remains good law. Therefore even if an ERISA plan loses its tax exemption, it still is excluded from the bankruptcy estate. But for a non-ERISA plan, the tax-exempt status can be crucial or purposes of the new exemption, although a spendthrift provision may otherwise provide relief. Generally, if a plan has received a favorable determination letter from the IRS that is still in effect when the debtor files for bankruptcy, the plan will be presumed to be exempt from the bankruptcy estate. 11 U.S.C. § 522(b)(4)(A). If the plan has no determination letter, the funds will be exempt from the estate if the debtor demonstrates that (1) no adverse determination as to the fund's tax-exempt status has been made

by a court or the IRS, and (2) either the fund is in substantial compliance with the applicable IRC requirements or, if it is not, the debtor is not materially responsible for the failure. 11 U.S.C. § 522(b)(4)(B). This rule provides still another incentive for a plan sponsor to obtain a written determination regarding the qualified status of a plan.

3.   *Benefits already distributed.* Can bankruptcy creditors reach a pension benefit once it has been paid? In Guidry v. Sheet Metal Workers Nat'l Pension Fund, 39 F.3d 1078 (10th Cir.1994) (en banc), discussed in Section E, supra, as *Guidry Remand Appeal II,* the court allowed the garnishment of funds in a bank account that had been received from a pension fund. The court relied on Treas.Reg. § 1.401(a)–13(c)(1)(ii), which defines the terms "assignment" or "alienation" as "[a]ny [arrangement] whereby a party acquires from a participant or beneficiary a right or interest enforceable against the plan." See also Trucking Employees of North Jersey Welfare Fund, Inc. v. Colville, 16 F.3d 52 (3d Cir.1994) (anti-alienation rule does not apply to funds distributed to beneficiaries). In Hoult v. Hoult, 373 F.3d 47 (1st Cir.2004), the court upheld an order requiring a plan participant to deposit his monthly pension benefit in a specified bank account, a portion of which would be made available to a judgment creditor.

Under BAPCPA, certain distributions are now protected from creditors in bankruptcy. Any distribution that qualifies as an "eligible rollover distribution within the meaning of section 402(c) of the Internal Revenue Code of 1986" continues to qualify for the bankruptcy exemption. 11 U.S.C. 522(b)(4)(D)(i). Eligible rollover distributions are discussed in detail in Chapter 11, infra, but generally any distribution from a qualified plan, 403(b) plan, or a governmental 457(b) plan qualifies, except for annuity type payments, minimum required distributions, or hardship distributions. See IRC §§ 402(c)(4), 403(b)(8), and 457(e)(16). For example, a lump sum distribution from a profit-sharing plan would be protected, even though it is no longer in the plan. However, a monthly pension benefit, as in *Hoult*, is not protected. The statute leaves unclear exactly how this exemption will apply if the distribution is commingled with other funds or transferred to another asset, such as a mutual fund account. A distribution from an IRA receives similar protection, but with a significant additional requirement: it must actually be rolled over into another tax-exempt retirement fund within 60 days of the distribution. 11 U.S.C. 522(b)(4)(D)(ii).

Even if a distribution from a plan is unprotected from creditors, a bankruptcy decree will extinguish typical creditor claims, leaving the creditors with no basis to seize future plan distributions. But note that there is no discharge in bankruptcy for debts arising from "fraud or defalcation while acting in a fiduciary capacity, embezzlement, or larceny." 11 U.S.C. § 523(a)(4).

4.   *Federal tax liens and levies.* Although pension benefits may be excluded or exempted from the bankruptcy estate, the benefits under the plan are property (or at least a right to property) to which a federal tax lien can attach. See Anderson v. United States, 149 Bankr. 591 (Bankr. 9th Cir.1992). This result follows from the general rule that ERISA does not supersede any law of the United States. See ERISA § 514(d). Section 6321 of the Internal Revenue Code creates a lien "upon all property and

rights to property" under specified circumstances and does not exempt pension benefits. Similarly, pension plans are not exempt from an IRS levy. See IRC § 6334(c); McIntyre v. United States, 222 F.3d 655 (9th Cir.2000) ("IRS's authority to proceed against a delinquent taxpayer's interest in benefits from an ERISA-governed plan is not constrained by ERISA's anti-alienation provision").

Other federal statutes have been construed to create the functional equivalent of a tax lien. For example, the Mandatory Victims Restitution Act makes certain restitution orders in criminal cases "a lien in favor of the United States on all property and rights to property of the person fined as if the liability of the person fined were a liability for a tax assessed under the Internal Revenue Code of 1986." 18 U.S.C. § 3613(c). As already noted, such orders can therefore be used to seize assets in a pension plan. See, e.g., United States v. James, 312 F.Supp.2d 802 (E.D.Va. 2004)("criminal defendants owing restitution to the government cannot protect their pension benefits from being used to satisfy their monetary obligation to the government"); United States v. Tyson, 265 F.Supp.2d 788 (E.D.Mich.2003).

Even though a tax lien or its equivalent has attached to a pension benefit, the government must wait to collect until the participant or beneficiary has a right to a distribution. If the participant or beneficiary can elect to receive a distribution currently, presumably the government by reason of its lien can make the same election. In a Field Service Advice, the IRS has stated that a plan may refuse to honor an IRS tax levy if the participant is not currently entitled to a distribution. See FSA 199930039. However, according to a later Chief Counsel Advice, the IRS may elect a distribution, on behalf of the participant, if he or she has a present right to a distribution. See CCA 199936042. However, the IRS concedes that the government is subject to the joint and survivor annuity rules and other plan provisions just as the participant or beneficiary would be. See Letter Ruling 200426027.

Suppose Employee retires with a monthly pension benefit payable for life. If Employee dies before receiving 120 payments, the remainder of the 120 payments are to be paid to a beneficiary designated by Employee. Employee has named his son the beneficiary. Shortly after retiring, a tax lien is placed against the pension benefit and the IRS begins collecting a portion of each benefit payment. A few years later, Employee dies, having received 61 payments. May the IRS continue to collect a portion of the remaining 59 monthly payments payable to the son based on its lien? In Asbestos Workers Local No. 23 Pension Fund v. United States, 303 F.Supp.2d 551, 559 (M.D.Pa.2004), the district court rejected the IRS claim:

> The mere right to designate a beneficiary, however, is not a sufficiently "beneficial interest" to satisfy the federal definition of property. As the Supreme Court stated nearly fifty years ago in the context of life insurance policies, the power of designation offers the owner no ability to use the funds for his or her personal benefit. United States v. Bess, 357 U.S. 51, 59–60 (1958). Because disposition of the funds occurs after the death of the owner, that party cannot enjoy the asset or otherwise use it to his or her advantage. Only the beneficiary stands to gain.

Whatever incidental benefits the owner may obtain from the authority to designate is simply insufficient to meet the federal definition of "property."

5.   *Fraudulent transfers.* Could a transfer be made to a plan just prior to bankruptcy in order to shield the transferred funds from creditors? In Velis v. Kardanis, 949 F.2d 78, 82 (3d Cir.1991), the court noted: "Presumably, substantial or unusual contributions to a self-settled pension trust made within the preference period, or with intent to defraud creditors, should receive no protection."

PART 2

PENSION TAXATION

CHAPTER 8

OVERVIEW OF THE TAXATION OF QUALIFIED PLANS

[handwritten: Pension Taxation]

[handwritten: - Income tax]

Analysis

Introduction.
A.   The Statutory Basis for Tax-Favored Retirement Saving.
    1.   Qualified Plans.
    2.   403(b) Plans, Traditional IRAs, SEPs, and SIMPLE Plans.
    3.   Roth IRAs and "Roth Contributions" to 401(k) and 403(b) Plans.
    4.   Nondeductible Contributions.
B.   The Economics of Tax Deferral.
C.   Summary of Requirements for Qualified Plans.
    1.   Qualification Requirements with ERISA Counterparts.
    2.   Qualification Requirements with No ERISA Counterpart.
    3.   The Mechanics of Qualification.
    4.   Remedial Amendment Period.
    5.   IRS Programs to Avoid the Disqualification Sanction.
D.   Nonqualified Plans.
    1.   Unfunded Plans.
    2.   ERISA Limitations: "Top Hat" Plans and Excess Benefit Plans.
    3.   Funded Nonqualified Plans.
    4.   Rabbi Trusts and Funding Triggers.
    5.   Deferred Compensation Plans of Tax Exempt Employers: IRC § 457.
E.   Employment Taxes.
F.   State Income Taxation.

Introduction

The next four chapters are devoted to pension taxation. This is a broad topic, encompassing not only a variety of taxpayers, such as employers, pension and profit-sharing trusts, employees, and beneficiaries, but also several different taxes, including income, estate and gift, and Social Security taxes. We shall focus mainly on the income tax, which is by far the most important tax in the pension area, but a brief discussion of Social Security taxes is found in Section E. Estate and gift taxation is considered at the end of Chapter 11.

There were certainly pension plans before there was an income tax, but there can be little doubt that the growth of the income tax has also spurred the growth of tax-favored pension plans. The interaction between the pension system and the tax system has been complex and continuous. *[handwritten: Definitional + computational]*

Pension taxation can be divided into two principal subjects—the definitional and the computational. The definitional concerns the requirements for qualifying for special tax treatment. The computational deals with the timing and method whereby contributions to deferred compensation arrangements are deducted and distributions are taxed.

The two subjects sometimes overlap, as in the case of the limitations on deductions and the special tax rules for distributions.

Chapter 8 provides an overview of the taxation of qualified plans and other tax-favored retirement saving. Section A reviews the statutory basis for the tax benefits provided to such plans and Section B explores the economics of these tax benefits. Section C outlines the definitional requirements for qualified plans. An important aspect of these requirements is the distinction between requirements imposed by federal law on all plans, not just qualified plans, and requirements that the tax law imposes only on qualified plans. In the former case the tax system serves as an enforcement aid to the regulatory law, but in the latter case the tax system functions independently, channeling tax benefits toward certain favored arrangements and controlling the cost in lost revenue of such benefits.

Section D considers the tax treatment of nonqualified plans. These are typically unfunded plans for top management, which are often designed to avoid some of the limitations on qualified plans. However, funded plans can also be nonqualified, either deliberately or more likely because they were disqualified by the IRS due to improper structure or operation.

Section E discusses how the Social Security and unemployment taxes operate in connection with both qualified and nonqualified plans. Finally, in Section F we examine the federal legislation limiting the ability of states to tax the pension income of former residents.

The remaining chapters of Part II explore the distinctive features of the tax structure for qualified plans and other forms of tax-favored retirement saving. Chapter 9 considers the rules prohibiting discrimination in favor of the highly compensated employees, which play a crucial role in determining the coverage and benefits of every plan and are central to understanding the modern rationale for continuing the favorable tax treatment of qualified plans. Chapter 10 deals with a variety of limitations on contributions, benefits, deductions, and funding, most of which are designed to control the cost of the tax subsidy. Chapter 11 discusses in detail the complex system for taxing and timing distributions to participants and beneficiaries.

As you study these materials, and in particular as you try to decipher the statute, you may feel overpowered by the unbearable complexity of it all. This is a natural reaction that is shared by most practitioners. The following comments of Judge Learned Hand seem especially applicable to the task ahead. "In my own case the words of such an act as the Income Tax [merely] dance before my eyes in a meaningless procession: crossreference to crossreference, exception upon exception—couched in abstract terms that offer no handle to seize hold of—leave in my mind only a confused sense of some vitally important, but successfully concealed, purport, which it is my duty to extract, but which is within my power, if at all, only after the most inordinate expenditure of time. I know that these monsters are the result of fabulous industry and ingenuity, plugging up this hole and casting out that net, against all possible evasion; yet at times I cannot help recalling a saying of William James about certain passages of Hegel: that they were no doubt written with a passion of rationality; but that one cannot help wondering whether to the reader they have any significance save that the words are strung together with syntactical correctness." L. Hand, Thomas Walter Swan, 57 Yale L.J. 167, 169 (1947).

A. THE STATUTORY BASIS FOR TAX-FAVORED RETIREMENT SAVING

[handwritten: Tax-Favored Retirement Saving]

1. QUALIFIED PLANS *[handwritten: - Requirements on pg. 304 + 306]*

The Internal Revenue Code provides substantial tax advantages to a wide variety of retirement savings devices. The most important of these devices is the "qualified plan." The term "qualified plan" is not actually used in the Internal Revenue Code; it means an employer-sponsored pension, profit-sharing, or stock bonus plan that meets the requirements established by IRC § 401(a) or an annuity plan that meets the requirements of IRC § 404(a)(2). Annuity plans, which purchase annuities directly and do not have a trust, must meet essentially all of the requirements of IRC § 401(a) and are taxed in an identical fashion. Accordingly, we shall not distinguish between annuity and other qualified plans in these materials.

[handwritten margin: Qualified Plan definition — hold the most money]

The qualification requirements imposed by IRC § 401(a), summarized below in Section C of this chapter, are extraordinarily complex. Assuming an employer's plan is qualified, the relevant taxpayers—the employer, the employee, and the trust holding the funds—are taxed in a fashion that in combination proves highly favorable. There are three main advantages:

[handwritten margin: - only taxed when amounts are distributed from the trust]

[handwritten margin: Pros of this plan]

(1) The employee (or in some cases a beneficiary of the employee) is subjected to income tax only when amounts are actually distributed from the trust. IRC § 402(a). If the distribution is an "eligible rollover distribution", income taxation can be deferred further to the extent that the payee makes a "rollover" to an "eligible retirement plan." IRC § 402(c)(1). Chapter 11 infra describes the rules governing rollovers.

[handwritten margin: unless defer taxation if the distribution is an "eligible rollover distribution" and the payee makes a "rollover" to an "eligible retirement plan"]

(2) The employer receives a current income tax deduction for contributions to the trust. IRC § 404(a)(1), (2), (3).

(3) The trust itself is exempt from tax on its investment income. IRC § 501(a). As is the case with other tax-exempt organizations, the trust is subject to tax only on its "unrelated business taxable income," which is essentially the income from any trade or business regularly carried on by the trust or by a partnership of which it is a member. IRC §§ 511(b), 512, 513(b).

The use of a trust is not essential to achieve the tax advantage of deferral. A qualified plan can be funded without a trust by using a custodial account or an annuity contract, provided that the account or annuity meets all of the other requirements of a qualified trust. IRC § 401(f). Since the yield on these investments is not taxed to the employee until distributed, the tax benefit remains the same.

Under one type of qualified plan, employees are given the option of voluntarily deferring part of their salary by directing the employer to contribute the funds to the plan. These plans are governed by IRC § 401(k) and are commonly referred to as "401(k) plans" or "cash or deferred arrangements (CODAs)." The salary voluntarily deferred is generally excluded from the employee's income and treated as an employer contribution. IRC § 402(e)(3).

Before 1962, participation in qualified plans was limited to employees. Self-employed persons, such as sole proprietors and partners, could not participate, even if they had established a plan for their employees. In 1962 legislation was enacted to permit qualified plans to cover the self-employed. Under IRC § 401(c)(1) such individuals are treated as "employees" and they (or the partnership, in the case of a partner) are treated as their own employer for qualified plan purposes. The net result is that contributions to the plan are currently deductible and income is deferred until distribution. Plans covering the self-employed are often referred to as "Keogh" plans (after the sponsor of the 1962 legislation). Note that almost all limited liability companies (LLCs) and similar entities are taxed either as sole proprietorships (if they have only one member) or as partnerships (if they have two or more members). Accordingly, the term "self-employed" generally includes members of an LLC.

Keogh Plans

(Plans covering the self-employed)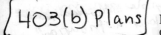

2.   403(b) PLANS, TRADITIONAL IRAS, SEPS, AND SIMPLE PLANS

Similar tax benefits have been extended to several retirement savings arrangements that are not qualified plans. It must always be kept in mind that these arrangements have their own governing statutory provisions, which may differ from those governing qualified plans. These distinctions will be highlighted in the following chapters.

403(b) plans. Under IRC § 403(b), tax-exempt organizations and public educational organizations can purchase annuities or contribute to certain custodial accounts for their employees. The amount the employer ① pays is excluded from the employee's gross income; taxation is deferred ② until distributions are actually made. IRC § 403(b)(1). These plans (known as "403(b) plans" or "tax-sheltered annuities") often operate as "salary reduction" arrangements, under which the employee and the employer agree that the employee's salary will be reduced in the future, and the amount of the reduction is contributed to the 403(b) plan. These salary reduction arrangements function much like 401(k) plans, in that the amount voluntarily deferred is not included in the employee's income.

403(b) Plans

Traditional IRAs. Individual retirement accounts and individual retirement annuities (IRAs) provide the same tax deferral benefits as a qualified plan. Contributions to IRAs are generally deductible and the IRA is itself tax-exempt. IRC §§ 219(a), 408(e)(1). Thus, the funds in the IRA can accumulate tax-free and the owner of the IRA is taxed only when amounts are actually distributed. IRC § 408(d). Employees who (or whose spouses) are active participants in a qualified plan may not deduct their IRA contributions unless their incomes are below a specified threshold. IRC § 219(g). IRA contributions are generally limited to $5,500 for 2015 (adjusted for inflation thereafter), but this limit is increased by $1,000 for individuals who have attained age 50. IRC § 219(b)(5). The vast

Traditional IRA's

- contributions limited to $5,500 per year

- Post-tax plans (pg. 295)

majority, by value, of IRA contributions are rollover contributions from other tax-favored retirement plans: rollover contributions are not deductible but have the effect of deferring what would otherwise be the receipt of taxable income.

Since 2001, qualified plans, section 403(b) plans, and even governmental 457 plans have been allowed to set up separate IRA accounts (so-called "deemed IRAs") within the plan, although to date most plans have not done so because of the added administrative cost. IRC § 408(q).

SEPs. An employer may also establish a simplified employee pension (SEP) under IRC § 408(k). Under a SEP, the employer contributes to an IRA established on behalf of each participant. The employer receives a deduction for the contributions and the employee is taxed only upon distribution. IRC §§ 402(h), 404(h). SEPs are subject to fewer of the limitations imposed on qualified plans and are easier to administer. The advantage of a SEP over a conventional IRA is that larger contributions are permitted.

SEP's
- good for small employees (simple)
- defer taxation + no obligations of operating the plan

SIMPLE IRA plans. Since 1996 certain small businesses have been allowed to create another type of simplified retirement plan called the savings incentive match IRA plan for employees (SIMPLE IRA). IRC § 408(p). An employer is eligible to contribute to a SIMPLE IRA if it does not maintain another retirement plan and has 100 or fewer employees who received $5,000 or more in compensation during the previous year. A SIMPLE plan allows employees to make tax-deferred elective contributions to an IRA, much like 401(k) plans. The employer is required to make a minimum matching or nonelective contribution. One can think of a SIMPLE IRA plan as a SEP with a salary reduction arrangement. As with SEPs, the employer receives a deduction for the contributions and the employee is taxed only upon distribution. IRC §§ 402(k), 404(m).

SIMPLE IRA plans
- like a SEP but with a salary reduction arrangement

3. ROTH IRAs AND "ROTH CONTRIBUTIONS" TO 401(k) AND 403(b) PLANS

The Taxpayer Relief Act of 1997 created a second type of IRA, the "Roth IRA." Unlike traditional IRAs, contributions to Roth IRAs are nondeductible but "qualified" distributions are not taxable. A qualified distribution in one that is made on or after the date the individual attains age 59 ½; or is made to a beneficiary (or to the individual's estate) after the death of the individual; or that is attributable to the individual being disabled, as defined in IRC § 72(m)(7); or which is a qualified first-time homebuyer distribution, as defined in IRC § 72(t)(2)(F). The distribution will *not* be a qualified distribution if it is made within the 5 taxable year period beginning with the first taxable year for which a contribution was made to a Roth IRA for the individual's benefit. IRC § 408A(d)(2). The maximum Roth IRA contribution is the same as the maximum allowable IRA deduction, reduced by any contributions to traditional IRAs. For 2015, the maximum contribution to Roth IRAs is phased out for single taxpayers with adjusted gross income between $116,000 and $131,000 and for joint filers with AGI between $183,000 and $193,000. A taxpayer who is covered by a qualified plan is nevertheless eligible for the full tax benefit of a Roth IRA, unlike the rule for traditional IRAs.

Roth IRA
- Pre-tax plans
(pg. 295)

Beginning in 2006, employers sponsoring 401(k) and 403(b) plans can give participants the option of treating elective deferrals as after-tax "Roth contributions." IRC § 402A. Employers that elect to do so will have to establish separate accounts under the plan and make significant payroll accounting changes. As discussed in Part B infra, even though "Roth-type" vehicles provide no deduction for contributions, they can often provide greater economic benefits than traditional IRAs and elective deferrals. For this reason many employers are expected to allow Roth contributions despite the added administrative burden.

The Small Business Jobs Act of 2010 provides for 401(k) and 403(b) plans to allow in-plan Roth conversions and, beginning in 2011, allows governmental 457 plans to accept Roth contributions. The American Taxpayer Relief Act of 2012 expands rollover opportunities for distributions from a plan that includes a designated Roth contribution program.

4. NONDEDUCTIBLE CONTRIBUTIONS

Howell v. United States

775 F.2d 887 (7th Cir.1985).

■ EASTERBROOK, CIRCUIT JUDGE. An employer that establishes a pension plan for its employees sometimes contributes funds to the plan on top of the employees' stated salaries. These are "employers' contributions" and are not taxable income for the employee until the plan pays benefits to the employee. [IRC] §§ 401(a), 403, 501(a). The employer alternatively may give the employees higher stated salaries but dedicate some of the salaries to the pension plan. These deductions are "employees' contributions" and are taxable income to the employee, but corresponding amounts of pension disbursements will not be taxed. [IRC] §§ 72, 402.

The distinction between "employers' contributions" and "employees' contributions" to qualified pension plans is almost wholly nominal. It is a matter of indifference to an employer whether it pays $30,000 salary to the employee plus $3,000 to a pension plan on the employee's behalf, or instead $33,000 to the employee, of which it sends $3,000 to a pension plan. In either event the employee receives $30,000 at once and $3,000 in deferred compensation, and the employer may deduct the whole $33,000 as an ordinary and necessary business expense. [IRC] § 404. But the tax consequences of the distinction are substantial. The tax on employers' contributions is deferred until retirement, and the discounted present value of the deferred tax is less than the value of tax paid today.

The distinction between employers' and employees' contributions is one example of the dominance of form over substance in the tax code. Perhaps aware that there was no substance—but substantial consequences for the revenue—in this distinction, Congress allowed governmental bodies (but not private employers) to select still a third label. A section added in 1974, [IRC] § 414(h)(2), provides that if a state or local government's contributions "are designated as employee contributions but [the] employing unit picks up the contributions, the contributions so picked up shall be treated as employer contributions." ...

Under the Commissioner's interpretation § 414(h)(2) permits a government to treat contributions as "employees' contributions" for its own purposes but "employers' contributions" for purposes of federal income taxation. The government establishes two "salaries." One, for state purposes, is the base from which contributions are withheld; the other, for federal purposes, is a lower salary from which nothing is withheld; the difference between the salary for state purposes and the salary for federal purposes is the "picked up" contribution. In order to use this option, a government announces that the employees' contributions have been "picked up" and reduces their salaries—or more accurately the amounts shown as wages on their W-2 forms. So long as the employer forecloses the employees' "option of choosing to receive the contributed amounts directly instead of having them paid by the employer to the pension plan" (Rev.Rul. 81–35, 1981 Cum.Bull. 255), it meets the requirements of § 414(h)(2).

— Commissioner interpretation of law

court disagrees (next page)

In 1980 Illinois enacted a statute providing that after January 1, 1981, each governmental unit "may pick up the employee contributions required" by the state's pension laws. Ill.Rev.Stat. ch. 108 1/2 § 18–133.1. The Commissioner then issued a private letter ruling that contributions "picked up" by the state after December 31, 1981, and paid to the retirement system would not be includable in the employees' gross income.

Snyder Howell, a circuit judge in Williamson County, Illinois, is covered by the Judges' Retirement System of Illinois. Judge Howell then filed amended tax returns for 1978–80. He claimed a refund for taxes paid on the sums that had been withheld from his pay and turned over to the Retirement System. These sums, he maintained, had been "picked up" by the state fully as much as the sums turned over to the Retirement System starting in 1982. There was no substantive difference and therefore, he maintained, there should be no tax difference. The IRS denied the request, and Howell filed this suit. The suit is financed by the Illinois Judges Association, whose members have an interest in common with Judge Howell.

The district court concluded that the pension contributions before 1982 were "employees' contributions" within the meaning of federal law. State law designated them this way, and under federal law the employer's designation controls. The proviso allowing employers to "pick up" employees' contributions gives them a way to reverse the effect of their own designation, but they must avail themselves of the privilege. Illinois did not do so until 1982, so Howell lost. We agree with both the result and the reasoning.

The starting point for income taxation is that all sums paid to, or on behalf of, an employee are taxable income. [IRC] § 61.

As an economic matter, employers' contributions and employees' contributions are identical; they differ in name only. Under the tax law the name matters, and the employer picks the name.

The employee is stuck with the employer's designation, no matter what it is. Until 1981 Illinois by statute called the contributions to the Judges' Retirement System employees' contributions. This remitted Judge Howell to the presumptive rule that the whole salary is taxable.

We could not accept his argument that the state "picked up" his contributions even before 1982 because he never saw the money either before or after the new law and never has had any choice about its destination without either reversing one of the most venerable principles of taxation (that he who earns the money pays the full tax) or disregarding the rule that permits the employer to designate a contribution as made by it or by the employee. Illinois made one choice for years before 1982, and now (using the right to "pick up" contributions) it has made another. Judge Howell is bound by both.

Ruling —

This exalts form over substance, no doubt. In tax, however, form and substance often coincide. The election between employers' and employees' contributions is nothing but form, and the new designation option in § 414(h)(2) simply continues the practice.

NOTES

1. *Employee contributions.* Qualified plans may provide for mandatory or voluntary employee contributions. Plans that provide for such contributions are frequently referred to as thrift plans. Employee contributions generally are not deductible from the employee's gross income. However, even though the employee's contribution is made on an after-tax basis, the earnings on such contributions are not taxed until they are distributed from the plan. Thus, there is a tax advantage to making employee contributions, but it is not as great as that for the employer contributions, which are made on a pretax basis.

As the *Howell* court indicates, the distinction between employee and employer contributions is often devoid of any economic significance. But for tax purposes, form in this context controls over substance. Recognizing that governmental entities are often less able to control the form of their employee compensation, ERISA added IRC § 414(h)(2), which permits such entities to convert employee contributions to employer contributions by nothing more than an announcement. State and local governments have almost uniformly done so. This "pick-up" rule is not available to private employers, although as a practical matter few private plans require employee contributions.

2. *Cash or deferred arrangements.* It is important to distinguish employee contributions from employer contributions under "salary reduction" plans, whereby an employee elects to have an employer make contributions to a 401(k) plan (technically known as a cash or deferred arrangement), 403(b) plan, or a SIMPLE IRA. Although employees view these contributions as their own, for tax purposes they are employer contributions, albeit subject to some special limitations not applicable to normal employer contributions. Since substantial tax benefits can be achieved by this mere relabeling, it is not surprising that beginning in 1978, when 401(k) plans were first expressly permitted by statute, many of the former thrift plans that used after-tax employee contributions have switched over to 401(k) plans.

3. *Nondeductible IRAs.* Contributions to traditional IRAs can also be made on an after-tax basis, even by individuals who could not deduct contributions to an IRA by reason of their participation in a qualified plan. IRC § 408(o). Although after-tax contributions do not produce as large a tax advantage as deductible contributions, they may still be attractive since the

income on the contributions is not taxed until it is withdrawn. But a contribution to a Roth IRA, also nondeductible, would generally be preferable, since the income need never be taxed. Thus, nondeductible IRA contributions will usually only be made by individuals who are not eligible to contribute the maximum amount to Roth IRAs, such as taxpayers filing a joint return with adjusted gross income in excess of $150,000 (indexed— $183,000 for 2015). See IRC § 408A(c)(3).

B. THE ECONOMICS OF TAX DEFERRAL

The basic tax advantage of qualified plans is income tax deferral. Employer contributions to qualified plans are not taxed to the employee as they are made; the earnings on the assets in the plan are permitted to accumulate tax-free; the employee includes the benefits of the plan in income only when distributed. The first advantage is lost when employee contributions to the plan are made on an after-tax basis, such as in the older thrift plans, but the advantage of postponed taxation of the investment earnings remains. Examples of these tax benefits are shown in the table below, taken (with minor modification) from Congressional Budget Office, Tax Policy for Pensions and Other Retirement Saving 4 (1987).

TABLE 8.1

TAX ADVANTAGES OF A $1000 CONTRIBUTION TO A QUALIFIED RETIREMENT PLAN

	Example 1: Tax Rate of 0.15 in Working Years (15% tax rate)			Example 2: Tax Rate of 0.40 in Working Years (40% tax rate)		
	Regular Account	Qualified Plan (after tax)	Qualified Plan (pretax)	Regular Account	Qualified Plan (after tax)	Qualified Plan (pretax)
Contribution	$1,000	$1,000	$1,000	$1,000	$1,000	$1,000
Tax on Contribution	150	150	—	400	400	—
Deposit	850	850	1,000	600	600	1,000
Value at Withdrawal Retirement	2,280	2,696	3,172	1,212	1,903	3,172
Tax Rate	—	0.15	0.15	—	0.40	0.40
Tax on Withdrawal	0	277	476	0	521	1,269
Net Withdrawal	2,280	2,419	2,696	1,212	1,382	1,903
Gain Over Regular Account	—	139	416	—	170	691
Percent Gain	—	6	18	—	14	57
Alternative Retirement Tax Rate	—	0	0	—	0.30	0.30
Tax on Withdrawal	0	0	0	0	391	952
Net Withdrawal	2,280	2,696	3,172	1,212	1,512	2,221

[Handwritten annotations: "Net investment accrues at 8% a yr."; "tax b4 + after contribution"; "best deal" (under 3,172 column); "best deal" (under 2,221 column)]

Gain Over Regular Account	—	416	892	—	300	1,008
Percent Gain	—	18	39	—	25	83

3 scenarios:

① –EER direct payment to EEE +EEE contributes to a Savings Account

② –Eer direct payment to EEE + EEF contributes to Qualified Plan

③ –Eer contributes directly to Qualified Plan

Table 8.1 compares three arrangements: (1) a direct payment of $1,000 to the employee who then contributes it (after taxes) to a savings account ("Regular Account"); (2) a direct payment of $1,000 to the employee, who then contributes it to a qualified plan ("Qualified Plan (after-tax)"); and (3) an employer contribution of $1,000 to a qualified plan for an employee's benefit ("Qualified Plan (pretax)"). The interest rate on the savings account and on the plan investments is assumed to be a constant 8 percent. The table assumes that after fifteen years the employee retires and the qualified plan distributes the accumulated fund to the employee.

1. *The essence of the tax benefit: a tax-free rate of return on after-tax compensation.* Consider Example 1 in the table, which assumes that the employee is in the 15 percent income tax bracket during the employee's working years. If the $1,000 is paid directly to the employee, the employee would have $850 after taxes to deposit in the savings account or contribute to the plan. Although the savings account earns 8 percent interest, the interest is subject to income tax, which means the after-tax rate of return is only 6.8 percent. The $850 in the account compounded at 6.8 percent over 15 years yields $2,280. If the $850 were contributed to the qualified plan it would compound at the 8 percent rate, unreduced by any taxes, and yield $2,696. If instead of paying the employee the $1,000 the employer had placed the $1,000 in a qualified plan, the full $1,000 would compound at the 8 percent pretax rate and yield $3,172 at the end of 15 years.

The amounts in the three accounts cannot yet be directly compared, since the savings account can be withdrawn without any additional tax, whereas any distribution from the qualified plan would be taxed as income to the extent not previously taxed. Thus, in order to compare the hypotheticals we need to know the employee's tax rate at the time of the distribution. Assuming that the employee's tax rate in retirement is unchanged, the distribution of the $3,172 from the employer funded qualified plan would result in a tax of $476, leaving the employee with a net amount of $2,696 after taxes. This is $416 more than would be yielded by the direct cash compensation and investment in the savings account. The distribution of the $2,696 from the employee after-tax funded plan produces a tax of $277 (15 percent of $2,696 less $850), leaving the employee with a net amount of $2,419. This is more than the savings account but less than the employer funded plan.

This example illustrates the essence of the tax benefits of the various forms of tax-favored retirement savings. The example applies equally to traditional IRAs. A deductible contribution to a traditional IRA is equivalent to a pretax employer contribution to a qualified plan. A nondeductible traditional IRA contribution is equivalent to an after-tax employee contribution to a qualified plan. It is also important to note that the employer's tax rate plays no role in determining the relative tax benefits. The employer receives a $1,000 deduction whether the cash is paid directly to the employee or contributed to the qualified plan.

It can be shown that if tax rates remain constant, the benefits of pretax contributions to qualified plans and traditional IRAs are equivalent to taxing the contributions when they are made and permitting the *after-tax remainder* to earn investment income tax free. Example 1 provides a nice illustration. The "Value at Withdrawal" in the after-tax plan is $2,696. This is exactly what one would have if one received $1,000 in compensation, paid the $150 income tax, and invested the remaining $850 at the tax-free rate of return of 8 percent. But this $2,696 figure is precisely equal to the "Net Withdrawal" from the qualified plan if the $1,000 had instead been contributed to the plan.

The employee already has the option of investing after-tax compensation in tax-free municipal bonds, but the advantage of the qualified plan is that the investment yields for taxable investments are higher than taxfree yields. The reason for this difference is that the market for tax-favored investments, such as municipal bonds, reflects the tax benefits. It is therefore generally disadvantageous for a qualified plan to invest in tax-favored returns.

These calculations do not reflect the effect of Social Security taxes, discussed in Section E of this chapter. An employee who contributes to a regular account, or makes an after-tax contribution to a qualified plan, must pay Social Security taxes (7.65% of wages up to the wage base, $118,500 for 2015, and 1.45% on any excess) on his or her full salary. An employer contribution to a qualified plan is not subject to these taxes. However, payment of the taxes will increase the employee's Social Security earnings and may result in higher Social Security benefits. In addition, if the employee pays state or local income taxes, this increases the benefit of deferral, particularly as many states allow partial exclusions from taxable income for pension payments. See National Conference of State Legislatures, Fiscal Affairs Program-State Personal Income Taxes on Pensions and Retirement Income: Tax Year 2007 (July 2007), available at www.ncsl.org.

In calculating the tax benefits of deferral, Medicare taxes will be increasingly important. For 2015, the basic Medicare tax for employees is 2.90% of wages, half paid by the employer and half by the employee, with no cap. Self-employed individuals pay 2.90% of their net earnings from self-employment.

For taxable years beginning after 2012, there is an additional Medicare tax on individuals who receive more than a certain amount of wages or earned income during the year: $250,000 for married taxpayers filing a joint return, $200,000 for a single taxpayer, and $125,000 for a married taxpayer filing separately. The tax is equal to 0.9 percent of the excess. [Code §§ 3101(b)(2), 1401(b)(2), as amended by PPACA § 9015 and HCERA § 1402(b).] For a self-employed individual, no part of the additional tax is deductible. Unlike the basic 1.45 percent tax, in the case of a joint return, the additional 0.9 percent tax is on the combined wages and earned income of both spouses. [Joint Committee on Taxation, Technical Explanation of the Revenue Provisions of the "Reconciliation Act of 2010," as amended, in combination with the "Patient Protection and Affordable Care Act," JCX–18–10, Mar. 21, 2010.]

Historically, employment taxes, including Medicare tax, have applied only to income received in the form of wages or self-employment income. For taxable years beginning after 2012, the Affordable Care Act also adds new Code Section 1411, which imposes on individuals a Medicare tax equal to 3.8 percent of the lesser of (1) net investment income for the year or (2) the excess (if any) of (a) the modified adjusted gross income (MAGI) for the year over (b) the threshold amount. A similar tax applies to estates and trusts. The threshold amount is $250,000 for a joint return or a surviving spouse, $125,000 for a married taxpayer filing a separate return, and $200,000 in any other case. Net investment income includes income from passive activities, a trade or business of trading in financial instruments or commodities, and investment of working capital, subject to an exception for certain active interests in partnerships and S corporations. Net investment income does not include any distribution from a tax-favored retirement plan or any item taken into account in determining self-employment income.

The dollar thresholds for the imposition of these two new taxes are not indexed for inflation.

2. *Roth IRAs and "Roth contributions" to 401(k) plans: an added advantage?* Since contributions to Roth IRAs and Roth contributions to 401(k) plans are made after-tax (i.e., no deduction), and the income on the contributions is tax-free (if taken as a "qualified distribution"), they appear to offer essentially the same economic benefit as the traditional IRA or qualified plan. For example, assume in Example 1 that the employee paid the $150 tax on the $1,000 and contributed the after-tax remainder of $850 to a Roth IRA with an 8 percent tax-free interest rate of return. After 15 years, the investment would be worth $2,696, exactly the same amount as the pretax contribution of the $1,000 to a qualified plan would yield after withdrawing the account and paying the appropriate tax.

But in fact Roth type plans have two significant advantages over traditional plans. First, Roth IRAs are not subject to the age 70 1/2 minimum distribution requirements that apply to other IRAs. Second, although the contribution limit for Roth IRAs is the same as the limit for traditional IRAs (and the limit for Roth contributions to 401(k) plans is the same as the limit for traditional contributions), a contribution to the Roth type arrangement is actually worth more because it is in after-tax dollars. The table below illustrates this advantage.

TABLE 8.2

Roth IRAs v. Traditional IRAs			
	Roth IRA	Traditional IRA	
Contribution	$5,000	$5,000	
Tax savings on contribution			$2,000
IRA return (8% tax free)	10,861	10,861	
Tax savings return (8% taxable)			2,040
Value at withdrawal	15,861	15,861	4040
Tax on withdrawal	0	6,344	0
Net withdrawal	15,861	9,517	4,040
Total gain on $5,000 contribution	10,861	8,557	

Assumptions: 8 percent investment return, withdrawal after 15 years; constant 40 percent marginal tax rate

3.   *After-tax contributions.* Examples 1 and 2 in Table 8.1 illustrate that after-tax contributions to qualified plans (and nondeductible contributions to traditional IRAs) are less advantaged than equivalent pretax contributions. The tax is merely postponed until the income is distributed. This is certainly an improvement over the normal investment in a savings account, but it is not a unique benefit. Other types of investments receive similar tax treatment. For example, the yearly appreciation in value of real estate and corporate stock (as opposed to rental or dividend income) is not taxed until the asset is sold. Similarly, the gain on an individual deferred annuity contract is not taxed until annuity payments begin. Of course, the market, quite analogously to the situation of municipal bonds, may reduce the yield of such investments to reflect this tax benefit. If in fact the yield is lower than an investment of equivalent risk paying current taxable income, investing after-tax contributions to a qualified plan or IRA in the latter investment would produce a greater rate of return after taxes.

4.   *Changing tax rates.* Both examples in Table 8.1 also illustrate that the advantage of a qualified plan increases when the tax rate in retirement is less than that during the working years. In Example 2, if the employee's 40 percent tax rate declines to 30 percent at retirement, the qualified plan yields $1,008 more than the savings account, which represents 83 percent of the amount in the savings account. Similarly, in Example 1, if the employee's 15 percent tax rate drops to zero, the percent gain of using a qualified plan increases from 18 percent to 39 percent. Thus the advantage of shifting income from high tax rate years to low tax rate years can be even greater in magnitude than the rather substantial benefits of tax deferral alone.

In the case of Roth IRAs and designated Roth accounts, the situation is reversed. The advantage of Roth-type accounts is greater if contributions are made in low tax rate years and withdrawals occur in high tax rate years. Roth-type accounts are therefore the preferred savings vehicle for children, students, and others with part-time or entry-level jobs who expect to be in higher tax brackets when withdrawal occurs.

5.   (*Social security benefit tax trap.*) Due to the wide variety of phase-outs of various deductions, exclusions, and credits, a taxpayer's real marginal rate is not a monotonically increasing function of income. The marginal rate over certain lower income ranges can be far higher than the marginal rate at a higher income level. In addition, the phase-outs can in certain cases result in a higher marginal rate at retirement than during a taxpayer's working years, making deferrals into traditional IRAs and 401(k) plans uneconomic.

A common and striking example of this phenomenon is the phase-out of the exclusion of social security benefits from gross income. Under IRC § 86, at low income levels, social security benefits are tax-free, but once a certain threshold is reached, an increasing portion of the benefit is taxed until a maximum of 85% of the benefit is taxed. For example, assume an unmarried individual earned a steady $70,000 a year before retirement, putting her in the 25% marginal tax bracket. She has just retired and will have an annual income of $30,000 in pension benefits and another $20,000 in social security benefits. Under IRC § 86, only

$9,600 of the social security benefits would be taxable. But if the taxpayer were to increase her annual income by withdrawing $1,000 from her 401(k) plan, an additional $850 of social security benefits would become taxable. Since her taxable income in retirement puts her in the 25% tax bracket, the additional $1,000 of income, by increasing her taxable income by another $850 due to the phase-out of the social security exclusion, increases her income tax by 25% of ($1,000 plus $850), or $462.50. Her marginal tax rate on additional income is therefore 46.25%!

Is it sensible for this taxpayer to contribute to a 401(k) plan during her working years, thereby deferring income that would be taxed currently at 25% into a future year when it will be taxed at 46.25%? What advice would you give a taxpayer in this situation? Would it make a difference if the employer provided a matching 401(k) contribution? Note that the marginal tax rate for high income taxpayers is unaffected by IRC § 86, since the taxation of their social security benefits is already fully phased-in.

6. *Taxpayers in higher tax brackets receive a greater benefit*. Example 2 in Table 8.1 illustrates the important fact that the benefits of investing in a qualified plan are even greater for taxpayers in a higher bracket. Although an employee paying a 40 percent marginal tax rate is able to accumulate less after taxes than one paying 15 percent, the relative advantage of the qualified plan over the savings account is greater. There is a $691 advantage to an employer contribution to the plan as compared with only $416 in Example 1. Another way to express the difference is that the employee with a 40 percent marginal rate has 57 percent more money if a qualified plan is used, while the 15 percent employee has only 18 percent more. This advantage is merely a reflection of the fact that tax-free income is more valuable to someone in a higher tax bracket. Thus, an 8 percent tax-free rate of return is equivalent to a 9.41 percent taxable return for a person in the 15 percent tax bracket, but it is equivalent to a 13.3 percent taxable return for a person in the 40 percent bracket. Many individuals pay no federal income tax; according to one recent study, 43.3% of "tax units" had zero (or negative) income tax for 2013, and 14.4% had zero (or negative) income and payroll tax. Tax Policy Center, Tax Units With Zero or Negative Liability Under Current Law, 2004–2024, Aug. 29, 2013, www.taxpolicycenter.org.

This "upside-down" nature of the tax benefit of tax-favored retirement saving is problematic in two distinct ways. First, the tax incentive is greatest for those individuals with the highest incomes, who are already likely to be saving and investing a significant portion of their income. Many will simply shift savings from normal investments to qualified plans, without any significant increase in their overall level of savings. Thus, to the extent the government loses revenue due to increased investment in tax-favored retirement saving, the revenue is wasted, because it did not promote enhanced retirement saving. Second, lower-income individuals face greater pressure to use their income for current consumption. The correspondingly reduced tax incentive due to their lower tax bracket may simply be inadequate to persuade them to increase their retirement savings. This characteristic is not unique to retirement saving, but applies in all situations (such as home mortgage interest) where the tax benefit takes the form of a deduction or exclusion rather than a credit.

We shall see when we examine the discrimination rules (mainly IRC §§ 401(a)(4) and 410(b)) in Chapter 9 that Congress has tried to solve these two problems by allowing qualified plans to benefit highly-compensated employees only if sufficient benefits flow to nonhighly-compensated employees. Unfortunately, the economic reality is such that these rules are largely ineffective in generating sufficient retirement saving for lower-income workers.

7. *Limited tax credit for elective deferrals and IRA contributions.* Recognizing the "upside-down" nature of the traditional tax subsidy for retirement saving, Congress in 2001 decided to try something new: an incentive for retirement saving that is targeted at lower and moderate-income workers. IRC § 25B. This provides a nonrefundable tax credit (the "saver's credit") for elective contributions to a section 401(k) plan, section 403(b) annuity, governmental section 457 plan, SIMPLE, or SEP; contributions to a traditional or Roth IRA; and voluntary after-tax employee contributions to a qualified plan. The maximum annual contribution eligible for the credit is $2,000 per person. The maximum credit is $1,000 ($2,000 for a married couple filing jointly).The credit rate depends on the adjusted gross income of the taxpayer. Married couples earning less than $36,000 in 2014 ($18,000 for singles, $27,000 for heads of households) get a 50 percent credit. The credit phases down to 20 percent, then 10 percent and disappears for married couples earning over $60,000 ($30,000 for singles, $45,000 for heads of households). See http://www.irs.gov/Retirement-Plans/Plan-Participant,-Employee/Retirement-Topics-Retirement-Savings-Contributions-Credit-%28Saver%E2%80%99s-Credit%29. The credit is available to individuals who are 18 or over, other than fulltime students or those claimed as dependents by another taxpayer. As a practical matter, relatively few individuals will be able to take advantage of the full 50 percent credit since it is nonrefundable and most of the taxpayers who meet the adjusted gross income test pay no income tax. Preliminary data from 2003 returns indicate that 5.3 million returns claimed the credit, amounting to a total slightly in excess of $1 billion. For an excellent overview of § 25B, as in effect before enactment of the Pension Protection Act of 2006, see William G. Gale, J. Mark Iwry, and Peter R. Orszag, The Saver's Credit: Issues and Options, Tax Notes, May 3, 2004, p. 597.

8. *Revenue effects.* The special tax advantages of qualified plans and other tax-favored retirement savings cause tax revenue to be lost. Both the Staff of the Joint Committee on Taxation and the Office of Management and Budget treat these tax advantages as "tax expenditures" and prepare annual estimates as part of the budget process. The Joint Committee on Taxation's estimates are set forth in the following table.

ESTIMATED TAX EXPENDITURE ON TAX-FAVORED
RETIREMENT SAVINGS (in billions)

	2014	2015	2016	2017	2018
Employer Plans	70.9	103.6	131.6	160.1	181.1
IRAs	16.7	18.3	20.0	21.6	23.2
Keogh Plans	5.8	8.7	110.0	111.4	16.2
Tax Credit (§ 25B)	1.2	1.2	1.2	1.2	1.2

Source: Joint Committee on Taxation, Estimates of Federal Tax Expenditures for Fiscal Years 2014–2018 JCX–97–14, Aug. 5, 2014.

This tax expenditure is one of the largest in the entire tax expenditure budget, exceeding the tax expenditure due to the deduction of home mortgage interest ($67.8 billion in 2014) but less than the exclusion of employer provided health benefits ($143.0 billion in 2014). The cost of the tax credit is fairly realistic, but the other numbers represent only the annual revenue loss and ignore future tax liabilities. They are computed by estimating for a given year the foregone taxes due to the exclusion of plan contributions and plan earnings from income and subtracting from this an estimate of the taxes paid on pension benefit distributions made during the year. This method overstates the true cost of the tax advantage, since it fails to offset the present value of the future tax collections arising from the current contributions. This present value is likely to be far higher than the current aggregate revenue from pension distributions, since current distributions derive from contributions and service in earlier years when plan participation, both in absolute numbers and as a percentage of the work force, was lower.

An alternative cost measure would be the revenue loss over the lifetime of each taxpayer. For example, $1,000 contributed to a plan on behalf of an employee in the 28 percent tax bracket gives rise to a current revenue loss of $280. Yet when this $1,000 is distributed to the employee in a future year, the $280 is repaid, assuming an unchanged employee tax bracket. The real loss to the Treasury is the difference between $280 now and the present value of the $280 to be paid in the future. Similar losses occur as income is earned by the plan and tax is deferred until distributions are made. Measuring the aggregate amount of these losses for all taxpayers is not an easy task.

The true cost of the tax advantage of a Roth IRA (or a designated Roth account) is much easier to compute because there is no need to consider the present value of future tax collections. Since most distributions from a Roth IRA are tax free, there are no future taxes to be collected. Unlike a traditional IRA or a qualified plan, a contribution to a Roth-type account causes no revenue loss in the year of the contribution. This feature made Roth IRAs very attractive to politicians who were seeking ways to subsidize increased savings, but were faced with severe spending constraints under the balanced budget rules then in effect. Since the revenue loss from a Roth IRA contribution is initially small but grows exponentially, the bulk of the revenue loss occurs beyond the usual budget-scoring window.

As is the case with all tax expenditures, the estimated revenue losses cannot be equated with the actual revenue gain that would occur by repealing the special tax treatment of qualified plans. Repeal would certainly cause changes in employer and employee behavior. Employers might increase the use of other tax-favored fringe benefits. Employees might seek out other tax-favored investments, such as deferred annuities or other assets that tend to produce unrealized appreciation.

9. *Alternatives to the current tax structure.* Although no serious Congressional proposals have been made to eliminate the tax subsidy for qualified plans, one could in principle do so by taxing them in the same manner as funded nonqualified plans. See Section D, infra. Another alternative would be to tax the contributions and plan earnings at some appropriate rate. See Alicia H. Munnell, Current Taxation of Qualified Pension Plans: Has the Time Come?, New England Economic Review, 12 (March/April 1992).

Some commentators believe that the present tax treatment, with all of its flaws, should not be viewed as a subsidy, but rather as normatively correct and preferable to the alternatives, when considerations of administrability, liquidity, valuation, acceptability, and the like are taken into account. See, e.g., Edward A. Zelinsky, The Tax Treatment of Qualified Plans: A Classic Defense of the Status Quo, 66 N.C.L.Rev. 315 (1988). Stein's challenge to Zelinsky's views and Zelinsky's rejoinder provide a thorough airing of the issues. See Norman P. Stein, Qualified Plans and Tax Expenditures: A Reply to Professor Zelinsky, 9 Am. J. Tax Pol'y 225 (1991) and Edward A. Zelinsky, Qualified Plans and Identifying Tax Expenditures: A Rejoinder to Professor Stein, 9 Am. J. Tax Pol'y 257 (1991).

The status quo has also been supported on efficiency grounds: "[T]here is nothing in the current treatment of pensions that obviously results in a misallocation of resources. The current tax rules may indeed be substantially more efficient than a straightforward income tax. Therefore, from the standpoint of public policy, there is no scientific basis on which to form a recommendation that the current special tax treatment of pensions should be eliminated. Unless empirical evidence is developed that reestablishes the income tax as a more efficient means of taxation, the deferral of pension savings for tax purposes should be maintained." Richard A. Ippolito, Pensions, Economics, and Public Policy 209 (Pension Research Council 1986).

C. SUMMARY OF REQUIREMENTS FOR QUALIFIED PLANS

In order to receive the favorable tax benefits made available under the Internal Revenue Code, a qualified plan must meet a complex set of requirements, generally contained in IRC §§ 401, 410–417, and amplified in an elaborate set of Treasury Regulations. Many of these requirements are duplicated in Title I of ERISA and hence also apply to some nonqualified plans. In addition, Title I of ERISA imposes some requirements that are not found in the Internal Revenue Code. Most qualified plans must satisfy these requirements as well, even though they have nothing to do with the plan's qualified status under the Internal Revenue Code.

The following is a summary of the basic requirements of plan qualification. Some of these requirements, such as the vesting and accrual provisions, have been discussed earlier in their ERISA versions. Others will be considered in the next few chapters on pension taxation. These chapters omit many IRC provisions dealing with more esoteric aspects of plan qualification or with specific types of plans, e.g., the special requirements for employee stock ownership plans (ESOPs). This chapter groups the IRC requirements into two categories: those with ERISA counterparts and those without. Where a parallel ERISA provision applies, the citation is provided.

Note that violation of an IRC qualification requirement merely disqualifies the plan, which may produce unfavorable tax consequences to both the employer and the employee. A violation of ERISA, however, can affect the substantive rights of participants. For example, a pension plan that does not by its terms provide a qualified preretirement survivor annuity to the spouse of a deceased participant is not only disqualified, but pursuant to ERISA must also provide the benefit, even though the plan language does not. See Lefkowitz v. Arcadia Trading Co., 996 F.2d 600 (2d Cir.1993), discussed supra in Chapter 7.

1. QUALIFICATION REQUIREMENTS WITH ERISA COUNTERPARTS

1. *Written employer plan.* There must be a "definite written program and arrangement which is communicated to the employees and which is established and maintained by an employer." Treas.Reg. § 1.401–1(a)(2). ERISA also requires every employee benefit plan to be established and maintained pursuant to a written instrument. ERISA § 402(a)(1).

2. *Trust.* ERISA generally requires all assets of employee benefit plans, other than insurance contracts, to be held in trust. ERISA § 403(a), (b). Except for annuity plans under IRC § 404(a)(2) and certain custodial accounts and annuity contracts under IRC § 401(f), only contributions to a trust qualify for the favorable tax rule permitting the employer to deduct the contribution before the employee includes it in gross income. IRC § 404(a)(1), (3), (5). Although IRC § 401(a) requires that a qualified trust be created or organized in the United States, other provisions permit a foreign trust to receive most of the benefits of qualified status. See IRC § 404(a)(4).

3. *Exclusive benefit.* A plan must be operated for the exclusive benefit of employees or their beneficiaries. IRC § 401(a) (introductory language); ERISA § 404(a)(1)(A). Furthermore, in the case of a trust forming part of a plan, it must be impossible under the trust instrument, at any time prior to the satisfaction of all liabilities with respect to employees and their beneficiaries under the trust, for any part of the corpus or income to be used for, or diverted to, purposes other than for the exclusive benefit of the employees or their beneficiaries. IRC § 401(a)(2); ERISA § 403(c)(1). An important feature of these rules is that upon termination of a plan, after all liabilities to participants and beneficiaries have been satisfied, any remaining assets may be distributed to the employer, provided the plan so provides. Treas.Reg. § 1.401–2(b)(1); ERISA § 4044(d)(1). The issue of asset reversions to employers is considered in Chapter 7, supra.

4. *Age and Service Eligibility Requirements* As discussed in Chapter 4, a plan is limited in its ability to impose minimum age, minimum service, or maximum age conditions. A plan may generally not require, as a condition of participation, that an employee complete a period of service with the employer extending beyond the later of age 21 or one year of service. IRC § 410(a)(1)(A); ERISA § 202(a)(1)(A). The minimum service requirement can be extended to two years if the plan provides for 100 percent vesting of accrued benefits after two years. IRC § 410(a)(1)(B)(i); ERISA § 202(a)(1)(B)(i). A plan may not exclude from participation (on the basis of age) employees who have attained a specified age. IRC § 410(a)(2); ERISA § 202(a)(2). Age discrimination is discussed in Chapter 18. Note that there is no requirement that every employee who meets the minimum age and service requirements must be covered by the plan. A plan can exclude such persons for other reasons. For example, it may be possible to cover only those employees in certain job categories or in certain geographic locations.

[handwritten: (4) Age + Service Requirements]

5. *Minimum accrual and vesting.* As noted in Chapter 4, benefits must accrue (i.e., be earned) at certain minimum rates and vest (i.e., become nonforfeitable) after certain time periods. IRC §§ 401(a)(7), 411; ERISA §§ 203, 204.

[handwritten: (5) Minimum accrual and Vesting]

6. *Commencement of benefits.* A plan must provide that, unless the participant otherwise elects, the payment of benefits will begin not later than the 60th day after the close of the plan year in which the latest of the following occurs: (A) the participant reaches the earlier of age 65 or the normal retirement age under the plan; (B) the participant's 10th anniversary of participation; or (C) the participant terminates his service with the employer. IRC § 401(a)(14); ERISA § 206(a). The plan may, however, permit the employee to defer distribution to a later date. Although ERISA does not restrict such voluntary deferrals, Internal Revenue Code limitations, noted below, prevent overly lengthy periods of deferral.

[handwritten: (6) Commencement of Benefits (plan document must specify when this will happen)]

7. *Spousal annuities.* A plan must provide retirement benefits to a married participant in the form of a qualified joint and survivor annuity (QJSA), unless both spouses elect another form of benefit. IRC §§ 401(a)(11), 417; ERISA § 205(a). In addition, when a vested participant dies before retirement, a plan must provide the surviving spouse (if any) with a qualified preretirement survivor annuity (QPSA). Profit-sharing and stock bonus plans are exempt from these rules, provided that upon the death of the participant the participant's vested benefits are payable in full to the surviving spouse. IRC § 401(a)(11)(B)(iii); ERISA § 205(b)(1)(C). The spousal annuity rules are discussed in Chapter 7.

[handwritten: (7) Spousal Annuities]

8. *Plan mergers.* A plan must provide that after a merger or consolidation with, or transfer of assets or liabilities to, another plan, each participant must have a benefit such that if the plan then terminated the benefit would be equal to or greater than the benefit that the participant would have had if the plan had terminated immediately prior to the merger, consolidation, or transfer. IRC § 401(a)(12), 414(*l*); ERISA § 208. Multiemployer plans covered by Title IV of ERISA are exempt from this requirement.

[handwritten: (8) Plan Mergers]

9. *Assignment and alienation.* A plan must provide that its benefits may not be assigned or alienated. IRC § 401(a)(13); ERISA

[handwritten: (9) Assignment + Alienation]

§ 206(d). There are three exceptions to this antialienation rule: (1) a voluntary and revocable assignment not exceeding 10 percent of any payment; (2) using vested benefits as security for a plan loan to a participant or beneficiary meeting the requirements of IRC § 4975(d)(1); and (3) assignments under a qualified domestic relations order (QDRO). Participant loans are discussed in Chapter 11, infra. QDROs and creditor access to plan benefits are discussed in Chapter 7, supra.

10. *Diversification of employer securities.* A defined contribution plan that holds publicly traded employer securities (other than certain ESOPs) generally must allow participants to diversify their accounts. IRC § 401(a)(35); ERISA § 204(j).

11. *In-service pension distributions.* Beginning in 2007, pension payments may be made to a participant who has attained age 62 and continues in employment. IRC § 401(a)(36); ERISA § 3(2)(A).

2. QUALIFICATION REQUIREMENTS WITH NO ERISA COUNTERPART

1. *Permanency.* The IRS takes the position that a plan "implies a permanent as distinguished from a temporary program." Treas.Reg. § 1.401–1(b)(2). The requirement does not appear in the Code. The Regulation recognizes that plans can be terminated, but warns that "the abandonment of the plan for any reason other than business necessity within a few years after it has taken effect will be evidence that the plan from its inception was not a bona fide program." Id. For profit-sharing plans, the Regulation requires that there be "recurring and substantial contributions." Courts have expressed doubts as to whether the statute requires this. See Lincoln Electric Co. v. Commissioner, 190 F.2d 326 (6th Cir.1951). The danger is that when a plan is terminated the IRS could retroactively disqualify it.

2. *Incidental benefits.* The IRS interprets the term "pension plan" as a plan primarily providing retirement benefits and the terms "profit-sharing plan" and "stock bonus plan" as plans primarily providing deferred compensation. Treas.Reg. § 1.401–1(b)(1). Other benefits, such as death benefits, life insurance, and health insurance, must be "incidental." Pension and annuity plans may provide benefits for sickness, accident, hospitalization, and medical expenses only if the requirements of IRC § 401(h) are met. Incidental benefits are discussed further in Chapter 11.

3. *Minimum coverage and participation.* A qualified plan can exclude nonhighly compensated employees from benefiting under the plan only if the plan's coverage of nonhighly compensated employees meets certain minimum standards. IRC §§ 401(a)(3), 410(b)(1). In addition, a defined benefit plan must benefit at least the lesser of (i) 50 employees of the employer or (ii) the greater of (A) 40 percent of all employees of the employer or (B) 2 employees (or 1, if there is only one employee). The number of employees is determined on a controlled group basis. IRC § 401(a)(26). These coverage requirements are discussed in Section B of Chapter 9.

4. *Nondiscrimination.* The contributions or benefits provided under a qualified plan must not discriminate in favor of highly

compensated employees. IRC § 401(a)(4). This requirement is extensively discussed in Section C of Chapter 9.

5.   *Full vesting upon plan termination.* As discussed in Chapter 4, a qualified plan must provide that upon termination, partial termination, or—in the case of profit-sharing plans—discontinuance of contributions, all accrued benefits must become 100 percent vested to the extent funded. IRC § 411(d)(3). *—do this to disincentivize ER's just terminating plans to the detriment of EEE's* ⑤ (*Fullfillment of*)

6.   *Minimum distributions.* Qualified plans are not free to delay the payment of benefits beyond certain time periods, even if the employee ⑥ consents. A qualified plan must commence distributions by April 1 of the calendar year following the calendar year in which the employee attains age 70½ or retires, whichever is later. If the entire interest of the employee is not distributed by that date, it must be distributed over the life (or period not greater than the life expectancy) of the employee (or of the employee and a designated beneficiary). IRC § 401(a)(9). There are also special rules applicable when the employee dies before his entire interest is distributed. IRC § 401(a)(9)(B). These requirements are discussed in Chapter 11.

7.   *Limitations on contributions, benefits, and elective deferrals.* A qualified plan must provide for benefits or contributions that do not exceed the limitations of IRC § 415 and must not allow elective deferrals to exceed the limitations of IRC § 402(g)(1). IRC § 401(a)(16), (30). These limitations are discussed in Section A of Chapter 10. ⑦

8.   *Limitation on includible compensation.* A qualified plan must also limit the amount of the annual compensation of each employee that is taken into account under the plan ($260,000 in 2014, $265,000 in 2015). IRC § 401(a)(17). This requirement is discussed in Section C.3 of Chapter 9. ⑧

9.   *Top-heavy plans.* A qualified plan must provide that if it becomes "top-heavy," i.e., key employees have more than 60 percent of the accrued benefits under the plan, the plan will meet certain minimum vesting and benefit requirements specified by IRC § 416. IRC § 401(a)(10)(B). The top-heavy rules are discussed in Chapter 9. ⑨

10. *Defined benefit plan forfeitures.* A qualified defined benefit plan may not use forfeitures to increase benefits. IRC § 401(a)(8). Forfeitures must instead be used to reduce future employer contributions. Treas.Reg. § 1.401–7. This requirement seems tautological since the essence of a defined benefit is that the benefit is specified independently of the plan's experience with employee turnover, investment income, mortality, and the like. Defined contribution plans, such as profit-sharing plans, may and generally do reallocate forfeitures to the accounts of the remaining participants, although such forfeitures can also be used to reduce employer contributions that would otherwise be made. See Rev.Rul. 71–313, 1971–2 C.B. 203. ⑩

11. *Direct transfer of eligible rollover distributions.* A qualified plan must allow participants to elect to have certain distributions ("eligible rollover distributions") made in the form of a direct trustee-to-trustee transfer to an IRA or a defined contribution plan. IRC § 401(a)(31)(A). In addition, plans that require cash-outs of benefits not exceeding $5,000 are required to transfer any such distribution in excess of $1,000 to an ⑪

IRA, unless the participant elects to receive it directly. IRC § 401(a)(31)(B). Such transfers are discussed in Section B of Chapter 11.

12. *Cost-of-Living Adjustments.* Many of the dollar limitations in the Internal Revenue Code are adjusted annually to reflect inflation or statutory phase-ins. The qualified plan limitations for 2015 are referred to throughout the text. IRS News Release IR–2014–99, Oct. 23, 2014.

13. *Death benefits under USERRA-qualified active military service.* In the case of a participant who dies while performing qualified military service, the survivors must be entitled to any additional benefits (other than benefit accruals relating to the period of qualified military service) provided under the plan had the participant resumed and then terminated employment on account of death. IRC § 401(a)(37).

NOTES AND QUESTIONS

1. *Minimum funding.* Title I of ERISA establishes minimum funding requirements for most plans, other than profit sharing plans, stock bonus plans, and certain other exempted plans. ERISA §§ 301–306. This is a requirement of regulatory law and has nothing to do with a plan's status under the Internal Revenue Code. At the same time, IRC § 412 imposes the same minimum funding requirements on plans that are (or were ever) qualified plans, again subject to similar exceptions. It is important to note that failing to meet the IRC § 412 minimum funding standards does not disqualify a plan. Instead, IRC § 4971 imposes an excise tax on an employer who fails to meet the standard. The tax is generally 10 percent of the funding deficiency, but becomes 100 percent if the funding deficiency is not corrected within a specified period. The minimum funding requirements are considered in detail in Chapter 6.

2. *Contrasting Title I of ERISA with the IRC.* The curious duplicate structure of many provisions of Title I of ERISA and the Internal Revenue Code has already been noted in Chapter 3. Compare the qualified plan requirements that have ERISA counterparts with those that do not. Is there a rationale common to the unique IRC requirements that warrants applying them only to qualified plans?

3. THE MECHANICS OF QUALIFICATION

There is no requirement in the Internal Revenue Code or Treasury regulations that the sponsor of a plan must seek an advance determination that a plan meets the qualification requirements of IRC § 401. In practice sponsors of individually designed plans almost always request a determination letter, since the rules are complex, and failing to qualify results in serious tax consequences, discussed in Section D, infra. Additionally, as discussed in Note 5, infra, plans with a current favorable determination letter have greater leeway to correct plan qualification failures using the IRS's Employee Plans Compliance Resolution System. Applicants for determination letters must give appropriate notice to certain "interested parties," generally the applicant's current employees with accrued benefits and vested former employees. Treas. Reg. § 1.7476–2; ERISA § 3001.

The IRS also issues opinion and determination letters relating to the qualification of master, prototype and volume submitter plans. These are plans made available by sponsoring organizations—mostly trade or professional organizations and financial intermediaries, such as banks, insurance companies, mutual funds—for adoption by employers. A master plan uses a single funding medium (e.g., a trust) for all adopting employers, while a prototype or volume submitter plan uses a separate funding medium (e.g., a separate trust) for each employer. The plan consists of an adoption agreement, which generally allows an adopting employer various options, and a basic plan document. In some cases, the adopting employer can rely on the opinion letter issued to the sponsoring organization. In other cases, the employer should apply for its own determination letter, though the process is simpler because the basic plan has already been approved.

If the IRS refuses to qualify a plan or revokes the qualification of a plan, a proceeding can be brought in the United States Tax Court for a declaratory judgment regarding the plan's qualification. IRC § 7476. The declaratory judgment proceeding is available only if the plan has been put into effect before the action is brought. The petitioner can be the employer, the plan administrator, an employee who qualifies as an interested party, or even the PBGC.

4. REMEDIAL AMENDMENT PERIOD

there's — No longer a Remedial Amendment Period for New Plans

If after a plan has been adopted or amended, it is later discovered that the plan's provisions do not meet the requirements of IRC § 401(a), a retroactive amendment may be possible. Under IRC § 401(b), a retroactive amendment can be made as late as the last day (including extensions) for filing the employer's tax return for the tax year in which the plan or amendment was adopted, provided that the amendment is made retroactively effective for all purposes.

Pursuant to authority granted in IRC § 401(b), the Treasury has issued regulations permitting extensions under other circumstances. Treas. Reg. § 1.401(b)–1. For example, if a determination letter has been requested, the remedial amendment period is generally extended to 91 days following the later of the IRS disposition of the request or the date a decision by the Tax Court in a declaratory judgment proceeding becomes final. Treas. Reg. § 1.401(b)–1(e)(3).

The most common use of a remedial amendment period is in connection with efforts to comply with statutes that change the plan qualification requirements. Following legislation, new interpretive regulations are often slow to appear. Until they do there can be uncertainty regarding precisely what plan amendments are appropriate. Under Treas. Reg. § 1.401(b)–1(b)(3), the IRS may designate two distinct types of plan provisions as a "disqualifying provision" and extend the remedial amendment period for retroactive amendments of such a provision. One is a plan provision that causes a plan to fail to satisfy the qualification requirements because of changes made to those requirements. The other is a plan provision that is "integral to a qualification requirement" that has been changed.

A good example of a plan provision "integral to a qualification requirement" is the provision specifying the maximum amount of the accrued benefit that is subject to involuntary distribution, a provision that all qualified plans must have pursuant to IRC § 411(a)(11). The Taxpayer Relief Act of 1997 increased the IRC § 411(a)(11) limit from $3,500 to $5,000, effective for plan years beginning after August 5, 1997. A qualified plan containing the $3,500 limit would not be disqualified if the $3,500 figure were not amended; a plan could provide more protection against involuntary distribution than the amended statute required. But in the IRS's view, the $3,500 limit was integral to a qualification requirement that has been changed. Thus, the IRS allowed plans to use the new $5,000 figure during the remedial amendment period in anticipation of a retroactive amendment reflecting the increase in the limit.

It should be emphasized that the remedial amendment period does not provide a plan with any relief from complying with the new rules as soon as they come into effect. The amendment must be retroactive and, even more importantly, the plan must be operated in accordance with the new qualification requirement prior to the adoption of the amendment. This will often mean that a plan will be operated in a fashion inconsistent with its terms, but this is inevitable if retroactive changes are to be allowed.

If a statute affects the qualification provisions, the statute itself will typically state the date by which plan amendments, to comply with the newly enacted requirements, must be made. For example, section 1107 of the Pension Protection Act of 2006 required plans to be amended by the last day of the first plan year beginning on or after January 1, 2009 to effectuate the changes made by the Act. Governmental plans were given until 2011. Also, IRS routinely uses its discretion under IRC § 401(b) to provide plan sponsors with additional time to make plan amendments to disqualifying provisions. In the past, these remedial amendment periods were frequently extended and often stretched to five years and beyond. This created severe workload problems for the IRS, since most plan administrators tend to wait until near the end of the remedial amendment period to apply for a new determination letter. The IRS has now adopted a radical new system of staggered remedial amendment cycles. See Rev. Proc. 2007–44, 2007–2 C.B. 54 (superseding Rev. Proc. 2005–66, 2005–2 C.B. 509). Different plans have different five-year cycles, depending on the employer's taxpayer identification number, so that the cycle for only one-fifth of the plans will end in any given year. All cycles end on January 31. A plan will be expected to apply for a new determination letter during the last 12 months of its five-year cycle.

A key feature of the new system is that there will be an automatic remedial amendment period for all disqualifying provisions arising out of a statutory change. The remedial amendment period with respect to such a disqualifying provision will be extended to the end of the first five-year cycle that ends at least 12 months after the change is first listed on the "Cumulative List of Changes in Plan Requirements." The IRS will publish this list around mid-November of each year. The list will also identify those items of published guidance, such as regulations and revenue rulings, that the IRS will consider in reviewing a plan's compliance with the changes. The most recent (2014) Cumulative List appears in Notice 2014–77, 2014–52 I.R.B. 974, December 05, 2014.

For example, assume a plan's current remedial amendment cycle ends January 31, 2016. This means that the employer must file its request for a determination letter between February 1, 2015 and January 31, 2016. In reviewing the plan, the IRS will consider only the changes published in the 2014 Cumulative List or earlier. If in January 2015, guidance is published requiring plans to be amended effective for plan years beginning in 2014, that guidance would first appear on the 2015 Cumulative List. In reviewing the plan for the cycle ending January 31, 2016, any amendments required by the January 2015 guidance would not be considered by the IRS. Instead, they would be considered as part of the cycle ending January 31, 2021.

This does not mean that an employer is free to wait until the end of the five-year cycle before amending the plan. The new procedure specifies that interim amendments must be adopted on a timely basis. Rev. Proc. 2007–44. An interim amendment is generally considered timely if it is adopted by the later of (1) the due date (including extensions) of the employer's tax return for the tax year in which the change became effective, or (2) the last day of the plan year in which the change became effective. Id., § 5.05. Thus, even under the new procedure, an employer may not be able to avoid periodic plan amendments between applications for a new determination letter.

Using the example above, the January 2015 guidance required a change in the plan to commence in 2014. Assuming the employer's taxable year and the plan year are both the calendar year, an interim amendment implementing the guidance would need to be adopted by the due date of the employer's 2014 tax return. The interim amendment would have to be retroactive to the first day of the 2014 plan year, and the plan would have to operate in compliance with the amendment provisions beginning on that date. If it turns out that a timely interim amendment must itself be amended, the employer will have until the end of the five-year cycle to do so.

The new procedure provides so-called "preapproved plans" (i.e., master/prototype or volume submitter plans) with a six-year amendment/approval cycle. All defined contribution plans would have the same six-year cycle and all defined benefit plans would have a different six-year cycle, with the two cycles spaced roughly two years apart.

It is important to note that the remedial amendment period procedures do not provide relief from the anti-reduction requirements of IRC § 411(d)(6) and ERISA § 204(g). See Rev. Proc. 2007–44, § 6.05. Thus, plan amendments adopted as a result of changes in the plan qualification requirements are forbidden from decreasing a participant's accrued benefit or reducing or eliminating early retirement benefits or optional forms of benefits. However, sometimes in connection with a statutory change, Congress will specify a statutory remedial amendment period and provide that as to any permitted retroactive plan amendments, the plan will be treated as operated in accordance with its terms and will not fail to satisfy the anti-reduction rules of IRC § 411(d)(6) and ERISA § 204(g) by reason of the amendment. In such circumstances, a plan is protected not only against disqualification, but also against claims by participants that a retroactive amendment violates ERISA.

5. IRS PROGRAMS TO AVOID THE DISQUALIFICATION SANCTION

Beginning in 1990 the IRS began to develop several programs under which the IRS would refrain from disqualifying a plan, provided the plan made appropriate corrections of the plan defects. The challenge in constructing such programs is to avoid undermining the incentives to prevent plan violations in the first place. These programs have evolved and expanded over time and have now been consolidated into the Employee Plans Compliance Resolution System (EPCRS), the latest version of which is set forth in Rev. Proc. 2013–12, 2013–1 C.B. 313. EPCRS covers qualified plans, 403(b) plans, SEPs, and SIMPLE IRA plans. There are three distinct correction programs: the Self Correction Program (SCP), the Voluntary Correction Program (VCP), and the Audit Closing Agreement Program (Audit CAP).

There are limits to what EPCRS can do. It is not available for failures relating to the diversion or misuse of plan assets. Furthermore, excise taxes and additional taxes are generally not waived merely because the underlying failure has been corrected or because the taxes result from the correction. For example, amounts contributed in excess of the IRC § 404 deduction limit (see Chapter 10, infra) may be subject the IRC § 4972 excise tax and excess contributions to highly compensated employees in 401(k) plans (see Chapter 9, infra) may be subject to the IRC § 4979 excise tax. Previously, the only exception was for minimum required distribution failures under IRC § 401(a)(9): as part of VCP, the Service in appropriate cases would waive the excise tax under IRC § 4974. The latest version of EPCRS expands the list of taxes that may be waived, in appropriate cases, as part of VCP. Rev. Proc. 2013–12, section 6.09(2) through (6).

The existence of EPCRS has sparked a lucrative "plan audit" business among accounting firms and pension consultants, who for a substantial fee will review a plan's operation for possible defects. But even when defects are discovered, plan sponsors will sometimes choose not to make use of EPCRS because the cost of retroactive correction is too high. For this reason, care is usually taken to cloak the self-audit with the attorney-client privilege. Serious professional responsibility issues can arise.

A plan sponsor who fails to use EPCRS will find little solace in the courts. Disqualification of a plan that lacks the proper form is routinely upheld, even if no participant was harmed and the plan operated in compliance with the statute. See, e.g., Basch Engineering, Inc. v. Commissioner, T.C. Memo. 1990–212; Tionesta Sand & Gravel, Inc. v. Commissioner, 73 T.C. 758, 764 (1980), aff'd, 642 F.2d 444 (3d Cir.1981). Also, the courts have generally held that even an inadvertent operational violation will disqualify a plan. See, e.g., Ludden v. Commissioner, 68 T.C. 826 (1977), aff'd, 620 F.2d 700 (9th Cir.1980) (administrative error excluded an eligible employee resulting in discrimination in favor of the highly compensated); Buzzetta Construction Corp. v. Commissioner, 92

T.C. 641 (1989) (inadvertent contribution in excess of the IRC § 415 maximum).

1.   *Self Correction Program (SCP)*. SCP is the simplest of all the correction programs. It provides formal IRS approval of what many plan administrators and sponsors had been doing all along. There is no fee or sanction and no requirement to report the correction to the IRS. All that is required is that full correction be made with respect to all participants and beneficiaries, no matter how far back the violation extended.

SCP is available provided three conditions are met. First, the violation must be an operational failure, i.e., a failure to follow plan provisions. Thus, a defect in the wording of the plan (a "document failure") cannot be corrected using SCP. Similarly, a violation of the discrimination rules due to the nature of the employer's workforce and the scope of the plan's coverage (a "demographic failure") is also ineligible.

Second, the operational failure must not be egregious. Egregious failures include: (a) a plan that has consistently and improperly covered only highly compensated employees; (b) a plan that provides more favorable benefits for an owner of the employer based on a purported collective bargaining agreement where there has in fact been no good faith bargaining between bona fide employee representatives and the employer; or (c) a defined contribution plan where a contribution is made on behalf of a highly compensated employee that is several times greater than the dollar limit set forth in § 415 (c). VCP and Audit CAP (discussed below) are available to correct egregious failures. Rev. Proc. 2008–50, section 4.11.

Third, the plan sponsor or administrator must have established practices and procedures (formal or informal) reasonably designed to promote and facilitate overall compliance with the qualification rules. Thus, the operational failure must have occurred through an oversight or mistake in applying the procedures, or because of an inadequacy in the procedures.

If the operational failure is "insignificant," there is no time limit for making the correction, and SCP remains available even if the plan is under audit. If the operational failure is "significant," SCP is available only if the plan has a current favorable determination letter from the IRS regarding its qualified status, which is a powerful incentive to obtain a determination letter. In addition, the correction of "significant" operational failures must generally occur within a two-year period and before the plan comes under audit. Rev. Proc. 2013–12, § 8.04 sets forth a few examples to illustrate what the Service considers insignificant violations. For example, if excess contributions totaling $4,550 (out of a $3.5 million plan contribution) were made to 3 participants (out of 50), the violation would be insignificant, but if the excess contributions were instead made to 18 of the participants and totaled $150,000, the failure would be significant.

SCP, though simple and inexpensive, has the disadvantage that there is no confirmation by the Service that the failure is eligible for correction under SCP and that the correction procedure is appropriate. However, the Service has assured plan sponsors that the extent to which corrections occurred before audit will be taken into account in reducing any potential sanction under Audit CAP. For this reason, if there is any uncertainty whether an operational failure is significant, many practitioners will treat it as insignificant and correct it under SCP. If it gets picked up on an audit, the plan sponsor will likely get credit for the correction.

Rev. Proc. 2013–12 establishes general principles to be used in making the necessary corrections and provides examples of correction procedures for certain specified defects. This guidance is fairly elaborate and gives plan sponsors specific methods that they can use to correct the operational failures typically encountered under EPCRS.

2. *Voluntary Correction Program* (VCP). The VCP program permits a plan sponsor to correct almost any type of plan qualification defect, whether it is an operational, plan document, or demographic failure. The VCP program applies only to plans that are not under audit (hence the term "voluntary"). The price is that the plan sponsor must pay a "compliance fee," which varies based on the number of plan participants. For plans with 20 or fewer participants the fee is generally $750, rising to $25,000 for plans with more than 10,000 participants. For an egregious failure, the compliance fee can be as high as 40 percent of the "maximum payment amount," i.e., essentially 40 percent of what the Service could collect in taxes and penalties upon plan disqualification.

Common operational failures that have been corrected under VCP include: failure to make timely minimum distributions under IRC § 401(a)(9); excess annual additions in violation of the IRC § 415(c) limits; failure to meet the 401(k) actual deferral percentage test; and top-heavy plan violations under IRC § 416. Common non-operational failures include neglecting to make timely plan amendments required by statutory changes and violations of the anti-discrimination rules due to changes in the composition of the plan sponsor's workforce

A plan sponsor initiates a request under the VCP program by filing with the Service a submission that provides a description of the failures, a description of the proposed methods of correction, and supporting information and documentation. The plan sponsor, often following some negotiation with the Service, then receives a "compliance statement" describing the terms of the acceptable correction. If the sponsor satisfies those terms in a timely manner, the Service will not disqualify the plan on account of the admitted and corrected defects.

VCP also allows a sponsor of a master or prototype plan to obtain a compliance statement affecting a group of plan sponsors. Moreover, VCP even permits a plan sponsor to make a submission on an anonymous basis. Anonymous submissions account for 20 percent of all submissions. At some point, of course, the plan must be identified, but this will only occur when the plan sponsor decides to go forward with the correction.

3. *Audit Closing Agreement Program (Audit CAP).* If a plan is under audit, VCP is unavailable, although SCP may still be used if the plan failure is an insignificant operational one. Once under audit, the only way to avoid disqualification is to reach a closing agreement with the Service, which requires correction of the failures and the payment of a "sanction," a deliberate change in terminology from the VCP's

"compliance fee." The sanction is a negotiated percentage of the maximum payment amount, but the Service promises that it "will not be excessive and will bear a reasonable relationship to the nature, extent, and severity of the failures." Rev. Proc. 2013–12, § 14.01.

In section 1101(a) of the Pension Protection Act of 2006, Congress gave explicit statutory authority for the establishment and implementation of EPCRS and any successor program, "and any other employee plan correction policies, including the authority to waive income, excise, or other taxes to ensure that any tax, penalty, or sanction is not excessive and bears a reasonable relationship to the nature, extent, and severity of the failure."

D. NONQUALIFIED PLANS

Although qualified plans are a useful device for providing deferred compensation, they are subject to numerous and complex requirements that severely restrict their flexibility. Qualified plans cannot discriminate in favor of highly compensated employees, nor can they provide for benefits or contributions in excess of certain amounts. These limitations prevent an employer from using a qualified plan to provide special benefits to key employees. For example, an employer may wish to provide a pension at retirement to key executives equal to 80 percent of their final average compensation, as opposed to 70 percent for the rank and file; or perhaps the employer wants only modest benefits for the key employees, but none for the rank and file. Even if the percentages were identical, the compensation of key executives may be so high that the specified percentage of compensation could not be paid from a qualified plan without violating the limitation on maximum annual benefits in IRC § 415 ($210,000 in 2015). Thus, a top executive earning $1,000,000 a year is not permitted to receive a $700,000 annual pension from a qualified plan, although an employee earning $100,000 is permitted to receive a $70,000 annual pension. Given these limitations, an employer will often provide its key executives with an employer-paid nonqualified plan, sometimes referred to as a supplemental executive retirement plan ("SERP"). Many employers will also allow their executives to defer a portion of their current salary or bonuses to future years.

The employer's deduction under any form of nonqualified deferred compensation plan is governed by IRC § 404(a). If contributions are made to a nonqualified stock bonus, pension, profit-sharing, or annuity plan, or if compensation is paid or accrued on account of any employee under any other plan deferring the receipt of compensation, the employer may deduct the contribution or compensation only in the taxable year in which an amount attributable to the contribution is includible in the gross income of employees participating in the plan. IRC § 404(a)(5). The same rule applies even if there is no "plan," as long as there is a method or arrangement of employer contributions or compensation that has the effect of a stock bonus, pension, profit-sharing, or annuity plan, or other plan deferring the receipt of compensation. IRC § 404(b). Thus, no matter what arrangement is used, the employer receives a deduction only when the employee recognizes income from the arrangement. This is often referred to as the "matching" principle. As we shall see in the materials below, the timing of the employee's recognition of income depends on the nature of the plan's funding and the extent to which the employee's rights are forfeitable.

1. UNFUNDED PLANS

Revenue Ruling 60–31
1960–1 C.B. 174.

Advice has been requested regarding the taxable year of inclusion in gross income of a taxpayer, using the cash receipts and disbursements method of accounting, of compensation for services received under the circumstances described below.

(1) On January 1, 1958, the taxpayer and corporation X executed an employment contract under which the taxpayer is to be employed by the corporation in an executive capacity for a period of five years. Under the contract, the taxpayer is entitled to a stated annual salary and to additional compensation of $10x$ dollars for each year. The additional compensation will be credited to a bookkeeping reserve account and will be deferred, accumulated, and paid in annual installments equal to one-fifth of the amount in the reserve as of the close of the year immediately preceding the year of first payment. The payments are to begin only upon (a) termination of the taxpayer's employment by the corporation; (b) the taxpayer's becoming a part-time employee of the corporation; or (c) the taxpayer's becoming partially or totally incapacitated. Under the terms of the agreement, corporation X is under a merely contractual obligation to make the payments when due, and the parties did not intend that the amounts in the reserve be held by the corporation in trust for the taxpayer.

The contract further provides that if the taxpayer should fail or refuse to perform his duties, the corporation will be relieved of any obligation to make further credits to the reserve (but not of the obligation to distribute amounts previously contributed); but, if the taxpayer should become incapacitated from performing his duties, then credits to the reserve will continue for one year from the date of the incapacity, but not beyond the expiration of the five-year term of the contract. There is no specific provision in the contract for forfeiture by the taxpayer of his right to distribution from the reserve; and, in the event he should die prior to his receipt in full of the balance in the account, the remaining balance is distributable to his personal representative at the rate of one-fifth per year for five years, beginning three months after his death.

(2) The taxpayer is an officer and director of corporation A, which has a plan for making future payments of additional compensation for current services to certain officers and key employees designated by its board of directors. This plan provides that a percentage of the annual net earnings (before Federal income taxes) in excess of $4,000x$ dollars is to be designated for division among the participants in proportion to their respective salaries. This amount is not currently paid to the participants; but, the corporation has set up on its books a separate account for each participant and each year it credits thereto the dollar amount of his participation for the year, reduced by a proportionate part of the corporation's income taxes attributable to the additional compensation.

Each account is also credited with the net amount, if any, realized from investing any portion of the amount in the account.

Distributions are to be made from these accounts annually beginning when the employee (1) reaches age 60, (2) is no longer employed by the company, including cessation of employment due to death, or (3) becomes totally disabled to perform his duties, whichever occurs first. The annual distribution will equal a stated percentage of the balance in the employee's account at the close of the year immediately preceding the year of first payment, and distributions will continue until the account is exhausted. However, the corporation's liability to make these distributions is contingent upon the employee's (1) refraining from engaging in any business competitive to that of the corporation, (2) making himself available to the corporation for consultation and advice after retirement or termination of his services, unless disabled, and (3) retaining unencumbered any interest or benefit under the plan. In the event of his death, either before or after the beginning of payments, amounts in an employee's account are distributable in installments computed in the same way to his designated beneficiaries or heirs-at-law. Under the terms of the compensation plan, corporation *A* is under a merely contractual obligation to make the payments when due, and the parties did not intend that the amounts in each account be held by the corporation in trust for the participants. . . .

Section 1.451–1(a) of the Income Tax Regulations provides in part as follows:

> Gains, profits, and income are to be included in gross income for the taxable year in which they are actually or constructively received by the taxpayer unless includible for a different year in accordance with the taxpayer's method of accounting.

And, with respect to the cash receipts and disbursements method of accounting, section 1.446–1(c)(1)(i) provides in part—

> Generally, under the cash receipts and disbursements method in the computation of taxable income, all items which constitute gross income (whether in the form of cash, property, or services) are to be included for the taxable year in which actually or constructively received.

As previously stated, the individual concerned in each of the situations described above employs the cash receipts and disbursements method of accounting. Under that method, as indicated by the above-quoted provisions of the regulations, he is required to include the compensation concerned in gross income only for the taxable year in which it is actually or constructively received. Consequently, the question for resolution is whether in each of the situations described the income in question was constructively received in a taxable year prior to the taxable year of actual receipt.

A mere promise to pay, not represented by notes or secured in any way, is not regarded as a receipt of income within the intendment of the cash receipts and disbursements method. . . .

This should not be construed to mean that under the cash receipts and disbursements method income may be taxed only when realized in cash. For, under that method a taxpayer is required to include in income that which is received in cash or cash equivalent. And, as stated in the above-quoted provisions of the regulations, the "receipt" contemplated by the cash method may be actual or constructive.

With respect to the constructive receipt of income, section 1.451–2(a) of the Income Tax Regulations [provides], in part, as follows:

> Income although not actually reduced to a taxpayer's possession is constructively received by him in the taxable year during which it is credited to his account or set apart for him so that he may draw upon it at any time. However, income is not constructively received if the taxpayer's control of its receipt is subject to substantial limitations or restrictions. Thus, if a corporation credits its employees with bonus stock, but the stock is not available to such employees until some future date, the mere crediting on the books of the corporation does not constitute receipt.

Thus, under the doctrine of constructive receipt, a taxpayer may not deliberately turn his back upon income and thereby select the year for which he will report it. Nor may a taxpayer, by a private agreement, postpone receipt of income from one taxable year to another.

However, the statute cannot be administered by speculating whether the payor would have been willing to agree to an earlier payment. See, for example, *Amend v. Commissioner,* 13 T.C. 178, acq., 1950–1 C.B. 1; and *Gullett v. Commissioner,* 31 B.T.A. 1067, in which the court, citing a number of authorities for its holding, stated:

> It is clear that the doctrine of constructive receipt is to be sparingly used; that amounts due from a corporation but unpaid, are not to be included in the income of an individual reporting his income on a cash receipts basis unless it appears that the money was available to him, that the corporation was able and ready to pay him, that his right to receive was not restricted, and that his failure to receive resulted from exercise of his own choice.

Consequently, it seems clear that in each case involving a deferral of compensation a determination of whether the doctrine of constructive receipt is applicable must be made upon the basis of the specific factual situation involved.

Applying the foregoing criteria to the situations described above, the following conclusions have been reached:

(1) The additional compensation to be received by the taxpayer under the employment contract concerned will be includible in his gross income only in the taxable years in which the taxpayer actually receives installment payments in cash or other property previously credited to his account. To hold otherwise would be contrary to the provisions of the regulations and the court decisions mentioned above.

(2) For the reasons in (1) above, it is held that the taxpayer here involved also will be required to include the deferred compensation concerned in his gross income only in the taxable years in which the taxpayer actually receives installment payments in cash or other property previously credited to his account. . . .

With respect to deductions for payments made by an employer under a deferred compensation plan, see section 404(a)(5) of the 1954 Code and section 1.404(a)–12 of the Income Tax Regulations.

In the application of those sections to unfunded plans, no deduction is allowable for any compensation paid or accrued by an employer on account of any employee under such a plan except in the year when paid and then only to the extent allowable under section 404(a). Thus, under an unfunded plan, if compensation is paid by an employer directly to a former employee, such amounts are deductible under section 404(a)(5) when *actually* paid *in cash or other property to the employee,* provided that such amounts meet the requirements of section 162 or section 212.

NOTES

1.   *Economics of tax deferral in unfunded plans.* Recall that if tax rates are unchanged, a contribution to a qualified plan provides an economic benefit equivalent to paying tax on the contribution and receiving a tax-free rate of return on the after-tax amount. The economics of unfunded deferred compensation are generally quite different. If tax rates are unchanged, a deferral of compensation is economically equivalent to paying tax on the original compensation at the employee's tax rate, but paying tax on the income from investing the after-tax amount at the *employer's* tax rate. A useful analysis of the economics of unfunded deferred compensation can be found in Daniel I. Halperin, Interest in Disguise: Taxing the "Time Value of Money," 95 Yale L.J. 506 (1986).

To illustrate this result, consider an employer who can pay an employee $1,000 currently. But instead of making that payment, the employer puts the money in its bank account and lets it accumulate for five years. The employer pays tax on the interest each year and pays that tax out of the interest. At the end of five years, the employer gives the account to the employee. If r is the *employer's* after-tax rate of return and t is the employee's tax rate, then after taxes the employee will have $1,000 × $(1+r)^5$ × $(1-t)$. But this is precisely the same amount that the employee would have if the employee received the $1,000 currently, paid tax at rate t, and invested what was left at an after-tax rate of return of r, i.e., $1,000 × $(1-t)$ × $(1+r)^5$. It should be emphasized that this arrangement is almost costless to the employer, apart from the transaction costs of setting up the arrangement. Few arrangements are actually structured in this fashion, but it captures the essence of the economics.

Is this deferral a good deal for the employee? If the employer's tax rate is higher than the employee's, the employee is worse off than if there were no deferral. But if the employer's tax rate is lower, the employee is better off deferring. Historically the top individual tax rates have been much higher than the top corporate tax rates, but in recent years the difference has narrowed. In fact, a quick glance at the rate tables reveals that the top individual rate for 2015 is 39.6 percent and the top corporate rate is 35 percent. Compare IRC § 1 with § 11. When marginal rates of the employer and employee are equal, the decision to defer is purely a financial one: If the employer can offer a marginally higher rate of return than an equivalent investment available to the employee, then deferred compensation may be a good investment: some employers credit deferred compensation with "interest" or similar credits that, in addition to being tax-deferred, are significantly higher than a market rate of return. The marginal rates shown in the tables do not, however, provide a full picture. State income taxes must be taken into account, as well as various deduction phase outs, especially IRC § 68, the overall limitation on itemized deductions. For example, in a state such as California, with a top corporate tax rate of 8.84 percent and a top individual tax rate of 12.3 percent, the highest combined federal/state corporate marginal rate is 40.7 percent and the combined individual rate is 47.0 percent. Thus, in California and other states with relatively high individual tax rates, highly-paid corporate executives still have an economic incentive to defer income.

So far the analysis has assumed constant tax rates, but if marginal tax rates fluctuate, there may be an incentive or disincentive to defer income, even if the rates for the employer and employee are identical. For example, if marginal rates are expected to be lower in the future, deferring income can create significant benefits for the employee. This prospect was once a major reason for deferring income, but because tax rates are much flatter now, highly-paid executives (the main beneficiaries of unfunded deferred compensation) are not likely to have a lower marginal rate after retirement than before. On the other hand, deferral might be foolish if tax rates were expected to increase significantly.

2. *Statutory limits on constructive receipt: IRC § 409A.* Rev. Rul. 60–31 provided a basic roadmap for structuring unfunded deferred compensation plans so that constructive receipt (and therefore taxation of the deferrals) could be avoided until the benefits were actually received. Over time, companies became quite aggressive in pushing the limits of constructive receipt. Determined to rein in these abuses, early in 1978 the IRS proposed a regulation providing that if payment of part of a taxpayer's fixed, basic, or regular compensation is deferred at the taxpayer's individual election (other than as part of a qualified retirement plan) to a future taxable year, the deferred amount will be treated as received in the earlier year. Prop. Treas. Reg. § 1.61–16. At the same time the IRS indicated that it would reexamine its holding in Rev.Rul. 60–31.

Intense lobbying by corporate interests persuaded Congress to intervene. In the Revenue Act of 1978, Congress nullified the proposed regulation by providing that the taxable year for including deferred compensation shall be determined by the principles in effect before the proposed regulation was announced. Since the IRS was precluded from changing the rules administratively, its only recourse was to engage in case-by-case battles with taxpayers over the interpretation of pre-1978 regulations, rulings and cases. The conflict involved issues such as how late an election could be made to defer compensation, whether and when distribution options could be selected or modified, and under what circumstances payment could be accelerated. The IRS suffered a number of notable defeats in the courts, which encouraged some companies to take even more aggressive positions. See, e.g., Martin v. Commissioner, 96 T.C. 814 (1991).

Congress ignored the situation for many years, until the highly-publicized collapse of Enron and several other large corporations in 2001–02. In some of these cases top executives had been able to accelerate receipt of their deferred compensation while lower-paid workers suffered huge losses when the employer stock in their qualified plan accounts became essentially worthless. See Joint Committee on Taxation, Report of Investigation of Enron Corporation and Related Entities Regarding Federal Tax and Compensation Issues, and Policy Recommendations (JCS–3–03), February 2003. Congress responded to these concerns as part of the American Jobs Creation Act of 2004 by adding IRC § 409A, which places new restrictions on the design and operation of nonqualified deferred compensation plans. The House Ways and Means Committee Report (H.R. Rep. No. 548, 108th Cong., 2d Sess.) states:

> The Committee believes that many nonqualified deferred compensation arrangements have developed which allow improper deferral of income. Executives often use arrangements that allow deferral of income, but also provide security of future payment and control over amounts deferred. For example, nonqualified deferred compensation arrangements often contain provisions that allow participants to receive distributions upon request, subject to forfeiture of a minimal amount (i.e., a "haircut" provision). . . .

> While the general tax principles governing deferred compensation are well established, the determination whether a particular arrangement effectively allows deferral of income is generally made on a facts and circumstances basis. There is limited specific guidance with respect to common deferral arrangements. The Committee believes that it is appropriate to provide specific rules regarding whether deferral of income inclusion should be permitted.

> The Committee believes that certain arrangements that allow participants inappropriate levels of control or access to amounts deferred should not result in deferral of income inclusion.

IRC § 409A represents a major change in the rules regarding nonqualified deferred compensation. Treasury and IRS issued final regulations in 2007 (72 Fed. Reg. 19234, April 17, 2007). In 2008, additional proposed regulations were issued on the calculation of amounts includible in income under § 409A and the additional taxes imposed by that section with respect to certain service providers (73 Fed. Reg. 74380, Dec. 8, 2008). The statute is exceptionally complex, and potentially applies to many arrangements that have not typically been thought of as deferred compensation arrangements. The IRS has implemented a correction program for certain operational and document failures. Notices 2008–113, 2008–2 C.B. 1305, 2010–6, 2010–1 C.B. 275, 2010–80, 2010–2 C.B. 853 Following is a brief summary of the key provisions, except for the rules relating to funding, which are discussed in Section D.4 below.

Distribution limitations. IRC § 409A(a)(2) permits a distribution from a nonqualified deferred compensation plan only upon six specified events: (1) separation from service, (2) disability, (3) death, (4) a time specified under the plan at the date of deferral, (5) a change in the ownership or effective control of the corporation, or in the ownership of a substantial portion of the assets of the company, but only to the extent provided by the IRS, or (6) an unforeseeable emergency. The legislative history makes it clear that amounts payable upon the occurrence of an event, such as marriage, a child attending college, and the like, are not treated as amounts payable at a "specified time."

A key employee (as defined in IRC § 416(i)) of a publicly-traded company may not receive a distribution upon separation from service, but must wait six months. IRC § 409A(2)(B)(i). The purpose is to prevent insiders who see the coming collapse of the company from resigning and immediately grabbing their cash. "Unforeseeable emergency" is defined quite narrowly to mean a severe financial hardship resulting from illness, accident, a casualty loss, or other similar extraordinary and unforeseeable circumstances beyond the control of the participant. IRC § 409A(2)(B)(ii).

Accelerations prohibited. IRC § 409A(a)(3) generally prohibits any acceleration of distributions, although the IRS may by regulations allow certain accelerations. Many companies had allowed participants to elect a distribution at any time, provided they forfeited some specified percentage (known as the "haircut"), often 10 percent. The asserted justification was that the haircut was a substantial limitation upon access to the funds that avoided constructive receipt, although there was no direct authority for that position. Such haircut provisions are now forbidden. Similarly, the new rule prohibits converting an annuity or installment payments into a lump sum. The regulations authorize plans to permit acceleration in a number of limited circumstances, including payments necessary to fulfill a domestic relations order and cash-outs of $10,000 or less accompanying the participant's separation from service. Treas. Reg. § 1.409A–3(j)(4).

Timing of deferral elections. An election to defer compensation for services performed during a taxable year must be made before the year begins, or within 30 days after the participant becomes eligible to participate in the plan. IRC § 409A(a)(4)(B). However, if the compensation is performance-based and relates to services over a period of at least 12 months, the deferral election may be made as late as six months prior to the end of the period. IRC § 409A(a)(4)(B)(iii). For example, if an employer provides a bonus on January 15 based on performance during the preceding calendar year, a plan could allow an employee to elect to defer the bonus as late as June 30. The statute does not define the term "performance-based compensation," but the regulations do so. Treas. Reg. § 1.409A–1(e).

Before the enactment of IRC § 409A, it was common for plans to allow participants to elect to extend the time of payment or otherwise change the form of future distributions. The IRS had never approved such plans, but practitioners relied on case law, which they interpreted to allow such plans as long as the election was not made too close to the originally scheduled payment date. Under IRC § 409A(a)(4)(C) such elections are now highly constrained. First, no such election may take effect until at least 12 months after it is made. Second, in the case of a payment to be made based on separation from service or scheduled at a specified time (or pursuant to a fixed schedule), the election must defer the first scheduled payment for at least five years. Third, in the case of payments scheduled at a specified time (or pursuant to a fixed schedule), the election must be made at least 12 months before the first scheduled payment.

Sanctions. If a plan fails to comply in form or operation with the new limitations, all compensation deferred under the plan (including deferrals in prior years) is includible in gross income to the extent not subject to a substantial risk of forfeiture and not previously included in gross income. IRC § 409A(a)(1)(A). The amount of deferred compensation includes any income attributable to the deferred compensation or such income. IRC

§ 409A(d)(5). The participant must also pay an additional tax equal to 20 percent of the amount included in gross income. Moreover, the participant must pay interest on the underpayments that would have occurred had the deferrals been included in income in the year of deferral or, if later, the first taxable year in which the compensation was not subject to a substantial risk of forfeiture. IRC § 409A(a)(1)(B). These consequences will apply only to those participants "with respect to whom the failure relates," so that an operational failure affecting only a few participants will not cause tax sanctions for the other participants. IRC § 409A(a)(1)(A)(ii).

The meaning of "substantial risk of forfeiture" is well-established under IRC § 83, and Congress appears to have carried over the definition. Compare IRC § 83(c)(1) with IRC § 409A(d)(4). The regulations set forth the following definition, which is similar to the one in Treas.Reg. § 1.83–3(c)(1):

> Compensation is subject to a substantial risk of forfeiture if entitlement to the amount is conditioned on the performance of substantial future services by any person or the occurrence of a condition related to a purpose of the compensation, and the possibility of forfeiture is substantial. [A] condition related to a purpose of the compensation must relate to the service provider's performance for the service recipient or the service recipient's business activities or organizational goals (for example, the attainment of a prescribed level of earnings, or equity value or completion of an initial public offering). For purposes of this paragraph (d), if a service provider's entitlement to the amount is conditioned on the occurrence of the service provider's involuntary separation from service without cause, the right is subject to a substantial risk of forfeiture if the possibility of forfeiture is substantial. An amount is not subject to a substantial risk of forfeiture merely because the right to the amount is conditioned, directly or indirectly, upon the refraining from the performance of services. Treas. Reg. § 1.409A–1(d).

Plans subject to IRC § 409A. The definition of nonqualified deferred compensation plan in IRC § 409A is extremely broad. It includes any plan that provides for the deferral of compensation, other than (1) a "qualified employer plan" and (2) any bona fide vacation leave, sick leave, compensatory time, disability pay, or death benefit plan. IRC § 409A(d)(1). Here the term "qualified employer plan" includes not only qualified plans under IRC § 401(a), but also 403(b) plans, SEPs, SIMPLE IRA plans, 457(b) eligible plans, and qualified governmental excess benefit arrangements under IRC § 415(m). The most common plans subject to IRC § 409A include elective deferrals of salary or bonuses, SERPs (whether defined benefit or defined contribution), and severance pay and change-in-control plans with income deferral aspects. The term "plan" is much broader than the meaning under ERISA, because it includes "any agreement or arrangement." IRC § 409A(d)(3). A plan is subject to IRC § 409A even if it covers nonemployees, such as directors or independent contractors.

A short-term deferral, generally up to 2½ months after the end of the taxable year in which a payment vests, is not considered a deferral of compensation for IRC § 409A purposes. Treas. Reg. § 1.409A–1(b)(4). Thus, an arrangement under which a calendar year employer awards a bonus on November 1 of Year 1, but delays payment of the bonus until January of Year

2, is not subject to IRC § 409A. A similar 2½ month rule exempts such brief deferrals from the matching rule of IRC § 404 as well. Treas.Reg. § 1.404(b)–1T, Q & A–2. Thus, if the employer in the above example used the accrual method of accounting, it could deduct the bonus in Year 1, even though the employee, who uses the cash method of accounting, would be taxable on the bonus in Year 2.

Recognizing that an enormous number of noncomplying plans were already in existence, Congress made IRC § 409A effective generally for amounts deferred after December 31, 2004. Amounts deferred prior to that date will not be subject to the new rules unless the plan under which the deferral was made is materially modified after October 3, 2004. The regulations are generally applicable for taxable years beginning on or after January 1, 2008, but the regulations and other IRS guidance provide a number of transitional rules and delayed effective dates.

3. *Offshore entities: IRC § 457A.* The Emergency Economic Stabilization Act of 2008 enacted § 457A, which significantly limits the ability of certain offshore entities to allow U.S. taxpayers to defer taxation by deferring the receipt of compensation from such entities. Section 457A generally applies to any amounts deferred that are attributable to services performed after 2008. IRS provided guidance in Notice 2009–8, 2009–1 C.B. 347.

2. ERISA LIMITATIONS: "TOP-HAT" PLANS AND EXCESS BENEFIT PLANS

Although nonqualified plans are not subject to the Internal Revenue Code limitations on qualified plans, such plans are potentially subject to the requirements of ERISA. There are, however, a number of important exceptions. A plan that is "unfunded and is maintained by an employer primarily for the purpose of providing deferred compensation for a select group of management or highly compensated employees" (commonly referred to as a "top-hat" plan) is exempt from the participation, vesting, funding, fiduciary responsibility, and plan termination insurance provisions of ERISA. ERISA §§ 201(2), 301(a)(3), 401(a)(1), 4021(b)(6). Top-hat plans are subject to the reporting and disclosure requirements of Part 1 of Title I of ERISA, but the Department of Labor permits such plans to comply with these requirements by filing a fairly simple notice. DOL Reg. § 2520.104–23. Top-hat plans are also subject to the enforcement provisions of ERISA. See Barrowclough v. Kidder, Peabody & Co., 752 F.2d 923 (3d Cir.1985). Thus, benefit disputes are federal claims, and state laws relating to such plans are preempted.

The inapplicability of ERISA's protective rules is a major reason why employers adopt top-hat plans. For example, the payments under the plan can be tied to future corporate performance, such as achieving a certain stock price or level of earnings. In addition, top-hat plans can have forfeiture provisions forbidden by ERISA, such as a requirement that the employee work for a certain number of years and not engage in certain prohibited activities. Prohibitions against working for a competitor of the employer or committing crimes involving the employer are common. The ability to impose such conditions can make top-hat plans attractive to employers even absent any significant benefit from tax deferral. Also employers do not have to set aside funds currently to pay for the projected benefits as would be the case if ERISA's minimum funding rules applied.

The language of ERISA's top-hat exception is not a model of clarity. For example, in ERISA § 201(2), does the word "primarily" modify the "providing deferred compensation" clause or the "select group" clause? The Department of Labor takes the position that the term "primarily" refers to the "purpose of the plan (i.e., the benefits provided) and not the participant composition of the plan. Therefore, a plan that extends coverage beyond 'a select group of management or highly compensated employees' would not constitute a 'top hat' plan." DOL ERISA Advisory Opinion 90–14A, n.1. In this view even allowing only one employee to participate who is not in a select group of management or other highly compensated employees would violate ERISA.

The Department of Labor's position is based upon ERISA's underlying protective policy. "It is the view of the Department that in providing relief for 'top-hat' plans from the broad remedial provisions of ERISA, Congress recognized that certain individuals, by virtue of their position or compensation level, have the ability to affect or substantially influence, through negotiation or otherwise, the design and operation of their deferred compensation plan, taking into consideration any risks attendant thereto, and, therefore, would not need the substantive rights and protections of Title I." Id.

Yet a number of courts have rejected the Department's interpretation. For example, in Demery v. Extebank Deferred Compensation Plan (B), 216 F.3d 283, 289 (2d Cir.2000), the Second Circuit stated:

> [We] think it significant that the statute defines a top hat plan as "primarily" designed to provide deferred compensation for certain individuals who are management or highly compensated. It suggests that if a plan were principally intended for management and highly compensated employees, it would not be disqualified from top hat status simply because a very small number of participants did not meet that criteria or met one of the criteria but not the other.

Demery also dealt with another ambiguity of the top-hat definition: What constitutes a "select group"? The plan in *Demery* was unusually broad, covering assistant vice-presidents, managers, and other senior officers, representing approximately 15 percent of the employer's workforce. The plaintiffs, who were seeking forfeited benefits that would not have been forfeitable had ERISA's vesting rules applied, argued that 15 percent of employees was more than a select group. In rejecting the plaintiffs' claims, the Second Circuit noted:

> While this number is probably at or near the upper limit of acceptable size for a "select group," we cannot say that it alone made [the plan] too broad to be a top hat plan without considering the positions held [by] the Plan's participants. It is clear [that] a "select group of management" could include senior management and high-level executives.

Plaintiffs also claim that despite the fact that [all] participants were officers of Extebank, they did not constitute a select group because they were neither key executives nor highly compensated. We do not find this argument compelling. While [the] participants did include assistant vice presidents and branch managers, and therefore swept more broadly than a narrow range of top executives, it was nonetheless limited to highly valued managerial employees. Moreover, unlike other situations in which plans were found not to satisfy the "select group" requirement, participation [was] not offered to employees at widely varying levels. Furthermore, the average salary of plan participants was more than double that of the average salary of all Extebank employees.

Lacking clear guidance from the courts, there is a risk in offering an unfunded plan to too broad a group. Some employers will limit participation to employees with compensation above a certain level, frequently somewhere between the Internal Revenue Code definition of highly compensated ($120,000 in 2015, $115,000 in 2014) and the maximum compensation that a plan can take into account in computing benefits or contributions ($ 265,000 in 2015, $ 260,000 in 2014). Another strategy is to have two separate plans, one for a group that is clearly select, and the other for a broader group that reaches into the gray area. If the broader plan's exemption from ERISA were successfully challenged, at least the ERISA exemption for the select plan could be salvaged.

Another form of plan generally exempt from ERISA's requirements is an unfunded "excess benefit" plan. An excess benefit plan is a "plan maintained by an employer solely for the purpose of providing benefits for certain employees in excess of the limitations on contributions and benefits" imposed by IRC § 415. ERISA § 3(36). A plan that replaces benefits restricted by another limitation, such as IRC § 401(a)(17), cannot qualify as an excess benefit plan. See Garratt v. Knowles, 245 F.3d 941 (7th Cir.2001). Unlike top-hat plans, unfunded excess benefit plans are completely exempt from Titles I and IV of ERISA, and thus need not be limited to a select group of employees. ERISA §§ 4(b)(5), 4021(b)(8).

3. FUNDED NONQUALIFIED PLANS

1. *General rules.* A major difference between funded and unfunded nonqualified plans is that under a funded plan the employee may be taxed on contributions to the plan before the employee actually receives distributions. Under IRC § 83, the fair market value of property transferred in connection with the performance of services is includible in the employee's gross income in the year in which the property first becomes transferable or not subject to a substantial risk of forfeiture. Property, for this purpose, includes a beneficial interest in assets (including money) transferred or set aside from the claims of creditors of the transferor, such as a trust or escrow account. Treas.Reg. § 1.83–3(e). Contributions to a nonqualified trust or premium payments on a nonqualified annuity are explicitly subject to the IRC § 83 rules, except that the value of the employee's interest in the trust or annuity contract is substituted for the fair market value of the property for IRC § 83

purposes. IRC §§ 402(b), 403(c). Actual distributions from the trust are taxed generally under the usual rules for taxing annuities. Id.

The general matching rule of IRC § 404(a)(5) governs the employer deduction for contributions to a funded nonqualified plan, with the additional proviso that no deduction is allowable unless separate accounts are maintained for each employee. Treas. Reg. § 1.404(a)–12(b)(3). Thus, an employer cannot deduct any contribution to a funded nonqualified defined benefit plan that benefits more than one employee. For this reason the disqualification of a defined benefit plan can have especially devastating tax consequences. A defined contribution plan, by contrast, fits the requirement easily, since all defined contribution plans have separate accounts.

The trust that holds the assets of a funded nonqualified plan is fully taxable on the trust income. The mechanics of this taxation are not wholly clear from the statute, but the IRS has fleshed out the rules in regulations and rulings. The usual trust rules in Subchapter J "have no application to beneficiaries of nonexempt employees' trusts." Treas. Reg. § 1.641(a)–0(b). However, in Rev. Rul. 74–299, 1974–1 C.B. 154, the IRS held that the trust deduction for distributions, IRC § 661(a), remains applicable. Funded nonqualified trusts are not grantor trusts. Prop.Treas. Reg. § 1.671–1(g). Thus, in principle and ignoring some of the fine points of trust taxation, a nonqualified trust is basically taxable on its undistributed income.

As an illustration of these rules, assume that the employer contributes $1,000 to a trust on behalf of an employee in Year One. The trust provides that the employee's interest is forfeitable until the employee works an additional five years. The accounts under the trust are distributable only upon the employee's death, retirement, or separation from service. The trust would be taxable each year on any taxable income earned by the trust. Assume that in Year Six, when the employee becomes vested, the account is worth $5,000. Under these facts the employee would include $5,000 in income in Year Six and the employer would be entitled to a deduction of $1,000 in Year Six. See Treas. Reg. § 1.404(a)–12(b). Once taxed on the $5,000, the employee would have a basis in his interest in the trust equal to $5,000. Note that the employer only deducts the actual contribution, which may, depending on the investment experience of the trust, be more or less than the amount the employee takes into income. Thus, if the account were worth only $500 in Year Six, the employer would still receive a deduction of $1,000.

2. *Disqualified plans.* Because the employees are taxed on their vested interests prior to actual distribution and the trust is taxed on the trust income, funded nonqualified plans are unattractive from a tax viewpoint. In addition, even though a funded plan is disqualified for tax purposes, it still generally must meet all of the requirements of Title I of ERISA. Accordingly, plan sponsors seldom intentionally create such a trust, but it can arise whenever a qualified plan becomes disqualified.

Disqualified plans are taxed under the general rules applicable to funded nonqualified plans. The only issue unique to disqualified plans is the tax treatment of the benefits that accrued during the time that the plan was qualified. For example, assume A is 60 percent vested in a profit-sharing plan that becomes disqualified in Year 1. A's account is worth $10,000. A was never taxed on this amount since the plan was qualified. Now that the trust is no longer exempt, how should A be taxed on the accumulated $10,000?

Prior to 1986 the answer was simple: A was not taxable on any part of the $10,000 until it was distributed, even though A was fully vested in $6,000. Under the general rule of IRC § 402(b)(1), an employee can be taxed on his vested interest in a nonqualified trust, prior to distributions from the trust, only if the interest arises out of contributions made while the trust is nonqualified. Thus, disqualification was relatively painless to the employees, if future contributions were anticipated to be minimal.

Since 1986 special rules have applied to plans that fail to meet the minimum coverage rules of IRC § 410(b) or 401(a)(26). First, a highly compensated employee (as defined in IRC § 414(q)) is taxable on the value of the vested accrued benefit (other than the investment in the contract) as of the close of the taxable year of the trust. IRC § 402(b)(4)(A). The employee's investment in the contract is equal to the sum of all amounts taxed as the employee's vested accrued benefit in the trust in prior years, less amounts that have been distributed to the employee but not taxed at that time. For an example of a highly-compensated employee who ran afoul of these provisions, see Gant v. Commissioner, T.C. Memo. 1998–440.

Thus, if A in the example above is highly compensated and if one of the reasons for the plan's disqualification was a failure to meet the minimum coverage rules of IRC § 410(b), A will be taxed on the $6,000 vested accrued benefit in Year 1. A will also be taxed in future years on any increases in the vested accrued benefit. Thus, even if A's vesting percentage is unchanged in Year 2, A would be taxed on 60 percent of any increase in the value of his account.

The second special rule added in 1986 provides that if the *only* reason for the trust's lack of tax-exempt status in any taxable year is a failure by the plan to satisfy IRC § 410(b) or IRC § 401(a)(26), IRC § 402(b)(1) does not apply to any employee who was not a highly compensated employee during such taxable year or any preceding period for which service was creditable to the employee. Under such circumstances a nonhighly compensated employee would be taxed only as distributions were made, i.e., the same timing rule that would apply if the plan were qualified. IRC § 402(b)(4)(B). Why did Congress limit the special rule in IRC § 402(b)(4) only to disqualification under IRC § 410(b) or 401(a)(26)?

4.   RABBI TRUSTS AND FUNDING TRIGGERS

From the employee's point of view, a major drawback of unfunded deferred compensation is precisely that it is unfunded. Without dedicated assets backing up the employer's promise, there is an increased risk of not being paid. To reduce that risk, an arrangement known as a "rabbi trust" was developed. These trusts take their name from the IRS's first ruling on the arrangement, Letter Ruling 8113107, December 31, 1980, which was issued to a congregation that had set up a trust to provide retirement benefits to its rabbi. Typically a rabbi trust is an irrevocable trust that allows its assets to be used solely to provide deferred compensation, with one crucial and explicit exception: the assets remain subject to the claims of the employer's creditors in the event of the employer's bankruptcy or insolvency. It is this exception that makes the trust "unfunded" for tax purposes, avoiding both constructive receipt and the application of the economic benefit doctrine. The exception also makes the trust "unfunded" for ERISA purposes. See, e.g., Demery v. Extebank Deferred Compensation Plan (B), 216 F.3d 283, 287 (2d Cir.2000); DOL Advisory Opinions 91–16A and 92–13A.

Because of the insolvency exception, rabbi trusts still present a risk to the employee. For example, in Goodman v. Resolution Trust Corp., 7 F.3d 1123 (4th Cir.1993), the court held that former executives of an insolvent employer were not entitled to recover assets of a rabbi trust from the receiver of the employer. The court described the executives as "unsecured creditors, who took the risks of being subject to the claims of general creditors for the benefits of favorable tax treatment—a gamble which failed to pay off in this case." Id. at 1129.

Nevertheless, because insolvency risk is not large in most enterprises that pay executive-level compensation, rabbi trusts have become quite popular as a means to provide a measure of protection for the employee beyond an employer's mere promise to pay. In particular, they protect the employee against a "change of heart," which can often occur when there is a change in control of the employer. For many years there was uncertainty regarding which features of a trust were necessary to (or fatal to) achieving the desired tax result. In Rev. Proc. 92–64, 1992–2 C.B. 422, the IRS issued a model rabbi trust and announced that rulings would generally not be issued on trusts other than the model trust.

Over time, aggressive techniques were developed which attempted to protect the assets of the rabbi trust from creditors despite the express terms of the trust. One of the most common was the use of offshore trusts. Although creditors would have a nominal right to obtain the trust assets, they would have greater difficulty and expense in doing so. Also certain foreign jurisdictions could be relied upon to be creditor unfriendly, with procedural rules in place that present creditors with costly hurdles.

Another aggressive technique was to create a funding trigger based on the financial health of the employer. For example, if the employer's debt/equity ratio or some other financial measure reached a specified level indicating increased risk of nonpayment, an otherwise unfunded plan would provide for the transfer of funds to a trust, or if the funds were already in a rabbi trust, the plan would provide that the creditor rights would be eliminated. Such funding would of course cause immediate taxation, but it would reduce the chance that creditors would obtain the funds ahead of the employee-beneficiaries.

Whether the use of offshore trusts or funding triggers could really avoid constructive receipt is questionable but now irrelevant. Under IRC § 409A(b), added by the American Jobs Creation Act of 2004, both techniques are heavily penalized. Assets set aside in an offshore trust used to provide nonqualified deferred compensation and any amount deferred under a plan that has a trigger based on the "employer's financial health" will be treated as property transferred for IRC § 83 purposes, whether or not the assets are available to satisfy the claims of general creditors. There is also a 20 percent penalty and an interest charge identical to the penalty and interest charge imposed on unfunded plans that do not comply with the IRC § 409A(a) requirements discussed in Section D.1, supra. Compare IRC § 409A(b)(4) with IRC § 409A(a)(1)(B). IRC § 457A, discussed in section D.3 of this chapter, supra, limits the ability to defer taxation of compensation to be received from certain foreign entities.

As long as offshore trusts and funding triggers are avoided, rabbi trusts remain a viable tool for executive compensation, and IRS challenges can be effectively eliminated by using the model trust set forth in Rev. Rul. 92–64.

5. DEFERRED COMPENSATION PLANS OF TAX EXEMPT EMPLOYERS: IRC § 457

As discussed above, the economic effects of a qualified plan and an unfunded nonqualified plan are usually different. Assuming tax rates remain constant, both are equivalent to receiving the deferred amount, paying tax on it at the employee's tax rate, and subjecting the return on the after-tax amount to taxation at another rate, which differs for each type of plan. In the case of a qualified plan, the return on the after-tax amount is *tax free*, while in the case of the unfunded plan the return is taxed at the *employer's* tax rate.

Although it is true that a taxable employer will normally face a positive tax rate, at least over the long term, there is a class of employers whose tax rate is always zero: state and local governments and nongovernmental tax-exempt organizations such as colleges and universities, charities, labor unions, and the like. An unfunded plan established by such employers provides precisely the same tax benefit as a qualified plan. For many years these entities were able to provide their employees with tax-favored retirement saving, unconstrained by any of the myriad limitations on qualified plans, especially the rules limiting the amount of contributions or benefits.

Eventually Congress recognized and limited the unique advantage of tax-exempt entities. In the Revenue Act of 1978, Congress enacted IRC § 457, which permitted the usual rules to apply to an unfunded deferred compensation plan of a state or local government only if the plan met certain eligibility requirements. In 1986, IRC § 457 was extended to cover nongovernmental tax-exempt organizations as well.

The requirements of IRC § 457 are similar to those imposed on qualified retirement plans and are designed to achieve the same goal, namely to "ensure that tax-favored savings are used primarily for retirement purposes." H.R. Rep. No. 426, 99th Cong., 1st Sess. 701 (1985). For example, deferrals each year are generally limited to a maximum amount equal to the maximum deferral under a 401(k) plan: however, this limit differs from the 401(k) limit because it applies to all deferrals under the plan, including employer-funded contributions. IRC § 457(b)(2),(e)(15). Amounts may not be made available prior to the earlier of the calendar year in which the participant attains age 70½, severance from employment, or an "unforeseeable emergency." IRC

§ 457(d)(1)(A). The usual minimum distribution rules under IRC § 401(a)(9) apply. IRC § 457(d)(2). A plan that meets these requirements is sometimes referred to as an "eligible 457 plan" or often simply as a "457 plan."

Initially, employees were taxed on their 457 plan accounts when the amounts were "made available," even if they were not yet distributed. Since 2001, this rule has applied only to employees of nongovernmental tax-exempt employers. IRC § 457(a)(1)(B). Participants in governmental 457 plans are taxed only when a distribution is made, which is the rule for qualified plans. This distinction is extremely important, because as we shall see in Chapter 11, infra, participants in nongovernmental 457 plans cannot avoid taxation by rolling over a distribution into an IRA or another plan. Why does the statute treat nongovernmental 457 plans less favorably?

Participants in nongovernmental 457 plans can avoid taxation in certain circumstances, even though they have a right to a distribution. First, if an amount becomes available due to the attainment of age 70½, severance from employment, or an unforeseeable emergency, a participant can elect, but only once, to defer commencement of distributions under the plan and avoid taxation until the amounts are ultimately made available, provided that the payments have not actually begun. IRC § 457(e)(9)(B). Second, the fact that a participant may elect to receive a distribution of the total amount payable under the plan does not make such amount available (and therefore subject to tax), provided such amount does not exceed $5,000, the participant has not deferred any amount under the plan for two years, and no such election has previously been made. IRC § 457(e)(9)(A).

If a plan does not meet the IRC § 457(b) requirements, the present value of the compensation is included in the gross income of the participant or beneficiary when there is no substantial risk of forfeiture. IRC § 457(f). Such noncomplying plans are often referred to as "457(f) plans." Because employees generally dislike paying tax on compensation they have yet to receive, almost all 457(f) plans provide for distribution when the deferred compensation vests. For example, an executive of a nonprofit corporation might be given a bonus of $100,000, payable in three years together with interest, provided that the executive remains employed for that period. The $100,000 amount exceeds the maximum permitted by IRC § 457(b), so this is a 457(f) plan. However, because the executive must continue to work for three years in order to receive the payment, it is subject to a substantial risk of forfeiture and is therefore not taxable until the end of the three year period, at which point it will be paid and would have been taxable anyway.

Although 457(b) eligible plans are exempt from IRC § 409A, 457(f) plans are not. IRC § 409A(d)(2)(B). Thus, 457(f) plans must take care to comply with the IRC § 409A restrictions on the timing of distributions, accelerations, and deferral elections. For example, if the nonprofit corporation in the example above retained the right to terminate the plan and accelerate the payment of any deferred bonuses, the plan might not satisfy IRC § 409A. The penalty here is not the premature taxation of the deferral, since the timing of taxation under IRC § 457(f) and IRC § 409A(a)(1)(A) is the same, i.e., the deferral is taxed when there is no longer a substantial risk of forfeiture. The real penalty is the additional tax of 20 percent of the deferred compensation. See IRC § 409A(a)(1)(B)(ii).

There is one special type of plan that is exempt from the requirements of IRC §§ 457 and 409A: the "qualified governmental excess benefit arrangement" defined in IRC § 415(m). Basically, this is a governmental plan maintained solely for the purpose of providing annual benefits that exceed the IRC § 415 limits and which does not provide for any type of elective deferral. For example, a public university might have a qualified defined benefit plan with a formula based on age and years of service. For some highly-paid employees this formula produces an annual benefit in excess of the IRC § 415(b) limit. It is not uncommon for the university to set up a qualified governmental excess benefit plan to make up the difference. Private tax-exempt employers do not have this opportunity. Can the exception for qualified governmental excess benefit arrangements be justified?

Bona fide vacation leave, sick leave, compensatory time, severance pay, disability pay, and death benefit plans are not subject to IRC § 457. IRC § 457(e)(11). Consider the following severance pay plan set up by a public university for its top administrators. Each year a participant earns a severance pay credit of 5 percent of compensation. Each year the accumulated severance pay credit is also increased by a specified rate of interest. When separation from employment occurs, the participant receives a lump sum payment of the accrued severance pay credit and interest earnings. The payment is limited to twice the participant's salary in the year preceding separation. Is this arrangement subject to IRC § 457? See DOL Reg. § 2510.3–2(b). Is this plan subject to IRC § 409A? Compare IRC § 409A(d)(1)(B) with IRC § 457(e)(11).

Funded 457 plans. Recall that ERISA does not permit pension plans to be unfunded unless they are top-hat or excess benefit plans. Thus, a private tax-exempt employer can establish an unfunded plan only for a select group of employees, unless the plan takes the form of an excess benefit plan, which is quite limited in the benefit it can provide. However, public employers are not constrained by ERISA and can extend the benefits of any type of unfunded plan to rank and file employees.

Many public employees participated in these plans oblivious to the risk of an unfunded plan, although in the case of a governmental entity such risk would seem negligible. The magnitude of the risk became apparent as a result of the bankruptcy of Orange County, California, in late 1994. Millions of dollars in unfunded deferred compensation accounts of the county employees under the county's 457 plan were potentially subject to the claims of the county's general creditors. Ultimately, the employees were able to retain their accounts as part of the bankruptcy settlement, but in 1996 Congress established a new requirement that all amounts deferred under a section 457 plan maintained by a state or local governmental employer have to be held in trust (or a custodial account or an annuity contract) for the exclusive benefit of employees. IRC § 457(g). The trust (or custodial account or annuity contract) is provided tax-exempt status. The rules under section 457 are to govern the taxation of participants and beneficiaries, rather than the usual rules of IRC § 83 and 402(b) applicable to funded nonqualified plans. Thus, the tax treatment of such plans will remain the same as if the plan were unfunded, but the employees will have the added security of a funded trust.

Why does the statute permit this type of funded nonqualified plan to receive special tax benefits? Why exclude plans of private tax-exempt employers from the funding requirement?

E. EMPLOYMENT TAXES

1. *Qualified plans.* Both employer contributions to and distributions from qualified plans, SEPs, SIMPLE plans, and 403(b) plans are generally not treated as wages subject to Social Security (FICA) and unemployment (FUTA) taxes. IRC §§ 3121(a)(5), 3306(b)(5). However, this exemption from employment taxes does not apply to elective deferrals under such plans. IRC §§ 3121(v)(1), 3306(r)(1).

The FICA tax has two components: (1) the old-age, survivors, and disability insurance (OASDI) portion is 6.2 percent of wages up to the Social Security wage base ($118,500 in 2015), and (2) the hospital insurance ("Medicare") portion is 1.45 percent of wages, unlimited by any cap. The tax is withheld from the employee's wages and the employer pays an equal amount. For 2011 and 2012 only, the employee's OASDI share was reduced to 4.2 percent. For 2015, the FUTA tax is 6.0 percent on the first $7,000 of wages, reduced by a credit of up to 5.4 percent, and is paid only by the employer. The $7,000 is the federal wage base; the state unemployment tax wage base may be different. The FICA and FUTA taxes are generally referred to as the "payroll" taxes.

For taxable years beginning after 2012, there is an additional Medicare tax on individuals who receive more than a certain amount of wages during the year: $250,000 for married taxpayers filing a joint return, $200,000 for a single taxpayer, and $125,000 for a married taxpayer filing separately. I.R.C. §§ 1401, 3101. The tax is equal to 0.9% of the excess. The thresholds are not adjusted for inflation. Unlike the basic 1.45 percent tax, in the case of a joint return, the additional 0.9% tax is on the combined wages and earned income of both spouses.

Historically, employment taxes, including Medicare tax, have applied only to income received in the form of wages. For taxable years beginning after 2012, there is also imposed on individuals a new Medicare tax equal to 3.8% of the lesser of (1) net investment income for the year or (2) the excess (if any) of (a) the modified adjusted gross income (MAGI) for the year over (b) the threshold amount. I.R.C. § 1411. A similar tax applies to estates and trusts. The threshold amount is $250,000 for a joint return or a surviving spouse, $125,000 for a married taxpayer filing a separate return, and $200,000 in any other case. Net investment income does not include any distribution from a tax-favored retirement plan or any item taken into account in determining self-employment income.

The exclusion of contributions to retirement plans from the FICA tax is a significant additional incentive to shift compensation into qualified plans. For example, assume Employer pays Employee a salary of $70,000 a year. If Employer pays Employee a cash bonus of $1,000 at the end of the year, Employer must pay a FICA tax of $76.50 (7.65 percent of

$1,000). Employer must also withhold an equivalent amount from Employee's bonus, so that Employee receives only $923.50. If instead Employer contributed the $1,000 to a profit-sharing plan on Employee's behalf, no FICA taxes would be paid, nor would any FICA taxes be paid when distributions from the plan were made. This result makes the bonus in the form of the profit-sharing contribution attractive to both Employer and Employee. Even if Employee's compensation were above the Social Security wage base, Employer and Employee would each save the Medicare portion of the FICA tax (at least 1.45 percent of compensation). Note that if this were a 401(k) plan and the employee elected to defer the $1,000, the $1,000 would be fully subject to FICA taxation. IRC § 3121(v)(1).

2. *Plans for the self-employed.* A self-employed person, such as a sole proprietor or a partner, has no employer and is not an employee for FICA purposes. Instead of FICA taxes, a self-employed person pays a special self-employment tax on "self-employment income." See IRC §§ 1401–1403. The rate is twice the rate of the employer FICA tax, hence a self-employed person pays the equivalent of both the employer and the employee share of the FICA tax, amounting to 15.3 percent of income up to the wage base and 2.9 percent thereafter. For 2011 and 2012 only, the rate was reduced to 13.3 percent of income up to the wage base and 2.9 percent thereafter. The individual is allowed a federal income tax deduction for 50% of the self-employment tax.

For taxable years beginning after 2012, the new and additional Medicare taxes described in the preceding section also apply to self-employed individuals.

Although contributions to qualified plans by an employer on behalf of an employee are not subject to the FICA tax, contributions to qualified plans and SEPs on behalf of a self-employed person do not reduce self-employment income and are thus fully subject to the SECA tax. What is the justification for treating the self-employed differently?

3. *Nonqualified plans.* Since 1984, amounts deferred under a nonqualified deferred compensation plan have been subject to the payroll taxes as of the *later* of the date the services are performed or the date on which there is no substantial risk of forfeiture of the rights to such amount. IRC §§ 3121(v)(2), 3306(r)(2). Thus, if the services have already been performed, the payroll taxes are payable when the benefits *vest*, not when they are actually paid. As discussed above, for income tax purposes, benefits from unfunded plans are not taxable until they are actually paid, unless the plan runs afoul of IRC § 409A. A nonqualified deferred compensation plan is defined for these purposes to be "any plan or other arrangement for deferral of compensation" other than qualified plans, certain exempt government deferred compensation plans, supplemental pension benefits, and certain "cafeteria plans" under IRC § 125. IRC § 3121(v)(2)(C).

Prior to 1994, this provision drew little attention, because both portions of the FICA tax were levied on earnings only up to the wage base and most employees receiving unfunded deferred compensation had earnings above the wage base. But in 1994 the hospital insurance portion of the FICA tax was made applicable to all wages, and now all nonqualified deferred compensation is subject to at least some FICA tax.

Applying the payroll taxes to nonqualified deferred compensation has proven to be complex. The complexity arises in part from the requirement, known as the "nonduplication rule," that once an amount is subjected to FICA taxation, that amount and any attributable income is not to be treated as wages for FICA tax purposes at any time thereafter. IRC § 3121(v)(2)(B). Distinguishing between additional deferred compensation and income on previously taxed deferred amounts is not always easy. In addition, given the extraordinary variety of deferred compensation plans, computing the "amount deferred" can in some cases be exceedingly difficult.

Highly technical regulations now provide guidance. Treas. Reg. § 31.3121(v)(2)–1. The following examples illustrate how the FICA tax applies under the regulations to a number of common plans.

Example 1: defined contribution plan. Employer M establishes a nonqualified deferred compensation plan for Employee A. Under the plan, 10 percent of annual compensation is credited on behalf of Employee A on December 31 of each year. In addition, a reasonable rate of interest is credited quarterly on the balance credited to Employee A as of the last day of the preceding quarter. All amounts credited under the plan are 100 percent vested, and the benefits payable to Employee A are based solely on the balance credited to Employee A's account.

The "amount deferred" (i.e., subject to FICA tax) for a calendar year is equal to 10 percent of A's compensation. When A ultimately receives the value of the amounts credited to A under the plan, there will be no FICA tax on that amount. If the interest rate were "unreasonable," the interest in excess of a presumed reasonable rate defined in the regulations is treated as an additional amount deferred and subject to FICA tax in the year it is credited.

Example 2: defined benefit plan with ascertainable benefits. Employer O establishes a nonqualified deferred compensation plan for Employee C. Under the plan, Employee C has a fully vested right to receive a life annuity, payable monthly beginning at age 65, equal to the product of (a) 2 percent for each year of service and (b) Employee C's highest average annual compensation for a three-year period. The plan also provides that, if Employee C dies before age 65, the present value of the future payments will be paid to his or her beneficiary. As of the end of Year One, Employee C has 25 years of service and high three-year average compensation of $100,000. As of the end of Year Two, Employee C is age 61, has 26 years of service, and has high three-year average compensation of $104,000.

As of the end of Year One, Employee C has a legally binding right to receive lifetime payments of $50,000 (2 percent x 25 years x $100,000) per year. As of the end of Year Two, Employee C has a legally binding right to receive lifetime payments of $54,080 (2 percent x 26 years x $104,000) per year. Thus, during Year Two, Employee C has earned a legally binding right to additional lifetime payments of $4,080 ($54,080–$50,000) per year beginning at age 65. The amount subject to FICA tax for Year Two is the present value, as of the end of Year Two, of these additional payments, using reasonable actuarial assumptions.

Example 3: a defined benefit plan with nonascertainable benefits. Assume the same facts as in Example 2, except that the benefits under the plan are to be reduced by the amount payable to Employee C from Employer O's qualified plan. Under the regulations, the amount deferred is not reasonably ascertainable prior to termination of employment and therefore no FICA tax need be paid until Employee C terminates employment. At that time, the present value of the payments under the nonqualified plan would be treated as an amount deferred and subject to FICA tax. The regulations allow the employer to elect to take amounts into account and pay FICA taxes before the amounts are reasonably ascertainable. If such an election is made, complex actuarial calculations are required to determine the proper FICA tax when the amounts eventually become ascertainable at a later date.

F. STATE INCOME TAXATION

Generally those states that impose income taxes have adopted tax provisions that parallel the Internal Revenue Code and provide essentially the same tax treatment to qualified plans and other forms of retirement savings. The National Conference of State Legislatures has issued, and periodically updates, a study of the state income taxation of retirement benefits, State Personal Income Taxes on Pensions and Retirement Income, available at www.ncsl.org. For many years there was quite a controversy about the state tax treatment of migratory retirees. The question was whether a state in which deferred compensation was earned should be able to tax the distributions if the distributee no longer resided in the state. In the late 1980s, California began aggressively to audit recipients of public pensions who were not filing California income tax returns. The courts consistently upheld the constitutionality of this so-called "source-based" taxation of deferred compensation, but its use by California and several other states sparked a great deal of grassroots opposition, particularly in Nevada, a California neighbor that has no income tax.

In response to lobbying by retiree groups, and by business groups concerned about the administrative and recordkeeping burdens of multistate taxation of pensions, in 1996 Congress enacted 4 U.S.C. § 114, which provides that "[n]o State may impose an income tax on any retirement income of an individual who is not a resident or domiciliary of such State (as determined under the laws of such State)." Retirement income is broadly defined to include all the statutory tax-favored arrangements such as qualified plans, IRAs, 403(b) plans, 457 plans, SEPs, and the like.

Even nonqualified plans are covered, as long as they are (1) maintained solely for the purpose of providing retirement benefits in excess of the IRC limits on statutory tax-favored arrangements, *or* (2) structured in the form of substantially equal periodic payments payable either as a life annuity or over a minimum of at least 10 years. The latter rule is designed to prevent abusive arrangements. For example, assume Employee in State A will be retiring in two years and is planning on a move to State B, which has no income tax. Employee agrees with his employer to defer 50 percent of his compensation over the next two years, to be paid to him (with specified interest) in a lump sum

6 months after he retires and moves to State B. State A is permitted to tax the lump sum payment.

Is the ban on source-based taxation imposed by 4 U.S.C. § 114 fair to the source state?

CHAPTER 9

THE ANTIDISCRIMINATION NORM

Analysis

[handwritten note: Two components of the Non-Discrimination Norm: ① ②]

Introduction

Employers are not completely free to pick and choose which employees may participate in a qualified plan or to vary the level of contributions or benefits among the participants. Well before ERISA, the favorable tax treatment accorded to qualified plans was denied to plans that discriminated in favor of highly compensated employees. These rules have evolved into the complex web of restrictions that is the subject of this chapter.

Section A explores the background and purpose of the nondiscrimination rules. Since retirement plans are voluntary arrangements, there is a fundamental tension between stricter nondiscrimination rules and the willingness of firms to offer plans. The antidiscrimination norm has two distinct components: (1) minimum coverage and participation requirements that limit an employer's ability to exclude employees from the plan; and (2) limitations on the extent to which contributions or benefits under a plan can vary from participant to participant. These rules are considered in Sections B and C.

The remainder of the chapter examines the antidiscrimination requirements that are applicable only to certain types of plans. Section D reviews the special statutory rules for those plans that direct a relatively high percentage of their benefits to key employees, the so-called "top heavy" plans. Section E describes how the antidiscrimination rules apply to those plans, such as 401(k) plans, that accord the employees some degree of choice about the level of contributions. The antidiscrimination rules that apply to employee welfare benefit plans are discussed in Chapter 19.

A. PURPOSE OF THE ANTIDISCRIMINATION RULES

Bruce Wolk, Discrimination Rules for Qualified Retirement Plans: Good Intentions Confront Economic Reality

70 Va.L.Rev. 419, 426–433 (1984).

The first specific statutory reference to retirement plans appeared in the Revenue Act of 1921. This legislation provided that a trust created by an employer as part of a stock bonus or profit-sharing plan would be tax-exempt and that beneficiaries would be taxed when distributions were made, but only if the plan was for the "exclusive benefit of some or all of [the] employees."

Under the "some or all" requirement, carried forward in successive revenue acts, it was certainly textually plausible that a plan could benefit only selected groups of employees to the exclusion of others and still remain qualified. Perhaps because tax rates declined to a relatively low level during the 1920's, the propriety of such plans was not a serious issue. With the onset of the Depression and the resulting sharply reduced tax yields, however, tax rates began rising, beginning with the Revenue Act of 1932.

Increased tax rates inevitably led taxpayers to seek tax avoidance devices of all kinds. In 1937 the Treasury Department listed pension trusts as one of the principal devices used to avoid income taxes. The Treasury was concerned that a company could create a plan that covered only a select group of high-salaried employees who would benefit from tax deferral on large amounts of income. When it enacted the loophole-closing Revenue Act of 1937, Congress, nevertheless, declined to deal with this perceived problem, ostensibly because little apparent revenue loss had resulted. The Treasury then took a more aggressive position in its regulations and began to challenge plans benefiting only stockholder-employees and key employees on the theory that these plans were not for the "exclusive benefit" of the company's employees as required by the statute. These attacks proved largely unsuccessful.

The World War II era brought even higher tax rates. According to the Treasury, these increased rates stimulated the use of retirement plans as tax-saving devices for key employees. The Treasury viewed the favorable tax treatment of retirement plans as a tax subsidy granted by Congress out of a desire to improve the welfare of employees by encouraging the creation of such plans. The Treasury argued that plans covering only a few favored high-salaried employees were inconsistent with Congress' goal and therefore undeserving of any subsidy.

In 1942 Congress responded to the Treasury's concerns by enacting a novel set of nondiscrimination requirements. A plan could no longer qualify for favorable tax treatment unless it covered either a sufficient statutory percentage of the firm's employees or those employees who qualified under a classification set up by the employer and found by the Commissioner not to be discriminatory in favor of officers, shareholders, supervisors, or highly compensated employees. To prevent employers from evading this minimum coverage requirement by providing employees with nominal benefits, Congress also required that the contributions and benefits provided under the plan not discriminate in favor of the officers, shareholders, supervisors, or highly compensated employees.

This nondiscrimination concept has been carried forward in the present law [with some modifications. Currently the "prohibited group" is defined just to be "highly compensated employees."] The House Ways and Means Committee Report accompanying the Revenue Act of 1942 refers to the nondiscrimination requirements as preventing "the trust device from being used for the benefit of shareholders, officials, or highly paid employees." In actual practice it has been possible to structure plans to make the prohibited group a substantial, if not the principal, beneficiary of the plan. A straightforward analysis of the subsidy's operation in its economic setting reveals that significant benefits *must* flow to the prohibited group if the tax incentive for qualified retirement plans, as it currently exists, is to succeed in increasing retirement benefits for rank-and-file employees. . . .

Modern law

[The] employer is the one who makes the decision to establish a retirement plan. From its own income tax viewpoint, the employer is theoretically indifferent to the plan's creation. Whether as a $1,000 wage payment or as a $1,000 contribution to a qualified retirement plan, the employer can deduct the total amount as a business expense. Yet by contributing to the plan, the employer channels a government subsidy to the plan participants. Providing this subsidy is not cost free. Establishment and maintenance of a qualified plan involve significant administrative costs. If paid by the plan, these costs reduce the value of the subsidy. If paid by the employer, they serve to reduce the employee's nominal wage. For example, if it costs the employer $10 per $1,000 contribution to the plan, the employer would have to reduce the employee's compensation by $10 in order to keep the employer's total real wage cost constant. This wage reduction therefore also reduces the value of the subsidy.

At first glance it might appear that, as long as the potential subsidy to an employee exceeded the administrative costs of including the employee in the plan, the employer would choose to include the employee in the plan. This ignores the fact that savings and consumption patterns are not identical across the compensation spectrum.

Low-paid employees, for example, may be less willing to save than others because of pressing current consumption needs. Moreover, even if the savings level were appropriate, the illiquid nature of retirement plan savings and the lack of investment vehicle choice make such plans less desirable than investment plans employees could arrange on their own. The enhanced rate of return on their savings generated by the tax subsidy may not be sufficient to overcome their preference for consumption or other forms of savings. For such employees a mere dollar-for-dollar substitution of retirement savings for wages would not maintain their level of satisfaction; wages would have to be increased. For example, an employee who was paid $10,000 before the plan's establishment might demand $9,500 after establishment even though the employer contributes an additional $1,000 to the plan. All other things being equal, an employer would not want to include such an employee in the plan because the total wage cost to the employer would increase from $10,000 to $10,500.

On the other hand, a high bracket employee is quite likely to be more interested in savings and would also receive a greater tax incentive to shift income to the retirement plan. To this employee a dollar of retirement contribution is worth more than a dollar of compensation. Thus, such employees would be willing to accept some level of actual wage reduction as a cost of plan participation. For example, an employee who was paid $50,000 before the plan's establishment might only demand a salary of $44,500 if an additional $5,000 is contributed to the retirement plan. The total wage cost to the employer would therefore actually drop from $50,000 to $49,500. In effect the employer would receive a portion of the tax subsidy. Once the tradeoff between wages and retirement benefits had occurred and equilibrium was established, the tax subsidy would be distributed in some fashion among numerous potential recipients, including high-paid employees, low-paid employees, the employer, or perhaps even the consumer in the form of lower prices for the employer's products.

This rather basic analysis suggests that given the choice to select employees for retirement plan coverage, employers would generally cover only highly compensated employees. Although the discrimination rules were enacted to prevent an employer's doing this, the rules must operate in the real economic world. As the discrimination rules require more in the way of contributions for lower paid employees, the employer's costs increase. For any given employer, the costs may eventually exceed the benefits of covering the highly paid employees. At that point, the employer would decline to establish or continue a retirement plan. Thus, an aggressive congressional stance against discrimination might effectively preclude many lower paid employees from receiving retirement benefits. This result seems contrary to Congress' goal of adequate retirement income for employees.

Congress could avoid the adverse effect of aggressive discrimination rules by designing rules to ensure a high level of tax subsidy in relation to employer costs. Presumably this would result in a larger number of employers establishing or maintaining plans. Rules bringing about this result, however, would risk wasting the tax subsidy. To the extent that such rules would encourage employers to establish plans by excluding lower paid employees, the subsidy would be applied ineffectively. Inefficient application would result where the employer would have covered low bracket employees even if the subsidy were lower. For such plans, the higher level of subsidy would be a windfall for high bracket employees.

From Congress' perspective, the optimum level of tax subsidy is that which encourages the establishment of a retirement plan only if the social benefit of the plan equals or exceeds its costs. By relying on a tax deferral mechanism tied to the employer's decision to establish a retirement plan, Congress has chosen to pay a tax subsidy to high bracket employees to induce employers to establish plans also covering low bracket employees. The subsidy must be large enough for the employer to share in an amount sufficient to cover administrative costs and the additional wage cost of covering the low bracket employees yet not so large as to create wasted revenue loss. To control the level of the subsidy, Congress has relied upon a few very blunt instruments. One of these, the discrimination rules (supplemented by the relatively new top-heavy plan rules), limits the ability to shift contributions and benefits to the highly compensated employees.

Modern law

B. COVERAGE

Testing for Discrimination within a Plan

1. BASIC COVERAGE TESTS

An employer often seeks to cover fewer than all employees under a plan. The employer may wish to limit participation to a particular type of employee, such as salaried employees (as opposed to hourly employees) or clerical employees; or the employer may find it advantageous to have a plan just for employees of a given division or even for employees in a given geographic area. By limiting participation in this manner, an employer could discriminate against lower paid employees, even though such discrimination is not an explicit goal.

EER's tend to want to limit Plan Participation

however, this can discriminate against lower paid employees

Prior to the Tax Reform Act of 1986, a plan could satisfy the minimum coverage rule by meeting either a percentage or a classification test. A plan met the percentage test if (1) it benefited at least 70 percent of all employees, or (2) it benefited at least 80 percent of the employees eligible to benefit under the plan and at least 70 percent of all employees were eligible. A plan met the classification test if the IRS determined that it covered a classification of employees that did not discriminate in favor of employees who were officers, shareholders, or highly compensated (the "prohibited group"). The Congressional pension oversight committees became concerned that these tests were permitting too large a disparity in the coverage percentages of highly and nonhighly compensated employees and were therefore insufficient to ensure broad, nondiscriminatory coverage of rank-and-file employees. In addition, there was a concern that the definition of the prohibited group was imprecise and difficult to administer.

Plans should adhere to one or both of these tests so as to avoid discriminating against lower-paid/compensated employees

The Tax Reform Act of 1986 established new ① minimum coverage tests and redefined ② the prohibited group to include only "highly compensated employees," an objectively determined category discussed below. Under IRC § 410(b)(1), a plan is not qualified unless it satisfies one of two tests: the IRC § 410(b)(1)(A) and (B) *ratio percentage test* or the IRC § 410(b)(2) *average benefits test*. The average benefits test is itself composed of two prongs: the *nondiscriminatory classification test* and the *average benefit percentage test*.

Tax Reform Act of 1986 est. new minimum Coverage Tests: (① or ②)

1. *Ratio percentage test.* A plan satisfies the ratio percentage test if the percentage of nonhighly compensated employees who benefit under the plan is at least 70 percent of the percentage of highly compensated employees who benefit under the plan. To illustrate, consider an

① Ratio Percentage Test

small businesses usually just try to satisfy this test

employer with 100 employees, 20 of whom are highly compensated and 80 of whom are nonhighly compensated. A plan that benefits 18 of the highly compensated (90 percent) and 52 of the nonhighly compensated (65 percent) satisfies the test since 65 percent divided by 90 percent is 72.2 percent. If the plan benefited only 50 nonhighly compensated employees (62.5 percent), the plan would fail the test since 62.5 percent divided by 90 percent is less than 70 percent. A plan that fails the ratio percentage test must satisfy both prongs of the average benefits test to avoid disqualification.

2.   *Nondiscriminatory classification test.* The first prong of the average benefits test requires that a plan benefit "such employees as qualify under a classification set up by the employer and found by the Secretary not to be discriminatory in favor of highly compensated employees." IRC § 410(b)(2)(A)(i). The statute provides no guidance regarding what classifications are discriminatory. Fortunately, the Treasury has issued regulations providing a fairly objective approach to the nondiscriminatory classification test. Treas. Reg. § 1.410(b)–4. There are two requirements. First, the classification must be "reasonable" and "established under objective business criteria." According to the regulations, reasonable classifications "generally include specified job categories, nature of compensation (i.e., salaried or hourly), geographic location, and similar bona fide business criteria." Merely enumerating employees by name or using criteria having substantially the same effect is not acceptable. Although this is a facts and circumstances test, for most bona fide plans there will be no uncertainty.

Second, the regulations provide both an objective safe harbor and an objective unsafe harbor for determining whether a classification is nondiscriminatory. Both harbors rely on two factors: (1) the plan's ratio percentage (i.e., the same number as is used in the ratio percentage test) and (2) the percentage of all of the employees of the employer who are not highly compensated employees (the concentration percentage).

For a given concentration percentage a table in the regulations provides the respective safe and unsafe harbor for the ratio percentage. Treas. Reg. § 1.410(b)–4(c)(4)(iv). The following example, taken from the regulations, illustrates the test. Employer A has 200 employees; 120 are nonhighly compensated and 80 are highly compensated. The concentration percentage is 60 percent (120/200). For this concentration percentage the table in the regulations specifies a safe harbor ratio percentage of 50 percent and an unsafe harbor ratio percentage of 40 percent. Employer A maintains a plan that benefits 72 highly compensated employees (90 percent of the highly compensated). If the plan benefits at least 45 percent (the safe harbor percentage of 50 percent times 90 percent) of the nonhighly compensated employees, or 54 employees, the plan is considered nondiscriminatory. If the plan benefits less than 36 percent (the unsafe harbor percentage of 40 percent times 90 percent) of the nonhighly compensated employees, or 44 employees, the plan is considered discriminatory.

If a plan's coverage falls between the safe and unsafe harbors, the IRS will determine whether the classification is discriminatory based on all relevant facts and circumstances. Among the factors that will be considered are (1) the business reason for the classification, (2) the percentage of employees benefiting under the plan, (3) whether the number of employees benefiting in each salary range is representative of the total number of employees in each range, (4) how close the classification comes to satisfying the safe harbor percentage, and (5) the extent to which the plan's average benefit percentage exceeds 70 percent. Treas. Reg. § 1.410(b)–4(c)(3)(ii).

3. *Average benefit percentage test.* In order to meet the minimum coverage requirements, a plan that fails the ratio percentage test must satisfy not only the nondiscriminatory classification test, but also the average benefit percentage test. IRC § 410(b)(2)(A)(ii). A plan satisfies this test if the average benefit percentage for the nonhighly compensated employees is at least 70 percent of the average benefit percentage for the highly compensated employees. The term "average benefit percentage" means, with respect to any group of employees, the average of the benefit percentages calculated separately with respect to each employee in the group (*whether or not a participant in any plan*). IRC § 410(b)(2)(B). The term "benefit percentage" means the employer-provided contribution or benefit of an employee under all plans in the so-called "testing group" of the employer, expressed as a percentage of such employee's compensation. The "testing group" of plans is defined in Treas. Reg. § 1.410(b)–7(e) and generally includes all of the employer's qualified plans, with some limited exceptions (e.g., collectively bargained plans are not part of the testing group for a non-collectively bargained plan).

Applying the average benefit percentage test can be quite complex, particularly if the employer has both defined contribution and defined benefit plans. The regulations provide detailed guidance on how to calculate employee benefit percentages. Treas. Reg. § 1.410(b)–5(d). These rules are generally the same as the rules for calculating allocation and accrual rates for IRC § 401(a)(4) benefit and contribution discrimination purposes.

For typical plans, the average benefit percentage test will prove to be a more difficult hurdle than the nondiscriminatory classification test. For example, consider Employer A in the safe harbor example above. Assume Employer A's plan is a defined contribution plan and that each participant's contribution is ten percent of compensation. By covering 54 nonhighly compensated employees, the plan meets the nondiscriminatory classification safe harbor. However, the average benefit percentage of the nonhighly compensated employees is only 4.5 percent (10 percent times 54/120), since all employees in the group have to be averaged in, including those who do not participate. The average benefit percentage of the highly compensated employees is 9 percent (10 percent times 72/80). Since 4.5 percent is less than 70 percent of 9 percent, the plan fails the average benefits percentage test and is not qualified.

Employer A has a number of options. It could cut back on the coverage of highly compensated employees or increase the coverage of nonhighly compensated employees, or both, and thereby meet the ratio percentage test. Another option would be to establish a second, less generous plan for the remaining 55 percent of nonhighly compensated employees that is sufficient to enable the first plan to meet the average benefits percentage test. For example, if the second plan were a defined contribution plan allocating 3.28 percent of compensation to each participant's account, the average benefit percentage of the nonhighly compensated employees would be 6.3 percent (i.e., 45 percent of 10 percent plus 55 percent of 3.28 percent). Since 6.3 percent is 70 percent of 9 percent, the first plan meets the average benefits percentage test. Since the second plan benefits only nonhighly compensated employees, it satisfies the ratio percentage test.

4. *Minimum participation requirement for defined benefit plans.* In addition to the coverage tests imposed by IRC § 410(b), defined benefit plans must also meet the minimum participation requirement of IRC § 401(a)(26). This requires each qualified defined benefit plan to benefit at least the lesser of (1) 50 employees or (2) the greater of (a) 40 percent of all employees or (b) two employees (one employee if there is only one employee). Unlike the minimum coverage rule, which need be satisfied on only one day in each quarter of a plan year (IRC § 401(a)(6)), the minimum participation rule must be met on each day of the plan year. Although the minimum participation requirement was added by the Tax Reform Act of 1986 to deal mainly with employers who had established multiple plans, each plan covering a small number of employees, the rule operates to create a minimum number of employees who must be covered even by an employer with just a single defined benefit plan.

Applied literally, IRC § 401(a)(26) would preclude a small employer from establishing a defined benefit plan that covered only nonhighly compensated employees. For example, an employer with 2 highly compensated employees and 8 nonhighly compensated employees would seem to be precluded from establishing a defined benefit plan that covered only 3 nonhighly compensated employees. However, the regulations, consistent with a statement in the legislative history, deem a plan to satisfy IRC § 401(a)(26) if the plan does not currently benefit any employee or former employee who is a highly compensated employee. Treas. Reg. § 1.401(a)(26)–1(b)(1). This special rule does not apply if the plan must be aggregated with another plan of the employer in order for the other plan to satisfy IRC §§ 401(a)(4) or 410(b).

5. *Multiple plans.* An employer may wish to cover one group of employees with one type of plan and another group of employees with a different plan. For example, there may be a profit-sharing plan for the salaried employees and a pension plan for the hourly employees. One of the plans, considered separately, might be unable to meet the minimum coverage requirements of IRC § 410(b), even though the plans taken together cover a group of employees that would satisfy the requirements.

Under IRC § 410(b)(6)(B), an employer may designate two or more plans as a single plan for purposes of satisfying the coverage requirements. However, those designated plans, considered as a single plan, must satisfy the requirements of IRC § 401(a)(4); i.e., they must provide contributions or benefits that do not discriminate in favor of highly compensated employees. Thus, an employer may not establish a lavish plan for the highly compensated and a modest plan for the remaining workers. The rather complex determination of whether multiple plans discriminate in favor of highly compensated employees is considered in connection with the discussion of IRC § 401(a)(4) in Section C below.

Although plans may be aggregated for purposes of the minimum coverage rule, they may not be aggregated for purposes of the minimum participation requirement of IRC § 401(a)(26). Congress was worried about the potential for discrimination when an employer maintained multiple plans, each of which covered a small number of employees: "Although such arrangements were vulnerable to challenge as discriminatory under prior law, Congress was concerned that because of the large number of these arrangements, the inherent complexity of the comparability analysis, and the difficulties in discovering all differences in funding levels and benefit options, the IRS lacked sufficient resources to monitor compliance with the nondiscrimination standards by small aggregated plans." Staff of the Joint Comm. on Taxation, 100th Cong., 1st Sess., General Explanation of the Tax Reform Act of 1986, at 683 (Joint Comm.Print 1987).

6. *Employees who benefit under a plan.* Under both the minimum coverage and the minimum participation requirement, an employee generally is treated as benefiting for a plan year only if, in the case of a defined contribution plan, the employee receives an allocation of contributions or forfeitures or, in the case of a defined benefit plan, the employee accrues a benefit. The regulations provide a number of exceptions to this allocation or accrual requirement. For example, an employee is treated as benefiting under a plan if the employee fails to accrue a benefit solely because of a uniformly applicable benefit limit or solely because of the IRC § 415 limits on benefits and annual additions. Thus, if a plan takes into account only the first 30 years of service for accrual purposes, a participant who has completed more than 30 years of service is still treated as benefiting under the plan. See Treas. Reg. § 1.410(b)–3(a)(2).

In the case of a 401(k) plan or a plan providing for employee contributions or employer matching contributions, employees are treated as benefiting under the plan if they are eligible to contribute, even if they elect not to participate. IRC §§ 410(b)(6)(E), 401(a)(26)(C). These elective arrangements have their own special nondiscrimination tests, discussed in Section E below, which preclude a plan from excessively favoring the highly compensated.

7. *Consequences of minimum coverage violations.* The minimum coverage rules of IRC § 410(b) and the minimum participation rule of IRC § 401(a)(26) are requirements of a qualified plan, but not requirements of Title I of ERISA. Thus, an employee may not bring an ERISA claim for benefits under a plan based on allegations that the plan violated the minimum coverage or participation rules. Also, unlike many other plan qualification requirements, the minimum coverage rules do not impose a requirement to add specific provisions to the language of the trust or plan. They are demographic requirements and may cause a plan that was initially qualified to become disqualified due to changes in the work force.

[handwritten margin note: Beneficiary/Participant can NOT bring suit]

Disqualification normally has unpleasant effects on participants in a plan. Under IRC § 402(b)(1) a participant is taxable on employer contributions to the extent the participant is vested in the benefits generated by such contributions. As discussed in Section E of Chapter 8, supra, Congress has altered the normal treatment of disqualification for violations of the minimum coverage rules, relieving the nonhighly compensated employees of the burden of current taxation and imposing significant additional tax burdens on the highly compensated employees. IRC § 402(b)(4).

8. *Governmental and church plans.* The minimum coverage rules of IRC § 410(b) and the minimum participation requirement of IRC § 401(a)(26) do not apply to governmental or to non-electing church plans. IRC §§ 401(a)(26)(G), 401(c) and 410(d). Why not?

QUESTIONS

1. The minimum coverage requirement adopts a relative percentage test, comparing the percentage of highly compensated employees covered with the percentage of nonhighly compensated employees covered. Why not frame the requirement in absolute terms? For example, why not require a plan to cover a certain number of nonhighly compensated employees for each covered highly compensated employee? If a tax subsidy is appropriate for a plan that benefits 10 highly compensated and 30 nonhighly compensated employees when that is the entire work force, why does it become inappropriate if there are an additional 30 nonhighly compensated employees in the work force who are not covered by the plan?

2. Why not require 100 percent coverage in all plans?

3. A plan maintained by an employer that has no employees other than highly compensated employees is treated as meeting the minimum coverage requirements of IRC § 410(b). IRC § 410(b)(6)(F). Is this consistent with the policies supporting the favorable tax treatment of qualified plans?

4. Employer B has 15 employees, 8 of whom are nonhighly compensated. Under IRC § 401(a)(26), Employer B is not permitted to establish a defined benefit plan that covers 3 nonhighly compensated employees and 2 highly compensated employees, even though such a plan would meet the ratio percentage test of IRC § 410(b)(1). On the other hand, Employer C, with 150 employees, 80 of whom are nonhighly compensated, is permitted to establish a defined benefit plan that covers 30 nonhighly compensated employees and 20 highly compensated employees. Why are small employers treated differently than large employers? Note that Employer B could satisfy IRC § 401(a)(26) by covering an additional highly compensated employee and still meet the ratio percentage test. Is this sound tax policy? Should IRC § 401(a)(26) apply only if the employer has more than one plan?

2. | HIGHLY COMPENSATED EMPLOYEES |

The statute's focus on strict numerical tests for discrimination requires an objective classification of each employee as either highly compensated or nonhighly compensated. The term "highly compensated employee" as defined in IRC § 414(q) is only applicable to those provisions that incorporate it by reference. These include not only the discrimination rules for qualified plans, but also the discrimination rules for many other employee benefit arrangements, such as health and group-term life insurance. IRC § 414(q) is not determinative with respect to the provisions of Title I of ERISA providing exceptions for top-hat plans (i.e., ERISA §§ 201(2), 301(a)(3), and 401(a)(1)), which also use the term "highly compensated."

1.   *Definition of highly compensated.* A highly compensated employee is an employee who:

(1) was a 5-percent owner of the employer at any time during the year or the preceding year; or

(2) for the preceding year, had compensation from the employer in excess of the IRC § 414(q)(1)(B) amount ($115,000 in 2014, $120,000 in 2015), and, if the employer elects for that year, was also in the "top-paid group," defined as the highest paid 20 percent of all employees.

[handwritten: Definition of "Highly compensated"]

2.   *Compensation.* The definition of the term compensation is essential to numerous provisions in the pension area. Because definitions of the term vary, care must be taken in determining which definition is applicable to a given provision. For purposes of determining whether an employee is highly compensated, "compensation" means compensation within the meaning of IRC § 415(c)(3). IRC § 414(q)(4). We shall examine the IRC § 415(c)(3) compensation definition in more detail in Chapter 10, but in general it includes only those items of compensation that are includible in the employee's gross income. However, under IRC § 415(c)(3)(D), elective deferrals under 401(k) plans, 403(b) annuities, and SIMPLE plans, as well as salary reduction contributions to cafeteria plans (IRC § 125), qualified transportation fringe benefits (IRC § 132(f)(4))and 457 plans are treated as compensation, even though they are not included in the employee's gross income. For example, an employee whose salary is $105,000, but who elects to have $15,000 contributed to her 401(k) plan account, has compensation of $105,000, while an employee whose salary is $90,000, but whose employer makes a nonelective $15,000 contribution to a profit-sharing plan on his behalf, has compensation of $90,000.

QUESTIONS

1.   Is the definition of highly compensated employee too broad? Assume a law firm has 50 partners and 80 associates with compensation in excess of the IRC § 414(q)(1)(B) limit and 20 associates and 150 secretaries and other support staff with compensation below the limit. Could the law firm establish a plan that excluded all associates? Assuming the associates were excluded, what percentage of the support staff could be excluded and still permit the plan to meet the ratio percentage test of IRC § 410(b)(1)?

[handwritten right margin: –Highly compensated (130) –Not highly compensated (170) –cannot eliminate the 100 partners associates –but can have min. of 76 support staff to have legit plan]

2.   Is the definition of highly compensated employee too narrow? Employer X has two officers who earn $150,000. Both officers are covered by a nonqualified deferred compensation plan. X has twenty other employees, 5 of whom have compensation of $90,000 and 15 of whom have compensation between $25,000 and $40,000. May X establish a qualified profit-sharing plan just for the 5 employees earning $90,000?

3.   Does the top-paid group election under IRC § 414(q)(1)(B)(ii) permit too narrow a definition of highly compensated employee? Assume an employer has 10 employees: 2 support staff earning $35,000, 6 technical staff earning $120,000, and 2 owners earning $175,000. Can the employer establish a qualified plan that covers everyone but the support staff?

3.   EXCLUDABLE EMPLOYEES

The coverage rules are a game of numbers, made even more complicated by rules permitting certain employees to be excluded from the various coverage computations.

1.   *Minimum age and service.* If a plan has a minimum age or service requirement, employees not meeting the requirement can be excluded under the minimum participation test and all of the minimum coverage tests except the average benefit percentage test. IRC §§ 401(a)(26)(B)(i), 410(b)(2)(D)(i), 410(b)(4)(A). However, if the employer elects, the average benefits percentage test can be applied by excluding those employees who do not meet the lowest age and service requirements of all qualified plans maintained by the employer. Thus, if the employer has only one plan, or all plans have the same age and service requirement, employees not meeting the requirement can be excluded for purposes of the average benefit percentage test.

The exclusion of employees not meeting the minimum service requirement is extremely significant, since it permits plans to exclude part-time employees without risk of violating the minimum coverage rule. A plan is permitted to exclude employees who have not completed one year of service. IRC § 410(a)(1)(A); ERISA § 202(a)(1)(A). A year of service is defined as a 12-month period during which the employee has at least 1,000 hours of service. IRC § 410(a)(3)(A); ERISA § 202(a)(3)(A). Thus, an employee who worked 18 hours a week on a permanent basis would never reach 1,000 hours of service in any year and could therefore be excluded from participating in the plan and from all coverage tests. A plan may compute service on an elapsed time basis, rather than by counting hours of service. See Treas. Reg. § 1.410(a)–7. Measuring service is discussed in Chapter 4, Section B.2.9, supra.

Note that an employee who has previously met the minimum age and service requirements of a plan may nevertheless fail to accrue a benefit during a given plan year because he or she either did not have 1000 hours of service during the year or was not employed on the last day of the year. Such employees must be taken into account in testing the plan under IRC § 410(b), but are treated as not benefiting under the plan. The regulations provide a limited exception for employees who terminate employment during the plan year with not more than 500 hours of service. Treas. Reg. § 1.410(b)–6(f). This important exception permits a plan to impose a limited minimum service requirement without risking possible disqualification on account of employee turnover.

2.   *Collective bargaining agreements.* Employees who are included in a unit of employees covered by a collective bargaining agreement are also excluded from the minimum participation and coverage tests, provided that there is evidence that retirement benefits were the subject of good faith bargaining. IRC §§ 401(a)(26)(B)(i), 410(b)(3)(A). For example, assume an employer wishes to establish a profit-sharing plan for its 5 noncollectively bargained employees, 4 of whom are highly compensated. It has 10 collectively bargained employees, all of whom are nonhighly compensated. As long as the employer has previously bargained about retirement benefits, even if no plan or a less advantageous plan were established for the collectively bargained

employees, the employer can exclude the collectively bargained employees from all of the coverage tests. Without the collective bargaining agreement exclusion, the profit-sharing plan would fail both the ratio percentage test of IRC § 410(b)(1) and the minimum participation test of IRC § 401(a)(26).

A plan that benefits only collectively bargained employees automatically meets the minimum coverage test of IRC § 410(b). See Treas. Reg. § 1.410(b)–2(b)(7). The statute reaches this result in a somewhat cryptic fashion through the application of IRC § 413(b)(1). This rule allows collectively bargained plans to be negotiated without worrying about minimum coverage issues.

Collectively bargained plans do not automatically satisfy the minimum participation rule. However, in testing a collectively bargained plan, employees who are not covered by the collective bargaining agreement can be excluded. IRC § 401(a)(26)(C). For example, assume that an employer has 30 collectively bargained employees who benefit under a defined benefit plan and 70 non-collectively bargained employees who are not covered by a plan. The employer can disregard the non-collectively bargained employees in applying IRC § 401(a)(26) to the collectively bargained plan. Excluding those employees, the plan covers 100 percent of the remaining employees and therefore satisfies IRC § 401(a)(26). Without this special rule, the plan would cover only 30 percent of the employees and would be disqualified.

The statute also contains protective language to discourage misuse of the collective bargaining exceptions through the use of artificial collective bargaining. See IRC § 7701(a)(46). Moreover, an employee is not considered covered by a collective bargaining agreement if more than 2 percent of the employees who are covered pursuant to such an agreement are "professionals." Treas. Reg. § 1.410(b)–6(d)(2)(iii)(B); IRC § 413(b)(9).

[handwritten marginal note: – Exception to collective bargaining Agreements]

The collective bargaining exception was enacted in 1974 with ERISA. The apparent rationale was to mitigate the "hardship" that might arise if employees represented by a union preferred current compensation or other nonpension benefits to coverage under a pension plan. If most of the low-paid personnel were members of the collective bargaining unit, the coverage rules might make it impossible to establish a qualified plan for the remaining employees, a greater number of whom might be members of the prohibited group. The courts had encountered this problem prior to ERISA but had refused to create a judicial exception for collectively bargained plans. See, e.g., Loevsky v. Commissioner, 55 T.C. 1144, 1151 (1971).

The collective bargaining agreement exclusion is directly contrary to the congressional goal of increasing pension plan participation for lower income employees. As already noted, such employees, particularly younger employees, have less tax incentive to save for retirement and often may prefer current consumption over savings. Consequently, an employer can entice such employees to accept a retirement plan only at the cost of additional compensation. The collective bargaining exception allows the employer to avoid this cost by placing a retirement plan on the bargaining table and then agreeing to alternative nonpension benefits. Even if such benefits cost the employer more than the retirement plan, the employer will still have an incentive to provide them so long as this additional cost is less than the benefits realized from providing a retirement plan to the remaining employees outside the bargaining unit. As one commentator has put it, "no one at the bargaining table [represents] the collective, societal interest for which the favorable tax treatment is granted." Nancy Altman, Rethinking Retirement Income Policies: Nondiscrimination, Integration, and the Quest for Worker Security, 42 Tax L.Rev. 435, 473 (1987). This concern may be more theoretical than real: coverage data have consistently shown a significantly higher rate of retirement plan coverage among union members than non-union employees. "Overall, union workers' rate of participation in retirement plans—at 80 percent—was greater than that of nonunion workers, which was 48 percent." U.S. Bureau of Labor Statistics, Perspectives on Retirement Benefits, Issue 3, March 2009, www.bls.gov/opub/perspectives/issue3.pdf. The collective bargaining exclusion is also consistent with the principles of federal labor law, under which the union represents the interests of the members of the collective bargaining unit, and the employer generally may not unilaterally provide benefits that have not been negotiated with the union.

3. *Miscellaneous excludable employees.* Employees who are nonresident aliens and who receive no earned U.S. source income from the employer are not considered. IRC 410(b)(3)(C); IRC § 401(a)(26)(B)(i). A plan established under a collective bargaining agreement between air pilots and their employers is tested by excluding all employees not covered by the agreement. IRC § 410(b)(3)(B); IRC § 401(a)(26)(B)(i).

QUESTIONS

1.   What is the justification for allowing permanent part-time employees to be excluded from the coverage tests? Does this rule encourage employers to hire part-time employees rather than fulltime employees as a means of cutting benefit costs?

2.   Hospital has 250 employees, 60 of whom are highly compensated. There are 50 physicians on the staff, all of whom are highly compensated. The physicians are members of a union and are covered by a collective bargaining agreement with Hospital. The agreement establishes a money purchase pension plan for the physicians. None of the other employees participate in a qualified plan.

(a)   Assuming that none of the other employees is covered by a collective bargaining agreement, is the pension plan qualified?

(b)   Assuming that all of the nonhighly compensated employees are covered by a collective bargaining agreement, is the pension plan qualified?

(c)   Would the result in (a) change if instead of a hospital, the employer was an airline, and instead of physicians, the plan covered airline pilots? See IRC § 410(b)(3)(B).

3.   Employer A provides a defined contribution plan to all of its employees. The plan provides that an employee will not receive an allocation of contributions for a plan year unless the employee is employed by A on the last day of the plan year. At the beginning of the plan year, A had 9 employees, 3 of whom were highly compensated. During the year, 2 of the

nonhighly compensated employees terminated employment and were not replaced. They had each worked 750 hours during the plan year. Does the plan satisfy IRC § 410(b)?

4.   X Corp. operates in two locations: its headquarters in San Diego (20 employees) and its manufacturing operation in Mexico (100 employees). The headquarters personnel are covered by a pension plan. The three top managers of its operation in Mexico, all of whom are Mexican nationals, are also covered by the same pension plan, but none of the other employees in Mexico is covered. Does X need to consider the Mexican employees in determining whether the plan is qualified? Is the U.S. taxpayer subsidizing the pensions for the high paid managers?

4. CONTROLLED GROUPS AND AFFILIATED SERVICE GROUPS

The coverage rules could easily be circumvented by splitting employees among a number of related employers. Thus, a corporation could set up two subsidiaries. One would employ the bulk of the nonhighly compensated workers and have no plan, the other would employ mainly the highly compensated employees and have a generous plan. The plan might easily meet the coverage tests if only the subsidiary's own employees were considered. For example, the subsidiary might cover all of its employees, thereby meeting the ratio percentage test.

To prevent this and similar abuses, there are a variety of rules that treat all employees of certain related employers as employed by a single employer. These rules are extremely important since they apply not only to the coverage tests but to numerous other Internal Revenue Code provisions, including IRC §§ 401, 408(k) (simplified employee pensions), 411 (vesting requirements), 415 (maximum contributions and benefits), 416 (top-heavy plan rules), and a variety of employee welfare benefit provisions. IRC § 414(b), (c), (m), (n), (o) and (t). Careful attention to these rules is essential to the proper design of almost every type of employee benefit plan.

1.   *Controlled groups of corporations and trades or businesses under common control.* All employees of the members of a "controlled group of corporations" or of trades or businesses (whether or not incorporated) that are under "common control" are treated as employed by a single employer. IRC § 414(b), (c). Treas.Reg. §§ 1.414(c) and 1.1563–1 provide a detailed interpretation of the rules. Under the regulations, employers are under common control if they are members of a parent-subsidiary group, a brother-sister group, or a combined group.

A parent-subsidiary group is one or more chains of organizations connected with a common parent if each organization is at least 80 percent owned by another organization in the chain. For example, if Corporation A owns 90 percent of the stock of corporations B and C, and Corporation C owns 80 percent of the stock of Corporation D, all four corporations are members of a parent-subsidiary group.

A brother-sister group is composed of two or more organizations that are (1) at least 80 percent owned by the same 5 or fewer persons, *and* (2) more than 50 percent owned by the same 5 or fewer persons if the stock ownership of each person is taken into account only to the extent the ownership is identical with respect to each organization. "Person" for this purpose includes only individuals, estates, and trusts. Complex rules attribute interests owned by corporations, partnerships, trusts, or estates to the shareholders, partners, and beneficiaries, respectively. If a common parent of a parent-subsidiary group is also a member of a brother-sister group, all of the organizations in both groups form a combined group.

As an illustration, if unrelated individuals A, B, and C each own 1/3 of the stock of corporation X and A and B each own 10 percent and C owns 80 percent of the stock of corporation Y, then X and Y form a brother-sister group and the employees of both corporations are treated as employed by a single employer. The overlapping ownership is 10 percent, 10 percent, and 1/3 respectively, which totals to more than 50 percent. Note that if A and B each owned only 5 percent of the Y stock and C owned 90 percent, then X and Y would not form a brother-sister group. The 50 percent requirement would not be met.

These same rules, often referred to as the "controlled group" or "common control" regulations, also apply in connection with an employer's liability under Title IV of ERISA for plan terminations or withdrawals from multiemployer plans. ERISA § 4001(b)(1). Thus, all members of a group of trades or businesses under common control are jointly and severally liable for any member's plan termination or withdrawal liability. This issue is discussed in Chapter 6, supra.

2. *Affiliated service groups.* Consider the following arrangement. A and B are equal partners in a law firm employing two secretaries and a paralegal. A forms a separate professional corporation, with A as the sole shareholder and employee. The corporation replaces A as a partner in the law partnership. Can A's corporation set up a qualified plan for A and ignore the employees of the partnership? In 1979 the Tax Court held that the common control regulations would not treat A's corporation and the law partnership as being under common control. Garland v. Commissioner, 73 T.C. 5 (1979). A's corporation and the partnership simply did not meet the definition of parent-subsidiary group or brother-sister group since the corporation lacked a greater than 50 percent interest in the partnership.

Rather than amending the definition of common control, in 1980 Congress responded by enacting a special rule which treats all employees of an "affiliated service group" as employed by one employer. IRC § 414(m). The rule clearly covers the partnership of professional corporations and other arrangements. For example, consider the following facts, taken from Prop. Treas. Reg. § 1.414(m)–2(c)(8), Example (4):

> Individual M owns one-third of an employee benefit consulting firm. M also owns one-third of an insurance agency. A significant portion of the business of the consulting firm consists of assisting the insurance agency in developing employee benefit packages for sale to third persons and providing services to the insurance company in connection with employee benefit programs sold to other clients of the insurance agency. Additionally, the consulting firm frequently provides services to

clients who have purchased insurance arrangements from the insurance company for the employee benefit plans they maintain. The insurance company frequently refers clients to the consulting firm to assist them in the design of their employee benefit plans. The percentage of the total gross receipts of the consulting firm that represent gross receipts from the performance of these services for the insurance agency is 20 percent.

Under these facts the insurance agency and the consulting firm would be an affiliated service group under IRC § 414(m)(2)(B). A significant portion of the business of the consulting firm is the performance of services for the agency of a type historically performed by employees in the insurance service field and more than 10 percent of the interests in the consulting firm is held by owners of the insurance agency.

Although the affiliated service group rules have been in effect for more than 30 years, it is often difficult to determine whether employers are affiliated, because the determination is inherently factual. Treasury regulations were proposed in the 1980s, but have never been finalized.

Tax-exempt employers do not have owners, but regulations have extended the trades or businesses under common control concept to them. See Treas. Reg. § 1.414(c)–5.

3. *Broad regulatory authority.* Concerned that it may have neglected to close some loophole that ever clever practitioners might exploit, Congress in IRC § 414(o) granted the Treasury authority to prescribe such regulations as may be necessary to prevent the use of separate organizations, employee leasing, or "other arrangements" to avoid the coverage and other specified statutory requirements. Proposed Regulations deal with a number of potentially abusive arrangements. Prop.Treas. Reg. § 1.414(o)–1.

QUESTIONS

1. X and Y, both publicly held corporations, have negotiated two joint investments, which they will structure in the form of two corporations, P and Q. The stock of P and Q will be held equally by X and Y. Are P and Q part of a controlled group of corporations which includes X and Y?

2. Mother owns 55 percent of the stock of X Corporation, which manufactures furniture. Her son owns 25 percent of the stock and an unrelated third party owns the remaining 20 percent. Mother has a separate consulting business which she operates as a sole proprietorship. Mother wishes to establish a retirement plan based on her consulting income. Can she do so without taking into account the pension coverage of the X Corporation employees? See Treas.Reg. § 1.414(c)–2(c), –4(b)(6)(ii).

3. Husband and Wife each operate a separate business. Do the businesses form a brother-sister group? See Treas.Reg. § 1.414(c)–4(b)(5). Does the answer change if Husband and Wife are the parents of a minor child? See Treas.Reg. § 1.414(c)–4(b)(6). What if the two businesses constitute community property of the spouses? See Treas.Reg. § 1.414(c)–4(b)(5)(ii)(A).

[Handwritten margin note: No, a minor child's stock is attributed to a parent OR if not a minor child and parent has more than 50% stock then it's also attributable to a parent]

4.   Unrelated individuals A, B, and C each own a one-third interest in partnership X, and A and B each own a one-half interest in partnership Y. Do X and Y form a brother-sister group of businesses under common control? Under United States v. Vogel Fertilizer, 455 U.S. 16 (1982), in determining whether two organizations are members of a brother-sister group, a person can be one of the five or fewer persons whose ownership is considered only if the person owns an interest in *both* organizations.

5. INDEPENDENT CONTRACTORS AND LEASED EMPLOYEES

Businesses can avoid coverage rules by hiring Independent Contractors + not Employees

One way for a business to avoid the coverage rules is to hire independent contractors instead of employees. For example, a business might engage a law firm to do its legal work, rather than hire in-house counsel, or it might contract with a landscape maintenance company instead of having its employees do landscape work. By using independent contractors a business can also avoid employment taxes and withholding responsibilities. Workers may sometimes also prefer independent contractor status, since independent contractors have a greater ability to deduct work-related expenses. "In February, 2005, there were about 10.3 million independent contractors, accounting for 7.4 percent of the employed." They were much less likely to be covered by health insurance, and less likely to be eligible for a pension plan, than workers in traditional arrangements. U.S. Bureau of Labor Statistics, Contingent and Alternative Employment Arrangements, February 2005, www.bls.gov/news.release/pdf/conemp.pdf.

The Supreme Court has applied what it calls the common-law test to determine who qualifies as an "employee" under ERISA. Nationwide Mutual Ins. Co. v. Darden, 503 U.S. 318, 324 (1992). See Chapter 3, supra. According to *Darden*, the common-law test is whether the "hiring party [has the] right to control the manner and means by which the product is accomplished." The IRC and ERISA definitions of the term "employee" appear to be identical. *Darden* cited Rev. Rul. 87–41, 1987–1 C.B. 296 for guidance as to the factors relevant to the test. Rev. Rul. 87–41 sets forth 20 factors as guides in determining whether an individual qualifies as a common-law employee in various tax law contexts. Long-standing Treasury Regulations in the employment tax context also adopt a "right to control and direct [the] details and means" test. Treas.Reg. § 31.3121(d)–1(c)(2).

Merely labeling someone as an independent contractor does not decide the question. For example, in Kenney v. Commissioner, T.C. Memo. 1995–431, a corporation's pension plan covered only the owner. Several other individuals worked for the corporation, but were told when they were hired that they would be treated as independent contractors. The Tax Court applied the common-law test and reclassified the individuals as employees. Since the individuals in question were not highly compensated, the plan failed to meet the minimum coverage test and was disqualified.

Likewise, an individual who is labeled an "employee," but who is actually an independent contractor, cannot participate in a qualified plan and is not counted in any of the discrimination tests. A plan that covered such a worker would violate the exclusive benefit rule of IRC § 401(a)(2) and be disqualified. See Professional & Executive Leasing, Inc. v.

Commissioner, 89 T.C. 225 (1987), aff'd 862 F.2d 751 (9th Cir.1988). Thus, misclassification in either direction has the potential to disqualify a plan.

In the early 1980's Congress became concerned about employee leasing arrangements being used as a device to evade the coverage rules. Suppose a firm needs clerks. Rather than hiring clerks directly, it contracts with an unrelated staffing firm to provide them. The staffing firm employs the clerks, paying their wages and fringe benefits.

Congress sought to eliminate this maneuver by enacting the employee leasing rules of IRC § 414(n). Under IRC § 414(n), a "leased employee" who performs services for any person (the "recipient") pursuant to an agreement between the recipient and any other person (the "leasing organization") is treated for certain purposes, including discrimination testing, as an employee of the recipient. A "leased employee" is defined as any person who provides services to the recipient but who is not an employee of the recipient, if such services (1) have been performed on a substantially fulltime basis for a period of at least one year, and (2) are performed "under primary direction or control by the recipient." There is a limited safe harbor exception for leased employees who are covered by a sufficiently generous money purchase pension plan of the leasing organization, provided that leased employees do not constitute more than 20 percent of the recipient's nonhighly compensated work force. IRC § 414(n)(5).

The following excerpt from the House Ways and Means Committee Report, H.Rep. No. 104–586, 104th Cong. 2d Sess. 125 (1996), describes the primary direction or control test:

> Whether services are performed by an individual under primary direction or control by the service recipient depends on the facts and circumstances. In general, primary direction and control means that the service recipient exercises the majority of direction and control over the individual. Factors that are relevant in determining whether primary direction or control exists include whether the individual is required to comply with instructions of the service recipient about when, where, and how he or she is to perform the services, whether the services must be performed by a particular person, whether the individual is subject to the supervision of the service recipient, and whether the individual must perform services in the order or sequence set by the service recipient. Factors that generally are not relevant in determining whether such direction or control exists include whether the service recipient has the right to hire or fire the individual and whether the individual works for others.

The definition of leased employee has led to a great deal of confusion. The statute says that to be a leased employee a person cannot be an employee of the recipient. But as noted above, the right to direct and control the means and details of the work is the key element of the common-law definition of employee. How does the new "primary direction or control" test, which makes an individual a leased employee, differ from the common-law employee test? In the typical arrangements, such as the hiring of temporary secretaries or clerks, both tests would seem to be met.

Since a plan is not permitted to cover individuals who are not employees of the plan sponsor, a staffing firm that provides a qualified plan for its workers risks potential disqualification of the plan. If the workers are actually the common-law employees of the firm's clients and not the firm, the plan violates the exclusive benefit rule. In Rev. Proc. 2002–21, 2002–1 C.B. 911, the IRS offered staffing firms a way to avoid disqualification: Get their clients to join as adopting employers of the plan and thereby turn the plan into a multiple employer plan. See IRC § 413(c)(2).

ERISA issues. In a number of cases employees who were nominally independent contractors or leased employees but who claimed status as common-law employees have sought to be covered under the employer's employee benefit plans. Although employees have sometimes succeeded in obtaining benefits, perhaps most notably in the highly publicized *Microsoft* case, see Vizcaino v. Microsoft Corp., 120 F.3d 1006 (9th Cir.1997), discussed in Chapter 3, supra, most courts have rejected the argument that such "misclassified" employees are automatically entitled to coverage. Wolf v. Coca-Cola Co., 200 F.3d 1337 (11th Cir.2000); Bronk v. Mountain States Tel. & Tel., Inc., 140 F.3d 1335 (10th Cir.1998); Abraham v. Exxon Corp., 85 F.3d 1126 (5th Cir.1996). The issue is whether, once recognized as employees, they also meet the eligibility criteria of the plan. Nothing in ERISA requires an employer to cover all of its employees. In the wake of cases such as *Vizcaino*, many plans now include language providing that an individual who is not classified as an employee by the employer will not be eligible for plan participation, even if he or she is determined to be an employee by a court or administrative agency.

Suppose an employer lays off its landscaping crew and outsources the work to a landscaping company in large part because of employee benefit costs. Is this a violation of ERISA § 510? See Chapter 3, supra. Could the employer avoid ERISA § 510 by retaining its landscaping crew but simply amending its employee benefit plans to exclude its landscaping crew?

6. SEPARATE LINES OF BUSINESS

The controlled group, common control, affiliated service group, and employee leasing rules treat all employees (including leased employees) of related employers as if they were employed by a single employer. However, if this single employer is treated as operating separate lines of business, the employer may apply the minimum coverage requirement of IRC § 410(b) and the minimum participation requirement of IRC § 401(a)(26) separately with respect to the employees in each separate line of business. IRC §§ 401(a)(26)(G), 410(b)(5).

For example, assume A is the sole shareholder of two corporations, X Corp. and Y Corp. X operates a baseball team and Y operates a restaurant. X employs 10 highly compensated and 50 nonhighly compensated employees and has a pension plan covering all of its employees. Y has one highly compensated and 50 nonhighly compensated employees and has no qualified plan. Since X and Y are part of a brother-sister group of controlled corporations, the minimum coverage rules would normally be applied to the X and Y employees as if they were employed by a single employer. The X Corp. pension plan would then fail the ratio percentage test, since 50 percent of the nonhighly compensated employees are covered compared with 91 percent of the highly compensated. But if X Corp. and Y Corp. could be treated as separate lines of business, the Y employees could be ignored, and the X Corp. plan would easily satisfy the ratio percentage test of IRC § 410(b) since the plan benefits 100 percent of the nonhighly compensated employees.

Without a separate line of business exception, diversified companies might be placed at a competitive disadvantage. If qualified plans with a certain level of benefits were the industry norm in one line of business, but were nonexistent or offered lower benefits in the other line, the company could not meet the industry norm for both lines. The coverage rules would force it to provide a qualified plan to both lines or neither line. Either way its costs or its employee benefits would differ from its competitors in one of the lines, making its product more expensive or the recruitment of employees more difficult.

1.　*The employer-wide nondiscriminatory classification test.* An employer who wishes to apply the minimum coverage requirement of IRC § 410(b) separately with respect to the employees of each separate line of business must meet an initial statutory hurdle. Each plan of the employer must benefit "such employees as qualify under a classification set up by the employer and found by the Secretary not to be discriminatory in favor of highly compensated employees." IRC § 410(b)(5)(B). Because this employer-wide nondiscriminatory classification test is a prerequisite to separate line of business testing, it is sometimes referred to as the "Gateway."

The Gateway is applied in the same basic manner as the similarly-worded nondiscriminatory classification test under the IRC § 410(b) regulations, discussed above in Section B.1. Treas. Reg. § 1.414(r)–8(b)(2). Thus, in the X Corp. and Y Corp. example discussed above we would apply the Gateway by using the test set forth in Treas. Reg. § 1.410(b)–4. First, we compute the "nonhighly compensated employee concentration percentage", which is equal to the percentage of all employees of the employer who are nonhighly compensated, 100/111 (90 percent) in our example. Next, we compute the "ratio percentage", which is the percentage of nonhighly compensated employees who benefit under the plan, divided by the percentage of highly compensated employees who benefit under the plan, 50/91 (54.95 percent) in our example. Looking up the 90 percent concentration percentage in the table in Treas. Reg. § 1.410(b)–4(c)(4)(iv), we find that the safe harbor percentage is 27.50. Since the ratio percentage exceeds the safe harbor percentage, the X Corp. plan meets the nondiscriminatory classification test. If X Corp. can qualify as a qualified separate line of business, the plan will satisfy IRC § 410(b).

2.　*Qualified separate line of business ("QSLOB").* The statute does not define the term "separate line of business," but it does establish some minimum criteria. A line of business is not to be treated as separate unless (1) it has at least 50 employees (excluding certain categories of employees); (2) the employer notifies the IRS that the line is being treated as separate; and (3) the line meets guidelines prescribed by the IRS, or the employer receives a determination from the IRS that the line may be treated as separate. IRC § 414(r)(2). Requirement (3) can be avoided if the percentage of employees working in the line of business who are highly compensated falls within a safe harbor range (not less than one-half, nor more than twice) of the same percentage applied on an employer-wide basis. IRC § 414(r)(3).

The Treasury has issued regulations (dubbed the "SLOB" regulations by practitioners) defining when an employer will be treated as operating "qualified" separate lines of business (QSLOB), which would enable the minimum coverage and participation rules to be applied separately with respect to the employees of each QSLOB. Treas. Reg. § 1.414(r). The regulations begin with a useful flowchart that graphically summarizes the three step procedure.

First, the employer determines the lines of business it operates by designating the property or services that each of its lines of business provides to its customers. The regulations provide employers with a great deal of discretion in making this determination. Treas. Reg. § 1.414(r)–2(b)(3).

Second, the employer must show that its lines of business are organized and operated separately from one another, i.e., that they are truly "separate" lines of business. The regulations set forth objective criteria that "generally require that the line of business be organized into one or more separate organizational units (e.g., corporations, partnerships, or divisions), that the line of business constitute one or more distinct profit centers within the employer, and that no more than a moderate overlap exist between the employee workforce and management employed by the line of business and those employed by the remainder of the employer." Treas. Reg. § 1.414(r)–1(b)(2)(iii). Several of these criteria involve strict numerical tests and require the employer to allocate employees among the various separate lines of business using fairly elaborate rules.

Finally, once the employer establishes that it has SLOBs, it must determine whether they are "qualified," i.e., whether they meet the three statutory requirements of IRC § 414(r)(2) noted above. The fifty-employee and notice requirements present little difficulty. The requirement of IRC § 414(r)(2)(C) that the SLOB must satisfy administrative scrutiny is more troublesome to practitioners. A separate line of business can meet this requirement in one of two ways. First, the regulations establish a number of safe harbors, including the statutory safe harbor of IRC § 414(r)(3) noted above. Treas. Reg. § 1.414(r)–5. Second, even if none of the safe harbors applies, the employer can request an individual determination that the SLOB may be treated as a qualified SLOB. Treas. Reg. § 1.414(r)–6.

QUESTIONS

1.   If the justification for the line of business exception is to avoid disadvantaging diversified businesses, what is the rationale for requiring plans to meet an employer-wide nondiscriminatory classification test (the "Gateway")?

2. If the Internal Revenue Code were amended to require a qualified plan to cover all employees, should an exception be made for separate lines of business?

3. P Corp. manufactures wood shingles in Maine and has 200 employees, 50 of whom are highly compensated. All of the employees participate in a generous defined benefit pension plan. P Corp. proposes to acquire S Corp. as a wholly owned subsidiary. S Corp. manufactures asphalt shingles in Alabama and has 100 employees, 5 of whom would be highly compensated within the P Corp. structure after the proposed acquisition. S Corp. does not maintain a pension plan. Can P Corp. exclude the S Corp. employees from its plan? If not, must the S Corp. employees be covered as of the date of the acquisition? See IRC § 410(b)(6)(C).

C. DISCRIMINATION IN CONTRIBUTIONS OR BENEFITS

Even if a plan's coverage is sufficiently broad to meet the coverage and participation requirements, discrimination could result if the plan's contributions or benefits were allocated so as to favor highly compensated employees. Nominal benefits could be given to the low-paid workers. For example, a plan might base contributions on one percent of the first $25,000 of compensation and 15 percent of the excess over $25,000. Similarly, a plan might provide certain benefit options (such as lump sum or early retirement options) only to highly compensated participants. To counter these and other possibilities, Congress has required qualified plans to provide "contributions *or* benefits" that do not discriminate in favor of highly compensated employees. IRC § 401(a)(4). The use of the term "or" is significant; "it need not be shown that both the contributions and the benefits provided are nondiscriminatory in amount, but only that either the contributions alone or the benefits alone are nondiscriminatory in amount." Treas. Reg. § 1.401(a)(4)–1(b)(2).

[margin note: — Possible to discriminate with the allocation of the plan's benefits or contributions to just the highly compensated]

1. THE NONDISCRIMINATION REGULATIONS

Although IRC § 401(a)(4) and its predecessors have been a part of the tax law since 1942, comprehensive regulations were never issued until 1991. Beyond the statement in IRC § 401(a)(5)(B) that a plan shall not be considered discriminatory merely because the contributions or benefits under the plan bear a uniform relationship to compensation, the statute provides almost no guidance as to what is discriminatory. Although the Tax Reform Act of 1986 triggered the Treasury's interest in developing the 401(a)(4) regulations, the Act did not change the basic wording of IRC § 401(a)(4), beyond redefining the group in whose favor discrimination was prohibited. The entire regulatory edifice is built essentially on a single sentence in the statute: "A trust [shall] constitute a qualified trust [if] the contributions or benefits provided under the plan do not discriminate in favor of highly compensated employees."

[margin note: —IRC does NOT say what is considered Discriminatory]

The regulations, contained in Treas. Reg. § 1.401(a)(4), span over 100 pages and are intended to set forth the exclusive rules for determining whether a plan meets the requirements of IRC § 401(a)(4). A plan must satisfy three requirements: (1) either the contributions or the benefits must be nondiscriminatory in amount; (2) the benefits, rights, and features provided under a plan must be made available to employees

[margin note: 3 Requirements for Plans: ① ② ③]

covered by the plan in a nondiscriminatory manner; and (3) the effect of certain special circumstances (e.g., plan amendments and the use of past service credits) must be nondiscriminatory.

1. *Defined contribution plans.* The regulations provide two safe harbors for testing whether the contributions to a defined contribution plan are discriminatory. The first safe harbor is satisfied if the plan uses a uniform allocation formula that allocates either the same percentage of compensation, the same dollar amount, or the same dollar amount for each unit of service (not to exceed one week) to each employee under the plan. Treas. Reg. § 1.401(a)(4)–2(b)(2). This is a "design-based" safe harbor, because compliance does not require any testing; the design of the plan guarantees compliance.

The following example illustrates a profit-sharing plan that satisfies the uniform allocation formula safe harbor. Assume that the plan covers all four of the employees compensated as shown in the table below and that contributions are allocated in proportion to each employee's compensation. The employer has decided to contribute to the plan an amount equal to 15 percent of employee compensation.

TABLE 9.1
PROFIT-SHARING PLAN EXAMPLE

	Compensation	Contribution Allocated to Employees	Percent of Total Contribution
A	$250,000	$37,500	62.5
B	90,000	13,500	22.5
C	40,000	6,000	10.0
D	20,000	3,000	5.0
	$400,000	$60,000	100.0

Even though A receives over 60 percent of the contribution, and more than twelve times that received by the lowest paid employee, the plan qualifies because the allocation rate (i.e., amount of contribution divided by compensation) is uniform. There is nothing astonishing about this result; it is clearly contemplated by IRC § 401(a)(5)(B).

The second safe harbor covers a rather narrowly defined class of "uniform points allocation" formulas. The formula must take either age or years of service (or both) into account, and may take compensation into account in a specified manner. Treas. Reg. § 1.401(a)(4)–2(b)(3). However, the average of the allocation rates for the highly compensated employees must not exceed the average of the allocation rates for the nonhighly compensated employees. This safe harbor is not design-based, since it does require testing by the employer.

For example, using the second safe harbor a plan might grant each employee 10 points for each year of service and one point for each $100 of compensation Thus, employee H with 20 years of service and compensation of $150,000 would receive 1,700 points. The allocation to each employee's account is based on the ratio of the employee's points to the total points for all employees in the plan. If the total number of points for all employees is 17,000 and the employer's total contribution is $100,000, H would receive an allocation of $10,000 (i.e., 10 percent of

$100,000). H's allocation rate is therefore 6.67 percent ($10,000 divided by H's compensation of $150,000). Such an allocation meets the safe harbor as long as the average of the allocation rates for the highly compensated employees does not exceed the average of the allocation rates for the nonhighly compensated employees.

A plan that does not qualify under one of the safe harbors must meet a complex general test: each "rate group" under the plan must satisfy the minimum coverage test of IRC § 410(b) as if it were a separate plan that benefits only the employees in the rate group. Treas. Reg. § 1.401(a)(4)–2(c). A "rate group" exists under a plan for each highly compensated employee in the plan and consists of the highly compensated employee and all other employees in the plan who have an allocation rate greater than or equal to the highly compensated employee's allocation rate. An employee's allocation rate is basically the sum of the allocations of employer contributions and forfeitures to the employee's account, expressed either as a percentage of compensation or as a dollar amount.

To understand the general test, consider the following example, taken from Treas. Reg. § 1.401(a)(4)–2(c)(4), Example 4. Assume Employer Y has a profit-sharing plan covering all 6 of its employees: H1 and H2 are highly compensated employees and N1 through N4 are nonhighly compensated employees. Their allocation rates are:

Employee	Allocation Rate (%)
H1	5.0
H2	7.5
N1	5.0
N2	5.0
N3	5.0
N4	8.0

Before the nondiscrimination regulations were issued, it was unclear whether these facts would cause a violation of IRC § 401(a)(4). H2 has an allocation rate higher than three out of the four nonhighly compensated employees, but a nonhighly compensated employee (N4) has the highest allocation rate. Employer Y can now know for certain where it stands. It turns out that N4's higher allocation rate saves the plan from disqualification.

First, we must determine the rate groups. There are two. Rate group 1 consists of H1 and all those employees who have an allocation rate greater than or equal to H1's allocation rate. Thus, rate group 1 consists of H1, H2, and N1 through N4. Rate group 2 consists of H2 and all those employees who have an allocation rate greater than or equal to H2's allocation rate. Thus, rate group 2 consists of H2 and N4.

Second, we must test each rate group to see whether standing alone it satisfies IRC § 410(b). Rate group 1 easily satisfies the ratio percentage test since 100 percent of the nonhighly compensated employees are in the rate group. Testing rate group 2 is more difficult. It does not satisfy the ratio percentage test because only 25 percent of the nonhighly compensated employees are in the rate group, compared to 50 percent of the highly compensated employees. This produces a ratio percentage of 50 percent (25/50), which is less than the required 70 percent.

Since rate group 2 does not satisfy the ratio percentage test, we must determine whether it satisfies the average benefits test of IRC § 410(b). As discussed in Section B.1 above, this two-prong test consists of the nondiscriminatory classification test and the average benefit percentage test.

As for the first prong, the nondiscriminatory classification test, the regulations deem the test to be satisfied if the ratio percentage of the rate group is at least the lesser of the ratio percentage of the entire plan or the midpoint between the safe and unsafe harbor percentages applicable to the plan. Treas. Reg. § 1.401(a)(4)–2(c)(3)(ii). Since the nonhighly compensated employee concentration percentage of the plan is 66 percent (4/6), the safe harbor percentage is 45.50 percent, using the table in Treas. Reg. § 1.410(b)–4(c)(4)(iv). Since the ratio percentage of rate group 2 is 50 percent (see above), it is greater than the safe harbor percentage and therefore rate group 2 satisfies the nondiscriminatory classification test of Treas. Reg. § 1.410(b)–4.

The second prong of the average benefits test is the average benefit percentage test. Under Treas. Reg. § 1.401(a)(4)–2(c)(3)(iii), this test is to be applied to the plan as a whole, not just the rate group. Assuming that this is the only plan of Employer Y, the average benefit percentage of the nonhighly compensated employees is 5.75 percent ((8+5+5+5)/4) and the average benefit percentage of the highly compensated employees is 6.25 percent ((7.5+5)/2). Since 5.75 percent is at least 70 percent of 6.25 percent, the average benefits percentage test is satisfied. Thus, rate group 2 does indeed satisfy IRC § 410(b).

Since both rate groups satisfy IRC § 410(b), the plan meets the general test for nondiscrimination in amount of contributions and therefore satisfies IRC § 401(a)(4). In this example an increase in the allocation rate of one nonhighly compensated employee allows an increase in the allocation rate of one of the two highly compensated employees. If N4's allocation rate were only 5 percent, the plan would not meet the general test. See Treas. Reg. § 1.401(a)(4)–2(c)(4), Example 3. Assume N4's compensation is $10,000 and H2's compensation is $150,000. By increasing N4's allocation from $500 to $800 (5 percent to 8 percent), Employer Y can increase H2's allocation from $7,500 to $11,250 (5 percent to 7.5 percent). Thus, H2 can be given an extra $3,750 at a cost of only $300 in increased contributions to others. In fact, as an exercise you can verify that H2 could have an allocation rate of 8 percent and the plan would still meet the general nondiscrimination test. If H2's allocation rate exceeds N4's, the plan would fail the test. Can you see why?

2. *Defined benefit plans.* The regulations establish three design-based safe harbors for testing defined benefit plans under IRC § 401(a)(4). To qualify for any of the safe harbors, a plan must satisfy a uniformity requirement. The plan must have uniform normal and post-normal retirement benefits, uniform subsidized optional forms of benefits, and uniform vesting and service crediting; the plan may not require employee contributions. The most significant safe harbor covers the commonly used unit credit plans (i.e., plans that compute benefits as a percentage of compensation relative to length of service). Such plans will satisfy IRC § 401(a)(4) if the benefits accrue under a unit benefit

formula that is uniform for all employees under the plan and the accrual rate satisfies the anti-backloading requirement of IRC § 411(b)(1)(B). Treas. Reg. § 1.401(a)(4)–3(b)(3). For example, a plan that provides a benefit equal to a percentage of average annual compensation based on 1.5 percent for the first five years of service and 2.0 percent for all additional years of service satisfies the unit credit safe harbor. The other safe harbors cover fractional accrual plans and insurance contract plans.

Defined benefit plans that do not meet a safe harbor must satisfy a complex general test similar to the general test for defined contribution plans. Each "rate group" under the plan must satisfy IRC § 410(b) as if it were a separate plan that benefits only the employees in the rate group. For defined benefit plans, however, the determination of the rate groups is more complicated. A rate group exists for each highly compensated employee and consists of the highly compensated employee and all other employees in the plan who have a "normal accrual rate" greater than or equal to that of the highly compensated employee, and who also have a "most valuable accrual rate" greater than or equal to that of the highly compensated employee. Treas. Reg. § 1.401(a)(4)–3(c).

The determination of accrual rates can be one of the more difficult aspects of performing the general test. The normal accrual rate is basically the yearly rate at which the employee's normal retirement benefit under the plan accrues. The most valuable accrual rate is the yearly rate at which the employee's most valuable optional form of benefit under the plan accrues. For example, an employee who would be eligible in the future for a subsidized early retirement benefit will have his or her most valuable accrual rate based on that benefit. Employers have a choice of three measuring periods to calculate accrual rates: the current plan year, the current plan year and all prior years, or the current plan year and all prior and future years. For a taste of the complexity of doing these calculations, skim Treas. Reg. § 1.401(a)(4)–3(d).

3. *Compensation.* The definition of "compensation" is crucial to applying the nondiscrimination tests since the computation of allocation rates and accrual rates is based upon compensation. The nondiscrimination regulations adopt the definition of compensation used in IRC § 414(s). See Treas. Reg. § 1.401(a)(4)–12 (Definition of plan year compensation). This choice is supported by the statute, since the statutory safe harbor for plans in which the contributions or benefits bear a uniform relationship to compensation, IRC § 401(a)(5)(B), uses the IRC § 414(s) definition.

In general, "compensation" under IRC § 414(s) is defined to mean "compensation" within the meaning of IRC § 415(c)(3). The definition in IRC § 415(c)(3) is extremely important, because it is used for a variety of plan qualification purposes, notably (1) to determine whether a plan satisfies any applicable discrimination requirement, including IRC § 401(a)(4); (2) to determine which employees are highly compensated; and (3) to apply the limits on contributions and benefits under IRC § 415.

IRC § 415(c) provides only a circular definition, defining compensation to mean compensation, somewhat the way the income tax statute defines income to mean income. The regulations, however, furnish a lengthy list of what is included and excluded from the definition, and provide a number of safe harbor provisions and alternative definitions. Treas. Reg. § 1.415(c)–2. In particular, a plan may define compensation to mean either "wages" for purposes of income tax withholding or the wages and other compensation reported on the W-2 form; such definition will be considered automatically to satisfy IRC § 415(c)(3). Treas. Reg. § 1.415(c)–2(d)(3) and (4). These alternatives were designed to simplify the task of computing compensation.

Although pension plan contributions are generally not considered compensation, IRC § 415(c) was amended to provide that compensation shall include elective deferrals to 401(k) plans, 403(b) plans, and SIMPLE plans; elective contributions to section 457 plans; salary reduction contributions under a qualified transportation fringe benefit program; and salary reduction contributions to cafeteria plans. IRC § 415(c)(3)(D). However, IRC § 414(s)(2) allows employers to elect to exclude these amounts as compensation, for nondiscrimination purposes. Since most plans base their benefits on the participant's compensation before any elective deferrals or salary reductions, IRC § 414(s)(2) elections will not be common.

Pursuant to the authority granted in IRC § 414(s)(3), the Treasury has provided a number of possible alternative definitions of compensation. See Treas. Reg. § 1.414(s)–1(c). Most importantly, the regulations allow any definition of compensation with respect to employees who are not self-employed if it (1) is reasonable, (2) does not by design favor highly compensated employees, and (3) satisfies a special nondiscrimination requirement. Treas. Reg. § 1.414(s)–1(d)(1). A definition of compensation is nondiscriminatory if the average percentage of total compensation included under the definition for an employer's highly compensated employees as a group does not exceed by more than a de minimis amount the average percentage of total compensation included under the definition for the employer's other employees as a group. Treas. Reg. § 1.414(s)–1(d)(3)(i).

Note that there is no express requirement that plans allocate contributions or accrue benefits based on an IRC § 414(s) definition of compensation. However, a plan that defines compensation in some other fashion cannot use the safe harbors under the IRC § 401(a)(4) regulations and must be tested for nondiscrimination under the general test. For example, assume Employer X has two employees, H, a highly compensated employee, and N, a nonhighly compensated employee. H earns a salary of $120,000 and N earns a regular salary of $30,000, but also receives $3,000 in overtime pay. Assume that Employer X's profit-sharing plan defines compensation as regular salary, excluding overtime, and allocates contributions in proportion to compensation. The plan's definition of compensation would not satisfy IRC § 414(s) and the plan would have to be tested for nondiscrimination using the general test. We shall see when we consider the topic of integration with Social Security below that the plan may indeed be able to satisfy the general test.

4. *Compliance.* Substantiating compliance with the nondiscrimination rules can be an enormous burden for employers, particularly large employers with thousands of employees who may be scattered among numerous divisions with separate payroll administration. The IRS has sought to find ways to reduce this burden

without compromising its goal of strong enforcement of the statute. In Rev. Proc. 93–42, 1993–2 C.B. 540, the IRS issued guidelines that attempt to simplify the substantiation process in a number of significant ways including permitting employers that do not have precise data available at reasonable cost to use a reliable substitute; allowing employers to test on a single representative day (so-called "snapshot" testing); and requiring a plan to be tested only once every three years provided it undergoes no significant change.

In recognition of the complexity of the nondiscrimination rules and the risk of inadvertent noncompliance, the regulations permit retroactive corrections to be made up to 9 1/2 months after the end of the plan year. Treas. Reg. § 1.401(a)(4)–11(g). The retroactive amendments may be made not only to satisfy IRC § 401(a)(4), but also to cover additional employees so that the plan may satisfy the IRC § 410(b) minimum coverage requirements or the IRC § 401(a)(26) minimum participation requirements. Two important limitations apply. First, the amendment cannot reduce any employee's benefits (including any benefit, right, or feature). Thus, the employer may not cut back benefits for the highly compensated employees; instead, the employer must increase benefits for the nonhighly compensated employees. Second, the additional benefits created by the retroactive amendment must separately satisfy IRC § 401(a)(4) and must benefit a group of employees that separately satisfies IRC § 410(b).

This liberal correction mechanism allows employers to adjust coverage and benefits on a year-by-year basis to maximize the benefits available to the highly compensated employees. One can envision an employer retroactively increasing the benefits of a small group of low paid workers by the lowest possible amount to justify much larger benefits for a small group of highly paid employees.

NOTES AND QUESTIONS

1.   University provides a defined benefit pension plan to all of its employees. The benefit is a uniform formula based on the average annual regular compensation over the three years with the highest such compensation. Regular compensation is defined to include all compensation except faculty summer research stipends. Is the plan likely to satisfy IRC § 401(a)(4) if (a) all, (b) most, (c) a few, or (d) none of the faculty receiving stipends are highly compensated? What data would University need to make this determination?

2.   Employer has 4 employees. H1 and H2 are highly compensated employees and N1 and N2 are nonhighly compensated employees. Employer has established two profit-sharing plans. Plan A covers H1 and N1 and Plan B covers H1 and N2. H2 is not covered by any plan. For the current year, each plan allocates 7.5 percent of compensation to each employee's account. Thus, H1 (who happens to own Employer) has a combined allocation of 15 percent and N1 and N2 each have a combined allocation rate of 7.5 percent. Does this violate IRC § 401(a)(4) or § 410(b)? Should it?

3.   *Plan amendments.* The timing of a plan amendment, including the establishment or termination of a plan, can often have a discriminatory effect. For example, an employer who is winding up its business and has

terminated all its nonhighly compensated employees, might decide to increase benefits for the remaining highly compensated employees just prior to terminating the plan. The regulations apply a facts and circumstances test to determine whether the timing of a plan amendment is discriminatory. See Treas. Reg. § 1.401(a)(4)–5(a).

Assume that a personal service corporation has two employees, the owner and a nonhighly compensated employee. The owner has decided to establish a defined benefit plan providing a benefit of 2 percent of average annual compensation per year of service, including years of service prior to the establishment of the plan. The owner has ten years of prior service, but the other employee has only one. Does the grant of past service credit violate IRC § 401(a)(4)? Would it be relevant whether there were former nonhighly compensated employees of the corporation who would have benefited had the plan been in effect for the prior ten years? See Treas. Reg. § 1.401(a)(4)–5(a)(2), (3) & (4), Examples 7, 8, & 9.

4. *Collectively bargained plans.* Under Treas. Reg. § 1.401(a)(4)–1(c)(5), a collectively bargained plan automatically satisfies the nondiscrimination requirement of IRC § 401(a)(4), just as it automatically satisfies the minimum coverage rule of IRC § 410(b). This exemption of collectively bargained plans from IRC § 401(a)(4) testing is statutory. See IRC § 413(b)(2). As with the minimum coverage rule, the exemption for collectively bargained plans does not apply to a plan if more than 2 percent of the covered employees are "professionals." Why should a discriminatory plan become acceptable for purposes of controlling and targeting the tax subsidy merely because it is negotiated by a union?

5. *Governmental Plans.* Governmental plans enjoy a complete exemption from the nondiscrimination rules. IRC §§ 401(a)(5)(G), 401(a)(26)(G), and 401(k)(3)(G). Should they?

2. BENEFITS V. CONTRIBUTIONS: THE CROSS-TESTING Plans PROBLEM — popular in 1990's

Recall that either the contributions or the benefits must be nondiscriminatory, not both. Treas. Reg. § 1.401(a)(4)–1(b)(2). To see how nondiscriminatory benefits could produce what might appear to be overwhelmingly discriminatory contributions, consider the following hypothetical. Assume that a professional service corporation establishes a defined benefit plan for its two employees: (1) H, the owner, age 55 with a salary of $100,000, and (2) N, age 30, with a salary of $50,000. The plan is a unit credit plan providing for a normal retirement benefit at age 65 equal to 5 percent of final average compensation multiplied by years of plan participation.

This plan easily satisfies IRC § 401(a)(4) because each employee has the same 5 percent accrual rate. At the end of the first year H has accrued a benefit of $5,000 per year payable for life commencing at age 65. Similarly, N has accrued a benefit of $2,500 per year payable for life commencing at age 65. But the present values of these accrued benefits are not the same percentage of compensation. Although N's accrued benefit is one-half of H's, because N is 25 years younger, N's benefit will commence 25 years after H's. Assuming an interest rate of 8.5 percent, the present value of N's benefit is only 6.5 percent of H's. Put another way, if the present value of the accrued benefits were contributed to the plan, H's allocation would be more than 15 times N's, even though H's salary is only twice N's.

Pre-termination restrictions. As a practical matter, when H retires, N is not likely to continue to accrue benefits. Furthermore, H will begin receiving benefits 25 years before N. The Treasury has long been concerned about the possibility of highly compensated employees retiring and receiving the bulk of the assets of a plan, leaving insufficient assets to pay the benefits for the remaining, often nonhighly compensated, employees. The danger is particularly great if the highly compensated employee can receive a lump-sum benefit.

For this reason, the nondiscrimination regulations require defined benefit plans to impose certain restrictions on distributions. Treas. Reg. § 1.401(a)(4)–5(b). A plan must provide that the annual payments to highly compensated current and former employees are restricted to an amount equal to the payments under a single life annuity that is actuarially equivalent to the employee's benefits under the plan (other than a Social Security supplement) plus any Social Security supplement. No such restriction need apply, however, if either (1) after payment of all of the employee's benefits the value of the plan assets equals or exceeds 110 percent of the value of current liabilities; (2) the value of the employee's benefits is less than 1 percent of the value of current liabilities; or (3) the value of the employee's benefits does not exceed $5,000. The plan may limit the restriction to a group of not less than 25 highly compensated employees and highly compensated former employees, provided the group consists of those employees with the greatest compensation. Treas. Reg. § 1.401(a)(4)–5(b)(3)(B)(ii).

The IRS will permit distributions to exceed these restrictions if the plan requires "adequate security to guarantee any repayment of the restricted amount upon plan termination." Rev. Rul. 92–76, 1992–2 C.B. 76. Adequate security can be the deposit in escrow of property with a fair market value of at least 125 percent of the restricted amount, or the posting of a bond or letter of credit in an amount equal to at least 100 percent of the restricted amount.

Cross-testing. In the professional service corporation hypothetical above we examined a defined benefit plan that had nondiscriminatory benefits and therefore was qualified, even though the equivalent allocations would be discriminatory. Suppose instead that the corporation sponsored a defined contribution plan that made discriminatory allocations, but the benefit accruals equivalent to the allocations were not discriminatory. Would the defined contribution plan nevertheless be qualified? The regulations say yes. A defined benefit plan is nondiscriminatory if its equivalent allocations are nondiscriminatory and a defined contribution plan is nondiscriminatory if its equivalent benefits are nondiscriminatory. Treas. Reg. § 1.401(a)(4)–1(b)(2).

The rules for this "cross-testing" are found in Treas. Reg. § 1.401(a)(4)–8. A benefit is converted to an equivalent allocation by taking the present value, using standard interest rates and mortality tables specified in the regulations, of the increase in the participant's benefit over the plan year, expressed as either a dollar amount or as a percentage of the employee's compensation. An allocation is converted into an equivalent accrual rate by converting the allocation into an actuarially equivalent straight life annuity commencing at the normal retirement age, expressed either as a dollar amount or as a percentage of the employee's average annual compensation.

Consider the professional service corporation hypothetical discussed above. Although H and N accrue benefits under the defined benefit plan at the same rate, H's accrued benefit is far more valuable because H will reach normal retirement age and commence receiving benefits 25 years before N. Such a defined benefit plan, while it allows a disproportionate amount of the contributions to the plan to be allocated toward providing H's benefit, has the usual drawbacks of a defined benefit plan: strict annual funding standards, employer liability for underfunding, and the survivor annuity requirements. With cross-testing permitted, H has another more flexible option: an "age-weighted" profit-sharing plan. This type of plan allocates contributions among the participants such that when the contributions are expressed as a benefit at normal retirement age, they produce the same accrual rates. Thus, H's allocation rate could be 7.7 times N's, assuming an 8.5 percent interest rate. If H decided to have the corporation contribute $22,500 to the plan in the current year, $21,126 could be allocated to H and $1,374 could be allocated to N. (Actually, the top-heavy rules of IRC § 416, discussed in Section D infra, would require N to receive a minimum of $1,500 (three percent of compensation), but H would still receive more than 90 percent of the total employer contribution.)

Obviously, this type of plan works best, from the owner's perspective, if the owner is much older than the lower-paid employees. Such a demographic is actually quite common, and many small businesses have adopted this type of plan. Defined contribution plans that rely on the cross-testing rules to meet the nondiscrimination rules are sometimes referred to as "new comparability plans." Using cross-testing in this fashion is viewed by some as an abuse. Why should economically equivalent benefits be discriminatory if provided through a defined contribution plan, but nondiscriminatory if provided through a defined benefit plan?

Reacting to Congressional concern about the aggressive use of new comparability plans, the Treasury revised the cross-testing regulations in 2001 to add an additional hurdle. Under Treas. Reg. § 1.401(a)(4)–8(b)(1), a defined contribution plan can demonstrate compliance with the nondiscrimination requirements based on plan benefits rather than contributions only if it meets one of the following three conditions:

(1) The plan has "broadly available" allocation rates (i.e., each allocation rate is currently available to a group of employees satisfying the minimum coverage test of IRC § 410(b) (without regard to the average benefits percentage test));

(2) The plan has age-based allocation rates that are based on either a gradual age and service schedule or a uniform target benefit allocation; or

(3) Each nonhighly compensated employee has an allocation rate that is at least 5 percent of compensation or at

least one third of the allocation rate of the highly compensated employee with the highest allocation rate (the "Gateway" test).

Consider the following example of an aggressive plan design. Employer has 55 employees, of whom 5 are highly compensated. The plan covers just one of the highly compensated employees and the seven lowest paid employees, each of whom earned less than $2,000. The highly compensated employee receives an allocation of 20% of compensation and the others receive an allocation of 5% (less than $100). Does the plan satisfy the minimum coverage requirement of IRC § 410(b)? If the low paid employees are all young, and the highly compensated employee is much older, the plan could literally satisfy the nondiscrimination in amount general test by using cross-testing under Treas. Reg. § 1.401(a)(4)–8. However, the IRS has warned that such a plan design may violate Treas. Reg. § 1.401(a)(4)–1(c)(2), which states that the regulations under IRC § 401(a)(4) "must be interpreted in a reasonable manner consistent with the purpose of preventing discrimination in favor of HCEs."

Multiple plans. When an employer elects to designate two or more plans to be treated as one plan for minimum coverage purposes, the plans must meet the nondiscrimination requirements of IRC § 401(a)(4) as if they were a single plan. IRC § 410(b)(6)(B). This determination presents little difficulty if the plans are all defined contribution plans or all defined benefit plans. However, if the employer offers both defined benefit and defined contribution plans, cross-testing is unavoidable. The regulations refer to such aggregated plans as "DB/DC" plans and provide complex rules for determining whether such plans discriminate in the amount of contributions or benefits. Treas. Reg. § 1.401(a)(4)–9.

3. LIMITATION ON INCLUDIBLE COMPENSATION

As noted in the previous sections, a plan that provides a uniform allocation or accrual rate is not discriminatory, even though the highly compensated employees receive more valuable benefits. But if the compensation of the highly compensated employee is high enough, even uniform contributions or benefits may seem abusive. For example, a 5.3 percent contribution on behalf of employees earning $1,000,000 and $10,000 would result in contributions of $53,000 and $530 respectively. As we shall see in Chapter 10, the maximum dollar amount of contribution to a defined contribution plan is $53,000 (in 2015). Thus, by setting the contribution percentage at the 5.3 percent figure the highly compensated employee could receive the maximum contribution and the low paid employee would receive very little.

Congress dealt with this problem in 1986 by establishing a limit on the amount of compensation that may be taken into account under any qualified plan. The limit has fluctuated over the years, but most recently in 2001 it was set at $200,000, indexed for inflation in $5,000 increments ($260,000 in 2014, $265,000 in 2015). IRC § 401(a)(17). Thus, in the example above, the highly compensated employee would be permitted to receive only a $14,045 contribution (5.3 percent of $265,000). If the employer wanted to contribute the maximum of $53,000 on behalf of the high paid employee, it must (1) set the contribution percentage at 20 percent for all employees or (2) establish that a lower rate for the nonhighly compensated employees satisfies the nondiscrimination requirement (e.g., by using permitted disparity or cross-testing).

The regulations under IRC § 401(a)(17) make it clear that compensation in excess of the annual limit must be disregarded not only for purposes of determining contributions or benefits, but also in computing allocation or accrual rates for purposes of applying the nondiscrimination rules. Treas. Reg. § 1.401(a)(17)–1(c). Thus, an employee whose compensation is $1,000,000 and who receives a defined contribution allocation of $26,500 has an allocation rate of 10 percent ($26,500/$265,000) for discrimination testing purposes.

In setting the IRC § 401(a)(17) level, Congress faces essentially the same quandary as in setting the minimum coverage level, discussed in Section A, supra. The current system of voluntary pension plans relies on the tax benefits to high income employees as a means of encouraging the creation of pension plans. If these benefits are cut back, there is the risk that the plans themselves will be cut back, depriving lower income workers of pension benefits. Of course, it is possible that for some plans the subsidy to the high income employees is in excess of what it would take to maintain the plans and therefore the reduction will simply save the government money without affecting coverage for lower income employees. But certainly there will be plans that will no longer make economic sense and some coverage for lower income workers will undoubtedly be lost. Some employers have responded to the IRC § 401(a)(17) limit not by terminating plans, but rather by establishing nonqualified plans to make up the lost benefits for top management.

4. INTEGRATION WITH SOCIAL SECURITY

From the time the nondiscrimination concept became part of the law in 1942, Congress has permitted plans to take Social Security benefits into account. Plans that do so are said to be "integrated." Over the years the IRS developed complex integration rules based mainly on the premise that Social Security benefits are in part attributable to employer contributions under the Federal Insurance Contributions Act. The employer was viewed as providing two plans, the employer's plan and the employer-financed portion of Social Security. As long as these two plans taken together produced contributions or benefits that bore a uniform relationship to compensation, the employer's plan would not be discriminatory. Subject to IRS guidelines, integration allowed plans to reduce contributions or benefits based on wages below the Social Security taxable wage base.

Beginning with the Tax Equity and Fiscal Responsibility Act of 1982, Congress began to establish statutory rules for permissible integration. These rules were initially quite liberal and even permitted plans to provide no benefits to low-paid workers, provided the benefits to the high-paid workers were not too high. The requirements were significantly revised by the Tax Reform Act of 1986. Under IRC § 401(a)(5)(C), a plan that integrates with Social Security will not be considered discriminatory under IRC § 401(a)(4) merely because of the disparity caused by the integration, provided the method of integration satisfies the requirements of IRC § 401(l). This provision establishes separate numerical tests for both defined contribution and defined benefit plans.

1. *Defined contribution plans.* Defined contribution plans may integrate with Social Security by specifying an "integration level," which is not permitted to exceed the taxable wage base under the Social Security Act ($118,500 for plan years beginning in 2015). The percentage of compensation contributed under the plan with respect to compensation below the integration level (the "base contribution percentage") is set at a rate lower than the percentage of compensation contributed with respect to compensation above the integration level (the "excess contribution percentage"). The plan is properly integrated if the excess contribution percentage does not exceed the base contribution percentage by more than the lesser of

(1) the base contribution percentage, or

(2) the greater of   *— the other 0.5 percent is for Disability is also added on*

    (i) 5.7 percentage points, or

    (ii) the percentage equal to the employer portion of the FICA tax attributable to old-age insurance.   *— So 6.2% of your salary up to $130,700 goes towards Social Security (then EER also adds 6.2% equivalent)*

IRC § 401(*l*)(2)(A). The legislative history indicates that the Social Security Administration is to advise the IRS when the rate of tax attributable to old-age insurance rises above 5.7 percent. Conference Report, H.R.Rep. No. 841, 99th Cong., 2d Sess. II–436 (1986). This figure cannot be directly determined from the FICA statute (IRC § 3111), because the tax rate includes a portion attributable to disability benefits.

A typical money purchase pension plan will integrate with Social Security by providing a contribution to each participant's account equal to X percent of the participant's total compensation plus Y percent of the participant's compensation in excess of the selected integration level. Under IRC § 401(*l*), Y may not exceed the lesser of X or 5.7. For example, a plan could choose X to be 10 and Y to be 5.7. If such a plan used the Social Security taxable wage base ($118,500 in 2015) as its integration level, an employee with compensation of $265,000 would receive a contribution of $34,850.50 (10 percent of $265,000 plus 5.7 percent of $146,500).

Integrating profit-sharing plans is somewhat more complex. The problem is that the employer's contribution to the plan can vary from year to year. A traditional nonintegrated plan would simply allocate to each participant's account a fraction of the employer's contribution equal to the participant's compensation divided by the total compensation of all participants. An integrated plan must use a two-step allocation. A plan that wanted to comply with the integration rules, but at the same time maximize the allocation to compensation above the integration level, could allocate contributions based on the following scheme. First, compute an allocation percentage (not to exceed 5.7 percent) equal to the employer contribution divided by the sum of the total compensation of all participants and the total "excess compensation" of all participants. Excess compensation is the compensation of the participant which exceeds the selected integration level. Second, allocate to each participant's account an amount equal to this percentage of the participant's excess compensation. Third, allocate the remainder of the employer contribution to each participant in proportion to the total compensation earned by all participants.

The profit-sharing plan example from Table 9.1 of the previous section can be used to illustrate this type of integration formula. Assume that the Social Security wage base ($118,500 in 2015) is selected as the integration level and that the employer makes the same $60,000 contribution. The resulting allocation is shown in Table 9.2.

TABLE 9.2

INTEGRATED PROFIT-SHARING PLAN EXAMPLE

Compensation	First Allocation	Second Allocation	Total Contribution	Percent of Total
A	$250,000	$7,496	$32,815	$40,311	67.2
B	90,000	0	11,813	11,813	19.7
C	40,000	0	5,250	5,250	8.8
D	20,000	0	2,625	2,625	4.4
	$400,000	$7,496	$52,504	$60,000	100.0

A comparison of the contributions with the nonintegrated plan reveals that integration has benefited employee A to the detriment of the others. Yet this plan passes the nondiscrimination test because the allocation method guarantees that the difference between the excess contribution percentage and the base contribution percentage will not exceed 5.7 percent or the base contribution percentage, if lesser. In the example this difference is 5.7 percent. A little arithmetic would show that the base contribution percentage is 13.1 percent and the excess contribution percentage is 18.8 percent. As the example illustrates, integrated plans can be used to skew benefits toward the owners and managers and away from lower-paid workers. A study that examined data from 1993 to 1997 found that about 25 percent of all defined contribution plans are integrated. See Pamela Perun, Social Security and the Private Pension System: The Significance of Integrated Plans, Center for Retirement Research, Working Paper 2002–02.

Although the integration level is not permitted to exceed the Social Security wage base, the level may be set lower. However, a lower integration level may discriminate in favor of the highly compensated employees. In particular, choosing the integration level to be just above the level of the bulk of the lower paid employees has been used as a device for shifting contributions away from that group. The regulations provide that the 5.7 percent factor in the maximum excess allowance must be reduced, in some cases to as low as 4.3 percent, if the integration level is selected within certain ranges below the Social Security wage base. Treas. Reg. § 1.401(*l*)–2(d)(4).

2.   *Defined benefit plans.* The rules for integrating defined benefit plans are extraordinarily complex. See Treas. Reg. § 1.401(*l*)–3. The root of the complexity is the difficulty in determining the appropriate portion of the social security benefit attributable to the contributions of the employer whose plan is to be integrated. The employee may have worked for many other employers at various salaries. In addition, the social security wage base and tax rate, which determine the employer FICA contributions, also have changed over the years.

Section 401(l) permits two forms of integration: Excess plans and offset plans. An excess plan is similar to an integrated defined contribution plan. For example, a plan could provide a benefit of 1.25 percent ("base benefit percentage") of the participant's highest three-year average compensation up to "covered compensation" and 2 percent ("excess benefit percentage") of the participant's highest three-year average compensation in excess of covered compensation, multiplied by the participant's years of credited service (up to a maximum of 35). The excess benefit percentage may not exceed the base benefit percentage by more than the lesser of .75 percent or the base benefit percentage. IRC § 401(l)(4)(A). Covered compensation is defined as the average of the Social Security taxable wage bases for each year in the 35-year period ending with the year in which the employee attains the Social Security retirement age. IRC § 401(l)(5)(E). A plan is not required to use covered compensation as the integration level, but if it does not, it generally must adjust the .75 maximum disparity to a lower figure.

An offset plan integrates by reducing the participant's accrued benefit by an amount (the offset) specified in the plan. A common arrangement under the prior law was to reduce the benefit by some fraction of the participant's Social Security benefit. Under the current law such a direct connection between a permissible offset and Social Security benefits no longer exists. The permissible offsets are severely limited. See IRC § 401(l)(3)(B).

An example of an offset plan formula that meets the requirements of IRC § 401(l) is a normal retirement benefit equal to 2 percent of the participant's highest three-year average compensation for each year of credited service up to a maximum of 40 years, reduced by .75 percent of the participant's final average compensation (up to covered compensation) for each year of credited service (up to 35 years). "Final average compensation" means the participant's average annual compensation for the 3-consecutive year period ending with the current year, or if shorter, the participant's full period of service. However, in determining annual compensation, only compensation up to the Social Security wage base is considered.

Note that the reductions permitted by IRC § 401(l) are derived from statutory formulas and do not relate to the employee's actual Social Security benefit. A special rule permits a plan to take account of actual benefits, but only in a very limited way. Under IRC § 401(a)(5)(D), a defined benefit plan can limit the maximum employer provided benefit to the excess of the participant's final pay over 50 percent of the employee's projected Social Security primary insurance amount attributable to service with the employer. See Treas. Reg. § 1.401(a)(5)–1(e). In a typical plan such a limit would likely affect only a small number of employees if any, although they probably would be the lowest paid due to the progressive nature of the Social Security benefit.

3. *Imputed disparity.* It should be emphasized that a plan will not necessarily violate the IRC § 401(a)(4) nondiscrimination requirement merely because it fails to satisfy IRC § 401(l) or IRC § 401(a)(5)(D). The effect of IRC §§ 401(a)(5) and 401(l) is to permit certain disparities in the allocation or benefits to be disregarded in applying IRC § 401(a)(4). However, even if the form of the plan does not satisfy IRC § 401(l), the

plan may still be found to be nondiscriminatory under the tests of IRC § 401(a)(4). In particular, the IRC § 401(a)(4) regulations provide an elaborate method for imputing the disparity permitted by IRC § 401(*l*) for purposes of testing for discrimination. Treas. Reg. § 1.401(a)(4)–7.

For example, assume Employer X has two employees, H, a highly compensated employee, and N, a nonhighly compensated employee. H has compensation of $150,000 and has $9,000 (i.e., 6 percent) allocated to his profit-sharing account. N has compensation of $30,000 and has $1,500 (i.e., 5 percent) allocated to his profit-sharing account. The regulations allow Employer X to "impute disparity" even though the plan is not directly integrated with Social Security in a form permitted by IRC § 401(*l*).

Under the regulations, the plan is permitted to treat N as having an "adjusted" allocation rate of 10 percent for purposes of testing for discrimination. Treas. Reg. § 1.401(a)(4)–7(b)(2). The logic is that the plan would have been permitted under IRC § 401(*l*) to contribute 5 percent of compensation for compensation below the Social Security wage base ($118,500 in 2015) and 10 percent for compensation above the wage base. Since all of N's compensation is below the wage base, his allocation would have only been 5 percent of compensation, exactly what he actually received.

Similarly, we are permitted to treat H as having an "adjusted" allocation rate of 10 percent as well. Treas. Reg. § 1.401(a)(4)–7(b)(3). Again, a plan would be permitted under IRC § 401(*l*) to contribute 5 percent of compensation for compensation below the social security wage base ($118,500 in 2015) and 10 percent for compensation above the wage base. Thus, 5 percent of $118,500 ($5,925) plus 10 percent of $31,500 ($3,150) equals $9,075, slightly more than H actually received. Applying the general nondiscrimination test, the plan is not discriminatory since H actually has the same adjusted allocation rate as N.

One way different allocation rates can arise is when a plan uses a definition of compensation that does not satisfy IRC § 414(s). For example, assume that Employer X's plan discussed above defined compensation to exclude overtime and allocated 7 percent of compensation to each employee's account. Assume that H had no overtime, but that N had $21,429 in regular salary and $8,571 in overtime. N's allocation of $1,500 is 7 percent of $21,429 (N's compensation as defined by the plan). But the $1,500 is just 5 percent of N's $30,000 of IRC § 414(s) compensation, which is what must be used to test for discrimination.

A similar, but far more complex, method of imputing permitted disparity is applicable to defined benefit plans. See Treas. Reg. § 1.401(a)(4)–7(c). Relying on imputed disparity to save a plan from disqualification is risky, since it requires periodic testing. In any given year the plan might not qualify.

4. *Policy perspective.* Consider the following critique of the integration rules.

Nancy J. Altman, Rethinking Retirement Income Policies: Nondiscrimination, Integration, and the Quest for Worker Security

42 Tax L.Rev. 435, 476 (1987).

From a taxpayer abuse perspective, [the rule requiring contributions or benefits to bear a uniform relationship to compensation] is sound. Providing all employees with benefits or contributions that are uniform proportions of their compensation is not an act of favoritism towards the prohibited group. Rather, the deferred compensation is an extension of, and is consistent with, the employer's overall pattern of compensation. From a worker security perspective, however, the proportionate rule would be troubling, if it were not for Social Security. Lower income workers generally need a higher percentage of their final salaries than higher paid workers to be able to retire without sacrificing their current standards of living. Moreover, higher salaried people have a greater ability to save for retirement.

In recognition that lower income workers need higher percentages of their incomes replaced from government supported programs in order to maintain comparable standards of living in retirement, Social Security has, since its enactment, provided benefits that constitute a larger proportion of the wages of lower income workers than higher income workers. . . .

Progressivity is produced in another way as well. Social Security benefits are based on covered taxable wages only, not all wages. As a consequence, with every dollar of additional wages a worker earns above the taxable wage base, the percentage of wages replaced by the Social Security benefit declines. . . .

Integration in Light of the Two Perspectives. Viewed from a concern to limit taxpayer abuse, the integration rules are understandable. An employer's decision to provide benefits to higher paid employees that are simply comparable to benefits received by lower paid employees from Social Security does not, by itself, evidence an improper motive; it may be consistent with a genuine interest in providing supplemental pensions.

Consistent with a taxpayer abuse perspective, the current integration rules focus on the employer-taxpayer. They concern the proper accounting of the portion of Social Security attributable to employer contributions. In contrast, a worker security perspective shifts the focus from the taxpayer to the worker.

When viewed from a worker security perspective, the integration rules clearly constitute bad policy. The current rationale for the favorable tax treatment of private pensions is that it is an inducement to employers to provide rank-and-file workers with supplemental pensions. The integration rules operate in a manner contrary to this goal. . . .

The problem is that the integration rules are built on a political fiction. Social Security is designed, through the use of trust funds, an earmarked payroll tax labeled a contribution, and other devices, to appear to be a program identical to private pension plans. This appearance is important in that it contributes to the earned right quality of the program, provides a level of security to beneficiaries, and encourages governmental fiscal responsibility. Nevertheless, the fiction is misemployed when it is used to justify regressive benefit or contribution payments under qualified private pensions.

Employers are paying a percentage of their workers' salaries into Social Security. However, the payment is a *tax,* not a pension contribution. The benefits for which the employer is contributing are not for its current workers, but for workers now retired, from an earlier generation, perhaps before this employer was even in business. To construe the employer's contribution as something other than a general tax and the employee's benefit as somehow purchased in part by the employee's employer is carrying a useful political fiction to an illogical extreme. . . .

For purposes of the nondiscrimination rules, the employer's Social Security costs should be construed no differently from costs incurred in the payment of property taxes or income taxes. . . .

A Worker Security Proposal. Social Security and qualified private retirement plans are each part of one system of retirement income delivery. They are both major sources of income for retirees. They should be coordinated. Without coordination, the rules and regulations surrounding their provision could inadvertently provide incentives for overpensioning some workers, which might influence them to leave the work force too early, or for underpensioning other workers, thereby failing to accomplish the goals of the retirement income system. . . .

In order to coordinate private pensions and Social Security on this basis, a definition of complete and full retirement income must be established. Social Security and most private pension plans implicitly define retirement income needs in terms of replacement of wages. Under this measure, complete and full retirement would be the amount necessary to permit people to cease work at a particular age without reduction in their standards of living.

At retirement, most people need less than 100% of their final compensation to maintain their preretirement standards of living. The precise percentage that people need varies with individual expenses and income levels. The government should specify, for purposes of integration, a percentage towards which its retirement policies are aimed.

QUESTIONS

1.   For purposes of determining whether a plan discriminates in favor of the highly compensated, is it appropriate to treat a portion of the Social Security benefit program as provided by the employer?

2.   If integration were forbidden, would nonhighly compensated employees be better off?

5. AVAILABILITY OF BENEFITS, RIGHTS, AND FEATURES

The prohibition against discrimination extends not only to the amount of contributions and benefits, but also to the availability of benefits, rights, and features under a plan. Treas. Reg. § 1.401(a)(4)–4.

The regulations provide that each benefit, right, or feature must be "currently available" to a group of employees that satisfies either the ratio percentage test of Treas. Reg. § 1.410(b)–2(b)(2) or the nondiscriminatory classification test of Treas. Reg. § 1.410(b)–4 (without regard to the average benefit percentage test). Treas. Reg. § 1.401(a)(4)–4(b)(1). In addition, the "effective availability" of the benefit, right, or feature must not substantially favor highly compensated employees. Treas. Reg. § 1.401(a)(4)–4(c)(1).

For example, assume Employer X has 6 employees, 2 highly compensated employees and 4 nonhighly compensated employees, all of whom participate in a defined benefit pension plan. The plan provides a lump sum optional form of benefit, but only to one of the highly compensated employees and one of the nonhighly compensated employees. The group of employees to whom the lump sum benefit is available does not satisfy the ratio percentage test, since 50 percent of the highly compensated employees are eligible but only 25 percent of the nonhighly compensated employees are eligible. This ratio percentage of 50 percent (i.e., 25/50) is somewhat shy of the required 70 percent, but is sufficient to satisfy the objective safe harbor of the nondiscriminatory classification test of Treas. Reg. § 1.410(b)–4. Thus, if the classification of employees eligible for the optional benefit is "reasonable and established under objective business criteria" (see Treas. Reg. § 1.410(b)–4(b)), the optional lump sum benefit will not be discriminatory.

Window plans. It is common for an employer seeking to reduce its work force to offer certain groups of employees special early retirement subsidies, provided the employees retire within a certain time period (the "window"). Such plan provisions are known as "early retirement window benefits." For example, an employer may have a defined benefit plan that provides for a normal retirement benefit commencing at age 65 and for an actuarially reduced early retirement benefit commencing at age 55 or later. The employer might decide to allow employees age 55 and over with more than 20 years of service to retire early with no actuarial benefit reduction, provided the employees retire within a specified four-month period. A plan that waives actuarial reduction in such a fashion is said to offer a "subsidized" early retirement benefit. ERISA fiduciary issues arising in connection with window plans are discussed in Chapter 13, infra.

Such window benefits raise a potential discrimination issue. For example, consider the extreme case of the owner of a business who establishes a window benefit, but it turns out that only the owner is eligible to retire during the window period. The way a plan with a window benefit is tested under the nondiscrimination regulations is to restructure the plan into two components, the window plan and its eligible employees, and the normal plan and the remaining employees. If each component can separately satisfy IRC § 401(a)(4) and the minimum coverage requirement of IRC § 410(b), then the plan will satisfy IRC § 401(a)(4). Treas. Reg. § 1.401(a)(4)–9(c)(1). For this purpose, in many cases the regulations deem the average benefit percentage test to be satisfied, leaving only the nondiscriminatory classification test to be satisfied in order to qualify the component plans. See Treas. Reg. § 1.401(a)(4)–9(c)(4), –9(c)(6) , Example 2. This rule is of immense practical importance to an employer in structuring an early retirement incentive plan.

QUESTIONS

1.   Employer A has an existing defined benefit plan for its 25 employees that permits a retiring employee to elect a lump sum payment instead of an annuity. A has amended the plan to eliminate the lump sum option for new employees. Two years later, A's plan covers 5 highly compensated employees and 20 nonhighly compensated employees. All 5 of the highly compensated employees are eligible to elect a lump sum distribution, but only one of the nonhighly compensated employees is eligible. All the other nonhighly compensated employees were hired after the plan was amended. Does the plan currently violate IRC § 401(a)(4)? Could A have avoided this problem by amending the plan to eliminate the lump sum option for all employees, new and existing? See IRC § 411(d)(6)(B); ERISA § 204(g)(2)(B). Is there any way for A to eliminate the lump sum option without risking disqualification? See Treas. Reg. § 1.401(a)(4)–4(b)(3).

2.   Employer X maintains a defined benefit plan that covers all ten of its employees, two of whom are highly compensated. The normal retirement age under the plan is 65. The employer wants to amend the plan to add an early retirement option, which would be payable to employees who terminate from service on or after age 55 with 30 or more years of service. Each highly compensated employee will have 30 years of service by the time he or she reaches 55, but only one of the nonhighly compensated employees will meet this requirement. Would you advise the employer to amend the plan? See Treas. Reg. § 1.401(a)(4)–4(c)(2), Example 1.

3.   University has a defined benefit plan that covers all of its employees, consisting of 100 faculty and 300 staff. University wishes to offer an early retirement window plan to the faculty, but not the staff. Of the faculty, 60 are highly compensated employees, of whom 4 would be eligible for the window, and 40 are nonhighly compensated employees, of whom 6 are eligible for the window. Of the staff, 30 are highly compensated employees and 270 are nonhighly compensated employees. Does the window plan violate IRC § 401(a)(4)? See Treas. Reg. § 1.401(a)(4)–9(c)(4)(i).

D. TOP-HEAVY PLANS

— when key employees have more than 60% of the plan's benefits

The discrimination rules do not prevent employers from structuring plans primarily favoring highly compensated employees, thanks to generous coverage standards, the collective bargaining exception, the uniform percentage rule, and the integration rules. Delayed vesting may also tend to favor the highly compensated if employee turnover is higher among the nonhighly compensated employees. Since 1982 a plan that skews too much of its benefits toward the employer's owners and officers is required under IRC § 416 to meet additional qualification requirements that are intended to shift more benefits back to the general employee group.

1.   *Definition of top-heavy plan.* Every qualified plan, other than governmental plans, must include the "top-heavy" provisions of IRC § 416, which take effect when the plan becomes top-heavy. A plan is top-heavy if more than 60 percent of the plan's benefits are for statutorily

defined "key employees." For defined benefit plans, the benefits are measured by the present value of the cumulative accrued benefits; for defined contribution plans, the benefits are measured by the account balances of the employees. IRC § 416(g)(1)(A). A plan's status for a given plan year is generally decided on the last day of the preceding plan year, except that in the first plan year the last day of the first plan year is used. IRC § 416(g)(4)(C).

An employee is considered a key employee if, during the prior plan year, the employee was:

(1) an officer of the employer with an annual compensation greater than $130,000, adjusted for inflation ($170,000 for 2014 and 2015);

(2) a more than 5-percent owner of the employer; or

(3) a more than 1-percent owner of the employer with an annual compensation greater than $150,000.

Regulations have been issued fleshing out the highly technical rules and definitions contained in the statute. Treas. Reg. § 1.416–1. Many a plan sponsor, faced with intricacies of determining whether a plan is top-heavy, has decided simply to assume so and conform the plan to the top-heavy requirements.

2. *Top-heavy plan requirements.* When a plan is top-heavy, two additional qualification requirements apply. First, a top-heavy plan must provide specified minimum contributions or benefits for plan participants who are not key employees. IRC § 416(c). For defined contribution plans, the employer contribution for non-key employees must generally equal at least 3 percent of compensation. The contribution may be less than 3 percent provided that it is not less than the highest percentage of compensation made for any key employee. An employee's own elective deferrals cannot be counted toward this minimum contribution, but any employer matching contributions are counted. IRC §§ 401(k)(4)(C) & 416(c)(2)(A). For defined benefit plans, non-key employees must accrue a minimum benefit that, when expressed as an annual retirement benefit, equals the lesser of 2 percent of the employee's average compensation multiplied by years of service or 20 percent of the employee's average compensation. Average compensation is determined by reference to the period of the employee's most highly compensated consecutive years of service (not exceeding five). The required minimum contribution or benefit may not be integrated with Social Security or offset by any other benefits under other federal or state laws. IRC § 416(e).

Second, top-heavy plans must provide more rapid vesting than is generally required of qualified plans: either three-year full vesting or graded vesting beginning at 20 percent after two years of service and reaching 100 percent after six years. IRC § 416(b)(1). Note that, since the top heavy rules were enacted in 1982, this vesting schedule has been extended to employer matching contributions and, more recently, to other employer contributions to defined contribution plans.

3. *Multiple plans.* When an employer has more than one plan, all plans covering at least one key employee, together with any plans which enable any of such key employee plans to meet the discrimination rules, must be combined and tested as one plan for top-heavy purposes. In addition, an employer may elect to add any other plans to this group for

top-heavy testing, provided the resulting group would continue to satisfy the discrimination rules taking into account such plans. IRC § 416(g)(2). If the group is top-heavy, all plans required to be included in the group are top-heavy; if the group is not top-heavy, none of the plans in the group is top-heavy.

When an employer has more than one plan that is top-heavy, it is not necessary for each plan to provide the required minimum benefits or contributions. IRC § 416(f). The regulations provide guidance on preventing duplication or omission of the top-heavy requirements. Treas. Reg. § 1.416–1, M–12.

4. *Collective bargaining agreements.* The top-heavy minimum vesting and minimum benefits requirements do not apply to employees covered by a collective bargaining agreement, provided that retirement benefits were the subject of good faith bargaining between employee representatives and the employer. IRC § 416(i)(4).

QUESTIONS

1. Consider the profit-sharing plan examples in Tables 6.1 and 6.2 above. Assume that A is the only key employee (i.e., B, C, and D have no ownership interest and are not officers). Which of the plans is currently top-heavy? Assuming that each plan already uses the 6-year graded vesting schedule in IRC § 416(b)(1)(B) and that the employer has no defined benefit plan, do the top-heavy plan requirements alter the distribution of plan benefits?

2. Why do the top-heavy plan limitations focus on officer or stock ownership status in determining whether the plan is top-heavy? A plan set up to benefit mainly those who control the business certainly appears abusive of the tax subsidy. Yet those who control the business may, for obvious business reasons, choose to provide plan benefits to a wider group of highly compensated employees. Such a plan would seem to be equally wasteful of the subsidy if only a relatively small proportion of plan benefits flowed to rank-and-file employees. Why not include highly compensated employees in the key employee group?

3. The top-heavy plan requirements were enacted at a time when the integration and vesting rules were less strict than today and when there was no limit on the amount of compensation that could be taken into account under a plan. A plan was able to delay any vesting for ten years and then integrate with Social Security in a fashion that totally eliminated benefits for low-paid workers. Are the top-heavy plan rules still warranted? Are some plans so top-heavy that they should be disqualified even if they provide a certain level of benefits to non-key employees?

E. ELECTIVE CONTRIBUTIONS TO 401(k) PLANS — tax deferred

Normally it is the employer who structures the coverage of a plan and determines its benefits and contributions. However, certain plans may provide for elective employee contributions (either after-tax or before-tax) and may also provide for some form of matching employer contributions. These plans raise the same tax policy problem as those without employee discretion. Lower paid employees will frequently prefer cash wages over retirement saving. The tax benefits, which are more modest the lower one's income, may not be sufficient to alter this preference. The highly compensated, who are more likely to have disposable income to save, will more often find the tax benefits of retirement saving attractive. Thus, Congress faces the same problem: structuring discrimination rules that will enhance the rank-and-file retirement saving without giving excessive tax subsidies to the highly compensated.

The most common type of elective arrangement is the qualified cash or deferred arrangement (CODA) under a profit-sharing or stock bonus plan, usually referred to as a 401(k) plan. Under such an arrangement an employee may elect to have the employer make contributions either to the plan or directly in cash to the employee. If a CODA is not "qualified" under IRC § 401(k), the employee will be taxed on the elective contributions made to the plan. See IRC § 402(e)(3); 1.402(a)–1(d)(1). As discussed more fully in Chapter 10, infra, elective contributions to 401(k) plans are subject to a more stringent dollar limitation ($17,500 in 2014, $18,000 in 2010) than contributions to regular profit-sharing plans ($52,000 in 2014 and $53,000 in 2010).

In order to be "qualified," a CODA must satisfy a number of special requirements. Unlike a normal profit-sharing plan, which may permit in-service withdrawals merely by reason of the lapse of a fixed number of years or the attainment of a certain age, a qualified CODA may not permit in-service withdrawals prior to age 59½ except under a limited number of specified circumstances. IRC § 401(k)(2)(B). These distribution limitations are discussed in Chapter 11. The employee must be immediately vested in amounts attributable to elective contributions. IRC § 401(k)(2)(C). Also, no more than one year of service may be required as a condition of participation in the plan. IRC § 401(k)(2)(D). In addition, no employer-provided benefit may be conditioned on the employee electing to contribute to a CODA, except for employer matching contributions. IRC § 401(k)(4)(A).

Although normally an employee is not taxed on any elective contribution to a 401(k) plan, such plans can allow an employee to designate irrevocably all or a part of the elective deferral as a "designated Roth contribution." See IRC § 402A. A designated Roth contribution is taxable in the year of the deferral. Apart from being taxable, a designated Roth contribution is treated as an elective deferral for all other purposes, including all of the limitations discussed in this section. IRC § 402A(a)(1).

1. *Coverage and nondiscrimination requirements.* A qualified CODA must also meet participation and nondiscrimination standards. First, the employees eligible to benefit under the arrangement must satisfy the minimum coverage requirements of IRC § 410(b)(1). Second, unless the CODA meets one of the design-based safe harbors discussed infra, the "actual deferral percentage" (ADP) for eligible highly compensated employees must meet either of the following tests: (1) it is not more than 1.25 times the ADP of all other eligible employees in the *preceding* year (the "125 percent test"); or (2) it does not exceed the ADP of all other eligible employees in the *preceding* year by more than 2 percentage points and it is not more than twice that ADP (the "alternative limitation"). IRC § 401(k)(3)(A). A CODA which meets this

ADP test is deemed to satisfy the IRC § 401(a)(4) nondiscrimination requirement. IRC § 401(k)(3)(C).

By comparing the ADP of the highly compensated employees for the current year with the ADP of the nonhighly compensated employees for the *previous* year, the statute permits the employer to control more easily the amount of deferral by the highly compensated so that the ADP test can be met. The employer can elect to use the current year in computing the ADP of the nonhighly compensated employees, but such an election, if made, may only be changed with the IRS's permission. For newly established plans, the employer has the option of using either 3 percent or the ADP in the current year as the ADP for the previous year.

The ADP for a specified group of employees for a plan year is defined as the average of the ratios (calculated separately for each employee in the group) of the amount of elective contributions made on behalf of the employee for the plan year to the employee's compensation for the plan year. "Compensation" for this purpose is determined according to IRC § 414(s). The compensation limitation of IRC § 401(a)(17), $265,000 in 2015 and $260,000 in 2014, applies to this computation. Treas.Reg. § 1.401(a)(17)–1(c)(1). Thus, an employee who earns $1 million in compensation and elects to defer $18,000 in 2015has a 6.79 percent individual deferral percentage, not 1.8 percent.

For an illustration of how the test works, assume the compensation and amounts deferred under 401(k) plan are as follows:

TABLE 9.3

CASH OR DEFERRED ARRANGEMENT

Employee	Compensation	Elective Contribution	Individual Deferral Percentage
A*	$150,000	$5,250	3.50
B	30,000	600	2.00
C	15,000	150	1.00

* The figures for A are the *current* year; the figures for B and C are for the *preceding* year.

Assuming that employee A is the only highly compensated employee, the ADP for the highly compensated group is 3.50 percent. The ADP for the other employees is 1.50 percent (the average of 2.00 and 1.00 percent). Because 3.50 exceeds 1.875 percent (1.50 times1.25), the 125 percent test is not satisfied. Moreover, since 3.50 percent is more than twice 1.50 percent, the alternative limitation is also not met. The most that A can defer and still meet the ADP test is 3 percent. Under a traditional 401(k) plan, the "excess contribution" of $750 would normally have to be returned to A. The handling of excess contributions is described below. Note that if employee C had contributed $225, instead of $150, the ADP test would have been satisfied. This illustrates how important it may be for some plans to encourage the participation of lower-paid employees.

Note that a qualified plan is not automatically disqualified under IRC § 401(a) merely because it includes a nonqualified CODA. See Treas. Reg. § 1.401(k)–1(a)(5)(iv). However, the elective deferrals would be treated as employer contributions for purposes of applying the general nondiscrimination test under IRC § 401(a)(4). Treas. Reg. § 1.401(k)–1(a)(5)(ii). In a typical plan that had no or at best uniform nonelective employer contributions, this would make the employer contributions nonuniform in favor of the highly compensated employees, which would generally disqualify the plan under IRC § 401(a)(4).

2.   *Catch-up contributions for individuals age 50 or over.* A plan can allow participants who have attained age 50 by the end of the year to make additional elective deferrals above the otherwise applicable limits. IRC § 414(v). These "catch-up contributions" were introduced in 2002 and are limited to $5,000, adjusted for inflation in years after 2006. The 2014 maximum is $5,500 and the 2015 maximum is $6,000. The term "catch-up" is a bit of a misnomer, since there is no requirement that catch-up contributions make up for lower contributions in the past.

A key feature of catch-up contributions is that they are not subject to any of the usual contribution or deduction limitations and are not taken into account in applying the contribution or deduction limits to other contributions or benefits under any plan. IRC § 414(v)(3). For example, catch-up contributions are ignored for purposes of ADP testing. Thus, in the example illustrated in Table 9.3, if A were 50 or over, the excess contribution of $750 would not have to be returned. In fact, A could have deferred an additional $5,250 during the year (in 2015).

Would you expect the catch-up contribution rule to benefit primarily highly compensated employees? A recent study by a major plan provider revealed that only 13% of those eligible to make a catch-up contribution actually did so and "as expected, participants with high household incomes were more likely to take advantage of this plan feature than their less affluent coworkers." Catch-Up Contributions in 2004: Plan Sponsor and Participant Adoption, Vanguard Center for Retirement Research, April 2005, p. 1.

3.   *Matching contributions.* One way to encourage participation in a 401(k) plan is to provide for employer matching contributions. The match can be structured in a fashion that provides a higher match on smaller elective contributions. For example, the employer might match the first one percent of pay contributed by the employee on a dollar-for-dollar basis, but match additional contributions on a 50 cents-on-the-dollar basis or on some declining scale. These matching contributions must themselves satisfy a special nondiscrimination rule known as the actual contribution percentage (ACP) test, which largely parallels the ADP test. See IRC § 401(m); Treas. Reg. § 1.401(m)–1.

Unlike elective deferrals, matching contributions do not have to be immediately vested, although they are subject to a slightly more accelerated vesting schedule than applied to contributions for years prior to 2002: either 3-year cliff vesting or 6-year graded vesting. IRC § 411(a)(12). However, if an employer is willing to vest the matching contributions immediately and subject them to the same in service withdrawal limitations imposed on elective deferrals, the matching contributions can be treated as elective contributions for purposes of the ADP test. These are referred to as qualified matching contributions (QMACs). See Treas. Reg. §§ 1.401(k)–2(a)(6) & 1.401(k)–6. This rule is crucial for many plans, since QMACs can enable a plan to qualify, even though the elective deferrals alone would fail the ADP test.

For example, assume that the CODA in Table 9.3 contained a dollar-for-dollar employer match up to the first one percent of pay. Taking into account the matching contributions, the individual deferral percentages would be the following:

TABLE 9.4

CASH OR DEFERRED ARRANGEMENT

Employee	Compensation	Qualified Matching Contribution	Elective Deferral	Individual Deferral Percentage
A*	$150,000	$1,500	$5,250	4.50
B	30,000	300	600	3.00
C	15,000	150	150	2.00

* The figures for A are the *current* year; the figures for B and C are for the *preceding* year.

The ADP for the nonhighly compensated employees is 2.50 percent. Since the highly compensated employee ADP meets the alternative limitation (200 percent/2 percentage points), the ADP test is just satisfied. $5,250 is the maximum deferral that A can make given the deferrals made by B and C.

4.   *Nonelective contributions.* Often 401(k) plans consist only of elective deferrals and a limited employer matching contribution. But 401(k) plans are profit-sharing plans and employers may also make contributions that are not tied to employee elective deferrals. If an employer is willing to vest these nonelective contributions immediately and subject them to the same in-service withdrawal limitations imposed on elective deferrals, these contributions may also be treated as elective contributions for ADP test purposes, just like QMACs. Such contributions are referred to as qualified nonelective contributions (QNECs). See Treas. Reg. §§ 1.401(k)–2(a)(6) & 1.401(k)–6.

Thus, in the example in Table 9.4 above, if instead of making matching contributions, the employer simply contributed one percent of salary on behalf of each participant and these contributions were fully vested and subject to same in-service withdrawal limitations as the elective contributions, the plan would meet the ADP test. The nonelective contributions must, however, satisfy the discrimination rules of IRC § 401(a)(4). Treas. Reg. § 1.401(k)–2(a)(6)(ii). In this example, since the nonelective contribution is a uniform percentage of compensation, the requirements of IRC § 401(a)(4) are easily met.

5.   *Design-based safe harbors.* The ADP test for 401(k) plans is complex and costly. An employer must do the record keeping necessary to monitor employee elections, perform the required calculations to apply the test, and administer the correction mechanism. Employer groups lobbied for many years for a design-based safe harbor test, and one was enacted as part of the Small Business Job Protection Act of 1996; it became effective in 2000. IRC § 401(k)(12).

A plan can satisfy the safe harbor by meeting one of two contribution requirements: (1) a minimum nonelective contribution requirement, or (2) a matching contribution requirement. IRC § 401(k)(12). The minimum nonelective contribution requirement is met if the employer makes a nonelective contribution to a defined contribution plan of at least 3 percent of an employee's compensation on behalf of each nonhighly compensated employee who is eligible to participate in the arrangement, without regard to whether the employee makes elective contributions under the arrangement. The matching contribution requirement is met if (1) the employer makes a matching contribution on behalf of each nonhighly compensated employee that is equal to (a) 100 percent of the employee's elective contributions up to 3 percent of compensation, and (b) 50 percent of the employee's elective contributions from 3 to 5 percent of compensation; and (2) the match rate for highly compensated employees is not greater than the match rate for nonhighly compensated employees at any level of compensation. The employer matching and nonelective contributions used to satisfy the safe harbor requirement must be fully vested and subject to the same restrictions on withdrawals as apply to the employee's elective deferrals.

There is flexibility in selecting the safe harbor matching formula, as long as the rate of the employer's matching contribution does not increase as the employee's rate of elective contribution increases, and the aggregate amount of matching contributions at least equals the amount that would be made using the formula above. IRC § 401(k)(12)(B)(iii). For example, an employer match of 100 percent of the employee's elective contributions up to 4 percent of compensation would satisfy the contribution requirement.

As long as the employer makes the safe harbor minimum contribution or minimum match for every nonhighly compensated participant, there is no ADP testing and the highly compensated employees are free to contribute up to the maximum permitted by IRC §§ 402(g) and 415. To illustrate this significant relaxation of the usual ADP test, assume that the matching contribution in Table 9.4 were changed to the minimum matching contribution under the safe harbor— i.e., a dollar-for-dollar match up to the first 3 percent of pay and a 50 cents match for each additional dollar deferred between 3 and 5 percent of pay. A would thereby be permitted to contribute up to the maximum $18,000 (in 2015) which would produce the following allocation:

TABLE 9.5

SAFE HARBOR CASH OR DEFERRED ARRANGEMENT

Employee	Compensation	Safe Harbor Matching Contribution	Elective Contribution	Individual Deferral Percentage
A	$150,000	$6,000	$18,000	16.00
B	30,000	600	600	4.00
C	15,000	150	150	2.00

Without the safe-harbor test, A's maximum permitted deferral would have been much less. The nonhighly compensated employee ADP (including the QMAC) is 3 percent, which under the standard ADP test would limit A's percentage (including the QMAC) to 5 percent. Thus, A could have deferred only $3,750, for a total contribution, including the equal employer match, of $7,500—i.e., only 1/3 of what the safe harbor allows.

Note that A's permitted contributions and employer match in Table 9.5 would be the same even if B and C elected to defer $0. In addition, if

A is 50 or older, A can make an additional catch-up contribution of $6,000 (in 2015). So A might end up with a $30,000 contribution even if no nonhighly compensated employee benefited at all. Concerned about precisely such scenarios, the Clinton Administration was opposed to the minimum matching contribution safe harbor, unless the safe harbor also required the employer to make a minimum nonelective contribution of one percent of compensation for nonhighly compensated employees. The safe harbor was ultimately enacted without the one percent minimum.

Before the safe harbors were enacted, employers had an incentive to encourage low-paid workers to elect deferrals, because such deferrals enabled the highly-compensated employees to defer more. Since under the safe harbors the actual deferrals by the low-paid workers are irrelevant, and under the matching contribution safe harbor such deferrals are actually costly to the employer, would you expect employers to publicize their 401(k) plans vigorously and encourage their employees to participate? To use the safe harbor, the employer must, within a reasonable period before any year, give to each employee eligible to participate in the arrangement written notice of the employee's rights and obligations under the arrangement. IRC § 401(k)(12)(D). Does this solve the problem?

6. *SIMPLE plans for small employers.* Small employers (100 or fewer employees who receive $5,000 or more in compensation) have still another way to provide elective deferrals without having to meet the ADP test: the savings incentive match plan for employees ("SIMPLE") 401(k) plan. See IRC § 401(k)(11). Such a plan is much like a safe harbor 401(k) plan, but with a few key differences. First, the required nonelective or matching contributions are lower. The nonelective contribution must be 2 percent of compensation for each eligible employee earning $5,000 or more; the matching contribution must be 100 percent of the elective deferral up to 3 percent of compensation. Second, the maximum employee elective deferral is also lower ($12,500 for a SIMPLE plan v. $18,000 for a regular 401(k) plan in 2015) and the deferral itself must be expressed as a percentage of compensation. Third, the employer cannot provide any other qualified plan to the employees eligible to participate in the SIMPLE plan. IRC § 401(k)(11)(C). Fourth, a SIMPLE plan is exempt from treatment as a top-heavy plan under IRC § 416, whereas other 401(k) plans are not exempt. IRC § 401(k)(11)(D)(ii).

A SIMPLE plan need not be a qualified plan, but can simply be an IRA for each employee, just like a SEP. IRC § 408(p). At one time SEPs themselves were permitted to provide employees with a cash or deferred election, but since 1996 the creation of new salary reduction SEPs ("SARSEPs") has been forbidden. A SIMPLE IRA plan must meet essentially the same requirements as a SIMPLE 401(k) plan, with two important exceptions. First, instead of matching elective deferrals up to 3 percent of compensation, the employer may elect a lower percentage contribution (but not less than one percent), for up to two years out of any five year period. IRC § 408(p)(2)(C)(ii). Second, a SIMPLE IRA plan must cover each employee who received at least $5,000 in compensation from the employer during any two prior years and who is reasonably expected to receive at least $5,000 in compensation in the current year.

7. *Automatic enrollment.* Another strategy some employers use to increase 401(k) coverage is to reverse the default rule and enroll employees automatically as soon as they become eligible to participate in the 401(k) plan. Employees are deemed to have elected to defer a specified percentage of compensation unless they elect otherwise. Although there was initially some concern that such an arrangement might not preserve enough employee choice to constitute a cash or deferred arrangement, automatic enrollment is now expressly authorized in the regulations. See Treas. Reg. § 1.401(k)–1(a)(3)(ii).

A new participant in such automatic (or "autopilot") 401(k) plans is free to opt out, but research from the field of behavioral finance indicates that many participants are not active decision-makers. They tend to follow the default set by the plan, so if the default is to save, they will save, and if the default is to do nothing, they will do nothing. Thus, "automatic enrollment has been shown to be remarkably effective in raising participation rates among eligible workers [from about] 75 percent of eligible employees to between 85 percent and 95 percent." William Gale, J. Mark Iwry, and Peter Orzag, The Automatic 401(k): A Simple Way to Strengthen Retirement Saving, Tax Notes 1207 (March 7, 2005).

Although automatic enrollment can increase participation, it may not increase the overall level of employee saving. In one study, researchers concluded that

> automatic enrollment added to savings by encouraging more people to save in their plan. At the same time, it subtracted from savings by encouraging individuals to remain at too-conservative savings rates and in too-conservative investment defaults. Put another way, some people (those who would have never enrolled) saved more, while others (those who would have saved at a higher rate or invested in different options on their own) saved less. In the end, the two effects were a virtual wash, and automatic enrollment did little to enhance aggregate savings.

Lessons From Behavioral Finance and the Autopilot 401(k) Plan, The Vanguard Center for Retirement Research, April 2004, p. 6. This undesirable effect of employee inertia can be mitigated by providing for gradual automatic increases in employee contributions over time. Even though participants can opt out of scheduled increases, they tend not to, and automatic enrollment coupled with automatic escalation has been shown to increase the overall level of contribution. Richard Thaler and Shlomo Benartzi, Save More Tomorrow: Using Behavioral Economics to Increase Employee Saving, 112 Journal of Political Economy, 164–187 (2004).

The Pension Protection Act of 2006 adds a new design-based safe harbor for a "qualified automatic contribution arrangement", or QACA, which is treated as meeting the ADP test with respect to elective deferrals and the ACP test with respect to matching contributions. IRC §§ 401(k)(13), 401(m)(12). In addition, like traditional safe harbor plans, a plan consisting solely of contributions made pursuant to a QACA is not subject to the top-heavy rules. IRC § 416(g)(4)(H).

To be qualified, the arrangement must meet three requirements: (1) automatic deferral, (2) matching or nonelective contributions, and (3) notice. The automatic deferral requirement is satisfied if employees are deemed to elect to contribute a qualified percentage of their compensation, unless they elect otherwise. A qualified percentage is one that applies uniformly to all eligible employees and does not exceed 10 percent and is not less than 3 percent during their first year of participation, 4 percent during their second, 5 percent during their third and 6 percent during each subsequent year. IRC § 401(k)(13)(C)(iii). The automatic election need not apply to existing employees who have already made an election to participate (or not to participate).

QACA is simple ✓ but vested (not good)

The matching or nonelective contribution requirement is met if the employer makes, on behalf of each nonhighly compensated employee, either (1) a nonelective contribution of at least 3 percent of compensation or (2) a matching contribution of 100 percent of the first one percent of compensation that is deferred and 50 percent of the next 5 percent of compensation deferred. IRC § 401(k)(13)(D)(i), The required matching or nonelective contributions must be 100 vested after no more than two years of service. IRC § 401(k)(13)(D)(iii)(I).

The notice requirement is met if each eligible employee receives a written notice of the employee's rights and obligations under the arrangement within a reasonable period before the beginning of each plan year. IRC § 401(k)(13)(E). The notice must be sufficiently accurate and comprehensive to apprise the employee of those rights and obligations and must be written in a manner calculated to be understood by the average employee. The notice must explain the employee's right not to have automatic contributions made, or to elect a different percentage, and must also explain how contributions will be invested, if the employee does not make an investment election. Employees must be given a reasonable time, after receipt of the notice and before the first elective contribution is made, to make an election with respect to contributions or investments.

Reasons for QACA:
①

A QACA may be more attractive to employers than the original safe harbor. First, the matching contribution requirement is generally lower. For example, if the employee deferred 6 percent or more, an employer using the original safe harbor would need to make a matching contribution of 4 percent of compensation. Under a QACA, the required match would be 3.5 percent. Second, the original safe harbor requires full and immediate vesting of the employer contributions. A QACA allows the plan to require two years of service before employer contributions are fully vested.

②

Beginning in 2010, an employer with 500 or fewer employees can offer an "eligible combined plan", a combined defined benefit and automatic enrollment 401(k) plan ("DB(k) plan") that would automatically satisfy the nondiscrimination rules, provided that certain safe-harbor benefits and contributions are provided. IRC § 414(x). The legislative history indicates that Congress' goal was to encourage smaller employers to maintain defined benefit plans. IRS has not yet issued guidance, but has requested comments on issues relating to eligible combined plans. Notice 2009–71, 2009–35 I.R.B. 262.

The defined benefit part of the eligible combined plan must provide to each participant a minimum employer-provided accrued benefit equal to the lesser of: (1) 1 percent of final average pay multiplied by the participant's years of service with the employer or (2) 20 percent of final average pay. Under a hybrid plan, each participant must receive a minimum pay credit to his or her hypothetical account. A participant must be fully vested after three years of service.

The defined contribution part of the eligible combined plan must include a qualified cash or deferred arrangement, which must also constitute an automatic contribution arrangement. The employer must make matching contributions on behalf of each employee eligible to participate in the qualified CODA: 50 percent of the elective contributions of the employee to the extent such elective contributions do not exceed 4 percent of compensation. The plan may provide for a different rate of matching contribution, provided that the rate of matching contribution does not increase as the participant's rate of elective contribution increases, and the aggregate amount of matching contributions at each rate of elective contribution is no less than the aggregate amount of matching contributions that would be provided under the basic matching contribution requirement. In no case may the rate of matching contribution for any elective contribution of a highly compensated employee at any rate of elective contribution be higher than the rate of matching contribution for a nonhighly compensated employee. All participants must be fully vested in any matching contributions, including any matching contributions that exceed the required matching contributions. A participant must be fully vested in any nonelective contributions after three years of service.

8. *Correction of excess contributions.* Although QMACs or QNECs can enable an employer to satisfy the ADP test or the safe harbors, such contributions may increase the cost of a 401(k) plan beyond an acceptable level. An alternative method of meeting the ADP test is to return the "excess contributions" (and allocable income) to the highly compensated employees within 12 months of the end of the plan year. IRC § 401(k)(8). The term "excess contributions" is defined to mean the excess of the aggregate amount of employer contributions paid on behalf of the highly compensated employees over the maximum amount of such contributions permitted under the ADP test. IRC § 401(k)(8)(B). This maximum amount is determined by reducing contributions made on behalf of the highly compensated employees in order of their individual deferral *percentages*, beginning with the highest of those percentages. However, the distribution of the excess contributions is made to the highly compensated employees on the basis of the *amount* of their contributions. IRC § 401(k)(8)(C). Thus, distributions are made first to those highly compensated employees with the highest dollar amount of deferral, even if their percentage deferral is lower than that of other highly compensated employees due to their higher salaries. See Treas. Reg. § 1.401(k)–2(b)(2).

The distribution of excess contributions may be made "without regard to any other provision of law." IRC § 401(k)(8)(A). Thus, the limitation on involuntary cash-outs in IRC § 411(a)(11) and the requirement of spousal consent to cash-outs in IRC § 417(e) do not apply.

In addition, the distributions are not subject to the tax on early withdrawals under IRC § 72(t).

The tax treatment of the return of excess contributions can be complex. If the distribution of the excess contributions (and any allocable income) occurs within 2½ months of the end of the plan year, it will generally be taxable to the employee in the contribution year, not the distribution year. IRC § 4979(f)(2). Taxation in the distribution year occurs only if the excess contribution is less than $100. However, if the distribution includes a return of designated Roth contributions, that amount is not taxable since it never reduced the employee's income to begin with. Plans can allow employees to elect which type of contribution is returned if both pre-tax and Roth contributions have been made during the year. See Treas. Reg. § 1.401(k)–2(b)(1)(ii), –2(b)(2)(vi)(C).

If the distribution is not made within 2½ months of the end of the plan year, it will be taxable in the year of distribution, but the employer must pay a 10 percent excise tax on the excess contributions. IRC § 4979.

The distribution of excess contributions must also include any income allocable to the excess contributions, through the end of the plan year for which the contribution was made. IRC § 401(k)(8)(A)(i). The distribution of the excess contributions and allocable income is treated as if it were earned and received by the payee in the year of the distribution. IRC § 4979(f)(2). If the distribution is not made within 2 ½ months (6 months in the case of a QACA) after the end of the plan year, the employer must pay a 10 percent excise tax on the excess contributions. IRC § 4979.

9.   *Recharacterization.* As an alternative to distributing the excess contributions, an employer can elect to recharacterize them as an amount distributed to the employee and then contributed by the employee to the plan. IRC § 401(k)(8)(A)(ii); Treas. Reg. § 1.401(k)–2(b)(3). Recharacterization must take place within 2½ months of the end of the plan year and recharacterized excess contributions are taxed to the employee in the year to which the contributions relate. For nondiscrimination purposes, recharacterized amounts are treated as employee after-tax contributions for the year in which the elective contributions would have been received (but for the deferral election). Since employee after-tax contributions, together with employer matching contributions, must themselves satisfy a special nondiscrimination rule known as the actual contribution percentage (ACP) test, which largely parallels the ADP test, recharacterization will rarely be an alternative to distribution. See IRC § 401(m); Treas. Reg. § 1.401(m)–1.

QUESTIONS

1.   Consider the examples in Tables 6.4 and 6.5. If an employer were to establish a nonelective plan that contributed 4.5 (or 14) percent on behalf of the highly compensated and 2.5 (or 3) percent on behalf of the nonhighly compensated, the plan would be disqualified for violating IRC § 401(a)(4). Why is such a difference acceptable when it is part of a 401(k) plan? Is it significant that 401(k) plans require full and immediate vesting, but standard plans do not?

2. A regular IRA has no discrimination rules and the contribution limit is $5,500 (in 2015). A SIMPLE plan has a modest minimum employer contribution (or match) and the contribution limit is $12,500 (in 2015). A regular 401(k) plan either has a more substantial minimum employer contribution (or match) than a SIMPLE plan or by means of the ADP test precludes highly compensated employees from deferring too much more than other employees; the contribution limit is $18,000 (in 2015). A defined contribution plan (other than a 401(k) plan) has the strictest discrimination rules of all, but as discussed in Chapter 10, contributions can be as high as $53,000 (in 2015). Can you explain this pattern?

3. A and B are equal partners in a partnership that operates a restaurant. All of the employees of the restaurant are covered by a collective bargaining agreement that provides a pension plan through a multiemployer pension fund. May A and B establish a profit-sharing plan for themselves that also has a qualified CODA? Assume that A and B disagree on the percentage of income to be contributed to the plan. Is there a way, other than a 401(k) plan, for A and B to have different percentages contributed? See Treas. Reg. § 1.401(k)–1(a)(6).

CHAPTER 10

LIMITATIONS ON BENEFITS, CONTRIBUTIONS, AND DEDUCTIONS

Analysis

Introduction

In Chapter 9 we discussed the Internal Revenue Code's attempt to prevent retirement plans from unduly favoring highly compensated employees. These discrimination rules focus on the coverage and level of contributions or benefits of the highly compensated employees compared with the nonhighly compensated employees. The standard is a relative one, the goal being to encourage benefits for the lower paid by providing substantial tax benefits to the higher paid.

This chapter deals with limitations on the absolute level of contributions and benefits, as well as limitations on the deduction of plan contributions. Despite the obvious revenue loss, until the enactment of ERISA in 1974 there were no direct limits either on the benefits or on the contributions that a qualified plan could provide to a participant. There were (and still are) maximum limitations on the employer's total deduction for plan contributions, but these were not terribly restrictive. As to profit-sharing and stock bonus plans, an employer could not deduct contributions in excess of 15 percent of the total compensation of all participants. Pension plans were even less restricted; employers could deduct essentially whatever level of contribution was actuarially necessary to fund the benefits promised by the plan. Plan contributions had to be "ordinary and necessary" under IRC § 162 or IRC § 212, but this required only that the total compensation package (i.e., plan contributions plus actual compensation) be reasonable. The benefits

[handwritten margin note: Deduction Limitations Started with ERISA in 1974]

themselves were subject to no specific limitation. Firms could provide enormous pensions to employees whose enormous salaries were themselves "reasonable" for this purpose.

Section A of this chapter focuses mainly on IRC § 415, which establishes individual limitations either on contributions or on benefits, depending on the type of plan. Section B examines IRC § 404, which places limits on the deductibility of the employer's annual contribution. Section C discusses how these limitations apply to plans for self-employed individuals.

Both IRC §§ 415 and 404 are pure tax rules; they have no counterparts in Title I of ERISA. However, the tax system coordinates with ERISA's minimum funding rules by allowing the employer's deductible contribution to be at least as great as the required minimum contribution. But the tax law has a concern that the ERISA regulatory law does not share: preventing overfunding. By overfunding a plan, an employer would gain substantial tax benefits. Thus, IRC § 404 limits the employer's defined benefit plan contribution deduction to an amount which depends on the relationship between a plan's assets and its liabilities. This limitation, which Congress significantly tightened in 1987 and then later loosened, highlights the tension between the goal of more secure pensions (as well as less risk for the PBGC) and the need to control the enormous cost of the tax subsidy for qualified plans.

A. LIMITATIONS ON CONTRIBUTIONS AND BENEFITS

Since 1974, IRC § 415 has set maximum limits on contributions to defined contribution plans and on benefits from defined benefit plans. A plan that exceeds these limits is disqualified. IRC § 401(a)(16). The legislative history indicates that the purpose of ERISA's limitation on contributions and benefits was to prevent partial public financing of excessively large retirement benefits through tax subsidies. H.R. Rep. No. 807, 93d Cong., 2d Sess. 35 (1974). In reviewing these limitations below, consider whether excessively large benefits continue to be subsidized and if so, why.

Limitation Year. The limitations are applied on the basis of a "limitation year" that does not necessarily coincide with the plan year or the employer's taxable year. If the limitation year is other than the calendar year, the dollar limitations which are in effect for a calendar year apply for limitation years beginning in that calendar year. Treas. Reg. § 1.415(j)–1.

Compensation. As we shall see, the maximum limits depend in part on the employee's compensation. The statute itself does not define the term compensation, but the regulations furnish a lengthy list of what is included and excluded. Treas. Reg. § 1.415(c)–(2). Generally, compensation includes wages, salaries, and other amounts received for personal services, but excludes tax-free employee benefits. Although contributions to deferred compensation plans, both qualified and nonqualified, that are excluded from gross income are generally not treated as compensation, IRC § 415(c)(3)(D) specifically includes in compensation elective deferrals under 401(k) plans, 403(b) annuities, and SIMPLE plans, as well as salary reduction contributions to cafeteria plans (IRC § 125), 457 plans and qualified transportation fringe benefit programs.

A distribution from a plan of deferred compensation (whether or not qualified) is generally not compensation for § 415 purposes. However, if the plan so provides, a distribution from an unfunded nonqualified plan will be considered as compensation in the year the distribution is received, to the extent includible in gross income. Treas. Reg. § 1.415(c)–2(c)(1).

[handwritten: What counts as "Compensation"]

Amounts realized from the exercise of nonqualified stock options or from the disposition of stock acquired under a qualified stock option are not includible as compensation. Treas. Reg. § 1.415(c)–2(c)(2).

The regulations also provide a number of safe harbor provisions and alternative definitions. In particular, a plan may define compensation to mean either "wages" for purposes of income tax withholding or the wages and other compensation reported on the W-2 form, with elective deferrals added back in. Treas. Reg. § 1.415(c)–2(d).

Payments made after severance from employment are generally not treated as compensation. The only exceptions are payments made within 2½ months after the later of severance from employment or the end of the limitation year that includes the date of severance, that are for (1) accrued bona fide sick, vacation, or other leave, or (2) normal compensation, overtime, commissions, or bonuses that would have been paid to the employee absent a severance from employment. Treas. Reg. § 1.415(c)–(2)(e)(3).

Multiple plans. The limitations on contributions and benefits are applied to an employer that sponsors multiple plans by treating all defined benefit plans of an employer as one defined benefit plan and treating all defined contribution plans as one defined contribution plan. IRC § 415(f). The controlled group, common control, affiliated service group, and employee leasing rules also apply so that plans of various separate employers may be aggregated. In addition, the controlled group and common control definitions are broadened by reducing the 80 percent test for determining parent-subsidiary groups to 50 percent. IRC § 415(h). If the limits of § 415 are exceeded when plans are aggregated, the regulations provide the order in which one or more of the plans will be disqualified. Treas. Reg. § 1.415(g)–1(b)(3).

[handwritten: Limitations apply to EER's that sponsor multiple plans]

When it was first enacted, § 415 had a provision that prevented a plan sponsor from taking complete advantage of both of the separate limits on defined contribution and defined benefit plans. The provision was extraordinarily complex, making it difficult for plan sponsors to comply and for the IRS to audit. Although some commentators sought to mend it rather than end it, see Norman P. Stein, Simplification and IRC § 415, 2 Fla. Tax Rev. 69 (1994), the provision was repealed in 1996, effective in 2000. The repeal has allowed some employers, particularly small employers and the self-employed, to take maximum advantage of both the defined benefit and defined contribution plan limits.

1. DEFINED CONTRIBUTION PLANS *[handwritten: Annual Addition Contribution Limits]*

The "annual additions" to a participant's defined contribution account must not exceed the lesser of (a) $40,000 indexed for inflation in

[handwritten: 1]

$1,000 increments ($52,000 in 2014, $53,000 in 2015), or (b) 100 percent of the participant's compensation. "Annual additions" include not only employer contributions, but also employee contributions and forfeitures. IRC § 415(c)(2). Rollovers to a plan from other qualified plans or IRAs are not treated as contributions for this purpose.

It is important to emphasize that § 415 limits only what is contributed to a participant's account, not what ultimately accumulates in it. Thus, shrewd (or lucky) investing can generate unlimited wealth in such accounts without fear of disqualification.

1. *Elective deferrals.* Elective deferrals are subject not only to the § 415 limit, but also to an additional limitation on the amount of such deferrals that an individual can exclude from gross income in any year. IRC § 402(g). This limit, sometimes referred to as the "402(g) limit" or the "exclusion amount", is $17,500 in 2014 and $18,000 in 2015, indexed for inflation in $500 increments. Elective deferrals include not only employer contributions to a 401(k) plan under a cash or deferred arrangement, but also similar salary deferrals under a SEP, a SIMPLE IRA, or a 403(b) plan. A special rule permits elective deferrals under a 403(b) plan to exceed this limitation somewhat under certain circumstances. IRC § 402(g)(7).

Note that the limitation on excess deferrals is applicable to the individual employee. Thus, unlike the general § 415 limitation on contributions and benefits, employees who have multiple employers may not make multiple use of the limitation. Employers are not responsible for monitoring the deferrals of their employees with respect to other employers. However, it is a requirement of plan qualification that a plan provide that any elective deferrals under the plan and all other plans, contracts, or arrangements of the employer maintaining the plan may not exceed the 402(g) limit. IRC § 401(a)(30).

2. *Catch-up contributions.* Individuals who have attained age 50 by the end of the year are permitted to make additional elective deferrals (so-called "catch-up" contributions) above the otherwise applicable limits under both § 415 and § 402(g). IRC § 414(v). The additional amount is $5,500 in 2014 and $6,000 in 2015, indexed for inflation in $500 increments, but cannot exceed the participant's compensation reduced by any other elective deferrals. For participants in SIMPLE plans, this additional amount is $2,500 in 2014 and $3,000 in 2015.

For example, in 2015 the § 415(c) contribution limit is $53,000 for a participant earning $53,000 or more. Normal elective deferrals are subject to this limit, so if an employer makes a nonelective contribution of $35,000 on behalf of a participant, the participant could normally make a maximum elective deferral of $18,000. If the participant were age 50 or over, the participant could defer an additional $6,000 under the catch-up provision.

3. *Excess deferrals.* The amounts exceeding the 402(g) limitation and not qualifying as catch-up contributions (the "excess deferrals") are taxable to the employee in the year of the deferral, but if designated Roth contributions have been made they will offset the taxable amount. IRC § 402(g)(1)(A). This makes sense since the designated Roth contributions are taxable in any event.

As long as the excess deferrals (plus any allocable income) are returned to the employee by April 15 of the following year, only the allocable income will be taxable in the distribution year. IRC § 402(g)(2)(C). But if the April 15 deadline is not met, the excess deferrals will be taxed a second time when they are distributed. IRC §§ 402(g)(6), 402A(d)(3).

— Excess Deferrals and when to tax

4. *SEPs, SIMPLE IRAs, and 403(b) plans.* The limitations of § 415 also apply to SEPs and 403(b) plans, even though they are technically not qualified plans. IRC § 415(a)(2). The § 415 rules for 403(b) plans differ from those applicable to qualified plans and can be a trap for the unwary. Generally, a 403(b) plan is not aggregated with other plans that are maintained by the participant's employer, because the 403(b) plan is deemed to be maintained by the participant, not by the employer, for purposes of section 415. However, if a participant in a 403(b) plan is in control of any employer for a limitation year, the 403(b) plan is treated as a defined contribution plan maintained by both the controlled employer and the participant for that limitation year and so the 403(b) plan is aggregated with all other defined contribution plans maintained by the employer. For example, assume that a physician is employed by a tax-exempt hospital and participates in its 403(b) plan. The physician also has her own professional practice, entirely separate from the hospital, which she owns and thus controls. For § 415 purposes, any contributions for her to the practice's 401(k) plan are aggregated with contributions made for her to the hospital's 403(b) plan. IRC § 415(k); Treas. Reg. § 1.415(f)–1(f). The limitations of § 415 do not expressly apply to SIMPLE IRAs. Is this an oversight?

5. *Section 457 plans.* Under IRC § 457(b)(2), in order to be an eligible deferred compensation plan of a tax-exempt or state or local governmental employer, the maximum amount that can be deferred is the lesser of (1) $17,500 in 2014 and $18,000 in 2015, indexed for inflation in $500 increments, or (2) the participant's compensation. Unlike other plans, the § 457(b) limit applies to employer contributions as well as employee deferrals. Unlike 403(b) plans, 457 plans are not subject to the limitations of § 415. The dollar limit can be up to twice the otherwise applicable amount in the three years prior to reaching normal retirement age under the plan, provided the participant did not take full advantage of the limit in prior years. IRC § 457(b)(3). "Catch-up" elective deferrals under IRC § 414(v) for employees age 50 or older are also available under governmental 457 plans, but the participant cannot take advantage of both the special increase in the dollar limit and the catch-up rule. Although at one time the § 457 dollar limit was coordinated with the 402(g) limit on elective deferrals, since 2001 this is no longer the case. This is a very significant advantage that 457 plan participants have over participants in 401(k) and 403(b) plans. In 2015 an eligible employee could defer $18,000 under a section 401(k) or 403(b) plan and an additional $18,000 under a 457 plan (and if at least age 50, an additional $6,000 catch-up contribution to each). Recall that ERISA generally precludes unfunded plans in the private sector unless they qualify as top-hat plans. Thus, this form of "double-dipping" can be made available to rank-and-file employees only in the public sector.

6.   *Coordination of IRAs with qualified plans.* Traditional IRAs are a form of do-it-yourself deferral. The maximum deductible contribution that can be made to an IRA generally is the lesser of $5,500 in 2014 and 2015, or 100 percent of an individual's compensation. IRC § 219(b). The dollar limitation is indexed for inflation in $500 increments, is increased by a "catch-up" amount of $1,000 for individuals age 50 and over, and is not directly coordinated with other forms of tax-deferred savings. However, the dollar limitation may be reduced if the individual or the individual's spouse is an "active participant" in any qualified plan, 403(b) annuity, SEP, or SIMPLE IRA. IRC § 219(g).

The amount of the reduction depends on the individual's modified adjusted gross income (MAGI). For a married individual filing jointly, a reduction in the dollar limitation is made if the MAGI (computed without the IRA deduction) exceeds $98,000 in 2015, and the limit reduces down to zero for a MAGI in excess of $118,000 in 2015. For singles the phaseout begins at $61,000 and is complete at $71,000. If only one of the spouses is an active participant, the phaseout for the *nonactive* participant spouse begins at $183,000 in 2015. IRC § 219(g)(7). For example, assume H and W are married and file jointly and that H is an active participant in his employer's qualified plan, but that W's employer has no plan. If H and W have a MAGI of $120,000, H cannot make a deductible IRA contribution, but W can make the maximum $5,500 deductible contribution.

Unlike traditional IRAs, contributions to Roth IRAs are not affected by participation in qualified plans, 403(b) annuities, SEPs, or SIMPLE IRAs. However, the maximum contribution to a Roth IRA, which is essentially the same as the maximum contribution to a traditional IRA (reduced by any IRA contributions), is reduced or eliminated for high-income taxpayers. IRC § 408A(c)(3). For a married taxpayer filing jointly the phaseout begins at an AGI of $183,000 and for singles at $116,000 in 2015. Thus, in the example of H and W above, H could contribute $5,500 to a Roth IRA, even though H cannot contribute to a traditional IRA because of his participation in his employer's qualified plan. Since for many taxpayers a contribution to a Roth IRA is preferable to a contribution to a traditional IRA, the restriction on an active participant's deduction of IRA contributions is largely irrelevant except for a small percentage of taxpayers. Also, contributions can be made to a Roth IRA after age 70½, though deductible contributions to a regular IRA would no longer be allowed. IRC §§ 408A(c)(4), 219(d)(1).

QUESTIONS

1.   Assuming an 8% rate of return, a 35-year-old who has an annual addition of $53,000 each year to a profit-sharing plan would have more than $6 million in her account at age 65. Is the IRC § 415(c) limit too high?

2.   What is the justification for a special limit on the amount of elective deferrals? Would lowering the limit encourage traditional pension plans? Does a higher limit encourage employers who do not have a pension plan, particularly small employers, to adopt elective plans, such as 401(k) plans and SIMPLE IRAs?

3.   Should regular and Roth IRA contributions be coordinated with the IRC § 402(g) limit on elective deferrals? With the IRC § 415 limit? Is it relevant that contributions by high-income taxpayers are limited?

2. DEFINED BENEFIT PLANS *Benefit Limits*

Annual Benefit

A defined benefit plan must not provide benefits that, when expressed as an "annual benefit" exceed the lesser of (a) $160,000 (the ① "dollar limitation"), indexed for inflation in increments of $5,000 ($210,000 in 2014 and 2015), or (b) 100 percent of the participant's ② average compensation for his high 3 consecutive years of service. IRC § 415(b). "Annual benefit" is defined to mean a benefit payable annually in the form of a straight life annuity, excluding benefits attributable to employee contributions.

Benefits payable in a form other than a straight life annuity must be actuarially adjusted to an equivalent straight life annuity. The statute provides guidance as to how the various actuarial computations are to be made, including limitations on the permissible interest rates that may be used. IRC § 415(b)(2)(E).

There is an important exception for qualified joint and survivor *Exceptions* annuities (QJSAs), the normal form of benefit payable to a married participant. QJSAs are discussed in Chapter 7, supra. Under IRC § 415(b)(2)(B), QJSAs do not have to be actuarially adjusted, which may in some cases permit a married participant to receive a more valuable benefit than an unmarried participant with the same accrued benefit. For example, assume that under the benefit formula used by the plan, a participant in 2015 has accrued an annual normal retirement benefit of $230,000. If the participant is single, the benefit is limited to $210,000 by § 415. Assume further that if the participant were married, the qualified joint and survivor annuity that is actuarially equivalent to the single life annuity of $230,000 would be $200,000, payable annually for the joint lives of the participant and the participant's spouse. Because of IRC § 415(b)(2)(B), this joint and survivor annuity satisfies § 415. Because it is payable over two lives instead of one, a joint and survivor annuity of $200,000 is worth far more than a single life annuity of $200,000.

The dollar limitation is itself to be adjusted downward if benefits begin before age 62 and upward if benefits begin after age 65. IRC § 415(b)(2)(C), (D). For example, assume a plan permits retirement at age 50 and the current dollar limitation is $210,000. An annuity of $210,000 commencing at age 62 is actuarially equivalent to an annuity of a much smaller amount, say $90,000, commencing at age 50, and thus $90,000 would be the maximum annual benefit for a 50-year-old retiree. However, no reduction is required for qualified police and firefighters who retire before age 62 or for commercial airline pilots who are compelled to retire between age 60 and 62. IRC § 415(b)(2)(G),(b)(9).

Limitation Adjusted Downward if benefits begin before age 62
+ Adjust Upward if benefits begin after age 65

In the case of an employee with less than ten years of participation, the dollar limitation, as adjusted by these rules, must be reduced by multiplying it by a fraction equal to the number of years of participation divided by 10. IRC § 415(b)(5)(A). This rule prevents an employer from creating a large pension over a brief time period. The concern is to prevent the pension plan from being used more as a tax shelter than as a bona fide device for retirement saving. Funding large pensions over a brief time period would produce enormous tax deductions for the employer. The employer's deduction is discussed in Section B, infra. The 100-percent-of-compensation limit is similarly reduced, except that years of service are used in applying the rule and computing the fraction. Although the statute authorizes the IRS to issue regulations applying the same reduction with respect to each change in the benefit structure of a plan, and the IRS initially did so, the IRS no longer requires such reductions. Rev. Proc. 92–42, 1992–1 C.B. 872. The IRS decided that the nondiscrimination regulations under IRC § 401(a)(4), which preclude discriminatory plan amendments, are sufficient to prevent abuse.

Notwithstanding any of these adjustments or limitations, a plan may provide a $10,000 annual benefit to an employee who has not at any time participated in a defined contribution plan of the employer. IRC § 415(b)(4). However, in the case of employees with less than ten years of service, the $10,000 limitation is fractionally reduced. In addition, the 100 percent limit does not apply to governmental plans, multiemployer plans, and to certain lower paid employees under collectively bargained plans with at least 100 participants. IRC § 415(b)(7), (11).

Cost-of-living adjustments. Suppose that A retires in 2015 with an accrued annual benefit of $240,000 according to the plan's benefit formula, but is restricted to receiving $210,000 a year, the maximum permitted under IRC § 415(b)(1) in 2015. In 2017 the IRS adjusts the dollar limitation to $220,000 to reflect an increase in the cost of living. May A then begin receiving $220,000? The regulations allow such an increase, provided that the plan specifically provides for it. Treas. Reg. § 1.415(d)–(1)(a)(4).

Suppose that B retires in Year One with an accrued annual benefit of $60,000, representing 100 percent of his average compensation for his high three years. B's plan provides for an annual cost-of-living adjustment to the pensions of retired participants, amounting to two percent in Year Two. May B receive the adjustment? The answer depends on how the plan computes the adjustment. The regulations allow B's compensation limitation for the year B separated from service to be adjusted annually by a cost-of-living factor computed by the IRS annually. See Treas. Reg. § 1.415(d)–1(a)(7), Example 1. Note that these adjustments take place each year, whereas adjustments to the dollar limitation occur less frequently because they are required to be made in $5,000 increments. IRC § 415(d)(4).

QUESTIONS

1. Only a small percentage of individuals earn $210,000 or more a year. Why should the tax system subsidize pensions as high as the current (2015) § 415 limit of $210,000?

2. Would a 35-year-old employee prefer $53,000 contributed annually to a defined contribution plan until age 65 or an annuity of $210,000 per year commencing at age 65? Suppose the employee were 55 years old?

B. LIMITATIONS ON THE DEDUCTION OF CONTRIBUTIONS *by the Employer*

1. GENERAL RULES

All deductions for contributions to deferred compensation plans, both qualified and nonqualified, are governed by IRC § 404. To be deductible under IRC § 404, contributions must be "otherwise deductible." Thus, generally the contributions would have to constitute "ordinary and necessary" trade or business or profit-seeking activity expenses under IRC §§ 162 or 212. Under these provisions, compensation must be reasonable in order to be deductible. What constitutes reasonable compensation depends on the facts and circumstances of each case. Treas. Reg. § 1.404(a)–(1)(b).

Reqs to be deductible:
① *Ordinary + necessary*
② *Reasonable*

1. *Timing.* Contributions to qualified plans are generally deductible in the taxable year when paid. The requirement of actual payment is a significant feature of IRC § 404. Typically, an accrual method taxpayer can deduct expenses when they accrue, rather than when they are actually paid, but as regards pension contributions, all taxpayers are placed on the cash method of accounting. For example, delivery of a check to the plan's trustee constitutes payment, provided the check is not dishonored. On the other hand, a contribution of the employer's own note, even an interest bearing demand note, is not a payment until the note is paid. See Don E. Williams Co. v. Commissioner, 429 U.S. 569 (1977).

The statute does, however, permit a limited type of retroactive deduction. Contributions made after the close of the taxable year "on account of" such taxable year but no later than the due date (including extensions) of the employer's tax return may be deemed to have been made on the last day of the preceding taxable year. IRC § 404(a)(6). Since the due date for corporate income tax returns is 2½ months after the close of the taxable year and an automatic extension of six months is available (and almost universally used), contributions made within the first 8½ months of the following taxable year can be deducted on the prior year's return. The deadline for making a deductible contribution to a pension plan does not necessarily coincide with the deadline for satisfying the minimum funding rules, and thus avoiding the excise tax under IRC § 4971.

Details concerning retroactive contributions can be found in Rev.Rul. 76–28, 1976–1 C.B. 106. The ruling notes that the plan must have been in existence on the last day of the taxable year with respect to which a contribution is made. Thus, an employer (including a self-employed individual) may not retroactively establish a plan and take a retroactive deduction. In addition, the courts have uniformly held that the "on account of" language in IRC § 404(a)(6) permits a retroactive deduction only if the contribution is attributable to compensation earned by participants during the prior taxable year. See American Stores Co. v. Commissioner, 170 F.3d 1267 (10th Cir.1999); Lucky Stores, Inc. v. Commissioner, 153 F.3d 964 (9th Cir.1998). Similarly, in Rev. Rul. 90–105, 1990–2 C.B. 69, the IRS ruled that an employer who makes contributions to a 401(k) plan based on compensation in Year 2 does not have the option of deducting that contribution in Year 1.

2. [*Capitalization* Rule] Pension contributions are not immune from the usual rules regarding the capitalization of the direct and indirect costs of producing or acquiring property. Under IRC § 263A, such costs generally must be added to the basis of the property, rather than be deducted currently. See Treas. Reg. § 1.263A(1)(e)(3)(ii)(C). Just as the wages of assembly line workers must be added to the inventory cost of the product, so must their pension contributions. The loss of the deduction for the pension contribution will be offset by a reduction in the gain when the inventory is sold, but that tax benefit may occur in a later taxable year.

Pension contributions are added to the inventory cost of the product (aka added to the basis of the property, rather than deducted currently)

A different capitalization issue can arise when a business is purchased. As a general rule, when an obligation is assumed in connection with the purchase of an asset, the payments satisfying the obligation are nondeductible capital expenditures. The obligation is viewed as part of the cost of the asset and is used to increase the asset's basis. Theoretically, a purchaser of a business who assumes an unfunded pension liability could be subject to similar treatment.

In David R. Webb Co. v. Commissioner, 708 F.2d 1254 (7th Cir.1983), the court held that a purchaser's assumption of a seller's obligation under an unfunded nonqualified death benefit plan must be capitalized. The court stated that "[t]here is no indication that Congress has intended to exclude pension plans from the general rule that the assumption of a seller's liability constitutes part of the acquisition costs." Id. at 1257. It is unclear exactly how this general principle should be applied to qualified plans. In PLR 8411106 the IRS ruled that the liability under IRC § 412 to fund prospectively an unfunded past service liability is not the type of liability that must be capitalized. On the other hand, the IRS noted that if the plan's funding standard account had an accumulated funding deficiency, i.e., there were past due contributions, or if the plan had already terminated and there were actual liabilities to the PBGC or plan participants, such liabilities would have to be capitalized.

2. CONTRIBUTION V. EXPENSE

Revenue Ruling 86–142
1986–2 C.B. 60.

Restorative (ex. from a lawsuit) Contributions/Payments are NOT included/subject under §404 payment

[Issue] Are additional contributions made by the employer to reimburse the trust of a qualified plan for brokers' commissions on transactions involving plan assets deductible under [IRC] § 162 or 212? . . .

[Facts] A corporation established a plan for its employees. The plan is qualified under § 401(a) and the related trust is exempt from tax under § 501(a). The plan year and the taxable year of the employer are the calendar year.

The plan provides that the employer will reimburse the trust for brokers' commissions charged in connection with the purchase and sale of securities for the employees' trust. The employer, over the plan year, makes the maximum deductible contribution to the plan under § 404.

During the plan year, the employer makes additional contributions to reimburse the trust for the brokers' commissions paid by the trust. . . .

[Law and Analysis] Section 1.404(a)(3)(d) of the regulations provides that expenses incurred by the employer in connection with a qualified employees' plan, such as trustee's fees and actuary's fees, that are not provided for by contributions under the plan are deductible by the employer under § 162 (relating to trade or business expenses), or § 212 (relating to expenses for production of income), to the extent that such expenses are ordinary and necessary. Amounts that are not ordinary and necessary expenses are not deductible under § 162.

Rev.Rul. 68–533, 1968–2 C.B. 190, holds that a sole proprietor's payment of trustee's fees that were expenses not provided for by contributions under a qualified plan are deductible by the sole proprietor under § 162 or 212 to the extent that they are ordinary and necessary. Such expenses are deductible in addition to the maximum deduction for employer contributions under the plan allowable by § 404.

The principles enunciated in the regulations under § 162 are equally applicable to § 212, except that the production of income requirement is substituted for the business requirement. Section 1.212(1)(e) of the regulations provides in part that § 212 does not allow the deduction of any expenses which are disallowed by any of the provisions of Subtitle A (relating to Income Taxes) even though such expenses may be paid or incurred for one of the purposes specified in § 212.

Brokers' commissions are not recurring administrative or overhead expenses, such as trustee or actuary fees, incurred in connection with the maintenance of the trust or plan. Rather, brokers' commissions are intrinsic to the value of a trust's assets: buying commissions are part of the cost of the securities purchased and selling commissions are an offset against the sales price. Accordingly, employer contributions to reimburse the trust for brokers' commissions are used to provide benefits under the plan of which the trust is a part and thus are not deductible under § 162 or 212. Similarly, if instead of making additional contributions to the trust, the employer paid the brokers' commissions directly to the broker, such amounts are treated as though they had been contributed to the trust and used to provide benefits under the plan. Such direct payments thus are not deductible under § 162 or 212.

Amounts contributed (or treated as contributed) to a plan are deductible subject to the rules and limits in § 404. This is the case without regard to whether the amounts are used to pay brokers' commissions, administrative or overhead expenses (such as trustee or actuary fees), or cash benefits.

[The] employer's contributions to reimburse the trust for brokers' commissions are not deductible as a separate expense under § 162 or 212. Also, because such contributions result in the employer's total contributions exceeding the amount deductible under § 404 for the taxable year, such additional contributions are not deductible under § 404. . . .

Revenue Ruling 2002–45

2002–2 C.B. 116.

Under the facts described below, are payments to the trust of a defined contribution plan qualified under § 401(a) of the Internal Revenue Code (the Code) treated as contributions for purposes of § 401(a)(4), 401(k)(3), 401(m), 404, 415(c), or 4972?

[Facts] Situation 1. Employer M maintains Plan X, a defined contribution plan, for the benefit of M's employees. The plan is qualified under § 401(a). Employer M caused an unreasonably large portion of the assets of Plan X to be invested in Entity G, a high-risk investment. It is later determined that the investment has become worthless.

A group of participants in Plan X files a suit against Employer M alleging a breach of fiduciary duty in connection with the investment in Entity G. Following the filing of the suit, the parties agree to a settlement pursuant to which Employer M does not admit that a breach of fiduciary duty occurred but makes a payment to Plan X equal to the amount of the losses (including an appropriate adjustment to reflect lost earnings) to Plan X from the investment in Entity G. The settlement also provides that the payment will be allocated among the individual accounts of all of the participants and beneficiaries in proportion to each account's investment in Entity G over the appropriate period. The court approves the settlement and enters a consent order. Employer M makes the payment to Plan X and the payment is allocated to the appropriate accounts.

Situation 2. The facts are the same as in Situation 1, except that no lawsuit is filed against Employer M. However, Employer M becomes aware that participants in Plan X are concerned about the investment in Entity G and are considering taking legal action. Employer M also learns that lawsuits alleging fiduciary breach have been filed against other companies by those companies' employees over losses to their qualified retirement plans due to investment in Entity G. Employer M decides to make the payment to Plan X before a lawsuit is filed, after reasonably determining that it has a reasonable risk of liability for breach of fiduciary duty based on all of the relevant facts and circumstances.

[Law and Analysis] The provisions of the Code that apply to contributions to qualified defined contribution plans include §§ 401(a)(4), 401(k)(3), 401(m), 404, 415 and 4972. . . .

A payment made to a qualified defined contribution plan is not treated as a contribution to the plan, and accordingly is not subject to the Code provisions described above, if the payment is made to restore losses to the plan resulting from actions by a fiduciary for which there is a reasonable risk of liability for breach of a fiduciary duty under Title I of [ERISA] and plan participants who are similarly situated are treated similarly with respect to the payment. For purposes of this revenue ruling, these payments are referred to as "restorative payments."

The determination of whether a payment to a qualified defined contribution plan is treated as a restorative payment, rather than as a contribution, is based on all of the relevant facts and circumstances. As a general rule, payments to a defined contribution plan are restorative payments for purposes of this revenue ruling only if the payments are made in order to restore some or all of the plan's losses due to an action (or a failure to act) that creates a reasonable risk of liability for breach of fiduciary duty. In contrast, payments made to a plan to make up for losses due to market fluctuations and that are not attributable to a fiduciary breach are generally treated as contributions and not as restorative payments. In no case will amounts paid in excess of the amount lost (including appropriate adjustments to reflect lost earnings) be considered restorative payments. Furthermore, payments that result in different treatment for similarly situated plan participants are not restorative payments. The failure to allocate a share of the payment to the account of a fiduciary responsible for the losses does not result in different treatment for similarly situated participants.

Payments to a plan made pursuant to a Department of Labor order or court-approved settlement to restore losses to a qualified defined contribution plan on account of a breach of fiduciary duty generally are treated as having been made on account of a reasonable risk of liability.

In no event are payments required under a plan or necessary to comply with a requirement of the Code considered restorative payments, even if the payments are delayed or otherwise made in circumstances under which there has been a breach of fiduciary duty. Thus, for example, while the payment of delinquent elective deferrals or employee contributions is part of an acceptable correction under the VFC Program, such payment is not a restorative payment for purposes of this revenue ruling. Similarly, payments made under the Employee Plans Compliance Resolution System (EPCRS), or otherwise, to correct qualification failures are generally considered contributions and do not constitute restorative payments for purposes of this revenue ruling. However, the payment of appropriate adjustments to reflect lost earnings required under EPCRS is generally treated in the same manner as a restorative payment.

In Situation 1, the payment by Employer M to restore losses to Plan X on account of the investment in Entity G is made pursuant to a court-approved settlement of the suit filed against it by plan participants and is not in excess of the amount lost (including appropriate adjustments to reflect lost earnings). In Situation 2, the payment by Employer M is made after it reasonably determines, based on all of the relevant facts and circumstances, that it has a reasonable risk of liability for breach of fiduciary duty even though no suit has yet been filed. In reaching this determination, the following facts are taken into account: that Entity G was a high-risk investment, that a large portion of the plan assets had been invested in Entity G, that participants expressed concern about the investment, and that several lawsuits had been filed against other employers alleging fiduciary breach in connection with the investment of plan assets in Entity G.

In both Situation 1 and Situation 2, therefore, the payment is made based on a reasonable determination that there is a reasonable risk of liability for breach of fiduciary duty and to restore losses to the plan. In addition, the payment is allocated among the individual accounts of the participants and beneficiaries in proportion to each account's investment in Entity G so that similarly situated participants are not treated differently.

In both Situation 1 and Situation 2, the payment is a restorative payment (as defined in this revenue ruling) and, as such, is not a contribution to a qualified plan. . . .

NOTES AND QUESTIONS

1.   Although an employer will often pay plan expenses to obtain an additional deduction, if a plan is overfunded, the employer will often seek to have the plan pay as much of the administrative expense as possible. Some employers are quite aggressive, charging not only external expenses (legal fees, investment management fees, etc.) to the plan, but also allocable internal expenses, such as the salary and fringe benefits of the employees who perform services for the plan, telephone expense, utilities, continuing education expenses, and the like. Care must be taken to avoid a violation of the "exclusive benefit" rule of IRC § 401(a)(2) and the prohibited transaction rules of IRC § 4975 and ERISA § 406. In particular, a plan is permitted to pay only "reasonable compensation" to the employer for such administrative expenses. IRC § 4975(d)(2); ERISA § 408(b)(2).

May a plan pay all or part of the cost of maintaining its qualified status? Is it relevant that a plan benefits from its qualified status by remaining tax exempt? See DOL ERISA Advisory Opinion 2001–10A (plan may pay costs of drafting plan amendments required by tax law changes, nondiscrimination testing, and requesting IRS determination letters).

2.   *Tax credit for new retirement plan expenses.* Small employers (fewer than 100 employees who earn over $5,000) receive a 50 percent tax credit for the first $1,000 of administrative or employee-education expenses connected with a new qualified plan, a SIMPLE IRA plan, or a SEP. IRC § 45E. The credit is available for up to three years. A plan does not qualify if it does not cover at least one nonhighly compensated employee or if within the previous three years the employer maintained a plan for substantially the same employees. No deduction is allowed for that portion of the plan expenses equal to the amount of the credit.

3.   CONTRIBUTIONS OF PROPERTY AND EMPLOYER SECURITIES

Unlike a contribution to an IRA, which must be made in cash, nothing in the Internal Revenue Code prohibits a deduction for a contribution of property to a qualified plan. For tax purposes this is treated as a sale of the property to the plan for an amount equal to its fair market value and a contribution of that amount to the plan. See United States v. General Shoe Corp., 282 F.2d 9 (6th Cir.1960). This treatment is identical to what happens when an employer pays compensation in the form of property. For example, suppose the employer owns some land worth $40,000 that was purchased several years earlier for $10,000. If the land is contributed to the employer's qualified profit-sharing plan, the employer must recognize $30,000 gain on the sale of the land, but receives a $40,000 contribution deduction under IRC § 404, assuming the usual requirements for the deduction are met. If instead the land had been purchased for $50,000, there would be a $10,000 loss on the sale. However, such a loss would not be deductible, because IRC § 267 denies a deduction for losses on sales or exchanges between related parties and the trust and the employer are related parties under IRC § 267(b)(4). See Rev.Rul. 61–163, 1961–2 C.B. 58.

1. *Property contributions as prohibited transactions.* Contributions of property may, however, constitute a prohibited transaction under IRC § 4975. The sale or exchange of property between a plan and an employer is a prohibited transaction. IRC § 4975(c)(1)(A). The issue is whether a contribution of property to a plan amounts to a "sale or exchange" for this purpose. In Commissioner v. Keystone Consolidated Industries, Inc., 508 U.S. 152 (1993), the Supreme Court held that the transfer of property by an employer to a defined benefit plan in satisfaction of a funding obligation is indeed a prohibited transaction. Note that there was no dispute in the case as to the adequacy of the value of the property. Is the value relevant to the question whether the transaction should be prohibited?

Although *Keystone* left open the question whether a property transfer to a defined benefit plan in excess of any minimum funding obligation would be permitted, the Department of Labor in DOL Interpretive Bulletin 94–3 took the view that such transfers would be prohibited as well "because the contribution would result in a credit against funding obligations which might arise in the future." In contrast, Interpretive Bulletin 94–3 also concluded that a property transfer to a discretionary profit-sharing plan would not be prohibited:

> For example, where a profit sharing or stock bonus plan, by its terms, is funded solely at the discretion of the sponsoring employer, and the employer is not otherwise obligated to make a contribution measured in terms of cash amounts, a contribution of unencumbered real property would not be a prohibited sale or exchange between the plan and the employer.

Is it sensible to draw a distinction between the transfer of an identical piece of property to a discretionary profit-sharing plan (permitted) and to a defined benefit plan (prohibited)? For a critique of the holding in *Keystone* see Edward A. Zelinsky, The *Keystone* Decision: The Case for Legislative Repeal, 60 Tax Notes 1025 (1993).

The holding in *Keystone* does not absolutely preclude a contribution of property to a plan in satisfaction of a funding obligation. If the transaction is in the interest of the plan and its beneficiaries, it may be possible to obtain an individual administrative exemption from the prohibited transaction rules. IRC § 4975(c)(2). Under ERISA Reorganization Plan § 102 the authority to grant such an exemption has been transferred to the Department of Labor. Prohibited transactions are discussed in more detail in Chapter 13, infra.

2. *Qualifying employer securities.* The most common form of noncash contribution is employer stock or certain other employer securities that qualify under ERISA § 407(d)(5). Provided a plan is permitted by ERISA § 407 to acquire and hold such "qualifying employer securities," the prohibited transaction rules do not apply so long as the acquisition is for adequate consideration and no commission is charged.

ERISA § 408(e); IRC § 4975(d)(13). Although qualifying employer securities are generally held by employee stock ownership plans (ESOPs) and profit-sharing plans, a defined benefit plan is allowed to hold up to 10 percent of its assets in such securities, ERISA § 407, but only if the holding can be justified under ERISA's duties of prudence and diversification, ERISA § 404(a)(1)(B)–(C), discussed infra in Chapter 14.

Under IRC § 1032 no gain or loss is recognized by a corporation on the sale or exchange of its stock. This is not a special rule for retirement plans; a corporation's transfer of its own stock is generally a nonrecognition transaction. Thus, an employer whose common stock is worth $100 per share can contribute the stock to a plan and deduct $100 for each share contributed. Obviously, difficult valuation questions can arise in the case of closely held corporations. The legal and policy implications of plan investments in employer securities are discussed in detail in Chapter 14, infra.

4. DEFINED CONTRIBUTION PLANS

The total deduction for contributions to all of an employer's defined contribution plans is limited to 25 percent of the compensation of the employees covered by the plans. IRC § 404(a)(3)(A). This rule applies to covered participants and their compensation in the aggregate. Allocations to a particular participant's account in excess of 25 percent of that participant's compensation are deductible, although the discrimination rules under IRC § 401(a)(4) preclude skewing contributions too heavily in favor of the highly compensated. Contributions to SEPs and SIMPLE IRAs are subject to the same 25 percent limitation in a coordinated fashion. IRC § 404(h)(1)(C), (m)(1).

Compensation for purposes of determining the maximum deduction is defined to include salary reduction amounts treated as compensation under IRC § 415, such as elective deferrals, deferrals under 457 plans, and cafeteria plan reductions. IRC § 404(a)(12). Furthermore, only compensation up to $265,000 (in 2015, indexed for inflation in $5,000 increments) can be taken into account for each covered employee. IRC § 404(*l*). Thus, if a plan covered two employees, A earning $300,000 and B earning $50,000, in 2015 the employer deduction would be limited to 25 percent of $315,000.

1. *Special treatment of elective deferrals.* Contributions in the form of elective deferrals are not subject to the IRC § 404 deduction limit and are not to be taken into account in applying the deduction limit to any other employer contribution to a qualified plan. IRC § 404(n). Thus, using the above example of the plan covering A and B, if the plan had a 401(k) component and A deferred $15,000 and B deferred $10,000, the employer could deduct the $25,000 in elective deferrals without regard to the 25 percent limit. In addition, the employer could deduct up to 25 percent of the total includible compensation of $315,000. Of course, this would be relevant only if the employer actually made additional contributions, such as matching or nonelective contributions.

2. *Interaction with IRC § 415.* IRC § 415 limits the total annual addition to each participant's account. The annual addition includes not only the employer contribution, but also any forfeitures allocated to the

account and after-tax employee contributions. If the IRC § 415 limit is exceeded, the plan is disqualified unless the violation is appropriately corrected under EPCRS, discussed in Chapter 8, supra. In addition, in computing the amount of the allowable employer deduction, the amount of contributions taken into account must be reduced by the excess annual addition. IRC § 404(j). For example, if in 2015 an employee with compensation of $220,000 receives an allocation to her profit-sharing account of $55,000, the IRC § 415 limit of $53,000 is exceeded. Only $53,000 would be deductible.

Assume an employer has 6 employees, one earning $100,000 and 5 earning $40,000 during the year. Assume further that the employer has had a banner year and would like to contribute $20,000 to each participant's profit-sharing account. Such contributions are well within the IRC § 415 limit, but the $120,000 contribution is well above the maximum deductible amount of $75,000 (25% of $300,000). As long as the IRC § 415 limit is met, why should there be a separate limitation on deductions?

5. DEFINED BENEFIT PLANS

The question of how to fund a defined benefit plan, discussed in Chapter 6, supra, is distinct from the question of how to take such funding into account for purposes of computing the employer's taxable income. The minimum funding rules require a certain level of funding as a protection against default, but suppose an employer is interested in funding the plan beyond the bare minimum. Should there be a limitation on the amount of the contribution that can be deducted?

1. *Economic advantage of accelerated funding.* To see the economics of the problem, consider the following example. Assume that an employee is hired at the beginning of Year One and will be entitled to a lump-sum pension of $5,000 at the end of Year Five. For simplicity, we shall ignore mortality risk and employee turnover. Assume that the employer decides to fund this pension by contributing a level amount to the plan at the end of each year (a permissible method under ERISA) and that the expected investment yield is 6 percent. The yearly contribution would be $887. However, by contributing $3,960 at the end of Year One, the employer could fully fund the $5,000 payment; at a yield of 6 percent the $3,960 would grow to $5,000 at the end of Year Five.

Assuming such accelerated funding were permitted, it would give the employer a significant tax benefit. By investing in the plan, the employer in effect has the use of a tax-free savings account to accumulate part of its future payment obligation. For example, if the employer is in the 34 percent tax bracket, fully funding the pension at the end of Year One would have an after-tax cost of $2,614 (.66 times $3,960). The after-tax cost of each level payment would be $585 (.66 times $887). The total cost of these payments, discounted to present value at the end of Year One, assuming an after-tax discount rate of 3.96 percent (.66 times 6 percent), is $2,710. Thus, the employer saves nearly $100 by pre-funding the pension. The advantage arises because the funds are generating tax-free income in the plan, but would be generating taxable income had the employer held on to the funds outside the plan and used them to make the level payments in later years.

2. *General deduction limitation.* To prevent the abusive use of a defined benefit plan as a tax-free employer savings account, IRC § 404(a)(1) imposes a limitation on the amount of the deduction for contributions to defined benefit plans. At a minimum an employer may always deduct the amount necessary to make the minimum required contribution under IRC § 430. IRC § 404(*o*)(1)(B). But in many cases IRC § 404(*o*)(1)(A) allows the deduction to exceed the minimum funding standard. The PPA greatly simplified this limitation, consistent with the changes to the funding requirements for pension plans. The maximum deductible contribution is the excess (if any) of the sum of the plan's funding target, the plan's target normal cost, and a "cushion amount" for a plan year, over the value of plan assets (unreduced by any credit balances). The cushion amount is the sum of 50 percent of the plan's funding target plus the amount the plan's funding target would increase if projected increases in compensation were taken into account. In making this latter computation, plans covered by the PBGC may take into account expected future increases in the 401(a)(17) limitation. Why did Congress permit plans insured by the PBGC to create a larger cushion?

The deduction limitation has fluctuated over time, reflecting the tension between worker security and revenue loss. Allowing some measure of overfunding provides a measure of insurance against a sudden decline in asset value. But permissive pre-funding creates a significant revenue loss. The impetus for the PPA was largely a plan funding crisis that threatened the solvency of the PBGC, so it is not surprising that the PPA liberalized the deduction limitation, allowing employers to create an overfunding cushion.

The higher funding limit put in place by the PPA has created significant tax planning opportunities, particularly for small businesses and the self-employed. To prevent manipulation, plans with 100 or fewer participants must calculate the 50 percent cushion without taking into account benefit increases for highly compensated employees that were adopted within the prior two years. Why did Congress limit this rule to small plans? However, in view of the profound economic recession that developed after the 2006 PPA was enacted, the real concern is not employers contributing too much, but employers not being able to contribute enough to satisfy the new minimum funding rules.

3. *Interaction with IRC § 401(a)(17) and IRC § 415 limitations.* In applying the IRC § 404(a) limitations on deductions, no more than $265,000 (in 2015, indexed in $5,000 increments) of annual compensation may be taken into account. IRC § 404(*l*). An important feature of this limitation is that for purposes of computing the maximum deduction under IRC § 404 for contributions to pension trusts, projected inflation adjustments may not be taken into account. This rule can affect the current funding of pensions for employees earning well below the $265,000 limit.

For example, assume that in 2015 A currently earns $60,000, is 35 years old, and is expected to retire at age 65. Assume that under the pension plan A's expected benefit will be 50 percent of his final salary. In order to decide how much to fund A's pension currently, an actuary must project what A's final salary will be. If the actuary assumes an annual

5.5 percent wage growth, A would be projected to earn $299,038 at retirement, which translates into a projected annual pension of $149,569. The employer would normally begin to fund this obligation currently, but IRC § 404(*l*) does not permit the employer to use the full $299,038 in computing the funding. Only $265,000 of A's compensation can be taken into account. Thus, instead of being allowed to fund a $149,569 pension, the employer can only fund a $132,500 pension. Of course, in later years, as the $265,000 figure is indexed, the employer will be able to fund the larger pension. The effect is to skew the employer's contributions toward the later years, thereby reducing the tax deferral available to the employer and making the plan more expensive.

Similarly, in computing the amount of the employer's deduction under IRC § 404(a), any benefits in excess of the IRC § 415 limitation may not be taken into account. IRC § 404(j)(1). The IRC § 415(b) limitation on the maximum annual benefit payable by defined benefit plans is indexed and for 2015 is $210,000. Here, too, for purposes of computing the maximum deduction under IRC § 404(a), projected inflation adjustments may not be taken into account. This rule does not affect the result in the example above because the $265,000 limitation causes A's projected permitted pension of $132,500 to fall below the current $210,000 limit. But change the facts in the example and assume that under the plan A would be entitled to a pension equal to 90 percent of final salary. The $265,000 limitation of IRC § 404(*l*) would allow the employer to fund for a $238,500 pension. Since this amount exceeds the current IRC § 415(b) limitation of $210,000, IRC § 404(j) permits the employer to fund only for a $210,000 pension.

Why does the statute not permit employers to take into account the projected inflation adjustments to the IRC § 415 and IRC § 401(a)(17) limits in determining current funding? Is inflation not a legitimate actuarial factor to consider?

6. CONTRIBUTIONS TO MORE THAN ONE TYPE OF PLAN

There is an important additional limitation on the total amount deductible if an employer contributes to either (1) one or more defined contribution plans and one or more defined benefit plans, or (2) trusts or plans described in two or more of the paragraphs of IRC § 404(a), and at least one employee is a beneficiary under more than one of the plans. IRC § 404(a)(7). The limitation is the greater of (1) 25 percent of the compensation of the employees who benefit under the plans, or (2) the amount of contributions needed to meet the minimum funding standard under IRC § 412 for the defined benefit plans. For underfunded plans, the limitation under (2) is not less than the plan's funding shortfall. IRC § 404(a)(7)(A)(last sentence).This latter provision is designed to encourage the funding of unfunded liabilities, despite the revenue losses.

The PPA liberalizes the combined limit in two significant ways. First, any plan covered by the PBGC is excluded from the calculation. Thus, an employer with a defined benefit plan covered by the PBGC and a defined contribution plan need not worry about the combined limit at all. IRC § 404(a)(7)(C)(iv). Second, the combined limit applies only if the employer contributions (excluding elective deferrals) to the defined contribution plans exceed 6 percent of the total participant compensation, and even then only the excess over 6 percent is subject to the combined limit. IRC § 404(a)(7)(C)(iii).

For example, assume a professional service employer, such as a law firm, with fewer than 25 employees, has a defined benefit plan and a profit-sharing plan. The PBGC does not insure the defined benefit plan of such an employer. ERISA § 4021(a)(13). If the contribution to the defined benefit plan is 15 percent of payroll, the most that could be contributed to the profit-sharing plan is 16 percent of payroll. Note that any deduction for elective deferrals is not subject to this combined plan limit. IRC § 404(n). Thus, in this example, it is only the nonelective and matching contributions that are limited to 16 percent of payroll; employee elective deferrals are always deductible.

Assume that a small professional employer with a $1 million payroll has a defined benefit plan with a funding target of $2.5 million, target normal cost of $150,000, and assets of $2.5 million. If there is no defined contribution plan, the employer would be able to contribute and deduct enough to fund the current year's target cost ($150,000) plus a cushion amount of $1.25 million (50 percent of the plan's funding target). This is over 100 percent of payroll. Now assume that the employer also sponsors a defined contribution plan and contributes 7 percent of payroll. The combined limit applies and the maximum deduction is limited to 25 percent of payroll, i.e., just $250,000. The first 6 percent of payroll contributed to the defined contribution plan can be deducted without regard to this limit.

Note that, in applying these payroll-based limitations, only the compensation of the employees who actually benefit under the plan or plans can be taken into account. Accordingly, compensation paid to employees who are not eligible to receive a contribution or accrue a benefit for the year in question is disregarded.

7. ·CONTRIBUTIONS TO FUND RETIREE HEALTH BENEFITS

Although a pension plan may provide for a disability pension and for incidental death benefits, "a plan is not a pension plan if it provides for the payment of benefits not customarily included in a pension plan such as layoff benefits or benefits for sickness, accident, hospitalization, or medical expenses." Treas. Reg. § 1.401–1(b)(1)(i). Health benefits may, however, be provided to retired employees, their spouses, and their dependents, but only if the special requirements of IRC § 401(h) are met. Basically, a separate account must be established, to which the employer makes reasonable and ascertainable contributions that may only be used to pay such benefits. Any amount remaining in the separate account after paying all such benefits must be returned to the employer; it may not remain in the plan to be used to fund retirement benefits.

The most significant limitation on these retiree health benefits is the requirement that such benefits be "subordinate" to the plan's retirement benefits. IRC § 401(h)(1). Retiree health benefits are subordinate only if at all times the aggregate of contributions (made after the date on which the plan first includes such benefits) to provide such benefits, as well as life insurance protection, does not exceed 25 percent of the aggregate contributions (made after such date) other than contributions to fund past service credits. IRC § 401(h) (last sentence). This rule makes it impossible to establish a 401(h) plan if a retirement plan is fully funded. A fully funded plan cannot receive any contributions toward its retirement component and therefore any contribution to fund the 401(h) component would exceed 25 percent of the actual contributions.

The deductibility of contributions to fund IRC § 401(h) benefits is governed by IRC § 404. The regulations clarify that the 401(h) component of the plan is not taken into account in determining the amount deductible with respect to contributions to provide the retirement benefits under the plan. Treas. Reg. § 1.404(a)–3(f)(1). Thus, for both funding and deduction purposes, the two components of the pension plan are treated as separate plans. The minimum funding limitation of IRC § 412 does not apply to the 401(h) benefits. Treas. Reg. § 1.412(c)(3)–1(f)(5).

The regulations limit the amount deductible with respect to retiree health contributions to the total cost of providing the health benefits, determined in accordance with any generally accepted and reasonable actuarial method. However, paralleling the usual IRC § 404(a)(1) limitation under pre-PPA law, the amount deductible for any year with respect to such cost may not exceed the greater of (a) an amount determined assuming level funding (either in amount or as a percentage of contribution) of the remaining unfunded costs of past and current service credits over the remaining future service of each employee, or (b) 10 percent of the cost required to completely fund the health benefits. Treas. Reg. § 1.404(a)–3(f)(2). If this limitation is exceeded, the excess can be carried forward and deducted in succeeding years; however, the excise tax of IRC § 4972, discussed below, would apply.

The requirement that the retiree health benefits be subordinate to the retirement benefits is a far more significant limitation on contributions than the IRC § 404 deduction restriction. If most of the employees are modestly paid, limiting the contributions to fund health benefits to no more than 25 percent of the total contributions to the plan makes it impossible to fund full medical coverage at retirement. This impediment may help explain why very few employers have chosen to fund retiree health benefits using an IRC § 401(h) separate account.

NOTES

1.   *Key employees.* Although the separate account for 401(h) plans is generally maintained on an aggregate, rather than a per-participant basis, separate accounts must be established for each "key employee." The key employee's benefits (including benefits for a spouse or dependents) may be paid only from this separate account. Furthermore, under IRC § 415(*l*), contributions allocated to such an account are treated as annual additions to a defined contribution plan for IRC § 415(c) limitation purposes, except that the 100 percent of compensation limitation of IRC § 415(c)(1)(B) does not apply.

2.   *Voluntary employees' beneficiary associations (VEBAs).* An employer can also prefund retiree health (and life insurance) benefits by establishing a welfare benefit fund. Under IRC §§ 419 and 419A, an employer is permitted to deduct contributions to fund a reserve for postretirement

medical and life insurance benefits, but funding must be actuarially determined on a level basis, computed using current medical costs (i.e., no adjustment for inflation). In addition, the investment income from such a reserve is treated as unrelated business taxable income, which is subject to tax at the usual corporate rates. IRC § 512(a)(3). This rule eliminates the tax-shelter potential of such funded retiree health plans. Despite the earlier deduction, pre-funding creates no special tax advantage if the employer's tax rate and the VEBA's tax rate are the same. Why? The rule does not apply to a VEBA maintained pursuant to a collective-bargaining agreement. IRC §§ 419A(f)(5) & 512(a)(3)(E).

Funded retiree health plans are also subject to special discrimination rules and must maintain separate accounts for key employees (and coordinate with the IRC § 415 limitations) in the same fashion as 401(h) plans. These rules are enforced by a 100 percent excise tax under IRC § 4976.

Recent concerns about retiree health benefits, particularly in the public sector and the automobile industry, have led to a resurgence of interest in VEBAs as a funding vehicle. For discussions of the issues, see Phyllis C. Borzi, Retiree Health VEBAs: A New Twist On An Old Paradigm, Implications for Retirees, Unions and Employers, March 2009, http://www. kff.org/medicare/upload/7865.pdf; Aaron Bernstein, Can VEBAs Alleviate Retiree Health Care Problems, Pension Research Council Working Paper 2009–24, http://www.pensionresearchcouncil.org/publications/document.ph p?file=817; AARP Public Policy Institute, Retiree Health Care: What Do the New Auto Industry VEBAs Mean for Current and Future Retirees?, http:// assets.aarp.org/rgcenter/econ/i4_veba.pdf.

3.   *Transfers of excess pension assets to 401(h) accounts*. A defined benefit plan is permitted to transfer tax-free some of its "excess pension assets" into a 401(h) account in the plan to fund retiree health benefits. IRC § 420. Excess pension assets are defined to be assets in excess of a statutory cushion, generally 125 percent of the sum of the plan's funding target and target normal cost determined under IRC § 430. Various conditions apply to such transfers, including the requirement that all participants be vested as if the plan terminated, and the requirement that the employer maintain existing health benefits at a minimum level. IRC § 420(c)(2), (3).

IRC § 420 was originally enacted in 1990 as a temporary revenue raiser. Can you see why? Extended several times, it is currently scheduled to expire in 2021. Plan surpluses and reversions are discussed in Chapter 6, supra.

8.   NONDEDUCTIBLE CONTRIBUTIONS: CARRYFORWARDS, PENALTIES AND CORRECTION

1.   *Carryforward of nondeductible contributions*. IRC §§ 404(a)(1) & (a)(3) do not actually prohibit an employer from contributing more than the maximum deductible amount to a qualified plan; they simply disallow a deduction in the current year. Any excess may be carried over and deducted in succeeding years subject to the normal deduction limitations. IRC § 404(a)(1)(E), (3)(A)(ii).

2.   *Excise tax on nondeductible contributions*. Even though a deduction for contributions to a plan in excess of the IRC § 404 limitation is delayed, by placing the funds in the trust the employer still has the advantage of tax-free accumulation of income. To discourage the use of

this tax advantage, there is a 10 percent excise tax on nondeductible contributions to qualified plans, SEPs and SIMPLE IRAs. IRC § 4972(a). The excise tax is not deductible. IRC § 275(a)(6).

As noted in Section 6, supra, there is an overall limit on the amount of deductible contributions if an employer sponsors both a defined benefit and a defined contribution plan that cover some of the same employees. Contributions to one or more defined contribution plans that are nondeductible because they exceed this overall limit are not subject to the excise tax to the extent such contributions are employer matching contributions. IRC § 4972(c)(6)(A).

The excise tax is cumulative in that it applies not only to the nondeductible contributions for the current year, but also to nondeductible contributions for prior years that have not yet become deductible or been returned to the employer. IRC § 4972(c)(1)(B). In some situations, nondeductible contributions might not become deductible for several years. For example, if an employer contributed $100,000 to a pension plan in a year in which the maximum deduction was $40,000, $60,000 would be nondeductible and an excise tax of $6,000 would be payable. The excise tax is due even if the extra contribution was made in good faith. A $60,000 carryover deduction is available as a deduction for the following year, but subject to the IRC § 404 limitations. Nothing can actually be deducted in the following year or any future year until the deduction limitations permit. Accordingly, a $6,000 excise tax would potentially be payable in each succeeding year until the amount becomes deductible.

Nondeductible Contributions are Non-Refundable (bc of the no reversion rule)

3. (*Return of nondeductible contributions.*) An obvious solution would be to have the plan return the nondeductible portion of the contribution. Yet this appears to be forbidden by the no reversion rule contained in IRC § 401(a)(2). In contrast, the ERISA version of the no reversion rule, ERISA § 403(c), expressly permits the return of a contribution if (1) the contribution is made by reason of a mistake of fact (or law, in the case of a multiemployer plan); (2) the contribution is conditioned on initial qualification of the plan, the application for determination is made in a timely fashion, and the plan received an adverse determination with respect to its initial qualification; or (3) the contribution is conditioned on its deductibility under IRC § 404. The return to the employer of the amount involved must generally be made within one year of the mistaken payment of the contribution, the date of denial of qualification, or disallowance of the deduction.

ERISA allows an exception to the general rule

In Rev. Rul. 91–4, 1991–1 C.B. 57, the IRS ruled that it would allow a plan to provide for a return of contributions under the circumstances specified in ERISA § 403(c). The Ruling provides the following guidance:

> The determination of whether a reversion due to a mistake of fact or the disallowance of a deduction with respect to a contribution that was conditioned on its deductibility is made under circumstances specified in § 403(c)(2)(A) and (C) of ERISA, and therefore will not adversely affect the qualification of an existing plan, will continue to be made on a case by case basis. In general, such reversions will be permissible only if the surrounding facts and circumstances indicate that the contribution of the amount that subsequently reverts to the

employer is attributable to a good faith mistake of fact, or in the case of the disallowance of the deduction, a good faith mistake in determining the deductibility of the contribution. A reversion under such circumstances will not be treated as a forfeiture in violation of § 411(a) of the Code, even if the resulting adjustment is made to the account of a participant that is partly or entirely nonforfeitable.

The maximum amount that may be returned to the employer in the case of a mistake of fact or the disallowance of a deduction is the excess of (1) the amount contributed, over, as relevant, (2) (A) the amount that would have been contributed had no mistake of fact occurred, or (B) the amount that would have been contributed had the contribution been limited to the amount that is deductible after any disallowance by the Service. Earnings attributable to the excess contribution may not be returned to the employer, but losses attributable thereto must reduce the amount to be so returned. Furthermore, if the withdrawal of the amount attributable to the mistaken or nondeductible contribution would cause the balance of the individual account of any participant to be reduced to less than the balance which would have been in the account had the mistaken or nondeductible amount not been contributed, then the amount to be returned to the employer must be limited so as to avoid such reduction. In the case of a reversion due to initial disqualification of a plan, the entire assets of the plan attributable to employer contributions may be returned to the employer.

Plans almost always include provisions permitting the reversion of contributions under the circumstances set forth in ERISA§ 403(c). Thus, plans generally condition contributions on deductibility and require any nondeductible contributions to be returned to the employer within one year of the disallowance. Similarly, plan language typically permits employer contributions made under a mistake of fact to be returned to the employer within one year of payment. Plans also universally condition contributions on the initial IRS approval of the plan's qualified status.

In order for a nondeductible contribution to be returned it must be "disallowed." Rev. Proc. 90–49, 1990–2 C.B. 620, provides a procedure whereby an employer can obtain a ruling from the IRS disallowing a deduction for a plan contribution. Rev. Proc. 90–49 also provides for a "disallowance" of deductions without the need for a ruling if the amount is less than $25,000 and certain conditions are met.

There is no right to the return of nondeductible contributions unless the plan provides for it. An employer cannot avoid making a contractually required contribution to a plan, even if the plan's fully funded condition renders the contribution nondeductible. See Bituminous Coal Operators' Ass'n v. Connors, 867 F.2d 625 (D.C.Cir.1989). Thus, proper drafting of plans and collective bargaining agreements is crucial to avoiding overcontributions and any resulting excise taxes.

C. LIMITATIONS ON THE SELF-EMPLOYED — count as EEEs

Under IRC § 401(c)(1), self-employed individuals, such as partners, members of a limited liability company and sole proprietors, are treated as "employees" for qualified plan purposes and may participate in a qualified plan. This presents a problem in applying the limitation on contributions and benefits under IRC § 415 and the limitation on deductions under IRC § 404 because both limitations depend to some extent on participant compensation, yet self-employed participants do not have compensation in the normal sense of the word. Instead, the self-employed have profits (or perhaps losses!) from their business.

(margin note: Problems w/ this)

Under both IRC § 415 and 404, "compensation" is defined as the participant's "earned income" within the meaning of IRC § 401(c)(2). IRC §§ 404(a)(8), 415(b)(3), 415(c)(3)(B). "Earned income" is itself defined as the "net earnings from self-employment" as defined in IRC § 1402(a), determined "only with respect to a trade or business in which personal services of the taxpayer are a material income-producing factor." IRC § 401(c)(2)(A). Thus, a partner who is simply an investor and not actually working in the business does not have any earned income and is not an "employee" under IRC § 401(c)(1). In addition, in computing the "compensation" of self-employed participants, two key adjustments must be made. First, earned income is computed *after* taking into account the deductions under IRC § 404 for contributions to the plans. IRC § 401(c)(2)(A)(v). Second, there is a deduction from earned income equal to one-half the self-employment (Social Security and Medicare) taxes imposed by IRC § 1401 for the year. IRC §§ 164(f), 401(c)(2)(A)(vi).

(margin notes: ① ②)

In the case of any "owner-employee", contributions may be made only with respect to earned income derived from the trade or business with respect to which the plan is established. IRC § 401(d). An owner-employee is a sole proprietor or a partner (or LLC member) who owns more than 10 percent of either the capital interest or the profits interest in the firm. IRC § 401(c)(3).

(margin note: Self Employed CASH)
(margin calculations:)
100,000 CASH
−7,650 EEE pays in Taxes FICA
14,130 −7,650 EER pays in Taxes FICA
85,870 cash in
−18,587 retirement acct
67,292 in bank

These adjustments complicate the determination of the maximum contribution for a self-employed individual, but they are needed to ensure that the owners of businesses conducted in corporate form are treated approximately the same as sole proprietors and partners. The main source of the complexity is the circularity of the definition of compensation. IRC § 404 limits the deduction to 25 percent of compensation, but compensation depends on the amount of the deductible contribution. A little algebra (i.e., solving x = .25 * (1–x)) reveals that the maximum IRC § 404 deduction is 20 percent of [net profits minus one-half the self-employment tax].

(margin calculations:)
100,000
−7,650 (Deduct the FICA taxes)

(margin note: Self Employed Earnings)
92,350
×20% (IRC § 404 Deduction)
18,587
73,763

To illustrate, assume an individual has $100,000 of net profits from a consulting business carried on as a sole proprietor. First, the self-employment (SECA) tax must be computed. Pursuant to IRC § 1402(a)(12), the tax is imposed on .9235 times the net profits, here $92,350. The SECA tax in 2015 is 15.3 percent of the first $118,500 (the Social Security wage base), plus 2.9 percent of any excess. Assuming that the individual does not have wage income from other employment, the SECA tax is $14,130. The IRC § 404 deduction limit is therefore $18,587 (20% of ($100,000 minus 1/2 of $14,130)).

(margin note: this goes on his tax return + he pays income taxes on this)

Elective deferrals neither affect this limit, nor are they subject to it. See IRC § 404(c)(12), (n). Our self-employed individual can therefore contribute $18,587 to a profit-sharing plan on top of a maximum 401(k) deferral of $18,000 (in 2015), for a total of $36,587. If the individual is 50 or over, a further $6,000 (in 2015) catch-up contribution can be made.

IRC § 404 is not the only limitation. Recall that IRC § 415(c) limits the annual addition with respect to a participant to the lesser of $53,000 (in 2015) or 100 percent of the participant's compensation. Here again there is circularity, because compensation depends on the amount of the contribution. Unlike the IRC § 404 limit, elective deferrals are subject to the IRC § 415 limit, but like the IRC § 404 limit, elective deferrals are considered part of compensation. See IRC § 415(c)(3)(D). A little algebra reveals that the profit-sharing contribution (apart from the elective deferrals) is limited to 50 percent of [net profits minus one-half the self-employment tax minus the elective deferrals] and the total of the profit-sharing contribution and the elective deferrals is limited to $53,000 (in 2015). This limit presents no problem for our consultant, since 50 percent of ($100,000 minus 1/2 of $14,130 minus $18,000) is $37,468, well above the $18,587 permitted by IRC § 404. Once again, catch-up contributions are not subject to the IRC § 415(c) limit and do not play a role in its computation. IRC § 414(v)(3)(A).

This example illustrates why 401(k) plans for the self-employed, often referred to as "solo-k" or "individual-k" plans, have become so popular since 2001. Before then, elective deferrals counted against the IRC § 404 deduction limit and also reduced the earned income used to compute that limit. Without a 401(k) component, our consultant would be limited to a maximum profit-sharing contribution of $18,587, but with a 401(k) component the total contribution can be as high as $36,587, plus an additional $6,000 if she is 50 or older.

Normally a cash or deferred election can only be made with respect to an amount that is not yet currently available. Treas. Reg. § 1.401(k)–1(a)(3)(iii). Obviously, since a sole proprietor does not receive a paycheck and has ready access to business funds, the usual concept of current availability will not work. The Regulations solve the problem by deeming a sole proprietor's compensation to be currently available on the last day of the individual's taxable year and a partner's compensation to be currently available on the last day of the partnership's taxable year. Treas. Reg. § 1.401(k)–1(a)(6)(iii).

QUESTIONS

1.   E, age 48, is an employee with a salary of $300,000. E's employer has a profit-sharing plan and contributes $30,000 to E's account under the plan for the current year. In addition, E elects to defer an additional $14,000 under the 401(k) component of the plan. E also is an artist and has $10,000 net income from the sale of E's paintings in the current year. Could E establish a profit-sharing plan based on E's income as an artist? If so, what is the maximum contribution that E can make to the plan?

2.   What is the minimum amount of net income that a self-employed person would need in order to contribute the maximum dollar amount permitted under IRC § 415?

3.   Partnership M has adopted a money purchase plan that allocates 15 percent of compensation to each employee's account. Each partner was given a one-time irrevocable election to specify the percentage of compensation (up to 15 percent) to be contributed on his behalf. Are these elective contributions subject to the limitation of IRC § 402(g)? See Treas.Reg. § 1.401(k)–1(a)(3)(v). Instead of such an election, could Partnership M establish a schedule of percentages for each partner (e.g., 5 percent for Partner A, 7 percent for Partner B, etc.) and change the schedule on an annual basis? See Treas. Reg. § 1.401(k)–1(a)(6)(i).

4.   If a partnership provides matching contributions for elective deferrals under a 401(k) plan, are the matching contributions made with respect to an individual partner's elective deferrals subject to the IRC § 402(g) limit? See IRC § 402(g)(9).

CHAPTER 11

TAXATION OF PARTICIPANTS AND BENEFICIARIES

Analysis

- No social security tax on Retirement Plan income

- But, must pay Income Tax (+ Estate Tax once they die - if over $11 million exemption) (unless donate it to a Charity

---

Introduction

In Chapter 8 we discussed the basic tax advantages of qualified plans: Neither the contributions to the plan nor the earnings on the plan assets are taxed to the participant, and the participant is generally taxed only when distributions are actually made. In this chapter we examine some important aspects of the taxation of participants and their beneficiaries.

Section A explains the normal method for taxing distributions. The key issue is timing the recovery of any after-tax contributions that the participant made. Under prior law it was often possible for the participant to recover these contributions first and thereby delay taxation until this after-tax investment was fully recovered. The current law generally spreads the recovery of the participant's investment over specified time periods in the case of annuities. For non-annuity distributions, the investment is recovered pro rata.

Certain distributions, mainly those not in the form of an annuity, can avoid taxation, if they are transferred to another plan or IRA, either directly or within 60 days of the original distribution to the participant or beneficiary. These so-called "rollovers," covered in Section B, are an important planning device for gaining flexibility over the choice of investment and the timing of taxable distributions.

For many years, a "lump sum distribution," a term of art that is not necessarily a distribution in one lump sum, received special favorable averaging treatment. Lump sum averaging was repealed in 1996, but

Section C describes the transitional rule that preserves it for employees who were born before 1936.

Not every distribution from a plan is taxable immediately. Section D discusses the special treatment of employer securities. The appreciation on employer securities that are received in a lump sum distribution is not taxed when the securities are distributed; taxation is postponed until the securities are ultimately sold. Section E examines plan loans to participants. A loan is generally not taxed as income, provided it meets certain limitations regarding the amount and timing of the repayment.

The timing and amount of plan distributions are severely restricted in a variety of ways that are discussed in Section F. In order to target the tax subsidy to retirement saving, as opposed simply to short-term saving, there is a penalty on most distributions made prior to age 59½, as well as prohibitions against certain early distributions from specified types of plans. On the other hand, there is also a prohibition against delaying distributions for too long, and thus prolonging the tax subsidy. The logic of the minimum distribution rules is that the purpose of the tax subsidy is to encourage retirement benefits, not wealth accumulation for one's heirs. The complex rules reviewed in Section F can be summed up as follows: not too soon and not too late.

In Section G, we note some of the estate and gift tax implications of retirement saving.

The edifice described in this chapter has a variety of flaws, not the least of which is its overwhelming complexity. As you read these materials, an important question to ask yourself is which rules (and which exceptions to the rules) are truly worth the complexity that they engender.

A. BASIC INCOME TAX TREATMENT

As a general rule, distributions from qualified plans, tax-sheltered annuities, SEPs, and IRAs are all subject to taxation under IRC § 72. See IRC §§ 402(a)(1), 403(a)(1), (b)(1), 408(d)(1). If, as is increasingly the norm, only employer contributions have been made (or in the case of an IRA, only deductible contributions) all distributions from the plan are fully taxable. Remember that pre-tax elective deferrals under 401(k) plans, SIMPLE plans, and 403(b) plans are *employer* contributions. However, when nondeductible employee contributions have indeed been made, the employee must be permitted to recover such contributions tax-free if double taxation is to be avoided. Taking account of employee contributions is a major source of complexity. IRC § 72 provides two methods for recovering the participant's cost basis in the plan, depending on whether or not the payment is periodic. The special rules for Roth contributions are discussed in notes 5 and 6 of this section, infra.

1. *Periodic payments from qualified plans.* Periodic payments (technically "amounts received as an annuity," see Treas. Reg. § 1.72–2(b)(2)) from qualified plans and from 403(b) plans are taxed under a special simplified method. Basically, the annuity recipient excludes from income an amount of each monthly annuity payment equal to the "investment in the contract" (as of the annuity starting date) divided by

the number of anticipated payments determined from the tables set forth in IRC § 72(d)(1)(B).

If the annuity is payable over the life of a single individual, or over the lives of more than one individual, the number of anticipated payments is determined from the tables.

If the annuity is payable over a fixed number of years, the number of anticipated payments is simply the number of monthly payments under the annuity. If the annuitant is 75 or over on the annuity starting date and there are 5 or more years of guaranteed payments, a more complicated method must be used. IRC § 72(d)(1)(E).

The investment in the contract is the participant's cost basis in the plan, which will generally be the participant's after-tax contributions to the plan plus any employer contributions that were includible in the participant's gross income. IRC § 72(f). The cost basis in the plan is reduced by amounts received before the annuity starting date that were excludable from gross income. IRC § 72(c)(1)(B).

Once the participant's cost basis is recovered, all amounts paid are fully taxable. If annuity payments cease on account of the death of the annuitant, and not all the investment has been recovered, a deduction for the unrecovered investment is allowed on the annuitant's final income tax return. IRC § 72(b)(3). This deduction is treated as if it were attributable to a trade or business for purposes of IRC § 172, which allows the deduction to be carried back to a prior year as part of a net operating loss deduction if there is insufficient income in the final year to absorb the deduction.

2. *Nonperiodic payments.* The treatment of amounts not received as an annuity is governed by IRC § 72(e), which specifies that the participant's investment in the trust or contract is recovered on a pro rata basis. The participant excludes that portion of the payment that bears the same ratio to the total payment as the investment in the trust or contract bears to the value of the vested portion of the participant's account balance. Distributions from defined contribution plans and traditional IRAs are governed by this method. If a defined benefit plan makes nonperiodic payments, the present value of the accrued benefit is treated as the account balance for purposes of computing the ratio. See IRS Notice 87–13, 1987–1 C.B. 432.

[handwritten margin note: NonPeriodic Payments]

For example, assume a participant receives a $5,000 distribution from a defined contribution plan to which the participant has made $1,000 in nondeductible contributions. If the vested portion of the participant's account balance is $20,000, 1/20 of the $5,000 payment would be received tax-free. The statute provides that this computation is to be made on the date of distribution or such other time as the IRS may prescribe. The IRS gives plans a choice of several alternative valuation dates, provided that the choice is made on a reasonable and consistent basis. Id. at A–12.

3. *Separate contracts.* Under IRC § 72(d)(2), employee contributions and allocable income under a defined contribution plan can be treated as a separate contract for IRC § 72 purposes, provided a strict separate accounting is maintained. The employee can then achieve a faster tax-free recovery of his or her contributions, and thus pay less tax

on the distributions that are received first, by taking distributions from the employee contribution account. See the example in IRS Notice 87–13, A–14.

4. *Traditional IRAs.* There is a special rule for applying IRC § 72 to IRAs. Under IRC § 408(d)(2), all the taxpayer's IRAs (including SEPs and rollover IRAs, but excluding Roth IRAs) are treated as a single IRA, taken at fair market value at the end of the calendar year in which the distributions are made, with the amount of the distributions added back in. Thus, the nontaxable fraction of the amount distributed during the year is the ratio of the unrecovered nondeductible contributions to the sum of the (1) IRA account balances on December 31 and (2) the total amount distributed during the year. For this purpose, the account balance includes any outstanding rollovers (i.e., amounts distributed within 60 days of the end of the year but which are rolled over in the following year). IRS Notice 87–16, 1987–1 C.B. 446, provides guidance on the taxation of IRA distributions.

5. *Roth IRAs.* All Roth IRAs are aggregated together and treated separately from traditional IRAs for IRC § 72 purposes. There is no tax on "qualified distributions" from Roth IRAs, which are distributions that are (1) made after the end of the five-taxable-year period beginning with the first taxable year for which the individual made a contribution to a Roth IRA, *and* (2) made on or after age 59 1/2, made after the death of the individual, attributable to the individual's being disabled, or used for a first-time home purchase (subject to a $10,000 lifetime limit). IRC § 408A(d)(2). A nonqualified distribution is taxable under IRC § 72, except that there is a special basis recovery rule that is very favorable to the taxpayer: distributions are treated as made from contributions first. IRC § 408A(d)(4)(B). Thus, until the total of the distributions exceeds the Roth IRA contributions, no portion of the distribution is taxable.

6. *Roth 401(k)s.* 401(k) plans and 403(b) plans are now permitted to allow participants to designate some or all of their contributions as "Roth contributions." See IRC § 402A. A plan that does so must establish separate "designated Roth accounts" and maintain separate recordkeeping with respect to the two types of accounts. Distributions from designated Roth accounts are tax-free if they are "qualified distributions." IRC § 402A(d)(1). The definition of qualified distribution is the same as the Roth IRA definition noted above, with two important differences. First, the five-taxable-year period begins with the first taxable year for which a designated Roth contribution is made to a designated Roth account under the plan or to a designated Roth account under another plan that has been rolled over into a designated Roth account under the plan. Second, unlike a Roth IRA, a distribution from a Roth 401(k) to finance a first-time home purchase is not treated as a qualified distribution.

IRC § 72 is "applied separately with respect to distributions and payments from a designated Roth account and other distributions and payments from the plan." IRC § 402A(d)(4). Regulations clarify that plans are permitted to allow an employee to determine whether a distribution is made from a designated Roth account or another account. Treas. Regs. §§ 1.401(k)–i(f), 1.402A–1. However, there is as yet no guidance regarding the proper basis recovery rule if nonqualified distributions are made from a designated Roth account. Presumably, the usual IRC § 72 rule would apply, and the after-tax contributions would be recovered pro rata. As noted above, Roth IRAs are subject to a special favorable rule that treats distributions as coming from after-tax contributions first, but IRC § 402A lacks such a provision. This discrepancy may have been a Congressional oversight, especially since, as we shall discuss below, a designated Roth account can be rolled over into a Roth IRA.

The Small Business Jobs Act of 2010 allows 401(k) and 403(b) plans to provide for in-plan Roth conversions [IRC § 402A (c) (4)] and, beginning in 2011, allows governmental 457 plans to accept Roth contributions. IRS issued guidance in Notice 2010–84, 2010–2 C.B. 872.

In-plan Roth rollovers of amounts currently distributable have been allowed since 2010, while rollovers of otherwise nondistributable balances have been allowed since 2013. Later guidance confirmed that these nondistributable balances still must be vested to be eligible for an in-plan Roth 401(k) conversion. IRS Notice 2013–74, 2013–52 I.R.B. 819, Q&A–1.

Plan sponsors can restrict the type of participant contributions eligible for, and the frequency of, in-plan Roth conversions. Id., Q&A–6. Plan sponsors can discontinue an in-plan Roth conversion feature at any time, as long as the timing of the plan amendment does not discriminate against nonhighly compensated employees.

In-plan Roth rollovers are also available for annual deferrals made to a governmental 457(b) plan.

7.   *Withholding.* Although distributions from qualified plans are subject to income tax withholding, the recipient can elect not to have withholding apply. IRC § 3405. That election is not permitted for distributions that are "eligible rollover distributions" (see Section B, infra). Periodic payments are withheld at the rate applicable to wages. Nonperiodic payments are withheld at a 10 percent rate, except for "eligible rollover distributions," which are withheld at a 20 percent rate.

QUESTIONS

1.   What purpose is served by allowing after-tax contributions to qualified plans?

2.   E has two IRAs, A and B. Only deductible contributions have been made to IRA A. IRA B was established in Year One and the only contribution was a $2,000 nondeductible contribution in Year One. In Year Two E withdrew everything from IRA B, which at that time amounted to $2,500. On December 31 of Year Two, IRA A had a fair market value of $97,500. Assuming that E is over 59 1/2 and thereby avoids the IRC § 72(t) tax on early withdrawals, how is the distribution from IRA B taxed? Is this fair? What would the result be if IRA B were a Roth IRA?

3.   Over a four-year period Hardluck made $4,000 in nondeductible contributions and $4,000 in deductible contributions to his only IRA. Hardluck's choice of IRA investments proved to be poor and his account is now worth only $2,000. What are the tax consequences if Hardluck withdraws the $2,000?

B. ROLLOVERS

immediately

— not taxing distributions if distributions are transferred to another Qualified Plan (Tax Deferral)

1. ROLLOVERS FROM QUALIFIED PLANS

1. *Eligible rollover distributions.* An "eligible rollover distribution" from a qualified plan is not taxed currently if it is transferred to another qualified plan, IRA, 403(b) plan, or governmental 457 plan within 60 days after receipt. IRC § 402(c). A similar rule applies to distributions from 403(b) plans and governmental 457 plans. IRC §§ 403(b)(8), 457(e)(16). The advantage of a rollover is not only the deferral of tax liability on the distribution, but also the continuing deferral of tax liability on the future earnings of the rolled over assets. Why are rollovers from 457 plans of private tax-exempt employers not permitted?

General Rule:
— Any distribution from a qualified plan is an eligible rollover distribution

Generally, any distribution from a qualified plan is an eligible rollover distribution, unless it is one of the following: (1) substantially equal life annuity payments; (2) substantially equal installment payments payable over ten years or more; (3) a required minimum distribution under the rules of IRC § 401(a)(9) (see Section F.3, infra); or (4) a hardship distribution from 401(k) and 403(b) plans (see Section F.1, infra). IRC § 402(c)(4). Certain corrective and deemed distributions are also excluded. Treas. Reg. § 1.402(c)–2, Q & A 4.

Exceptions to the rule that any distribution from a qualified plan is an eligible rollover distribution

Allowing rollovers of required minimum distributions would defeat the purpose of IRC § 401(a)(9), which is to preclude the unwarranted deferral of taxation. Similarly, a rollover would be inconsistent with a hardship distribution, which is meant to provide the recipient with immediately needed funds. Why not allow annuity and installment distributions to be rolled over?

2. *Nontaxable portion.* Prior to 2002 only the taxable portion of an eligible rollover distribution could be rolled over. Currently, after-tax contributions can be rolled over into an IRA, a qualified plan, or a 403(b) plan. The portion of any such distribution that is rolled over is attributed first to amounts includible in gross income. IRC § 402(c)(2)(flush language). For example, assume that a $10,000 distribution is made from a qualified plan, of which $1,000 is nontaxable, and that only $5,000 is rolled over into an IRA. The $5,000 is treated as coming from the $9,000 taxable portion of the distribution, leaving only $4,000 to be taxed.

In the case of a rollover of after-tax contributions from a qualified plan to another qualified plan or a 403(b), the rollover must be a direct rollover (see infra). Furthermore, the plan accepting a rollover of after-tax contributions must provide a separate accounting for such contributions. IRC § 402(c)(2)(A).

In September, 2014, IRS issued proposed regulations [79 Fed. Reg. 56,310] and a Notice [Notice 2014–54, 2014–41 IRB 670] that are applicable to distributions made after 2014, However, the new rules can be relied on immediately. Under the new guidance, a participant can (1) roll over pre-tax amounts (401(k) deferrals, employer contributions and investment earnings) to a traditional IRA or an employer plan, and continue the tax deferral, and (2) receive and retain after-tax amounts, tax-free, or roll over these amounts to a Roth IRA.

3. *Rollovers by nonspousal beneficiaries limited.* In general, only distributions to the employee may be rolled over. IRC § 402(c)(1)(A). There are, however, two important exceptions. First, a spouse may roll over distributions paid after the employee's death in the same manner as if the spouse were the employee. IRC § 402(c)(9). Second, if an alternate payee who is the spouse or former spouse of the participant receives a distribution under a qualified domestic relations order (QDRO), the alternate payee is treated for rollover purposes in the same manner as if the alternate payee were the employee. IRC § 402(e)(1)(B). QDROs are discussed at length in Chapter 7, supra.

Suppose that plan proceeds are payable to the participant's estate or a trust. If the executor (or trustee) distributes the proceeds or the IRA account to the surviving spouse as beneficiary of the estate or trust, may the spouse roll over the distribution? Generally, if the proceeds pass through a third party and then are distributed to the decedent's spouse, the surviving spouse is not permitted to roll over the proceeds. However, in an important concession to the complexities of real-world estate planning, the IRS has allowed such rollovers in a number of private letter rulings, provided that the surviving spouse has a right to receive the proceeds that is not subject to the trustee's or executor's discretion, or the discretion is in the hands of the surviving spouse. Compare PLR 200509034 (rollover permitted) with PLR 9416045 (rollover denied).

The 2006 PPA for the first time allowed plan distributions to be rolled over by nonspouse beneficiaries, subject to important limitations. IRC § 402(c)(11)(A). First, the rollover must be accomplished by means of a direct trustee-to-trustee transfer from the plan to the IRA. Second, the IRA must be established to receive the distribution. Third, the IRA is treated as an inherited IRA of the nonspouse beneficiary.

The pre-PPA rule regarding nonspousal beneficiaries created a significant trap for the unwary. Many qualified plans limit the types of distributions that are permitted. For example, many profit sharing plans require that the account must be distributed within one year after the death of the participant. Prior to the PPA, if the beneficiary were not a spouse, the account could not be rolled over when the participant died; it would be fully taxable within a year. But as we shall see in Section F.3, infra, if the participant had rolled over the funds into an IRA, the funds could have been distributed over the life of the beneficiary. For large plan balances the tax savings from the additional tax deferral can be enormous. For this reason most planners urged their clients to make a rollover into an IRA at the earliest possible time. Under the 2006 PPA there is no need to make the rollover before the death of the participant.

Undoubtedly some beneficiaries, through mistake or due to bad advice, will take a distribution in cash from a decedent's plan and try to roll it over to an IRA. Unlike missing the 60-day limit on rollovers, an error which the IRS can waive, there is no mechanism that allows such a distribution to be undone and then redone as a trustee-to-trustee transfer to an inherited IRA. Should there be?

4. *The rollover decision.* In the case of an involuntary distribution, which can occur as part of a plan termination or the distribution of a small (less than $5,000) account balance when one leaves a job, a rollover is an obvious way to avoid current taxation and continue to achieve the

benefits of tax deferral. But if a participant has the option of leaving the funds in a qualified plan, why would the participant want to transfer them to an IRA? The answer is that an IRA gives the participant maximum control over investments and the timing of future distributions.

Although the conventional wisdom is to make a rollover at the earliest possible date, there are some caveats:

(1) A participant who is not a 5 percent owner of the business and who works past age 70½ is not required to commence receiving distributions from the employer's qualified plan. In contrast, an IRA account owner must commence minimum distributions at age 70½ even if he is still employed. See Section F.3, infra.

(2) As discussed in Chapter 7, spousal rights in ERISA plans and IRAs differ. For example, a nonparticipant spouse cannot bequeath his or her community property interest in a qualified plan, but it is likely that such a bequest of a similar interest in a spouse's IRA would not be preempted. Also, distributions and beneficiary designations in connection with qualified plans are subject to strict spousal consent rules, but IRAs have no spousal consent rules.

(3) A participant can borrow from a qualified plan account (if the plan permits), but a loan from an IRA is treated as a distribution. See Section E, infra.

(4) The investment options in the qualified plan may be superior to what a participant could obtain through an IRA and may place less of the responsibility for investment selection on the participant.

(5) The rights of the participant against the fiduciaries of the plan, who are subject to ERISA, are almost certainly stronger than the rights of an IRA owner against the trustee or custodian of the IRA. See, e.g., Diana B. Henriques, Questions for a Custodian After Scams Hit I.R.A.'s, New York Times, July 25, 2009 at 1.

As before, no plan is required to accept rollovers. Rev. Rul. 2014–9, 2014–17 I.R.B. 975, provides two new safe harbor procedures that an administrator of a qualified plan may use in order to be deemed to have reasonably concluded that an amount is a valid rollover contribution under Treas. Reg. § 1.401(a)(31)–1.

Rollovers to IRAs from employer plans have received considerable recent scrutiny. A March 2013 General Accountability Office report [GAO 13–30, 401(k) Plans—Labor and IRS Could Improve the Rollover Process for Participants, http://www.gao.gov/assets/660/652881.pdf] found that rollover processes are inefficient, that IRAs are heavily marketed, and that participants are often given incomplete, misleading, or false information about IRA rollovers. In some cases, the advice was given by a party that had a direct financial interest in steering the participant to a particular IRA provider.

The report recommended action by DOL and IRS, including (1) standard guidance for participants about distribution options and (2) guidance for plans about accepting rollovers that are later found not to be qualified. In a letter to the GAO, Assistant Secretary of Labor Phyllis Borzi said that "We believe our work regarding the definition of fiduciary is key to addressing conflicted investment advice and related problems your report identifies."

The Center for Retirement Research at Boston College issued a report in February 2013. [Alicia H. Munnell, Anthony Webb & Francis M. Vitagliano, Will Regulations to Reduce IRA Fees Work?, http://crr.bc.edu/briefs/will-regulations-to-reduce-ira-fees-work/] Its recommendations included: making all rollover transactions subject to ERISA; extending ERISA protections to all rollover IRAs; and controlling fees.

The Financial Industry Regulatory Authority (FINRA), which regulates broker-dealers, issued an investor alert, [The IRA Rollover: 10 Tips to Making a Sound Decision, http://www.finra.org/Investors/Protect Yourself/InvestorAlerts/RetirementAccounts/P436001] In December 2013, FINRA issued Regulatory Notice 13–45, Rollovers to Individual Retirement Accounts, which notes that a recommendation to roll over plan assets to an IRA typically involves securities recommendations subject to FINRA rules regarding suitability, and that related marketing must be "fair, balanced and not misleading." [https://www.finra.org/web/groups/industry/@ip/@reg/@notice/documents/notices/p418695.pdf] FINRA released its 2014 regulatory and examination priorities on January 2, 2014, [http://www.finra.org/web/groups/industry/@ip/@reg/@guide/documents/industry/p419710.pdf], and the SEC released its examination priorities on January 9, 2014, [http://www.sec.gov/about/offices/ocie/national-examination-program-priorities-2014.pdf]. Both sets of priorities include practices related to recommendations to roll over assets from an employer-sponsored plan to an IRA.

In its examination priorities, FINRA stated that it "shares the GAO's concerns that investors may be misled about the benefits of rolling over assets . . . to an IRA." and that it will evaluate securities recommendations to determine whether they comply with FINRA's suitability standards. The SEC's examination priorities indicate that it will focus on the practices of broker-dealers, as well as investment advisers, with respect to IRA rollovers. See generally John V. Ayanian, Lindsay B. Jackson, Daniel R. Kleinman & Michael B. Richman, FINRA and SEC to Focus on IRA Rollover Practices in 2014, Feb. 6, 2014, http://www.morganlewis.com/pubs/EB_IM_LF_FINRAandSECFocusOn IRARolloverPractices_06feb14?source=homepg.

5. *Rollovers from Roth 401(b) and Roth 403(b) plans.* A rollover of an eligible rollover distribution from a designated Roth account under a 401(k) or a 403(b) plan can only be made to another designated Roth account or to a Roth IRA. IRC §§ 402A(c)(3)(A), 408A(e). The ability to roll over a designated Roth account into a Roth IRA can be significant, because a Roth IRA is not subject to the age 70½ required beginning date for minimum distributions. IRC § 408A(c)(5). As noted above, the Small Business Jobs Act of 2010 allows 401(k) and 403(b) plans to provide for in-plan Roth conversions. [IRC § 402A (c) (4)] and IRS issued guidance in Notice 2010–84, 2010–2 C.B. 872.

6. *Direct rollovers.* A qualified plan must permit a participant (or other distributee) to elect to have any eligible rollover distribution paid directly to another qualified defined contribution plan, IRA, 403(b) plan, or governmental 457 plan. IRC § 401(a)(31). Similar rules apply to 403(b) annuities. IRC § 403(b)(10). These "direct rollovers" are important because they are not subject to the standard 20 percent withholding tax applicable to eligible rollover distributions, discussed below. The statute does not, however, require plans to accept direct rollovers, and many plans do not. For purposes of applying the qualification requirements of IRC § 401(a), a direct rollover is considered to be a distribution followed by an immediate rollover. Treas.Reg. § 1.401(a)(31)–1, Q & A–14. Accordingly, any applicable spousal consent rules (see Chapter 7, supra) must be satisfied.

Requiring a plan to provide the option of a direct rollover is an added administrative burden. The regulations provide guidance about the mechanics of electing and accomplishing such rollovers. Treas.Reg. § 1.401(a)(31)–1. For example, the regulations allow the actual transfer to be made by "any reasonable means of direct payment." A reasonable means is expressly defined to include providing the check to the distributee with instructions to deliver the check to the eligible retirement plan, provided that the check is made payable to the trustee of the receiving plan for the benefit of the distributee. Treas.Reg. § 1.401(a)(31)–1, Q & A–4.

7. *Automatic rollovers.* If the value of an employee's vested accrued benefit exceeds $5,000, a qualified plan is not permitted to make an immediate distribution of the employee's benefit without the employee's consent. IRC § 411(a)(11). An immediate distribution is one that is made prior to the later of age 62 or the normal retirement age under the plan. Treas.Reg. § 1.411(a)–11(c)(4). Because maintaining small accounts for former employees is administratively expensive, most plans mandate distribution of benefits valued at $5,000 or less when an employee terminates employment. Because the portion of a benefit attributable to any rollovers is not counted toward the $5,000 limit, in some cases a mandatory cash-out can exceed $5,000. IRC § 411(a)(11)(D).

Prior to 2005, a qualified plan was permitted to make such a mandatory distribution directly to a terminating employee. Although former participants had the option of rolling over the cash-out into an IRA or into another employer's qualified plan, very few did. Now a plan must roll over a mandatory distribution in excess of $1,000 into a designated IRA, unless the departing employee elects to receive the distribution directly or elects a direct rollover of the distribution into another IRA, another qualified plan, a 403(b) plan, or a governmental 457 plan. IRC § 401(a)(31)(B). A similar rule applies to 403(b) plans and governmental 457 plans. Under the new regime the employee's ultimate options are unchanged, but the default has shifted from cashing out to rolling over. Would you expect this to increase the level of retirement savings?

Employers have been concerned about the administrative burden of selecting an IRA provider and arranging for the direct rollovers, and about possible fiduciary liability for taking those steps. Some employers have simply lowered the plan's mandatory cash-out level to $1,000, but most have established automatic rollovers for account balances between $1,000 and $5,000. The Department of Labor has provided a safe harbor under which the employer's designation of (1) the institution to receive the automatic rollover and (2) the initial investment for the rolled over funds, would be deemed to satisfy ERISA's fiduciary requirements. See DOL Reg. § 2550.404a–2. Generally, the safe harbor requires that such an IRA be invested in an investment product designed to preserve principal and to provide a reasonable rate of return consistent with liquidity. The safe harbor specifies that "preserving principal" requires an investment that seeks "to maintain, over the term of the investment, the dollar value that is equal to the amount invested." DOL Reg. § 2550.404a–2(c)(3)(ii). The IRA fees must not exceed the fees charged by the IRA provider for comparable IRAs that are not established for automatic rollovers. Are the safe harbor investments the best place to put long-term retirement savings? Why not allow investment in equities, such as broad stock market index funds?

8. *Withholding requirements.* There is a 20 percent withholding tax on any eligible rollover distribution that is not directly rolled over. IRC § 3405(c). For example, assume that a participant receives a $10,000 distribution from a qualified plan and that the distribution is an eligible rollover distribution. If the participant elects to have the distribution paid directly to an IRA or a qualified plan that will accept it, nothing is withheld and nothing is included in the participant's income. If the participant does not elect a direct rollover, the plan must withhold $2,000 and the participant receives only $8,000.

To avoid taxation of the distribution completely, the participant must roll over the full $10,000 distribution, not just the 80 percent left after withholding, within 60 days. If the participant can do so, which requires the participant to come up with $2,000 from some other source, the distribution will not be includible in income. The $2,000 withheld will be available as an income tax credit on the participant's tax return. Note that if the participant rolls over only the $8,000 actually received from the plan, $2,000 of the distribution will be taxable to the participant. Furthermore, if the participant is under age 59½ at the time of the distribution, the participant may also have to pay a 10 percent additional early withdrawal tax under IRC § 72(t) on the $2,000 (see Section F, infra).

One way around the withholding requirement is to make a direct rollover to an IRA and then withdraw the funds from the IRA. There is no mandatory withholding on distributions from IRAs. Why are IRAs treated more favorably than qualified plans with respect to withholding?

9. *Distributions of property.* If property other than money is distributed, the property must be rolled over in order to avoid taxation. It is not sufficient to contribute cash in an amount equivalent to the value of the property. Rev.Rul. 87–77, 1987–2 C.B. 115. However, the property may be sold and the proceeds (including any appreciation after the date of distribution) rolled over. IRC § 402(c)(6). No gain or loss is recognized on the sale to the extent the proceeds are rolled over. IRC § 402(c)(6)(D). Note that one cannot receive money in an eligible rollover distribution, purchase property with the money, and then deposit the

property into an eligible plan. See Lemishow v. Commissioner, 110 T.C. 110 (1998).

Why not permit the cash equivalent of distributed property to be rolled over? Note that certain property (such as collectibles and life insurance policies) cannot be held by an IRA. If a plan distributes these they must first be sold and the proceeds rolled over.

There is no exception from withholding if property is received in an eligible rollover distribution. If the distribution does not include sufficient cash to pay the withholding, the payor must sell enough of the assets to satisfy the withholding obligation. Treas.Reg. § 35.3405–1, F–2. However, the payor can instead arrange for the payee to provide sufficient cash from nonplan assets to satisfy the withholding obligation and thereby avoid the need for a sale. The statute protects employer securities from such forced sales by limiting the maximum amount of the withholding to the cash and fair market value of property (other than employer securities) distributed. IRC § 3405(e)(8). Thus, nothing is required to be withheld from a distribution consisting only of employer securities.

10. *Waiver of the 60-day limitation.* The IRS can waive the 60-day rollover period "where the failure to waive such requirement would be against equity or good conscience, including casualty, disaster, or other events beyond the reasonable control of the individual subject to such requirement." IRC § 402(c)(3)(b). Rev. Proc. 2003–16, 2003–1 C.B. 359, provides that in determining whether to grant a waiver, the IRS will consider all relevant facts and circumstances, including: (1) errors committed by a financial institution; (2) inability to complete a rollover due to death, disability, hospitalization, incarceration, restrictions imposed by a foreign country or postal error; (3) the use of the amount distributed (for example, in the case of payment by check, whether the check was cashed); and (4) the time elapsed since the distribution occurred. The IRS has been generous with waivers, even allowing a taxpayer whose tax preparer provided "incomplete and erroneous information regarding the tax effects of a rollover" and who later "discovered the advantages of [a] rollover" to complete a rollover well beyond the 60-day limit. PLR 200418048.

11. *Taxation of the "failed" rollover.* A purported rollover contribution to an IRA that turns out not to be eligible for rollover treatment can have significant tax consequences. First, the distribution from the plan that generated the failed rollover is taxable in the year of the distribution as if no rollover had occurred. Second, the contribution to the IRA is subject to the usual rules for IRA contributions, in particular, the maximum dollar limit. To the extent the failed rollover exceeds the IRA contribution limit it constitutes an "excess contribution." As long as the contribution (together with any attributable income) is withdrawn from the IRA on or before the due date (including extensions) of the contributor's tax return, the contribution will be treated as if it had never been contributed to the IRA. The net income attributable to the contribution, however, is includible in income in the year in which the contribution is made and is potentially subject to the 10 percent premature distribution penalty (see Section F, infra) if made before age 59½. IRC § 408(d)(4)(flush language).

If the excess contribution is not withdrawn by the due date of the return, there is a nondeductible excise tax of 6 percent on the amount of the excess. IRC § 4973(a). The tax applies each year to any excess amounts that remain in the IRA. Any excess can be treated as a contribution in a later year, thereby reducing the amount of the remaining excess, up to the maximum allowable contribution for that year. IRC § 4973(b)(2), (f)(2).

The taxation of a withdrawal of an excess contribution *after* the due date of the return is a matter of some dispute. The IRS has taken the position that an excess contribution is not added to the taxpayer's investment in the contract, arguing that when Congress amended IRC § 408(d)(1) to allow a taxpayer to have a basis in an IRA, Congress did not intend to provide a basis for any excess contribution. The Tax Court rejected this position in Campbell v. Commissioner, 108 T.C. 54 (1997), reasoning that "double taxation is to be avoided unless expressly intended by Congress." Is it relevant that excess deferrals made to a 401(k) plan and not withdrawn in a timely fashion are expressly *not* treated as an investment in the contract and hence subject to double taxation? See IRC § 402(g)(7).

12. *Notice requirement.* The plan administrator of any plan that makes a distribution eligible for rollover treatment must, within a reasonable period of time before the distribution, provide a written explanation of the opportunity for tax-free rollover treatment (and, if applicable, for electing special lump sum averaging). IRC § 402(f). The IRS has published safe harbor explanations that may be provided to recipients of eligible rollover distributions in order to satisfy § 402 (f). The most recent versions appear in Notice 2009–68, 2009–39 I.R.B. 423.

2. ROLLOVERS FROM IRAS

1. *General rule.* Generally, all or part of any distribution from a traditional IRA may be rolled over tax-free into another traditional IRA, a qualified plan, 403(b) plan, or governmental 457 plan within 60 days of receipt. IRC § 408(d)(3)(A)(i), (D)(i). As with qualified plan distributions, required minimum distributions (see Section F.3, infra) are not eligible for rollover treatment.

2. *Nontaxable portion.* The nontaxable portion of an IRA distribution can be rolled over only into another IRA, but not a qualified plan, 403(b) plan, or governmental 457 plan. In applying this limitation, the distribution is attributed first to amounts other than after-tax contributions. IRC § 408(d)(3)(H). For example, if the IRA consists of $4,000, $2,000 of which are after-tax contributions, $2,000 can be rolled over into a qualified plan, leaving $2,000 of after-tax contributions still in the IRA. Compare this with what would happen if $2,000 were simply withdrawn from the IRA and not rolled over. In that case the usual § 72 pro rata rule would treat 50 percent (i.e., $1,000) of the distribution as taxable.

3. *One-year waiting period between rollovers.* Only one rollover may be made from an IRA during any one-year period. IRC § 408(d)(3)(B). Although the statute could easily be read to the contrary, proposed

regulations issued in 1981 applied this one year rule separately to each IRA. "Thus, if an individual maintains two [IRAs], IRA-1 and IRA-2, and rolls over the assets of IRA-1 into IRA-3, he is not precluded [from] making a tax-free rollover from IRA-2 to IRA-3 or any other IRA within one year after the rollover from IRA-1 to IRA-3." Prop.Treas.Reg. § 1.408–4(b)(4)(ii).

However, in Bobrow v. Commissioner, T.C. Memo. 2014–21, the Tax Court recently held that the limitation applies on an aggregate basis, so that only one IRA-to-IRA rollover may be made in any 1-year period with respect to all IRAs. The Court held that the taxpayer was taxable on the full amount of the second rollover. In the above example, the Tax Court's ruling means that, after the tax-free rollover from IRA-1 to IRA-3, no tax free rollover from IRA-1, IRA-2, IRA-3 or any newly established IRA into any other IRA would be permitted within the 1-year period beginning on the date of the rollover from IRA-1 to IRA-3.

In Announcement 2014–15, 2014–16 I.R.B. 973, IRS indicated that it intends to follow the Bobrow decision and withdraw the proposed regulation, but will not apply the aggregate one IRA-to-IRA rollover rule to rollovers which occur prior to January 1, 2015. See also Announcement 2014–32, which clarifies this transitional rule.

Note that a direct transfer from the trustee of one IRA to the trustee of another does not count as a rollover contribution since it is not considered a distribution to the participant. Rev.Rul. 78–406, 1978–2 C.B. 157. Thus, an unlimited number of such trustee-to-trustee transfers may be made without any tax consequences. Why then are rollovers limited to one per year?

4. *Inherited IRAs.* An inherited IRA, other than an IRA inherited by a surviving spouse, is not eligible to receive rollovers or make rollover distributions. IRC § 408(d)(3)(C). The reason such rollovers are not permitted is that they would circumvent the minimum distribution rules of IRC § 401(a)(9) (made applicable to IRAs by IRC § 408(a)(6)). These rules are discussed in Section F, infra.

Suppose an IRA owner withdraws funds from her IRA just before her death. Can her executor roll those funds back into the IRA if the executor does so within the 60-day period? The IRS says no. See PLR 200415011. However, at least one court has held that the personal representative of taxpayer's estate has the authority to effect a tax-free rollover of a distribution from the decedent's profit sharing plan to an IRA, within the 60-day period that would have been applicable to the decedent, had he lived. Gunther v. United States, 573 F.Supp. 126 (W.D.Mich.1982). Is the court correct? Who should the beneficiary of the IRA be? In a number of rulings the IRS has allowed a post-death rollover of a pre-death distribution by a surviving spouse who was the sole beneficiary of the decedent's IRA. See, e.g., PLR 200520038 and 200415012. These latter rulings seem inconsistent with the language of the statute, which suggests that a rollover can only be made by the person who received the distribution from the IRA. See IRC § 408(d)(3)(A).

Although rollovers of inherited IRAs are generally prohibited, a direct trustee-to-trustee transfer of a decedent's IRA is allowed, provided it is to a new IRA maintained in the decedent's name as an inherited IRA. IRC § 402(c)(11)(A). This is an extremely important planning tool since it allows the nonspousal beneficiary to spread distributions from the IRA over his or her remaining life expectancy. See Section F.3, infra.

Why not allow rollovers of inherited IRAs (and inherited qualified plan accounts as well) and require appropriate reporting and beneficiary designations to avoid manipulation of the minimum distribution rules?

5. *IRA to Roth IRA rollovers.* A Roth IRA can be rolled over into another Roth IRA under the usual rules for IRA rollovers. A traditional IRA can also be rolled over (or converted) into a Roth IRA, but only if the taxpayer's adjusted gross income (AGI) does not exceed $100,000 and the taxpayer is not a married individual filing a separate return. IRC § 408A(c)(3)(B). These restrictions have been repealed for taxable years beginning after 2009. For purposes of determining whether the $100,000 AGI limit is exceeded, amounts included in gross income as a result of the rollover (or conversion) or by reason of a required minimum distribution under IRC § 401(a)(9) are *not* taken into account. IRC § 408A(c)(3)(C)(i).

The rollover (or conversion) of a traditional IRA is treated as a distribution of the assets in the IRA and is taxable under the usual rules for IRA distributions. IRC § 408A(d)(3). However, the 10 percent additional tax on early withdrawals does not apply. IRC § 408A(d)(3)(A)(ii).

Why would anyone be willing to pay a potentially large tax currently for the privilege of converting a traditional IRA to a Roth IRA? The answer is that for most taxpayers it makes economic sense, provided that the full IRA distribution is rolled over. The motivation is essentially the same as the reason why taxpayers prefer to contribute to a Roth IRA rather than a traditional IRA: greater effective deferral. See Chapter 8, supra. The table below assumes that a taxpayer has $100,000 in a traditional IRA and compares two situations: (1) taxpayer maintains the traditional IRA, and (2) taxpayer rolls over the traditional IRA into a Roth IRA. In the second case, the taxpayer must pay tax on the rollover, which the table assumes to be 40 percent and paid out of non-IRA assets. Thus, in comparing the Roth IRA to the traditional IRA, the non-IRA assets that would be used to pay the tax on the rollover must be considered together with the traditional IRA.

The following table illustrates that even with the large initial tax payment, the rollover to the Roth IRA has a significant economic benefit. Note that the 2006 PPA allows distributions from qualified plans, 403(b) plans, and governmental 457 plans to be rolled over from such plans into a Roth IRA, subject to the same rules that apply to rollovers from a traditional IRA into a Roth IRA. Thus, the numbers in the table would be the same if instead of a traditional IRA, the $100,000 came from a qualified plan.

ECONOMICS OF ROLLOVER FROM TRADITIONAL IRA TO ROTH IRA

	Maintain IRA		Rollover to Roth IRA
	Traditional IRA	Non-IRA Investments	Roth IRA
Starting account balance	$100,000	$40,000	$100,000
IRA return (6% tax free)	$139,656		$139,656
Non-IRA return (6% taxable)		$27,992	
Value at withdrawal	$239,656	$67,992	$239,656
Tax on withdrawal	$95,862	$0	$0
Net withdrawal	$143,794	$67,992	$239,656
Ending balance	$211,786		$239,656

Assumptions: 6 percent investment return; withdrawal after 15 years; constant 40 percent marginal tax rate.

Even nondeductible contributions that have been made to a traditional IRA can be rolled over to a Roth IRA. Is this a windfall or a sensible policy choice?

As noted above, the Small Business Jobs Act of 2010 allows 401(k) and 403(b) plans to provide for in-plan Roth conversions. [IRC § 402A (c) (4)] and IRS issued guidance in Notice 2010–84, 2010–2 C.B. 872.

6. *SIMPLE plan rollovers.* An IRA that is part of a SIMPLE plan (see Section A.2 of Chapter 8) can be rolled over only to another SIMPLE IRA during the two-year period beginning on the date the employee first participated in the SIMPLE plan. IRC § 408(d)(3)(G). After this period it can be rolled over just like any other IRA.

C. TRANSITIONAL LUMP SUM AVERAGING

Prior to the Tax Reform Act of 1986, a "lump sum distribution" from a qualified plan could qualify for a special 10-year forward income averaging. In addition, the portion of the lump sum distribution attributable to contributions prior to January 1, 1974, could qualify for treatment as long-term capital gains. When the tax structure was made less progressive in 1986, Congress repealed the capital gains treatment, substituted less generous 5-year averaging for 10-year averaging, and narrowed the availability of the averaging election to employees age 59½ or over. A transitional rule permitted individuals who were born before 1936 to make a one-time election to use 10-year averaging (using 1986 tax rates) and to have the capital gains portion taxed at a special 20 percent tax rate.

The Small Business Job Protection Act of 1996 Act repealed the special 5-year income averaging rule, effective for taxable years beginning after December 31, 1999. The Ways and Means Committee gave as reasons for the change the following:

> The original intent of the income averaging rules for pension distributions was to prevent a bunching of taxable income because a taxpayer received all of the benefits in a qualified plan in a single taxable year. Liberalization of the rollover rules [in] 1992 increased taxpayers' ability to determine the time of the income exclusion of pension distributions, and eliminates the

need for special rules such as 5-year forward income averaging
to prevent bunching of income.

H.R. Rep. No. 586, 104th Cong., 2d Sess. 98 (1996). The existing
transitional rules were retained and remain significant for the many plan
participants born before 1936. The details of the computation of the tax
on lump sum distributions can be found in IRS Form 4972. One
important planning point is that a rollover from an IRA into a qualified
plan account will preclude the use of the transitional rules for that
account unless all of the funds in the IRA are attributable to qualified
plan sources.

Although lump sum averaging will eventually disappear, the
definition of lump sum distribution is still relevant in connection with
distributions of employer securities, which are discussed in the next
section.

D. EMPLOYER SECURITIES

The distribution of employer securities from a qualified plan receives
special favorable treatment. The term "securities" for this purpose means
not only shares of stock but also bonds or debentures issued by a
corporation with interest coupons or in registered form. IRC § 402(e)(4).
The securities can also be securities of a parent or subsidiary corporation,
as defined in IRC § 424(e) and (f). The special treatment involves deferral
of gain on the unrealized appreciation of the securities and depends on
whether the distribution is made as part of a lump sum distribution or
otherwise.

In the case of a lump sum distribution, the net unrealized
appreciation (NUA) of the employer securities during the time they were
held in the trust is not taxed at the time of the distribution. IRC
§ 402(e)(4)(B). For determination of the cost basis of the securities in the
hands of the trust, see Treas.Reg. § 1.402(a)–1(b)(2). Generally,
purchased stock has a basis equal to its cost and contributed stock has a
basis equal to its fair market value on the date of contribution. The basis
of the securities in the hands of the recipient is the average basis of the
securities distributed. Rev.Rul. 57–514, 1957–2 C.B. 261.

The unrealized appreciation that avoids taxation will not go untaxed
forever, but rather will be taxed at the time the stock is sold. As an
example, assume that the employer has contributed $1,000 of employer
stock (valued at the time of contribution) to a qualified plan. If at the
time of its distribution in a lump sum distribution to the participant the
employer stock is worth $10,000, only $1,000 is taxable to the participant.
The participant then has a basis of $1,000 in the stock. If the stock is
later sold for $12,000, there will be a gain of $11,000, of which $9,000 is
attributable to the untaxed NUA. The $9,000 is taxed as long-term
capital gain, regardless of how long the recipient has held the stock. The
$2,000 gain in excess of the excluded NUA is long or short-term capital
gain, depending on the holding period after distribution. Treas. Reg.
§ 1.402(a)–1(b); Rev. Rul. 81–122, 1981–1 C.B. 202. In addition, the IRS
takes the position that the $9,000 of NUA is income in respect of a
decedent, and therefore no step-up in basis at death under IRC § 1014 is
available for the $9,000 of NUA. Rev.Rul. 75–125, 1975–1 C.B. 254. Thus,

in the above example, if the employee died when the securities were worth $14,000, the beneficiary would take a basis equal to $5,000, the fair market value reduced by the NUA.

Under IRC § 402(e)(4)(D)(i), a "lump sum distribution" is defined as a distribution from a qualified plan, within one taxable year of the recipient, of the balance to the credit of the employee, which becomes payable to the recipient: (i) on account of the employee's death; (ii) after the employee attains age 59½; (iii) on account of the employee's separation from service (except for self-employed individuals); or (iv) in the case of self-employed individuals, after the employee has become disabled.

The term "lump sum" is somewhat deceiving, since a lump sum distribution can be made in several installments, provided they are made within the same taxable year. For purposes of determining the balance to the credit of the employee, all pension plans are treated as a single plan, all profit-sharing plans are treated as a single plan, and all stock bonus plans are treated as a single plan; nonqualified plans are ignored. IRC § 402(e)(4)(D)(ii).

A distribution can qualify as a lump sum distribution even though a portion of the distribution is rolled over into an IRA. See PLR 200302048. Thus, if a participant receives a lump sum distribution of employer stock and cash, the participant could roll over the cash into an IRA and still qualify for the special treatment of NUA on the employer stock. Once employer stock is rolled over into an IRA, the NUA will no longer receive any special tax treatment. Given that the maximum federal tax rate on long term capital gains is 15 percent and the maximum rate on ordinary income is 35 percent, is it ever advisable to roll over a distribution of employer stock?

In the case of distributions other than lump sum distributions, only the NUA of employer securities attributable to nondeductible employee contributions is excluded from income. IRC § 402(e)(4)(A). Thus, in noncontributory plans, employer securities are fully taxable unless distributed as part of a lump sum distribution. The regulations provide rules for allocating the NUA between the nondeductible employee contributions and the other assets of the trust. Treas.Reg. § 1.402(a)–1(b). The basis of the stock in the hands of the distributee is the trust's basis, increased by that portion of the NUA required to be recognized. The computation of income and basis can get quite complex for contributory plans. See IRS Notice 89–25, Q–1, 1989–1 C.B. 662; Kirk F. Maldonado, Basis Issues Complicate Qualified Plan Distributions of Employer Securities, 77 J. Taxation 334 (1992).

The original reason for the favorable tax treatment of NUA on employer securities was the same as for 10 year averaging: to avoid a bunching of taxable income. As pointed out in the Ways and Means Committee report quoted supra, this reason no longer exists. Accordingly, there is no longer any good policy reason for preserving the exclusion.

E. LOANS

Sometimes a distribution from a qualified plan is simply not possible, or even if permissible, is disadvantageous due to penalties and/or the loss of significant future tax deferral. As discussed in Section F, infra, the IRC forbids early distributions from certain types of plans and subjects most permitted distributions made to employees under age 59½ to a 10 percent additional tax under IRC § 72(t). However, an employee may be able to make use of the accrued benefit without regard to these limitations, albeit in a limited fashion, by means of a loan from the plan.

Although a loan between a plan and a participant or beneficiary is potentially a prohibited transaction, there is an important exemption for any loan that (1) is available to all participants and beneficiaries on a reasonably equivalent basis, (2) is not made available to highly compensated employees in an amount greater than the amount made available to other employees, (3) is made in accordance with specific provisions regarding such loans set forth in the plan, (4) bears a reasonable rate of interest, and (5) is adequately secured. ERISA § 408(b)(1); IRC § 4975(d)(1). The regulations elaborate on these requirements. See DOL Reg. § 2550.408b–1. For example, the regulations permit up to 50 percent of a participant's vested accrued benefit under a plan to be used as security for a participant loan. Note that a loan to a participant or beneficiary that does not satisfy IRC § 4975(d)(1) and is secured by the plan benefit is a violation of the antialienation provision of IRC § 401(a)(13) and therefore disqualifies the plan. See Treas. Reg. § 1.401(a)–13(d)(2).

In addition, under IRC § 72(p), a loan from a plan (including a 403(b) annuity) to a participant or beneficiary (or the pledge or assignment of an interest in a plan or 403(b) annuity) will be treated as a distribution (referred to as a "deemed distribution") unless the loan meets certain requirements. The loan (together with all other loans to the participant from the plan) may not exceed the lesser of (1) $50,000, or (2) the greater of $10,000 or one-half the present value of the nonforfeitable accrued benefit of the participant under the plan. The loan must be repayable within 5 years (longer for certain home loans), with the payments made at least quarterly and in substantially level installments. All plans of an employer are treated as one plan and "employer" for this purpose includes businesses under common control. IRC § 72(p)(2)(D).

Generally a violation of IRC § 72(p), either in form or in operation, will cause a deemed distribution of the entire outstanding balance of the loan (including accrued interest). For example, this would occur if there were a failure to pay an installment payment by the end of the plan's grace period. However, if the only violation of IRC § 72(p) is that the loan exceeds the maximum permissible amount, only the excess amount of the loan is a deemed distribution. Treas. Reg. § 1.72(p)–1, Q & A–4(a).

Although IRC § 72(p) theoretically permits a plan to loan $10,000 to a participant whose vested account balance is under $20,000, such a loan would not be adequately secured (as required by ERISA § 408(b)(1) and IRC § 4975(d)(1)) if the only security were the participant's vested benefit. Most plans avoid the administrative burden of determining the adequacy of possible additional collateral by limiting loans to the lesser of $50,000 or one-half the present value of the nonforfeitable accrued benefit of the participant. For administrative reasons many plans will also limit the number of loans a participant may take in any year. Many plans will require that the loan repayments be made by payroll withholding, which generally avoids a deemed distribution as long as the participant remains employed. Most plans require immediate repayment once a participant leaves employment. Due to the obvious administrative burdens, participant loan programs are more commonly found in plans of large employers. In 2002, over 90 percent of plans with more than 5,000 participants had loan programs, but they were present in less than 50 percent of plans with fewer than 50 participants.

NOTES AND QUESTIONS

1. *Why allow loans?* Do loans undermine the purpose of the tax subsidy for retirement saving? Does the availability of loans lead to fewer pre-retirement distributions? Would a prohibition on loans discourage the adoption of plans or participation in voluntary plans such as 401(k) plans?

A GAO study in 1997 found that participation rates in 401(k) plans were 6 percent higher in plans with loan provisions than in plans without such provisions. Furthermore, participants in plans that permit borrowing against account balances contribute, on average, 35 percent more to their pension accounts than participants in plans that do not allow borrowing. On the other hand, the GAO also pointed out that borrowing can reduce retirement income, since the interest rate on the loan is usually lower than the typical rate of return on a diversified portfolio. GAO, 401(k) Pension Plans, October 1, 1997. See also GAO, 401(k) Plans: Policy Changes Could Reduce the Long-term Effects of Leakage on Workers' Retirement Savings, GAO–09–715 August 28, 2009 (finding that "The incidence and amount of the principal forms of leakage from 401(k) plans—that is, cashouts of account balances at job separation that are not rolled over into another retirement account, hardship withdrawals, and loans—have remained relatively steady, with cashouts having the greatest ultimate impact on participants' retirement preparedness. Approximately 15 percent of participants initiated some form of leakage from their retirement plans, according to an analysis of U.S. Census Bureau survey data collected in 1998, 2003, and 2006. In addition, the incidence and amount of hardship withdrawals and loans changed little through 2008, according to data GAO received from selected major 401(k) plan administrators. Cashouts of 401(k) accounts at job separation can result in the largest amounts of leakage and the greatest proportional loss in retirement savings. Most plans that GAO contacted used plan documents, call centers, and Web sites to inform participants of the short-term costs associated with the various forms of leakage, such as the tax and associated penalties. However, few plans provided them with information on the long-term negative implications that leakage can have on their retirement savings, such as the loss of compounded interest and earnings on the withdrawn amount over the course of a participant's career.")

2. *IRAs.* Unlike a loan from a qualified plan or a tax-sheltered annuity, a loan from an IRA to its owner or to a member of his or her family is always a prohibited transaction. IRC § 4975(d); ERISA § 408(d). If such a

loan were made, the IRA would lose its exemption and all assets would be treated as distributed. IRC § 408(e)(2). Furthermore, the assignment or pledge of an IRA is a deemed distribution to the owner. IRC § 408(e)(4). The inability to borrow from an IRA is a potential drawback of rolling over assets from a qualified plan to an IRA.

3.   *Multiple plans.* Employee has a vested account balance of $50,000 in Employer's profit-sharing plan. Employee also participates in Employer's defined benefit pension plan and Employee's vested benefits under that plan have a present value of $50,000. How much can Employee borrow from the profit-sharing plan?

4.   *Interest deduction.* The usual rules regarding the deductibility of interest generally apply to plan loans to participants or beneficiaries. However, no interest deduction is allowed for interest on a plan loan during any period (1) on or after the first day on which the recipient of the loan is a key employee (as defined in IRC § 416(i)) or (2) the loan is secured by elective deferrals under a 401(k) plan or a 403(b) annuity. IRC § 72(p)(3). Why should deductibility be limited in these instances and not others?

Assume that an employee in the 25-percent tax bracket wishes to borrow to finance the purchase of a car. Assuming that the employee can borrow from his 401(k) plan (with the loan secured by his elective deferrals) at 6 percent or from a bank (with the loan secured by the car) at 7 percent, which would be more economical? See IRC § 163(h)(1). Would the choice be different if instead the bank loan were secured by a second mortgage on the employee's principal residence? See IRC § 163(h)(2)(D), (h)(3).

5.   *Loans as eligible rollover distributions.* A deemed distribution of a loan due to a failure to satisfy IRC § 72(p)(2) is a distribution only for federal income tax purposes and is not a distribution of the participant's accrued benefit. Thus, it is not an eligible rollover distribution and is therefore not subject to mandatory 20 percent withholding. Treas.Reg. § 1.402(c)(2), Q & A–4. However, many plans require that a participant's benefit be reduced (offset) by the amount of the loan under certain circumstances. For example, some plans require automatic offsets when an employee terminates employment; others have no automatic offset, but provide for an offset if full repayment of the loan is not made within 30 days of termination of employment. Some plans provide for an offset whenever the participant requests a distribution. All such offset amounts are considered distributions and are eligible rollover distributions if they otherwise would qualify as such. Treas.Reg. § 1.402(c)–2, Q & A–8.

Since a direct rollover is impossible, the offset amount is subject to mandatory 20 percent withholding under IRC § 3405(c). But how can the plan withhold from something it doesn't have? Although the statute is silent on this issue, the IRS has announced that withholding with respect to an offset amount that is an eligible rollover distribution is to be limited in the same manner as in the case of a distribution of employer securities. IRS Notice 93–3, 1993–1 C.B. 293. "In other words, although the offset amount must be included in the amount that is multiplied by 20 percent, the total amount required to be withheld for an eligible rollover distribution does not exceed the sum of the cash and the fair market value of property received by the participant, excluding any amount of the distribution that is an offset amount or [employer securities]." Id. at 294. For example, assume Employee A has an account balance of $11,000, of which $10,000 is invested in a plan loan to Employee A. Employee A elects a distribution of his entire account balance, which causes the plan to offset the loan against the account balance. If Employee A does not elect a direct rollover, the plan will withhold $1,000. Employee A is taxable on $11,000, but Employee A can avoid taxation by contributing $11,000 to an IRA or another plan within 60 days. If Employee A elects a direct rollover of the $1,000, there is no withholding, but Employee A is taxable on the $10,000 offset amount. However, Employee A can avoid taxation by contributing $10,000 to an IRA or another plan within 60 days.

F. LIMITATIONS ON DISTRIBUTIONS

Both ERISA and the Internal Revenue Code impose limitations on the nature and timing of distributions from qualified plans. Some of these rules protect participants or their spouses. For example, distributions may not be postponed beyond a specified date unless the employee consents. IRC § 401(a)(14); ERISA § 206(a). A participant with a vested accrued benefit worth more than $5,000 cannot be "cashed-out" of the plan prior to normal retirement age without his or her consent. IRC § 411(a)(11); ERISA § 203(e). Moreover, subject to exceptions for certain defined contribution plans, a plan must provide benefits in the form of a "qualified joint and survivor annuity" and a "qualified preretirement survivor annuity," unless the participant and the participant's spouse elect otherwise. IRC §§ 401(a)(11), 417; ERISA § 205(a); see Chapter 7, supra.

The Internal Revenue Code also contains limitations on distributions that are not protective in purpose. These limitations, discussed in the materials below, are designed to ensure that qualified plans and other forms of tax-favored retirement savings operate to provide retirement income, rather than serve as a form of tax-subsidized saving for other purposes.

1. RESTRICTIONS ON EARLY DISTRIBUTIONS

A distribution of benefits from a plan during the working life of an individual enables the individual to expend those benefits on current consumption. Such benefits, unless they are saved, will not be available to support the individual in retirement. Since the purpose of the tax subsidy for retirement plans is to increase old age security by encouraging retirement saving, it is not surprising that Congress has imposed limitations on an employee's access to retirement benefits prior to retirement age. Thus, certain types of plans are required by the IRC to limit early distributions, if they are to retain their favorable tax status.

a. PENSION PLANS

Revenue Ruling 74–254
1974–1 C.B. 91.

Advice has been requested whether a plan, containing the provision described below, qualifies as a pension plan under section 401(a) of the Internal Revenue Code of 1954.

An employer established a noncontributory money purchase plan that permits distributions to be made to participants, to the extent their rights have vested, when they are transferred to job locations outside the area covered by the plan and, for that reason, become ineligible to participate in the plan. These participants are not considered to have terminated their service upon transfer and have no control as to the time and place of transfer.

Section 401(a) of the Code prescribes the requirements which must be met for qualification of a pension, profit-sharing, or stock bonus plan.

Section 1.401–1(b)(1)(i) of the Income Tax Regulations provides that a pension plan, within the meaning of section 401(a) of the Code, is a plan established and maintained by an employer primarily to provide systematically for the payment of definitely determinable benefits to his employees over a period of years, usually for life, after retirement. The regulations provide further, however, that a plan is not a pension plan if it provides for the payment of benefits not customarily included in a pension plan such as layoff benefits or benefits for sickness, accident, hospitalization, or medical expenses, except as described in section 401(h).

Disability and death benefits, although incidental to the primary purpose of providing benefits after normal retirement, are essentially a form of "retirement" benefits, since they are payable upon severance or termination of employment. Contingencies such as layoff, sickness, and accident generally do not involve a termination of employment, and payments for such contingencies from a qualified pension plan are prohibited by section 1.401–1(b)(1)(i) of the regulations.

Revenue Ruling 56–693, 1956–2 C.B. 282, as modified by Rev.Rul. 60–323, 1960–2 C.B. 148, holds that a pension plan fails to meet the requirements for qualification under section 401(a) of the Code if it permits employees to withdraw prior to normal retirement any part of the funds accumulated on their behalf which consist of employer contributions or increments thereon prior to the severance of employment or the termination of the plan. That Revenue Ruling deals with a situation in which withdrawals are at the option of, or subject to the control of, the employee and does not deal with the case in which an employee is being dropped from participation in the plan under conditions beyond his control. . . .

In this case, [the] payment of an annuity or lump-sum distribution from employer contributions or increments thereon when an employee ceases his plan participation but continues his employment, is analogous to payments for contingencies such as layoff, sickness, and accident and does not satisfy the requirements of section 1.401–1(b)(1)(i) of the regulations. Therefore, a pension plan does not qualify if it permits distributions prior to normal retirement and prior to termination of employment or termination of the plan, and this requirement does not depend on whether withdrawals of employer contributions are at the discretion of the employee.

Accordingly, this plan does not qualify as a pension plan under section 401(a) of the Code since it permits distributions to be made to participants prior to normal retirement and prior to their termination of employment or the termination of the plan.

IRS General Counsel Memorandum 39824
August 15, 1990.

[One] of the principles that underlies the definition of pension plan in Reg. § 1.401–1(b)(1)(i) and thus is relevant in construing the term "severance from employment" as used in Rev. Rul. 56–693 is that only employees (within the meaning of section 401) of the employer maintaining a pension plan may benefit under the plan. Treas. Reg. § 1.401–1(b)(1)(i) provides that a pension plan is a plan maintained by an employer to provide benefits to his employees. Consequently, when the employment relationship between an employee and the employer maintaining a pension plan is severed before the employee retires, a distribution of benefits to the employee from that pension plan after severance of the employment relationship with that employer is not inconsistent with the concept of a pension plan that meets all of the requirements of section 401(a). However, the determination of whether the employment relationship between an employee and the employer maintaining the plan has been severed is not based simply on whether, under common law, the employee has terminated employment with the employer. The rules for making this determination must be consistent with the provisions of section 401(a) and the definition of pension plan in Reg. § 1.401–1(b)(1)(i).

In determining whether the employment relationship with the employer maintaining the plan has been severed for purposes of section 401(a), the employer includes all members of any controlled group as defined in section 414(b), partnerships, proprietorships, etc. under common control as defined in section 414(c), and members of an affiliated service group as defined in section 414(m), of which the employer maintaining the plan is a member. Each of these sections provides that all employers described in that section are generally treated as the same employer for purposes of section 401(a), 408(k), 410, 411 and 415, and 416. Consequently, if the employer of an employee changes from the employer maintaining the plan to another employer who is treated as the same employer pursuant to section 414(b), (c), or (m), no severance from employment will be treated as having occurred for purposes of section 401(a).

Further, a severance of employment does not always occur when the common law employer of an employee changes to an employer that is not treated as the same employer of the employee pursuant to section 414(b), (c), or (m). If the new employer is substituted as the sponsor of the former employer's pension plan (or the subsidiary now under the control of a new parent retains the plan) or there is otherwise a transfer of plan assets and liabilities relating to any portion of the employee's benefit under the pension plan of the employee's former employer to a plan being maintained or created by the new employer, then the employment relationship with the employer maintaining the plan has not been severed with respect to that employee. . . .

If the new employer of an employee is not treated as the same employer as the employee's former employer under section 414(b), (c), or (m), and the new employer is not treated as maintaining the pension plan of the former employer with respect to the employee, a severance of the employment relationship between the employee and the employer maintaining the plan may be found to have occurred even though the employee has not separated from service for purposes of section [402(e)(4)(D)(i)(III)]. In the case of a liquidation, merger, or consolidation, etc. of an employee's employer, severance of the employment relationship with the employer maintaining the plan may be found to have occurred even though the employee continues at the same job with the new employer.

Further, a severance of the employment relationship between an employee and the employer maintaining a pension plan may also be found to have occurred for purposes of section 401(a) under certain circumstances when the stock in a subsidiary is sold by a parent (resulting in loss of control) even though there is no change in the common law employer of the employee. A severance of employment with respect to the employees of the subsidiary will be found to have occurred for purposes of section 401(a) if three conditions are met: the pension plan continues to be maintained by the original parent but is no longer maintained by the subsidiary in the hands of its new owner; no assets or liabilities are transferred to the subsidiary in the hands of the new owner or to any other employer who is treated as the same employer as the subsidiary under 414(b), (c), or (m); and the subsidiary in the hands of the new owner is not treated as the same employer as the original parent under section 414(b), (c), or (m). If these conditions are met, the pension plan is no longer being maintained by the subsidiary for the benefit of that employee.

NOTE

For decades, Treas. Reg. § 1.401–1(b)(1)(i) has precluded a distribution from a defined benefit plan before an employee reaches normal retirement age, usually age 65, unless the employee terminates employment. Recently, both employers and employees have shown increased interest in the possibility of "phased retirement," whereby employees nearing retirement could reduce their workload (and their pay), and at the same time begin receiving a portion of their pension benefits. Employers see this as a way to encourage older, more experienced workers to remain in the workforce. Employees who do not have the resources or the desire to retire completely see phased retirement as a way to increase their leisure time with less reduction in income. An employee who lacks access to a phased retirement program can construct a "do-it-yourself" program by retiring from Employer No. 1, receiving his or her pension, and then taking employment with another Employer No. 2 part-time.

In 2004, the IRS proposed regulations that would allow certain phased retirement programs. See Prop. Treas.Reg. § 1.401(a)(3). The regulations would permit a pro rata share of an employee's accrued benefit to be paid under a bona fide phased retirement program. The pro rata share is based on the extent to which the employee has reduced hours under the program. Payment of phased retirement benefits is permitted only if the program meets certain conditions, including that employee participation is voluntary and that the hours worked by the employee be reduced by at least 20 percent. A phased retirement program must be limited to employees who have attained age 59½. An employee must be entitled to continue to earn additional accrued benefits under the plan, but the service credit is proportionately reduced to reflect the part-time status. When the employee fully retires, the benefit would be the total of the original phased retirement benefit plus the remaining accrued benefit.

The proposed regulations note that the right to receive a phased retirement benefit is a "benefit, right, or feature" that is subject to the usual nondiscrimination rules discussed in Section C.5 of Chapter 9, supra. This may complicate matters for employers who do not want to make phased retirement available to all employees. The proposed regulations prohibit key employees (as defined under the top-heavy rules of IRC § 416) from participating in a phased retirement program. The regulations also clarify that a phased retirement program would be a protected benefit under IRC § 411(d)(6). Would this make employers reluctant to experiment with a phased retirement program? Would it be possible to set up a program that was available for employees who elect it during a brief (say three month) time period?

The proposed regulations have not yet been finalized.

Why limit phased retirement to employees who have attained age 59½? Why not allow an employee to opt to receive a full benefit while continuing to work part-time? As you will see in the following materials, profit-sharing plans can in general make in-service distributions long before normal retirement age. Why should defined benefit plans be treated differently?

The 2006 PPA allows pension plans to make in-service distributions to a participant who has attained age 62, without regard to the normal retirement age under the plan and without any need to comply with the work reduction and pro-rata benefit requirements under the proposed regulations. IRC § 401(a)(36).

The IRS has also closed a perceived loophole in § 1.401–1(b)(1)(i). To avoid the limitations on in-service distributions, some plans, particularly cash balance plans, have established a very young normal retirement age, such as age 50 or 55. Can you see why the normal retirement age is largely irrelevant in a cash balance plan? The regulations now provide that "The normal retirement age under a plan must be an age that is not earlier than the earliest age that is reasonably representative of the typical retirement age for the industry in which the covered workforce is employed." Treas.Reg. § 1.401(a)–1(b)(2)(i).

b.   PROFIT SHARING AND STOCK BONUS PLANS

Revenue Ruling 68–24
1968–1 C.B. 150.

Advice has been requested whether a profit-sharing plan will fail to qualify under section 401(a) of the Internal Revenue Code of 1954 because it allows members with no less than 60 months of participation to withdraw all employer contributions, including contributions which have been made within the last 24 months.

An employer adopted a plan intended to qualify as a profit-sharing plan under section 401(a) of the Code. The plan provides that a member with no less than 60 months of participation may withdraw all amounts credited to his account, including employer contributions made within the last 24 months. The plan also provides that any withdrawals will result in the suspension of participation in the plan for a period which will depend on the amount of the withdrawal. In any event the suspension will be for a period of at least six months.

Section 1.401–1(b)(1)(ii) of the Income Tax Regulations states that a profit-sharing plan must provide a definite predetermined formula for allocating the contributions made to the plan among the participants and for distributing the funds accumulated under the plan after a fixed number of years, the attainment of a stated age, or upon the prior occurrence of some event such as layoff, illness, disability, retirement, death, or severance of employment. A profit-sharing plan, within the meaning of section 401 of the Code, is primarily a plan of deferred compensation.

Revenue Ruling 54–231, [1954–1 C.B. 150], holds that the term "fixed number of years" is considered to mean at least two years. That Revenue Ruling also holds, in effect, that a plan which permits an employee to withdraw any portion of his share of the employer's contribution 18 months after it has been made (or within any period of less than two years) before the attainment of a stated age or the occurrence of some event such as layoff, illness, disability, retirement, death, or severance of employment, is not a profit-sharing plan within the purview of section 165(a) of the Internal Revenue Code of 1939 (now section 401(a) of the 1954 Code).

Neither section 1.401–1(b)(1)(ii) of the regulations nor Revenue Ruling 54–231 contains an exhaustive listing of events, the occurrence of which may permit distributions of funds from a profit-sharing plan before they have been accumulated for at least two years. Sixty months of participation under the instant plan will result in a significant deferral of compensation. The attainment of such a period of participation is an event within the meaning of section 1.401–1(b)(1)(ii) of the regulations and Revenue Ruling 54–231, and withdrawals may then be permitted.

Accordingly, it is held that the employees' profit-sharing plan will not fail to qualify under section 401(a) of the Code solely because it contains a provision allowing members with no less than 60 months of participation to withdraw all employer contributions, including those which have been made within the last 24 months.

Revenue Ruling 71–224

1971–1 C.B. 124.

Advice has been requested whether a profit-sharing plan that permits distributions to participants under the circumstances described below may qualify under section 401(a) of the Internal Revenue Code of 1954.

The plan, which otherwise meets the requirements of section 401(a) of the Code, provides that in the case of hardship a participant may apply in writing to the trustee for payment of part or all of his then vested interest in the trust. Subject to the discretion of the trustee, the participant may be paid a portion or all of such vested interest as the trustee determines is necessary to alleviate the hardship. The trustee is required to follow uniform and nondiscriminatory rules in his determination and his conclusion is to be final. "Hardship" is defined in the plan as "circumstances of sufficient severity that a participant is confronted by present or impending financial ruin or his family is clearly endangered by present or impending want or privation." Such hardship must be shown by positive evidence submitted to the trustee. The plan sets forth examples of circumstances wherein hardship may be found but does not limit such finding to those listed. . . .

The distribution of a part or all of an employee's vested interest because of the existence of bona fide hardship is an event within the ambit of section 1.401–1(b)(1)(ii) of the regulations. Therefore, provision may be made in profit-sharing plans for accelerated distributions because of such hardship provided that the term "hardship" is defined, the rules with respect thereto are uniformly and consistently applied, and the distributable portion does not exceed the employee's vested interest.

Based on the foregoing, it is held that this profit-sharing plan qualifies under section 401(a) of the Code.

———

1.   *401(k) and 403(b) plans: elective contributions.* 401(k) plans and 403(b) plans are not generally permitted to distribute amounts attributable to elective contributions prior to an employee's severance from employment, death, disability, or attainment of age 59½. IRC §§ 401(k)(2)(B)(i), 403(b)(11)(A). A significant exception to this rule is that in the case of "hardship," a distribution of the amount of the employee's elective contributions (but not the earnings) is permitted. IRC §§ 401(k)(2)(B)(i)(IV), 403(b)(11)(B). Although the statute does not define the term "hardship," the IRS has issued regulations, which apply to both 401(k) and 403(b) plans. Treas. Regs. § 1.401(k)–1(d)(3), § 1.403(b)–6(d)(2).

The regulations establish a two-part test. The employee must have an "immediate and heavy financial need" and the distribution must be "necessary" to satisfy the need. The first requirement will normally be easy to satisfy. The regulations provide a liberal list of "deemed" immediate and heavy financial needs, which include (1) medical expenses, (2) college tuition, (3) the purchase of a principal residence, (4) the prevention of eviction from, or foreclosure on, the employee's principal residence, (5) funeral expenses for an employee's parent, spouse, child, or dependent, and (6) repairs of damage to employee's principal residence caused by a casualty loss.

The "necessary" requirement is potentially more troublesome, since it demands that the immediate and heavy financial need cannot be met by alternative means. However, Treas. Reg. § 1.401(k)–1(d)(3)(iv)(E) provides an extraordinarily liberal safe harbor, under which a distribution will be deemed to be necessary to satisfy an immediate and heavy financial need of an employee if (1) The employee has obtained all distributions, other than hardship distributions, and all nontaxable loans currently available under all plans maintained by the employer; and (2) The employee is prohibited from making elective contributions and employee contributions to the plan and all other plans of the employer for at least 6 months after receipt of the hardship distribution.

Section 826 of the 2006 PPA directed Treasury to publish regulations allowing distributions from a 401(k), 403(b) or 457(b) plan, or a plan subject to section 409A, for hardship or unforeseeable emergencies of a participant's beneficiary, to the same extent as for a hardship or unforeseeable emergency of the participant, spouse, or dependent. See Section III of IRS Notice 2007–7, 2007–1 C.B. 395.

Aside from hardship distributions, plans are permitted to make payments to an alternate payee pursuant to a qualified domestic relations order, even if the participant is under age 59½ and still working. IRC § 414(p)(10). Cases have arisen in which the participant has obtained a QDRO in sham divorce proceedings in order to receive an otherwise unpermitted early distribution of benefits, and also avoid the otherwise applicable 10 percent penalty on early distributions. DOL Advisory Opinion 99–13A advises plan administrators on how to handle "questionable" QDROs.

Finally, a 401(k) plan can permit in-service distributions prior to age 59½ if (1) the plan terminates and no other defined contribution plan (other than an ESOP) is established or maintained, and (2) the balance to the credit of the employee is distributed within one taxable year of the recipient. IRC § 401(k)(10).

2. *401(k) and 403(b) plans: other contributions.* Amounts attributable to other contributions (employer matching and nonelective contributions) are generally subject to the same distribution rules as apply to profit sharing and stock bonus plans. See Section F.1.2, supra; Treas.Reg. § 1.403(b)–6(b). However, contributions to a safe harbor 401(k) plan, and contributions that are used to help the plan satisfy the special 401(k) nondiscrimination rules, are subject to the same distribution restrictions as elective deferrals. IRC § 401(k)(12)(E)(i); Treas. Regs. §§ 1.401(k)–2(a)(6), 1.401(k)–6.

In addition distributions from a 403(b) custodial account (as opposed to an annuity contract) may not be paid before the participant has a severance from employment, dies, becomes disabled or attains age 59½. Treas. Reg. § 1.403(b)–6(c). The 403(b) regulations now provide for a potential termination of a 403(b) plan and distribution of its assets, but this procedure is not always feasible. Treas. Reg. § 1.403(b)–10(a).

3. *457 plans.* Although not classified as qualified plans, eligible deferred compensation plans of governmental and tax-exempt employers (457 plans) are similarly tax-advantaged (see Chapter 8, supra) and are subject to early distribution limitations as well. Amounts deferred under a 457 plan may not be made available to an employee before the earlier of (1) the calendar year in which the participant attains age 70½, (2) when the participant has a severance of employment, or (3) when the participant is faced with an unforeseeable emergency. IRC § 457(d)(1)(A).

The definition of an unforeseeable emergency is much narrower than the term "hardship" under a 401(k) or 403(b) plan. Treas. Reg. § 1.457–6(c). Also, unlike other tax-favored retirement arrangements, the doctrine of constructive receipt still applies to eligible plans of private tax-exempt employers. IRC § 457(a)(1)(B).

2. ADDITIONAL TAX ON EARLY DISTRIBUTIONS

Even if a plan is permitted to make early distributions, the IRC discourages such distributions by subjecting them to an additional tax. The House Ways and Means Committee justified the tax as follows: "Although the committee recognizes the importance of encouraging taxpayers to save for retirement in order to take pressure off the social security system, the committee believes that tax incentives for retirement savings are inappropriate unless the savings generally are not diverted to nonretirement uses. One way to prevent such diversion is to impose an additional income tax on early withdrawals from tax-favored retirement savings arrangements in order to discourage withdrawals and to recapture a measure of the tax benefits that have been provided." H.R.Rep. No. 426, 99th Cong., 1st Sess. 728–29 (1985).

Under IRC § 72(t), a 10-percent additional tax is generally imposed on the taxable portion of any distribution made before the employee attains age 59½, other than a distribution made after the employee's death or attributable to disability. The tax applies to a distribution from any plan, contract, account, or annuity, which is (or was at any time determined by the IRS to be) a "qualified retirement plan" under IRC § 4974(c), which includes qualified plans, IRAs, and 403(b) plans. Section 457 plans are not subject to the additional tax, except to the extent the distribution is attributable to rollovers from plans that are subject to the additional tax. IRC § 72(t)(9).

Certain types of distributions are exempt from the additional tax:

(1) Distributions that are part of a series of substantially equal periodic payments (not less frequently than annually) made for the life (or life expectancy) of the employee or the joint lives (or joint life expectancies) of such employee and his designated beneficiary, but, except for IRAs, only if the series begins after separation from service;

(2) Distributions made to an employee after separation from service after attainment of age 55 (age 50 for public safety employees);

(3) Distributions made to the employee that do not exceed the amount of allowable medical expense deductions (determined without regard to whether the employee itemizes deductions);

(4) Payments to an alternate payee under a qualified domestic relations order;

(5) Distributions of certain dividends paid with respect to stock in an ESOP;

(6) Distributions of excess deferrals under IRC § 402(g), excess contributions to 401(k) plans or to IRAs, and excess

aggregate contributions (excess employee or employer matching contributions under IRC § 401(m));

(7) Distributions on account of an IRS levy;

(8) Any qualified reservist distribution.

Special IRA rules. The separation from service after age 55, and alternate payee exceptions do not apply to IRAs. IRC § 72(t)(3)(A). However, certain exceptions from the 10-percent additional tax apply *only* to IRAs:

IRA 10%. *penalty Exceptions:*

(1) Qualified first-time homebuyer distributions (as defined in IRC § 72(t)(8)), which are subject to a lifetime limit of $10,000;

(2) Distributions that do not exceed the amount of the taxpayer's qualified higher education expenses for the taxpayer, the taxpayer's spouse, or the taxpayer's children and grandchildren;

(3) Distributions made to certain unemployed individuals that do not exceed the amount paid for health insurance.

Why are these three exceptions limited to IRAs?

Certain distributions from SIMPLE accounts are subject to a 25 percent additional tax rather than the usual 10 percent. IRC § 72(t)(6).

NOTES AND QUESTIONS

1. *IRS levies.* The exception for IRS levies was added in 1998, although an earlier Tax Court case, Larotonda v. Commissioner, 89 T.C. 287 (1987), nonacq. 1988–2 C.B. 1, had held that such an exception was implied, arguing that "to impose the penalty [would] be like throwing salt into a wound." Isn't it reasonable for the Treasury to receive some compensation for its lost revenue, even when the withdrawal is compelled by the need to pay taxes? Note that the exception does not apply to a taxpayer who withdraws funds to pay taxes in order to avoid a levy. Suppose your 50-year-old client's only major asset is $800,000 in an IRA and the client owes the IRS $500,000. What advice would you give? Is this regime sensible?

2. *Other involuntary or hardship distributions.* In Aronson v. Commissioner, 98 T.C. 283 (1992), the taxpayer had deposited funds in an IRA at a financial institution that was taken over by the state banking authorities and liquidated. The taxpayer received an involuntary distribution of the funds in the IRA. The court upheld the imposition of the additional tax, noting that, unlike a tax levy, the distribution was eligible to be rolled over. Other than levies by third parties, most involuntary early distributions are eligible for rollover treatment. Common examples include the involuntary distribution of a vested accrued benefit of less than $5,000 (see IRC § 411(a)(11)) or a distribution upon termination of a plan.

"Hardship" distributions from 401(k) plans and 403(b) salary reduction plans are not eligible for rollover treatment. Nevertheless, they are subject to the IRC § 72(t) additional tax. Should they be? Does the existing exemption of distributions up to the amount of allowable medical expense deductions reflect a concern for hardship? Note that distributions pursuant to a qualified domestic relations order (see Chapter 7, supra) are not subject to the additional tax. IRC § 72(t)(2)(C). Why not? This discrepancy has apparently encouraged some participants to engage in sham divorces in order to obtain early distribution of plan benefits, free of the additional tax and the usual 401(k) and 403(b) plan limitations on early distributions. See DOL Advisory Opinion 99–13A.

3. *Prohibiting cash-outs.* If promoting retirement saving is the purpose of the tax subsidy for qualified plans and other tax-favored retirement plans, why not simply prohibit distributions prior to retirement or some specified age (perhaps the earliest age for receiving Social Security benefits)? To accomplish this goal, would it make sense to increase the IRC § 72(t) additional tax to 50 or even 100 percent? In addition, why not require that every distribution be in the form of a life annuity? What retirement policy is served by tax-subsidized saving that is withdrawn at age 65 and squandered on immediate consumption, leaving the participant with nothing but Social Security benefits? On the other hand, given the voluntary nature of our private pension system, would restrictions on access to retirement funds discourage the adoption of plans and thereby reduce the overall amount of retirement savings? "Experts that GAO contacted said that certain provisions had all likely reduced the overall incidence and amount of leakage, including those that imposed a 10 percent tax penalty on most withdrawals taken before age 59 1/2, required participants to exhaust their plan's loan provisions before taking a hardship withdrawal, and required plan sponsors to preserve the tax-deferred status of accounts with balances of more than $1,000 at job separation. However, experts noted that a provision requiring plans to suspend contributions to participant accounts for 6 months following a hardship withdrawal may exacerbate the long-term effect of leakage by barring otherwise able participants from contributing to their accounts. GAO also found that some plans are not following current hardship rules, which may result in unnecessary leakage." GAO, 401(k) Plans: Policy Changes Could Reduce the Long-term Effects of Leakage on Workers' Retirement Savings, GAO–09–715 August 28, 2009.

Another issue was recently identified by the SEC: "Self-directed IRAs are tax-deferred retirement accounts that carry a financial penalty for prematurely withdrawing money before a certain age. This financial penalty may induce self-directed IRA investors to keep funds in a fraudulent scheme longer than those investors who invest through other means. Also, the prospect of an early withdrawal penalty could encourage an investor to become passive with a lesser degree of oversight than a managed account might receive, allowing a fraud promoter to perpetrate his fraud longer." Investor Alert issued by the SEC's Office of Investor Education and Advocacy (OIEA) and the North American Securities Administrators Association (NASAA), Self-Directed IRAs and the Risk of Fraud, available at www. investor.gov.

4. *Spousal rollovers.* Since the 10-percent additional tax applies only to taxable distributions, a rollover avoids the tax. However, in some cases a rollover may create a later additional 10-percent tax that might otherwise not have been due. For example, assume H dies at age 58, survived by his spouse W, age 50. W can receive distributions from H's profit-sharing plan free of any 10-percent additional tax, since the payments are made after H's death. If a distribution is rolled over into an IRA, distributions from the IRA before W reaches age 59½ will be subject to the 10-percent additional tax.

5. *Substantially equal periodic payments and recapture.* The exception to the 10-percent additional tax for substantially equal periodic payments is subject to a form of recapture should the payments be modified within the later of five years of the date of the first payment or the attainment of age 59½. The tax for the year of the modification is to be increased by the amount of the 10-percent additional tax that (but for the substantially equal periodic payment exception) would have been imposed, plus interest. IRC § 72(t)(4).

The IRS has provided detailed guidance regarding what constitutes substantially equal periodic payments. See Rev. Rul. 2002–62, 2002–2 C.B. 710. There are three acceptable methods:

(1) *Required minimum distribution method*: The annual payment for each year is determined by dividing the account balance for that year by the remaining life expectancy of the taxpayer (or joint life expectancy if there is a designated beneficiary).

(2) *Fixed amortization method*: The annual payment is determined by amortizing in level amounts the account balance over the taxpayer's life expectancy (or joint life expectancy of the taxpayer and a designated beneficiary).

(3) *Fixed annuitization method*: The annual payment is determined by dividing the account balance by an annuity factor that is the present value of an annuity of $1 per year beginning at the taxpayer's age and continuing for the life of the taxpayer (or the joint lives of the taxpayer and a designated beneficiary).

The chosen interest rate for the second and third methods can be any rate not in excess of 120 percent of the federal mid-term rate (determined in accordance with § 1274(d) for either of the two months immediately preceding the month in which the distribution begins).

Note that the annual payment under last two methods is determined once in the first year and remains the same for each succeeding year. Such a fixed distribution could prove to be a poor choice if the value of assets in the account changes dramatically. For example, suppose in Year 1, A, age 44, rolls over a $2.5 million distribution from a qualified plan into an IRA and begins receiving $175,000 per year, representing the amount calculated to exhaust the IRA over the joint life expectancy of A and A's spouse under the fixed amortization method. Due to extraordinary investment success, the IRA is worth $9 million in Year 5. A might like to increase the annual payment, but the recapture rule presents a costly barrier. Rev. Rul. 2002–62 provides A with a way to increase the annual payment, by allowing an individual who begins taking distributions under either the fixed amortization or fixed annuitization method to switch to the required minimum distribution method for all future distributions. Switching back is not permitted.

A significant decline in the account value can also make fixed withdrawals undesirable. Thus, instead of $9 million in Year 5, A might have $500,000. Continuing to withdraw the $175,000 annual payment would quickly exhaust the account. The one-time switch is available in that case as well, allowing a reduction in the payment without penalty.

6. *Employer securities.* Employee A, age 40, has terminated his employment with M and has received his account balance from M's profit-sharing plan, consisting of $40,000 of M common stock, of which $20,000 represents net unrealized appreciation. Several months after receiving the distribution, A sells the stock for $50,000. How does IRC § 72(t) apply to the distribution of the stock and its later sale?

3. MINIMUM DISTRIBUTIONS

Just as premature distribution can be viewed as defeating the purpose of the tax subsidy for retirement savings, so can undue deferral of distribution. Imagine an employee with a large profit-sharing plan account who simply lets the funds accumulate for her heirs. After the employee's death, the beneficiaries might let the funds accumulate further, prolonging the tax deferral to take advantage of the tax subsidy. Even before ERISA, the Treasury had required that the primary purpose of a qualified plan must be to provide retirement benefits or deferred compensation. Treas. Reg. § 1.401–1(b)(1). Any other benefits had to be incidental. A number of revenue rulings were issued interpreting the term "incidental" as applied to death benefits. These rulings established the minimum distribution incidental benefit requirement (MDIB requirement), which limited the portion of the participant's benefit that could be paid after the participant's (and spouse's) death. In addition, there were detailed statutory rules that applied only to plans for the self-employed, requiring distributions to commence by age 70½.

These minimum distribution rules, now set forth in IRC § 401(a)(9), were eventually extended in the 1980's to all tax favored retirement arrangements, including IRAs, 403(b) plans, and even eligible deferred compensation plans of governmental and tax exempt employers (457 plans). See IRC §§ 403(b)(10), 408(a)(6), 457(d)(2)(A). The minimum distribution rules establish the permissible periods over which benefits from these arrangements may be distributed. The Congressional goal is to encourage the replacement of a portion of a participant's preretirement income stream at retirement, not the indefinite deferral of tax on a participant's accumulation under the plan. See Staff of the Joint Comm. on Taxation, 100th Cong., 1st Sess., General Explanation of the Tax Reform Act of 1986, at 710 (1987). Nevertheless, as discussed below, the rules permit quite lengthy deferrals, often far beyond the life of the participant. Because the deferral of distributions produces such significant tax benefits, financial and estate planners have an exceptionally keen interest in the details of the minimum distribution rules. See, e.g., Natalie B. Choate, Life and Death Planning for Retirement Benefits, 6th ed., 2006, particularly Chapter 1.

Following the enormous decline in the stock market in 2008, there was concern that the minimum distribution rules would compel individuals to take distributions (and therefore sell shares) at a time when prices were unusually low. In response, Section 201 of the Worker, Retiree, and Employer Recovery Act of 2008 suspended the minimum distribution requirements for defined contribution plans, including IRAs, for calendar year 2009. IRC § 401(a)(9)(H) Critics of the suspension argued that it favored high income taxpayers, since low and moderate income taxpayers frequently need the distributions to cover living expenses and would take them even if they were not required.

1.   *Pre-death minimum distributions.* Under IRC § 401(a)(9)(A), the entire interest of each employee must be distributed not later than the "required beginning date," or alternatively, payments must begin by that date. The required beginning date is generally April 1 of the calendar year following the later of the calendar year in which the employee attains age 70½, or the calendar year in which the employee retires from employment with the employer maintaining the plan. IRC § 401(a)(9)(C). In the case of IRAs or 5-percent owners of the employer, distribution must commence by April 1 of the calendar year following the year in which the owner attains age 70½.

The statute specifies that payments must be made over the life of the employee or over the lives of the employee and a designated beneficiary (or over a period not extending beyond the life expectancy of the employee or the joint life expectancy of the employee and a designated beneficiary). The precise determination of the minimum amount that must be distributed each year is left to the regulations. The typical annuity paid from a defined benefit plan will normally satisfy IRC § 401(a)(9). See Treas.Reg. § 1.401(a)(9)–6. On the other hand, in the case of individual account plans, the minimum distribution will be a series of unequal installments.

The regulations now provide a fairly simple rule for calculating the required minimum distribution for any given "distribution calendar year" beginning prior to the employee's death. The required minimum distribution is the employee's account balance (generally determined as of the end of the prior calendar year) divided by the "applicable distribution period." The applicable distribution period is generally determined from a uniform lifetime table in Treas.Reg. § 1.401(a)(9)–9, A–2, based solely on the employee's age as of the employee's birthday in the relevant distribution calendar year.

Note that the applicable distribution period does not depend on the identity of the beneficiary of the employee's account. It could be anyone, including an estate or a charitable organization.

The numbers in the table represent the joint life expectancy of an employee of a given age and a beneficiary 10 years younger. Obviously if a beneficiary were more than ten years younger the joint life expectancy would be longer (e.g., the joint life expectancy of a 70-year-old and a 1-year-old is 81.6 years!). But allowing distributions to be spread over such a long time period would cause the bulk of the account to be distributed after the employee's death. Congress prevented such prolonged deferrals by incorporating the minimum distribution incidental benefit (MDIB) requirement into the minimum distribution rules. See IRC § 401(a)(9)(G). The policy justification for tax subsidized death benefits is much weaker than for subsidized retirement benefits. The 10-year rule that is built into the uniform lifetime table is the current embodiment of the MDIB requirement.

The only exception to using the uniform lifetime table is when the employee's sole beneficiary at all times during the distribution calendar year is the employee's spouse and the spouse is more than 10 years younger than the employee. In that case, the applicable distribution period will be the longer joint life expectancy of the employee and the spouse, not the shorter number in the table. Treas. Reg. § 1.401(a)(9)–5, A–4(b). The MDIB rules never applied to spousal beneficiaries, because payments to a spouse are conceptually lifetime distributions when the couple is viewed as the appropriate retirement unit. The relevant joint life expectancies are set forth in Treas. Reg. § 1.401(a)(9)–9, A–3. Note that the longer the applicable distribution period is, the less is required to be distributed in any given year. Because marital status is determined on January 1 of the distribution year, divorce or death of the spouse later in the year does not affect the calculation for that year. Treas. Reg. § 1.401(a)(9)–5, A(4)(b)(2).

For distributions required before the death of the employee, the first "distribution calendar year" is the year before the year containing the required beginning date. The distribution for this first year must be made by the required beginning date. The distribution for each later year must be made by December 31 of that year. For example, assume that employee E was born on March 1, 1936, and that E's spouse, S, was born on September 1, 1931. S is designated as E's beneficiary under E's profit-sharing plan. E's first distribution year is 2006, the year E reaches 70½. Assume E's account balance in the plan was $1,000,000 on December 31, 2005. Using the applicable distribution period table, the divisor is 27.4 since E attained age 70 during 2006. The required minimum distribution for 2006 is therefore $1,000,000/27.4, or $36,496, and it must be distributed by April 1, 2007.

For 2007, the second distribution year, the divisor is 26.5, since E will be 71 in 2007. Assume the account balance at the end of 2006 has grown to $1,100,000. The required minimum distribution for 2007 is $1,100,000/26.5, or $41,509. It must be made by December 31, 2007. If the required distributions are large, the permitted bunching of the first two required distributions into one year may lead to a high marginal income tax rate. In such cases it may be preferable to make the required minimum distribution for the first distribution year by December 31 of that year, instead of waiting until the following April 1.

Each year a similar calculation would be repeated, applying the new denominator from the table to the account value as of December 31 of the prior year. Note that if the participant dies after reaching age 70½ but before the required beginning date, the pre-death minimum distribution that would otherwise have been required is excused. See Treas. Reg. § 1.401(a)(9)–2, A–6(a). In such a case the required minimum distributions are determined under the usual rules applicable to a participant who dies before the required beginning date, discussed in Note 3 below.

2. *Death on or after the employee's required beginning date.* Identifying the employee's beneficiary is largely irrelevant while the employee is alive, but important after the employee's death. If an employee dies on or after the required beginning date, the applicable distribution period for distribution years after the year of the employee's death is the greater of (1) the remaining life expectancy of the employee's "designated beneficiary" (if there is a designated beneficiary); or (2) the remaining life expectancy of the employee. Treas. Reg. § 1.401(a)(9)–5, Q

& A–5. As discussed more fully below, only individuals can be designated beneficiaries; neither estates nor charities qualify.

Unless the surviving spouse of the employee is the sole beneficiary, the remaining life expectancy of a beneficiary is determined using the beneficiary's age as of the beneficiary's birthday in the year following the year of the employee's death. In subsequent calendar years, the applicable distribution period is reduced by one for each year that has elapsed since the year immediately following the year of the employee's death.

For example, assume that Employee D, born on October 1, 1930, has named D's grandchild, G, born on December 1, 1982, as the beneficiary of D's profit-sharing account. D dies on September 1, 2006. The minimum required distribution for distribution year 2006, the year of D's death, is determined under the usual uniform table used for lifetime distributions, i.e., it is simply the account balance at the end of 2005 divided by 22.0, which is the applicable divisor for a 76-year-old. This distribution must be made by December 31, 2006, if it has not already been made prior to D's death. The minimum required distribution for 2007 is based on G's life expectancy, as of G's birthday in 2007, determined using the Single Life Table of Treas. Reg. § 1.401(a)(9)–9, A–1. Since G will be 25 in 2007, G's life expectancy is 58.2. Thus, the minimum required distribution for 2007 is the account balance at the end of 2006 divided by 58.2. This amount must be distributed by December 31, 2007. In 2008, the denominator will be 57.2 and each year thereafter the denominator will be further reduced by one. G's death would not cause any acceleration of distributions. This process would continue until 2065, when whatever is left in the account will have to be withdrawn.

If the employee's spouse is the sole beneficiary, the denominator is the spouse's life expectancy, redetermined each year based on the spouse's attained age in the year. For years after the year of the spouse's death, the denominator is the life expectancy determined using the spouse's age in the year of the spouse's death, reduced by 1 for each subsequent year.

To illustrate, assume in the above example that D's spouse had been named as the beneficiary of the account and that D's spouse turned 72 in 2006, the year of D's death. The spouse's life expectancy is 14.8 years in 2007 (i.e., the life expectancy of a 73-year-old) and therefore the minimum required distribution for 2007 is the account balance at the end of 2006 divided by 14.8. In 2008 the divisor would be 14.1, the life expectancy of a 74-year-old. If the spouse dies in 2008, then the divisor in 2009 is 13.1 (the life expectancy in the year of the spouse's death, reduced by 1). However, we shall see shortly that it is usually more advantageous for the spouse to roll over the account into her own plan.

If the employee does not have a designated beneficiary, the applicable distribution period is based on the life expectancy of the employee, using the age of the employee as of the employee's birthday in the year of death, reduced by 1 for each year subsequent to the year of death. In the above example, assume that D had named D's estate as the beneficiary of the account. D would have been 76 in 2006 had D survived to D's birthday. The life expectancy of a 76-year-old, determined using the Single Life Table of Treas. Reg. § 1.401(a)(9)–9, A–1, is 12.7 years.

The minimum required distribution for 2007, the year following D's death, is the account balance at the end of 2006 divided by 11.7 (i.e., the life expectancy in the year of death, reduced by one). In each subsequent year the divisor is reduced by 1. Thus, the account must be fully distributed after just 12 years, as opposed to the 59-year period that would have applied had the grandchild been the beneficiary. This example illustrates why estate planners avoid having an estate named as a beneficiary of a pension plan or IRA and why younger beneficiaries are preferable to older beneficiaries.

Why should any deferral be allowed beyond the lives of the employee and the employee's spouse? By allowing the benefits to be paid out over the life expectancy of a designated beneficiary who may be many years younger than the participant, wealthy participants (those who do not need the plan benefits to meet current living expenses) can ensure that the tax shelter continues for decades after they are dead. For instance, assume that a 65 year old decedent names her six-year-old grandson as the designated beneficiary of her IRA, which is worth $1 million at her death. The rules allow the IRA to be paid out over the grandchild's life expectancy, 76.7 years [Treas. Reg. § 1.401(a)(9)–9, Q & A 1]. With a constant 8% annual return, the total payments, if the grandchild takes only the required minimum each year, would be more than $800 million. This is patently absurd.

Would it be feasible politically (and fiscally) simultaneously (1) to repeal the minimum distribution rules for distributions during the lives of the employee and the employee's spouse, and (2) to require all amounts to be distributed within one year of their deaths?

3.   *Death before the required beginning date.* If an employee dies before the employee's required beginning date, the employee's benefit must be distributed under one of two methods. Treas. Reg. § 1.401(a)(9)–3, Q & A–1. The first method (the "life expectancy rule" set forth in IRC § 401(a)(9)(B)(iii)) is to use an applicable distribution period equal to the remaining life expectancy of the designated beneficiary, as if the employee had died after the required beginning date. Under this method the first distribution year is the year following the death of the employee, and distributions would have to commence by December 31 of that year. This method is only available if in fact there is a designated beneficiary.

The second method (the "5-year rule" set forth in IRC § 401(a)(9)(B)(ii)) requires that the employee's entire interest be distributed by December 31 of the fifth calendar year after the year of the employee's death. Id., Q & A–2. A plan may specify which method is to apply or allow employees or their beneficiaries to select the method. The default method in the absence of a plan specification or employee election is the life expectancy rule, provided that the employee has a designated beneficiary. Id., A–4(a).

For example, assume that the employee dies on April 30, 2006, at age 54. The employee has designated her son, born on June 9, 1982, as the beneficiary of her profit-sharing plan account. The son's life expectancy based on his age in 2007, the year following the employee's death, is 58.2 years. Thus, under the life expectancy rule, 1/58.2 of the plan account (valued on December 31, 2006) would have to be distributed by December 31, 2007. For each future year, the divisor would be reduced by 1. Alternatively, under the 5-year rule, annual distributions would not be required, but the entire account would have to be distributed by December 31, 2011. Section 201 of the Worker, Retiree, and Employer Recovery Act of 2008 provides that the 5-year period "shall be determined without regard to calendar year 2009." See IRC § 401(a)(9)(H)(ii)(II). Thus, in the above example, the entire account would not have to be distributed until December 31, 2012.

There is a special exception if a surviving spouse is the sole designated beneficiary. In that case, under the life expectancy rule, distributions need not commence before December 31 of the calendar year in which the employee would have attained age 70½. Treas. Reg. § 1.401(a)(9)–3, A–3(b). Furthermore, if the surviving spouse dies before such benefits are required to begin, the minimum distribution rules are to be applied as if the surviving spouse were the employee. IRC § 401(a)(9)(B)(iv). Thus, benefits could be distributed over the life of the surviving spouse's designated beneficiary. If the surviving spouse is younger than the deceased employee, even greater deferral can be achieved by rolling over the account balance into the surviving spouse's IRA, as discussed next.

4. *Spousal rollovers.* As noted in Section B, supra, a surviving spouse may elect to roll over an eligible rollover distribution from a decedent's plan. IRC § 402(c)(9). Once in the surviving spouse's account, the surviving spouse is treated as the owner for all purposes, including the minimum distribution requirements. Thus, a surviving spouse would not be required to begin receiving distributions from the account until April 1 of the year following the year in which he or she attains age 70½. Furthermore, distributions after the surviving spouse's death can be based on a designated beneficiary's life expectancy, thereby allowing a much longer time period for distributions. Since few qualified plans permit the surviving spouse to designate a beneficiary to whom lifetime payments are to be made if the surviving spouse should die, a rollover to a spousal IRA is a crucial tax-planning tool.

In the case of an inherited IRA, a spouse who is the sole beneficiary of the IRA can elect to treat it as his or her own without actually having to make a rollover distribution to another IRA. The election can be made by (1) redesignating the account as an account in the name of the surviving spouse as IRA owner, (2) making contributions to the IRA, or (3) not making distributions that would be required if the IRA were the decedent's. Treas. Reg. § 1.408–8, A–5(b).

For example, assume H dies at age 73 in 2006 and W, H's spouse, is the beneficiary of H's profit-sharing plan. The minimum required distribution for 2006 based on H's age using the uniform table must be made by December 31 of 2006. The remainder of the account can be rolled over into an IRA owned by W. If W has reached age 70½ by 2006, the distributions from the IRA for 2007 and later years will be determined based on W's age and the uniform table. If W has not turned 70½ by 2006, then minimum distributions from the IRA do not have to be made until W's required beginning date, which will be April 1 of the year following the year in which W reaches age 70½.

Effective for distributions after December 31, 2006, section 829 of the 2006 PPA allows a non-spouse beneficiary to make a direct transfer (not a rollover) to an IRA from a qualified plan, a governmental section 457 plan, or a 403(b) plan. Unlike spouses, non-spouse beneficiaries may only move funds to an IRA. The amounts transferred to an IRA will be treated as amounts held in an inherited IRA, and the beneficiary will be subject to the same required minimum distribution rules as apply to the non-spouse beneficiary of an IRA.

5.   *Designated beneficiary.* When a participant dies, the identity of the designated beneficiary is crucial, because distributions may be made over that person's life expectancy. The statute defines "designated beneficiary" to mean "any individual designated as a beneficiary by the employee." IRC § 401(a)(9)(E). The regulations make it clear that a person that is not an individual, such as an estate, is not a "designated beneficiary." Treas. Reg. § 1.401(a)(9)–4, Q & A–3. For this reason, naming an estate as a beneficiary of a qualified plan is generally not advisable, since the plan account would have to be distributed over a much shorter period after the employee's death. Trusts are treated differently, as is discussed below.

If there is more than one designated beneficiary, the beneficiary with the shortest life expectancy is generally the designated beneficiary for purposes of determining the distribution period. Treas. Reg. § 1.401(a)(9)–5, Q & A–7. If any beneficiary is not an individual (e.g., an estate or a charity), the employee is treated as having no designated beneficiaries, even if there are also individual beneficiaries. Treas. Reg. § 1.401(a)(9)–4, Q & A–3. For example, suppose the owner of an IRA writes in the beneficiary designation of the IRA the following: "$50,000 to Charity X and the remainder of my account to my daughter, Gwen." There is no designated beneficiary.

Post-mortem events can affect the identity of the designated beneficiary. The regulations specify that the employee's designated beneficiary is determined based on the beneficiaries designated as of the date of death who remain beneficiaries as of September 30 of the year following the year of the employee's death. Treas. Reg. § 1.401(a)(9)–4, Q & A–4. Consequently, a person who was a beneficiary as of the date of death, but who is not a beneficiary as of this later date (e.g., because the beneficiary has already received the entire benefit to which the beneficiary is entitled), is not taken into account in determining the employee's designated beneficiary. Thus, in the example above of the charity entitled to part of an IRA, as long as the charity receives its share of the IRA in a timely fashion, the remaining individual beneficiary will qualify as the designated beneficiary. The regulations expressly provide that if a designated beneficiary dies before the September 30 date, the individual continues to be treated as the designated beneficiary for purposes of determining the distribution period, rather than any successor beneficiary. Id., A–4(c).

The regulations specifically allow a beneficiary's disclaimer to be given effect for minimum distribution purposes, provided the disclaimer satisfies IRC § 2518 by the September 30 date. Id., A–4(a). Section 2518 specifies that a disclaimer with respect to an interest in property will be recognized for estate and gift tax purposes only if:

1.   the disclaimer is in writing;

2.   the holder of legal title to the property to which the interest relates receives the writing within 9 months after the later of (A) the date of the transfer creating the interest, or (B) the day on which the person disclaiming turns 21;

3.   the person disclaiming has not accepted the property or any of its benefits; and

4.   as a result of the disclaimer, the interest passes without any direction on the part of the person making the disclaimer, and passes either (A) to the spouse of the decedent, or (B) to a person other than the person making the disclaimer.

For example, a participant names Son, age 40, as the beneficiary and names Son's children as alternate beneficiaries should Son predecease her. Son could timely disclaim Son's interest and Son's children would then become the designated beneficiaries, thereby allowing distributions to be made over a much longer period.

6.   *Separate accounts.* As noted above, if there are multiple beneficiaries, the beneficiary with the shortest life expectancy determines the distribution period. However, if the plan maintains separate accounts for each beneficiary, the minimum required distribution is determined separately for each separate account, based on the life expectancy of the designated beneficiary of each separate account. The plan can set up the separate accounts after the death of the employee, provided the separate accounts are established by December 31 of the year following the year of the employee's death. All post-death investment gains and losses, contributions, and forfeitures, for the period prior to the establishment of the separate accounts, must be allocated among the separate accounts "on a pro rata basis in a reasonable and consistent manner." Treas. Reg. § 1.401(a)(9)–8, A–3. Any post-death distribution to a beneficiary must be allocated to that beneficiary's account.

To illustrate, assume a participant's account is payable to "my three children, A, B, and C" in event of the participant's death. If the plan divides the account into three separate accounts by December 31 of the year following the participant's death, each child will be considered the designated beneficiary with respect to his or her account. In the absence of a division into separate accounts, the oldest child is deemed to be the designated beneficiary.

7. |Trusts| Like an estate, a trust is not an individual and cannot be a designated beneficiary. However, the regulations treat trusts far more liberally, allowing the beneficiaries of a trust to be treated as designated beneficiaries with respect to the trust's interest in the employee's benefit, provided the following requirements are met:

Trusts can't be a designated beneficiary

(1)   The trust is a valid trust under state law, or would be but for the fact that there is no corpus;

(2)   The trust is irrevocable or will, by its terms, become irrevocable upon the death of the employee;

— *Use "Conduit Trust (next page)"*

(3)   The beneficiaries are identifiable from the trust instrument; and

(4)   Proper documentation (such as a list of all the beneficiaries) has been provided to the plan administrator. See Treas. Reg. § 1.401(a)(9)–4, Q & A–5.

These trusts have become known as "see through" trusts, because the regulations see through the trust and treat the individual beneficiaries as the designated beneficiaries. If the trust has multiple beneficiaries, the usual rule that the beneficiary with the shortest life expectancy is the designated beneficiary for minimum distribution purposes applies. In applying this rule, someone who is merely a potential successor to the interest of another beneficiary upon that beneficiary's death is not treated as a beneficiary. Treas. Reg. § 1.401(a)(9)–5, A–7(c).

See Through Trust

The "see through" trust rules have important implications for trust drafting. For example, in PLR 200228025, a grandmother named a trust as the beneficiary of her IRA. The trustee had discretion to distribute funds to each of her two minor grandchildren or to accumulate them in the trust. When each grandchild reached age 30, he could withdraw his share of the IRA. If both children died before reaching age 30, a 67-year-old contingent beneficiary would become the beneficiary of the trust assets. The IRS ruled that because distributions from the IRA could be accumulated in the trust and ultimately distributed to the contingent beneficiary, the contingent beneficiary qualified as a designated beneficiary and therefore the life expectancy of the 67-year-old had to be used.

Conduit Trust

The way around this problem is to make the trust a "conduit trust," which is a trust that provides that all amounts distributed from the retirement plan account to the trustee must be distributed to the current beneficiaries. See Treas. Reg. § 1.401(a)(9)–5, A–7(c)(3), Example 2.

As noted in Note 6, supra, if there are multiple beneficiaries of a qualified plan or IRA and the plan maintains separate accounts, the minimum required distribution can be determined separately for each account. Can one leave the entire benefit to a conduit trust and create valid separate accounts in the trust? The regulations and a number of private rulings say no. See Treas. Reg. § 1.401(a)(9)–4, A–5(c)(last sentence); PLR 200329048. This restriction has irritated practitioners considerably because it would be much simpler to name the trust as the plan beneficiary and create the separate accounts within the trust.

Despite their tax advantage, separate accounts may not be consistent with particular estate planning goals. For example, a participant with several children who may have dramatically different and not wholly predictable needs may decide to name a family trust as the plan beneficiary, and to give the trustee discretion regarding what distributions to make to or for each child, depending on each child's needs. Lacking separate accounts, the plan would have to make required minimum distributions based on the life expectancy of the oldest child.

8.   *Multiple plans.* The minimum required distribution must be calculated separately for each plan. Each qualified plan must be considered individually in satisfying its distribution requirement. However, if there are multiple IRA accounts, the IRS will permit the required distribution from each to be totaled and the resulting total

amount withdrawn from any one or more of the IRAs. Treas. Reg. § 1.408–8, Q & A–9. A similar rule applies to 403(b) accounts and Roth IRAs, but a distribution from one type of account cannot be used to meet a minimum required distribution from another type. For example, a distribution from a Roth IRA will not count toward satisfying the minimum required distribution from a traditional IRA.

9.   *Annuity payments.* Under IRC § 401(a)(9), annuity distributions under a defined benefit plan must be made at intervals not longer than one year. The payments must be made over the life (or lives), or over a period certain not to exceed the life expectancy (or joint life expectancy), of the employee (or the employee and the designated beneficiary). The payments must either not increase or increase only on account of the following: (1) cost of living adjustments, (2) an increase in a joint and survivor annuity by reason of the death of the nonemployee annuitant or the divorce of the participant and spouse, (3) cash refunds of employee contributions upon death, (4) increases in benefits under the plan. Treas. Reg. § 1.401(a)(9)–6, Q & A–14. Annuity contracts purchased from insurance companies are permitted to have certain other increases in benefits, including dividends or other payments resulting from actuarial gains. See Id., Q & A–14(c).

Suppose employee, age 75, retires and receives a joint and survivor annuity for the joint life of the employee and a grandchild, age 2. If the grandchild's annuity upon the death of the employee were allowed to be 100 percent of the employee's annuity, most of the value of the benefit would be payable as a death benefit to the grandchild, hence not as a retirement benefit to the employee or the employee's spouse. Recall that the minimum distribution incidental benefit (MDIB) rule, incorporated into the minimum distribution rule by IRC § 401(a)(9)(G), is designed to defeat such outcomes.

For joint and survivor annuities, the MDIB rule limits the percentage of the employee's annuity that can be paid to a survivor who is not the employee's spouse. The applicable percentage is specified in a table in the regulations based on the "adjusted employee/beneficiary age difference." See Treas. Reg. § 1.401(a)(9)–6, A–2(c)(2). The adjusted employee/beneficiary age difference is defined as the excess of the age of the employee over the age of the beneficiary, reduced by the number of years (if any) that the employee is younger than age 70. A survivor annuity of 100 percent is allowed if the adjusted age difference is 10 years or less, but for adjusted age differences greater than 43 years the survivor annuity is limited to 52 percent. Thus, the 75-year-old employee in the example above may elect a joint and survivor annuity with the 2-year-old grandchild as beneficiary, but the survivor annuity must not exceed 52 percent of the employee's annuity. The effect of the MDIB rule is to skew more of the benefit to years prior to the employee's death.

10.   *Enforcing the minimum distribution rules: Excise taxes and reporting requirements.* If a distribution from a plan subject to the minimum distribution requirement is less than the required minimum, a 50 percent nondeductible excise tax is imposed on the amount of the shortfall. IRC § 4974. The tax is imposed on the payee of the required distribution. However, the IRS is authorized to waive the tax if the payee

can establish that the shortfall was due to reasonable error and that reasonable steps are being taken to remedy it. IRC § 4974(d).

The Staff of the Joint Committee on Taxation has explained the rationale for the excise tax and its relation to the disqualification sanction:

> The sanction of disqualification of a plan [was] too onerous for a plan's failure in operation to satisfy technical distribution requirements with respect to any one participant. Disqualification might result in adverse tax consequences to all plan participants or all highly compensated plan participants, even though the plan administrator was responsible for the failure to make a required distribution, and the failure may have occurred with respect to only a single participant. Plan disqualification procedures also imposed a significant administrative burden on the IRS. Although Congress believed that a plan should, by its terms, prohibit the violation of the minimum distribution rules, Congress also believed an operational error should not cause plan disqualification.

Staff of the Joint Comm. on Taxation, 100th Cong., 1st Sess., General Explanation of the Tax Reform Act of 1986, at 710 (1987).

To improve compliance, the IRS has imposed a reporting requirement on IRA custodians and trustees, who must, by January 31 of each year, either inform the IRA owner of the amount required to be distributed from the IRA and the date by which it is required, or offer to calculate the amount of the required minimum distribution upon request. In addition, IRA custodians and trustees must identify to the IRS each IRA for which a minimum distribution is required. See Notice 2002–27, 2002–1 C.B. 814. These rules apply only to lifetime distributions. Moreover, in computing the required minimum distribution, the trustee or custodian may presume that the IRA owner does not have a spouse more than ten years younger.

11. *Rollovers.* As noted in Section B.1 supra, a required minimum distribution is not an eligible rollover distribution. See IRC § 402(c)(4)(B). The purpose of the minimum distribution rules is to prevent unwarranted deferral, and a rollover would extend the deferral period. This rule can affect distributions even before the required beginning date. Any distribution made on or after January 1 of the year in which the participant will reach age 70½ is considered part of the required minimum distribution (up to the amount of the required minimum distribution). Such a distribution cannot be rolled over. Treas. Reg. § 1.402(c)–2, A–7.

A rollover from one plan to another will reduce the assets of the distributing plan and increase the assets of the receiving plan for purposes of computing the following year's required minimum distribution. To preclude an obvious tax avoidance scheme, a rollover that straddles two years is treated as if it had been completed in the earlier year. Treas. Reg. § 1.401(a)(9)–7, A–2. Thus, if an individual withdraws $10,000 from IRA A on December 15 of Year 1 and rolls it over into IRA B on January 15 of Year 2, for purposes of computing the required minimum distribution for Year 2, IRA B is considered to have an additional $10,000 on December 31 of Year 1.

12. *Roth IRAs.* The pre-death minimum distribution rules of IRC § 401(a)(9)(A) and the minimum distribution incidental death benefit rules do not apply to Roth IRAs. IRC § 408A(c)(5). Thus, no distribution from a Roth IRA is required until after the death of the owner. This distribution rule is a significant advantage of a Roth IRA compared to a traditional IRA. When the Roth IRA owner dies, the minimum distribution rules apply as though the Roth IRA owner died before his or her required beginning date. Thus, distribution must be made under either the "five-year rule" or the "life expectancy rule" described in Note 3, supra. Treas. Reg. § 1.408A–6, Q & A–14(b).

13. *Changes to the Minimum Distribution Rules*: *Qualifying Longevity Annuity Contracts.*

Under the prior regulations, an immediate annuity purchased in a plan or IRA were required to satisfy the following requirements: [Treas. Reg. § 1.401(a)(9)–6, A–1(a)]

> Payments under the contract must begin no later than the participant's required beginning date; [Treas. Reg. § 1.401(a)(9)–6, A–1(c)(7)]
>
> Payments must be made at least annually; and
>
> Payments must be non-increasing, subject to exceptions (e.g., cost-of-living increases). [Treas. Reg. § 1.401(a)(9)–6, A–14]

There were also limitations on the period over which the annuity payments are made. [Treas. Reg. § 1.401(a)(9)–5, A–1(e)]

Under those regulations, a longevity annuity (i.e., a deferred annuity under which payments do not begin until an advanced age, such as 80 or 85) could not be used to satisfy the minimum distribution requirements because of the rule that payments under an annuity contract must begin by the required beginning date.

On February 3, 2012, IRS issued proposed regulations [77 Fed. Reg. 5443] providing for the purchase of "qualifying longevity annuity contracts" (QLACs) by IRAs and individual account plans. According to the preamble to the regulations:

> The Treasury Department and the IRS have concluded that there are substantial advantages to modifying the required minimum distribution rules in order to facilitate a participant's purchase of a deferred annuity that is scheduled to commence at an advanced age—such as age 80 or 85—using a portion of his or her account. Under the proposed amendments to these rules, prior to annuitization, the participant would be permitted to exclude the value of a longevity annuity contract that meets certain requirements from the account balance used to determine required minimum distributions. Thus, a participant would never need to commence distributions from the annuity contract before the advanced age in order to satisfy the required minimum distribution rules and, accordingly, the contract could be designed with a fixed annuity starting date at the advanced

age (and would not need to provide an option to accelerate commencement of the annuity).

Treasury and the IRS issued final regulations on July 1, 2014. See http://www.treasury.gov/press-center/press-releases/Pages/jl2448.aspx. The final rules are largely consistent with the proposed regulations, but expand the permitted longevity annuities in several respects, including:

Increasing the maximum permitted investment: Under the final rules, a plan or IRA may permit plan participants to use up to 25 percent of their account balance or (if less) $125,000 (up from $100,000 in the proposed regulations) to purchase a qualifying longevity annuity without concern about noncompliance with the age 70 1/2 minimum distribution requirements. The dollar limit will be adjusted for cost-of-living increases.

Allowing "return of premium" death benefit: Under the final rules, a longevity annuity can provide that, if the retiree dies before (or after) the age when the annuity begins, the premiums they paid but have not yet received as annuity payments, will be returned to their accounts.

Protecting individuals against accidental payment of longevity annuity premiums exceeding the limits: The final rules permit individuals who inadvertently exceed the 25 percent or $125,000 limits to correct the excess without disqualifying the annuity purchase.

Providing more flexibility in issuing longevity annuities: The proposed regulations provided that a contract is not a qualifying longevity annuity contract unless it states, when issued, that it is intended to be one. The final rules facilitate the issuance of longevity annuities by allowing the alternatives of including such a statement in an insurance certificate, rider, or endorsement relating to a contract.

According to the Committee of Annuity Insurers, the median IRA balance of about $54,000 in 2008 for individuals between the ages of 65 and 69 would support a maximum QLAC premium of about $13,500. Based on information provided in the preamble to the proposed regulation, a QLAC purchased at age 70 would produce about $290 in monthly joint and survivor annuity payments commencing at age 85. "Assuming 3% annual inflation, the purchasing power of this monthly payment would be about $185 at age 85," an amount that may be insufficient to motivate individuals to purchase QLACs, the annuity insurers said." [BNA Snapshot, Qualified Longevity Annuity Contract Rules Should Allow More Options, Commenters Say]

G. ESTATE AND GIFT TAXATION

The proceeds of qualified plans, 403(b) annuities, and IRAs payable as a result of the death of the participant are fully includable in the participant's gross estate. IRC § 2039. Similarly, the irrevocable designation of a beneficiary is a completed gift for gift tax purposes. Typically, a beneficiary designation becomes irrevocable only when the participant dies or begins to receive benefits under an annuity. Recall that most 401(k) plans do not offer annuities, and that many participants do not elect annuities where offered. When an irrevocable beneficiary designation is made, the annual per donee gift tax exclusion ($13,000 in 2009) is not available, since the beneficiary's interest is a future interest. IRC § 2503(b). The annual gift tax exclusion remained at $ 13,000 for 2010, 2011 and 2012, but increased to $ 14,000 for 2013 and 2014.

The following notes explore some of the estate and gift tax issues raised by retirement benefits.

1. *Transfers to spouses.* Transfers to spouses receive uniquely favorable treatment under the estate and gift taxes. Such transfers generally qualify for the unlimited marital deduction, unless they are in the form of certain nonqualifying terminable interests, a highly technical concept that we can only touch upon here. See IRC §§ 2056, 2523. Thus, if an employee dies having named his spouse as the beneficiary of the balance of his profit-sharing plan account, the value of the account is included in the gross estate, but there is a marital deduction for an equal amount.

Special provisions also permit transfers of spousal joint and survivor annuity interests to qualify for the deduction, even though such transferred interests would normally be treated as nonqualifying terminable interests. Under IRC § 2503(f), a spouse's waiver of her rights under a qualified joint and survivor annuity (QJSA) or qualified preretirement survivor annuity (QPSA) is not treated as a transfer of property by gift. QPSAs and QJSAs are discussed in Chapter 7, supra. In addition, if under a joint and survivor annuity no one other than the spouses has the right to receive payments before both spouses die, all of the interests created by the annuity qualify for the gift tax marital deduction, unless the donor spouse elects otherwise. IRC § 2523(f)(6).

If the donee (nonemployee) spouse dies first, nothing is included in that spouse's gross estate. If the donor spouse dies first, the annuity is treated as qualified terminable interest property (QTIP) and therefore eligible for the estate tax marital deduction, unless the donor spouse's executor elects otherwise. IRC § 2056(b)(7)(C). This means that only the remaining value of the annuity, if any, will be subject to estate taxation when the surviving spouse dies. IRC § 2044.

The net result of these rules is that the typical joint and survivor annuity, which ceases payments when both spouses die, is free of estate and gift taxation. An annuity with a refund or guaranteed payment feature may be subject to tax after the death of both spouses. For example, assume that H retires in Year One and elects a $10,000 per year joint and survivor annuity for the life of himself and his wife, W, with payments guaranteed for ten years, to be paid to X if both H and W die within ten years. If W dies first and then in Year Five H dies, the value of the remaining payments to X is included in H's gross estate. Similarly, if H dies first and W dies in Year Five, the value of the remaining payments to X is included in W's gross estate.

As discussed earlier in the chapter, it is generally advantageous for income tax purposes to name a spouse as the beneficiary of a retirement plan. By making a surviving spouse the designated beneficiary, required distributions under the minimum distribution rules can generally be postponed for a longer period than if other beneficiaries were named. Moreover, only a surviving spouse can roll over distributions into her own IRA.

Nevertheless, in some cases there may be good estate tax planning reasons for making someone other than the spouse the beneficiary, for example, in order to maximize use of the so-called "credit shelter." In general, the first $5,340,000 (in 2014) of transferred wealth is free of estate or gift tax due to the operation of the applicable exclusion amount under IRC § 2010. It is important not to waste this exclusion. Under the 2010 legislation, the Tax Relief, Unemployment Insurance Authorization, and Job Creation Act of 2010, any portion of the exclusion that was not used when the first spouse dies may be added to the exclusion available to, and may be used by, the estate of the second spouse to die. For example, assume that H dies with $6,000,000 in a profit-sharing plan and no other assets. If H leaves all of the plan assets to W, H avoids all estate taxes because of the marital deduction. But now it appears that W's estate will have to pay estate taxes, since her estate will probably be larger than her $5,000,000 indexed exclusion amount, unless her assets are reduced by consumption or a decline in market value. However, under the new portability provision, W can use not only her own exclusion but also the exclusion that was not used in H's estate.

Estate tax planning is complicated by several factors. First, many state estate tax laws have much lower exclusion amounts, often $1 million. Second, most state laws do not provide for portability of the exclusion.

2.   *Spousal trusts as plan beneficiaries.* Frequently a decedent does not devise assets directly to a spouse, but establishes a trust eligible for the marital deduction. These so-called "marital deduction trusts" must meet fairly strict requirements set forth in IRC § 2056(b) in order to avoid being classified as nondeductible terminable interests. Today the most common form of the marital deduction trust is the qualified terminable interest property (QTIP) trust, which requires that the trust income be distributed to the surviving spouse annually or at more frequent intervals. Exactly how this requirement applies to plan proceeds is not wholly clear.

In Rev. Rul. 2006–26, 2006–22 I.R.B. 939, IRS ruled that, in order for a marital trust named as beneficiary of a retirement account to qualify for the estate tax marital deduction, the trust document must require distribution to the spouse of the account's income, or must disallow use of the 10% rule of the 1999 Uniform Principal and Income Act, which would otherwise allow the trustee to treat only 10% of each minimum required distribution as income of the trust distributable to the spouse. With some degree of complexity, it is possible to structure a QTIP trust so that the excess income can stay inside the plan account, subject to a withdrawal right by the spouse. On April 11, 2008, Steven B. Gorin of Thompson Coburn LLP forwarded to Treasury a memorandum on proposed changes to section 409 of the Uniform Principal & Income Act. See Writer Seeks Treasury's Response To Proposed Changes To Uniform

Principal And Income Act, Tax Notes Today, April 23, 2008, 2008 TNT 79–23.

3. *Income in respect of a decedent (IRD).* Distributions from retirement plans, including IRAs, are treated as income in respect of a decedent (IRD). IRD does not receive a new date-of-death basis, as would normally be the case for a decedent's property. IRC § 1014(c). Thus, as discussed in Section A supra, the beneficiary is taxed in the same fashion as the participant would have been taxed, had the participant survived.

The fact that distributions from retirement plans generate taxable income creates some important estate planning opportunities. First, by making a surviving spouse the beneficiary of the plan, the income tax payments reduce the amount of the surviving spouse's property that will be subjected to estate taxation when the property passes to the next generation. The nonmarital bequest, typically a credit shelter trust, can be funded primarily with other assets that, unlike the plan benefits, received a stepped up basis at death.

Second, retirement plan distributions are an ideal bequest to a charitable beneficiary. For example, assume that D has $1,000,000 in a profit-sharing plan and $1,000,000 in other assets. D wishes to leave half of his estate to charity and half to his family. If the plan assets were left to his family, they would be subjected to income tax when distributed, which could reduce them by 40 percent or more if high state income taxes are also applicable. On the other hand, the charity is exempt from tax; when it collects the plan proceeds it receives the full $1,000,000. Similarly, if the family beneficiaries liquidate the other assets they will receive the full $1,000,000 tax-free because of the step-up in basis rules of IRC § 1014.

In an attempt to equalize the treatment of income collected before a decedent's death with income collected after death, IRC § 691(c) provides a special income tax deduction for the estate (or generation-skipping) tax attributable to the IRD. The computation of the appropriate deduction is complex, and there are special rules for joint and survivor annuities. See Treas. Reg. § 1.691(d)–1. The deduction is an itemized deduction, but is not subject to the 2-percent floor for miscellaneous deductions. IRC § 67(b)(7).

4. *Effect of estate taxes on planning.* For wealthy decedents the overall tax burden on pension saving can be enormous. For example, assume that W dies after H in 2014 and leaves $3,000,000 in a profit-sharing plan to her children. Assume further that her estate tax exclusion is used to shelter other assets, and that the family is wealthy enough to face the highest marginal estate and income tax rates. To simplify the calculation, we will assume that the $3,000,000 is withdrawn in a lump sum, perhaps because it was one of the few liquid assets available to pay the estate taxes. Table 8.2 illustrates the overall tax burden, which under the assumptions noted leaves the heirs with only about one-third of the assets in the plan.

TABLE 11.2

Combined Effect of Estate and Income Taxes

Account Balance at Death	$3,000,000
Federal & State Estate Taxes	$1,350,000
Federal & State Income Taxes	$676,500
Balance to heirs	$973,500

Assumptions: combined federal and state income tax rate of 41%; combined federal and state estate tax rate of 45%; IRD income tax deduction for amount of net federal estate tax.

Using retirement plan assets to pay estate taxes results in the loss of a significant tax deferral opportunity. For an estate in which there is no other source of liquid assets, estate planners will often recommend the creation of an irrevocable life insurance trust. Such a trust invests in a life insurance policy on the decedent's life, sufficient to cover all or at least part of the estate tax. It is possible to structure the policy and trust such that the insurance proceeds would not be subject to estate tax, but would nevertheless be available to pay the estate tax. Although such insurance can be expensive, the cost is usually more than offset by the benefit of the increased tax deferral on the retirement plan assets.

5. *Uncertainty*. EGTRRA, the Economic Growth and Tax Relief Reconciliation Act of 2001, repealed the federal estate tax for decedents who died during 2010, but reinstated it for those dying after 2010. The Tax Relief, Unemployment Insurance Authorization, and Job Creation Act of 2010 (1) gave estates of decedents dying in 2010 a choice- federal estate tax plus a full step up in basis or no federal estate tax and only a limited step up- and (2) reinstated the federal estate tax for decedents dying in 2011 and 2012, with a $ 5 million exemption and a 35% top estate tax rate.

The American Taxpayer Relief Act of 2012 ("ATRA") was signed by President Obama on January 2, 2013. The new law generally makes permanent the changes enacted in 2010 with regard to federal estate taxes, gift taxes and generation skipping transfer taxes, ending the uncertainty that previously prevailed.

PART 3

ERISA FIDUCIARY LAW

CHAPTER 12

FIDUCIARY STATUS

Analysis

Introduction.
A. Who Is a Fiduciary Under ERISA?
    1. *Blatt v. Marshall & Lassman.*
    2. ERISA's Many Fiduciaries.
    3. Plan Assets: Mutual Fund Shares and Insurance Contracts.
B. The Employer as Fiduciary.
    1. *Varity Corp. v. Howe (I).*
    2. The Employer's Two Hats.

Introduction

There are numerous fields of fiduciary law, including trusts, estate administration, guardianship, conservatorship, agency, corporations, and partnership. What these fields share is the obligation placed upon the fiduciary—that is, upon the person who is given power over the property or affairs of others—to use that power only for the benefit of those other persons. ERISA, drawing on earlier pension practice, makes pension and benefit law another field of fiduciary law.

[handwritten: Areas of Fiduciary Law]

This book devotes four chapters and part of a fifth to ERISA fiduciary law. The present chapter explores the question of fiduciary status—when and why someone becomes an ERISA fiduciary. Chapter 13 examines substantive fiduciary law, emphasizing the main fiduciary duties of loyalty and prudence. Chapter 14 treats the challenges of investing and managing plan assets. Chapter 15 deals with the requirements of fiduciary decisionmaking in cases of benefit denial. Special problems associated with applying ERISA fiduciary law to health insurance plans, including health maintenance organizations ("HMOs"), are discussed at the end of Chapter 19.

Federal trust law. ERISA fiduciary law derives from the law of trusts. The Supreme Court has remarked that ERISA's fiduciary responsibility provisions, which are found in Part 4 of Title 1, §§ 401–14, "codif[y] and mak[e] applicable to [ERISA] fiduciaries certain principles developed in the evolution of the law of trusts." Firestone Tire & Rubber Co. v. Bruch, 489 U.S. 101, 110–11 (1989). The congressional conference report accompanying the enactment explained that ERISA would "apply rules and remedies similar to those under traditional trust law to govern the conduct of fiduciaries." H.R. Conference Report No. 1280, 93d (1974), reprinted in 1974 U.S.Code Cong. & Admin. News 5038, 5076.

ERISA subjects pension and benefit plans to a double dose of trust fiduciary law. The statute imposes a rule of mandatory trusteeship, which requires that "all assets of an employee benefit plan shall be held in trust by one or more trustees." ERISA § 403(a). More importantly, ERISA extends the ambit of fiduciary duty far beyond the plan's trustees, because ERISA requires every plan to "provide for one or more named fiduciaries," who are empowered "to control and manage the operation and administration of the plan." ERISA § 402(a). Section 3(21)(A), discussed extensively below, treats anyone as a fiduciary to the extent that the person exercises material discretion over the administration of the plan, or "exercises any authority or control respecting management or disposition of its assets."

Although the Supreme Court has emphasized that it is "guided by principles of trust law" when interpreting ERISA, *Bruch*, 489 U.S. at 111, the Court has also cautioned "that trust law does not tell the entire story. After all, ERISA's standards and procedural protections partly reflect a congressional determination that the common law of trusts did not offer completely satisfactory protection." Varity Corp. v. Howe, 516 U.S. 489, 497 (1996) (substantially reproduced infra in Section B of this chapter). It follows, the Court said in that case, "that the law of trusts often will inform, but will not necessarily determine the outcome of, an effort to interpret ERISA's fiduciary duties."

Pension and other employee benefit funds took juridical shape in the trust form decades before ERISA. The Taft-Hartley Act mandated the trust for multiemployer plans in 1947. Labor-Management Relations Act, § 302(c)(5), 29 U.S.C. § 186(c)(5). Since 1921 the Internal Revenue Code has insisted upon the use of the trust as a condition for what we now call "qualifying" a pension plan for tax benefits. Revenue Act of 1921, ch. 136, § 219(f), 42 Stat. 227, 247. The modern version is IRC § 401(a). The requirement of mandatory trusteeship does not pertain to a plan funded exclusively by insurance or annuity contracts. ERISA § 403(a); IRC §§ 403(a), 404(a)(2).

Pension funds typically take the trust form in other common law countries. See, e.g., Noel Davis, The Law of Superannuation in Australia (2005 ed.); Richard Nobles, Pensions, Employment and the Law (1993) (England). For discussion of why trust prevails over corporation as a means of organizing pension and benefit plans, see John H. Langbein, The Secret Life of the Trust: The Trust as an Instrument of Commerce, 107 Yale L.J. 165, 179–85 (1997).

Trust and contract. As you study ERISA fiduciary law, be alert to the question, which surfaces prominently in Chapter 15, of whether it is wholly accurate to see pension and benefit plans in trust-law terms. These plans have contractual as well as trust dimensions. They arise in the employment relationship, which is fundamentally contractual, and some plans, especially welfare benefit plans that provide insurance benefits, are implemented by means of contracts with third-party insurers. When a dispute arises about the meaning or application of a term in an employment contract, contract law normally governs. When the particular term of the contract that comes into contention happens to concern an employee benefit plan rather than some other aspect of the contract of employment, what law should govern, contract or trust, and why?

A. WHO IS A FIDUCIARY UNDER ERISA?

The multifaceted definition of "fiduciary" in ERISA § 3(21)(A) reflects the expectation that a large cast of characters may be at work in administering a pension or welfare benefit plan. The definition directs attention away from labels and toward the function of each actor.

A person is a fiduciary under § 3(21)(A) "to the extent" that (i) "he exercises any discretionary authority or discretionary control" in the management of the plan "or exercises any authority or control respecting management or disposition of [plan] assets" or (ii) renders paid investment advice; or (iii) "has any discretionary authority [in] the administration" of the plan. ERISA's definition is discretion-centered. If a person has discretion over assets, investment, or administration, that person is a fiduciary in respect of those discretionary powers; and if a person renders compensated investment advice, fiduciary-level discretion is presumed.

The Supreme Court has emphasized that this provision of ERISA "defines 'fiduciary' not in terms of formal trusteeship, but in *functional* terms of control and authority over the [plan]." Mertens v. Hewitt Associates, 508 U.S. 248, 262 (1993).

By defining fiduciary status so broadly, ERISA allows plan designers to have considerable flexibility in allocating plan functions among different persons, while still preserving the protective principle that persons exercising material discretion must be responsible as fiduciaries for their conduct.

The fiduciary responsibility rules of ERISA's Title 1, Part 4, apply to persons deemed to be fiduciaries. Persons who fall within the definition of ERISA fiduciaries are subject to the substantive fiduciary obligations of § 404, the co-fiduciary rules of § 405, the prohibited transaction rules of §§ 406–408E and 502.

From the standpoint of someone who is sued in an action for breach of fiduciary duty, defending on the ground that one is not a fiduciary is particularly attractive. If fiduciary status is defeated, any claim based on breach of fiduciary duty is precluded. Accordingly, denying fiduciary status is a defense commonly raised in motions to dismiss under Fed. R. Civ. P. § 12(b)(6), or in motions for summary judgment.

1. BLATT V. MARSHALL & LASSMAN

812 F.2d 810 (2d Cir.1987).

■ ALTIMARI, CIRCUIT JUDGE. Abbey E. Blatt appeals from an order of the United States District Court for the Eastern District of New York granting summary judgment for defendants on the ground that they could not be considered fiduciaries under [ERISA §] 3(21)(A). We reverse and remand for the entry of summary judgment in favor of appellant.

Abbey Blatt joined the accounting firm of Marshall, Dym and Lassman in 1968. He became a partner in 1977 and remained with the firm, which is now known as Marshall and Lassman, until October 3, 1983, when he left the firm.

During the entire period of Blatt's association, Marshall and Lassman (and its predecessors in interest) participated in a retirement plan sponsored by the American Institute of Certified Public Accountants ("AICPA"). The plan is administered by an AICPA Retirement Committee and is insured by the Mutual Life Insurance Company of New

York ("MONY"). The plan allows employees of different accounting firms to pool their funds toward retirement.

An accounting firm that wishes to make the AICPA plan available to its employees must apply to the Retirement Committee. If the firm's application is accepted, employees who wish to take advantage of the plan may become participants. An employee's participation in the plan terminates upon the termination of that employee's services with the particular employer.

In its application to the Retirement Committee an employer must make several elections regarding the plan's applicability to its particular firm. These elections include: (1) the formula by which employer contributions are to be computed, and the frequency of those contributions; (2) the number of years of service required for an employee to be eligible to participate; (3) whether employees have the option to make voluntary contributions; (4) the formula for determining number of hours of service performed by employees; and (5) whether to adopt a minimum contribution provision.

The employer's contributions must be paid in cash to MONY at least once a year. The employer also must pay entry fees and a share of the administrative expenses, as determined by the Retirement Committee. All contributions are exclusively for the benefit of employee-participants; no plan assets ever revert to the employer. The employer may defer paying its contributions for up to one year and may, subject to conditions established by the Retirement Committee, direct MONY to transfer all the accounts of its employee-participants into another retirement plan. Finally, the employer must agree to furnish all information necessary for the convenient administration of the plan.

Appellant Blatt had been a participant in the AICPA plan sponsored by Marshall and Lassman. On December 9, 1983, Blatt wrote to MONY, informing them that he had left the employ of Marshall and Lassman and requesting a lump-sum distribution of the amount in his AICPA retirement account. MONY informed Blatt that no funds would be released to him until Marshall and Lassman delivered to MONY a "Notice of Change" form reflecting Blatt's status as a former member of the firm. MONY subsequently sent a Notice of Change form to Marshall and Lassman, but despite repeated requests by both Blatt and his attorney, Marshall and Lassman never executed the form. After Blatt commenced the instant federal action in April 1985, Marshall and Lassman finally executed the Notice of Change on May 17, 1985, more than one and one-half years after Blatt had left the firm.

Blatt's complaint alleged that the defendants were fiduciaries under ERISA, and that they had breached their fiduciary duty to Blatt by intentionally failing to execute the Notice of Change, thereby preventing Blatt's access to his fully vested retirement funds. *See* [ERISA § 404]. According to Blatt, the defendants' refusal to execute the Notice of Change was motivated by a desire to gain advantage over him in an unrelated suit then pending in state court which defendants had filed shortly after Blatt left the firm.

In a memorandum and order dated May 1, 1986, 633 F.Supp. 712, the district court found that Marshall and Lassman could not be considered fiduciaries with respect to the AICPA retirement plan under [ERISA § 3(21)(A)]. The opinion first notes that Marshall and Lassman did not render investment advice to the plan for a fee, or have the authority to do so, *see* § 3(21)(A)(ii). Second, appellees had no discretionary role in administering the plan, *see id.* § 3(21)(A)(iii). After reviewing the various elections which Marshall and Lassman made in their application to the Retirement Committee, the court concluded that appellees' responsibility for making a limited number of choices respecting contributions to the plan was merely a ministerial one. The court found no other provision of the plan which conferred any *discretionary* authority over plan administration. Finally, appellees were found not to possess any discretionary authority with respect to management of the plan or disposition of its assets, *see id.* § 3(21)(A)(i). Accordingly, the court directed that summary judgment be entered for defendants.

The term "fiduciary" is defined in Section 3(21)(A) of ERISA. . . .

Congress intended the term to be broadly construed. "[T]he definition includes persons who have authority and responsibility with respect to the matter in question, regardless of their formal title." H.R.Rep. No. 1280, 93d Cong., 2d Sess., *reprinted in* 1974 U.S. Code Cong. & Admin. News 4639, 5038, 5103. According to an interpretive bulletin issued by the Department of Labor, someone who performs purely "ministerial" functions for a benefit plan is not a fiduciary. *See* 29 C.F.R. § 2509.75–8. Such ministerial functions include the application of rules determining eligibility for participation, calculation of services and benefits, and collection of contributions.

Thus, whether or not an individual or entity is an ERISA fiduciary must be determined by focusing on the function performed, rather than on the title held. An entity need not have absolute discretion with respect to a benefit plan in order to be considered a fiduciary; rather, fiduciary status exists with respect to any activity enumerated in the statute over which the entity exercises discretion or control.

We conclude that Marshall and Lassman acted as fiduciaries in this case because they exercised *actual* control over the disposition of plan assets. The definition of "fiduciary" under ERISA focuses on the exercise, as well as the possession, of authority or control. Thus, "a person is a fiduciary with respect to a plan *to the extent (i) he exercises . . . any authority or control* respecting . . . disposition of its assets." [ERISA § 3(21)(A)(i)] (emphasis added).

The return of contributions to plan participants is one method of disposition of plan assets. When Marshall and Lassman ignored Blatt's requests and delayed executing the Notice of Change form, they effectively prevented the Retirement Committee from returning Blatt's vested contributions to him. Therefore, within the plain meaning of the statute, Marshall and Lassman exercised actual control respecting disposition of plan assets. We hold that Marshall and Lassman are indeed fiduciaries to the extent of this actual control.

We now consider whether Marshall and Lassman breached their fiduciary duty to Blatt when they delayed executing the Notice of Change for one and one-half years. There is no need for us to remand for consideration of this issue, even though the district court did not reach it, because all parties agree on the pertinent facts.

An ERISA fiduciary is obligated to "discharge his duties with respect to a plan solely in the interest of the participants and beneficiaries and . . . for the exclusive purpose of . . . providing benefits to participants and their beneficiaries." [ERISA § 404(a)(1)(A)(i)]. The fiduciary is held to a "prudent man" standard of care, id. § [404(a)(1)(B)].

A fiduciary breaches his § [404] duty to a plan participant by preventing or interfering with the receipt of benefits to which the participant is entitled. *See Kann v. Keystone Resources, Inc.,* 575 F.Supp. 1084, 1091 (W.D.Pa.1983) (company pension plan's decision to withhold payment of benefits to which former executive was entitled was made with only the company's interest in mind, and was therefore breach of fiduciary duty); *Frary v. Shorr Paper Products, Inc.,* 494 F.Supp. 565, 569 (N.D.Ill.1980) (pension plan manager's refusal to pay vested benefits to former employee because employee had accepted job with competitor was breach of fiduciary duty).

We therefore conclude that Marshall and Lassman breached their fiduciary duty to Blatt by failing to deliver the Notice of Change form to MONY until more than one and one-half years after Blatt left the firm. Appellees' unreasonable delay in performing such a simple function was decidedly not "solely in the interest of [Blatt]," nor did it serve "the exclusive purpose of providing benefits to [Blatt]." [ERISA § 404(a)(1)(A)(i).]

We reverse and remand for entry of summary judgment in favor of Blatt on the issue of liability, and for consideration of any fees, costs, and damages to which Blatt may be entitled.

2.   ERISA'S MANY FIDUCIARIES

1.   *How much discretion suffices to make a person a fiduciary under § 3(21)(A)?* In contrast to the Second Circuit opinion reproduced above, the district court in *Blatt* maintained that the defendants were not fiduciaries. Which opinion is better reasoned?

Interpretative regulations issued by the Department of [Labor], 29 C.F.R. § 2509.75–8 (1985), [make] clear that a person who performs purely ministerial functions for an employee benefit plan within a framework of policies, interpretations, rules, practices, and procedures is not a fiduciary.

[The] Court concludes that defendants are not fiduciaries under the AICPA Plan. First, defendants do not render any investment advice, either for a fee or otherwise, and have no control over the assets of the Plan, which, as the Plan makes clear, never revert to the employer. At best, an employer sends contributions to MONY as an agent of the participant.

Second, defendants have no discretionary role in the administration of the AICPA Plan. By the terms of the Plan the employer has almost no discretion in the Plan's administration. The Plan specifically requires the employer to furnish to MONY all information necessary to the Plan's administration.

Although MONY or the [AICPA] Retirement Committee may delegate administrative functions to an employer, there is no evidence that this has occurred here. The employer clearly administers the Plan with respect to each of its employees, but even here, the employer's role is limited largely to communication and contact with the participant employee on behalf of MONY. To the extent that the Plan gives defendants any administrative authority, the Court concludes that these activities are largely ministerial. . . .

Third, defendants have no discretionary authority with respect to the management of the Plan or the disposition of its assets. The Plan has no provision for employers to control, disperse, or invest any of the assets of the fund. Employers have no involvement in the choice of investments, investment advisors, plan managers, fiduciaries, administrators, or members of the Retirement Committee. Moreover, viewed from the perspective of an accounting firm, the Plan is essentially a take it or leave it proposition. The functioning of the Plan as a whole leaves an employer little management discretion. Aside from the limited election provisions available to an eligible firm, nearly all of the Plan's provisions are set by the Retirement Board, without any provision for input by the employer. Moreover, the Retirement Committee is free to make changes in the Plan unilaterally and without the consent of any employer.

Plaintiff argues that the election provisions available to the employer create a fiduciary relationship between the employer and the employee/participant. The Court disagrees. ERISA does not contemplate the imposition of a fiduciary duty on an employer because the employer selects from among several, pre-determined options.

Blatt v. Marshall & Lassman, 633 F.Supp. 712, 716–17 (E.D.N.Y.1986).

ERISA's discretion-centered definition of "fiduciary" in § 3(21)(A) is one of the most important features of the Act. The issue in *Blatt* was whether the defendant partners' power over the filing of the "Notice of Change" form made the defendants ERISA fiduciaries with respect to the exercise or nonexercise of that power. Although the defendants had little or no authority with respect to most of the rest of the plan, the Second Circuit found that their control over the filing of the notice caused them to be exercising control over the "disposition" of plan assets within the meaning of ERISA § 3(21)(A)(i).

2. *ERISA's fractionation of trusteeship.* ERISA's definition of "fiduciary" in § 3(21)(A) is far more complex than the conventional definition of a trustee. The Restatement defines a trustee simply as "the person holding property in trust." Restatement (Third) of Trusts § 3(3) (2003). The Restatement definition reflects the traditional pattern of trust administration, in which a single trustee (either an individual or a corporate fiduciary such as a bank trust department) exercises all trust functions. When a trust provides for co-trustees, they perform the trust functions jointly, unless the trust instrument provides otherwise. Id. § 39.

ERISA, by contrast, envisions multiple fiduciary service providers, and the complexity of ERISA's definition of fiduciary in § 3(21)(A) responds to the dispersion of fiduciary functions that ERISA permits.

ERISA's fractionation of traditional trusteeship reflects the complexity of the modern pension trust. Because millions, even billions of dollars can be involved, great care is required in investing and safekeeping plan assets. Administering such plans—computing and honoring benefit entitlements across decades of employment and retirement—is also a complex business. A plan sponsor may choose to keep all these functions in-house, designating its own personnel as trustees and named fiduciaries. Since, however, neither the sponsor nor any other single entity has a comparative advantage in performing all these functions, the tendency has been for pension plans to use a variety of specialized providers. A consulting actuary, a plan administration firm, or an insurance company may assist in the design of a plan. Sometimes the processing of benefit claims is delegated to an outside entity. Investment industry professionals manage the portfolio (the largest plans spread their pension investments among dozens of money management firms). Another entity, commonly a bank or an investment company, may serve as trustee, handling the safekeeping of plan assets, responding to investment managers' directions, collecting plan contributions and investment income, and making benefit payments. Legal, accounting, actuarial, and other advisers have their niches.

3. *Named fiduciary.* Section 402(a)(1) requires every plan to provide for one or more "named fiduciaries," who have "authority to control and manage the operation and administration of the plan." The plan sponsor, typically the employer, chooses the named fiduciaries, § 402(a)(2), usually naming itself. Section 403(a) allows the plan to subject the trustee to the direction of the named fiduciary; this so-called directed trustee is discussed below and again in Chapter 14. Section 403(a)(2) invites the plan to allocate investment responsibility away from the trustee, by delegating to investment managers the "authority to manage, acquire, or dispose of" plan assets. Section 402(c)(2) authorizes the named fiduciary to employ other service providers "to render advice with regard to any responsibility such fiduciary has under the plan." (Bear in mind that, as seen in *Blatt*, a person who is not named as a fiduciary may still be found to have functioned as one.)

4. *Co-fiduciaries.* Section 405(a), which governs the relations of co-fiduciaries, follows the common law of trusts in prescribing that a co-fiduciary can become liable for a breach committed by another fiduciary if the co-fiduciary (1) participates in or conceals the breach; or (2) facilitates the breach by his own breach; or (3) fails to make appropriate efforts to remedy a known breach committed by a co-fiduciary. Section 405(b)(1)(B), governing the relations of co-fiduciaries, prescribes that co-fiduciaries must act jointly, unless the pension trust instrument allocates specific responsibilities among them. However, § 405(c)–(d) protects a fiduciary who has properly delegated responsibilities to other fiduciaries. The logic of this system is to facilitate specialization of function while always leaving the participant with a fiduciary who owes the participant ERISA fiduciary responsibilities with respect to plan functions that entail material discretion.

[handwritten margin note: Plan Administrator / Makes sure that Plan is administered as the document OR Law prescribes]

5. *The plan administrator.* A central figure in ERISA's cast of fiduciaries is the plan administrator (the PA). ERISA authorizes the plan to designate the PA; in default of such a designation, ERISA makes the plan sponsor the PA. ERISA § 3(16)(A)(i)–(ii). ERISA treats plan administration as a fiduciary function, saying that the plan "shall provide for one or more named fiduciaries who jointly or severally shall have authority to control and manage the operation and administration of the plan." ERISA § 402(a)(1). Among the responsibilities of the PA is the work of applying plan benefit formulas, hence resolving benefit claims. (Chapter 15 of this book examines the process of judicial review of these determinations.)

Not all administrative tasks are sufficiently discretionary to make the person performing them a fiduciary. "[T]here is some exercise of discretion 'in even the most innocuous of clerical acts.' It seems clear, however, that discretion in the statutory sense means more than the options reposed in every functionary. Instead, discretion implies the 'power to make . . . decisions as to plan policy, interpretations, practices or procedures.' " Daniel C. Knickerbocker, Jr., Trust Law with a Difference: An Overview of ERISA Fiduciary Responsibility, 23 Real Property, Probate & Trust J. 633, 642 (1988) (quoting 29 C.F.R. § 2509.75–8 (D–2) (1987)). Notice, however, that "[t]he word 'discretionary' is pointedly absent [in] respect of plan assets. The exercise of any power at all over the disposition of assets imports fiduciary status." Id. at 639 (citing *Blatt*).

(a) *Employer.* ERISA § 3(16)(ii) treats the plan sponsor, normally the employer, as the plan administrator unless the plan designates somebody else. The issue of when the employer is or is not acting in a fiduciary capacity is a subject of critical importance in ERISA law, discussed below in Section B in the principal case, *Varity Corp. v. Howe*, and the notes following. As in *Blatt*, in a case in which the plan documents designate a separate plan administrator, an employer may still be a fiduciary if the employer actively administers the plan. See, e.g., Hamilton v. Allen-Bradley Co., Inc., 217 F.3d 1321, 1326 (11th Cir.2000), vacated on other grounds, 244 F.3d 819 (2001) (employer that required "employees to go through its human resources department in order to obtain an application for disability benefits [was] in sufficient control over the process to qualify as the plan administrator notwithstanding" contrary language in plan literature); Law v. Ernst & Young, 956 F.2d 364 (1st Cir.1992); Rosen v. TRW, Inc., 979 F.2d 191 (11th Cir.1992).

(b) *Corporate officers.* Even when the employer is not serving as fiduciary, its agents often are. ERISA § 408(c)(3), discussed extensively in Chapter 14, infra, underscores the expectation that employers will designate their officers and other personnel as ERISA fiduciaries. The question of when the officer's service should be attributed to the employer under the doctrine of vicarious liability (*respondeat superior*) has been raised in a few cases. Most, but not all, find that the doctrine applies in ERISA settings. See, e.g., In re Cardinal Health, Inc. ERISA Litig., 424 F.Supp.2d 1002, 1048–49 (S.D.Ohio 2006) (reviewing the case law and holding that the doctrine "is applicable to claims brought under ERISA"); Horn v. Cendant Operations, Inc., 69 Fed.Appx. 421, 427 (10th Cir.2003) (employer's "fiduciary 'obligations cannot be circumvented by building a

"Chinese wall" around those employees on whom plan participants reasonably rely for information and guidance' "). See Bradley P. Humphreys, Assessing the Viability and Virtues of *Respondeat Superior* for Nonfiduciary Responsibility in ERISA Actions, 75 U. Chicago L. Rev. 1683 (2008).

The reverse question also arises, whether corporate officers acting in the scope of employment are individually liable as ERISA fiduciaries, or whether the corporation alone is the fiduciary. In Bell v. Executive Committee of United Food & Commercial Workers Pension Plan, 191 F.Supp.2d 10, 14 (D.D.C.2002), the court observed "widespread disagreement among courts [about] the circumstances under which the officers or employees of a corporate fiduciary might also acquire fiduciary status under ERISA." The court pointed to Confer v. Custom Engineering Co., 952 F.2d 34, 37 (3d Cir.1991), as the leading case against fiduciary status. *Confer* held "that when an ERISA plan names a corporation as a fiduciary, the officers who exercise discretion on behalf of the corporation are not fiduciaries within the meaning of section 3(21)(A)(iii), unless it can be shown that these officers have *individual* discretionary roles as to plan administration." 952 F.2d at 37 (emphasis original). Contrary cases have found that corporate officers and employees who acted in the course of their employment may be ERISA fiduciaries, depending on the amount of authority or control that they exercise over the plan and its assets. See, e.g., Kayes v. Pacific Lumber Co., 51 F.3d 1449, 1461 (9th Cir.1995), in which the Ninth Circuit expressly "reject[ed] the Third Circuit's interpretation in *Confer* that an officer who acts on behalf of a named fiduciary corporation cannot be a fiduciary if he acts within his official capacity and if no fiduciary duties are delegated to him individually." Accord, Musmeci v. Schwegmann Giant Super Markets, 332 F.3d 339, 350–51 (5th Cir.2003) (personal liability for firm's breach).

(c) *Third party administrator.* When an employer designates an external service provider, that entity is commonly called a third party administrator (TPA). A DoL interpretive bulletin excludes from fiduciary status under § 3(21)(A) a person who does not have the power to make or interpret plan policies, and who performs ministerial functions such as processing claims, applying plan eligibility rules, communicating with employees, and calculating benefits. 29 C.F.R. § 2509.75–8 D–2. "The policy behind this exception to fiduciary status is to encourage professionals to provide their necessary services without fear of incurring fiduciary liability or feeling the need to charge a higher price to compensate for such risk." CSA 401(k) Plan v. Pension Professionals, Inc., 195 F.3d 1135, 1139 (9th Cir.1999). Is that policy sound? Fiduciary liability only arises for breach of fiduciary duty. Isn't the better policy to protect plan participants and beneficiaries by casting the net of fiduciary responsibility widely?

The case law varies with the facts of the cases, sometimes finding the TPA to be a fiduciary, sometimes not. Cases finding on the particular facts that the TPA was acting as an ERISA fiduciary include Rud v. Liberty Life Assurance Co. of Boston, 438 F.3d 772, 774 (7th Cir.2006) (citing TPA's authority to construe the policy terms and to determine benefit eligibility "conclusively"); Briscoe v. Fine, 444 F.3d 478, 492 (6th Cir.2006) (citing TPA's unilateral control over plan assets). By contrast, in Oliver v. Coca Cola Co., 497 F.3d 1181 (11th Cir.2007), a TPA that was not authorized to make final decisions on benefit claims, but merely processed initial applications, was held not to be a fiduciary. For a recent example of a case finding fiduciary status of a TPA, see Pipefitters Local 636 Insurance Fund v. Blue Cross & Blue Shield of Michigan, 722 F.3d 861 (6th Cir. 2013) (finding fiduciary status based on TPA's "discretion in the way it collected the funds to defray its one-percent Medigap obligation to the State").

Circumstances decide whether an insurer is or is not acting as a plan fiduciary. An insurer may be nothing more than a vendor of claims-processing services, or the insurer may be exercising discretionary authority over benefit determinations. Compare, e.g., Cotton v. Massachusetts Mutual Life Ins. Co., 402 F.3d 1267 (11th Cir.2005) (not fiduciary), with Ruiz v. Continental Casualty Co., 400 F.3d 986 (7th Cir.2005) (fiduciary, on account of authority to determine benefits). In Baker v. Big Star Div. of the Grand Union Co., 893 F.2d 288 (11th Cir.1989), involving an occupational disability plan, an insurance company processed claims and disbursed benefits under an administrative services agreement with the employer, but did not insure the plan benefits. The employer both self-insured the plan and reserved the right to review benefit determinations. A participant whose claim for benefits was denied sued both the employer and the insurance company. The court held that the insurer was not a fiduciary. Grand Union, the employer, "did no more than 'rent' the claims processing department of [the insurance company] to review claims and determine the amount payable 'in accordance with the terms and conditions of the Plan.' " Accord, Witt v. Allstate Ins. Co., 50 F.3d 536 (8th Cir.1995).

Given ERISA's functional definition of a fiduciary, a TPA may be a fiduciary for some purposes and not others. Thus, in DeLuca v. Blue Cross Blue Shield of Mich., 628 F.3d 743 (6th Cir. 2010), the Sixth Circuit held that, although Blue Cross Blue Shield acted as a fiduciary when it acted as the administrator and claims-processing agent for the plan, it was not acting as a fiduciary when it negotiated reimbursement rates with hospitals that were more favorable to its HMO clients than to its self-funded health plan clients. The court concluded that "those business dealings were not directly associated with the benefits plan at issue here but were generally applicable to a broad range of health-care consumers." Id at 747.

The dissent objected to the majority's disposing of the question on summary judgment, finding that the record was such that a jury could find that the defendant "agreed to provide services rather than a product. Those services—'[e]stablishing, arranging, and maintaining provider networks . . . through contractual arrangements' with hospitals and other health-care providers—are highly discretionary and have a direct impact on the Plan's bottom line." Id at 751. Thus, Blue Cross Blue Shield was acting as a fiduciary if it provided those services. The Sixth Circuit declined a request that it rehear the case. Deluca v. Blue Cross Blue Shield of Mich., 2011 U.S. App. LEXIS 3518 (6th Cir. Feb. 17, 2011).

Given ERISA's functional approach to the question of who is a fiduciary, the fact that portions of the service agreement between a benefits administrator and the plan sponsor expressly state that the administrator is not a fiduciary is not dispositive of the question. If the administrator exercises authority and control over plan assets, it is a fiduciary. See Guyan Int'l v. Professional Benefits Administrators, Inc., 689 F.3d 793 (6th Cir. 2012) (holding PBA liable for breach of fiduciary duty for using funds it received from plan sponsors for its own purposes rather than solely paying plan claims).

In HealthSouth Rehabilitation Hospital v. American Nat'l Red Cross, 101 F.3d 1005 (4th Cir.1996), one of the defendants, Aetna Insurance, provided claims administration services to a health plan for which the employer, the Red Cross, was the plan administrator. A Red Cross employee failed to enroll his son in the plan. When the boy's mother took the child to the hospital for rehabilitation therapy, she represented that the son was covered by the father's plan. The hospital contacted Aetna, which erroneously confirmed that the son was covered. Some weeks later, after the hospital had provided $82,967 in services to the son, Aetna notified the hospital that the earlier confirmation had been an error and the son had no coverage. The hospital sued Aetna on the theory that Aetna was a fiduciary, that it had amended the plan to include the son, and that the son had assigned his rights to the hospital. The Fourth Circuit held that Aetna did not have authority to amend the plan. Further: "Given Aetna's limited role in processing claims under the plan and reading a computer screen to determine who is and who is not covered, it is clear that Aetna is not a fiduciary under the plan." Id. at 1009. Was Aetna just "reading a computer screen," or was Aetna determining coverage? Should Aetna's behavior on behalf of the plan estop the plan to deny coverage? Regarding the difficulties in basing liability for denying ERISA benefits on estoppel grounds, see infra Chapter 15.

The fiduciary status of health maintenance organizations (HMOs), which perform insurance functions as well as provide health care, is discussed infra in Section C of this chapter. Case law is collected in Annot., When Is Insurer Fiduciary Under [ERISA], 181 A.L.R. Fed. 269 (2002 & Supp. 2009).

One consequence of a determination that a TPA was acting in a fiduciary role is that the plan fiduciary who delegated the function to the TPA may be treated as no longer a fiduciary for the delegated function. In Jones v. Unum Provident, 2007 WL 2609791 (N.D.N.Y.2007), for example, the employer (who was the PA) was held relieved of fiduciary responsibility in a case in which it had delegated the decision-making authority to an insurer as TPA. In such a case, the PA's selection of the TPA is a fiduciary function, even when the PA ceases to be a fiduciary with respect to the performance of the functions prudently delegated to the TPA. This point is further discussed below in Section B.2.6 of this chapter ("Appointing a fiduciary is a fiduciary function") in the text following *Varity I*; and in connection with the employer stock cases, infra in Chapter 14.

6. [*Attorneys, accountants, actuaries, and consultants*] DoL's interpretive bulletin, 29 C.F.R. § 2509.75–5 D–1, states that "attorneys, accountants, actuaries and consultants performing their usual professional functions will ordinarily not be considered fiduciaries," unless (tracking ERISA § 3(21)(A)) the particular professional exercises

[handwritten margin note:] Attorneys, Accountants, Actuaries, and consultants

[handwritten bottom note:] Usually NOT Fiduciaries, unless they overstep + influence (be just offer advice) too much

discretionary authority or control respecting the management of the plan, the plan assets, or the plan administration; or unless the person renders investment advice for a fee. The courts routinely follow this regulation, exempting these professionals from being treated as fiduciaries. E.g., Mellon Bank, N.A. v. Levy, 71 Fed.Appx. 146 (3d Cir.2003) (attorney); Custer v. Sweeney, 89 F.3d 1156 (4th Cir.1996) (attorney); Painters of Philadelphia District Council No. 21 Welfare Fund v. Price Waterhouse, 879 F.2d 1146 (3d Cir.1989) (accountant); Pension Plan of Public Service Co. of New Hampshire v. KPMG Peat Marwick, 815 F.Supp. 52 (D.N.H.1993) (accountant); Pappas v. Buck Consultants, Inc., 12 E.B.C. 1984 (N.D.Ill.1989), aff'd, 923 F.2d 531 (7th Cir.1991) (actuary).

In exceptional circumstances, such service professionals sometimes exercise sufficient discretion that the courts find them to be fiduciaries. E.g., Martin v. Feilen, 965 F.2d 660 (8th Cir.1992) (accountant); Bouton v. Thompson, 764 F.Supp. 20 (D.Conn.1991) (lawyer). In Iron Workers Local 25 Pension Fund v. Watson Wyatt & Co., 2009 WL 3698562 (E.D.Mich.), the court refused to dismiss a claim against a law firm for breach of fiduciary duty. The plaintiffs alleged that the law firm initiated a lawsuit on behalf of the plan, then refused but later accepted an offer of settlement of the suit, all without authorization. The court concluded that the law firm "exceeded the bounds of the functions [that the firm] was hired to perform, *i.e.,* the provision of legal advice, and . . . thereby crossed the line from usual professional functions to discretionary control." Id. at 11. See Annot., When Is Attorney, Accountant, or Other Professional Service Provider Fiduciary Within Meaning of § 3(21)(A)(i) of [ERISA], 166 A.L.R. Fed. 596 (2000 & Supp. 2009).

Reflecting on "[j]ust why a pension plan's lawyer should be excused from ERISA fiduciary status," and finding the answer "a little obscure," Judge Posner pointed out that service providers do not exercise direct decisionmaking authority. "Moreover, a professional who renders services to an ERISA plan is subject to whatever fiduciary or other duties his profession imposes upon him." Health Cost Controls of Illinois, Inc. v. Washington, 187 F.3d 703, 709 (7th Cir.1999). Regarding the circumstances in which state malpractice law survives ERISA's preemption law, see below in this chapter in the notes following Pegram v. Herdrich, 530 U.S. 211 (2000); and in Chapter 17, infra.

7. *Investment advisers.* ERISA singles out investment advisers for special treatment. Unlike professionals who render legal, actuarial, or accounting advice, persons who render investment advice are ipso facto fiduciaries. Under § 3(21)(A)(ii), a person is a fiduciary to the extent that "he renders investment advice for a fee or other compensation, direct or indirect, with respect to any moneys or other property of such plan, or has any authority or responsibility to do so."

[handwritten margin note: Investment Advisors/Managers — Always Fiduciaries]

Thus, a person who serves as an investment adviser for plan assets is always an ERISA fiduciary. Bearing in mind that lawyers and other professionals are not categorically deemed fiduciaries, why did ERISA's drafters decide to treat investment advisers oppositely?

Who is an "adviser?" The question here has been largely one of distinguishing a mere salesperson. For example, a broker touting a particular stock seems just to be someone who is trying to sell you something. On the other hand, if you visit the same broker repeatedly, and both you and the broker know that you generally follow the broker's investment suggestions, the broker seems in substance to have become your adviser. The DoL's early regulation defining "fiduciary," promulgated in 1975, shortly after ERISA's enactment, drew the distinction along similar lines: An investment adviser within ERISA's meaning "render[s] individualized investment advice to the plan based on [its] particular needs," and does so "on a regular basis" pursuant to an agreement or undertaking that "such services will serve as a primary basis for [the plan's] investment decisions." 29 C.F.R. § 2510.3–21(c).

For case law arising under this definition see Annot., When Is Third-Party Administrator or Other Person or Entity Providing Administrative or Investment Services to ERISA Plan Fiduciary under [ERISA], 175 A.L.R. Fed. 129 (2002 & Supp. 2009); Annot, When is Individual or Entity Fiduciary Within Meaning of § 3(21)(A)(ii) of [ERISA] Defining "Fiduciary" to Include Paid Investment Advisors, 167 A.L.R. Fed. 595 (2001 & Supp. 2009). For an example of the operation of the DOL's regulations on when an investment adviser is a fiduciary see Tiblier v. Dlabal, 2014 U.S. App. LEXIS 3897 (5th Cir. Feb. 28, 2014) (holding that an investment adviser was not a fiduciary with respect to an investment where trustees made the ultimate decision to buy the bonds in question, they did so based on the advice of the adviser and another adviser, and they rejected some of the adviser's other investment proposals).

More recently, DoL has become concerned that this definition is too narrow; that it excludes people and entities who hold themselves out as "financial consultants" or the like, whom a plan might reasonably consider as advisers, but whose contact with the plan is not, for example, "regular." Often such consultants' interests conflict with those of their clients, unbeknownst to the latter, as a result of commission-based fee or similar arrangements. In the Department's words, "Instead of ensuring that trusted advisers give prudent and unbiased advice in accordance with fiduciary norms, the current regulation erects a multi-part series of technical impediments to fiduciary responsibility." Proposed Rules, Department of Labor, Definition of the Term "Fiduciary," 80 FR 21927, 21933 (Apr. 20, 2015).

Accordingly the Department has been attempting to revise the scope of the "investment adviser" definition, in the face of stiff opposition from the financial industry. An initial attempt at new proposed regulations, released in 2010, was withdrawn following industry outcry. As of April, 2015, the DoL has tried again. Newly proposed regulations (cited just above) expand the definition of investment adviser to include anyone who makes an investment "recommendation" to a plan, if either (1) the person making the recommendation acknowledges ERISA fiduciary status; or (2) the recommendation is made pursuant to an understanding—written or otherwise—that advice is to be "individualized," or "specifically directed to" the plan. The requirement that the advice be "regular" is deleted.

At the same time the newest proposed regulations sweeten the pill for financial advisers by including a set of carve-outs from the definition for specific situations, including for providers of plan "platforms" through which plan investments may be made, as well as for persons who merely provide or evaluate objective investment data or criteria, or who provide general "investment education." Significantly, the regulation also carves out from the definition of investment adviser any employee of the plan sponsor, provided the employee provides plan advice only in her employment capacity and receives no extra compensation for doing so.

Despite these carve-outs, the financial industry has expressed continued opposition to the change in regulatory definition, and it remains to be seen whether the new rules will become final.

In Smith v. Harrang, 8 E.B.C. 2279 (9th Cir.1987) (opinion withdrawn for mootness upon settlement by the parties, 841 F.2d 1466 (9th Cir.1988)), the plan trustee made loans from plan assets to certain borrowers, who pledged real property as security. The plan's lawyer, Rubenstein, counseled the trustee that the real estate made the plan "well secured." When the borrowers defaulted, it was discovered that the value of the collateral was insufficient to secure the loan. The trustee sued the lawyer not only for professional negligence, but also for violation of his fiduciary duty under ERISA, on the theory that Rubenstein had acted as an investment adviser for the plan. Was Rubenstein rendering "investment advice" as the term is used in ERISA § 3(21)(A)(ii)?

8. *Investment managers.* ERISA invites the named fiduciary to appoint a so-called "investment manager" to manage plan assets, §§ 402(c)(3), 403(a)(2). Section 405(d)(1) absolves the trustee of responsibility for plan assets that have been responsibly committed to the direction of an investment manager. An investment manager is necessarily a fiduciary under ERISA § 3(21)(A)(i).

ERISA § 3(38) defines the term "investment manager" as "any fiduciary [other] than a trustee or named [fiduciary] who has the power to manage" plan assets. An investment manager that is not a bank or an insurance company must be registered as an investment adviser under the Investment Advisers Act of 1940. The definition also requires the manager to "acknowledge[ ] in writing that he is a fiduciary with respect to the plan."

Selecting an investment manager is itself a fiduciary responsibility, and the duty of prudent administration requires the appointing fiduciary to investigate and evaluate a potential manager with suitable care. See In re Masters, Mates & Pilots Pension Plan, 11 E.B.C. 2629 (S.D.N.Y.1990) (whether the retention of a manager was imprudent is a fact issue that cannot be resolved on motion for summary judgment), discussed in Bernard M. Baum, Trustees and Their Professionals, 18 Employee Benefits J. 7 (Mar. 1993); Whitfield v. Cohen, 682 F.Supp. 188 (S.D.N.Y.1988) (discussing factors bearing on fiduciary selection of investment managers, including credentials, expertise, past performance, third-party evaluations, and registration as an advisor with the SEC).

A trustee or fiduciary who has made an improper investment may be tempted to claim that the person with whom the money was invested was an investment manager, hence that under § 405(d)(1) liability rests upon the manager and not upon the trustee or other fiduciary. Notice, however, that the requirements of § 3(38) are bright-line-type factors. Someone either is or is not registered under the 1940 Act, and a written acknowledgement that one is an ERISA fiduciary is not likely to be executed casually.

9. *Self-directed accounts.* The facts in *Stanton v. Shearson Lehman/American Express,* supra, instance what ERISA § 404(c) describes as "a pension plan which provides for individual accounts and permits a participant or beneficiary to exercise control over the assets in his [account]." Section 404(c)(1)(B) provides that "no person who is otherwise a fiduciary shall be liable under this part for any loss, or by reason of any breach, which results from such participant's or beneficiary's exercise of control." See, e.g., Schwartz v. Gordon, 5 E.B.C. 1189 (S.D.N.Y.1983), sustained on other grounds, 761 F.2d 864 (2d Cir.1985), exonerating a broker who executed orders from the participant in such an account. Section 404(c) and associated regulations are discussed infra in Chapter 14.

10. *Directed trustees; custodians.* As previously mentioned, ERISA § 403(a)(1) allows a plan to provide that the trustee be "subject to proper directions" of a named fiduciary who is not a trustee. In such cases, the trustee will not be a fiduciary with respect to the functions for which proper direction was accepted. E.g., Maniace v. Commerce Bank of Kansas City, 40 F.3d 264 (8th Cir.1994).

The claim has been asserted that when a directed trustee or custodian takes more initiative than the plan documents require, fiduciary status attaches. The courts have not welcomed these cases. "A financial institution cannot be deemed to have volunteered itself as a fiduciary simply because it undertakes reporting responsibilities that exceed its official mandate. [A] rule that would dampen any incentive on the part of depository institutions voluntarily to make relevant information available to fund administrators and other interested parties is counter-intuitive." Beddall v. State Street Bank & Trust Co., 137 F.3d 12, 21 (1st Cir.1998). Accord Arizona State Carpenters Pension Trust Fund v. Citibank, 125 F.3d 715 (9th Cir.1997).

The scope of a directed trustee's duty under a 401(k) plan to resist instructions to buy or retain employer stock has become a central issue in many of the employer stock plans cases that have been brought in recent years, including those resulting from the Enron and WorldCom bankruptcies. DoL has addressed the subject in a Field Assistance Bulletin, "Fiduciary Responsibilities of Directed Trustees," DoL FAB 2004–03 (2004), discussed in Chapter 14, infra.

11. *"Party in interest."* ERISA's prohibited transaction rules, § 406, discussed in Chapter 13, infra, forbid certain transactions between an ERISA fiduciary and any person defined in § 3(14) as a "party in interest." In addition to fiduciaries, parties in interest include service providers, employers, and unions. Thus, a person who is not liable as a fiduciary may be liable as a party in interest for conduct that violates the prohibited transaction rules of § 406. Comparable provisions under IRC § 4975 impose a tax on prohibited transactions with respect to a "disqualified person," who is defined under § 4975(e)(2).

12. *Veil piercing.* If a corporation is liable as a fiduciary or otherwise under ERISA, are the shareholders immune from personal liability? In Alman v. Danin, 801 F.2d 1, 4 (1st Cir.1986), the First Circuit imposed

personal liability in a case in which the individual defendants "had not respected [the corporation's] separate existence even minimally."

Greenblatt v. Prescription Plan Services Corp., 783 F.Supp. 814 (S.D.N.Y.1992), concerned two corporations that were conceded to be ERISA fiduciaries. The dispute was whether two controlling shareholders of the corporations were also ERISA fiduciaries in their individual capacities. They were held to be, on account of their extensive management and control of the two corporations. The Second Circuit has said that "at least to the extent that a controlling corporate official defrauds or conspires to defraud a benefit fund of required contributions, the official is individually liable [under ERISA]." Leddy v. Standard Drywall, Inc., 875 F.2d 383, 388 (2d Cir.1989).

3. PLAN ASSETS: MUTUAL FUND SHARES AND INSURANCE CONTRACTS

One branch of ERISA's definition of a fiduciary, § 3(21)(A)(i), makes a person a fiduciary of a plan to the extent of the person's discretion over the plan's assets. It is usually easy enough to know what plan assets are—fortunately, since ERISA does not define this component of the definition of a fiduciary.

[handwritten margin note: look at underlying K to see if Insurer can be held as a Fiduciary]

In the prototypical trusteed pension plan, the trustees invest contributions, and they reinvest investment gains and investment income; these investments constitute the plan assets. Difficulty about whether to characterize particular assets as plan assets has arisen on two fronts. Certain types of investments in pooled vehicles such as mutual funds raise the problem of whether or not ERISA looks through the intermediating entity to treat the underlying assets in the pool as the plan assets. Second, certain investment vehicles operated by insurance companies raise the question of whether the arrangement qualifies for ERISA's exclusion from its fiduciary responsibility rules for guaranteed benefit policies; if not, the insurer is an ERISA fiduciary for the assets.

1. *Mutual fund shares.* Suppose a pension plan invests in mutual fund shares. For example, suppose that the plan invests in an extremely well-diversified fund, such as an index fund that tracks the Standard & Poor's 500. The pension plan effectively owns a pro rata share of the mutual fund's holdings of the securities in 500 issuers. Are the pension fund's proportionate interests in the mutual fund's holdings of the 500 securities "plan assets" within the meaning of ERISA fiduciary law, thereby making the investment company an ERISA fiduciary for the pension plan and its beneficiaries? Section 401(b)(1) treats the security issued by the investment company (in our example, the pension trust's shares of the index mutual fund) as the plan asset, but not the underlying assets owned by that index fund. Thus, ERISA § 3(21)(B) generally excludes the investment company from the reach of ERISA fiduciary law.

Both §§ 401(b)(1) and 3(21)(B) limit this dispensation from ERISA fiduciary law to securities issued by an investment company that is registered under the Investment Company Act of 1940, implying that the regulatory regime of the 1940 Act is to some extent a *quid pro quo* for exclusion from ERISA's regime.

2. *The plan asset regulations.* An important DoL regulation, 29 C.F.R. § 2510.3–101, deals with comparable issues that arise in a variety of pooled vehicles other than investment company funds—limited partnerships, venture capital operating companies, real estate operating companies, and mortgage pools.

3. *Insurance contracts.* In certain circumstances the question of whether an insurer is a fiduciary turns on ERISA's exclusion of certain insurance products from the coverage of the fiduciary responsibility rules. Section 401(b)(2) treats an insurance product that is a "guaranteed benefit policy" as the plan asset, rather than the underlying assets of the insurer. If the exclusion applies, the plan cannot look behind the insurance contract to the assets in the account of the insurance company, hence cannot deem the company to be a fiduciary for the plan and for the plan's participants and beneficiaries with respect to those assets. Section 401(b)(2)(B) defines a guaranteed benefit policy as one that "provides for benefits the amount of which is guaranteed by the insurer."

Investment and annuity vehicles operated by insurance companies for pension plans run the gamut from products that leave all investment risk on the plan and are functionally indistinguishable from an investment management contract, to pure annuity contracts that guarantee fixed lifetime payouts and thus absorb all investment (and mortality) risk. In the prominent case of Peoria Union Stock Yards Co. v. Penn Mutual Life Ins. Co., 698 F.2d 320 (7th Cir.1983), dealing with a species of insurance company product called a group deposit administration annuity (GDAA), the Seventh Circuit determined that the GDAA in question did not satisfy the ERISA § 401(b)(2)(B) definition of a guaranteed benefit policy, because too much of the investment risk remained with the pension plan. The court saw the GDAA contract as more like the hiring of an investment adviser than the purchase of an insurance product. The trustees surrendered "the assets of the pension plan to [the insurance company] to manage with full investment discretion, subject only to a modest income guaranty."

It can be objected that the mode of analysis in *Peoria Union* proves too much. Most insurance products shift much of the investment risk to the policyholder. Under a so-called "participating" policy, that is, a policy that pays dividends to the policyholder based in part upon the insurance company's investment experience, the policyholder bears a material component of the investment risk. The insurance industry strenuously resisted the analysis in *Peoria Union* that treats the absence of investment risk as the test for whether an insurance product qualifies as an ERISA-exempt guaranteed benefit policy. See Stephen H. Goldberg & Melvin S. Altman, The Case for the Nonapplication of ERISA to Insurers' General Account Assets, 21 Tort & Insurance Law J. 475, 476–77 (1986).

4. *Harris Trust.* The Third Circuit disapproved *Peoria Union* in Mack Boring & Parts v. Meeker Sharkey Moffitt, 930 F.2d 267 (3d Cir.1991). The Second Circuit followed *Peoria Union* in Harris Trust & Savings Bank v. John Hancock Mutual Life Ins. Co., 970 F.2d 1138 (2d Cir.1992). On certiorari in 1993, the Supreme Court resolved the conflict, determining to "follow the Seventh Circuit's lead" in *Peoria Union*. John Hancock Mutual Life Ins. Co. v. Harris Trust & Savings Bank, 510 U.S. 86, 102 (1993). "[We] hold that to determine whether a contract qualifies

as a guaranteed benefit policy, each component of the contract bears examination. A component fits within the guaranteed benefit policy exclusion only if it allocates investment risk to the insurer." Id. at 106. The Court concluded that the funds in the deposit administration contract "are 'plan assets,' and that [the insurance company's] actions in regard to their management and disposition must be judged against ERISA's fiduciary standards." Id.

    5. *Regulatory and legislative responses to Harris Trust.* In 1996 Congress enacted the so-called ERISA Clarification Act, as part of the Small Business Job Protection Act of 1996. This legislation supplied new ERISA § 401(c), which provides retroactive protection against the consequences of the *Harris Trust* decision. Conforming DoL regulations were issued in 2000, see 29 C.F.R. § 2550.401c–1. For discussion, see Linda K. Shore, DoL's Final Rule on Insurance Company General Accounts: How Much Does It Resolve?, 28 Tax Management Compensation Planning J. 208 (2000).

    6. *Timing.* The question has arisen whether contributions that an employer owes to an employee benefit plan become ERISA "plan assets" at the point at which the contributions become due, or only after they have been paid to the plan. Federal prosecutors have won several cases against employers charged with criminal conversion, in circumstances in which the employer has withheld proceeds from employees' paychecks for contribution to an ERISA plan, but then pocketed the funds. The defendants in these cases have unsuccessfully argued that the misappropriated funds, not having reached the plan, were not plan assets. E.g., United States v. Whiting, 471 F.3d 792 (7th Cir.2006); United States v. Grizzle, 933 F.2d 943, 947 (11th Cir.1991).

    The Fourth Circuit held similarly in United States v. Jackson, 524 F.3d 532 (4th Cir.2008). On certiorari, however, the Supreme Court vacated the judgment and remanded the case "for further consideration in light of the position asserted by the Solicitor General in his brief for the United States. . . ." 129 S.Ct. 1307 (2009). In that brief the Solicitor confessed error, saying that "[a]lthough the government argued in the courts below that unpaid employer contributions are plan assets, the government now agrees with" the convicted defendants who were seeking certiorari, arguing that the funds were not plan assets. Brief for the United States, 2009 WL 133443, at 9–10. The Solicitor endorsed the longstanding view of DoL "that, absent provisions in plan documents giving the plan a beneficial interest in unpaid contributions, the contributions themselves are not assets of the plan until the contributions are paid to the plan." The Solicitor reasoned that "[i]f unpaid contributions were plan assets, ERISA's requirements would govern the normal operations of an employer's business whenever it failed to timely pay contributions. As soon as contributions were past due, an undifferentiated part of the employer's assets would become plan assets, and the employer would find itself in the unmanageable position of being a plan fiduciary in its general business activities." Id. at 15. The DoL regulation on which the Solicitor relied provides that "the assets of the plan include amounts . . . that a participant or beneficiary pays to an employer, or amounts that a participant has withheld from his wages by an employer, for contribution to the plan as of the earliest date on which such contributions can reasonably be segregated from the employer's general assets." 29 CFR § 2510.3–102.

In In re Halpin, 566 F.3d 286 (2d Cir.2009), a bankruptcy case in which the issue was whether withheld but unpaid contributions were assets of the bankrupt employer's estate or plan assets not subject to the bankruptcy, the Second Circuit followed the Solicitor's position in *Jackson*. The court held that the proceeds were not plan assets, saying that "if unpaid employer contributions were plan assets, the employer would automatically become an ERISA fiduciary once it failed to make the payments. As such, the employer would owe the plan undivided loyalty at the expense of competing obligations—some fiduciary—to the business, and to others such as employees, customers, shareholders and lenders, and an undifferentiated portion of the company's assets would be held in trust for the plan. It is difficult to envision how proprietors could ever operate a business enterprise under such circumstances. It is highly unlikely—indeed inconceivable—that Congress intended such a result." Id. at 292.

B. THE EMPLOYER AS FIDUCIARY

1. VARITY CORP. V. HOWE (I)

516 U.S. 489 (1996).

■ BREYER, J., delivered the opinion of the Court, in which REHNQUIST, C. J., and STEVENS, KENNEDY, SOUTER, and GINSBURG, JJ., joined. THOMAS, J., filed a dissenting opinion, in which O'CONNOR and SCALIA, JJ., joined.

A group of beneficiaries of a firm's employee welfare benefit plan, protected by the Employee Retirement Income Security Act of 1974 (ERISA), have sued their plan's administrator, who was also their employer. They claim that the administrator, through trickery, led them to withdraw from the plan and to forfeit their benefits. They seek, among other things, an order that, in essence, would reinstate each of them as a participant in the employer's ERISA plan. The lower courts entered judgment in the employees' favor, and we agreed to review that judgment.

In conducting our review, we do not question the lower courts' findings of serious deception by the employer, but instead consider three legal questions. First, in the factual circumstances (as determined by the lower courts), was the employer acting in its capacity as an ERISA "fiduciary" when it significantly and deliberately misled the beneficiaries? Second, in misleading the beneficiaries, did the employer violate the fiduciary obligations that ERISA § 404 imposes upon plan administrators? Third, does ERISA § 502(a)(3) authorize ERISA plan beneficiaries to bring a lawsuit, such as this one, that seeks relief for individual beneficiaries harmed by an administrator's breach of fiduciary obligations?

We answer each of these questions in the beneficiaries' favor, and we therefore affirm the judgment of the Court of Appeals.

I

The key facts, as found by the District Court after trial, include the following: Charles Howe, and the other respondents, used to work for Massey-Ferguson, Inc., a farm equipment manufacturer, and a wholly-owned subsidiary of the petitioner, Varity Corporation. (Since the lower courts found that Varity and Massey-Ferguson were "alter egos," we shall refer to them interchangeably.) These employees all were participants in, and beneficiaries of, Massey-Ferguson's self-funded employee welfare benefit plan—an ERISA-protected plan that Massey-Ferguson itself administered. In the mid-1980's, Varity became concerned that some of Massey-Ferguson's divisions were losing too much money and developed a business plan to deal with the problem.

The business plan—which Varity called "Project Sunshine"—amounted to placing many of Varity's money-losing eggs in one financially rickety basket. It called for a transfer of Massey-Ferguson's money-losing divisions, along with various other debts, to a newly created, separately incorporated subsidiary called Massey Combines. The plan foresaw the possibility that Massey Combines would fail. But it viewed such a failure, from Varity's business perspective, as closer to a victory than to a defeat. That is because Massey Combine's failure would not only eliminate several of Varity's poorly performing divisions, but it would also eradicate various debts that Varity would transfer to Massey Combines, and which, in the absence of the reorganization, Varity's more profitable subsidiaries or divisions might have to pay.

Among the obligations that Varity hoped the reorganization would eliminate were those arising from the Massey-Ferguson benefit plan's promises to pay medical and other nonpension benefits to employees of Massey-Ferguson's money-losing divisions. Rather than terminate those benefits directly (as it had retained the right to do), Varity attempted to avoid the undesirable fallout that could have accompanied cancellation by inducing the failing divisions' employees to switch employers and thereby voluntarily release Massey-Ferguson from its obligation to provide them benefits (effectively substituting the new, self-funded Massey Combines benefit plan for the former Massey-Ferguson plan). Insofar as Massey-Ferguson's employees did so, a subsequent Massey Combines failure would eliminate—simply and automatically, without distressing the remaining Massey-Ferguson employees—what would otherwise have been Massey-Ferguson's obligation to pay those employees their benefits.

To persuade the employees of the failing divisions to accept the change of employer and benefit plan, Varity called them together at a special meeting and talked to them about Massey Combines' future business outlook, its likely financial viability, and the security of their employee benefits. The thrust of Varity's remarks (which we shall discuss in greater detail) was that the employees' benefits would remain secure if they voluntarily transferred to Massey Combines. As Varity knew, however, the reality was very different. Indeed, the District Court found that Massey Combines was insolvent from the day of its creation and that it hid a $46 million negative net worth by overvaluing its assets and underestimating its liabilities.

After the presentation, about 1,500 Massey-Ferguson employees accepted Varity's assurances and voluntarily agreed to the [transfer]. Unfortunately for these employees, Massey Combines ended its first year with a loss of $88 million, and ended its second year in a receivership, under which its employees lost their nonpension benefits. Many of those employees [brought] this lawsuit, seeking the benefits they would have been owed under their old, Massey-Ferguson plan, had they not transferred to Massey Combines.

After trial, the District Court found, among other things, that Varity and Massey-Ferguson, acting as ERISA fiduciaries, had harmed the plan's beneficiaries through deliberate deception. The court held that Varity and Massey-Ferguson thereby violated an ERISA-imposed fiduciary obligation to administer Massey-Ferguson's benefit plan "solely in the interest of the participants and beneficiaries" of the plan. ERISA § 404(a). [The] Court of Appeals later affirmed the District Court's determinations. . . .

Varity points out that the relevant ERISA section imposes liability only upon plan fiduciaries; and it argues that it was acting only as an employer and not as a plan fiduciary when it deceived its employees. Second, it argues that, in any event, its conduct did not violate the fiduciary standard that ERISA imposes. . . .

II

ERISA protects employee pensions and other benefits by providing insurance (for vested pension rights, see ERISA § 4000 et seq.), specifying certain plan characteristics in detail (such as when and how pensions vest, see §§ 201–211), and by setting forth certain general fiduciary duties applicable to the management of both pension and nonpension benefit plans. See § 404. In this case, we interpret and apply these general fiduciary duties and several related statutory provisions.

In doing so, we recognize that these fiduciary duties draw much of their content from the common law of trusts, the law that governed most benefit plans before ERISA's enactment.

We also recognize, however, that trust law does not tell the entire story. After all, ERISA's standards and procedural protections partly reflect a congressional determination that the common law of trusts did not offer completely satisfactory protection. See ERISA § 2(a). And, even with respect to the trust-like fiduciary standards ERISA imposes, Congress "expected that the courts will interpret this prudent man rule (and other fiduciary standards) bearing in mind the special nature and purpose of employee benefit plans" as they "develop a 'federal common law of rights and obligations under ERISA-regulated plans.' "

Consequently, we believe that the law of trusts often will inform, but will not necessarily determine the outcome of, an effort to interpret ERISA's fiduciary duties. In some instances, trust law will offer only a starting point, after which courts must go on to ask whether, or to what extent, the language of the statute, its structure, or its purposes require departing from common-law trust requirements. And, in doing so, courts may have to take account of competing congressional purposes, such as Congress' desire to offer employees enhanced protection for their benefits, on the one hand, and, on the other, its desire not to create a system that is so complex that administrative costs, or litigation expenses, unduly discourage employers from offering welfare benefit plans in the first place. Compare ERISA § 2 with *Curtiss-Wright Corp. v. Schoonejongen*, 514 U.S. 73, 78–81 (1995), and *Mertens v. Hewitt Associates*, 508 U.S. 248, 262–263 (1993).

We have followed this approach when interpreting, and applying, the statutory provisions here before us.

A

We begin with the question of Varity's fiduciary status. In relevant part, the statute says that a "person is a fiduciary with respect to a plan," and therefore subject to ERISA fiduciary duties, "to the extent" that he or she "exercises any discretionary authority or discretionary control respecting management" of the plan, or "has any discretionary authority or discretionary responsibility in the administration" of the plan. ERISA § 3(21)(A).

Varity was both an employer and the benefit plan's administrator, as ERISA permits. [Varity] argues that when it communicated with its Massey-Ferguson workers about transferring to Massey Combines, it was not administering or managing the plan; rather, it was acting only in its capacity as an employer and not as a plan administrator.

The District Court, however, held that when the misrepresentations regarding employee benefits were made, Varity was wearing its "fiduciary," as well as its "employer," hat. In reviewing this legal conclusion, we give deference to the factual findings of the District Court, recognizing its comparative advantage in understanding the specific context in which the events of this case occurred. We believe that these factual findings (which Varity does not challenge) adequately support the District Court's holding that Varity was exercising "discretionary authority" respecting the plan's "management" or "administration" when it made these misrepresentations, which legal holding we have independently reviewed.

[The Court's opinion reviews "relevant factual circumstances," including the terms of a] side-by-side benefits comparison [that] contained a fairly detailed description of the benefit plans. Its object was to show that after transfer, the employees' benefits would remain the same. [In addition, a question-and-answer sheet read:]

"Q. 3. What happens to my benefits, pension, etc.?

"A. 3. When you transfer to MCC [Massey Combines], pay levels and benefit programmes will remain unchanged. There will be no loss of seniority or pensionable service. . . ."

[Similar representations were made in a 90-second videotape message, which] repeated much of the information in the question-and-answer sheet, adding assurances about Massey Combines' viability. . . .

The District Court concluded that the basic message conveyed to the employees was that transferring from Massey-Ferguson to Massey Combines would not significantly undermine the security of their benefits. And, given this view of the facts, we believe that the District Court reached the correct legal conclusion, namely, that Varity spoke, in significant part, in its capacity as plan administrator.

To decide whether Varity's actions fall within the statutory definition of "fiduciary" acts, we must interpret the statutory terms which limit the scope of fiduciary activity to discretionary acts of plan "management" and "administration." ERISA § 3(21)(A). These words are not self-defining, and the activity at issue here neither falls clearly within nor outside of the common understanding of these words. . . . [We] look to the common law, which, over the years, has given to terms such as "fiduciary" and trust "administration" a legal meaning to which, we normally presume, Congress meant to refer. The ordinary trust law understanding of fiduciary "administration" of a trust is that to act as an administrator is to perform the duties imposed, or exercise the powers conferred, by the trust documents. See Restatement (Second) of Trusts § 164 (1957). Cf. ERISA § 404(a). The law of trusts also understands a trust document to implicitly confer "such powers as are necessary or appropriate for the carrying out of the purposes" of the trust. 3 A. Scott & W. Fratcher, Law of Trusts § 186, p. 6 (4th ed. 1988). Conveying information about the likely future of plan benefits, thereby permitting beneficiaries to make an informed choice about continued participation, would seem to be an exercise of a power "appropriate" to carrying out an important plan purpose. After all, ERISA itself specifically requires administrators to give beneficiaries certain information about the plan. See, e.g., ERISA §§ 102, 104(b)(1), 105(a). And administrators, as part of their administrative responsibilities, frequently offer beneficiaries more than the minimum information that the statute requires—for example, answering beneficiaries' questions about the meaning of the terms of a plan so that those beneficiaries can more easily obtain the plan's benefits. To offer beneficiaries detailed plan information in order to help them decide whether to remain with the plan is essentially the same kind of plan-related activity. Cf. Restatement (Second) of Agency § 229(1) (1957) (determining whether an activity is within the "scope of . . . employment" in part by examining whether it is "of the same general nature as that authorized").

Moreover, as far as the record reveals, [the information summarized above] came from those within the firm who had authority to communicate as fiduciaries with plan beneficiaries. . . .

Finally, reasonable employees, in the circumstances found by the District Court, could have thought that Varity was communicating with them both in its capacity as employer and in its capacity as plan administrator. Reasonable employees might not have distinguished consciously between the two roles. But they would have known that the employer was their plan's administrator and had expert knowledge about how their plan worked. The central conclusion ("your benefits are secure") could well have drawn strength from their awareness of that expertise, and one could reasonably believe that the employer, aware of the importance of the matter, so intended.

We conclude, therefore, that the factual context in which the statements were made, combined with the plan-related nature of the activity, engaged in by those who had plan-related authority to do so, together provide sufficient support for the District Court's legal conclusion that Varity was acting as a fiduciary.

Varity raises three contrary arguments. First, Varity argues that it was not engaged in plan administration because neither the specific disclosure provisions of ERISA, nor the specific terms of the plan instruments, required it to make these statements. But that does not mean Varity was not engaging in plan administration in making them. . . . There is more to plan (or trust) administration than simply complying with the specific duties imposed by the plan documents or statutory regime; it also includes the activities that are "ordinary and natural means" of achieving the "objective" of the plan. Indeed, the primary function of the fiduciary duty is to constrain the exercise of discretionary powers which are controlled by no other specific duty imposed by the trust instrument or the legal regime. If the fiduciary duty applied to nothing more than activities already controlled by other specific legal duties, it would serve no purpose.

Second, Varity says that when it made the statements that most worried the District Court—the statements about Massey Combines' "bright future"—it must have been speaking only as employer (and not as fiduciary), for statements about a new subsidiary's financial future have virtually nothing to do with administering benefit plans. But this argument parses the meeting's communications too finely. The ultimate message Varity intended to convey—"your benefits are secure"—depended in part upon its repeated assurances that benefits would remain "unchanged," in part upon the detailed comparison of benefits, and in part upon assurances about Massey Combines' "bright" financial future. Varity's workers would not necessarily have focused upon each underlying supporting statement separately, because what primarily interested them, and what primarily interested the District Court, was the truthfulness of the ultimate conclusion that transferring to Massey Combines would not adversely affect the security of their benefits. And, in the present context, Varity's statements about the security of benefits amounted to an act of plan administration. That Varity intentionally communicated its conclusion through a closely linked set of statements (some directly concerning plan benefits, others concerning the viability of the corporation) does not change this conclusion.

We do not hold . . . that Varity acted as a fiduciary simply because it made statements about its expected financial condition or because "an ordinary business decision turned out to have an adverse impact on the plan." Instead, we accept the undisputed facts found, and factual inferences drawn, by the District Court, namely that Varity *intentionally* connected its statements about Massey Combines' financial health to statements it made about the future of benefits, so that its intended communication about the security of benefits was rendered materially misleading. And we hold that making intentional representations about the future of plan benefits in that context is an act of plan administration.

Third, Varity says that an employer's decision to amend or terminate a plan (as Varity had the right to do) is not an act of plan administration. How then, it asks, could conveying information about the likelihood of termination be an act of plan administration? While it may be true that amending or terminating a plan (or a common-law trust) is beyond the power of a plan administrator (or trustee)—and, therefore, cannot be an act of plan "management" or "administration"—it does not follow that making statements about the likely future of the plan is also beyond the scope of plan administration. As we explained above, plan administrators often have, and commonly exercise, discretionary authority to communicate with beneficiaries about the future of plan benefits.

B

The second question—whether Varity's deception violated ERISA-imposed fiduciary obligations—calls for a brief, affirmative answer. ERISA requires a "fiduciary" to "discharge his duties with respect to a plan solely in the interest of the participants and beneficiaries." ERISA § 404(a). To participate knowingly and significantly in deceiving a plan's beneficiaries in order to save the employer money at the beneficiaries' expense, is not to act "solely in the interest of the participants and beneficiaries." As other courts have held, "lying is inconsistent with the duty of loyalty owed by all fiduciaries and codified in section 404(a)(1) of ERISA." Because the breach of this duty is sufficient to uphold the decision below, we need not reach the question of whether ERISA fiduciaries have any fiduciary duty to disclose truthful information on their own initiative, or in response to employee inquiries. . . .

We are aware, as Varity suggests, of one possible reason for a departure from ordinary trust law principles. In arguing about ERISA's remedies for breaches of fiduciary obligation, Varity says that Congress intended ERISA's fiduciary standards to protect only the financial integrity of the plan, not individual beneficiaries. This intent, says Varity, is shown by the fact that Congress did not provide remedies for individuals harmed by such breaches; rather, Congress limited relief to remedies that would benefit only the plan itself. This argument fails, however, because, in our view, Congress did provide remedies for individual beneficiaries harmed by breaches of fiduciary duty, as we shall next discuss.

C

The remaining question before us is whether or not the remedial provision of ERISA that the beneficiaries invoked, ERISA § 502(a)(3), authorizes this lawsuit for individual relief. [This portion of the opinion is reproduced in Chapter 16, infra, as *Varity Corp. v. Howe (II).*—Eds.]

■ JUSTICE THOMAS, with whom JUSTICE O'CONNOR and JUSTICE SCALIA join, dissenting. . . .

Under ERISA, an employer is permitted to act both as plan sponsor and plan administrator. § 408(c)(3). Employers who choose to administer their own plans assume responsibilities to both the company and the plan, and, accordingly, owe duties of loyalty and care to both entities. In permitting such arrangements, which ordinary trust law generally forbids due to the inherent potential for conflict of interest, Congress understood that the interests of the plan might be sacrificed if an employer were forced to choose between the company and the plan. Hence, Congress imposed on plan administrators a duty of care that requires them to "discharge [their] duties with respect to a plan solely in the interest of the participants and beneficiaries." § 404(a)(1). Congress also understood, however, that virtually every business decision an employer makes can have an adverse impact on the plan, and that an employer would not be able to run a company profitably if every business decision had to be made in the best interests of plan participants. . . .

Even business decisions that directly affect the plan and plan participants, such as the decision to modify or terminate welfare benefits, are not governed by ERISA's fiduciary obligations because they do not involve discretionary administration of the plan. In contrast, the discretionary interpretation of a plan term, or the discretionary determination that the plan does not authorize a certain type of procedure, would likely qualify as plan administration by a fiduciary. There is no claim in this case, however, that Varity failed to implement the plan according to its terms, since respondents actually received all of the benefits to which they were entitled under the plan, as the courts below found.

An employer will also make countless representations in the course of managing a business about the current and expected financial condition of the corporation. Similarly, an employer may make representations that either directly or impliedly evince an intention to increase, decrease, or maintain employee welfare benefits. Like the decision to terminate or modify welfare benefits, the decision to make, or not to make, such representations is made in the employer's "corporate nonfiduciary capacity as plan sponsor or settlor," and ERISA's fiduciary rules do not apply. Such communications simply are not made in the course of implementing the plan or executing its terms. Rather, they are the necessary incidents of conducting a business, and Congress determined that employers would not be burdened with fiduciary obligations to the plan when engaging in such conduct. See § 3(21)(A)(iii). . . .

Because an employer's representations about the company's financial prospects or about the possible impact of ordinary business transactions on the security of unvested welfare benefits do not involve execution or implementation of duties imposed by the plan or the Act, and because these are the types of representations employers regularly make in the ordinary course of running a business, I would not hold that such communications involve plan administration. The untruthfulness of a statement cannot magically transform it from a nonfiduciary representation into a fiduciary one; the determinative factor is not truthfulness but the capacity in which the statement is made.

NOTES AND QUESTIONS

1. *Conduct and status.* Does the majority opinion respond effectively to Justice Thomas' observation in dissent that "[t]he untruthfulness of a statement cannot magically transform it from a nonfiduciary representation into a fiduciary one; the determinative factor is not truthfulness but the capacity in which the statement is made"?

2. *Employer as de facto or functional fiduciary. Varity* has come to stand for the distinction between the two ways in which an employer can become an ERISA fiduciary. An employer may become an ERISA fiduciary by being named as such in the plan documents, pursuant to the procedures contained in ERISA §§ 402–403. Moreover, as in *Varity,* an employer can become an ERISA fiduciary by virtue of conduct, that is, by exercising

particular functions that are fiduciary in character under ERISA § 3(21)(A), even if that person has not been formally named a fiduciary, or named to discharge those functions. The Supreme Court held that when Varity made misrepresentations on which employees foreseeably relied in making grievously disadvantageous plan elections, "Varity was exercising 'discretionary authority' respecting the plan's 'management' or 'administration.'" 516 U.S. at 498. The central message of *Varity* is estoppel-like: The courts will protect the justified reliance of plan participants by construing material misrepresentation regarding plan affairs as fiduciary conduct.

3.   *Transforming tort?* It is easy to understand that intentional misrepresentation ought to be actionable. Intentional misrepresentation (deceit, fraud) is an ancient category of liability in tort. Why, therefore, not remedy the conduct in *Varity* in tort? Why twist a familiar tort into a problematic claim for breach of fiduciary duty? The shortcomings of ERISA remedy law as interpreted by the Supreme Court, discussed infra in Chapter 16, bear on the matter. ERISA supplies no tort law of its own, and the Supreme Court has been hostile to implying causes of action under federal statutes. Moreover, ERISA's preemption provision, § 514(a), preempts much of state tort law under the *Pilot Life* doctrine, discussed infra in Chapter 17.

4.   *Substantive fiduciary law.* In Section II.B of its opinion in *Varity* the Court gave "a brief, affirmative answer" to the question whether, if Varity were a fiduciary, its conduct violated ERISA fiduciary law. The Court cited ERISA fiduciary's duty of loyalty, which requires that a fiduciary "discharge his duties with respect to a plan solely in the interest of the participants and beneficiaries." ERISA § 404(a). ERISA's duty of loyalty figures centrally in Chapters 13–15 of this book, exploring ERISA's substantive fiduciary law.

5.   *Disclosure.* The lower court in *Varity* said that the duty of loyalty requires an ERISA fiduciary to communicate material facts that could adversely affect a plan member's interests. Howe v. Varity Corp., 36 F.3d 746, 754 (8th Cir.1994). The Supreme Court carefully refused to address "the question of whether ERISA fiduciaries have any fiduciary duty to disclose truthful information on their own initiative, or in response to employee inquiries." The scope of an ERISA fiduciary's duty of disclosure is discussed in Chapter 13, infra.

Could better disclosure about the employer's status have altered the result in *Varity*? Suppose the employer had prefaced every communication about future benefits with a notice saying that "this information is offered in our capacity as employer and not as plan fiduciary." Would such disclaimers have altered the result in *Varity*?

6.   *Remedy.* It will not help a plaintiff to succeed in having a defendant construed to be an ERISA fiduciary if ERISA's remedy provisions do not permit effective recovery for breach of fiduciary duty. The Supreme Court addressed that issue in a portion of its opinion in *Varity* that is reproduced separately (as *Varity II*) in Chapter 16, infra; and in several subsequent cases also extracted there.

2. THE EMPLOYER'S TWO HATS

The question in *Varity* was whether a particular function exercised by the employer was or was not fiduciary. ERISA does not require the employer (or other plan sponsor) to serve as plan administrator or to conduct most other fiduciary functions. The employer can delegate most fiduciary tasks, typically by contract with external service providers. Most employers choose to retain many fiduciary functions, in order to retain direct control over such major cost centers.

1. *Nomenclature.* Several labels have come into use to capture the distinction between an employer's fiduciary and nonfiduciary roles. ERISA lawyers contrast the employer's fiduciary work of *plan administration* with *plan design*, which is nonfiduciary. This nonfiduciary role is also referred to as the *settlor function*, a term taken from trust law, which evokes the unconstrained authority of the donor of property who creates ("settles") a trust. The Supreme Court spoke of "the settlor-fiduciary distinction" in Lockheed Corp. v. Spink, 517 U.S. 882, 891 (1996). Another such usage juxtaposes the employer's fiduciary role against its *business function.*

Yet another common formulation of the distinction is the *two hat* doctrine. "Generally, employers owe no fiduciary duty towards plan beneficiaries under ERISA. However, when employers choose to 'wear two hats,' i.e., act as both employer and plan administrator, ERISA fiduciary duties regarding plan administration attach. Yet, employers who act as plan administrators 'assume fiduciary status only when and to the extent that they function in their capacity as plan administrators, not when they conduct business that is not regulated by ERISA.'" Barnes v. Lacy, 927 F.2d 539, 544 (11th Cir.1991). In Pegram v. Herdrich, 530 U.S. 211, 225 (2000), reproduced below in this chapter, the Supreme Court remarked that ERISA requires "the fiduciary with two hats [to] wear only one at a time, and [to] wear the fiduciary hat when making fiduciary decisions."

2. *Rationale.* ERISA presupposes but does not articulate the distinction between an employer's fiduciary and nonfiduciary roles. Judge Easterbrook has observed:

> One subject conspicuously missing from [ERISA's definition of a fiduciary in § 3(21)(A)] is the establishment and amendment of the plan itself. Employers decide who receives pension benefits and in what amounts, select levels of funding, adjust myriad other details of pension plans, and may decide to terminate the plan altogether. In doing these things, we have held, they are no more "fiduciaries" than when they decide what wages to offer or whether to close the plant and lay the workers off. And no wonder. Defined-benefit plans create claims not just against the assets in the pension trust but against the employer's general assets. Excessive promises of benefits, or poor performance by the assets held in trust, oblige the employer to pay additional sums. As the entity with ultimate responsibility for satisfying the pension promises, the employer is entitled to control decisions about the level of benefits to be guaranteed and the means by which that is accomplished.

Johnson v. Georgia-Pacific Corp., 19 F.3d 1184, 1188 (7th Cir.1994).

3. *Setting benefit levels.* In a single employer plan, setting benefit levels is, like plan creation and plan amendment, a nonfiduciary function. "Nothing in ERISA requires employers to establish employee benefits plans. Nor does ERISA mandate what kind of benefits employers must provide if they choose to have such a plan." Lockheed Corp. v. Spink, 517 U.S. 882, 887 (1996).

4. *Amending a single-employer plan.* The logic that makes creating plans and setting benefit levels nonfiduciary extends more generally to plan amendments. "[E]mployers or other plan sponsors are generally free under ERISA, for any reason at any time, to adopt, modify, or terminate welfare plans." Curtiss-Wright Corp. v. Schoonejongen, 514 U.S. 73, 78 (1995). Moreover, "an employer's decision to amend a pension plan concerns the composition or design of the plan itself and does not implicate the employer's fiduciary duties, which consist of such actions as the administration of the plan's assets." Hughes Aircraft Co. v. Jacobson, 525 U.S. 432, 444 (1999). The Supreme Court cases are discussed in Dana M. Muir, The Plan Amendment Trilogy: Settling the Scope of the Settlor Doctrine, 15 Labor Lawyer 205 (1999). In Beck v. PACE International Union, 551 U.S. 96 (2007), the Supreme Court said: "It is well established in this Court's cases that an employer's decision whether to terminate an ERISA plan is a settlor function immune from ERISA's fiduciary obligations." Id. at 101 (emphasis deleted). Recall, however, from Chapters 4–5, supra, that under ERISA § 204(g) no plan amendment is permitted to reduce an accrued pension benefit.

In Sengpiel v. B.F. Goodrich Co., 156 F.3d 660, 666 (6th Cir.1998), the Sixth Circuit held that the transfer of welfare benefit plan liabilities to a successor entity was not a fiduciary activity. Citing *Varity,* the court said that "the fact that an action taken by an employer to implement a business decision may ultimately affect the security of employees' welfare benefits does not automatically render the action subject to ERISA's fiduciary duties. To adopt such a rule would, in effect, erode the well-established principle that employers are free to make decisions that modify, amend, or even terminate their employees' unvested welfare benefits."

5. *Multiemployer plans.* In dealing with multiemployer plans, as opposed to single employer plans, some courts have held that setting benefit levels and amending plans can be fiduciary conduct. A multiemployer plan is an entity distinct from the employers that contribute to it. Governance of such plans is remitted to trustees drawn equally from employer and union representatives, as required under the Taft-Hartley Act § 302(c)(5), 29 U.S.C. § 186. In NLRB v. Amax Coal Co., 453 U.S. 322 (1981), the Supreme Court held that although § 302(c) refers to the employer-designated trustees of a multiemployer plan as "the representatives of the employer," these persons are not agents of the employer but fiduciaries for the plan participants and beneficiaries. Because multiemployer plan trustees are fiduciaries, some courts have reasoned that setting benefit levels and amending other plan terms is fiduciary conduct under ERISA. E.g., Deak v. Masters, Mates & Pilots Pension Plan, 821 F.2d 572, 581 (11th Cir.1987); Geib v. New York State

Teamsters Conference Pension & Retirement Fund, 758 F.2d 973 (3d Cir.1985).

Following such precedents, the district court in Walling v. Brady, 917 F.Supp. 313 (D.Del.1996), concluded that multiemployer "plan trustees are treated as fiduciaries and plan amendments are regarded as fiduciary functions. Courts have not hesitated to invalidate amendments not made in furtherance of the participants' and beneficiaries' interests as breaches of fiduciary responsibility." Id. at 319–20. The Third Circuit, however, reversed, 125 F.3d 114 (3d Cir.1997), finding no basis in the structure of ERISA for treating plan amendment as a fiduciary function even in the case of a multiemployer plan. The court distinguished plan amendment from plan administration, finding only the latter to be a fiduciary function. Cases according with this view include Hartline v. Sheet Metal Workers' National Pension Fund, 286 F.3d 598 (D.C. Cir.2002); Gard v. Blankenburg, 33 Fed.Appx. 722 (6th Cir.2002); Milwaukee Area Joint Apprenticeship Training Committee v. Howell, 67 F.3d 1333 (7th Cir.1995).

6. *Appointing a fiduciary is a fiduciary function.* Although the employer may delegate fiduciary functions, the act of delegation is itself fiduciary. DoL has said when the employer's board of directors is responsible for the selection and retention of plan fiduciaries, the directors "exercise 'discretionary authority or discretionary control respecting management of such plan' " and are therefore fiduciaries with respect to their exercise of the function. 29 C.F.R. § 2509.75–8, at D4, quoting ERISA § 3(21)(A). The ERISA standard derives from trust law; see e.g., Uniform Trust Code § 807 (2000) (delegating important trust functions requires the trustee to exercise prudent care, skill, and caution in selecting, instructing, and monitoring the agent); accord Uniform Prudent Investor Act § 9 (1994) (same standard in delegating investment and management of trust assets). "A person with discretionary authority to appoint, maintain and remove plan fiduciaries is himself deemed [an ERISA] fiduciary with respect to the exercise of that authority." In re Xcel Energy, Inc., Securities, Derivative & "ERISA" Litig., 312 F.Supp.2d 1165, 1176 (D.Minn.2004). This principle has figured importantly in the employer stock plan litigation, discussed infra in Chapter 14.

CHAPTER 13

FIDUCIARY DUTIES

Analysis

A. SUBSTANTIVE FIDUCIARY LAW

1. THE MAIN PRINCIPLES

ERISA fiduciary law is derived from and patterned on the Anglo-American law of trusts, as discussed in Chapter 12, supra. That chapter emphasized that ERISA fiduciary law pertains not only to the trusteeship of plan assets required under ERISA § 403(a), but also to every aspect of plan administration that entails the "discretionary authority" or the "control" over plan assets that is contemplated under ERISA's definition of a fiduciary, § 3(21)(A).

1. *Trust law foundations.* Trust fiduciary law derives from two grand principles, the trustee's duties of *loyalty* and of *prudence.* ERISA fiduciary law carries forward both.

The duty of loyalty requires a trustee "to administer the trust solely in the interest of the beneficiaries. . . ." Restatement (Third) of Trusts § 78 (2007). This "sole interest" rule is widely regarded as " 'the most fundamental' " rule of trust law. Pegram v. Herdrich, 530 U.S. 211, 224 (2000), quoting 2A Austin W. Scott & William F. Fratcher, The Law of Trusts § 170, at 311 (4th ed. 1987).

The prudence norm is the trust-law standard of care. It resembles the reasonable person rule of tort law. A trustee "has a duty to administer the trust as a prudent person would, in light of the purposes, terms and other circumstances of the trust. The duty of prudence requires the exercise of reasonable care, skill, and caution." Restatement (Third) of Trusts § 77(1)–(2) (2007).

Subrules of fiduciary administration abound in trust law—for example, the duties to keep and render accounts, to segregate and earmark trust assets and accounts, to furnish information, to preserve

[handwritten margin note: Fiduciary's Duty of Loyalty + Prudence]

trust assets and make them productive, to enforce and defend claims, and to minimize costs. See Restatement (Third) of Trusts §§ 82–84, 88 (2007); Restatement (Second) of Trusts §§ 175–78 (1959). These subrules of fiduciary obligation ultimately derive from and implement the duties of loyalty and prudence.

In transposing the trust model as the regulatory regime for a new field of federal law, Congress chose not to replicate much of the detail of traditional trust law. Because pension and employee benefit plans are commercial arrangements arising from the employment relationship, there was no need in ERISA to carry over doctrines of trust law that speak mainly to intrafamilial wealth transfer. Congress intended that the courts would draw upon the law of trusts in giving shape to a " 'federal common law of rights and obligations under ERISA-regulated plans.' " Firestone Tire & Rubber Co. v. Bruch, 489 U.S. 101, 110 (1989) (quoting Pilot Life Ins. Co. v. Dedeaux, 481 U.S. 41, 56 (1987)). ERISA lodges extensive regulatory authority with the Department of Labor (DoL), which has produced an important body of regulations interpreting ERISA fiduciary law. Congress could be skeletal in absorbing the subordinate rules of trust fiduciary law, because the core principles of loyalty and prudence would allow DoL and the courts to import and to modify whatever else they might need as the field took shape.

2.   *ERISA § 404(a)*. The heart of ERISA fiduciary law is § 404(a)(1). Subsection A imposes ERISA's version of the duty of loyalty, the exclusive benefit rule. Subsection B imposes the requirement of prudent trust administration. Subsection C contains ERISA's duty to diversify trust investments, which is discussed in Chapter 14, infra. Subsection D, which obliges the fiduciary to obey plan terms to the extent consistent with ERISA, seems innocuous but in fact signals an important departure from the trust law model.

3.   *Loyalty: "sole interest/exclusive purpose."* ERISA's version of the duty of loyalty appears both in the stem language of § 404(a)(1), requiring the ERISA fiduciary to "discharge his duties with respect to a plan solely in the interest of the participants and beneficiaries"; and in § 404(a)(1)(A)(i), requiring the ERISA fiduciary to act "for the exclusive purpose [of] providing benefits to participants and their beneficiaries." In ERISA argot, this language constitutes the "sole interest/exclusive purpose" rule, sometimes called the "exclusive benefit" rule.

ERISA § 403(c)(1) supplies another and distinct formulation of the loyalty norm, the so-called "noninurement" rule. It requires that, subject to certain exceptions that become important in situations in which a pension plan is terminated, "the assets of a plan shall never inure to the benefit of any employer and shall be held for the exclusive [purpose] of providing benefits to participants in the plan and their [beneficiaries]."

ERISA's exclusive benefit rule had a half century of prehistory in other federal pension legislation. The Revenue Act of 1921 introduced an exclusive benefit requirement into the Internal Revenue Code as a condition for qualifying a pension trust for tax deferral. The Act required that the employer create the trust "for the exclusive benefit of some or all of his employees. . . ." Section 401(a) of the present Code carries forward the tax law version of the exclusive benefit rule. Further, since 1947, section 302(c)(5) of the Taft-Hartley Act has required that contributions to multiemployer plans regulated under that legislation be made "for the sole and exclusive benefit of the employees [and] their families and dependents. . . ."

The drafters of ERISA had a special mission for the duty of loyalty in pension fiduciary law. In the 1950s and 1960s, Congressional investigations led by Senator John McClellan into labor union racketeering, especially corruption in the Teamsters Union, achieved immense notoriety. The McClellan Committee uncovered looting of union-controlled pension and employee benefit funds, through sweetheart deals, kickbacks, and other forms of cronyism. See James A. Wooten, The Employee Retirement Security Act of 1974: A Political History 47–48, 117–18 (2005). By mandating the trust form and by transposing the loyalty and care (prudence) standards from trust to pension law, the drafters of ERISA were able to absorb a familiar fiduciary regime to protect plan funds against internal defalcation.

In the post-ERISA period, when cases of self-dealing have arisen, the exclusive benefit rule has proved an effective corrective. Although the exclusive benefit rule works well enough against thievery and self-dealing, the rule sweeps more broadly, and in some settings it has proven problematic. The leading case of Donovan v. Bierwirth, 680 F.2d 263 (2d Cir.1982), reproduced infra in Chapter 14, illustrates these tensions.

4. *Prohibited transactions.* ERISA contains a further regime for dealing with loyalty issues, the prohibited transaction rules of §§ 406–408, discussed infra in Section C of this chapter. Bear in mind that the prohibited transaction rules substantially overlap the exclusive benefit rule of § 404(a)(1)(A). Accordingly, in many circumstances, breaching one entails breach of the other.

5. *Impartiality.* Having originated as a branch of the law of donative transfers, the law of trusts has been particularly attuned to the problems associated with successive (usually life and remainder) estates. The law of trusts imposes a duty of impartiality upon trustees in such settings. "When there are two or more beneficiaries of a trust, the trustee is under a duty to deal impartially with them." Restatement (Third) of Trusts § 79 (2007) (trustee under a duty to "to act with due regard for the diverse beneficial interests created by the terms of the trust").

ERISA does not by its terms spell out the duty of impartiality. However, the assumption is widespread that ERISA's exclusive benefit rule implies the duty of impartiality, because a fiduciary cannot properly implement the duty of loyalty without taking into account the interests of all the affected beneficiaries. A Third Circuit panel, speaking in the context of a multiemployer plan, said: "In actions by individual claimants challenging the trustees' denial of benefits, the issue [is] whether the trustees have correctly balanced the interests of present claimants against the interests of future claimants." Struble v. New Jersey Brewery Employees' Welfare Trust Fund, 732 F.2d 325, 333 (3d Cir.1984). In Armstrong v. LaSalle Bank N.A., 446 F.3d 728, 734 (7th Cir.2006), the Seventh Circuit said that ERISA's prudence norm imposed a duty on the plan trustee to consider "how best to balance the interests of the various participants in the" plan.

The Second Circuit invoked impartiality concerns in Morse v. Stanley, 732 F.2d 1139, 1145 (2d Cir.1984). "[A] trustee has a duty to deal impartially with beneficiaries. In this case there are working Plan participants and retired beneficiaries and/or their families. The trustee must deal even-handedly among them, doing his best for the entire trust looked at as a whole. That is to say, a trustee's duty is not to prefer the present interest of one group, e.g., here the departing plan participants, but also not to unduly delay payment of benefits to such participants to their detriment."

6. *Prudence.* ERISA § 404(a)(1)(B), which imposes the "prudent man" standard of plan administration, codifies the duty of prudent administration long familiar in trust law. The term "prudence" is another word for "reasonableness." The prudence standard is relational, that is, it compares the behavior of the fiduciary in the present case to the practice of others similarly situated. ERISA's version calls for the fiduciary to exercise "the care, skill, prudence, and diligence under the circumstances then prevailing that a prudent man acting in a like capacity and familiar with such matters would use in the conduct of an enterprise of a like character and with like aims." ERISA § 404(a)(1)(B). The prudence norm supplies the basis for ERISA's standards for fiduciary investing of plan assets, discussed infra in Chapter 14.

The prudence norm is often expressed procedurally. For example, the prominent *Unisys I* case, dealing with fiduciary investing, speaks of prudence as "an objective standard, focusing on a fiduciary's conduct in arriving at an investment decision, not on its results, and asking whether a fiduciary employed the appropriate methods to investigate and determine the merits of a particular investment." In re Unisys Savings Plan Litigation (Unisys I), 74 F.3d 420, 434 (3d Cir.1996). This subject is discussed further in the note on process values in fiduciary investing in Chapter 14, infra, following the principal case, *Donovan v. Bierwirth*.

Although the prudence norm is often expressed procedurally, a mere allegation that a fiduciary did not follow particular procedures is not sufficient to establish fiduciary liability. See Plasterers' Local Union No. 96 Pension Plan v. Pepper, 663 F.3d 210 (4th Cir. 2011) (allegation that fiduciaries failed to research alternative investment vehicles or to consider certain aspects of the strategies' reasonableness is insufficient; remanding the case to allow district court to make necessary factual findings to determine what circumstances informed the fiduciaries' decision making).

7. *Diversification.* The duty to diversify plan investments, ERISA § 404(a)(1)(C), is a particular application of the duty of prudent investing. Restatement (Third) of Trusts § 90(b) (2007); Uniform Prudent Investor Act § 3 (1994). Modern portfolio theory, the dominant school of thought about contemporary investment practice, emphasizes diversification. The logic and the central importance of diversification in fiduciary investing are discussed infra in Chapter 14, treating plan investments.

8. *Liability and remedy.* Section 409(a) makes the fiduciary who commits a breach of the fiduciary responsibility rules "personally liable to make good to [the] plan any losses," as well as to restore any profits "made through use of assets of the plan." The section also subjects the breaching fiduciary "to such other equitable or remedial relief as the

court may deem appropriate. . . ." ERISA remedy law authorizes actions by participants, beneficiaries, fiduciaries, and the Secretary of Labor to enforce § 409. ERISA § 502(a). Regarding the complexities of ERISA remedy law, see Chapter 16, infra.

9. *Exculpation.* In a major departure from the law of private trusts, ERISA forbids the trust or other plan documents from "reliev[ing] a fiduciary from responsibility or liability." § 410(a). By contrast, trust law allows exculpation clauses, subject to some limitations. See Restatement (Second) of Trusts § 222 (1959); Uniform Trust Code § 1008 (2000). The Ninth Circuit applied § 410(a) in IT Corp. v. General American Life Ins. Co., 107 F.3d 1415, 1418 (9th Cir.1997), finding that "a contract exonerating an ERISA fiduciary from fiduciary responsibilities is void as a matter of law."

Although ERISA Section 410(a) prohibits a plan from relieving a fiduciary of liability, the fiduciary may nonetheless be indemnified for that liability. Section 410(b) permits a plan to purchase liability insurance for the plan fiduciaries, subject to various conditions. Moreover the DoL has interpreted the statute to permit the employer's (as opposed to the plan's) directly indemnifying fiduciaries for liability arising under ERISA. DoL Reg. Section 2509.75–4, 29 C.F.R. Section 2509.75–4. Is the allowance of indemnification consistent with the policy embodied in the prohibition against exculpation clauses in Section 410(a)?

10. *ERISA § 404(a)(1)(D): Adhering to plan terms and to ERISA.* Notice ERISA § 404(a)(1)(D) carefully. This provision requires an ERISA fiduciary to act "in accordance with the documents and instruments governing the plan," but subject to the important qualification that this requirement pertains only "insofar as such documents and instruments are consistent with the provisions of [ERISA's Titles 1 and 4]."

For a straightforward application of the requirement that ERISA fiduciaries obey lawful plan documents, see Dardaganis v. Grace Capital Inc., 889 F.2d 1237 (2d Cir.1989) (investment manager authorized by plan documents to invest no more than 50 percent of ERISA fund in equities held in violation of § 404(a)(1)(D) when it invested 80 percent in equities). Notice that the "documents and instruments" envisaged in § 404(a)(1)(D) include not only the plan and the trust required under §§ 403–404, but also ancillary documents such as the investment management agreement in *Dardaganis*.

The requirement that fiduciaries obey the plan documents is commonly invoked, along with the writing requirement of § 402(a)(1), as a defense to lawsuits in which a plan participant seeks to enforce a benefit claim based upon his or her reliance on an oral representation made by a plan fiduciary or agent regarding the plan's benefits. The troubled case law is discussed in Chapter 15, infra.

When a plan term conflicts with ERISA requirements, § 404(a)(1)(D) insists that the fiduciary prefer ERISA over the document. Thus, for example, DoL has said that when an investment manager determines that complying with voting instructions contained in a plan's statement of investment policy would be "imprudent or not solely in the interest of plan participants, the investment manager would be required to ignore the voting policy that would violate ERISA § 404(a)(1)(D) in that instance." Interpretive Bulletin 94–2, codified as 29 C.F.R. § 2509.94–2.

11. *Limits on plan autonomy?* The concluding portion of § 404(a)(1)(D), which requires that plan terms be "consistent with the provisions of [ERISA]," is a measure of potentially profound significance. The Supreme Court has interpreted the provision to mean "that trust documents cannot excuse trustees from their duties under ERISA, and that trust documents must generally be construed in light of ERISA's [policies]." Central States, Southeast & Southwest Areas Pension Fund v. Central Transport, Inc., 472 U.S. 559, 568 (1985).

In trust law, virtually all the rules are default rules that the trust instrument may override. See John H. Langbein, Mandatory Rules in the Law of Trusts, 98 Northwestern L. Rev. 1105 (2004). By forbidding plan drafters to depart from "the provisions of [ERISA]," § 404(a)(1)(D) transforms trust default law into ERISA mandatory law.

This branch of ERISA § 404(a)(1)(D) has had particular significance in fiduciary investment matters, notably in the employer stock plan cases discussed infra in Chapter 14. The Fifth Circuit has said: "In case of a conflict [between ERISA duties and plan terms], the provisions of the ERISA policies as set forth in the statute and regulations prevail over those of the Fund guidelines." Laborers Nat. Pension Fund v. Northern Trust Quantitative Advisors, Inc., 173 F.3d 313, 322 (5th Cir.1999) (holding that investment manager must disregard plan terms if investing plan assets as required by plan would violate its duty of prudence).

Can artful plan design trump ERISA fiduciary law? Consider Hamilton v. Air Jamaica, Ltd., 945 F.2d 74 (3d Cir.1991), which concerned a severance pay plan. The plan contained a term that reserved to the employer "the right, whether in an individual case or more generally, to alter, reduce or eliminate any pay practice, policy or benefit, in whole or in part, without notice." Id. at 76. The district court had refused to enforce the term, reasoning that the term conflicted with ERISA's requirement that plan terms be in writing. Hamilton v. Air Jamaica, Ltd., 750 F.Supp. 1259, 1270 (E.D.Pa.1990). The Third Circuit reversed, reasoning that "the reservation is part of the written promise and a limitation upon it. While ERISA was enacted to provide security in employee benefits, it protects only those benefits provided in the plan." 945 F.2d at 78. "Air Jamaica's reservation of the right to determine benefits on a case-by-case basis prevented Hamilton from having an enforceable claim to the severance benefits [that the plan otherwise provided]." Id. at 77. For criticism of *Air Jamaica*, see Catherine L. Fisk, *Lochner* Redux: The Renaissance of Laissez-Faire Contract in the Federal Common Law of Employee Benefits, 56 Ohio State L.J. 153, 185–86, 208–11 (1995). Fisk faults the courts for "hav[ing] accorded ERISA's voluntarist aspect more significance than its regulatory aspect—more significance than it deserves or was intended to have." Id. at 159. Might ERISA § 404(a)(1)(D) have provided a limiting principle in *Air Jamaica?*

12. *Co-fiduciary liability.* ERISA § 405 regulates the liability of co-fiduciaries. Under § 405(a)(1), an ERISA fiduciary who "participates knowingly" in a breach committed by a co-fiduciary is also liable for the breach. Under § 405(a)(3), a fiduciary who "has knowledge of [a co-fiduciary's] breach" is liable "unless he makes reasonable efforts under

the circumstances to remedy the breach." While these provisions appear to require actual knowledge, courts have held that a fiduciary can have constructive knowledge if he or she is on notice of a potential breach that reasonable investigation would have revealed. Diduck v. Kaszycki & Sons Contractors, Inc., 974 F.2d 270, 283 (2d Cir.1992); Silverman v. Mutual Benefit Life Ins. Co., 941 F.Supp. 1327, 1337 (E.D.N.Y.1996).

Under § 405(a)(2), a fiduciary will be liable if failure to fulfill his or her own fiduciary duties imposed under § 404(a)(1) "enable[s]" the co-fiduciary's breach. ERISA § 405(b) makes co-trustees jointly responsible for the management and control of plan assets and imposes a duty to use reasonable care to prevent a co-trustee from committing a breach. Liability may be imposed "whether or not [a co-fiduciary] actually knows or participates with other fiduciaries in the breach." PBGC v. Ross, 781 F.Supp. 415, 420 (M.D.N.C.1991).

Courts have found nonfeasance and inactivity sufficient to impose liability under §§ 405(a)(2) and 405(b) for breaches committed by a co-fiduciary. E.g., Free v. Briody, 732 F.2d 1331, 1335 (7th Cir.1984) (co-trustee's inaction facilitated the willful wrongdoing of the other trustee); Raff v. Belstock, 933 F.Supp. 909, 915 (N.D.Cal.1996) (co-trustee has "duty to monitor the conduct of another trustee and to intervene if he suspects improprieties"); Mazur v. Gaudet, 826 F.Supp. 188, 192 (E.D.La.1992) ("ERISA trustees have a duty to conduct their own independent investigation of [investments], even where experts have been consulted"); Russo v. Unger, 1991 WL 254570 (S.D.N.Y.1991) (widow of firm's founder liable as co-trustee where son misappropriated $500,000 from fund, notwithstanding that she was wholly ignorant of his malfeasance, because she had a duty to monitor). It can happen that a court will treat a co-fiduciary's inaction as a breach of the duty of prudence under ERISA § 404(a)(1)(B), without invoking the co-fiduciary liability provision of § 405(a). E.g., Barker v. American Mobil Power Corp., 64 F.3d 1397, 1402 (9th Cir.1995)

13. *Contribution.* Should breaching co-fiduciaries have a right of contribution or indemnity between or among themselves? Trust law allows contribution. Restatement (Second) of Trusts § 258 (1959). ERISA is silent on the matter, and the courts have split over whether to imply the principle as a matter of federal common law. The Second Circuit recognized a right of contribution in Chemung Canal Trust Co. v. Sovran Bank/Maryland, 939 F.2d 12 (2d Cir.1991), cert. denied, 505 U.S. 1212 (1992). Judge Altimari dissented, arguing that "if Congress had intended to include a right of action for contribution and indemnification it would have done so." The majority's answer: "A more likely inference is that when it came to remedies under ERISA, Congress simply did not focus its attention beyond the welfare of the plan's participants and beneficiaries." Accord, Site-Blauvelt Engineers, Inc. v. First Union Corp., 153 F.Supp.2d 707 (E.D.Pa.2001); Green v. William Mason & Co., 976 F.Supp. 298, 301 (D.N.J.1997).

By contrast, the Ninth Circuit declined to imply a right of contribution in Kim v. Fujikawa, 871 F.2d 1427, 1432–33 (9th Cir.1989), reasoning from Massachusetts Mutual Life Ins. Co. v. Russell, 473 U.S. 134 (1985), which is discussed in Chapter 16, infra, that ERISA's remedial scheme is comprehensive and not to be expanded by courts;

accord, Travelers Casualty & Surety Co. v. IADA Services, Inc., 497 F.3d 862 (8th Cir.2007). In Haddock v. Nationwide Financial Services, Inc., 570 F.Supp.2d 355 (D.Conn.2008), Judge Stefan Underhill criticized the reasoning in these cases. He emphasized language in ERISA's legislative history evidencing "Congress's explicit guidance that the courts may consider common law principles of trust law when interpreting and applying ERISA." Id. at 361. Moreover, he said, "I do not agree that contribution or indemnification among co-fiduciaries can be fairly described as a new 'right of action' under ERISA," and he followed "the *Chemung* decision that described such claims as procedural devices for apportioning costs among responsible parties. The right to contribution or indemnification among joint tortfeasors does not affect a plaintiff's ultimate right to, or amount of, recovery." Id. For discussion see Jeffrey A. Brauch, The Federal Common Law of ERISA, 21 Harvard J.L. & Public Policy 541, 585–592 (1998); Comment, Fairness and Efficiency: Allowing Contribution Under ERISA, 80 California L. Rev. 1543 (1992); Note, Bucking the Trend: An Argument in Favor of a Fiduciary's Implied Right to Contribution Under ERISA, 76 Virginia L. Rev. 1377 (1990).

14. *Standard of Review.* Section A of the next chapter addresses the standard of review of benefit determinations. With nuances addressed in that chapter, the abuse of discretion standard generally applies to determinations in the adjudication of claims for benefits. In Tussey v. ABB, Inc., 2014 US. App. LEXIS 5518 (8th Cir. Mar. 19, 2014), the Eighth Circuit held that that abuse of discretion standard also generally applies to fiduciary determinations regarding the administration of a plan. This ruling is consistent with other case law, although it makes the point more directly.

2. FIDUCIARY LAW IN ACTION: THE *MAZZOLA* CASE

Perhaps the best known case illustrating the application of ERISA's duties of prudence and loyalty is Donovan v. Mazzola, 716 F.2d 1226 (9th Cir.1983). *Mazzola* arose fairly soon after ERISA came into effect. The setting was a union-dominated multiemployer plan, and the facts instanced the sort of abuse of plan assets that had made some of the Teamsters plans notorious in the 1950s and 1960s. This time, however, ERISA was on the books, and DoL enforced it in exemplary fashion. The following account summarizes (and reorders some of the quoted passages) from the lengthy Ninth Circuit opinion.

In the 1950s, Local 38, a Northern California local of the Plumbers and Pipefitters Union, established a multiemployer pension plan (the Pension Plan) and a multiemployer welfare benefit plan (the Convalescent Fund).

> The Convalescent Fund owns and operates a hotel, the Konocti Harbor Inn, which provides rooms at discounted prices, a summer camp, and a low-cost retirement housing project for participants of the Convalescent Fund and their families. [The] participants of the Pension Fund and Convalescent Fund although substantially the same are not identical. [The] Convalescent Fund has had more participants than the Pension Fund. The eligibility requirements of the two funds have also differed. Moreover, some contributing employers of the Pension

Fund have not been at the same time contributing employers of the Convalescent Fund.

The trustees of the Pension Fund served as an "Advisory Committee" to the sole trustee of the Convalescent Fund.

DoL's action complained of two sorts of transactions, loans from the Pension Fund to the Convalescent Fund and to others; and overpayments in connection with a supposed contract for services, the so-called feasibility study.

1.   *Interfund loans; sweetheart loans to insiders.* In the later 1970s, after ERISA came into effect, the Pension Fund trustees

made a $1.5 million loan of Pension Fund assets to the Convalescent Fund. The following year, they granted a moratorium on that loan as well as all other loans that the Pension Fund had made to the Convalescent Fund. When granting the moratorium they did not request amendments favorable to the Pension Fund on the terms of the loans, nor did they require any additional security. In 1978 and 1979, the individual appellants also granted the Convalescent Fund two extensions to repay a $500,000 loan originally granted in December 1974 and due November 1, 1978. When these extensions were granted the amount owed on the final payment was in excess of $400,000. In spite of this, the individual appellants did not alter in any way the terms of that loan, nor did they seek or receive additional security. The Secretary [of Labor] charged that in making the above, the individual appellants violated ERISA §§ 404 and 406(b)(2).

[In] addition to the loans made to the Convalescent Fund, in 1975, the individual appellants made a loan of $650,000 of Pension Fund assets to a limited partnership known as S & F Spas for the conversion of a hotel to a health spa. One of the principals of the limited partnership was Dr. Schwartz [who figures in another transaction described below]. Prior to making this loan the Pension Fund trustees had approved a $2.25 million construction loan secured by the property on which the spa was to be constructed. The Secretary claimed that in approving the $650,000 loan, the individual appellants breached their fiduciary duties under [ERISA § 404].

[After a bench trial,] the district court found that the individual appellants violated § 404(a)(1)(B) because the challenged loans and extensions of credit were not ones that a reasonably competent lender would have made, nor were they made using accepted procedures used by such a lender. In addition, the district court found that the challenged loans and extensions of credit were in violation of [§ 404(a)(1)(A)] because they were not made for the exclusive purpose of benefiting the Pension Fund.

The Ninth Circuit sustained the district court, pointing to some of the shortcomings in the trustees' behavior:

When the $1.5 million loan was granted, the Convalescent Fund was in poor financial condition as evidenced by substantial operating losses and its inability to make regular payments on previous loans from the Pension Fund and a bank loan.

Before granting the loan the [defendant trustees] also failed to ascertain the value of the property which the Convalescent Fund deeded as security for the loan. Although the Convalescent Fund's total property holding was appraised at $16 million, the Pension Fund received as security only that part of the property which did not include the resort facilities. The value of the property actually given as security was never determined. Moreover, a portion of the property offered as security was subject to prior rights of a bank and already was security for the Pension Fund's $5.5 million loan to the Convalescent Fund. The individual appellants, in granting the $1.5 million loan, failed to ascertain the extent to which the Pension Fund's interest in the property deeded as security would be subordinate to other security interests.

A government witness, Joseph Azrack, gave expert testimony regarding the prevailing standards to be applied by competent real estate lenders in making, pricing, and managing real estate secured loans. After reviewing the individual appellants' actions with regard to the $1.5 million loan, the expert witness noted several deficiencies in the manner in which trustees approved the loan. He opined that the [trustees'] conduct regarding this loan did not meet industry standards.

The Ninth Circuit also endorsed the district court's finding that the trustees "violated their fiduciary obligations under ERISA by granting the loan below the prevailing interest rates for comparable mortgages at that time." The court said:

After reviewing the record we are convinced that the district court had ample basis to conclude that the trustees violated their fiduciary obligation by granting the loan at 8.5 percent interest. The Secretary's expert witness testified that the interest rate on long-term commercial mortgages at the time the $1.5 million loan was made ranged from 9.75 percent to ten percent. This was over one percent more than the interest rate actually allowed on the loan. The expert witness further testified that because the loan was secured by a resort, rather than an office building, shopping center or industrial property, the loan would have been priced one to three percent above the commercial rate. In addition, the expert testified that in light of California's usury law, a lender confronted with the possibility of making this loan would have chosen making the loan within the statutory ceiling of ten percent, making an out-of-state real estate loan, or making another sort of investment. Based on this evidence the district court properly concluded that the individual appellants breached their fiduciary duty by lending the money at 8.5 percent interest.

2.   *The feasibility study.* In March 1977, the Convalescent Fund retained one Dr. Schwartz, described as a friend of one of the trustees and the personal physician for another, and paid him $250,000 "to perform a feasibility study to determine the most profitable use of the

Convalescent Fund's Konocti Harbor Inn. [The] district court found that the trustees had not complied with accepted industry standards in selecting a consultant to perform the feasibility study of the Konocti Harbor Inn and had thereby imprudently discharged their duty in violation of [§ 404(a)(1)(B)]. By overpaying Dr. Schwartz for the study, the trustees also violated [§ 404(a)(1)(A)]." The Ninth Circuit found that the trustees

> never inquired into Dr. Schwartz's qualifications to prepare the study. The evidence shows that Dr. Schwartz had never made a feasibility study, or written a report on the potential markets and customers for a recreational facility, and had not specialized in advising others as to recreational resort properties or other specific types of real estate. Indeed, the individual appellants never discussed Dr. Schwartz's oral proposals with any consultants or experts, nor did they interview or solicit bids from other potential consultants. Although Dr. Schwartz did not complete the study until September 1977, the individual appellants paid him the entire $250,000 which he had requested as payment for the study in June 1977.
>
> In the proceedings below, the Secretary presented expert testimony regarding the prevailing standards for selection of a consultant to perform a feasibility study. In essence, the expert testified that the prevailing practice was to obtain bids and written proposals from several consultants and to withhold some portion of the consultant's fee pending satisfactory completion of the study.

Citing the Convalescent Fund trustees' "failure to inquire into Dr. Schwartz's qualifications and to follow accepted standards for hiring a consultant," the Ninth Circuit "agree[d] with the district court's conclusion that [the trustees] acted imprudently by paying Dr. Schwartz $250,000 for the feasibility study and thereby breached their fiduciary duty under [§ 404(a)(1)(B)] of ERISA."

The Ninth Circuit concluded that the record supported the district court's

> finding that the study was worth only $50,000. Dr. Schwartz kept no record of the amount of hours spent on the project. The Secretary's expert testified that a professionally completed feasibility study of acceptable quality, covering the same subject areas as the Schwartz study, would have cost the trustees no more than approximately $100,000 in 1977 dollars. The expert specified numerous deficiencies in the Schwartz study. He noted that it largely failed to reach specific conclusions regarding recommendations as to each key subject area; it did not provide any substantial market analysis; it did not develop a coordinated program for physical development of the many general proposals set forth in the study or for financing such development; it did not adequately assess the risks or probabilities of success of each proposal; it was not written in a sufficiently comprehensible fashion; and it failed to provide the trustees with sufficient analysis and grounds for making informed decisions. The expert also testified that approximately

$50,000 to $100,000 would have to be expended to raise the Schwartz study up to the level of a professionally competent document.

3. *Proving imprudence.* Because the prudence norm is comparative, the proofs in a prudence case typically contrast the behavior in question with that of other fiduciaries similarly situated. That standard is rooted in the text of ERISA, which requires the ERISA fiduciary to exercise "the care, skill, prudence, and diligence under the circumstances then prevailing that a prudent man acting in a like capacity and familiar with such matters would use in the conduct of an enterprise of a like character and with like aims." ERISA § 404(a)(1)(B).

The prudence norm inclines ERISA fiduciaries to use investment industry and other experts to advise them about industry standards in the exercise of their managerial discretion. Likewise, in litigation settings, the parties will often adduce expert evidence about the standards of good practice in a contested transaction. Although the courts commonly regard it as a sign of prudence that plan fiduciaries have taken expert advice, courts expect fiduciaries to exercise independent judgment in evaluating expert advice. See *Unisys I*, supra, 74 F.3d at 435–36 (fiduciary duty to investigate investment consultants' advice); Howard v. Shay, 100 F.3d 1484, 1489–90 (9th Cir.1996) (obtaining "independent appraisal" of the value of certain securities was "not a magic wand that fiduciaries may simply wave over a transaction to ensure that their responsibilities are fulfilled"). The courts are also uncomfortable about the dangers associated with partisan selection and preparation of testifying experts in litigation.

4. *Remedies.* The Ninth Circuit explained in *Mazzola* that the district court had ordered the trustees to make

> restitution for the losses the Pension Fund suffered as a result of the below-market-interest rate on the $1.5 million loan and the excess compensation for the feasibility study, [and it] found the Pension Fund trustees jointly and severally liable for potential losses in connection with the $1.5 million loan to the Convalescent Fund and the $650,000 loan to the S & F Spas. To insure the Pension Fund against such potential losses, the district court ordered the [trustees] to post a $1 million cash or corporate surety bond which [was] to remain in effect until the outstanding balance on [the various loans was worked down to prescribed levels]. The district court also ordered the appointment of an investment manager to manage the Pension Fund's assets for a term of ten years.

The Ninth Circuit approved these remedies, citing ERISA § 409, and saying:

> Where there has been a breach of fiduciary duty, ERISA grants to the courts broad authority to fashion remedies for redressing the interests of participants and beneficiaries. [In] effectuating this provision, Congress intended the courts to draw on principles of traditional trust law. "Traditional trust law provides for broad and flexible remedies in cases involving breaches of fiduciary duty." Courts also have a duty "to enforce

the remedy which is most advantageous to the participants and most conducive to effectuating the purposes of the trust."

The scope of remedy for cases of breach of fiduciary duty under ERISA is discussed in Chapter 16, infra; remedy issues are also central in the leading fiduciary investment case, Donovan v. Bierwirth, 680 F.2d 263 (2d Cir.1982), reproduced and discussed in Chapter 14, infra.

5.   *The duty of reasonableness in incurring costs.* A key theme in *Mazzola* is that overpaying for goods or services—in that case, for Dr. Schwartz' consulting services—is imprudent. This is a familiar principle of trust fiduciary law. Section 7 of the Uniform Prudent Investor Act (1994) codifies the common law standard thus: "In investing and managing trust assets, a trustee may only incur costs that are appropriate and reasonable in relation to the assets, the purposes of the trust, and the skills of the trustee." The official comment explains: "Wasting beneficiaries' money is imprudent. In devising and implementing strategies for the investment and management of trust assets, trustees are obliged to minimize costs." Accord, Restatement (Third) of Trusts § 88 (2007). For other ERISA authority, see Reich v. Lancaster, 843 F.Supp. 194 (N.D.Tex.), affirmed, 55 F.3d 1034 (5th Cir.1995) (excess insurance commissions). See generally Pamela D. Perdue, Satisfying ERISA's Fiduciary Duty Requirements with Respect to Plan Costs, 25 J. Pension Planning & Compliance 1 (Spr. 1999).

6.   *Advice of counsel.* The trustees in *Mazzola* defended in part by contending that even if their conduct might otherwise have been in violation of ERISA's fiduciary norms, "they did not violate ERISA by acting imprudently because they relied on counsel's advice that the $250,000 expenditure [for Dr. Schwartz's study] conformed to ERISA requirements." The court held that "[t]his asserted defense fails. Nothing in the record supports their contention that they received any advice from counsel on this matter. Even if such advice had been received, reliance on counsel's advice, without more, cannot be a complete defense to an imprudence charge. *See, e.g., Donovan v. Bierwirth,* 680 F.2d at 272." The Ninth Circuit quoted Scott's treatise on trust law for the proposition that a trustee may take professional advice but is "not justified [in] relying wholly upon the advice of others, since it is his duty to exercise his own judgment in the light of the information and advice which he receives." The court concluded that "in evaluating an allegation of imprudence under ERISA, reliance on counsel's advice is, at most, a single factor to be weighed in determining whether a trustee has breached his or her duty." Similarly, the Restatement says that although taking advice of counsel on a matters of legal difficulty in trust administration is widely understood to "evidence[ ] prudent conduct on the part of the trustee," acting in reliance on that advice "is not a complete defense to an alleged breach of trust. . . ." Restatement (Third) of Trusts § 77, cmt. b(2) (2007).

There is an inherent tension in this treatment of the advice-of-counsel defense, exemplified in *Mazzola*. Is it not a fiction to think that an inexpert fiduciary can bring to bear much independent judgment on counsel's advice? If so, why isn't reliance on counsel's advice a compete defense?

In Martin v. Schwab, 15 E.B.C. 2135 (W.D.Mo.1992), a company's board of directors relied upon a lawyer-member of the board, who wrongly told the board that, because the firm's retirement arrangement was unfunded, it was not an ERISA-covered pension plan. The court held that the board members were ERISA fiduciaries, and that they were liable for breach of fiduciary duty. The board members other than the lawyer-member argued that their good faith reliance upon the views of the lawyer-member should excuse them from liability. The court rejected the defense; reliance upon the casual advice of a board member who was not expert on the subject was not prudent.

3.   CLEANING UP THE MULTI'S

Cases of looting and cronyism such as *Mazzola* still surface in multiemployer plans on occasion, e.g., United States v. Mason Tenders District Council of Greater New York, 909 F.Supp. 882 (S.D.N.Y.1995). Indeed, two decades after the initial *Mazzola* case, DoL again sued Mazzola and Local 38 for diverting plan assets to renovate and operate the Konocti Harbor property. A consent decree settled the case, under which fiduciary liability insurers paid $3.5 million to the plans. Mazzola and others were permanently barred from serving as ERISA plan fiduciaries, and outside professionals were installed to manage the finances of the plans. Chao v. Mazzola, discussed in DoL Release No. 07–1004–SAN, Aug. 17, 2007.

For the most part, however, such cases have become rare in the wake of ERISA. The combination of ERISA's reporting and disclosure standards (Title 1, Part 1), fiduciary standards (Title 1, Part 4), and remedial measures (Title 1, Part 5), including both private and DoL enforcement, have deterred as well as remedied abuse.

The central objective of ERISA fiduciary law was to clean up the investment and administration of multiemployer plans, and in this respect ERISA has indeed been a success story. "Anyone working with plan trustees noted a change in awareness and attitude after ERISA's enactment. Also, the ability of the Department of Labor to enforce these [fiduciary] provisions did put the few bad apples (notably the Central States Teamsters Funds) under honest management and enable them to become today's models of pension fund administration." Kathleen P. Utgoff & Theodore R. Groom, The Regulation of Pensions: Twenty Questions After Twenty Years, 21 J. Pension Planning & Compliance 1, 10 (1995).

Violations of the duty of loyalty are by no means limited to multiemployer plan cases. See, e.g., Chao v. Malkani, 452 F.3d 290 (4th Cir.2006) (removing single-employer plan trustee for "repeated efforts to plunder the Plan's assets").

B.   DUTIES OF DISCLOSURE

Two relatively distinct bodies of disclosure law have developed under ERISA. In this book we distinguish between what we call the "regulatory" disclosure requirements imposed under ERISA Title 1, Part 1, and the "fiduciary" disclosure standards that have grown up in the case law applying the duties of loyalty and prudence under ERISA § 404(a).

1. REGULATORY DISCLOSURE

DoL-administered reporting and disclosure requirements for benefit plans trace back to the Welfare and Pension Plans Disclosure Act of 1958 (WPPDA) (also known as the Douglas-Ives Act). The origins of WPPDA are discussed in Michael Gordon's account of the inception of ERISA, extracted in Chapter 3, supra. See also Senate Rep. No. 1440, 85th Cong., 2d Sess., reprinted in 1958 U.S. Code Cong. & Adm. News 4137.

1. *The ERISA §§ 100s.* Title 1, Part 1 imposes reporting and disclosure rules that apply both to pension plans and to welfare benefit plans. ERISA §§ 101–110. These measures displace WPPDA, which ERISA § 111 repeals. Compliance with ERISA's reporting and disclosure rules is an important task of routine plan administration.

2. *COBRA disclosure.* In addition to the reporting and disclosure requirements of Part 1, Title 1 was amended in 1986 to add new Part 6, the §§ 600s, imposing notice and disclosure responsibilities regarding the continuation of benefits under health care plans. These so-called COBRA rules have been discussed in Chapter 3, supra.

3. *Reporting.* ERISA § 103 provides that financial statements (and in the case of defined benefit pension plans, actuarial statements) are to be prepared annually for each plan and filed with DoL. Section 104(a) requires the administrator of each ERISA-covered plan to file an annual report with DoL.

4. *Disclosing benefits.* Section 105 requires the plan administrator to supply information to the participant or beneficiary upon written request about that person's accrued benefits and vesting status.

5. *Summary plan description (SPD).* The most consequential feature of ERISA's reporting and disclosure regime has been § 102, which requires every plan administrator to prepare, periodically update, and furnish to plan participants and beneficiaries a so-called summary plan description (SPD). Section 102(b) identifies information that the SPD "shall contain." The SPD must, among other things, identify the administrator and trustees, set forth the eligibility and vesting rules, and describe the plan's claims and appeal procedures. See also the DoL regulations on SPD content, 29 C.F.R. § 2520.102–2, –3.

Section 102 requires that the SPD "shall be written in a manner calculated to be understood by the average plan participant," yet that it also "be sufficiently accurate and comprehensive to reasonably apprise such participants and beneficiaries of their rights and obligations under the plan." This provision sets up a tension between the conflicting goals of simplification and accuracy. SPDs tend to be written in defensive legalese, and few participants and beneficiaries read them.

DoL regulation requires the plan administrator to use "measures reasonably calculated to ensure actual receipt of the [SPD] by plan participants," 29 C.F.R. § 2520.104b–1(b)(1). In Leyda v. AlliedSignal, Inc., 322 F.3d 199, 208–09 (2d Cir.2003), the court held that making the SPD available at meetings that a busy employee might not attend was a procedure not reasonably calculated to achieve actual distribution. In Hunter v. Lockheed Martin Corp., 2002 WL 1492137 (N.D.Cal.2002), the court held that the employer's evidence of its routine practice of providing the SPD to each new employee upon hiring was sufficient to overcome the participant's claim that she had not received it. Accord, Brenner v. Johns Hopkins Univ., 88 Fed.Appx. 555 (4th Cir.2004).

6. *Variance between SPD and plan.* When the terms of the SPD appear more generous than the actual language of the plan, the SPD will govern. The Second Circuit has said that ERISA "contemplates that the summary will be an employee's primary source of information regarding employee benefits, and employees are entitled to rely on the descriptions contained in the summary. To allow the Plan to contain different terms that supersede the terms of the [SPD] would defeat the purpose of providing the employees with summaries." Heidgerd v. Olin Corp., 906 F.2d 903, 907–08 (2d Cir.1990). The rule preferring the SPD over the plan is estoppel-like, preventing the plan from recanting on the representation in the SPD. The rule is now accepted in all circuits that have addressed the question. The Third Circuit, which had resisted, capitulated in Burstein v. Retirement Account Plan for Employees of Allegheny Health Education & Research Foundation, 334 F.3d 365, 376–78 (3d Cir.2003).

In CIGNA Corp. v. Amara, 131 S. Ct. 1866 (2011), the Supreme Court held that a discrepancy between an SPD and a plan does not give rise to a contractual remedy under § 502(a)(1)(B), but that relief could be had under § 502(a)(3), which authorizes equitable remedies for violations of ERISA.

Amara dealt with CIGNA's conversion of its defined benefit plan into a cash balance plan. The district court found several ways in which the SPD was incomplete and inaccurate, and further, that CIGNA intentionally misled its employees. Its remedy was to reform the terms of the plan and to direct the plan administrator to enforce the plan as reformed.

The Supreme Court rejected the district court's conclusion that its relief was authorized by § 502(a)(1)(B). Justice Breyer, writing for the majority, asked:

> Where does § 502(a)(1)(B) grant a court the power to *change* the terms of the plan as they previously existed? The statutory language speaks of *"enforc[ing]"* the "terms of the plan," not of *changing* them. The provision allows a court to look outside the plans' written language in deciding what those terms are, *i.e.,* what the language means. But we have found nothing suggesting that the provision authorizes a court to alter those terms, at least not in present circumstances, where that change, akin to reformation of a contract, seems less like the simple enforcement of a contract as written and more like an equitable remedy.

Id. at 1876–77. The Court also rejected the argument of the Solicitor General that the SPD constituted part of the plan.

> Even if the District Court had viewed the summaries as plan "terms" (which it did not), however, we cannot agree that the terms of statutorily required plan summaries (or summaries of plan modifications) necessarily may be enforced (under § 502(a)(1)(B)) as the terms of the plan itself. For one thing, it is difficult to square the Solicitor General's reading of the statute

with ERISA § 102(a), the provision that obliges plan administrators to furnish summary plan descriptions. The syntax of that provision, requiring that participants and beneficiaries be advised of their rights and obligations "under the plan," suggests that the information about the plan provided by those disclosures is not itself part of the plan. Nothing in § 502(a)(1)(B) (or, as far as we can tell, anywhere else) suggests the contrary.

Nor do we find it easy to square the Solicitor General's reading with the statute's division of authority between a plan's sponsor and the plan's administrator. The plan's sponsor (e.g., the employer), like a trust's settlor, creates the basic terms and conditions of the plan, executes a written instrument containing those terms and conditions, and provides in that instrument "a procedure" for making amendments. The plan's administrator, a trustee-like fiduciary, manages the plan, follows its terms in doing so, and provides participants with the summary documents that describe the plan (and modifications) in readily understandable form. Here, the District Court found that the same entity, CIGNA, filled both roles. But that is not always the case. Regardless, we have found that ERISA carefully distinguishes these roles. See, e.g., Varity Corp., 516 U.S., at 498. And we have no reason to believe that the statute intends to mix the responsibilities by giving the administrator the power to set plan terms indirectly by including them in the summary plan descriptions. See Curtiss-Wright Corp. v. Schoonejongen, 514 U.S. 73 (1995).

Finally, we find it difficult to reconcile the Solicitor General's interpretation with the basic summary plan description objective: clear, simple communication. To make the language of a plan summary legally binding could well lead plan administrators to sacrifice simplicity and comprehensibility in order to describe plan terms in the language of lawyers. Consider the difference between a will and the summary of a will or between a property deed and its summary. Consider, too, the length of Part I of this opinion, and then consider how much longer Part I would have to be if we had to include all the qualifications and nuances that a plan drafter might have found important and feared to omit lest they lose all legal significance. The District Court's opinions take up 109 pages of the Federal Supplement. None of this is to say that plan administrators can avoid providing complete and accurate summaries of plan terms in the manner required by ERISA and its implementing regulations. But we fear that the Solicitor General's rule might bring about complexity that would defeat the fundamental purpose of the summaries.

For these reasons taken together we conclude that the summary documents, important as they are, provide communication with beneficiaries about the plan, but that their statements do not themselves constitute the terms of the plan for purposes of § 502(a)(1)(B). We also conclude that the District

Court could not find authority in that section to reform CIGNA's plan as written.

Id. at 1877–78. After rejecting the possibility of a contractual remedy under § 502(a)(1)(B), the Court went on to suggest that the remedy of reformation could be possible under § 502(a)(3). Thus, in at least some cases, harm caused by misrepresentations like the ones at issue in this case will be remediable. The portion of the Supreme Court's opinion addressing relief under § 502(a)(3) is reproduced in Chapter 16 of this Supplement.

Although the Court's assumption that an SPD is distinct from a plan document is sensible in the context of pension plans, the Court's decision does raise a question about health plans, which typically use the SPD as the plan document or incorporate the SPD into the plan document. Participants in such plans generally never see anything but an SPD. Although it makes some sense to conclude that a welfare plan SPD that is presented to participants as the plan document should serve as the basis for contractual recovery under § 502(a)(1)(B), the Court's language may suggest some discomfort with that approach. Nonetheless, in a decision rendered subsequent to the Supreme Court's decision in *Amara*, the Tenth Circuit held that courts have consistently held that an SPD can be part of a plan. In the view of the court, *Amara* has no relevance in situations where an SPD "unequivocally state[s] that it is part of the plan." Eugene S. v. Horizon Blue Cross Blue Shield of N.J., 663 F.3d 1124, 1131 (10th Cir. 2011).

Amara was cited by another circuit court, concluding that "silence in a summary plan description about some features of a pension plan does not override language in the plan itself." Sullivan v. CUNA Mut. Ins. Soc'y, 649 F.3d 553, 557–58 (7th Cir. 2011).

Courts are, however, reluctant to prefer the SPD over the plan when the SPD is less favorable to the participant than the plan, reasoning that the employer or other plan sponsor should adhere to the plan's ERISA-authorized procedures for amendment. Shaw v. Connecticut General Life Ins. Co., 353 F.3d 1276 (11th Cir.2003); Ludlow v. Advo-Systems, Inc., 2004 WL 1844843 (N.D.Cal.2004).

Employer-provided literature other than the SPD does not override the plan. Helfrich v. Carle Clinic Ass'n, P.C., 328 F.3d 915 (7th Cir.2003). Not every descriptive communication to employees about benefits qualifies as an SPD upon which a participant is entitled to rely. See Hicks v. Fleming Cos., Inc., 961 F.2d 537 (5th Cir.1992) (booklet was not an SPD, hence employee's reliance was not justified).

When the SPD is not prominently labeled as such, litigation can arise concerning what document constitutes the SPD, e.g., Administrative Com. of the Wal-Mart Stores, Inc. v. Gamboa, 479 F.3d 538 (8th Cir.2007) (concluding SPD was also the plan); Hughes v. 3M Retiree Medical Plan, 281 F.3d 786 (8th Cir.2002) (determining which of two documents was the SPD).

How comprehensive must the SPD be in disclosing plan terms? Compare Tocker v. Philip Morris Cos., Inc., 470 F.3d 481 (2d Cir.2006) (plan term providing for deferential standard of review of plan administrator's decisionmaking need not be disclosed in SPD), with

Wilkins v. Mason Tenders District Council Pension Fund, 445 F.3d 572 (2d Cir.2006) (SPD held deficient in not advising that plan participant had burden of proof regarding credited service). Consider Hillis v. Waukesha Title Co., 576 F.Supp. 1103 (E.D.Wis.1983). A profit sharing plan contained a clause forfeiting the interest of a participant who, after leaving the employer, worked for a competitor. The SPD did not, however, describe that term. The plaintiff, who worked for the employer for nearly five years before quitting to join a competitor, demanded payment of his profit-sharing account, alleging that failure of the SPD to describe the noncompetition clause should render the clause unenforceable against him. What result?

Can a plan be drafted to reverse the rule that the SPD prevails when plan and SPD conflict? Compare Hansen v. Continental Ins. Co., 940 F.2d 971, 982 (5th Cir.1991), with Bower v. Bunker Hill Co., 725 F.2d 1221, 1224 (9th Cir.1984). How might ERISA § 404(a)(1)(D), discussed supra, bear on this question?

7. *Reliance on the SPD.* Most courts have held that the plaintiff "must show some significant reliance upon, or possible prejudice flowing from, the faulty plan description." Govoni v. Bricklayers, Masons & Plasterers Int'l Union Pension Fund, 732 F.2d 250, 252 (1st Cir.1984). In Heffner v. Blue Cross and Blue Shield of Alabama, Inc., 443 F.3d 1330 (11th Cir.2006), the court held that because individual reliance on the SPD had to be proved, the case could not proceed as a class action.

In Burke v. Kodak Retirement Income Plan, 336 F.3d 103 (2d Cir.2003), the Second Circuit decided that requiring detrimental reliance imposed too heavy a burden on plaintiffs. The court adopted a likelihood-of-prejudice standard. If the plan participant makes an initial showing that he or she was likely to have been harmed as a result of the deficient SPD, the burden shifts to the employer to prove that "the deficient SPD was in effect a harmless error." 336 F.3d at 113.

By contrast, in *Burstein*, supra, the Third Circuit refused to impose any reliance or causation requirement, on analogy to the premise that "a court's enforcement of a contract does not require proof that the parties to the contract actually read, and therefore relied upon the particular terms of the [contract]." 334 F.3d at 381. Is that analogy persuasive? Which is the contract in these cases, the defective SPD that the Third Circuit's rule favors, or the underlying plan?

In Washington v. Murphy Oil USA, Inc., 497 F.3d 453 (5th Cir.2007), the Fifth Circuit refused to require proof of reliance, basing its result on the rule of insurance law that an ambiguity in a contract of insurance is resolved against the drafter. Is the court's reasoning sound? A rule resolving ambiguity establishes the meaning of a disputed term; how does that bear on the question of whether the term affected the conduct of one of the parties, which is what reliance is about?

Literature: Michael Cavadel, *Burke v. Kodak* and the SPD Circuit Split, 7 U. Pennsylvania J. Labor & Employment L. 139 (2004); "*Burstein*," 11 ERISA Litigation Rptr. 25 (2003).

The Supreme Court's decision in *Amara* will impact how courts analyze the reliance issue in the future. Now that any relief to be had for a discrepancy between an SPD and a plan document must be granted pursuant to § 502(a)(3), the question will be whether the specific remedy being contemplated requires a showing of detrimental reliance. The Court's discussion of this is addressed in Chapter 16.

8.   *Right to obtain documents.* Section 104(b)(4) obliges the plan administrator to furnish the participant or beneficiary, upon written demand, with the SPD, plan description, annual report, trust agreement, collective bargaining agreement, "or other instruments under which the plan is established or operated." The Ninth Circuit held in Hughes Salaried Retirees Action Committee v. Administrator of the Hughes Non-Bargaining Retirement Plan, 72 F.3d 686 (9th Cir.1995) (en banc), vacating 39 F.3d 1002 (9th Cir.1994), that the language of § 104(b) requiring the plan administrator to supply "other instruments" did not cover the plaintiffs' demand for a list of the names and addresses of other plan participants. The en banc opinion read § 104(b) to mean other instruments "similar in nature to the documents specifically listed in § 104(b)(4)." The plaintiffs wanted the list in order "to solicit financial support for future litigation," but the court held that Congress in enacting § 104(b)(4) did not intend "to help plan participants amass a litigation war chest." Really?

9.   *Remedies.* The common remedy in a variance case is to enforce the more generous benefit described in the SPD, under the "benefits due" remedial provisions of ERISA § 502(a)(1), but remedy can also take the form of "appropriate equitable relief" under § 502(a)(3). In Brown v. Aventis Pharmaceuticals, Inc., 341 F.3d 822 (8th Cir.2003), for example, the SPD for a life insurance plan failed to disclose certain options that the plan allowed the participant, who had neglected to make timely application. The court upheld as an equitable remedy a decree ordering that the participant be issued the insurance coverage, not disclosed in the SPD, for which she would have been eligible under the plan.

In Killian v. Concert Health Plan, 680 F.3d 749 (7th Cir. 2012), the Seventh Circuit granted summary judgment for a plan where a participant failed to show that she was harmed by the plan's failure to disclose plan documents. The participant was denied coverage under her employer's health plan when she sought treatment at an out-of-network facility. Although the plan had failed to disclose to the participant an SPD, the court was persuaded by the argument that the breach did not cause the participant any harm "because she would have sought treatment [from the out of network providers] even if she had received an SPD." Id. at 758. On July 12, 2012, the Seventh Circuit granted rehearing en banc and vacated its April 19, 2012 opinion and judgment. Killian v. Concert Health Plan, 742 F.3d 641 (7th Cir. 2013).

10.   *Penalties.* ERISA § 502(c) allows the court in its discretion to impose a penalty up to a statutory ceiling, now $110 per day, payable to the participant or beneficiary, against a plan administrator who "refuses to comply with a request for any information which such administrator is required by this title to furnish to a participant or [beneficiary]." This provision applies to the failure to supply an SPD. Because ERISA § 104(b)(4) requires a "written request" for the SPD, disregard of an oral request has been held insufficient for penalties under § 502(c). Graham v. Pactiv Corp. Benefits Comm., 301 F.Supp.2d 483 (E.D.Va.2004).

11. *Disclosure of reasons for benefit denial.* Apart from the regulatory disclosure duties in ERISA Title 1, Part 1, the statute imposes a further disclosure requirement in benefit denial cases. ERISA § 503(1), amplified in DoL Reg. 29 C.F.R. § 2560.503–1(f), requires the administrator to provide a written notice of and statement of reasons for a benefit denial. The purpose is "to afford the beneficiary an explanation of the denial of benefits that is adequate to ensure meaningful review of that denial." Halpin v. W.W. Grainger, Inc., 962 F.2d 685, 689 (7th Cir.1992). Judicial review of benefit denials is the subject of Chapter 15, infra.

2. FIDUCIARY DISCLOSURE

Trust law has long imposed a duty to inform or disclose, as an aspect of the trustee's fiduciary duties of loyalty and prudence.

1. *The trust standard.* The core principle is that the trustee has a duty to inform the beneficiaries "about significant developments concerning the trust and its administration, particularly material information needed by beneficiaries for the protection of their interests." Restatement (Third) of Trusts § 82(1)(c) (2007).

The duty to disclose entails both the duty to be truthful in what one says (that is, the duty not to misrepresent); and the affirmative duty to volunteer information that the beneficiary needs to know. In Justice Cardozo's pithy phrase, "[a] beneficiary, about to plunge into a ruinous course of dealing, may be betrayed by silence as well as by the spoken word." Globe Woolen Co. v. Utica Gas & Electric Co., 224 N.Y. 483, 489 (N.Y.1918). The leading modern case on the trust law duty of disclosure, Allard v. Pacific Nat'l Bank, 663 P.2d 104, 110–11 (Wash.1983), places particular weight on the need to alert beneficiaries in advance regarding matters of exceptional importance: "The trustee must inform beneficiaries . . . of all material facts in connection with a nonroutine transaction which significantly affects the trust estate and the interests of the beneficiaries prior to the transaction taking place."

2. *The ERISA duty.* Case law has been absorbing the trust standard into ERISA fiduciary law. Like ordinary trustees, ERISA fiduciaries "must also communicate material facts affecting the interests of the beneficiaries. The duty exists when a beneficiary asks for information, and even when he or she does not." Anweiler v. American Elec. Power Serv. Corp., 3 F.3d 986, 991 (7th Cir.1993).

ERISA's fiduciary duty of disclosure derives from the duties of loyalty and prudence, § 404(a)(1)(A)–(B), hence the fiduciary duty applies independently of the regulatory disclosure requirements of ERISA Title 1, Part 1. To be sure, the two sets of disclosure duties can overlap. In Becker v. Eastman Kodak Co., 120 F.3d 5, 9 (2d Cir.1997), for example, the court expressed doubt about the adequacy of the SPD but declined to decide the case on that ground, instead resting its decision on the ground that the plan administrator "breached its fiduciary duty to provide [the participant] with complete and accurate information."

In Kujanek v. Houston Poly Bag I, Ltd., 658 F.3d 483 (5th Cir.2011), the Fifth Circuit found a breach where a fiduciary failed to provide a plan participant with information on how to request a distribution from the plan. Although the SPD for the plan stated that requests for benefits "should be made in writing," the court was "not persuaded that the quoted provisions of the Summary Plan Description control the issue of Houston Poly's fiduciary duty." Id. at 488.

The Third Circuit has played a dominant role in developing the fiduciary disclosure standards under ERISA. The court has "repeatedly held that a fiduciary may not materially mislead those to whom [ERISA § 404(a)'s] duties of loyalty and prudence are owed." *Unisys I*, 74 F.3d at 440. "[A]n ERISA fiduciary has a duty under [ERISA § 404(a)] to convey complete and accurate information when it speaks to participants and beneficiaries regarding plan benefits." Id. at 441. "[The] duty to inform is a constant thread in the relationship between beneficiary and trustee; it entails not only a negative duty not to misinform, but also an affirmative duty to inform when the trustee knows that silence might be harmful." Bixler v. Central Pennsylvania Teamsters Health & Welfare Fund, 12 F.3d 1292, 1300 (3d Cir.1993) (citing Restatement (Second) of Trusts § 173 (1959), in interpreting "to what extent failure to provide relevant information constitutes a breach of fiduciary duty" under ERISA § 404(a)).

This chapter reproduces the Third Circuit's landmark *Fischer II* opinion; later developments are discussed in the note following. *Fischer* concerns a recurrent category of fiduciary disclosure litigation, regarding the scope of disclosure owed to a participant who is considering the timing of his or her retirement, and who might decide differently if he or she had knowledge of changes in future benefits, such as an early retirement bonus, that the plan sponsor is contemplating.

In considering the opinion in *Fischer II*, bear in mind that in the ERISA context, the employer commonly acts both in fiduciary and nonfiduciary roles. The fiduciary duty to disclose pertains solely to the employer's fiduciary role. Since, however, as discussed in Chapters 5 and 12, supra, the Supreme Court has repeatedly held that amending a plan is a nonfiduciary function, why does the fiduciary duty to disclose attach in such a case?

3. FISCHER V. PHILADELPHIA ELECTRIC CO. (II)

96 F.3d 1533 (3d Cir.1996).

■ ROTH, CIRCUIT JUDGE. In this appeal, we must review the application of a decision we reached when this case first came before us. In Fischer v. Philadelphia Elec. Co., 994 F.2d 130 (3d Cir.) (*Fischer I*), cert. denied, 510 U.S. 1020, 114 S.Ct. 622, 126 L.Ed.2d 586 (1993), we reversed the district court's grant of summary judgment to defendant Philadelphia Electric Co. ("PECo"), holding that there were genuine issues of material fact as to whether PECo, acting in its role as fiduciary under [ERISA], had made affirmative material misrepresentations to its employee-beneficiaries. The misrepresentations alleged were that PECo had denied, or failed to disclose when asked, that it was seriously considering an early retirement program. We remanded the case to the district court to determine when PECo began to give serious consideration to an early retirement program.

On remand, the district court concluded that PECo was seriously considering an early retirement program as of March 12, 1990. Applying *Fischer I*, the district court held that any employee who sought information about retirement benefits during the period from March 12, 1990, until the announcement of the plan on April 19, 1990, and who was told that no change was under consideration, had received material misinformation.

We find that the district court misunderstood the concept of "serious consideration." We will therefore reverse the decision of the district court, and we will enter judgment for defendants.

I.

This action arises out of PECo's efforts to cut costs and reduce its payroll by implementing an early retirement plan. On April 19, 1990, Joseph Paquette, PECo's President and Chief Operating Officer, announced in a letter to all employees that he would recommend to PECo's Board of Directors that the company cut its payroll through early retirement. On April 26, 1990, PECo sent a letter to all employees who had announced an intent to retire, suggesting that they delay their retirement until the company's early retirement package was finalized. On May 25, 1990, PECo's Board of Directors approved a plan, which included inducements such as a five year time-in-service credit, a five year age credit, and severance pay. These events caused much consternation among employees who had retired in the months preceding the plan's announcement.

Various pre-plan retirees filed suit in the U.S. District Court for the Eastern District of Pennsylvania, alleging that PECo had long known of its intent to offer an early retirement package, or at least that it was considering a package, and had breached its fiduciary duty under ERISA § 404, by providing material misinformation. The district court certified a class, then entered summary judgment for PECo. In *Fischer I*, we reversed, holding that PECo could be liable for breach of fiduciary duty if the company represented that no early retirement plan was being considered at a time when the plan was in fact under serious consideration. We remanded for a trial on the merits; a bench trial followed. The facts we recite here were found by the district court; the vast majority were stipulated.

PECo had long engaged in a practice of reviewing its retirement and pension benefits packages as part of its ordinary course of business. During one such review, on March 21, 1988, Fred Beaver, an Administrative Assistant in the Benefits Division of Human Resources, prepared a memorandum for Charles Fritz, Vice President of Personnel and Industry Relations, on the possibility of reducing the size of PECo's work force. The memorandum suggested that a modest "sweetener" could induce approximately 50% of a target group of workers to retire. During the same period, on May 5, 1988, Michael Crommie, PECo's Director of Benefits, contacted William Murdoch, a consultant with Towers, Perrin, Forster & Crosby (TPF&C), to discuss various early retirement options. Discussions between management and TPF&C continued into June.

Beaver's memorandum and the TPF&C consultations occurred roughly contemporaneously with Joseph Paquette's arrival at PECo as president and chief of operations. Paquette had a long term goal of reducing the number of PECo employees, and he would ultimately recommend the 1990 early retirement package. In June, 1988, however, Paquette decided against an early retirement plan. At trial, Paquette testified that PECo was then in the process of completing one nuclear plant and restarting another. He did not want to risk an early retirement program because personnel vital to the nuclear effort might leave. He believed that PECo could not legally institute an early retirement plan that excluded nuclear plant personnel. After deciding that no early retirement package would be considered, Paquette shifted his attention to promoting operational excellence at the company.

In July, 1989, PECo requested a rate increase from the Public Utility Commission ("PUC"). PUC staff made a preliminary recommendation that PECo be granted less than half its requested increase.

In November, 1989, as part of the operational excellence program, PECo hired McKinsey & Co. to explore long-term strategies and cost-cutting measures. Paquette used the McKinsey report to calculate the savings that an early retirement program could produce.

On December 13, 1989, Paquette held three meetings with employees to discuss the importance of the rate increase to the company. In response to questions, Paquette stated that an early retirement plan might be considered if the rate request was denied. He explained that the company had no plans for such a program because the outcome of the rate increase was in doubt. Paquette stated that PECo's first option in the event the increase was denied would be to appeal the decision but that the company would also consider cutting costs and reducing its stock dividend. On March 1, 1990, an Administrative Law Judge issued an interim decision recommending that PECo receive 21% of the rate increase it had requested.

Events accelerated rapidly following the ALJ's decision. On March 12, 1990, Kenneth Lefkowitz, Manager of Compensation & Benefits, contacted Murdoch at TPF&C. Lefkowitz stated PECo's concern about its rate case before the PUC and the need to reduce costs quickly. The question of an early retirement sweetener was mentioned as a possible method. TPF&C had done no work for PECo on early retirement plans since June, 1988, nor had TPF&C been asked to prepare contingency plans in case PECo's rate request was denied. On March 20, 1990, Lefkowitz asked TPF&C to develop a set of early retirement alternatives. On March 28, 1990, Murdoch proposed three alternative programs, the first of which resembled the 1988 program in some respects, although it targeted a different group of eligible employees and contained different severance provisions. On April 2, 5, and 6, Murdoch had further discussions with PECo personnel about the details of the early retirement sweetener. On April 7, senior PECo executives attended a corporate strategy meeting. Notes from the meeting indicated a statement by Paquette that on April 20 he would issue a letter announcing a $100 million cost cutting program. On April 13, 1990, TPF&C provided PECo with a survey of early retirement plans used by other utilities. On April 19, 1990, the PUC granted less than 50% of PECo's rate request. Paquette then sent the letter to PECo employees announcing his intent to recommend an early retirement package.

Based on these findings, the district court held that PECo began seriously considering an early retirement plan on March 12, 1990. The district court entered judgment for those retirees who asked about an early retirement plan and retired after March 12. It entered judgment for PECo on the claims of those retirees who asked about retirement and retired before that date. Both PECo and the plaintiff class appealed. The plaintiff class appeals the district court's determination that serious consideration of the early retirement plan did not begin before March 12, 1990. PECo, on the other hand, asserts that serious consideration did not begin until after March 12, 1990.

II.

Our analysis proceeds within the confines of *Fischer I*. In that decision, we established the general rule that governs interactions between a company-as-fiduciary and its employee-beneficiaries regarding changes in benefits: "A plan administrator may not make affirmative material misrepresentations to plan participants about changes to an employee pension benefits plan. Put simply, when a plan administrator speaks, it must speak truthfully." This overarching duty of truthfulness forms an important part of our ERISA jurisprudence. See In re Unisys Corp. Retiree Medical Benefit "ERISA" Litig., 57 F.3d 1255, 1266–67 (3d Cir.1995), cert. denied, 517 U.S. 1103, 116 S.Ct. 1316, 134 L.Ed.2d 469, 470 (1996); Bixler v. Central Pa. Teamsters Health & Welfare Fund, 12 F.3d 1292, 1302–03 (3d Cir.1993).

The rule of truthfulness that we announced in *Fischer I* focused on the materiality of a plan administrator's misrepresentations. We defined materiality as a mixed question of law and fact, ultimately turning on whether "there is a substantial likelihood that [the misrepresentation] would mislead a reasonable employee in making an adequately informed decision about if and when to retire." We further explained that

> [i]ncluded within the overall materiality inquiry will be an inquiry into the seriousness with which a particular change to an employee pension plan is being considered at the time the misrepresentation is made. All else equal, the more seriously a plan change is being considered, the more likely a misrepresentation, e.g., that no change is under consideration, will pass the threshold of materiality. . . .

Although the test we set out in *Fischer I* ultimately turned on "serious consideration," we paid little attention to the details of that term. We offered nothing in the way of a definition, standard, or even factors to consider. We simply remanded the case to the district court, leaving to the district judge the task of determining when PECo's consideration became serious. We commend his efforts to apply this amorphous concept. We will now provide further guidance on the meaning of "serious consideration."

The concept of "serious consideration" recognizes and moderates the tension between an employee's right to information and an employer's need to operate on a day-to-day basis. Every business must develop strategies, gather information, evaluate options, and make decisions. Full disclosure of each step in this process is a practical impossibility. Moreover, as counsel for PECo emphasized at oral argument, large corporations regularly review their benefit packages as part of an on-going process of cost-monitoring and personnel management. The various levels of management are constantly considering changes in corporate benefit plans. A corporation could not function if ERISA required complete disclosure of every facet of these on-going activities. Consequently, our holding in *Fischer I* requires disclosure only when a change in benefits comes under serious consideration.

Equally importantly, serious consideration protects employees. Every employee has a need for material information on which that employee can rely in making employment decisions. Too low a standard could result in an avalanche of notices and disclosures. For employees at a company like PECo, which regularly reviews its benefits plans, truly material information could easily be missed if the flow of information was too great. The warning that a change in benefits was under serious consideration would become meaningless if cried too often.

We demonstrated our awareness of these competing policies in *Fischer I*. Although our decision was clearly driven by an employee's need for truthful information, we nevertheless recognized a concomitant "right [of] an employer to make the business decision of how much and when to enhance pension benefits." Later in the opinion, we expressed similar sentiments, cautioning that

> ERISA does not impose a duty of clairvoyance on fiduciaries. An ERISA fiduciary is under no obligation to offer precise predictions about future changes to its plan. Rather, its obligation is to answer participants' questions forthrightly, a duty that does not require the fiduciary to disclose its internal deliberations nor interfere with the substantive aspects of the collective bargaining process.

Other courts of appeals have likewise emphasized the absence of any "duty of clairvoyance," as well as the fact that disclosure does not extend to internal deliberations.

In light of these concerns, we believe that the following formulation of serious consideration is appropriate: Serious consideration of a change in plan benefits exists when (1) a specific proposal (2) is being discussed for purposes of implementation (3) by senior management with the authority to implement the change. [Consistent] with our decision in [*Kurz I*], *Fischer I's* companion case, this formulation does not turn on any single factor; the determination is inherently fact-specific. Likewise, the factors themselves are not isolated criteria; the three interact and coalesce to form a composite picture of serious consideration. For purposes of discussion, we address each in turn.

The first element, a specific proposal, distinguishes serious consideration from the antecedent steps of gathering information, developing strategies, and analyzing options. A company must necessarily go through these preliminary steps before its deliberations can reach the serious stage. This factor does not mean, however, that the proposal must describe the plan in its final form. A specific proposal can contain several alternatives, and the plan as finally implemented may differ somewhat from the proposal. What is required, consistent with the overall test, is a specific proposal that is sufficiently concrete to support consideration by senior management for the purpose of implementation.

The second element, discussion for implementation, further distinguishes serious consideration from the preliminary steps of gathering data and formulating strategy. It also protects the ability of senior management to take a role in the early phases of the process without automatically triggering a duty of disclosure. This factor recognizes that a corporate executive can order an analysis of benefits alternatives or commission a comparative study without seriously considering implementing a change in benefits. Preliminary stages may also require interaction among upper level management, company personnel, and outside consultants. These discussions are properly assigned to the preliminary stages of company deliberations. Consideration becomes serious when the subject turns to the practicalities of implementation.

The final element, consideration by senior management with the authority to implement the change, ensures that the analysis of serious consideration focuses on the proper actors within the corporate hierarchy. As noted, large corporate entities conduct regular or on-going reviews of their benefit packages in their ordinary course of business. These entities employ individuals, including middle and upper-level management employees, to gather information and conduct reviews. The periodic review process may also entail contacting outside consultants or commissioning studies. During the course of their employment, the employees assigned these tasks necessarily discuss their duties and the results of their studies. These discussions may include issues of implementation. The employees may also make recommendations to upper level management or senior executives. As a general rule, such operations will not constitute serious consideration. These activities are merely the ordinary duties of the employees. Until senior management addresses the issue, the company has not yet seriously considered a change.

Consideration by senior management is also limited to those executives who possess the authority to implement the proposed change. This focus on authority can be used to identify the proper cadre of senior management, but it should not limit serious consideration to deliberations by a quorum of the Board of Directors, typically the only corporate body that in a literal sense has the power to implement changes in benefits packages. It is sufficient for this factor that the plan be considered by those members of senior management with responsibility for the benefits area of the business, and who ultimately will make recommendations to the Board regarding benefits operations. . . .

Our decision today [contrasts] markedly with a true bright-line rule, such as that recently adopted by the Court of Appeals for the Second Circuit[:] Pocchia v. NYNEX Corp., 81 F.3d 275, 278 (2d Cir.1996) (adopting bright-line rule where employee fails to request information about changes in benefits, finding no duty to disclose changes until new plan goes into effect).

We believe that our explanation of serious consideration maintains the balance struck in *Fischer I*. Our formulation respects the division of responsibility in corporate entities and the day-to-day realities of running a business. Even more importantly, it protects the right of employees to material information. Characterizing serious consideration in this fashion ensures that disclosures to employees about potential changes in benefits will be meaningful. Employees will learn of potential changes when the company's deliberations have reached a level where an employee should reasonably factor the potential change into an employment decision. This guarantees that employees will have the information they need, while avoiding a surfeit of meaningless disclosures. Finally, as a matter of policy, we note that imposing liability too quickly for failure to disclose a potential early retirement plan could harm employees by deterring employers from resorting to such plans. . . .

III.

Having explained our understanding of serious consideration, we now apply it to the case at bar. Although we would ordinarily remand to allow the district court to apply our standard in the first instance, we see no need in the current case. [The district court's] thoughtful opinion has set out clearly the necessary factual findings, and we can simply apply the law to reach the requisite conclusion. Based on our three factor test, we find that serious consideration began on April 7, 1990. We will therefore reverse the district court to the extent that it found serious consideration as of March 12, 1990.

The district court correctly dismissed events prior to March 12, 1990, as failing to rise to the level of serious consideration. Any potential consideration of an early retirement program prior to June, 1988, was conclusively ended by Paquette's decision to forego an early retirement option and focus on operational excellence. These events had no bearing on the subsequent decision to implement an early retirement plan in August, 1990.

The district court was equally correct to dispose of Paquette's statements during his speeches to employees on December 13, 1989. Paquette responded truthfully to employee questions regarding PECo's potential responses to an adverse decision in the rates case. Paquette explained that PECo would first appeal the decision but might also have to consider cutting costs by reducing its stock dividend or other methods. This is the type of frank response to employee concerns that should be encouraged. Paquette's statements will not support an inference that an early retirement plan was then under serious consideration.

The district court then concluded that PECo began seriously considering a plan sometime between December and April. Citing Lefkowitz's March 12, 1990, telephone call to TPF&C as the earliest example of affirmative action to implement the plan, the district court marked the start of serious consideration on that date. Under our three factor inquiry, this is incorrect.

As we have explained, serious consideration requires (1) a specific proposal (2) discussed for purposes of implementation (3) by senior management with the authority to implement the change. In the case at bar, these three factors did not coincide until April 7, 1990, when senior PECo management met to discuss the TPF&C report on staff reduction options. The TPF&C report is an excellent example of a specific proposal. This document outlined various early retirement alternatives and served as the basis for management's deliberations. Senior management was present at the meeting. The subject of the meeting was corporate strategy, and meeting notes indicate that Paquette disclosed his intent to announce $100 million in cost cuts. Both facts suggest that an early retirement plan was discussed for purposes of implementation at the April 7 meeting.

Events prior to April 7, by contrast, do not rise to the level of serious consideration. The March 12 Lefkowitz telephone call is clearly insufficient. First, the substance of the March 12 call involved nothing more than a general discussion of early retirement options. Lefkowitz was reestablishing contact on a subject where TPF&C had done no work since 1988. The subject matter of the contact was therefore preliminary. Second, Lefkowitz was a middle management employee in PECo's benefits department. His official duties entailed monitoring PECo's benefits package and exploring potential changes. Nothing in the record indicates that, when Lefkowitz made his March 12 telephone call to TPF&C, he was doing anything more than acting within the scope of his normal duties. This type of action by a middle management employee is preliminary. Third, even if Lefkowitz were acting on orders from senior management, his call to TPF&C would still fall under the rubric of gathering information. Senior management is free to start the process of exploration and evaluation without immediately triggering a duty of disclosure. For each of these reasons, the March 12 phone call took place prior to serious consideration. The district court was therefore incorrect.

The March 20 contact between Lefkowitz and TPF&C confirms this conclusion. It was on March 20 that Lefkowitz asked TPF&C to develop a set of options for staff reduction, including various early retirement plans. This is crucial. Serious consideration can only begin after information is gathered and options developed. The record indicates that the March 20 phone call assigned TPF&C the task of developing options. This contact therefore preceded serious consideration.

Events between March 20 and April 7 can similarly be categorized under preliminary stages such as information gathering and strategy formulation. The record indicates that Murdoch, a partner at TPF&C, met with Lefkowitz and other PECo executives during this period. These meetings are consistent with TPF&C's efforts to develop a report for PECo, the very task it had been assigned on March 20. The fact that TPF&C submitted its report on April 2 removes any lingering doubt. It was only after April 2 that a specific proposal existed.

Given that TPF&C submitted its report on April 2, the meetings that occurred on April 2, 5, and 6 between Murdoch, Paquette, and other PECo management present a closer question. A proposal had been developed and PECo management was involved in the meetings. However, details of the proposals were still being discussed. On April 7, a corporate strategy meeting was held. Paquette stated at the meeting that he would announce targets and programs on April 20. Based on this clear example of a meeting of senior PECo executives to address the early retirement issue at a time when a specific proposal had been submitted, we conclude that serious consideration began on April 7, 1990.

Under the rule established in *Fischer I*, any employee who asked about a potential early retirement plan after serious consideration began on April 7, 1990, but before the plan's formal announcement on April 19, 1990, received material misinformation. Such an employee would have established a claim for breach of fiduciary duty under ERISA. However, all of the members of the plaintiff class retired before this period. We will, therefore, enter judgment for PECo on the plaintiff's breach of fiduciary duty claim.

4. THE WINDOW PLAN LITIGATION

Fischer exemplifies a type of case known as "window plan" litigation:

> Under the typical claim of this type, the employer adopts an early retirement window program, under which employees who elect to retire during the "window" will receive enhanced pension benefits. Employees who retired shortly before the window opened then sue, claiming that they asked the employer's human resources staff whether there were any benefit improvements or window programs likely to be adopted, and that the staff members falsely told them that no such programs were coming, or simply denied any knowledge.

Susan Katz Hoffman, Fiduciary Misrepresentations after *Varity* and *Knudson*: Is There a Wrong, and Is There a Remedy?, 2002 N.Y.U. Rev. Employee Benefits § 4.03(1)(a), at 4–5/6.

Although the main development of ERISA's fiduciary duty of disclosure has occurred in window plan cases, such claims also arise in other settings, e.g., failing to disclose that an occupational disability plan had lapsed, Peralta v. Hispanic Business, Inc., 419 F.3d 1064 (9th Cir.2005); or failing to correct misinformation that plan personnel had given to a plan participant regarding his eligibility for a tax-free rollover. Griggs v. E.I. DuPont de Nemours & Co., 237 F.3d 371 (4th Cir.2001).

1. *Who won?* The Third Circuit recognized a fiduciary duty of disclosure, but the "serious consideration" test that the court devised defeated the plaintiffs. Commentators have written: "The Third Circuit's decision in *Fischer II* was an important victory for plan administrators, because the court defined 'serious consideration' narrowly enough so that only the latest stages of a plan administrator's decision-making process would trigger the fiduciary obligation not to mislead employees." Julie M. Edmond & Howard R. Rubin, When Talk Isn't Cheap: Scrutinizing Fiduciaries' Communications to ERISA Plan Participants, 23 J. Pension Planning & Compliance 1, 13 (Sum.1997).

Other prominent cases in which the courts treated *Fischer*'s "serious consideration" test as controlling but found that the claimants did not satisfy it include Vartanian v. Monsanto Co., 131 F.3d 264 (1st Cir.1997), and Hocket v. Sun Company, Inc., 109 F.3d 1515 (10th Cir.1997); but see McAuley v. IBM, 165 F.3d 1038 (6th Cir.1999), noted in 7 ERISA Litigation Rptr. 16 (Dec. 1998), which reversed a grant of summary judgment to the employer-fiduciary on the *Fischer* factors.

Literature: Valerie S. Grace & Gina M. Marsala, Planning Early Retirement Incentives—When Must Employers Disclose Future Window Benefits?, 24 Employee Relations L.J. 145 (No. 2, Autumn 1998); Note, 42 Villanova L. Rev. 1915 (1997); Note, 5 ERISA Litigation Rptr. 3 (Feb. 1997). The pre-*Fischer* case law is discussed in Howard Shapiro & Robert

Rachal, The Duty to Inform and Fiduciary Breaches: The "New Frontier" in ERISA Litigation, 14 Labor Lawyer 503 (1999).

2. *"Serious consideration."* The "serious consideration" rubric now associated with the Third Circuit's *Fischer* cases originated in Berlin v. Michigan Bell Tel. Co., 858 F.2d 1154, 1163–64 (6th Cir.1988). Evidence regarding when the employer began serious consideration of benefit alterations is treated in many circuits as only one issue in a multifactor inquiry about whether the conduct or the representations in question materially misled the plan participants. In Ballone v. Eastman Kodak Co., 109 F.3d 117 (2d Cir.1997), the Second Circuit held that an employer could be liable for misrepresentations that occurred before the point of serious consideration. Accord, Wayne v. Pacific Bell, 238 F.3d 1048 (9th Cir.2001), foreshadowed in Bins v. Exxon Co. U.S.A., 220 F.3d 1042 (9th Cir.2000) (en banc). Likewise, the Fifth Circuit has refused to "agree that misrepresentations are actionable only after the company has seriously considered the plan change." Martinez v. Schlumberger, Ltd., 338 F.3d 407, 425 (5th Cir.2003). "We therefore reject the *Fischer II* serious consideration approach to materiality, and adopt a fact-specific approach akin to that promulgated by the Second Circuit in *Ballone*." The central consideration "is whether there is a substantial likelihood that a reasonable person in the plaintiffs' position would have considered the information an employer-administrator allegedly misrepresented important in making a decision to retire." Id. at 428.

Keeping employee benefits personnel ignorant of pending benefits enhancements does not improve the employer's defensive posture in these cases. In Broga v. Northeast Utilities, 315 F.Supp.2d 212, 243 (D.Conn.2004), the court found the employer "not absolve[d] of liability" in a case in which the employer "withheld critical information from its human resources employees so that they could not technically lie to employees when responding to their questions."

Literature: William L. Belanger, The "Serious Consideration" Test: The Winding Path from *Fischer* to *Martinez*, 32 Tax Management Compensation Planning J. 247 (2004); Kyle Murray, Assumption-of-the-Risk Retirement?: A Survey of Recent "Serious Consideration" Case Law, 37 J. Marshall L. Rev. 159 (2003).

3. *Questioning the "serious consideration" test.* Does the rule in *Fischer* make policy sense? Why should employees have a right to disclosure of a pending change in a plan option when the employer begins to give it "serious consideration"? Employment is an arm's length relationship, and employers unilaterally make many decisions that affect employees' options under plans and otherwise. Since the employer has the power to alter the plan, why does the employer not have unrestricted authority over timing the disclosure of plan changes?

The "serious consideration" test and its "materiality" variants around the circuits share the drawback that they are fact-intensive. One can always litigate about when something became "serious" or how "material" it was or should have been to participant decision-making. Might the window plan cases be better resolved with a mechanical rule—for example, by conclusively presuming that developments occurring during the six months preceding the benefit enhancement offer were serious, and allow any participant or beneficiary who made a disadvantageous election within that period to rescind it?

4. *Varity.* The Supreme Court's opinion in Varity Corp. v. Howe, 516 U.S. 489 (1996), reproduced supra Chapter 12, which expanded the potential extent of an employer's fiduciary role, has given considerable impetus to the growth of ERISA disclosure law. *Varity* established that communication about plan benefits is a fiduciary function. The Court said: "Conveying information about the likely future of plan benefits, thereby permitting beneficiaries to make an informed choice about continued participation, would seem to be an exercise of a power 'appropriate' to carrying out an important plan purpose." *Varity,* 516 U.S. at 502. Furthermore, the Court observed, plan "administrators, as part of their administrative responsibilities, frequently offer beneficiaries more than the minimum information that the statute requires—for example, answering beneficiaries' questions about the meaning of the terms of a plan so that those beneficiaries can more easily obtain the plan's benefits. To offer beneficiaries detailed plan information in order to help them decide whether to remain with the plan is essentially the same kind of plan-related activity." Id. at 502–03.

Varity is commonly invoked in the ERISA fiduciary disclosure cases, e.g., *Bins,* supra, 220 F.3d at 1048; Matthews v. Chevron Corp., 362 F.3d 1172, 1178 (9th Cir.2004). The Supreme Court in *Varity* carefully avoided "reach[ing] the question whether ERISA fiduciaries have any fiduciary duty to disclose truthful information on their own initiative, or in response to employee inquiries." 516 U.S. at 506. *Varity* did, however, establish that speaking about plan benefits is fiduciary conduct, and hence that the duty of loyalty attaches. The duty of disclosure arises from the duty of loyalty, because " '[l]ying is inconsistent with the duty of loyalty owed by all fiduciaries and codified in section 404(a)(1) of ERISA.' " *Varity,* 516 U.S. at 506, quoting Peoria Union Stock Yards Co. v. Penn Mut. Life Ins. Co., 698 F.2d 320, 326 (7th Cir.1983).

In Beach v. Commonwealth Edison Co., 382 F.3d 656 (7th Cir.2004), a divided Seventh Circuit panel treated the employer's misrepresentations about the prospects of enhanced retirement benefits as relating to a new plan, not the existing plan under which the employer was a *Varity*-type fiduciary. Dissenting from a denial to rehear in banc, two judges accused the majority of "allow[ing] an employer-administrator to avoid the ramifications of its fiduciary status by simply attaching the label 'new plan'—as opposed to 'plan amendment'—to the subject of its misrepresentations." Id. at 662.

5. *Affirmative duties to disclose.* The *Fischer* cases develop a fiduciary duty not to conceal material information. Another line of cases, beginning with Eddy v. Colonial Life Ins. Co., 919 F.2d 747 (D.C.Cir.1990), and including Bixler v. Central Pa. Teamsters Health & Welfare Fund, 12 F.3d 1292 (3d Cir.1993), cited supra in *Fischer II,* require the fiduciary to volunteer relevant information. In *Bixler* the fiduciary accurately answered a widow's inquiry about her entitlement to a death benefit under her husband's plan, but the fiduciary did not volunteer information about COBRA benefits to which she was also entitled and from which she would have benefitted. The court held that the fiduciary had a duty to inform her of those rights even though she did

not ask about them. It said: the "duty to inform is a constant thread in the relationship between beneficiary and trustee; it entails not only a negative duty not to misinform, but also an affirmative duty to inform when the trustee knows that silence might be harmful." 12 F.3d at 1300.

Eddy involved an employee whose employer was terminating a health care plan. The participant contacted the plan fiduciary about whether he had the right to *continue* his group health coverage. He was told that he did not; the fiduciary did not volunteer the information that the employee did have the right to *convert* from group to individual coverage. The D.C. Circuit directed attention to Restatement (Second) of Trusts § 173, comment d (1959) (now slightly revised as Restatement (Third) of Trusts § 82(1)(c) (2007), quoted supra), which places a trustee "under a duty to communicate to the beneficiary material facts which he knows the beneficiary does not know and which the beneficiary needs to know for his protection in dealing with a third person." The court said that "[t]his duty to disclose and inform governs the case before us." The ERISA fiduciary was obliged "to convey correct and complete information material to Eddy's circumstance," including the availability of conversion and the inapplicability of continuation. 919 F.2d at 751.

As the cases suggest, although courts are reluctant to impose affirmative disclosure duties where doing so would create a significant burden on fiduciaries, "once an ERISA beneficiary has requested information from an ERISA fiduciary who is aware of the beneficiary's status and situation, the fiduciary has an obligation to convey complete and accurate information material to the beneficiary's circumstance, even if that requires conveying information about which the beneficiary did not specifically inquire." Kenseth v. Dean Health Plan, Inc., 610 F.3d 452 (7th Cir. 2010). See also Killian v. Concert Health Plan, 742 F.3d 651 (7th Cir.2012) (allowing plaintiff to go forward with his claim that fiduciary breached its duty by not informing him that the medical providers who were going to perform emergency surgery on his wife were out of network).

In Professional Helicopter Pilots Ass'n v. Denison, 804 F.Supp. 1447 (M.D.Ala.1992), officers of the employer who were plan fiduciaries were held liable for failing to notify employees of the employer's failure to make the requisite pension plan contributions. "A fiduciary, at the very least, has an obligation to notify employees of the employer's failure to contribute to the pension fund as required by the trust or collective bargaining agreement." Id. at 1454.

The concept of affirmative fiduciary duties to disclose or inform underlies many cases: Krohn v. Huron Memorial Hospital, 173 F.3d 542 (6th Cir.1999) (duty to advise about the availability of long-term disability benefits); Joyce v. RJR Nabisco Holdings Corp., 126 F.3d 166 (3d Cir.1997) (same); Farr v. U.S. West Communications, 151 F.3d 908 (9th Cir.1998) (duty accurately to inform participants regarding tax consequences of electing lump sum distribution under early retirement plan); Jordan v. Federal Express Corp., 116 F.3d 1005 (3d Cir.1997) (duty to inform participant of the irrevocable character of early retirement election).

Glaziers & Glassworkers Union Local No. 252 Annuity Fund v. Newbridge Securities, 93 F.3d 1171 (3d Cir.1996), concerned an investment firm that was a fiduciary to certain ERISA-covered pension plans. The firm dismissed an employee on grounds of suspected financial malfeasance. The plans then employed the dismissed employee, not knowing the circumstances of his dismissal. Subsequently, he stole half a million dollars of plan funds and wasted two million more in "bizarre and worthless investments." It was held that the investment firm had a fiduciary duty to the pension plans to disclose material information about the employee when the firm learned that the plans were engaging his services.

6. *Tension with benefit denial cases.* The courts' permissive attitude toward remedy for nondisclosure or misrepresentation in the window plan cases contrasts markedly with the courts' reluctance to remedy misrepresentation in benefit denial cases. It will be seen in Chapter 15, infra, treating judicial review of benefit denials, that the courts have mostly refused relief in cases in which oral misrepresentations about plan benefits by plan personnel have caused participants or beneficiaries to lose benefits or suffer other harm. What justifies remedy in *Fischer*-type cases but not in cases such as Schmidt v. Sheet Metal Workers' National Pension Fund, 128 F.3d 541 (7th Cir.1997), the principal case on benefit denial reproduced infra in Chapter 15?

In Kenseth v. Dean Health Plan, Inc., 610 F.3d 452 (7th Cir. 2010), the Seventh Circuit found a breach of fiduciary duty where a fiduciary encouraged participants to call its customer service representative with questions about coverage but failed to warn them that they could not rely on the answers they obtained and failed to inform participants how they could obtain reliable answers to their questions. What relief should a participant receive in such circumstances? The Seventh Circuit remanded the case so that the district court could consider the question, but suggested it was unclear whether the participants would be able to identify a form of equitable relief that would be appropriate. On remand, the district court determined that the plaintiff was requesting monetary relief, which did not fall within a category of "appropriate equitable relief." 784 F. Supp. 2d 1081 (W.D. Wis. 2011). However, in light of the Supreme Court's decision in *Cigna Corp. v. Amara* (discussed above and in Chapter 16), the Seventh Circuit vacated and remanded the case for further consideration. 722 F.3d 869 (7th Cir. 2013).

7. *Employer stock plan cases.* The fiduciary duty of disclosure that has been developed in the window plan cases is being applied extensively in the burgeoning case law involving 401(k) plans and ESOPs that offer employer stock as a plan investment. When, for example, a misrepresentation, such as the accounting frauds in the celebrated Enron and WorldCom insolvencies, causes the employer stock to be overvalued when purchased or held in the employees' ERISA-plan accounts, the claim is increasingly made that the employer, its officers and directors, and sometimes other persons should be liable as ERISA fiduciaries to make good the losses. See infra Chapter 14, Section D.

C. PROHIBITED TRANSACTIONS

1. THE PROHIBITED TRANSACTIONS RULES

The prohibited transactions regime of ERISA § 406 (and IRC § 4975), summarized in the extract from Kroll and Tauber below, embodies an alternative approach to constructing the fiduciary's duty of loyalty. The prohibited transaction rules of § 406(a) forbid categorically various transactions between a fiduciary and a "party in interest," a term defined in ERISA § 3(14) to include fiduciaries, service providers, plan sponsors, and substantial owners of sponsoring firms. The gist of § 406(a) is that every sale, loan, or transfer of plan assets to a party in interest is prohibited, as is the use of plan assets by a party in interest. The other main branch of the prohibited transactions scheme, § 406(b), forbids self-dealing by a fiduciary, as distinct from transactions with a party in interest.

The model for ERISA's prohibited transaction rules was a comparable set of prohibitions inserted in the Internal Revenue Code in 1969 to prevent insiders from abusing the assets of charitable entities.

The prohibitions of ERISA § 406 are so sweeping that they require an elaborate set of exemptions to rescue such innocent transactions as having the plan pay ordinary compensation to service providers or having the plan make a regular benefit payment to someone who is also a fiduciary. ERISA § 408(c)(1)–(2). In addition to the categoric exemptions, § 408(a) requires DoL to operate a procedure for individual exemptions ("administrative exemptions"). There are extensive DoL regulations, see 29 C.F.R. § 2550.408b–2 et seq. *Department of Labor*

Chapters 14 and 15, infra, emphasize that, of the statutory exemptions, one—§ 408(c)(3), which allows officers and employees of the plan sponsor to serve as ERISA fiduciaries—is centrally important in perpetuating the conflicts of interest that are so common in plan administration.

Arthur H. Kroll & Yale D. Tauber, Fiduciary Responsibility and Prohibited Transactions under ERISA

14 Real Property, Probate & Trust J. 657 (1979)
(edited to relocate citations from footnotes into text).

The excise taxes imposed under ERISA if a tax-qualified plan engages in certain prohibited transactions are collected by the IRS. IRC § 4975. The IRS also administers all requirements under the Code (including the "exclusive benefit" requirement) for plan qualification. If a plan (other than a tax-qualified plan) covered under Title 1 of ERISA engages in a prohibited transaction, then the Secretary of Labor may assess a "civil penalty" which will essentially be equal to the excise tax which would have been imposed by the IRS on a tax-qualified plan. ERISA § 502(i). [ERISA] specifically authorizes litigation to be brought by a participant or beneficiary or by the Department of Labor against a fiduciary who breaches any of his responsibilities, obligations or duties. ERISA § 502(a)(2), (5)–(6). Such litigation can be free of cost to participants and beneficiaries whenever the Labor Department commences an action on their behalf, and in any action brought by a participant or beneficiary (or class thereof) the court may in its discretion allow a reasonable attorney's fee and costs of the action. ERISA § 502(g).

ERISA contains provisions (similar to those contained in the Tax Reform Act of 1969 regarding private foundations) which generally prohibit certain classes of transactions between a plan and a "party in interest" or a "disqualified person" regardless of the fairness of the particular transaction involved. ERISA §§ 407 and 406(a)(1)(E), (2). The terms, "party in interest" and "disqualified person" generally include:

1.   any fiduciary including, without limitation, an administrator, trustee, officer or custodian, and any counsel to or employee of the plan;

2.   a person providing services to the plan;

3.   an employer any of whose employees are covered by the plan and any owner of 50 percent of such employer; and

4.   a "relative" (i.e., spouse, ancestor, lineal descendant or spouse of a lineal descendant) of any of the persons or organizations described in 1, 2 and 3 and any organization 50 percent or more controlled by any such persons or organizations and any highly compensated employees, directors, officers and 10 percent shareholders of the persons or organizations described in 2 and 3. ERISA § 3(14); IRC § 4975(e)(2).

Subject to certain exemptions (only some of which are discussed below), a fiduciary is prohibited from causing a plan to engage in a transaction if he knows or should have known that such transaction constituted a direct or indirect (i.) sale, exchange or lease of property between the plan and a party in interest; (ii.) extension of credit between the plan and a party in interest; (iii.) furnishing of goods, services or facilities between the plan and a party in interest; (iv.) transfer or use of plan assets for the benefit of a party in interest; or (v.) the acquisition or holding by the plan of excess employer securities (described above). ERISA § 406(a)(1)(A)–(E); IRC § 4975(C)(1)(A)–(D).

In addition, ERISA contains general prohibitions against fiduciary self-dealing. A fiduciary may not deal with plan assets in his own interest or for his own account or receive any personal consideration from any person dealing with the plan in a transaction involving plan assets. ERISA § 406(b)(1), (3); IRC § 4975(c)(1)(E)–(F). A fiduciary is also prohibited from acting, whether or not for personal consideration, in a transaction involving the plan on behalf of a person whose interests are adverse to the plan or its participants or beneficiaries. ERISA § 406(b)(2).

Presumably, a plan fiduciary who knowingly engages in a prohibited transaction would be liable for a breach of fiduciary duty. ERISA § 409(a).

The classes of specific transactions that are prohibited by ERISA are extensive, but there are also many exceptions. The exceptions include:

1.   contracting or making reasonable arrangements [with] a party in interest for office space or legal, accounting or other necessary services, provided that no more than reasonable

compensation is paid by the plan (where an employee is paid reasonable compensation by his employer he may not be paid compensation from the plan for the performance of fiduciary duties under the plan but he may be reimbursed for his expenses);

2. the investment of all or a part of the plan's assets in deposits which bear a reasonable interest rate in a bank or similar financial institution (such as a savings and loan association), if the plan covers employees of such bank or savings and loan association or of its affiliates or if the plan expressly authorizes such investment;

3. the providing of "ancillary" services by a bank or similar financial institution which is a plan fiduciary, for reasonable compensation, if appropriate internal standards have been adopted by such banks (as determined by the Secretary of Labor);

4. the purchase or sale by a plan of an interest in either (i) a common or collective trust fund maintained by a party in interest which is a bank or trust company or (ii) a pooled investment fund of a qualified insurance company (it should be noted that such insurance company would thereby become subject to the ERISA fiduciary rules with respect to the plan), if such bank or trust company or insurance company does not receive more than reasonable compensation and if the plan expressly authorizes such transaction; and

5. payment of benefits in accordance with the plan to a fiduciary who is also a participant or beneficiary. ERISA § 408(b)(2), (4), (6), (8), (c)(1)–(2); IRC § 4975(d)(2), (4), (6), (8)–(10).

In addition, the Secretary of Labor [is] granted broad authority to provide general or specific exemptions. ERISA § 408(a); IRC § 4975(c)(2).

Under the Labor provisions a fiduciary can only be held liable if he knows or should have known that he caused the plan to engage in a prohibited transaction. ERISA § 406(a)(1). Generally, in the case of a relatively large transaction, a fiduciary must make a thorough investigation of the other party's relationship to the plan in order to determine whether the transaction is a prohibited one. In view of the breadth of the definition of a party in interest, all fiduciaries will want to adopt some standards to avoid engaging in prohibited transactions.

The tax provisions on prohibited transactions do not apply to a fiduciary unless he has engaged in a prohibited transaction in some capacity other than, or in addition to, his fiduciary capacity. IRC § 4975(a), (b). Unlike the Labor provisions, the tax provisions do not include a knowledge requirement, but rather impose excise taxes on any "disqualified persons" (i.e., generally a party in interest), other than a fiduciary acting only as such, who engages in a prohibited transaction regardless of whether or not such person knew that the transaction was a prohibited one. IRC § 4975(a), (b), (e)(2).

An initial excise tax of 5 percent [subsequently increased to 15 percent for violations after August 5, 1997] of the "amount involved" in a prohibited transaction for each taxable year is imposed on the disqualified person. IRC § 4975(a). If, within 90 days after receiving appropriate notice from the IRS, the transaction is not corrected (e.g., rescinded), then an additional excise tax equal to 100 percent of the amount involved is imposed upon such person. IRC § 4975(b), (f)(5). The amount involved is the greater of the fair market value of the property given or received in the transaction or, where appropriate, the excess (i.e., unreasonable) compensation paid.

2. POLICY AND PRACTICE

ERISA's prohibited transactions regime has given rise to considerable discontent. Among the criticisms: The rules are harsh, complex, overbroad, costly to comply with (notice, for example, the word "indirect" in the stem language of § 406(a), which magnifies the reach of the provision); yet because the prohibited transactions rules serve the same purposes as the duties of loyalty and prudence in ERISA § 404(a), they are redundant.

Case law is collected in Jayne E. Zanglein, Lawrence A. Frolik & Susan J. Stabile, ERISA Litigation (4th ed.2011 and Supp. 2013); Annot., Construction and Application of [ERISA § 406] Enumerating Prohibited Transactions by Plan Fiduciaries, 103 A.L.R. Fed. 10 (1991 & Supp. 2009).

1. *Triple enforcement.* "Violation of the prohibited transaction rules was not only made actionable in suits by plan participants and the Department of Labor, but to add still another layer of protection, the Internal Revenue Service was given authority to levy excise taxes on these transactions." Kathleen P. Utgoff & Theodore R. Groom, The Regulation of Pensions: Twenty Questions After Twenty Years, 21 J. Pension Planning & Compliance 1, 12 (1995).

Clasby v. Commissioner, 77 Tax Ct. Memo (CCH) 1546 (1999), concerned a pension plan trustee who steered the plan's insurance purchases to an agency in which he and his wife had interests. DoL and several participants sued, and the trustee settled the action by paying $345,000. "Despite the settlement, the DoL apparently informed the IRS of the prohibited transaction." The Tax Court sustained the IRS in imposing a $360,732 fine under the excise tax of IRC § 4975(a). See Note, Fiduciaries Liable for Prohibited Transaction Excise Taxes Regardless of Civil Suit Settlement, 27 Tax Management Compensation Planning J. 152 (1999).

2. *Exemptions.* In addition to the exemptions contained in ERISA § 408(b)–(e), § 408(a) authorizes DoL, in consultation with Treasury (that is, the IRS), to exempt particular transactions or classes of transactions. A number of so-called class exemptions have been granted over the years. See generally Donald J. Myers & Michael B. Richman, ERISA Class Exemptions (3d ed. 2006 & 2008 Supp.). Class exemptions are numbered serially, e.g. PTE 76–1, the first issued in 1976, which allows multiemployer plans to share office space and administrative services

with parties in interest (typically, with the union that promotes the plan for its members) despite § 406(a).

Objection can be made to the prohibited transactions regime not simply on the ground that it is redundant and costly, but also on the view that it needlessly aggrandizes the power of the DoL. Ought a regulatory scheme to be so overinclusive that it is unworkable without an extensive law of exemptions to minimize such trivial, routine, and innocuous transactions?

On February 12, 2012, The DoL issued final regulations under Section 408(b)(2) requiring that certain service providers disclose to pension plan fiduciaries information about their compensation and potential conflicts of interest. The final regulations provide greater disclosure of "indirect compensation" as well as additional investment related disclosure. The regulations aim at providing fiduciaries with information necessary to assess both the reasonableness of the total (direct and indirect) compensation received by service providers and any potential conflicts of interest. 77 Fed. Reg. 5632 (Feb. 3, 2012). The regulations are discussed further in Chapter 14.

3. *Allocating burdens in prohibited transaction cases.* In New York State Teamsters Council Health & Hospital Fund v. Estate of DePerno, 816 F.Supp. 138 (N.D.N.Y.1993), De Perno Sr. was trustee and the principal manager of the pension fund. De Perno Jr., his son, a lawyer, was counsel to the fund. De Perno Jr. also owned a seasonal restaurant, the Inn, that operated from spring to early fall. During an interval of five years, De Perno Sr. caused the pension fund to employ two cooks from the Inn during the months that the Inn was closed. The cooks did maintenance work at the pension fund building. Successor trustees as plaintiffs alleged that the cooks were hired for this work for the benefit of De Perno Jr., in order to guarantee that the cooks would return to the Inn each spring, and that the work they did for the pension fund was make-work. The defendants claimed that the work was needed and that the compensation was reasonable, hence that the employment was prudent and for the exclusive benefit of the pension fund. The court found that De Perno Jr. was a party in interest under ERISA § 3(14)(B), as were the cooks, under § 3(14)(H); and that De Perno Sr.'s hiring of the cooks for the fund was a prohibited transaction in violation of § 406(a)(1)(C) and (D). The defendants argued that § 408(b)(2), excusing transactions that are necessary and at reasonable rates, provided a defense. The court held that the burden of proving that the cooks' services were necessary was upon De Perno Sr., the defendant trustee, and that he failed to prove that "it was 'necessary for the . . . operation of the plan' to hire *these particular* cooks, who were parties in interest." 816 F.Supp. at 146. The court also found that the arrangement violated § 406(b)(1) and (2). Damages were assessed at $1.00, because the plaintiffs failed in their burden to show any harm to the Fund. The cooks' services were beneficial to the fund and fairly priced. "Therefore the hirings did not create any tangible loss to the Fund."

On appeal to the Second Circuit, the district court's opinion was sustained on liability but reversed on damages. 18 F.3d 179, 180 (2d Cir.1994). "[A]fter the plaintiffs sustained their burden of showing the defendants' violation of their fiduciary duty to the Fund and the payment of money as a result of that violation, the burden should have shifted to the defendants to demonstrate factors mitigating the costs incurred by the [fund]."

4.   *"Reasonable compensation."* ERISA § 408(c)(2) exempts from liability a fiduciary's receipt of "reasonable compensation" for services provided to the plan. In Patelco Credit Union v. Sahni, 262 F.3d 897 (9th Cir.2001), the court followed a DoL regulation, 29 CFR § 2550.408b–2(a), in concluding that the exemption " 'applies only to transactions with parties in interest (in violation of [ERISA § 406(a)]) and not to fiduciary self-dealing (in violation of [§ 406(b)]) or a breach of the general duty of loyalty (in violation of [§ 404(a)(1)(A)]). [Section 406(a)] prohibits fiduciaries from causing the plan to engage in specified transactions with parties in interest '[e]xcept as provided in [§ 408].' But [§ 406(b)], which prohibits fiduciary self-dealing, makes no mention of the exceptions in § [408]. Department of Labor regulations indicate that the exception in § [408(b)(2)] applies only to § [406(a)], not to § [406(b)] or § [404(a)].' " 262 F.3d at 910. Is there any functional justification for limiting the "reasonable compensation exemption" to party-in-interest transactions prohibited under § 406(a), as opposed to self-dealing under § 406(b)?

In Danzas v. Fidelity Management Trust Company, 533 Fed.Appx. 120 (3rd Cir. Jul. 29, 2013), the Third Circuit held that a service provider did not breach its fiduciary duties or engage in a prohibited transaction by allegedly charging excessive fees for reviewing QDROs because it was not an ERISA fiduciary when it negotiated the fee. The court acknowledged that at the point in time when Fidelity actually charged its fee it did have a fiduciary duty to the plan and its participants, but said that Fidelity "did not then control the fee structure, as it was set in the agreement with A&P and Fidelity did not have unilateral discretion to change it." Likewise, at the time the agreement was signed, Fidelity was not yet a plan service provider. Is there a danger to the court's analysis?

5.   *Employer personnel.* Among the statutory exemptions, ERISA § 408(c)(3), authorizes "an officer, employee, agent, or other representative of a party in interest" to serve as an ERISA fiduciary. Section 408(c)(3) figures centrally in *Donovan v. Bierwirth*, the leading case on fiduciary investment issues under ERISA, reproduced infra in Chapter 14.

6.   *Participant investment advice.* The prohibited transaction rules have long interfered with efforts by plan sponsors or plan investment providers to assist plan participants in making choices among the investment options offered in defined contribution plans. The Pension Protection Act of 2006 created a new exemption, ERISA § 408(g), to facilitate participant investment advice, which is discussed in Chapter 14, infra.

7.   *Duplication and expense.* The duty of loyalty under ERISA's exclusive benefit rule, § 404(a)(1)(A), in principle reaches any transaction that evinces self-dealing or improper conflict of interest. E.g., Stuart Park Associates Ltd. Partnership v. Ameritech Pension Trust, 51 F.3d 1319 (7th Cir.1995) (fiduciary accepting kickbacks for steering plan funds to real estate partnership interests violated both the anti-kickback rule of ERISA § 406(b) and the exclusive benefit rule of § 404(a)(1)(A)).

Does ERISA need the prohibited transactions scheme? Or is ERISA prohibited transaction law redundant? In 1997 the Uniform Law Commission promulgated the Uniform Management of Public Employee Retirement Systems Act (1997) (UMPERS), a model act to govern ERISA-exempt state and local pension plans. Sections 7(1)–(2) of UMPERS track the "solely in the interest" and "exclusive purpose" language of ERISA's exclusive benefit rule, § 404(a)(1)(A). The Official Comment explains that the Act declined to imitate ERISA's prohibited transactions scheme because of its complexity, and because it "would add little to the affirmative fiduciary duties of the Act." UMPERS § 7, cmt.

Kathleen Utgoff, former executive director of the PBGC, wrote with a coauthor that the prohibited transaction rules "prevent plans from engaging in beneficial investment transactions"; and that, because of compliance costs, the prohibited transactions rules "increase the marginal cost of nearly every investment transaction that does not take place in public [markets]." The authors reported asking "[s]everal experienced ERISA attorneys [if] they were aware of any case in which these rules had prevented or punished some abusive act that was not also proscribed by the general fiduciary rules. None could identify a single case. If there are any such cases, the DoL should identify them so that it would be possible to weigh the beneficial value against the easily identifiable cost these rules exact." Kathleen P. Utgoff & Theodore R. Groom, The Regulation of Pensions: Twenty Questions After Twenty Years, 21 J. Pension Planning & Compliance 1, 13 (1995).

8.   *Spink*. In Lockheed Corp. v. Spink, 517 U.S. 882 (1996), the Supreme Court dealt with the claim that Lockheed, the employer, engaged in a prohibited transaction by amending its pension plan to offer enhanced retirement benefits conditioned on the employee agreeing to release any employment-related claims against Lockheed. The Ninth Circuit found the plan amendments "unlawful under IRC § 406(a)(1)(D), which prohibits a fiduciary from causing a plan to engage in a transaction that transfers plan assets to a party in interest or involves the use of plan assets for the benefit of a party in interest." The Ninth Circuit " 'reasoned that because the amendments offered increased benefits in exchange for a release of employment claims, they constituted a use of Plan assets to "purchase" a significant benefit for Lockheed.' " 517 U.S. at 886. The Supreme Court reversed, saying "[p]lan sponsors who alter the terms of a plan do not fall into the category of fiduciaries." Id. at 890. "Lockheed acted not as a fiduciary but as a settlor when it amended the terms of the Plan to include the retirement programs. Thus, § 406(a)'s requirement of fiduciary status is not met." Id. at 891. The Court also rejected Spink's prohibited transaction theory, reasoning that

> the payment of benefits is in fact not a "transaction" in the sense that Congress used that term in § 406(a). Section 406(a) forbids fiduciaries from engaging the plan in the "sale," "exchange," or "leasing" of property; the "lending of money" or "extension of credit"; the "furnishing of goods, services, or facilities"; and the "acquisition . . . of any employer security or employer real property" with a party in interest. These are commercial bargains that present a special risk of plan underfunding because they are struck with plan insiders, presumably not at

arms-length. What the "transactions" identified in § 406(a) thus have in common is that they generally involve uses of plan assets that are potentially harmful to the plan. The payment of benefits conditioned on performance by plan participants cannot reasonably be said to share that characteristic.

According to Spink and the Court of Appeals, however, Lockheed's early retirement programs were prohibited transactions within the meaning of § 406(a)(1)(D) because the required release of employment-related claims by participants created a "significant benefit" for Lockheed. Spink concedes, however, that among the "incidental" and thus legitimate benefits that a plan sponsor may receive from the operation of a pension plan are attracting and retaining employees, paying deferred compensation, settling or avoiding strikes, providing increased compensation without increasing wages, increasing employee turnover, and reducing the likelihood of lawsuits by encouraging employees who would otherwise have been laid off to depart voluntarily.

We do not see how obtaining waivers of employment-related claims can meaningfully be distinguished from these admittedly permissible objectives. [We] thus hold that the payment of benefits pursuant to an amended plan, regardless of what the plan requires of the employee in return for those benefits, does not constitute a prohibited transaction.

9. *Nonfiduciary liability.* Despite the emphasis in *Spink* on fiduciary status as a prerequisite for responsibility under ERISA's prohibited transactions regime, the Supreme Court held in Harris Trust & Savings Bank v. Salomon Smith Barney, 530 U.S. 238 (2000), that liability for participation in a prohibited transaction could also attach to a nonfiduciary who was assumed to be an ERISA party in interest. The case involved an ERISA-covered pension fund that had purchased an investment from Salomon Smith Barney, a firm that, having also provided some broker-dealer services to the fund, would have been a party in interest under ERISA § 3(14)(B). In *Harris Trust* the Court conceded "that § 406(a) imposes a duty only on the fiduciary that causes the plan to engage in the transaction." Id. at 245. Nevertheless, the Court reasoned that the provision of ERISA remedy law under which the suit had been brought, § 502(a)(3), "itself imposes certain duties, and [therefore] liability under that provision does not depend on whether ERISA's substantive provisions [i.e., the prohibited transaction rules] impose a specific duty on the party being sued. [Indeed] § 502(a)(3) makes no mention at all of which parties may be proper [defendants]." Id. at 245–46. *Harris Trust* is further discussed infra in Chapter 16.

Harris Trust was a unanimous decision. Is the opinion persuasive in resting nonfiduciary liability for a prohibited transaction on ERISA remedy law?

For a garden variety nonfiduciary liability case, consider Chao v. Johnston, 2007 WL 2847548 (E.D.Tenn.2007), which involved a lawyer who was alleged to have assisted an ERISA fiduciary and others to loot an ERISA plan. The court held that nonfiduciary liability would lie if DoL could establish, as it alleged in the complaint, that the lawyer knew or should have known that he was facilitating the fiduciary breaches of the others. The case law is reviewed in Jayne E. Zanglein & Susan J. Stabile, ERISA Litigation 260–62 (3d ed. 2008).

CHAPTER 14

FIDUCIARY INVESTING

Analysis

In Chapters 12 and 13, concerning fiduciary status under ERISA and the duties of ERISA fiduciaries, it was emphasized that ERISA's fiduciary regime applies equally to pension and to welfare benefit plans. The present chapter, concerning the fiduciary responsibilities of investing plan assets, is centered on pension funds, because single-employer welfare benefit plans, being unfunded, conduct no investment function. However, multiemployer welfare plans such as the Convalescent Fund in *Mazzola*, discussed supra in Chapter 13, are funded, and ERISA's rules for fiduciary investing do apply in such cases.

Section A of this chapter provides an introduction to the investment function under ERISA. Section B, centered on the leading case of *Donovan v. Bierwirth*, examines ERISA fiduciary law in the setting of the defined benefit plan. Section C deals with the investment challenges of defined contribution plans. Section D reviews the special problems that have arisen in plans that invest in employer stock.

A. THE INVESTMENT FUNCTION

1. *Magnitudes*. Because pension wealth constitutes a significant share of the nation's capital stock, the regulation of pension fund investing is a matter of exceptional importance. At December 31, 2014, total U.S. retirement plan assets stood at $24.7 trillion, up from $18 trillion in 2007. Investment Company Institute, Retirement Assets Total $24.7 Trillion in Second Quarter 2014, http://www.ici.org/research/stats/retirement/ret_14_q4. Of this amount, IRAs held $7.4 trillion, employer sponsored defined contribution plans $6.8 trillion, private-sector defined benefit pension plans $3.2 trillion, governmental defined benefit plans $5.2 trillion; the remainder was in annuity reserves. Retirement plan

assets constituted 36 percent of U.S. household assets. Id. In 1985, the total was $2.4 trillion. EBRI, Assets in Qualified Retirement Plans, 1985–2002, Facts from EBRI 1–2 (Sept. 2004).

Pension funds are the largest holders of American financial assets. As of year-end 2006 institutional investors held 21 percent of American financial assets and 66.3 percent of total equity; pension funds owned nearly two-fifths of institutional assets. Conference Board, Institutional Investment Report: Trends in Institutional Assets and Equity Ownership of U.S. Corporations 9, 11, 20 & tbls. 1, 3, 10 (2008) [hereafter 2008 Conference Board Report]. By contrast, in 1950, pension funds held less than 1 percent of all equities. Richard A. Ippolito, Pensions, Economics and Public Policy 123 (Pension Research Council) (1986). Institutional investors held 76.4 percent of the equity in the largest 1,000 American companies in 2007, up from 46.6 percent in 1987. 2008 Conference Board Report, at 6, 26 & tbl. 18.

Despite the stupendous amounts at stake, ERISA supplies no explicit direction for investing ERISA-covered assets. There are no categoric requirements that pension wealth be invested in particular types of assets. ERISA's regulation of the investment function rests on § 404(a), the all-purpose fiduciary duties of loyalty, prudence, and diversification, as reinforced by the prohibited transactions regime of §§ 406–408, all discussed supra in Chapter 13.

Broadly speaking, ERISA's regulation of investing has unfolded in two phases. The earlier phase, in the 1980s, centered on the leading case of *Donovan v. Bierwirth*, reproduced below, concerned the investment responsibilities of fiduciaries under defined benefit plans. As defined contribution plans have become prevalent, plan participants have become increasingly responsible for investing the assets in their accounts. Section C of this chapter examines the rules that guide participant-directed investing. Section D is devoted to the burgeoning case law arising from defined contribution plans in which participants' accounts are allowed or required to be invested in the stock of the employer.

2.   *Monitoring and control.* Investment in equities carries with it the power to vote the shares. If pension funds and other institutional shareholders were to coordinate their voting power, they could control the fate of most large publicly traded corporations. The burgeoning of fiduciary shareholdings was a crucial factor in the increasing number of hostile tender offers and the other manifestations of the active market for corporate control that intensified across the last quarter of the twentieth century.

A relatively few institutional investors (pension funds, investment companies, insurance companies, bank and trust companies, foundations and other charitable endowments) now command a controlling interest in most large companies. These investors act under a fiduciary duty to maximize the interest of the beneficial owners. This phenomenon has been labeled "fiduciary capitalism." James P. Hawley & Andrew T. Williams, The Emergence of Fiduciary Capitalism, 5 Corporate Governance 206 (1997). "[The] rise of fiduciary capitalism with its great concentrations of wealth in the hands of relatively few institutional investors raises serious concerns about the monitoring of the monitors." Id. at 211.

In contrast to the fear that the institutional investors will capture control of the economy is the opposite concern, that institutional investors may have too little incentive to do adequate monitoring. There is concern that the broad diversification characteristic of institutional portfolios has dispersed shareholder voting power so widely that the monitoring function of shareholders vis-a-vis corporate management has been impaired:

> Institutions with well diversified portfolios cannot take [the traditional shareholder's interest in improving individual companies] because they hold too many companies. Monitoring every company would mean sacrificing most of the transaction cost savings that motivated adopting an indexing strategy in the first place. Moreover, institutions *should not* take such an interest because they stand to gain much less from it than traditional owners might gain. Many improvements affecting the value of one company in an indexed portfolio come only at the expense of other companies in the portfolio. For example, the institutional investor does not gain when one of its portfolio companies acquires market share at the expense of another. From the portfolio holder's point of view, this improvement merely transfers money from one pocket to another in the same pair of pants.

Ronald J. Gilson & Reinier Kraakman, Reinventing the Outside Director: An Agenda for Institutional Investors, 43 Stanford L. Rev. 863, 866 (1991). "The prevailing watchword [for fiduciaries under ERISA and under the common law of trusts] is caution. Broad diversification and passivity are safe; concentrated ownership and activism are dangerous. [Diversifying] widely, owning small percentage stakes in hundreds or even thousands of companies, is safe, since it is what others 'in a like capacity' [ERISA § 404(a)(1)(B)] are doing. In contrast, owning large stakes in a smaller number of companies, which could increase the gains from monitoring, is risky because it isn't what others are doing, and doesn't 'minimize' the risk of 'large losses' [ERISA § 404(a)(1)(C)]." Bernard S. Black, Shareholder Passivity Reexamined, 89 Michigan L. Rev. 520, 553 (1990).

Corporate governance issues arising from institutional investment patterns are discussed in Chapter 1, supra, in connection with Peter Drucker's "Pension Fund Socialism"; and below in Section B of this chapter, in connection with the fiduciary standards for shareholder voting under ERISA.

3. *Prudent investing.* As discussed in Chapter 12, supra, the prudence norm is expressed as a comparative standard: "the care, skill, prudence, and diligence under the circumstances then prevailing that a prudent man acting in a like capacity and familiar with such matters would use in the conduct of an enterprise of a like character and with like aims." ERISA § 404(a)(1)(B). It seems unlikely that anybody reading that standard would feel particularly instructed in how to invest a pension fund—even in conjunction with § 404(a)(1)(C), which calls for diversification of investments in order to minimize "large losses, unless

under the circumstances it is clearly prudent not to do so." ERISA's prudent investor should be doing about what other prudent investors are doing.

The Seventh Circuit has observed that "the ultimate outcome of an investment is not proof of imprudence. We cannot say that [a particular manager] was imprudent merely because [the fund] lost [money]. The fiduciary duty of care [requires] prudence, not prescience." DeBruyne v. Equitable Life Assurance Soc., 920 F.2d 457, 465 (7th Cir.1990) (fund manager not responsible for consequences of Black Monday stock-market decline in October 1987). In a similar vein, § 8 of the Uniform Prudent Investor Act of 1994 says: "Compliance with the prudent investor rule is determined in light of the facts and circumstances existing at the time of a trustee's decision or action and not by hindsight."

Nor does the mere fact that a fiduciary continues to hold a security in the face of a declining market price in the security constitute a violation of the duty of prudence. In PBCG v. Morgan Stanley Investment Mngmt Inc., 712 F.3d 705 (2d Cir.2013) the Second Circuit held that the fact that a plan administrator purchased and continued to hold mortgage-backed securities despite a decline in the market price of the securities does not give rise to a reasonable inference that it was imprudent to purchase or hold the securities. The court rejected plaintiffs' claim that there were "warning signs" throughout 2007 and 2008 that the investment was imprudent. In the eyes of the court, none of the identified warning signs "gives rise to a plausible inference that Morgan Stanley knew, or should have known, that the securities in the Portfolio were imprudent investments, or that Morgan Stanley breached its fiduciary duty by not selling those investments at whatever unspecified prices existed during the unspecified period in which it was imprudent to maintain those unspecified investments." Id. at 721. The court admitted that a "rapid decline in the price of a security" should lead a prudent fiduciary to investigate whether continuing to hold the securities was prudent, but there was no allegation Morgan Stanley failed to conduct such an investigation. Id. Section D discusses this claim in connection with investments in employer securities.

4.   *Modern portfolio theory (MPT)*. In Laborers National Pension Fund v. Northern Trust Quantitative Advisors, 173 F.3d 313 (5th Cir.1999), the trustees of a multiemployer plan sued one of the plan's investment managers for imprudence in respect of a disappointing investment in a mortgage-backed security that was AAA-rated at the time of purchase. The Fifth Circuit held that the investment was authorized by the plan's investment guidelines and was consistent with ERISA. The court faulted the lower court for failing to judge the investment "according to the modern portfolio theory required by ERISA" as interpreted in DoL regulation, 29 C.F.R. § 2550.404a–1. 173 F.3d at 322.

Modern Portfolio Theory (MPT) is a body of theoretical and empirical knowledge about the behavior of securities prices and securities markets that began developing in the late 1950s, and that has reshaped the conduct of professional investing. Six Nobel Prizes in economics have thus far been awarded for scholarly contributions to MPT. As the Fifth Circuit's opinion in *Laborers National Pension Fund* illustrates, the courts have increasingly come to the view that the prudence norm in trust law and in ERISA has absorbed the main precepts of MPT.

MPT, which is sometimes called efficient market theory, rests on the understanding that organized securities markets are so efficient at discounting securities prices that the current market price of a security is highly likely already to impound the information that is known or knowable about the future prospects of that security. Even expert investment professionals have enormous difficulty outsmarting the market, that is, identifying overpriced securities to sell and underpriced securities to buy. Evidence has accumulated that professional investors managing large portfolios have regularly underperformed the broad market averages such as the Standard & Poor's 500 or the Wilshire 5000.

Professionally managed mutual fund portfolios have been extensively studied. Adjusting for costs, the average mutual fund underperforms the broad market averages for securities of the type that the fund contains. For the ten years ending in 1993, the Morningstar mutual fund research organization found that "diversified U.S. stock funds returned an average 12.8%, compared with 14.9% for the Standard & Poor's 500-stock index." Jonathan Clements, Boggled by Fund Picking?, Wall St. J., May 20, 1994, at C1. Another Morningstar study released in 2009 found that more that 60 percent of these professionally managed funds underperformed the indexes over the previous three years, and that the numbers were "similar for five and ten year returns." Sam Mamudi, Active Management Loses in Risk Study, Wall St. J., Oct. 6, 2009, at C9. Consistent exceptions are very rare. Some funds do better than others, but across long periods of time few have outperformed the market with a consistency greater than the law of averages would predict. In a sense these findings flow naturally from the magnitude of pension and mutual fund holdings. It is hard to beat the market when you are the market.

Literature: Frank J. Fabozzi & Pamela Peterson Drake, Finance: Capital Markets, Financial Management, and Investment Management (2009); Burton G. Malkiel, A Random Walk Down Wall Street (9th ed. 2007); Jonathan R. Macey, An Introduction to Modern Financial Theory (2d ed. 1998); Roger G. Ibbotson & Gary P. Brinson, Investment Markets (1987); R.A. Brealey, An Introduction to Risk and Return from Common Stocks (2d ed. 1983) [hereafter Brealey, Stocks].

5. *Diversification.* In addition to the efficiency of the organized securities markets, another great theme of MPT has been the discovery of the importance of broad diversification, both across and within asset classes.

MPT isolates three distinct components of the risk of owning any security: market risk, industry risk, and firm risk. Market risk is common to all securities; it reflects general economic and political conditions, interest rates, and so forth. The 2008–2009 disruption of world credit markets, for example, affected virtually all asset classes. Industry risk refers to factors common to the firms in a particular industry or an industry grouping, in contrast to firm risk, which refers to factors that touch the fortunes only of the individual firm. Take the international oils as an example: All the producers suffered from the 1973

Arab oil embargo (industry risk), but only Exxon incurred the liabilities arising from the great Alaskan oil spill of March 1989 (firm risk).

The finance scholars have been able to compute the approximate weight of the three elements that comprise the risk of securities ownership. In round numbers, market risk has been reckoned at 30 percent; the risk of industry and other groupings at about 50 percent; and firm risk at about 20 percent. See Brealey, Stocks, supra, at 117. These numbers underlie the intense preoccupation with diversification in modern investment practice. Although market risk cannot be eliminated, since it is common to all securities, industry risk and firm risk can be greatly reduced through diversification.

The gains from diversification pertain not only to domestic equities but also to other asset classes, including fixed income securities, real estate, and non-dollar-denominated assets. For discussion, see John H. Langbein, The Uniform Prudent Investor Act and the Future of Trust Investing, 81 Iowa L. Rev. 641, 646–49 (1996).

A telling expression has been coined to describe what is wrong with underdiversification: *uncompensated risk*. Nobody pays the investor for owning too few asset classes or too few issues within an asset class. Underdiversification entails needless risk, risk that can be avoided by constructing a sufficiently large and representative portfolio.

Andrew Carnegie, who lived before anybody ever heard of MPT, was not a believer in diversification. He is reported to have said that there's nothing wrong with putting all your eggs in one basket, provided that you select the right basket and keep watching your eggs. MPT has shown us why Carnegie's intuitively attractive dictum is wrong. We now know that no amount of selecting and watching can protect an investor against certain risks of securities ownership against which diversification does protect. Even a blue chip can suffer catastrophic and wholly unpredictable losses—as happened, for example, to the shares of the Union Carbide Company in the wake of the 1984 Bhopal disaster; or to Texaco, one of the major international oil companies, when a fluke lawsuit forced it into bankruptcy in 1987. The accounting frauds that reduced Enron and WorldCom to bankruptcy in 2001 and 2002 were so sophisticated that virtually all investment professionals failed to detect them until the harm had been done. Precisely because it is so hard to foresee the next Bhopal, or the next WorldCom, the prudent fiduciary investor diversifies so broadly that if catastrophe befalls one holding, the loss will be lessened or offset in the rest of the portfolio.

Trust investment law recognizes a strong duty to diversify. In 1992 the American Law Institute revised the Restatement of Trusts to take account of the rise of MPT, incorporating the duty to diversify as a subprinciple of the prudence norm. Restatement (Third) of Trusts § 90(b) (2007) (formerly § 227(b) of 1992 revision). Section 3 of the Uniform Prudent Investor Act (1994), which tracks the Restatement standard, has been enacted in 45 states and the District of Columbia; the other states have broadly comparable nonuniform legislation.

ERISA's duty to diversify is sometimes applied straightforwardly, e.g., Meyer v. Berkshire Life Ins. Co., 250 F.Supp.2d 544, 565 (D.Md.2003) (breach found where defendants "conceded that the plans were not diversified and did not conform [to] Modern Portfolio Theory"). Some courts, however, have confused diversification with other aspects of prudent investing. For example, in Metzler v. Graham, 112 F.3d 207 (5th Cir.1997), the court rejected a DoL action for breach of the duty to diversify in a case in which an ERISA plan trustee had invested 63% of the plan's assets in a single tract of undeveloped real estate. There was conflicting evidence about whether the property, which the plan still owned, had subsequently declined in value. The court cited the following factors in support of its conclusion that not diversifying was "clearly prudent": (1) the plan had enough other assets to make projected payouts for the next 20 years; (2) the trustee feared the return of high inflation and esteemed real estate as a protection against inflation; (3) the trustee paid less than appraised value for the parcel; and (4) the trustee had expertise in this type of property. What is wrong with the court's reasoning?

ERISA contains special provisions dealing with investments in employer securities or employer realty. Section 407(a) limits a defined benefit plan from investing more than 10 percent in such assets. In *Donovan v. Bierwirth*, reproduced infra, the 10 percent limit was held to be a ceiling, not an authorization, and the plan fiduciaries who bought employer stock up to that ceiling were held to have acted imprudently in the circumstances.

ERISA's duty to diversify is subject to an exception for investments in employer stock in individual account plans. ERISA § 404(a)(2), cross-referencing § 407(d)(3); see also § 407(b)(1). Employer stock plans are discussed below in Section D of this chapter.

Literature: Rali Wakeman, ERISA's Duty of Diversification, 22 J. Pension Planning & Compliance 67 (1996).

6. *Spread of market-matching vehicles.* A prominent scholarly study of the performance of professional investment managers conducted some years ago concluded that "pension fund equity managers seem to subtract rather than add value relative to the performance of the Standard & Poor's 500 Index." Josef Lakonishok, Andrei Schleifer, & Robert W. Vishny, The Structure and Performance of the Money Management Industry, in Brookings Papers on Economic Activity: Microeconomics 339, at 378 (M. Baily & C. Winston eds., 1992). The authors computed that pension funds underperformed the average by about 1.5 percent a year, or $15 billion per trillion of assets, money "that [goes] to the brokerage industry, the money management industry, and the smart investors who trade against the funds." Id. at 379.

In response to the growing awareness of how difficult and costly it is to try to outperform the broad market averages, so-called index or market funds—portfolios that attempt to match rather than to beat the averages—have become commonplace. Index funds are relatively passive; the fund buys and holds the market-matching portfolio, eschewing the research and trading costs of active management. Large pension funds commonly place a portion of their assets into such vehicles, while devoting the remainder to active management (the so-called "core/noncore" strategy). As of 1998 it was reported that all the 200 largest U.S. pension funds were indexing some portion of their equity investments. Pensions & Investments, Jan. 25, 1999, at 26. As of 2006, the 200 largest defined benefit plans had indexed more than a third of their equities. 2008 Conference Board Report, supra, at 8.

7. *The changed conventions of fiduciary investment law.* Older trust law understood the prudence norm to direct the trustee (1) to make investment decisions with respect to the merits of each security in isolation, and (2) to avoid "speculative" investments. MPT emphasizes that the fiduciary investor should view any investment in relation to the total portfolio and the risk tolerance of the investor. No investment is per se too risky for fiduciary investing if the risk is properly compensated and is undertaken as part of an appropriately diversified portfolio. Thus, MPT has directed attention away from the selection of individual securities and toward the composition of the portfolio as a whole. Absorbing the lessons of MPT, the 1992 Restatement revised the standard of prudent investment to "require[ ] the exercise of reasonable care, skill, and caution . . . to be applied to investments not in isolation but in the context of the trust portfolio and as a part of an overall investment strategy, which should incorporate risk and return objectives reasonably suitable to the trust." Restatement (Third) of Trusts § 90 (2007) (formerly § 227(a) of 1992 revision). The Uniform Prudent Investor Act § 2(b) (1994) amplified and codified the Restatement formulation.

MPT has led to a more refined understanding of the risk/return relationship in investing by emphasizing the volatility of returns as the key measure of risk. An ERISA fiduciary who exposes plan funds to excessive risk can be found liable for imprudent investing under § 404(a)(1)(b). See, e.g., California Ironworkers Field Pension Trust v. Loomis Sayles & Co., 259 F.3d 1036 (9th Cir.2001) (imprudent to invest 30 percent of welfare plan in inverse floaters, a volatile type of collateralized mortgage obligation); Toledo Blade Newspaper Unions Blade Pension Plan v. Investment Performance Services, Inc., 565 F.Supp.2d 879, 889 (S.D.Ohio 2008) (investment "overly risky" for the benchmark chosen).

The DoL has recognized the spread of MPT. DoL promulgated the regulation at 29 C.F.R § 2550.404a–1, cited in *Laborers National Pension Fund,* supra, with an official commentary that endorsed MPT concepts of fiduciary investing: "The Department is of the opinion that (1) generally, the relative riskiness of a specific investment or investment course of action does not render such investment or investment course of action either *per se* prudent or *per se* imprudent, and (2) the prudence of an investment decision should not be judged without regard to the role that the proposed investment or investment course of action plays within the overall plan portfolio. Thus, although securities issued by a small or new company may be a riskier investment than securities issued by a 'blue chip' company, the investment in the former company may be entirely proper under the Act's 'prudence' rule." 44 Fed. Reg. 37,221, at 37,222 (Jun. 26, 1979).

Although various forms of active management continue to be widespread in fiduciary investing, the growth of passive, index-matching investing from a trickle in the mid-1970s to the trillions of dollars in modern practice has been a dominant trend in the period since the enactment of ERISA.

8. *Promoting professional investment management.* Most people are not well suited to engage in investment management. Investing is time-consuming and specialized. Many unsophisticated investors make palpably unwise decisions. The defined benefit pension plan, by placing the responsibility for investment on the employer, promotes the use of professionals. The employer either has investment professionals on its finance staff, or engages suitable external service providers. Although the evidence suggests that the professionals are not very good at outsmarting the broad market averages, which is to say that they are not very good at outsmarting each other, they do the job of investing much better than the average worker on the shop floor. Not only do professionals seldom fall victim to such obvious blunders as load funds and boiler-room fraud scams, the professionals are more sensitive to the importance both of diversifying and of placing the portfolio appropriately on the risk return curve. Alicia Munnell and co-authors have computed based on 2007 data that "14 percent of [401(k)] participants held no equity and 28 percent held all their balances in equity. . . ." Alicia Munnell et al., An Update on 401(k) Plans: Insights from the 2007 SCF 5 (Mar. 2009) (Boston College Center for Retirement Research).

Whereas a defined benefit plan lodges investment responsibility with the employer or other sponsor, the typical defined contribution plan leaves considerable investment responsibility with the plan participant. DoL regulations under ERISA § 404(c), discussed below in Section C, restrict most participants in defined contribution plans to choosing among broadly diversified and professionally managed portfolios, commonly mutual funds. Thus, most defined contribution plans tend to limit the participant to asset allocation among professionally constructed portfolios. Some 401(k) plans, and many IRAs, however, do allow so-called self-directed accounts, enabling the participant to select individual securities. See Donna Rosato, "Investments: New 401(k) Tool, but Who Needs It?," N.Y. Times, Feb. 2, 2003, at 9.

Much of ERISA is protective in character. ERISA's tendency to encourage professional investment management also manifests a protective policy. However, ESOPs and those 401(k) and other profit sharing plans that allow or require investment in the employer's stock constitute important departures from the general trend of pension investment policy under ERISA to encourage the use of professionally managed and broadly diversified portfolios. As of the year 2000, 19 percent of all 401(k) plan assets were invested in employer stock. Alicia H. Munnell & Annika Sunden, Coming Up Short: The Challenge of 401(k) Plans 102 & tbl. 5–3 (2004). By 2007 that figure had declined to 11 percent. Jack VanDerhei et al., 401(k) Plan Asset Allocation, Account Balances, and Loan Activity in 2007, EBRI Issue Brief No. 324 (Dec. 2008), at 20 & Fig. 17. Although relatively few sponsors offer employer stock plans, those who do tend to be large employers. According to EBRI data for 2007, "less than 1 percent of participants in small plans were offered company stock as an investment option, while 64 percent of participants in plans with more than 5,000 participants were offered company stock as an investment option. . . ." Id. at 21. (Fiduciary issues associated with employer stock plans are discussed infra in Section D of this chapter.)

QUESTIONS

1.   If an investment manager invests a pension fund entirely in a portfolio of long term U.S. Treasury bonds—instruments that are presumed to have no risk of default—can the manager ever be liable for imprudent investing? For underdiversification? See GIW Industries, Inc. v. Trevor, Stewart, Burton & Jacobsen, Inc., 895 F.2d 729 (11th Cir.1990).

2.   ERISA's prudence norm, like the trust-law rule from which it is derived, is relational or comparative in character, asking what "a prudent man acting in a like capacity and familiar with such matters would use in the conduct of an enterprise of a like character and with like aims." ERISA § 404(a)(1)(B). This standard, by measuring investment performance against investment-industry benchmarks, is sometimes thought to result in a preoccupation on the part of fiduciary investors with measurable returns that are excessively short-term. Former Senators Nancy Kassebaum (R. Kans.) and Robert Dole (R. Kans.) once proposed legislation—which they labeled the Excessive Churning and Speculation Act—that would have placed an excise tax on capital gains realized by pension funds on the sale of an asset that the fund had held for less than 180 days. See Current Investment Issues, EBRI Issue Brief 1, 12 (Apr. 1990). What are the merits and demerits of this proposal?

B. DEFINED BENEFIT PLANS

ERISA's main principles of fiduciary investing, loyalty and prudence, apply nominally both to defined benefit and to defined contribution plans, except (as discussed below in Section D) that defined contribution plans offering employer stock can escape the duty to diversify. Although most of the current controversy about fiduciary investing under ERISA concerns defined contribution plans, the leading precedent arose in a defined benefit plan sponsored by the Grumman Corporation, a military aircraft manufacturer that became caught up in a contest for corporate control.

1. DONOVAN V. BIERWIRTH

680 F.2d 263 (2d Cir.1982).

■ FRIENDLY, CIRCUIT JUDGE. This action was brought on October 19, 1981, by the Secretary of Labor (the Secretary) under § 502(e)(1) of [ERISA] in the District Court for the Eastern District of New York, against John C. Bierwirth, Robert G. Freese and Carl A. Paladino, Trustees of the Grumman Corporation Pension Plan (the Plan). The action stems from the unsuccessful tender offer by LTV Corporation (LTV) in the fall of 1981 for some 70% of the outstanding common stock and convertible securities of Grumman Corporation (Grumman) at $45 per share. At the time of the offer the Plan owned some 525,000 shares of Grumman common stock, which it had acquired in the mid-1970's. As hereafter recounted, the Plan not only declined to tender its stock but purchased an additional 1,158,000 shares at an average price of $38.27 per share, at a total cost of $44,312,380. These acts, the Secretary's complaint alleged, constituted a violation of §§ 404(a) and 406(b) of ERISA. . . .

No testimony was taken [in the district court]; the matter was submitted on affidavits, depositions, public filings and a stipulation of background facts. A number of participants in the Plan were allowed to intervene as defendants; a supporting affidavit of one of the Plan participants alleged that:

> [S]pontaneously and within days after this suit was commenced, Grumman employees at all levels and in all departments began to circulate petitions expressing their approval of the trustees' actions, as participants in the Pension Plan. To date, petitions have been signed by approximately 17,000 of the 22,000 employees who are Plan participants and beneficiaries.

On December 3, 1981, the district court, 538 F.Supp. 463, rendered an opinion containing its findings of fact and conclusions of law. After rejecting the Secretary's contention that the trustees committed *per se* violations of ERISA and making a detailed survey of the evidence, the judge concluded that the Secretary had "shown a likelihood of success on his claim that each of the trustees has acted imprudently with respect to their recent investment decisions concerning Grumman stock". He invited suggestions with respect to the form of preliminary relief. The trustees proposed that if the court felt it necessary to go beyond a preliminary injunction with respect to dealings in Grumman securities, it should adopt a proposal of the Grumman board, embodied in a resolution passed on December 17, 1981, that the board, with all management directors abstaining, should appoint three non-management directors as interim trustees. Declining this proposal the judge entered an order which preliminarily enjoined the trustees from buying, selling or exercising any rights with respect to Grumman securities except upon further order of the court and directed the appointment of a receiver to serve as an "Investment Manager" for Grumman securities owned by the Plan, with "power to sell, tender for sale, or otherwise dispose of all or part of such stock or securities." The order contained elaborate provisions concerning the qualifications, method of appointment and compensation of the Investment Manager. The provisions with respect to the Investment Manager were stayed on condition "that defendant promptly request and diligently pursue an expedited appeal" to this court, which was done.

The LTV tender offer followed a scenario that has become familiar. On September 21, 1981, in the absence of defendant Bierwirth, Chairman of the Board of Grumman, who was on vacation, Joseph O. Gavin, Jr., President of Grumman, received a telephone call from Paul Thayer, Chairman of the Board and Chief Executive Officer of LTV, inviting him to discuss a possible merger. Gavin rejected the invitation. Evidently unsurprised, LTV, prior to the opening of trading on the New York Stock Exchange on September 23, issued a press release announcing that it was planning to make a cash tender offer at $45 per share for up to 70% of Grumman's common stock and securities representing or convertible into common stock. According to the press release, the offer constituted "the first step in a plan to acquire 100% of the voting equity of the Grumman Corporation". On September 21 and 22 Grumman stock had sold on the New York Stock Exchange at prices ranging between 23$\frac{7}{8}$ and 27$\frac{1}{4}$.

Later in the morning of September 23 Grumman put out a release on the Dow Jones News Service in Bierwirth's name stating that the Grumman directors would promptly consider the proposed offer. The release noted that the board would "consider legal factors including antitrust implications,"[2] warned stockholders not to act hastily and said that Dillon, Read & Co. had been retained to provide advice regarding the LTV offer. On the same day LTV delivered to Bierwirth's office a letter expressing regret at the lack of a meeting in which LTV would have had an "opportunity to spell out in a personal way how . . . combination would be beneficial to the shareholders, employees, and communities served by Grumman", and stating that "[t]he headquarters of a combined Grumman-Vought aerospace operation would be established in Bethpage, Long Island [Grumman's headquarters] under a top management team that would include you as CEO as well as Joe Gavin and George Skurla from Grumman and Bob Kirk from Vought." Thayer continued to hope for "the opportunity to explain to you in more detail the advantages of the synergistic combination" he had proposed and enclosed a copy of the press release.

The LTV offer was made on September 24. It was conditioned upon the tender of a minimum of 50.01% of Grumman's common stock and securities representing or convertible into common stock. The withdrawal/proration date was 12:01 A.M. on October 16, 1981; the termination date was 12:01 A.M. on October 23. Bierwirth cut short his vacation and reached the Grumman office at midday on September 24.

Although SEC Rule 14e–2 gave the Grumman board 10 business days from the commencement of the offer to communicate its position, if any, the board lost no time in going into action. It met on September 25. By then the LTV offer had caused the price of Grumman stock to rise to a range of $32^5/_8$ to $34\frac{1}{4}$. The board had before it a two page letter of Dillon, Read & Co., Inc., which had served Grumman as investment banker, stating in a conclusory fashion that it was "of the opinion that the offer is inadequate from a financial point of view to holders of the Grumman securities." The letter said this conclusion was based on "certain information of a business and financial nature regarding Grumman which was either publicly available or furnished to us by Grumman and [on] discussions with the management of Grumman regarding its business and prospects." The letter made no attempt at quantification of these factors, and no representative of Dillon, Read attended the meeting for questioning, although apparently there were some supporting financial materials available. Defendant Robert G. Freese had also prepared some projections which are not in the record. The board unanimously adopted a resolution to oppose the tender offer, and issued a press release to that effect, saying that the board had concluded that "the offer is inadequate, and not in the best interests of Grumman, its shareholders, employees or the United States."

On September 28 Grumman began the previously mentioned [lawsuit] which was to lead to the injunction of the tender offer. On the same day defendant Bierwirth, Chairman of the Board of Grumman, sent

---

[2]   These arose from the fact that one of LTV's subsidiaries was Vought Corporation which, like Grumman, was a manufacturer of military aircraft and airframe subassemblies.

a letter to the company's shareholders seeking their help in defeating the offer. The letter stated:

> We're very optimistic about our chances of defeating the takeover bid. About a third of all shares are held by Grumman's employee investment and pension plans. These plans are managed by Grummanites who will look long and hard at how well their fellow members would be served by selling off Grumman stock. Much of the rest is owned by Grumman people who, I believe, understand their future is worth more than a quick return on a block of shares.

The reasons given for opposing LTV's offer were the inadequacy of the price and others, relating to the pension [fund].[3] The letter concluded by announcing that "Grumman's management is totally committed to defeating this takeover attempt," and by pleading "If you own Grumman shares, don't sell out to LTV."

On September 30, at the invitation of George Petrilak, President of the Grumman Retirees Club, Bierwirth met with 300 retirees to discuss the LTV offer. An affidavit of Petrilak avers that "there was great concern expressed by the members as to the possible impact of LTV succeeding in their tender offer upon their pensions," and said that "[t]he overwhelming attitude of the retirees was 'what is good for Grumman is good for retirees.'" The Club purchased an advertisement appearing in Newsday, a Long Island newspaper, on October 13, headed, "Grumman retirees protect your pension. Do not tender your stock to LTV."

Expectably, Bierwirth spent about 90% of his time during the next fortnight in activity directed to opposing the LTV offer. Freese devoted at least half his time to arranging an "additional bank credit facility". This was done "without any specific plans as to the use of the proceeds" in order "to have as much borrowing capability as possible in the event the Board wanted to take some action. . . ." Two borrowings had been made as of the date Freese's deposition was taken. One was for "compensating balances that are required under the agreement itself"; the second was "to have the funds available to pay for . . . up to a million shares of Grumman common stock."

The Grumman Pension Plan, established in 1943, is a "defined benefit plan" within the meaning of § 3(35) of ERISA, meeting the requirements for qualification under § 401(a) of the Internal Revenue Code and covering both salaried and hourly employees. Initially banking institutions had acted as trustees of the Plan. However, in 1973 Grumman adopted a policy of having officers of Grumman or its affiliates serve as trustees, as permitted by § 408(c)(3) of ERISA. The trustees in the fall of 1981 were Bierwirth; Freese, chief financial officer of Grumman since 1972; and Carl A. Paladino, Treasurer of Grumman Aerospace Corporation since 1969. John Mullan, associate general counsel of Grumman, has served as counsel to the trustees and regularly

---

[3]   There's one other factor to keep in mind: your pension fund. It's Grumman's policy to fully fund its employee pension fund. In contrast, LTV's pension fund right now is underfunded by almost a quarter of a billion dollars. Grumman people could lose if the two funds were to be merged.

attended their meetings. Sometime prior to January 1, 1975, the Plan had acquired 525,000 Grumman shares.

On September 28 Freese mentioned to Bierwirth that the trustees "are going to have to get together here at some point and decide what [to] do in regard to the holdings of Grumman stock." Bierwirth agreed and said he would call Paladino. During the next ten days, the three trustees had casual conversations as they happened to meet each other. Nothing was said about the Plan's buying Grumman shares and no financial data were assembled for the meeting. Bierwirth had been informed by Mullan that if LTV succeeded, it could "merge the pension Plan though it may take them some time" and also "could cancel the Plan to the extent that they eliminate the Fund although of course they would retain the corporate obligation to pay", and by unidentified other sources that changing the presumed earnings rate would permit the declaration of some of the fund as surplus and recapture for the corporation.

What occurred at the Plan trustees' meeting, which was held on October 7, was described in the depositions of the three trustees. Freese's is the most detailed; we shall follow it, with supplementation from the others when required. Mullan made a ten minute presentation dealing with ERISA, pointing out that the trustees' decisions "as far as the Grumman stock was concerned had to be predicated solely upon the best interests of the participants of the Plan." There was then a general discussion of how the trustees felt about LTV, the Dillon, Read opinion letter, and Freese's five year financial projections for Grumman. Elaborating on the discussion of LTV, Freese mentioned concern about the underfunding of "their pension plan," LTV's highly leveraged debt situation which would be aggravated by the need for borrowing to finance the acquisition of Grumman, contingent liability with respect to environmental problems and a large number of pending lawsuits and alleged SEC violations, all of which was revealed in a recent LTV prospectus. The same information was contained in LTV's annual report and in its other publicly available filings. Freese expressed concern that the assumed rate of return used by LTV's pension plan was higher than that used by other companies and that LTV would have trouble making contributions to their pension plan. Bierwirth testified that the trustees "were aware of" a report about Grumman by Lehman Brothers Kuhn Loeb Inc. (Lehman Brothers). This report, dated July 8, 1981, which recommended purchase of Grumman common stock, then selling at $28 per share, projected a 1981–84 earnings progression of $2.75, $5.00, $6.50 and $7.50, and contained financial analysis supporting the estimates. The report's projection of greater sales was stated to be based primarily on "[i]ndications . . . that [President] Reagan's request [for increased expenditures for military aircraft] will be approved by Congress" and Grumman's "promising diversification into aerospace subcontracting. . . ."

After a half hour's discussion the trustees voted not to tender the 525,000 Grumman shares held by the Plan. According to Bierwirth the trustees "then discussed whether we should take a second step. If we did not want to tender the stock at $45 a share, should we then consider buying additional shares, the market then being in the 30's?" A merit of such a purchase would be in making it more difficult for LTV to gain control of the pension fund. However, "it was also important that a further investment in Grumman shares be the right thing for us to do." "[A] number of fortuitous events had occurred during the summer and early in September which greatly enhanced the outlook for Grumman" and had made Bierwirth "feel earlier that a further investment in Grumman was desirable and should be recommended to the Trustees come this fall." While it had been "very difficult to accumulate substantial positions in Grumman stock," which ordinarily traded at volumes of 20,000 shares a day, the daily volume of half a million shares induced by the LTV offer made it "possible to accumulate a major position in Grumman stock without affecting the price all that much." Bierwirth was then of the view that "probably a majority of the stock would not be tendered" but could not feel confident about it. He recognized that if the LTV tender offer were abandoned, selling by arbitrageurs would push the price down. Following their discussion of these ideas, the trustees concluded that purchases of Grumman stock up to the maximum of 10% of the value of the Plan's assets permitted by § 407(a)(2) of ERISA would be prudent.

Two steps were taken shortly after the meeting: Grumman applied to the SEC for an exemption from rule 10b–6, which was thought necessary to permit the Plan to purchase additional Grumman shares. Grumman and the trustees executed an amendment of the trust agreement adding a new paragraph which, among other things, provided that Grumman should indemnify and hold harmless each trustee from any liability or expense arising out of any act or failure to act pursuant to the trust unless the liability or expense resulted from willful misconduct or lack of good faith. Authorization of the planned purchases was deferred until the SEC had acted on Grumman's request for an exemption from SEC rule 10b–6. On October 8 a press release announced the decision of the trustees not to tender the Plan's shares.

The request to the SEC was granted on Friday, October 9. The trustees met briefly on Monday, October 12, and authorized the Plan's purchase of 1,275,000 additional Grumman shares—just short of ERISA's 10% limitation. A press release issued on October 13 stated that use of the authorization would increase the Plan's ownership of Grumman stock from 3.8% to approximately 8% of the outstanding fully diluted shares. The Plan, acting through Dillon, Read, purchased 958,000 shares at an average price of $38.61 per share on October 12 and an additional 200,000 shares on October 13 at an average price of $36.62, for a total cost of $44,312,380.

On the next day, October 14, [Judge Mishler in] the district court temporarily enjoined the LTV offer, thereby drastically reducing its chances for success. The price of Grumman stock fell on October 15 to a range of 28¼–29½. After this court affirmed the temporary injunction, the price of Grumman shares was 28–28¾; the market value of the newly purchased shares was approximately $32,500,000. . . .

We deal first with the contention, advanced by the Secretary in passing, that the result reached by the district judge was compelled on a ground rejected by him, namely, that the trustees, at least in their purchase of Grumman stock, violated the specific prohibitions of § 406(b) of ERISA. The only such prohibition that is arguably applicable is § 406(b)(2).

We hold that the section does not apply. The "party" that the trustees are claimed to have been acting on the behalf of or to have been representing presumably is Grumman. We read this section of the statute as requiring a transaction between the plan and a party having an adverse interest. Such was the case in the only appellate decision cited to us by the Secretary, *Cutaiar v. Marshall,* 590 F.2d 523, 529 (3d Cir.1979). [We] see no reason to think Congress intended the expansive interpretation of the various specific prohibitions of § 406 urged by the Secretary, particularly in light of the inclusion of the sweeping requirements of prudence and loyalty contained in § 404.

Sections 404(a)(1)(A) and (B) impose three different although overlapping standards. A fiduciary must discharge his duties "solely in the interests of the participants and beneficiaries." He must do this "for the exclusive purpose" of providing benefits to them. And he must comply "with the care, skill, prudence, and diligence under the circumstances then prevailing" of the traditional "prudent man."

The trustees urge that the mandates of § 404(a)(1)(A) and (B) must be interpreted in the light of two other sections of ERISA. One is § 408(c)(3), which permits the appointment of officers of the sponsoring corporation as trustees. The other is § 407(a)(3), which, as here applicable, permitted the Plan to acquire Grumman stock having an aggregate fair market value not exceeding 10% of the fair market value of the assets of the Plan. This provision, the trustees point out, was the result of a lengthy debate in which the Department of Labor played an important role; they rely especially on the following passage from its statement to the Senate Finance Committee:

> Especially significant among the expressly allowed transactions is that which permits, in most types of plans, investment of up to ten percent of the fund assets in securities issued by the employer of the employees who are participants in the plan. Since such an employer will often be an administrator of his plan, or will function as a trustee or in some other fiduciary capacity, this provision creates a limited exception to the listed proscription against self-dealing. The exception is made in recognition of *the symbiotic relationship* existing between the employer and the plan covering his employees (emphasis supplied).

Appellants do not contend that these provisions relieve corporate officers or directors who are trustees of a plan of the duties imposed by § 404(a) when dealing with stock of the corporation which is an asset of the Plan. They argue rather that, despite the words "sole" and "exclusive", such officers or directors do not violate their duties by following a course of action with respect to the plan which benefits the corporation as well as the beneficiaries.

We accept the argument but not the conclusion which appellants seem to think follows from it. Although officers of a corporation who are trustees of its pension plan do not violate their duties as trustees by taking action which, after careful and impartial investigation, they reasonably conclude best to promote the interests of participants and beneficiaries simply because it incidentally benefits the corporation or, indeed, themselves, their decisions must be made with an eye single to the interests of the participants and beneficiaries. Restatement of Trusts 2d § 170 (1959). This, in turn, imposes a duty on the trustees to avoid placing themselves in a position where their acts as officers or directors of the corporation will prevent their functioning with the complete loyalty to participants demanded of them as trustees of a pension plan.

There is much to be said for the Secretary's argument that the participation of Bierwirth and Freese in the directors' decision of September 25 press release announcing the unanimous decision of the board to do this on the ground, *inter alia,* of its inadequacy; the sending of Bierwirth's letter of September 28 repeating this and also announcing that the LTV offer was a threat to the pension fund; and the other activities of Bierwirth and Freese in opposing the offer precluded their exercising the detached judgment required of them as trustees of the Plan, and that the only proper course was for the trustees immediately to resign so that a neutral trustee or trustees could be swiftly appointed to serve for the duration of the tender offer. Looking at the matter realistically we find it almost impossible to see how Bierwirth and Freese, after what they had said and done between September 24 and October 7, could have voted to tender or even to sell the Plan's stock, no matter how compelling the evidence for one or the other of those courses might have been.[9] Grumman shareholders who had acted in accordance with the company's pleas would have had every reason to consider such action a breach of faith. Even though the district judge had not seen or heard Freese, he was not required to accept Freese's deposition testimony that his mind "was not absolutely made up" until he got to the October 7 meeting and that he "hadn't predecided" what his answer would be. . . .

We are not, however, required to go so far in this case. The record contains specific instances of the trustees' failure to observe the high standard of duty placed upon them. Bierwirth and Freese should have been immediately aware of the difficult position which they occupied as a result of having decided as directors some of the same questions they would have to decide as trustees, and should have explored where their duty lay. Instead the question of a trustees' meeting was treated quite casually—something to be attended to when the hectic pace of fighting the tender offer would permit. One way for the trustees to inform themselves would have been to solicit the advice of independent counsel; Mullan, a junior Grumman employee, was under disabilities similar to those of the trustees themselves. He could hardly have been expected to tell the trustees that the better course would be to resign or even to suggest investigations which might alter the judgment of total

---

[9] We are not impressed with the defendants' argument that they, and particularly Bierwirth, had nothing to fear from the LTV offer in light of LTV's announced intention to make Grumman's office the headquarters of its aerospace division and to retain Bierwirth as C.E.O. of that division. No offer was made with respect to Freese or Paladino. Even as to Bierwirth there have been countless instances where, even when a proposal to retain the chief executive of the target was wholly sincere, he will have disappeared within a year or so. Moreover, being C.E.O. of a division of LTV was not the same thing as being C.E.O. of an independent Grumman. The press currently recounts how high corporate executives are equipping themselves with "golden parachutes" providing large benefits in the event that the executive is dismissed or even if he quits on his own volition after a takeover.

commitment to defeating the LTV offer that management had already expressed. We do not mean by this either that trustees confronted with a difficult decision need always engage independent counsel or that engaging such counsel and following their advice will operate as a complete whitewash which, without more, satisfies ERISA's prudence requirement. But this was, and should have been perceived to be, an unusual situation peculiarly requiring legal advice from someone above the battle. . . .

An even more telling point against the trustees is their swift movement from a decision not to tender or sell[15] the shares already in the fund to a decision to invest more than $44,000,000 in the purchase of additional Grumman shares up to the 10% maximum permitted by § 407(a)(2) of ERISA. Their argument is that once they had reasonably decided not to tender the shares already in the fund since success of the offer would run counter to the interests of the beneficiaries, it followed that they should do everything else they lawfully could do to thwart the offer. This, however, should have involved a calculation of the risks and benefits involved. Bierwirth properly conceded that a further investment in Grumman shares had to be "the right thing for us to do." The trustees' consideration of this was woefully inadequate. Although Grumman shares may have seemed attractive when selling in the high 20's, with what appeared a good chance of appreciation, [they] were not necessarily attractive when, under the impetus of the tender offer, they had risen to the high 30's. Moreover, and even more important, in purchasing additional shares when they did, the trustees were buying into what, from their own point of view, was almost certainly a "no-win" situation. If the LTV offer succeeded, the Plan would be left as a minority stockholder in an LTV-controlled Grumman—a point that seems to have received no consideration. If it failed, as the Plan's purchase of additional 8% of the outstanding Grumman stock made more likely, the stock was almost certain to sink to its pre-offer level, as the trustees fully appreciated. Given the trustees' views as to the dim future of an LTV-controlled Grumman, it is thus exceedingly difficult to accept Bierwirth's testimony that the purchase of additional shares was justified from an investment standpoint—or even to conclude that the trustees really believed this. Investment considerations dictated a policy of waiting. If LTV's offer were accepted, the trustees would not want more Grumman shares; if it failed, the shares would be obtainable at prices far below what was paid. Mid-October 1981 was thus the worst possible time for the Plan to buy Grumman stock as an investment.[16] It is almost

---

[15] The record does not indicate that sale was even considered, although that course had some attractions. It would have eliminated the possibilities that if the Plan did not tender and the offer succeeded, the Plan might be left as a minority stockholder in an LTV controlled Grumman, and that, if the Plan did tender and the offer succeeded, the Plan might be left with some Grumman stock, because of the 70% maximum in the tender offer.

[16] The judge was not bound to accept the trustees' claim that purchases of considerable amounts of Grumman stock could not be made (and that their failure to purchase Grumman stock earlier although their belief in its attractiveness was claimed to go back to the summer of 1981 was thereby explained) on the ground that, with a daily volume of only 20,000 shares, substantial purchases would have greatly increased the price. No expert testified to that effect and no explanation was offered how the Plan had managed to accumulate 525,000 shares when, as Bierwirth stated, the market had been much thinner. Even if we assume that a carefully executed buying program would have somewhat boosted the price, there was no testimony that

impossible to believe that the trustees did not realize this and that their motive for purchasing the additional shares was for any purpose other than blocking the LTV offer. Moreover, even if we were to make the dubious assumption that a purchase for this purpose would have been permissible despite all the investment risks that it entailed, the trustees should at least have taken all reasonable steps to make sure the purchase was necessary. As indicated, Bierwirth was under the impression that the necessary 50.01% would not be tendered—an expectation not unnatural in view of the fact that Grumman's investment and pension plans already owned nearly a third of the shares—although he could not be sure. The record gives no explanation why, if additional shares were to be purchased, this could not have been done by Grumman, in some way that would not reduce the number of outstanding shares, with the bank credit Freese had negotiated in part for that very purpose, rather than by the Plan. There is also nothing to indicate that the trustees, or other Grumman officers or directors, had been willing to risk their own funds in buying additional Grumman shares in the interval before the Plan was free to act. While the trustees did wait over the week-end of October 10 and 11 to see whether the judge's decision on Grumman's application for a preliminary injunction would come down, there is nothing to indicate any effort to ascertain from the judge's chambers when this could be expected, although such an inquiry would have been entirely proper. To be sure, the trustees could not have foretold what the decision would have been but if they had known that it was expected to be filed on October 14, they could well have decided to postpone the expenditure of $44,000,000 of the Plan's money in buying Grumman shares even if denial of the injunction might have somewhat increased the price of the stock.

We do not join in all of the district judge's pejorative adjectives concerning the trustees. They were caught in a difficult and unusual situation—apparently, so far as shown in the briefs, one that had not arisen before. We accept that they were honestly convinced that acquisition of Grumman by the debt-ridden LTV would mean a less bright future for Grumman and also that an LTV acquisition posed some special dangers to the participants of the Plan. However, they should have realized that, since their judgment on this score could scarcely be unbiased, at the least they were bound to take every feasible precaution to see that they had carefully considered the other side, to free themselves, if indeed this was humanly possible, from any taint of the quick negative reaction characteristic of targets of hostile tender offers displayed at the September 24 board meeting, and particularly to consider the huge risks attendant on purchasing additional Grumman shares at a price substantially elevated by the tender offer. We need not decide whether even this would have sufficed; perhaps, after the events of late September, resignation was the only proper course. It is enough that, for the reasons we have indicated, as well as others, the district judge was warranted in concluding, on the materials before him, that the trustees had not measured up to the high standards imposed by

---

this would have been anything like the increase of ten points that had resulted from LTV's $45 offer.

§ 404(a)(1)(A) and (B) of ERISA. How the situation will appear after a trial is a different matter which we cannot now decide.

2. LIABILITY ISSUES

1. *Provisional relief.* The opinion in *Bierwirth* reproduced above is the appeal to the Second Circuit from Judge Mishler's decisions in the district court, 538 F.Supp. 463 (E.D.N.Y.1981), and 2 E.B.C. 2430 (E.D.N.Y.1982). Judge Mishler provisionally enjoined the trustees from further dealings with the pension plan's holdings of Grumman securities except with court approval, and he appointed an investment manager to act as a receiver of the plan's Grumman shares *pendente lite.* In a portion of the Second Circuit opinion not reproduced above, Judge Friendly reversed the lower court's decision to appoint an investment manager, reasoning that the preliminary injunction against further dealings with Grumman securities sufficiently protected the plan.

The time pressures in takeover contests frequently cause the issues to arise—at least initially—on a motion for preliminary injunction or for a temporary restraining order. In such cases the court often works from provisional evidence, such as the depositions, affidavits, and related exhibits in *Bierwirth,* rather than from trial evidence and findings. In the particular case, Judge Mishler treated "[t]he material facts [as] either conceded or beyond dispute;" hence he was prepared to dispense with an evidentiary hearing and he made "findings of fact and conclusions of law as required by Rule 52(a) of the Federal Rules of Civil Procedure." 538 F.Supp. at 465. The Second Circuit, knowing that trial evidence would have to be taken on damages issues on remand, seemed to view the findings as provisional; see the concluding line of the opinion as reproduced above.

2. *ERISA's authorization of nonneutral fiduciaries.* It has been emphasized in Chapter 13 that the duty of loyalty is a centerpiece of ERISA fiduciary law. The exclusive benefit rule of § 404(a)(1)(A) requires an ERISA fiduciary to "discharge his duties with respect to a plan solely in the interest of the beneficiaries [and] for the exclusive purpose [of] providing benefits to participants and their beneficiaries." The noninurement rule of § 403(c)(1) has a similar purport; so do the prohibited transaction rules of § 406(a)–(b).

Bierwirth and his co-trustees were both plan trustees and corporate officers. The two roles gave rise to a serious conflict of interest. The three trustees were required to act for the exclusive benefit of the plan participants and beneficiaries in circumstances in which zealous performance of that duty might have cost them their jobs with the corporation (as explained in footnote 9 of the opinion).

How can such nonneutral persons serve as ERISA fiduciaries, consistent with their ERISA duty of loyalty? The starting point is § 408(c)(3), which effectively authorizes such conflicts. It overrides the prohibited transaction rules to allow "an officer, employee, agent or other representative of a party in interest" to serve as fiduciary. Section 408(c)(3) is, as a practical matter, one of the most important provisions in ERISA, because it legitimates conflict-of-interest situations that would otherwise be per se violations of ERISA's prohibited transaction rules.

Judge Friendly tried to reconcile § 408(c)(3) with ERISA's duties of loyalty and prudence by minimizing the conflict. While insisting that the interested trustees had to make their decisions "with an eye single to the interests of the participants and beneficiaries," he nevertheless found that the conflicted trustees "do not violate their duties as trustees by taking action [to] promote the interests of participants and beneficiaries simply because [the action] *incidentally* benefits the corporation or, indeed, [themselves]" (emphasis supplied). How might one resist that argument?

By its terms, § 408(c)(3) negates liability under the prohibited transaction rule of § 406, but does not speak to a fiduciary's duties of loyalty under §§ 404(a)(1)(A) and 403(c)(1). Does § 408(c)(3) apply to those rules by implication? In other circumstances, the courts have said that a prohibited transaction exemption under § 408(c) does not create a defense under § 404(a). See, e.g., Patelco Credit Union v. Sahni, 262 F.3d 897, 910 (9th Cir.2001) (sustaining DoL regulation, that § 408(c) exemption for "reasonable compensation" bears only on party in interest transactions under § 406(a) and does not excuse self-dealing under § 406(b) or § 404(a)(1)(A)).

Section 408(c)(3) is a stunning departure from ERISA's main principles of fiduciary responsibility. Why did the drafters allow it? And why do plan sponsors want to have their officers and employees serve as trustees or in other fiduciary capacities? What might be the effects of not having § 408(c)(3), or of repealing it?

3.   *When conflict arises.* The ordinary fiduciary has a duty to avoid conflicts of interest. How should the § 408(c)(3) fiduciary, who has a structural conflict of interest, act in circumstances in which a serious conflict arises?

DoL argued in *Bierwirth* that the conflict in that case was so intense that the trustees should have resigned in favor of neutral trustees. Under a typical pension trust instrument, the trustees would have selected their successors. Whom could they have chosen? Would a corporate fiduciary, such as a bank trust department, chosen by the trustees have been adequately neutral?

In recent years, firms that serve as independent ERISA fiduciaries have developed. See, e.g., www.fiduciarycounselors.com (website of one such provider).

In some circumstances the act of resigning can itself amount to a breach of fiduciary duty. An ERISA fiduciary may not resign for the purpose of ignoring or facilitating a breach of trust; see Ream v. Frey, 107 F.3d 147 (3d Cir.1997). See also Allison v. Bank One-Denver, 289 F.3d 1223, 1239 (10th Cir.2002) (endorsing earlier authority that "a resignation is valid only when [the resigning fiduciary] has made adequate provision for continued prudent management of the plan assets").

Even if the trustees in *Bierwirth* were not obliged to resign, the Second Circuit said, they should have discharged their fiduciary responsibility differently. In lieu of casual meetings with a junior Grumman lawyer, the trustees might have "solicit[ed] the advice of independent counsel [from] someone above the battle." Can you suggest any reason for thinking that such a step would have been an illusory safeguard?

Another path open to conflicted fiduciaries in the trust tradition is to seek instruction from the court. The Restatement provides: "The trustee is entitled to apply to the court for instructions as to the administration of the trust if there is reasonable doubt as to his duties or powers as trustee." Restatement (Second) of Trusts § 259 (1959). In modern civil practice such a petition usually takes the form of an action for a declaratory judgment, see e.g. Central Trust Co. v. American Avents Corp., 771 F.Supp. 871 (S.D.Ohio 1989) (granting declaratory judgment approving ESOP trustee's tender of plan shares in response to a tender offer).

4. *Process values.* Judge Friendly expressed his discomfort about the way the *Bierwirth* trustees had conducted their deliberations. He remarked that "the question of a trustees' meeting was treated quite casually—something to be attended to when the hectic pace of fighting the tender offer would permit." Process values—that is, adhering to procedures of orderly investigation, consultation with advisors, deliberation, and recordation—loom large in professional fiduciary practice. "In cases involving the propriety of investments, the decision-making process may be as important as the decision itself, at least for purposes of determining the trustee's responsibility." A. Walter Nossaman et al., Trust Administration and Taxation § 29.05[2] (1976 & 2009 Supp.). In Donovan v. Mazzola, 716 F.2d 1226, 1232 (9th Cir.1983), the court said that the question posed under the prudence norm was "whether the individual trustees, at the time they engaged in the challenged transactions, employed the appropriate methods to investigate the merits of the investment and to structure the investment."

In routine investment matters, best practice is for the trustees or other investment fiduciaries to develop an investment policy statement, which is a written document prepared with expert advisors, establishing risk/return objectives and other investment policies, and allocating responsibilities. See, e.g., Foundation for Fiduciary Studies, Prudent Investment Practices: A Handbook for Investment Fiduciaries 9, 25 (2004 ed.), identifying "preparation of the investment policy statement [as] one of the most critical functions" of the fiduciary, among the "[p]ractices that define a prudent investment management process." See also Eugene B. Burroughs, The Investment Policy Statement, 41 Benefits & Compensation Digest 1 (Dec. 2004). DoL's recommendation, 29 C.F.R. § 2509.94–2, that named fiduciaries adopt formal "statements of investment policy" to guide investment managers investing in voting proxies on behalf of the plan is discussed below, in the note on voting plan shares.

5. *ERISA's 10 percent ceiling on employer securities.* ERISA § 407(a) limits a defined benefit plan to investing no more than 10 percent of its assets in employer securities or realty. Although Bierwirth and his co-trustees kept the Grumman plan's investment in employer stock below that ceiling, they were held to have acted imprudently. Thus, the court read § 407(a) to set a ceiling but not an authorization. The prudence and

diversification rules of § 404(a) govern the question of how much less than 10 percent may be appropriate.

As of 2003 employer stock constituted about 1.5 percent of the assets of the thousand largest defined benefit plans. See "Average Asset Mix of the Top 1,000 Plans," Pension & Investments, Jan. 26, 2004, at 22. The corresponding figure for the largest thousand defined contribution plans, which are exempt from ERISA's diversification rules for employer stock, was 27.2%. Id. Employer stock plan issues are discussed below in Section D of this chapter.

6. *Prohibited transactions.* The Second Circuit refused to apply the prohibited transaction rule of § 406(b)(2) to the trustees' dealings in the *Bierwirth* case, although the point did not much matter, since the court thought the trustees breached their duties of loyalty (exclusive benefit) and prudence, §§ 404(a)(1)(A) and (B). Do you agree with the court that it is difficult to view the trustees as acting on behalf of a party whose interests are adverse to the plan? In a later case Judge Cudahy disagreed. Leigh v. Engle, 727 F.2d 113, 126–27 (7th Cir.1984). DoL policymakers insist that Judge Friendly erred in not applying ERISA § 406(b) in *Bierwirth*. Morton Klevan, The Fiduciary's Duty of Loyalty under ERISA Section 406(b)(1), 23 Real Property, Probate & Trust J. 561, 565–67 (1988).

7. *Protecting the wrong interests?* The court's analysis seems unanswerable that purchasing the additional 1,158,000 shares of Grumman was a "no-win" move; either the takeover would be defeated and the Grumman shares would fall in value; or, if the LTV takeover succeeded despite the defensive efforts, the plan would have paid a premium for a minority position in a Grumman Corp., which was about to be captured by an acquiring corporation that the trustees mistrusted. "Mid-October 1981 was thus the worst possible time for the plan to buy Grumman stock as an investment. It is almost impossible to believe that the trustees did not realize this and that their motive for purchasing the additional shares was for any purpose other than blocking the LTV offer." Accordingly, the trustees "had not measured up to the high standards imposed by § 404(a)(1)(A) and (B) of ERISA"—the exclusive benefit rule and the duty of prudence.

Notice, however, the reaction of the plan participants. The Second Circuit opinion says near the outset: "A number of participants in the Plan were allowed to intervene *as defendants*" (emphasis supplied), and that as of the date of the litigation petitions in support of the trustees had been signed by 17,000 of the plan's 22,000 Grumman employee participants. (Ultimately, some plan beneficiaries did sue, sub nom. Ford v. Bierwirth, 636 F.Supp. 540 (E.D.N.Y.1986)).

Why did participants, whom the rules of prudent investing and exclusive benefit mean to protect, side with the trustees who broke the rules? Fischel and Langbein have written:

> Because the plan was a well funded defined benefit plan—the sort of plan in which almost all of the investment risk incides on the sponsor—Grumman's stockholders would bear the capital losses from adverse investment results. Pension plan participants, by contrast, would be relatively unaffected by

investment losses. In their capacity as active employees, however, many of these same participants might have been harmed by the takeover if, for example, LTV would have closed Grumman plants or transferred or terminated Grumman employees. Thus, it was rational for workers to oppose the LTV offer and support plan purchases of Grumman stock to defeat the offer. This is precisely the position that most Grumman employees apparently took; recall that it was the Secretary of Labor, not the employees, who brought the *Bierwirth* lawsuit.

From the perspective of Grumman's stockholders, the situation was different. Not only did they bear the investment losses incurred by the plan, but they would have received a substantial premium for their shares had LTV been able to complete its offer.

The irony of the *Bierwirth* case should now be clear. The Secretary of Labor sued to redress an injury allegedly suffered by the participants and beneficiaries of the plan. Most of them, however, thought that they benefited from the defeat of LTV's offer and supported the trustees' actions. And in any event, because the plan in question was a well funded defined benefit plan, the investment risk was borne by the employer, not by the employees, or the government insurer, the PBGC. The shareholders of the firm, by contrast, on whom the risk did incide, suffered the true injury, yet they went unrepresented in the case.

Daniel Fischel & John H. Langbein, ERISA's Fundamental Contradiction: The Exclusive Benefit Rule, 55 U.Chicago L.Rev. 1105, 1139–40 (1988). Indeed, it has been contended:

The simple truth is that *investment policy is seldom of concern to the participants in a single-employer defined benefit plan.* So long as the plan is significantly overfunded, as many are, the shareholders bear all the risk. In [a significantly overfunded plan, the] participants would be unaffected if the trustees were to go out to Aqueduct [a horse track] tonight and bet a billion on the third nag in the opening race. The victims of the trustees' imprudent investing would be [the sponsor's] shareholders. In the private trust, by contrast, every penny of gain or loss is at the beneficiaries' risk. Yet ERISA fiduciary law ignores the shareholders and gives the protections to the plan participants. ERISA woodenly transposes to pension law the fiduciary rule that makes sense for the private trust, even though the allocation of risk in a pension trust is dramatically altered.

John H. Langbein, The Conundrum of Fiduciary Investing under ERISA, in Proxy Voting of Pension Plan Equity Securities 128, 132 (Pension Research Council) (D. McGill ed. 1989) (emphasis original).

8. *Shareholders.* If, as the foregoing analysis indicates, the real grievance in *Bierwirth* was the shareholders', why did no shareholders intervene in the case or sue independently? See Panter v. Marshall Field & Co., 646 F.2d 271 (7th Cir.1981) (holding as a matter of Delaware law

that the business judgment rule exonerates directors who defeat a hostile takeover and cause the price of the company's shares to plummet).

Because directors and officers fare so well under the doctrines of corporate law that govern in shareholder litigation about defensive tactics, it appears puzzling, as the Second Circuit in *Bierwirth* remarked, that Bierwirth and his co-trustees did not have Grumman purchase the additional shares "with the bank credit Freese had negotiated in part for that very purpose," but rather they had the plan buy the shares. Why might it sometimes be more effective in a takeover defense for the plan to own company shares than the company? See, e.g., Delaware General Corporation Law § 160(c), Del.Code Ann. tit. 8, § 160(c) (1989) (treasury stock not entitled to vote).

Suppose that the *Bierwirth* litigation had resulted in damages against the three defendants. Who would have paid the judgment? Who would have paid if the three had insurance in their capacities as Grumman officers? As plan fiduciaries? See ERISA § 410(b). Suppose that the three defendants had negotiated an indemnity agreement with Grumman, that Grumman would make them whole in the event of liability arising from their service as plan fiduciaries. Would the agreement be valid under § 410(a)? Section 410(a) is discussed in connection with exculpation issues in Chapter 13, supra. If such an agreement were valid, would it be fair to describe the result in *Bierwirth* as shareholders paying to have management use corporate assets to defeat shareholder interests?

9. *Retirement income security versus employment income security.* Most of the plan participants in the *Bierwirth* case did not want the pension assets protected; they preferred to see the pension assets used to fend off a takeover that many perceived as a threat to their employment continuity. 680 F.2d at 265. Should ERISA's protective policy (manifested in such places as the antialienation rule of § 206(d)(1), discussed supra in Chapter 7) prevent a plan fiduciary from trading the participants' retirement income security in exchange for employment income security? Since employment security yields the income stream that funds present consumption, using pension wealth to promote employment security can be seen to be merely a two-step path around the antialienation rule. On the other hand, continued employment is the source of continued contributions to the employee's retirement account.

10. *Conflicts of interest among plan participants and beneficiaries.* Most plan participants sided with management's use of plan assets to defeat the takeover of Grumman, but not all. Some participants could not have benefited from protecting Grumman jobs—for example, plan participants and beneficiaries who were already retired and in "pay status," that is, presently drawing retirement benefits; and those active (typically senior) participants whose employment was most secure. They had no interest in impairing their retirement income security to enhance the employment prospects of younger workers.

ERISA's exclusive benefit rule does not by terms direct ERISA fiduciaries to take account of such conflicts of interests among plan participants and beneficiaries. The common law of trusts imposes upon the trustee a duty of impartiality, that is, to give due regard to the interests of all the beneficiaries of the trust. Restatement (Third) of

Trusts § 79 (2007). Assuming that the duty of impartiality applies by implication from the duty of loyalty, how should plan fiduciaries balance such strongly adverse interests as those in *Bierwirth?*

11. *Underfunded plans: the interest of the PBGC.* Suppose the Grumman plan had been underfunded:

> [E]ven if the Grumman pension plan had been underfunded, the participants would have borne little risk. The employer is liable to make up a funding deficiency, which means that the primary risk still incides on the firm's shareholders. In the rare case in which insolvency results in employer default, Title 4 of ERISA has arranged that the Pension Benefit Guaranty Corporation [PBGC] will stand in for the firm, in order to honor the firm's defined benefit pension promises. [ERISA § 4022(a).]
>
> If the employer defaults, the PBGC must pay the defaulted benefits. When PBGC pays, it has recourse against the employer for the amount paid, up [to] the employer's net worth [ERISA § 4062], but an employer that defaults on pension promises usually has little net worth. A sick company that pays workers with extravagant pension promises in lieu of cash wages creates contingent liabilities for the PBGC. In such circumstances, the party with the greatest interest in the management of the plan's assets is, therefore, not the participants (whom ERISA fiduciary law needlessly protects), but the PBGC. . . . The existing scheme presents a classic moral hazard problem, encouraging sick companies to take excessive risk in pension affairs. If the coin turns up heads for the firm that makes risky pension promises, the managers and shareholders win. [If] the coin comes up [tails], PBGC does a giant share of the losing.
>
> In private trust law, by contrast, only the beneficiaries of the trust fund are at risk from trustee misconduct, which is why trust fiduciary law protects only the beneficiaries. The insight that ERISA's drafters failed to capture in their fiduciary law is that in the ERISA pension trust the nominal trust beneficiaries (that is, the plan participants and their beneficiaries) are seldom at risk; accordingly, the fiduciary rules should have been more concerned to protect the employer's stockholders and the PBGC than the plan participants.

Langbein, The Conundrum of Fiduciary Investing under ERISA, supra, at 131–33.

ERISA fiduciary law takes no account of the interest of the PBGC. Should it? The argument has been made, id. at 133 n.21: "PBGC should have the ability to restrict corporate spending, dividends, and plan investments when severe underfunding puts the PBGC at serious risk." Issues affecting the soundness of PBGC are discussed supra in Chapter 6, treating plan termination.

12. *Harley: Does overfunding excuse breach of fiduciary duty?* Harley v. Minnesota Mining & Manufacturing Co., 284 F.3d 901 (8th Cir.2002), cert. denied, 537 U.S. 1106 (2003), concerned a $20 million investment made on behalf of a defined benefit pension plan in a hedge

fund, which became insolvent. The fund's managers had violated contractual risk limits with the plan. On behalf of the plan, a class of participants sued 3M, the employer, which had acted as investment manager for the plan. The class alleged that 3M breached its ERISA duties as a prudent investor to investigate and monitor the investment appropriately. Although finding that these counts would otherwise have stated a cause of action, the district court dismissed the case, reasoning that because "the Plan's portfolio [was] in a surplus position, [the] investment [in question] has not caused [plaintiffs] or the Plan any cognizable harm." Harley v. Minnesota Mining & Manufacturing Co., 42 F.Supp.2d 898, 912 (D.Minn.1999). The Eighth Circuit sustained the outcome but reformulated the rationale, rejecting the views of the DoL, which had filed an amicus brief. The court recognized that the $20 million investment was a loss that "reduced the pool of Plan assets," hence that the district court erred in finding that the loss did not cause the plan harm. 284 F.3d at 905. Because, however, the plan was overfunded, and because "a relatively modest loss to Plan surplus is a loss only to 3M, the Plan's sponsor," the Eighth Circuit concluded that the plaintiffs lacked standing "under § [502(a)(2)] to seek relief under § [409] for this particular breach of duty." 284 F.3d at 906. Dismissal was warranted because "the Plan's surplus was sufficiently large that [the] investment loss did not cause actual injury to plaintiffs' interests in the Plan." Id. at 907.

What, if anything, is wrong with the Eighth Circuit's reasoning? See Dana Muir, ERISA and Investment Issues, 65 Ohio St. L.J. 199, 206–30 (2004); Vineeta Anand, Court Says Overfunded Plan Safe from Participant Suit: Appellate Ruling Seems at Odds with ERISA, Pensions & Investments, Apr. 1. 2002, at 1; Note, Harley v. 3M: Eighth Circuit Takes a Constitutional, 10 ERISA Litigation Rptr. 18 (Apr. 2002). In 2009 an Eighth Circuit panel was asked to reconsider *Harley* but refused. McCullough v. AEGON USA Inc., 585 F.3d 1082 (8th Cir.2009).

13. *Duty to tender.* The ERISA agencies issued a statement in 1989 saying that ERISA fiduciary law does not require "the plan fiduciary automatically to tender shares held by the plan to capture the premium over market represented by the tender offer." "Joint Department of Labor/Department of Treasury Statement on Pension Investments," Jan. 31, 1989, reprinted in 16 BNA Pension Rptr. 215 (1989). "It would also be proper to weigh the long-term value of the company against the value presented by the tender offer and the ability to invest the proceeds elsewhere. In making these determinations, the long-term business plan of the target company's management would be relevant." Is the Joint Statement sound?

14. *Aftermath.* In April 1994, more than a decade after the *Bierwirth* litigation, Grumman agreed to be acquired by Northrop Corporation, after a bidding war between Northrop and Martin Marietta. Northrop Offer of $2.17 Billion Wins Grumman, Wall St. J., Apr. 5, 1994, at A3. Northrop paid $62 a share for Grumman, which, adjusted for a 2-for-1 Grumman stock split in 1983, amounted to $124 per share for shares that the *Bierwirth* defendants had purchased for $38.27. Equity prices in general tripled between the early 1980s and the mid-1990s.

Paul Thayer left LTV in January 1983 to become Deputy Secretary of Defense in the Reagan Administration. He resigned from that post when the SEC charged him with insider trading violations under the Securities Acts. Thayer confessed to having tipped his friends, Billy Bob Harris, a Dallas stockbroker, and Sandra K. Ryno, a former LTV receptionist, with whom the SEC alleged that Thayer had a "private personal relationship." These associates and others were alleged to have made profits exceeding $1.9 million trading on Thayer's tips. Thayer, who served on the boards of Anheuser-Busch and Allied Corporation, was also alleged to have leaked information regarding various merger and acquisition plans of those two companies, and to have leaked information on LTV's unsuccessful tender offer to acquire Grumman in 1981. In May 1985, Thayer, Billy Bob Harris, and another associate settled the civil suit brought by the SEC for a then-record figure in excess of $1 million. Thayer, Others to Settle Case for $1 Million, Wall St. J., May 8, 1985. In the related criminal case, both Thayer and Harris pled guilty to lying to the SEC and otherwise obstructing justice. Both were sentenced to four years in prison and fined the maximum $5,000. Thayer, Friend Are Sentenced to Four Years, Wall St. J., May 9, 1985. At the time these sentences were the longest ever imposed in an insider-trading case. Thayer served fourteen months of the sentence, the latter part in a half-way house in Dallas, where he apparently worked as a trainee at a property-management concern. After the Fall: Fates are Disparate for Those Charged With Insider Trading, Wall St. J., Nov. 18, 1987.

3. DAMAGES ISSUES

1. *Computing the loss in Bierwirth.* On March 10, 1983, with the district court's consent, the plan trustees sold 1,200,000 shares of Grumman at $47.50 per share, "producing a profit of $13,212,780 above the cost of the [1,158,000] shares acquired on October 12 and 13, 1981." Donovan v. Bierwirth, 4 E.B.C. 2173, 2174 (E.D.N.Y.1983).

DoL argued that the trustees' misconduct in spending $44,397,720 to buy the 1,158,000 shares of Grumman in October 1981 produced an initial loss of $18,562,740 (the difference between the average price of $38.34 per share that the plan paid and the fair market value of $22.31, calculated on the price range before LTV's offer and immediately after its defeat). Donovan v. Bierwirth, 5 E.B.C. 1065 (E.D.N.Y.1984). Relying on ERISA § 409(a), which makes a breaching fiduciary liable to make "good to such plan any losses to the plan resulting from each such breach," DoL sought as the measure of damages the investment return that the plan would have made had it invested the $44,397,720 in any of three benchmark portfolios during the period in question, from the purchase in 1981 to the sale in 1983. On this theory, the trustees would have been liable for between $20.3 and $23.2 million.

The Second Circuit endorsed the use of benchmark damages, saying that "the district court should presume that the funds would have been treated like other funds being invested during the same period in proper transactions. Where several alternative investment strategies were equally plausible, the court should presume that the funds would have been used in the most profitable of these. The burden of proving that the funds would have earned less than that amount is on the fiduciaries found to be in breach of their duty. Any doubt or ambiguity should be resolved against them." 754 F.2d 1049, 1056 (2d Cir.1985). For a later instance of resort to benchmark portfolios to measure damages arising in the case of a wrongful underperforming investment, see GIW Industries v. Trevor, Stewart, Burton & Jacobsen, Inc., 10 E.B.C. 2290, 2298–99, 2305 (S.D.Ga.1989).

Although the Second Circuit reversed Judge Mishler's finding that "the plan suffered no loss as a result of the trustees' violation of their fiduciary obligation," 5 E.B.C. at 1066, the Second Circuit allowed the trial court discretion to "pick a date on which the relative performance of the plan and the improper investment may fairly be compared." 754 F.2d 1049, 1058 (2d Cir.1985). Judge Mishler used that discretion to reinstate his result. He found that because the plan investment in Grumman shares outperformed the benchmark portfolios during the period between the breach and the sale of the Grumman shares in 1983, the trustees were not liable to the plan. Ford v. Bierwirth, 636 F.Supp. 540 (E.D.N.Y.1986).

The key issue in the *Bierwirth* damages litigation was whether, as DoL urged, to determine the trustees' initial liability as of the October 1981 purchase and drop in value of the shares; or whether, as Judge Mishler permitted, to fix the liability as of the time of the sale of the shares in 1983. Commentators have criticized Judge Mishler's solution: "Grumman stock, like other defense stocks, rose in value during the early 1980s as a result of the defense build-up. This increase in the value of defense stocks should have been irrelevant in determining whether the plan incurred any losses at the time of the trustees' decision to oppose the offer. Instead, the Second Circuit allowed the trustees to appropriate by way of set off the appreciation in trust assets." Fischel & Langbein, supra, 55 U.Chicago L.Rev. at 1140 n.126.

Consider the Restatement rule: "A trustee who is liable for a loss caused by a breach of trust may not reduce the amount of the liability by deducting the amount of a profit that accrued through another and distinct breach of trust; but if the breaches of trust are not separate and distinct, the trustee is accountable only for the net gain or chargeable only with the net loss resulting therefrom." Restatement (Second) of Trusts § 213 (1959). Judge Mishler held that the trustees' purchase and retention of the Grumman stock from 1981 to 1983 was "one distinct breach of trust and the Trustees may therefore offset any losses to the Plan for such purchases against the profit from the sale of such stock." 4 E.B.C. 2173, 2177 (E.D.N.Y.1983). Assuming that Restatement § 213 reflects the standard that ought to be applied to determine the trustees' liability under ERISA § 409(a), how might one resist the judge's application of the standard?

Would it be fair to say that the wrongdoers in *Bierwirth* escaped scot free? If the duty of loyalty intends a deterrent policy, was that policy well-served? Compare Dardaganis v. Grace Capital Inc., 889 F.2d 1237 (2d Cir.1989), which involved an investment manager who had exceeded the 50 percent cap on equities contained in its investment agreement with an ERISA fund. The Second Circuit approved the district court's conclusion "that the measure of the damages caused by investing more than 50% of the Fund's assets in equities was the difference between the earnings of the Fund as invested and what the earnings would have been if the 50% limit had been observed and the assets had been invested in non-equity securities instead." 889 F.2d at 1243. The Second Circuit sustained this measure against the argument that no actual harm resulted from the breach, since the excess equity holdings had increased somewhat in value, although not as much as the non-equities. Citing *Bierwirth*, the Second Circuit said: "If, but for the breach, the fund would have earned more than it actually earned, there is a 'loss' for which the breaching fiduciary is liable." Id. Damages in the case were ultimately calculated at about $1.5 million. 18 BNA Pension Rptr. 183 (1991).

2. *Disgorging profits.* Leigh v. Engle, 727 F.2d 113 (7th Cir.1984), presents a situation that is in one sense the reverse of *Bierwirth:* not the target company using pension assets for a takeover defense, but the acquiring firm using plan assets to conduct takeovers.

Large pension funds sometimes participate as lenders or equity investors in takeover ventures. What proved problematic in *Leigh v. Engle* was that the acquiring firm employed assets of *its own* profit sharing plan as a small part of the funds that the firm used to conduct takeover campaigns against three small companies. As in *Bierwirth,* the trustees in *Leigh v. Engle* were insiders of the firm. Unlike *Bierwirth,* the plan's investments in *Leigh v. Engle* turned out to be exceptionally profitable. Roughly 30 percent of the plan's assets were used. The takeovers produced an average annualized rate of return on the plan assets of 72 percent; one investment produced a 66 percent gain, another a 141 percent gain, the third (in shares of Hickory Furniture Company) a skimpy 4 percent gain.

Notwithstanding the profitability of the investments, certain plan participants sued the trustees for breach of ERISA § 404(a)(1)(A) (the exclusive benefit rule) and § 406(a)(1)(D) and (b)(1) (prohibited transactions). The district court found no violations, but the Seventh Circuit reversed, saying that "the district court clearly erred when it concluded that plan assets were used exclusively in the interests of the beneficiaries." Id. at 124. The plaintiffs contended that they were entitled to all the profits that the firm and its insiders made in the three takeover campaigns, including profits that these defendants made using their own investment capital. The Seventh Circuit resisted the claim, citing the language of ERISA's liability standard, § 409(a), authorizing recovery of profits "made through use of assets of the plan." "We believe that this language of section [409] permits recovery of a fiduciary's profits only where there is a causal connection between the use of the plan assets and the profits made by fiduciaries on the investment of their own assets." Id. at 137. How might the plaintiffs have argued that there was the requisite "causal connection"?

On remand the district court analyzed the three investments separately and found liability for $6,704—the amount by which the 4 percent return on the Hickory Furniture shares underperformed a benchmark portfolio. Leigh v. Engle, 669 F.Supp. 1390, 1395–96, 1405 (N.D.Ill.1987), aff'd 858 F.2d 361 (7th Cir.1988), cert. denied, 489 U.S. 1078 (1989). Liability in *Leigh v. Engle* was predicated solely on breach of the duty of loyalty. Might other grounds have been present? See Fischel & Langbein, supra, 55 U.Chicago L.Rev. at 1143.

Leigh v. Engle was followed in Sandoval v. Simmons, 622 F.Supp. 1174 (C.D.Ill.1985), another case in which an ERISA fiduciary, who was waging a contest for corporate control with non-pension assets, caused the pension fund to invest in support of his takeover activities. The court found that he violated both the duty of loyalty, ERISA § 404(a)(1)(A), and the prohibited transaction rules §§ 406(a)(1)(D) and 406(b)(1)–(2), notwithstanding that he acted in good faith and that the transactions "ultimately 'paid off well' for the [pension funds]." Accord, Felber v. Estate of Regan, 117 F.3d 1084 (8th Cir.1997) (self-dealing fiduciary must disgorge all profits even though plan benefitted from transaction).

3. *Injunctive relief.* ERISA § 409 authorizes restitutionary relief for breach of fiduciary duty, together with "such other equitable or remedial relief as the court may deem appropriate, including removal of [the] fiduciary." Section 502(a)(2) authorizes a suit for equitable relief to enforce § 409; and § 502(a)(3) authorizes injunctive relief or "other appropriate equitable relief" to enforce ERISA requirements or plan terms. Beck v. Levering, 947 F.2d 639 (2d Cir.1991), involved fiduciaries of a multiemployer plan who had been found responsible for serious self-dealing that resulted in losses of more than $20 million to the plan. The Second Circuit approved DoL's suit to enjoin the defendants permanently from acting as plan fiduciaries or providing services to ERISA plans, finding "that such a remedy may be appropriate where individuals participate in the kind of egregious self-dealing proved in [this case]." 947 F.2d at 641.

4. VOTING PLAN SHARES

In *Bierwirth* the purchase of the additional 1,158,000 shares was such an astonishing step that it deflected attention away from the other aspect of the trustees' behavior: their decision not to vote (in this instance, not to tender) or not to sell the 525,000 shares that the plan already owned. Does it follow that if the trustees were disloyal and imprudent in buying the additional shares, they were disloyal and imprudent in not selling or tendering the plan's original holdings? If, as the court concluded, the takeover period was the worst time to buy more Grumman shares, was that period for the same reasons the most advantageous moment for the plan to sell or to tender the shares that the plan already owned?

1. *Avon Products Letter: Voting is fiduciary.* There has been some concern that managers of companies that sponsor pension plans, and who are aware that they may someday find themselves in the shoes of Mr. Bierwirth, defending a hostile takeover with their jobs at stake, do not view with favor investment managers who rigorously extract top dollar for plan assets in takeover contests. In 1988 DoL issued its so-called *Avon Products Letter*, emphasizing the fiduciary character of proxy voting (and hence the duty of investment fiduciaries to exercise proxy rights for the exclusive benefit of plan participants and beneficiaries). DoL said: "In general, the fiduciary act of managing plan assets which are shares of corporate stock would include the voting of proxies appurtenant to those shares of stock. For example, it is the Department's position that the decision as to how proxies should be voted . . . are fiduciary acts of plan

asset [management]." DoL, Letter on Proxy Voting by Plan Fiduciaries, Feb. 23, 1988, 15 BNA Pension Rptr. 391 (1988).

2.   *Interpretive Bulletin IB 94–2.* Plan shareholding gives rise to voting rights quite apart from the exceptional event of a contest for corporate control. An important difference between investments in equity (shares) and in debt (bonds) is that holders of debt have no voting rights, save in exceptional circumstances. Shareholders vote on the election of directors, and on corporate transactions that, pursuant to state law or to the corporate bylaws, require shareholder approval. This routine proxy voting is regarded as a nuisance by many pension fund trustees and investment managers, especially those operating passive, market-matching portfolios.

DoL's Interpretive Bulletin IB 94–2, codified as 29 C.F.R. § 2509.94–2, encourages named fiduciaries to adopt formal "statements of investment policy" to guide investment managers investing on behalf of the plan. "Since the fiduciary act of managing plan assets that are shares of corporate stock includes the voting of proxies appurtenant to those shares of stock, a statement of proxy voting policy would be an important part of any comprehensive statement of investment policy." DoL reasoned that "a named fiduciary's determination of the terms of a statement of investment policy is an exercise of fiduciary responsibility and, as such, statements may need to take into account factors such as the plan's funding policy and its liquidity needs as well as issues of prudence, diversification and other fiduciary requirements of ERISA."

The Interpretive Bulletin endorses what it calls "shareholder activism" on matters such as contests for control, election of directors, and executive compensation:

> An investment policy that contemplates activities intended to monitor or influence the management of corporations in which the plan owns stock is consistent with a fiduciary's obligations under ERISA where the responsible fiduciary concludes that there is a reasonable expectation that such monitoring or communication with management, by the plan alone or together with other shareholders, is likely to enhance the value of the plan's investment in the corporation, after taking into account the costs involved.

In a preamble to the Interpretive Bulletin not incorporated in the text, DoL opined that this responsibility for shareholder activism "would not be different for portfolios designed to match the performance of market indexes (sometimes referred to as 'index funds'). In such funds, the investments are often held on a long-term basis and the prudent exercise of proxy voting rights or other forms of corporate monitoring or communication may be the only method available for attempting to enhance the value of the portfolio." 59 Fed. Reg. at 38,862 n.6.

Does a fiduciary remain free to determine that the particular plan should not engage in shareholder activism, on the ground that the costs of investigation incident to active monitoring outweigh the potential gain to the plan?

5. SOCIAL INVESTING

Proposals that trustees or other investment fiduciaries take into account noneconomic factors in investing plan funds exemplify what is known as "social investing" or "socially responsible investing." In the 1990s the term "economically targeted investments" came into use, an odd euphemism for projects about which the main concern has been the risk of insensitivity to economic returns.

Social investing raises questions about the bounds of law and morality. As pension (and other institutional) portfolios grow ever more important, interest in the ethical and political ramifications of such large pools of capital also increases. On the other hand, reservations have been voiced about the dangers of politicizing the investment process. Which causes should social investors embrace? Which companies' shares should be excluded, which included? Was opposition to apartheid better served when companies withdrew from commerce in South Africa, or when they remained there under the Sullivan Principles or similar programs as a force for economic and educational opportunity? Because people of good will differ on such questions, it can be difficult to discern what social investing should entail.

The most intense social investing pressures have been directed at non-ERISA fiduciaries, that is, at the endowment funds of educational and religious organizations; and at the pension funds of state and local governments, which are excluded from ERISA under § 4(b)(1). In the world of ERISA-covered plans, there have been a few efforts at investing multiemployer plan pension funds to stimulate demand for union labor, especially in the construction trades, but in general very little social investing has taken place.

1. *Costlessness.* In 1980, the then chief administrator of the DoL's pension section, Ian Lanoff, and his predecessor, James Hutchinson, each published articles emphasizing that ERISA interposed major legal obstacles to many social investing proposals. Ian D. Lanoff, The Social Investment of Private Pension Plan Assets: May It Be Done Lawfully under ERISA?, 31 Labor L.J. 387 (1980); James D. Hutchinson & Charles G. Cole, Legal Standards Governing Investment of Pension Assets for Social and Political Goals, 128 U. Pennsylvania L. Rev. 1340 (1980). These articles directed attention to ERISA's duties of loyalty and prudent investing and to ERISA's prohibited transaction rules.

Lanoff's paper, based upon his testimony as DoL administrator before a Senate committee, has been especially influential. Lanoff warned that "the adoption of a plan policy which excludes investment opportunities for so-called social purposes would be difficult to defend against challenges raised under the 'solely in the interest and exclusive purpose tests—the basic duty of loyalty tests in ERISA.' " (Presumably, including an investment for noneconomic purposes would be as suspect as excluding an investment for such reasons.) Nonetheless, Lanoff observed that ERISA contained no bar to costless social investing: It would be unobjectionable for plan fiduciaries to pursue "investment opportunities which are economically competitive with other investment opportunities which may not contain similar socially beneficial features." 31 Labor L.J. at 391–92.

The official comment to the Uniform Prudent Investor Act § 5 (1994) accords: "No form of so-called 'social investing' is consistent with the duty of loyalty if the investment activity entails sacrificing the interests of trust beneficiaries—for example, by accepting below-market returns—in favor of the interests of the persons supposedly benefitted by pursuing the particular social cause."

2. *Implementing costlessness.* DoL restated the costlessness standard in an interpretive bulletin (IB 94–1) in 1994, and again in 2008 in IB 08–1, replacing IB–94–1, codified as 29 C.F.R. § 2509.08–1. The regulation reviews DoL's prior analysis of social investing questions and restates the position that plan fiduciaries may engage in social investing only in conformity with the prudence and loyalty standards of ERISA §§ 403–404:

> ERISA's plain text does not permit fiduciaries to make investment decisions on the basis of any factor other than the economic interest of the plan. Situations may arise, however, in which two or more investment alternatives are of equal economic value to a plan. . . .

> Given the significance of ERISA's requirement that fiduciaries act "solely in the interest of participants and beneficiaries," the Department believes that, before selecting an economically targeted investment, fiduciaries must have first concluded that the alternative options are truly equal, taking into account a quantitative and qualitative analysis of the economic impact on the plan. . . . The Department rejects a construction of ERISA that would render the Act's tight limits on the use of plan assets illusory, and that would permit plan fiduciaries to expend ERISA trust assets to promote myriad public policy preferences.

In some settings, compliance with the costlessness standard can be hard to determine. Varieties of social investing designed to pass the costlessness test, such as some union-sponsored construction projects, can be hard to value, because each project is unique. Such deals do not have market prices listed in the published or online tables. Proving whether such a deal was ex ante uneconomic can be difficult. Who bears the burden of showing that a socially motivated investment was costless?

3. *Brock v. Walton.* In Brock v. Walton, 794 F.2d 586 (11th Cir.1986), an Eleventh Circuit panel sustained an investment designed to stimulate construction activity in the then-depressed market in Broward County (Fort Lauderdale), Florida. The trustees of the Operating Engineers Local 675 Pension Fund, a construction industry multiemployer plan, undertook to develop a tract of real estate, employing union labor. Bargain-rate mortgage loans were offered to plan participants, apparently in order to stimulate demand. DoL sued, complaining that the program violated the duties of loyalty and prudent investing as well as the prohibited transaction rules. The Eleventh Circuit concluded that the trustees acted prudently in lending mortgage money for the project at $2^1/_8$ percentage points below the area norm.

The court reasoned that the trustees consulted experts and went through the motions of deliberation, and that the interest rates on the loans were higher than on other parts of the fund's portfolio. Is the court's rationale persuasive? Would you advise other pension fiduciaries that it is now prudent to accept below-market returns on mortgage investments? On other investments?

If a pension trustee were given the choice of investing in two different federal government bond issues that were identical in maturities and in all other respects, save that one issue pays six percent and the other pays four percent, would it be imprudent to forego the higher interest investment? If your answer is yes, have you necessarily decided that the court in *Brock v. Walton* erred in approving the below-market mortgage lending program?

DoL regards *Brock v. Walton* as seriously mistaken and has effectively refused to attribute precedential force to the decision. "[R]egulations promulgated since *Walton* was decided would treat the extension of loans bearing a below-market interest rate as prohibited transactions. 29 C.F.R. § 2550.408b–1 (1991). The regulations squarely contradict the holding in *Walton*." Norman Stein, ERISA and the Limits of Equity, 56 Law & Contemporary Probs. 71, 85 n. 93 (1993).

4. *Defined benefit versus defined contribution.* Whereas the plan sponsor bears the investment risk in a defined benefit plan, the participant bears that risk in a defined contribution plan. Accordingly, the risks incident to social investing strategies will fall on different parties depending upon which type of plan is in question.

Some defined contribution plans offer among their permitted investment options one or more mutual funds that pursue stated social investing criteria. Provided that the plan satisfies the requirements of ERISA § 404(c), which are discussed later in this chapter, making such an option available does not raise fiduciary concerns, because the decision about whether or not to invest any of the participant's account in such a fund is left entirely to the participant. In a private letter ruling in 1991, the IRS said that an IRC § 403(b) plan would not endanger its status as a qualified plan by offering its participants the option to invest in a fund that is restricted to investing in companies that have no ties with a particular foreign country (presumably at that time South Africa). Private Letter Ruling 91–22–081 (Mar. 8, 1991).

5. *Proxy voting.* Social investing issues arise not only in the design of a portfolio (deciding what securities to include and exclude), but also in administering the portfolio, when it comes time to vote plan-owned shares. Shareholder proposals not infrequently raise environmental, foreign policy, or other social concerns. The *Avon Products Letter*, supra, makes it clear that proxy voting is a fiduciary function. How should a pension fiduciary decide what position to take on a shareholder proposal that management opposes? What factors should be considered? What procedures should be employed in deciding how to vote?

Researching the merits of shareholder proposals can be a costly activity, especially for a broadly diversified portfolio that contains hundreds or thousands of different issuers' securities. How should the fiduciary take account of the cost of investigating these proposals in deciding upon its proxy voting procedures?

In 2008, DoL issued an opinion on the question of using "plan assets to promote union organizing campaigns and union goals in collective bargaining negotiations." It said:

> The Department believes the use, or threat of use, of pension plan assets or plan management to achieve a particular collective bargaining objective is activity that subordinates the interests of participants and beneficiaries in their retirement income to unrelated objectives. Although union representation of plan participants and benefit related provisions of collective bargaining agreements may in some sense affect a plan, the fiduciaries may not, consistent with ERISA, increase expenses, sacrifice investment returns, or reduce the security of plan benefits in order to promote or oppose union organizing goals or collective bargaining objectives. In addition, expenditures of plan assets to urge union representation of employees in the collective bargaining process or to promote a particular collective bargaining demand may constitute a prohibited transfer of plan assets for the benefit of a party in interest, under section 406(a)(1)(D) and potentially an act of self-dealing under section 406(b)(1).

DoL Advisory Opinion 2008–05A. The previous year DoL issued a similar opinion disapproving "the use of pension plan assets by plan fiduciaries to further public policy debates and political activities through proxy resolutions that have no connection to enhancing the value of the plan's investment in a company." DoL Advisory Opinion 2007–07A.

6.   *Lobbying.* Does ERISA fiduciary law prevent organized labor from threatening to blacklist a financial services firm that supports changes in the Social Security program opposed by organized labor? In March 2005 two prominent Republican Congressmen complained to DoL that the AFL-CIO was pressuring financial service firms to cease supporting President George W. Bush's proposal to introduce private accounts within the Social Security program, by threatening such firms with the loss of business from union-influenced pension fund accounts. See "Boehner, Johnson Seek Investigation of AFL-CIO's Efforts Targeting Financial Firms," 32 BNA Pension & Benefits Rptr. 718 (2005).

DoL responded by meeting with AFL-CIO representatives, then issuing a letter cautioning that DoL "is very concerned about the potential use of plan assets to promote particular policy positions." Citing *Donovan v. Bierwirth* for the observation that plan fiduciaries must act with an "eye single to the interests of the participants and beneficiaries," the letter cautioned that under ERISA § 404(a)(1)(A) "[a] fiduciary may never increase a plan's expenses, sacrifice the security of promised benefits, or reduce the return on plan assets, in order to promote its views on Social Security or any other broad policy issue." Letter from Alan D. Lebowitz, DoL, to Jonathan P. Hiatt, General Counsel, AFL-CIO, CCH Pension Plan Guide ¶ 19,980OU, May 3, 2005, at 1, 3. The letter conceded that in "certain very narrow circumstances, such as where a legislative proposal is near enactment and closely tied to plan issues, a fiduciary could decide to spend plan assets to educate participants about the need to take legislation into account in making particular decisions about their options under the plan." Id. at 2.

May plan fiduciaries expend plan assets to recommend to participants that they lobby Congress against pending legislation that the fiduciaries regard as adverse to the interests of the participants? Suppose the sponsor is a defense contractor, and the fiduciaries engage lobbyists to oppose (1) threatened cancellation of a weapons system that would result in job losses among participants; and (2) threatened changes in retirement plan taxation that might impair plan funding. Do such differences in the nature of the affected interests bear on the question?

7. *ERISA-exempt plans.* Because ERISA fiduciary law has effectively constrained social investing in the private pension system, the main episodes occur in state and local plans. In Connecticut, the state pension fund lost $25 million attempting to shore up Colt Industries, the Hartford-based manufacturer of guns. The firm went bankrupt two years after the fund bought a 47 percent stake in the company, ostensibly to protect against job losses. Anne Schwimmer, Connecticut's Deal a Bust, Pensions & Investments, Mar. 30, 1992, at 4. The Kansas state pension fund lost between $100 and $200 million on a program of in-state investing, including defaulted loans to a chain of video stores, a steel mill, a failed savings-and-loan bank, and some supposedly high-tech enterprises named Tallgrass Technologies and Hydrogen Energy Corp. James A. White, Picking Losers: Back-Yard Investing Yields Big Losses, Roils Kansas Pension System, Wall St. J., Aug. 21, 1991, at A1. See generally, David L. Gregory, Public Employee Pension Funds: A Cautionary Essay, 41 Labor L.J. 700 (1990).

On June 30, 2010, the SEC approved new rules effectively banning the influence of so-called "pay to play" practices by investment advisers, significantly curtailing their ability to make political contributions to those elected officials with decision-making authority over public pension fund assets. 17 C.F.R. § 275.206(4)–5 (2010). The new rule responds to some recent scandals, including one involving the New York State Common Retirement Fund, in which investment advisers allegedly made campaign contributions with the intention of influencing the recipients' selection of state pension fund asset managers. Rule 206(4)–5.

C. DEFINED CONTRIBUTION PLANS

The drafters of ERISA were preoccupied with the problems of defined benefit plans. The plan termination insurance system of Title 4, which developed in reaction to the Studebaker default, excludes defined contribution plans. ERISA fiduciary law was largely a response to scandal-riddled multiemployer defined benefit plans. (Regarding the origins of ERISA, see supra Chapter 3.) Only a small fraction of plan assets in 1974 were in defined contribution plans, mostly in supplementary profit-sharing plans for the affluent, or in IRC 403(b) plans for academia. Defined contribution plans were at that time relatively problem-free. ERISA would not have been enacted but for the problems of defined benefit plans. Because defined contribution plans did exist, however, Congress made provision for them in ERISA § 404(a)(2) and 404(c), discussed below.

Today's picture is very different. By introducing IRA accounts and ESOPs, ERISA innocuously planted the seeds of the defined contribution future. See Edward A. Zelinsky, The Defined Contribution Paradigm, 114 Yale L.J. 451, 471–82 (2004) (expanded in book form as The Origins of the Ownership Society: How the Defined Contribution Paradigm Came to America (2007)); see generally EBRI, "History of 401(k) Plans: An Update," Facts from EBRI (Feb. 2005). The 401(k) revolution began with modest legislative and regulatory changes in 1978–1980, see Zelinsky, supra, 114 Yale L.J. at 483–84. The number of active participants in defined contribution plans that constituted the participant's primary plan grew from 4 million in 1975 to 19 million in 1993. EBRI, Databook (Mar. 2005), ch. 1, at 5. In 2012, about 52 million American workers were active 401(k) participants, and there were about 515,000 401(k) plans. Investment Company Institute, Frequently Asked Questions About 401(k) Plans, http://www.ici.org/policy/retirement/plan/401k/faqs_401k. At June 30, 2014, 2008, 401(k) plans held $4.4 trillion in assets (up from $2.3 trillion in 2008). Id.

The shift from defined benefit plans to defined contribution plans, discussed supra in Chapter 2, has had many causes and many consequences. The implications for the investment function have been particularly profound. In a defined contribution plan, the participants and beneficiaries bear investment responsibility and investment risk. The employer or other plan sponsor makes no promise to pay any particular level of benefits. Because the employer no longer has obligations for which to invest, the employer no longer invests the plan's assets. The incentives of a defined benefit plan encourage the plan sponsor to develop internally (or to obtain from external providers) professional investment management for the challenges of investing plan assets. The defined contribution plan, by contrast, imposes significant investment responsibility on ordinary workers, who only exceptionally have the skill, experience, interest, and resources needed to engage in portfolio management.

Evidence for the twelve-year period 1995–2006 compiled by Watson Wyatt, a benefits consulting firm, indicates that defined benefit plans outperformed defined contribution plans in investment returns by an average of one percent a year, "a cumulative dollar difference of nearly 14 percent for money invested at the start of the period." CCH, Pension Plan Guide, Jul. 8, 2008, at 1. Wilson Wyatt attributed the difference in performance to the superior skills and resources of the investment professionals who conduct the investing of defined benefit plan assets. Id. Accord, Beth Almeida & William B. Fornia, A Better Bank for the Buck: The Economic Efficiencies of Defined Benefit Pension Plans (Nat'l Institute for Retirement Security, Aug. 2008). A 2013 report found that from 1995 to 2011, DB plans outperformed DC plans by an annual average of 76 basis points. DB plans outperformed DC plans in 13 of the 17 years analyzed. But in 2011, the performance gap between DB and DC plans narrowed by nearly 50%, primarily due to strong DC investment results in 2009. Towers Watson, Defined Benefit Plans Outperform Defined Contribution Plans Again, http://www.towers watson.com/en-US/Insights/Newsletters/Americas/us-finance-matters/2013/Defined-Benefit-Plans-Outperform-Defined-Contribution-Plans-Again.

Not only does the employer bring greater skill to the investment function, the employer operating a defined benefit plan also has superior capability to bear and to spread investment risk. "[T]he employer can average out investment results among cohorts of retirees, so it need not worry about temporary market downturn." Daniel Halperin, Employer-Based Retirement Income—The Ideal, The Possible, and the Reality, 11 Elder L.J. 37, 61 (2003).

1. THE FIDUCIARY REGIME UNDER ERISA § 404(c)

1. *ERISA provisions.* ERISA's main provisions for defined contribution plans are found in § 404(c). ERISA calls them "individual account plans," defined in § 3(34) as a plan that "provides for an individual account for each participant and for benefits based solely upon the amount contributed to the participant's account, and any income, expenses gains and losses, and any forfeitures of accounts of other participants which may be allocated to such participant's account."

Section 404(c) provides that when "a participant or beneficiary exercises control over the assets in his account," the participant or beneficiary does not as a result become an ERISA fiduciary. More importantly, such an "exercise of control" relieves "persons who are otherwise plan fiduciaries" from liability "for any [resulting] loss [or breach]." Thus, § 404(c) is primarily concerned to redraw the lines of fiduciary responsibility under ERISA § 404(a) to clarify that when the participant conducts his or her own investing, the plan fiduciaries are not responsible for decisions that the participant or beneficiary "controls." The question arises, in what circumstances the participant or beneficiary exercises such control.

Another provision, ERISA § 404(a)(2), modifies the duty to diversify for those individual account plans that offer employer stock.

2. *The 404(c) regulations.* Section 404(c) directs DoL to produce regulations regarding the circumstances in which "a participant or beneficiary exercises control over the assets in his [account]." In 1992 DoL promulgated the so-called 404(c) regulations, 29 C.F.R. § 2550.404c–1, also known as the individual account regulations, superseding earlier provisional drafts.

3. *Control.* One branch of the 404(c) regulations focuses on the conditions constituting sufficient participant control. To come within the protection of § 404(c), a plan must "[provide] an opportunity for a participant or beneficiary to exercise control over assets in his individual [account]." 29 C.F.R. § 2550.404c–1(b)(1)(i). But the participant or beneficiary does not exercise the requisite control unless he or she is "provided or has the opportunity to obtain sufficient information to make informed decisions with regard to investment alternatives available under the [plan]." 29 C.F.R. § 2550.404c–1(b)(2)(B).

This concept of informed participant decisionmaking figures centrally in the employer stock plan litigation discussed below in Section D of this chapter: If disclosure is inadequate, the participant or beneficiary has not been sufficiently well informed to be regarded as having exercised the control necessary to allow the plan fiduciary to invoke the § 404(c) defense.

The regulations require various disclosures, including information about the investment managers, the fees and expenses of various options, any restrictions on frequency of sales or exchanges, and so forth. With respect to "an investment alternative which is subject to the Securities Act of 1933," the participant or beneficiary must be provided with "a copy of the most recent prospectus provided to the [plan]." 29 C.F.R. § 2550.404(c)–1, (b)–1 viii. Accordingly, in an employer stock plan case, a deficient Securities Act filing can undercut the 404(c) defense.

The SEC now allows mutual funds to provide only a Summary Prospectus to investors, so long as both the Summary Prospectus and the regular prospectus are available. In FAB 2009–03, DoL concluded that a fiduciary can satisfy its obligation to provide a prospectus under section 404(c) by providing the Summary Prospectus, if that is the most recent prospectus provided to the plan.

4. *The "broad range."* The other main emphasis of the 404(c) regulations is the requirement that the plan provide the "participant or beneficiary an opportunity to choose, from a broad range of investment alternatives, the manner in which some or all of the assets in his account are invested." 29 C.F.R. § 2550.404c–1(b)(1)(ii).

The "broad range" requirement is connected to the control requirement, in the sense that the investor who has too little choice is not adequately in control. The "broad range" requirement implements the view that a participant or beneficiary investing retirement assets needs sufficient choice to enable him or herself to position the account appropriately on the risk/return curve. The regulation provides that:

A plan offers a broad range of investment alternatives only if the available investment alternatives are sufficient to provide the participant or beneficiary with a reasonable opportunity to:

(A) Materially affect the potential return on amounts in his individual account with respect to which he is permitted to exercise control and the degree of risk to which such amounts are subject;

(B) Choose from at least three investment alternatives:

(1) Each of which is diversified;

(2) Each of which has materially different risk and return characteristics;

(3) Which in the aggregate enable the participant or beneficiary by choosing among them to achieve a portfolio with aggregate risk and return characteristics at any point within the range normally appropriate for the participant or beneficiary; and

(4) Each of which when combined with investments in the other alternatives tends to minimize through diversification the overall risk of a participant's or beneficiary's [portfolio].

29 C.F.R. § 2550.404c–1(b)(3)(B)(i).

5. *Constructing the menu is a fiduciary function.* Although § 404(c) and the accompanying DoL regulations establish that the participant is

not acting as a fiduciary when choosing investments for his or her account from among the plan's "broad range" of alternatives, the underlying work of selecting, monitoring, and altering this menu of investment options is the responsibility of the plan's fiduciaries. Selecting and reviewing investment options is inevitably fiduciary, because it entails the "exercise[ ] [of] authority or control respecting management or disposition of [plan assets]" under ERISA § 3(21)(A)(i). Regarding the fiduciary duties of loyalty and prudence as they apply to the selection of investment options for 401(k) plans, see Colleen E. Medill, Stock Market Volatility and 401(k) Plans, 34 U. Michigan J.L. Reform 470 (2001).

A recurrent issue in employer stock plan litigation, discussed below in Section D of this chapter, is the extent to which plan terms mandating the use of employer stock defeat fiduciary responsibility by falling under the plan design defense.

6. *Excessive fees.* The duty of cost-sensitivity in investment matters is a familiar subprinciple of the duty of prudent administration in trust investment law, codified in most states in the Uniform Prudent Investor Act § 7 (1994). The official comment to that measure remarks: "Wasting beneficiaries' money is imprudent. In devising and implementing strategies for the investment and management of trust assets, trustees are obliged to minimize costs." Id., cmt.

In recent years there has been a wave of plaintiffs' class-action lawsuits under ERISA directed at sponsors of large defined contribution plans, alleging that the sponsor has breached its duty of prudent investing by selecting plan investment options that entail excessive fees or costs; in some of the cases, there is also a count alleging deficient disclosure of fees or expenses. See Litigation Trends: ERISA Plan Fees Cases Face Uphill Battle After Seventh Circuit Ruling, 36 BNA Pension & Benefits Rptr. 589 (2009) (circuit-by-circuit review of pending cases).

In the most prominent of the cases, Hecker v. Deere & Co., 556 F.3d 575 petition for rehearing and for rehearing en banc denied, 569 F.3d 708 (7th Cir.2009), a Seventh Circuit panel sustained the lower court in dismissing such a case on the pleadings for failure to state a claim, on the ground that a plan sponsor's choice of funds was within the § 404(c) safe harbor protection from fiduciary liability. The court's decision was contrary to the position taken by DoL, which filed an amicus brief in the case. DoL contended that "[i]f . . . the funds offered to the participants were imprudently selected or monitored, the fiduciary retains liability for the losses attributable to the fiduciary's own imprudence." DoL, Brief in Hecker v. Deere & Co., 2008 WL 5731147.

In Renfro v. Unisys Corp., 2010 U.S. Dist. LEXIS 41563 (E.D. Pa.Apr. 26, 2010), a district court in the Eastern District of Pennsylvania adopted *Hecker* in full, holding that plaintiffs' claim that the fiduciaries caused them to pay excessive fees for investments in their retirement savings plan failed to state a claim of breach of ERISA's fiduciary duties. The court argued:

> Sophisticated workers, seeing their compensation unnecessarily siphoned off to a plan administrator, would demand changes and possibly gravitate to other employers whose savvier

> behavior would ensure that workers took home a greater compensation package. Thus, it would seem that plan sponsors, when negotiating with potential trustees, would seek out the best deal possible for plan participants and would negotiate lower investment fees or administrative fees based on their market power if possible.

Id. at 22. The district court's assessment of the effectiveness of labor market forces to police excessive fees seems somewhat optimistic. According to a recent study 62% of plan participants are unaware of how much they pay in fees for their plans and 32% have no knowledge of the impact that fees can have on their retirement savings. AARP, 401(k) Participants' Awareness and Understanding of Fees, Feb. 2011, at p.1.

The district court's opinion in *Renfro* was affirmed by the Third Circuit. Renfro v. Unisys Corp., 671 F.3d 314 (3d Cir.2011). The DoL had filed an amicus brief arguing that the participants' allegations that the plan's fiduciaries imprudently selected investment choices that charged excessive fees plausibly stated a claim for breach of fiduciary duty. "Because the complaint alleges that the fees charged by many of the Plan's investments were excessive compared to the services provided and that these investments were selected pursuant to an imprudent process, it is akin to the complaint that the Eighth Circuit held sufficient to state a fiduciary breach claim in Braden v. WalMart, 588 F.3d 585 (8th Cir.2009) and distinguishable from the complaint that was dismissed in [*Hecker*]." Brief of Secretary of Labor, Hilda L. Solis, as Amicus Curiae in Support of Plaintiffs-Appellants and Requesting Reversal, Renfro v. Unisys, 671 F.3d 314 (3d Cir.2011) (No. 10–2447), 2010 WL 4160882 at *6.

The Third Circuit was not persuaded by the DoL's position, finding that the range of investment options offered by the plan in question, which offered a number of funds "with a variety of risk and fee profiles including low-risk and low-fee options," was "much closer to the characteristics of the plan evaluated by the *Hecker* court than to the scanty mix and range of selections in the plan reviewed by the *Braden* court." *Renfro* 671 F.3d 314 at 327. The Seventh Circuit reaffirmed its commitment to *Hecker* in Loomis v. Exelon Corp., 658 F.3d 667 (7th Cir.2011). But see also Tibble v. Edison Int'l, 2010 U.S. Dist. LEXIS 69119 (C.D. Cal. July 8, 2010), aff'd 711 F.3d 1061 (9th Cir. 2013) (finding violation of duty of prudence, but not loyalty, where fiduciaries caused plan to invest in the retail share classes of three mutual funds rather than the institutional share classes of those funds, causing plan participants to incur "wholly unnecessary fees").

According to Mercer Bullard, the courts that have accepted the "large menu" defense "have substituted their free market ideology for fiduciary duties under ERISA in dismissing claims against plan sponsors on the ground that the menu offered was so large as to abrogate the sponsors' ERISA duties. . . . The courts' interpretation of the control safe harbor contradicts the plain meaning of the statute. Far worse, the courts' free market assumption that large menus will increase participants' wealth is empirically false. Research has shown that large 401(k) menus result in lower participation rates, overly conservative allocations, inferior investment options and other adverse effects that, collectively, cost workers billions of dollars every year. [Mercer Bullard, The Social Costs of Choice, Free Market Ideology and the Empirical Consequences of the 401(k) Plan Large Menu Defense May 10, 2013, http://ssrn.com/abstract=2263353] He argues that: "This choice-for-choice's sake view misunderstands that the broad-range requirement is designed to promote diversification, not large menus." As the ERISA Industry Committee noted in a November 19, 2014 comment letter to DoL, "some plans have a very large number of designated investment alternatives, which may confuse less knowledgeable participants. Research suggests that participants benefit from fewer investment choices. A recent research paper found that the more investments offered, the lower the participation rate. Another study indicated that "larger menus are objectively worse than smaller menus" in 401(k) plans. Research has also found that "the presence of more funds in an individual's 401(k) plan is associated with a greater allocation to money market and bond funds at the expense of equity funds.""

Is it sufficient for a fiduciary to engage independent consultants for advice as to the reasonableness of recordkeeping fees or must he solicit competitive bids for recordkeeping services to satisfy the duty of prudence? In George v. Kraft Foods Global, Inc., 641 F.3d 786 (7th Cir.2011), the Seventh Circuit reversed the district court's summary judgment ruling in favor of the defendants, believing there to be a genuine issue of material fact whether the defendants acted prudently. The court observed that "[a]lthough the fact that defendants engaged consultants and relied on their advice with respect to Hewitt's fee is certainly evidence of prudence, it is not sufficient to entitle defendants to judgment as a matter of law." Id. at 799. Should reliance on the advice of consultants be sufficient?

Does a service provider become a plan fiduciary by limiting the mutual funds it makes available to a plan sponsor and failing to disclose to the plan, plan sponsor and participants its revenue sharing arrangements with mutual funds offered to the plan? The Seventh Circuit said no in Leimkuehler v. Amer. United Life Ins. Co., 713 F.3d 905, 912 (7th Cir. 2013), holding that "standing alone, the act of selecting both funds and their share classes for inclusion on a menu of investment options offered to 401(k) plan customers does not transform a provider of annuities into a functional fiduciary." The Seventh Circuit also rejected the view of the DoL, which filed an amicus brief in the case, that the provider's contractual reservation of the right to substitute or delete funds made available to plan participants is itself an exercise of authority or control over plan assets, even if it never affirmatively exercised those contractual rights. The "non-exercise" theory, in the view of the court, "conflicts with a common-sense understanding of the meaning of 'exercise.' " The Supreme Court has declined to review the Seventh Circuit's decision.

In recent years concern has also developed about the issue of "hidden" fees in participant-directed 401(k) plans; particularly under so-called "bundled" arrangements. The issue typically arises where a financial company—often one of the large, well-known mutual fund providers—offers to take on the entire job of administering an employer's 401(k) plan. Plan administration entails a number of things, including maintaining a website and phone center through which participants can make and change their investment elections, as well as keeping track of which participants are invested in which options and the value of their accounts—so-called "recordkeeping" functions. In a bundled arrangement, the financial service provider says to the employer: We will undertake to perform these plan recordkeeping and other administrative functions for you at a very low—in some cases zero—cost, so long as the plan's menu of investment choices includes only or mostly those mutual funds of which we are the sponsor. Under such an arrangement the financial service provider receives its compensation, effectively, through the mutual fund management fees charged to participant accounts that are invested in the provider's mutual funds. In recent years it has emerged that not only have the details of such bundled arrangements not been disclosed to plan participants, they have often not been well understood even by employers, and they have resulted in participants unwittingly bearing the full cost of plan administration through unnecessarily high mutual fund "loads" being charged to their accounts.

Toward the end of the George W. Bush Administration, DoL drafted a regulation that would have required certain disclosures respecting investment fees and costs. See 74 Fed. Reg. 3822 (Jan. 21, 2009). Under the Obama Administration, the effective date of the regulation was several times delayed. In late 2009, reciting the receipt of criticisms that the regulation "does not adequately protect against investment advice that is influenced by the financial interests of the fiduciary adviser's affiliates," DoL withdrew the regulation. 74 Fed. Reg. 60156 (Nov. 20, 2009). The notice of withdrawal said DoL intends to propose a revised regulation. Id. As of fall 2009, bills on the subject were also pending in Congress. See "House Subcommittee Approves 401(k) Fee Disclosure, Investment Advice Bills," CCH Pension Plan Guide No. 1861, Jun. 29, 2009, at 1.

In October 2010, the DoL issued final regulations requiring the disclosure of certain plan and investment-related information, including fee and expense information, to participants and beneficiaries in participant-directed individual account plans such as 401(k) plans. 75 Fed. Reg. 64909 (Oct. 20, 2010). The regulations require that participants be provided with sufficient information regarding the plan, including plan fees and expenses, and regarding the designated investment alternatives available under the plan, including fees and expenses attendant thereto, to make informed decisions with regard to the management of their individual accounts. With respect to plan administrative expense information, participants must be provided with an explanation of any fees and expenses for general plan administrative services that may be charged against their individual accounts and that are not reflected in the total annual operating expenses of any investment option, as well as the basis upon which the charge will be allocated to individual accounts. The regulations also require that participants be given an explanation of any fees and expenses that may be charged against their individual account on an individual basis and that are not reflected in the total annual operating expense of an investment option (such as fees for investment advice, commissions, front or back-end loads, as well as fees for processing plan loans or QDROs).

DoL has also issued regulations under section 408(b)(2) of ERISA, requiring extensive disclosure of fees from service providers to plan sponsors. 77 Fed. Reg. 5632 (Feb. 3, 2012), proposed amendment at 79 Fed. Reg. 13949 (March 12, 2014). A schedule to Form 5500 (the annual IRS filing required of all plans) requires plans to provide information regarding fees paid by the plan.

7. *The "broad range" in practice.* Most defined contribution plans offer a far larger menu of investment choices than the minimum three required under the 404(c) regulations. The choices offered are most commonly mutual funds, but can be plan-specific funds offered through banks, investment companies, or insurance companies. Stock fund offerings include indexed and actively managed funds; funds concentrating on larger and smaller capitalization stocks; international funds; funds investing in real estate; and so-called "growth" and "value" funds. The usual plan menu also contains fixed-income offerings, commonly government and corporate bond funds of varying maturities and issuer quality. A plan offering employer stock offers a separate fund devoted solely to that option.

Although the "broad range" requirement encourages the plan sponsor to provide the defined contribution plan investor with a set of choices that would allow him or her to make wise allocations for a retirement savings program, many such participants fail to make effective use of these options because the participant is "not familiar with the fundamentals of investment allocation." Kathleen P. Utgoff & Theodore R. Groom, The Regulation of Pensions: Twenty Questions After Twenty Years, 21 J. Pension Planning & Compliance 1, 11 (1995). Many participants tend to be excessively risk-averse, holding less equity than most financial planning experts recommend in the early decades of their careers. By clumping themselves too conservatively on the risk/return curve, that is, by slighting equities and overemphasizing low-risk, low-return fixed-income investments, they tend "over the long run [to] produce lower retirement income." Id.

The U.S. General Accounting Office reported in 2002 that "most plans are offering over 10 investment choices for participants." GAO, Private Pensions: Participants Need Information on the Risks of Investing in Employer Securities and the Benefits of Diversification 6 (GAO–02–943)(2002). Munnell & Sunden, writing in 2004, reported that about half of all 401(k) participants can choose among more than 16 alternatives. Alicia H. Munnell & Annika Sunden, Coming Up Short: The Challenge of 401(k) Plans 94 (2004). Certain large plans are reported to have offered an average of 38 investment options. Id. at 70. Empirical study indicates high levels of investment choice under some plans can become counterproductive. Participants "do not end up any better off with a vast array of choices, and in fact a large number of choices can be demotivating." Id. at 73. "[L]ow-wage participants are more likely to hold no equities and invest their entire 401(k) accounts in interest-earning assets, such as guaranteed investment contracts issued by insurance companies and money market funds. That means that they are more likely to see a return of about 2.4 percent (adjusted for inflation) instead of the historical 7.2 percent return on stocks." Id. at 81.

Susan Stabile has contended that participant control under 404(c) is illusory, because the employer has so much influence over the choice of the plan's permitted investment alternatives, and because plan participants are so ill suited to exercise investment discretion effectively. Susan J. Stabile, Freedom to Choose Unwisely: Congress' Misguided Decision to Leave 401(k) Plan Participants to Their Own Devices, 11 Cornell J.L. & Public Policy 361, 401–02 (2002).

8. *Target maturity funds.* One response to the problems of participant investing has been the emergence of so-called "life cycle" or "target maturity" funds as plan options. Such funds are designed for persons who project an approximate retirement date. The funds are tailored to the circumstances of similarly situated retirement cohorts, but not to the precise circumstances of particular retirees. The major mutual fund providers offer them in five year intervals, that is, as separate funds for persons aiming to retire about 2015, 2020, 2025, 2030, and so forth. The managers of such funds invest heavily in equities in the early years, then rebalance with greater use of less risky fixed-income assets as the retirement date approaches and the participants are projected to begin taking distributions. By selecting such a fund, the investor effectively transfers to the fund managers the responsibility for a lifetime course of investment management. See generally Marcia S. Wagner, Fiduciary Issues Associated with Life Cycle Funds in Individual Account Plans, 33 Tax Management Compensation Planning J. 162 (2005); Munnell & Sunden, supra, at 93–94.

Target maturity funds, along with virtually all other investment classes, suffered large losses in the 2008–2009 financial crisis. See Mina Kimes, "Target Funds Miss the Mark," Fortune, May 11 2009, at 27. Investment performance varies significantly among such funds. In one study of target-date 2010 funds, the worst performer lost 35 percent of its value in the year 2008, the best was down only 13 percent. "Taking Aim at Target-Date Funds," Trust Regulatory News, Apr. 2009, at 1, 2–3. What is the fiduciary responsibility of a plan sponsor whose plan offered the 2010 fund that lost 35 percent of its worth in 2008?

Despite the investment reverses of 2008, target maturity funds have continued to grow. In 2008, they attracted a further $60 billion in contributions. "Target Practice," Pensions & Investments, Sept. 21, 2009, at 3. Target-date products now make up an estimated 20% of the defined-contribution retirement market, up from 7% in 2007. Target-date funds also are found in individual retirement accounts. Barron's, Target-Date Funds Take Over, July 5, 2014, http://online.barrons.com/articles/SB500 01424053111904544004579651134019266274.

9. *Brokerage Windows.* According to a November 19, 2014 letter from the ERISA Industry Committee to DoL, "ERIC's survey of its members who sponsor large retirement plans found that 58% of responding companies include brokerage windows as options in their 401(k) plans. The survey also found that the brokerage window option is used by a relatively small number of participants; with 77% of these responding companies indicating that the brokerage window is used by 5% or fewer participants. Additionally, the investments in the brokerage window represented less than 20% of plan assets for 100% of the

respondents; with the vast majority (77%) of plans having 5% or less assets in the brokerage window."

DoL is concerned that plan sponsors may add brokerage windows to retirement plans to avoid having designated investment alternatives (DIAs) and thus avoid fee disclosure to participants. DoL's Field Assistance Bulletin 2012–02R does *not* prohibit brokerage-window only plans, but not having any DIAs raises DOL concerns. DOL noted that, while plans are not required to have a particular number of DIAs, the failure to designate any investment alternatives would raise questions under the general fiduciary duties of prudence and loyalty. On August 20, 2014, DOL released a request for information (RFI) concerning brokerage windows in 401(k) plans. [79 Fed. Reg. 49,469] Assistant Secretary Phyllis Borzi said: "Our goal in issuing this RFI is to determine whether, and to what extent, regulatory standards or other guidance concerning the use of brokerage windows may be necessary to adequately protect participants' retirement savings." [http://www.dol.gov/opa/media/press/ebsa/EBSA20141523.htm]

What is another reason employers might want to add a brokerage window as a plan investment option? Some sponsors and advisors have argued that offering such an alternative represents the ultimate form of disclaiming employer responsibility for investment decisions—of allocating the responsibility for choosing plan investments to participants themselves. At minimum the presence of such an option—allowing as it does almost any investment, at least in publicly traded securities—seems to preclude a participant from arguing the plan's menu of investment choices is insufficiently diversified. What are the potential pitfalls of such an approach to retirement investment, from a policy perspective?

10. *Managed Accounts* Under a managed account, a provider makes investment decisions for specific participants to allocate their retirement savings among a mix of assets that the provider has determined to be appropriate for the participant, based on his or her personal information. According to providers and sponsors, participants in managed accounts receive improved diversification and experience higher savings rates; however, they pay additional fees, which vary considerably.

DoL has not issued specific guidance on how sponsors should select and oversee managed account providers. In a 2014 report, 401(k) Plans: Improvements Can Be Made to Better Protect Participants in Managed Accounts, GAO–14–310 (June 2014), GAO found that the absence of guidance has led to inconsistency in sponsors' procedures for selecting and overseeing providers. Without better guidance, plan sponsors may be unable to select a provider who offers an effective service for a reasonable fee.

2. THE PROBLEMS OF PARTICIPANT INVESTING: THE PPA (2006) REFORMS

As experience with participant-directed investment grew, concern developed in pension policy circles that alterations were needed to adapt ERISA to the defined contribution world. In the Pension Protection Act of 2006 (PPA), Congress made several important changes.

1. *Automatic enrollment; QDIA.* Defined contribution plans leave much more discretion to eligible employees than do defined benefit plans about whether to participate and how much to contribute. As of 2004 it was reported that "[a]bout a quarter of workers who are offered a 401(k) plan at work don't participate in it. Those who do participate rarely make the maximum contribution: Well under 10 percent of participants contribute as much as is allowed by law." John C. Goodman & Peter Orszag, Retirement Savings Reforms on Which the Left and the Right Can Agree, National Center for Policy Analysis Brief No. 495 (Dec. 1, 2004), at 1. The lowest participation and contribution rates have tended to be among young and low-paid workers. Jack VanDerhei & Craig Copeland, The Impact of PPA on Retirement Savings for 401(k) Participants, ERI Issue Brief No. 318 (Jun. 2008), at 1.

Empirical studies have shown that large gains in participation rates result when plan participation is automatic, that is, when eligible workers have to opt out rather than opt in. See, e.g., Brigitte C. Madrian & Dennis F. Shea, The Power of Suggestion: Inertia in 401(k) Participation and Savings Behavior, 116 Quarterly J. Econ 1149 (2001). When automatic enrollment takes effect in a plan, participation increases from about 75 percent to between 85 and 95 percent. William G. Gale et al., The Automatic 401(k): A Simple Way to Strengthen Retirement Saving, 106 Tax Notes 120, 1210 (2005). Because employees "tend[ ] to follow whatever retirement planning path provides the least resistance . . . benefit plan architects and administrators effectively direct and pave that path, . . . especially . . . when it comes to establishing plan default provisions, the 'rules' governing what happens when workers fail to make active decisions about their retirement plan." Jodi DiCenso, Behavioral Finance and Retirement Plan Contributions, EBRI Issue Brief No. 301 (Jan. 2007), at 3.

To promote greater participation among eligible workers, the Pension Protection Act 2006 amended ERISA in 2006 to add § 404(c)(5), which authorizes defined contribution plans to provide for automatic enrollment in the plan and in the plan's default investment option, called a "qualified default investment alternative" (QDIA), subject to the condition that the plan notify affected employees how their accounts will be invested, how they may opt out of participation, and how they may choose the plan's other investment options. Section 404(c)(5) requires the DoL to issue regulations to "provide guidance on the appropriateness of designating default investments," which DoL did in 2007. See 29 C.F.R. § 2550.404c–5.

The relatively few plans that provided for automatic enrollment before the 2006 legislation had used money-market or other low risk, low return, fixed-income funds as the default investment. The 2007 regulations limit the use of such a fund to a 120-day transition period. Otherwise, the regulations require that the plan use one of three types of diversified investment program that applies generally accepted investment theories, is diversified, and is designed to provide varying degrees of long-term appreciation and capital preservation through a mix of equity and fixed income exposures: (1) a fund or product with a mix of investments that takes into account the individual's age, retirement date, or life expectancy, such as a life cycle or target maturity fund; (2) a fund or product with a mix of investments that takes into account the characteristics of the group of participants as a whole, such as a balanced fund; or (3) an investment service that allocates contributions among existing plan options to provide an asset mix that takes into account the individual's age or retirement date, that is, a professionally managed account. 29 C.F.R. § 2550.404c–5(e).

When a plan provides for automatic enrollment and investment in a QDIA, and complies with the notice requirements of the statute and regulations, the plan fiduciaries are immunized from fiduciary liability under ERISA. 29 C.F.R. § 2550.404c–5(b).

Literature: Linda K, Shore, Qualified Default Investment Alternatives: Emerging Issues, 37 Tax Management Compensation Planning J. 87 (2009); Anne E. Moran, Automatic Enrollment and Default Features for 401(k) Plans: Do They Work for You?, 34 Employee Relations L.J. 69 (Sum. 2008).

2.   *Investment advice.* Plan fiduciaries have "no obligation under [ERISA fiduciary law] to provide investment advice to a participant or beneficiary" in a defined contribution plan. 29 C.F.R. § 2550.404c–1(c)(4).

Although disposed to help participants get better investment results, plan sponsors and fiduciaries have been reluctant to take steps to deliver investment advice, for fear of being exposed to potential liability as investment advisers under ERISA's expansive definition of a fiduciary. Providing investment advice for a fee falls unambiguously within ERISA's definition of a fiduciary, § 3(21)(A)(ii). Moreover, many plausible advisory arrangements would violate the prohibited transaction rules, for example, in the situation in which the person offering advice was an agent of a mutual fund organization that provided plan investment options. In 1996 DoL issued Interpretive Bulletin IB 96–1, which encouraged plan fiduciaries to supply participants with some rudimentary education about plan investment choices without becoming investment advisers. 29 C.F.R. 2509.96–1, discussed in William A. Schmidt, Recent ERISA Fiduciary Developments: Participant Advice, 28 J. Pension Planning & Compliance 62, 63–66. (Jun. 2002). Because the DoL-approved measures stopped short of protecting individuated recommendations—the step that would most help the participant to make investment choices appropriate to his or her particular family and financial circumstances—there has been considerable dissatisfaction with IB 96–1; see, e.g., Dana M. Muir, The Dichotomy Between Investment Advice and Investment Education: Is No Advice Really the Best Advice?, 23 Berkeley J. Employment & Labor L. 1, 21–24 (2002). "Sex education and 401(k) education have a lot in common: No one can agree on how much students can be told." Ellen E. Schultz, Employees Looking for Advice on 401(k)s Often Face Obstacles, Wall St. J., Feb. 6, 1998, at C1, quoted in Colleen E. Medill, The Individual Responsibility Model of Retirement Plans Today: Conforming ERISA Policy to Reality, 49 Emory L.J. 1, 14 (2000).

The Pension Protection Act of 2006 amended ERISA in the hope of encouraging plans to provide better advising without fear of fiduciary liability. The act added a prohibited transaction exemption, ERISA §§ 408(b)(14), 408(g)(5), IRC § 4975(f)(8), which permits a fiduciary that is a bank, registered investment advisor, or registered broker-dealer to provide investment advice, if (1) the advice is based on an unbiased computer model certified by an independent third party; or (2) the advisor's compensation does not vary with the investment option recommended. ERISA § 408(g)(2)–(3). See David A. Pratt, Focus on Investment Advice Under the Pension Protection Act of 2006, 14 J. Pension Benefits 42 (Win. 2007).

Allowing an otherwise conflicted entity such as a mutual fund company to advise plan participants about the choice of investment options without fiduciary responsibility has been controversial. DoL regulations (proposed as 29 C.F.R. § 2550.408g–1) implementing various aspects of the PPA-approved advisory regime have been postponed several times.

3.   *Promoting annuitization.* The movement from defined benefit to defined contribution plans has not only transferred to plan participants and beneficiaries the responsibility for investing retirement savings, but also for managing the timing and amounts of distribution. Traditionally, a defined benefit plan paid benefits solely in the form of an annuity for the lives of the participant and his or her spouse, although in recent years the rise of cash balance plans has led to increasing provision of lump sum alternatives in defined benefit plans. Defined contribution plans typically provide for lump sum distribution as the only mode of payout, thereby placing on the plan participant or beneficiary the responsibility both for determining the rate at which to receive distributions from the plan, and for making plan-permitted investment decisions throughout their retirement years. (When a participant or beneficiary takes a lump sum withdrawal from an employer-sponsored plan and rolls over the proceeds to an IRA, the investment alternatives will be those available under the IRA rather than the plan.)

Annuitization has great advantages as a mode of distribution. Annuitization effectively transfers mortality risk from the individual to the annuity pool, thereby eliminating uncertainty about the rate at which the plan participant (and his or her spouse if any) may safely consume retirement savings. Annuitization eliminates the danger of outliving one's retirement savings. See generally GAO, Private Pensions: Participants Need Information on Risks They Face in Managing Pension Assets at and During Retirement (GAO–03–810) (2003); Lawrence A. Frolik, Protecting Our Aging Retirees: Converting 401(k) Accounts into Federally Guaranteed Lifetime Annuities, 47 San Diego L. Rev. 277; David Pratt, Retirement in a Defined Contribution Era: Making the Money Last, 41 J. Marshall L. Rev. 1091, 1135 (2008). However, despite numerous proposals from policy experts advocating the annuitization of defined contribution account balances, there has been very little progress toward attaining this goal. See, e.g., David C. John, J. Mark. Iwry, Lina Walker and William G. Gale, Increasing Annuitization of 401(k) Plans with Automatic Trial Income, Hamilton Project Discussion Paper, June 2008, available at www.brookings.edu; John Beshears, James J. Choi, David Laibson, Brigitte C. Madrian, and Stephen P. Zeldes, What Makes Annuitization More Appealing?, available at http://papers.ssrn.com/sol3/papers.cfm?abstract_id=2183035 (describing the results of research that explains why ERISA plan participants fail to take advantage of annuities and suggests what might be done to convince them to do so); Robert J.

Toth, Jr. and Evan Giller, Regulatory and Fiduciary Framework for Providing Lifetime Income from Defined Contribution Plans, NYU Review of Employee Benefits and Executive Compensation (2013).

In a defined contribution plan that offers an annuitization option, the participant may convert his or her individual account into a payment stream resembling that of a defined benefit plan. That conversion is typically effected by using the participant's account balance (or as much of it as he or she wishes to annuitize) to purchase a single-premium annuity from an insurance company. Although the lifetime payment streams from a defined benefit plan and from an annuitized defined contribution account are functionally identical, the defined benefit stream is guaranteed against sponsor default under the Pension Benefit Guaranty Corporation's plan termination insurance program. Insurance company annuity promises are not PBGC-covered in the event of insurer default. Some such obligations may be protected under state insurance guaranty programs, which have widely varying eligibility rules and other shortcomings. "[S]tate guaranty funds are not pre-funded. Instead, funds must be found to cover the cost of an insurance company failure after it occurs, by making assessments on (that is, taxing) other companies doing business in the state. In general, these guaranty funds provide insurance coverage for annuities up to a net present value of $100,000. To the extent that an annuitant has a policy or policies above the coverage limit, the uninsured portion would represent a claim on the receivership of the failed insurance company and, in all likelihood, would not be paid in full." National Academy of Social Insurance, Uncharted Waters: Paying Benefits from Individual Accounts in Federal Retirement Policy 87 (2005).

In pension policy circles, there has been growing concern that ordinary workers are even less adept at managing the draw-down phase of retirement finance than they are at the investment accumulation phase. In consequence, it is feared, many participants will overspend in their early retirement years, leaving themselves (and especially their widows) destitute in their last years. Various proposals to encourage or mandate annuitization have been formulated. See, e.g., Mark Iwry & John A. Turner, Automatic Annuitization: New Behavioral Strategies for Expanding Lifetime Income in 401(k)s, (Retirement Security Project, Jul. 2009), available at www.brookings.edu/about/projects/retirement security#recent_rr/; David A. Pratt, Focus on Decumulation, 16 J. Pension Benefits 8 (Aut. 2008); Teresa Ghilarducci, Guaranteed Retirement Accounts: Toward Retirement Income Security (Economic Policy Institute, Nov. 2007), available at www.sharedprosperity.org/bp204/bp204.pdf; Hazel Bateman et al., Forced Saving: Mandating Private Retirement Incomes (2001) (discussing the Australian system); Jeffrey R. Brown et al., The Role of Annuity Markets in Financing Retirement (2001). In October, 2014, the Treasury Department and IRS approved the use of annuities in target date funds in 401(k) plans. IRS Notice 2014–66. The DoL has issued an advance notice of proposed rulemaking regarding new disclosure requirements to help workers in the draw-down phase of retirement. Concerned that defined contribution plan participants do not have sufficient information to make decisions regarding the spending and management of their plan assets upon retirement, the DoL is considering additional disclosure on quarterly or annual benefit statements containing lifetime income illustrations. The proposal would require that participants be provided with not only their current account balance and a projected account balance, but also two lifetime income illustrations (one based on the current account balance and another based on the projected balance).

As remarked supra in Chapter 6 in connection with the Executive Life insolvency, there is reason to think that ERISA's fiduciary rules have deterred plan sponsors from offering annuities, for fear of liability in the event that the annuity provider should fail. See Pamela Perun, "Putting Annuities Back in Savings Plans," in Employee Pensions: Policies, Problems, and Possibilities 143 (Teresa Ghilarducci & Christian E. Weller, eds. 2007). Responding to this concern, Congress in 2006 directed DoL to revise its previous regulation at 29 C.F.R § 2509.95–1, to clarify that the selection of an annuity contract as an optional form of distribution from an individual account plan need not be "the safest available annuity," but must still be selected in accord with prudent procedures of risk and cost analysis. Pension Protection Act, § 625, Pub. L. 109–280, 120 Stat.780 (2006). DoL made the modification in 2007. Whether this modest change will have much effect on the trend away from annuitization remains to be seen.

D. EMPLOYER STOCK PLANS

The most problematic aspect of investment policy associated with the increasing primacy of the defined contribution plan in the American private pension system has been the catastrophic experience with employer stock funds in some plans. In such notorious cases as the Enron and WorldCom bankruptcies of the early 2000s, thousands of participants and beneficiaries lost much or all of their retirement accumulations.

This unit directs attention, first, to the diversification waiver that allows significant accumulations of employer stock in defined contribution plans, then to the issues of ERISA fiduciary law that have arisen in the burst of employer stock plan litigation commencing in the early 2000s, with particular attention to the litigation arising from the bankruptcy of Enron Corp. in 2001.

1. *Plan types.* Employer stock plans come in several varieties, previously discussed supra in Chapter 2. For present purposes, be alert to the three main patterns by which a plan may offer employer stock:

(1) *ESOP.* The employee stock ownership plan (ESOP), which must be "designed to invest primarily in" employer stock, see ERISA § 407(d)(6), IRC § 4975(e)(7), usually provides nothing but employer stock. In larger companies, ESOPs have tended to be secondary or supplementary plans, offered in addition to the core defined benefit or 401(k) plan. IRC § 401(a)(28) provides that a participant who has completed 10 years of service under the ESOP and has reached age 55 must be allowed to diversify out of employer stock at the rate of 25 per cent per year, or 50 percent in the plan year in which the participant is allowed to make his or her last election.

(2) *Employer match.* Within the 401(k) universe, employer stock funds show up in two ways. Most 401(k) plans have an employer match feature, by which the employer contributes to the participant's account (the match) in some proportion to the employee's contribution, up to a stated ceiling. In many such plans, the match is contributed solely in employer stock.

Before the 2006 Pension Protection Act amendments to ERISA, some plans required the match shares to be kept in employer stock until the participant terminated employment or reached a plan-stated age. The PPA amended ERISA to require that a defined contribution plan holding publicly-traded employer securities must allow a participant to divest those securities and invest the proceeds in other plan options. With respect to elective deferrals and after-tax participant contributions, this right to diversify takes effect when the participant begins participation in the plan. The plan can continue to postpone the right to diversify employer contributions until the participant has three years of service. (An ESOP that has no 401(k) component is exempt from this diversification requirement, but remains subject to the age 55 requirements noted above.) ERISA § 204(j); IRC § 401(a)(35).

(3) *Participant election.* A 401(k) plan may also offer as an investment option alongside the plan's mutual funds and other options a fund consisting solely of employer stock.

The three types can be combined in various ways. It is quite common for a 401(k) plan to feature both an employer match and an employee election. Munnell and Sunden report that about 45 percent of sponsors that offer company stock as an employee election also make matching contributions exclusively in company stock. In such cases, the average concentration of employer stock in the accounts of plan participants is 53 percent. Munnell & Sunden, supra, at 101. Empirical investigation has shown that employees are more likely to invest their own funds in employer stock when the plan mandates that the employer match be paid in employer stock. Regarding this so-called endorsement effect, see Susan J. Stabile, The Behavior of Defined Contribution Plan Participants, 77 New York U.L. Rev. 71, 87 (2002).

A 401(k) plan can also be designed to use ESOP shares for the employer match.

Employer stock funds of all types almost always provide for the fund to hold cash or cash-equivalent investments in addition to employer stock, as a short-term suspense account for funds awaiting investment in or divestment from employer stock.

2. *The Enron plan.* Enron Corp.'s 401(k) plan was reasonably typical of the genre. The plan permitted a participant to contribute up to 15 percent of salary, subject to a ceiling. Enron contributed a 50 percent match, up to 6 percent of base pay, entirely in Enron stock. The participant could choose to invest his or her contribution among a variety of options, including well-diversified mutual funds, or in the Enron stock fund. See Enron Corp. Savings Plan as Amended and Restated Effective July 1, 1999, § III.1, 4, V.16(a). The plan required the participant to retain

the match shares until age fifty, at which time he or she could direct that the shares be sold and the proceeds be redirected into other plan options. Id., § IV–16(b). As explained above, the 2006 ERISA amendments now cap any plan-required involuntary holding period at three years.

At year-end 2000, about 60 percent of the Enron 401(k) plan's assets were invested in the Enron company stock fund; 89 percent of the assets in the company stock fund derived from employee contributions, and 11 percent from the employer's matching contributions. Patrick J. Purcell, Congressional Research Service: The Enron Bankruptcy and Employer Stock in Retirement Plans, Jan. 3, 2002, at 3. The market price of a share of Enron stock declined from a high of $88 in September 2000 to less than a dollar in late 2001. Munnell & Sunden, supra, at 113.

1.   THE DIVERSIFICATION WAIVER

ERISA requires fiduciaries to "diversify[ ] the investments of the plan so as to minimize the risk of large losses, unless under the circumstances it is clearly prudent not to do so." ERISA § 404(a)(1)(C).

As discussed in *Donovan v. Bierwirth*, supra, ERISA § 407(a) limits a defined benefit plan to investing not more than 10 percent of its assets in employer securities or employer realty. In *Bierwirth*, the 10 percent limit was held to be a mere ceiling, not an affirmative authorization, and plan fiduciaries who bought employer stock up to that ceiling were held to have acted imprudently in the circumstances.

The centrality of diversification in modern investment practice and the corresponding importance of the duty to diversify in modern trust and pension fiduciary law have been emphasized in Section A of this chapter. It is astonishing to see, therefore, that the drafters of ERISA, having so insistently imposed the duty to diversify on the defined benefit plans that were uppermost in their minds, then waived that requirement for defined contribution plan investments in employer securities (and employer realty).

ERISA's waiver provision is § 404(a)(2), which says: "In the case of an individual account plan as defined in section 407(d)(3), the diversification requirement of [§ 404(a)(1)(C)] and the prudence requirement (only to the extent it requires diversification) of [§ 404(a)(1)(B)] is not violated by acquisition or holding [of] qualifying employer securities. . . ."

Testifying at the Senate Enron hearings in 2002, one of the authors of this book explained why employer stock plans offend conventional principles of good investment practice for retirement accounts:

> A pension fund portfolio holding a massive part of its assets in any one stock is bad; but holding such a concentration in the stock of the employer is worse. For the employees of any firm, diversification away from the stock of that employer is even more important. The simple reason is that the employee is already horrifically underdiversified by having his or her human capital tied up with the employer. The employee is necessarily exposed to the risks of the employer by virtue of the employment relationship. The last thing in the world that the employee needs is to magnify the intrinsic underdiversification

of the employment relationship, by taking his or her diversifiable investment capital and tying that as well to the fate of the employer. The Enron debacle illustrates this point poignantly. Just when many of the employees have lost their jobs, they have also lost their pension savings. . . .

John H. Langbein, Testimony to Senate Committee on Governmental Affairs, Jan. 24, 2002, reprinted as "What's Wrong with Employer Stock Pension Plans," in Enron and Other Corporate Fiascos: The Corporate Scandal Reader 487 (Nancy B. Rapoport & Bala G. Dharan eds., 2d ed. 2009); accord, Munnel & Sunden, supra, at 96–98, 111–17. Langbein recommended eliminating the diversification waiver for employer stock plans, hence effectively forbidding such plans. In an article published well before Enron imploded, another of the authors, Susan Stabile, recommended that Congress impose a ten-percent ceiling on the amount of employer stock in any participant's 401(k) account. Susan J. Stabile, Pension Plan Investments in Employer Securities: More Is Not Always Better, 15 Yale J. Regulation 61, 88 (1998). She also proposed limiting ESOPs to the role of secondary savings plans, by amending ERISA to prohibit an employer from offering an ESOP unless the employer also provided a primary plan that supplies "meaningful retirement benefits backed by a diversified investment portfolio. . . ." Id. at 89. See also Andrew Stumpff and Norman Stein, Repeal Tax Incentives For ESOPs, 125 Tax Notes 337 (2009).

Compare the position of the ERISA Industry Committee (ERIC), a lobbying organization of large-plan sponsors, which has opposed change. In a statement to the House Committee investigating ERISA issues raised by the Enron collapse, ERIC argued:

> Employer stock plans serve the important purpose of aligning the interests of employees with the interests of the employer's business, [thus serving] important business purposes in addition to providing a safety net for retirement. . . .

> Employer stock plans give employees the opportunity to purchase employer stock economically, conveniently, and tax-efficiently. Employees highly value the opportunity to invest [pension assets] in employer stock, the stock they know best. . . .

> Congress should allow employees to make their own decisions regarding the diversification of their employee-directed accounts. . . .

> Congress should preserve an employer's freedom to require that its own contributions to a defined contribution plan be invested in employer stock. If employers are prohibited from requiring their contributions to defined contribution plans to be invested in employer stock, they are likely to curtail their contributions, thereby reducing employees' retirement savings.

ERISA Industry Committee, Statement on Investments in Employer Stock, House Committee on Education and the Workforce, 109th Cong. (2002).

Can you answer ERIC's arguments? What reasons not mentioned in the ERIC statement might the managers of a large firm have for wanting to place shares of the company's stock in the hands of its employees?

Recall the takeover contest in *Donovan v. Bierwirth*: Which side did the plan participants support?

Despite the Enron calamity and comparable losses at WorldCom and other troubled firms in the years since, Congress has left in place the diversification waiver that gives rise to employer stock plans. Regarding suggested reforms to ERISA that were proposed in connection with the Enron events, see Susan J. Stabile, 401(k) Answer Book: Special Supplement: Lessons from Enron 9–1/9–13 (2002); Janice Kay Lawrence, Pension Reform in the Aftermath of Enron: Congress' Failure to Deliver the Promise of Secure Retirement to 401(k) Plan Participants, 92 Kentucky L. Rev. 1 (2003).

The percentage of employer stock in 401(k) plans has declined somewhat, from an estimated 15 percent in 2002 to an estimated 11 percent in 2007. See Alicia H. Munnell et al., An Update on 401(k) Plans: Insights from the 2007 SCF 5 & fig. 8 (Boston College Center for Retirement Research, Mar. 2009). A 2013 Morningstar report found that "Within our dataset we see an aggregate dollar-weighted reduction in the assets invested in employer stock from 17% at the beginning of 1999 to 10% at the end of 2011." Employer Stock Ownership in 401(k) Plans and Subsequent Company Stock Performance, http://corporate.morningstar. com/us/documents/MethodologyDocuments/ResearchPapers/Employer-Stock-Ownership-in-401k-Plans.pdf.

2. THE EMPLOYER STOCK LITIGATION: *ENRON* AND BEYOND

ERISA allows employers to offer employer stock plans, but ERISA fiduciary law imposes many responsibilities on the fiduciaries who administer such plans. Over the past decade, hundreds of lawsuits have been brought that have caused the courts to spell out standards of fiduciary obligation for such plans. The financial crisis and the resulting decline in stock and bond prices in 2008–2009 gave rise to a further wave of such cases. See, e.g., BofA [Bank of America] Faces ERISA Class Action Over Losses Connected to Countrywide, Merrill Purchases, 36 BNA Pension & Benefits Rptr. 308 (2009); Bear Stearns Hit with Three Class Actions within Days of Purchase by J.P. Morgan, 35 BNA Pension & Benefits Rptr. 671 (2008); Financial Industry Hit Hard by Subprime Mortgage Meltdown Becomes New Target of ERISA 'Stock Drop' 401(k) Litigation, 35 BNA Pension & Benefits Rptr. 2188 (2008)

Most of the reported decisions in the employer stock plan cases have been district court opinions responding to pretrial motions, e.g., In re Enron Corp. Securities, Derivative & ERISA Litigation (Tittle v. Enron Corp.), 284 F.Supp.2d 511 (S.D.Tex.2003) [hereafter *Enron*]. A case that resists a motion to dismiss or for summary judgment tends thereafter to settle; see, e.g., Tittle v. Enron Corp., 228 F.R.D. 541 (S.D.Tex.2005) (approving $85 million settlement of the liability of various fiduciaries in *Enron* two years after the court sustained plaintiffs' case against a motion to dismiss). For a compilation of settled ERISA class action cases, mostly employer stock cases, see Fiduciary Counselors, "ERISA Class Action Litigation Settlements and Attorney Fees," available at http:// www.erisasettlements.com/press/ERISA-Chart.pdf; a compilation of reported employer stock cases as of 2005 appears in Craig C. Martin & Elizabeth L. Fine, ERISA Stock Drop Cases: An Evolving Standard, 38 John Marshall L. Rev. 889, 919–51 (2005).

There has been relatively little guidance at the appellate level about many of the issues presented in the employer stock cases. The district courts, sensitive to the importance and novelty of the cases, have produced many thoughtful opinions. Judge Melinda Harmon's 173-page opinion in *Enron* in 2003 is emphasized in the discussion following. The case law is reviewed in Robert Rachal, Howard Shapiro & Nicole Eichberger, "Fiduciary Duties Regarding 401(k) and ESOP Investments in Employer Stock," in Jayne E. Zanglein, Lawrence A. Frolik & Susan J. Stabile, ERISA Litigation (4th ed. 2011 and 2013 Supp.)

The employer stock plan cases exhibit many similarities. Most are brought as class actions, on behalf of all affected participants and beneficiaries. The cases arise both from 401(k) plans and from ESOPs. Remedy is usually sought under ERISA § 409(a), the provision that makes fiduciaries "personally liable to make good to such plan any losses to the plan resulting from" breach of fiduciary duty; and under various provisions of § 502(a), especially § 502(a)(2), which provides for relief under § 409. In LaRue v. DeWolff, Boberg, & Associates, Inc., 552 U.S. 248 (2008), the Supreme Court confirmed that § 502(a)(2) authorizes recovery for fiduciary breaches that impair the value of plan assets in participants' individual accounts.

1. *Disclosure.* The cases commonly allege that the company and various of its officers and directors engaged in wrongful or ill-advised business practices and in wrongful financial reporting practices. They further allege that these practices were wrongfully concealed, thereby inflating the price of the stock, and inducing participants to purchase or retain the employer shares at the wrongfully bloated price. In *Enron*, for example, the plaintiffs alleged that the plan fiduciaries "breached their duty of loyalty [by] affirmatively and materially misleading them about Enron's financial condition and performance and its accounting manipulations, while inducing them to hold and purchase additional Enron stock." 284 F.Supp.2d at 555. There is a duty not to "mislead or fail to disclose information that [certain plan fiduciaries] knew or should have known would be needed for the . . . participants to prevent losses." In re Merck & Co. Inc. Securities Derivative & ERISA Litigation, 2006 WL 2050577, at 17 (D.N.J.2006) (failure to disclose adverse information about Merck's drug Vioxx, which had to be withdrawn from the market, resulting in a sharp decline in the price of Merck shares).

The employer stock cases rest squarely upon the fiduciary duty of disclosure (discussed in Chapter 13, supra) that the courts have derived from ERISA's core duties of loyalty (exclusive benefit) and prudence, § 404(a)(1)(A)–(B). The *Enron* opinion reviews that case law and sustains the plaintiffs' claim for breach of the duty to disclose "Enron's alleged fraudulent accounting, concealment of its deceitful business practices and of the company's precarious, swiftly deteriorating financial [condition]." Id. at 562.

2. *Prudence.* Congress waived ERISA's diversification requirement for employer stock plans in § 404(a)(2), but that provision expressly declares that the duty of prudence abides for such plans.

Because concentrated investing in one stock, especially employer stock, is so risky for retirement accounts, the prudence standard may be correspondingly heightened. Speaking of an ESOP trustee, Judge Posner observed:

> The duty to diversify is an essential element of the ordinary trustee's duty of prudence, given the risk aversion of trust beneficiaries, but the absence of any general such duty from the ESOP setting does not eliminate the trustee's duty of prudence. If anything, it demands an even more watchful eye, diversification not being in the picture to buffer the risk to the beneficiaries should the company encounter adversity. There is a sense in which, because of risk aversion, an ESOP is imprudent per se, though legally authorized. This built-in "imprudence" (for which the trustee is of course not culpable) requires him to be especially careful to do nothing to increase the risk faced by the participants still further.

Armstrong v. La Salle Bank Nat'l Ass'n, 446 F.3d 728, 732 (7th Cir.2006).

In cases such as *Enron* and In re WorldCom, Inc. ERISA Litigation, 263 F.Supp.2d 745 (S.D.N.Y.2003), in which ERISA fiduciaries knew or had reason to know that massive accounting frauds had inflated the share prices, it was easy for the courts to conclude that the plan fiduciaries had not used appropriate "care, skill, prudence, and diligence" as required by ERISA § 404(a)(1)(A) when deciding to offer the fraud-affected shares as investments for employees' retirement accounts. But "ERISA imposes no duty on plan fiduciaries to continuously audit operational affairs. Rather, courts have held that a duty to investigate only arises when there is some reason to suspect that investing in company stock may be imprudent—that is, there must be something akin to a 'red flag' of misconduct." Pugh v. Tribune Co., 521 F.3d 686 (7th Cir.2008). In a similar vein, Judge Easterbrook has cautioned against the "assertion that pension fiduciaries have a duty to outsmart the stock market, a contention with little prospect of success." Rogers v. Baxter Int'l, Inc., 521 F.3d 702, 705 (7th Cir.2008).

In Majed v. Nokia, Inc., 528 Fed. Appx. 52 (2nd Cir. Jun. 25, 2013), the Second Circuit observed that the "prudence analysis does not turn on whether information disclosed to the market caused a share price decline, even a substantial one." Rather, the court "must consider the extent to which plan fiduciaries at a given point in time reasonably could have predicted the outcome that followed." Using that analysis, the court found no breach of the duty of prudence in the fiduciaries' continued investment in Nokia's parent company's stock despite certain warning signals.

3.   *Loyalty.* In addition to challenging the prudence of employer stock as a plan investment, some cases also allege that the plan "fiduciaries had conflicting interests in using company stock in the plan because either their compensation was stock-based or they owned substantial amounts of company stock." Dana M. Muir & Cindy A. Schipani, 43 Harvard J. Legislation 437, 463 (2006). These claims have not been well received. In the *WorldCom* case, for example, it was alleged that the main fraudster, "Bernard Ebbers, a WorldCom director as well as its President and CEO, breached his duty of loyalty by receiving stock-

based compensation that created an incentive for him to keep the stock price high and ignore the best interests of plan participants and beneficiaries. The court rejected the claim, relying on both ERISA's explicit provision for conflicted fiduciaries and its limitation of liability to only those acts taken while in the role of an ERISA fiduciary. The plaintiffs had not shown that the conflict of interest caused Ebbers to act other than in the best interests of plan participants and beneficiaries when making decisions as a plan fiduciary." Id., citing In re WorldCom, Inc. ERISA Litigation, 354 F.Supp.2d 423 (S.D.N.Y.2005).

4.   *Who is a fiduciary?* Because the theory of liability in employer stock cases is breach of fiduciary duty, the cases must have fiduciary defendants. Plaintiffs attempt to cast a wide net of purported fiduciaries, commonly including the company, the named fiduciaries, and various officers and directors. (Some of the suits also name the trustee, who is usually a directed trustee. The liability of directed trustees is discussed below.)

The fiduciary status of various persons named as defendants has been among the most contested issues in the employer stock cases. Outcomes vary with particular plan terms and with the conduct of particular persons in the setting of particular cases. Especially when the company has become insolvent, as in *Enron* and *WorldCom*, the individuals (and their fiduciary insurers) may be the only defendants worth suing. Judge Harmon said in *Enron*:

> Courts are divided about if and under what circumstances the officers or employees of a corporation that is the named fiduciary in plan instruments may be personally liable for a breach of their fiduciary duty. In light of the traditional rule that the employees of a corporation acting within the course and scope of their employment cannot be personally liable for their actions, some courts have held that the individual corporate employee must have an individual discretionary role in the plan administration to be liable as a fiduciary under ERISA. [Other] courts, stressing the functional definition of a fiduciary under ERISA, have held that the individuals within the corporations who actually exercised the fiduciary discretionary control or authority in their official capacity may also be personally liable, depending on the facts of the particular case.

Enron, 284 F.Supp.2d at 567–68. Judge Harmon took the view that ERISA fiduciary law required her to side with "with those courts which reject a *per se* rule of nonliability for corporate [officers.]" Id. at 569. Instead, she endorsed "a functional, fact-specific inquiry to assess 'the extent of responsibility and control exercised by the individual with respect to the [plan].' " Id.

The mirror image question also arises when the issue is whether to impute an officer's conduct to the employer. "The majority of courts to have considered this issue . . . have held that an employer/principal may be held vicariously liable under ERISA for the acts of its employee when the employee breaches fiduciary duties while acting within the scope of his employment." Wasley Products, Inc. v. Bulakites, 2006 WL 3834240 (D.Conn.2006).

In *In re Citigroup ERISA Litig.*, 662 F.3d 128 (2d Cir. 2011), the Second Circuit held that Citigroup and its former CEO did not have fiduciary liability for alleged misstatements made to employees, including those contained in SEC disclosure documents filed by the company because they had no responsibility for communicating with participants and were not acting as plan fiduciaries.

5.   *Appointing and monitoring.* It is widely understood that appointing fiduciaries to administer an ERISA plan is itself a fiduciary function. Judge Harmon reiterated the point in *Enron*: "A person or entity that has the power to appoint, retain and/or remove a plan fiduciary from his position has discretionary authority or control over the management or administration of a plan and is a fiduciary to the extent that he or it exercises that power." 284 F.Supp.2d at 552.

The duty to appoint imports the duty to monitor those whom one appoints (and whom one can remove). DoL has long taken the position that, among the "ongoing responsibilities of a fiduciary who has appointed trustees," is that "[a]t reasonable intervals the performance of trustees and other fiduciaries should be reviewed by the appointing fiduciary in such manner as may be reasonably expected to ensure that their performance has been in compliance with the terms of the plan and statutory standards, and satisfies the needs of the plan." 29 C.F.R. § 2509.75–8, at FR–17.

The effect of the principle that appointing fiduciaries is a fiduciary function has been in some cases to impute fiduciary responsibility to persons such as directors and officers who exercised appointing authority under the plan, even when those persons were not directly implicated in the alleged improprieties and concealment. "[T]he fiduciary power to appoint and remove trustees to a plan carries with it a concomitant and ongoing duty to monitor those trustees' performance." Cannon v. MBNA Corp., 2007 WL 2009672, at 4 (D.Del.2007). The case law is reviewed in James F. Carey et al., The Employer Stock Cases: Does an Appointing Fiduciary Have a Duty to Disclose?, 13 ERISA Litigation Rptr. (Jun./Jul. 2005), at 16.

6.   *The 404(c) defense.* ERISA § 404(c), discussed supra in Section C of this chapter, can shift responsibility for investment decisions in defined contribution plans from the plan fiduciaries to the participant or beneficiary who has exercised control over the investment. When the 404(c) defense is invoked in employer stock plan litigation, it is commonly met with the response that the fiduciaries' breach of the duty of disclosure renders the defense inapplicable. If the fiduciaries mislead the participants about plan investments, the participants are not in control for purposes of ERISA § 404(c). See In re Unisys Sav. Plan Litig., 74 F.3d 420, 447 (3d Cir.1996). DoL has endorsed this position in its § 404(c) regulations, which provide that the participant or beneficiary does not exercise the requisite control unless he or she "has the opportunity to obtain sufficient information to make informed decisions with regard to investment alternatives available under the [plan]." 29 C.F.R. § 2550.404c–1(b)(2)(B). DoL's authority to issue the regulation was questioned by the majority in a divided Fifth Circuit panel opinion, Langbecker v. Electronic Data Systems Corp., 476 F.3d 299, 310–13 (5th Cir.2007). The district court in Tyco Int'l Multidistrict Litig., 606

F.Supp.2d 166, 169 (D.N.H.2009), refused to follow *Langbecker*, "agree[ing] with the dissent in that case that the DOL's interpretation of its own regulations is reasonable and should not be ignored."

In Howell v. Motorola, Inc., 633 F.3d 552 (7th Cir. 2011), the Seventh Circuit held that although § 404(c) is a defense against claims that a fiduciary failed to disclose material information or failed to monitor fiduciaries, it is not available as a defense against claims of imprudent fund selection, which is also the position taken by the DoL. The court reasoned that the language of § 404(c)

> creates a safe harbor only with respect to decisions that the participant can make. The choice of which investments will be presented in the menu that the plan sponsor adopts is not within the participant's power. It is instead a core decision relating to the administration of the plan and the benefits that will be offered to participants.

Id. at 567. The Seventh Circuit reached the same conclusion regarding 404(c) in Lingis v. Dorazil, a companion case to *Howell*. However, the court also concluded that the imprudence claim failed on the merits because other investment options were offered and the company was not facing imminent collapse. The Supreme Court denied certiorari in both cases in Lingis v. Dorazil, 132 S. Ct. 96 (2011).

7.   *The Securities Act*. Fiduciary defendants in *WorldCom* argued that imposing ERISA disclosure duties on them as employer stock plan fiduciaries would compel them to violate the Securities Act prohibitions against insider trading. The court rejected the argument, saying that the duty to disclose does not "require[ ] ERISA fiduciaries to convey non-public material information to Plan participants. What is required, is that any information that is conveyed to participants be conveyed in compliance with the standard of care that applies to ERISA fiduciaries." In re WorldCom, Inc. ERISA Litigation, 263 F.Supp.2d 745, 767 (S.D.N.Y.2003). Rejecting a similar defense, the *Enron* court quoted DoL's amicus brief, which contended that " 'nothing in the securities laws would have prohibited [the fiduciaries] from disclosing the information to other shareholders and the public at large, or from forcing Enron to do so.' " 284 F.Supp.2d at 566. The court asserted the principle that "[as] a matter of public policy, the statutes should be interpreted to require that persons *follow* the laws, not undermine them." Id. at 565. Regarding the overlap of ERISA with the Securities Acts in employer stock cases, see Susan J. Stabile, I Believed My Employer and Didn't Sell My Company Stock: Is There an ERISA (or '34 Act) Remedy for Me?, 36 Connecticut L. Rev. 385 (2004).

8.   *Plan design, fiduciary duty, and ERISA § 404(a)(1)(D)*. Under the "two hat" doctrine discussed supra in Chapter 12, plan design is nonfiduciary, plan administration is fiduciary. A recurrent problem in employer stock cases is the question of whether plan terms requiring the use of employer stock immunize the plan fiduciaries from responsibility for conduct that would otherwise breach their fiduciary duties. This so-called plan design defense has been particularly urged when the plan is an ESOP or a 401(k) plan in which the terms mandate the use of company stock. How does the fiduciary duty to administer a plan prudently and for the exclusive benefit of the participants and beneficiaries apply in a

plan whose terms require investing in employer stock that the fiduciaries know or should know is imprudent and not in the interests of the participants and beneficiaries?

Similar issues had arisen in the 1980s in share voting cases, in circumstances in which plan terms required plan fiduciaries to vote the employer shares in a manner that appeared to be contrary to the interests of plan participants. A celebrated takeover battle occurred in 1982 involving Martin Marietta's tender offer for Bendix. The Bendix plan contained a term prohibiting the trustee from tendering Bendix shares in a hostile tender offer. "When Martin Marietta announced its offer to purchase Bendix shares, however, [the trustee] decided that the risk of violating ERISA Section 404(a)(1)(D) by failing to tender the Bendix shares was so great that it had a duty to tender the shares in violation of the plan." See Edward A. Landry, Fiduciary Responsibility under ERISA in a Takeover Situation, 12 Probate Notes 148, 151 (American College of Probate Counsel) (1986). The courts sustained the trustee's position. Id.

The issue of fiduciary limits on plan-directed conduct arose in the prominent case of Moench v. Robertson, 62 F.3d 553, 571 (3d Cir.1995), involving the question of whether an ESOP fiduciary must desist from further investing in the employer's shares when the firm becomes imperilled. The Third Circuit held that "an ESOP fiduciary who invests the assets in employer stock is entitled to a presumption that it acted consistently with ERISA by virtue of that decision. However, the plaintiff may overcome that presumption by establishing that the fiduciary abused its discretion by investing in employer securities." 62 F.3d at 571.

In an amicus brief in *Enron*, DoL emphasized the controlling importance, in its view, of ERISA § 404(a)(1)(D), the measure (discussed supra in Chapter 13) that requires plan fiduciaries to obey plan documents only "insofar as [they] are consistent with the provisions of [ERISA]." DoL argued that § 404(a)(1)(D) places plan fiduciaries under a duty "to ignore the terms of the plan document where those terms require[ ] them to act imprudently in violation of ERISA § 404(a)(1)(B)." Amended Brief of the Secretary of Labor as Amicus Curiae Opposing the Motions to Dismiss, Aug. 30, 2002, at 30–31. "Even if the plan document requires an investment, the fiduciaries must override it if it violates ERISA." Id. at 32. In an employer stock plan case arising from the insolvency of Polaroid Corp., the district court held that "the fact that the Plan required investments in Polaroid stock does 'not ipso facto relieve [Defendants] of their fiduciary obligations.' [By] force of statute, Defendants had the fiduciary responsibility to disregard the Plan and eliminate Plan investments in Polaroid stock if the circumstances warranted. *See* [ERISA § 404(a)(1)(D)]. As such, to the extent Polaroid stock was an imprudent investment, Defendants possessed the authority as a matter of law to exclude Polaroid stock from the ESOP or as a 401(k) investment alternative, regardless of the Plan's dictates." In re Polaroid ERISA Litigation, 362 F.Supp.2d 461, 474–75 (S.D.N.Y.2005).

The *Enron* court concluded that the plaintiff plan participants "have stated a claim for breach of their fiduciary duties of loyalty and prudence based on Defendants' alleged inducement of the plan participants to direct the trustee to invest in Enron [stock]. They also state a claim for breach of fiduciary duty in causing and allowing the [Plan] to purchase or accept Enron's matching contributions in the form of Enron stock once the fiduciaries allegedly knew or should have known of the inherent risk of such [stock]." 284 F.Supp.2d at 656 (emphasis deleted).

In circuits following *Moench*, two questions arose. First, how compelling need the evidence of imprudence be to overcome the *Moench* presumption, and second, at what stage of the proceedings does the presumption applies. The dispute among the circuits on these issues set the stage for the 2014 Supreme Court decision in Fifth Third Bancorp. v. Dudenhoeffer, No. 12–751, 134 S. Ct. 2459 (June 25, 2014) reproduced at D.3. below.

9.   *Directed trustees.* As discussed supra in Chapter 12, ERISA § 403(a)(1) allows a plan to make the trustee "subject to the proper directions" of some other named fiduciary. The trustee for the typical large 401(k) plan is a bank or investment company that provides record keeping services, but which is directed with respect to investments. Plan fiduciaries select the investment options, from which individual plan participants and beneficiaries make their investment choices. The directed trustee executes their instructions.

The directed trustee, usually a flourishing financial intermediary, has deep pockets that make it a tempting target for liability in employer stock cases, especially when the employer has become insolvent. The question has thus been presented in some of the employer stock cases, what responsibility does the directed trustee have to ascertain that the directions under which it acts are "proper" within the meaning of ERISA § 403(a)(1)? ERISA does not define the term "proper." Because the directed trustee is an ERISA fiduciary, ERISA's core fiduciary duties of prudence and loyalty apply. The legislative history is explored in Patricia Wick Hatamyar, See No Evil? The Role of the Directed Trustee under ERISA, 64 Tennessee L. Rev. 1, 22–32 (1996), concluding that Congress intended ERISA fiduciary duties to apply to directed trustees. The *Enron* court concluded that "even where the named fiduciary appears to have been granted full control, [the] directed trustee still retains a degree of discretion, authority, and responsibility that may expose him to liability, as reflected in the structure and language of provisions of ERISA." 284 F.Supp.2d at 601.

In *Worldcom*, at the motion to dismiss stage, the court held that a directed trustee is an ERISA fiduciary, 263 F.Supp.2d at 761–62. In a later opinion, the court reaffirmed its holding, saying: "A directed trustee must discharge its own duties in conformity with the prudent man standard of care, and avoid prohibited transactions. It may not comply with a direction from a named fiduciary that it knows or ought to know is violating that fiduciary's obligations to plan beneficiaries." 354 F.Supp.2d 423, 445 (S.D.N.Y.2005). On summary judgment motions after discovery the court found that the directed trustee in *Worldcom* had not breached its duty. The Court followed a recent DoL Field Assistance Bulletin, FAB 2004–03 (2004), reprinted in CCH Pension Plan Guide ¶ 19,980R. "[W]hen a directed trustee does not possess material non-public information, it will '*rarely* have an obligation under ERISA to question the prudence of a direction to purchase publicly traded securities at the market price solely on the basis of publicly available information.'" 354 F.Supp.2d at 447 (quoting FAB 2004–03, emphasis by the court). The court held that the *Worldcom* plaintiffs had not satisfied that standard.

In Summers v. State Street Bank & Trust Co., 453 F.3d 404 (7th Cir.2006), State Street was the directed trustee of the United Airlines ESOP. State Street continued to obey instructions from the plan fiduciaries to invest in United shares across a two-year period during which the shares declined from about $44 per share to near zero in December 2001, when United declared bankruptcy. The court sustained State Street's conduct, reasoning that "at *every* point in the long slide of United's stock price, that price was the best estimate available either to State Street or to the [plan] Committee of the company's value, [and] so neither fiduciary was required to act on the assumption that the market was overvaluing United." Id. at 408.

10. *The McKesson defense: no harm?* In In re McKesson HBOC, Inc. ERISA Litigation, 2002 WL 31431588 (N.D.Cal.2002), an employer stock case that was decided against the participants, the court endorsed the defendants' argument that concealing alleged financial improprieties did not harm the plan participants:

> Defendants argue that plaintiffs have failed to allege a claim here because there can be no damages flowing from the alleged breach. Specifically, defendants could not have sold company stock and not disclosed the financial improprieties without violating the federal securities laws, and disclosing the information publicly prior to selling the stock would itself have resulted in the same precipitous decline in stock value. If McKesson disclosed the financial improprieties before selling McKesson stock, the alleged loss to the Plan assets would have occurred before any sale could have occurred at the inflated pre-disclosure price. Under the "efficient capital markets hypotheses" such disclosure would have swiftly resulted in a market adjustment. Thus, the Plan would not have been able to sell the stock at the artificially high price, and there was no way for the Plan Fiduciaries to have lawfully avoided the drop that [occurred]. Thus, even if defendants breached a fiduciary duty by failing to divest the Plan of McKesson stock after the merger, plaintiffs have not alleged facts to establish that any damages were caused by such breach.

Id. at 6. Similar reasoning appears in Edgar v. Avaya, Inc., 503 F.3d 340, 350 (3d Cir.2007). Is this analysis sound?

11. *Lockdowns.* The typical claim a against directed trustee in an employer stock plan case is that the trustee knew or should have known enough about the wrongdoing and nondisclosure to have given the trustee cause to suspend or terminate investments in the employer stock fund. In *Enron*, however, there was an added grievance. During the last weeks before Enron's insolvency, the plan fiduciaries had, consistent with plan terms, imposed a so-called lockdown period, instructing the directed trustee to allow no trading within the Enron stock fund, thus suspending the right to sell or exchange out of company stock for those participants who were otherwise so entitled. The purpose of the lockdown period was to facilitate a change of record keepers. The plaintiffs

contended that the directed trustee "breached its fiduciary duties in following the lockdown instructions, because the directions were contrary to ERISA and [the trustee] knew or should have known that the lockdown instructions violated ERISA." 284 F.Supp.2d at 582. The court held that the plaintiffs stated a claim that the timing of the lockdown was sufficiently suspect that the directed trustee's duties of prudence and loyalty should have caused the trustee to question the instruction. Id. at 602.

Irritation at the lockdown led to one of the few legislative reforms of ERISA to result from the debacle of the Enron and WorldCom plans. The Sarbanes-Oxley Act of 2002 added the elaborate regulation of so-called blackout periods that is now codified as ERISA § 101(i). See James E. Hickmon, Sarbanes-Oxley Produces Complex Blackout Notice Requirements and Imposes Civil Liability for Plan Administrators, 31 Tax Management Compensation Planning J. 219 (2003).

3.   FIFTH THIRD BANCORP V. DUDENHOEFFER

134 S. Ct. 2459 (2014).

■ JUSTICE BREYER delivered the opinion for a unanimous Court. ERISA requires the fiduciary of a pension plan to act prudently in managing the plan's assets. This case focuses upon that duty of prudence as applied to the fiduciary of an "employee stock ownership plan" (ESOP), a type of pension plan that invests primarily in the stock of the company that employs the plan participants.

We consider whether, when an ESOP fiduciary's decision to buy or hold the employer's stock is challenged in court, the fiduciary is entitled to a defense-friendly standard that the lower courts have called a "presumption of prudence." The Courts of Appeals that have considered the question have held that such a presumption does apply, with the presumption generally defined as a requirement that the plaintiff make a showing that would not be required in an ordinary duty-of-prudence case, such as that the employer was on the brink of collapse.

We hold that no such presumption applies. Instead, ESOP fiduciaries are subject to the same duty of prudence that applies to ERISA fiduciaries in general, except that they need not diversify the fund's assets.

I

Petitioner Fifth Third Bancorp, a large financial services firm, maintains for its employees a defined contribution retirement savings plan. Employees may choose to contribute a portion of their compensation to the Plan as retirement savings, and Fifth Third provides matching contributions of up to 4% of an employee's compensation. The Plan's assets are invested in 20 separate funds, including mutual funds and an ESOP. Plan participants can allocate their contributions among the funds however they like; Fifth Third's matching contributions, on the other hand, are always invested initially in the ESOP, though the participant can then choose to move them to another fund. The Plan requires the ESOP's funds to be "invested primarily in shares of common stock of Fifth Third."

Respondents, who are former Fifth Third employees and ESOP participants, filed this putative class action in Federal District Court in Ohio. They claim that petitioners, Fifth Third and various Fifth Third officers, were fiduciaries of the Plan and violated the duties of loyalty and prudence imposed by ERISA. We limit our review to the duty-of-prudence claims.

The complaint alleges that by July 2007, the fiduciaries knew or should have known that Fifth Third's stock was overvalued and excessively risky for two separate reasons. First, publicly available information such as newspaper articles provided early warning signs that subprime lending, which formed a large part of Fifth Third's business, would soon leave creditors high and dry as the housing market collapsed and subprime borrowers became unable to pay off their mortgages. Second, nonpublic information (which petitioners knew because they were Fifth Third insiders) indicated that Fifth Third officers had deceived the market by making material misstatements about the company's financial prospects. Those misstatements led the market to overvalue Fifth Third stock—the ESOP's primary investment—and so petitioners, using the participants' money, were consequently paying more for that stock than it was worth.

The complaint further alleges that a prudent fiduciary in petitioners' position would have responded to this information in one or more of the following ways: (1) by selling the ESOP's holdings of Fifth Third stock before the value of those holdings declined, (2) by refraining from purchasing any more Fifth Third stock, (3) by canceling the Plan's ESOP option, and (4) by disclosing the inside information so that the market would adjust its valuation of Fifth Third stock downward and the ESOP would no longer be overpaying for it.

Rather than follow any of these courses of action, petitioners continued to hold and buy Fifth Third stock. Then the market crashed, and Fifth Third's stock price fell by 74% between July 2007 and September 2009, when the complaint was filed. Since the ESOP's funds were invested primarily in Fifth Third stock, this fall in price eliminated a large part of the retirement savings that the participants had invested in the ESOP. (The stock has since made a partial recovery to around half of its July 2007 price.)

The District Court dismissed the complaint for failure to state a claim. The court began from the premise that where a lawsuit challenges ESOP fiduciaries' investment decisions, "the plan fiduciaries start with a presumption that their 'decision to remain invested in employer securities was reasonable.' " The court next held that this rule is applicable at the pleading stage and then concluded that the complaint's allegations were insufficient to overcome it.

The Court of Appeals for the Sixth Circuit reversed. Although it agreed that ESOP fiduciaries are entitled to a presumption of prudence, it took the view that the presumption is evidentiary only and therefore does not apply at the pleading stage. Thus, the Sixth Circuit simply asked whether the allegations in the complaint were sufficient to state a claim for breach of fiduciary duty. It held that they were.

In light of differences among the Courts of Appeals as to the nature of the presumption of prudence applicable to ESOP fiduciaries, we granted the fiduciaries' petition for certiorari. . . .

II

A

. . .

B

Several Courts of Appeals have gone beyond ERISA's express provision that ESOP fiduciaries need not diversify by giving ESOP fiduciaries a "presumption of prudence" when their decisions to hold or buy employer stock are challenged as imprudent. Thus, the Third Circuit has held that "an ESOP fiduciary who invests the [ESOP's] assets in employer stock is entitled to a presumption that it acted consistently with ERISA" in doing so. *Moench v. Robertson.* The Ninth Circuit has said that to "overcome the presumption of prudent investment, plaintiffs must . . . make allegations that clearly implicate the company's viability as an ongoing concern or show a precipitous decline in the employer's stock . . . combined with evidence that the company is on the brink of collapse or is undergoing serious mismanagement." And the Seventh Circuit has described the presumption as requiring plaintiffs to "allege and ultimately prove that the company faced 'impending collapse' or 'dire circumstances' that could not have been foreseen by the founder of the plan."

The Sixth Circuit agreed that some sort of presumption favoring an ESOP fiduciary's purchase of employer stock is appropriate. But it held that this presumption is an evidentiary rule that does not apply at the pleading stage. It further held that, to overcome the presumption, a plaintiff need not show that the employer was on the "brink of collapse" or the like. Rather, the plaintiff need only show that "'a prudent fiduciary acting under similar circumstances would have made a different investment decision.'"

Petitioners argue that the lower courts are right to apply a presumption of prudence, that it should apply from the pleading stage onward, and that the presumption should be strongly in favor of ESOP fiduciaries' purchasing and holding of employer stock.

In particular, petitioners propose a rule that a challenge to an ESOP fiduciary's decision to hold or buy company stock "cannot prevail unless extraordinary circumstances, such as a serious threat to the employer's viability, mean that continued investment would substantially impair the purpose of the plan." . . . This is because the goal of employee ownership will be substantially impaired only if the employer goes out of business, leaving the employees with no company to own.

We must decide whether ERISA contains some such presumption.

III

A

In our view, the law does not create a special presumption favoring ESOP fiduciaries. Rather, the same standard of prudence applies to all ERISA fiduciaries, including ESOP fiduciaries, except that an ESOP fiduciary is under no duty to diversify the ESOP's holdings. This conclusion follows from the pertinent provisions of ERISA, which are set forth above.

Section 1104(a)(1)(B) "imposes a 'prudent person' standard by which to measure fiduciaries' investment decisions and disposition of assets." Section 1104(a)(1)(C) requires ERISA fiduciaries to diversify plan assets. And § 1104(a)(2) establishes the extent to which those duties are loosened in the ESOP context to ensure that employers are permitted and encouraged to offer ESOPs. Section 1104(a)(2) makes no reference to a special "presumption" in favor of ESOP fiduciaries. It does not require plaintiffs to allege that the employer was on the "brink of collapse," under "extraordinary circumstances," or the like. Instead, § 1104(a)(2) simply modifies the duties imposed by § 1104(a)(1) in a precisely delineated way: It provides that an ESOP fiduciary is exempt from § 1104(a)(1)(C)'s diversification requirement and also from § 1104(a)(1)(B)'s duty of prudence, but *only to the extent that it requires diversification.*"

Thus, ESOP fiduciaries, unlike ERISA fiduciaries generally, are not liable for losses that result from a failure to diversify. But aside from that distinction, because ESOP fiduciaries are ERISA fiduciaries and because § 1104(a)(1)(B)'s duty of prudence applies to all ERISA fiduciaries, ESOP fiduciaries are subject to the duty of prudence just as other ERISA fiduciaries are.

B

Petitioners make several arguments to the contrary. First, petitioners argue that the special purpose of an ESOP—investing participants' savings in the stock of their employer—calls for a presumption that such investments are prudent. Their argument is as follows: ERISA defines the duty of prudence in terms of what a prudent person would do "in the conduct of an enterprise of a like character and with like aims." § 1104(a)(1)(B). The "character" and "aims" of an ESOP differ from those of an ordinary retirement investment, such as a diversified mutual fund. An ordinary plan seeks (1) to maximize retirement savings for participants while (2) avoiding excessive risk. But an ESOP also seeks (3) to promote employee ownership of employer stock. For instance, Fifth Third's Plan requires the ESOP's assets to be "invested primarily in shares of common stock of Fifth Third." In light of this additional goal, an ESOP fiduciary's decision to buy more shares of employer stock, even if it would be imprudent were it viewed solely as an attempt to secure financial retirement benefits while avoiding excessive risk, might nonetheless be prudent if understood as an attempt to promote employee ownership of employer stock, a goal that Congress views as important. Thus, a claim that an ESOP fiduciary's investment in employer stock was imprudent as a way of securing retirement savings should be viewed unfavorably because, unless the company was about to go out of business, that investment was advancing the additional goal of employee ownership of employer stock.

We cannot accept the claim that underlies this argument, namely, that the content of ERISA's duty of prudence varies depending upon the specific nonpecuniary goal set out in an ERISA plan, such as what petitioners claim is the nonpecuniary goal here. Taken in context, § 1104(a)(1)(B)'s reference to "an enterprise of a like character and with like aims" means an enterprise with what the immediately preceding provision calls the "exclusive purpose" to be pursued by all ERISA fiduciaries: "providing benefits to participants and their beneficiaries" while "defraying reasonable expenses of administering the plan." Read in the context of ERISA as a whole, the term "benefits" in the provision just quoted must be understood to refer to the sort of *financial* benefits (such as retirement income) that trustees who manage investments typically seek to secure for the trust's beneficiaries. The term does not cover nonpecuniary benefits like those supposed to arise from employee ownership of employer stock.

Consider the statute's requirement that fiduciaries act "in accordance with the documents and instruments governing the plan *insofar as such documents and instruments are consistent with the provisions of this subchapter.* " This provision makes clear that the duty of prudence trumps the instructions of a plan document, such as an instruction to invest exclusively in employer stock even if financial goals demand the contrary. This rule would make little sense if, as petitioners argue, the duty of prudence is defined by the aims of the particular plan as set out in the plan documents, since in that case the duty of prudence could never conflict with a plan document.

Consider also § 1104(a)(2), which exempts an ESOP fiduciary from § 1104(a)(1)(B)'s duty of prudence but "only to the extent that it requires diversification." What need would there be for this specific provision were the nature of § 1104(a)(1)(B)'s duty of prudence altered anyway in the case of an ESOP in light of the ESOP's aim of promoting employee ownership of employer stock?

Petitioners are right to point out that *Congress,* in seeking to permit and promote ESOPs, was pursuing purposes other than the financial security of plan participants. Congress pursued those purposes by promoting ESOPs with tax incentives. And it also pursued them by exempting ESOPs from ERISA's diversification requirement, which otherwise would have precluded their creation. But we are not convinced that Congress *also* sought to promote ESOPs by further relaxing the duty of prudence as applied to ESOPs with the sort of presumption proposed by petitioners.

Second, and relatedly, petitioners contend that the duty of prudence should be read in light of the rule under the common law of trusts that "the settlor can reduce or waive the prudent man standard of care by specific language in the trust instrument." The argument is that, by commanding the ESOP fiduciary to invest primarily in Fifth Third stock, the plan documents waived the duty of prudence to the extent that it comes into conflict with investment in Fifth Third stock—at least unless "extraordinary circumstances" arise that so threaten the goal of employee ownership of Fifth Third stock that the fiduciaries must assume that the settlor would want them to depart from that goal under the common-law "deviation doctrine." This argument fails, however, in light of this Court's holding that, by contrast to the rule at common law, "trust documents cannot excuse trustees from their duties under ERISA."

Third, petitioners argue that subjecting ESOP fiduciaries to a duty of prudence without the protection of a special presumption will lead to conflicts with the legal prohibition on insider trading. The potential for conflict arises because ESOP fiduciaries often are company insiders and because suits against insider fiduciaries frequently allege, as the complaint in this case alleges, that the fiduciaries were imprudent in failing to act on inside information they had about the value of the employer's stock.

This concern is a legitimate one. But an ESOP-specific rule that a fiduciary does not act imprudently in buying or holding company stock unless the company is on the brink of collapse (or the like) is an ill-fitting means of addressing it. While ESOP fiduciaries may be more likely to have insider information about a company that the fund is investing in than are other ERISA fiduciaries, the potential for conflict with the securities laws would be the same for a non-ESOP fiduciary who had relevant inside information about a potential investment. And the potential for conflict is the same for an ESOP fiduciary whose company is on the brink of collapse as for a fiduciary who is invested in a healthier company. (Surely a fiduciary is not obligated to break the insider trading laws even if his company is about to fail.) The potential for conflict therefore does not persuade us to accept a presumption of the sort adopted by the lower courts and proposed by petitioners. We discuss alternative means of dealing with the potential for conflict in Part IV, *infra*.

Finally, petitioners argue that, without some sort of special presumption, the threat of costly duty-of-prudence lawsuits will deter companies from offering ESOPs to their employees, contrary to the stated intent of Congress. ESOP plans instruct their fiduciaries to invest in company stock, and § 1104(a)(1)(D) requires fiduciaries to follow plan documents so long as they do not conflict with ERISA. Thus, in many cases an ESOP fiduciary who fears that continuing to invest in company stock may be imprudent finds himself between a rock and a hard place: If he keeps investing and the stock goes down he may be sued for acting imprudently in violation of § 1104(a)(1)(B), but if he stops investing and the stock goes up he may be sued for disobeying the plan documents in violation of § 1104(a)(1)(D). Petitioners argue that, given the threat of such expensive litigation, ESOPs cannot thrive unless their fiduciaries are granted a defense-friendly presumption.

Petitioners are basically seeking relief from what they believe are meritless, economically burdensome lawsuits. We agree that Congress sought to encourage the creation of ESOPs. And we have recognized that "ERISA represents a " 'careful balancing" between ensuring fair and prompt enforcement of rights under a plan and the encouragement of the creation of such plans.' "

At the same time, we do not believe that the presumption at issue here is an appropriate way to weed out meritless lawsuits or to provide the requisite "balancing." The proposed presumption makes it impossible for a plaintiff to state a duty-of-prudence claim, no matter how meritorious, unless the employer is in very bad economic circumstances. Such a rule does not readily divide the plausible sheep from the meritless goats. That important task can be better accomplished through careful, context-sensitive scrutiny of a complaint's allegations. We consequently stand by our conclusion that the law does not create a special presumption of prudence for ESOP fiduciaries.

IV

We consider more fully one important mechanism for weeding out meritless claims, the motion to dismiss for failure to state a claim. That mechanism, which gave rise to the lower court decisions at issue here, requires careful judicial consideration of whether the complaint states a claim that the defendant has acted imprudently. Because the content of the duty of prudence turns on "the circumstances . . . prevailing" at the time the fiduciary acts, § 1104(a)(1)(B), the appropriate inquiry will necessarily be context specific.

The District Court in this case granted petitioners' motion to dismiss the complaint because it held that respondents could not overcome the presumption of prudence. The Court of Appeals, by contrast, concluded that no presumption applied. And we agree with that conclusion. The Court of Appeals, however, went on to hold that respondents had stated a plausible duty-of-prudence claim. The arguments made here, along with our review of the record, convince us that the judgment of the Court of Appeals should be vacated and the case remanded. On remand, the Court of Appeals should apply the pleading standard as discussed in *Twombly* and *Iqbal* in light of the following considerations.

A

Respondents allege that, as of July 2007, petitioners knew or should have known in light of publicly available information, such as newspaper articles, that continuing to hold and purchase Fifth Third stock was imprudent. The complaint alleges, among other things, that petitioners "continued to allow the Plan's investment in Fifth Third Stock even during the time that the stock price was declining in value as a result of [the] collapse of the housing market" and that "[a] prudent fiduciary facing similar circumstances would not have stood idly by as the Plan's assets were decimated."

In our view, where a stock is publicly traded, allegations that a fiduciary should have recognized from publicly available information alone that the market was over- or undervaluing the stock are implausible as a general rule, at least in the absence of special circumstances. Many investors take the view that " 'they have little hope of outperforming the market in the long run based solely on their analysis of publicly available information,' " and accordingly they " 'rely on the security's market price as an unbiased assessment of the security's value in light of all public information.' " ERISA fiduciaries, who likewise could reasonably see "little hope of outperforming the market . . . based solely on their analysis of publicly available information," may, as a general matter, likewise prudently rely on the market price.

In other words, a fiduciary usually "is not imprudent to assume that a major stock market . . . provides the best estimate of the value of the stocks traded on it that is available to him."

We do not here consider whether a plaintiff could nonetheless plausibly allege imprudence on the basis of publicly available information by pointing to a special circumstance affecting the reliability of the market price as " 'an unbiased assessment of the security's value in light of all public information' " that would make reliance on the market's valuation imprudent. In this case, the Court of Appeals held that the complaint stated a claim because respondents "allege that Fifth Third engaged in lending practices that were equivalent to participation in the subprime lending market, that Defendants were aware of the risks of such investments by the start of the class period, and that such risks made Fifth Third stock an imprudent investment." The Court of Appeals did not point to any special circumstance rendering reliance on the market price imprudent. The court's decision to deny dismissal therefore appears to have been based on an erroneous understanding of the prudence of relying on market prices.

B

Respondents also claim that petitioners behaved imprudently by failing to act on the basis of *nonpublic* information that was available to them because they were Fifth Third insiders. In particular, the complaint alleges that petitioners had inside information indicating that the market was overvaluing Fifth Third stock and that they could have used this information to prevent losses to the fund by (1) selling the ESOP's holdings of Fifth Third stock; (2) refraining from future stock purchases (including by removing the Plan's ESOP option altogether); or (3) publicly disclosing the inside information so that the market would correct the stock price downward, with the result that the ESOP could continue to buy Fifth Third stock without paying an inflated price for it.

To state a claim for breach of the duty of prudence on the basis of inside information, a plaintiff must plausibly allege an alternative action that the defendant could have taken that would have been consistent with the securities laws and that a prudent fiduciary in the same circumstances would not have viewed as more likely to harm the fund than to help it. The following three points inform the requisite analysis.

First, in deciding whether the complaint states a claim upon which relief can be granted, courts must bear in mind that the duty of prudence, under ERISA as under the common law of trusts, does not require a fiduciary to break the law. Federal securities laws "are violated when a corporate insider trades in the securities of his corporation on the basis of material, nonpublic information." As every Court of Appeals to address the question has held, ERISA's duty of prudence cannot require an ESOP fiduciary to perform an action—such as divesting the fund's holdings of the employer's stock on the basis of inside information—that would violate the securities laws. To the extent that the Sixth Circuit denied dismissal based on the theory that the duty of prudence required petitioners to sell the ESOP's holdings of Fifth Third stock, its denial of dismissal was erroneous.

Second, where a complaint faults fiduciaries for failing to decide, on the basis of the inside information, to refrain from making additional stock purchases or for failing to disclose that information to the public so that the stock would no longer be overvalued, additional considerations arise. The courts should consider the extent to which an ERISA-based obligation either to refrain on the basis of inside information from making a planned trade or to disclose inside information to the public could conflict with the complex insider trading and corporate disclosure requirements imposed by the federal securities laws or with the objectives of those laws. The U. S. Securities and Exchange Commission has not advised us of its views on these matters, and we believe those views may well be relevant.

Third, lower courts faced with such claims should also consider whether the complaint has plausibly alleged that a prudent fiduciary in the defendant's position could not have concluded that stopping purchases—which the market might take as a sign that insider fiduciaries viewed the employer's stock as a bad investment—or publicly disclosing negative information would do more harm than good to the fund by causing a drop in the stock price and a concomitant drop in the value of the stock already held by the fund.

* * *

We leave it to the courts below to apply the foregoing to the complaint in this case in the first instance. The judgment of the Court of Appeals for the Sixth Circuit is vacated and the case is remanded for further proceedings consistent with this opinion. *It is so ordered.*

NOTE

In the immediate aftermath of the Supreme Court's decision, several commentators suggested that employers will think twice before offering stock as an investment option in their plans. It is too early to tell whether that will be the case. While plaintiffs no longer have to overcome a presumption of prudence, the Court's language in Part IV of its opinion suggests they still have a significant hurdle in demonstrating lack of prudence as well as indicating what the fiduciary could have done that would not violate the securities laws. As Justice Breyer pointed out, ERISA's duty of prudence "does not require a fiduciary to break the law." Still, the effect of the Court's decision may be to make it easier to plaintiff to get past a motion to dismiss. See, e.g., Groom Law Group, Supreme Court Strikes Down ESOP Presumption of Prudence and Imposes New Limits and Standards for Stock Drop Claims, http://www.groom.com/media/publication/1473_Investment_Lawyer_Oct_2014.pdf; Wilson Elser, U.S. Supreme Court Issues Important Decision Affecting Fiduciaries of ESOPs, http://www.wilsonelser.com/news_and_insights/client_alerts/1977-u_s_supreme_court_issues_important_decision; American Benefits Council, ERISA Litigation & Company Stock: Supreme Court's Decision in Fifth Third v. Dudenhoeffer, http://www.americanbenefitscouncil.org/documents2014/presentation_blb_stockplans 081114.pdf.

BENEFIT DENIALS

Analysis

Introduction

ERISA plan administrators are routinely called upon to decide whether benefit claims fall within plan terms. The "vast majority of ERISA cases are simple benefit claim disputes in which a federal judge is reviewing the decision of a plan fiduciary." Peter M. Kelly, Blunt Judicial Guidance on ERISA Benefit Claims, Probate & Property (Sept.– Oct. 2000), at 49. Plan-level benefit determinations are made by the millions every month under health care plans alone. Most benefit determinations are routine and uncontested. Nevertheless, because the volume is so large, the tiny fraction of benefit denials that are contested produces an immense caseload (and case law).

Contested benefit issues are litigated as federal-law claims under ERISA. Section 503 obliges every plan to have a written claims procedure, including an internal review process conducted "by the appropriate named fiduciary." DoL regulations amplify these requirements, see 29 C.F.R. § 2560.503–1. The determination of benefits is, therefore, a fiduciary function, consistent with ERISA's definition of a fiduciary as one who exercises "any discretionary authority or discretionary responsibility in the administration of [the] plan." ERISA § 3(21)(A)(iii).

Judicial review of benefit denials follows from ERISA § 502(a)(1)(B), which empowers the participant or beneficiary to sue to recover or to enforce rights under the plan. (ERISA remedy law is the subject of Chapter 16, infra.)

Although most benefit denial cases arise from welfare benefit plans, disputes regarding pension claims also occur, e.g., Gilley v. Monsanto

Co., Inc., 490 F.3d 848 (11th Cir.2007) (whether participant satisfied plan's length-of-service requirement); Gallo v. Madera, 136 F.3d 326 (2d Cir.1998) (how to apply break in service rules).

Frequently, denials of benefits claims regarding pension plans involve calculation of pension benefits. See, e.g., Fortier v. Principal Life Ins. Co., 666 F.3d 231 (4th Cir.2012); Novella v. Westchester Cnty., New York Carpenters' Pension Fund, 661 F.3d 128 (2d Cir. 2011).

Especially under a welfare benefit plan such as one providing health care, accident insurance, or disability pay, the issue in a benefit dispute can be quite fact-intensive, often requiring investigation into the claimant's physical condition or other circumstances.

A. JUDICIAL REVIEW OF FIDUCIARY DECISIONMAKING

ERISA § 503(1) requires the plan to provide written reasons for a benefit denial. This provision "afford[s] the beneficiary an explanation of the denial of benefits that is adequate to ensure meaningful review of that denial." Halpin v. W.W. Grainger, Inc., 962 F.2d 685, 689 (7th Cir.1992). The measure "ensure[s] that a plan participant is protected from arbitrary or unprincipled decision-making." Ellis v. Metropolitan Life Ins. Co., 126 F.3d 228, 236–37 (4th Cir.1997). In VanderKlok v. Provident Life & Accident Ins. Co., 956 F.2d 610, 616 (6th Cir.1992), the court found that a letter denying benefits was defective under ERISA § 503 "because it fails to provide the specific reason or reasons for denial and the specific reference to pertinent plan provisions on which the denial is based."

Neither ERISA § 503 nor the DoL regulations require the plan administrator to afford the participant a hearing, and the courts have refused to imply such a requirement. "[A] trial-like atmosphere" is not required, nor need the decisionmaker hear oral testimony; a written record will suffice. Grossmuller v. UAW, 715 F.2d 853, 858 n. 5 (3d Cir.1983); accord, DuMond v. Centex Corp., 172 F.3d 618, 623 (8th Cir.1999). (The concern of the courts with procedural regularity, so-called process values, in benefit denial matters is further discussed later in this chapter.)

Apart from the remedy and preemption issues dealt with in Chapters 16 and 17, infra, two main difficulties have arisen with regard to judicial review of benefit denials. ERISA did not address the standard of review, that is, the extent of deference, if any, that a reviewing court should give to the plan's internal decisionmaking. Section A examines the troubled case law dealing with that question, centered on the Supreme Court's opinions in Firestone Tire & Rubber Co. v. Bruch, 489 U.S. 101 (1989), and Metropolitan Life Ins. Co. v. Glenn, 554 U.S. 105, 128 S.Ct. 2343 (2008).

Section B of this chapter deals with the recurrent problem of the plan participant who fails to comply with some plan requirement, or who acts in reliance upon a misunderstanding of plan provisions, oftentimes because plan personnel have misinformed the participant. The courts have mostly insisted upon compliance with the plan's written terms, but limited excusing doctrines, examined here, have developed.

1. THE STANDARD OF REVIEW: DEFERENTIAL OR DE NOVO?

Although ERISA provides for judicial review of plan decisionmaking about benefit denials, ERISA neglected to supply any express guidance about what standard of review courts should apply in reviewing the decisions of plan fiduciaries. The fundamental choice is between deferential review, which casts upon the participant or beneficiary the burden of showing that the benefit denial was unjustified; or nondeferential review, sometimes called de novo review, in which no presumption of correctness attaches to the plan's decisionmaking.

Deferential review is commonly called the "arbitrary and capricious" (A&C) standard. The issue is "not which side we believe is right, but whether the [decisionmaker] has substantial evidentiary grounds for a reasonable decision in its favor." Doyle v. Paul Revere Life Ins. Co., 144 F.3d 181, 184 (1st Cir.1998). Under the A&C standard, "[a] court may overturn a plan administrator's decision to deny benefits only if the decision was 'without reason, unsupported by substantial evidence, or erroneous as a matter of law.' " Celardo v. GNY Automobile Dealers Health & Welfare Trust, 318 F.3d 142, 146 (2d Cir.2003).

Lacking statutory direction, the courts had to devise the standard of review as a matter of ERISA common law. Early in their encounter with ERISA, the courts transposed the standard of review that they had developed in litigation challenging benefit determinations made by multiemployer plan trustees. The Taft-Hartley Act of 1947, 29 U.S.C. § 186 et seq., requires that multiemployer plans be governed by joint boards of union- and industry-selected trustees. Unlike ERISA § 503(1), however, Taft-Hartley does not contain an express authorization for judicial review of benefit denials. The federal courts implied the authorization anyhow. Taft-Hartley § 302(c)(5) imposes an exclusive benefit rule, comparable to the later such rule in ERISA § 404(a)(1)(A). The courts rested judicial review of benefit denials in Taft-Hartley plans mainly on implication from § 302(c)(5). They reasoned that when plan fiduciaries denied benefits unreasonably, the plan exhibited a "structural defect" that conflicted with the requirement of § 302(c)(5) that the plan be "for the sole and exclusive benefit of the employees."

In part because the basis for review of benefit denials under the Taft-Hartley Act was so tenuous, the courts applied the deferential A&C standard of review. The decisions of multiemployer plan trustees could be "reversed only [when] arbitrary, capricious or made in bad faith, not supported by substantial evidence, or erroneous on a question of law." Rehmar v. Smith, 555 F.2d 1362, 1371 (9th Cir.1976). This policy of deferential review also reflected a longstanding concern to minimize the courts' involvement in labor-management struggles.

Because ERISA's exclusive benefit rule was nearly identical to the Taft-Hartley rule, it was a simple step for the federal courts to apply the familiar A&C standard of review to benefit denial cases arising under ERISA's express authorization of judicial review. The effect was to extend the A&C standard from the world of Taft-Hartley-governed multiemployer plans (for which it had been tailored) to the prevailingly single-employer world of ERISA-covered plans. For background, see

Comment, The Arbitrary and Capricious Standard under ERISA: Its Origins and Application, 23 Duquesne L. Rev. 1033, 1035–41 (1985).

In 1989 in *Firestone*, excerpted below, the Supreme Court unexpectedly substituted nondeferential review in place of deferential A&C review as ERISA's default regime. Four years after deciding *Firestone*, the Supreme Court effectively abrogated A&C review even for multiemployer plans under Taft-Hartley, in part because ERISA fiduciary law provides a later and better statutory foundation for judicial review of plan benefit denials of all sorts. Local 144 Nursing Home Pension Fund v. Demisay, 508 U.S. 581 (1993). Justice Scalia's opinion emphasizes that Taft-Hartley fiduciaries are subject to the exclusive benefit requirement of ERISA § 404(a)(1). 508 U.S. at 592. The logic of *Demisay* appears to be that this explicit authority for reviewing plan decisionmaking under ERISA obviates the need for the comparable regime that the courts read into Taft-Hartley in the decades before ERISA.

Remarkably, although *Firestone* makes de novo review the default norm for judicial review of benefit denial cases, most such cases continue to be decided under the old A&C standard. The reason is that the decision in *Firestone* allows the ERISA plan documents to defeat the default standard and to substitute deferential review by granting a fiduciary discretionary authority. Since most plans elect that option, A&C review prevails just as it did before *Firestone* purported to disapprove it.

2. CONFLICT OF INTEREST: DEVELOPMENTS BEFORE *FIRESTONE*

"Welfare benefit plans and defined benefit pension plans affect the employer's bottom line more or less directly. When a benefit claim is denied, the employer's liability is reduced." Daniel Fischel & John H. Langbein, ERISA's Fundamental Contradiction: The Exclusive Benefit Rule, 55 U. Chicago. L. Rev. 1105, 1131 (1988) [hereafter Fischel & Langbein].

Recall that ERISA effectively lodges the power to choose fiduciaries with the employer or other sponsor. See ERISA §§ 402, 403; see also § 3(16)(A)(ii), designating the plan sponsor as the default plan administrator in the event the plan documents do not delegate the function to another fiduciary. Recall, further, the discussion from Chapter 14, supra, emphasizing that because ERISA § 408(c)(3) allows management officers to serve as plan fiduciaries, ERISA all but invites conflicts of interest in plan administration.

Another recurrent setting of embedded conflict occurs when an ERISA plan purchases insurance to cover promised benefits, and the insurance contract makes the insurance company responsible for benefit determinations under the policy. Such arrangements are common in ERISA plans that provide health care, occupational disability insurance, and life and accident insurance. In such cases the insurer is an ERISA fiduciary; see, e.g., Blue Cross & Blue Shield v. Sanders, 138 F.3d 1347, 1354 (11th Cir.1998) (administrators "are fiduciaries if they have the authority to make ultimate decisions regarding benefits eligibility").

In the 1980s, a number of courts began to grapple with the concern that in some circumstances, the conflict of interest between management-selected plan fiduciaries and plan participants might dictate some adjustment to the deferential A&C standard of review, which was then the default standard. In Dockray v. Phelps Dodge Corp., 801 F.2d 1149, 1152–53 (9th Cir.1986), the court concluded that the "countervailing tugs of divided loyalty" pulling at the plan administrator made it "unrealistic to grant the same substantial deference to [the firm's] management as we would to the decision of a wholly independent fund trustee in similar circumstances." In another Ninth Circuit case, the court held: "Where, as here, the employer's denial of benefits to a class avoids a very substantial outlay, the reviewing court should consider that fact in applying the arbitrary and capricious standard of review. Less deference should be given to the trustee's decision." Jung v. FMC Corp., 755 F.2d 708, 711–12 (9th Cir.1985).

The Third Circuit opinion in *Firestone* also emphasized the conflict of interest of plan fiduciaries as a factor that justified restricting the deference that was otherwise due plan decisionmakers. Bruch v. Firestone Tire & Rubber Co., 828 F.2d 134 (3d Cir.1987). In that case, the employees who claimed severance benefits under the Firestone plan were terminated when Firestone sold their division, but the successor employer continued their employment. Firestone rejected the claims. Judge Becker said that "under ERISA courts must be cognizant of the features that distinguish the ERISA arrangements from the paradigmatic common law [trust] situation," in particular that in this unfunded severance pay plan, "every dollar saved by the administrator on behalf of his employer is a dollar in Firestone's pocket." Id. at 144.

3.   FIRESTONE TIRE & RUBBER CO. V. BRUCH

489 U.S. 101 (1989).

■ JUSTICE O'CONNOR delivered the opinion of the Court. . . .

Late in 1980, petitioner Firestone Tire and Rubber Company (Firestone) sold, as going concerns, the five plants comprising its Plastics Division to Occidental Petroleum Company (Occidental). Most of the approximately 500 salaried employees at the five plants were rehired by Occidental and continued in their same positions without interruption and at the same rates of pay. At the time of the sale, Firestone maintained three pension and welfare benefit plans for its employees: a termination pay plan, a retirement plan, and a stock purchase plan. Firestone was the sole source of funding for the plans and had not established separate trust funds out of which to pay the benefits from the plans. All three of the plans were either "employee welfare benefit plans" or "employee pension benefit plans" governed (albeit in different ways) by ERISA. By operation of law, Firestone itself was the administrator [ERISA § 3(16)(A)(ii)] and fiduciary [ERISA § 3(21)(A)] of each of these "unfunded" plans. At the time of the sale of its Plastics Division, Firestone was not aware that the termination pay plan was governed by ERISA, and therefore had not set up a claims procedure [ERISA § 503], nor complied with ERISA's reporting and disclosure obligations [ERISA §§ 101–111] with respect to that plan.

Respondents, six Firestone employees who were rehired by Occidental, sought severance benefits from Firestone under the termination pay plan. In relevant part, that plan provides as follows:

"If your service is discontinued prior to the time you are eligible for pension benefits, you will be given termination pay if released because of a reduction in work force or if you become physically or mentally unable to perform your job.

"The amount of termination pay you will receive will depend on your period of credited company service."

Several of the respondents also sought information from Firestone regarding their benefits under all three of the plans pursuant to certain ERISA disclosure provisions. See [ERISA §§ 104(b)(4), 105(a)]. Firestone denied respondents severance benefits on the ground that the sale of the Plastics Division to Occidental did not constitute a "reduction in work force" within the meaning of the termination pay plan. . . .

Respondents then filed a class action on behalf of "former, salaried, non-union employees who worked in the five plants that comprised the Plastics Division of Firestone." The action was based on [ERISA § 502(a)(1)], which provides that a "civil action may be brought . . . by a participant or beneficiary [of a covered plan to] recover benefits due to him under the terms of his plan." In Count I of their complaint, respondents alleged that they were entitled to severance benefits because Firestone's sale of the Plastics Division to Occidental constituted a "reduction in work force" within the meaning of the termination pay plan.

The District Court granted Firestone's motion for summary judgment. With respect to Count I, the District Court held that Firestone had satisfied its fiduciary duty under ERISA because its decision not to pay severance benefits to respondents under the termination pay plan was not arbitrary or capricious.

The Court of Appeals reversed the District Court's grant of summary [judgment]. With respect to Count I, the Court of Appeals acknowledged that most federal courts have reviewed the denial of benefits by ERISA fiduciaries and administrators under the arbitrary and capricious standard. It noted, however, that the arbitrary and capricious standard had been softened in cases where fiduciaries and administrators had some bias or adverse interest. The Court of Appeals held that where an employer is itself the fiduciary and administrator of an unfunded benefit plan, its decision to deny benefits should be subject to *de novo* judicial review. It reasoned that in such situations deference is unwarranted given the lack of assurance of impartiality on the part of the employer. . . .

Respondents' action asserting that they were entitled to benefits because the sale of Firestone's Plastics Division constituted a "reduction in work force" within the meaning of the termination pay plan was based on the authority of [ERISA § 502(a)(1)(B)]. That provision allows a suit to recover benefits due under the plan, to enforce rights under the terms of the plan, and to obtain a declaratory judgment of future entitlement to benefits under the provisions of the plan contract. The discussion which follows is limited to the appropriate standard of review in [§ 502(a)(1)(B)] actions challenging denials of benefits based on plan interpretations. We express no view as to the appropriate standard of review for actions under other remedial provisions of ERISA.

Although it is a "comprehensive and reticulated statute," ERISA does not set out the appropriate standard of review for actions under [§ 502(a)(1)(B)] challenging benefit eligibility determinations. To fill this gap, federal courts have adopted the arbitrary and capricious standard developed under [Taft-Hartley Act § 302(c), Labor Management Relations Act (LMRA)]. . . .

Unlike the LMRA, ERISA explicitly authorizes suits against fiduciaries and plan administrators to remedy statutory violations, including breaches of fiduciary duty and lack of compliance with benefit plans. See [ERISA §§ 502(a), 502(f)].

Thus, the *raison d'être* for the LMRA arbitrary and capricious standard—the need for a jurisdictional basis in suits against trustees— is not present in ERISA. Without this jurisdictional analogy, LMRA principles offer no support for the adoption of the arbitrary and capricious standard insofar as [§ 502(a)(1)(B)] is concerned.

ERISA abounds with the language and terminology of trust law. See, e.g., [ERISA §§ 3(7)] ("participant"), [3(8)] ("beneficiary"), [3(21)(A)] ("fiduciary"), [403(a)] ("trustee"), [404] ("fiduciary duties").

ERISA's legislative history confirms that the Act's fiduciary responsibility provisions, [ERISA §§ 401–414] "codif[y] and make[ ] applicable to [ERISA] fiduciaries certain principles developed in the evolution of the law of trusts." Given this language and history, we have held that courts are to develop a "federal common law of rights and obligations under ERISA-regulated plans." In determining the appropriate standard of review for actions under [ERISA § 502(a)(1)(B)], we are guided by principles of trust law.

Trust principles make a deferential standard of review appropriate when a trustee exercises discretionary powers. See Restatement (Second) of Trusts § 187 (1959) ("[w]here discretion is conferred upon the trustee with respect to the exercise of a power, its exercise is not subject to control by the court except to prevent an abuse by the trustee of his discretion"). A trustee may be given power to construe disputed or doubtful terms, and in such circumstances the trustee's interpretation will not be disturbed if reasonable. Whether "the exercise of a power is permissive or mandatory depends upon the terms of the trust." 3 W. Fratcher, Scott on Trusts § 187, p. 14 (4th ed. 1988). Hence, over a century ago we remarked that "[w]hen trustees are in existence, and capable of acting, a court of equity will not interfere to control them in the exercise of a *discretion vested in them by the instrument* under which they act." *Nichols v. Eaton,* 91 U.S. 716, 724–725, 23 L.Ed. 254 (1875) (emphasis added). Firestone can seek no shelter in these principles of trust law, however, for there is no evidence that under Firestone's termination pay plan the administrator has the power to construe uncertain terms or that eligibility determinations are to be given deference.

Finding no support in the language of its termination pay plan for the arbitrary and capricious standard, Firestone argues that as a matter of trust law the interpretation of the terms of a plan is an inherently discretionary function. But other settled principles of trust law, which point to *de novo* review of benefit eligibility determinations based on plan interpretations, belie this contention. As they do with contractual provisions, courts construe terms in trust agreements without deferring to either party's interpretation. "The extent of the duties and powers of a trustee is determined by the rules of law that are applicable to the situation, and not the rules that the trustee or his attorney believes to be applicable, and by the terms of the trust *as the court may interpret them,* and not as they may be interpreted by the trustee himself or by his attorney." 3 W. Fratcher, Scott on Trusts § 201, at 221 (emphasis added). A trustee who is in doubt as to the interpretation of the instrument can protect himself by obtaining instructions from the court. Restatement (Second) of Trusts § 201, Comment b (1959). The terms of trusts created by written instruments are "determined by the provisions of the instrument as interpreted in light of all the circumstances and such other evidence of the intention of the settlor with respect to the trust as is not inadmissible." Restatement (Second) of Trusts § 4, Comment d (1959).

The trust law *de novo* standard of review is consistent with the judicial interpretation of employee benefit plans prior to the enactment of ERISA. Actions challenging an employer's denial of benefits before enactment of ERISA were governed by principles of contract law. If the plan did not give the employer or administrator discretionary or final authority to construe uncertain terms, the court reviewed the employee's claim as it would have any other contract claim—by looking to the terms of the plan and other manifestations of the parties' intent.

Despite these principles of trust law pointing to a *de novo* standard of review for claims like respondents', Firestone would have us read ERISA to require the application of the arbitrary and capricious standard to such claims. ERISA defines a fiduciary as one who "exercises any discretionary authority or discretionary control respecting management of [a] plan or exercises any authority or control respecting management or disposition of its assets." [ERISA § 3(21)(A)(i)]. A fiduciary has "authority to control and manage the operation and administration of the plan," [§ 402(a)(1)], and must provide a "full and fair review" of claim denials, [§ 503(2)]. From these provisions, Firestone concludes that an ERISA plan administrator, fiduciary, or trustee is empowered to exercise *all* his authority in a discretionary manner subject only to review for arbitrariness and caprice. But the provisions relied upon so heavily by Firestone do not characterize a fiduciary as one who exercises *entirely* discretionary authority or control. Rather, one is a fiduciary to the extent he exercises *any* discretionary authority or control.

ERISA was enacted "to promote the interests of employees and their beneficiaries in employee benefit plans" and "to protect contractually defined benefits." Adopting Firestone's reading of ERISA would require us to impose a standard of review that would afford less protection to employees and their beneficiaries than they enjoyed before ERISA was enacted. . . .

Firestone and its *amici* also assert that a *de novo* standard would contravene the spirit of ERISA because it would impose much higher administrative and litigation costs and therefore discourage employers from creating benefit plans. Because even under the arbitrary and capricious standard an employer's denial of benefits could be subject to judicial review, the assumption seems to be that a *de novo* standard would encourage more litigation by employees, participants, and beneficiaries who wish to assert their right to benefits. Neither general principles of trust law nor a concern for impartial decisionmaking, however, forecloses parties from agreeing upon a narrower standard of review. Moreover, as to both funded and unfunded plans, the threat of increased litigation is not sufficient to outweigh the reasons for a *de novo* standard that we have already explained.

As this case aptly demonstrates, the validity of a claim to benefits under an ERISA plan is likely to turn on the interpretation of terms in the plan at issue. Consistent with established principles of trust law, we hold that a denial of benefits challenged under [§ 502(a)(1)(B)] is to be reviewed under a *de novo* standard unless the benefit plan gives the administrator or fiduciary discretionary authority to determine eligibility for benefits or to construe the terms of the plan. Because we do not rest our decision on the concern for impartiality that guided the Court of Appeals, we need not distinguish between types of plans or focus on the motivations of plan administrators and fiduciaries. Thus, for purposes of actions under [§ 502(a)(1)(B)], the *de novo* standard of review applies regardless of whether the plan at issue is funded or unfunded and regardless of whether the administrator or fiduciary is operating under a possible or actual conflict of interest. Of course, if a benefit plan gives discretion to an administrator or fiduciary who is operating under a conflict of interest, that conflict must be weighed as a "factor[ ] in determining whether there is an abuse of discretion." Restatement (Second) of Trusts § 187, Comment d (1959). . . .

For the reasons set forth above, the decision of the Court of Appeals [is] reversed [and] the case is remanded for proceedings consistent with this opinion.

4. INTERPRETING *FIRESTONE*

Since *Firestone* was decided in 1989, it has been the most cited ERISA case. A search conducted on November 23, 2009, found nearly 6,600 case citations in the Westlaw database. Virtually every case in which a court deals with a benefit denial begins with a recital that *Firestone* governs the standard of review.

1. *Disturbing the prior consensus.* In purporting to disapprove the arbitrary-and-capricious (A&C) standard for ERISA cases, the *Firestone* opinion only hints at the extent of the Supreme Court's departure from settled law. Toward the end of the opinion as extracted above, the Court mentions that "most federal courts had adopted the arbitrary and capricious standard of review." Actually, all twelve circuits had adopted the A&C standard, and the Third Circuit was undertaking to depart from the A&C standard only in conflict-of-interest cases.

2. *Distinguishing Taft-Hartley.* The Court distinguishes review in ERISA cases from review in Taft-Hartley cases on the ground that ERISA §§ 502(a) and 502(e) contain unmistakable grants of jurisdiction to remedy breaches by fiduciaries. "Thus, the *raison d'être* for the [Taft-Hartley] arbitrary and capricious standard—the need for a jurisdictional basis in suits against trustees—is not present in ERISA."

Actually, in Taft-Hartley cases the A&C doctrine did double duty. It supplied the standard of review—deference to fiduciary decisionmaking—as well as the jurisdictional basis. But on the question of what deference the courts should give to the decisionmaking of plan fiduciaries, ERISA is as silent as Taft-Hartley. As Justice O'Connor elsewhere says in *Firestone,* "ERISA does not set out the appropriate standard of review for actions [challenging] benefit eligibility determinations."

3. *Why, or why not, defer?* The Supreme Court reasons from authority—the supposed authority of trust law—in concluding that reviewing courts should give no deference to fiduciary decisionmaking. The Court gave no mention to the functional justifications for deferring to fiduciary decisionmaking that were commonplace in the pre-*Firestone* case law. Consider, for example, Judge Wilkinson's formulation in Berry v. Ciba-Geigy Corp., 761 F.2d 1003, 1006 (4th Cir.1985): "While the [A&C] standard is perhaps more commonly associated with appellate court review of administrative findings, deference is likewise due when a district court reviews the action of a private plan trustee. Here, as in other contexts, the standard exists to ensure that administrative responsibility rests with those whose experience is daily and continuous, not with judges whose exposure is episodic and occasional."

With Judge Wilkinson's view, contrast Judge Becker's position in the Third Circuit opinion in *Firestone* that a benefit denial case does not ordinarily "turn on information or experience which expertise as a claims administrator is likely to produce." Rather, the case "is likely to turn on a question of law or of contract interpretation. Courts have no reason to defer to private parties to obtain answers to these kinds of questions." He reasoned that the "significant danger that the plan administrator will not be impartial [offsets] any remaining benefit which the administrators' expertise might be thought to produce." Bruch v. Firestone Tire & Rubber Co., 828 F.2d 134, 144 (3d Cir.1987).

4. *Trust law.* The Supreme Court purported to derive its no-deference rule in *Firestone* from the trust law principles that underlie ERISA fiduciary law. "In determining the appropriate standard of review for actions under [§ 502(a)(1)(B)], we are guided by principles of trust law." The Court acknowledged the authority of Restatement (Second) of Trusts § 187 (1959), which calls for deference to trustee decisionmaking. "The exercise of a power is discretionary except to the extent to which its exercise is required by the terms of the trust or by the principles of law applicable to the duties of trustees." Id., cmt. a. "Where discretion is conferred upon the trustee with respect to the exercise of a power, its exercise is not subject to control by the court, except to prevent an abuse by the trustee of his discretion." Id. Since "abuse of discretion" is the A&C standard by another name, shouldn't the Restatement provision have led the Court to decide *Firestone* oppositely, that is, sustaining A&C review as the default standard?

Indeed, the court in *Firestone,* citing Restatement § 187, says that "[t]rust principles make a deferential standard of review appropriate when a trustee exercises discretionary powers." How, then, did the Court manage both to invoke § 187 and to refuse the deference to fiduciary decisionmaking that § 187 requires? The Court underscored language from a century-old trust case, Nichols v. Eaton, 91 U.S. 716 (1875), which, according to the Court in *Firestone*, endorsed deference to trustees' "exercise of a *discretion vested in them by the instrument* under which they act" (emphasis supplied in *Firestone*). From this passage the Court then drew a negative inference. "Firestone can seek no shelter in these principles of trust law, however, for there is no evidence that under Firestone's termination pay plan the administrator has the power to construe uncertain terms or that eligibility determinations are to be given deference." In other words, the *Firestone* opinion reasons that trust law defers to the trustee's decisionmaking not as a matter of default law, but only when the trust power in question is particularly granted by the trust instrument.

Legislation such as the Uniform Trustees' Powers Act (1964) and the Uniform Trust Code §§ 815–816 (2000) bestows extensive powers to manage and invest trust assets upon the trustees of private trusts. Under the reasoning in *Firestone,* if a trust instrument happens to incorporate these powers expressly, the courts should defer to the trustee's decisionmaking, but not in the case in which the trust instrument is silent on the matter and relies upon the statute book authorizing the same powers.

Although the Supreme Court said that it was instituting "the trust law *de novo* standard of review," that standard is not in fact particularly characteristic of trust law. There may be functional justifications for preferring such nondeferential review, but the Court's preference is hard to rest on trust law, which routinely gives deference to trustee decisionmaking about matters of trust administration. Indeed, pre-*Firestone* cases had rested A&C review on the trust tradition, for example, in a prominent Fifth Circuit case in which Judge Brown observed that the A&C standard has been "traditionally used for review of trusts," because it "prevents excessive judicial intervention in trust operations." Dennard v. Richards Group, Inc., 681 F.2d 306, 313 (5th Cir.1982).

5.   *Trust or contract?* Would it have been better for the Court to have said that it was preferring the contract standard of review to the trust standard? The Court remarked in *Firestone* that ERISA's remedy provision, § 502(a)(1)(B), allows participants to enforce their rights "under the provisions of the plan contract." The Court's willingness to allow the plan instrument to defeat the de novo standard of review that the Court otherwise imposes is premised on the contract that the plan supposedly embodies.

Other courts have matter-of-factly described themselves as engaged in applying contract law when interpreting ERISA plans. In Santaella v. Metropolitan Life Ins. Co., 123 F.3d 456, 461 (7th Cir.1997), the Seventh Circuit said: "Because this insurance plan was established under ERISA, federal common law rules of contract interpretation govern the disposition of this case." In a later case the Seventh Circuit remarked that although "the starting point in resolving an issue of interpretation of an ERISA pension plan is the general law of contracts, the ending point may be different if the general law doesn't fit the issue because of something either in ERISA or in the nature of a pension plan." Mathews v. Sears Pension Plan, 144 F.3d 461 (7th Cir.1998).

Professor Bogan has suggested that the distinction between welfare benefit plans and pension plans should bear on the choice between contract-based and trust-based theories of review. Welfare benefit plans can be unfunded, whereas the funding rules of ERISA §§ 302–305 require that pension plans be funded. Bogan points to the so-called *res* rule of trust law, that "[a] trust cannot be created unless there is trust property in existence and ascertainable at the time of the creation of the trust." Restatement (Third) of Trusts § 2, cmt. i (2003). Accordingly, Bogan reasons, a standard of review based on trust law ought not to be applied to welfare benefit plans. "When a plan is totally unfunded, which is a typical occurrence in welfare benefit plans, employees have no place to look but to the employer to satisfy plan promises because there is no trust *res* to [satisfy] judgments obtained to recover benefits due under the plan." Donald T. Bogan, ERISA: Rethinking Firestone in Light of *Great-West*—Implications for Standard of Review and the Right to Jury Trial in Welfare Benefit Claims, 37 John Marshall L. Rev. 629, 645 (2004).

Does it follow that because trust law generally adheres to the *res* rule, Congress must have presupposed the *res* rule in ERISA? In recent decades the *res* rule has been partially abrogated in most American states, as a result of the Uniform Testamentary Additions to Trust Act (1960, revised 1991), which validates unfunded trusts for certain purposes. See also Rev. Rul. 81–114, which concerned an employee benefit trust that was valid under local law in all respects except that it lacked a corpus at the end of the employer's tax year. The IRS deemed the trust to have been in existence as of the last day of the tax year for purposes of the deduction under section 404.

Although many welfare benefit plans are unfunded, some, especially multiemployer plans, are funded. Would it be wise to have a different standard of review for benefit denials for funded as opposed to unfunded plans?

Bogan would subordinate trust to contract, reasoning that "in ERISA, the trust, when employed, serves as a security instrument to guarantee separate contract promises made by the employer to its employees." Bogan, supra, at 650. Conceptualizing ERISA benefit denials as breach of contract would result in a de novo standard of review, no different from the Supreme Court's questionable reading of the trust law standard. The attraction of contract is that it contains a richer tradition of limits on contrary plan terms, for example, the unconscionability doctrine, and the rules restricting adhesion-type terms.

Professor Muir has also suggested redrawing the trust/contract line. She would distinguish what she calls benefit administration from what she regards as the more characteristic fields of trust law, such as investing plan assets. Accordingly, in benefit denial matters she would give less weight to trust principles and more to contract. Dana M. Muir, Fiduciary Status as an Employer's Shield: The Perversity of ERISA Fiduciary Law, 2 U. Pennsylvania J. Labor & Employment L. 391, 441ff (2000).

Is it fair to say that although ERISA plans partake of both trust and contract law, neither category is very illuminating about the question of how much deference the courts should give to plan decisionmaking in particular benefit denial cases?

Regarding the intrinsic overlap of trust and contract, see John H. Langbein, The Contractarian Basis of the Law of Trusts, 105 Yale L. J. 625 (1995).

6. *Allowing the plan drafter to reinstate the A&C standard*. The most striking feature of *Firestone* is the largely self-defeating character of the decision. *Firestone* called for de novo review, yet effectively entrenched the deferential review it purported to abrogate. *Firestone* allows plan sponsors to opt out of de novo review and back into the pre-*Firestone* standard of deferential review, merely by inserting some boilerplate to that effect in the plan documents. Indeed, the final paragraph (as edited above) of the *Firestone* opinion seems to invite plan drafters to make that move, by emphasizing that the de novo standard of review applies "unless the benefit plan gives the administrator or fiduciary discretionary authority to determine eligibility for benefits or to construe the terms of the plan."

"[The] puzzle about the Supreme Court's handling of the *Firestone* case [is] easy to state but impossible to solve. If the Court was right to think that the arbitrary-and-capricious standard worsened the situation of plan participants and beneficiaries unacceptably, why did the Court permit plan drafters to reinstitute the arbitrary-and-capricious standard by means of boilerplate grants of discretion? [It] seems transparently counterproductive to allow the employer to bootstrap around the safeguards of the statute by inserting boilerplate in the plan ordering the courts not to pay much attention to the misbehavior of an employer-dominated fiduciary." John H. Langbein, The Supreme Court Flunks Trusts, 1990 Supreme Court Rev. 207, 221–22 (1991).

In Comrie v. IPSCO, 636 F.3d 839 (7th Cir. 2011), the Seventh Circuit rejected the claim that the decisions of the administrators of a top-hat plan were not entitled to deference under *Firestone* because they were not ERISA fiduciaries. Although the Third Circuit has taken the position that interpretations of non-fiduciaries are not entitled to deference, see Goldstein v. Johnson & Johnson, 251 F.3d 433 (3d Cir. 2001), the Seventh Circuit believed that view to be a misunderstanding of *Firestone*. The court observed that under *Firestone*,

> fiduciary status leads to independent judicial decisions, unless the contract specifies otherwise. To hold, as *Goldstein* does, that non-fiduciary status *requires* independent judicial decisions, *despite* a contract, is to turn *Firestone* on its head. *Firestone* tells us that a contract conferring interpretive discretion must be respected, *even when* the decision is to be made by an ERISA fiduciary. It is easier, not harder as *Goldstein* thought, to honor discretion-conferring clauses in contracts that govern the actions of non-fiduciaries.

Id. at 842.

7. *Default or mandatory law?* If the Supreme Court was right to think that the A&C standard worsens the situation of plan participants and beneficiaries unacceptably, was there any functional justification for allowing plan drafters to reinstitute the A&C standard by means of boilerplate grants of discretion? Is it consistent with the purposes of

ERISA fiduciary law to permit a plan sponsor to have the power to impose a standard of review that disadvantages plan participants?

Judge Posner, in Hawkins v. First Union Corp. Long-Term Disability Plan, 326 F.3d 914, 917 (7th Cir.2003), asserted that "the procedures followed by plan administrators are matters of contract," and that *Firestone* allows a plan to "specify the degree of deference due the plan administrator's benefit determination." Accordingly he asked rhetorically: "Why can't [the plan] equally specify the procedures and rules of evidence, including presumptions, that the plan's administrator shall use to evaluate claims?" Can you answer his question?

The Supreme Court in *Firestone*, purporting to follow the law of trusts, assumed that the standard of review was a matter of default law that the plan terms could alter. However, ERISA is a regulatory statute, in which Congress resorted to trust law principles in order to protect the interests of plan participants, as discussed supra in Chapter 3. As the Court remarked a few years later, "trust law does not tell the entire story. After all, ERISA's standards and procedural protections partly reflect a congressional determination that the common law of trusts did not offer completely satisfactory protection." Varity Corp. v. Howe, 516 U.S. 489, 497 (1996).

Although in *Firestone* the Court did not address the question of whether permitting a plan drafter to impose a self-serving standard of review intrudes upon ERISA's protective purpose, ERISA does in fact contain three distinct statutory bases that might justify treating the plan's standard of review as a matter of mandatory rather than default law, hence not open to contrary plan drafting:

(1) Section 404(a)(1)(D), discussed supra in Chapters 13 and 14, requires plan instruments to be "consistent with the provisions of" ERISA. Since the Supreme Court in *Firestone* read ERISA to envisage de novo review, should the Court have treated plan terms substituting A&C review as "[in]consistent with the provisions of" ERISA?

(2) Section 410(a) forbids exculpation clauses. It says that "any provision in [an] instrument which purports to relieve a fiduciary from responsibility or liability for any responsibility, obligation, or duty under [ERISA Part 4] shall be void as against public policy." When the plan document insists upon deferential A&C review, the instrument is instructing reviewing courts not to probe too deeply into benefit denials that save money for the plan sponsor. Should a self-serving plan term of this sort be understood to "relieve a fiduciary [from] liability," contrary to 410(a)?

(3) Section 503(2) requires the plan to have internal review procedures that "afford a reasonable opportunity to any participant whose claim for benefits has been denied for a full and fair review by the appropriate named fiduciary of the decision denying the claim." Does a plan term demanding deferential external review of such procedures impermissibly interfere with the purpose of § 503(2)? Consider the dictum in a Fourth Circuit case, in which the court said that it would enforce

a plan whose "language provided that pain could never support a finding of disability." Smith v. Continental Casualty Co., 369 F.3d 412, 420 (4th Cir.2004). Would that term conflict with the requirement of "full and fair review" under § 503(2)?

When the Supreme Court revisited *Firestone* in 2008 in Metropolitan Life Ins. Co. v. Glenn, 554 U.S. 105, 128 S.Ct. 2343 (2008), discussed below, the Court confronted none of these fundamental objections to *Firestone*'s premise that an ERISA plan sponsor should be allowed to dictate a self-serving standard of judicial review of plan decisionmaking. For the view that the standard of review ought not to be treated as a matter within plan autonomy, see John H. Langbein, Trust Law as Regulatory Law: The Unum/Provident Scandal and Judicial Review of Benefit Denials under ERISA, 101 Northwestern U.L. Rev. 1315, 1336–40, 1342 (2007).

8. *What language trumps?* Considerable litigation has arisen about the question of what language suffices for the plan to overcome *Firestone*'s default regime of de novo review in favor of deferential review. The Seventh Circuit said at the outset that "magic words (such as 'the committee has discretion to . . .') are unnecessary." Sisters of the Third Order of St. Francis v. SwedishAmerican Group Health Benefit Trust, 901 F.2d 1369, 1371 (7th Cir.1990). The problem has been, therefore, one of construction: Does the particular language used in the instrument oust de novo review and institute deferential review?

In a prominent case decided shortly after *Firestone*, the Fourth Circuit was faced with a plan that granted the fiduciary the authority "to determine all benefits and resolve all questions pertaining to the administration, interpretation and application of Plan provisions, either by rules of general applicability or by particular decisions." The court found that this language justified applying "the deferential 'abuse of discretion' standard" even though "the word discretion appears nowhere in the Plan documents." De Nobel v. Vitro Corp., 885 F.2d 1180, 1186–87 (4th Cir.1989). Accord, Block v. Pitney Bowes Inc., 952 F.2d 1450 (D.C.Cir.1992).

Language "to the effect that benefits shall be paid when the plan administrator upon proof (or satisfactory proof) determines that the applicant is entitled to them" is usually treated as not effective to defeat de novo review. Herzberger v. Standard Ins. Co., 205 F.3d 327, 329 (7th Cir.2000); accord, Hoover v. Provident Life & Acc. Ins. Co., 290 F.3d 801 (6th Cir.2002); Walke v. Group Long Term Disability Ins., 256 F.3d 835 (8th Cir.2001). Does it make a difference when the language requires proof satisfactory "to us," that is, to the insurer or administrator? Compare Nance v. Sun Life Assurance Co. of Canada, 294 F.3d 1263 (10th Cir.2002) (deferential review granted), with Kinstler v. First Reliance Standard Life Ins. Co., 181 F.3d 243 (2d Cir.1999) (de novo review).

See also Gross v. Sun Life Assurance Co., 734 F.3d 1 (1st Cir.2013) (holding that de novo is the proper standard of review where a plan requires proof of disability "satisfactory to us"; such language "is inadequate to confer the discretionary authority that would trigger deferential review"). Accord Cosey v. Prudential, 735 F.3d 161 (4th Cir.2013). In contrast, the Sixth Circuit held in Frazier v. Life Ins. Co.,

725 F.3d 560 (6th Cir.2013) that "satisfactory proof" is sufficiently clear to grant discretionary authority. Likewise, in Prezioso v. Prudential Ins. Co., 748 F. 3d 797 (8th Cir. Apr. 4, 2014), the Eighth Circuit held that proof satisfactory to the plan administrator grants discretionary authority and thus warrants use of the abuse of discretion standard.

In some settings the plan drafter may prefer not to oust the de novo standard. "Among these, in our experience," write the seasoned ERISA lawyers who author the *ERISA Litigation Reporter*, "are collectively bargained single-employer plans involving a union which is willing to have the employer administer the plan but not to enjoy broad interpretive discretion." Note, "Firestone Tire & Rubber Co. v. Bruch: Three Years After—Part I," 1 ERISA Litigation Rptr. (Dec. 1991), at 17, 18. When the plan drafter does intend to provide for deferential review, the authors recommend language that claims discretion for the plan decisionmaker both on questions of eligibility for benefits and on the interpretation of plan terms, including the power to construe doubtful terms. This authority should be described as within the fiduciary's sole discretion, and fiduciary decisionmaking should be declared to be conclusive on all parties. Id. at 19. The Seventh Circuit "drafted and commend[ed] to employers" the following purported safe harbor language: "Benefits under this plan will be paid only if the plan administrator decides in his discretion that the applicant is entitled to them." *Herzberger*, 205 F.3d at 331.

9. *Does the summary plan description (SPD) need to disclose the standard of review?* In Mario v. P & C Food Markets, Inc., 313 F.3d 758 (2d Cir.2002), the court considered but did not have to decide the question of whether the SPD must disclose that the plan contains a term imposing deferential in place of de novo review. Judge Calabresi pointed to ERISA § 102(b), which requires the SPD to include information on all "circumstances which may result in disqualification, ineligibility, or denial or loss of benefits," as seeming to require such disclosure. "On the other hand," he wrote, "one might as forcefully maintain that the standard of judicial review is not such a circumstance because it simply fixes the procedure to be followed *after* a denial has occurred, and therefore a plan participant cannot be prejudiced by a lack of knowledge about that procedure." 313 F.3d at 764.

On the other hand, putting a grant of discretion only in an SPD and not a plan is not sufficient. In Ringwald v. Prudential Ins. Co., 609 F.3d 946 (8th Cir. 2010), the Eighth Circuit held that a federal district court had erred in reviewing a plan's denial of disability benefits under an abuse of discretion standard. Although the SPD granted the plan administrator discretion to interpret the plan and determine benefit eligibility, the plan neither granted such discretion nor provided that the SPD could amend the plan. Thus, de novo review was appropriate. Accord. Jobe v. Med. Life Ins. Co., 598 F.3d 478 (8th Cir. 2010).

10. *Nord.* The Supreme Court returned to the subject of judicial review of ERISA plan benefit denials in Black & Decker Disability Plan v. Nord, 538 U.S. 822 (2003), but the Court did not use the occasion to rethink *Firestone*'s premises or to deal with the main problems that the lower courts have been confronting as they have tried to apply *Firestone*.

In *Nord* the Court unanimously reversed a Ninth Circuit decision that would have imported into ERISA from the law of Social Security disability plans a principle called "the treating physician rule," discussed below. The Supreme Court held that rule to be inconsistent with *Firestone*'s rule honoring plan-dictated grants of deferential review. The case involved the question of whether a participant in an ERISA-covered occupational disability plan had become disabled. The plan document remitted such determinations to the "sole and exclusive discretion" of the plan administrator.

The Social Security Administration (SSA) operates an immense program of disability compensation as part of the Social Security system. In 2008 the program provided disability payments averaging $1,063 per month to 8.5 million beneficiaries. SSA, Annual Statistical Report on the Social Security Disability Insurance Program, 2008, available at www.ssa.gov/policy/docs/statcomps/di_asr/2008/index.html. The treating physician rule gives special weight or deference to the opinion of the physician who treated the patient for the condition giving rise to the disability claim. SSA has promulgated a regulation to that effect. As a matter of Social Security law, the Court has held that SSA's interpretation of the Social Security Act's definition of disability is entitled to so-called *Chevron* deference. See Barnhart v. Thomas, 540 U.S. 20 (2003), invoking Chevron U.S.A., Inc. v. Natural Resources Defense Council, Inc., 467 U.S. 837, 843 (1984).

In *Nord*, the Ninth Circuit applied SSA's treating physician rule to the ERISA plan, requiring a plan decisionmaker who rejects the opinions of the claimant's treating physician "to come forward with specific reasons for decision, based on substantial evidence in the record." 538 U.S. at 822. The Ninth Circuit thus used the treating physician rule to overcome the plan term reserving "sole and exclusive discretion" to the plan administrator. Id. at 826. Other circuits had refused to give such presumptive force to the treating physician's opinion. The Seventh Circuit worried that "the patient's regular physician may want to do a favor for a friend and client, and so the treating physician may too quickly find disability." Dixon v. Massanari, 270 F.3d 1171, 1177 (7th Cir.2001). Justice Ginsburg's opinion reversing the Ninth Circuit in *Nord* pointed to differences between Social Security and ERISA-plan disability determinations, including the voluntary nature of ERISA plans, and their variety of terms.

Despite *Nord*, the findings in an SSA disability determination remain highly probative in determining disability under an ERISA plan. See, e.g., Bennett v. Kemper National Service, Inc., 514 F.3d 547 (6th Cir.2008); Gannon v. Metropolitan Life Ins. Co., 360 F.3d 211 (1st Cir.2004).

However, medical evidence that post-dates an SSA determination of disability may be good reason to avoid giving deference to the SSA determination. See Nugent v. Aetna Life Ins. Co., 540 Fed. Appx. 473 (5th Cir. Jan. 3, 2014) (termination of benefits based on medical evidence that post-dated an SSA disability determination was not an abuse of discretion).

11. *State insurance law.* The California Department of Insurance, interpreting Cal. Ins. Code § 10291, has taken the position that state

insurance law forbids an insurer from imposing contract provisions that would grant the insurer "discretionary authority to determine eligibility for benefits or to interpret the terms or provisions of the contract." 11 ERISA Litigation Rptr. (Feb. 2004), at 10. The Department reasoned that such provisions deprive insureds of "the protections of California insurance law, including the covenant of good faith and fair dealing. . . ." Id. The National Association of Insurance Commissioners (NAIC) has encouraged the states to take this position. See 2002–1 NAIC Proceedings 12 (2002); see generally Henry Quillen, State Prohibition of Discretionary Clauses in ERISA-Covered Benefit Plans, 32 J. Pension Planning & Compliance 67 (Sum. 2006). Should DoL or the federal courts take a similar view of the protective purposes of ERISA, and require that ERISA plans be interpreted to contain a nonwaivable covenant of good faith and fair dealing?

Consider in light of Chapters 17 and 19, infra, treating ERISA's preemption clause, whether state insurance law can forbid discretionary review provisions that the Supreme Court authorized in *Firestone,* or whether ERISA § 514(b)(2)(A), the exception for state insurance law, preserves state law from preemption. "According to the NAIC, as of 2008, a dozen states had limited or barred the use of discretionary clauses in at least some form of insurance." Standard Ins. Co. v. Morrison, 584 F.3d 837, 841 (9th Cir.2009). In *Morrison,* the Ninth Circuit sustained the Montana insurance commissioner's rule disapproving such contracts, concluding that the provision fell within the insurance exception. Likewise, in American Council of Life Insurers v. Ross, 558 F.3d 600 (6th Cir.2009), the Sixth Circuit sustained a regulation issued by the Michigan commissioner of insurance forbidding insurance contracts in that state from requiring deferential review.

5. CONFLICT OF INTEREST AFTER *FIRESTONE*

1. *"Conflict must be weighed."* Judge Becker's opinion for the Third Circuit in *Firestone,* previously discussed, favored departing from deferential A&C review (which at that time was the default standard) in cases in which the plan decisionmaker was operating under a conflict of interest. *Firestone* involved a single employer plan. In such a plan, as Judge Becker observed regarding the severance pay plan in *Firestone,* "every dollar saved by the administrator on behalf of his employer is a dollar in the employer's pocket." 828 F.2d at 144. The Supreme Court, however, expressly refused to rest its decision in *Firestone* "on the concern for impartiality that guided the Court of Appeals." 489 U.S. at 115. Rather, the Supreme Court authorized de novo review as the default rule "regardless of whether the administrator or fiduciary is operating under a possible or actual conflict of interest." Id. Because, however, the Supreme Court allowed plan drafters to evade de novo review by so drafting the plan documents, the Court still had to confront the Third Circuit's concern about the intrinsic danger of deferential review by a conflicted decisionmaker. The Court took account of the point in a single sentence, saying: "Of course, if a benefit plan gives discretion to an administrator or fiduciary who is operating under a conflict of interest, that conflict must be weighed as a 'factor[ ] in determining whether there

is an abuse of discretion.' " Id., citing Restatement (Second) of Trusts § 187, comment d (1959).

Thus, the Supreme Court in *Firestone* acknowledged that in cases in which the plan provides for deferential review, the courts should "weigh" the conflict, but the Court gave no guidance about how much weight to give or in what circumstances. A large case law developed, in which the "circuits agree[d] that a conflict of interest trigger[ed] a less deferential standard of review [but] differ[ed] over how this lesser degree of deference alter[ed] their review process." Chambers v. Family Health Plan Corp., 100 F.3d 818, 825 (10th Cir.1996). For the case law a decade after *Firestone*, see Kathryn J. Kennedy, Judicial Standard of Review in ERISA Benefit Claim Cases, 50 American U.L. Rev. 1083 (2001).

Several circuits developed burden of proof rules, requiring the plaintiff to show not only that the decisionmaker was conflicted, but that the conflict resulted in improper decisionmaking. E.g., Pulvers v. First Unum Life Ins. Co., 210 F.3d 89, 92 (2d Cir.2000) (conflict "is alone insufficient as a matter of law to trigger stricter review"); Schatz v. Mutual of Omaha Ins. Co., 220 F.3d 944, 948 (8th Cir.2000). The Eleventh Circuit, by contrast, held that "when a plan beneficiary demonstrates a substantial conflict of interest on the part of the fiduciary responsible for benefits determinations, the burden shifts to the fiduciary to prove that its interpretation of plan provisions committed to its discretion was not tainted by self-interest." Brown v. Blue Cross & Blue Shield of Alabama, 898 F.2d 1556, 1566 (11th Cir.1990). The Tenth Circuit adopted a rule that shifted to the conflicted fiduciary the burden "to establish by substantial evidence that the denial of benefits was not arbitrary and capricious." Fought v. Unum Life Ins. Co., 379 F.3d 997, 1005 (10th Cir.2004).

2. *What is a conflict?* Speaking of the attributes of conflict that result in diminished deference, the Tenth Circuit has said that "the mere fact that the plan administrator was a [company] employee is not enough *per se* to demonstrate a conflict. Rather, a court should consider various factors including whether: (1) the plan is self-funded; (2) the company funding the plan appointed and compensated the plan administrator; (3) the plan administrator's performance reviews or level of compensation were linked to the denial of benefits; and (4) the provision of benefits had a significant economic impact on the company administering the plan." Kimber v. Thiokol Corp., 196 F.3d 1092, 1098 (10th Cir.1999).

A rule of heightened sensitivity to the dangers of a conflicted decisionmaker will not help the claimant if the court refuses to see any conflict. A string of Seventh Circuit cases minimized conflicts that other courts have found to be acute. With *Brown*'s premise that an insurance company's "fiduciary role lies in perpetual conflict with its profit-making role as a business," 898 F.2d at 1561–62, compare Cozzie v. Metropolitan Life Ins. Co., 140 F.3d 1104, 1108 (7th Cir.1998), in which the Seventh Circuit said: "Although MetLife acts as both administrator and insurer of the plan, that factor, standing alone, does not constitute a conflict of interest." In 2008 the Supreme Court resolved that question, holding in *Glenn* that when "the entity that administers the plan, such as an employer or an insurance company, both determines whether an employee is eligible for benefits and pays benefits out of its own pocket[,] this dual role creates a conflict of interest. . . ." 128 S.Ct. at 2346.

3.   *Reputational incentives.* "[Most] plan decision making occurs in the setting of long term or repeat player relations. Management dominated fiduciaries typically have strong incentives not to acquire a reputation for sharp practice that would harm morale and cause employees to assign lower value to plan benefits." Fischel & Langbein, supra, 55 U. Chicago L. Rev., at 1132. On the other hand, "the employer's reputational interest [is] not likely to be effective when the long term relationship [is] dissolving, as in plant closings or in corporate reorganizations. In these cases, the gains from self-interested action by nonneutral fiduciaries may outweigh the usual inhibiting future costs." One factor that distinguishes severance plan cases "from routine plan administration disputes is that, since the employer is shedding the aggrieved employees (and sometimes their union as well), the long term relational incentives no longer pertain." Id.

Even as regards an ongoing plan, the magnitude of the contested benefit can tempt a conflicted fiduciary to subordinate reputational good will. As Judge Posner remarked in a case in which $125 million turned on the plan fiduciaries' decision about what compensation was covered under a benefit accrual formula: "Of course, a loss of reputation might be a price worth paying to avoid $125 million in unanticipated expense." Gallo v. Amoco Corp., 102 F.3d 918, 921 (7th Cir.1996). Some years before, Judge Posner, dealing with a pension case, pointed to other reasons why reputational incentives may be inadequate to protect plan participants:

> [Pension] rights are too important these days for most employees to want to place them at the mercy of a biased tribunal subject only to a narrow form of "arbitrary and capricious" review, relying on the company's interest in its reputation to prevent it from acting on its bias. Nor is it clear that the contractual perspective is the correct one in which to view claims under ERISA. A Congress committed to the principles of freedom of contract would not have enacted a statute that interferes with pension arrangements voluntarily agreed on by employers and employees. ERISA is paternalistic; and it seems incongruous therefore to deny disappointed pension claimants a meaningful degree of judicial review on the theory that they might be said to have implicitly waived it.

Van Boxel v. Journal Co. Employees' Pension Trust, 836 F.2d 1048, 1053 (7th Cir.1987).

Later Seventh Circuit cases have been more accepting of the argument that long term reputational incentives deter conflicted decisionmakers from abusing their authority. In Perlman v. Swiss Bank Corp. Comprehensive Disability Protection Plan, 195 F.3d 975, 981 (7th Cir.1999), Judge Easterbrook reasoned that an insurer might not be conflicted if the policy it was administering was "retrospectively-rated," that is, a policy in which the insurer was able to pass its expenditures through to the employer whose plan purchased the coverage. 195 F.3d at 981. Another tack in some Seventh Circuit cases has been to belittle the severity of the conflict by comparing the amount of the claim in issue with the gross revenue of the defendant firm, e.g., Mers v. Marriott International Group Accidental Death and Dismemberment Plan, 144 F.3d 1014, 1020–21 (7th Cir.1998); Chojnacki v. Georgia-Pacific Corp., 108 F.3d 810, 815 (7th Cir.1997); Chalmers v. Quaker Oats Co., 61 F.3d 1340, 1344 (7th Cir.1995).

In *Perlman* Judge Easterbrook expressed the further view that the claims processing employees of Unum Life Insurance Company, the plan administrator in that case, lacked any personal stake in the outcome of the disability denials they decided, because getting employees to identify with the interests of their employer "is a daunting challenge for any corporation." 195 F.3d at 981. You may test that conjecture against the evidence regarding the behavior of claims processing employees at Unum/Provident, discussed next.

6.   THE UNUM/PROVIDENT SCANDAL

1.   *Disability insurance.* Occupational disability insurance is an important tool of personal and family financial planning for anyone whose livelihood depends upon employment. Disability insurance replaces employment income for an insured who becomes unable to work. Such insurance is commonly made available through the workplace, in ERISA-covered employee benefit plans.

Benefit claims under disability insurance policies give rise in some cases to disputes about how impaired or how employable an insured actually is. The genre is intrinsically fact-intensive. The recurrent question is whether, on the facts regarding this worker's medical and occupational circumstances, he or she is occupationally disabled. Oftentimes, the reviewing court will not find much guidance regarding that determination in the terms of the policy, or in background rules or case law. The amount in issue in a disability claim can be quite large, because under the policy the insurer contracts to replace some fraction of the worker's employment income for life. (The amount payable under a disability insurance contract is commonly integrated with and thus offset by the amount of any Social Security disability payments).

A disability insurer's claims review process needs to strike a balance between paying meritorious claims and detecting and denying exaggerated or fraudulent claims. The danger that an insured may exaggerate or falsify conditions of disability poses a constant concern to the insurer. This danger is more acute with disability insurance than with other forms of insurance, such as life insurance, in which it is more costly to qualify for the insurable event and harder to falsify it. The insurer commonly limits the coverage to an amount well short of a worker's full salary, as a way to reduce the moral hazard. "[People] who know that their full income will continue after they stop working may take more risks in their daily lives and will not try as hard to return to work after injury or illness. . . ." Hall v. Life Ins. Co. of North America, 317 F.3d 773, 775 (7th Cir.2003).

2.   *The rise of Unum/Provident.* Through various subsidiary companies, Unum/Provident Corp. became by the early 2000s the largest American provider of disability insurance. In 2003 Unum/Provident issued 40 percent of the individual disability policies and 25 percent of

the group disability policies sold in the U.S., covering more than 17 million persons. Dean Frost, "Disability Claim Denied!," Business Week, Dec. 22, 2003, at 62. Most of the group policies were issued under ERISA-covered plans.

3. *Bad faith claims denial.* In the early 2000s, evidence mounted that Unum/Provident Corp. had been engaged in a deliberate program of denying meritorious benefit claims brought by its policyholders.

The growth of Unum/Provident was engineered by J. Harold Chandler, who became CEO of Provident in 1993, and who ran the merged companies until his dismissal in 2003. Under Chandler, Unum/Provident instituted cost-containment measures that pressured claims-processing employees to deny valid claims. Pressures on employees to deny claims peaked in the last month of each quarter, called the "scrub months," when claims managers put extra pressure on staff to deny claims, in order to meet or surpass budget goals. Frost, supra. Word of these practices emerged in lawsuits by former employees, in investigative reports broadcast by NBC's "Dateline" (Oct. 13, 2002) and CBS' "60 Minutes" (Nov. 17, 2002), and in the 2003 *Business Week* report by Frost, supra. Employees interviewed for the Dateline program said that the claims that were "the most vulnerable" to pressures for bad faith termination were those of insureds "with so-called subjective illnesses, illnesses that don't show up on x-rays or MRIs, like mental illness, chronic pain, migraines, or even Parkinsons." The Dateline story disclosed an internal company e-mail cautioning a group of claims staff that they had one week remaining to close (i.e., deny) 18 more claims in order to meet projections.

Unum/Provident claims evaluation personnel who questioned the company's practices contended they were intimidated into acquiescing, or else they were dismissed. Some of those dismissed brought wrongful dismissal suits; Unum/Provident defended, alleging that the dissidents were dismissed for cause. In the most prominent of the suits, Dr. Patrick McSharry, who worked as a staff physician in the company's claims review operations, alleged that he was required to review so many claims that he could not analyze them properly; that he was instructed "to use language [to] support the denial of disability insurance"; that he was not allowed "to request further information or suggest additional medical tests"; and that he was "not supposed to help a claimant perfect a claim for disability insurance benefits." McSharry v. UnumProvident Corp., 237 F.Supp.2d 875, 877 (E.D.Tenn.2002). In Bennett v. Unum Life Ins. Co., 321 F.Supp.2d 925, 934–35 (E.D.Tenn.2004), the court found that "internally generated memoranda from Unum/Provident [executives] appear to support the plaintiff's claim that one of Unum/Provident's corporate goals was to terminate as many ongoing claims and deny as many new claims as possible. . . ."

ERISA remedy law, as discussed infra in Chapter 16, has been interpreted to preclude punitive damages. In several non-ERISA cases, large punitive damage awards were made against Unum/Provident companies for bad faith claims denials. See Frost, supra. In one, Hangarter v. Paul Revere Life Ins. Co., 236 F.Supp.2d 1069, 1082 (N.D.Cal.2002), the judge who sustained a trial jury's award of $5 million in punitive damages found that the "jury heard more than enough evidence to conclude that Plaintiff was totally disabled and that Defendants in bad faith terminated her benefits and caused her damages."

In a number of ERISA cases, federal courts remarked on Unum/Provident's aggressive claims denial practices. See, e.g., Moon v. Unum Provident Corp., 405 F.3d 373, 381 (6th Cir.2005) (denial based on "selective review of the administrative record"); Stup v. Unum Life Ins. Co., 390 F.3d 301, 310 (4th Cir.2004) (denial rested on "[a]n equivocal opinion [based] on ambiguous test results"); Lain v. Unum Life Ins. Co., 279 F.3d 337, 347 (5th Cir.2002) (denial of claim "reflects plain lack of objectivity and an abuse of discretion by Unum"); Dandurand v. Unum Life Ins. Co., 284 F.3d 331, 338 (1st Cir.2002) (Unum's handling of claim "defies common sense"). Chief Judge Young found the benefit denial in Radford Trust v. First Unum Life Ins. Co., 321 F.Supp.2d 226, 247 (D.Mass.2004), "entirely inconsistent with the company's public responsibilities and with its obligations under the [ERISA-covered disability] Policy." He collected citations to a mass of reported cases that he characterized as "reveal[ing] a disturbing pattern of erroneous and arbitrary benefits denials, bad faith contract misinterpretations, and other unscrupulous tactics."

4. *The multistate investigation and settlement.* As complaints, litigation, and media accounts grew, several state insurance commissions began to investigate the company's claims denial practices. The Georgia commissioner concluded that Unum/Provident had been "looking for every technical legal way to avoid paying a claim." Mike Pare, Georgia Insurance Commissioner Fines UnumProvident $1 Million, Chattanooga Times Free Press, Mar. 19, 2003, at C1.

In 2003–2004, the Maine, Massachusetts, and Tennessee state insurance regulatory authorities ("the Lead States"), acting also on behalf of most other states, conducted a coordinated investigation of Unum/Provident's disability claims practices. The Lead States filed a report that accused Unum/Provident of systematic irregularities in evaluating medical evidence of disability. Unum/Provident agreed to pay a $15 million fine, to reopen several years' worth of denied claims, and to make detailed changes in its claims review procedures and its corporate governance. Report of the Targeted Multistate Market Conduct Examination, available at www.state.me.us/pfr/ins/Unum_Multistate_ExamReport.htm (Feb. 29, 2004).

In Keir v. UnumProvident Corp., 2010 U.S. Dist. LEXIS 95560 (S.D.N.Y. Sept. 14, 2010), a federal district judge ruled that this regulatory settlement agreement rendered moot an action brought under ERISA by disability plan participants. In the absence of any evidence that the new procedures adopted by UnumProvident do not fully comply with ERISA, plaintiffs no longer had a viable claim for injunctive relief.

5. *ERISA's role.* In the course of litigation against Unum/Provident, a remarkable internal memorandum was unearthed, in which a company executive emphasized the company's perception of how ERISA helped the company resist paying benefit claims:

  A [company] task force has recently been established to promote the identification of [disability] policies covered by

ERISA and to initiate active measures to get new and existing policies covered by ERISA. The advantages of ERISA coverage in litigious situations are enormous: state law is preempted by federal law, there are no jury trials, there are no compensatory or punitive damages, relief is usually limited to the amount of benefit in question, and claims administrators may receive a deferential standard of review. The economic impact on Provident from having policies covered by ERISA could be significant. As an example, [a company employee] identified 12 claim situations where we settled for $7.8 million in the aggregate. If these 12 cases had been covered by ERISA, our liability would have been between zero and $0.5 million.

In order to take advantage of ERISA protection, we need to be diligent and thorough in determining whether a policy is covered. [While] our objective is to pay all valid claims and deny invalid claims, there are gray areas, and ERISA applicability may influence our course of action.

"Provident Internal Memorandum," titled "Re: ERISA," from Jeff McCall to IDC Management Group & Glenn Felton, Oct. 2, 1995, reprinted at Ray Bourhis, Insult to Injury: Insurance, Fraud, and the Big Business of Bad Faith (2005), at 225.

Contrast the passage from the Provident internal memorandum reproduced above, exulting in the ways ERISA disadvantages the benefit claims of ERISA plan participants, with the Supreme Court's observation in *Firestone* that "ERISA was enacted 'to promote the interests of employees and their beneficiaries in employee benefit plans' and 'to protect contractually defined benefits,'" 489 U.S. at 113. An important question to ask when you have concluded studying Chapters 15–17 of this book (treating benefit denials, ERISA remedy law, and ERISA preemption) is what changes would be needed to achieve greater fidelity to ERISA's protective purposes. As regards the fiduciary law dimension, see Dana M. Muir, Fiduciary Status as an Employer's Shield: The Perversity of ERISA Fiduciary Law, 2 U. Pennsylvania J. Labor & Employment L. 391 (2000).

6. *What lessons?* Broadly speaking, there are two plausible interpretations of the Unum/Provident scandal. On one view, Unum/Provident was such an outlier that the scandal is without policy implications. On this view, a rogue insurance company behaved exceptionally badly; it got caught and sanctioned; and its fate will deter others.

The other reading of the story is less sanguine. Unum/Provident has not been the only conflicted ERISA fiduciary that has yielded to the temptation to line its own pockets at the expense of the claimants whose meritorious benefit claims it denied. Consider, for example, Zanny v. Kellogg Co., 2006 WL 1851236, at *9 (W.D.Mich.2006), in which the court found that Metropolitan Life Insurance Co. "regularly reviewed the client's file with an open intention to deny benefits despite the profound and compelling evidence of serious and prolonged mental illness." In Loucks v. Liberty Life Assurance Co., 337 F.Supp.2d 990, 995 (W.D.Mich.2004), the court characterized the insurer's evaluation of the disability claim as "unprincipled, bias[ed] and craven[,] grossly negligent and driven by financial motives." In Wible v. Aetna Life Ins. Co., 375 F.Supp.2d 956, 969 (C.D.Cal.2005), the court found that "the record reflects unrebutted material, probative evidence tending to show that Aetna's self-interest caused a breach of its fiduciary obligations to" the disability claimant. The implication from these cases is that the danger of bias on the part of conflicted fiduciaries in ERISA benefit denial cases is severe and systemic, perhaps severe enough to call into question the wisdom of that branch of the decision in *Firestone* allowing plan documents to overturn *Firestone*'s default standard of de novo review.

7.   *Glenn.* In Metropolitan Life Ins. Co. v. Glenn, 554 U.S. 105, 128 S.Ct. 2343 (2008), discussed further below, the Supreme Court took note of the Unum/Provident scandal, but did not take the opportunity to reconsider *Firestone*'s endorsement of plan terms dictating deferential review. Rather, the Court said, "where an insurance company administrator has a history of biased claims administration," that fact "should prove more important (perhaps of great importance)" in deciding the weight that the reviewing court should give to the plan decisionmaker's conflict of interest. 128 S.Ct. at 2351, citing John H. Langbein, Trust Law as Regulatory Law: The Unum/Provident Scandal and Judicial Review of Benefit Denials under ERISA, 101 Northwestern U. L. Rev. 1315, 1317–21 (2007).

QUESTIONS

1.   Recall the discussion of reputational incentives at the outset of this chapter and again in the note on "Conflict of Interest after *Firestone*," supra. Does the evidence of bad faith claims denial just reviewed undermine Judge Easterbrook's assumption in *Perlman*, 195 F.3d at 981, that the claims-processing employees of Unum/Provident Corp. would have had no personal stake in the outcome of the disability denials they decided, because getting employees to identify with the interests of their employer "is a daunting challenge for any corporation"?

2.   In a later case Judge Easterbrook offered a slightly different economic explanation of why insurance companies wouldn't cheat: "[M]ost insurers are well diversified, so that the decision in any one case has no perceptible effect on the bottom line. There is correspondingly slight reason to suspect that they will bend the rules. Unless an insurer or plan administrator pays its staff more for denying claims than for granting them, the people who actually implement these systems are impartial." Leipzig v. AIG Life Ins. Co., 362 F.3d 406, 409 (7th Cir.2004). Judging from the Unum/Provident scandal, this account is wrong. What did Judge Easterbrook's economic analysis fail to capture?

7.   *GLENN*: RESTATING THE CONFLICT STANDARD

In 2008 in *Glenn*, the Supreme Court revisited the question of the appropriate standard of review in ERISA benefit denials, for the first time since *Firestone*. The case arose from an insurer's denial of disability benefits. The Court largely reiterated its position in *Firestone*, but did so in a way that has required the lower courts to reformulate somewhat the way they evaluate the significance of a plan decisionmaker's conflict of interest. As previously mentioned, the Court's opinion, by Justice Breyer, confirms that when "the entity that administers the plan, such as an employer or an insurance company, both determines whether an employee is eligible for benefits and pays benefits out of its own pocket[,] this dual role creates a conflict of interest. . . ." 128 S.Ct. at 2346. Regarding the standard of review in such cases, the Court in effect reiterated the *Firestone* standard, saying that "a reviewing court should consider that conflict as a factor in determining whether the plan administrator has abused its discretion in denying benefits. . . ." Id.

Addressing the question of how a reviewing court should take account of such a conflict, the Court refused to "overturn *Firestone* by adopting a rule that in practice could bring about near universal review by judges *de novo—i.e.*, without deference—of the lion's share of ERISA plan claims denials." 128 S.Ct. at 2350. The Court continued:

> Neither do we believe it necessary or desirable for courts to create special burden-of-proof rules, or other special procedural or evidentiary rules, focused narrowly upon the evaluator/payor conflict. In principle, as we have said, conflicts are but one factor among many that a reviewing judge must take into account. Benefits decisions arise in too many contexts, concern too many circumstances, and can relate in too many different ways to conflicts-which themselves vary in kind and in degree of seriousness-for us to come up with a one-size-fits-all procedural system that is likely to promote fair and accurate review. Indeed, special procedural rules would create further complexity, adding time and expense to a process that may already be too costly for many of those who seek redress.

> We believe that *Firestone* means what the word "factor" implies, namely, that when judges review the lawfulness of benefit denials, they will often take account of several different considerations of which a conflict of interest is one. This kind of review is no stranger to the judicial system. Not only trust law, but also administrative law, can ask judges to determine lawfulness by taking account of several different, often case-specific, factors, reaching a result by weighing all together.

> In such instances, any one factor will act as a tiebreaker when the other factors are closely balanced, the degree of closeness necessary depending upon the tiebreaking factor's inherent or case-specific importance.

The Court concluded by remarking that its "elucidation of *Firestone's* standard does not consist of a detailed set of instructions." Analogizing the issue to the standard of "review of agency factfinding" in administrative law, the Court quoted with approval from a precedent in that field, to the effect that "there 'are no talismanic words that can avoid the process of judgment,' bearing in mind 'the intractability of any formula to furnish definiteness of content for all the impalpable factors involved in judicial review.'" 128 S.Ct. at 2352.

Chief Justice Roberts resisted the majority's rationale, saying that he "would instead consider the conflict of interest on review only where there is evidence that the benefits denial was motivated or affected by the administrator's conflict." Id. at 2353. Similarly, Justice Scalia, joined by Justice Thomas, rejected "the Court's totality-of-the-circumstances (so-called) 'test,' in which the existence of a conflict is to be put into the mix and given some (unspecified) 'weight.' " In Scalia's view, trust law should govern the question, and "[u]nder that law, a fiduciary with a conflict does not abuse its discretion unless the conflict *actually* and *improperly motivates* the decision." Id. at 2357. Justice Scalia dismissed the majority opinion as fostering "a judge-liberating totality-of-the-circumstances 'test' " that is "nothing but *de novo* review in sheep's clothing." Id. at 2357, 2358.

QUESTIONS

1.   How is a reviewing court to decide what weight to give to the many competing "factors" that may be taken into account under *Firestone* and *Glenn*?

2.   Does *Glenn* provide true guidance, or is the post-*Glenn* standard illusory? Is it "anything goes"?

3.   Might the Supreme Court's continued willingness to allow plan documents to authorize deferential review of benefit denials be motivated by fear of the caseload consequences of mandating de novo review in all such cases? If fear of caseload pressures has been a core policy concern motivating the Supreme Court not to be more alert to the danger of conflicts of interest in benefit denial cases, should Congress remove these cases from the ordinary courts to an administrative agency?

8.   APPLYING *FIRESTONE* AFTER *GLENN*

1.   *Questioning the analogy to judicial review of administrative proceedings.* The Court in *Glenn* asserted an analogy between judicial deference to ERISA plan decisionmaking and judicial deference to the decisionmaking of administrative agencies. There are, however, significant institutional and procedural differences between the two reviewing functions. Courts and commentators have pointed to these differences over the years, but *Glenn* took no account of these differences.

One major ground of difference concerns the personnel. "[T]he individuals who occupy the position of ERISA fiduciaries are less well-insulated from outside pressures than are decisionmakers at government agencies." Brown v. Blue Cross & Blue Shield of Alabama, Inc., 898 F.2d 1556, 1564 (11th Cir.1990). Moreover, as the Third Circuit observed in Luby v. Teamsters Health, Welfare, and Pension Trust Funds, 944 F.2d 1176, 1183 (3d Cir.1991), ERISA plan administrators are often laypersons, that is, neither lawyers nor ERISA experts, and accordingly, their factual determinations are not entitled to the deference that courts grant to the factual determinations of administrative agencies staffed by experts.

Another important difference is that the procedural regime for benefit denials in administrative proceedings such as those conducted by the Social Security Administration (SSA) is more deliberative. Comparing ERISA benefit denial procedure with those of SSA, the Seventh Circuit has emphasized that SSA "is a public agency that denies benefits, only after giving the applicant an opportunity for a full and fair adjudicative hearing. The procedural safeguards thus accorded, designed to assure a full and fair hearing, are missing from determinations by [ERISA] plan administrators." Herzberger v. Standard Ins. Co., 205 F.3d 327, 332 (7th Cir.2000). For discussion, see Mark D. DeBofsky, The Paradox of the Misuse of Administrative Law in ERISA Benefit Claims, 37 John Marshall L. Rev. 727, 738–43 (2004).

2.   *What Glenn changed.* The main effect of *Glenn* has been to cause many circuits to abandon rules that they had developed under *Firestone* treating conflict of interest as altering the deferential standard of review. The Second Circuit, for example, understands *Glenn* to have "rejected the notion that the conflict of interest justifies changing the standard of review from deferential to *de novo.*" McCauley v. First Unum Life Ins. Co., 551 F.3d 126, 132 (2d Cir.2008). Similarly, the Third Circuit has treated *Glenn* as holding that courts "should take the conflict into account not in formulating the standard of review, but in determining whether the administrator or fiduciary abused its discretion." Estate of Schwing v. The Lilly Health Plan, 562 F.3d 522, 525 (3d Cir.2009), citing *Glenn*'s observation, 128 S.Ct. at 2350, that "conflicts are but one factor among many that a reviewing judge must take into account." In Doyle v. Liberty Life Asur. Co. of Boston, 542 F.3d 1352, 1360 (11th Cir.2008), superseding 511 F.3d 1336, the Eleventh Circuit held that *Glenn* effectively overruled the circuit's former rule that required "district courts to review benefit determinations by a conflicted administrator under [a] heightened standard." Instead, under *Glenn*, "the existence of a conflict of interest should merely be a factor for the district court to take into account when determining whether an administrator's decision was arbitrary and capricious." 542 F.3d at 1360.

In Miller v. Am. Airlines, Inc., 632 F.3d 837 (3d Cir. 2011), the Third Circuit held that *Glenn* affected its determination of whether a conflict existed. Prior to *Glenn*, the Third Circuit had "consistently held" that no conflict existed where an employer operated an actuarially grounded plan that paid claims through a trust, based on the view that the employer gained no direct benefit in denying claims. The court observed, however, that in light of the Supreme Court's decision

> this approach is no longer valid. *Glenn* instructs that a conflict arises where an employer both funds and evaluates claims. The Supreme Court's broad view of whether a conflict of interest exists, therefore, encompasses an arrangement where an employer makes fixed contributions to a plan, evaluates claims, and pays claims through a trust. Even in an actuarially grounded plan, the employer provides the monetary contribution and any money saved reduces the employer's projected benefit obligation.

Id. at 847. In *Miller* the Third Circuit determined that termination of a claimant's disability benefits was arbitrary and capricious "in light of the numerous substantive deficiencies and procedural irregularities that pervaded [the plan's] decision-making process." Id. at 841.

The harder task for the courts will be determining how heavily to weight the conflict. See Beverly Cohen, Divided Loyalties: How the Metlife v. Glenn Standard Discounts ERISA Fiduciaries' Conflicts of Interest, 3 Utah Law Review 956 (2009), arguing that *Glenn* discounts a fiduciary's conflict of interest as a determining factor in the review, meaning that conflicted decision making will continue to be a key feature of ERISA health and disability plans. One commentator has suggested that the "combination of factors" approach of *Glenn* has "left the circuits just as confused post-*Glenn* as they were pre-*Glenn*, as predicted by Chief Justice Roberts in the *Glenn* dissent." Kathryn J. Kennedy, Prime ERISA Areas for Supreme Court Review, 54 Tax Management Memorandum 55, 58 (2013).

3. *Process values.* In many fields of law, when the substantive legal standards do not provide much guidance, reviewing courts tend to emphasize process values, that is, the court examines whether the decisionmaker followed sound investigative and deliberative procedures. ERISA benefit denial cases often invoke such concerns. In such cases, the courts commonly invoke ERISA § 503, which requires (1) that the plan provide a plain-language notice to the participant or beneficiary of the reasons for the denial, and (2) "afford a reasonable opportunity [for] a full and fair review by the appropriate named fiduciary of the decision denying the claim."

Cases abound in which the courts have reversed benefit denials for failure of the decisionmaker to provide suitable reasons for denying a benefit claim. In Love v. National City Corp. Welfare Benefits Plan, 574 F.3d 392, 396 (7th Cir. 2009), the plan sent two letters to the participant denying her claim for disability benefits. The court found both letters inadequate because, although each "asserted that all relevant medical evidence had been considered, [neither] explained *why* the reviewer chose to discredit the evaluations of Love's treating physicians." Accord, Hackett v. Xerox Corp. Long-Term Disability Income Plan, 315 F.3d 771, 774–75 (7th Cir.2003) ("Even under the deferential review we will not uphold a [benefits] termination when there is an absence of reasoning in the record to support [it]. Conclusions without explanations [do] not allow for effective review."); Calvert v. Firstar Finance, Inc., 409 F.3d 286 (6th Cir.2005) (failure to state the factual basis for decision held A&C).

For example, in Abram v. Cargill, Inc., 395 F.3d 882 (8th Cir.2005), the court reversed a benefit denial because the plan's review procedure failed to provide an opportunity for the claimant to reply to a medical examiner's report that the decisionmaker used as the basis for denying benefits. A plan decisionmaker's failure properly to investigate medical evidence submitted to it was treated as arbitrary and capricious in Gaither v. Aetna Life Ins. Co., 388 F.3d 759 (10th Cir.2004). The Ninth Circuit reversed a denial of disability benefits in a case in which "virtually all of the evidence" supported the claim, and the decisionmaker rested its denial upon the single opinion of a vocational consultant, who contradicted the medical evidence. Spangler v. Lockheed Martin Energy Systems, Inc., 313 F.3d 356, 362 (6th Cir.2002). Accord, Cook v. Liberty Life Assurance Co., 320 F.3d 11, 23 (1st Cir.2003) (insurer failed to develop any medical evidence to contradict medical evidence of disability submitted by the claimant); Torres v. Unum Life Ins. Co., 405 F.3d 670, 681 (8th Cir.2005) (same).

In Miller v. Am. Airlines, Inc., 632 F.3d 837 (3d Cir. 2011), the Third Circuit catalogued a number of procedural irregularities in reaching the conclusion that a plan's termination of disability benefits was arbitrary and capricious: an administrator's reversal of its decision to award benefits without any new medical information to support its change in position; the imposition of requirements extrinsic to the plan in evaluating benefit eligibility; the failure of the denial letter sent to the participant to set forth "specific reasons," as required by ERISA § 503; the administrator's failure to address all relevant diagnoses in terminating benefits; and the administrator's failure to address the claimant's ability to perform his or her job requirements in light of the relevant diagnosis. See also Durakovic v. Bldg. Serv. 32 BJ Pension Fund, 609 F.3d 133 (2d Cir. 2010) (finding that the fund's summary dismissal of a report by the claimant's vocational expert "bespeak[s] the influence of a conflict of interest").

By contrast, following good procedures buttresses the decisionmaker against reversal under the deferential A&C standard. See, e.g., Boardman v. Prudential Ins. Co., 337 F.3d 9, 17 (1st Cir.2003) (lauding administrator for advising the applicant of the weaknesses of her claim and informing her of her right to submit additional evidence). Similarly, the Supreme Court in *Glenn* suggested that "where the administrator has taken active steps to reduce potential bias and to promote accuracy, for example, by walling off claims administrators from those interested in firm finances, or by imposing management checks that penalize inaccurate decisionmaking irrespective of whom the inaccuracy benefits," the existence of a conflict of interest "should prove less important (perhaps to the vanishing point). . . ." 128 S.Ct. at 1351.

When a plan that calls for deferential review commits a procedural irregularity, does the plan cease to qualify for deferential review? Compare Jebian v. Hewlett-Packard Co. Employee Benefits Organization Income Protection Plan, 349 F.3d 1098 (9th Cir.2003) (yes), with Finley v. Hewlett-Packard Co. Employee Benefits Organization Income Protection Plan, 379 F.3d 1168 (10th Cir.2004) (no). Hewlett-Packard sought certiorari in *Jebian*. The Supreme Court invited the Solicitor General to file a brief. 542 U.S. 935 (2004). The brief, available at 2005 WL 1277853 (May 27, 2005), reviewed the case law and recommended against certiorari, which was denied, see 545 U.S. 1139 (2005).

What effect should an incorrect interpretation of a plan by a plan administrator have on the standard of review applied by the courts? In Frommert v. Conkright, 433 F.3d 254 (2d Cir. 2006), after an appellate remand determined that the administrator of a pension plan unreasonably interpreted the plan in calculating benefits for rehired employees, the administrator's second interpretation was rejected. The Court of Appeals held that the second interpretation was properly reviewed without deference.

In 2010, the Supreme Court reversed and remanded the *Frommert* case, 559 U.S. 506, 130 S. Ct. 1640 (2010), holding that "a single honest mistake in plan interpretation [does not justify] stripping the administrator of . . . deference for subsequent related interpretations of the plan." Id. at 1644. The Court rejected the "one-strike-and-you're-out" approach as inconsistent with *Firestone*. The interests in "efficiency, predictability, and uniformity" promoted by *Firestone* deference "do not suddenly disappear simply because a plan administrator made a single honest mistake." Id. at 1649. Writing for the majority, Chief Justice

Roberts also observed that "[i]f, as we held in [*Glenn*], a systemic conflict of interest does not strip a plan administrator of deference, . . . it is difficult to see why a single honest mistake would require a different result." Id. at 1647.

The Court acknowledged that "[m]ultiple erroneous plan interpretations of the same plan provision, even if issued in good faith, might well support a finding that a plan administrator is too incompetent to exercise his discretion fairly, cutting short the rounds of costly litigation that respondents fear," Id. at 1651, but it did not believe the case before it justified such a finding.

Justice Breyer, joined by Justices Stevens and Ginsberg, wrote in dissent that a finding that an administrator's interpretation of a plan was arbitrary and capricious allows a court to "exercise its own discretion rather than defer to a trustee's interpretation of trust language." Id. at 1655. Which of the majority or dissent better promote ERISA's aims? For a criticism of the Court's analysis, see Kathryn J. Kennedy, Conkright: A Conundrum for Future Courts, An Opportunity for Congress, NYU Rev. of Employee Benefits Law & Executive Compensation 2010, 16–70–16–71 (2010) (suggesting that the Court's decision "forsakes trust law").

On remand, the district court applied a more deferential review and held that the plan administrator's proposed offset was a reasonable interpretation of the plan, a ruling that was vacated by the Second Circuit, which found the offset unreasonable because it was inconsistent with the plan's terms. 738 F.3d 522 (2nd Cir.2013).

4.   *Distinguish plan interpretation from fact-based determinations?* One of Judge Becker's reasons for declining to defer to plan decisionmaking in the Third Circuit's opinion in *Firestone*, it will be recalled, was the supposition that a benefit denial case does not ordinarily "turn on information or experience which expertise as a claims administrator is likely to produce." When the case "turn[s] on a question of law or of contract interpretation, [courts] have no reason to defer to private [parties]." 828 F.2d at 144. This distinction between benefit denials based on fact-finding and those turning on the interpretation of plan terms has resurfaced in the case law applying *Firestone*.

Firestone was an interpretation case. The Supreme Court remarked: "As this case aptly demonstrates, the validity of a claim to benefits under an ERISA plan is likely to turn on the interpretation of terms in the plan at issue." 489 U.S. at 115.

Shortly after *Firestone,* the Fifth Circuit attempted to limit *Firestone*'s de novo standard of review to plan interpretation questions, thus preserving routine deferential review in cases involving factual determinations. Pierre v. Connecticut General Life Ins. Co., 932 F.2d 1552 (5th Cir.1991), cert. denied, 502 U.S. 973 (1991). "Unlike plan term interpretations," the court said, "factual determinations do not involve contract interpretations." The Fifth Circuit feared the caseload consequences of routine de novo review of fact-finding. "The courts simply cannot supplant plan administrators, through *de novo* review, as resolvers of mundane and routine fact disputes."

The Fifth Circuit's initiative in *Pierre* is "very much the minority view, and numerous circuits have declined to adopt it." Shaw v.

Connecticut General Life Ins. Co., 353 F.3d 1276, 1285 (11th Cir.2003) (citing cases). The Ninth Circuit has questioned *Pierre*'s premise, contending that "factual findings and plan interpretations are often intertwined. For example, determining eligibility for disability benefits almost always involves an interpretation of the plan's term 'disabled,' but it also involves the fact of whether the claimant is disabled." Walker v. American Home Shield Long Term Disability Plan, 180 F.3d 1065, 1070 (9th Cir.1999). Cases in the Seventh Circuit have emphasized that the terms of the Supreme Court's opinion in *Firestone* leave no room for restricting de novo review to factual determinations. Petrilli v. Drechsel, 910 F.2d 1441, 1446 (7th Cir.1990), reaffirmed in Ramsey v. Hercules, Inc., 77 F.3d 199, 204 (7th Cir.1996).

The Fifth Circuit, however, adheres to *Pierre*. "[F]actual determinations made by the administrator during the course of a benefits review will be rejected only upon the showing of an abuse of discretion." Meditrust Financial Services Corp. v. Sterling Chemicals, 168 F.3d 211, 213 (5th Cir.1999).

5. *New evidence.* May the plan participant present the reviewing court with evidence that was not brought to the attention of the plan fiduciary whose decision the court is reviewing? In Moon v. American Home Assurance Co., 888 F.2d 86, 89 (11th Cir.1989), the Eleventh Circuit held that such evidence could be offered. The court reasoned that limiting evidence to that presented to the plan administrator is contrary to the concept of de novo review (the default standard of review in *Firestone*). Accord, Luby v. Teamsters Health, Welfare, and Pension Trust Funds, 944 F.2d 1176, 1184–85 (3d Cir.1991). Supporting this view, Judge Easterbrook has written that what *Firestone* calls de novo review "is not 'review' of any kind; it is an independent decision." In such a case, "we cannot imagine any justification for refusing to admit evidence that one party has procured at its own [expense]." Krolnik v. Prudential Ins. Co., 570 F.3d 841, 843 (7th Cir.2009). By contrast, "[when] review is deferential—when the plan's decision must be sustained unless arbitrary and capricious—*then* review is limited to the administrative record." Id.

The Sixth Circuit has developed the opposite view. "*Bruch* does not contemplate a de novo *hearing*, but rather a de novo consideration of the proper interpretation of the plan and whether an employee is entitled to benefits under [it]." The federal court would become a "substitute plan administrator" were it to consider evidence regarding benefit entitlement that had not been presented to the plan administrator. Perry v. Simplicity Engineering, 900 F.2d 963, 966 (6th Cir.1990). Similarly, the First Circuit has said: "The decision to which judicial review is addressed is the final ERISA administrative decision. It would offend interests in finality and exhaustion of administrative procedures required by ERISA to shift the focus from that decision to a moving target by presenting extra-administrative record evidence going to the substance of the decision." Orndorf v. Paul Revere Life Ins. Co., 404 F.3d 510, 519 (1st Cir.2005). "Confining review in general to the administrative record [encourages] the parties to develop the factual record as fully and as early as [possible]." Jewell v. Life Ins. Co. of North America, 508 F.3d 1303, 1308 (10th Cir.2007).

The Fourth Circuit has followed a middle path, leaving to judicial discretion the decision of whether or not to admit such evidence. Quesinberry v. Life Ins. Co. of North America, 987 F.2d 1017 (4th Cir.1993). The Tenth Circuit follows a version of that standard, saying that review should "ordinarily" be restricted to the administrative record, but "the district court [may] supplement the record 'when circumstances clearly establish that additional evidence is necessary to conduct an adequate *de novo* [review].'" Hall v. Unum Life Ins. Co., 300 F.3d 1197, 1202 (10th Cir.2002). The Second Circuit allows extra-record evidence in cases involving plan interpretation, Masella v. Blue Cross & Blue Shield, Inc., 936 F.2d 98 (2d Cir.1991); and for "good cause" in other cases. Zervos v. Verizon N.Y., Inc., 277 F.3d 635, 646 (2d Cir.2002).

The Fifth Circuit holds that claimants should be permitted to introduce evidence that questions "the completeness of the administrative record; whether the plan administrator complied with ERISA's procedural regulations; and the existence and extent of a conflict of interest created by a plan administrator's dual role in making benefits determinations and funding the plan." Crosby v. La. Health Serv. & Indem. Co., 647 F.3d 258, 263 (5th Cir. 2011). Accord. Eugene S. v. Horizon Blue Cross Blue Shield of NJ, 663 F.3d 1124 (10th Cir. 2011).

When the plan documents impose deferential A&C review, most courts exclude extra-record evidence—the distinction voiced by Judge Easterbrook in *Krolnik*, quoted above. "Permitting a district court to examine evidence outside the administrative record would open the door to the anomalous conclusion that a plan administrator abused its discretion by failing to consider evidence not before it." Jones v. Laborers Health & Welfare Trust Fund, 906 F.2d 480, 482 (9th Cir.1990); accord, McKenzie v. General Telephone Co. of California, 41 F.3d 1310 (9th Cir.1994). However, when the decisionmaker under a plan-provided deferential standard of review is operating under a conflict of interest, the conflict may justify consideration of non-record evidence, especially evidence about whether the conflict of interest affected the decision being challenged. See Tremain v. Bell Industries, 196 F.3d 970 (9th Cir.1999).

In Helton v. AT&T Inc., 709 F.3d 343 (4th Cir. 2013), the Fourth Circuit held that a federal district court properly considered extrinsic evidence in making an award of retroactive benefits to a pension plan participant even though the standard of review was arbitrary and capricious. In the case at hand, the limited evidence considered by the district court was evidence that had been known to AT&T when it made the determination to deny benefits to the participant. The court observed that "we have long recognized that certain types of extrinsic evidence often are necessary for a court to assess whether an administrator abused its discretion in denying a plan member's request for benefits." Id at 353. In the view of the court, a failure to allow review of such evidence "effectively surrender[s] our ability to review ERISA benefit determinations because plan administrators could simply omit any evidence from the administrative record that would suggest their decisions were unreasonable." Id.

6. *Contra proferentum.* Some post-*Firestone* cases have undertaken to apply in benefit denial cases as a rule of federal common law the constructional principle of contract law that the court should

construe ambiguities (both in the plan and in the summary plan description) against the drafter. This so-called *contra proferentum* rule has had a particularly close association with the construction of insurance contracts; see generally Kenneth S. Abraham, A Theory of Insurance Policy Interpretation, 95 Michigan L. Rev. 531 (1996). The Fifth Circuit has said:

> In contracts of insurance generally, ambiguities are resolved against the drafter. The same rule should apply [to ERISA plan documents; in this case] the ambiguity in the summary plan description must be resolved in favor of the employee and made binding against the drafter. Any burden of uncertainty created by careless or inaccurate drafting of the summary must be placed on those who do the drafting, and who are most able to bear that burden, and not on the individual employee, who is powerless to affect the drafting of the summary or the policy and ill equipped to bear the financial hardship that might result from a misleading or confusing document. Accuracy is not a lot to ask. And it is especially not a lot to ask in return for the protection afforded by ERISA's preemption of state law causes of action—causes of action which threaten considerably greater liability than that allowed by ERISA.

Hansen v. Continental Ins. Co., 940 F.2d 971, 982 (5th Cir.1991). The Second Circuit has remarked that ERISA's protective policy reinforces this result, since "ERISA is not to be interpreted to afford employees and their beneficiaries less protection than they enjoyed before ERISA was [enacted]." Critchlow v. First Unum Life Ins. Co., 378 F.3d 246, 256 (2d Cir.2004); cf. *Firestone*, 489 U.S. at 113 ("ERISA was enacted 'to promote the interests of employees and their beneficiaries in employee benefit plans' and 'to protect contractually defined benefits' ").

The leading case applying the *contra proferentum* principle in ERISA settings is Kunin v. Benefit Trust Life Ins. Co., 910 F.2d 534 (9th Cir.1990), cert. denied, 498 U.S. 1013 (1990), rehearing denied, 498 U.S. 1074 (1991), noted in 77 Minnesota L. Rev. 1219 (1993). Accord, Lee v. Blue Cross/Blue Shield of Alabama, 10 F.3d 1547 (11th Cir.1994); Heasley v. Belden & Blake Corp., 2 F.3d 1249 (3d Cir.1993); Phillips v. Lincoln National Life Ins. Co., 978 F.2d 302 (7th Cir.1992); contra, Brewer v. Lincoln National Life Ins. Co., 921 F.2d 150, 154 (8th Cir.1990) ("neither party's construction should be favored").

The *contra proferentum* rule places great weight upon the court's determination that a plan provision is indeed ambiguous. E.g., Shanks v. Blue Cross & Blue Shield United of Wisconsin, 979 F.2d 1232, 1233 (7th Cir.1992) ("The law concerning ambiguities in contracts [does] not come into play in this case because the term 'treatment' as used here is not ambiguous"); accord, Weir v. Federal Asset Disposition Ass'n, 123 F.3d 281 (5th Cir.1997). In deciding whether a term is ambiguous, extrinsic evidence is normally admissible. Moriarty v. Svec, 164 F.3d 323, 331 (7th Cir.1998); Farley v. Benefit Trust Life Ins. Co., 979 F.2d 653, 657 (8th Cir.1992).

Because *contra proferentum* is a rule of deference to the claimant in a case of ambiguity, it is in tension with a plan provision that requires deference to plan decisionmaking. Several courts have concluded that the plan's grant of discretion trumps *contra proferentum*, which is a mere constructional rule, hence default law. E.g., Marrs v. Motorola, Inc., 577 F.3d 783, 787 (7th Cir.2009); Kimber v. Thiokol Corp., 196 F.3d 1092 (10th Cir.1999); Winters v. Costco Wholesale Corp., 49 F.3d 550 (9th Cir.1995). Under this view, there is room to apply *contra proferentum* only when the court undertakes de novo review. Morton v. Smith, 91 F.3d 867, 871 n. 1 (7th Cir.1996); Pagan v. NYNEX Pension Plan, 52 F.3d 438, 443 (2d Cir.1995); Miller v. Monumental Life Ins. Co., 502 F.3d 1245 (10th Cir.2007). By contrast, in Bailey v. Blue Cross & Blue Shield of Virginia, 67 F.3d 53, 58 (4th Cir.1995), the court insisted "that ambiguous language must be construed against the drafter" even in a case in which the plan called for deferential review. Accord, White v. Coca-Cola Co., 542 F.3d 848, 855 (11th Cir.2008).

A rule of construing strictly against benefit denials could be justified on grounds other than ambiguity. Professor Fisk has criticized the federal courts in benefit denial cases for being "oblivious to the disparities of bargaining power," and for ignoring "that individual bargaining over the terms of the employee benefit plan never [occurs]." Catherine L. Fisk, *Lochner* Redux: The Renaissance of Laissez-Faire Contract in the Federal Common Law of Employee Benefits, 56 Ohio St. L.J. 153, 186–87 (1995).

In Murphy v. Deloitte & Touche Grp. Ins. Plan, 619 F.3d 1151 (10th Cir. 2010), the Tenth Circuit overturned a magistrate's determination that discovery could not be had because the defendant Met Life had conceded that it acted as both administrator and insurer. Acknowledging that its past instructions to lower courts had been unclear, the court clarified that there are circumstances under which it may be appropriate to allow a plaintiff to engage in discovery to determine "the seriousness of the inherent conflict and the likelihood that it jeopardized MetLife's decisionmaking process." Id. at 1164. In determining when discovery is appropriate, district courts must consider ERISA's competing goals of seeking a fair and informed resolution of claims and seeking to ensure a speedy, inexpensive and efficient resolution of claims. For an example of a district court application of the rule established in *Murphy*, see Jaremko v. ERISA Admin. Comm., 2011 U.S. Dist. LEXIS 1399 (D. Kan. Jan. 6, 2011). But see Atkins v. Prudential Ins. Co., 404 Fed. Appx. 82 (8th Cir. Dec. 13, 2010) (upholding the district court in denying motion for discovery into an insurer's conflict of interest where the administrative record was sufficient to permit the court to fairly evaluate the fiduciary's decision to deny benefits).

7.   *Federal common law.* In construing plan terms, the courts have developed a federal common law of ERISA. "In fashioning federal common law under ERISA, including principles that govern the legal effect of plan terms, courts may look to state law for guidance so long as the state law is not contrary to the provisions of ERISA." Mansker v. TMG Life Ins. Co., 54 F.3d 1322, 1326 (8th Cir.1995). The federal courts "look to state law as a model because of the states' greater experience in interpreting insurance contracts and resolving coverage disputes. To decide whether a particular rule should become part of ERISA's common law, courts must examine whether the rule, if adopted, would further

ERISA's scheme and goals." Horton v. Reliance Standard Life Ins. Co., 141 F.3d 1038, 1041 (11th Cir.1998).

Literature: George L. Flint, Jr., ERISA: Reformulating the Federal Common Law for Plan Interpretation, 32 San Diego L. Rev. 955 (1995); Jay Conison, Foundations of the Common Law of Plans, 41 DePaul L. Rev. 575 (1992). See Chapter 17, infra, treating preemption, for discussion of when ERISA preemption should lead to the creation of federal common law.

9. SEVERANCE AND ACCIDENT PLANS

Four types of welfare plans feature centrally in the benefit denial case law: occupational disability plans, severance pay plans, health care plans, and plans that insure against accidental death and injury. See generally Peter A. Myers, Discretionary Language, Conflicts of Interest, and Standard of Review for ERISA Disability Plans, 28 Seattle L. Rev. 925 (2005). Disability plan issues have been extensively discussed earlier in this chapter, in connection with the Unum/Provident scandal. Health plans are discussed in chapter 19.

1. *Severance pay plans.* A severance pay plan (sometimes called a termination plan) commonly provides a lump sum payment, calculated with reference to the length of an employee's service with the firm, when the employee is terminated other than for cause.

When there is a change of ownership of the employing entity, but with employment continuity for the employee, has the employee been terminated within the meaning of the severance plan? That question was presented in *Firestone*, and it arose frequently in the 1980s and 1990s. Many severance plans drafted before the large-scale corporate downsizings of the 1980s had not foreseen the question. Most courts have sustained the fiduciary's decision to deny severance benefits in these cases, whether the standard of review is A&C or de novo, but because these cases interpret particular plan language, the issue is seldom closed to litigation. E.g., Smith v. United Television, Inc., Special Severance Plan, 474 F.3d 1033 (8th Cir.2007) (against participant, deferential review); Hickey v. Digital Equipment Corp., 43 F.3d 941 (4th Cir.1995) (against participants, deferential review); Bradwell v. GAF Corp., 954 F.2d 798 (2d Cir.1992) (against participants, de novo review); Bellino v. Schlumberger Technologies, Inc., 944 F.2d 26 (1st Cir.1991) (for participants, de novo review).

Regarding the question of how employment continuity with the successor firm affects a claim to severance pay under the former employer's plan, the First Circuit in *Bellino* summarized the case law thus: "Federal courts have established no hard and fast rule that an individual must suffer a period of unemployment to qualify for severance benefits under ERISA. Those courts that have deemed unemployment a prerequisite to such benefits have predicated their decisions on the particular terms of the ERISA plan at issue and its application to the specific facts before them." 944 F.2d at 31.

When the language of the plan does not supply precise guidance, should the decisionmaker try to ascertain whether the circumstances of the termination fit the purpose of the plan? What is the purpose of a severance plan? On one view, severance pay represents a kind of contingent deferred compensation—a bonus that is paid to workers who are laid off or otherwise dismissed without fault. A more common view is that severance pay serves as a species of preliquidated unemployment compensation. Unlike state unemployment compensation programs, which vary the amount of the payment with the length of the period after termination that the worker is unable to find employment, severance plans provide a lump sum payment and dispense with the need to monitor the terminated worker's efforts at reemployment.

Should a court that is reviewing a severance benefit denial case consider whether the acquiring firm offers less generous compensation or benefits to the workers? See Bedinghaus v. Modern Graphic Arts, 15 F.3d 1027 (11th Cir.1994), in which the court awarded severance pay to the rehired employees under the former employer's plan, emphasizing that the new owner's severance plan did not recognize credits accrued with the former owner, and hence that the plaintiffs had "lost substantial severance benefits."

Should the financial condition of the acquiring firm be taken into account—for example, if the employing entity is being sold by a strong corporation to one that is highly leveraged and thus more subject to the risk of insolvency? (Recall *Varity v. Howe*, supra in Chapter 12, in which a weakened successor firm defaulted on welfare benefit plans.)

The question sometimes arises whether a particular terminal arrangement for a departing employee or group of employees is or is not an ERISA plan. That issue, which figured in Fort Halifax Packing Co. v. Coyne, 482 U.S. 1 (1987), has been discussed in Chapter 3, supra. Compare Simas v. Quaker Fabric Corp. of Fall River, 6 F.3d 849 (1st Cir.1993) (finding a plan), with James v. Fleet/Norstar Financial Group, Inc., 992 F.2d 463 (2d Cir.1993) (no plan).

2.   *Accidental death and injury.* Accident plans need to decide what is accidental. E.g., Santaella v. Metropolitan Life Ins. Co., 123 F.3d 456 (7th Cir.1997) (death from overdose of prescription pain medication was accidental rather than intentionally self-inflicted); Ford v. Metropolitan Life Ins. Co., 834 F.Supp. 1272 (D.Kan.1993) (death of employee who was shot by police while holding third person hostage deemed not accidental); McLain v. Metropolitan Life Ins. Co., 820 F.Supp. 169 (D.N.J.1993) (death from cocaine-related cardiac arrest not accidental); Finley v. Special Agents Mutual Benefit Ass'n, Inc., 957 F.2d 617 (8th Cir.1992) (drug enforcement agent killed in air crash in Peru held not to have died in a "confrontational" situation, which would have entitled his survivor to a higher level of benefits).

A large number of cases of benefit denials under plans providing for accidental death and injury benefits concern people who have been driving while intoxicated, with courts coming to different conclusions as to whether injury or death in such cases is the result of an accident or was reasonably foreseeable and, therefore, not accidental. The Tenth Circuit, in LaAsmar v. Phelps Dodge Corp. Life, Accidental Death & Dismemberment and Dependent Life Ins. Plan, 605 F.3d 789 (10th Cir. 2010), ruled that a participant's death from a single-vehicle crash was an "accident." The participant, who was driving the vehicle, had a blood alcohol level of 2.8 times the legal limit and was driving 20 miles an hour over the speed limit at the time of the crash.

Finding the term "accident" to be ambiguous, the court said that "[i]t is not too much to ask of ERISA insurers to set forth explicitly what is and is not an accident covered by their AD&D policy, and to state unambiguously whether death and disability caused by an insured's drunk driving is an accident and, if not, to include a workable definition of drunkenness and of causation attributed to such drunkenness." 605 F.3d at 805. Although the court explicitly stated that it was not suggesting "that there are no circumstances where an insured would be so drunk that a resulting wreck could no longer be deemed an accident," id. at 808, it found that "a reasonable person in [the participant's] position would have understood the term 'accident' as used in this AD&D plan, to cover the crash at issue." Id. at 802.

Regardless of whether you agree with the court's conclusion on these facts, is its suggestion sound? How would you articulate in an AD&D policy the circumstances under which death and disability caused by drunk driving is an accident? The Eighth Circuit has ruled that death caused by drunk driving of a motorcycle is an accident "if the decedent did not subjectively expect to suffer 'an injury similar in type or kind to that suffered' and the suppositions underlying that expectation were reasonable." McClelland v. Life Ins. Co. of N. Am., 679 F.3d 755, n.2 (8th Cir. 2012) (citing Wickman v. Nw. Nat'l Ins. Co., 908 F.2d 1077 (1st Cir.1990)). Is that a reasonable test to apply? See also Johnson v. American United Life Ins. Co., 716 F.3d 813 (4th Cir.2013) (finding the undefined term "accident" to be ambiguous and construing it against the drafting party, concluding that a reasonable plan participant under similar circumstances would have understood an alcohol-related crash to be an "accident" under the policy language). A plan can, of course, avoid uncertainty by how it drafts its plan. See, e.g., Green v. Life Ins. Co., 754 F. 3d 324 (5th Cir. June 11, 2014) (upholding denial of benefits based on plan exclusion for injuries caused by operating a vehicle under the influence of alcohol or drugs); Shaw v. Prudential Ins. Co., 566 Fed. Appx. 536 (8th Cir. June 3, 2014) (upholding denial of benefits based on plan exclusion for losses resulting from accidents occurring while operating a motor vehicle involving illegal use of alcohol).

Accidental death policies sometimes exclude death caused by accidental overdose of prescription drugs. See, e.g., Brimer v. Life Ins. Co. of N.A., 462 Fed. Appx. 804 (10th Cir. Feb. 10, 2012); Smith v. Life Ins. Co. of N. Am., 459 Fed. Appx. 480 (5th Cir. Feb. 6, 2012) (both upholding benefit denials pursuant to exclusions). See also Hernandez v. Hartford Life & Accident Ins. Co., 462 Fed. Appx. 583 (6th Cir. Feb. 17, 2012) (upholding denial of benefits pursuant to exclusion of coverage of losses caused by "circulatory malfunctioning").

Accidental death plans sometimes contain a moral hazard exclusion for suicide. In Reinking v. Philadelphia American Life Ins. Co., 910 F.2d 1210 (4th Cir.1990), the court, operating under de novo review, refused to apply the exclusion, reasoning that the participant lacked adequate mental capacity to understand that she was attempting suicide. Does such an exclusion apply to an insured who is asphyxiated while engaged in autoerotic activity? Compare Critchlow v. First Unum Life Ins. Co.,

378 F.3d 246 (2d Cir.2004) (no), with Hamilton v. AIG Life Ins. Co., 182 F.Supp.2d 39 (D.D.C.2002) (yes). Does an insurance policy's exclusion of double indemnity coverage for "intentionally self-inflicted injury" or suicide apply to a participant-insured who was killed operating a motorcycle while intoxicated? See King v. Hartford Life & Accident Ins. Co., 414 F.3d 994 (8th Cir.2005) (en banc).

The participant in an ERISA-covered accidental death insurance plan suffered from serious heart disease; he died of a heart attack suffered moments after an auto accident. Was his death within the policy terms that covered only losses resulting "directly" from an accident? See Dixon v. Life Ins. Co. of North America, 389 F.3d 1179 (11th Cir.2004).

A participant was injured in a workplace elevator on her way to a scheduled coffee break. Does she qualify for benefits under a plan that compensates accidental injury suffered "during and in direct connection with the performance of duties" of employment? Recupero v. New England Telephone & Telegraph Co., 118 F.3d 820 (1st Cir.1997).

A participant is rendered permanently quadriplegic in an accident. Does he qualify for benefits under an accidental death and dismemberment plan that provides for benefits in the case of "dismemberment by severance"? In Fier v. Unum Life Ins. Co., 629 F.3d 1095 (9th Cir. 2011), the Ninth Circuit rejected the participant's argument that although his hands and feet remained physically attached to his body, he lost them from a functional standpoint due to the severance of his spinal cord. The court held that reading the policy language in its "ordinary and popular sense" compelled the conclusion that "dismemberment by severance" required "actual, physical separation." Id. at 1099.

B. ERISA'S REQUIREMENT OF WRITTEN TERMS

ERISA § 402(a)(1) requires that "every employee benefit plan shall be maintained pursuant to a written instrument." Other ERISA provisions echo the expectation that ERISA plan terms will be in writing. The courts' reading of these ERISA provisions as imposing a mini-Statute of Frauds has produced a large and disquieting case law.

1. SCHMIDT V. SHEET METAL WORKERS' NATIONAL PENSION FUND

128 F.3d 541 (7th Cir.1997).

■ ILANA DIAMOND ROVNER, CIRCUIT JUDGE.

Richard A. Schmidt ("Richard") initiated this ERISA action against the Sheet Metal Workers' National Pension Fund ("NPF" or "Fund") and its Board of Trustees ("Trustees") to recover the portion of his father's death benefit that the Fund disbursed to Richard's sister. Although Richard's father failed to designate a beneficiary for his death benefit, Richard contends that his father intended that he be the sole beneficiary and that the proper designation was never made only because a benefit analyst employed by the Fund sent the wrong form after speaking with Richard and his father over the telephone. Richard therefore argues that he is entitled to the contested benefits either under an estoppel or breach of fiduciary duty theory. [The] district court granted summary judgment to defendants on each of Richard's claims. Richard now challenges that disposition here, and [we] affirm the judgment below.

On March 4, 1994, Allen J. Schmidt ("Allen") was told by his doctors that he had pancreatic cancer and that he had but a few months to live. Allen was not married at the time, and he therefore wished to designate his son Richard as the sole beneficiary of the pension benefit that would be payable upon his death by the NPF, a multi-employer benefit trust fund maintained under ERISA. On March 10, Allen called the Fund's administrative office to inquire about the procedure for designating his son as the sole beneficiary of his death benefit. He spoke on that occasion to Eunjae Lee, an NPF benefit analyst. Allen explained to Lee that he was terminally ill and that he wished to designate his son as the sole beneficiary of his pension death benefit. Because Allen believed that Lee was not fully understanding his request, he asked Richard to attempt to explain it to her. Richard reiterated to Lee that Allen was terminally ill and that he wished to designate Richard as the sole beneficiary of his death benefit. Lee indicated to Richard that she understood and that she would send the proper paperwork. Several days later, the Schmidts received a "Pension or Vesting Application," which they promptly completed and returned to the Fund. On that application, Allen designated Richard as his primary beneficiary and his daughter, Ginger Riphahn, as the successor beneficiary. It turned out, however, that Lee had sent the Schmidts the incorrect form. The "Pension or Vesting Application" was exactly that—an application for pension benefits, and was not the proper mechanism for designating a beneficiary for a pension plan death benefit. A death benefit beneficiary was properly designated only once a plan participant submitted to the Fund the "benefit designation card" included in the front of the Fund's pension plan booklet (the "Booklet").[2] This Booklet had been mailed to all plan participants in 1990.

Allen died on April 16, 1994, and on August 29, 1994, Richard received a letter from Lee explaining that because his father had failed to name a beneficiary for his death benefit, the $22,693.13 benefit would be divided evenly between Allen's surviving children in accordance with section 7.01 of the pension plan. Lee included with this letter another copy of the Booklet, which sets out the death benefit eligibility rules and an individual's appeal rights. Upon receiving Lee's letter, Richard called the Fund's administrative office and this time spoke with Barry Sweger, an assistant benefits coordinator. Richard explained to Sweger that Lee had sent his father the wrong form after their March 10 telephone conversation, and Sweger indicated that Richard should write down exactly what had happened and note that his letter was to be considered an appeal to the Fund's Board of Trustees. Sweger explained that all information substantiating Richard's position should be included in the

---

[2]   The summary included in the Booklet explains:

Use the card attached in this booklet to name your beneficiary for this [death] benefit. File it with your local union after completion. The Plan does not accept any beneficiary card other than its own.

If no Plan beneficiary card is filed with your local union, the Death Benefit will be paid to your legal spouse. If you have no spouse, it will be paid to your children.

letter and that any supporting documentation should be appended. Sweger told Richard to mail the letter to him and that the Trustees then would consider Richard's appeal at their next meeting. Richard did as he was told, mailing his letter to Sweger on September 30, 1994. He received a letter in response which indicated that his appeal had been received and that it would be considered at the next meeting of the Fund's Trustees. By letter dated May 30, 1995, Richard was notified that the Appeals Committee of the Board of Trustees, consisting of two of the six trustees, had considered his appeal at their May 2 meeting and had determined to deny it. The letter provided the following explanation of the Appeals Committee's [decision]:

> Mr. Schmidt did not have [a Death Benefit] designation on file at the time of his death. The designation of beneficiary section completed by Mr. Schmidt on the pension application received shortly before his death is not the form required by the Trustees to designate beneficiaries for a Death Benefit, but is a designation of beneficiary for *pension* benefits, in the event any such payments are payable after the death of the retiree. . . .

Richard does not dispute that the Trustees' decision to distribute his father's death benefit to him and his sister in equal shares is consistent with the explicit terms of the Plan and the Booklet describing [it].[4] He argues instead that defendants should be estopped from adhering to the literal terms of the Plan because of the misrepresentation of its benefit analyst.

We agree with the district court, however, that defendants are not estopped from applying the literal terms of the Plan by any oral representation made by Lee in the course of the March 10, 1994 telephone conversation. As we have noted on many occasions, oral representations that conflict with the terms of a written plan will not be given effect, as the written instrument must control. Although a subsequent modification to a written plan may equitably estop the plan administrator from denying benefits if the alleged modification is in writing (*see Black v. TIC Investment Corp.*, 900 F.2d 112, 116 (7th Cir.1990)), we do not think the writing requirement was satisfied here by the fact that Lee subsequently mailed to the Schmidts the "Pension or Vesting Application." That application did not itself indicate that it was the appropriate mechanism for designating a death benefit beneficiary. Richard's estoppel claim instead depends on what transpired during the March 10 telephone conversation—specifically on what he and his father may have told Lee about Allen's intent, and on Lee's alleged statement that she would send Allen the proper paperwork for designating a death benefit beneficiary. The oral representation upon which Richard's claim is based clearly conflicts with the designation method prescribed by the Plan Booklet, and the Plan itself requires all beneficiary designations to be in the proper form. That is presumably to avoid beneficiary disputes like this one, which only will arise upon a participant's death, when it is too late for his intent to be clarified. It is in precisely this situation, then, that we must refuse to apply estoppel principles to give effect to oral

---

[4] Because the Plan provides the Trustees with discretion in interpreting its terms, we would be required to defer to the Trustees' judgment unless we were to find it arbitrary and capricious.

representations that contradict written Plan terms. For these reasons, we agree with the district court that Richard's estoppel claim must fail.

Richard also contends that the Trustees breached their fiduciary duties when Lee advised the Schmidts, erroneously it turned out, that the beneficiary designation could be made on the "Pension or Vesting Application." Lee's misstatement, according to Richard, breached the Trustees' duty to provide plan participants with complete and accurate material information regarding their status and options under an ERISA plan.

In *Anweiler v. American Elec. Power Serv. Corp.*, 3 F.3d 986, 991 (7th Cir.1993), we explained that "[f]iduciaries breach their duties of loyalty and care [when] they mislead plan participants or misrepresent the terms or administration of a plan." A plan fiduciary may violate its duties, we said, either by affirmatively misleading plan participants about the operations of a plan, or by remaining silent in circumstances where silence could be considered misleading. In this case, Richard contends that he and his father were affirmatively misled by Lee's directions for designating a death benefit beneficiary. The district court did not doubt that the Schmidts had been misled, but in granting summary judgment, the court focused on whether Lee's misstatement could be said to have breached the duties owed to plan participants by the Trustees themselves, as they were the only ERISA fiduciaries named as defendants in this case. We therefore turn to that question now.

It goes without saying that a claim for breach of fiduciary duty lies only against an individual or entity that qualifies as an ERISA "fiduciary." And to be a fiduciary, the individual or entity involved must exercise a degree of discretion over the management of the plan or its assets, or over the administration of the plan itself. *See* [ERISA § 3(21)(A)] (defining "fiduciary"). It is clear that Lee herself was not an ERISA fiduciary, as she merely performed ministerial and clerical functions relating to the administration of the Plan; she had no discretionary authority or control in the tasks she was assigned. *See* 29 C.F.R. § 2509.75–8, D–2 ("a person who performs purely ministerial functions [for] an employee benefit plan within a framework of policies, interpretations, rules, practices and procedures made by other persons is not a fiduciary . . ."). Indeed, Richard has not even made Lee's status an issue, as she is not named as a defendant. The Trustees alone are alleged to have breached their fiduciary duties, and given their discretionary authority over the management and administration of the Fund, we agree that they would qualify as ERISA fiduciaries.

Yet the Trustees did not make the misstatement on which Richard's fiduciary duty claim is based—Lee did. Significantly, no evidence suggests that the Trustees either authorized, participated in, or had knowledge of Lee's misstatement, or that the Trustees deliberately withheld information from Lee about the proper means of making a beneficiary designation. Rather, this is a case in which the Trustees provided complete and correct information to participants both in the Plan itself and in the Plan Booklet only to have a ministerial employee make a negligent misrepresentation in response to a single question from a single participant. The district court concluded that absent evidence that the Trustees had participated in Lee's misstatement or had failed to exercise care in hiring her, the Trustees could not be said to have breached their fiduciary duties solely by virtue of Lee's misstatement. We believe that in general, the district court was correct, but we would add that the Trustees may also breach their fiduciary duties by failing to exercise care in training someone like Lee, or by retaining her in circumstances where they should know her performance to be inadequate. There is no evidence that the Trustees in this case were involved in any way with Lee's misstatement. Nor has Richard attempted to show that the Trustees failed to exercise due care either in hiring or retaining Lee, or in training her to respond to inquiries from plan participants. We therefore agree with the district court that Lee's misstatement would not in these circumstances support a breach of fiduciary duty claim against the Trustees.

We hasten to add, however, that our resolution of this case depends in large measure on the fact that the Trustees provided complete and accurate information in the Plan and Plan Booklet they distributed to all participants. [We] believe that the adequacy of the relevant disclosures in the written plan materials is an important consideration in a circumstance like this where a non-fiduciary agent subsequently provides erroneous information in response to a question from a single participant.

NOTES AND QUESTIONS

1. *Defeating intent.* The pension plan in *Schmidt* was a multiemployer defined benefit plan. The plan promised a death benefit for survivors in the event that the participant did not survive until retirement, as happened in the case. The plan allowed the participant, Allen Schmidt, to designate a person or persons to receive the death benefit; or, if he failed to designate a beneficiary, the plan's rules directed the benefit to his spouse, if any, or if none, as in *Schmidt*, equally among his children. Allen wanted to direct the entire sum to his son Richard, who had been caring for him. Because Allen's effort at designating Richard was treated as ineffective, the account proceeds passed in accordance with the plan's rule for cases in which no designation was in effect, half to Richard and half to a sister. Accordingly, the result in the case was to defeat the transferor's intent with respect to half the sum in issue.

2. *Beneficiary designations.* The option to designate a beneficiary to receive the assets on the owner's death is now a pervasive feature of accounts with financial intermediaries of many sorts, including life insurance companies, banks, brokerage houses, and investment companies (mutual funds), as well as pension plans. The terms of such accounts typically arrange for the financial intermediary rather than a probate court to transfer the account balance at death. See John H. Langbein, The Nonprobate Revolution and the Future of the Law of Succession, 97 Harvard L. Rev. 1108 (1984).

The terms of such an account commonly provide for default beneficiaries (e.g., spouse if any, otherwise to children, then to more remote relatives) in the event that the decedent did not designate particular death beneficiaries. Such terms mimic but displace the otherwise applicable intestacy law.

3. *Transferor's intent.* The reason for allowing an account owner to name nonprobate death beneficiaries is the same as the reason for allowing a testator to designate devisees under a will. The dominant substantive principle of the law of gratuitous transfers is to carry out the transferor's intent, in recognition of the transferor's property interest. "The donor's intention is given effect to the maximum extent allowed by law." Restatement (Third) of Property: Wills and Other Donative Transfers § 10.1 (2003) [hereafter Wills Restatement].

4. *Formalities of transfer.* All systems of wealth transfer on death impose formal requirements. In the law of wills, most states require the testator's will to be in writing, signed, and witnessed by two attesting witnesses. Wills Restatement § 3.1. In the nonprobate system, the terms of the account impose formal requirements as a matter of contract, typically (as in the pension plan in *Schmidt*) that the transferor complete and sign a written beneficiary designation form. Compliance with these formalities of written terms and signature serves several functions, especially evidentiary and cautionary. Id., § 3.3, cmt. a. Signing a written document directing how account proceeds are to be transferred on the owner's death supplies evidence of the decedent's intent that can be relied upon when the decedent is no longer alive to express that intent. Signing such a form also cautions the potential transferor about the seriousness of executing the designation.

5. *No stakeholder interest.* The question in *Schmidt* was not whether the plan would pay the death benefit but to whom. The plan's financial integrity was not at stake in the choice between paying the beneficiary whom the participant wanted to pay, or paying the default beneficiaries who take when the transferor is treated as not having had a proper designation in effect. Should a court be more attentive to implementing transferor's intent when neither the interests of the plan nor those of other plan participants are affected?

6. *Construction.* Did the court have to treat the form that Allen filled out and executed as ineffective? As a matter of construction, was it open to the court in the circumstances of the case to treat the language of the form that Allen did sign as adequately evidencing his intent to designate Richard as the death beneficiary? Compare Wills Restatement § 11.2: "An ambiguity [is] resolved by construing the text of the donative document in accordance with the donor's intention," including evidence of intention extrinsic to the document.

7. *Reformation.* Even if the court determined that the language of the form could not be construed to effectuate Allen's intention, could the court have applied the equitable remedy of reformation to correct the form's mistaken contents? Courts of equity have long exercised a jurisdiction to reform errors in written instruments, such as conveyances, life insurance policies and other contracts, deeds of gift, and trusts. That remedy has been extended to wills in Restatement (Third) of Property: Wills and Other Donative Transfers § 12.1 (2003) (allowing reformation to conform the writing to the terms intended, on showing of clear and convincing evidence); accord, Uniform Probate Code § 2–805; Uniform Trust Code § 415 (trusts). The Restatement provides that a court may reform a donative document in order to "conform the text to the donor's intention if it is established by clear and convincing evidence (1) that a mistake of fact or law, whether in expression or inducement, affected specific terms of the document; and

(2) what the donor's intention was." Wills Restatement § 12.1. In International Union v. Murata Erie North America, 980 F.2d 889 (3d Cir.1992), the court sustained the application of reformation to correct a drafting mistake in an ERISA plan document, "provided the evidence [of mistake] is 'clear, precise, convincing, and of the most satisfactory character'" Compare Aramony v. United Way Replacement Benefit Plan, 191 F.3d 140, 150 (2d Cir.1999) (refusing to remedy alleged mistake when plan term unambiguous). For discussion of case law and other sources, see Craig C. Martin & William L. Scogland, Attempting to Undo the Scrivener's Error in *Young v. Verizon's Bell Atlantic Cash Balance Plan*, 34 Employee Relations L.J. 75 (Spr. 2009); David A. Pratt & Martin M. Heming, Focus on Scrivener's Errors, 15 J. Pension Benefits 19 (Sum. 2008); Rosina B. Barker, Is There a Scrivener's Error Doctrine in ERISA?, 13 Benefits L.J. 59 (Spr. 2000).

In Young v. Verizon's Bell Atlantic Cash Balance Plan, 615 F.3d 808 (7th Cir. 2010), rehearing denied, 2010 U.S. App. LEXIS 19299 (7th Cir. Sept. 8, 2010), the Seventh Circuit upheld a district court opinion allowing reformation to correct a mistake that would otherwise have resulted in a billion dollar loss to the plan sponsor. In so doing, the court set a high standard for reformation with the aim of deterring employers from seeking reformation merely because the language leads to an unfavorable result. The court held that there must be "clear and convincing" evidence that the language is contrary to the parties' expectations and that the evidence must be objective and not dependent on the credibility of the testimony of an interested party.

2. ORAL MODIFICATIONS AND ESTOPPEL CLAIMS

The court's starting point for denying relief in *Schmidt* was the principle that "oral representations that conflict with the terms of a written plan will not be given effect, as the written instrument must control." On this view, Richard Schmidt was asking the court to prefer the mistaken words of Lee, the plan employee who misled Allen Schmidt, over the written term of the plan, which required Allen to submit a different form than the one he executed. Richard wanted the court to estop the plan from pleading its written term against the oral term (Lee's instruction) on which Allen relied.

Similar issues arise in a variety of settings, for example, when a health plan employee mistakenly assures a participant or a third-party health care provider that the plan covers a particular procedure or person. The case law as of the early 1990s is collected in Comment, Estoppel Claims Against ERISA Employee Benefit Plans, 25 U.C. Davis L. Rev. 487 (1992). A notable series of essays on such cases ran in the *ERISA Litigation Reporter* in the 1990s; the title, "Betrayal Without Remedy," conveys the uneasiness about these cases that pervades the ERISA bar. E.g., "Betrayal Without Remedy—Part I: Employees Bound by Plan Descriptions at Odds with Employer's Oral Representations," 1 ERISA Ligation Rptr. (Mar.-Apr. 1991), at 9; "Betrayal Without Remedy—Part VII: The Recent Non-3d Circuit Decisions," 3 ERISA Litigation Rptr. (Jun. 1994), at 9.

1. *ERISA's writing requirement.* ERISA § 402(a)(1) says: "Every employee benefit plan shall be maintained pursuant to a written

instrument." Section 402(b)(3) requires that every plan "provide a procedure for amending such plan." The requirement of § 402(a)(1) that the plan be in writing is thought to carry over to this "procedure for amending such plan," hence to mean that plan amendments must be in writing. Other provisions of ERISA underscore the expectation of writing, e.g., § 404(a)(1)(D), requiring fiduciaries to act "in accordance with the documents and instruments governing the plan"; and § 403(a), providing for trustees to be "named in the trust instrument or in the plan instrument" or appointed by a named fiduciary.

The Supreme Court has emphasized the importance of ERISA's writing requirement in various settings, notably in Kennedy v. Plan Administrator for DuPont Savings & Investment Plan, 555 U.S. 285, 129 S.Ct. 865 (2009), applying the so-called "plan documents rule" that prefers an ERISA plan's beneficiary designation directing payment of proceeds on death over contrary terms in a marital property agreement. In that case, the Court remarked that "by giving a plan participant a clear set of instructions for making his own instructions clear, ERISA forecloses any justification for enquiries into nice expressions of intent, in favor of the virtues of adhering to an uncomplicated rule: 'simple administration, avoid[ing] double liability, and ensur[ing] that beneficiaries get what's coming quickly, without the folderol essential under less-certain rules.' " 129 S.Ct. at 875–76, quoting Fox Valley & Vicinity Const. Workers Pension Fund v. Brown, 897 F.2d 275, 283 (7th Cir.1990) (Easterbrook, J., dissenting).

Judge Easterbrook has characterized the written plan requirement of § 402(a)(1) as "a long way toward a statute of frauds." Frahm v. Equitable Life Assurance Soc., 137 F.3d 955, 958 (7th Cir.1998), invoking the Supreme Court's observation in Curtiss-Wright Corp. v. Schoonejongen, 514 U.S. 73, 83 (1995), that under ERISA "every employee may, on examining the plan documents, determine exactly what his rights and obligations are under the plan."

Was ERISA's requirement of written terms meant to foreclose remedy in a case such as *Schmidt*?

2.   *Nachwalter: The protective rationale for the rule against oral modifications.* The federal courts have developed a rule against enforcing oral modification of ERISA plan terms. The rule traces to Nachwalter v. Christie, 805 F.2d 956 (11th Cir.1986), a case of first impression for all circuits. In that case, the court refused to entertain the claim made by the widow of a deceased plan participant that the participant had, during his lifetime, negotiated with the trustees an oral understanding allowing him a more favorable valuation date than that provided in the plan for the withdrawal of his shares. The court rested its decision on ERISA's writing requirement, saying:

> A central policy goal of ERISA is to protect the interests of employees and their beneficiaries in employee benefit plans. This goal would be undermined if we permitted oral modifications of ERISA plans because employees would be unable to rely on these plans if their expected retirement benefits could be radically affected by funds dispersed to other employees pursuant to oral agreements. This problem would be

exacerbated by the fact that these oral agreements often would be made many years before any attempt to enforce them.

805 F.2d at 960–61. Thus, reading ERISA to contain a rule against oral modifications was said to protect plan participants against abuse.

Cases do indeed occur in which the writing requirement protects plan participants against sharp practices. For example, in Confer v. Custom Engineering Co., 952 F.2d 41 (3d Cir.1991), the employer's president announced in a speech on April 1 that the employer intended to exclude motorcycle accidents from coverage under the firm's health care plan. In May the firm executed a new health care plan that did not in fact exclude motorcycle accidents. On June 1 the plaintiff, a plan participant, was injured in a motorcycle accident. When the president discovered that the plan had not been altered to exclude motorcycle accidents, he arranged for an amendment to the plan excluding coverage for such accidents, with a backdated effective date of April 10. The Third Circuit sustained the district court's holding that the plaintiff was entitled to coverage. "Only a formal written amendment, executed in accordance with the Plan's own procedure for amendment, could change the Plan. Moreover, the change by means of a formal amendment could operate only prospectively." Id. at 43.

The rule against oral modifications also protects plan sponsors, as Judge Easterbrook underscored in *Frahm*, supra: "Havoc would ensue if plans meant different things for different participants, depending on what someone said to them years earlier. Memory is weak compared to the written word, and there is the substantial risk that participants will not correctly recall what was said, will exaggerate (in their favor) what they heard, or will simply prevaricate in order to improve their position. Employers could do little to protect themselves against such claims— which is why ERISA calls for [writings]." 137 F.3d at 960. The writing requirement "protect[s] the financial integrity of pension and welfare plans by confining benefits to the terms of the plans as [written]." Pohl v. National Benefits Consultants, Inc., 956 F.2d 126, 128 (7th Cir.1992).

Summing up the policies that have led the courts to be hostile to claimed oral modifications, a commentator has identified "(1) ensuring the stability and reliability of written plans; (2) avoiding the evidentiary problems involved with enforcing oral modifications; (3) avoiding the agency problems of determining who has power to bind the plan or fund; (4) preventing financial harm to third parties whose interests could be impaired if oral modifications were allowed; (5) preserving the actuarial soundness of the plans; and (6) protecting employees against unexpected, informal employer modifications." Andrew Y.S. Cheng, Oral Modifications of ERISA-Covered Pension and Benefit Plans: Protection or Deception?, 18 J. Pension Planning & Compliance 28, 33 (1992) [hereafter Cheng, Oral Modifications].

3. *Estoppel: the elements.* However much the writing requirement may be meant to protect plan participants and beneficiaries, it undoubtedly disserves them in cases such as *Schmidt*, where it shields misrepresentation against remedy. The doctrine of estoppel (sometimes called equitable or promissory estoppel), if applied in such cases, has the potential to protect the reliance of the participant in preference to the literal terms of the plan. The elements of the black letter law of estoppel

are that "(1) the party to be estopped misrepresented material facts; (2) the party to be estopped was aware of the true facts; (3) the party to be estopped intended that the misrepresentation be acted on or had reason to believe the party asserting the estoppel would rely on it; (4) the party asserting the estoppel did not know, nor should it have known, the true facts; and (5) the party asserting the estoppel reasonably and detrimentally relied on the misrepresentation." National Companies Health Benefit Plan v. St. Joseph's Hospital of Atlanta, 929 F.2d 1558, 1572 (11th Cir.1991).

The leading case applying estoppel to an ERISA plan is a Seventh Circuit precedent that *Schmidt* cited and distinguished, Black v. TIC Investment Corp., 900 F.2d 112 (7th Cir.1990). *Black* concerned an undertaking by a bankrupt employer to pay certain severance benefits, on which it subsequently reneged. The participant, Black, contended that the plan was estopped to deny the promised benefits. Judge Cummings wrote:

> To determine whether estoppel is applicable to ERISA actions, our first resort would ordinarily be to the statute itself. In this case, the statute is silent. This is not so much a question of statutory interpretation as a question of public policy. . . .

> [E]stoppel principles generally apply to all legal actions. It is an exception to that general rule to deny the use of the doctrine. The reasons for the general application of estoppel are simple enough—the doctrine prevents a party from benefitting from its own misrepresentations. Yet even among courts that recognize the availability of estoppel in ERISA cases, there is real resistance to the use of that doctrine. The reason ordinarily cited for this reluctance (and for earlier refusals to allow estoppel at all) is a concern for the actuarial soundness of the ERISA plan. There are two types of ERISA plans: pension plans, which are funded and have strict vesting and accrual requirements; and welfare plans such as the one involved in this case, which have no such requirements. In the case of an unfunded welfare plan, there is no particular fund which is depleted by paying benefits. Thus there is no need for concern about the Plan's actuarial soundness. . . .

> In cases [where] there is no danger that others associated with the Plan can be hurt, there is no good reason to breach the general rule that misrepresentations can give rise to an estoppel. There is no reason for the employee who reasonably relied to his detriment on his employer's false representations to suffer. There is no reason for the employer who misled its employee to be allowed to profit from the misrepresentation. We hold, therefore, that estoppel principles are applicable to claims for benefits under unfunded single-employer welfare benefit plans under ERISA. We express no opinion as to the application of estoppel principles in other situations.

900 F.2d at 114–15. In a subsequent case, Judge Cummings reaffirmed the holding in *Black* and glossed its policy basis. "The concern [in *Black*] was both for detriment to the relying party and for [preventing] unjust enrichment on the part of the party to be estopped." Thomason v. Aetna

Life Ins. Co., 9 F.3d 645, 649 (7th Cir.1993). *Schmidt* distinguished *Black* on the ground that "the alleged modification [in that case was] in writing," but *Black* expressed no such limitation. Most estoppel cases involve oral representations.

4.   *Actuarial soundness. Black*'s theme of concern for third-party effects pervades the case law. The fear is expressed that enforcing oral claims might jeopardize the funds needed to pay the claims of the other beneficiaries. "That prospect would threaten the stability and solvency of many plans upon which so many other employees are dependent." Degan v. Ford Motor Co., 869 F.2d 889, 895 (5th Cir.1989). In Shields v. Local 705, Int'l Brotherhood of Teamsters Pension Plan, 188 F.3d 895, 900 (7th Cir.1999), the court expressed doubt "whether estoppel principles could ever apply to multi-employer, funded benefit plans." Judge Posner, concurring in the case, was prepared to "hold that promissory estoppel can *never* be used to alter the terms of a defined-benefit plan, especially when it is a multiemployer plan." Id. at 903.

The courts have been more willing to entertain estoppel claims against single-employer welfare benefit plans. In Armistead v. Vernitron Corp., 944 F.2d 1287 (6th Cir.1991), Judge Boggs explained: "In this case, there is no fund from which retiree insurance benefits are drawn, because the issue here is Vernitron's obligation to pay health and life insurance premiums, not to maintain a fund from which retirees or their dependents are compensated in the event of death or illness. We conclude that in these circumstances, estoppel principles are applicable." However, the Fourth Circuit has resisted this notion. Judge Wilkinson wrote that "the statutory emphasis on adherence to the written terms of ERISA plans leaves [no] room for this distinction between pension and welfare benefits plans." Coleman v. Nationwide Life Ins. Co., 969 F.2d 54 (4th Cir.1992). "Congress knew how to exempt welfare benefit plans from ERISA requirements when it wished to do so." 969 F.2d at 59, citing ERISA §§ 201(1) and 301(1), which exempt welfare benefit plans from the vesting and funding rules. "The financial integrity of a group health insurer could be quickly compromised if courts compelled the insurer to assume risks for which no premium was ever paid. Moreover, if courts allowed estoppel to be used to modify ERISA plans, plan assets could also be chewed up in costly, litigious disputes over what informal modifications may have been made to a written instrument." 969 F.2d at 60.

5.   *Estoppel: the quality of the reliance.* In Coker v. Trans World Airlines, 165 F.3d 579, 586 (7th Cir.1999), the plaintiff had been mistakenly continued on her husband's former employer's health care plan after her entitlement expired, and was then dropped when the error was discovered. She insisted that she had relied upon the erroneous determination of coverage. The Seventh Circuit rejected her claim. Judge Diane Wood pointed out that the plaintiff's husband had copies of the collective bargaining agreement creating the plan, the summary plan description (SPD), and another writing summarizing the coverage. Accordingly, the plaintiff "could not have reasonably relied" on the mistaken notifications of coverage "in light of her easy access to convenient ways of ascertaining the true facts about her medical coverage." Accord, Livick v. Gillette Co., 524 F.3d 24, 32 (1st Cir.2008)

(estoppel claim rejected "because it was unreasonable for [participant] to rely on informal communications which contradicted clear plan terms"); Mello v. Sara Lee Corp., 431 F.3d 440 (5th Cir.2005) (same).

Based on a calculation of a participant's expected pension plan benefit, the participant's spouse retired from her job. A subsequent calculation revealed that the participant was entitled to a smaller benefit. Should the spouse's retirement constitute sufficient detrimental reliance in an action for breach of fiduciary duty based on the erroneous calculation? See Shook v. Avaya Inc., 625 F.3d 69, 75 (3d Cir. 2010) ("This type of reliance is simply too attenuated to hold Avaya liable as a fiduciary.") Similarly, in Pearson v. Voith Paper Rolls, Inc., 656 F.3d 504 (7th Cir. 2011), the Seventh Circuit refused to find detrimental reliance, ruling that a plaintiff's claim that he would have negotiated better severance terms but for the misrepresentation of projected pension benefits was entirely speculative. As a general matter, it will be difficult to demonstrate reliance on incorrect benefits estimates. See, e.g., Stark v. Mars, Inc., 518 Fed. Appx. (6th Cir. May 9, 2013).

Even if a court finds reliance, the lack of *reasonable* reliance may doom a plaintiff's claim. In Jenkins v. Union Labor Life Co., 543 Fed. Appx. 180 (3d Cir. Sept. 16, 2013), the Third Circuit held that any reliance plaintiffs put on a question and answer document distributed to them before they were offered employment was not reasonable. Several other communications with the plaintiffs, before and after their receipt of the Q&A document, clarified any confusion that document might have created about what benefits they would be provided.

6. *ERISA's fiduciary duty of disclosure.* We have seen, in Chapter 13 supra, treating the disclosure duty that has developed in ERISA fiduciary law, that plan fiduciaries can be liable for misrepresentations made to plan participants. Can an oral modification be enforced by means of an action for breach of fiduciary duty? Richard Schmidt attempted it in *Schmidt*, but the court resisted the claim on the ground that Lee, the plan employee who misled Allen Schmidt, was not a fiduciary. Would the outcome have been different had she been, and if so, why?

Granted that Lee was not a fiduciary, she was acting in the course of employment on behalf of the fiduciaries and in the discharge of their fiduciary duties of plan administration. Should not ordinary agency notions of vicarious responsibility attribute Lee's misconduct to those who engaged her? The court says "no evidence suggests that the Trustees either authorized, participated in, or had knowledge of Lee's misstatement." Is that the test? Shouldn't there be a cause of action against the trustees for their imprudence in failing to select, train, and monitor their agent appropriately? For supporting authority, see Gifford v. CALCO, 2005 WL 984518 (D. Alaska 2005) ("the doctrine of *respondeat superior* is viable under ERISA"); Broga v. Northeast Utilities, 315 F.Supp.2d 212, 246 (D.Conn.2004) (fiduciaries have duty to take appropriate steps to see to it that benefits counselors advise plan participants truthfully). Compare Frahm v. Equitable Life Assurance Soc., 137 F.3d 955, 959 (7th Cir.1998), in which Judge Easterbrook said that "slip-ups in managing any complex enterprise are inevitable, and negligence—a violation of the duty of care—is not actionable." Why not?

When the fiduciary makes the misrepresentation, courts have often been willing to protect participant reliance. For example, in Jones v. American General Life & Accident Ins. Co., 370 F.3d 1065 (11th Cir.2004), the participants claimed that repeated misrepresentations from the ERISA plan fiduciary caused them to believe, contrary to the plan term, "that if they stayed with the company until they were eligible for retirement, they would receive free, lifetime life insurance coverage." They contended that they relied on these misrepresentations to their detriment in making financial plans for themselves and their families. Id. at 1071. In sustaining the claim against dismissal on summary judgment, the court reviewed the authorities, saying that it had previously "recognized that an ERISA participant has a right to accurate information, and that an ERISA plan administrator's withholding of information may give rise to a cause of action for breach of fiduciary duty. Our sister circuits have reached the same conclusion, consistently holding that ERISA plan participants may state a cause of action for breach of fiduciary duty based on a plan administrator's material misrepresentations or omissions." Id. at 1072 (citing cases).

The bases for remedying *Schmidt* and other misrepresentation cases under ERISA fiduciary law are developed in Jill M. Perry, A Fiduciary Solution to ERISA's Problem of Inconsistent Oral Promises, 28 J. Pension Planning & Compliance 1 (Win. 2003).

The strategy of recharacterizing a claim for benefits as an action for breach of fiduciary duty in a misrepresentation case has become materially more difficult as a result of the limitations on monetary relief that the Supreme Court has read into ERISA remedy law in *Mertens* and *Great-West*, cases that are emphasized in Chapter 16, infra. See generally Susan Katz Hoffman, Fiduciary Misrepresentation After *Varity* and *Knudson*: Is There a Wrong, and Is There a Remedy?, 2002 New York U. Rev. Employee Benefits 4–1.

7. *Distinguishing interpretation from modification.* In Kane v. Aetna Life Ins., 893 F.2d 1283 (11th Cir.1990), the prospective adoptive parents of a newborn child were covered under an ERISA-regulated health care plan. Aetna administered the plan for the employer. The child had been born prematurely and suffered serious medical complications. The prospective parents telephoned the regional Aetna customer service office and were assured that the child's medical expenses would be covered under the plan if the couple adopted the child. Another Aetna employee gave similar assurances to the hospital administration. The couple adopted the child and filed under the plan for the medical expenses. "Aetna denied the claim. As justification, Aetna cited the provision of the Plan stating that medical expenses for a continuous hospitalization are not covered under the Plan where the hospitalization began prior to the effective date of coverage. Because the formal adoption proceedings did not begin until after the commencement of the infant's hospitalization, Aetna maintained, it was not obligated to pay for any of the medical expenses." 893 F.2d at 1285. The court applied equitable estoppel as federal common law "because the representations made by Aetna to Mrs. Kane and the hospital were *interpretations* of the plan and not modifications." Id. (emphasis original). Thus, the Eleventh Circuit, which had first framed the rule against oral modifications in *Nachwalter*,

effectively limited the reach of its precedent by distinguishing between alteration and interpretation.

The stratagem in *Kane* places considerable weight upon the question of whether the disputed plan term is sufficiently ambiguous to require interpretation. An Eleventh Circuit panel emphasized that "*Kane* only comes into play when the terms of a plan are ambiguous. In addition, equitable estoppel may only be used where the communications constituted an interpretation of that ambiguity." Alday v. Container Corp. of America, 906 F.2d 660, 666 (11th Cir.1990). Thus, an employee who contends that a plan fiduciary waived a term of the plan is seeking to change the plan rather than interpret it, and such a case falls outside the *Kane* exception. E.g., Ramsom v. Administrative Committee for Lightnet/WTG, 820 F.Supp. 1429 (N.D.Ga.1993).

A commentator has observed with regard to *Kane*'s distinction between interpretation and modification: "On the one hand, the distinction may succeed too well for those who believe that ambiguity inheres in all written instruments: it will be too easy for courts to disguise all modifications as 'interpretations.' On the other hand, the distinction may not go far enough when the plan provision is wholly unambiguous." Cheng, Oral Modifications, supra, at 51.

In its first decision recognizing an estoppel claim in the pension benefit context, the Sixth Circuit in Bloemker v. Laborers' Local 265 Pension Fund, 605 F.3d 436 (6th Cir. 2010), rehearing denied, 2010 U.S. App. LEXIS 17244 (6th Cir. Aug. 13, 2010) declined to apply the rule that estoppel cannot be applied to vary the terms of an unambiguous plan document. In the case before it, the participant had received a document stating the amount of pension benefits he could elect to receive upon early retirement, along with a certification by the plan administrator that he was entitled to that benefit. Two years later, he was notified that the certified calculation was incorrect, that his monthly benefits would be decreased and that he was required to repay the excess payments he had received.

The Sixth Circuit held that the plaintiff alleged a valid claim for equitable estoppel, finding that the certified document constituted "conduct or language amounting to a representation of material fact." Id. at 442. In the view of the court, the actions of the defendants contained "an element of fraud, either intended deception or such gross negligence as to amount to constructive fraud," Id. at 443, convincing the court that the defendants intended the participant to rely on their representations.

While the court accepted the general propositions that reliance is typically not reasonable in the case of an unambiguous plan and that enforcing something inconsistent with the plan documents is inconsistent with ERISA, those general rules fell before the "extraordinary circumstances presented by this case," i.e., that it would have been impossible for the participant to make an independent calculation of his pension benefit given the complexity of the actuarial calculations and his lack of knowledge of the relevant actuarial assumptions. Given that impossibility, the court believed that "a fact finder could determine that his reliance on the certification of his pension benefits was reasonable." Id. Did the court incorrectly ignore concerns about the actuarial soundness of the plan?

Notwithstanding *Bloemker*, as noted in the Text, courts will generally not find reliance to be reasonable where an oral misrepresentation is inconsistent with clear written plan documents. For a recent case see Watson v. Consol. Edison, 374 Fed. Appx. 159 (2d Cir. Apr. 20, 2010).

8. *Apply the writing requirement asymmetrically?* The argument has been made that because ERISA's writing requirement was meant to protect plan participants, "[r]efusing to estop an ERISA plan because of ERISA's written instrument provision is inconsistent with Congress's goals in enacting the provision. Congress enacted the provision to enhance employees' ability to enforce their rights, not to allow employers to escape responsibility for their representations. Courts should view ERISA's written instrument provision solely as Congress intended: as a mechanism to aid and protect employees." Comment, Estoppel Claims Against ERISA Employee Benefit Plans, 25 U.C. Davis L. Rev. 487, 536–37 (1992).

Why might courts incline to resist the argument that they should be more liberal in allowing only employees to assert oral modifications to ERISA plans?

9. *Interaction with ERISA preemption.* ERISA preemption of state law lurks in the background in the estoppel area, as in so many fields of ERISA litigation law. The state law of fraud, misrepresentation, and estoppel would afford remedy in many of the cases that turn on whether or not to enforce ERISA's writing requirement. Initially, preemption, especially as interpreted by the Supreme Court in *Pilot Life*, discussed in Chapter 17, infra, was treated as suppressing most such state law claims, e.g., Fisher v. Combustion Engineering, Inc., 976 F.2d 293 (6th Cir.1992); Cromwell v. Equicor-Equitable HCA Corp., 944 F.2d 1272 (6th Cir.1991). There were some contrary decisions, reasoning that the state-law estoppel claim was too tenuously related to the ERISA plan, e.g., Hospice of Metro Denver, Inc. v. Group Health Ins. of Oklahoma, Inc., 944 F.2d 752 (10th Cir.1991); Pizlo v. Bethlehem Steel Corp., 884 F.2d 116 (4th Cir.1989). Later developments, including the Supreme Court's revision of the preemption standard in *Travelers*, the leading case, decided in 1995, which is reproduced infra in Chapter 17, and the Court's implied endorsement of state court medical malpractice actions in *Pegram* in 2000, supra Chapter 12, may afford more scope for state law causes of action, but subject to the continuing limitations on state interference with plan administration that the Court enunciated afresh in 2004 in *Davila*, infra Chapter 17.

10. *Estoppel as federal common law?* The question arises repeatedly in different settings whether, if ERISA preempts state law on a topic, under what circumstances may the federal court replicate that cause of action as federal common law of ERISA. Cases such as *Black* that enforce estoppel claims under ERISA are creating federal common law on the subject, whether they so describe it or not. Because, however, the Supreme Court has been hostile to implied causes of action in the *Russell-Mertens-Great-West* line of cases discussed in Chapter 16, infra, many courts are uneasy about having to base decisions on ERISA common law. For example, in HealthSouth Rehabilitation Hospital v. American National Red Cross, 20 E.B.C. 2230, 2235 (4th Cir.1996), the court

refused "estoppel arguments which would serve to vary the terms of a written plan," on the ground that "ERISA simply does not recognize the validity of oral or non-conforming written modifications to ERISA plans." For contrasting views on the proper scope of federal common law under ERISA, compare Jeffrey A. Brauch, The Federal Common Law of ERISA, 21 Harvard J. L. & Public Policy 541, 572–74 (1998) (limiting federal common law to gap-filling role), with Catherine L. Fisk, Lochner Redux: The Renaissance of Laissez-Faire Contract in the Federal Common Law of Employee Benefits, 56 Ohio St. L.J. 153 (1995) (urging expansive protective role); and Jayne E. Zanglein, Closing the Gap: Safeguarding Participants' Rights by Expanding the Federal Common Law of ERISA, 72 Washington U.L.Q. 671 (1994) (same).

11. *Analogizing to the informal plan cases.* A large case law has developed regarding the question of whether some arrangement, such as a recurrent pattern of severance payments, was or was not an employee benefit plan. See the discussion in Chapter 3, supra, in the note following *Massachusetts v. Morash* ("What Is a Plan?"). The courts have been willing in these cases to infer the existence of a plan from the totality of circumstances even if the plan was not reduced to writing. See, e.g., the leading case, Donovan v. Dillingham, 688 F.2d 1367, 1373 (11th Cir.1982), identifying factors that help decide what is a plan. The state of the law is, therefore, that an oral plan can be enforced but an oral modification cannot. Is the distinction sound? Why does ERISA's writing requirement not defeat the enforcement of wholly oral plans? One court has reasoned: "The writing requirement becomes important only when it is determined that ERISA covers a plan, because it is [at] this point in time that plan administrators and fiduciaries are charged with various fiduciary and reporting responsibilities." Moeller v. Bertrang, 801 F.Supp. 291, 294–95 (D.S.D.1992).

A few courts have been prepared to treat an oral representation by employer representatives about coverage not as a plan modification, but as creating a new plan. See, e.g., Adler v. Aztech Chas. P. Young Co., 807 F.Supp. 1068 (S.D.N.Y.1992); Lipscomb v. Transac, Inc., 749 F.Supp. 1128 (M.D.Ga.1990).

12. *Conflicting writings.* An estoppel case involving a supposed oral modification should be distinguished from a case instancing a discrepancy between plan documents and the summary plan description (SPD). SPDs are discussed in Chapter 13, supra. In the event of conflict between the SPD and other plan documents, the courts protect reliance upon the SPD, e.g., Hansen v. Continental Ins. Co., 940 F.2d 971 (5th Cir.1991).

Suppose an employee contemplating retirement receives from the plan administrator a written statement mistakenly calculating retirement benefits that are larger than the employee is actually entitled to receive. If the employee retires and the plan then pays the correct but lower benefits, can the employee obtain the higher benefits based on equitable estoppel? Such claims have been rejected on the grounds that estoppel only applies to plausible interpretations, not to modifications; and that a plan cannot be modified by a writing that is not a formal amendment. See, e.g., Slice v. Sons of Norway, 34 F.3d 630 (8th Cir.1994); Law v. Ernst & Young, 956 F.2d 364 (1st Cir.1992). Are these cases consistent with the cases that protect reliance upon a mistaken SPD? Which reliance is more worthy of protection—reliance on the boilerplate language in an SPD, or reliance on an individuated communication to the participant from an agent of the plan administrator?

3. SUBSTANTIAL COMPLIANCE

Suppose that the facts in *Schmidt* had occurred in a non-ERISA setting: For example, suppose that the beneficiary designation concerned a life insurance policy, and that Lee, the person who misled Allen Schmidt about which form to complete, had been an employee of the insurance company. Would the case have been decided differently?

1. *Substantial compliance doctrine for defective beneficiary designations.* Under Illinois law (which would have governed the case) as under the law of most states, the courts follow a substantial compliance doctrine, which excuses some departures from the formalities required to effect a change of beneficiary designation in a life insurance policy. The Illinois version of the doctrine requires that the party seeking to validate the defective change of beneficiary designation must establish (1) that the insured intended to make the change; and (2) "that the insured did everything he could have reasonably done under the circumstances to carry out his intention to change the beneficiary." Aetna Life Ins. Co. v. Wise, 184 F.3d 660, 663 (7th Cir.1999), citing Dooley v. James A. Dooley Assoc. Employees Ret. Plan, 442 N.E.2d 222, 227 (Ill.1982). Voluminous case law on substantial compliance with insurance policy change of beneficiary requirements is collected in Annots., 78 A.L.R. 3d 466 (1977 & Supp.2009); 19 A.L.R. 2d 5 (1951 & Supp.2009).

Over the past generation a comparable excusing doctrine has been developed for cases in which a testator fails to comply fully with the formalities of the governing Statute of Wills. Wills Restatement § 3.3 (1999); Uniform Probate Code § 2–503 (1990 rev.); Restatement (Third) of Trusts § 19(c)(i) (2003).

Schmidt would have been an easy case for application of a substantial compliance doctrine. There was no doubt that the moribund Allen intended to name Richard as the beneficiary, nor that Allen did all that he could have done to effect the designation, given that he acted in reasonable reliance on Lee's instruction to use the wrong form. Evidence that his failure of compliance was the result of third-party wrongdoing (Lee's negligent misrepresentation) would have made the case particularly compelling for application of the substantial compliance doctrine.

Why, then, did the court in *Schmidt* not consider applying the doctrine, in order to excuse Allen's defective compliance with the plan's beneficiary designation rules? The answer seems to be, because nobody thought about it.

2. *Substantial compliance for ERISA-plan designation cases.* There are two possibilities for applying the doctrine: as a matter of state law, on the theory that designating a beneficiary is sufficiently remote from the purposes of ERISA to escape ERISA preemption; or, if preemption does defeat state law, then as a matter of federal common law. There is case support for both positions.

In BankAmerica Pension Plan v. McMath, 206 F.3d 821, 829 (9th Cir.2000), the Ninth Circuit enforced the California substantial compliance rule in an ERISA plan setting. The court avoided preemption on the ground that the state law merely "aid[ed] in determining the identity of the proper recipient of the proceeds," and hence that California's rule did not impermissibly "affect the administration of the plan." Accord, Peckham v. Gem State Mut. of Utah, 964 F.2d 1043 (10th Cir.1992). In Metropolitan Life Ins. Co. v. Kubichek, 83 Fed.Appx. 425 (3d Cir.2003), the Third Circuit applied New Jersey substantial compliance law to an ERISA plan case without mention of the preemption problem.

The contrary view, that a beneficiary designation does indeed "relate to" an ERISA plan for purposes of preempting state law, and that the substantial compliance doctrine must take the form of federal common law, was developed in Phoenix Mutual Life Ins. Co. v. Adams, 30 F.3d 554, 559–60 (4th Cir.1994). That position has gained considerable strength from the Supreme Court's decision in Egelhoff v. Egelhoff, 532 U.S. 141 (2001), discussed infra in Chapter 17. *Egelhoff* held that ERISA preempted the Washington version of a common type of state statute, which treats divorce as impliedly revoking prior a beneficiary designation of the former spouse. In Metropolitan Life Ins. Co. v. Johnson, 297 F.3d 558, 566 (7th Cir.2002), the Seventh Circuit treated *Egelhoff* as controlling on the question of whether ERISA also preempted state substantial compliance law. However, both in *Johnson* and in Davis v. Combes, 294 F.3d 931 (7th Cir.2002), the Seventh Circuit applied the substantial compliance doctrine in ERISA beneficiary designation cases as federal common law. See also Tinsley v. General Motors Corp., 227 F.3d 700 (6th Cir.2000) (reasoning that ERISA preempts state undue influence law as applied to an ERISA plan beneficiary designation, although the federal court looks to state law principles for guidance in crafting federal common law).

Even where the substantial compliance doctrine is recognized as federal common law, there will be cases in which the evidence of transferor's intent is too weak to satisfy the requirements of the doctrine. See, e.g., Prudential Ins. Co. v. Schmid, 337 F.Supp.2d 325 (D.Mass.2004); SunTrust Bank v. Aetna Life Ins. Co., 251 F.Supp.2d 1282 (E.D.Va.2003); Life Ins. Co. of North America v. Leeson, 2002 WL 483563 (S.D.Ohio 2002).

In Prudential Ins. Co. v. Giacobbe, 2009 WL 3644121 (D.N.J.2009), the insured under an ERISA-covered plan attempted to change the beneficiary designation from his spouse to his parents and brother, but neglected to supply their Social Security numbers as required on the form. The court refused to find substantial compliance, reasoning that the "[d]ecedent had the opportunity and ability to fully complete the change of beneficiary form yet he failed to do so." Id. at 8. What is wrong with the court's reasoning?

Literature: Meredith H. Bogart, Comment, State Doctrines of Substantial Compliance: A Call for ERISA Preemption and Uniform Federal Common Law Doctrine, 25 Cardozo L. Rev. 447 (2003).

3.   *Other spheres of substantial compliance under ERISA.* Federal courts applying ERISA have made use of the substantial compliance

concept in two circumstances distinct from remedying defective compliance with beneficiary designation requirements.

A number of decisions have invoked substantial compliance to excuse minor plan administrative lapses in complying with DoL regulations that specify notice or internal review procedures for benefit denials under ERISA § 503, 29 C.F.R. § 2650.503–1. See, e.g., Lacy v. Fulbright & Jaworski, 405 F.3d 254 (5th Cir.2005); but see Wenner v. Sun Life Assurance Co. of Canada, 482 F.3d 878 (6th Cir.2007) (plan administrator did not substantially comply with notice requirements for communicating benefit denial reasons under ERISA § 503); Nichols v. Prudential Ins. Co., 406 F.3d 98, 107 (2d Cir.2005) (doctrine not allowed when effect would be to permit a plan administrator to "block or delay a plaintiff's access to the federal courts").

A rule of substantial compliance has also been applied to defects in form and content in state-court qualified domestic relations orders (QDROs); the QDRO rules are discussed in Chapter 7, supra. Some of the substantial compliance cases excuse defects in state domestic relations orders that predate the ERISA amendments, e.g., Metropolitan Life Ins. Co. v. Bigelow, 283 F.3d 436 (2d Cir.2002); Metropolitan Life Ins. Co. v. Marsh, 119 F.3d 415 (6th Cir.1997). The courts have been divided on whether defects in post-REAct state decrees qualify for substantial compliance. Compare Stewart v. Thorpe Holding Co. Profit Sharing Plan, 207 F.3d 1143, 1151–53 (9th Cir.2000) (yes), with Hawkins v. C.I.R., 86 F.3d 982 (10th Cir.1996) (no). As always, a court otherwise favorably disposed to the doctrine may conclude that the particular facts of a case do not evidence substantial compliance. E.g., Butler v. Encyclopedia Brittanica, Inc., 41 F.3d 285, 295 (7th Cir.1994), refusing to find that compliance was substantial when the decree lacked the attestation required for spousal waiver under ERISA's survivor annuity rules, § 205(c)(2)(A)(iii), discussed supra in Chapter 7.

The Eighth Circuit recently held that the substantial compliance doctrine does not interfere with the discretion granted to a plan administrator in an ERISA plan. In Hall v. Metropolitan Life Ins. Co., 750 F. 3d 995 (8th Cir. May 8, 2014), the court held that even assuming the continued validity of the substantial compliance doctrine after the Supreme Court's decision in Kennedy v. Plan Administrator for DuPont Savings & Investment Plan, 555 U.S. 285 (2009), a plan administrator who is given discretion to determine eligibility for benefits has the power to require strict compliance with plan terms.

PART 4

ERISA LITIGATION

CHAPTER 16

ENFORCEMENT AND REMEDIES

Analysis

Introduction

This chapter 16 reviews recurrent issues that have arisen in litigating ERISA claims, including the question of what remedies are available for statutory violations, who may seek those remedies and from whom they may be sought. Chapter 17 addresses a question central to the enforcement of participants' rights, ERISA's preemption of state law. In the absence of an ERISA claim, or in situations in which a participant wishes to escape the limited remedies available under ERISA, the participant will be tempted to seek relief under state law. Accordingly, determining what state law claims survive ERISA's preemptive effect is of paramount importance. Chapter 18 addresses the relation between ERISA and federal employment discrimination statutes (prohibiting discrimination on the basis of age, gender and disability), which often figures in litigation involving employee benefit claims.

A. THE STATUTORY REGIME

A disproportionate share of appellate resources has been devoted to working out the remedies available to various plaintiffs under ERISA. One potential explanation has to do with the way the drafters organized the statute's enforcement scheme. ERISA does not contain one single catch-all enforcement authorization, along the lines of "any person may bring suit in federal court to enforce a violation of the statute." Instead the drafters attempted to *itemize* all the types of claims that may be brought, and the categories of claimants who may bring them. One result has been the emergence, as the statute has been laboriously parsed by courts over the decades, of apparent, and significant, gaps in available claims and remedies,

1. *Section 502.* Part 5 of ERISA's Title 1 is devoted to "Administration and Enforcement," and the centerpiece of ERISA's enforcement system is § 502, which deals with who can sue to enforce ERISA claims and how. The several subsections of ERISA § 502(a) should be studied with special care. Section 502 applies to all ERISA civil actions.

2. *Recovering benefits.* Section 502(a)(1)(B) authorizes the participant or beneficiary to bring a civil action "to recover benefits due to him under the terms of his plan, to enforce his rights under the terms of the plan, or to clarify his rights to future benefits under the terms of the plan."

3. *Enforcing § 409.* Section 502(a)(2) provides for suits to enforce the liability-creating provisions of § 409 (fiduciary requirements), concerning harm to the plan. In such a case § 502(a)(2) allows suit "for appropriate equitable relief under section 409." The right to sue is given to the Secretary of Labor or to a plan fiduciary as well as to a plan participant or beneficiary. Section 409 makes a fiduciary personally liable for breach of ERISA's fiduciary duties. The fiduciary is liable to make good any losses to the plan, and to restore any profits made from plan assets. Section 409 also authorizes removal of a fiduciary, and "such other equitable or remedial relief as the court may deem appropriate."

4. *Equitable remedies.* Section 502(a)(3) authorizes a participant, beneficiary, or fiduciary to seek equitable remedies—injunctive relief against "any act or practice which violates" ERISA or the plan terms, or "other appropriate equitable relief (i) to redress such violations or (ii) to enforce any provisions" of ERISA or the plan. Efforts to use the category of "other appropriate equitable relief" to extend the reach of ERISA, for example, to consequential or punitive damages and to nonfiduciary liability, constitute a major topic of this chapter.

5. *Statutory penalty.* Section 502(c)(1) of ERISA authorizes a statutory penalty of up to $100 per day against a plan administrator who refuses to supply information that is required to be supplied under ERISA. ERISA § 502(a)(1)(A) authorizes a participant or beneficiary to sue to enforce the statutory penalty. The maximum penalty is now $110. 68 Fed. Reg. 2875.

6. *Criminal sanctions.* Section 501 imposes criminal sanctions for willful violation of ERISA's reporting and disclosure rules.

7. *Jurisdiction and venue.* ERISA §§ 502(e) and 502(f) create federal jurisdiction and make it exclusive save in one class of case. The exception: § 502(e)(1) grants concurrent jurisdiction to state and federal courts in actions under § 502(a)(1)(B)—that is, actions "to recover benefits due" or to enforce or clarify rights "under the terms of the plan." The conference committee explained that Congress intended to grant the federal courts "exclusive jurisdiction with respect to actions involving breach of fiduciary responsibility as well as exclusive jurisdiction over other actions to enforce or clarify benefit rights provided under Title 1. However, with respect to suits to enforce benefit rights under the plan or to recover benefits under the plan which do not involve application of the

Title 1 provisions," Congress allowed concurrent jurisdiction. H.R. Conf. Rep. No. 1280, 93rd Cong., 2d Sess., reprinted in 1974 U.S. Code Cong. & Admin. News 5038, 5107. Section 502(e) has been amended to extend concurrent jurisdiction to claims under § 502(a)(7) to enforce compliance with qualified medical child support orders.

Why did ERISA's drafters provide for state court jurisdiction over this corner of a field that they were otherwise choosing to federalize?

Section 502(e)(2) grants liberal choice of venue and nationwide service of process—important advantages by comparison with pre-ERISA state jurisdiction over pension trusts and plans.

8. *Lacunae.* As subsequent litigation has made clear, the statutory text of ERISA § 502 left many questions unanswered, including the scope of consequential damages (so-called "extracontractual" damages); whether punitive damages can be obtained in ERISA cases; whether litigants have the right to jury trial in ERISA actions; the standards for recovering attorney fees; and the applicable statutes of limitation.

B. SCOPE OF AVAILABLE REMEDIES

1. *RUSSELL* AND THE LIMITATIONS ON EXTRACONTRACTUAL DAMAGES

Much of the jurisprudence regarding the remedies available under ERISA is based on language in Massachusetts Mutual Life Ins. Co. v. Russell, 473 U.S. 134 (1985). The plaintiff in *Russell* sued under ERISA § 502(a)(2), alleging that the improper processing of her benefit claim exacerbated her physical and psychological condition and entitled her to extracontractual and punitive damages under ERISA § 409(a). The Court concluded that any recovery under ERISA § 409 must inure to the plan, not to any individual beneficiary. In doing so, the Court made much broader observations regarding available remedies under ERISA (id. at 144):

> Significantly, the statutory provision explicitly authorizing a beneficiary to bring an action to enforce his rights under the plan—§ 502(a)(1)(B)[—says] nothing about the recovery of extracontractual damages, or about the possible consequences of a delay in the plan administrators' processing of a disputed claim. Thus, there really is nothing at all in the statutory text to support the conclusion that such a delay gives rise to a private right of action for compensatory or punitive relief. And the entire text of § 409 persuades us that Congress did not intend that section to authorize any relief except for the plan itself.

Responding to the plaintiff's argument that a private right of action for extracontractual damages should be implied, the Court delivered what is probably *Russell's* most influential dictum (id. at 146):

> The six carefully integrated civil enforcement provisions found in § 502(a) of the statute as finally enacted . . . provide strong evidence that Congress did *not* intend to authorize other remedies that it simply forgot to incorporate expressly. The assumption of inadvertent omission is rendered especially

suspect upon close consideration of ERISA's interlocking, interrelated, and interdependent remedial scheme, which is in turn part of a "comprehensive and reticulated statute."

Russell arose from an ERISA § 502(a)(2) claim. The narrow wording of ERISA § 502(a)(1)(B), which allows a participant or beneficiary "to recover benefits due him under the terms of his plan" and "to enforce his rights under the terms of the plan," makes that provision an even more unlikely basis for seeking damages for consequential injury. The Courts of Appeals have read *Russell* to hold that § 502(a)(1)(B) provides no recourse for consequential damages. See, e.g., Paese v. Hartford Life & Accident Ins. Co., 449 F.3d 435 (2d Cir.2006); Kerr v. Charles F. Vatterott & Co., 184 F.3d 938 (8th Cir.1999); Harsch v. Eisenberg, 956 F.2d 651 (7th Cir.1992). As one court emphatically stated, *"[n]owhere does [ERISA] allow consequential or punitive damages."* Allison v. Unum Life Ins. Co. of Am., 381 F.3d 1015 (10th Cir.2004) (emphasis supplied by the court).

Many of the opinions denying damages for consequential injury involve appalling fiduciary behavior. In Harsch v. Eisenberg, 956 F.2d 651 (7th Cir.1992), plaintiffs who left their jobs in a law firm sought distribution of their profit sharing accounts. The owner of the firm, who was the named trustee and administrator of the plan, ignored with evident hostility their requests for information and for distribution of their benefits. In one letter rejecting a meeting with a participant, he wrote that "I understand Peking, China, is nice at this time of year, and I might consider meeting you there but only if you can speak Chinese." Responding to another letter, he wrote: "Thank you for the marvelous collection of dog sled stamps on the envelope. The thought of your staff putting their 'little' tongues on the backs of those stamps is just mind boggling; boggle, boggle, boggle." The plaintiffs received their benefits only after filing suit, more than two years after they should have been paid: nevertheless, their recovery was limited to the actual benefits they were owed, with no avenue available to be compensated for the deliberate delay or the consequences thereof.

Other cases involve lapses in plan administration, sometimes with appalling consequences. In Huss v. Green Spring Health Services, Inc., 1999 WL 455666 (E.D.Pa.1999), the plaintiff sought a psychiatric referral from a plan's mental health benefits coordinator for her 16-year-old son. The coordinator denied the request, because its records neglected to show that the son was covered under the plan. Several days later the coordinator discovered its error, but the son committed suicide several hours before the coordinator called to authorize the referral. Should there be a remedy for such inadvertent error? Suppose it were discovered that the plan had a policy of delaying referrals to try to reduce its costs?

Russell has been called "the single most important decision under ERISA," not only because it is understood to preclude extracontractual damages, but also because it is commonly "read for the proposition that, unless a remedy is expressly provided in ERISA, it does not exist." Note, The ERISA Supreme Court, 1 ERISA Litigation Reporter 1, 2 (Oct. 1992). The Supreme Court's premise in *Russell* has been challenged as a "myth," on the ground that ERISA § 502(a) contains both duplications and omissions, evidencing that it is "not so carefully crafted nor comprehensive." George L. Flint, ERISA: Extracontractual Damages Mandated for Benefit Claims Actions, 36 Arizona L.Rev. 611, 639 (1994).

Russell has also had an influence on the Supreme Court's preemption jurisprudence. In Pilot Life Ins. Co. v. Dedeaux, 481 U.S. 41 (1987), the Court relied heavily on *Russell*'s interpretation of ERISA § 502(a) in reaching its conclusion that state tort and contract damage claims for improper claims processing are preempted. The question whether to imply a corresponding federal cause of action as ERISA common law when ERISA preempts a state cause of action is discussed in the note on Federal Common Law in Chapter 17, infra.

Russell continues to influence the courts to deny relief in cases in some cases where there is a clear ERISA violation. In Smith v. Med. Benefit Adm'r. Group, Inc., 639 F.3d 277 (7th Cir. 2011), a health plan participant alleged breach of fiduciary duty where the plan's third-party administrator preapproved his gastric bypass surgery and then later denied coverage based on the plan's exclusion for surgery and other medical services related to obesity. The participant sought "an appropriate award of damages, restitution, and/or other monetary relief", Id. at 280, to compensate him for the financial injury suffered in undergoing the surgery.

The Seventh Circuit agreed that the participant stated a viable theory of recovery. However, the participant could not obtain relief under 502(a)(1)(B) because the plan excluded his surgery from coverage and could not obtain relief under 502(a)(2) because he sought relief for personal rather than plan injuries. The court observed that *Russell*, rather than the court's later decision in *LaRue* (reproduced in the text at p. 717) governed because the plan held "no assets in trust for any individual participant." 639 F.3d at 284. Nor was the participant entitled to equitable relief under 502(a)(3) since the restitution sought clearly was not equitable in nature.

A consequence of *Russell* and the cases that followed has been that plaintiffs in employee benefit cases now frequently seek to style and bring their complaints under state law, where remedies such as extracontractual damages would remain available. Hundreds of preemption cases are handled by the federal courts each year, and in nearly all of them the employer/plan sponsor, ironically, is the party seeking to have ERISA apply, in order to limit exposure to damages. See Andrew Stumpff, Darkness at Noon: Judicial Interpretation May Have Made Things Worse for Benefit Plan Participants under ERISA than had the Statute Never Been Enacted 23 St. Thomas L. Rev. 101, 103 n.10 (2011).

2. MERTENS V. HEWITT ASSOCIATES

508 U.S. 248 (1993).

■ JUSTICE SCALIA delivered the opinion of the Court.

The question presented is whether a nonfiduciary who knowingly participates in the breach of a fiduciary duty imposed by [ERISA] is liable for losses that an employee benefit plan suffers as a result of the breach.

I

According to the complaint, the allegations of which we take as true, petitioners represent a class of former employees of the Kaiser Steel Corporation (Kaiser) who participated in the Kaiser Steel Retirement Plan, a qualified pension plan under ERISA. Respondent was the plan's actuary in 1980, when Kaiser began to phase out its steelmaking operations, prompting early retirement by a large number of plan participants. Respondent did not, however, change the plan's actuarial assumptions to reflect the additional costs imposed by the retirements. As a result, Kaiser did not adequately fund the plan, and eventually the plan's assets became insufficient to satisfy its benefit obligations, causing the Pension Benefit Guaranty Corporation (PBGC) to terminate the plan pursuant to [ERISA § 4041]. Petitioners now receive only the benefits guaranteed by ERISA, see [§ 4022], which are in general substantially lower than the fully vested pensions due them under the plan.

Petitioners sued the fiduciaries of the failed plan, alleging breach of fiduciary duties. They also commenced this action against respondent, alleging that it had caused the losses by allowing Kaiser to select the plan's actuarial assumptions, by failing to disclose that Kaiser was one of its clients, and by failing to disclose the plan's funding shortfall. Petitioners claimed that these acts and omissions violated ERISA by effecting a breach of respondent's "professional duties" to the plan, for which they sought, inter alia, monetary relief. [The] District Court for the Northern District of California dismissed the complaint, and the Court of Appeals for the Ninth Circuit affirmed in relevant part, 948 F.2d 607 (1991). . . .

II

ERISA is, we have observed, a "comprehensive and reticulated statute," the product of a decade of congressional study of the Nation's private employee benefit system. The statute provides that not only the persons named as fiduciaries by a benefit plan, see [ERISA § 402(a)], but also anyone else who exercises discretionary control or authority over the plan's management, administration, or assets, see [§ 3(21)(A)], is an ERISA "fiduciary." Fiduciaries are assigned a number of detailed duties and responsibilities, which include "the proper management, administration, and investment of [plan] assets, the maintenance of proper records, the disclosure of specified information, and the avoidance of conflicts of interest." *Massachusetts Mut. Life Ins. Co. v. Russell*, 473 U.S. 134, 142–143 (1985); see [ERISA § 404(a)]. Section 409(a) makes fiduciaries liable for breach of these duties, and specifies the remedies available against them: the fiduciary is personally liable for damages ("to make good to [the] plan any losses to the plan resulting from each such breach"), for restitution ("to restore to [the] plan any profits of such fiduciary which have been made through use of assets of the plan by the fiduciary"), and for "such other equitable or remedial relief as the court may deem appropriate," including removal of the fiduciary. Section 502(a)(2)—the second of ERISA's "six carefully integrated civil enforcement provisions," *Russell*—allows the Secretary of Labor or any plan beneficiary, participant, or fiduciary to bring a civil action "for appropriate relief under section [409]."

The above described provisions are, however, limited by their terms to fiduciaries. The Court of Appeals decided that respondent was not a fiduciary, and petitioners do not contest that holding. Lacking equivalent provisions specifying *non*fiduciaries as potential defendants, or damages as a remedy available against them, petitioners have turned to § 502(a)(3), which authorizes a plan beneficiary, participant, or fiduciary to bring a civil action:

> "(A) to enjoin any act or practice which violates any provision of [ERISA] or the terms of the plan, or (B) to obtain other appropriate equitable relief (i) to redress such violations or (ii) to enforce any provisions of [ERISA] or the terms of the plan. . . ."

See also § 502(a)(5) (providing, in similar language, for civil suits by the Secretary based upon violation of ERISA provisions). Petitioners contend that requiring respondent to make the Kaiser plan whole for the losses resulting from its alleged knowing participation in the breach of fiduciary duty by the Kaiser plan's fiduciaries would constitute "other appropriate equitable relief" within the meaning of § 502(a)(3).

We note at the outset that it is far from clear that, even if this provision does make money damages available, it makes them available for the actions at issue here. It does not, after all, authorize "appropriate equitable relief" *at large*, but only "appropriate equitable relief" for the purpose of "redress[ing any] violations or . . . enforc[ing] any provisions" of ERISA or an ERISA plan. No one suggests that any term of the Kaiser plan has been violated, nor would any be enforced by the requested judgment. And while ERISA contains various provisions that can be read as imposing obligations upon nonfiduciaries, including actuaries, no provision explicitly requires them to avoid participation (knowing or unknowing) in a fiduciary's breach of fiduciary duty. It is unlikely, moreover, that this was an oversight, since ERISA *does* explicitly impose "knowing participation" liability on cofiduciaries. See § 405(a). That limitation appears all the more deliberate in light of the fact that "knowing participation" liability on the part of *both* cotrustees *and* third persons was well established under the common law of trusts. In *Russell* we emphasized our unwillingness to infer causes of action in the ERISA context, since that statute's carefully crafted and detailed enforcement scheme provides "strong evidence that Congress did *not* intend to authorize other remedies that it simply forgot to incorporate expressly." All of this notwithstanding, petitioners and their *amicus* the United States seem to assume that respondent's alleged action (or inaction) violated ERISA, and address their arguments almost exclusively to what forms of relief are available. And respondent, despite considerable prompting by its *amici*, expressly disclaims reliance on this preliminary point. Thus, although we acknowledge the oddity of resolving a dispute over remedies where it is unclear that a remediable wrong has been alleged, we decide this case on the narrow battlefield the parties have chosen, and reserve decision of that antecedent question.

Petitioners maintain that the object of their suit is "appropriate *equitable* relief" under § 502(a)(3). They do not, however, seek a remedy traditionally viewed as "equitable," such as injunction or restitution. (The Court of Appeals held that restitution was unavailable, and petitioners have not challenged that.) Although they often dance around the word, what petitioners in fact seek is nothing other than compensatory *damages*—monetary relief for all losses their plan sustained as a result of the alleged breach of fiduciary duties. Money damages are, of course, the classic form of *legal* relief. And though we have never interpreted the precise phrase "other appropriate equitable relief," we have construed the similar language of Title VII of the Civil Rights Act of 1964 (before its 1991 amendments)—"any other equitable relief as the court deems appropriate,"—to preclude "awards for compensatory or punitive damages."

Petitioners assert, however, that this reading of "equitable relief" fails to acknowledge ERISA's roots in the common law of trusts, see *Firestone Tire & Rubber Co. v. Bruch*, 489 U.S. 101, 110–111 (1989). "[A]lthough a beneficiary's action to recover losses resulting from a breach of duty superficially resembles an action at law for damages," the Solicitor General suggests, "such relief traditionally has been obtained in courts of equity" and therefore "is, by definition, 'equitable relief.' " It is true that, at common law, the courts of equity had exclusive jurisdiction over virtually all actions by beneficiaries for breach of trust. It is also true that money damages were available in those courts against the trustee, and against third persons who knowingly participated in the trustee's breach.

At common law, however, there were many situations—not limited to those involving enforcement of a trust—in which an equity court could "establish purely legal rights and grant legal remedies which would otherwise be beyond the scope of its authority." 1 J. Pomeroy, Equity Jurisprudence § 181, p. 257 (5th ed. 1941). The term "equitable relief" can assuredly mean, as petitioners and the Solicitor General would have it, whatever relief a court of equity is empowered to provide in the particular case at issue. But as indicated by the foregoing quotation—which speaks of "legal remedies" granted by an equity court—"equitable relief" can also refer to those categories of relief that were *typically* available in equity (such as injunction, mandamus, and restitution, but not compensatory damages). As memories of the divided bench, and familiarity with its technical refinements, recede further into the past, the former meaning becomes, perhaps, increasingly unlikely; but it remains a question of interpretation in each case which meaning is intended.

In the context of the present statute, we think there can be no doubt. Since *all* relief available for breach of trust could be obtained from a court of equity, limiting the sort of relief obtainable under § 502(a)(3) to "equitable relief" in the sense of "whatever relief a common-law court of equity could provide in such a case" would limit the relief *not at all*. We will not read the statute to render the modifier superfluous. Regarding "equitable" relief in § 502(a)(3) to mean "all relief available for breach of trust at common law" would also require us either to give the term a different meaning there than it bears elsewhere in ERISA, or to deprive of all meaning the distinction Congress drew between "equitable" and "remedial" relief in § 409(a), and between "equitable" and "legal" relief in the very same section of ERISA, see [§ 502(g)(2)(E)]; in the same subchapter of ERISA, see [§ 104(a)(5)(C)]; and in the ERISA subchapter dealing with the PBGC. Neither option is acceptable. The authority of courts to develop a "federal common law" under ERISA, see *Firestone*, is not the authority to revise the text of the statute. . . .

In the last analysis, petitioners and the United States ask us to give a strained interpretation to § 502(a)(3) in order to achieve the "purpose of ERISA to protect plan participants and beneficiaries." They note, as we have, that before ERISA nonfiduciaries were generally liable under state trust law for damages resulting from knowing participation in a trustee's breach of duty, and they assert that such actions are now preempted by ERISA's broad preemption clause, § 514(a). Thus, they contend, our construction of § 502(a)(3) leaves beneficiaries like petitioners with *less* protection than existed before ERISA, contradicting ERISA's basic goal of "promot[ing] the interests of employees and their beneficiaries in employee benefit plans."

Even assuming (without deciding) that petitioners are correct about the preemption of previously available state-court actions, vague notions of a statute's "basic purpose" are nonetheless inadequate to overcome the words of its text regarding the specific issue under consideration. This is especially true with legislation such as ERISA, an enormously complex and detailed statute that resolved innumerable disputes between powerful competing interests—not all in favor of potential plaintiffs. See, e.g., *Pilot Life Ins. Co. v. Dedeaux*, 481 U.S. 41, 54–56 (1987). The text that we have described is certainly not nonsensical; it allocates liability for plan-related misdeeds in reasonable proportion to respective actors' power to control and prevent the misdeeds. Under traditional trust law, although a beneficiary could obtain damages from third persons for knowing participation in a trustee's breach of fiduciary duties, only the trustee had fiduciary duties. ERISA, however, defines "fiduciary" not in terms of formal trusteeship, but in *functional* terms of control and authority over the plan, see [§ 3(21)(A)], thus expanding the universe of persons subject to fiduciary duties—and to damages—under § 409(a). Professional service providers such as actuaries become liable for damages when they cross the line from advisor to fiduciary; must disgorge assets and profits obtained through participation as parties-in-interest in transactions prohibited by § 406, and pay related civil penalties, see § 502(i); and (assuming nonfiduciaries can be sued under § 502(a)(3)) may be enjoined from participating in a fiduciary's breaches, compelled to make restitution, and subjected to other equitable decrees. All that ERISA has eliminated, on these assumptions, is the common law's joint and several liability, for *all* direct and consequential damages suffered by the plan, on the part of persons who had no real power to control what the plan did. Exposure to that sort of liability would impose high insurance costs upon persons who regularly deal with and offer advice to ERISA plans, and hence upon ERISA plans themselves. There is, in other words, a "tension between the primary [ERISA] goal of benefitting employees and the subsidiary goal of containing pension costs." *Alessi v. Raybestos-Manhattan, Inc.*, 451 U.S. 504, 515 (1981). We will not attempt to adjust the balance between those competing goals that the text adopted by Congress has struck.

The judgment of the Court of Appeals is *Affirmed*.

■ JUSTICE WHITE, with whom THE CHIEF JUSTICE, JUSTICE STEVENS, and JUSTICE O'CONNOR join, dissenting.

The majority candidly acknowledges that it is plausible to interpret the phrase "appropriate equitable relief" as used in § 502(a)(3), at least standing alone, as meaning that relief which was available in the courts of equity for a breach of trust. The majority also acknowledges that the relief petitioners seek here—a compensatory monetary award—was available in the equity courts under the common law of trusts, not only against trustees for breach of duty but also against nonfiduciaries knowingly participating in a breach of trust. Finally, there can be no dispute that ERISA was grounded in this common-law experience and that "we are [to be] guided by principles of trust law" in construing the terms of the statute. Nevertheless, the majority today holds that in enacting ERISA Congress stripped ERISA trust beneficiaries of a remedy against trustees and third parties that they enjoyed in the equity courts under common law. Although it is assumed that a cause of action against a third party such as respondent is provided by ERISA, the remedies available are limited to the "traditional" equitable remedies, such as injunction and restitution, and do not include compensatory damages—"the classic form of *legal* relief." Because I do not believe that the statutory language requires this result and because we have elsewhere recognized the anomaly of construing ERISA in a way that "would afford *less* protection to employees and their beneficiaries than they enjoyed before ERISA was enacted," *Firestone*, (emphasis added), I must dissent.

I . . .

As we have noted previously, "ERISA's legislative history confirms that the Act's fiduciary responsibility provisions, [ERISA §§ 401–414], 'codif[y] and mak[e] applicable to [ERISA] fiduciaries certain principles developed in the evolution of the law of trusts.' " *Firestone* (quoting H. R. Rep. No. 93–533, p. 11 (1973)). ERISA, we have explained, "abounds with the language and terminology of trust law" and must be construed against the background of the common law of trusts. Indeed, absent some express statutory departure—such as ERISA's broader definition of a responsible "fiduciary,"—Congress intended that the courts would look to the settled experience of the common law in giving shape to a " 'federal common law of rights and obligations under ERISA-regulated plans.' " *Firestone*.

Accordingly, it is to the common law of trusts that we must look in construing the scope of the "appropriate equitable relief" for breaches of trust contemplated by § 502(a)(3). As the majority notes, at common law the courts of equity were the predominant forum for beneficiaries' claims arising from a breach of trust. These courts were not, however, the exclusive forum. In some instances, there was jurisdiction both in law and in equity and it was generally (although not universally) acknowledged that the beneficiary could elect between her legal and equitable remedies. Indeed, the Restatement of Trusts sets out in separate, successive sections the "legal" and "equitable" remedies available to beneficiaries under the common law of trusts. See Restatement (Second) of Trusts §§ 198, 199 (1959).

The traditional "equitable remedies" available to a trust beneficiary included compensatory damages. Equity "endeavor[ed] as far as possible to replace the parties in the same situation as they would have been in, if no breach of trust had been committed." This included, where necessary, the payment of a monetary award to make the victims of the breach whole.

Given this history, it is entirely reasonable in my view to construe § 502(a)(3)'s reference to "appropriate equitable relief" to encompass what was equity's routine remedy for such breaches—a compensatory monetary award calculated to make the victims whole, a remedy that was available against both fiduciaries and participating nonfiduciaries. Construing the statute in this manner also avoids the anomaly of interpreting ERISA so as to leave those Congress set out to protect—the participants in ERISA-governed plans and their beneficiaries—with "less protection . . . than they enjoyed before ERISA was enacted." Indeed, this is precisely how four Justices of this Court read § 502(a)(3)'s reference to "appropriate equitable relief" in *Russell*.

II

The majority, however, struggles to find on the face of the statute evidence that § 502(a)(3) is to be more narrowly construed. First, it observes that ERISA elsewhere uses the terms "remedial relief" and "legal relief" and reasons that Congress must therefore have intended to differentiate between these concepts and "equitable relief." Second, it is noted that the crucial language of § 502(a)(3) describes the available relief as *equitable* relief. It is then asserted that "[s]ince *all* relief available for breach of trust could be obtained from a court of equity, limiting the sort of relief obtainable under § 502(a)(3) to 'equitable relief' in the sense of 'whatever relief a common-law court of equity could provide in such a case' would limit the relief *not at all*," rendering Congress' imposition of the modifier "equitable" a nullity. Searching for some way in which to give "appropriate equitable relief" a limiting effect, the majority feels compelled to read the phrase as encompassing only "those categories of relief that were *typically* available" in the broad run of equity cases, without regard to the particular equitable remedies available in trust cases. This would include injunction and restitution, for example, but not money damages. As I see it, however, the words "appropriate equitable relief" are no more than descriptive and simply refer to all remedies available in equity under the common law of trusts, whether or not they were or are the exclusive remedies for breach of trust.

I disagree with the majority's inference that by using the term "legal . . . relief" elsewhere in ERISA, Congress demonstrated a considered judgment to constrict the relief available under § 502(a)(3). To be sure, § 502(g)(2)(E) of the statute empowers courts to award appropriate "legal or equitable relief" where a fiduciary successfully sues an employer for failing to make required contributions to a "multiemployer plan." Likewise, § 104(a)(5)(C) authorizes the Secretary of Labor to bring "a civil action for such legal or equitable relief as may be appropriate" to force the administrator of an employee benefit plan to file certain plan documents with the Secretary. And finally, §§ 4003(e)(1) and 4301(a)(1) of the statute, also cited by the majority, empower courts to dispense "appropriate relief, legal or equitable or both," in actions brought by the Pension Benefit Guaranty Corporation (PBGC) or by plan fiduciaries, participants, or beneficiaries with respect to the peculiar statutory duties relating to the PBGC. Significantly, however, none of the causes of action described in these sections—relating to the financing of "multiemployer plans," administrative filing requirements, and the PBGC—had any discernible analogue in the common law of trusts. Accordingly, there being no common-law tradition either in law or in equity to which Congress might direct the courts, it is not at all surprising that Congress would refer to both legal and equitable relief in making clear that the courts are free to craft whatever relief is most appropriate. It seems to me a treacherous leap to draw from these sections a congressional intention to foreclose compensatory monetary awards under § 502(a)(3) notwithstanding that such awards had always been considered "appropriate equitable relief" for breach of trust at common law. . . .

III

Although the trust beneficiary historically had an equitable suit for damages against a fiduciary for breach of trust, as well as against a participating nonfiduciary, the majority today construes § 502(a)(3) as not affording such a remedy against any fiduciary or participating third party on the ground that damages are not "appropriate equitable relief." The majority's conclusion, as I see it, rests on transparently insufficient grounds. The text of the statute supports a reading of § 502(a)(3) that would permit a court to award compensatory monetary relief where necessary to make an ERISA beneficiary whole for a breach of trust. Such a reading would accord with the established equitable remedies available under the common law of trusts, to which Congress has directed us in construing ERISA, and with Congress' primary goal in enacting the statute, the protection of beneficiaries' financial security against corrupt or inept plan mismanagement. Finally, such a reading would avoid the perverse and, in this case, entirely needless result of construing ERISA so as to *deprive* beneficiaries of remedies they enjoyed prior to the statute's enactment. For these reasons, I respectfully dissent.

NOTES

1. *Limitations on remedies available under ERISA § 502(a)(3).* "Equitable" can be a consequential word to deploy in a statute. To the layperson (and perhaps to a harried legislator) the term might be expected to suggest, simply, "fair." In a statute, at least as interpreted by the likes of Justice Scalia, the word is distinguished from "legal" and means something like: "relating to the Court of Chancery in England prior to the administrative merger, during the 1800s, of English courts of equity and courts of law." The result is that the remedies an ERISA plaintiff may now pursue depend upon historical examination of Baroque-era British judicial practices, as *Mertens* and following cases illustrate. (Similarly remarkable situations continue to arise in interpreting "equitable" rights in contexts other than ERISA. See Robert W. Phillips, Case Note: Cass County Music Co. v. C.H.L.R., Inc.: Law, Equity, and the Right to Jury Trial in Copyright Infringement Suits Seeking Statutory Damages, 51 Ark. L. Rev. 117 (1998).) Justice Scalia's decision to interpret the statute as requiring this result has been the subject of blistering criticism. See, e.g., John H. Langbein, What ERISA Means by "Equitable": The Supreme Court's Trail of Error in Russell, Mertens, and Great-West, 103 Colum. L. Rev. 1317 (2003).

2. Robert Nagle was General Counsel to the Senate Labor Committee during the negotiation and enactment of ERISA, and was heavily involved in drafting the statute's text. In 2013, Mr. Nagle participated in an ERISA retrospective conference at Drexel Law School, where he engaged, at one point, in the following colloquy with other conferees (including Frank Cummings, also a former congressional staff member who had been heavily involved in ERISA's drafting):

> Robert Nagle: We were talking about section 502(a)(3), which was clearly intended to be a total catch-all provision and to provide any sort of appropriate relief.
>
> Frank Cummings: Equitable relief.
>
> * * *
>
> Robert Nagle: This is the problem, and I feel a certain *mea culpa* about all this because I would say drafting carelessness gave [Justice] Scalia the opening to do what he did.
>
> * * *
>
> Robert Nagle: Well, yeah, well, this is where it all gets silly. 502(a)(3) refers specifically to equitable relief. [Justice] Scalia, in trying to determine for us what equitable relief is, saying, "Well, in other sections there are references to 'legal or equitable' relief, and Congress didn't put the term 'legal' in 502(a)(3)." This is the *mea culpa* part. And therefore Congress must have intended in 502(a)(3) to provide only those forms of equitable relief which were typically available in courts of equity, notwithstanding that courts of equity would also award legal relief. And so he said, "So consequently Congress must not have intended to allow that type of relief in 502(a)(3)," and then I think he went on to imagine plausible reasons why Congress may have reached that conclusion. And I keep thinking, this is ridiculous. If only we had thought to put "legal" in there, this whole issue would have been avoided.
>
> [laughter]
>
> Scott Macey: And Bob, do you think he's right or wrong? Was it just an inadvertent mistake that it wasn't in there, or was it intended not to be in there?
>
> Robert Nagle: Oh, it was an inadvertent mistake. If anybody had said in our drafting group, "Wait a minute, we've got legal and equitable everywhere else, let's put . . ." we would have said, "Of course." I mean there was no intention whatsoever to restrict the sort of relief.

Symposium: ERISA at 40: What Were They Thinking? 6 Drexel L. Rev. 257, 421–422 (2014).

3. Although *Mertens* dealt with a claim against a *nonfiduciary*, the same statutory language applies to suits against fiduciaries, as the dissenting justices recognized: "Although the trust beneficiary historically had an equitable suit for damages against a fiduciary for breach of trust, [the] majority today construes § 502(a)(3) as not affording such a remedy against any fiduciary [on] the ground that damages are not 'appropriate equitable relief.'" The lower courts have generally applied the holding in *Mertens* to suits against fiduciaries. See, e.g., McLeod v. Oregon Lithoprint

Inc., 102 F.3d 376, 378 (9th Cir.1996), cert. denied, 520 U.S. 1230 (1997)("the status of the defendant, whether fiduciary or nonfiduciary, does not affect the question of whether damages constitute 'appropriate equitable relief' under § 502(a)(3)"). The DoL rejects this application, and has taken the position in several amicus briefs that the limitation on remedies established by *Mertens* and Great-West Life & Annuity Ins. Co. v. Knudson, 534 U.S. 204 (2002), reproduced infra, applies only to nonfiduciaries. See, e.g., Tittle v. Enron Corp., Civ. Act. No. H–01–3913, Amended Brief of the Secretary of Labor as Amicus Curiae Opposing the Motions to Dismiss, p.64 (S.D. Tex. Aug. 30, 2002).

4. *Punitive damages.* In *Russell,* four justices joined in Justice Brennan's concurring opinion emphasizing that *Russell's* holding leaves open the question of whether punitive damages lie under § 502(a)(3). However, *Mertens'* holding that "appropriate equitable relief" under ERISA § 502(a)(3) is limited to traditional equitable remedies has been read as resolving the issue. See, e.g., Zavala v. Trans-System, Inc., 258 Fed.Appx. 155 (9th Cir.2007).

5. *Judicial balancing of participant rights versus perceived deterrence to employer plan adoption.* It appeared important to Justice Scalia's conclusion that, as the Court had put it in the earlier *Alessi* case, ERISA reflects a "tension between the primary goal of benefitting employees and the subsidiary goal of containing pension costs." See Brendan S. Maher, Creating a Paternalistic Market for Legal Rules Affecting the Benefit Promise," 2009 Wis. L. Rev. 658, for a summary of the many contexts—not limited to consequential damages—in which courts have similarly explicitly based denial of participants' ERISA claims, at least in part, on a concern over increasing the cost to employers of plan sponsorship. Professor Maher argues judges are not ideally placed to make that cost-benefit determination.

6. *Did ERISA leave participants worse off?* Justice Scalia specifically acknowledged the possibility, emphasized by the dissent, that "our construction of § 502(a)(3) leaves beneficiaries like petitioners with less protection than existed before ERISA," but concluded that "vague notions of a statute's 'basic purpose' are nonetheless inadequate to overcome the words of its text regarding the specific issue under consideration." Does Justice Scalia's contention that the words of the statute are sufficiently clear to supersede ERISA's purpose survive scrutiny? Or is the more appropriate characterization that the issue before the Court was the intended meaning of unclear text, an issue as to which consulting statutory purpose would have been, in fact, necessary? See Langbein, note 1 above, at 1363–64.

3. POST-*MERTENS* DEVELOPMENTS

1. *Great-West.* In Great-West Life & Annuity Ins. Co. v. Knudson, 534 U.S. 204 (2002), Justice Scalia elaborated upon the "equitable damages" constraint on § 502(a)(3) that the Court had located in *Mertens.* *Great-West* involved a subrogation claim brought by the insurer of an employer medical plan. A plan participant had been injured in a car accident and received medical reimbursements through the plan; the insurer, Great-West, sought to recoup from the participant, under the plan's subrogation clause, part of the damages recovered by the participant from third parties in a tort case arising out of the accident. The participant and her attorney, seeking to avoid this result, had

(arguably fraudulently) arranged to have the tort settlement allocate nearly all the awarded amount to attorney fees and to a trust established to provide for the participant's future medical benefits, rather than to already incurred medical claims.

Trying to avoid the limitations of *Mertens* despite the fact it was seeking money damages, Great-West characterized its claim as, alternatively, for "injunction" or for "restitution," historically equitable remedies. Writing for the majority, Justice Scalia denied both arguments. "An injunction to compel the payment of money past due under a contract, or specific performance of a past due monetary obligation, was not typically available in equity," he wrote. Meanwhile restitution, Scalia noted, could historically be had in *either* courts of law or equity—but in the latter case only through a constructive trust or equitable lien, where the recovery sought was of assets in the defendant's possession. That was not the situation in *Great-West*, because the amounts in question were in the hands of the participant's attorney and a trust for future medical costs. Great-West was therefore unable to recover, even for amounts arguably withheld from it through fraud, because the recovery sought could not be characterized as "equitable." In a strongly worded dissent Justice Ginsburg, for a four-justice minority, stated that she was "unprepared to agree that Congress chose to infuse § 502(a)(3) with the recondite distinctions on which the majority relies."

For a historical summary of the doctrine of restitution, see Douglas Laycock, The Scope and Significance of Restitution, 67 Tex. L. Rev. 1277 (1989). A sense of the difficulty in untangling which aspects of this remedy might be equitable and which legal can be gleaned from this introductory sentence by Professor Laycock: "In every major remedies book, *three* of the largest subdivisions are some variation of damages, equity, and restitution." (Emph. added.)

2. *Sereboff.* Sereboff v. Mid Atlantic Medical Services, Inc., 547 U.S. 356 (2006), involved facts similar to *Great-West*, except that the tort recovery had been paid directly to the plan participant, and the insurer sought to impose a lien on those assets to the extent of the asserted subrogation right. This time the Court, in an opinion by Justice Roberts, concluded the remedy was available. The relief sought, an equitable lien on assets in the hands of the defendant, was indeed "equitable," the Court concluded. Justice Roberts rejected, on historical grounds, the participant's argument that the equitable remedy of restitution was confined to situations involving a specific *res* or asset specifically "traceable" to the breach in order for equitable restitution to obtain.

Does demanding that the funds be physically in the defendant's possession serve any purpose or does it elevate a formal fortuity over substance? In Bauhaus USA, Inc. v. Copeland, 292 F.3d 439 (5th Cir. 2002), a medical plan that paid expenses for injuries to a participant's daughter caused by a third party sought to recover under the plan's reimbursement provision from a monetary award paid to the participant in a tort case. The funds, however, were in the possession of the Chancery Court in Mississippi pending resolution of the claim. The Sixth Circuit said that because the funds were not in the defendant's possession, the relief sought was legal and not equitable. Subsequently, the plan sued the bank into which the Chancery Court had deposited the funds being held. This time, a district court ruled that the plaintiff was entitled to seek equitable restitution in the form of a constructive trust, since the funds were in the hands of the defendant. Bauhaus USA, Inc. v. Copeland, 2003 WL 25886543 (E.D.La.2003), withdrawn and substituted with 2003 WL 24207524 (E.D.La.2003). What is served by forcing the second lawsuit in this situation?

In Bilyeu v. Morgan Stanley Long Term Disability Plan, 683 F.3d 1083 (9th Cir. 2012) the Ninth Circuit held that a plan fiduciary may not enforce an equitable lien under ERISA against a beneficiary who agreed to reimburse the plan for any benefit overpayment if the funds are no longer in the beneficiary's possession. The court acknowledged that "a number of circuits have interpreted *Sereboff's* discussion of tracing rules as a signal that a fiduciary can assert an equitable lien—presumably against a beneficiary's general assets—even if the beneficiary no longer possesses the specifically identifiable funds." Id. at 1094. However, it was unpersuaded by those other circuits because "[t]he tracing issue in *Sereboff* was whether Mid Atlantic could obtain an equitable lien against specifically identified funds when Mid Atlantic never had possessed those funds itself—an issue that has no relevance here." Id. at 1095. The court also observed that its conclusion that a fiduciary must recover from specifically identified funds in the beneficiary's possession is consistent, not only with *Sereboff*, but with *Amara*.

The "funds possession" requirement of *Great-West* and *Sereboff* has resulted in decisions that seem anomalous at best. For example, a son hides the death of his father from the plan from which the father had been receiving pension benefits. The son continues to receive and cash the checks for a decade, during which he executes numerous false affidavits that his father is still alive. May the plan seek relief from the son? In Kroop v. Rivlin, 2004 WL 2181110 (S.D.N.Y.2004), a district court held that the plan may not recover under § 502(a)(3) because the funds are no longer in the possession of the son. In contrast, in Lumenite Control Technology, Inc. v. Jarvis, 252 F.Supp.2d 700 (N.D.Ill.2003), an employer mistakenly overpaid pension benefits to a former employee, who deposited the funds into an IRA and subsequently used the money to purchase a home. The court held that because the overpayment was potentially traceable to the new home, the employer could seek a constructive trust in a share of it, allowing the relief to be properly characterized as equitable restitution. Does it make sense to allow recovery in the latter case but not the former?

In inviting a focus on whether the recovery sought by the plaintiff is traceable to actual funds still held in the hands of the defendant, *Great-West* encourages courts to ignore "the doctrinal basis upon which restitution has come to rest," that is, unjust enrichment. John H. Langbein, *The Later History of Restitution*, in RESTITUTION PAST, PRESENT AND FUTURE 57–58 (W.R. Cornish, et. al., eds. 1998). Is there any difference in the extent to which the defendants in *Kroop* and *Jarvis* have been unjustly enriched? Disallowing relief in either case would seem to ignore the core equitable principle of preventing unjust enrichment.

3.   *Varity.* The facts and first part of the Supreme Court's opinion in Varity Corp. v. Howe, 516 U.S. 489 (1996), dealing with the scope of

fiduciary duty, are reproduced in Chapter 12. In the second part of the opinion the Court confirmed that the plaintiffs could recover for individual, equitable relief under § 502(a)(3). The Court rejected Varity's argument that, given that the Court in *Russell* had interpreted Congress as intending to deny the right to individual—as opposed to plan—equitable relief for fiduciary breach under § 502(a)(2), it was illogical to believe Congress could have simultaneously intended to authorize that relief under § 502(a)(3).

A number of *amicus* briefs were filed in *Varity* expressing concern that a participant who was denied benefits would routinely claim that the benefit denial was a breach of fiduciary duty. As we saw in Chapter 15, supra, courts review most benefit denial claims under the so-called "arbitrary and capricious" standard, which presumes the correctness of plan decisionmaking. The *amici* were concerned that the judicial standard of review for breach of fiduciary duty under ERISA § 502(a)(3) would accord administrators less deference.

The majority in *Varity* questioned whether the two standards differed, and also observed that "where Congress elsewhere provided adequate relief for a beneficiary's injury, there will likely be no need for further equitable relief, in which case such relief normally would not be appropriate." Responding to this admonition, numerous courts have held that if a beneficiary has a claim under ERISA § 502(a)(1)(B), equitable relief under ERISA § 502(a)(3) is inappropriate, and have refused to allow plaintiffs to reframe what are essentially claims for benefits as claims for breach of fiduciary duty. See, e.g., Tolson v. Avondale Industries, Inc., 141 F.3d 604, 610 (5th Cir.1998).

4.   *Remedies for § 510 violations: back pay.* ERISA § 510 makes it unlawful for any person to interfere with a participant or beneficiary's rights under ERISA or the plan. But ERISA § 510 can be enforced only under ERISA § 502(a), which as we have seen has the effect of limiting the participant or beneficiary to appropriate equitable relief. Suppose an employer discharges an employee for exercising the employee's rights under ERISA. What are the available remedies? Prior to *Great-West*, some courts had characterized both backpay and frontpay awards as equitable remedies under ERISA. See, e.g., Schwartz v. Gregori, 45 F.3d 1017 (6th Cir.1995) (analogizing to Supreme Court precedents that had characterized back pay awards under the Fair Labor Standards Act as restitutionary).

Does the view that back pay constitutes equitable relief survive *Great-West*? Dicta in Great-West raised the question, with the Court suggesting that the fact that back pay is viewed as equitable in the Title VII context does not necessarily mean it should be treated as equitable in nature. In Millsap v. McDonnell Douglas Corp., 368 F.3d 1246 (10th Cir.2004), the Tenth Circuit answered the question in the negative. Millsap involved a class action by former employees who alleged that McDonnell Douglas closed a plant to prevent employees from becoming eligible for pension and health care benefits. The district court concluded that the defendant's behavior violated Section 510 and that back pay was appropriate equitable relief. After engaging in an extensive discussion of the Supreme Court's decision in *Great-West*, the Tenth Circuit identified the question to be whether back pay was a remedy typically available in equity. As to that question, the court said back pay "is a creature of positive law; that is, the remedy of back pay did not exist at common law." Citing several treatises on remedies, the court opined that back pay claims " 'do not differ remedially from the personal injury claim for lost wages, or the contract claim for past wages due' " and are "remedially analogous to personal injury or breach of contract claims because back pay awards compensate employees for lost wages and benefits before trial." The Third Circuit has agreed. Eichorn v. AT & T Corp., 484 F.3d 644, 655–56 (3d Cir. 2007). Does *Millsap* deprive plaintiffs of any meaningful remedy under § 510?

5.   *The "Specificity Myth."* In *Mertens* and *Russell*, the Court stressed the idea of ERISA as a "comprehensive and reticulated statute," with a set of "carefully integrated civil enforcement provisions." This comprehensiveness justified the view, for example, that the word "equitable" must be taken seriously as a limit on the types of remedies Congress meant to authorize. The idea has been brought into question:

> Professor George Flint has disparaged this argument from ERISA's supposed comprehensiveness as the "specificity myth." Flint directed attention to the cumbersome duplication of language in the six subsections of section 502(a). One can point to other evidence that reinforces his point. The Court's claim in these ERISA remedy cases that ERISA is so perfectly drafted that it already expresses every detail of its intended coverage conflicts with the Court's incessant complaining about the bad drafting of section 514(a), ERISA's preemption measure. In truth, ERISA's procedure and remedy provisions suffer from major omissions that the courts have had to supply from context.

John H. Langbein, What ERISA Means by "Equitable": The Supreme Court's Trail of Error in Russell, Mertens, and Great-West, 103 Colum. L. Rev. 1317, 1344 (2003), citing George L. Flint, Jr. ERISA: Extracontractual Damages Mandated for Benefit Claims Actions, 36 Ariz. L. Rev. 611, 638 (1994).

6.   *Subrogation cases.* Reimbursement provisions such as those at issue in *Great-West* and *Sereboff* are common features of health plans, and litigation involving such provisions is correspondingly common. Subsequent to the Supreme Court's decision in *Great-West*, courts struggled in numerous cases over whether subrogation claims gave rise to a claim for equitable relief. In one of them, Scholastic Corp. v. Najah Kassem & Casper & De Toledo LLC, 389 F.Supp.2d 402 (D. Conn.2005), the court bemoaned the challenge of applying *Great-West* to subrogation claims, observing that "despite Justice Scalia's cheery assurance that the dissenters in *Great-West* 'greatly exaggerate[d] . . . the difficulty of the [t]ask' of determining the types of remedies typically available in equity, the Supreme Court's decision has created real challenges for those of us who have little training, let alone experience, in the subtleties of ancient writs."

4. CIGNA CORP. V. AMARA

131 S. Ct. 1866 (2011).

■ JUSTICE BREYER delivered the opinion of the Court. In 1998, petitioner CIGNA Corporation changed the nature of its basic pension plan for employees. Previously, the plan provided a retiring employee with a defined benefit in the form of an annuity calculated on the basis of his preretirement salary and length of service. The new plan provided most retiring employees with a (lump sum) cash balance calculated on the basis of a defined annual contribution from CIGNA as increased by compound interest. Because many employees had already earned at least some old-plan benefits, the new plan translated already-earned benefits into an opening amount in the employee's cash balance account.

Respondents, acting on behalf of approximately 25,000 beneficiaries of the CIGNA Pension Plan (which is also a petitioner here), challenged CIGNA's adoption of the new plan. They claimed in part that CIGNA had failed to give them proper notice of changes to their benefits, particularly because the new plan in certain respects provided them with less generous benefits.

The District Court agreed that the disclosures made by CIGNA violated its obligations under ERISA. In determining relief, the court found that CIGNA's notice failures had caused the employees "likely harm." The Court then reformed the new plan and ordered CIGNA to pay benefits accordingly. It found legal authority for doing so in ERISA § 502(a)(1)(B)(authorizing a plan "participant or beneficiary" to bring a "civil action" to "recover benefits due to him under the terms of his plan").

We agreed to decide whether the District Court applied the correct legal standard, namely, a "likely harm" standard, in determining that CIGNA's notice violations caused its employees sufficient injury to warrant legal relief. To reach that question, we must first consider a more general matter—whether the ERISA section just mentioned (ERISA's recovery-of-benefits-due provision, § 502(a)(1)(B)) authorizes entry of the relief the District Court provided. We conclude that it does not authorize this relief. Nonetheless, we find that a different equity-related ERISA provision, to which the District Court also referred, authorizes forms of relief similar to those that the court entered.

Section 502(a)(3) authorizes "appropriate equitable relief" for violations of ERISA. Accordingly, the relevant standard of harm will depend upon the equitable theory by which the District Court provides relief. We leave it to the District Court to conduct that analysis in the first instance, but we identify equitable principles that the court might apply on remand.

I. . .

A

Under CIGNA's pre-1998 defined-benefit retirement plan, an employee with at least five years service would receive an annuity annually paying an amount that depended upon the employee's salary and length of service. Depending on when the employee had joined CIGNA, the annuity would equal either (1) 2 percent of the employee's average salary over his final three years with CIGNA, multiplied by the number of years worked (up to 30); or (2) 1 2/3 percent of the employee's average salary over his final five years with CIGNA, multiplied by the number of years worked (up to 35). Calculated either way, the annuity would approach 60 percent of a longtime employee's final salary. A well-paid longtime employee, earning, say, $ 160,000 per year, could receive a retirement annuity paying the employee about $ 96,000 per year until his death. The plan offered many employees at least one other benefit: They could retire early, at age 55, and receive an only-somewhat-reduced annuity.

In November 1997, CIGNA sent its employees a newsletter announcing that it intended to put in place a new pension plan. The new plan would substitute an "account balance plan" for CIGNA's pre-existing defined-benefit system. The newsletter added that the old plan would end on December 31, 1997, that CIGNA would introduce (and describe) the new plan sometime during 1998, and that the new plan would apply retroactively to January 1, 1998. Eleven months later CIGNA filled in the details. Its new plan created an individual retirement account for each employee. (The account consisted of a bookkeeping entry backed by a CIGNA -funded trust.) Each year CIGNA would contribute to the employee's individual account an amount equal to between 3 percent and 8.5 percent of the employee's salary, depending upon age, length of service, and certain other factors. The account balance would earn compound interest at a rate equal to the return on 5-year treasury bills plus one-quarter percent (but no less than 4.5 percent and no greater than 9 percent). Upon retirement the employee would receive the amount then in his or her individual account—in the form of either a lump sum or whatever annuity the lump sum then would buy. As promised, CIGNA would open the accounts and begin to make contributions as of January 1, 1998.

But what about the retirement benefits that employees had already earned prior to January 1, 1998? CIGNA promised to make an initial contribution to the individual's account equal to the value of that employee's already earned benefits. And the new plan set forth a method for calculating that initial contribution. The method consisted of calculating the amount as of the employee's (future) retirement date of the annuity to which the employee's salary and length of service already (i.e., as of December 31, 1997) entitled him and then discounting that sum to its present (i.e., January 1, 1998) value. . . .

B

1

The District Court found that CIGNA's initial descriptions of its new plan were significantly incomplete and misled its employees. In November 1997, for example, CIGNA sent the employees a newsletter that said the new plan would "significantly enhance" its "retirement program," would produce "an overall improvement in . . . retirement benefits," and would provide "the same benefit security" with "steadier benefit growth." CIGNA also told its employees that they would "see the growth in [their] total retirement benefits from CIGNA every year," that its initial deposit "represent[ed] the full value of the benefit [they] earned for service before 1998," and that "[o]ne advantage the company will not get from the retirement program changes is cost savings."

In fact, the new plan saved the company $10 million annually (though CIGNA later said it devoted the savings to other employee benefits). Its initial deposit did not "represen[t] the full value of the benefit" that employees had "earned for service before 1998." And the plan made a significant number of employees worse off. . . .

The District Court concluded, as a matter of law, that CIGNA's representations (and omissions) about the plan, made between November 1997 (when it announced the plan) and December 1998 (when it put the plan into effect) violated: ERISA §§ 204(h), . . . 102(a) and 104(b).

2

The District Court then turned to the remedy. First, the court agreed with CIGNA that only employees whom CIGNA's disclosure failures had harmed could obtain relief. But it did not require each individual member of the relevant CIGNA employee class to show individual injury. Rather, it found (1) that the evidence presented had raised a presumption of "likely harm" suffered by the members of the relevant employee class, and (2) that CIGNA, though free to offer contrary evidence in respect to some or all of those employees, had failed to rebut that presumption. It concluded that this unrebutted showing was sufficient to warrant class-applicable relief.

Second, the court noted that § 204(h) had been interpreted by the Second Circuit to permit the invalidation of plan amendments not preceded by a proper notice, prior to the 2001 amendment that made this power explicit. But the court also thought that granting this relief here would harm, not help, the injured employees. That is because the notice failures all concerned the new plan that took effect in December 1998. The court thought that the notices in respect to the freezing of old-plan benefits, effective December 31, 1997, were valid. To strike the new plan while leaving in effect the frozen old plan would not help CIGNA's employees.

The court considered treating the November 1997 notice as a sham or treating that notice and the later 1998 notices as part and parcel of a single set of related events. But it pointed out that respondents "ha[d] argued none of these things." And it said that the court would "not make these arguments now on [respondents'] behalf."

Third, the court reformed the terms of the new plan's guarantee. It erased the portion that assured participants who retired the greater of "A" (that which they had already earned as of December 31, 1997, under the old plan, $ 11,667 in our example) or "B" (that which they would earn via CIGNA's annual deposits under the new plan, including CIGNA's initial deposit). And it substituted a provision that would guarantee each employee "A" (that which they had already earned, as of December 31, 1997, under the old plan) plus "B" (that which they would earn via CIGNA's annual deposits under the new plan, excluding CIGNA's initial deposit). In our example, the District Court's remedy would no longer force our employee to choose upon retirement either an $ 11,667 annuity or his new plan benefits (including both CIGNA's annual deposits and CIGNA's initial deposit). It would give him an $ 11,667 annuity plus his new plan benefits (with CIGNA's annual deposits but without CIGNA's initial deposit).

Fourth, the court "order[ed] and enjoin[ed] the CIGNA Plan to reform its records to reflect that all class members . . . now receive [the just described] 'A + B' benefits," and that it pay appropriate benefits to those class members who had already retired.

Fifth, the court held that ERISA § 502(a)(1)(B) provided the legal authority to enter this relief. That provision states that a "civil action may be brought" by a plan "participant or beneficiary . . . to recover benefits due to him under the terms of his plan." The court wrote that its orders in effect awarded "benefits under the terms of the plan" as reformed.

At the same time the court considered whether ERISA § 502(a)(3) also provided legal authority to enter this relief. . . . The District Court decided not to answer this question because (1) it had just decided that the same relief was available under § 502(a)(1)(B), regardless; and (2) the Supreme Court has "issued several opinions . . . that have severely curtailed the kinds of relief that are available under § 502(a)(3)."

The parties cross-appealed the District Court's judgment. The Court of Appeals for the Second Circuit issued a brief summary order, rejecting all their claims, and affirming "the judgment of the district court for substantially the reasons stated" in the District Court's "well-reasoned and scholarly opinions." The parties filed cross-petitions for writs of certiorari in this Court. We granted the request in CIGNA's petition to consider whether a showing of "likely harm" is sufficient to entitle plan participants to recover benefits based on faulty disclosures.

II

CIGNA in the merits briefing raises a preliminary question. It argues first and foremost that the statutory provision upon which the District Court rested its orders, namely, the provision for recovery of plan benefits, § 502(a)(1)(B), does not in fact authorize the District Court to enter the kind of relief it entered here. And for that reason, CIGNA argues, whether the District Court did or did not use a proper standard for determining harm is beside the point. We believe that this preliminary question is closely enough related to the question presented that we shall consider it at the outset.

A

[This portion of the Court's opinion is discussed in Chapter 13—Eds.]

B

If § 502(a)(1)(B) does not authorize entry of the relief here at issue, what about nearby § 502(a)(3)? That provision allows a participant, beneficiary, or fiduciary "to obtain other *appropriate equitable relief* " to redress violations of (here relevant) parts of ERISA "or the terms of the plan." The District Court strongly implied, but did not directly hold, that it would base its relief upon this subsection were it not for (1) the fact that the preceding "plan benefits due" provision, § 502(a)(1)(B), provided sufficient authority; and (2) certain cases from this Court that narrowed the application of the term "appropriate equitable relief." Our holding in Part II-A, *supra*, removes the District Court's first obstacle. And given the likelihood that, on remand, the District Court will turn to and rely upon this alternative subsection, we consider the court's second concern. We find that concern misplaced.

We have interpreted the term "appropriate equitable relief " in § 502(a)(3) as referring to " 'those categories of relief' " that, traditionally speaking (i.e., prior to the merger of law and equity) " 'were *typically* available in equity.' " In *Mertens*, we applied this principle to a claim seeking money damages brought by a beneficiary against a private firm that provided a trustee with actuarial services. We found that the plaintiff sought "nothing other than compensatory damages" against a nonfiduciary. And we held that such a claim, traditionally speaking, was legal, not equitable, in nature.

In *Great-West*, we considered a claim brought by a fiduciary against a tort-award-winning beneficiary seeking monetary reimbursement for medical outlays that the plan had previously made on the beneficiary's behalf. We noted that the fiduciary sought to obtain a lien attaching to (or a constructive trust imposed upon) money that the beneficiary had received from the tort-case defendant. But we noted that the money in question was not the "particular" money that the tort defendant had paid. And, traditionally speaking, relief that sought a lien or a constructive trust was legal relief, not equitable relief, unless the funds in question were "*particular* funds or property in the defendant's possession."

The case before us concerns a suit by a beneficiary against a plan fiduciary (whom ERISA typically treats as a trustee) about the terms of a plan (which ERISA typically treats as a trust). It is the kind of lawsuit that, before the merger of law and equity, respondents could have brought only in a court of equity, not a court of law.

With the exception of the relief now provided by § 502(a)(1)(B), the remedies available to those courts of equity were traditionally considered equitable remedies.

The District Court's affirmative and negative injunctions obviously fall within this category. And other relief ordered by the District Court resembles forms of traditional equitable relief. That is because equity chancellors developed a host of other "distinctively equitable" remedies— remedies that were "fitted to the nature of the primary right" they were intended to protect. Indeed, a maxim of equity states that "[e]quity suffers not a right to be without a remedy." And the relief entered here, insofar as it does not consist of injunctive relief, closely resembles three other traditional equitable remedies.

First, what the District Court did here may be regarded as the reformation of the terms of the plan, in order to remedy the false or misleading information CIGNA provided. The power to reform contracts (as contrasted with the power to enforce contracts as written) is a traditional power of an equity court, not a court of law, and was used to prevent fraud.

Second, the District Court's remedy essentially held CIGNA to what it had promised, namely, that the new plan would not take from its employees benefits they had already accrued. This aspect of the remedy resembles estoppel, a traditional equitable remedy. Equitable estoppel "operates to place the person entitled to its benefit in the same position he would have been in had the representations been true." And, as

Justice Story long ago pointed out, equitable estoppel "forms a very essential element in . . . fair dealing, and rebuke of all fraudulent misrepresentation, which it is the boast of courts of equity constantly to promote."

Third, the District Court injunctions require the plan administrator to pay to already retired beneficiaries money owed them under the plan as reformed. But the fact that this relief takes the form of a money payment does not remove it from the category of traditionally equitable relief. Equity courts possessed the power to provide relief in the form of monetary "compensation" for a loss resulting from a trustee's breach of duty, or to prevent the trustee's unjust enrichment. Indeed, prior to the merger of law and equity this kind of monetary remedy against a trustee, sometimes called a "surcharge," was "exclusively equitable."

The surcharge remedy extended to a breach of trust committed by a fiduciary encompassing any violation of a duty imposed upon that fiduciary. Thus, insofar as an award of make-whole relief is concerned, the fact that the defendant in this case, unlike the defendant in *Mertens*, is analogous to a trustee makes a critical difference. In sum, contrary to the District Court's fears, the types of remedies the court entered here fall within the scope of the term "appropriate equitable relief " in § 502(a)(3).

III

Section 502(a)(3) invokes the equitable powers of the District Court. We cannot know with certainty which remedy the District Court understood itself to be imposing, nor whether the District Court will find it appropriate to exercise its discretion under § 502(a)(3) to impose that remedy on remand. We need not decide which remedies are appropriate on the facts of this case in order to resolve the parties' dispute as to the appropriate legal standard in determining whether members of the relevant employee class were injured.

The relevant substantive provisions of ERISA do not set forth any particular standard for determining harm. They simply require the plan administrator to write and to distribute written notices that are "sufficiently accurate and comprehensive to reasonably apprise" plan participants and beneficiaries of "their rights and obligations under the plan." Nor can we find a definite standard in the ERISA provision, § 502(a)(3) (which authorizes the court to enter "appropriate equitable relief " to redress ERISA "violations"). Hence any requirement of harm must come from the law of equity.

Looking to the law of equity, there is no general principle that "detrimental reliance" must be proved before a remedy is decreed. To the extent any such requirement arises, it is because the specific remedy being contemplated imposes such a requirement. Thus, as CIGNA points out, when equity courts used the remedy of estoppel, they insisted upon a showing akin to detrimental reliance, i.e., that the defendant's statement "in truth, influenced the conduct of" the plaintiff, causing "prejudic[e]." Accordingly, when a court exercises its authority under § 502(a)(3) to impose a remedy equivalent to estoppel, a showing of detrimental reliance must be made.

But this showing is not always necessary for other equitable remedies. Equity courts, for example, would reform contracts to reflect the mutual understanding of the contracting parties where "fraudulent suppression[s], omission[s], or insertion[s]," 1 Story § 154, at 149, "material[ly] . . . affect[ed]" the "substance" of the contract, even if the "complaining part[y]" was negligent in not realizing its mistake, as long as its negligence did not fall below a standard of "reasonable prudence" and violate a legal duty.

Nor did equity courts insist upon a showing of detrimental reliance in cases where they ordered "surcharge." Rather, they simply ordered a trust or beneficiary made whole following a trustee's breach of trust. In such instances equity courts would "mold the relief to protect the rights of the beneficiary according to the situation involved." This flexible approach belies a strict requirement of "detrimental reliance."

To be sure, just as a court of equity would not surcharge a trustee for a nonexistent harm, a fiduciary can be surcharged under § 502(a)(3) only upon a showing of actual harm—proved (under the default rule for civil cases) by a preponderance of the evidence. That actual harm may sometimes consist of detrimental reliance, but it might also come from the loss of a right protected by ERISA or its trust-law antecedents. In the present case, it is not difficult to imagine how the failure to provide proper summary information, in violation of the statute, injured employees even if they did not themselves act in reliance on summary documents—which they might not themselves have seen—for they may have thought fellow employees, or informal workplace discussion, would have let them know if, say, plan changes would likely prove harmful. We doubt that Congress would have wanted to bar those employees from relief.

The upshot is that we can agree with CIGNA only to a limited extent. We believe that, to obtain relief by surcharge for violations of §§ 102(a) and 104(b), a plan participant or beneficiary must show that the violation injured him or her. But to do so, he or she need only show harm and causation. Although it is not always necessary to meet the more rigorous standard implicit in the words "detrimental reliance," actual harm must be shown.

We are not asked to reassess the evidence. And we are not asked about the other prerequisites for relief. We are asked about the standard of prejudice. And we conclude that the standard of prejudice must be borrowed from equitable principles, as modified by the obligations and injuries identified by ERISA itself. Information-related circumstances, violations, and injuries are potentially too various in nature to insist that harm must always meet that more vigorous "detrimental harm" standard when equity imposed no such strict requirement.

IV

We have premised our discussion in Part III on the need for the District Court to revisit its determination of an appropriate remedy for the violations of ERISA it identified. Whether or not the general principles we have discussed above are properly applicable in this case is for it or the Court of Appeals to determine in the first instance. Because the District Court has not determined if an appropriate remedy may be imposed under § 502(a)(3), we must vacate the judgment below and remand this case for further proceedings consistent with this opinion.

NOTES

Justice Scalia, joined by Justice Thomas, concurred in the Court's judgment that § 502(a)(1)(B) of ERISA does not authorize relief for misrepresentations in an SPD. However, he saw "no need and no justification for saying anything more than that." In his view, there was no reason for the Court to speculate about equitable remedies, observing that the Court's opinion on this issue is "purely dicta, binding neither on us nor the district court." Clearly he is correct that the portion of the opinion reproduced here is dicta. Nonetheless, the Court's analysis represents a dramatic change in ERISA remedies and has been considered by lower courts as important guidance in determining appropriate equitable relief in cases of this type.

"Cash balance" conversions, the subject of the complaint in this case, are discussed in some detail in Chapter 18.

1.   *Equitable remedies.* The *Amara* opinion again illustrated the extent to which, given the Court's earlier decisions in *Russell* and *Mertens*, ERISA remedies have come to depend on parsing the historical distinction between courts of law and courts of equity. The resulting difficulties arise partly from the arbitrary nature of that distinction: What was "legal" or "equitable" was always a function of largely accidental and political events, not amenable to capture by conceptual formulation. A leading British authority described thusly the problematic nature, even in the early 20th Century, of defining "equity":

> [W]e are driven to say that Equity now is that body of rules administered by our English courts of justice which, were it not for the operation of the Judicature Acts [which during the 1870s merged the English law and equity systems], would be administered only by those courts which would be known as Courts of Equity.
>
> This, you may well say, is but a poor thing to call a definition. . . . Still I fear that nothing better than this is possible.

F.W. Maitland, Equity 1 (1936).

2.   *Surcharge.* Amara left the ERISA bar scrambling to learn more, in particular, about the historical remedy of "surcharge," by which the Court's opinion appeared to extend to ERISA fiduciary plaintiffs the most promising generally available route to obtaining monetary relief since the Mertens decision.

Surcharge was a remedy applied by courts of equity characteristically in the context of trusts, against trustees who breached their fiduciary duty:

> Damages in equity, especially for breach of trust, are sometimes called "surcharge." The concept, evoking the days when English lawyers still spoke law French, is that the Chancellor grants monetary relief by a charge on (*sur*) the account filed by the breaching trustee.

John H. Langbein, What ERISA Means by "Equitable": The Supreme Court's Trail of Error in Russell, Mertens, and Great-West, 103 Colum. L. Rev. 1317, 1352–53 (2003).

Post-*Amara,* several Courts of Appeals appear to have read broadly the possibility of a surcharge remedy against breaching fiduciaries under ERISA, treating *Amara* as a "striking development" "that significantly altered the understanding of equitable relief available under" § 502(a)(3). McCravy v. Metro. Life Ins. Co., 690 F.3d 176, 180 (4th Cir. 2012) and Kenseth v. Dean Health Plan, Inc., 722 F.3d 869, 876 (7th Cir. 2013). The Court of Appeals for the Seventh Circuit in *Kenseth,* for example, remanded to the District Court to consider whether a plaintiff who had undergone surgery in reliance on a plan representative's incorrect representation that the procedure would be covered could recover under a surcharge theory, characterizing the remedy sought, and allowed by *Amara,* as "make-whole money damages." In the *McCravy* case, above and in Gearlds v. Entergy Services, Inc., 709 F.3d 448 (5th Cir. 2013), Silva v. Metro. Life Ins. Co., 762 F.3d 711 (8th Cir.2014, and Gabriel v. Alaska Electrical Pension Fund, 773 F.3d 945 (9th Cir.2014), the Courts of Appeals for the Fourth, Fifth, Eighth and Ninth Circuits remanded similar cases to District Courts, which had dismissed on the grounds the relief sought was not "equitable," to determine whether surcharge might apply in light of *Amara.*

The Ninth Circuit, by contrast, has determined—pending the outcome of a petition for hearing *en banc*—that surcharge is limited to situations where the fiduciary itself benefited from the alleged breach or caused a loss to the plan, a reading that would deny claims for, for example, the value of benefits or their equivalent—the type of claim at issue in *Kenseth, McCravy, Gearlds* and, indeed, *Amara* itself. *Gabriel* thus appears to raise a nascent conflict among the circuits as to how to apply *Amara,* a conflict that may ultimately require recourse yet again to the Supreme Court to resolve.

3. *Reformation.* "Reformation" is another equitable possibility discussed by the *Amara* majority. "The traditional grounds justifying reformation of an instrument are either mutual mistake or unilateral mistake by one party and fraud or unconscionable conduct by the other." St. Pius X House of Retreats, Salvatorian Fathers v. Diocese of Camden, 88 N.J. 571, 577 (1982)).

The conclusion that reformation may have been an appropriate equitable remedy on the facts before the *Amara* Court does not mean reformation will always be an appropriate remedy in a suit under 502(a)(3) based on an inaccurate SPD description. See *Gabriel,* note 2 above; Skinner v. Northrop Grumman Ret. Plan B, 673 F.3d 1162 (9th Cir. 2012) (refusing to grant reformation as an equitable remedy on the facts before it, finding reformation to be proper only in cases of fraud and mistake and finding neither on the facts before it). It appears, however, that some courts will find reformation to be an appropriate equitable remedy even in the absence of actual harm. See Osberg v. Foot Locker, Inc., 555 Fed. Appx. 77 (2d Cir. 2014) (suggesting that reformation could be an appropriate remedy for a former participant challenging the conversion of a traditional defined benefit plan to a cash balance plan without showing actual harm).

4. *McCutchen.* Given that § 502(a)(3) permits a claim for "traditionally equitable" remedies, does that mean the defendant is also free to raise "traditionally equitable" *defenses* to such a claim? No, according to the Court's decision in US Airways, Inc., v. McCutchen, 133 S. Ct. 1537 (2013), a case involving facts essentially identical to *Sereboff* (see Part A.3.2 above). In *McCutcheon* the question that reached the Court was whether the

participant could defeat the plan's subrogation claim for the participant's tort recovery—either fully, on the basis of a theory of "double recovery" under which subrogation would be limited to amounts for which the participant had been compensated twice, by the plan and the third party tortfeasor; or at least partly, under the "common fund" doctrine, by which the plan would be required at least to bear its share of the attorney's fees incurred by the participant to obtain the tort recovery. Both the "double recovery" and "common fund" doctrines were historically equitable.

Writing for the majority, Justice Kagan concluded neither defense could be raised by the participant. The double recovery and common fund doctrines, she reasoned, historically applied where the underlying claim arose entirely through the operation of equity—not where the claim was based on the written instrument's terms—"the modern-day equivalent of an 'equitable lien by agreement' ", the way the claim at issue in *McCutchen* was based on the terms of the plan. Thus, while the plan could seek equitable *remedies* under § 502(a)(3), because the claim was based on the terms of the plan rather than on "freestanding" equitable principles, freestanding equitable principles could not be invoked to defeat those claims in contravention of the plan terms. (Nonetheless the Court went on to hold, as a matter of textual interpretation, that the plan in question should be read as incorporating the "common fund" doctrine to require the employer to bear its share of the attorney's fees incurred in obtaining the tort recovery.)

C. ERISA PARTIES: WHO CAN SUE?

1. ENUMERATED PARTIES

ERISA enumerates four parties as having standing to sue under Section 502(a): participants, beneficiaries, fiduciaries and the Secretary of Labor.

1. *Participant or beneficiary.* ERISA envisages that the plan participant or beneficiary will be the usual plaintiff in ERISA litigation. Under § 502(a)(1)(B), a participant or a beneficiary may sue "to recover benefits due to him under the terms of his plan," or otherwise to enforce or clarify rights under the terms of the plan. Section 502(a)(3) allows a participant or beneficiary to obtain injunctive and other equitable relief. Section 502(a)(2) authorizes a participant or beneficiary to sue to enforce § 409, which is the section imposing liability in favor of the plan for breach of the fiduciary responsibility rules. Section 502(a)(1), cross-referencing to § 502(c), allows a participant or beneficiary to recover the statutory penalty, up to $110 per day, against an administrator (the term is defined, see § 3(16)(A)) who willfully denies information that the participant or beneficiary is entitled to obtain. Section 3(7) defines "participant" and § 3(8) defines "beneficiary."

Does a spouse who is not named as a beneficiary of a plan have standing? In Sladek v. Bell System Management Pension Plan, 880 F.2d 972 (7th Cir.1989), the employee spouse elected as the mode of distribution of his pension proceeds a single-life annuity, which would cease on his death without providing survivor's coverage for his spouse. (The case arose prior to REA, which amended ERISA in 1984 to prevent the employee spouse from making such an election without the consent of the nonemployee spouse; see Chapter 7, supra.) The nonemployee spouse sued, alleging that her husband was so afflicted with Alzheimer's disease at the time he made the election that he lacked capacity to make a valid election. The Seventh Circuit held that she had standing as a "beneficiary" to bring this claim, because the plan's default rule treated the employee as having elected a joint and survivor annuity for himself and his spouse unless he elected the single life-annuity. The Seventh Circuit has applied the same reasoning to ex-spouses, holding in Riordan v. Commonwealth Edison Co., 128 F.3d 549 (7th Cir.1997), that an ex-spouse, who had been named as a plan beneficiary pursuant to a separation order and who claimed that a subsequent election of the participant's new spouse as beneficiary was void, was "just as much a potential beneficiary" as the nonemployee spouse in *Sladek*. However, where a spouse is not named as a beneficiary, some courts have refused to find standing. See Weinreb v. Hospital for Joint Diseases Orthopaedic Inst., 285 F.Supp.2d 382 (S.D.N.Y.2003), aff'd, 404 F.3d 167 (2d Cir.2005) (determining that a widow of a beneficiary lacked standing to make a claim for life insurance benefits in her individual capacity, because she was never designated as a beneficiary).

Similarly, children not actually named as beneficiaries have frequently been denied standing. See, e.g., Coleman v. Champion Int'l Corp., 992 F.2d 530 (5th Cir.1993) (son not designated as beneficiary claimed that plan administrator had failed to send required notices, thereby preventing his father from exercising his options to make the son the beneficiary under the plan; held, son did not have standing to recover his father's pension); Weber v. Damin Sales, 106 F.Supp.2d 459 (E.D.N.Y.2000) (children not named as beneficiaries had no standing to seek disability benefits and damages for period preceding death of their father).

For a more recent decision denying standing to children not named as beneficiaries, see A.J. v. UNUM, 696 F.3d 788 (8th Cir. 2012). In *A.J.*, the plan provided that if a participant did not name a beneficiary UNUM could pay the benefits to the estate or the participant's children. The estate filed a claim for life insurance benefits, which UNUM denied on the ground that the participant contributed to his death. The estate, of which the children were the sole beneficiaries, did not appeal the benefit denial. The children sued Unum for wrongful denial of benefits and breach of the policy. The Eighth Circuit affirmed the district court's dismissal of the claim for lack of standing. It rejected the argument that the children were beneficiaries because they "may become entitled" to benefits, finding that "[t]he estate's decision not to appeal precludes the children from having a reasonable or colorable claim to benefits." Id. at 790.

It is common for health care service providers to obtain an assignment of benefits from a patient before extending care. (The antiassignment or antialienation rule of ERISA § 206(d)(1) applies only to pension benefits, not to benefits under a welfare benefit plan.) There is a split of authority on the question of whether the assignee has the "derivative standing" that the participant would have had. Cases so holding include City of Hope National Medical Center v. Healthplus, Inc., 156 F.3d 223 (1st Cir.1998) and Cagle v. Bruner, 112 F.3d 1510 (11th

Cir.1997). By contrast, the Third Circuit has argued that "Congress simply made no provision [in § 502(a)(1)(B)] for persons other than participants and beneficiaries to sue, including persons purporting to sue on their behalf." Northeast Dept. ILGWU Health & Welfare Fund v. Teamsters Local Union No. 229 Welfare Fund, 764 F.2d 147, 154 n. 6 (3d Cir.1985). Can you answer the Third Circuit's argument? Note that the plan itself may preclude assignment, and such provisions have generally been upheld. See Long Beach Memorial Medical Center v. California Mart Employee Benefit Plan, 172 F.3d 57 (9th Cir.1999); Davidowitz v. Delta Dental Plan, Inc., 946 F.2d 1476 (9th Cir.1991).

In Eden Surgical Ctr. v. Rudolph Foods Co., Inc., 420 Fed. Appx. 696 (9th Cir. Mar. 9, 2011), the Ninth Circuit ruled that an assignment to a health care provider to pursue "any legal process, necessary to collect claims" did not confer standing to seek statutory penalties from a plan for failing to disclose documents required to be provided under ERISA. Although the dissent viewed "[t]he rights to seek disclosure of information under ERISA and to sue for an administrator's failure to disclose [to be] part of the legal process by which ERISA plan participants appeal their denied benefit claims," the majority did not view the action as a process "necessary to collect claims." Id. at 697–98. Similarly, in several other recent cases, courts have held that assignment language was insufficient to confer ERISA standing. See Middlesex Surgery Center v. Horizon, 2013 U.S. Dist. LEXIS 27542, 10–11 (D.N.J. Feb. 28, 2013) (finding that the language in question could be read merely as a "grant of a power of attorney for the limited purposes of allowing [Middlesex] to represent the patient-insured in appealing the Fund's decision"); MHA LLC v. Aetna Health Inc., 2013 U.S. Dist. LEXIS 25743 (D.N.J. Feb. 25, 2013) (language in question merely authorizes an insurer to make payments to Meadowlands directly rather than through the patient as an intermediary). See also Medicomp, Inc. v. United Healthcare Ins. Co., 562 Fed. Appx. 754 (11th Cir. Apr. 1, 2014) (the mere possibility of direct payment for medical services, without an actual assignment, is insufficient to establish standing to sue).

Does the heir of a beneficiary have standing to claim the beneficiary's rights under a plan? ERISA § 3(8) makes no express provision for an heir of a beneficiary. Nonetheless, in Yarde v. Pan Amer. Life Ins. Co., 67 F.3d 298 (4th Cir.1995)(unpublished opinion), the Fourth Circuit held that the sole heir of the deceased beneficiary of a life insurance policy had standing, stating that "an insurance company should not be allowed to deny [benefits] merely because the participant and beneficiary of the [plan] have died."

2. *Former participants.* ERISA § 3(7) defines "participant" as "any employee or former employee [who] is or may become eligible to receive a benefit" from a plan. In Firestone Tire & Rubber Co. v. Bruch, 489 U.S. 101, 116–17 (1989), the Supreme Court interpreted § 3(7) to include "either 'employees in, or reasonably expected to be in, currently covered employment,' or former employees who 'have [a] reasonable expectation of returning to covered employment' or who have 'a colorable claim' to vested benefits."

The Supreme Court further explained in *Firestone*, that "[i]n order to establish that he or she 'may become eligible' for benefits, a claimant must have a colorable claim that (1) he or she will prevail in a suit for benefits, or that (2) eligibility requirements will be fulfilled in the future." 489 U.S. at 117–18. In that case, Firestone, as plan administrator, determined that the plaintiffs, former employees, were not entitled to benefits under Firestone's severance pay plan. The plaintiffs asked the court to impose the discretionary $100-per-day liability under ERISA § 502(c) for refusing to give them information they sought as participants. The Third Circuit was prepared to allow anyone "who claims to be a participant or beneficiary" to sue under § 502(c). The Supreme Court rejected this reading, saying that "it strays far from the statutory language. Congress did not say that all 'claimants' could receive information about benefit plans. To say that a 'participant' is any person who claims to be one begs the question of who is a 'participant' and renders the definition set forth in § [3(7)] superfluous." Id. at 117. Courts in all circuits have applied this two-part framework for determining standing.

Since the test for whether a former participant has standing is whether the former participant has a colorable claim to vested benefits, a former employee who has received all benefits to which he or she is entitled has no standing. In Kuntz v. Reese, 785 F.2d 1410 (9th Cir.1986), cert. denied, 479 U.S. 916 (1986), the issue was whether former employees who had already received lump sum distribution of their vested benefits had standing to sue for breaches of fiduciary duty committed while they were participants. Reversing itself and vacating an earlier reported opinion, the Ninth Circuit panel decided that a former employee did not qualify under the definition of participant as a person "eligible to receive a benefit." ERISA § 3(7). The court reasoned: "Because, if successful, the plaintiffs' claim would result in a damage award, not in an increase of vested benefits, they are not plan participants." 785 F.2d at 1411. A contrary holding, the court said, "would have the effect of converting claims of all types, whether colorable or not, into 'potential benefits' within the meaning of ERISA." 785 F.2d at 1412.

Should such reasoning be used to deny standing in cases in which an employee takes early retirement, missing out on subsequently sweetened plan benefits, based on a concealment or misrepresentation by a fiduciary regarding the likelihood or character of future benefit changes? In such cases, a number of courts have held that an employee has standing to sue an employer for fraudulently inducing retirement, since the plaintiff would have been entitled to additional benefits "but for" the defendant's action. E.g., Jordan v. Tyson Foods, Inc., 257 Fed.Appx. 972, 977 (6th Cir.2007) ("if the employer's breach of fiduciary duty causes the employee to either give up his right to benefits or to fail to participate in a plan, then the employee has standing to challenge that fiduciary breach"); Vartanian v. Monsanto, 14 F.3d 697 (1st Cir.1994); Mullins v. Pfizer, Inc., 23 F.3d 663 (2d Cir.1994).

The need for a broad interpretation of "participant" in § 510 claims is illustrated by McBride v. PLM International, Inc., 179 F.3d 737, 743–44 (9th Cir.1999). McBride led an effort to oppose the termination of his employer's ESOP, including an attempt to involve the Department of Labor. PLM fired McBride and later terminated the ESOP, making a lump sum distribution to all participants, including McBride. McBride then filed suit against PLM, alleging a violation of ERISA § 510 and making state law claims for wrongful termination, defamation, and breach of contract. The district court dismissed the action on the basis that McBride was not a participant or beneficiary, as he had no expectation of reinstatement to a position covered by plan benefits, nor additional benefits under the plan. The Ninth Circuit reversed. Writing for the majority, Judge Trott noted that requiring that "claimants like McBride be plan participants at the time of suit would create a race to the courthouse. Standing would depend upon which event occurred first: the plan's termination, or the claimant's filing of a lawsuit. In this case, McBride alleged that his discharge was caused by his criticism of PLM's proposed ESOP termination. Ironic it would be indeed to hold that the plan's termination itself then deprived McBride of standing to sue." A similar result was reached by the Third Circuit in Graden v. Conexant Systems Inc., 496 F.3d 291, 302 (3d Cir.2007), where the court found that denying standing "would allow an employer who had mismanaged individual account plan assets to avoid liability by cashing out the participants."

Is the policy-based approach of the court in *McBride* and *Graden* consistent with the literalist interpretation of ERISA § 502(a) suggested by the Supreme Court in *Russell*? See Massachusetts Mutual Life Ins. Co. v. Russell, 473 U.S. 134, 146 (1985) ("The six carefully integrated civil enforcement provisions found in [ERISA § 502(a)] provide strong evidence that Congress did not intend to authorize other remedies that it simply forgot to incorporate expressly."). In Kwatcher v. Massachusetts Serv. Employees Pension Fund, 879 F.2d 957, 965 (1st Cir.1989), the First Circuit observed that "since Congress has carefully catalogued a selected list of persons eligible to sue under ERISA, there is no plausible rationale for us gratuitously to enlarge the roster." Does the problem of former participant standing illustrate that perhaps Congress did not think through the wording of ERISA as carefully as the courts have sometimes assumed?

If *McBride* had been decided oppositely, would ERISA § 510 have been rendered inoperative? In a spirited dissent in *McBride*, Judge Beezer accused the majority of ignoring *Russell*, and he pointed out that Congress had indeed created a remedy: "[A] victim of wrongdoing who lacks standing may still indirectly seek redress through the Secretary of Labor," who is empowered to bring an action under ERISA § 502(a)(5). 179 F.3d at 752. Judge Beezer also suggested that because McBride did not have standing, there could be no preemption of his state law causes of action, and hence that McBride could bring those claims in state court, an issue that will be taken up in Chapter 17.

Comparable issues arise upon plan termination, when former employees assert claims upon residual plan assets. Compare Amalgamated Clothing & Textile Workers Union, AFL-CIO v. Murdock, 861 F.2d 1406, 1411 (9th Cir.1988) (finding that giving the participants standing was the "only means available to give effect to the goals of ERISA") with Teagardener v. Republic-Franklin Inc. Pension Plan, 909 F.2d 947 (6th Cir.1990) (participant status denied).

When a pension plan terminates, a fiduciary may purchase annuities from an insurance company for the participants. The standing of former participants to bring a claim against the former fiduciary for a breach of fiduciary duty in the event the insurance company that sold the annuities becomes insolvent is addressed supra in Chapter 6.

3. *Fiduciary.* Under § 502(a)(2), a fiduciary may sue for relief under § 409. A fiduciary may also seek equitable relief under § 502(a)(3). Persons who may not sue in a personal capacity may sue as fiduciaries. Regarding fiduciary status under ERISA, see Chapter 12, supra.

4. *DoL.* The Secretary of Labor may sue to enforce fiduciary liability under § 409, see § 502(a)(2). The Secretary may collect a variety of civil penalties assessable under § 502(c), see § 502(a)(6). The Secretary may sue to enforce certain penalties under § 406, see §§ 502(a)(6), 502(i). Section 502(h) facilitates DoL intervention by requiring that private parties serve copies of complaints (other than in actions to recover benefits) on the Secretary. Section 504 grants extensive investigative authority to the Secretary. And § 502(a)(5) grants the Secretary broad authority to seek to "enjoin any act or practice which violates any provision of this title, or [to] obtain other appropriate equitable relief [to] redress such violation or [to] enforce any provision of [Title 1 of ERISA]." Finally, § 502(*l*) allows the Secretary to assess penalties against both fiduciaries and other persons who knowingly participate in a fiduciary breach.

5. *Class Actions.* Whether an ERISA cause of action may proceed as a class action is governed by Fed. R. Civ. P. 23. Although issues regarding such certification are generally outside of the scope of this course, be aware that the Supreme Court's 2011 decision in Wal-Mart, Inc. v. Dukes, 131 S. Ct. 2541 (2011) will make it more difficult for plaintiffs to obtain class certification in ERISA actions. E.g., Matz v. Household Int'l Tax Reduction Inv. Plan, 2012 U.S. Dist. LEXIS 32412 (N.D. Ill. Mar. 12, 2012), appeal denied and dismissed 687 F.3d 824 (7th Cir. 2012) (decertifying a class in a pending ERISA action, finding that plaintiff failed to demonstrate commonality required by the Supreme Court's decision in *Wal-Mart*).

2. LARUE V. DEWOLFF, BOBERG & ASSOCIATES, INC.

552 U.S. 248 (2008).

■ JUSTICE STEVENS delivered the opinion of the Court.

In *Massachusetts Mut. Life Ins. Co. v. Russell*, 473 U.S. 134 (1985), we held that a participant in a disability plan that paid a fixed level of benefits could not bring suit under § 502(a)(2) of the Employee Retirement Income Security Act of 1974 (ERISA) to recover consequential damages arising from delay in the processing of her claim. In this case we consider whether that statutory provision authorizes a participant in a defined contribution pension plan to sue a fiduciary whose alleged misconduct impaired the value of plan assets in the participant's individual account. Relying on our decision in *Russell,* the Court of Appeals for the Fourth Circuit held that § 502(a)(2) "provides remedies only for entire plans, not for individuals. . . . Recovery under this subsection must 'inure[ ] to the benefit of the plan *as a whole,*' not to particular persons with rights under the plan." While language in our *Russell* opinion is consistent with that conclusion, the rationale for *Russell's* holding supports the opposite result in this case.

I

Petitioner filed this action in 2004 against his former employer, DeWolff, Boberg & Associates (DeWolff), and the ERISA-regulated 401(k) retirement savings plan administered by DeWolff (Plan). The Plan permits participants to direct the investment of their contributions in accordance with specified procedures and requirements. Petitioner alleged that in 2001 and 2002 he directed DeWolff to make certain changes to the investments in his individual account, but DeWolff never carried out these directions. Petitioner claimed that this omission "depleted" his interest in the Plan by approximately $150,000, and amounted to a breach of fiduciary duty under ERISA. The complaint sought " 'make-whole' or other equitable relief as allowed by [§ 502(a)(3)]," as well as "such other and further relief as the court deems just and proper."

Respondents filed a motion for judgment on the pleadings, arguing that the complaint was essentially a claim for monetary relief that is not recoverable under § 502(a)(3). Petitioner countered that he "d[id] not wish for the court to award him any money, but . . . simply want[ed] the plan to properly reflect that which would be his interest in the plan, but for the breach of fiduciary duty." The District Court concluded, however, that since respondents did not possess any disputed funds that rightly belonged to petitioner, he was seeking damages rather than equitable relief available under § 502(a)(3). Assuming, *arguendo,* that respondents had breached a fiduciary duty, the District Court nonetheless granted their motion.

On appeal petitioner argued that he had a cognizable claim for relief under §§ 502(a)(2) and 502(a)(3) of ERISA. The Court of Appeals stated that petitioner had raised his § 502(a)(2) argument for the first time on appeal, but nevertheless rejected it on the merits.

Section 502(a)(2) provides for suits to enforce the liability-creating provisions of § 409, concerning breaches of fiduciary duties that harm plans. The Court of Appeals cited language from our opinion in *Russell* suggesting that these provisions "protect the entire plan, rather than the rights of an individual beneficiary." It then characterized the remedy sought by petitioner as "personal" because he "desires recovery to be paid into his plan account, an instrument that exists specifically for his benefit," and concluded:

> "We are therefore skeptical that plaintiff's individual remedial interest can serve as a legitimate proxy for the plan in its entirety, as [§ 502(a)(2)] requires. To be sure, the recovery plaintiff seeks could be seen as accruing to the plan in the narrow sense that it would be paid into plaintiff's plan *account,* which is part of the plan. But such a view finds no license in the statutory text, and threatens to undermine the careful limitations Congress has placed on the scope of ERISA relief."

The Court of Appeals also rejected petitioner's argument that the make-whole relief he sought was "equitable" within the meaning of

§ 502(a)(3). Although our grant of certiorari encompassed the § 502(a)(3) issue, we do not address it because we conclude that the Court of Appeals misread § 502(a)(2).

II

As the case comes to us we must assume that respondents breached fiduciary obligations defined in § 409(a), and that those breaches had an adverse impact on the value of the plan assets in petitioner's individual account. Whether petitioner can prove those allegations and whether respondents may have valid defenses to the claim are matters not before us.[3] Although the record does not reveal the relative size of petitioner's account, the legal issue under § 502(a)(2) is the same whether his account includes 1% or 99% of the total assets in the plan.

As we explained in *Russell,* and in more detail in our later opinion in *Varity Corp. v. Howe,* 516 U.S. 489 (1996), § 502(a) of ERISA identifies six types of civil actions that may be brought by various parties. The second, which is at issue in this case, authorizes the Secretary of Labor as well as plan participants, beneficiaries, and fiduciaries, to bring actions on behalf of a plan to recover for violations of the obligations defined in § 409(a). The principal statutory duties imposed on fiduciaries by that section "relate to the proper management, administration, and investment of fund assets," with an eye toward ensuring that "the benefits authorized by the plan" are ultimately paid to participants and beneficiaries. *Russell,* 473 U.S., at 142; see also *Varity,* 516 U.S., at 511–512 (noting that § 409's fiduciary obligations "relat[e] to the plan's financial integrity" and "reflec[t] a special congressional concern about plan asset management"). The misconduct alleged by the petitioner in this case falls squarely within that category.[4]

The misconduct alleged in *Russell,* by contrast, fell outside this category. The plaintiff in *Russell* received all of the benefits to which she was contractually entitled, but sought consequential damages arising from a delay in the processing of her claim. In holding that § 502(a)(2) does not provide a remedy for this type of injury, we stressed that the text of § 409(a) characterizes the relevant fiduciary relationship as one "with respect to a plan," and repeatedly identifies the "plan" as the victim of any fiduciary breach and the recipient of any relief. The legislative history likewise revealed that "the crucible of congressional concern was misuse and mismanagement of plan assets by plan administrators." Finally, our review of ERISA as a whole confirmed that §§ 502(a)(2) and

---

[3] For example, we do not decide whether petitioner made the alleged investment directions in accordance with the requirements specified by the Plan, whether he was required to exhaust remedies set forth in the Plan before seeking relief in federal court pursuant to § 502(a)(2), or whether he asserted his rights in a timely fashion.

[4] The record does not reveal whether the alleged $150,000 injury represents a decline in the value of assets that DeWolff should have sold or an increase in the value of assets that DeWolff should have purchased. Contrary to respondents' argument, however, § 502(a)(2) encompasses appropriate claims for "lost profits." Under the common law of trusts, which informs our interpretation of ERISA's fiduciary duties, see *Varity,* 516 U.S., at 496–497, trustees are "chargeable with . . . any profit which would have accrued to the trust estate if there had been no breach of trust," including profits forgone because the trustee "fails to purchase specific property which it is his duty to purchase." 1 Restatement (Second) Trusts § 205, and Comment *i,* § 211 (1957); see also 3 A. Scott, Law on Trusts §§ 205, 211 (3d ed.1967).

409 protect "the financial integrity of the plan," whereas other provisions specifically address claims for benefits. We therefore concluded:

> "A fair contextual reading of the statute makes it abundantly clear that its draftsmen were primarily concerned with the possible misuse of plan assets, and with remedies that would protect the entire plan, rather than with the rights of an individual beneficiary."

Russell's emphasis on protecting the "entire plan" from fiduciary misconduct reflects the former landscape of employee benefit plans. That landscape has changed.

Defined contribution plans dominate the retirement plan scene today. In contrast, when ERISA was enacted, and when *Russell* was decided, "the [defined benefit] plan was the norm of American pension practice." J. Langbein, S. Stabile, & B. Wolk, Pension and Employee Benefit Law 58 (4th ed.2006); see also Zelinsky, The Defined Contribution Paradigm, 114 Yale L.J. 451, 471 (2004) (discussing the "significant reversal of historic patterns under which the traditional defined benefit plan was the dominant paradigm for the provision of retirement income"). Unlike the defined contribution plan in this case, the disability plan at issue in *Russell* did not have individual accounts; it paid a fixed benefit based on a percentage of the employee's salary.

The "entire plan" language in *Russell* speaks to the impact of § 409 on plans that pay defined benefits. Misconduct by the administrators of a defined benefit plan will not affect an individual's entitlement to a defined benefit unless it creates or enhances the risk of default by the entire plan. It was that default risk that prompted Congress to require defined benefit plans (but not defined contribution plans) to satisfy complex minimum funding requirements, and to make premium payments to the Pension Benefit Guaranty Corporation for plan termination insurance.

For defined contribution plans, however, fiduciary misconduct need not threaten the solvency of the entire plan to reduce benefits below the amount that participants would otherwise receive. Whether a fiduciary breach diminishes plan assets payable to all participants and beneficiaries, or only to persons tied to particular individual accounts, it creates the kind of harms that concerned the draftsmen of § 409. Consequently, our references to the "entire plan" in *Russell,* which accurately reflect the operation of § 409 in the defined benefit context, are beside the point in the defined contribution context.

Other sections of ERISA confirm that the "entire plan" language from *Russell,* which appears nowhere in § 409 or § 502(a)(2), does not apply to defined contribution plans. Most significant is § 404(c), which exempts fiduciaries from liability for losses caused by participants' exercise of control over assets in their individual accounts. See also 29 CFR § 2550.404c–1 (2007). This provision would serve no real purpose if, as respondents argue, fiduciaries never had any liability for losses in an individual account.

We therefore hold that although § 502(a)(2) does not provide a remedy for individual injuries distinct from plan injuries, that provision does authorize recovery for fiduciary breaches that impair the value of plan assets in a participant's individual account. Accordingly, the judgment of the Court of Appeals is vacated, and the case is remanded for further proceedings consistent with this opinion.[6]

■ CHIEF JUSTICE ROBERTS, with whom JUSTICE KENNEDY joins, concurring in part and concurring in the judgment.

[LaRue's] right to direct the investment of his contributions was a right granted and governed by the plan. In this action, he seeks the benefits that would otherwise be due him if, as alleged, the plan carried out his investment instruction. LaRue's claim, therefore, is a claim for benefits that turns on the application and interpretation of the plan terms, specifically those governing investment options and how to exercise them.

It is at least arguable that a claim of this nature properly lies only under § 502(a)(1)(B) of ERISA. That provision allows a plan participant or beneficiary "to recover benefits due to him under the terms of his plan, to enforce his rights under the terms of the plan, or to clarify his rights to future benefits under the terms of the plan." It is difficult to imagine a more accurate description of LaRue's claim. . . .

If LaRue may bring his claim under § 502(a)(1)(B), it is not clear that he may do so under § 502(a)(2) as well. Section 502(a)(2) provides for "appropriate" relief. Construing the same term in a parallel ERISA provision, we have held that relief is not "appropriate" under § 502(a)(3) if another provision, such as § 502(a)(1)(B), offers an adequate remedy. See *Varity Corp. v. Howe,* 516 U.S. 489 (1996). . . .

The significance of the distinction between a § 502(a)(1)(B) claim and one under § 502(a)(2) is not merely a matter of picking the right provision to cite in the complaint. Allowing a § 502(a)(1)(B) action to be recast as one under § 502(a)(2) might permit plaintiffs to circumvent safeguards for plan administrators that have developed under § 502(a)(1)(B). Among these safeguards is the requirement, recognized by almost all the Courts of Appeals that a participant exhaust the administrative remedies mandated by ERISA § 503, before filing suit under § 502(a)(1)(B). Equally significant, this Court has held that ERISA plans may grant administrators and fiduciaries discretion in determining benefit eligibility and the meaning of plan terms, decisions that courts may review only for an abuse of discretion. *Firestone Tire & Rubber Co. v. Bruch,* 489 U.S. 101, 115 (1989).

These safeguards encourage employers and others to undertake the voluntary step of providing medical and retirement benefits to plan participants, see *Aetna Health Inc. v. Davila,* 542 U.S. 200, 215 (2004), and have no doubt engendered substantial reliance interests on the part of plans and fiduciaries. Allowing what is really a claim for benefits under a plan to be brought as a claim for breach of fiduciary duty under § 502(a)(2), rather than as a claim for benefits due "under the terms of

---

[6]   After our grant of certiorari respondents filed a motion to dismiss the writ, contending that the case is moot because petitioner is no longer a participant in the Plan. While his withdrawal of funds from the Plan may have relevance to the proceedings on remand, we denied their motion because the case is not moot. A plan "participant," as defined by § 3(7) of ERISA, may include a former employee with a colorable claim for benefits.

[the] plan," § 502(a)(1)(B), may result in circumventing such plan terms. . . .

[I] see nothing in today's opinion precluding the lower courts on remand, if they determine that the argument is properly before them, from considering the contention that LaRue's claim may proceed only under § 502(a)(1)(B). In any event, other courts in other cases remain free to consider what we have not—what effect the availability of relief under § 502(a)(1)(B) may have on a plan participant's ability to proceed under § 502(a)(2).

■ JUSTICE THOMAS, with whom JUSTICE SCALIA joins, concurring in the judgment.

I agree with the Court that petitioner alleges a cognizable claim under § 502(a)(2), but it is ERISA's text and not "the kind of harms that concerned [ERISA's] draftsmen" that compels my decision. . . .

Although I agree with the majority's holding, I write separately because my reading of §§ 409 and 502(a)(2) is not contingent on trends in the pension plan market. Nor does it depend on the ostensible "concerns" of ERISA's drafters. Rather, my conclusion that petitioner has stated a cognizable claim flows from the unambiguous text of §§ 409 and 502(a)(2) as applied to defined contribution plans. . . .

The plain text of § 409(a), which uses the term "plan" five times, leaves no doubt that § 502(a)(2) authorizes recovery only for the plan. Likewise, Congress' repeated use of the word "any" in § 409(a) clarifies that the key factor is whether the alleged losses can be said to be losses "to the plan," not whether they are otherwise of a particular nature or kind. On their face, §§ 409(a) and 502(a)(2) permit recovery of *all* plan losses caused by a fiduciary breach.

The question presented here, then, is whether the losses to petitioner's individual 401(k) account resulting from respondents' alleged breach of their fiduciary duties were losses "to the plan." In my view they were, because the assets allocated to petitioner's individual account were plan assets. . . .

[Because] a defined contribution plan is essentially the sum of its parts, losses attributable to the account of an individual participant are necessarily "losses to the plan" for purposes of § 409(a). Accordingly, when a participant sustains losses to his individual account as a result of a fiduciary breach, the plan's aggregate assets are likewise diminished by the same amount, and § 502(a)(2) permits that participant to recover such losses on behalf of the plan.

NOTES

1.   *Individual vs. plan relief.* Prior to the Supreme Court's decision in *LaRue*, some courts read *Russell* as precluding relief to participants for losses to their defined contribution plan accounts attributable to fiduciary breaches. For example, in Milofsky v. American Airlines, Inc., 404 F.3d 338 (5th Cir.2005), the Fifth Circuit held that a plaintiff lacked standing to seek relief under ERISA 502(a)(2) in a claim relating to an individual account plan where the plaintiff was not seeking planwide relief. The court held that "this suit concerns individualized relief for the particularized harm suffered by a

subset of plan participants and does not seek to vindicate the rights or interests of the plan as a whole." On rehearing, the Fifth Circuit reversed itself, deciding that the plaintiffs were entitled to further development of their fiduciary claims. 442 F.3d 311 (5th Cir.2006).

The Court's decision in *LaRue* recognizes the difference between defined contribution and defined benefit plans; in a defined contribution plan, damage to a participant's individual account is damage to the plan. The "entire plan" language of *Russell* simply does not accurately reflect the reality of defined contribution plans. In the wake of *LaRue*, courts are consistent in holding that "participants in defined-contribution plans may use § 502(a)(2), and thus § 409(a), to obtain relief if losses to an account are attributable to a pension plan fiduciary's breach of a duty owed to the plan." Rogers v. Baxter International, Inc., 521 F.3d 702 (7th Cir.2008).

2. *State causes of action and preemption.* If a cause of action under ERISA does not provide an adequate remedy, might there be a cause of action under state law that does? This raises the vexing issue of ERISA preemption, which is discussed in detail in Chapter 17, infra. For now we note that the Supreme Court has clearly stated that "ERISA pre-empts state laws that [provide] alternative enforcement mechanisms." New York State Conference of Blue Cross & Blue Shield Plans v. Travelers Ins. Co., 514 U.S. 645, 646 (1995). Nevertheless, a few courts have been willing to permit state causes of action in this context.

For example, a participant covered by an employer's health plan hides his divorce from the plan. His ex-wife incurs significant medical expenses, which the plan dutifully pays. In Trustees of AFTRA Health Fund v. Biondi, 303 F.3d 765 (7th Cir.2002), the Seventh Circuit held that the plan's state common law fraud claim against the participant is not preempted. "It would, in our opinion, elevate 'uncritical literalism' to a new level to characterize the Trustees' common law fraud claim as an 'alternative enforcement mechanism' of ERISA when ERISA's civil enforcement provisions neither address nor provide a remedy for situations where an employee benefit trust fund has been defrauded by a non-fiduciary." Id. at 782.

3. *Interest.* Although ERISA is silent on the issue of prejudgment interest, the lower courts have generally concluded that prejudgment interest is available in the discretion of the court. In Dunnigan v. Metropolitan Life Ins. Co., 277 F.3d 223, 229 (2d Cir.2002), the Second Circuit rejected the argument that interest may never be awarded as an equitable remedy under § 502(a)(3), holding that an award of interest in circumstances when benefits are paid after the date on which a beneficiary is entitled to receive them "serves as an equitable make-whole remedy." Similarly, in Fotta v. Trustees of the United Mine Workers of America, Health and Retirement Fund of 1974, 165 F.3d 209, 213 (3d Cir.1998), the Third Circuit held that a "claim for interest is appropriately raised under § 502(a)(3)(B)" because it serves to "prevent unjust enrichment," even when the delayed benefits were paid prior to the lawsuit and the suit is solely to obtain interest. The D.C. Circuit has gone further, suggesting that prejudgment interest is "presumptively appropriate." Moore v. CapitalCare, Inc., 461 F.3d 1 (D.C.Cir.2006). Are these cases consistent with *Great-West*, which disregarded the unjust enrichment resulting from failure to enforce the plan's subrogation clause?

Other courts that have awarded prejudgment interest have not relied on § 502(a)(3), but rather have viewed the interest as part of benefits due under § 502(a)(1)(B). See, e.g. Dobson v. Hartford Financial Services Group, Inc., 389 F.3d 386 (2d Cir.2004) (holding that the terms of an ERISA plan may impliedly obligate an insurer to pay interests on delayed benefits). The Sixth Circuit observed in Ford v. Uniroyal Pension Plan, 154 F.3d 613, 618 (6th Cir.1998), that "awards of prejudgment interest pursuant to [§ 502(a)(1)(B)] . . . simply compensate a beneficiary for the lost interest value of money wrongfully withheld from him or her." But see Devito v. Pension Plan of Local 819 I.B.T. Pension Fund, 975 F.Supp. 258 (S.D.N.Y.1997)(claim of extracontractual interest is not permitted under § 502(a)(1)(B)).

Courts use different standards to calculate awards of prejudgment interest. Any reasonable means of calculation should be permissible, so long as the award is not punitive. In Rybarczyk v. TRW, Inc., 235 F.3d 975, 981 (6th Cir. 2000), the Sixth Circuit adopted the unusual approach of awarding an amount equal to the greater of the fifty-two week Treasury bill rate or "interest equal to the rate of return actually earned on the principal amount of the underpayment during the prejudgment period." Why might such an approach be appealing? In Holmes v. Pension Plan of Bethlehem Steel Corp., 213 F.3d 124, 132 (3d Cir.2000), the Third Circuit rejected the "greater of" approach, noting that "any return the Plan realized in excess of the risk-free yield on Treasury Bills [would] be the result of the Plan's investment expertise and labor, as well as additional risk that the Plan, not Appellants, bore." See Michael D. Grabhorn, ERISA & Prejudgment Interest: Calculating Interest in the Wake of Rybarczyk, 41 Brandeis L.J. 659 (2003).

4. *Statutory penalty*. ERISA § 502(c), as amended, authorizes a statutory penalty, in the court's discretion, of up to $110 per day on an administrator who fails to comply with a request for information that the administrator is required to furnish to a participant or beneficiary. The penalty is payable to the participant or beneficiary who requested the information. Although necessarily extracontractual, the penalty is expressly authorized by statute and recoverable under ERISA § 502(a)(1). One way to view the $110 per day penalty of ERISA § 502(c) is as a species of statutorily liquidated punitive damages. In Faircloth v. Lundy Packing Co., 91 F.3d 648, 659 (4th Cir.1996), the Fourth Circuit noted that "[t]he purpose of § 502(c)(1) is not to compensate participants for injuries, but to punish noncompliance with ERISA. Accordingly, prejudice to the party requesting the documents is not a prerequisite to the imposition of penalties. But prejudice is a factor that a district court may consider in deciding whether to impose a penalty. The district court may also consider whether the administrator acted in bad faith."

3. NONENUMERATED PARTIES.

1. *The plan*. Section 409 creates liability to the plan. Section 502(d)(1) endows a plan with the capacity to "sue or be sued [as] an entity." However, § 502(a) by its terms authorizes only participants, beneficiaries, fiduciaries, and the Secretary of Labor, to bring the various civil actions to enforce § 409 and otherwise to redress or prevent breach. May a plan or fund sue under § 502(a)? Most courts have read the statute literally and held that plans do not have standing to sue. See Flynn v. Anthony Mion & Son, 112 Fed.Appx. 101 (2d Cir.2004); Local 159, 342,

343 & 444 v. Nor-Cal Plumbing, Inc., 185 F.3d 978 (9th Cir.1999); but see Louisiana Bricklayers & Trowel Trades Pension Fund & Welfare Fund v. Alfred Miller Gen. Masonry Contracting Co., 157 F.3d 404, 406 n. 3 (5th Cir.1998) (treating ERISA action brought by benefit plan as action brought by plan's trustees).

2. *Labor unions.* Does a labor union, which is neither a participant nor a beneficiary, have standing to sue on behalf of the plan participants? Although not an enumerated party, some courts have permitted a union to bring suit on behalf of its members who are participants in the plan. See Southern Ill. Carpenters Welfare Fund v. Carpenters Welfare Fund of Ill., 326 F.3d 919 (7th Cir.2003)(Congress did not intend to prevent union from suing on behalf of plan participants, who are the real "plaintiffs in interest").

3. *Employers.* Most courts have held that an employer does not have standing to sue under ERISA in its capacity as employer. E.g., Jamail, Inc. v. Carpenters Dist. Council of Houston Pension & Welfare Trusts, 954 F.2d 299 (5th Cir.1992). However, an employer that serves as a plan fiduciary may sue in that capacity. See Coyne & Delany Co. v. Selman, 98 F.3d 1457 (4th Cir.1996).

Should an employer be able to recover a mistaken overpayment of plan contributions? Compare Award Service v. Northern California Retail Clerks Unions & Food Employers Joint Pension Trust Fund, 763 F.2d 1066 (9th Cir. 1985) finding that employer has an implied right of action under ERISA to recover overpayments with Plucinski v. I.A.M. National Pension Fund, 875 F.2d 1052 (3d Cir.1989).

D. NONFIDUCIARY LIABILITY

1. *Impact of* Mertens*: What* Mertens *did not decide.* In *Mertens*, reproduced in Section B, supra, the plaintiffs were suing the actuary that had provided services to the plan. Chapter 12, supra, reviews the authorities that make it difficult to treat a service provider, especially an actuary, as an ERISA fiduciary. In *Mertens*, the plaintiffs sought to attach nonfiduciary liability. Notice that *Mertens* involved the terminated plan of a failed employer; there was no prospect of a significant recovery from the employer. The actuary, by contrast, was solvent.

ERISA § 502(a)(3) authorizes a participant, beneficiary, or fiduciary to sue "(A) to enjoin any act or practice which violates any provision of [ERISA's Title 1] or the terms of the plan, or (B) to obtain *other appropriate equitable relief* (i) to redress such violations or (ii) to enforce [ERISA] or the terms of the plan" (emphasis supplied). *Mertens* holds, by a 5–4 margin, that the phrase "other appropriate equitable relief" in § 502(a)(3) does not authorize a suit for *money damages* against a *nonfiduciary* who allegedly participated knowingly in a fiduciary's breach of duty.

There are two components to the issue in *Mertens*: whether damages constitute equitable relief (the issue addressed in Section B supra), and if so, whether such relief can be had from a nonfiduciary. The case was fought essentially on the ground that divided the majority and the dissenters, that is, whether damages can be fairly characterized as equitable relief. The majority records its irritation with having to "decide this case on the narrow battlefield that the parties have chosen." The majority observes that "no provision [of ERISA] explicitly requires [nonfiduciaries] to avoid participation (knowing or unknowing) in a fiduciary's breach of fiduciary duty. It is unlikely, moreover, that this was an oversight, since ERISA *does* explicitly impose 'knowing participation' liability on cofiduciaries [under] § 405(a)." Thus, the opinion in *Mertens* carefully reserved for future decision the question of whether nonfiduciary liability would lie in an action other than for money damages, although the majority hinted in the dicta just quoted that such an action might not lie.

2.   *Extending Mertens.* In Reich v. Rowe, 20 F.3d 25 (1st Cir.1994), the First Circuit took the hint from *Mertens* and held that ERISA provides no remedy against a nonfiduciary for knowing participation in a fiduciary breach. "All things considered, judicial remedies for nonfiduciary participation in a fiduciary breach fall within the line of cases where Congress deliberately omitted a potential cause of action rather than the cases where Congress has invited the courts to engage in interstitial lawmaking." Id. at 31. The court expressed special concern to spare actuaries, lawyers, accountants and consultants from the threat of ERISA litigation. "We do not mean to countenance the action of someone who advises a fiduciary to break the law, but we are concerned that extending the threat of liability over the heads of those who only lend professional services to a plan without exercising any control over, or transacting with, plan assets will deter such individuals from helping fiduciaries navigate the intricate financial and legal thickets of ERISA." The court recognized that its "decision to limit liability for nonfiduciaries may provide less protection than existed before ERISA was enacted and that the decision may appear contrary to ERISA's purpose of protecting the interests of plan participants and beneficiaries," but the court attributed this result to congressional line drawing. "Congress decided that the best approach was to limit liability for nonfiduciaries, especially service providers, while at the same time increasing the number of fiduciary parties and the scope of fiduciary responsibility. See *Mertens.*" Id. at 32–33. Other circuits came to the same conclusion. Reich v. Continental Casualty Co., 33 F.3d 754 (7th Cir.1994); Reich v. Compton, 57 F.3d 270 (3d Cir.1995).

3.   *The protective policy.* The dissenters in *Mertens* drew upon language from Firestone Tire & Rubber Co. v. Bruch, 489 U.S. 101 (1989), reproduced in Chapter 15, supra, that in construing ERISA "we are guided by principles of trust law"; and that, on account of ERISA's protective purpose, the statute ought not to be construed to "afford less protection to employees and their beneficiaries than they enjoyed before ERISA was enacted." Accordingly, the dissent reasoned, since conventional trust law allows the plaintiff to sue a nonfiduciary who knowingly participates in the trustee's breach of trust, the ERISA plaintiff ought to have a similar cause of action. On what grounds might this analogy to private trust law be resisted?

4.   *State law remedies against nonfiduciaries.* If ERISA provides no remedy against nonfiduciaries who participate in fiduciary breaches, are there potential state law remedies that are not preempted? Although the

majority in *Mertens* declined to decide whether "previously available state court actions" against a nonfiduciary are preempted by ERISA, the dissenters remarked in a footnote that "it is difficult to imagine how any common-law remedy for the harm alleged here—participation in a breach of fiduciary duty concerning an ERISA-governed plan—could have survived enactment of ERISA's 'deliberately expansive' preemption provision."

Suppose the actuary in *Mertens* had been negligent in performing its duties and that when the plan trustees discovered the negligence they sued the actuary for professional malpractice under state law. Would the dissenters in *Mertens* treat such a suit as preempted? As will be discussed in Chapter 17, infra, the lower courts have generally held state law remedies against nonfiduciary service providers not to be preempted.

Could a participant bring an actuarial malpractice claim directly or would a participant be limited to bringing an action under ERISA § 502(a)(3) to compel the plan fiduciary to do so?

5. *Party-in-interest liability for prohibited transactions.* Although the issue before the Supreme Court in *Mertens* was only whether a nonfiduciary is liable for damages suffered as a result of a fiduciary breach, near the end of the majority's opinion in *Mertens*, the Court states that "[p]rofessional service providers such as actuaries [must] disgorge assets and profits obtained through participation as parties-in-interest in transactions prohibited by § 406." Even pre-*Mertens*, a number of courts distinguished between participation by a nonfiduciary in a fiduciary breach and participation by a nonfiduciary party in interest in a prohibited transaction, finding liability in the case of the latter, but not the former. See, e.g., Nieto v. Ecker, 845 F.2d 868 (9th Cir.1988). Most of the circuits adopted this view post-*Mertens*. However, some read *Mertens* as foreclosing such liability.

6. *Harris Trust.* In Harris Trust and Savings Bank v. Salomon Smith Barney, 530 U.S. 238 (2000), the Supreme Court resolved the above disagreement in favor of the proposition that ERISA authorizes suit under § 502(a)(3) against a nonfiduciary who "knowingly participates" in a fiduciary violation. *Harris Trust* involved a defendant, Salomon, who, though not a fiduciary, was a "party in interest" to the plan who was alleged to have participated in a prohibited transaction with the plan at the direction of a fiduciary. Nonetheless Justice Thomas's opinion did not limit the class of potential nonfiduciary "other parties" who could be sued to parties in interest. To the concern that this result might open the ERISA floodgates to suits against even innocent third parties, Justice Thomas reemphasized that the Court was merely authorizing "appropriate equitable relief":

[I]t has long been settled that when a trustee in breach of his fiduciary duty to the beneficiaries transfers trust property to a third person, the third person takes the property subject to the trust, *unless he has purchased the property for value and without notice of the fiduciary's breach of duty.* The trustee or beneficiaries may then maintain an action for restitution of the property (if not already disposed of) or disgorgement of proceeds (if already disposed of), and disgorgement of the third person's profits derived therefrom.

530 U.S. 250 (emph. added).

The implication, then, is that a nonfiduciary third party risks liability under *Harris Trust* only if the nonfiduciary's "knowingly" participates in the breach.

7.   *Fiduciary and party-in-interest liability as rationale.* Although the majority opinion in *Mertens* turned mainly upon constructional grounds, in *Harris Trust* Justice Thomas also pointed to a broader policy basis. ERISA § 3(21)(A) expands "the universe of persons subject to fiduciary duties," whereas under the original law of trusts only the trustee risked liability as a fiduciary. Further, the result of *Harris Trust* is to allow some recovery against those nonfiduciaries who come within the party-in-interest definition of § 3(14) and who participate in a prohibited transaction. These bases of liability strengthen the position of the plaintiff by comparison with the remedies available to a plaintiff under the law of trusts, and thus help explain why ERISA's drafters may have chosen not to impose liability on nonfiduciaries who are not parties-in-interest. That is, ERISA can narrow nonfiduciary liability because ERISA greatly expands fiduciary liability and party-in-interest liability. This rationale appears in *Reich v. Rowe*, in the extract supra, extending *Mertens* to exclude nonfiduciary liability.

8.   *A proposal for vicarious liability.* Professor Colleen Medill has proposed that federal courts should adopt a federal common law rule of vicarious fiduciary liability under ERISA, pursuant to which corporate principals whose employees or agents are plan fiduciaries would be held strictly liable for breaches of fiduciary duty committed in the course of their employment. She examines the theoretical, policy and statutory bases for imposing such liability in Colleen E. Medill, The Federal Common Law of Vicarious Fiduciary Liability Under ERISA, 44 Mich. J. L. Ref. 249 (2011).

E. ATTORNEY FEES UNDER ERISA

1.   *The text.* ERISA § 502(g)(1) provides: "In any action under this title . . . by a participant, beneficiary, or fiduciary, the court in its discretion may allow a reasonable attorney's fee and costs of action to either party."

This measure departs from the ordinary "American rule" against shifting the costs of litigation, yet it supplies no guidance to the court about how to exercise this discretionary power to allocate the cost of attorney fees. Accordingly, case law has had to work out the cost-shifting regime. The main source of difficulty is that ERISA's cost-shifting regime is not automatic ("the court in its discretion may allow"). The grant of discretion has been taken to mean that the statute does not contemplate routine loser-pays cost-shifting.

2.   *The five-factor test.* In an early ERISA case, Eaves v. Penn, 587 F.2d 453, 465 (10th Cir.1978), involving prevailing plaintiffs, the Tenth Circuit devised a five-factor test for "determining whether or not to award fees from the Plan fund or against the offending parties [personally.]" Versions of this test have been adopted in the other circuits. In exercising its discretion to award attorney fees, the court should consider "(1) the degree of the offending parties' culpability or bad

faith; (2) the degree of the ability of the offending parties to personally satisfy an award of attorneys fees; (3) whether or not an award of attorneys fees against the offending parties would deter other persons acting under similar circumstances; (4) the amount of benefit conferred on members of the pension plan as a whole; and (5) the relative merits of the parties' position."

The five-factor test has generated considerable litigation—not surprisingly, since it is fact-oriented and does not manifest a dominant principle. Some courts have suggested that it is an abuse of discretion to refuse to award fees when all five factors are satisfied. See First Trust Corp. v. Bryant, 410 F.3d 842 (6th Cir.2005); Chambless v. Masters, Mates & Pilots Pension Plan, 815 F.2d 869 (2d Cir.1987). The Seventh Circuit has suggested that the five-factor test is not determinative, but is merely a method of determining whether the defendant's position was substantially justified. Sullivan v. William A. Randolph, Inc., 504 F.3d 665 (7th Cir.2007).

3.   *Presumption in favor of the prevailing plaintiff?* Should there be a presumption in favor of awarding attorney fees to prevailing plaintiffs in ERISA cases, as there is in civil rights cases? In Kayes v. Pacific Lumber Co., 51 F.3d 1449, 1469 (9th Cir.1995), the Ninth Circuit held that interim attorney's fees were available under ERISA "to the extent they are available under civil rights statutes." In Reinking v. Philadelphia Am. Life Ins. Co., 910 F.2d 1210, 1218 (4th Cir.1990), the Fourth Circuit recalled the analogy to attorney fee awards under the Civil Rights Acts and concluded that the five-factor test was but a guide, a guide that should not obscure "the remedial purposes of ERISA to protect employee rights and to secure effective access to federal courts." The court held that "in order to effectuate the remedial purposes of ERISA, a prevailing individual beneficiary should ordinarily recover attorney's fees unless special circumstances would render such an award unjust." Accord, Elliot v. Fortis Benefits Ins. Co., 337 F.3d 1138, 1148 (9th Cir.2003) ("[s]uccessful plaintiffs in ERISA suits should ordinarily recover fees unless special circumstances would render such an award unjust").

Is the analogy to civil rights cases a sound one? Judge Gee argued against the analogy in Iron Workers Local No. 272 v. Bowen, 624 F.2d 1255, 1265 (5th Cir.1980): "The policies underlying ERISA are certainly important ones, but they simply do not rise to the level of assuring that all citizens are accorded their civil rights." Furthermore, "the need for attorneys' fees as an enforcement incentive is less under ERISA" because participants and beneficiaries have monetary incentives to vindicate their ERISA rights, and ERISA fiduciaries "may have a statutory duty to bring ERISA suits."

In a similar vein, Judge Posner contrasted ERISA with the Civil Rights Attorney's Fees Awards Act, whose legislative history indicates an unmistakable intent "to encourage meritorious civil rights litigation by allowing prevailing plaintiffs to obtain an award of attorney's fees almost as a matter of course but prevailing defendants only if the suit was frivolous. . . . There is nothing comparable in the legislative history of ERISA; nor do pension plan participants and beneficiaries constitute a vulnerable group whose members need special encouragement to exercise their legal rights, like a racial minority." Bittner v. Sadoff & Rudoy Industries, 728 F.2d 820, 829 (7th Cir.1984).

In evaluating Judge Posner's view that the ERISA plaintiffs are not particularly vulnerable, consider that "most participants who pursue a claim are supported by limited means." Jessica Michelle Westbrook, Resolving the Dispute Over When Attorney's Fees Should be Awarded Under ERISA in Two Words: Plaintiff Prevails, 53 Ala. L. Rev. 1311, 1321 (2002). See also Ann C. Bertino, The Need for a Mandatory Award of Attorney's Fees for Prevailing Plaintiffs in ERISA Benefits Cases, 41 Catholic U.L. Rev. 871, 884–85 (1992) (observing that "most potential plaintiffs are low-income pensioners" and commenting on the impossibility of ERISA plaintiffs retaining an attorney on a contingency fee basis). "Few would-be ERISA plaintiffs have the ability or desire to finance their own litigation, particularly in view of the fact that the magnitude of an individual's claim may well be under $50,000 or $25,000, or $10,000. Litigation fees and expenses can easily surpass the potential recovery, and it is not necessarily sensible for a would-be ERISA plaintiff to agree to finance litigation of this kind. [Given] the economics of the practice, it is difficult for claimants to find experienced counsel who are willing to take individual ERISA litigation on a contingent fee basis." Alan M. Sandals, ERISA Class Actions and Strategic Issues: The Plaintiff's Perspective, 11th Annual ERISA Litigation Conference 661, 674–75 (1998).

A prominent critique of the presumption in favor of awarding fees in ERISA cases is that of Judge Wilkinson, dissenting in Rodriguez v. MEBA Pension Trust, 956 F.2d 468, 472–73 (4th Cir.1992). He observed that because "the attorney fees will be paid from pension plan assets, the real losers [will] be the plan's intended beneficiaries. Indeed, the very prospect of automatic fee shifting in favor of prevailing plaintiffs (but not prevailing defendants) is likely to create many more lawsuits under ERISA and cause many more trust assets to be consumed in litigation costs." Judge Wilkinson also disputed the "private attorney general" analogy from civil rights law. "[T]he benefits of private suits under ERISA often flow exclusively and directly to the plaintiff, as in this case where Rodriguez sued for and received an award of pension benefits, In such cases, fee shifting is not necessary to ensure enforcement of the statute." Id. at 476. In view of Judge Wilkinson's concerns about consuming trust assets, should the standard for awarding fees differ in cases where there is no trust, such as a claim against an unfunded health plan?

In Quesinberry v. Life Ins. Co. of North America, 987 F.2d 1017 (4th Cir.1993) (en banc), the Fourth Circuit effectively overruled *Reinking*, supra. Sitting en banc, the court said that it did "not agree that *Reinking* establishes [a] presumption in favor of a prevailing insured or beneficiary, but [to] the extent that *Reinking* supports a mandatory presumption in favor of granting attorneys' fees, it is overruled." 987 F.2d at 1029–30. The court said that "the foremost principle which guides our review of attorneys' fees awards under ERISA is the discretion the statute grants to the district court." Is that a principle? Should discretion have standards? Most of the circuits have now expressly rejected any presumption in favor of the plaintiff. See Martin v. Arkansas Blue Cross and Blue Shield, 299 F.3d 966 (8th Cir.2002) (reviewing status of the law in the various circuits).

For a more recent denial of fees to a prevailing plaintiff see *Weitzenkamp v. Unum Life Ins. Co.*, 500 Fed. Appx. 506 (7th Cir. Jan. 8, 2013) (affirming district court denial of fees to prevailing plaintiff because Unum's position had a reasonable basis in law and fact and its interpretation was a literal reading of a clause in the plan that gave Unum discretion to interpret plan terms).

Although prevailing plaintiffs commonly recover attorney fees under the five-factor test, losing defendants do sometimes succeed in resisting the award, see, e.g., Davidson v. Canteen Corp., 957 F.2d 1404 (7th Cir.1992); McBride v. PLM International, Inc., 179 F.3d 737, 746 (9th Cir.1999).

4. *Fees in administrative proceedings.* As discussed in Section H, infra, ERISA requires participants to exhaust internal plan remedies before they may bring a lawsuit. Does ERISA allow the award of attorney's fees for pre-litigation administrative proceedings? The circuits have uniformly disallowed such fees. See, e.g., Hahnemann University Hospital v. All Shore, Inc., 514 F.3d 300, 313 (3d Cir.2008) (citing five circuits disallowing fees in such cases and joining their view).

5. *Awarding fees to prevailing defendants.* Section 502(g)(1) says that a court may award costs to "either party," thus allowing a court the discretion to award fees to a prevailing defendant. Although courts have historically been reluctant to award attorney's fees to prevailing defendants, e.g., Salovaara v. Eckert, 222 F.3d 19 (2d Cir.2000); Maune v. International Brotherhood of Electrical Workers, Local #1, Health and Welfare Fund, 83 F.3d 959 (8th Cir.1996), there are decisions awarding such fees, particularly when the plaintiff acted in bad faith. See, e.g., Seitzman v. Sun Life Assurance Co. of Can., 311 F.3d 477 (2d Cir.2002) (ordering plaintiff who acted in bad faith to pay defendant's attorney fees of over $100,000); Estate of Shockley v. Alyeska Pipeline Service Co., 130 F.3d 403 (9th Cir.1997) (applying the five-factor test to award ten percent of requested attorney fees to the defendant plan against an estate that sued unsuccessfully to recover survivor's benefits).

6. *Nonprevailing plaintiffs.* Should attorney fees ever be awarded to a plaintiff in a case in which the plaintiff is not the prevailing party?

Over time, a consensus developed among the courts that success in the entirety is not required, but that an award was permissible so long as the plaintiff received at least some relief on the merits of his claim.

The Supreme Court has adopted the consensus position. In Hardt v. Reliance Standard Life Ins. Co., 560 U.S. 242 (2010), the Court held that a fee claimant need not be a prevailing party to be eligible for an award of attorney's fees under § 502(g)(1). Citing its decision in Ruckelshaus v. Sierra Club, 463 U.S. 680, 694 (1983), the Court held fees and costs may be awarded so long as the fee claimant has achieved "some degree of success on the merits." In the wake of the Supreme Court's decision, several circuits have considered its effect, holding that courts must follow a two-step approach, examining first whether the fee claimant has achieved "some degree of success on the merits" and then evaluating the claim using the traditional five-factor test. See Williams v. Metro. Life

Ins. Co., 609 F.3d 622 (4th Cir.2010); Simonia v. Glendale Nissan/Infiniti Disability Plan, 608 F.3d 1118 (9th Cir.2010); Gross v. Sun Life Assur. Co., 763 F.3d 73 (1st Cir. 2014); Bender v. Newell Window Furnishings, Inc., 560 Fed. Appx. 469 (6th Cir. 2014); Temme v. Bemis Co., 762 F.3d 544 (7th Cir. 2014).

In Scarangella v. Scarangella & Sons, Inc., 731 F.3d 146 (2nd Cir.2013), a health plan was sued by its insurer. After the court granted summary judgment on the first claim, the insurer voluntarily dismissed its remaining claims. In light of *Hardt*, the Second Circuit held that the plan had obtained some degree of success on the merits on the first claim, and that "the district court erred in classifying this success on the merits as merely a procedural victory." It also found that the voluntary dismissal of the remaining claims could give rise to a claim for attorney's fees, giving this guidance on how to determine when voluntary conduct by another party should be sufficient:

> Certainly a party that obtains relief due to the voluntary conduct of another party after minimal litigation in the district court is unlikely to succeed in demonstrating that the impetus for relief was some action by the court related to the merits of the case. Where, however, the parties already have received a tentative analysis of their legal claims within the context of summary judgment, a party may be able to show that the court's discussion of the pending claims resulted in the party obtaining relief.

7.   *Computation issues.* The "lodestar" method, common in other areas in which fee shifting occurs, is also employed to compute reasonable attorney's fees in ERISA cases. See, e.g., Hahnemann University Hospital v. All Shore, Inc., 514 F.3d 300, 310 (3d Cir.2008) (describing the lodestar calculation as a "useful starting point for determining the reasonableness" of attorney's fees); Welch v. Metropolitan Life Ins. Co., 480 F.3d 942, 945–46 (9th Cir. 2007) (explaining lodestar approach). The formula takes the hours that the attorneys reasonably spent on the case, and multiplies that figure by a prevailing rate for comparable legal services in the relevant market.

Courts have discretion to make adjustments to the lodestar amount in appropriate circumstances. For example, in Brown v. Aventis Pharmaceuticals, Inc., 341 F.3d 822, 829 (8th Cir.2003), the court reduced the lodestar award "to eliminate any duplication of efforts or redundancy." In Motion Picture Industry Pension Plan v. Klages Group, 757 F.Supp. 1082 (C.D.Cal.1991), the court reduced the lodestar award because the plaintiff multiemployer plan recovered only a portion of the contributions it sought from the defendant employer. Accord Sheehan v. Metropolitan Life Ins. Co., 450 F.Supp.2d 321 (S.D.N.Y.2006) (reducing lodestar amount to reflect fact that plaintiff achieved only a partial success on his claims). Nonetheless courts treat adjustments as exceptions to be applied only in "rare and exceptional" circumstances. *Welch*, 480 F.3d at 946. Accord D'Emanuele v. Montgomery Ward & Co., Inc., 904 F.2d 1379, 1383 (9th Cir.1990) (in ERISA action, adjustments to lodestar are exception rather than rule because lodestar is presumed to be a reasonable fee). Should a plaintiff ever be awarded attorney's fees in an amount that exceeds the amount of the plaintiff's recovery? See

Maryland Electric Industry Health Fund v. Triangle Sign & Service Div., 814 F.Supp. 15 (D.Md.1993).

For a recent example of a downward adjustment of the lodestar amount, see Central Pension Fund v. Ray Haluch Gravel Co., 745 F.3d 1 (1st Cir. Mar. 11, 2014). There the First Circuit found that the federal district court did not abuse its discretion in considering proportionality as a factor in setting the fee award. Moreover, the modest size of the damage award, the disparity between the amount of the award sought and the amount received, and the lack of success in a major part of the case, justified the reduction in the lodestar amount.

In a non-ERISA case, City of Burlington v. Dague, 505 U.S. 557, 112 S.Ct. 2638 (1992), concerning an award of attorney fees under the Solid Waste Disposal Act, 42 U.S.C. § 6972(e), and the Clean Water Act, 33 U.S.C. § 1365(d), the Supreme Court held that enhancing the multiplier to reflect the risk of nonrecovery in a contingent fee case was inappropriate. The Ninth Circuit has held "that we should apply *Dague* to the ERISA fee shifting statute. Thus, the award of attorneys' fees in this case could not properly have been enhanced for contingency." Cann v. Carpenters' Pension Trust Fund for Northern California, 989 F.2d 313, 318 (9th Cir.1993). Accord, Murphy v. Reliance Standard Life Ins. Co., 247 F.3d 1313 (11th Cir.2001).

While the lodestar approach gives the court some discretion in determining the amount of fees, where the language of a plan entitles a participant to attorney fees and provides for the method of calculating fees, the amount of those fees has been held to be a matter of contract interpretation, ousting judicial discretion under ERISA's general attorney fee provision. See Bowles v. Quantum Chemical Co., 266 F.3d 622 (7th Cir.2001).

F. RIGHT TO JURY TRIAL

One of ERISA's more lamentable shortcomings is the failure of Congress to prescribe whether or not causes of action arising under the statute are meant to be triable by jury.

The question whether a federally created cause of action is triable by jury has two dimensions, constitutional and statutory. The Seventh Amendment guarantees the right to trial by jury "in suits at common law, where the value in controversy shall exceed twenty dollars." The reference to suits at common law preserves the eighteenth-century distinction between cases cognizable in the English courts of common law, where juries decided disputes of fact; and suits triable in the juryless procedure of the equity court, the chancery. When dealing with a cause of action unknown in the eighteenth century, the Supreme Court has undertaken to discern whether the particular issue resembles more closely a case at common law or in equity. This method applies to statutory causes of action.

Congress can extend the right to jury trial by statute, either expressly, or by implication. When Congress creates a cause of action without deciding whether to make it juryable, as it did in ERISA, the courts are left under the Seventh Amendment to analogize the action either to common law or to equity.

1.   *Benefit denial cases.* The circuit courts have ruled uniformly against juryability for benefit denial litigation arising under § 502(a)(1)(B). In the leading case of Wardle v. Central States, Southeast and Southwest Areas Pension Fund, 627 F.2d 820, 829 (7th Cir.1980), the Seventh Circuit noticed that pre-ERISA pension cases were typically treated as trust cases, hence equitable and nonjuryable. "Congress' silence on the jury right issue reflects an intention that suits for pension benefits by disappointed applicants are equitable. Such suits under the law of trusts have existed for quite a while in state courts and have been entertained in federal courts under their diversity jurisdiction. These suits have been considered equitable in character." See, e.g., Vegter v. Canada Life Assurance Co., 311 Fed.Appx. 248 (11th Cir.2009) (no right to jury trial for claim for denial of disability benefits, which is equitable in nature); DeLong v. Aetna Life Ins. Co., 232 Fed.Appx. 190, 193 n.3 (3d Cir.2007) (claim for benefits is equitable in nature); Adams v. Cyprus Amax Minerals Co., 149 F.3d 1156 (10th Cir.1998)(plaintiffs have no entitlement to benefits unless and until a court exercises its equitable powers to declare them eligible beneficiaries and orders the fiduciary to pay benefits, thus making "their claim for monetary damages . . . inextricably tied with equitable relief").

Although a pure ERISA benefits claim is not juryable, some courts have permitted jury trials in so-called "hybrid" actions brought under both § 301 of the Labor Management Relations Act (LMRA) and ERISA. Section 301 of the LMRA allows suits for violations of collective bargaining agreements. In Chauffeurs, Teamsters and Helpers, Local 391 v. Terry, 494 U.S. 558 (1990), the Supreme Court concluded that a jury trial right exists in some situations under § 301. In *Terry*, the relief sought was back pay, which the court, after reviewing the eighteenth century sources, concluded was legal in nature. In Senn v. United Dominion Industries, Inc., 951 F.2d 806 (7th Cir.1992), retirees brought an action under LMRA § 301 and ERISA §§ 502(a)(1)(B) and 502(a)(3) against their former employer alleging entitlement to lifetime welfare benefits and seeking prospective injunctive relief and damages for the employer's prior refusal to pay for the benefits. Relying on *Terry* for the proposition that the retirees' damage claim under LMRA § 301 was legal, not equitable, the Seventh Circuit upheld the right to a jury trial:

> It is well settled that when legal and equitable relief are separately authorized by statute, and the "legal claim is joined with [the] equitable claim, the right to jury trial on the legal claim, including all issues common to both claims, remains intact. The right cannot be abridged by characterizing the legal claim as 'incidental' to the equitable relief sought." Tull v. United States, 481 U.S. 412, 424–25 (1987). Because the plaintiffs instituted a legal claim for breach of contract and sought legal relief in the form of compensatory damages pursuant to Section 301 of the LMRA, in addition to injunctive relief pursuant to Sections 404(a)(1), 502(a)(1)(B) and 502(a)(3) of ERISA, the Seventh Amendment provided them with a right to a jury trial.

Id. at 813–14; accord, Stewart v. KHD Deutz of America Corp., 75 F.3d 1522 (11th Cir.1996).

In contrast to *Senn*, the Sixth Circuit has held that an action under LMRA § 301 to reinstate health benefits and obtain damages sustained as a result of the employer's failure to pay the benefits is equitable in nature. See Golden v. Kelsey-Hayes Co., 73 F.3d 648, 661 (6th Cir.1996). Relying on *Golden*, the Sixth Circuit later held that retirees making similar hybrid claims under both LMRA and ERISA are not entitled to a jury trial. Bittinger v. Tecumseh Products Co., 123 F.3d 877 (6th Cir.1997)(request for monetary relief is incidental and intertwined with equitable claim for declaratory relief).

It has been argued that the strongest case for juryability would be a "narrow class [in] which there are no questions of trust administration— that is, cases in which the trustee admits his currently due monetary obligation to the beneficiary." Note, The Right to Jury Trial in Enforcement Actions under Section 502(a)(1)(B) of ERISA, 96 Harvard L. Rev. 737, 757 (1983); cf. id. at 751. What makes such facts inviting for juryability?

2. *Other ERISA claims.* Courts typically hold that there is no right to a jury trial under § 502(a)(2) for breach of fiduciary duty, because such claims have traditionally been characterized as equitable and Section 409 provides for restitution and other equitable remedies. E.g., Borst v. Chevron Corp., 36 F.3d 1308 (5th Cir.1994); Karr v. Central States, Southeast & Southwest Areas Pension Fund, 215 F.3d 1326 (6th Cir.2000). But see Bona v. Barasch, 2003 WL 1395932 (S.D.N.Y.2003) (arguing based on Great-West that a demand for monetary relief in a breach of fiduciary duty action gives rise to a jury trial). Similarly, because relief under § 502(a)(3) resonates in the juryless tradition of equity, post-*Mertens* courts have had no trouble denying the right to jury trial in such cases. E.g., Helwig v. Kelsey-Hayes Co., 907 F.Supp. 253, 255 (E.D.Mich.1995).

Prior to *Mertens*, several district courts took the position that ERISA § 510 actions should be juryable, because they resemble common law actions for wrongful termination or breach of contract, which are traditionally legal in nature. E.g., McDonald v. Artcraft Electric Supply Co., 774 F.Supp. 29 (D.D.C.1991). However, most courts have held that a plaintiff has no right to a jury trial in § 510 claims for interference or retaliation. E.g., Langlie v. Onan Corp., 192 F.3d 1137 (8th Cir.1999). In Spinelli v. Gaughan, 12 F.3d 853 (9th Cir.1993), which alleged retaliation against the plaintiff for exercising rights under ERISA, the Ninth Circuit suggested that because Congress chose to limit remedies under ERISA "to those available in equity," the right created by Congress was "essentially equitable in nature" Thus, a jury trial was not required.

3. *Evaluating juryability of ERISA claims.* What are the arguments for and against juryability? Do the issues of fact that arise in ERISA litigation seem to lend themselves well to determination by lay persons? Might jury trial be more appropriate for some issues than for others, and if so, which? If you were an employer, would you be more or less inclined to create or to enhance a pension or benefit plan if you thought that disputes arising under the plan would be tried to a jury? For a lament about the effects of courts increasingly interpreting ERISA to deny a jury trial to participants, see Radford Trust v. First Unum Life Ins. Co., 321 F.Supp.2d 226, 241–42 (D. Mass. 2004). If an ERISA plan

contains a term conditioning participation on waiver of jury trial, should the term be enforceable?

G. STATUTES OF LIMITATIONS

ERISA contains quite inadequate limitations provisions. The main ERISA limitations measure, § 413, pertains only to fiduciary litigation, hence not to the benefit claims and other causes of action created under ERISA Title 1, Part 5. There is also a special limitations measure, § 4003(e)(6), for actions affecting the Pension Benefit Guaranty Corporation; and another, § 4301(f), governing withdrawal liability issues in the multiemployer plan system.

Broadly speaking, two sorts of limitations issues arise in ERISA litigation. There is constructional case law concerning the application of the § 413 limitations provisions for fiduciary litigation, and there is a substantial body of law directing federal courts to apply state-law limitations periods for the topics on which ERISA does not provide a federal standard.

Regarding litigation complaining of breach of fiduciary duties, ERISA § 413 provides that the action must be commenced within six years of the breach, or within three years of plaintiff's obtaining actual knowledge of the breach, whichever is earlier. However, if the defendant has concealed the breach, or if the breach entails fraud, action may be commenced up to six years after the date of discovery of the breach. ERISA § 413.

Does a fiduciary's failure to remove allegedly imprudent investment options from a 401(k) plan constitute a cognizable breach separate from the alleged improper selection of the options in the first instance? The Eleventh Circuit said no in Fuller v. SunTrust Banks, Inc., 744 F.3d 685 (11th Cir. Feb. 26, 2014). Although the court viewed it to be a close question, it said that because the allegations concerning the defendants' failure to remove the funds "are in all relevant respects identical to the allegations concerning the selection process, [the] complaint contains no factual allegation that would allow us to distinguish between the alleged imprudent acts occurring at selection from the alleged imprudent acts occurring thereafter." Is that a defensible result? See also Tibble v. Edison International, 729 F. 3d 1110 (9th Cir. 2013). On October 2, 2014, the U.S. Supreme Court granted a petition for certiorari in Tibble, limited to the following question: "Whether a claim that ERISA plan fiduciaries breached their duty of prudence by offering higher-cost retail-class mutual funds to plan participants, even though identical lower-cost institution-class mutual funds were available, is barred by 29 U.S.C. § 1113(1) when fiduciaries initially chose the higher-cost mutual funds as plan investments more than six years before the claim was filed." 189 L. Ed. 2d 895 (2014).

The question of whether a particular plaintiff had actual knowledge, or suffered fraud or concealment, is highly fact-intensive and has produced a large body of case law. E.g., Tinley v. Gannett Co., 55 Fed.Appx. 74, 78–79 (3d Cir.2003) (plaintiff had actual knowledge of breach when company sent notice of exclusion from plan, thus triggering three year period); Babcock v. Hartmarx Corp., 182 F.3d 336, 339 (5th

Cir.1999)(actual knowledge requires not only that plaintiff know of the events constituting the breach, but also "that those events supported a claim for breach of fiduciary duty"). Some courts hold that when there are multiple breaches, the clock begins to run when the plaintiff learned of any. E.g., Phillips v. Alaska Hotel & Restaurant Employees Pension Fund, 944 F.2d 509 (9th Cir.1991) ("if the breaches are of the same kind and nature and the plaintiff had actual knowledge of one of them more than three years before commencing suit, § 413(a)(2) bars the action"). Should a fiduciary be free to engage in repeated violations of ERISA once one violation has been discovered and become time-barred? See generally Annot., Limitation of Actions, under § 413 of [ERISA], with Respect to Action for Breach of Fiduciary Duty, 118 A.L.R. Fed. 377 (1994 & Supp. 2000).

When does a plaintiff have actual knowledge of a breach? In Fish v. GreatBanc Trust Co., 749 F.3d 671 (7th Cir. May 14, 2014), the Seventh Circuit found plaintiff's lack of knowledge of the defendant fiduciaries' decisionmaking process sufficient to allow them to proceed. Even though the harm to the plaintiffs resulted from the substance of the fiduciary's decision, "knowledge of an unwise decision does not amount to 'actual knowledge' of an imprudent process, which is an independent breach of fiduciary duty."

For an example of a recent case applying the fraudulent concealment exception to the statute of limitations see Chaaban v. Criscito, 468 Fed. Appx. 156 (3d Cir. Mar. 7, 2012) (extending statute of limitations in fiduciary claim against a former trustee to six years from the date of discovery). Note also that the circuits are split on the issue of whether ERISA's "fraud or concealment" exception applies only in cases of fraudulent concealment of the breach or to any situation where the underlying allegation sounds in fraud, even without an allegation of an attempt to conceal the breach. Cataldo v. US Steel, 676 F.3d 542 (6th Cir. 2012) (observing that the issue is an open one in the Sixth Circuit).

For benefits claims and other ERISA litigation not invoking the § 413 limitations provisions for fiduciary matters, the federal courts apply the most analogous limitations statute of the state in which the federal court sits. This standard places a premium on characterizing the claim. Most benefit claims are treated as contract suits, e.g., Johnson v. State Mutual Life Assur. Co., 942 F.2d 1260, 1262–63 (8th Cir.1991), applying Missouri's ten year limitations period for written contracts rather than its five year period for breach of trust. When the jurisdiction has different limitations periods for written and oral contracts, the former pertains. E.g., Lumpkin v. Envirodyne Industries, Inc., 933 F.2d 449 (7th Cir.1991); Arena v. ABB Power T & D Co., 31 EB Cases (BNA) 1465 (S.D.Ind.2003). The Eighth Circuit, in selecting among statutes of limitations for various types of contracts, concluded that the statute for recovery of wages pertains. See Adamson v. Armco, Inc., 44 F.3d 650 (8th Cir.1995). These wage recovery statutory periods are often much shorter than the breach of contract periods. See Syed v. Hercules Inc., 214 F.3d 155 (3d Cir.2000) (Delaware's one-year wage recovery statute applies instead of the three-year statute applicable to general contract claims).

The statute of limitations on a 502(a)(1)(B) action begins to run when the benefit denial occurs. In Brothers v. Miller Oral Surgery, Inc.

Retirement Plan, 230 F.3d 1348 (3d Cir.2000), the employer amended its plan eight years earlier, but the plan administrator failed to provide participants with a 204(h) notice. The court allowed a challenge to the amendment to be brought when the plaintiffs did not receive benefits due under the terms of the old plan. The court found that the action was properly characterized as a claim for benefits under 502(a)(1)(B), and thus that the limitation period did not begin to run until the plaintiff had been denied his benefits.

A number of courts have held that actual denial of a benefit is not necessary to start the running of the statute of limitations; a "clear repudiation" by the fiduciary is sufficient. See, e.g., Romero v. Allstate Corp., 404 F.3d 212 (3d Cir.2005)(cause of action accrued when "employee knew or should have known that the amendment has brought about a clear repudiation of certain rights that the employee believed he or she had under the plan"). See also Withrow v. Bache Halsey Stuart Shield Inc., 655 F.3d 1032 (9th Cir.2011) (finding evidence insufficient to establish a "clear and continuing repudiation" in multiple communications between participant and benefit manager regarding calculation of the participant's benefits).

Could a plan provide its own statute of limitations by providing, for example, that with respect to benefit claims, no action may be commenced or maintained against the plan more than 90 days after the plan trustees' decision on review? Such a term was upheld in Northlake Regional Medical Center v. Waffle House System Employee Benefit Plan, 160 F.3d 1301 (11th Cir.1998) (contractual limitations periods on ERISA actions are enforceable, provided they are reasonable). The key to whether a court will apply a shorter contractual period turns appears to turn on whether the period is reasonable based on "the totality of the circumstances surrounding the plaintiff's filing." Steelworkers v. Rohm & Haas Co., 35 EB Cases (BNA) 2271 (E.D.Pa.2005). In Abena v. Metropolitan Life Insurance Co., 544 F.3d 880 (7th Cir.2008), the Seventh Circuit determined that a contractual limitation period shorter than the statute of limitations was reasonable, and therefore enforceable, as applied to a disability claim. In the course of its discussion, the court gave two examples of situations where shorter contractual periods would not be upheld:

> For example, if the employer paid the claim for three or more years and then terminated payments, it would be unreasonable to enforce a limitations period that ended before the claim could have ever accrued. Or if the appeals process was so protracted that the claimant was unable to file suit within the contractual period, the application of this provision would not be reasonable.

Id. at 884.

Apart from the reasonability of the period, a participant needs to be given notice that a shorter period is applicable. In Rumpf v. Metro. Life Ins. Co., 2010 U.S. Dist. LEXIS 74388 (E.D. Pa. July 23, 2010), a federal district court refused to give effect to a contractual limitation contained in a certificate of insurance. The contractual limitation period was not listed in the summary plan description of the plan and a copy of the certificate was not given to the participant until after she brought suit against Metropolitan Life. Accord. Ortega Candelaria v. Orthobiologics,

661 F.3d 675 (1st Cir.2011) (shorter plan period did not apply because of lack of notice).

In Scharff v. Raytheon Co. Short Term Disability Plan, 581 F.3d 899 (9th Cir.2010), the Ninth Circuit upheld a one-year contractual limitation period for the bringing of a claim for disability benefits. The court found that the placement and display of the limitation period in the plan's SPD met participant's "reasonable expectations." In so doing, it rejected the participant's argument that the contractual limitation period should have been disclosed in correspondence she received from the insurer. In the view of the court, the insurer had no obligation to inform the participant of the limitation period in its correspondence with her, finding "no need to supplement the comprehensive scheme already in place for regulating plan administrators' disclosures to participants." The Supreme Court has declined to review the Ninth Circuit's decision. Scharff v. Raytheon Co. Short Term Disability Plan, 130 S. Ct. 3508 (2010).

How should courts deal with time periods contained in an SPD but not in the plan in the wake of the Supreme Court's decision in *Amara*? Contrast Tetreault v. Reliance Stan. Life Ins. Co., 2011 U.S. Dist. LEXIS 152252 (D. Mass. Nov. 28, 2011) (participant bound by time periods in SPD even if they are not mentioned in plan) with Merigan v. Liberty Life Assur. Co., 826 F. Supp. 2d 388 (D. Mass. 2011) (time limit contained in SPD but not plan was not binding).

Can a contractual limitation period affect when action begins to accrue? In Heimeshoff v. Hartford Life & Accident Insurance Co. 134 S.Ct. 604 (2013), the Supreme Court unanimously said yes. The Hartford plan provided that no legal action could be brought challenging a benefit denial more than "3 years after the time written proof of loss is required to be furnished according to the terms of the policy." Plaintiff's application for long-term disability benefits was denied in December of 2005 on the grounds that she failed to provide satisfactory proof of her disability. After an informal appeal, Hartford issued a "last and final denial letter" on November 25, 2008. Plaintiff filed suit on Nov. 18, 2010, within three years of the final denial of benefits, but more than three years after her proof of loss was submitted to Hartford.

The Second Circuit affirmed a district court ruling in favor of Hartford, finding that ERISA does not prohibit a contractual limitation period that begins to run before a final claims denial, that is, before the plaintiff has the ability to bring suit. In the view of the court, "[t]he policy language is unambiguous and it does not offend [ERISA] to have the limitations period begin to run before the claim accrues." Id at 130. Thus, the limitation period for filing suit can be running while the plaintiff is going through the administrative review process, a conclusion several circuits have come to.

The Supreme Court upheld the Second Circuit's opinion, holding that a contractual limitation period in a plan is enforceable. It relied on the rule established in Order of United Commercial Travelers of Am. v. Wolfe, 331 U.S. 586 (1947) holding that a contractual limitations period is enforceable so long as the limitations period is reasonable in length and there is no controlling statute to the contrary. The Court also observed that courts can apply traditional equitable doctrines such as waiver or estoppel or equitable tolling if necessary to protect participant interests.

How short a period is reasonable? In Claeys v. Aetna Ins. Co., 548 Fed. Appx. 344 (6th Cir. Dec. 17, 2013), the Sixth Circuit found a six-month limitation period in a welfare benefit plan to be reasonable. The SPD for the plan provided that legal action must commence the earlier of "six months from the date a determination is made" or "three years from the date the service or treatment was provided or the date the claim arose, whichever, is earlier." The court found no ambiguity in the provision and no reason the period should have been equitably tolled.

In ERISA § 510 cases the courts generally have applied the state limitations period for wrongful termination. See, e.g., McClure v. Zoecon, Inc., 936 F.2d 777 (5th Cir.1991); Felton v. Unisource Corp., 940 F.2d 503 (9th Cir.1991). In a case where the state did not recognize a cause of action for wrongful termination, the Second Circuit looked to the statute of limitations under a workers' compensation statute that prohibited retaliatory discharge or discrimination against employees for making workers' compensation claims or testifying in proceedings. Sandberg v. KPMG Peat Marwick, LLP, 111 F.3d 331 (2d Cir.1997). In Lopez v. Premium Auto Acceptance Corp., 389 F.3d 504, 507 (5th Cir.2004), the Fifth Circuit applied the two-year Texas statute of limitations "applicable to most torts and discrimination claims."

QUESTIONS

1.   What explains the resort to state limitations law in a field of law in which the emphasis on broad federal preemption of state law (infra Chapter 17) is otherwise so pronounced?

2.   In *Firestone Tire & Rubber Co. v. Bruch*, reproduced supra in Chapter 15, dealing with the standard of review that courts should apply to grievances regarding plan decisionmaking, the Supreme Court placed considerable weight on analogizing employee benefit plans to the law of trusts rather than the law of contracts. How is that view to be reconciled with the strong tendency in the limitations cases to characterize benefit claims as contract-like?

3.   How well did Congress do its job when it foresaw the limitations problem for fiduciary claims and for PBGC matters, but neglected to provide limitations law for the benefit claims litigation that Congress expressly authorized under ERISA Title 1, Part 5?

4.   When a federal court is applying an analogous state law statute of limitations, should it also apply the state's borrowing statute? See Muto v. CBS Corp., 668 F.3d 53 (2d Cir.2012).

H. EXHAUSTION REQUIREMENTS AND ARBITRATION

ERISA § 503 requires plans to provide plainly written notice of the reasons for denying a benefit claim, and "a reasonable opportunity [for the] participant [to obtain] a full and fair review by the appropriate named fiduciary of the decision denying the claim." Case law has derived from this language the requirement that a claimant should ordinarily

follow internal plan procedures and exhaust internal plan remedies
before seeking judicial relief under ERISA.

1. *Rationale.* Judge Wilkinson has summarized the justification
for the exhaustion requirement:

> ERISA does not contain an explicit exhaustion
> provision. . . . This exhaustion requirement rests upon the Act's
> text and structure as well as the strong federal interest
> encouraging private resolution of ERISA disputes.
>
> ERISA requires benefit plans covered by the Act to provide
> internal dispute resolution procedures for participants whose
> claims for benefits have been denied. [§ 503]. Employee benefit
> plans must provide adequate, written notice of the specific
> reasons for such a denial and must afford participants a
> reasonable opportunity for a "full and fair review" of the decision
> denying the claim. Congress' apparent intent in mandating
> these internal claims procedures was to minimize the number
> of frivolous ERISA lawsuits; promote the consistent treatment
> of benefit claims; provide a nonadversarial dispute resolution
> process; and decrease the cost and time of claims settlement. It
> would be "anomalous" if the same reasons which led Congress
> to require plans to provide remedies for ERISA claimants did
> not lead courts to see that those remedies are regularly utilized.
>
> ERISA also imposes broad fiduciary responsibilities on plan
> trustees and extensively regulates their conduct. Plan
> fiduciaries must perform their obligations with diligence and
> must discharge their duties "solely" in the interest of plan
> participants and their beneficiaries. By preventing premature
> interference with an employee benefit plan's remedial
> provisions, the exhaustion requirement enables plan fiduciaries
> to efficiently manage their funds; correct their errors; interpret
> plan provisions; and assemble a factual record which will assist
> a court in reviewing the fiduciaries' actions. Indeed, subsequent
> court action may be unnecessary in many cases because the
> plan's own procedures will resolve many claims. In short,
> Congress intended plan fiduciaries, not the federal courts, to
> have primary responsibility for claims processing.

Makar v. Health Care Corp. of Mid-Atlantic, 872 F.2d 80, 82–83 (4th
Cir.1989). Such reasoning has led courts to suggest that there is a
" 'firmly established policy favoring exhaustion of administrative
remedies in ERISA cases.' " Kennedy v. Empire Blue Cross & Blue
Shield, 989 F.2d 588, 594 (2d Cir.1993) (quoting Alfarone v. Bernie Wolff
Construction, 788 F.2d 76, 79 (3d Cir.1986)). See Vaught v. Scottsdale
Healthcare Corp. Health Plan, 546 F.3d 620, 626 (9th Cir.2008) (noting
that the court "long ago" concluded that exhaustion was appropriate in
ERISA cases).

2. *Frustration and futility.* Courts will refuse to apply the
exhaustion requirement if they conclude that the plan frustrated the
internal appeals process or that an internal appeal would be futile. See,
e.g., Lee v. California Butchers' Pension Trust Fund, 154 F.3d 1075, 1080
(9th Cir.1998)("The plan itself thwarted proper exhaustion procedures

for review by the trustees, so [the plaintiff] was relieved from following them."); Fallick v. Nationwide Mutual Ins. Co., 162 F.3d 410, 419 (6th Cir.1998)(a court is obliged to disregard the exhaustion doctrine when "resorting to the plan's administrative procedure would simply be futile or the remedy inadequate"). Plaintiffs must meet a high burden to demonstrate that exhaustion should be excused. For example, the Seventh Circuit held in Lindemann v. Mobil Oil Corp., 79 F.3d 647, 650 (7th Cir.1996) that in order to demonstrate futility, a plaintiff must establish that "it is certain that [his] claim will be denied on appeal, not merely that [he] doubts that an appeal will result in a different decision." Some courts have also excused exhaustion "if the claimant is threatened with irreparable harm." Majka v. Prudential Ins. Co. of Am., 171 F.Supp.2d 410, 414 (D.N.J.2001); Henderson v. Bodine, 70 F.3d 958 (8th Cir.1995) (excusing exhaustion where claimant was in immediate need of medical treatment). The decision to require exhaustion is a matter within the discretion of the trial court, reversible only for abuse of discretion. See, e.g., Harrow v. Prudential Ins. Co., 279 F.3d 244 (3d Cir. 2002).

3. *Inadequate claims procedures.* The Department of Labor first issued regulations interpreting the requirements of ERISA § 503 in 1977. In November 2000, it promulgated new final regulations significantly altering the claims procedure rules. See DOL Reg. § 2560.503–1. The regulations impose procedural requirements on claims processing, including more rapid timeframes for claims decisionmaking by health and disability plans as well as several additional notice requirements. If a plan fails to establish or follow claims procedures consistent with the requirements in the regulations, the regulations deem the claimant to have exhausted the administrative remedies available under the plan and authorize the claimant "to pursue any available remedies under section 502(a)." DOL Reg. § 2560.503–1(*l*). See Nichols v. Prudential Ins. Co., 406 F.3d 98 (2d Cir.2005) (failure of plan administrator to adhere to regulatory deadlines results in conclusion that claimant's administrative remedies have been exhausted by operation of law). Where a plan provision detailing its claims procedure is not clear, such that participants could reasonably interpret the plan terms not to require exhaustion, failure to exhaust may be excused. Kirkendall v. Halliburton, Inc., 707 F.3d 173 (2d Cir. 2013).

4. *Distinguishing statutory violations.* Courts are divided on whether to require exhaustion when the plaintiff asserts a statutory violation, for example, breach of fiduciary duty. Illustrative of those courts finding no exhaustion requirement is Smith v. Sydnor, 184 F.3d 356 (4th Cir.1999). Smith alleged that plan fiduciaries breached their duty to the plan by selling preferred stock held by the plan at a below-market price and engaging in self-dealing and other prohibited transactions. After receiving a distribution, Smith did not seek an internal appeal, but filed suit in federal court. The district court granted the defendants' motion to dismiss on the basis that Smith had not exhausted internal appeals. On appeal, the Fourth Circuit reversed.

> There is no statutory mandate for benefit plans to provide review of claims for violation of ERISA itself. [It] follows, therefore, that if there is no statutory requirement for an

> appeals procedure respecting claims not involving benefits, the logic of the exhaustion requirement no longer applies.
>
> Unlike a claim for benefits under a plan, which implicates the expertise of a plan fiduciary, adjudication of a claim for a violation of an ERISA statutory provision involves the interpretation and application of a federal statute, which is within the expertise of the judiciary.

184 F.3d at 364–65. Recognizing that it may not always be easy to distinguish a claim for benefits from a breach of fiduciary duty, the Fourth Circuit remarked that "a claim for breach of fiduciary duty is actually a claim for benefits where the resolution of the claim rests upon an interpretation and application of an ERISA-regulated plan rather than upon an interpretation and application of ERISA." Id. at 362. In contrast, several circuits have ruled that exhaustion is required in cases alleging breach of fiduciary duty. E.g., Wilson v. Kimberly-Clark Corp., 254 Fed.Appx. 280, 285 (5th Cir.2007); Bickley v. Caremark Rx, Inc., 461 F.3d 1325 (11th Cir.2006). In circuits not requiring exhaustion of fiduciary claims, plaintiffs sometimes try to recast benefit denial claims as fiduciary claims in order to avoid exhaustion. Courts, however, are vigilant in not allowing such artful pleading. E.g. Madera v. Marsh USA, Inc., 426 F.3d 56 (1st Cir.2005).

Courts are also divided on whether to apply the exhaustion doctrine to ERISA § 510 claims, in which a plaintiff alleges that he or she was discharged or otherwise penalized for exercising rights established by the plan or by ERISA. Compare Chailland v. Brown & Root, Inc., 45 F.3d 947, 950–51 (5th Cir.1995); Zipf v. AT & T, 799 F.2d 889 (3d Cir.1986) (declining to apply exhaustion); with Lindemann v. Mobil Oil Corp., 79 F.3d 647, 649–50 (7th Cir.1996); Mason v. Continental Group, Inc., 763 F.2d 1219 (11th Cir.1985)(exhaustion is required both for breach of fiduciary duty and for § 510 claims); Hannah v. American Republic Ins. Co., 416 F.Supp.2d 605 (W.D.Tenn.2006) (exhaustion required in § 510 action). Are you persuaded that statutory violations should be treated differently from denial of benefit claims?

5. *Preclusion.* Not only can the exhaustion requirement delay judicial review, judicial review can be wholly extinguished if internal plan procedures are not carefully followed. For example, it is common for plans to require that a dissatisfied claimant make a timely request for internal review. See, e.g., Tiger v. AT & T Technologies, 633 F.Supp. 532 (E.D.N.Y.1986), involving a rejected disability claim. When denying the claim, the administrator gave notice to the employee that the plan provided that any appeal from an adverse determination had to be lodged in writing within 60 days. The plaintiff delayed beyond the 60-day period. The court held the plaintiff's suit for review precluded, in view of the plan's interest in obtaining timely evidence of the facts in claim disputes.

In Edwards v. Briggs & Stratton Ret. Plan, 639 F.3d 355 (7th Cir. 2011), the Seventh Circuit rejected a plaintiff's argument that her untimely appeal should be excused because "she was in 'substantial compliance' with administrative review procedures under the plan." The court explained that "[t]o import into the exhaustion requirement the substantial compliance doctrine" "would render it effectively impossible for plan administrators to fix and enforce administrative deadlines while involving courts incessantly in detailed, case-by-case determinations as to whether a given claimant's failure to bring a timely appeal from a denial of benefits should be excused." Id. at 362.

6. *Arbitration.* An arbitration clause can be even more potent than an exhaustion requirement in restricting or defeating judicial review. In Kramer v. Smith Barney, 80 F.3d 1080 (5th Cir.1996), the Fifth Circuit held that an arbitration clause in a customer agreement signed by Kramer when opening his account mandated arbitration of his ERISA claims of account mismanagement. The court followed Shearson/ American Express, Inc. v. McMahon, 482 U.S. 220 (1987), which sustained the pro-arbitration-clause policy of the Federal Arbitration Act against a challenge brought under the Securities Exchange Act of 1934. See generally Annot., Enforceability of Predispute Agreements to Arbitrate Claims Arising under [ERISA], 116 A.L.R. Fed. 525 (1993). For a thorough discussion of arbitration in the context of employment disputes, see David Sherwyn, J. Bruce Tracey, and Zev J. Eigen, In Defense of Mandatory Arbitration of Employment Disputes: Saving the Baby, Tossing Out the Bath Water, and Constructing a New Sink in the Process, 2 U.Pa.J.Labor & Employment L. 73 (1999).

In Gilmer v. Interstate/Johnson Lane, 500 U.S. 20 (1991), the Supreme Court upheld an arbitration clause against an ADEA claim. *Gilmer* was influential in causing the Third Circuit to abandon its original decision that ERISA claims were not subject to arbitration. Pritzker v. Merrill Lynch, Pierce, Fenner & Smith, Inc., 7 F.3d 1110 (3d Cir.1993) (arbitration clause enforced), overruling Barrowclough v. Kidder Peabody & Co., Inc., 752 F.2d 923 (3d Cir.1985) (arbitration clause not enforced). The issue now appears well-settled. See Peruvian Connection, Ltd. v. Christian, 977 F.Supp. 1107, 1110 (D.Kan.1997) ("The circuit courts that have considered the arbitrability of an ERISA claim have uniformly concluded that nothing in the text of the statute evinces a Congressional intent to preclude arbitration.")

Although the DoL's proposed regulations on plan claims specifically precluded plans from requiring benefits claimants to submit to binding arbitration, the final rules regulate (although do not preclude) mandatory arbitration only with respect to group health and disability benefits.. DoL Reg. § 2560.503–1(c)(4). Under the final rules, a claims procedure that requires arbitration will be considered reasonable only if (i) the arbitration counts as one of the maximum of two internal appeals a plan may require before a plaintiff can sue under § 502(a)(1)(B) and is conducted in accordance with the requirements applicable to such appeals, and (ii) the claimant is not precluded from challenging the arbitration decision under § 502(a) or other applicable law.

If an employer provides a benefit plan pursuant to a collective bargaining agreement ("CBA") and the CBA has an arbitration clause, the question can arise whether a coverage dispute under the plan is subject to arbitration under the CBA. The answer depends on the exact wording of the CBA. Compare Schweizer Aircraft Corp. v. Local 1752, Intl. Union, United Auto., Aero. & Agric. Implement Workers of America, 29 F.3d 83 (2d Cir.1994) (arbitrable under the CBA) with International Assoc. of Machinists and Aerospace Workers, Dist. No. 10 v. Waukesha

Engine Division, Dresser Industries, Inc., 17 F.3d 196 (7th Cir.1994) (not arbitrable).

ERISA requires arbitration of disputes between employers and multiemployer plans regarding the amount of employer withdrawal liability. ERISA § 4221. If the employer fails to request arbitration, the amounts demanded by the plan become due and owing and the plan may bring an action in state or federal court for collection.

For recent cases upholding an obligation to arbitrate ERISA claims see Hendricks v. UBS Financial Services, Inc., 546 Fed. Appx. 514 (5th Cir. 2013) (requiring former employees to arbitrate claims related to ERISA plan); VanPamel v. TRW Vehicle Safety Systems, Inc., 723 F.3d 664 (6th Cir.2013) (upholding arbitration of retirees challenging changes to their health care benefits based on collective bargaining provision).

7.   *Propriety of the requirement.* The judicial inference that ERISA requires exhaustion of remedies has been questioned. Professor Brendan Maher, for example, argues:

> [N]owhere does ERISA's text require administrative exhaustion. The operative provision provides that plans "afford a reasonable *opportunity* to any participant whose claim for benefits has been denied for a full and fair review by the appropriate named fiduciary of the decision denying the claim." . . . By its terms, an opportunity is not a requirement. . . . Had Congress desired administrative review to be mandatory prior to commencement of suit, one suspects it would have said so (as it has elsewhere)."

Brendan S. Maher, Creating a Paternalistic Market for Legal Rules Affecting the Benefit Promise, 2009 Wis. L.Rev. 658, 674–75 (emph. in original).

CHAPTER 17

PREEMPTION

Analysis

Introduction

A central objective of ERISA was to federalize pension and employee benefit law. In the decades before ERISA, the qualified plan requirements of the IRC had set federal standards for certain aspects of pension and profit sharing plans. Otherwise, state law governed the basics of creating, construing, and administering pension and benefit plans.

This chapter treats ERISA's preemption provision, § 514, and the vast case law it has provoked—leaving, however, until Chapter 19 the preemption issues touching on state regulation of health insurance benefits

Even had ERISA contained no express preemption provision, ERISA would nevertheless have preempted inconsistent state law by implication, through the operation of the Supremacy Clause. U.S. Constitution, Article VI, § 2. As will be seen, however, the effect of § 514 is to preempt a broader range of state laws than would be preempted by the Supremacy Clause. ERISA preemption has proved to be astonishingly complex and highly contested, having provoked no less than fifteen Supreme Court cases—a remarkable quantum of judicial resources in view of the proportion of American law that ERISA (let alone its preemption section) represents.

A. Structure of the Statute

1. Overview

1. *Explicit preemption.* Congress chose to handle preemption under ERISA by means of an express provision, ERISA § 514. The core is § 514(a), which says that the provisions of Titles 1 and 4 of ERISA "shall supersede *any* and all State laws insofar as they may now or hereafter *relate to* any employee benefit plan. . . ." (emphasis supplied). This is language of remarkable breadth. The rest of § 514 subjects the preemption rule of § 514(a) to several exceptions.

2. *Insurance.* The most important exception to § 514(a) is § 514(b)(2)(A), which provides that "nothing in this title shall be construed to exempt or relieve any person from any law of any State which regulates insurance, banking, or securities." This provision, frequently called the insurance savings clause or insurance exception, continues the federal policy entrenched in the McCarran-Ferguson Act of 1945, 15 U.S.C. § 1011, that the federal government defers to the states in the regulation of the insurance industry. The insurance exception is discussed in Chapter 19.

The insurance exception is itself subject to an exception, the so-called "deemer clause" of § 514(b)(2)(B), whose main message is that an employee benefit plan is not to be considered an insurer for purposes of the insurance savings clause (even though, like insurance, such a plan often bears and spreads risk). In the absence of such a provision, it would have been open to argue, as some pre-ERISA cases did, that any plan is an insurer. See, e.g., Bost v. Masters, 235 Ark. 393, 361 S.W.2d 272 (1962) (union health plan treated as insurance company for purposes of serving process under unauthorized insurers process act). But for the deemer clause, the insurance savings clause would operate so broadly that it would largely negate the general preemption rule announced in § 514(a).

3. *Compliance plans.* Section 514(a) by its terms applies to plans "not exempt under section 4(b)." Section 4(b)(3) excludes from ERISA a plan "maintained solely for the purpose of complying with applicable workmen's compensation laws or unemployment compensation or disability insurance laws." In Shaw v. Delta Air Lines, 463 U.S. 85, 106–08 (1983), the Supreme Court refused to apply the exclusion to "multi-benefit plans" that provide both state-mandated disability benefits and other benefits. "A State may require an employer to maintain a disability plan complying with state law as a separate administrative unit. Such a plan would be exempt under [ERISA § 4(b)(3)]." 463 U.S. at 108. But if state law does not require this administrative separation, and the employer complies with state law through a plan that is broader, the § 4(b)(3) exemption does not apply and state law is preempted under § 514.

4. *Domestic relations orders.* The Retirement Equity Act of 1984 (REAct) amended ERISA's antialienation clause, § 206(d), to allow

enforcement of state domestic relations orders. See Chapter 7 supra. As a conforming amendment, REAct added § 514(b)(7), providing that § 514(a) shall not apply to such orders.

5. *Criminal Law.* Section 514(b)(4) precludes applying the § 514(a) preemption rule "to any generally applicable" state criminal law.

6. *Other federal law.* Section 514(d) stipulates that ERISA does not "supersede any law of the United States." It appears that this proviso was inserted in the statute for the purpose of assuring that ERISA would not be read to conflict with the antidiscrimination laws of Title VII of the Civil Rights Act of 1964, resulting in the Supreme Court's adopting a narrow reading of the exception. Discussing the background to § 514(d) in Shaw v. Delta Air Lines, 463 U.S. 85, 104 (1983), the Court concluded that "ERISA's structure and legislative history, while not particularly illuminating with respect to § 514(d), caution against applying it too expansively." In Guidry v. Sheet Metal Workers National Pension Fund, 493 U.S. 365, 375 (1990), the Court gave preference to ERISA's antialienation provision over general remedial provisions of earlier federal labor law. See also Patterson v. Shumate, 504 U.S. 753 (1992) (harmonizing the Bankruptcy Code with ERISA).

7. *Automatic contribution arrangements.* Many states have statutes that prohibit withholding from an employee's wages unless specific written consent is obtained. See, e.g., Cal. Lab. Code § 300(b). There had been some concern that these statutes might prevent employers from establishing automatic enrollment arrangements in connection with their 401(k) plans. ERISA § 514(e)(1), added to the statute in 2006, specifically preempts any state law that would directly or indirectly prohibit or restrict the inclusion in a plan of an automatic contribution arrangement, even those that are not "qualified" under IRC § 401(k)(13), provided there is an adequate annual notice to participants. The state laws presumably continue to apply to non-ERISA plans, such as church plans.

8. *The "plan" limitation.* There can be no preemption unless the law in question relates to an "employee benefit plan" subject to Title 1 of ERISA. In most cases, particularly those dealing with health or pension plans, it is clear that an ERISA plan is involved. But as discussed in Chapter 3, supra, not every benefit provided by an employer to its employees constitutes an employee benefit plan under ERISA § 3(3). For example, in Fort Halifax Packing Co. v. Coyne, 482 U.S. 1 (1987), a state statute requiring severance pay for workers terminated incident to a plant closing was held not to be preempted. In the Court's view, the one-time, contingent nature of the required payment did not amount to a "plan."

Another example, also discussed in more detail in Chapter 3, is vacation pay. Under DoL regulations, certain "payroll practices," including vacation pay paid from an employer's general assets, are excluded from the definition of employee benefit plan. See DoL Reg. § 2510.3–1(b)(3)(i). In Massachusetts v. Morash, 490 U.S. 107 (1989), the Court, relying on these regulations, held that a Massachusetts statute forbidding the forfeiture of accrued vacation pay when an employee terminates employment was not preempted, because the vacation pay was not a "plan" under ERISA.

Similarly, as discussed in Chapter 3, supra, to be an ERISA plan, a plan must be maintained by an employer and/or by an employee organization. Thus, a plan offered by an association to a group of persons that includes non-employees is not an ERISA plan, and a claim with respect to such a plan is not preempted. See, e.g., Marcella v. Capital District Physicians' Health Plan Inc., 293 F.3d 42 (2d Cir.2002) (no preemption of claim relating to health plan offered to members of chamber of commerce, because plan was not maintained by an employer for the benefit of employees).

2. LEGISLATIVE HISTORY

Daniel M. Fox & Daniel C. Schaffer, Semi-Preemption in ERISA: Legislative Process and Health Policy
7 American J. Tax Policy 47, 48–52 (1988).

The preemption clause of ERISA is unusual because it forbids the states to regulate employee benefits even when federal law is silent. It preempts state laws touching on pensions, for which ERISA has set federal standards. But it also preempts state laws relating to other employee benefit plans, like health insurance, whose content federal law does not regulate.

The resulting "regulatory vacuum," as one participant in drafting ERISA recalled it in retrospect, was not a deeply considered result of the years of planning, negotiating, and drafting the bill that was passed by Congress in 1974. On the contrary, the preemption clause of 1974 was inserted during the final negotiations in the conference committee, in response to strong opinions voiced by House conferees speaking for powerful interest groups.

The preemption language that had survived, without controversy, until the conference simply prevented the states from legislating about the "subject matters regulated by this Act." The new language, preempting state laws relating to "any employee benefit plan" including matters not regulated by the Act, was disclosed when the conference committee report was filed ten days before Congress took final action on ERISA.

The House and Senate sponsors of the bill made very different claims about the significance of the revised preemption clause. Representative Dent called the new clause the "crowning achievement of this legislation" because it eliminated the "threat of conflicting and inconsistent state and local regulation." Senators Javits and Williams were less expansive, no doubt because they were rationalizing a change from a position they had held during the long period of drafting the legislation. Javits looked forward to a future refining of ERISA preemption, saying that the "desirability of further regulation—at either the State or Federal level—undoubtedly warrants further attention." The conferees had created a Joint Pension Task Force and ordered it to study ERISA's preemption of state law: Javits thought that this might lead to "appropriate modifications."

Senator Williams offered the first suggestion that interest group politics had influenced the language of preemption. He claimed that the language made it impossible for "State professional associations" to prevent "unions and employers" from agreeing on particular benefit programs. He explained that this language would preempt states from imposing on prepaid legal service plans a requirement of [open] rather than [closed] panels. Unions favored [closed] panels; the American Bar Association was working for state regulation requiring [open] panels.

Our conversations with participants in the legislative process that produced ERISA suggest that Williams was telling only a part of the story. Lobbyists for the AFL-CIO, working through the Coordinating Committee for Multi-Employer Plans, did press for language that would thwart the state bar associations. But the stakes of labor and their allies in heavy industry were considerably larger. Both groups were eager to prevent the states from taxing and regulating the health and pension plans they had negotiated under the Taft-Hartley Act. Several states (notably Missouri and New York) had asserted in court cases that these plans were, for purposes of state law, insurance companies and therefore should be licensed as insurance businesses and pay taxes on premiums. . . .

The insurance industry seems to have been relatively quiet in 1974 about the effects of preemption on health insurance. Some major companies were ambivalent. On the one hand, they favored the preemption of state law, especially mandates, because it made it easier to offer uniform policies to national employers. On the other hand, they had relied for many years on the arrangement whereby Congress left regulation of insurance to the states and the insurance companies cultivated the goodwill of the state insurance commissioners. Another segment of the insurance industry, smaller companies, generally operating in regional and state markets, who were losing business to self-insured benefit plans negotiated and administered by unions and management, however, favored state regulation of employee benefit plans. As a result of both ambivalence and internal conflict, the insurance industry did not actively seek to influence the final language of ERISA preemption.

The health insurers appear not to have been aware of the significance of the preemption clause for their markets. A high official of the Blue Cross Association recalled that "very little was going on because nobody saw it; nobody in the health industry understood the implications of preemption." A lobbyist for the life insurance industry recalled that even though many of his largest companies wrote health insurance, they focused on other issues than preemption in the short period between the conference committee deliberations and final passage of the bill. Similarly, an eyewitness at the Health Insurance Association of America recalled that in 1974 his organization was still concerned mainly about national health insurance, cost-containment, Professional Standards Review Organizations, and the new Health Planning and Resource Development Act. Moreover, the chief lobbyist was recovering from coronary bypass surgery during the period of the final negotiations of ERISA. In sum, he recalled, "I don't think anybody was thinking of the health implications of ERISA."

Thus Congressional staff and a few lobbyists made a major decision about employee benefits policy—mainly, it turned out, about health insurance—as if it were a technical issue. Not only were major interest groups not involved, but the Department of Labor, which would administer ERISA, was apparently not consulted about the changes in the preemption clause. The Senate conferees were members of the Committee on Finance and the Committee on Labor and Public Welfare. The latter was responsible for health policy, but apparently neither the senators nor their staff discussed the implications of preemption with their counterparts on the health subcommittee.

Semi-preemption, the policy by which states could regulate insurance companies but not self-insured plans, has been enormously significant for health policy. The policy was made initially neither by accident nor quite by design. The policy was the result of a process which permitted only some of the implications of a proposed law to be known. The people who drafted the final preemption clause did not realize that, as one later recalled, preempting mandated benefits and preserving state regulation were "not watertight compartments." On this occasion nobody who could tell them where the leaks would come was motivated to participate in the political process.

NOTES

1.   *Prepaid legal service plans.* The decision to impose a preemption clause of great breadth appears to have been considerably influenced by the wish to encourage the development of prepaid legal services plans, a species of welfare benefit plan enumerated in ERISA § 3(1). "The ERISA preemption clause was broadened largely because organized labor and consumer groups feared that states and bar associations would block the formation of 'closed panel' prepaid legal plans, which provide legal services through a group of participating lawyers. These interest groups wanted to prevent states and professional associations from enacting regulations favoring 'open panel' prepaid legal plans, which allow all lawyers to participate." Note, ERISA Preemption of State Mandated-Provider Laws, 1985 Duke L.J. 1194, 1201.

Prepaid legal service plans have been quantitatively insignificant among the plethora of employee benefit plans, although there has been some interest in them. Regarding some of the issues surrounding such plans, see Brian Heid & Eitan Misolovin, The Group Legal Plan Revolution: Bright Horizon or Dark Future, 18 Hofstra Labor & Employment L.J. 335 (2000).

2.   *Interpreting the legislative history.* The tail seems to have wagged the dog when a squabble about regulatory control of something as peripheral as prepaid legal service plans was allowed to shape the scope of ERISA preemption for pension plans and for such major welfare benefit plans as those providing health care. Does the legislative history really show (as many tend to assume) that Congress rejected a narrow approach to preemption in favor of very broad preemption? Or might the legislative history instead suggest that ERISA's framers hastily devised overbroad language in attempting to achieve the relatively narrow purpose of protecting prepaid legal service plans from hostile regulation by the organized bar?

3.   *Critique.* ERISA's preemption scheme has produced a large literature, most of it highly critical of the preemption provision and especially the Supreme Court's jurisprudence. E.g., Edward Zelinsky, Travelers, Reasoned Textualism, and the New Jurisprudence of ERISA Preemption, 21 Cardozo Law Rev. 807 (1999); Robert N. Covington, Amending ERISA's Preemption Scheme, 8 Kan. J.L. & Pub. Pol'y 1 (1999). As an initial point of critical perspective on the preemption case law, reflect on the views of Leon E. Irish & Harrison J. Cohen, ERISA Preemption: Judicial Flexibility and Statutory Rigidity, 19 U.Michigan J.L. Reform 109, 110–12 (1985):

> [It] is clear that the inclusion of section 514(a) in ERISA was a mistake. Given well-established judicial doctrines of preemption, section 514(a) was unnecessary. And, while judicial doctrines have been molded by sensitivity to what is practicable and a reasonable balancing of competing interests, the categorical language and wider scope of section 514(a) has unavoidably at times called for unreasonable and impractical results. In short, the adoption of section 514(a) not only failed to fill any real need, but also created unnecessary problems for both the judiciary and those affected by private employee benefit plans.

> The language of section 514(a) sweeps as broadly as the English language allows. In view of this breadth, judicial refusal to hold preempted any state law that touches upon an employee pension or welfare benefit plan strains ordinary notions of the proper boundaries between the legislative and judicial domains. Anyone advocating that ERISA preempts a particular state law can present an impressive array of arguments for that position, from the need to obey plain legislative language to the clearly enunciated congressional intent to free employee benefit plans from all but the specifically excepted areas of state law and regulation. Strict adherence to the literal scope and language of section 514(a), however, deprives courts of the flexibility that has proven crucially important in addressing questions of federal preemption and in the development of a "federal common law." The literal approach also makes it embarrassingly clear that Congress enacted ERISA while still oblivious to numerous problems related to benefit plans that the states had already recognized and addressed. . . .

> [The] primary shortcoming of section 514 is that, although it establishes a good starting point for thinking about ERISA preemption, it falls short both as a practical rule and as a guide to principled decisionmaking. Courts have thus had little choice but to create a federal common law of ERISA, including preemption, in spite of, and to some extent hindered by, the literal language of the statute.

More recent criticism of ERISA's preemption measure has centered on the effect of preemption on states' efforts, prior to the Affordable Care Act, to address perceived problems with health insurance coverage. See, e.g., Edward A. Zelinsky, The New Massachusetts Health Law: Preemption and Experimentation, 49 Wm. & Mary L. Rev. 229 (2007); Susan J. Stabile, State Law Health Care Initiatives, 19 St. Thomas L. Rev. 87 (2006); David A. Pratt, State Laws Rush in Where ERISA Fears to Tread, 18 J. Pension Benefits 3

(2011); Michael Serota & Michelle Singer, Comment: Maintaining Healthy Laboratories of Experimentation: Federalism, Health Care Reform, and ERISA, 99 Calif. L. Rev. 557, 559 (2011).

B. THE SUPREME COURT'S INITIAL PREEMPTION JURISPRUDENCE

1. ALESSI V. RAYBESTOS-MANHATTAN, INC.

451 U.S. 504 (1981).

■ JUSTICE MARSHALL delivered the opinion of the Court.

Some private pension plans reduce a retiree's pension benefits by the amount of workers' compensation awards received subsequent to retirement. In these cases we consider whether two such offset provisions are lawful under [ERISA], and whether they may be prohibited by state law.

Raybestos-Manhattan, Inc., and General Motors Corp. maintain employee pension plans that are subject to federal regulation under ERISA. Both plans provide that an employee's retirement benefits shall be reduced, or offset, by an amount equal to workers' compensation awards for which the individual is eligible. In 1977, the New Jersey Legislature amended its Workers' Compensation Act to expressly prohibit such offsets. The amendment states that "[t]he right of compensation granted by this chapter may be set off against disability pension benefits or payments but shall not be set off against employees' retirement pension benefits or payments."

Alleging violations of this provision of state law, two suits were initiated in New Jersey state court. The plaintiffs in both suits were retired employees who had obtained workers' compensation awards subject to offsets against their retirement benefits under their pension plans. The defendant companies independently removed the suits to the United States District Court for the District of New Jersey. There, both District Court Judges ruled that the pension offset provisions were invalid under New Jersey law, and concluded that Congress had not intended ERISA to preempt state laws of this sort. The District Court Judges also held that the offsets were prohibited by § 203(a) of [ERISA]. The judges concluded that offsets based on workers' compensation awards would be forbidden forfeitures. . . .

The United States Court of Appeals for the Third Circuit consolidated the appeals from these two decisions and reversed. It rejected the District Court Judges' view that the offset provisions caused a forfeiture of vested pension rights forbidden by § [203]. Instead, the Court of Appeals reasoned, such offsets merely reduce pension benefits in a fashion expressly approved by ERISA for employees receiving Social Security [benefits.] [The] court concluded that the New Jersey statute forbidding offsets of pension benefits by the amount of workers' compensation awards could not withstand ERISA's general preemption provision, [ERISA § 514(a)]. [We] affirm the judgment of the Court of Appeals.

Retirees claim that the workers' compensation offset provisions of their pension plans contravene ERISA's nonforfeiture provisions. . . .

Retirees rely on [ERISA's] sweeping assurance that pension rights become nonforfeitable in claiming that offsetting those benefits with workers' compensation awards violates ERISA. . . .

Despite this facial accuracy, retirees' argument overlooks a threshold issue: what defines the content of the benefit that, once vested, cannot be forfeited? ERISA leaves this question largely to the private parties creating the plan. . . .

Rather than imposing mandatory pension levels or methods for calculating benefits, Congress in ERISA set outer bounds on permissible accrual practices, [§ 204(b)(1)], and specified three alternative schedules for the vesting of pension rights, [§ 203(a)(2)]. . . .

It is particularly pertinent for our purposes that Congress did not prohibit "integration," a calculation practice under which benefit levels are determined by combining pension funds with other income streams available to the retired employees. . . .

Following its extensive study of private pension plans before the adoption of ERISA, Congress expressly preserved the option of pension fund integration with benefits available under both the Social Security Act and the Railroad Retirement [Act]. Congress was well aware that pooling of nonpension retirement benefits and pension funds would limit the total income maintenance payments received by individual employees and reduce the cost of pension plans to employers. . . .

In setting [a] limitation on integration with Social Security and Railroad Retirement benefits, Congress acknowledged and accepted the practice, rather than prohibiting it. Moreover, in permitting integration at least with these federal benefits, Congress did not find it necessary to add an exemption for this purpose to its stringent nonforfeiture [protections]. Under these circumstances, we are unpersuaded by retirees' claim that the nonforfeiture provisions by their own force prohibit any offset of pension benefits by workers' compensation awards. Such offsets work much like the integration of pension benefits with Social Security or Railroad Retirement payments. The individual employee remains entitled to the established pension level, but the payments received from the pension fund are reduced by the amount received through workers' compensation. The nonforfeiture provision of § [203(a)] has no more applicability to this kind of integration than it does to the analogous reduction permitted for Social Security or Railroad Retirement payments. Indeed, the same congressional purpose—promoting a system of private pensions by giving employers avenues for cutting the cost of their pension obligations—underlies all such offset possibilities. . . .

The New Jersey Legislature attempted to outlaw the offset clauses by providing that "[t]he right of compensation granted by [the New Jersey Workers' Compensation Act] may be set off against disability pension benefits or payments but *shall not be set off against employees' retirement pension benefits or payments.*" N.J.Stat.Ann. § 34:15–29 (emphasis added). To resolve retirees' claim that this state policy should govern, we must determine whether such state laws are preempted by

ERISA. Our analysis of this problem must be guided by respect for the separate spheres of governmental authority preserved in our federalist system. Although the Supremacy Clause invalidates state laws that "interfere with, or are contrary to the laws of [Congress,]" the "exercise of federal supremacy is not lightly to be [presumed]." As we recently reiterated, "[p]reemption of state law by federal statute or regulation is not favored 'in the absence of persuasive reasons—either that the nature of the regulated subject matter permits no other conclusion, or that the Congress has unmistakably so ordained.'"

In this instance, we are assisted by an explicit congressional statement about the preemptive effect of its action. The same chapter of ERISA that defines the scope of federal protection of employee pension benefits provides that

> "the provisions of this subchapter . . . shall supersede any and all State laws insofar as they may now or hereafter relate to any employee benefit plan described in section [4(a)] of this title and not exempt under section [4(b)] of this title." [ERISA § 514(a)].

This provision demonstrates that Congress intended to depart from its previous legislation that "envisioned the exercise of state regulation power over pension funds," and meant to establish pension plan regulation as exclusively a federal concern. But for the preemption provision to apply here, the New Jersey law must be characterized as a state law "that relate[s] to any employee benefit plan." That phrase gives rise to some confusion where, as here, it is asserted to apply to a state law ostensibly regulating a matter quite different from pension plans. The New Jersey law governs the State's workers' compensation awards, which obviously are subject to the State's police power. As a result, one of the District Court Judges below concluded that the New Jersey provision "is in no way concerned with pension plans *qua* pension plans. On the contrary, the New Jersey statute is solely concerned with protecting the employee's right to worker's compensation disability benefits." Similarly, the other District Court Judge below reasoned that the New Jersey law "only has a collateral effect on pension plans." The Court of Appeals rejected these analyses on two grounds. It read the "relate to pension plans" language in "its normal dictionary sense" as indicating a broad preemptive intent, and it also reasoned that the "*only* purpose and effect of the [New Jersey] statute is to set forth an additional statutory requirement for pension plans," a purpose not permitted by ERISA.

We agree with the conclusion reached by the Court of Appeals but arrive there by a different route. Whatever the purpose or purposes of the New Jersey statute, we conclude that it "relate[s] to pension plans" governed by ERISA because it eliminates one method for calculating pension benefits—integration—that is permitted by federal law. ERISA permits integration of pension funds with other public income maintenance moneys for the purpose of calculating [benefits]. New Jersey's effort to ban pension benefit offsets based on workers' compensation applies directly to this calculation technique. We need not determine the outer bounds of ERISA's preemptive language to find this New Jersey provision an impermissible intrusion on the federal regulatory scheme.

It is of no moment that New Jersey intrudes indirectly, through a workers' compensation law, rather than directly, through a statute called "pension regulation." ERISA makes clear that even indirect state action bearing on private pensions may encroach upon the area of exclusive federal concern. For the purposes of the preemption provision, ERISA defines the term "State" to include: "a State, any political subdivision thereof, or any agency or instrumentality of either, which purports to regulate, *directly or indirectly,* the terms and conditions of employee benefit plans covered by this subchapter." [ERISA § 514(c)(2)] (emphasis added). ERISA's authors clearly meant to preclude the States from avoiding through form the substance of the preemption provision.

Another consideration bolsters our conclusion that the New Jersey provision is preempted insofar as it bears on pensions regulated by ERISA. ERISA leaves integration, along with other pension calculation techniques, subject to the discretion of pension plan designers. Where, as here, the pension plans emerge from collective bargaining, the additional federal interest in precluding state interference with labor-management negotiations calls for preemption of state efforts to regulate pension terms. As a subject of collective bargaining, pension terms themselves become expressions of federal law, requiring preemption of intrusive state law. . . .

The decision of the Court of Appeals is Affirmed.

NOTE

Alessi was the Supreme Court's first encounter with ERISA preemption. As the Court's unanimous affirmance of the Third Circuit suggests, *Alessi* was an easy case. The New Jersey statute undertook to regulate how ERISA-covered plans compute benefit accruals and protect against forfeitures. Since these are central components of ERISA's substantive regulation of pension plans, the state legislation necessarily "relate[d] to" the plans.

Alessi is the prototype of "substantive" or "content conflict" preemption. The content of the state law conflicts with ERISA's regulation of the matter in question. In areas in which ERISA does not propound substantive regulation, the decision whether state law "relates to" a plan has been a harder one.

2. AFTER *ALESSI*: THE BROAD READING OF PREEMPTION

1. *The expansive interpretation.* The Supreme Court's second encounter with ERISA preemption, *Shaw v. Delta Air Lines,* 463 U.S. 85 (1983), produced language that has had far-reaching effect. At issue in *Shaw* were two New York statutes: New York's Human Rights Law, which forbade discrimination in employee benefits plans on the basis of pregnancy, and its Disability Benefits Law, which required employers to pay sick leave benefits to employees unable to work due to pregnancy. ERISA itself does not require that employers provide employees with any particular benefits and, at the time of the complained of conduct, federal law did not forbid discrimination on the basis of pregnancy. Using language that would be cited in more than a thousand judicial opinions, 463 U.S. at 96–98, the Court adopted such a broad interpretation of

§ 514(a) that preemption of state statutes became, for a while, almost automatic.

> We have no difficulty in concluding that the [New York] Human Rights Law and Disability Benefits Law "relate to" employee benefit plans. The breadth of § 514(a)'s preemptive reach is apparent from that section's language. A law "relates to" an employee benefit plan, in the normal sense of the phrase, if it has a connection with or reference to such a plan. Employing this definition, the Human Rights Law, which prohibits employers from structuring their employee benefit plans in a manner that discriminates on the basis of pregnancy, and the Disability Benefits Law, which requires employers to pay employees specific benefits, clearly "relate to" benefit plans. We must give effect to this plain language unless there is good reason to believe Congress intended the language to have some more restrictive meaning. . . .

> In fact, however, Congress used the words "relate to" in § 514(a) in their broad sense. To interpret § 514(a) to preempt only state laws specifically designed to affect employee benefit plans would be to ignore the remainder of § 514. It would have been unnecessary to exempt generally applicable state criminal statutes from preemption in § 514(b), for example, if § 514(a) applied only to state laws dealing specifically with ERISA plans.

> Nor, given the legislative history, can § 514(a) be interpreted to preempt only state laws dealing with the subject matters covered by ERISA—reporting, disclosure, fiduciary responsibility, and the like. The bill that became ERISA originally contained a limited preemption clause, applicable only to state laws relating to the specific subjects covered by ERISA. The Conference Committee rejected these provisions in favor of the present language, and indicated that the section's preemptive scope was as broad as its language.

2. Regarding Congress' purpose in enacting such a broad preemption provision, the Court quoted statements made by two of ERISA's sponsors during the debates, Representative Dent and Senator Williams, that the purpose was to "[eliminate] the threat of conflicting and inconsistent State and local regulation." 463 U.S. at 99. It is true that absent preemption, an employer might have to provide certain benefits in one state and different benefits in another. But would that outcome amount to "conflicting and inconsistent" regulation? Could not the employer satisfy both states simultaneously by having two benefit structures, one for each state? It is not as if the employer used a truck in both states and one state required that it be painted green and the other red.

As a policy matter, it is certainly possible Congress was worried about the administrative burden on a plan of complying with each state's law. But why exactly is this concern so pressing in the employee benefit plan context? Multi-state companies have to deal, after all, with patchworks of potentially conflicting state rules in many other contexts, including building codes, environmental regulations, and wage and hour laws, among others. What is different about employee benefit plans?

3.   The Court in *Shaw* recognized a limit to the breadth of ERISA preemption in an oft-cited footnote, id. at 100 n.21:

> Some state actions may affect employee benefit plans in too tenuous, remote, or peripheral a manner to warrant a finding that the law "relates to" the plan. Cf. *American Telephone and Telegraph Co. v. Merry*, 592 F.2d 118, 121 (2d Cir.1979) (state garnishment of a spouse's pension income to enforce alimony and support orders is not preempted). The present litigation plainly does not present a borderline question, and we express no views about where it would be appropriate to draw the line.

Despite the breadth of the Court's interpretation of the "relate to" clause, the Court actually held the first of the two statutes at issue in *Shaw* to be only partially preempted and the second not to be preempted. It held New York's Human Rights Law preempted only insofar as that act prohibited practices that were lawful under federal law. In analyzing ERISA's exception from preemption for federal laws, the Court reasoned that "[g]iven the importance of state fair employment laws to the federal enforcement scheme, pre-emption of the Human Rights Law would impair Title VII to the extent that the Human Rights Law provides a means for enforcing Title VII's commands." Id. at 102. The Court held the Disability Benefits Law not to be preempted, because that act came under the exception from ERISA's coverage for plans "maintained solely for the purpose of complying with applicable . . . insurance laws," discussed supra.

4.   *Alessi* and *Shaw* were both unanimous decisions. The next two Supreme Court cases dealing with preemption, Metropolitan Life Insurance Co. v. Massachusetts, 471 U.S. 724 (1985), and Pilot Life Insurance Co. v. Dedeaux, 481 U.S. 41 (1987), were also unanimous in applying *Shaw's* broad interpretation of § 514(a) to conclude that the state laws in question "related to" ERISA plans. *Metropolitan Life*, which involved a state statute mandating mental health coverage in group health insurance policies, is reproduced in Chapter 19, in connection with the discussion of the insurance exception. *Pilot Life*, concerning a state law cause of action against insurers for bad faith denial of claims is also discussed in Chapter 19, in connection with the insurance exception, and later in this Chapter in connection with the question of the exclusivity of ERISA's remedial scheme.

5.   *The first close case: garnishment.* In Mackey v. Lanier Collection Agency & Service, 486 U.S. 825 (1988), the Court faced its first close preemption case, in which it divided 5–4. *Mackey* involved a creditor's attempt to use Georgia's garnishment statute to garnish payments owed to a participant by a multiemployer vacation benefit plan. The Court concluded that the garnishment was not preempted. The Court observed that an ERISA plan may be sued "for run-of-the-mill state-law claims such as unpaid rent, failure to pay creditors, or even torts committed by an ERISA plan," and that such suits are not preempted, "although obviously affecting and involving ERISA plans and their trustees." Id. at 833. But ERISA does not provide an enforcement mechanism for enforcing such judgments against a plan. "Consequently, state-law methods for collecting money judgments must, as a general matter, remain undisturbed by ERISA." Id. at 834.

The Court pointed out that "there is simply no logical way to construe the English language so that garnishment or attachment laws 'relate to' benefit plans when they are invoked by creditors of the beneficiaries, but not when they are invoked by beneficiaries or creditors of the [plan] itself." Id. at 836. But, the Court noted, ERISA § 206(d) specifically prohibits the assignment or alienation of pension, but not welfare, benefits. If creditors could not gain access to ERISA plan benefits because such actions were preempted, § 206(d) would be redundant.

The dissenters observed that "[c]ompliance with the state garnishment procedures subjects the plan to significant administrative burdens and costs." Id. at 842. The plan must "confirm the identity" of the participant who owes money to the judgment creditor, "calculate the participant's maximum entitlement from the fund for the period between the service date and the reply date of the summons of garnishment, determine the amount that each participant [owes], and make payments into state [court. . . . Further, [because the plan operates in several states, it is] potentially subject to multiple garnishment orders under varying or conflicting state laws." Because these effects "are not tenuous, remote, or peripheral," the dissenters would have found such laws preempted. The dissenters resisted the majority's inference that ERISA's authorization for plans to be sued impliedly excepted state garnishment laws from preemption. The dissent distinguished between situations in which the ERISA plan is the debtor and those in which it is the garnishee, reasoning that only "in the latter situation [do] plans face the repetitious and costly burden of monitoring controversies involving hundreds of beneficiaries and participants in various states." Id. at 844.

State statutes impose many burdens on plans. For example, a state fair labor standards law may require a plan to pay the plan's employees a minimum wage; state income tax laws may require the plan to withhold state income tax on the wages paid to its employees. Would you expect the dissenters to regard such laws as preempted? If not, would the dissenters find preempted a section of a state income tax requiring plans to withhold state income taxes from payments made to beneficiaries?

Retirement Fund Trust of the Plumbing Industry v. Franchise Tax Board, 909 F.2d 1266, 1280–81 (9th Cir.1990), held that ERISA does not preempt California tax collection legislation authorizing the state to attach welfare plan balances of delinquent taxpayers. Because the plans were welfare benefit plans, ERISA's antialienation provision, § 206(d)(1), did not apply. Following Mackey, the court reasoned that the statute was not preempted, because it did not single out the ERISA plans. "A 'neutral' state law of general application with a 'tangential' impact on a plan does not 'relate to' ERISA and is not preempted."

6. *Laws that specifically reference employee benefit plans.* In *Mackey,* the state garnishment statute had a further provision barring the garnishment of "[f]unds or benefits of [an] employee benefit plan or program subject to [ERISA]." 486 U.S. at 828. The court was unanimous that this provision of the statute was preempted. "[State] laws which make 'reference to' ERISA plans are laws that 'relate to' those plans within the meaning of § 514(a). In fact, we have virtually taken it for granted that state laws which are 'specifically designed to affect

employee benefit plans' are preempted under § 514(a). [The] possibility that [the statute] was enacted [to] help effectuate ERISA's underlying purposes [is] not enough to save the state law from preemption." 486 U.S. at 829.

The Georgia garnishment statute in *Mackey* specifically prohibited garnishment of employee benefit plans subject to ERISA. Would such a prohibition be preempted if it applied to all employee benefit plans, whether or not subject to ERISA? In a footnote the Supreme Court in *Mackey* notes that "any state law which singles out ERISA plans, by express reference, for special treatment is pre-empted. It is this 'singling out' that preempts the Georgia antigarnishment exception." 486 U.S. at 838, n.12.

All states that impose income taxes have provisions in their income tax statutes that provide the same tax-favored treatment to qualified plans as is provided under the Internal Revenue Code. Are these measures preempted because they deliberately affect employee benefit plans?

7. *Laws that indirectly affect plans.* In *Ingersoll-Rand Co. v. McClendon*, 498 U.S. 133 (1990), the Supreme Court addressed the question whether ERISA preempts a state common law claim that an employee was wrongfully discharged in order to prevent his attaining benefits under an ERISA plan. The employee, McClendon, was terminated after working for Ingersoll-Rand for nine years and eight months, allegedly on account of a company-wide reduction in force. The pension plan under which McClendon was covered had a ten-year vesting requirement. (ERISA permitted ten-year cliff vesting until 1986; see supra Chapter 4.) McClendon sued under state law for wrongful discharge, alleging that the company terminated him to prevent him from vesting in his benefits. (In fact, unbeknownst to McClendon, as a result of ERISA's break-in-service rules, he was already vested at the time of his termination.) The Texas Supreme Court held that under Texas law a plaintiff could recover in a wrongful discharge action if he established that "the principal reason for his termination was the employer's desire to avoid contributing to or paying benefits under the employee's pension fund." Id. at 136.

The Supreme Court disagreed, determining that whether analyzed as a case of express or implied preemption, the Texas cause of action was preempted. As a matter of the express language of the statute, the Court began by observing that

> a state law may "relate to" a benefit plan, and thereby be preempted, even if the law is not specifically designed to affect such plans, or the effect is only indirect. Preemption is also not precluded simply because a state law is consistent with ERISA's substantive requirements.

Id. at 139. The Court explained why limits on ERISA's preemptive effect recognized in its earlier decisions were inapplicable:

> We are not dealing here with a generally applicable statute that makes no reference to, or indeed functions irrespective of, the existence of an ERISA plan. Nor is the cost of defending this lawsuit a mere administrative burden. Here, the existence of a

pension plan is a critical factor in establishing liability under the State's wrongful discharge law. As a result, this cause of action relates not merely to pension benefits, but to the essence of the pension *plan* itself. . . .

[I]n order to prevail, a plaintiff must plead, and the court must find, that an ERISA plan exists and the employer had a pension-defeating motive in terminating the employment. Because the court's inquiry must be directed to the plan, this judicially created cause of action "relate[s] to" an ERISA plan.

498 U.S. at 139–140.

The Court further said that, even had § 514 not expressly preempted state law, the Texas cause of action would have been preempted for conflict with ERISA: "[T]he Texas cause of action purports to provide a remedy for the violation of a right expressly guaranteed by § 510 and exclusively enforced by § 502(a)." Id. at 145. Preemption based on the exclusivity of ERISA's enforcement scheme is discussed in Section E.1., infra.

Why did McClendon not bring a claim under ERISA § 510 in federal court, since his allegations fit squarely within the language and purpose of that provision? The likely answer is that he was seeking punitive and consequential damages, remedies not available under ERISA, as we saw in Chapter 16, supra.

The reasoning of the Court in *Ingersoll-Rand* has been applied to similar allegations of wrongful discharge, see, e.g. Bullock v. Equitable Life Assurance Society, 259 F.3d 395 (5th Cir.2001); Felton v. Unisource Corp., 940 F.2d 503, 509 (9th Cir.1991). By contrast, when loss of benefits is a mere consequence of, rather than a motivation for, termination, preemption need not result. See Campbell v. Aerospace Corp., 123 F.3d 1308 (9th Cir.1997).

C. *TRAVELERS*: REVISITING THE SCOPE OF PREEMPTION

1. NEW YORK STATE CONFERENCE OF BLUE CROSS & BLUE SHIELD PLANS V. TRAVELERS INSURANCE CO.

514 U.S. 645 (1995).

■ JUSTICE SOUTER delivered the opinion for a unanimous Court.

A New York statute requires hospitals to collect surcharges from patients covered by a commercial insurer but not from patients insured by a Blue Cross/Blue Shield plan, and it subjects certain health maintenance organizations (HMOs) to surcharges that vary with the number of Medicaid recipients each enrolls. This case calls for us to decide whether [ERISA] preempts the state provisions for surcharges on bills of patients whose commercial insurance coverage is purchased by employee healthcare plans governed by ERISA, and for surcharges on HMOs insofar as their membership fees are paid by an ERISA plan. We hold that the provisions for surcharges do not "relate to" employee benefit plans within the meaning of ERISA's preemption provision, § 514(a), and accordingly suffer no preemption.

New York's Prospective Hospital Reimbursement Methodology (NYPHRM) regulates hospital rates for all inpatient care, except for services provided to Medicare beneficiaries. The scheme calls for patients to be charged not for the cost of their individual treatment, but for the average cost of treating the patient's medical problem, as classified under one or another of 794 Diagnostic Related Groups (DRGs). The charges allowable in accordance with DRG classifications are adjusted for a specific hospital to reflect its particular operating costs, capital investments, bad debts, costs of charity care and the like.

Patients with Blue Cross/Blue Shield coverage, Medicaid patients, and HMO participants are billed at a hospital's DRG rate. Others, however, are not. Patients served by commercial insurers providing in-patient hospital coverage on an expense-incurred basis, by self-insured funds directly reimbursing hospitals, and by certain workers' compensation, volunteer firefighters' benefit, ambulance workers' benefit, and no-fault motor vehicle insurance funds, must be billed at the DRG rate plus a 13% surcharge to be retained by the hospital. For the year ending March 31, 1993, moreover, hospitals were required to bill commercially insured patients for a further 11% surcharge to be turned over to the State, with the result that these patients were charged 24% more than the DRG rate.

New York law also imposes a surcharge on HMOs, which varies depending on the number of eligible Medicaid recipients an HMO has enrolled, but which may run as high as 9% of the aggregate monthly charges paid by an HMO for its members' inpatient hospital care. This assessment is not an increase in the rates to be paid by an HMO to hospitals, but a direct payment by the HMO to the State's general fund. . . .

On the claimed authority of ERISA's general preemption provision, several commercial insurers, acting as fiduciaries of ERISA plans they administer, joined with their trade associations to bring actions against state officials in United States District Court seeking to invalidate the 13%, 11%, and 9% surcharge statutes. The New York State Conference of Blue Cross and Blue Shield plans, Empire Blue Cross and Blue Shield (collectively the Blues), and the Hospital Association of New York State intervened as defendants, and the New York State Health Maintenance Organization Conference and several HMOs intervened as plaintiffs. The District Court consolidated the actions and granted summary judgment to the plaintiffs. [The] Court of Appeals for the Second Circuit affirmed. [We] now reverse and remand.

Our past cases have recognized that the Supremacy Clause, U.S. Const., Art. VI, may entail preemption of state law either by express provision, by implication, or by a conflict between federal and state law. And yet, despite the variety of these opportunities for federal preeminence, we have never assumed lightly that Congress has derogated state regulation, but instead have addressed claims of preemption with the starting presumption that Congress does not intend to supplant state law. Indeed, in cases like this one, where federal law is said to bar state action in fields of traditional state regulation, we have worked on the "assumption that the historic police powers of the States were not to be superseded by the Federal Act unless that was the clear and manifest purpose of Congress."

Since pre-emption claims turn on Congress's intent, we begin as we do in any exercise of statutory construction with the text of the provision in question, and move on, as need be, to the structure and purpose of the Act in which it occurs. The governing text of ERISA is clearly expansive. Section 514(a) marks for preemption "all state laws insofar as they . . . relate to any employee benefit plan" covered by ERISA, and one might be excused for wondering, at first blush, whether the words of limitation ("insofar as they . . . relate") do much limiting. If "relate to" were taken to extend to the furthest stretch of its indeterminacy, then for all practical purposes preemption would never run its course, for "really, universally, relations stop nowhere." H. James, Roderick Hudson xli (New York ed., World's Classics 1980). But that, of course, would be to read Congress's words of limitation as mere sham, and to read the presumption against preemption out of the law whenever Congress speaks to the matter with generality. That said, we have to recognize that our prior attempt to construe the phrase "relate to" does not give us much help drawing the line here.

In *Shaw v. Delta Air Lines, Inc.*, 463 U.S. 85 (1983), we explained that "[a] law 'relates to' an employee benefit plan, in the normal sense of the phrase, if it has a connection with or reference to such a plan." The latter alternative, at least, can be ruled out. The surcharges are imposed upon patients and HMOs, regardless of whether the commercial coverage or membership, respectively, is ultimately secured by an ERISA plan, private purchase, or otherwise, with the consequence that the surcharge statutes cannot be said to make "reference to" ERISA plans in any manner. But this still leaves us to question whether the surcharge laws have a "connection with" the ERISA plans, and here an uncritical literalism is no more help than in trying to construe "relate to." For the same reasons that infinite relations cannot be the measure of preemption, neither can infinite connections. We simply must go beyond the unhelpful text and the frustrating difficulty of defining its key term, and look instead to the objectives of the ERISA statute as a guide to the scope of the state law that Congress understood would survive.

As we have said before, [ERISA] § 514 indicates Congress's intent to establish the regulation of employee welfare benefit plans "as exclusively a federal concern." . . .

Accordingly in *Shaw*, for example, we had no trouble finding that New York's "Human Rights Law, which prohibited employers from structuring their employee benefit plans in a manner that discriminated on the basis of pregnancy, and [New York's] Disability Benefits Law, which required employers to pay employees specific benefits, clearly 'related to' benefit plans." These mandates affecting coverage could have been honored only by varying the subjects of a plan's benefits whenever New York law might have applied, or by requiring every plan to provide all beneficiaries with a benefit demanded by New York law if New York law could have been said to require it for any one beneficiary. Similarly, Pennsylvania's law that prohibited "plans from . . . requiring reimbursement [from the beneficiary] in the event of recovery from a third party" related to employee benefit plans within the meaning of § 514(a). *FMC Corp. v. Holliday*, 498 U.S. 52, 60 (1990). The law "prohibited plans from being structured in a manner requiring reimbursement in the event of recovery from a third party" and "required plan providers to calculate benefit levels in Pennsylvania based on expected liability conditions that differ from those in States that have not enacted similar antisubrogation legislation," thereby "frustrating plan administrators' continuing obligation to calculate uniform benefit levels nationwide." Pennsylvania employees who recovered in negligence actions against tortfeasors would, by virtue of the state law, in effect have been entitled to benefits in excess of what plan administrators intended to provide, and in excess of what the plan provided to employees in other States. Along the same lines, New Jersey could not prohibit plans from setting workers' compensation payments off against employees' retirement benefits or pensions, because doing so would prevent plans from using a method of calculating benefits permitted by federal law. *Alessi, supra*, at 524. In each of these cases, ERISA preempted state laws that mandated employee benefit structures or their administration. Elsewhere, we have held that state laws providing alternate enforcement mechanisms also relate to ERISA plans, triggering preemption. See *Ingersoll-Rand*.

Both the purpose and the effects of the New York surcharge statutes distinguish them from the examples just given. The charge differentials have been justified on the ground that the Blues pay the hospitals promptly and efficiently and, more importantly, provide coverage for many subscribers whom the commercial insurers would reject as unacceptable risks. The Blues' practice, called open enrollment, has consistently been cited as the principal reason for charge differentials, whether the differentials resulted from voluntary negotiation between hospitals and payers as was the case prior to the NYPHRM system, or were created by the surcharges as is the case now. Since the surcharges are presumably passed on at least in part to those who purchase commercial insurance or HMO membership, their effects follow from their purpose. Although there is no evidence that the surcharges will drive every health insurance consumer to the Blues, they do make the Blues more attractive (or less unattractive) as insurance alternatives and thus have an indirect economic effect on choices made by insurance buyers, including ERISA plans.

An indirect economic influence, however, does not bind plan administrators to any particular choice and thus function as a regulation of an ERISA plan itself; commercial insurers and HMOs may still offer more attractive packages than the Blues. Nor does the indirect influence of the surcharges preclude uniform administrative practice or the provision of a uniform interstate benefit package if a plan wishes to provide one. It simply bears on the costs of benefits and the relative costs of competing insurance to provide them. It is an influence that can affect a plan's shopping decisions, but it does not affect the fact that any plan will shop for the best deal it can get, surcharges or no surcharges.

There is, indeed, nothing remarkable about surcharges on hospital bills, or their effects on overall cost to the plans and the relative attractiveness of certain insurers. Rate variations among hospital providers are accepted examples of cost variation. . . .

If the common character of rate differentials even in the absence of state action renders it unlikely that ERISA preemption was meant to bar such indirect economic influences under state law, the existence of other common state action with indirect economic effects on a plan's costs leaves the intent to preempt even less likely. Quality standards, for example, set by the State in one subject area of hospital services but not another would affect the relative cost of providing those services over others and, so, of providing different packages of health insurance benefits. Even basic regulation of employment conditions will invariably affect the cost and price of services.

Quality control and workplace regulation, to be sure, are presumably less likely to affect premium differentials among competing insurers, but that does not change the fact that such state regulation will indirectly affect what an ERISA or other plan can afford or get for its money. Thus, in the absence of a more exact guide to intended preemption than § 514, it is fair to conclude that mandates for rate differentials would not be preempted unless other regulation with indirect effects on plan costs would be superseded as well. The bigger the package of regulation with indirect effects that would fall on the respondent's reading of § 514, the less likely it is that federal regulation of benefit plans was intended to eliminate state regulation of health care costs.

Indeed, to read the pre-emption provision as displacing all state laws affecting costs and charges on the theory that they indirectly relate to ERISA plans that purchase insurance policies or HMO memberships that would cover such services, would effectively read the limiting language in § 514(a) out of the statute, a conclusion that would violate basic principles of statutory interpretation and could not be squared with our prior pronouncement that "preemption does not occur . . . if the state law has only a tenuous, remote, or peripheral connection with covered plans, as is the case with many laws of general applicability." *District of Columbia v. Greater Washington Board of Trade,* 506 U.S. 125 (1992). While Congress's extension of preemption to all "state laws relating to benefit plans" was meant to sweep more broadly than "state laws dealing with the subject matters covered by ERISA[,] reporting, disclosure, fiduciary responsibility, and the like," *Shaw,* nothing in the language of the Act or the context of its passage indicates that Congress chose to displace general health care regulation, which historically has been a matter of local concern.

In sum, cost-uniformity was almost certainly not an object of preemption, just as laws with only an indirect economic effect on the relative costs of various health insurance packages in a given State are a far cry from those "conflicting directives" from which Congress meant to insulate ERISA plans. Such state laws leave plan administrators right where they would be in any case, with the responsibility to choose the best overall coverage for the money. We therefore conclude that such state laws do not bear the requisite "connection with" ERISA plans to trigger preemption. . . .

It remains only to speak further on a point already raised, that any conclusion other than the one we draw would bar any state regulation of hospital costs. The basic DRG system (even without any surcharge), like any other interference with the hospital services market, would fall on a theory that all laws with indirect economic effects on ERISA plans are preempted under § 514(a). This would be an unsettling result and all the more startling because several States, including New York, regulated hospital charges to one degree or another at the time ERISA was passed. And yet there is not so much as a hint in ERISA's legislative history or anywhere else that Congress intended to squelch these state efforts. . . .

[We] do not hold today that ERISA preempts only direct regulation of ERISA plans, nor could we do that with fidelity to the views expressed in our prior opinions on the matter. We acknowledge that a state law might produce such acute, albeit indirect, economic effects, by intent or otherwise, as to force an ERISA plan to adopt a certain scheme of substantive coverage or effectively restrict its choice of insurers, and that such a state law might indeed be preempted under § 514. But as we have shown, New York's surcharges do not fall into either category; they affect only indirectly the relative prices of insurance policies, a result no different from myriad state laws in areas traditionally subject to local regulation, which Congress could not possibly have intended to eliminate.

2.   POST-*TRAVELERS* JURISPRUDENCE AND THE MEANING OF "RELATE TO"

1.   *Reducing Shaw's reach.* In *Ingersoll-Rand*, discussed supra, which relied on *Shaw*'s broad "relate to" approach, the Supreme Court had recognized that laws not specifically designed to affect benefit plans or laws affecting such plans only indirectly may "relate to" a benefit plan and therefore be preempted. *Travelers* abandoned the *Shaw* analysis, which resulted in nearly automatic preemption of state law. A number of courts have described *Travelers* as effecting a "sea change." See, e.g., Whitt v. Sherman Int'l Corp., 147 F.3d 1325, 1333 (11th Cir.1998). What is the new test? Would it be fair to summarize *Travelers* as follows: (1) there is a presumption against preemption and (2) only state laws that address the administration of employee benefit plans or provide alternate enforcement mechanisms are preempted? Or is the court required in each instance, as stated in *Travelers*, to "look [to] the objectives of the ERISA statute as a guide to the scope of the state law that Congress understood would survive"?

2.   *Direct v. indirect effect revisited: De Buono.* The statute involved in *Travelers* imposed a tax on health insurers who provided coverage to plans and their beneficiaries. Several times in the opinion, the Court emphasizes the "indirect economic influence" of such a statute. Would the result be different if the state imposed a tax directly on a plan?

In De Buono v. NYSA-ILA Medical and Clinical Services Fund, 520 U.S. 806, 814–16 (1997), the Supreme Court upheld a state tax on gross receipts for patient services at hospitals and similar facilities, even though the tax applied to a medical center owned and operated by an ERISA plan. The Court began by invoking the "historic police powers of the State," observing that those powers include the regulation of matters of health and safety. While the [state statute] is a revenue raising measure, rather than a regulation of hospitals, it clearly operates in a field that " 'has been traditionally occupied by the States.' " Respondents therefore bear the considerable burden of overcoming "the starting presumption that Congress does not intend to supplant state law."

There is nothing in the operation of the [state statute] that convinces us it is the type of state law that Congress intended ERISA to supercede. This is not a case in which New York has forbidden a method of calculating pension benefits that federal law permits, or required employers to provide certain benefits. Nor is it a case in which the existence of a pension plan is a critical element of a state law cause of action, or one in which the state statute contains provisions that expressly refer to ERISA or ERISA plans.

As does the IRC, many states impose taxes on the unrelated business taxable income of an otherwise tax-exempt organization. Is the imposition of such a tax on the income earned by a pension fund preempted by ERISA? In Hattem v. Schwarzenegger, 449 F.3d 423 (2d Cir. 2006), the Court of Appeals for the Second Circuit held that California's unrelated business income taxation of an ERISA trust is not preempted. A New York Tax Appeals Tribunal came to the opposite conclusion regarding New York's unrelated business income tax, which is substantially similar to California's. See Matter of McKinsey Master Retirement Plan Trust, 2003 WL 22110291 (N.Y. Tax App.Div.2003).

3.   *Inducement v. compulsion: Dillingham.* In California Division of Labor Standards Enforcement v. Dillingham Construction, N.A., Inc., 519 U.S. 316 (1997), the Supreme Court had before it not a tax statute, but a prevailing wage statute. California requires a contractor on a public works project to pay its workers the prevailing wage (usually the local union wage), but lower wages are permitted for apprentices in a state-approved apprenticeship program. An apprenticeship plan that is separately-funded is an ERISA plan. ERISA § 3(1). In *Dillingham* the Court, reversing the Ninth Circuit, held that the prevailing wage statute was not preempted.

We think that, in every relevant respect, California's prevailing wage statute is indistinguishable from New York's surcharge program [in *Travelers*]. At the outset, we note that apprenticeship standards and the wages paid on state public works have long been regulated by the States. . . .

That the States traditionally regulated these areas would not alone immunize their efforts; ERISA certainly contemplated the preemption of substantial areas of traditional state regulation. The wages to be paid on public works projects and the substantive standards to be applied to apprenticeship training programs are, however, quite remote from the areas with which ERISA is expressly concerned—"reporting, disclosure, fiduciary responsibility, and the like." A reading of § 514(a) resulting in the preemption of traditionally state-regulated substantive law in those areas where ERISA has nothing to say would be "unsettling." . . .

[It] cannot be gainsaid that [the California statute] has the effect of encouraging apprenticeship programs—including ERISA plans—to meet the standards set out by California, but it has not been demonstrated here that the added inducement created by the wage break available on state public works projects is tantamount to a compulsion upon apprenticeship programs.

[The] prevailing wage statute alters the incentives, but does not dictate the choices, facing ERISA plans. In this regard, it is "no different from myriad state laws in areas traditionally subject to local regulation, which Congress could not possibly have intended to eliminate." *Travelers*. We could not hold preempted a state law in an area of traditional state regulation based on so tenuous a relation without doing grave violence to our presumption that Congress intended nothing of the sort.

519 U.S. at 330–34.

The Ninth Circuit applied the *Dillingham* analysis to apprenticeship standards for private works projects in Associated Builders and Contractors of Southern California, Inc. v. Nunn, 356 F.3d 979 (9th Cir.2004), rejecting the claim that there should be any difference in the preemption analysis, whether the project is public or private.

Is the line between "altering incentives" and "dictating the choices" coherent? What would be the fate of a state statute that levied a special income tax surcharge on all businesses, but eliminated the tax for businesses that provided a specified minimum level of health benefits to all of its employees? See the discussion of Golden Gate Restaurant Association v. City and County of San Francisco, 546 F.3d 639 (9th Cir.2008), in Chapter 19.

Would a prevailing wage law that required a firm working on public contracts to provide its employees not only with the prevailing cash wage, but also with the prevailing benefits, be preempted? Recall the statement in *Travelers* that a plan that "mandate[s] employee benefit structures" is preempted. In General Electric Co. v. New York State Dep't of Labor, 891 F.2d 25 (2d Cir.1989), the Second Circuit found that ERISA preempted the New York prevailing wage statute. As The New York Statute was then interpreted by the New York Commissioner of Labor, it required an employer either to bring the cost of a benefit into equivalence with the cost of the local prevailing one or to pay the additional cost to the employee-beneficiaries. The employer was not permitted to substitute one form of benefit for another, and received no credit for the cost of benefits not deemed to be prevailing benefits by the Commissioner.

Following *General Electric*, New York revised its approach, and allowed employers to meet their prevailing wage liability in any form or combination of benefit plans or wages. In Burgio & Campofelice, Inc. v. New York State Dep't of Labor, 107 F.3d 1000 (2d Cir.1997), a post-*Dillingham* case, the Second Circuit distinguished *General Electric* and concluded that such a "total package" approach is not preempted, because it does not require any particular benefit and thereby avoids the possibility of conflicting directives. Prevailing wage statutes using a total package approach have also been upheld in several other circuits. See HMI Mechanical Systems v. McGowan, 266 F.3d 142 (2d Cir.2001); WSB Electric, Inc. v. Curry, 88 F.3d 788, 794–96 (9th Cir.1996); Minnesota Chapter of Associated Builders & Contractors v. Minnesota Dep't of Labor & Industry, 47 F.3d 975, 979 (8th Cir.1995); Keystone Chapter, Assoc. Builders and Contractors v. Foley, 37 F.3d 945 (3d Cir.1994).

4. *Field preemption.* In a concurrence in *Dillingham*, 519 U.S. at 335–36, Justice Scalia, joined by Justice Ginsburg, opined that

> it would greatly assist our function of clarifying the law if we simply acknowledged that our first take on [ERISA preemption] was wrong; that the "relate to" clause of the preemption provision is meant, not to set forth a test for preemption, but rather to identify the field in which ordinary field preemption applies—namely, the field of laws regulating "employee benefit plan[s] described in [ERISA § 4(a)] and not exempt under [ERISA § 4(b)]." [ERISA § 514(a)]. [I] think it accurately describes our current ERISA jurisprudence to say that we apply ordinary field preemption, and, of course, ordinary conflict preemption. Nothing more mysterious than that; and except as establishing that, "relates to" is irrelevant.

Is Justice Scalia's formulation of the test any more helpful than the Court's? Under traditional field preemption analysis, the inquiry is whether Congress meant to occupy a regulatory field. If Congress manifests such a purpose, then there is no room for states to supplement the federal law or to enforce state laws on the same subject. Apart from reporting, disclosure, and fiduciary duty requirements, ERISA provides little substantive regulation of welfare benefit plans. Did Congress manifest an intent to preclude states from regulating the level of welfare plan benefits? Outside the employee benefit context, the Supreme Court has noted that "[a] federal decision to forgo regulation in a given area may imply an authoritative federal determination that the area is best left unregulated." Arkansas Electric Cooperative Association v. Arkansas Public Service Comm'n, 461 U.S. 375 (1983).

For a useful discussion of the various types of preemption, see Kathleen M. Sullivan & Gerald Gunther, Constitutional Law 237–40 (17th ed. 2010).

5. *Market participant exception.* In Building & Construction Trades Council v. Associated Builders, 507 U.S. 218 (1993), a non-ERISA case usually referred to as *Boston Harbor*, the Supreme Court held that National Labor Relations Act preemption does not apply when a state or local government pursues its purely proprietary interests. In Associated General Contractors of America v. Metropolitan Water District of Southern California, 159 F.3d 1178 (9th Cir.1998), a contractors' association sought on the grounds of ERISA preemption to prevent a water district from enforcing a provision of a project labor agreement that required contractors to participate in employee benefit plans. The Ninth Circuit held that a provision of a labor agreement for a discrete project that was not a generally applicable law or regulation was not "state law" within the meaning of ERISA § 514(a) and was therefore not preempted. "[W]here the state merely acts as any private party might act, instead of

areas where it exercises lawmaking or law enforcement authority, ERISA preemption does not come in to play." Id. at 1182. But see Air Transport Association of America v. City & County of San Francisco, 992 F.Supp. 1149, 1178 (N.D.Cal.1998)(San Francisco ordinance prohibiting the city from contracting with companies whose employee benefit plans discriminate between employees with spouses and employees with domestic partners held preempted because San Francisco had passed the ordinance with "policy goals in mind").

D. STATE INHERITANCE, DOMESTIC RELATIONS AND PROPERTY-RIGHTS LAWS

1. EGELHOFF V. EGELHOFF

532 U.S. 141 (2001).

■ JUSTICE THOMAS delivered the opinion of the Court.

A Washington statute provides that the designation of a spouse as the beneficiary of a nonprobate asset is revoked automatically upon divorce. We are asked to decide whether [ERISA] preempts that statute to the extent it applies to ERISA plans. We hold that it does.

I

Petitioner Donna Rae Egelhoff was married to David A. Egelhoff. Mr. Egelhoff was employed by the Boeing Company, which provided him with a life insurance policy and a pension plan. Both plans were governed by ERISA, and Mr. Egelhoff designated his wife as the beneficiary under both. In April 1994, the Egelhoffs divorced. Just over two months later, Mr. Egelhoff died intestate following an automobile accident. At that time, Mrs. Egelhoff remained the listed beneficiary under both the life insurance policy and the pension plan. The life insurance proceeds, totaling $46,000, were paid to her.

Respondents Samantha and David Egelhoff, Mr. Egelhoff's children by a previous marriage, are his statutory heirs under state law. They sued petitioner in Washington state court to recover the life insurance proceeds. Respondents relied on a Washington statute that provides:

> "If a marriage is dissolved or invalidated, a provision made prior to that event that relates to the payment or transfer at death of the decedent's interest in a nonprobate asset in favor of or granting an interest or power to the decedent's former spouse is revoked. A provision affected by this section must be interpreted, and the nonprobate asset affected passes, as if the former spouse failed to survive the decedent, having died at the time of entry of the decree of dissolution or declaration of invalidity."

That statute applies to "all nonprobate assets, wherever situated, held at the time of entry by a superior court of this state of a decree of dissolution of marriage or a declaration of invalidity." It defines "nonprobate asset" to include "a life insurance policy, employee benefit plan, annuity or similar contract, or individual retirement account."

Respondents argued that they were entitled to the life insurance proceeds because the Washington statute disqualified Mrs. Egelhoff as a beneficiary, and in the absence of a qualified named beneficiary, the proceeds would pass to them as Mr. Egelhoff's heirs. In a separate action, respondents also sued to recover the pension plan benefits. Respondents again argued that the Washington statute disqualified Mrs. Egelhoff as a beneficiary and they were thus entitled to the benefits under the plan.

The trial courts, concluding that both the insurance policy and the pension plan "should be administered in accordance" with ERISA, granted summary judgment to petitioner in both cases. The Washington Court of Appeals consolidated the cases and reversed. It concluded that the Washington statute was not preempted by ERISA. Applying the statute, it held that respondents were entitled to the proceeds of both the insurance policy and the pension plan.

The Supreme Court of Washington affirmed. It held that the state statute, although applicable to "employee benefit plan[s]," does not "refe[r] to" ERISA plans to an extent that would require preemption, because it "does not apply immediately and exclusively to an ERISA plan, nor is the existence of such a plan essential to operation of the statute." It also held that the statute lacks a "connection with" an ERISA plan that would compel preemption. It emphasized that the statute "does not alter the nature of the plan itself, the administrator's fiduciary duties, or the requirements for plan administration." Nor, the court concluded, does the statute conflict with any specific provision of ERISA, including the antialienation provision, because it "does not operate to divert benefit plan proceeds from distribution under terms of the plan documents," but merely alters "the underlying circumstances to which the distribution scheme of [the] plan must be applied."

Courts have disagreed about whether statutes like that of Washington are preempted by ERISA. To resolve the conflict, we granted certiorari.

II

Petitioner argues that the Washington statute falls within the terms of ERISA's express preemption provision and that it is preempted by ERISA under traditional principles of conflict preemption. Because we conclude that the statute is expressly preempted by ERISA, we address only the first argument.

ERISA's preemption section, [ERISA § 514(a)], states that ERISA "shall supersede any and all State laws insofar as they may now or hereafter relate to any employee benefit plan" covered by ERISA. We have observed repeatedly that this broadly worded provision is "clearly expansive." But at the same time, we have recognized that the term "relate to" cannot be taken "to extend to the furthest stretch of its indeterminacy," or else "for all practical purposes preemption would never run its course." [*Travelers*, *supra*, at 655.]

We have held that a state law relates to an ERISA plan "if it has a connection with or reference to such a plan." *Shaw v. Delta Air Lines, Inc.*, 463 U.S. 85 (1983). Petitioner focuses on the "connection with" part of this inquiry. Acknowledging that "connection with" is scarcely more restrictive than "relate to," we have cautioned against an "uncritical literalism" that would make preemption turn on "infinite connections." *Travelers, supra*, at 656. Instead, "to determine whether a state law has the forbidden connection, we look both to 'the objectives of the ERISA statute as a guide to the scope of the state law that Congress understood would survive,' as well as to the nature of the effect of the state law on ERISA plans." *California Div. of Labor Standards Enforcement v. Dillingham Constr., N. A., Inc.*, 519 U.S. 316, 325 (1997).

Applying this framework, petitioner argues that the Washington statute has an impermissible connection with ERISA plans. We agree. The statute binds ERISA plan administrators to a particular choice of rules for determining beneficiary status. The administrators must pay benefits to the beneficiaries chosen by state law, rather than to those identified in the plan documents. The statute thus implicates an area of core ERISA concern. In particular, it runs counter to ERISA's commands that a plan shall "specify the basis on which payments are made to and from the plan," [ERISA § 402(b)(4)], and that the fiduciary shall administer the plan "in accordance with the documents and instruments governing the plan," [ERISA § 404(a)(1)(D)], making payments to a "beneficiary" who is "designated by a participant, or by the terms of [the] plan." [ERISA § 3(8)]. In other words, unlike generally applicable laws regulating "areas where ERISA has nothing to say," *Dillingham*, 519 U.S., at 330, which we have upheld notwithstanding their incidental effect on ERISA plans, this statute governs the payment of benefits, a central matter of plan administration.

The Washington statute also has a prohibited connection with ERISA plans because it interferes with nationally uniform plan administration. Uniformity is impossible, however, if plans are subject to different legal obligations in different States.

The Washington statute at issue here poses precisely that threat. Plan administrators cannot make payments simply by identifying the beneficiary specified by the plan documents. Instead they must familiarize themselves with state statutes so that they can determine whether the named beneficiary's status has been "revoked" by operation of law. And in this context the burden is exacerbated by the choice-of-law problems that may confront an administrator when the employer is located in one State, the plan participant lives in another, and the participant's former spouse lives in a third. In such a situation, administrators might find that plan payments are subject to conflicting legal obligations. . . .

We recognize that all state laws create some potential for a lack of uniformity. But differing state regulations affecting an ERISA plan's "system for processing claims and paying benefits" impose "precisely the burden that ERISA preemption was intended to avoid." *Fort Halifax, supra*, at 10. And as we have noted, the statute at issue here directly conflicts with ERISA's requirements that plans be administered, and benefits be paid, in accordance with plan documents. We conclude that the Washington statute has a "connection with" ERISA plans and is therefore preempted.

III

Respondents suggest several reasons why ordinary ERISA pre-emption analysis should not apply here. First, they observe that the Washington statute allows employers to opt out. According to respondents, the statute neither regulates plan administration nor impairs uniformity because it does not apply when "[t]he instrument governing disposition of the nonprobate asset expressly provides otherwise." We do not believe that the statute is saved from preemption simply because it is, at least in a broad sense, a default rule.

Even though the Washington statute's cancellation of private choice may itself be trumped by specific language in the plan documents, the statute does "dictate the choice[s] facing ERISA plans" with respect to matters of plan administration. *Dillingham, supra*, at 334. Plan administrators must either follow Washington's beneficiary designation scheme or alter the terms of their plan so as to indicate that they will not follow it. The statute is not any less of a regulation of the terms of ERISA plans simply because there are two ways of complying with it. Of course, simple noncompliance with the statute is not one of the options available to plan administrators. Their only choice is one of timing, *i.e.*, whether to bear the burden of compliance ex post, by paying benefits as the statute dictates (and in contravention of the plan documents), or *ex ante*, by amending the plan.

Respondents emphasize that the opt-out provision makes compliance with the statute less burdensome than if it were mandatory. That is true enough, but the burden that remains is hardly trivial. It is not enough for plan administrators to opt out of this particular statute. Instead, they must maintain a familiarity with the laws of all 50 States so that they can update their plans as necessary to satisfy the opt-out requirements of other, similar statutes. They also must be attentive to changes in the interpretations of those statutes by state courts. This "tailoring of plans and employer conduct to the peculiarities of the law of each jurisdiction" is exactly the burden ERISA seeks to eliminate. *Ingersoll-Rand*, supra, at 142.

Second, respondents emphasize that the Washington statute involves both family law and probate law, areas of traditional state regulation. There is indeed a presumption against preemption in areas of traditional state regulation such as family law. But that presumption can be overcome where, as here, Congress has made clear its desire for preemption. Accordingly, we have not hesitated to find state family law preempted when it conflicts with ERISA or relates to ERISA plans.

Finally, respondents argue that if ERISA preempts this statute, then it also must preempt the various state statutes providing that a murdering heir is not entitled to receive property as a result of the killing. In the ERISA context, these "slayer" statutes could revoke the beneficiary status of someone who murdered a plan participant. Those statutes are not before us, so we do not decide the issue. We note, however, that the principle underlying the statutes—which have been adopted by nearly every State—is well established in the law and has a long historical pedigree predating ERISA. And because the statutes are more or less uniform nationwide, their interference with the aims of ERISA is at least debatable.

The judgment of the Supreme Court of Washington is reversed, and the case is remanded for further proceedings not inconsistent with this opinion.

■ JUSTICE BREYER, with whom JUSTICE STEVENS joins, dissenting.

[I] believe that we should apply normal conflict preemption and field preemption principles where, as here, a state statute covers ERISA and non-ERISA documents alike. . . .

[I] do not agree [h]owever, that there is any plausible preemption principle that leads to a conclusion that ERISA preempts the statute at issue here. No one could claim that ERISA preempts the entire *field* of state law governing inheritance—though such matters "relate to" ERISA broadly speaking. Neither is there any direct conflict between the Washington statute and ERISA, for the one nowhere directly contradicts the other.

The Court correctly points out that ERISA requires a fiduciary to make payments to a beneficiary "in accordance with the documents and instruments governing the plan." But nothing in the Washington statute requires the contrary. Rather, the state statute simply sets forth a default rule for interpreting documentary silence. . . . This state-law rule is a rule of interpretation, and it is designed to carry out, not to conflict with, the employee's likely intention as revealed in the plan documents. . . .

[The] Court claims that the Washington statute "interferes with nationally uniform plan administration" by requiring administrators to "familiarize themselves with state statutes." But administrators have to familiarize themselves with state law in any event when they answer such routine legal questions as whether amounts due are subject to garnishment, *Mackey v. Lanier Collection Agency & Service, Inc.*, 486 U.S. 825, 838 (1988), who is a "spouse," who qualifies as a "child," or when an employee is legally dead. And were that "familiarizing burden" somehow overwhelming, the plan could easily avoid it by resolving the divorce revocation issue in the plan documents themselves, stating expressly that state law does not apply. The "burden" thus reduces to a one-time requirement that would fall primarily upon the few who draft model ERISA documents, not upon the many who administer them. So meager a burden cannot justify preempting a state law that enjoys a presumption against preemption . . .

Indeed, if one looks beyond administrative burden, one finds that Washington's statute poses no obstacle, but furthers ERISA's ultimate objective—developing a fair system for protecting employee benefits. The Washington statute transfers an employee's pension assets at death to those individuals whom the worker would likely have wanted to receive them. . . . Of course, an employee can secure this result by changing a beneficiary form; but doing so requires awareness, understanding, and time. That is why Washington and many other jurisdictions have created a statutory assumption that divorce works a revocation of a designation in favor of an ex-spouse. That assumption is embodied in the Uniform Probate Code; it is consistent with human experience; and those with expertise in the matter have concluded that it "more often" serves the cause of "[j]ustice." Langbein, The Nonprobate Revolution and the Future of the Law of Succession, 97 Harv. L.Rev. 1108, 1135 (1984).

In forbidding Washington to apply that assumption here, the Court permits a divorced wife, who *already* acquired, during the divorce proceeding, her fair share of the couple's community property, to receive in addition the benefits that the divorce court awarded to her former husband. . . . The State of Washington enacted a statute to prevent precisely this kind of unfair result. But the Court, relying on an inconsequential administrative burden, concludes that Congress required it.

Finally, the logic of the Court's decision does not stop at divorce revocation laws. The Washington statute is virtually indistinguishable from other traditional state-law rules, for example, rules using presumptions to transfer assets in the case of simultaneous deaths, and rules that prohibit a husband who kills a wife from receiving benefits as a result of the wrongful death. It is particularly difficult to believe that Congress wanted to preempt the latter kind of statute. But how do these statutes differ from the one before us? Slayer statutes—like this statute—"gover[n] the payment of benefits, a central matter of plan administration." And contrary to the Court's suggestion, slayer statutes vary from State to State in their details just like divorce revocation statutes. [I]ndeed, the "slayer" conflict would seem more serious, not less serious, than the conflict before us, for few, if any, slayer statutes permit plans to opt out of the state property law rule.

NOTES

1. *Field preemption revisited.* Justice Breyer's dissent echoes Justice Scalia's concurrence in Dillingham (see Section C.2.4 above), in asserting that applying the idea of "field preemption" would make the analysis easier. But Breyer's discussion unintentionally suggests the limitations of that approach: It begs the question "What is 'the field' in question?

No one could claim that ERISA preempts the entire *field* of state law governing inheritance—though such matters "relate to" ERISA broadly speaking.

In a preemption case, is it employee benefit plans, or is it the area of state law (e.g., that governing inheritance) said to encroach upon employee benefit plans, that is the relevant "field" we are to ask whether Congress intended to occupy? Where does one field end and the other begin?

2. *Divorce revocation laws.* In state probate and nonprobate settings, the Uniform Probate Code treats the disposition in any instrument in favor of the divorced ex-spouse as revoked, and the property passes to any contingent beneficiary named in the instrument or to the decedent's estate. UPC § 2–804(b). Most states have some such measure for probate (and in some states, for nonprobate) transfers. What is the premise behind such statutes?

Egelhoff establishes that such laws are preempted by ERISA. That result defeats the purpose of these laws, which is to effectuate the intent of the testator. Does the Court place too much importance on its concern for uniform administration of multistate plans? The Court's decision has been criticized by those who believe that "[b]ecause states have vast experience dealing with the questions of donative intent and family law that arise in matters of wealth transfer on death, and because divorce revocation statutes further the purposes of ERISA, it would have been wiser for the courts to defer to state experience in these areas." David S. Lebolt, Making the Best of *Egelhoff*: Federal Common Law for ERISA-Preempted Beneficiary Designations, 28 J. Pension Planning & Compliance 29, 38 (2002). See also T.P. Gallanis, ERISA and the Law of Succession, 65 Ohio St. L.J. 185, 189 (2004) (criticizing *Egelhoff's* "nullification of attempts at the state level to unify the law of probate and nonprobate transfers").

UPC § 2–804(h)(2) attempts to avoid the effects of ERISA preemption by providing that if federal law preempts a state divorce-revocation statute, the ex-spouse "is obligated to return" the property or benefit that passed to him or her, "or is personally liable for the amount of the payment or the value of the item of property or benefit, to the person who would have been entitled to it were this section or part of this section not preempted." The official comment to UPC § 2–804(h)(2) explains: "This provision respects ERISA's concern that federal law govern the administration of the plan, while still preventing unjust enrichment that would result if an unintended beneficiary were to receive the pension benefits. Federal law has no interest in working a broader disruption of state probate and nonprobate transfer law than is required in the interest of smooth administration of pension and employee benefit plans."

UPC § 2–804(h)(2) was promulgated in the 1990 revision of the UPC and thus far has been adopted by a number of states and the District of Columbia. No federal court has yet directly passed on the question of whether this provision will withstand ERISA preemption. However, the Supreme Court has held the provision preempted in the case of a federal employee's life insurance benefits by a different law, the Federal Employees' Group Life Insurance Act of 1954 (FEGLIA), 5 U.S.C.S. § 8701 et seq. Hillman v. Maretta, 133 S. Ct. 1943, 1952 (2013) ("It makes no difference whether state law requires the transfer of the proceeds . . . or creates a cause of action . . . that enables another person to receive the proceeds upon filing an action in state court. In either case, state law displaces the beneficiary selected by the insured in accordance with FEGLIA and places someone else in her stead."). *Hillman* strongly suggests such a law would be held preempted by ERISA as well. For criticism of *Hillman*, see John H. Langbein, Destructive Federal Preemption of State Wealth Transfer Law in Beneficiary Designation Cases: Hillman Doubles Down on Egelhoff, 67 Vand. L. Rev. 1665 (2014).

Egelhoff involved not only a pension plan, but also a life insurance plan. Recall that in *Mackey*, a welfare benefit plan was compelled to make payments to a judgment creditor pursuant to a garnishment order, even though by its terms the plan was supposed to pay the participant. Does *Egelhoff* effectively overrule *Mackey*? Is a garnishment statute, using Justice Thomas's language in *Egelhoff*, a "generally applicable" law or, to the contrary, is it a statute that "governs the payment of benefits, a central matter of plan administration?" Could the children in *Egelhoff* be considered creditors under state law?

3. *Domestic relations orders.* Until 1985 when REAct intervened to resolve the question, the most important area in which state law trenched on ERISA-covered plans was domestic relations. As originally enacted,

ERISA made no mention of how to deal with domestic relations claims against pension assets. When, therefore, an alimony, child-support, or marital-property decree of a state court purported to reach pension assets, the question arose: Did such a decree "relate to" an ERISA-covered plan, and was it in consequence preempted?

Although the case for preemption would have seemed particularly strong, both because a state court order dividing up a pension account would appear to "relate to" a plan in the ordinary sense, and because ERISA § 206(d)(1) sets forth a strict anti-alienation rule, as discussed in Chapter 7, supra, courts rapidly and almost—but not quite—universally declined to preempt state domestic relations orders. The Internal Revenue Service also endorsed the view that ERISA did not preclude enforcement of state domestic relations orders in certain circumstances.

REAct amended both the labor and tax titles in 1984 to provide for the enforcement of so-called qualified domestic relations orders (QDROs), discussed supra in Chapter 7. ERISA § 206(d)(3), IRC § 414(p). The QDRO rules have thus completely supplanted the usual preemption and antialienation rules in this special area. If a domestic relations order is a QDRO, it will be enforced; if the order is not a QDRO, the plan must ignore it.

As noted in the discussion of the legislative history of ERISA § 514(a), supra, the framers of ERISA rejected a content-conflict standard of preemption in favor of the broader language in § 514(a). The lesson of the pre-REAct domestic relations cases is that the courts incline to follow a content-sensitive standard anyhow. When the state interest is strong and the federal interest attenuated, the courts often find ways to avoid preemption.

4.   *Community property.* In California, Texas, and other community property states, the nonemployee spouse acquires under state law a present one-half interest in the earnings of an employee spouse. In the divorce context, court orders dividing pension benefits pursuant to community property law can qualify as QDROs under the usual QDRO rules and no longer raise any preemption issues. However, in Boggs v. Boggs, 520 U.S. 833 (1997), reproduced in Chapter 7, supra, the Supreme Court held that Louisiana's community property law, permitting a nonparticipant spouse to transfer by will an interest in undistributed pension plan benefits of a participant spouse, is preempted by ERISA.

The Court explained that preemption was required because of a conflict with ERISA, and that there was thus no need to inquire whether the law in question "relates to" an ERISA plan. "ERISA's solicitude for the economic security of surviving spouses would be undermined by allowing a predeceasing spouse's heirs and legatees to have a community property interest in the survivor's annuity. [States] are not free to change ERISA's structure and balance." 520 U.S. at 843–44. The QDRO rules are unavailing because an order regarding an attempted testamentary transfer does not constitute a QDRO.

Distinguishing *Boggs*, the Ninth Circuit held in Emard v. Hughes Aircraft Co., 153 F.3d 949 (9th Cir.1998), cert. denied, 525 U.S. 1122 (1999), that ERISA does not preempt California community property law and constructive trust law as applied to a surviving spouse's interest in his deceased spouse's employer-provided life insurance policy, which named a former spouse as beneficiary. *Egelhoff* implicitly overrules *Emerd*. Subsequent to *Egelhoff*, the Ninth Circuit held that ERISA preempts California's community property law. Branco v. UFCW-Northern California Employers Joint Pension Plan, 279 F.3d 1154 (9th Cir.2002). The Court observed that the "concerns in *Egelhoff* apply equally to the present case. Acceptance of the district court's ruling would impermissibly require the Plan Administrators to master California's probate law; to pay benefits to the beneficiaries chosen by state law (California's intestate scheme); and/ or to await the conclusion of probate litigation to establish [the predeceased spouse's] lawful heirs. Such eventualities clearly contravene *Egelhoff*'s holding." *Id.* at 1159. See also Schreffler v. Metropolitan Life Ins. Co., 2006 WL 1127096 (D.Ariz.2006) (preempting Arizona community property law as having an impermissible connection with an ERISA plan); Barnett v. Barnett, 67 S.W.3d 107 (Tex.2001) (preempting widow's claim against husband's estate for life insurance proceeds paid to estate, even though proceeds were community property under Texas law).

5. *Slayer statutes.* Contrast the federal courts' handling of state divorce-revocation statutes with the treatment of state slayer-revocation statutes. Most probate codes contain a provision such as UPC § 2–803 dealing with the case in which the beneficiary under a probate or nonprobate designation has slain the decedent feloniously and intentionally. The statutes cause the slayer's interest to be forfeited. As discussed supra in Chapter 7, the federal courts have mostly refused to treat these statutes as preempted.

On what principled basis can we justify preemption of a divorce-revocation statute but not a homicide-revocation statute? Each "relates to" the ERISA plan in the same way, treating the affected interest as though the decedent had revoked the beneficiary designation. The Court in *Egelhoff* responded to this question by suggesting that the principle underlying the slayer statutes "is well established in the law and has a long historical pedigree predating ERISA." It is not clear that slayer statutes have any greater historical pedigree than do divorce revocation laws. The Court also suggested that "because the statutes are more or less uniform nationwide, their interference with the aims of ERISA is at least debatable." However, as Justice Breyer pointed out in his dissenting opinion, slayer statutes do vary from state to state. For example, some states require that there be a conviction, at least if the slayer is still alive, see Va. Code Ann. § 55–401 (Michie 2005), others do not. See Mich. Stat. Ann. § 700.2803(6). An Ohio court that faced the question after the Supreme Court's decision in *Egelhoff* concluded that Ohio's slayer statute was preempted by ERISA. Ahmed v. Ahmed, 158 Ohio App.3d 527, 817 N.E.2d 424 (2004)("[W]e cannot distinguish slayer statutes from the statute at issue in *Egelhoff*.).

2. STATE PROPERTY LAW

1. *Assignment laws.* Arkansas' general assignment statute provides that all written contracts for the payment of money or property shall be assignable. Arkansas Blue Cross & Blue Shield (BCBS) inserted language in its policies conditioning assignability upon its approval. "BCBS used this contractual right to disapprove assignments made to health care providers who refused to sign a participation agreement with

BCBS." St. Mary's Hospital, a provider, sued BCBS in the Arkansas courts and won, the Arkansas Supreme Court holding that the assignment law gave insured persons the unconditional right to assign their BCBS benefits. BCBS sought declaratory relief in the federal court, alleging that ERISA preempted the Arkansas assignment law. The district court found no preemption, the Eighth Circuit reversed. Arkansas Blue Cross & Blue Shield v. St. Mary's Hospital, 947 F.2d 1341 (8th Cir.1991), cert. denied, 504 U.S. 957 (1992).

The Tenth Circuit reached a similar result with respect to Kansas assignment law in St. Francis Regional Medical Center v. Blue Cross and Blue Shield of Kansas, 49 F.3d 1460 (10th Cir.1995). The court concluded that "ERISA preempts state law on the issue of the assignability of benefits because material provisions in the employee benefits plans covered by ERISA would be directly affected if Kansas law were to be interpreted as prohibiting restrictions on assignment." Id. at 1464.

Why are general garnishment statutes, which may compel a plan to pay X instead of Y, not preempted (Mackey), but general assignment statutes, which also may compel the plan to pay X instead of Y, are preempted?

2. *Escheat and unclaimed property laws.* In Aetna Life Ins. Co. v. Borges, 869 F.2d 142 (2d Cir.1989), the Second Circuit considered the question of whether ERISA preempted a Connecticut abandoned property statute requiring insurance companies to turn over to the state unclaimed payments after a period of three years. Under the statute, Connecticut would hold the funds and begin formal escheat proceedings if the funds remained unclaimed for 20 years. Aetna, which provided group health and accident insurance coverage as part of employee welfare plans, filed suit in federal court seeking an injunction and a declaration that the Connecticut law was preempted by ERISA. The Second Circuit held that "the impact of Connecticut's escheat law on ERISA benefit plans is too tenuous, remote, and peripheral to require preemption." Id. at 147. In response to Aetna's claims that the law increases the cost of plan administration, the court stated that "[t]hese indirect economic and administrative effects are not substantial enough [to] persuade us that this is the type of law Congress intended to preempt." Id. The court further noted that the effects of this law were no more intrusive than those of state garnishment laws, which were found not to be preempted in *Mackey*.

Contrast *Borges* with Commonwealth Edison Co. v. Vega, 174 F.3d 870 (7th Cir.1999), in which Commonwealth Edison and its defined-benefit plan sought a declaration that ERISA preempts the Illinois Uniform Disposition of Unclaimed Property Act. The court noted that "[t]he Uniform Disposition of Unclaimed Property Act, in force in about a third of the states, requires anyone in possession of intangible property that is unclaimed by its owner for seven years (five under the Illinois version of the Act) to transfer the property to the custody of the state. [This is not an escheat statute.] The state does not acquire title to the property. It is merely a custodian. The owner can reclaim his property at any time. [In] effect, the property is an interest-free loan to the state—in perpetuity if the owner never shows up to claim it." Id. at 872. The court, in an opinion by Judge Posner, held that the Illinois law relates to an employee benefit plan "directly and substantially" and is preempted. "Not only does the state become the custodian of the assets, in violation of ERISA's provisions regarding plan administration, [it] depletes those assets by taking the interest that accrues on them." Id. at 873.

Judge Posner distinguished *Borges* on the basis that it dealt with an escheat law, which gives title to the state. "This case is different [from an escheat statute] because the state does not claim to have an ownership interest in unclaimed benefits. It doesn't want to step into the shoes of the beneficiary; it wants to step into the plan's shoes." Id. at 875. Similarly, in Blue Cross & Blue Shield of Florida, Inc. v. Department of Banking and Finance, 791 F.2d 1501 (11th Cir.1986), the Eleventh Circuit held that Florida's Unclaimed Property Act, which provided that property unclaimed for seven years must be turned over to the state, was preempted on the ground that the law "purports to direct the disposition of unclaimed health and welfare benefits still in the hands of the benefit provider."

Are you persuaded that the unclaimed property statutes in Illinois and Florida should be analyzed differently from the escheat statute in *Borges*? Would the results in *Vega* and *Department of Banking and Finance* be different today, after *Travelers*? See Steelman v. Prudential Ins. Co. of America, 2007 WL 4105975 (E.D.Cal.2007) (preempting California unclaimed property law).

3. *Nonclaim statutes.* Nonclaim statutes are routine in state probate codes. A nonclaim statute is an especially short statute of limitations, which overrides the ordinary limitations periods, in the event that a claim is brought against a decedent's estate. The purpose is to promote rapid administration of decedents' estates, facilitating (1) payment of the debts of creditors who file timely claims, and (2) distribution of the residue of the estate to survivors, who sometimes depend upon the estate proceeds for support. About 20 states have enacted the version in Uniform Probate Code § 3–803, which provides that claims are barred unless presented within four months of the date of publication of notice to creditors.

In Board of Trustees of Western Conference of Teamsters Pension Trust Fund v. H.F. Johnson, Inc., 830 F.2d 1009 (9th Cir.1987), the trustees of a multiemployer plan brought an action against the estate of a Montana decedent to collect withdrawal liability under the 1980 amendments to ERISA (the Multiemployer Pension Plan Amendments Act, MPPAA). The action was timely within the six-year MPPAA limitations period, ERISA § 4301(f), but it was filed outside the four-month period of the Montana nonclaim statute. The Ninth Circuit held that ERISA preempted the Montana nonclaim statute. The Montana statute "adds a condition not contemplated by Congress to collection of withdrawal liability. Montana's nonclaim statute plainly 'relates to' the Fund, and is preempted under ERISA [§ 514(a)]." 830 F.2d at 1016. The court emphasized the conflict with ERISA's statute of limitations for withdrawal liability, § 4301(f). It reasoned: "We are faced with the awkward task of developing a coherent body of federal common law around specific statutory provisions which were not designed with these circumstances in mind. The potentially disruptive effect of our decision on probate of decedents' estates—an area of special concern to states—

can hardly be understated. Our decision is the product of expansive statutory liability, sweeping preemption and a Congressional mandate for creation of federal common law. Disruptive or not, our interpretation of the Act and our formulation of federal common law follow clearly from the congressional dictates in ERISA." Id. at 1017.

Is the Ninth Circuit correct that the "disruptive effect" of ERISA preemption on the state-law-dominated sphere of succession and probate "clearly follow from the congressional dictates in ERISA"? Contrast the pre-REAct domestic relations cases in which the courts declined to enforce ERISA preemption in order not to disrupt another great sphere of state-dominated subject-matter jurisdiction, domestic relations. Is the difference that MEPPA includes a specific statute of limitations?

Administrative Committee of Wal-Mart Stores, Inc. Associates' Health & Welfare Plan v. Mooradian, 2006 WL 508041 (M.D.Fla.2006) suggests that the answer to the foregoing question might be yes. In *Mooradian* the court addressed the question whether ERISA preempts Florida's nonclaim statute, which required that a claim against an estate be filed within three months of the publication of the notice to creditors. The court distinguished *H.F. Johnson*, noting that whereas ERISA contains a specific statute of limitations for withdrawal liability actions, it does not contain a limitations period applicable to the action before it (a plan's efforts to secure reimbursement for benefits paid on behalf of a plan participant). Thus, applying the state period "would not run counter to a limitations period set forth by Congress, as was the case in *H.F. Johnson*." The court also noted that there was "no evidence to suggest that application of the state probate laws would tend to frustrate ERISA's objectives, or that there is any other basis for suggesting that Congress expected state probate laws would not survive enactment of ERISA." 2006 WL 508041 at *4.

4. *Mechanic's and public improvement lien laws.* State law commonly creates a security interest called a mechanic's lien on behalf of construction workers for the value of their labor in the structure upon which they work. In the case of public works projects, such liens usually attach to any sums that have been appropriated for the making of the improvement. In Plumbing Industry Board, Plumbing Local Union No. 1 v. E.W. Howell Co., 126 F.3d 61 (2d Cir.1997), Howell was the general contractor for a public school construction project. When a subcontractor on the project failed to make timely payments to its workers' multiemployer benefit plan, the plan sought to enforce its statutory lien under New York law against the payments due Howell. The Second Circuit held that the lien law was preempted because it "provides an alternative mechanism—filing a lien that attaches to improvement funds—for enforcing the rights protected by ERISA § 502(a)," citing *Travelers* as well as Pilot Life Ins. Co. v. Dedeaux, 481 U.S. 41, 54 (1987), which as we shall see in Section D, infra, emphasizes the preemptive power of ERISA's civil enforcement provision. Accord, EklecCo v. Iron Workers Locals 40, 361 & 417 Union Security Funds, 170 F.3d 353 (2d Cir.1999); McCoy v. Massachusetts Institute of Technology, 950 F.2d 13 (1st Cir.1991); Leo Finnegan Constr. Co., Inc. v. Northwest Plumbing & Pipefitting Industry Health Welfare & Vacation Trust, 2008 WL 2811319 (Wash.App.2008). In contrast, in Southern California IBEW-NECA Trust

Funds v. Standard Indus. Elec. Co., 247 F.3d 920 (9th Cir.2001), the Ninth Circuit held that the relationships in question were too tenuous, remote or peripheral to be preempted by ERISA. Other courts have reached the same conclusion. See also Board of Trustees of Cement Masons & Plasterers Health and Welfare Trust v. GBC Northwest, LLC, 2007 WL 1306545 (W.D.Wash.2007) (state lien claim supplemental to an ERISA suit not preempted); Forsberg v. Bovis Lend Lease, Inc., 184 P.3d 610 (Utah App.2008) (state lien statute did not affect relations among principal ERISA entities and thus is not preempted).

Suppose in *Plumbing Industry Board* the collective bargaining agreement between the union and the subcontractor required the subcontractor to furnish a surety bond in favor of the employee benefit plan to guarantee the subcontractor's obligation under the agreement to make plan contributions. Would an action by the plan against the surety to recover on the bond under state surety law be preempted? See Greenblatt v. Delta Plumbing & Heating, 68 F.3d 561, 574 (2d Cir.1995)("A claim on a surety bond is but a run-of-the-mill state law claim [that] does not conflict with any enforcement mechanism specified in ERISA").

E. STATE TORT AND CONTRACT CLAIMS INVOLVING PLANS

1. *PILOT LIFE* AND THE EXCLUSIVITY OF ERISA'S REMEDIES

ERISA preemption has been especially important in the area previously occupied by state tort and tort-related causes of action. *Ingersoll-Rand Co. v. McClendon*, discussed supra, was an easier case than most, because ERISA § 510 supplied a federal cause of action comparable to the state law being preempted. In many settings, however, ERISA supplies no federal alternative to the state cause of action that ERISA § 514 is read to suppress. In such cases when a plan fiduciary, plan employee, or plan service provider harms a participant or beneficiary, there is no remedy.

The leading case suppressing state tort law, even in the absence of a corresponding federal cause of action, is Pilot Life Ins. Co. v. Dedeaux, 481 U.S. 41 (1987). As will be discussed in Chapter 19, in *Pilot Life* the Court unanimously held that a state cause of action based on the tort of bad faith denial of a benefit claim was not a law regulating insurance and was therefore preempted. But the Court in *Pilot Life* was not content to focus solely on the insurance savings clause. It also emphasized the exclusivity of the civil enforcement provisions of ERISA § 502(a):

> [T]he detailed provisions of § 502(a) set forth a comprehensive civil enforcement scheme that represents a careful balancing of the need for prompt and fair claims settlement procedures against the public interest in encouraging the formation of employee benefit plans. The policy choices reflected in the inclusion of certain remedies and the exclusion of others under the federal scheme would be completely undermined if ERISA-

plan participants and beneficiaries were free to obtain remedies under state law that Congress rejected in ERISA. 'The six carefully integrated civil enforcement provisions found in § 502(a) of the statute as finally enacted . . . provide strong evidence that Congress did not intend to authorize other remedies that it simply forgot to incorporate expressly.' . . .

Congress' specific reference to § 301 of the [Labor-Management Relations Act of 1947] to describe the civil enforcement scheme of ERISA makes clear its intention that all suits brought by beneficiaries or participants asserting improper processing of claims under ERISA-regulated plans be treated as federal questions governed by § 502(a).

481 U.S. at 54–56.

A number of lower court decisions have held that even when a law regulates insurance, if it provides a remedy not provided for in ERISA, the law is preempted. Thus, for example, a number of courts have suggested that even if a state bad faith claim regulates insurance, it would still be preempted. Such a law would "supplement the ERISA civil enforcement provisions available to remedy improper claims processing." Kanne v. Connecticut General Life Ins. Co., 867 F.2d 489 (9th Cir.1988), cert. denied, 492 U.S. 906 (1989) (rejecting the argument that a state statutory bad faith claim should be distinguished from a state common law bad faith claim for preemption purposes). Accord, Barber v. Unum Life Ins. Co., 383 F.3d 134 (3d Cir.2004); Conover v. Aetna US Health Care, Inc., 320 F.3d 1076 (10th Cir.2003), cert. denied, 542 U.S. 936 (2004).

More broadly, the Third Circuit observed in *Barber* that "[r]eading *Pilot Life, Rush Prudential*, and [*Aetna Health Inc. v. Davila*, 542 U.S. 200 (2004)] together, a state statute is preempted by ERISA if it provides 'a form of ultimate relief in a judicial forum that added to the judicial remedies provided by ERISA', or stated another way 'if it duplicates, supplements, or supplants the ERISA civil enforcement remedy.' " 383 F.3d at 140 (citing *Rush* and *Davila*).

By contrast, a state law claim does not supplant ERISA's remedial scheme if it "does not depend on or derive from [a] claim for benefits in any meaningful way." Dishman v. Unum Life Ins. Co., 269 F.3d 974, 983 (9th Cir.2001). In *Dishman*, the plaintiff brought a state law privacy claim against an ERISA plan disability insurer, seeking to hold the insurer vicariously liable for a tortuous invasion of privacy allegedly committed by investigative firms that the insurer hired to determine if the plaintiff was still disabled. The Ninth Circuit rejected the defendant's argument that *Pilot Life* dictated the conclusion that the plaintiff's claim was preempted, finding that although the conduct in question occurred "in the course of its administration of the plan, under which [the plaintiff] was seeking benefits," the plaintiff was not seeking to obtain an additional state law remedy not otherwise obtainable under ERISA; damages for invasion of privacy would "remain whether or not Unum ultimately pays his [disability] claim."

In Fossen v. Blue Cross and Blue Shield of Montana, Inc., 660 F.3d 1102 (9th Cir. 2012) the Ninth Circuit held that ERISA does not preempt a cause of action alleging violation of Montana's Unfair Trade Practices Act, which regulates the setting of health insurance premiums. The court held that the state law "creates a right that is separate from and could not possibly be remedied under ERISA." Id at 1114. In the view of the court, the state statute applies more broadly than HIPAA's prohibition of plans from charging different premiums on account of health related factors, barring "any unfair discrimination with respect to premiums." Id. Because the statutes were not identical in scope, the court found no conflict preemption.

Suppose a participant intentionally fails to notify his health insurance plan that he has divorced and misrepresents himself as still married in order to allow his ex-wife to continue to receive coverage under his plan. Is a state law fraud claim brought by trustees seeking to recoup plan funds improperly expended as a result of the participant's fraudulent conduct preempted? See Trustees of AFTRA Health Fund v. Biondi, 303 F.3d 765 (7th Cir.2002) (no preemption; claim was not an alternative enforcement mechanism under ERISA and claim neither intrudes on the structure of the plan nor binds plan administrators to particular choices).

Consider this scenario. Plaintiff had health insurance through his wife's employee health benefit plan. He underwent hip replacement surgery, after conferring with an insurance representative, who assured him that his policy was in effect and would cover the surgery. After the surgery was complete, the insurer refused to pay the treating physician or the hospital, saying the policy had been canceled at an earlier date. Plaintiff conceded that his wrongful denial of coverage claim was preempted, but argued that since he was not covered as a plan participant or beneficiary at the time of denial of coverage, his independent cause of action for detrimental reliance should not be preempted. What result? See King v. BlueCross BlueShield of Ala., 439 Fed. Appx. 386 (5th Cir. Aug. 30, 2011).

2. FRAUD AND MISREPRESENTATION

1. *Fraudulent inducement actions against insurance agents.* In Perkins v. Time Ins. Co., 898 F.2d 470 (5th Cir.1990), it was alleged that an insurance agent, Davis, sold a Time Insurance group health contract to Perkins' firm. Perkins told Davis that his daughter needed eye surgery and asked whether she would be covered under the Time policy that Davis was offering. Davis said the child's surgery would be covered, because it would be considered as a congenital defect rather than an excluded preexisting condition. Perkins arranged for his firm to purchase the Time policy, he terminated his coverage under his former policy, which did cover the daughter's surgery, and he elected coverage with Time. Time then denied the benefit on the ground that the surgery related to a preexisting condition. Perkins sued both Time and Davis. The Fifth Circuit held that the suit against Time was preempted. "It cannot be gainsaid that Perkins' claims against Time 'relate to' an employee benefits plan and thus fall within the scope of ERISA's preemption clause. . . . Perkins' complaint, which alleged tortious breach of contract as its sole cause of action, clearly mirrors that which *Pilot Life* has held to be preempted under ERISA." Id. at 473.

Perkins' complaint against Davis, however, was held not preempted. "While ERISA clearly preempts claims of bad faith as against insurance companies for improper processing of a claim for benefits under an employee benefit plan, *Pilot Life*, and while ERISA plans cannot be modified by oral representations, we are not persuaded that this logic should extend to immunize agents from personal liability for their solicitation of potential participants in an ERISA plan prior to its formation." The court "conclude[d] that a claim that an insurance agent fraudulently induced an insured to surrender coverage under an existing policy, to participate in an ERISA plan which did not provide the promised coverage, 'relates to' that plan only indirectly" and is not preempted. Id. at 469. The Fifth Circuit took the same position in Hobson v. Robinson, 31 E.B.C. 1328 (5th Cir.2003).

The Eleventh Circuit followed *Perkins* in Morstein v. National Insurance Services, 93 F.3d 715 (11th Cir.1996), which involved a similar claim against an insurance agent and his agency. The court held that "when a state law claim brought against a non-ERISA entity does not affect relations among principal ERISA entities as such, then it is not preempted by ERISA." Id. at 722. Accord, Finderne Management Co. v. Barrett, 355 N.J.Super. 197, 809 A.2d 857 (App.Div.2002) (claim involving preplan misrepresentation does not interfere with the structure or administration of ERISA plan).

In Lion's Volunteer Blind Industries, Inc. v. Automated Group Administration, Inc., 195 F.3d 803 (6th Cir.1999), an employer and participant of a partially self-insured employee welfare benefit plan brought suit alleging that the administrator denied benefits to the employee after assuring the employer that all persons covered under the employer's old plan would be covered under the new plan. The Sixth Circuit held that ERISA preempted the state law claim of misrepresentation. The court rejected a "rigid chronological approach," finding that "regardless of the phrasing of the prayer for relief, a court entertaining the merits of this misrepresentation claim would be forced to calculate the benefits that would have been owed to [the participant]" under the plan. Id. at 807, 809.

2. *Fraudulent inducement actions against employers.* Although *Morstein* emphasized that the insurance agent was a "non-ERISA entity," other courts have permitted fraudulent inducement actions against one of the key ERISA entities, the employer who was the plan sponsor. In Perry v. P*I*E Nationwide Inc., 872 F.2d 157 (6th Cir.1989), plaintiffs sued their employer for rescission of an ESOP, alleging that their participation had been secured by means of fraud and in breach of the employer's state law fiduciary duty. The district court refused preemption, saying that preemption "applies once the benefit plan is in existence, and does not apply to alleged common law actions of fraud or misrepresentation" to induce the plaintiffs to join the plan. The Sixth Circuit affirmed: "Plaintiffs [do] not seek plan benefits or an increase in plan benefits; rather, they seek not to be bound as participants and thus to recoup their wage reductions." Id. at 162. Accord, Hobson v. Robinson, 75 Fed.Appx. 949 (5th Cir.2003).

Suppose you were convinced to change your job on the promise from your new employer that if you did so, your benefits would be the same as (or better than) those you had with your former employer. You change jobs, become disabled, and discover that the new employer's disability plan does not cover you, but your former employer's plan would have. Would a fraudulent inducement claim against the new employer be preempted? In Smith v. Texas Children's Hospital, 84 F.3d 152 (5th Cir.1996), the Fifth Circuit allowed such a state law cause of action to go forward. "Such a claim escapes ERISA preemption because it does not necessarily depend upon the scope of [the employee's] rights under [the new employer's] plan." Id. at 155.

3.   *Misrepresentation to a third-party provider.* Routine practice in the health care industry is for the hospital or other provider to verify in advance of supplying care that a patient's claim of plan coverage is accurate. When the ERISA-covered plan initially acknowledges the coverage, then reneges after the provider extends care, does ERISA preempt the provider's state law action against the plan? In Transitional Hospitals Corp. v. Blue Cross & Blue Shield of Texas, 164 F.3d 952, 955 (5th Cir.1999), the Fifth Circuit refused preemption on the grounds that the state misrepresentation claim was "not dependent on or derived from [the patient's] right to recover benefits under [the] plan." Accord, In In Home Health, Inc. v. Prudential Ins. Co., 101 F.3d 600 (8th Cir.1996); The Meadows v. Employers Health Insurance, 47 F.3d 1006 (9th Cir.1995); Hospice of Metro Denver, Inc. v. Group Health Ins. of Okla., Inc., 944 F.2d 752 (10th Cir.1991). Other circuits have come to the contrary conclusion. For example, in Variety Children's Hospital, Inc. v. Century Medical Health Plan, Inc., 57 F.3d 1040 (11th Cir.1995), the Eleventh Circuit held that a hospital's claim against the health plan that certified the participant's treatment to recover the costs of medical services was preempted because the claim was based on the plan's failure to pay benefits.

Suppose the health plan administrator mistakenly informs a participant that a particular procedure is covered under the plan, but when the participant seeks reimbursement the plan declines to pay on the ground that the plan excludes the procedure. As we saw in Chapter 15, courts have concluded that such estoppel claims are usually not allowed under ERISA, because ERISA precludes oral modification of plans, which leaves participants with no remedy. On the same theory, courts have also concluded that health care providers lack an estoppel claim under ERISA or federal common law. See, e.g., HealthSouth Rehabilitation Hospital v. American National Red Cross, 101 F.3d 1005 (4th Cir.1996).

Is there any logic to allowing a state law misrepresentation action by a health care provider but not by a participant?

3.   CLAIMS AGAINST PLAN SERVICE PROVIDERS

Although ERISA provides the exclusive basis for enforcing claims against ERISA fiduciaries, the weight of authority among circuit courts is that ERISA does not preempt state law claims by a plan or plan sponsor against a nonfiduciary providing services to the plan. See e.g. Kloots v. American Express Tax & Business Services, 233 Fed.Appx. 485 (6th Cir.2007) (ERISA does not preempt claims of professional negligence and negligent misrepresentation against nonfiduciary service provider);

Penny/Ohlmann/Nieman, Inc. v. Miami Valley Pension Corp., 399 F.3d 692 (6th Cir.2005) (preempting state law breach of contract and negligence claim against bank that was a fiduciary, but not preempting such claims against record keeper that was not a fiduciary); Gerosa v. Savasta & Co., 329 F.3d 317 (2d Cir.2003) (ERISA does not preempt state law claim against actuary whose negligence resulted in severe underfunding of ERISA plan).

The Tenth Circuit, in Airparts Co. v. Custom Benefit Services of Austin, Inc., 28 F.3d 1062 (10th Cir.1994), explained the reason for not preempting claims against nonfiduciary service providers. Co-trustees of the ERISA plan brought state law claims of negligence, implied indemnity, and common law fraud against FAC, a firm that the plaintiffs hired to provide expert benefit plan consultation, but which was not a fiduciary. Plaintiffs alleged that FAC failed to give them timely advice on the effects of the Omnibus Budget Reconciliation Act of 1987, improperly calculated pension benefits, proposed and drafted a useless plan amendment, and deliberately concealed the cost of the amendment and its eventual ineffectiveness. The court held the state law claims not preempted. "The state laws involved do not regulate the type of benefits or terms of the plan; they do not create reporting, disclosure, funding, or vesting requirements for the plan; they do not affect the calculation of benefits; and they are not common law rules designed to rectify faulty plan administration. Similarly, plaintiffs are not employees resorting to state law to avail themselves of an alternative cause of action to collect benefits, nor do the state laws here specifically apply to ERISA plans or interfere with the calculation of benefits." Id. at 1065. The court also observed that the Third Circuit has found that ERISA "does not generally preempt state professional malpractice actions," citing Painters of Phila. Dist. Council No. 21 Welfare Fund v. Price Waterhouse, 879 F.2d 1146, 1153 n. 7 (3d Cir.1989). "Painters [held] that, because malpractice is traditionally an area of state concern, and because there is absolutely no indication that Congress intended to imply a cause of action under ERISA for professional malpractice, state malpractice claims are not preempted." 28 F.3d at 1067. Similarly, the Fourth Circuit in Coyne & Delany Co. v. Selman, 98 F.3d 1457 (4th Cir.1996), observed that an employer's state law claim against an insurance consultant for professional malpractice did not "mandate an employee benefit structure or plan," "seek to bind a plan administrator to particular choices or preclude uniform administrative practice," or provide an "alternate enforcement mechanism to obtain ERISA benefits." The claim arose from a state law of general application, did not depend in any way on ERISA, did not implicate relations among the ERISA entities, and therefore was not preempted.

F. THE SCOPE OF ERISA PREEMPTION: A RECAPITULATION

1.   Taking the cases altogether, as Justice Souter complained aloud in *Travelers*, it can be difficult to identify an organizing principle that successfully distinguishes those state laws that are preempted by ERISA from those state laws that are not. In *Travelers* the Court effectively concluded the test could not be whether a state law literally "relates to"

an employee benefit plan—because if that were the test every state law would be preempted. Yet the statute itself offers no more guidance than the words "relate to." Alternate formulations—such as whether or not a state law "has a connection with" employee benefit plans, or whether a law interferes with Congress's preemption of "the field"—have succeeded only in restating the question. It might be argued the currently operative test is effectively something like: A state law is preempted if and only if it "relates too much" to employee benefit plans.

2.   We may be left simply to enumerate the ERISA preemption cases decided by the Supreme Court so far (including those that will be encountered in Chapter 19), and, when it comes to analyzing any given state law, to try to determine whether that law is most similar to those that have been held to be preempted, or to those that have been held not to be:

Preempted	Not Preempted
State law prohibiting pension plans from offsetting benefits by amount of workers' compensation. Alessi v. Raybestos-Manhattan, Inc., 451 U.S. 504 (1981).	State law requiring insured plans provide minimum mental health benefits. Metropolitan Life Ins. Co. v. Massachusetts, 471 U.S. 724 (1985).
State disability and pregnancy discrimination laws, as applied to benefits under a plan. Shaw v. Delta Air Lines, 463 U.S. 85 (1983).	State-law garnishment of benefits payable from plan. Mackey v. Lanier Collection Agency, 486 U.S. 825 (1988).
State tort claim for bad faith denial of benefits. Pilot Life Ins. Co. v. Dedeaux, 481 U.S. 41 (1987).	State hospital surcharges that apply only to non-Blue Cross-insured benefits. Blue Cross & Blue Shield v. Travelers, 514 U.S. 645 (1995).
State law precluding plan subrogation right with respect to claim against tortfeasor. FMC Corp. v. Holliday, 498 U.S. 52 (1990).	Application of state hospital tax to a hospital owned by a benefit plan. De Buono v. NYSA-ILA Medical and Clinical Services Fund, 520 U.S. 806 (1997).
State law prohibiting employers from firing employees to prevent vesting under an employee benefit plan. Ingersoll-Rand Co. v. McClendon, 498 U.S. 133 (1990).	State "prevailing wage" law, differentially applied to ERISA-covered plans. Calif. Div. of Labor Stds. Enforcement v. Dillingham Construction, 519 U.S. 316 (1997).
State law allowing a nonparticipant spouse to transfer by testamentary instrument an interest in undistributed pension plan benefits. Boggs v. Boggs, 520 U.S. 833 (1997).	State law requiring independent review of benefit denial by health maintenance organization (HMO). Rush Prudential HMO, Inc. v. Moran, 536 U.S. 355 (2002).

State law automatically revoking, upon divorce, a spouse's designation as plan death beneficiary. Egelhoff v. Egelhoff, 532 U.S. 141 (2001).

State law imposing duty of "ordinary care" on HMOs making benefit determinations. Aetna Health Inc. v. Davila, 542 U.S. 200 (2004) (above).

State law requiring insured plan [to reimburse "any willing provider." Ky. Assn. of Health Plans v. Miller, 538 U.S. 329 (2003).

G. FEDERAL COMMON LAW

As discussed supra in connection with *Egelhoff,* the decision to preempt state law invites the question of what if anything will replace it. In the prototypical case of "content conflict," in which state law collides with some inconsistent provision of federal law, preemption simply prefers the federal law. In other cases, however, preemption suppresses the state action without supplying federal law, leaving the plaintiff remediless unless the court creates suitable federal common law. *Pilot Life* and many other tort and tort-like preemption cases fall into this category.

When should the courts imply federal common law? Fidelity to supposed congressional design is the goal. Although courts should not "rewrite the statute," they should fill in the "gaps" needed to implement the statutory purpose. When does gap filling become rewriting? Might Congress have wanted the gap, or did Congress merely overlook the particular issue?

This subject touches on aspects of ERISA law that are dealt with elsewhere in this coursebook, especially the refusal to imply extracontractual and punitive damages, see Massachusetts Mutual Life Ins. Co. v. Russell, 473 U.S. 134 (1985), supra Chapter 16; the limits on nonfiduciary liability, Mertens v. Hewitt Associates, 508 U.S. 248 (1993), supra Chapter 16; the problems that have arisen in discerning the appropriate standard of judicial review of plan decisionmaking, Firestone Tire & Rubber Co. v. Bruch, 489 U.S. 101 (1989), supra Chapter 15; and the tension about whether to enforce oral modifications or to recognize other estoppel notions, supra Chapter 15.

1. *Construction.* Federal common law under ERISA has frequently been created for the purpose of absorbing from state law the traditional rules of construction pertaining to insurance contracts and other documents. The First Circuit has said that "it is well settled that federal common law applies both to interpret the provisions of an ERISA benefit plan and to resolve issues of relinquishment of rights and waiver when such side agreements affect the benefits provided by an ERISA plan. [The] relevant federal substantive law includes the common sense canons of contract interpretation derived from state law." Morais v. Central Beverage Corp. Union Employees' Supplemental Retirement Plan, 167 F.3d 709, 711 (1st Cir.1999). Thus, for example, in Santaella v. Metropolitan Life Ins. Co., 123 F.3d 456 (7th Cir.1997), the question was

whether the plaintiff's daughter's death was "accidental," in which case the daughter's beneficiaries would receive a benefit under an employer-provided accidental death insurance policy. The daughter died from taking an overdose of a painkiller drug. Under the policy, benefits would not be paid if death resulted from suicide, self-inflicted injury, illness, disease, bodily infirmity or infection. The court applied federal common law, which required the court to "interpret the terms of the policy in an ordinary and popular sense, as would a person of average intelligence and experience, and construe all plan ambiguities in favor of the insured." Id. at 461. Since there was no evidence indicating that the daughter intended to take an overdose or inflict injury on herself, the court directed entry of judgment for the plaintiffs. See also Young v. IMO Industries, Inc., 541 F.Supp.2d 433 (D.Mass.2008) (federal common law applies where parties seek to enforce a settlement agreement based upon federal labor law and ERISA).

Construction questions arising under ERISA fiduciary law are discussed further in Chapter 15, supra.

2. *Coordination of benefit clauses.* Insurance policies for health and casualty insurance commonly contain coordination of benefit (COB) clauses for situations in which more than one policy provides coverage. When such clauses conflict, litigation is common. When COB clauses are contained in ERISA-covered plans, several circuits have deemed the subject proper for the development of federal common law. Citizens Ins. Co. of America v. MidMichigan Health ConnectCare Network Plan, 449 F.3d 688 (6th Cir.2006); Trustees of Southern Illinois Carpenters Welfare Fund v. RFMS, Inc., 401 F.3d 847 (7th Cir.2005); Boston Mutual Insurance v. Murphree, 242 F.3d 899 (9th Cir.2001).

3. *Rescission.* As discussed earlier in this chapter, the courts have generally preempted state insurance contract rescission law, but have recognized a federal common law right of rescission for concealment or misrepresentation of material facts. See, e.g., Werdehausen v. Benicorp Ins. Co., 487 F.3d 660 (8th Cir.2007); Security Life Insurance Co. of America v. Meyling, 146 F.3d 1184 (9th Cir.1998). Why is it appropriate for the federal courts to imply a cause of action when an insured makes a misrepresentation to a plan, yet not, for example, to imply a cause of action when the plan acts in bad faith to deny a claim? Can the apparent readiness of courts to create federal common law *equitable* remedies such as rescission and restitution as opposed to *legal* remedies such as damages for bad faith claims denial be explained simply on the basis that, as discussed in Chapter 16, supra, ERISA § 502(a) permits participants to recover equitable relief, but not legal relief?

H. REMOVAL AND THE DOCTRINE OF COMPLETE PREEMPTION

A non-ERISA provision, 28 U.S.C. § 1441, allows a defendant to remove to federal court an action brought in state court over which the federal court has original jurisdiction. There has been a significant amount of litigation regarding the question of whether a claim brought in state court under state law may be removed to federal court on the basis that the claim arises under ERISA.

1. METROPOLITAN LIFE INS. CO. V. TAYLOR

481 U.S. 58 (1987).

■ JUSTICE O'CONNOR delivered the opinion of the Court.

In *Pilot Life Ins. Co. v. Dedeaux* the Court held that state common law causes of action asserting improper processing of a claim for benefits under an employee benefit plan regulated by [ERISA] are preempted by the Act. The question presented by this litigation is whether these state common law claims are not only preempted by ERISA, but also displaced by ERISA's civil enforcement provision, § 502(a)(1)(B), to the extent that complaints filed in state courts purporting to plead such state common law causes of action are removable to federal court under 28 U.S.C. § 1441(b).

[Taylor was a participant in a disability plan provided by his employer through Metropolitan Life Insurance Company. Taylor made claims under the plan that were denied. Taylor filed suit against his employer and Metropolitan in Michigan state court seeking compensatory damages for money contractually owed, compensation for mental anguish caused by breach of contract, and immediate restoration of all benefits and insurance coverages. The defendants removed the suit to federal court, alleging federal question jurisdiction over the disability benefits claim by virtue of ERISA.]

The century-old jurisdictional framework governing removal of federal question cases from state into federal courts is described in Justice Brennan's opinion for a unanimous Court in *Franchise Tax Board of Cal. v. Construction Laborers Vacation Trust for Southern Cal.*, 463 U.S. 1 (1983). By statute "any civil action brought in a State court of which the district courts of the United States have original jurisdiction, may be removed by the defendant or the defendants, to the district court of the United States for the district and division embracing the place where such action is pending." 28 U.S.C. § 1441(a). One category of cases over which the district courts have original jurisdiction are "federal question" cases; that is, those cases "arising under the Constitution, laws, or treaties of the United States." 28 U.S.C. § 1331. It is long settled law that a cause of action arises under federal law only when the plaintiff's well-pleaded complaint raises issues of federal law. The "well-pleaded complaint rule" is the basic principle marking the boundaries of the federal question jurisdiction of the federal district courts.

Federal pre-emption is ordinarily a federal defense to the plaintiff's suit. As a defense, it does not appear on the face of a well-pleaded complaint, and, therefore, does not authorize removal to federal court. One corollary of the well-pleaded complaint rule developed in the case law, however, is that Congress may so completely preempt a particular area that any civil complaint raising this select group of claims is necessarily federal in character. For 20 years, this Court has singled out claims preempted by § 301 of the [Labor Management Relations Act (LMRA)] for such special treatment. *Avco Corp. v. Machinists*, 390 U.S. 557 (1968).

There is no dispute in this litigation that Taylor's complaint, although preempted by ERISA, purported to raise only state law causes of action. The question therefore resolves itself into whether or not the

Avco principle can be extended to statutes other than the LMRA in order to recharacterize a state law complaint displaced by § 502(a)(1)(B) as an action arising under federal law. In *Franchise Tax Board*, the Court held that ERISA preemption, without more, does not convert a state claim into an action arising under federal law. The court suggested, however, that a state action that was not only preempted by ERISA, but also came "within the scope of § 502(a) of ERISA" might fall within the *Avco* rule. The claim in this case, unlike the state tax collection suit in *Franchise Tax Board*, is within the scope of § 502(a) and we therefore must face the question specifically reserved by *Franchise Tax Board*.

In the absence of explicit direction from Congress, this question would be a close one. [But] the language of the jurisdictional subsection of ERISA's civil enforcement provisions closely parallels that of § 301 of the LMRA. Section 502(f) says:

> "The district courts of the United States shall have jurisdiction, without respect to the amount in controversy or the citizenship of the parties, to grant the relief provided for in subsection (a) of this section in any action."

Cf. § 301(a) of the LMRA. The presumption that similar language in two labor law statutes has a similar meaning is fully confirmed by the legislative history of ERISA's civil enforcement provisions. The Conference Report on ERISA describing the civil enforcement provisions of § 502(a) says:

> "[W]ith respect to suits to enforce benefit rights under the plan or to recover benefits under the plan which do not involve application of the title I provisions, they may be brought not only in U.S. district courts but also in State courts of competent jurisdiction. *All such actions in Federal or State courts are to be regarded as arising under the laws of the United States in similar fashion to those brought under section 301 of the Labor-Management Relations Act of 1947*." H. R. Conf. Rep. No. 93–1280, p. 327 (1974) (emphasis added).

No more specific reference to the *Avco* rule can be expected and the rest of the legislative history consistently sets out this clear intention to make § 502(a)(1)(B) suits brought by participants or beneficiaries federal questions for the purposes of federal court jurisdiction in like manner as § 301 of the LMRA. . . .

Accordingly, this suit, though it purports to raise only state law claims, is necessarily federal in character by virtue of the clearly manifested intent of Congress. It, therefore, "arise[s] under the . . . laws . . . of the United States," 28 U.S.C. § 1331, and is removable to federal court by the defendants.

2. SCOPE OF THE COMPLETE PREEMPTION DOCTRINE

1. *Scope of Taylor. Taylor* was an easy case, as it dealt with a state law claim that unmistakably fell within ERISA § 502(a)(1)(B). Nevertheless, the case implies, and courts have subsequently held, that any claim that falls within any of the subsections of ERISA § 502(a) would fall within the *Avco* rule. In applying *Taylor*, the lower courts have come to label its exception to the well-pleaded complaint rule as

"complete preemption," sometimes also referred to as "superpreemption." See, e.g., McGowin v. ManPower, International, Inc., 363 F.3d 556 (5th Cir.2004) (regardless of how plaintiff characterizes claim, a claim that essentially seeks determination of eligibility of benefits under an ERISA plan is completely preempted); Singh v. Prudential Health care Plan, 335 F.3d 278 (4th Cir.2003) (finding claims that fell within the scope of § 502(a) to be completely preempted). As stated in Dukes v. U.S. Healthcare, 57 F.3d 350, 355 (3d Cir.1995):

> Section 514 of ERISA defines the scope of ERISA preemption, providing that ERISA "supersede[s] any and all State laws insofar as they may now or hereafter relate to any employee benefit plan." [The *Taylor*] complete-preemption exception, on the other hand, is concerned with a more limited set of state laws, those which fall within the scope of ERISA's civil enforcement provision, § 502. State law claims which fall outside of the scope of § 502, even if preempted by § 514(a), are still governed by the well-pleaded complaint rule and, therefore, are not removable under the complete-preemption principles established in [*Taylor*].

Observing that "courts and parties often confuse § 514 preemption with § 502(a) complete preemption," the Tenth Circuit explained that the term "complete preemption" is not to be read "as a crude measure of the breadth of the preemption (in the ordinary sense) of a state law by a federal law, but rather as a description of the specific situation in which a federal law not only preempts a state law to some degree but also substitutes a federal cause of action for the state cause of action, thereby manifesting Congress's intent to permit removal." Felix v. Lucent Technologies, Inc., 387 F.3d 1146 (10th Cir.2004).

A claim made by a plaintiff who could not bring any type of action under ERISA § 502(a) is not completely preempted, and thus not removable. For example, in Franchise Tax Board v. Construction Laborers Vacation Trust, 463 U.S. 1 (1983), the California Franchise Tax Board brought suit in California state court against an employee welfare benefit trust alleging two causes of action: (1) that because the trust failed to comply with certain tax levies it was liable for damages, and (2) that in light of the trust's contention that ERISA preempted state law, a judgment be issued declaring the parties' respective rights. The trustees sought to remove the case to federal court. The Supreme Court held unanimously that a suit by state tax authorities under a tax levy statute does not "arise under" ERISA.

> Unlike the contract rights at issue in *Avco*, the State's right to enforce its tax levies is not of central concern to the federal statute. [Furthermore], ERISA does not provide an alternative cause of action in favor of the State to enforce its rights, while § 301 expressly supplied the plaintiff in *Avco* with a federal cause of action to replace its preempted state contract claim. Therefore, even though the Court of Appeals may well be correct that ERISA precludes enforcement of the State's levy in the circumstances of this case, an action to enforce the levy is not itself preempted by ERISA.

Id. at 25–26.

Similarly if a plaintiff lacks standing to bring a claim under ERISA, the claim cannot be fully preempted and therefore cannot be removed. Tenet Health Sys. Phila., Inc. v. Diversified Admin. Corp., 2012 U.S. Dist. LEXIS 61395 (E.D. Pa. May 2, 2012).

More difficult are claims that relate to plan benefits but do not actually seek to recover benefits due under a plan. In Ervast v. Flexible Products Co., 346 F.3d 1007 (11th Cir.2003), the Eleventh Circuit held that ERISA did not completely preempt the claim of a former employee against his employer for breach of fiduciary duty under state corporate law. The employee claimed that the employer failed to disclose material information that would have affected the employee's decision to liquidate his ESOP stock account. Because the employer's duty arose only by virtue of state law, and because the claim did not seek to recover benefits, the claim was not completely preempted.

2. *Removal and remand.* Defendants in state court actions, typically plans and their fiduciaries, but also third-party service providers and others, are well aware of ERISA's broad preemptive effect and almost always remove a suit from state to federal court if there is even a remote connection with ERISA. Commonly, the plaintiff responds with a motion to remand, alleging lack of federal jurisdiction. The federal district court must then decide whether the state cause of action is removable under *Taylor*.

If the district court concludes that the plaintiff's claim is not completely preempted and consequently that no federal jurisdiction exists, the court must remand the case and may order the payment of "just costs." 28 U.S.C. § 1447(c). Except for certain civil rights cases not relevant, "an order remanding a case to the State court from which it was removed is not reviewable on appeal or otherwise." 28 U.S.C. § 1447(d). Thus, even if the federal district court has mistakenly remanded a state law claim that is surely preempted by ERISA, the defendant will have to continue the litigation in state court.

Can the defendant then seek to dismiss the claim by arguing the preemption issue to the state court, or does the federal district court's determination preclude the defendant from raising the issue? A number of circuits have held that a district court's jurisdictional finding that a claim is not completely preempted does not preclude a state court from considering the merits of ERISA preemption. See e.g., Baldridge v. Kentucky-Ohio Transportation, Inc., 983 F.2d 1341, 1345–46 (6th Cir.1993) (en banc); Glasser v. Amalgamated Workers Union Local 88, 806 F.2d 1539, 1541 (11th Cir.1986).

3. *Tax Injunction Act.* As discussed supra, state tax statutes that affect employee benefit plans have sometimes been challenged as preempted under ERISA. When the complaint for injunctive or declaratory relief is brought in federal court, the plaintiffs must overcome the Tax Injunction Act (TIA), 28 U.S.C. § 1341. The TIA provides: "The district courts shall not enjoin, suspend or restrain the assessment, levy or collection of any tax under State Law where a plain, speedy and efficient remedy may be had in the courts of such State." The TIA has been held to preclude declaratory judgments as well. Fair Assessment in Real Estate Ass'n v. McNary, 454 U.S. 100, 103 (1981).

The Supreme Court has expressly reserved the issue of whether the TIA bars challenges to state tax laws under ERISA in federal courts. See *Franchise Tax Board*, 463 U.S. at 20 n.21; *Travelers*, 514 U.S. at 652 n.4. Several circuits have held that the TIA does not bar such actions, because the grant of exclusive federal jurisdiction in ERISA § 502(e)(1), by divesting state courts of jurisdiction to hear such claims, forecloses any "plain, speedy, and efficient" state remedy. See, e.g., Hattem v. Schwarzenegger, 449 F.3d 423 (2d Cir.2006); Travelers Ins. Co. v. Cuomo, 14 F.3d 708, 714 (2d Cir.1993), rev'd on other grounds, 514 U.S. 645 (1995); Thiokol Corp. v. Department of Treasury, 987 F.2d 376, 378 (6th Cir.1993). By contrast, the Ninth Circuit held in Chase Manhattan Bank, N.A. v. City & County of San Francisco, 121 F.3d 557, 560 (9th Cir.1997), that ERISA does not enable a plaintiff to circumvent the TIA. The court said that "a plain, speedy, and efficient remedy exist[s] because a party [can] pursue its ERISA preemption claim in state court." Accord Darne v. State of Wisconsin, 137 F.3d 484 (7th Cir.1998).

4. *Anti-Injunction Act.* Suppose a state court assumes jurisdiction over a case in which the defendant claims that the state court's jurisdiction is preempted by ERISA. Can the defendant enjoin the state court proceedings in a federal action? The Anti-Injunction Act, with limited exceptions, generally prohibits federal courts from enjoining a state court from proceeding. "A court of the United States may not grant an injunction to stay proceedings in a State Court except as expressly authorized by Act of Congress, or where necessary in aid of its jurisdiction, or to protect or effectuate its judgments." 28 U.S.C. § 2283.

The courts have generally rejected claims that ERISA falls within the "expressly authorized" exception. See, e.g., Denny's, Inc. v. Cake, 364 F.3d 521 (4th Cir.2004); NSG American, Inc. v. Jefferson, 218 F.3d 519, 522 n.4 (6th Cir.2000); Total Plan Services v. Texas Retailers Ass'n, 925 F.2d 142 (5th Cir.1991). In *Total Plan Services*, 925 F.2d at 146, the Fifth Circuit said: "Although plaintiffs present good arguments that the proper tribunal for an ERISA fiduciary action is a federal court, the appropriate authority to decide the scope of the ERISA preemption issue in *this* case is the state court, where the action initially was filed and where this issue initially was presented and ruled upon." In contrast, some courts have held that ERISA does fall within the "expressly authorized" exception to the Anti-Injunction Act where the parties in the ERISA action are not identical to the parties in the state court action. Peacock v. Pace Intern. Union Pension Fund Plan, 2007 WL 4403689 (M.D.Tenn.2007).

5. *Abstention.* Suppose a state regulatory agency brings an administrative proceeding against a state licensed health care provider alleging violations of state statutes. The provider believes that ERISA preempts the regulatory action. Can the provider seek a declaratory judgment to that effect in federal district court? In Delta Dental Plan of California, Inc. v. Mendoza, 139 F.3d 1289, 1294 (9th Cir.1998), the court held that the *Younger* abstention doctrine (see Younger v. Harris, 401 U.S. 37 (1971)) applies to such a preemption claim and requires the district court to abstain from hearing such a case when "(i) the state proceedings are ongoing; (ii) the proceedings implicate important state interests; and (iii) the state proceedings provide an adequate opportunity to raise federal questions." In Kaplan v. CareFirst, Inc., 614 F.Supp.2d

587 (D.Md.2009), a federal district court reached the same conclusion with respect to a suit seeking a declaratory judgment that ERISA preempted a state insurance law regulating compensation of officers and employees of nonprofit health service plans.

CHAPTER 18

EMPLOYMENT LAW AND DISCRIMINATION ISSUES

Analysis

Introduction: Employment Law and Employee Benefits

Employment law is principally concerned with the employment relationship itself: Employers are prohibited, for example, from taking race or sex into account in deciding whether to hire someone. In pursuit of their larger purpose employment laws also, however, regulate compensation levels, of which employee benefits form a part.

Sources of employment laws. Among the federal statutes are laws prohibiting employment discrimination on the basis of age (the Age Discrimination in Employment Act, or "ADEA"), sex (Title VII of the Civil Rights Act of 1964), and disability (the Americans with Disabilities Act, or "ADA"). All of these are interpreted and enforced by the Equal Employment Opportunity Commission ("EEOC"). Each has implicated employee benefit plans. The Family and Medical Leave Act of 1993 ("FMLA") (administered, in contrast to the above statutes, by the Department of Labor) requires employers to provide employees the opportunity for an unpaid leave of absence without adverse employment ramifications in the case of birth (or adoption) of a child, or of serious family illness.

The Constitution has been more recently interpreted by the Supreme Court, in *U.S. v. Windsor* (discussed in Section D), to extend protection from discrimination to same-sex married couples. While the law in this area remains distinctly in flux, this development has immediate important implications for a range of benefit plan issues.

Specific federal legislation (the Uniformed Services Employment and Reemployment Rights Act, or "USERRA") exists to protect the rights of employees called up to active duty in the armed forces. Finally, laws of an entirely different type, state laws protecting employees' rights to earned wages, are also sometimes relevant.

Most states also have statutes or constitutions that prohibit discrimination on the basis of age, sex, etc., similar to the federal laws described above. To the extent these laws impinge on employee benefit plans subject to ERISA, however, they have been held by the Supreme Court to be preempted, as is discussed in connection with *Shaw v. Delta Airlines,* in Chapter 17.

A. AGE DISCRIMINATION

1. INTRODUCTION

A defined benefit pension plan specifies a "normal retirement age" (NRA) in the plan. ERISA § 3(24) defines NRA as whatever the plan provides, or age 65 (subject to some adjustments for employees who join the plan at advanced ages). The function of age, including NRA, in benefit calculation is examined in Section A of this chapter.

ERISA's presumptive NRA of 65 reflects the common assumption of the mid-1970s that employees would retire at that age. Age 65 as the presumptive NRA goes all the way back to Bismarck, and was adopted by Social Security in the 1930s. When ERISA was enacted in 1974, the Age Discrimination in Employment Act (ADEA) of 1967 permitted employers to require employees to retire at age 65 (the so-called mandatory retirement age). ADEA was amended in 1978 to raise the age cap from 65 to 70. In 1986, Congress again amended the ADEA, prohibiting mandatory retirement at any age, subject to some exceptions.

Thus, while pension law encourages the notion of a normal retirement age, the prohibition of discrimination on the basis of age circumscribes the imposition of age-related retirement requirements. These tensions are explored in this section.

2. NORMAL RETIREMENT AGE (NRA)

Dan M. McGill, Kyle N. Brown, John J. Haley, Sylvester
J. Schieber & Mark J. Warshawsky, Fundamentals of
Private Pensions
327–28 (9th ed. 2010).

The normal retirement age has traditionally been considered the earliest age at which participants are eligible to retire with full benefits.

However, ERISA established a statutory definition of normal retirement age, used for determining plan vesting limits, accrual of benefit standards, and plan funding requirements. As defined by ERISA, normal retirement age is specified in the plan but may not be later than age 65 with five years of participation. In addition to the statutory ceiling in a plan's normal retirement age, IRS guidance has set a floor, so that a plan's normal retirement age cannot be before the earliest age that is typical for the industry in which the covered workforce is employed. . . .

There are three essential components in the definition of a benefit accrual: the dollar amount of the benefit, the age at which the benefit is payable in full (i.e., the normal retirement age), and the form under which the benefit is payable. The annuity form of the benefit can be a single-life annuity, a joint and survivor annuity, or a single-life annuity with a refund feature. The dollar amount of prospective retirement benefits to be paid to two participants of the same age and sex under two separate pension plans may be identical, but the actuarial value of the accrued benefits (and, hence, their cost) can be quite different if they do not become payable at the same age and under the same annuity form.

Thus, the normal retirement age should be viewed more as an element in the definition of the retirement benefit than as a statement of when participants are expected to retire. Participants may retire over a wide range of ages, with appropriate adjustments in their benefits. Most plans permit retirement before the normal retirement age, usually subject to specified age and service restrictions, and most permit deferment of retirement beyond the normal retirement age.

Many retirement plans have linked eligibility to unreduced benefits to five or ten years of service or participation, but some have a much longer period if the minimum age is younger than 65. For example, the normal retirement age may be the earlier of age 65 with 5 years of service, 60 with 20 years of service, or 55 with 30 years of service. Discontinuities in benefit entitlement can be avoided by providing unreduced benefits by the employee's age whenever his or her age and service equal a specified number, such as 90. A provision of this sort is referred to as the "Rule of 90," although the concept may also be applied in establishing eligibility for vested benefits.

Under the Rule of 90, such combinations as age 60 and 30 years of service would entitle participants to full benefits for their credited years of service. The rule may, of course, be stated in terms of other numbers, such as 85 or 95. Some plans with a nominal normal retirement age permit retirement before that age, subject to minimum service requirements, with full benefits for the years of accrued service. Under some collectively bargained plans, participants are permitted to retire with full accrued benefits after a specified amount of service, such as 30 years, irrespective of age, a provision commonly referred to as a "30 and out" retirement. Some plans have alternative criteria for normal retirement age, such as the earlier of age 65 or the completion of 30 years of service. Under all these arrangements, the normal retirement age varies according to the related service requirement and the participant's age of entry into the plan.

In addition to its actuarial function, the normal retirement age serves as an instrument of personnel policy. In most companies, it indicates the age at which employees typically retire. Some plans previously specified a mandatory retirement age, usually 70, but mandatory retirement is generally no longer permitted.

NOTE: THE IMPORTANCE OF NRA

The observation that "the normal retirement age should be viewed more as an element in the definition of the retirement benefit than as a statement of when participants are expected to retire" was previously emphasized in Chapter 4, supra, in connection with benefit accrual. Though counterintuitive, it is a point of fundamental importance.

3. EARLY RETIREMENT

Dan M. McGill, Kyle N. Brown, John J. Haley, Sylvester J. Schieber & Mark J. Warshawsky, Fundamentals of Private Pensions
329–31 (9th ed. 2010).

It is customary to provide for retirement earlier than the normal retirement age, subject to attaining a specified age, typically 55, and possibly fulfilling a minimum period of service, such as 10, 15, or 20 years. At one time, some plans required employer consent for early retirement, but IRS regulations no longer permit this.

Some plans permit early retirement only upon total and permanent disability. . . . In such plans, age and service requirements are also imposed. Some of the plans provide a special disability benefit, while others pay only the same percentage of the regular accrued benefit that would normally be paid on early retirement.

Calculating an early retirement benefit involves two steps. The first is to determine the amount of benefit that would be payable at normal retirement age based on the participant's service and compensation at the date of early retirement. This determination is made in the same manner as the computation of the vested benefit. The second step is to multiply the accrued benefit payable at normal retirement age by an early retirement factor reflecting the facts that (1) benefit payments begin earlier than contemplated and, therefore, extend over a longer time; (2) the assets supporting the benefits earn less investment income before payments commence; and (3) there will be no gains to the plan from participants' dying before benefit payments commence (the benefit of survivorship).

When the accrued retirement benefits are reduced by a set of factors that reflect the foregoing elements, they are said to be "actuarially reduced" or "actuarially equivalent." The expression "full actuarial reduction" is frequently applied to the process that fully recognizes the longer payout period and loss of investment earnings (and benefit of survivorship) to distinguish it from the results obtained by applying a higher scale of percentages to the accrued benefits. Some plans now link eligibility for unreduced benefits to Social Security's full retirement age. Thus one set of reductions applies for workers born before 1938, another for those born between 1938 and 1954, and a third for those born after 1954.

The reduction in the accrued benefits for early retirement depends upon the mortality and interest assumptions that underlie the calculation of the actuarial value of the normal retirement benefits. The greater the assumed rates of mortality and the higher the interest-rate assumption, the greater the reduction for each year of early retirement. The percentage reduction in the accrued benefits for each year of early retirement slopes downward. When the actuarial value of the normal retirement benefits is computed on the basis of [a unisex mortality table] and a 6 percent interest assumption, the accrued normal retirement benefit is reduced about 8 percent per year, expressed as a percentage of the benefit for the next higher age. For example, the benefit payable at age 64 is about 92 percent of that payable at age 65; that payable at age 63 is about 92 percent of that payable at age 64; and so on. This relatively uniform progression continues down to at least age 55.

The proportion of the accrued normal retirement benefit that would be payable at ages 55 through 64, under the mortality and interest assumptions set forth above, are shown in [the following table]. It must be emphasized that the percentages are applied to the benefit credits accrued to the date of early retirement and not to the benefits that would have been paid at age 65 if the employee continued working to that age. No distinction is allowed between male and female employees because of the difference in their life expectancy.

Proportion of Accrued Normal Retirement Income Available at Early Retirement at Various Ages under a Plan with Normal Retirement Age 65

Age at Retirement	Benefit Percentage
64	91.4
63	83.7
62	76.8
61	70.6
60	65
59	59.9
58	55.4
57	51.2
56	47.4
55	43.9

Some plans have moved away from actuarially precise early retirement factors and instead provide for a stipulated percentage discount for each month by which actual retirement precedes the normal retirement date. These monthly factors may approximate the annual factors that are geared to a full actuarial reduction, or, more commonly, they may be clearly designed to produce a smaller reduction than if full weight were being given to actuarial considerations. . . .

[The] general practice of using early retirement factors more favorable than the actuarially equivalent ones is referred to as "subsidized early retirement." . . . Special provision may be made for employees who retire early because of poor health.

4. EARLY RETIREMENT TRENDS

a. *Early retirement as the norm.* In an important sense, "normal retirement age" is abnormal. Most pension plans authorize early retirement, that is, retirement before NRA, and during the 1970s and 1980s there was a pronounced tendency for workers to elect early retirement options. During the period 1970–85, "age 62 replaced age 65 as the typical retirement age for men and retirement before age 62 became increasingly common." Michael D. Packard & Virginia P. Reno, A Look at Very Early Retirees, 52 Social Security Bulletin 16 (Mar. 1989). "In 1985 [almost] 50 percent of 62-year-old men were out of the work force, up from about 25 percent in 1970." Id. at 18. In 2001, the average retirement age for men was 62, and for women, 61.4. Murray Gendell, Retirement Age Declines Again in 1990s, Monthly Labor Review, Dec. 2001, at p.14.

More recent evidence suggests that the trend toward ever-earlier retirement has stabilized or even reversed. "Until the mid-1980s, the age at which people retired had declined for decades. In the mid-1980s, the decline ceased. Between 1985 and 2002, the retirement age for men held steady." Alicia H. Munnell, Kevin E. Cahill & Natalia A. Jivan, Center for Retirement Research at Boston College, Issue in Brief No. 13, at 1 (Sept. 2003). By 2012 the average retirement age reported for men was back up to 64. Alicia H. Munnell, What is the Average Retirement Age?, Society of Actuaries Pension Section News (February 2012, Issue No. 76). Munnell suggests several possible explanations for the slowing of the trend toward earlier retirement, including the reduction of retirement incentives within Social Security, the shift from defined benefit to defined contribution plans, improved health and longevity, and the decline in prevalence of retiree medical insurance. Researchers disagree, however, over whether this is a temporary or permanent phenomenon. "One side concludes that the trend has stopped due to economic, policy, and demographic changes. The other side stresses that long-run growth in income and the desire for more leisure suggest only a pause." Leora Friedberg, The Recent Trend Towards Later Retirement, Center for Retirement Research at Boston College, Issue in Brief: Work Opportunities for Older Americans, Series 9, 1, 2 (March 2007).

b. *Effect of actuarial reduction.* Workers are quite sensitive to the cost of early retirement when it is unsubsidized (that is, when pension benefits are actuarially reduced to reflect the cost of providing the pension across more years, as explained in the extract from McGill et al., supra). A survey of medium and large companies that appeared in 1985 contrasted the retirement behavior of workers in firms that offered subsidized early retirement with firms that did not. "The average age of retirement was strongly influenced by these inducements. In firms offering both unreduced benefits and small early-retirement discounts, 80 percent of the workers retired at age 62 or earlier. In those firms offering either unreduced benefits *or* small early-retirement discounts, 56 percent of the employees retired at age 62 or younger. Finally, in those firms not offering early-retirement inducements, only 24 percent of the workers retired at age 62 or younger." Michael Packard, Note, Company Policies and Attitudes Toward Older Workers, 48 Social Security Bull. 45 (May 1985). Subsequent studies have found the same influence. As of

2003, workers whose employers provide an economic subsidy for early retirement are 9.5% more likely to retire before age 65, with the percentage increasing for middle income workers. Janemarie Mulvey, Retirement Behavior and Retirement Plan Designs; Strategies to Retain an Aging Workforce, Benefits Quarterly 25, 29–31 (4th Q. 2003) Interestingly, Mulvey found that more productive workers "have a higher probability of retiring when offered generous early retirement incentives as compared to lower performers. For every 10% increase in the present value of the early retirement benefit relative to the normal retirement benefit, the probability of retiring increases 3.5% for top performers vs. 1.9% for low performers." Id. at 30.

      c.   *The demographic crunch.* Earlier retirement exacerbates a problem that would in any event have become worrisome, on account of underlying demographic trends. Retirees have to be supported by active workers. Can the workforce of the future sustain the expectations of future retirees for transfer payments (Social Security) and investment yields (which fund the private pension system)? The huge twentieth-century increase in longevity is now being accompanied by a marked decline in fertility rates—the "baby bust" following the post-World War II "baby boom." In the year 1900, 12.5 persons aged 20–64 supported one person aged 65 or older. By 1930, the figure was 10 to 1, by 1950, it was 7.1 to 1, by 1975 it was 5.3 to 1. Stein, Social Security and Pensions in Transition, supra, at 202 (Table 6–9). The Board of Trustees of the Federal Old-Age and Survivors Insurance and Federal Disability Insurance Trust Funds reported in its 2014 Annual Report that there were about 2.8 workers for every OASDI beneficiary in 2013 and projects that the retirement of the baby-boomer generation will mean a ratio of workers to beneficiaries of 2.2 to 1 in 2030. 2014 Annual Report of The Board of Trustees of the Federal Old-Age and Survivors Insurance and Federal Disability Insurance Trust Funds, House Doc. 113–139, p. 57 (July 28, 2014).

      If the burden of retirees on active workers becomes intolerable, what adjustments are likely to occur in the Social Security system and in the private pension system?

      d.   *Generational equity: the merits of early retirement.* Consider the views of the late Kingsley Davis, formerly a sociologist at the University of Southern California:

> A retired American today is probably the freest human being ever to walk the earth. Assuming that basic needs are met by a pension, Social Security, Medicare and investment income, the retiree lives in a perpetual paradise of leisure and recreation. If the retiree stays healthy, this special status can be enjoyed for 15 to 20 years. There is time to fish all day or golf every afternoon.

> But retirement in the United States is also frightfully expensive—both for the nation and for those who pay the bills. The high cost comes not only in payments to the retired but from production lost when part of the labor force sits on its hands. This foregone production creates a serious problem that can only get bigger.

Considering only healthy [people], the United States loses about 17.5 million older workers through complete retirement— about 14 percent of the total civilian labor force. So far, however, this loss has been more than made up by the entry of married women into the labor force. But this bonanza will not last long.

Indeed, as the graying of America continues, fewer and fewer workers will pay for more and more senior citizens.

[These] retired Americans have been told they have worked hard and now deserve their leisure. The average person retiring at age 63 still has 18 years to live (16 for men). This is equivalent to 42 percent of the average person's working life. This is not only a considerable amount of time to spend fishing and golfing, but it is also a long time to spend dependent on others.

And what about the direct costs to support what could be called a privileged group of idle senior citizens? . . . [A]s the population grows older, the burden on the labor force will become even more onerous.

What should we do? Reducing retiree benefits is probably harder to achieve than getting people to remain in the work force. Once support of retirees becomes impersonal—a charge on the general public rather than on grown children—there is no moral constraint on their economic demands. Further, the elderly are so numerous, so articulate and experienced, and so possessed of free time (since they are not working) they can and do lobby powerfully for their own interests.

Kingsley Davis, "Our Idle Retirees Drag Down the Economy," New York Times, Oct. 18, 1987, at 31. Davis had Social Security more in mind than the private pension system, but the two systems combine to produce the effects that he criticized.

e.   *Phased Retirement.* Davis paints a picture of retirees spending their time fishing and golfing. To what extent does that picture accurately reflect the current reality? Increasingly, workers who retire from their career jobs continue to work. According to Social Security figures, "37 percent of men and 31 percent of women aged 55 to 64 who received income from private pension plans in 1999 were employed in March 2000. The process of retiring often occurs gradually over a number of years, with many workers retiring from year-round, full-time employment and moving to part-time or part-year work at another firm, often in a different occupation." Patrick J. Purcell, Older Workers: Employment and Retirement Trends, Monthly Labor Review 19, 25 (Oct. 2000).

The ability of companies to benefit from the phased retirement of their own workers was improved by the 2006 PPA, which allows pension plans to begin paying benefits to workers who have not yet separated from service at the earlier of age 62 or the plan's NRA. This provision and the IRS regulations addressing NRAs below the age of 65 are discussed in Chapter 11, supra.

5. BENEFIT ACCRUAL BEYOND NRA

Continued Accruals. It used to be, but is no longer, permissible for retirement plans to cease providing for further benefit accruals once an employee reached normal retirement age. Since 1986, plans have not been permitted to reduce benefit accrual "because of the attainment of any age." ERISA § 204(b)(1)(H), IRC § 411(b)(1)(H). However, a plan may still "[impose] (without regard to age) a limitation on the amount of benefits that the plan provides or a limitation on the number of years of service or years of participation which are taken into account for purposes of determining benefit accrual under the plan." ERISA § 204(b)(1)(H)(ii), IRC § 411(b)(1)(H)(ii). The argument that such a limitation, even though not prohibited by ERISA, amounts to age discrimination is expressly foreclosed by section 4(i)(2) of ADEA, which provides that the ADEA's prohibition of age discrimination does not forbid "any provision of an employee benefit plan to the extent that such provision imposes (without regard to age) a limitation on the amount of benefits that the plan provides or a limitation on the number of years of service or years of participation which are taken into account for purposes of determining benefit accrual under the plan."

Hence, a plan that ceases accruals at age 65 is forbidden, yet a plan that ceases benefit accruals after 30 years of covered service is allowed. Since both tend in the same direction, what did the reform achieve? Cf. Northwest Airlines, Inc., v. Phillips, 675 F.3d 1126 (8th Cir. 2012) (money purchase plan formula did not violate ERISA or ADEA where the formula for determining a participant's benefit level includes factors that are "correlated with age").

Although a participant must continue to accrue benefits after normal retirement age, he or she may be adversely affected if the plan does not actuarially adjust the benefits to reflect the decreased payout period. For example, assume A has an annual compensation of $100,000 and accrues a benefit of 2% of highest average compensation multiplied by A's years of service. If A retires at age 65 with 30 years of service, A is entitled to a pension of $60,000 per year. If A works another year and then retires, A is entitled to $62,000 per year. Thus, A receives an extra $2,000 per year, but loses the $60,000 A could have received from the pension plan. It will never be paid. Treas.Reg. § 1.411(c)–1(f)(2) specifically permits this, as does DoL Reg. § 2530.203–3(c)(1). A challenge to these regulations failed in Atkins v. Northwest Airlines, 967 F.2d 1197 (8th Cir.1992).

Congress modified the law in 1996 to require that a participant who works past age 70½ must have his or her accrued benefit adjusted to reflect the value of the benefits that would have been received if the participant had retired at age 70½ and had begun receiving benefits at that time. IRC § 401(a)(9)(C)(iii). Thus, in the example above, if A works until age 71½, then from age 65 until age 70½ he will continue to "lose" the benefits he would have received had he retired at age 65. However, the benefits that A would have received between age 70½ and 71½ had he not continued working will not be lost; rather, his accrued benefit must be increased by an amount that when paid over his lifetime is actuarially equivalent to that one year's worth of foregone benefits.

Focus on the feature of this regime that allows benefits to be lost between normal retirement age and age 70½. By not adjusting the benefits to reflect accruals in those years, a plan creates an inherent incentive for participants to retire at normal retirement age, which is a useful way for employers to encourage older employees to retire. Can one analogize this failure to adjust benefits to ERISA's permitting forfeitures upon death? The purpose of a pension is to provide a replacement for wage income when an employee is no longer able to work. Like payments to heirs after death, payments to employees who are still working increase plan costs, which ex ante would have the effect of lowering average benefit levels. If the analogy is sound, why require actuarial adjustments of benefits in the case of an employee who works past the age of 70½?

6. ADEA

The Age Discrimination in Employment Act (ADEA), 29 U.S.C. 621 et seq., enacted in 1967, is primarily directed to proscribing discrimination in hiring, firing, and conditions of employment. Practice under ADEA has become a legal specialty unto itself, and ADEA is a centerpiece of the law school course in employment discrimination. For purposes of the course in pension and employee benefit law, the object is simply to alert students to the ADEA's strictures against discrimination in employee benefits.

Few areas of employee benefits law have undergone so many tides of change over the past quarter century or so as the topics touched by ADEA. As mentioned at the outset of this section, the presumptive NRA of ERISA § 3(24)(B)—age 65—is the age that the ADEA of 1967 permitted employers to require employees to retire when ERISA was enacted in 1974. Congress amended ADEA in 1978 to raise the mandatory retirement age from 65 to 70, and in OBRA in 1986 Congress amended the ADEA to prohibit mandatory retirement at any age, subject to some exceptions. (In Lockheed Corp. v. Spink, 517 U.S. 882 (1996), the Supreme Court held that the 1986 OBRA amendments did not require retrospective accrual of pension benefits for employees lawfully excluded from a plan under pre-OBRA law.)

As with the other federal anti-discrimination statutes discussed in this chapter, ADEA does not apply to small businesses. In the case of ADEA, only those private entities with 20 or more employees meet the definition, in ADEA § 11(b), of "employer" covered by the statute.

This Section reviews the main provisions of the ADEA that address benefit plans, then recounts the twists and turns in interpreting the statute that led to the changes effected by the Older Workers Benefit Protection Act of 1990 (OWBPA). Subsequent sections summarize OWBPA and address the standards for liability under ADEA, the overlap of ADEA with employee benefit plans, and the main patterns of litigation.

Students are cautioned that these materials supply a mere introduction to the employee benefits aspects of a distinct regulatory scheme and are no substitute for the course in employment discrimination.

1. *Summary of ADEA.* Relevant sections of the Age Discrimination in Employment Act of 1967 as amended, 29 U.S.C. § 621–34, are normally contained in ERISA/IRC statutory compilations used in conjunction with this coursebook. Following is a summary of certain key ADEA provisions that touch pension and employee benefits issues. It is recommended that students consult the statutory text in preference to this summary.

Section 12 of the ADEA limits its prohibitions "to individuals who are at least 40 years of age." Section 4(a)(1) contains the basic proscription, forbidding employers from refusing "to hire or to discharge any individual or otherwise discriminate against any individual with respect to his compensation, terms, conditions, or privileges of employment, because of such individual's age. . . ."

Section 4(f) excuses from the prohibition a variety of practices. Section 4(f)(2)(A) allows the employers and unions "to observe the terms of a bona fide seniority system that is not intended to evade the purposes of this chapter, except that no such seniority system shall require or permit the involuntary retirement of [individuals 40 or older] because of the age of such [individual]."

Section 4(f)(2)(B) allows employers and unions "to observe the terms of a bona fide employee benefit plan (i) where, for each benefit or benefit package, the actual amount of payment made or cost incurred on behalf of an older worker is no less than that made or incurred on behalf of a younger worker, as permissible under [29 C.F.R. § 1625.10]; or (ii) that is a voluntary early retirement incentive plan consistent with the relevant purpose or purposes of this chapter." However, the so-called bona fide plan exclusion is itself sharply restricted under section 4(f)(2)(B). The statute says that under neither "clause (i) [nor clause] (ii) of subparagraph (B) [may] such employee benefit plan or voluntary early retirement incentive [plan] excuse the failure to hire any individual, [nor may] such employee benefit [plan] require or permit the involuntary retirement of any individual [aged 40 or older] because of the age of such individual."

Section 4(i)(1) makes it unlawful "to establish or maintain an employee benefit pension plan which requires or permits (A) in the case of a defined benefit plan, the cessation of an employee's benefit accrual, or the reduction of the rate of an employee's benefit accrual, because of age, or (B) in the case of a defined contribution plan, the cessation of allocations to an employee's account, or the reduction of the rate at which amounts are allocated to an employee's account, because of age." However, section 4(i)(2) allows such plans to contain a "provision impos[ing] (without regard to age) a limitation on the amount of benefits that the plan provides or a limitation on the number of years of service or years of participation which are taken into account for purposes of determining benefit accrual under the plan."

7. OVERVIEW OF DEVELOPMENTS THROUGH OWBPA (1990)

In Public Employees Retirement System v. Betts, 492 U.S. 158 (1989), the Supreme Court read the then-language of ADEA virtually to exempt employee benefit plans from the reach of the ADEA. After considerable political struggle, Congress enacted the Older Workers Benefit Protection Act of 1990 (OWBPA), revising ADEA to overturn *Betts* and to effect other changes. A good account of these developments appears in Gary M. Ford & Paul S. Horn, Assessing the Impact of the Older Workers Act and the ADA, 18 J. Pension Planning & Compliance 1 (1992). Following are extracts from another succinct account of the employee benefits ramifications of the amended ADEA.

David A. Niles, The Older Workers Benefit Protection Act

40 Buffalo L. Rev. 869, 870–913 (1992)
(subheadings altered and citations relocated to text).

The Age Discrimination in Employment Act (ADEA) was passed in 1967 in part to prohibit arbitrary age discrimination in the employment context. Section 4(f)(2) of the Act provides an exception to the ADEA's general prohibitions for differential treatment of older workers that occurs as part of a "bona fide employee benefit plan." In June 1989, the United States Supreme Court issued its first authoritative interpretation of the meaning of the section 4(f)(2) exception, in *Public Employees Retirement System v. Betts*, 492 U.S. 158 (1989). The *Betts* decision sharply reduced the burden of proof placed on employers under section 4(f)(2) by requiring no showing of a cost justification for any discriminatory treatment effected under an allegedly bona fide plan. In response, Congress passed the Older Workers Benefit Protection Act (OWBPA), [29 U.S.C. § 621 (1990)], which was drafted specifically to overturn the *Betts* decision. . . .

The ADEA was passed in 1967 "to promote employment of older persons based on their ability rather than age, to prohibit arbitrary age discrimination in employment, [and] to help employers and workers find ways of meeting problems arising from the impact of age on employment." The ADEA applies to public and private employers, labor unions, and employment agencies, and it prohibits them from discriminating against employees over the age of forty in most employment settings. As the Supreme Court has recognized, the ADEA is strikingly similar to Title VII of the Civil Rights Act of 1964. Indeed, much of the language of the ADEA was drawn from Title VII.

The ADEA's proscription of discriminatory behavior by employers is set forth in section 4(a)(1), which states: "It is unlawful to fail or refuse to hire or to discharge any individual or otherwise discriminate against any individual with respect to his compensation, terms, conditions, or privileges of employment, because of such individual's age." Older workers are given additional protections against invidious segregation or classification on account of age, age-based expulsion from labor organizations, and retaliatory discharge for revealing employer age-discrimination. Section 7 of the ADEA furnishes the victims of age discrimination with a variety of remedies which may be refined or implemented by regulations promulgated by the Equal Opportunity Employment Commission (EEOC).

3. *The bona fide plan exception.* In addition to the general prohibition of section 4(a)(1), the ADEA contained a safe harbor

provision, section 4(f)(2), which was created to prevent a chilling effect in the hiring and retention of older employees. Section 4(f)(2) read:

> It is not unlawful for an employer to observe the terms of . . . any bona fide employee benefit plan such as a retirement, pension, or insurance plan, which is not a subterfuge to evade the purposes of this chapter, except that no such employee benefit plan shall excuse the failure to hire any individual, and no such . . . employee benefit plan shall require or permit the involuntary retirement of any individual . . . because of the age of such individual.

Two years after the ADEA was adopted, the Department of Labor clarified this safe harbor provision by issuing an Interpretive Bulletin (IB) which explained the 4(f)(2) exception. The IB set forth the cost-justification rule, which is sometimes referred to as the "Equal Benefit or Equal Cost" rule. The rule stated:

> A retirement, pension, or insurance plan will be considered in compliance with the statute where the actual amount of payment made, or cost incurred, in behalf of an older worker is equal to that made or incurred in behalf of a younger worker, even though the older worker may thereby receive a lesser amount of pension or retirement benefits, or insurance coverage.

Ten years after its original issuance, the Interpretive Bulletin was amended in response to congressional requests for more comprehensive guidance regarding section 4(f)(2) of the ADEA. The resulting amendment to the IB stated that:

> The legislative history of [§ 4(f)(2)] indicates that its purpose is to permit age-based reductions in employee benefit plans where such reductions are justified by significant cost considerations . . . [W]here employee benefit plans do meet the criteria in section 4(f)(2), benefit levels for older workers may be reduced to the extent necessary to achieve approximate equivalency in cost for older and younger workers. A benefit plan will be considered in compliance with the statute where the actual amount of payment made, or cost incurred, in behalf of an older worker is equal to that made or incurred in behalf of a younger worker even though the older worker may thereby receive a lesser amount of benefits or insurance coverage.

Despite the clarity of agencies' interpretations of section 4(f)(2), courts remained uncertain as to: 1) which plans fell within the 4(f)(2) exclusion; and 2) the meaning and purpose of the term "subterfuge" in section 4(f)(2). The United States Supreme Court addressed these issues in *Public Employees Retirement System v. Betts.*

The Betts case. In 1985, June Betts, permanently disabled by advancing Alzheimer's disease, became too ill to perform her duties and retired from her position as a speech pathologist with the County of Hamilton, Ohio. Upon her retirement, the 61 year old Mrs. Betts was unable to receive disability benefits because Ohio's Public Employees Retirement System prohibited persons over sixty from applying for disability benefits. Although a 1976 amendment to the Ohio program guaranteed disability beneficiaries a minimum of thirty percent of salary, Mrs. Betts' discrimination claim arose because there was no corresponding minimum benefits provision covering ordinary pension benefits for which recipients become eligible at age sixty. As a result of the denial of disability benefits caused by the lopsided structure of these provisions, Mrs. Betts received only $158.50 per month in age-and-service retirement benefits rather than the $355 per month a similarly situated fifty-nine year old would have received under disability retirement.

The Supreme Court's response to Mrs. Betts' plight was significant in three respects. First, the majority held that employee benefit plans, including pensions, did not fall within the language of "compensation, terms, conditions, or privileges of employment" under section 4(a)(1) of the ADEA. The Court reasoned that to conclude otherwise would render section 4(f)(2) "nugatory with respect to post-Act plans."

Second, the Court proceeded to reject the cost-justification interpretation of the term "subterfuge" as it had been applied by the Department of Labor, the EEOC, and the federal courts of appeals. The Supreme Court, following the case of *United Air Lines, Inc. v. McMann*, 434 U.S. 192, 202 (1977), interpreted the term "subterfuge" in light of its "plain meaning." According to the Court, the plain meaning of "subterfuge" was a "scheme" reflecting a subjective intent to discriminate, and therefore the contemporaneous regulations and judicial interpretations of the ADEA were incorrect to adopt an objective cost justification requirement. The subterfuge language was read by the Court as providing a narrow prohibition within an otherwise broad exemption for benefit plans under ADEA.

Third, the Court determined that section 4(f)(2) did not constitute an affirmative defense for employers accused of distributing employee benefits in a discriminatory fashion. Rather, the Court ruled that "the employee bears the burden of proving that the discriminatory plan provision actually was intended to serve the purpose of discriminating in some non-fringe-benefit aspect of the employment relation." . . .

8.   THE OLDER WORKERS BENEFIT PROTECTION ACT OF 1990 (OWBPA)

OWBPA was enacted specifically to redress the perceived damage to age discrimination law caused by the *Betts* decision, through four specific means. First, OWBPA clearly places employee benefits within the prohibitions against age discrimination contained in section 4(a) of the ADEA. Second, OWBPA reaffirms that employers may offer a lesser amount of benefits *only* when there is a cost justification for so doing under a bona fide benefit plan. OWBPA also places the burden of proof on the employer who utilizes section 4(f)(2) as an affirmative defense. Finally, OWBPA retroactively applies the latest version of the ADEA to all employee benefit programs outside of federal and state employment programs. . . .

1.   *Inclusion of employee benefits in the ADEA.* Section 102 of OWBPA was specifically enacted to overturn the first aspect of the *Betts*⋅ holding, thereby placing employee benefits within the general

prohibitions contained in section 4(a)(1) of the ADEA. Section 102 amends section 11 of the ADEA (the ADEA's definitional section), by inserting a new subsection (1) which states that the term "compensation, terms, conditions, or privileges of employment" found in ADEA section 4(a)(1), "encompasses all employee benefits, including such benefits provided pursuant to a bona fide employee benefit plan." . . .

2.   *Reaffirmation of section 4(f)(2) as an affirmative defense.* Prior to the *Betts* decision, the ADEA's section 4(f)(2) exemption of bona fide benefit plans provided the employer with an affirmative defense to charges of age discrimination. Accordingly, once a plaintiff alleged that the employer discriminated through the use of unequal benefits, the employer bore the burden of proving that any benefit disparity was merely part of a bona fide employee benefit plan. The majority in *Betts,* however, held that section 4(f)(2) required the plaintiff employee to prove "that the discriminatory plan provision actually was intended to serve the purpose of discriminating in some non-fringe-benefit aspect of the employment relation."

OWBPA squarely rejects the *Betts* majority's interpretation of section 4(f)(2). Section 103(1) of OWBPA replaces 4(f)(2), and includes a new paragraph that explicitly and unequivocally states that the employer bears the burden of showing that any benefit differential is justified by a significant cost consideration. The proviso at the end of section 103 (1) of OWBPA states that "[a]n employer, employment agency, or labor organization acting [under the new 4(f)(2)] shall have the burden of proving that such actions are lawful in any civil enforcement proceeding brought under this Act. . . ."

3.   *Explicit incorporation of the cost-justification rule.* Having clarified that ADEA section 4(f)(2) operated as an affirmative defense, Congress expressly incorporated the cost-justification rule into the ADEA, and thereby followed the consistent interpretation of the Department of Labor, the Equal Employment Opportunity Commission and the federal circuit courts that had interpreted section 4(f)(2). Section 103(1) of OWBPA replaces section 4(f)(2) with new language in order to eliminate confusion as to the scope of the cost-justification rule and to convey forcefully that "the *only* justification for age discrimination in an employee benefit is the increased cost in providing the particular benefit to older individuals."

4.   *Incorporation of public policy exceptions.* The exceptions to the cost-justification rule contained in OWBPA are found in section 103(3), which adds section 4(*l*) to the ADEA. This new section 4(*l*) merely mirrors the loose consensus of pre-*Betts* decisions regarding a number of issues, and exempts certain variations in pension and insurance benefits from section 4(a)(1) of the ADEA. These exceptions to the cost-justification rule are, for the most part, uncontroversial. . . .

5.   *Voluntary early retirement incentives.* Prior to the enactment of OWBPA, some early retirement incentives had the potential to violate the ADEA if they provided similarly situated younger employees with greater amounts of wages and benefits than older employees. Section 103(1) of OWBPA authorizes employers to provide different amounts to employees of differing ages by exempting specifically defined early retirement incentives from the application of the cost-justification rule.

Section 103(1) of OWBPA states that it is not unlawful for an employer to follow a bona fide plan which "is a voluntary early retirement incentive plan consistent with the relevant purpose or purposes of this Act." This clause was inserted to explicitly protect voluntary early retirement programs, including the window programs thought to be threatened by the strict application of the cost-justification rule.

Most employers provide enhanced benefits or supplements for limited periods of time to encourage employees to elect early retirement—so-called "windows of opportunity." Early retirement supplements are frequently offered as part of defined benefit plans, and these supplements differ from temporary "early retirement subsidies." OWBPA purposefully avoids adding any new textual guidance to the ADEA regarding window or "sweetener" programs of this type, choosing instead to allow the analysis of these programs to continue on a "case-by-case" basis. OWBPA requires the courts to determine whether a voluntary early retirement incentive plan is "consistent with the relevant purpose or purposes of [the ADEA]." As Congress recognized, this language unequivocally places the courts back into the pre-*Betts* legal framework under which such incentives were judged according to both their voluntariness, and the legitimacy of the differentiations made between participants in terms of eligibility and/or level of participation.

Under the ADEA, claims that early retirement was involuntary turn on a factually-based, reasonable person analysis of whether the employees to whom retirement incentive was offered had no choice but to accept the incentive. Prior to OWBPA, the circuit courts applied slightly different tests to determine the legality of these early retirement incentives. To resolve this divergence, section 103(1) of OWBPA firmly places the burden of proving voluntariness on the employer.

6. *Pension supplements.* OWBPA allows employers to utilize two common retirement incentives—supplemental unemployment compensation benefit payments (SUBs) and social security bridge payments. SUBs are payments made to employees who are eligible for retirement prior to reaching their employer's normal retirement age, and who are thereby eligible to receive proportionately reduced retirement benefits. Employers often provide SUBs to close the gap between the amount of reduced pension pay an early retirement-eligible employee would receive and the full pension amount the employee will receive upon reaching the employer's normal retirement age. OWBPA section 103(2), which adds new section 4(*l*)(1)(B) to the ADEA, allows an employer to offer SUBs which are provided for as part of a "defined benefit plan" offered by that employer. Congress inserted this authorization of SUBs to explicitly provide a safe harbor for these payments, which would otherwise be invalidated by the cost-justification rule.

Similarly, OWBPA section 103(2), which adds new section 4(*l*)(1)(B)(ii) to the ADEA, expressly permits the use of social security bridge payments—pension supplements that are calculated to supplement an employee's social security benefits rather than his or her pension payments, so long as the total of the social security and supplement payments does not exceed the amount the employee would receive at age sixty-two. Social security supplements violate the cost-justification rule because an employer will pay more, for example, to a fifty-nine year old than a sixty year old in order to ensure that each receives the equivalent of his or her full social security benefits. Without an explicit exception protecting them from the scope of the cost-justification rule, bridge payments would not qualify for the section 4(f)(2) exemption.

7. *Integration of severance pay and retirement-related benefits.* In an effort to extend the maximum level of benefits to the largest number of workers, employers design plans which offset the payment of one type of benefit against an entitlement payment. The variety and complexity of benefit packages have increased over the last twenty years, as employers developed separate pieces of benefits packages designed to meet the demands of various employees whose needs were inadequately covered under preexisting compensation scales. Benefit integration can occur as a permanent feature of a company's pension plan or as a sudden cost-shaving tactic in the face of impending workforce reductions.

8. *Retiree health benefits.* The new ADEA section 4(*l*)(2)(A) allows severance pay to be reduced by the amount of retiree health benefits and/or pension benefits for which an employee is eligible following a "contingent event unrelated to age." The events unrelated to age contemplated by the Act are those which trigger the payment of severance pay, such as plant closings or layoffs.

9. *Definition of the temporal scope of the ADEA.* The final mission of OWBPA was to make clear that employee benefit plans would be subject to the ADEA regardless of when the benefit plans were created. Section 103(2) of OWBPA adds section 4(k) to the ADEA, which places all employee benefit plans under the purview of the Act "regardless of the date of [the plans'] adoption." This provision reaffirms Congress' unequivocal rejection of the *McMann* decision which had exempted plans constructed before the enactment of the ADEA, and overturns the *Betts* Court's resurrection of that rationale.

10. *Developments Subsequent to OWBPA.* The Pension Protection Act of 2006 (PPA) clarified the terms under which cash balance plans are not discriminatory on the basis of age. The relevant provisions are discussed in Section A.6, infra. Other regulatory developments are discussed as relevant, infra.

9. STANDARDS FOR LIABILITY UNDER ADEA

Hazen Paper Co. v. Biggins
507 U.S. 604 (1993).

■ JUSTICE O'CONNOR delivered the opinion of the Court.

In this case we clarify the standards for liability and liquidated damages under the Age Discrimination in Employment Act of 1967 (ADEA).

Petitioner Hazen Paper Company manufactures coated, laminated, and printed paper and paperboard. The company is owned and operated by two cousins, petitioners Robert Hazen and Thomas N. Hazen. The Hazens hired respondent Walter F. Biggins as their technical director in 1977. They fired him in 1986, when he was 62 years old.

Respondent brought suit against petitioners in the United States District Court for the District of Massachusetts, alleging a violation of the ADEA. He claimed that age had been a determinative factor in petitioners' decision to fire him. Petitioners contested this claim, asserting instead that respondent had been fired for doing business with competitors of Hazen Paper. The case was tried before a jury, which rendered a verdict for respondent on his ADEA claim and also found violations of [ERISA § 510] and state law. . . .

In affirming the judgments of liability, the [First Circuit] Court of Appeals relied heavily on the evidence that petitioners had fired respondent in order to prevent his pension benefits from vesting. [953 F.2d 1405 (1st Cir.1992)]. That evidence, as construed most favorably to respondent by the court, showed that the Hazen Paper pension plan had a 10-year vesting period and that respondent would have reached the 10-year mark had he worked "a few more weeks" after being fired. There was also testimony that petitioners had offered to retain respondent as a consultant to Hazen Paper, in which capacity he would not have been entitled to receive pension benefits. The Court of Appeals found this evidence of pension interference to be sufficient for ERISA liability, and also gave it considerable emphasis in upholding ADEA liability. After summarizing all the testimony tending to show age discrimination, the court stated:

> "Based on the foregoing evidence, the jury could reasonably have found that Thomas Hazen decided to fire [respondent] before his pension rights vested and used the confidentiality agreement [that petitioners had asked respondent to sign] as a means to that end. The jury could also have reasonably found that age was inextricably intertwined with the decision to fire [respondent]. If it were not for [respondent's] age, sixty-two, his pension rights would not have been within a hairbreadth of vesting. [Respondent] was fifty-two years old when he was hired; his pension rights vested in ten years." . . .

We granted certiorari to decide [whether] an employer's interference with the vesting of pension benefits violate[s] the [ADEA].

The courts of appeals repeatedly have faced the question whether an employer violates the ADEA by acting on the basis of a factor, such as an employee's pension status or seniority, that is empirically correlated with age. We now clarify that there is no disparate treatment under the ADEA when the factor motivating the employer is some feature other than the employee's age.

We long have distinguished between "disparate treatment" and "disparate impact" theories of employment discrimination.

> " 'Disparate treatment' . . . is the most easily understood type of discrimination. The employer simply treats some people less favorably than others because of their race, color, religion [or other protected characteristics.] Proof of discriminatory motive is critical, although it can in some situations be inferred from the mere fact of differences in treatment. . . .
>
> "[C]laims that stress 'disparate impact' [by contrast] involve employment practices that are facially neutral in their

treatment of different groups but that in fact fall more harshly on one group than another and cannot be justified by business necessity. Proof of discriminatory motive . . . is not required under a disparate-impact theory." *Teamsters v. United States*, 431 U.S. 324, 335, n. 15 (1977) (citation omitted) (construing Title VII of Civil Rights Act of 1964).

The disparate treatment theory is of course available under the ADEA, as the language of that statute makes clear. "It shall be unlawful for an employer . . . to fail or refuse to hire or to discharge any individual or otherwise discriminate against any individual with respect to his compensation, terms, conditions, or privileges of employment, *because of such individual's age.*" [ADEA § 4(a)(1)] (emphasis added). By contrast, we have never decided whether a disparate impact theory of liability is available under the ADEA, and we need not do so here. Respondent claims only that he received disparate treatment.

In a disparate treatment case, liability depends on whether the protected trait (under the ADEA, age) actually motivated the employer's decision. The employer may have relied upon a formal, facially discriminatory policy requiring adverse treatment of employees with that trait. Or the employer may have been motivated by the protected trait on an ad hoc, informal basis. Whatever the employer's decisionmaking process, a disparate treatment claim cannot succeed unless the employee's protected trait actually played a role in that process and had a determinative influence on the outcome.

Disparate treatment, thus defined, captures the essence of what Congress sought to prohibit in the ADEA. It is the very essence of age discrimination for an older employee to be fired because the employer believes that productivity and competence decline with old age. As we explained in *EEOC v. Wyoming*, 460 U.S. 226 (1983), Congress' promulgation of the ADEA was prompted by its concern that older workers were being deprived of employment on the basis of inaccurate and stigmatizing stereotypes.

"Although age discrimination rarely was based on the sort of animus motivating some other forms of discrimination, it was based in large part on stereotypes unsupported by objective fact. . . . Moreover, the available empirical evidence demonstrated that arbitrary age lines were in fact generally unfounded and that, as an overall matter, the performance of older workers was at least as good as that of younger workers."

Thus the ADEA commands that "employers are to evaluate [older] employees . . . on their merits and not their age." *Western Air Lines, Inc. v. Criswell*, 472 U.S. 400, 422 (1985). The employer cannot rely on age as a proxy for an employee's remaining characteristics, such as productivity, but must instead focus on those factors directly.

When the employer's decision *is* wholly motivated by factors other than age, the problem of inaccurate and stigmatizing stereotypes disappears. This is true even if the motivating factor is correlated with age, as pension status typically is. Pension plans typically provide that an employee's accrued benefits will become nonforfeitable, or "vested," once the employee completes a certain number of years of service with the employer. On average, an older employee has had more years in the work force than a younger employee, and thus may well have accumulated more years of service with a particular employer. Yet an employee's age is analytically distinct from his years of service. An employee who is younger than 40, and therefore outside the class of older workers as defined by the ADEA, may have worked for a particular employer his entire career, while an older worker may have been newly hired. Because age and years of service are analytically distinct, an employer can take account of one while ignoring the other, and thus it is incorrect to say that a decision based on years of service is necessarily "age-based."

The instant case is illustrative. Under the Hazen Paper pension plan, as construed by the Court of Appeals, an employee's pension benefits vest after the employee completes 10 years of service with the company. Perhaps it is true that older employees of Hazen Paper are more likely to be "close to vesting" than younger employees. Yet a decision by the company to fire an older employee solely because he has nine-plus years of service and therefore is "close to vesting" would not constitute discriminatory treatment on the basis of age. The prohibited stereotype ("Older employees are likely to be ___") would not have figured in this decision, and the attendant stigma would not ensue. The decision would not be the result of an inaccurate and denigrating generalization about age, but would rather represent an *accurate* judgment about the employee—that he indeed is "close to vesting."

We do not mean to suggest that an employer *lawfully* could fire an employee in order to prevent his pension benefits from vesting. Such conduct is actionable under § 510 of ERISA, as the Court of Appeals rightly found in affirming judgment for respondent under that statute. See *Ingersoll-Rand Co. v. McClendon*, 498 U.S. 133, 142–143 (1990). But it would not, without more, violate the ADEA. That law requires the employer to ignore an employee's age (absent a statutory exemption or defense); it does not specify *further* characteristics that an employer must also ignore. Although some language in our prior decisions might be read to mean that an employer violates the ADEA whenever its reason for firing an employee is improper *in any respect*, this reading is obviously incorrect. For example, it cannot be true that an employer who fires an older black worker because the worker is black thereby violates the ADEA. The employee's race is an improper reason, but it is improper under Title VII, not the ADEA.

We do not preclude the possibility that an employer who targets employees with a particular pension status on the assumption that these employees are likely to be older thereby engages in age discrimination. Pension status may be a proxy for age, not in the sense that the ADEA makes the two factors equivalent, but in the sense that the employer may suppose a correlation between the two factors and act accordingly. Nor do we rule out the possibility of dual liability under ERISA and the ADEA where the decision to fire the employee was motivated both by the employee's age and by his pension status. Finally, we do not consider the special case where an employee is about to vest in pension benefits as a result of his *age*, rather than years of service, and the employer fires the employee in order to prevent vesting. That case is not presented here.

Our holding is simply that an employer does not violate the ADEA just by interfering with an older employee's pension benefits that would have vested by virtue of the employee's years of service.

Besides the evidence of pension interference, the Court of Appeals cited some additional evidentiary support for ADEA liability. Although there was no direct evidence of petitioners' motivation, except for two isolated comments by the Hazens, the Court of Appeals did note the following indirect evidence: Respondent was asked to sign a confidentiality agreement, even though no other employee had been required to do so, and his replacement was a younger man who was given a less onerous agreement. In the ordinary ADEA case, indirect evidence of this kind may well suffice to support liability if the plaintiff also shows that the employer's explanation for its decision—here, that respondent had been disloyal to Hazen Paper by doing business with its competitors—is " 'unworthy of credence.' " But inferring age-motivation from the implausibility of the employer's explanation may be problematic in cases where other unsavory motives, such as pension interference, were present. . . . We therefore remand the case for the Court of Appeals to reconsider whether the jury had sufficient evidence to find an ADEA violation.

NOTES

Because ADEA is an imitation of Title VII of the Civil Rights Act of 1964, which is an exceptionally prominent piece of legislation, ADEA cases have tended to ape the Title VII litigation standards. See generally Al Holifield Jr., Tina Haley & Virginia Couch, Age Discrimination in Employee Benefits, in Jayne E. Zanglein, Lawrence A. Frolik & Susan J. Stabile, ERISA Litigation, Chapter 32 (4th ed. 2011). However, as the following discussion suggests, the courts have not blindly followed Title VII in evaluating ADEA claims.

1. *Disparate Treatment Claims.* The Court in *Hazen Paper* states that its opinion "clarif[ies] that there is no disparate treatment under the ADEA when the factor motivating the employer is some feature other than the employee's age." In 2009, a sharply divided Supreme Court held that a plaintiff bringing a disparate treatment ADEA claim must show that age was the "but-for" cause of the challenged action. In Gross v. FBL Financial Service, Inc., 129 S.Ct. 2343 (2009), the Court held that it is not enough for a plaintiff to demonstrate that age was "simply a motivating factor," id. at 2349, rejecting the analogy to Title VII's burden-shifting framework. The Court said that age had to be *the* reason for the employer's action and concluded that the ADEA does not authorize mixed-motives age discrimination claims. *Gross* will make it more difficult for plaintiffs to prevail on a disparate treatment theory.

2. *Disparate Impact Claims.* Disparate impact analysis (the use of statistical data to shift the burden of justification to the employer), a centerpiece of Title VII law, often shows up in ADEA litigation, characteristically in discharge cases. As the Court explained in *Hazen Paper*, disparate impact claims do not require a showing of discriminatory intent, but rather involve practices that, although facially neutral, have a disproportionate effect on a particular group, in this case, older employees.

The respondent in *Hazen Paper* claimed only that he received disparate treatment, with the result that the Court did not decide in that case whether a disparate impact theory of liability is available under the ADEA. The Supreme Court finally did address the issue in *Smith v. City of Jackson*, 544 U.S. 228 (2005), holding that the ADEA authorizes recovery in disparate impact cases. The majority opinion concluded that the language of the statute and EEOC regulations supported the disparate impact theory. The majority emphasized that the ADEA uses identical language to the language of Title VII, which does provide for liability based on disparate impact. Justice O'Connor dissented, and in an opinion joined by two other justices stated that "[i]n the nearly four decades since the ADEA's enactment . . . we have never read the statute to impose liability upon an employer without proof of intent." 544 U.S. at 248.

There is a significant difference between ADEA and Title VII, however, which significantly limits a plaintiff's ability to prevail. ADEA permits "otherwise prohibited" action "where the differentiation is based on reasonable factors other than age." Based on this language, although the Court in *Smith* recognized the disparate impact theory, it found that liability was precluded in the case before it. The case involved suit by a group of older police officers who were allegedly adversely affected by a change in their employer's pay plan. The result of the plan, which was adopted to make salaries more competitive, resulted in more generous pay raises to younger employees. Because the employer's decision to adopt the plan was "based on reasonable factors other than age," the Court found no ADEA liability. 544 U.S. at 251.

Thus, while the result of *Smith* is that a plaintiff may proceed under a disparate impact theory, an employer may avoid ADEA liability by showing that a reasonable factor other than age motivated the decision in question. In 2008, the Supreme Court held that the employer has both the burden of production and the burden of persuasion on the question whether a reasonable factor other than age motivated the behavior that created the disparate impact. Meachan v. Knolls Atomic Power Lab, 128 S.Ct. 2395 (2008).

In several post-*Smith* decisions, employers have been able to demonstrate that disparate impact was based on a reasonable factor other than age, and thus avoid liability. E.g., Allen v. Highlands Hosp. Corp., 545 F.3d 387 (6th Cir.2008); Wilson v. MVM, Inc., 2005 WL 1231968 (E.D.Pa.2005); Duggan v. Orthopaedic Inst. of Ohio, Inc., 365 F.Supp.2d 853 (N.D.Ohio 2005). On the difficulty of getting past the reasonable factor other than age defense, see Ann Marie Tracey & Norma Skoog, Is Business Judgment a Catch-22 for ADEA Plaintiffs? The Impact of Smith v. City of Jackson on Future ADEA Employment Litigation, 33 U. Dayton L. Rev. 231 (2008).

Smith will, however, make it easier for the ADEA plaintiff to resist a motion for summary judgment. The questions of whether the plaintiff suffered a disparate impact and whether the employer's decision was based on a reasonable factor other than age commonly turn on issues of fact that preclude summary judgment. The tendency of juries to sympathize with dismissed or otherwise aggrieved employees makes summary judgment a vital objective for the defendant in an ADEA case. As one commentator observed, "a [jury's field of vision may not be confined to] the narrow question of whether any unfairness was based on age discrimination." McMorrow, Retirement and Worker Choice: Incentives to Retire and the Age Discrimination in Employment Act, 29 Boston College L.Rev. 347, 376 (1988). Thus, a case that resists summary judgment is more likely to settle on terms that favor the employee, meaning that *Smith* enhances the litigation and settlement prospects of some plaintiffs.

10. ADEA LITIGATION INVOLVING EMPLOYEE BENEFITS

Kentucky Retirement Systems v. E.E.O.C
554 U.S. 135 (2008).

■ JUSTICE BREYER delivered the opinion of the Court.

The question before us is whether Kentucky's system [illegally discriminates] "because of . . . age." We conclude that it does not.

I

A

Kentucky has put in place a special retirement plan (Plan) for state and county employees who occupy "[h]azardous position[s]," e.g., active duty law enforcement officers, firefighters, paramedics, and workers in correctional systems. The Plan sets forth two routes through which such an employee can become eligible for what is called "normal retirement" benefits. The first makes an employee eligible for retirement after 20 years of service. The second makes an employee eligible after only 5 years of service provided that the employee has attained the age of 55. An employee eligible under either route will receive a pension calculated in the same way: Kentucky multiplies years of service times 2.5% times final preretirement pay.

Kentucky's Plan has special provisions for hazardous position workers who become disabled but are not yet eligible for normal retirement. Where such an employee has worked for five years or became disabled in the line of duty, the employee can retire at once. In calculating that employee's benefits Kentucky will add a certain number of ("imputed") years to the employee's actual years of service. The number of imputed years equals the number of years that the disabled employee would have had to continue working in order to become eligible for normal retirement benefits, i.e., the years necessary to bring the employee up to 20 years of service or to at least 5 years of service when the employee would turn 55 (whichever number of years is lower). Thus, if an employee with 17 years of service becomes disabled at age 48, the Plan adds 3 years and calculates the benefits as if the employee had completed 20 years of service. If an employee with 17 years of service becomes disabled at age 54, the Plan adds 1 year and calculates the benefits as if the employee had retired at age 55 with 18 years of service. . . .

B

Charles Lickteig, a hazardous position worker in the Jefferson County Sheriff's Department, became eligible for retirement at age 55, continued to work, became disabled, and then retired at age 61. The Plan calculated his annual pension on the basis of his actual years of service (18 years) times 2.5% times his final annual pay. Because Lickteig became disabled after he had already become eligible for normal retirement benefits, the Plan did not impute any additional years for purposes of the calculation.

Lickteig complained of age discrimination to the Equal Employment Opportunity Commission (EEOC); and the EEOC then brought this age discrimination lawsuit against the Commonwealth of Kentucky, Kentucky's Plan administrator, and other state entities (to whom we shall refer collectively as "Kentucky"). The EEOC pointed out that, if Lickteig had become disabled before he reached the age of 55, the Plan, in calculating Lickteig's benefits would have imputed a number of additional years. And the EEOC argued that the Plan failed to impute years solely because Lickteig became disabled after he reached age 55. . . .

II

The ADEA forbids an employer to "fail or refuse to hire or to discharge any individual or otherwise discriminate against any individual with respect to his compensation, terms, conditions, or privileges of employment, because of such individual's age." In Hazen Paper Co. v. Biggins, 507 U.S. 604 (1993), the Court explained that where, as here, a plaintiff claims age-related "disparate treatment" (i.e., intentional discrimination "because of . . . age") the plaintiff must prove that age "actually motivated the employer's decision." . . .

At the same time, Hazen Paper indicated that discrimination on the basis of pension status could sometimes be unlawful under the ADEA, in particular where pension status served as a "proxy for age." . . . Hazen Paper also left open "the special case where an employee is about to vest in pension benefits as a result of his age, rather than years of service." We here consider a variation on this "special case" theme.

III

Kentucky's Plan turns normal pension eligibility either upon the employee's having attained 20 years of service alone or upon the employees having attained 5 years of service and reached the age of 55. The ADEA permits an employer to condition pension eligibility upon age. Thus we must decide whether a plan that (1) lawfully makes age in part a condition of pension eligibility, and (2) treats workers differently in light of their pension status, (3) automatically discriminates because of age. The Government argues "yes." But, following Hazen Paper's approach, we come to a different conclusion. In particular, the following circumstances, taken together, convince us that, in this particular instance, differences in treatment were not "actually motivated" by age.

First, as a matter of pure logic, age and pension status remain "analytically distinct" concepts. That is to say, one can easily conceive of decisions that are actually made "because of" pension status and not age, even where pension status is itself based on age. Suppose, for example that an employer pays all retired workers a pension, retirement eligibility turns on age, say 65, and a 70-year-old worker retires. Nothing in language or in logic prevents one from concluding that the employer has begun to pay the worker a pension, not because the worker is over 65, but simply because the worker has retired.

Second, several background circumstances eliminate the possibility that pension status, though analytically distinct from age, nonetheless serves as a "proxy for age" in Kentucky's Plan. We consider not an individual employment decision, but a set of complex systemwide rules. These systemic rules involve, not wages, but pensions—a benefit that the ADEA treats somewhat more flexibly and leniently in respect to age. See, e.g., 29 U.S.C.A. § 623(l)(1)(A)(i) (explicitly allowing pension eligibility to turn on age); 29 U.S.C. § 623(l)(2)(A) (allowing employer to consider (age-related) pension benefits in determining level of severance pay); § 623(l)(3) (allowing employer to consider (age-related) pension benefits in determining level of long-term disability benefits). And the specific benefit at issue here is offered to all hazardous position workers on the same nondiscriminatory terms ex ante. That is to say, every such employee, when hired, is promised disability retirement benefits should he become disabled prior to the time that he is eligible for normal retirement benefits.

Furthermore, Congress has otherwise approved of programs that calculate permanent disability benefits using a formula that expressly takes account of age. For example, the Social Security Administration now uses such a formula in calculating Social Security Disability Insurance benefits. And until (and in some cases after) 1984, federal employees received permanent disability benefits based on a formula that, in certain circumstances, did not just consider age, but effectively imputed years of service only to those disabled workers younger than 60.

Third, there is a clear non-age-related rationale for the disparity here at issue. The manner in which Kentucky calculates disability retirement benefits is in every important respect but one identical to the manner in which Kentucky calculates normal retirement benefits. The one significant difference consists of the fact that the Plan imputes additional years of service to disabled individuals. But the Plan imputes only those years needed to bring the disabled worker's years of service to 20 or to the number of years that the individual would have worked had he worked to age 55. The disability rules clearly track Kentucky's normal retirement rules.

It is obvious, then, that the whole purpose of the disability rules is, as Kentucky claims, to treat a disabled worker as though he had become disabled after, rather than before, he had become eligible for normal retirement benefits. Age factors into the disability calculation only because the normal retirement rules themselves permissibly include age as a consideration. No one seeking to help disabled workers in the way that Kentucky's rules seek to help those workers would care whether Kentucky's normal system turned eligibility in part upon age or upon other, different criteria. . . .

Fourth, although Kentucky's Plan placed an older worker at a disadvantage in this case, in other cases, it can work to the advantage of older workers. Consider, for example, two disabled workers, one of whom is aged 45 with 10 years of service, one of whom is aged 40 with 15 years of service. Under Kentucky's scheme, the older worker would actually get a bigger boost of imputed years than the younger worker (10 years would be imputed to the former, while only 5 years would be imputed to the latter). And that fact helps to confirm that the underlying motive is not an effort to discriminate "because of . . . age."

Fifth, Kentucky's system does not rely on any of the sorts of stereotypical assumptions that the ADEA sought to eradicate. It does not rest on any stereotype about the work capacity of "older" workers relative to "younger" workers. . . .

Sixth, the nature of the Plan's eligibility requirements means that, unless Kentucky were severely to cut the benefits given to disabled workers who are not yet pension eligible (which Kentucky claims it will do if its present Plan is unlawful), Kentucky would have to increase the benefits available to disabled, pension-eligible workers, while lacking any clear criteria for determining how many extra years to impute for those pension-eligible workers who already are 55 or older. The difficulty of finding a remedy that can both correct the disparity and achieve the Plan's legitimate objective—providing each disabled worker with a sufficient retirement benefit, namely, the normal retirement benefit that the worker would receive if he were pension eligible at the time of disability—further suggests that this objective and not age "actually motivated" the Plan.

The above factors all taken together convince us that the Plan does not, on its face, create treatment differences that are "actually motivated" by age. . . .

It bears emphasizing that our opinion in no way unsettles the rule that a statute or policy that facially discriminates based on age suffices to show disparate treatment under the ADEA. We are dealing today with the quite special case of differential treatment based on pension status, where pension status—with the explicit blessing of the ADEA—itself turns, in part, on age. Further, the rule we adopt today for dealing with this sort of case is clear: Where an employer adopts a pension plan that includes age as a factor, and that employer then treats employees differently based on pension status, a plaintiff, to state a disparate treatment claim under the ADEA, must adduce sufficient evidence to show that the differential treatment was "actually motivated" by age, not pension status. And our discussion of the factors that lead us to conclude that the Government has failed to make the requisite showing in this case provides an indication of what a plaintiff might show in other cases to meet his burden of proving that differential treatment based on pension status is in fact discrimination "because of" age. . . .

■ JUSTICE KENNEDY, with whom JUSTICE SCALIA, JUSTICE GINSBURG, and JUSTICE ALITO join, dissenting.

The Court today ignores established rules for interpreting and enforcing one of the most important statutes Congress has enacted to protect the Nation's work force from age discrimination, the Age Discrimination in Employment Act of 1967. That Act prohibits employment actions that "discriminate against any individual with respect to his compensation, terms, conditions, or privileges of employment, because of such individual's age." In recent years employers and employees alike have been advised by this Court, by most Courts of Appeals, and by the agency charged with enforcing the Act, the Equal Employment Opportunity Commission, that the most straightforward reading of the statute is the correct one: When an employer makes age a factor in an employee benefit plan in a formal, facial, deliberate, and explicit manner, to the detriment of older employees, this is a violation of the Act. Disparate treatment on the basis of age is prohibited unless some exemption or defense provided in the Act applies.

The Court today undercuts this basic framework. In doing so it puts the Act and its enforcement on a wrong course. The decision of the en banc panel of the Court of Appeals for the Sixth Circuit, which the Court reverses, brought that Circuit's case law into line with that of its sister Circuits. . . .

As a threshold matter, all should concede that the paradigm offered to justify the statute is a powerful one: The young police officer or firefighter with a family is disabled in the heroic performance of his or her duty. Disability payments are increased to account for unworked years of service. What the Court overlooks, however, is that a 61-year-old officer or firefighter who is disabled in the same heroic action receives, in many instances, a lower payment and for one reason alone: By explicit command of Kentucky's disability plan age is an express disadvantage in calculating the disability payment.

This is a straightforward act of discrimination on the basis of age. Though the Commonwealth is entitled by the law, in some instances, to defend an age-based differential as cost justified, that has yet to be established here. What an employer cannot do, and what the Court ought not to do, is to pretend that this explicit discrimination based on age is somehow consistent with the broad statutory and regulatory prohibition against disparate treatment based on age.

I

. . . Kentucky operates dual retirement systems for employees in hazardous occupations. An employee is eligible for normal retirement if he or she has accumulated 20 years of service with the Commonwealth, or is over age 55 and has accumulated at least 5 years of service. If the employee can no longer work as a result of a disability, however, he or she is entitled to receive disability retirement. Employees who are eligible for normal retirement benefits are ineligible for disability retirement.

The distinction between normal and disability retirement is not just a difference of nomenclature. Under the normal retirement system benefits are calculated by multiplying a percentage of the employee's pay at retirement by years of service. Under the disability system the years-of-service multiplier includes not only the employee's actual years of service but also the number of years it would have taken the employee to become eligible for normal retirement (subject to a cap equal to the number of actual years served). In other words employees in the normal retirement system are compensated based solely on their actual years of service; but employees in the disability retirement system get a bonus, which accounts for the number of years the employee would have worked had he or she remained healthy until becoming eligible to receive normal retirement benefits.

Whether intended or not, the result of these divergent benefits formulae is a system that, in some cases, compensates otherwise similarly situated individuals differently on the basis of age. Consider two covered workers, one 45 and one 55, both with five years of service with the Commonwealth and an annual salary of $60,000. If we assume both become disabled in the same accident, the 45-year-old will be entitled to receive $1,250 in monthly benefits; the 55-year-old will receive $625, just half as much. The benefit disparity results from the Commonwealth's decision, under the disability retirement formula, to credit the 45-year-old with 5 years of unworked service (thereby increasing the appliable years-service-multiplier to 10 years), while the 55-year-old's benefits are based only on actual years of service (5 years). In that instance age is the only factor that accounts for the disparate treatment.

True, age is not a factor that reduces benefits in every case. If a worker has accumulated 20 years of service with the Commonwealth before he or she becomes disabled, age plays no role in the benefits calculation. But there is no question that, in many cases, a disabled worker over the age of 55 who has accumulated fewer than 20 years of service receives a lower monthly stipend than otherwise similarly situated workers who are under 55. The Court concludes this result is something other than discrimination on the basis of age only by ignoring the statute and our past opinions. . . .

1.   *Difficulty of applying age discrimination rules to retirement plans.* The 5–4 breakdown of justices in *Kentucky Retirement Systems* bears little relation to the Court's usual ideological fault lines:

Majority (pro-employer)	Dissent (pro-participant)
Breyer	Kennedy
Roberts	Scalia
Stevens	Ginsburg
Souter	Alito
Thomas	

The unusual grouping might reflect the inherent analytical difficulty of applying age discrimination rules to something like a retirement plan, which is, after all, expressly meant to condition the right to receive payments (and/or the amount thereof) upon attainment of a particular age. No matter how strong the ideological or other predilection you bring to the issue, it seems a hard question, given the paradoxes that inevitably arise, to identify in this context exactly what is age discrimination and what is just a necessary consequence of ordinary retirement plan design.

2.   *Discrimination on the basis of "retirement status."* The Court of Appeals for the Sixth Circuit has extended the principle that an employer may discriminate based on "retirement status,' as opposed to age, concluding that an employer's failure to hire an individual because he is currently receiving pension benefits does not violate ADEA. *McKnight v. Gates,* 282 Fed. Appx. 394, 2008 WL 2491626 (6th Cir. 2008) (unpublished). The EEOC strongly disagrees, viewing *McKnight* as an early realization of the agency's fears that with *Kentucky Retirement Systems* the Supreme Court has effectively enabled indirect age discrimination. *See* "Impact of Kentucky Retirement Systems Unknown," 35 Pension & Benefits Rep. (BNA) 1729–30 (July 22, 2008).

3.   Coordination of Retiree Medical Benefits with Medicare

Employers have responded in various ways to the rising costs of providing retiree health benefits to their former employees, as discussed in Chapter 19. Rather than terminating retiree health coverage completely, or limiting it for all retirees, one approach has been to coordinate retiree health benefits with Medicare. Under such a plan, the employer provides less generous benefits for retirees who are already eligible for Medicare than for those retirees not yet eligible for Medicare. Does such a plan violate ADEA?

Originally the EEOC took the position that such reductions constituted prohibited age discrimination, a position that found mixed success in court. In 2007 the EEOC issued new final regulations taking the opposite view. Practical considerations motivate the EEOC's ultimate position. Is it better for an employer desiring to reduce the costs of providing retiree benefits to reduce or eliminate benefits for all employees or only for those employees who are already eligible for Medicare or other government retiree benefits? For a contrary view, however, and an argument that the exemption exceeded the EEOC's statutory authority, see Mary Kaczorek, "No Country for Old Men:" AARP v. EEOC and Age Discrimination in Employer-Sponsored Retiree Health Benefits, 26 Law & Ineq. 435 (2008). Because the EEOC's regulation covers only retiree medical benefits, it does not permit an employer to engage in such coordination with respect to other benefits. See Fulghum v. Embarq Corp., 2008 WL 5109781 (D.Kan.2008) (EEOC 2007 regulations do not allow an employer to reduce or rescind life insurance benefits).

4.   Early Retirement Incentives and Age Discrimination.

Incentive offers to encourage early retirement have figured prominently in the age discrimination litigation concerning pensions. Under defined benefit plans such incentive programs commonly manipulate the benefit accrual formula to enrich the payout to the departing employee. The program may credit extra years of service (e.g., by treating the terminating employee as though he or she had worked three years longer than the actual period of service); or the program may assume extra years of age (e.g., by treating the employee as though he or she had attained an age four years older than the actual age at termination).

The OWBPA amendments to ADEA reiterate that it is lawful for an employer to offer "a voluntary early retirement incentive plan consistent with the relevant purpose or purposes of this Act." ADEA § 4(f)(2)(B)(ii). OWBPA's exceptions permit two common practices by defined benefit retirement plans. One is offering subsidized early retirement benefits; the other is reducing benefits once a retiree becomes eligible for Social Security benefits. Barring an exception both would constitute age discrimination because both result in a reduction of the value of benefits, on the basis of age, without a cost justification. This is obvious in the case of the Social Security offset. That it is also true of early retirement subsidies can be seen by considering what "subsidization" means in this context: It means that an employee retiring early (say at age 55, rather than the plan's normal retirement age of 65) will receive a benefit having an actuarial present value greater than that of an otherwise identically situated 65-year old. (See the discussion of early retirement in Section A.2 above.)

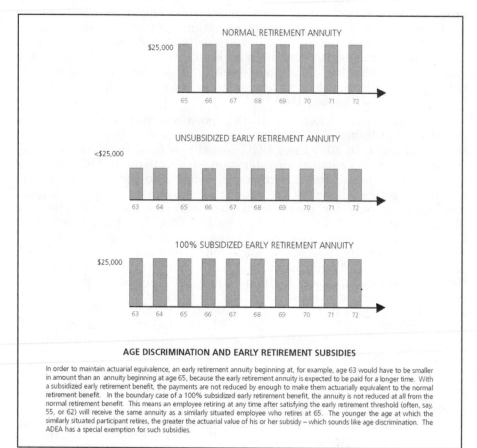

AGE DISCRIMINATION AND EARLY RETIREMENT SUBSIDIES

In order to maintain actuarial equivalence, an early retirement annuity beginning at, for example, age 63 would have to be smaller in amount than an annuity beginning at age 65, because the early retirement annuity is expected to be paid for a longer time. With a subsidized early retirement benefit, the payments are not reduced by enough to make them actuarially equivalent to the normal retirement benefit. In the boundary case of a 100% subsidized early retirement benefit, the annuity is not reduced at all from the normal retirement benefit. This means an employee retiring at any time after satisfying the early retirement threshold (often, say, 55, or 62) will receive the same annuity as a similarly situated employee who retires at 65. The younger the age at which the similarly situated participant retires, the greater the actuarial value of his or her subsidy – which sounds like age discrimination. The ADEA has a special exemption for such subsidies.

a. *Policies.* Should early retirement incentives be suspect under ADEA? In Karlen v. City Colleges of Chicago, 837 F.2d 314, 317 (7th Cir.1988), Judge Posner explained why he thought not:

> The question of the proper treatment of early-retirement programs is the most difficult question under the Age Discrimination in Employment Act. The purpose of such programs often is to ease out older employees, whether because they cost the employer more in salary or fringe benefits, or have gone stale, or are blocking advancement for the ambitious young. Often, therefore, the discussions leading up to the adoption of such programs will generate evidence of age discrimination. Yet the discrimination seems to be in favor of rather than against older employees, by giving them an additional option and one prized by many older employees. Nor can it seriously be argued that the concept of early retirement for workers over a specified age stigmatizes such workers, as would a program designed to change not the age but the racial composition of the work force by allowing blacks but not whites

to retire early. Entitlement to early retirement is a valued perquisite of age—an additional option available only to the older worker and only slightly tarnished by the knowledge that sometimes employers offer it because they want to ease out older workers.

Contrast the view of a commentator who argues that early retirement incentive programs should be suspect under ADEA:

> First, early retirement incentives arguably violate the ADEA because they harm older people as a group and society as a whole. Although they may benefit the individuals who receive them, they foster ageist stereotypes and reduce participation of older people in the workforce. Second, by making early retirement artificially attractive, the early retirement incentive is arguably a wolf in sheep's clothing—it may seem like a lovely fringe benefit at first, but ultimately it may harm the individuals who accept it by diminishing the length and quality of their lives. Third, early retirement incentives are arguably a mere disguise for mandatory retirement. No decision to accept an early retirement incentive is entirely voluntary and uncoerced, because of the power of the incentives and the contexts in which they arise.

Richard G. Kass, Early Retirement Incentives and the Age Discrimination in Employment Act, 4 Hofstra Labor L.J. 63, 66 (1986). See also Lorraine A. Schmall, Telling the Truth about Golden Handshakes: Exit Incentives and Fiduciary Duties, 5 Employee Rights & Employment Policy J. 169 (2001).

   b. *Constructive discharge: an offer you can't refuse.* Voluntariness is the customary justification for an age-specific early retirement program. Such a program does not offend ADEA's prohibition against age discrimination since, in Judge Posner's words above, "the discrimination seems to be in favor of rather than against older employees, by giving them an additional option, and one prized by many older employees."

   A number of so-called "constructive discharge" cases deal with the question of whether a seeming option is actually coercive—that is, whether a scheme of age-based mandatory retirement or dismissal is masquerading as optional early retirement. "Constructive discharge is appropriately found, for example, when the employer gives the older employees a choice of early retirement or termination, yet younger employees are also given the opportunity to transfer, or where an employee has previously been denied a promotion or raise, or received a significant reduction in work duties, or was transferred to an inferior sales territory and these conditions were not imposed upon younger, similarly-situated employees." McMorrow, supra, at 374.

   In Auerbach v. Board of Education of the Harborfields Central School District of Greenlawn, 136 F.3d 104 (1998), the Second Circuit suggested that in determining whether a retirement incentive is voluntary, "a court must consider whether, under the circumstances, a reasonable person would have concluded that there was no choice but to accept the offer." Older teachers were provided with what the court termed "an uncoerced, free choice." No one was forced to accept the plan, there was no evidence of fraud, or intimidation, no threats of imminent layoff and no subtle coercion. In the view of the court, this met the test for voluntariness.

Contrast Scott v. Goodyear Tire & Rubber Co., 160 F.3d 1121 (6th Cir.1998), in which the Sixth Circuit reversed a district court grant of summary judgment in favor of an employer in a case involving an ADEA claim of constructive discharge. The plaintiff alleged that after his job was eliminated, he was offered a choice between accepting layoff status and taking early retirement. The court found that what was told to the employee was sufficient to create in the employee the subjective belief that if he took layoff status he would not be recalled to work. The employee did not voluntarily choose retirement when he had no prospects of continued employment under either of the choices presented. Thus, he could maintain an ADEA claim based on a constructive discharge theory.

5. *Reverse Discrimination Claims*

ADEA prohibits discrimination against "individuals who are at least 40 years of age." The question has arisen whether the statute only prohibits discriminating against older employees in favor of younger employees or whether employees over the age of 40 can state an ADEA claim, even if the discrimination favors older employees.

In General Dynamics Land Systems, Inc. v. Cline, 540 U.S. 581 (2004), the Supreme Court concluded, 6–3, that the language of Section 4(a)(1) of ADEA does not prohibit favoring older workers over younger workers, even when the younger workers are in the protected class. *Cline* involved a collective-bargaining agreement that eliminated the employer's obligation to provide health benefits to future retirees, except as regards then-current workers at least 50 years old. A group of workers who were between age 40 and age 50 claimed that this violated the ADEA, since they were in the protected class and were being discriminated against because of their age. The EEOC agreed that the agreement violated ADEA and invited the parties to settle informally. When settlement efforts failed, suit was brought in federal court. The Supreme Court relied on the legislative history and the Court's "consistent understanding" in several earlier cases that "the text, structure, and history point to the ADEA as a remedy for unfair preference based on relative youth, leaving complaints of the relatively young outside the statutory concern."

The Supreme Court's decision is sensible as a matter of policy, but is difficult to square with the language of the statute and with traditional principles of deference to agency interpretations. In dissent, Justice Thomas (joined by Justice Kennedy) observed that the case before the court "should have been an easy case. The plain language of [ADEA] mandates a particular outcome: that the respondents are able to sue for discrimination against them in favor of older workers. The agency charged with enforcing the statute has adopted a regulation and issued an opinion as an adjudicator, both of which adopt this natural interpretation of the provision." For an analysis of the lower court rulings prior to the Supreme Court's decision and an argument that reverse discrimination claims should be permitted under ADEA, see Tracey A. Cullen, Note, Reverse Age Discrimination Suits and the Age

Discrimination in Employment Act, 18 St. John's J. Legal Commentary 271 (2003).

In 2007, the EEOC amended its age discrimination regulations to reflect the Supreme Court's decision in *Cline*. It added Section 1625.2, providing that "[f]avoring an older individual over a younger individual because of age is not unlawful discrimination under the ADEA."

Because ADEA does not protect against reverse age discrimination, an employer is free to structure amendments to a retiree medical plan in a way that grandfathers employees over a certain age but not other younger employees who are part of ADEA's protected class or to structure a special early retirement plan offered in connection with a reduction in force to provide enhanced benefits to older employees, but not to younger employees who are part of ADEA's protected class.

6.   *Cash Balance Plans*

During the 1990s and early 2000s, as discussed in Chapter 2, supra, a significant number of large firms converted existing defined benefit plans to cash balance plans. Because these conversions tend to reduce future accruals in a fashion that appears to disadvantage older workers, claims of age discrimination have resulted.

A cash balance plan is a defined benefit plan that specifies a participant's benefit as a hypothetical account balance. Each year the balance is credited with a hypothetical allocation and a hypothetical interest rate using whatever formula the plan provides. These hypothetical allocations and earnings are designed to mimic the actual contributions and earnings that would occur under a defined contribution plan.

Since a defined contribution plan does not discriminate on the basis of age, how can a cash balance plan that mimics a nondiscriminatory defined contribution plan be discriminatory? The charges of age discrimination have focused on two issues. The claim is made that under ERISA's accrual rules, cash balance plans are inherently discriminatory. Further, it is argued that even if ERISA does permit cash balance plans, the way in which some plan sponsors have converted their existing plans to cash balance plans, using a so-called "wear-away" formula, has resulted in age discrimination.

a.   *The claim that cash balance plans are inherently discriminatory on the basis of age.* To understand this claim, consider the following example. Assume the cash balance plan provides a hypothetical credit each year equal to 5 percent of the participant's salary, and an interest credit of 8 percent. The normal retirement age under the plan is 65. Upon reaching this age, a participant has the right to elect a lump sum distribution of an amount equal to the cash balance or an actuarially equivalent annuity. Assume that employee A is 34 and employee B is 64, that they began participating in the plan at the beginning of the year, and that they both earn $100,000. At the end of the year each of their hypothetical accounts will be credited with $5,000.

If this plan were a defined contribution plan, each employee would have an accrued benefit of $5,000 in his or her account. But for a defined benefit plan, accrued benefit is defined as "the individual's accrued benefit determined under the plan and . . . expressed *in the form of an annual benefit commencing at normal retirement age.*" ERISA § 3(23)(A)(emph. added). Thus, in the case of a cash balance plan, the accrued benefit, although fundamentally defined-contribution in its conceptual nature, must be converted into and expressed as its actuarially equivalent defined benefit—a conversion that increases the relative value for younger versus older employees of an equal "contribution."

In particular, since a participant's benefit under the cash balance plan is based on the account balance, and that balance includes amounts attributable to interest credits, the interest credits are part of the benefit and must be taken into account in determining whether the accrual of benefits satisfies one of the anti-backloading rules of ERISA § 204(b)(1)(A), (B), or (C). Thus, A's accrued benefit at the end of the year must include not only the $5,000 allocation, but also the future interest credits attributable to that allocation. If A terminates employment and defers distribution of his benefits until age 65, his lump sum benefit will be $50,313 (i.e., the $5,000 plus 30 years of compound interest at 8 percent). A plan that did not include future interest credits as a current accrued benefit would not be able to satisfy any of the accrual rules in ERISA § 204(b)(1)(A), (B), or (C). See IRS Notice 96–8, 1996–1 C.B. 359.

B has reached age 65, so unlike A, B's accrued benefit includes only the $5,000 allocation. The age discrimination claim arises because in the current year, A, a 35-year-old, has accrued a benefit equal to a $50,313 lump sum while B, a 65-year-old, has accrued only a $5,000 benefit. Recall that ERISA § 204(b)(1)(H)(i) provides that "a defined benefit plan shall be treated as not satisfying the requirements of this paragraph if, under the plan, an employee's benefit accrual is ceased, *or the rate of an employee's benefit accrual is reduced*, because of the attainment of any age." The term "rate of benefit accrual" is not defined in the statute or the regulations. If the rate of benefit accrual is determined by considering the increase in the projected benefit payable at normal retirement age, as the statute literally seems to require, then cash balance plans would violate the statute. The accrued benefit is a function of age and the yearly accrual is lower the older the employee.

Note that cash balance plans typically permit an employee who terminates employment to receive the current hypothetical account balance as a lump sum. Thus, if A and B quit at the end of the same future year they would each receive the identical benefit. Since a defined contribution plan would work in just this way, it is difficult to see how any real age discrimination is taking place.

Nonetheless a great deal of litigation ensued, based in some cases on evidence uncovered during discovery that one of the employer's specific goals, in converting to a cash-balance plan, was to allocate a higher share of future pension cost to younger employees. Ultimately, however, all the Circuit Courts of Appeals who were presented the issue ruled that cash balance plans are not inherently discriminatory on the basis of age.

b. *The claim of discrimination based on conversion formula.* The other potential age discrimination concern arises when a wear-away formula is used in connection with a plan's conversion to a cash balance plan. As an illustration, assume that the cash balance plan in the example above was created under an amendment to a preexisting defined benefit plan. Assume that the prior benefit formula provided a benefit equal to 2 percent of highest three-year average annual salary multiplied by years of participation. Assume further that both A and B have ten years of participation when the plan is amended.

A and B have each accrued a benefit under this formula equal to 20 percent of $100,000, payable at age 65. ERISA does not permit a plan amendment to decrease this accrued benefit. In converting the plan to a cash balance plan, the plan could provide that participants will receive this "frozen" accrued benefit plus future accruals under the cash balance formula. This is known as a fresh-start formula "without wear-away" and it raises no age discrimination issues aside from the first (accrued benefit) claim discussed above.

Many plan sponsors have chosen to provide a different formula. The participant's existing accrued benefit is converted to an actuarially equivalent cash balance, which is frozen. The participant's benefit is then defined as the *greater* of this balance or the balance that would have been accrued had the cash balance plan been in effect from the beginning of the participant's participation in the original plan. This is known as a fresh-start formula "with wear-away." Younger employees, who are farther from retirement age, have a smaller frozen existing accrued cash balance than similarly situated older employees. As a result younger employees, under the "greater of" wear-away formulation, begin accruing new benefits under the cash-balance formula sooner than older employees, whose benefits can remain at the frozen level for many years. Older employees thus argue that, looking only at new accruals, the wear-away formula results in age discrimination.

Although one might have expected the Supreme Court's endorsement in *Smith* of a disparate impact analysis for ADEA claims to make it easier for plaintiffs to challenge cash balance conversions, the Circuit Courts of Appeals that have addressed the issue have concluded that wear-away formulas in cash-balance plans are not discriminatory on the basis of age. See Cooper v. IBM Personal Pension Plan, 457 F.3d 636 (7th Cir.2006) and Register v. PNC Financial Services Group, Inc., 477 F.3d 56 (3d Cir.2007).

c.   *Congress acts.* The 2006 PPA clarifies that a defined benefit plan is not age discriminatory if a participant's accrued benefit under the terms of the plan is not less than the accrued benefit of any similarly situated younger employee. ERISA § 204(b)(5)(A)(i); IRC § 411(b)(5)(A)(i); ADEA § 4(i)(10)(A)(i). "Similarly situated" means identical in every respect except for age. The PPA specifically permits the accrued benefit under the plan to be determined not only as an annuity payable at normal retirement age, but also as the balance of a hypothetical account (e.g., a cash balance plan) or the current value of the accumulated percentage of the employee's final average compensation (e.g., so-called pension equity plans).

Although the PPA makes clear that cash balance and other hybrid plans are not inherently age discriminatory, the Act imposes a number of significant additional requirements. First, the interest credit (or equivalent amount) for any plan year must not be greater than a market rate of return and cannot be negative. ERISA § 204(b)(5)(B)(i). Second, the plan must provide that participants be fully vested after three years of service. ERISA § 203(f)(2). Third, there can be no "wear-away" of previously accrued benefits when a plan converts to a cash balance or other hybrid plan. ERISA § 204(b)(5)(B)(ii) & (iii). Thus, a participant will always begin to accrue new benefits after the conversion, which will be added to his existing accrued benefits under the old benefit formula.

11. WAIVER AND RELEASE OF ADEA CLAIMS

1.   *The statutory regime.* In 1990, OWBPA amended ADEA § 7 to add a new subsection (f)(1), which prescribes that "[a]n individual may not waive any right or claim under [ADEA] unless the waiver is knowing and voluntary." A purported waiver is presumed involuntary unless it meets seven statutorily specified criteria. However, compliance with the criteria does not create an automatic safe harbor on the question of whether the employee's waiver was knowing and voluntary. Courts have generally applied a "totality of circumstances" standard to the question of whether a waiver was knowing and voluntary.

The seven criteria of ADEA § 7(f)(1) are: (A) that the waiver is written in a manner calculated to be understood by the individual; (B) that the waiver specifically refers to rights or claims arising under ADEA; (C) that the waiver does not govern rights or claims arising after the date of the waiver—in other words, that the waiver does not have prospective effect; (D) that the individual receives fresh consideration for the waiver; (E) that the individual is advised in writing to consult an attorney before executing a waiver; (F) that the individual be allowed a 21-day cooling off period in which to deliberate on whether to accept the agreement embodying the waiver, or 45 days in the case of a group offer; and (G) that the agreement provide for a seven-day grace period following execution during which the employee can revoke the waiver.

In addition, in the case of a group offer, the employer must inform the individual in writing about (1) the groups covered by the program, any eligibility factors, and any time limits; and (2) the job titles and ages of all individuals eligible or selected for the program, and the ages of all individuals in the same job classification or organizational unit who are not eligible or selected for the program.

ADEA § 7(f)(2) softens (to "a reasonable period of time") the 21-day or 45-day waiting periods of § 7(f)(1) for cases in which the waiver settles litigation or EEOC proceedings. Section 7(f)(3) assigns the burden of proof on a contested waiver matter to the party asserting the validity of the waiver.

2.   *Written in a manner calculated to be understood by the participant.* In order to satisfy the "manner calculated to be understood" requirement, "waiver agreements must be drafted in a plain language geared to the level of understanding of the individual party to the agreement or individuals eligible to participate in a group termination plan, . . . [taking] into account such factors as the level of comprehension and education of typical participants" and avoiding technical legal jargon and long, complex sentences. Syverson v. IBM Corp., 472 F.3d 1072 (9th Cir.2007).

3.   *Fraud claims.* Can an employee challenge a waiver that otherwise meets the statutory requirements of ADEA § 7(f)(1) by

claiming that the waiver was procured by misrepresentation? Some courts have suggested that the ADEA criteria are not exclusive and that "non-statutory circumstances such as fraud, duress, or mutual mistake may render an ADEA waiver not 'knowing and voluntary' under the OWBPA," and therefore "void and unenforceable." Bennett v. Coors Brewing Company, 189 F.3d 1221, 1228 (10th Cir.1999). In *Bennett*, the Tenth Circuit indicated that courts must look "beyond the contract language and consider all relevant factors in assessing a plaintiff's knowledge and the voluntariness of the waiver." Id.

Suppose a plaintiff alleges that he or she signed a waiver under the economic duress of the threat of losing insurance benefits as well as his or her job? In Thiessen v. General Electric Capital Corp., 232 F.Supp.2d 1230 (D.Kan.2002), a district court determined this type of financial distress was insufficient to establish economic duress.

The question of whether and when an employer has a duty to disclose pending early retirement incentives and other plan amendments is discussed in Chapter 13, supra, treating fiduciary disclosure.

For a comprehensive review of the case law on "exit incentive program fraud claims," see Ethan Lipsig, Mary C. Dollarhide & Brit K. Seifert, Reductions in Force in Employment Law 712–29 (2007).

4.   *Oubre.* The Supreme Court has held that OWBPA's waiver and release requirements require strict adherence. Oubre v. Entergy Operations, 522 U.S. 422 (1998), involved a former employee who had signed a waiver that did not meet the statute's requirements for a 21-day consideration period or for a seven-day post-signing revocation period, and that failed specifically to mention claims arising under ADEA. Nonetheless, after signing the former employee received (and retained) several installments of severance pay she had received as part of her termination package, which had been conditioned on the release. The employer argued that by doing so she had equitably estopped herself from challenging the release's validity. A 7–2 majority of the Court rejected this argument, holding that "[t]he OWBPA sets up its own regime for assessing the effect of ADEA waivers, separate and apart from contract law. . . . The text of the OWBPA forecloses the employer's defense, notwithstanding how general contract principles would apply to non-ADEA claims."

5.   *Post-Oubre EEOC regulations.* Subsequent to the Supreme Court's decision in *Oubre*, the EEOC issued final regulations, effective January 10, 2001, regarding the waiver of ADEA claims. 29 C.F.R. 1625.23(a) provides that "[a]n individual alleging that a waiver agreement, covenant not to sue, or other equivalent arrangement was not knowing and voluntary under the ADEA is not required to tender back the consideration given for that agreement before filing either a lawsuit or a charge of discrimination with EEOC or any state or local fair employment practices agency acting as an EEOC referral agency for purposes of filing the charge with EEOC. Retention of consideration does not foreclose a challenge to any waiver agreement, covenant not to sue, or other equivalent arrangement; nor does the retention constitute the ratification of any waiver agreement, covenant not to sue, or other equivalent arrangement."

The regulation seems to go further than did *Oubre*. The Supreme Court addressed the question of the application of the common law tender-back doctrine in the context of an ADEA waiver that did not comply with OWBPA. The language of the regulation suggests that that the doctrine does not apply even in the case of a waiver agreement that fully complies with the OWBPA waiver requirements. For a discussion of the effect of the EEOC regulations on ADEA waivers, see Paul V. Lalli, Charles M. Rice & Tamisa N. Wertz, Reevaluating ADEA Waivers in Wake of New EEOC Final Regulations, 27 Employee Relations L.J. 43 (2001).

B. DISCRIMINATION ON THE BASIS OF GENDER

Arizona v. Norris
463 U.S. 1073 (1983).

■ PER CURIAM

Petitioners in this case administer a deferred compensation plan for employees of the State of Arizona. The respondent class consists of all female employees who are enrolled in the plan or will enroll in the plan in the future. Certiorari was granted to decide whether Title VII of the Civil Rights Act of 1964, 78 Stat. 253, as amended, 42 U. S. C. § 2000e et seq. (1976 ed. and Supp. V), prohibits an employer from offering its employees the option of receiving retirement benefits from one of several companies selected by the employer, all of which pay lower monthly retirement benefits to a woman than to a man who has made the same contributions; and whether, if so, the relief awarded by the District Court was proper. The Court holds that this practice does constitute discrimination on the basis of sex in violation of Title VII, and that all retirement benefits derived from contributions made after the decision today must be calculated without regard to the sex of the beneficiary. . . . Accordingly, the judgment of the Court of Appeals is affirmed in part, and reversed in part, and the case is remanded for further proceedings consistent with this opinion. The Clerk is directed to issue the judgment August 1, 1983.

CONCUR

■ JUSTICE MARSHALL, with whom JUSTICE BRENNAN, JUSTICE WHITE, and JUSTICE STEVENS join, and with whom JUSTICE O'CONNOR joins as to Parts I, II, and III, concurring in the judgment in part.

In *Los Angeles Dept. of Water & Power v. Manhart*, 435 U.S. 702 (1978), this Court held that Title VII of the Civil Rights Act of 1964 prohibits an employer from requiring women to make larger contributions in order to obtain the same monthly pension benefits as men. The question presented by this case is whether Title VII also prohibits an employer from offering its employees the option of receiving retirement benefits from one of several companies selected by the employer, all of which pay a woman lower monthly benefits than a man who has made the same contributions.

I A

Since 1974 the State of Arizona has offered its employees the opportunity to enroll in a deferred compensation plan administered by the Arizona Governing Committee for Tax Deferred Annuity and Deferred Compensation Plans (Governing Committee). Employees who participate in the plan may thereby postpone the receipt of a portion of their wages until retirement. By doing so, they postpone paying federal income tax on the amounts deferred until after retirement, when they receive those amounts and any earnings thereon.

After inviting private companies to submit bids outlining the investment opportunities that they were willing to offer state employees, the State selected several companies to participate in its deferred compensation plan. Many of the companies selected offer three basic retirement options: (1) a single lump-sum payment upon retirement, (2) periodic payments of a fixed sum for a fixed period of time, and (3) monthly annuity payments for the remainder of the employee's life. When an employee decides to take part in the deferred compensation plan, he must designate the company in which he wishes to invest his deferred wages. Employees must choose one of the companies selected by the State to participate in the plan; they are not free to invest their deferred compensation in any other way. At the time an employee enrolls in the plan, he may also select one of the pay-out options offered by the company that he has chosen, but when he reaches retirement age he is free to switch to one of the company's other options. If at retirement the employee decides to receive a lump-sum payment, he may also purchase any of the options then being offered by the other companies participating in the plan. Many employees find an annuity contract to be the most attractive option, since receipt of a lump sum upon retirement requires payment of taxes on the entire sum in one year, and the choice of a fixed sum for a fixed period requires an employee to speculate as to how long he will live.

Once an employee chooses the company in which he wishes to invest and decides the amount of compensation to be deferred each month, the State is responsible for withholding the appropriate sums from the employee's wages and channelling those sums to the company designated by the employee. The State bears the cost of making the necessary payroll deductions and of giving employees time off to attend group meetings to learn about the plan, but it does not contribute any moneys to supplement the employees' deferred wages.

For an employee who elects to receive a monthly annuity following retirement, the amount of the employee's monthly benefits depends upon the amount of compensation that the employee deferred (and any earnings thereon), the employee's age at retirement, and the employee's sex. All of the companies selected by the State to participate in the plan use sex-based mortality tables to calculate monthly retirement benefits. Under these tables a man receives larger monthly payments than a woman who deferred the same amount of compensation and retired at the same age, because the tables classify annuitants on the basis of sex and women on average live longer than men. Sex is the only factor that the tables use to classify individuals of the same age; the tables do not incorporate other factors correlating with longevity such as smoking habits, alcohol consumption, weight, medical history, or family history.

As of August 18, 1978, 1,675 of the State's approximately 35,000 employees were participating in the deferred compensation plan. Of these 1,675 participating employees, 681 were women, and 572 women had elected some form of future annuity option. As of the same date, 10 women participating in the plan had retired, and 4 of those 10 had chosen a lifetime annuity.

B

On May 3, 1975, respondent Nathalie Norris, an employee in the Arizona Department of Economic Security, elected to participate in the plan. She requested that her deferred compensation be invested in the Lincoln National Life Insurance Co.'s fixed annuity contract. Shortly thereafter Arizona approved respondent's request and began withholding $199.50 from her salary each month.

On April 25, 1978, after exhausting administrative remedies, respondent brought suit in the United States District Court for the District of Arizona against the State, the Governing Committee, and several individual members of the Committee. Respondent alleged that the defendants were violating § 703(a) of Title VII of the Civil Rights Act of 1964, by administering an annuity plan that discriminates on the basis of sex. Respondent requested that the District Court certify a class under Federal Rule of Civil Procedure 23(b)(2) consisting of all female employees of the State of Arizona "who are enrolled or will in the future enroll in the State Deferred Compensation Plan."

On March 12, 1980, the District Court certified a class action and granted summary judgment for the plaintiff class, holding that the State's plan violates Title VII. The court directed petitioners to cease using sex-based actuarial tables and to pay retired female employees benefits equal to those paid to similarly situated men. The United States Court of Appeals for the Ninth Circuit affirmed, with one judge dissenting. We granted certiorari to decide whether the Arizona plan violates Title VII and whether, if so, the relief ordered by the District Court was proper.

II

. . . Title VII makes it an unlawful employment practice "to discriminate against any individual with respect to his compensation, terms, conditions, or privileges of employment, because of such individual's race, color, religion, sex or national origin." There is no question that the opportunity to participate in a deferred compensation plan constitutes a "[condition] or [privilege] of employment," and that retirement benefits constitute a form of "compensation." The issue we must decide is whether it is discrimination "because of . . . sex" to pay a retired woman lower monthly benefits than a man who deferred the same amount of compensation.

In *Manhart*, we held that an employer had violated Title VII by requiring its female employees to make larger contributions to a pension fund than male employees in order to obtain the same monthly benefits upon retirement. Noting that Title VII's "focus on the individual is unambiguous," we emphasized that the statute prohibits an employer from treating some employees less favorably than others because of their race, religion, sex, or national origin. While women as a class live longer than men, we rejected the argument that the exaction of greater contributions from women was based on a "factor other than sex"—i.e., longevity—and was therefore permissible under the Equal Pay Act.

> "[Any] individual's life expectancy is based on a number of factors, of which sex is only one. . . . [One] cannot 'say that an actuarial distinction based entirely on sex is "based on any other factor than sex." Sex is exactly what it is based on.' "

We concluded that a plan requiring women to make greater contributions than men discriminates "because of . . . sex" for the simple reason that it treats each woman " 'in a manner which but for [her] sex would [have been] different.' "

We have no hesitation in holding, as have all but one of the lower courts that have considered the question, that the classification of employees on the basis of sex is no more permissible at the pay-out stage of a retirement plan than at the pay-in stage. We reject petitioners' contention that the Arizona plan does not discriminate on the basis of sex because a woman and a man who defer the same amount of compensation will obtain upon retirement annuity policies having approximately the same present actuarial value.[11] Arizona has simply offered its employees a choice among different levels of annuity benefits, any one of which, if offered alone, would be equivalent to the plan at issue in Manhart, where the employer determined both the monthly contributions employees were required to make and the level of benefits that they were paid. If a woman participating in the Arizona plan wishes to obtain monthly benefits equal to those obtained by a man, she must make greater monthly contributions than he. . . . For any particular level of benefits that a woman might wish to receive, she will have to make greater monthly contributions to obtain that level of benefits than a man would have to make.

In asserting that the Arizona plan is nondiscriminatory because a man and a woman who have made equal contributions will obtain annuity policies of roughly equal present actuarial value, petitioners incorrectly assume that Title VII permits an employer to classify employees on the basis of sex in predicting their longevity. Otherwise there would be no basis for postulating that a woman's annuity policy has the same present actuarial value as the policy of a similarly situated man even though her policy provides lower monthly benefits. This underlying assumption—that sex may properly be used to predict longevity—is flatly inconsistent with the basic teaching of *Manhart*: that Title VII requires employers to treat their employees as individuals, not "as simply components of a racial, religious, sexual, or national class." *Manhart*

---

[11] The present actuarial value of an annuity policy is determined by multiplying the present value (in this case, the value at the time of the employee's retirement) of each monthly payment promised by the probability, which is supplied by an actuarial table, that the annuitant will live to receive that payment. An annuity policy issued to a retired female employee under a sex-based retirement plan will have roughly the same present actuarial value as a policy issued to a similarly situated man, since the lower value of each monthly payment she is promised is offset by the likelihood that she will live longer and therefore receive more payments.

squarely rejected the notion that, because women as a class live longer than men, an employer may adopt a retirement plan that treats every individual woman less favorably than every individual man.

As we observed in *Manhart*, "[actuarial] studies could unquestionably identify differences in life expectancy based on race or national origin, as well as sex." If petitioners' interpretation of the statute were correct, such studies could be used as a justification for paying employees of one race lower monthly benefits than employees of another race. We continue to believe that "a statute that was designed to make race irrelevant in the employment market," could not reasonably be construed to permit such a racial classification. And if it would be unlawful to use race-based actuarial tables, it must also be unlawful to use sex-based tables, for under Title VII a distinction based on sex stands on the same footing as a distinction based on race unless it falls within one of a few narrow exceptions that are plainly inapplicable here. . . .

The use of sex-segregated actuarial tables to calculate retirement benefits violates Title VII whether or not the tables reflect an accurate prediction of the longevity of women as a class, for under the statute "[even] a true generalization about [a] class" cannot justify class-based treatment. An individual woman may not be paid lower monthly benefits simply because women as a class live longer than men.

NOTES

1.   The actuarial effect of gender is not small: The probability of death in any given year for women is, until extreme old age, quite significantly lower than that for men (for reasons that are, at this writing, not fully understood). As indicated by the following chart, for much of life men's death rates run about 50% higher than women's, which means that if you analyze otherwise equivalent defined benefit retirement or life insurance benefits for each sex as a group (that is, using just the type of analysis forbidden by Title VII as interpreted in *Norris*), participants of one sex will always be receiving benefits that are about 50% more costly than the benefits received by participants of the other sex, as a group.

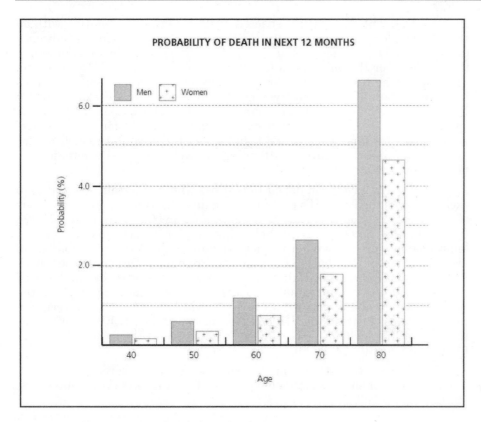

2.   Title VII proscribes discrimination respecting "the terms, conditions or privileges of employment." Accordingly, Title VII and the Supreme Court's decisions in *Manhart* and *Norris* address only employee benefit plans, and sex-distinct schedules remain common in annuity and insurance products offered outside the employment relationship.

3.   In 1976, the Supreme Court held that excluding women with pregnancy-related conditions from coverage under an employer's disability plan did not violate ERISA. General Electric Co. v. Gilbert, 429 U.S. 125. The opinion by Justice Rehnquist relied in part on the argument that the world could be divided into two groups: people who were pregnant and people who were not. Because the latter group included both men and women, the exclusion did not impermissibly discriminate on the basis of sex. Congress soon registered its disagreement with this conclusion by enacting the Pregnancy Discrimination Act of 1978, an amendment to Title VII which expressly prohibits employers from treating conditions associated with pregnancy less favorably from other conditions.

If an employer provides parental leave or other benefits on the basis of something other than medical condition (e.g., the mere fact of having recently become a parent), fathers must be treated as to those benefits the same as mothers.

More recently, beyond the issue of discrimination, Congress stepped in and specifically addressed the issue of providing new mothers the opportunity to take a leave of absence from their jobs without jeopardizing their employment. The FMLA, enacted in 1993, requires employers with 50 or more employees to provide up to 12 weeks of unpaid leave of absence following the birth or adoption of a child (or in the event of serious illness of the employee or the employee's family member). 29 U.S.C. §§ 2601 et seq. The FMLA was recently amended to require expanded leave opportunities for military families: An employer must provide up to 26 weeks of unpaid leave for an employee to care for a family member who is injured or ill while on active military duty; and must provide up to 12 weeks for an "exigency" arising out of a family member's being called to active duty (such as, for example, finding child care or attending farewell or arrival events for the family member).

4.   Courts have been asked to address whether certain medical plan exclusions violate Title VII's prohibition against discrimination on the basis of sex. For example, in *Saks v. Franklin Covey Co.*, 316 F.3d 337 (2d Cir.2003), the Second Circuit held that a plan's exclusion of surgical impregnation procedures does not violate Title VII's prohibition of discrimination on the basis of sex or the Pregnancy Discrimination Act's (PDA's) prohibition of discrimination on the basis of pregnancy and "related medical conditions." Courts and the EEOC have been more receptive to the claim that a medical plan's failure to provide coverage for prescription contraceptives violates Title VII. For a discussion of the EEOC's position, see U.S. Equal Employment Opportunity Commission, *Decision on Coverage of Contraception* (Dec. 14, 2000).

5.   As with the ADEA, small businesses are not covered by Title VII. The threshold for small private employers in Title VII's case is 15 employees. 42 U.S.C. § 2000e(b).

C. DISCRIMINATION ON THE BASIS OF DISABILITY

1. OVERVIEW

The Americans with Disabilities Act, or ADA, enacted in 1990, renders it illegal for employers with 15 or more employees to discriminate against a "qualified individual with a disability" in regard to, among other things, the "employee compensation, job training, and other terms, conditions, and privileges of employment." 42 U.S.C. § 12112(a). A "qualified person with a disability" is a person who has a "disability" but who can nonetheless (with the aid if need be of a "reasonable accommodation" by the employer) perform the "essential functions" of the job. "Disability" is itself defined as "a physical or mental impairment that substantially limits one or more of the major life activities," or having a record of, or being "regarded as having," such an impairment. 42 U.S.C. § 12102(2). It is also illegal to deny a job or benefits to a qualified individual because the individual is known to have a relationship with a disabled person (as in the case, for example, of an employee with a disabled child, whom an employer might want to exclude from the company health plan).

2. THE EMPLOYEE BENEFIT ISSUE

An exception in the ADA provides that the statute does not prohibit an employer from establishing "a bona fide benefit plan that [is] based on underwriting risks, classifying risks, or administering such risks that are based on or not inconsistent with State law," provided the plan is not a "subterfuge" to evade ADA's purposes. The EEOC has indicated that it interprets "subterfuge" as it did under the original version of the ADEA, to mean that distinctions in a plan must have a basis in demonstrable cost differences.

The question then reasonably arises: Why is it not permissible to exclude coverage for any disabled employee, or of any disability, under a plan such as a health or disability plan? Surely there is no difficulty in providing a cost justification for such an exclusion. On the other hand if such an exclusion is not permissible, what if a plan excludes or limits coverage for a certain type of benefits (which all plans do)? If people who have a condition that disproportionately calls for use of that benefit fall within the category of a "qualified person with a disability," isn't the exclusion a form of prohibited discrimination?

The government and the courts have resolved the seeming contradictions in the statute as follows: A limitation or exclusion is impermissible if it is "disability-based," but not otherwise. A limitation or exclusion is, in turn, "disability-based" if it specifically names, or effectively targets, a particular disability. General limitations such as coverage limits, or exclusions of experimental drugs or treatments, are not disability-based and hence permissible. This rationale is applied in the EEOC's regulations, among other things, to make clear that an employer may not include in a health plan lower maximum benefits for AIDS-related illnesses than for other illnesses. Guidance issued by the Justice Department is to similar effect:

> [A] health insurance plan that capped benefits for the treatment of all physical conditions at $50,000 per year does not make disability-based distinctions and does not violate the ADA. A plan that capped benefits for the treatment of all physical conditions, except AIDS, at $50,000 per year, and capped the treatment for AIDS-related conditions at $10,000 per year does distinguish on the basis of disability and probably violates the ADA.

U.S. Dept. of Justice, Civil Rights Division, Questions And Answers: The Americans With Disabilities Act And Persons With Hiv/Aids (http://www.ada.gov/archive/hivqanda.txt).

Questions of a "general cap" on health insurance benefits are now largely moot under the Affordable Care Act, discussed in Chapter 19. The "specific" vs. "blanket" rationale under the ADA nonetheless stands.

D. PROTECTION OF SAME-SEX MARRIAGE

United States v. Windsor

133 S.Ct. 2675 (2013).

■ JUSTICE KENNEDY delivered the opinion of the Court.

Two women then resident in New York were married in a lawful ceremony in Ontario, Canada, in 2007. Edith Windsor and Thea Spyer returned to their home in New York City. When Spyer died in 2009, she left her entire estate to Windsor. Windsor sought to claim the estate tax exemption for surviving spouses. She was barred from doing so, however, by a federal law, the Defense of Marriage Act, which excludes a same-sex partner from the definition of "spouse" as that term is used in federal statutes. Windsor paid the taxes but filed suit to challenge the constitutionality of this provision. The United States District Court and the Court of Appeals ruled that this portion of the statute is unconstitutional and ordered the United States to pay Windsor a refund. This Court granted certiorari and now affirms the judgment in Windsor's favor.

I

In 1996, as some States were beginning to consider the concept of same-sex marriage, see, e.g., Baehr v. Lewin, 74 Haw. 530, 852 P. 2d 44 (1993), and before any State had acted to permit it, Congress enacted the Defense of Marriage Act (DOMA), 110 Stat. 2419. DOMA contains two operative sections: Section 2, which has not been challenged here, allows States to refuse to recognize same-sex marriages performed under the laws of other States.

Section 3 is at issue here. It amends the Dictionary Act in Title 1, § 7, of the United States Code to provide a federal definition of "marriage" and "spouse." Section 3 of DOMA provides as follows:

> "In determining the meaning of any Act of Congress, or of any ruling, regulation, or interpretation of the various administrative bureaus and agencies of the United States, the word 'marriage' means only a legal union between one man and one woman as husband and wife, and the word 'spouse' refers only to a person of the opposite sex who is a husband or a wife."

1 U.S.C. § 7.

The definitional provision does not by its terms forbid States from enacting laws permitting same-sex marriages or civil unions or providing state benefits to residents in that status. The enactment's comprehensive definition of marriage for purposes of all federal statutes and other regulations or directives covered by its terms, however, does control over 1,000 federal laws in which marital or spousal status is addressed as a matter of federal law. . . .

While the [present] tax refund suit was pending, the Attorney General of the United States notified the Speaker of the House of Representatives, pursuant to 28 U.S.C. § 530D, that the Department of Justice would no longer defend the constitutionality of DOMA's § 3. . . .

In response to the notice from the Attorney General, the Bipartisan Legal Advisory Group (BLAG) of the House of Representatives voted to intervene in the litigation to defend the constitutionality of § 3 of DOMA. The Department of Justice did not oppose limited intervention by BLAG. The District Court denied BLAG's motion to enter the suit as of right, on the rationale that the United States already was represented by the Department of Justice. The District Court, however, did grant intervention by BLAG as an interested party. . . .

III

When at first Windsor and Spyer longed to marry, neither New York nor any other State granted them that right. After waiting some years, in 2007 they traveled to Ontario to be married there. It seems fair to conclude that, until recent years, many citizens had not even considered the possibility that two persons of the same sex might aspire to occupy the same status and dignity as that of a man and woman in lawful marriage. For marriage between a man and a woman no doubt had been thought of by most people as essential to the very definition of that term and to its role and function throughout the history of civilization. That belief, for many who long have held it, became even more urgent, more cherished when challenged. For others, however, came the beginnings of a new perspective, a new insight. Accordingly some States concluded that same-sex marriage ought to be given recognition and validity in the law for those same-sex couples who wish to define themselves by their commitment to each other. The limitation of lawful marriage to heterosexual couples, which for centuries had been deemed both necessary and fundamental, came to be seen in New York and certain other States as an unjust exclusion.

Slowly at first and then in rapid course, the laws of New York came to acknowledge the urgency of this issue for same-sex couples who wanted to affirm their commitment to one another before their children, their family, their friends, and their community. And so New York recognized same-sex marriages performed elsewhere; and then it later amended its own marriage laws to permit same-sex marriage. New York, in common with, as of this writing, 11 other States and the District of Columbia, decided that same-sex couples should have the right to marry and so live with pride in themselves and their union and in a status of equality with all other married persons. After a statewide deliberative process that enabled its citizens to discuss and weigh arguments for and against same-sex marriage, New York acted to enlarge the definition of marriage to correct what its citizens and elected representatives perceived to be an injustice that they had not earlier known or understood. See Marriage Equality Act, 2011 N. Y. Laws 749 (codified at N. Y. Dom. Rel. Law Ann. §§ 10–a, 10–b, 13 (West 2013)).

Against this background of lawful same-sex marriage in some States, the design, purpose, and effect of DOMA should be considered as the beginning point in deciding whether it is valid under the Constitution. By history and tradition the definition and regulation of marriage, as will be discussed in more detail, has been treated as being within the authority and realm of the separate States. Yet it is further established that Congress, in enacting discrete statutes, can make determinations that bear on marital rights and privileges. . . .

In order to assess the validity of that intervention it is necessary to discuss the extent of the state power and authority over marriage as a matter of history and tradition. State laws defining and regulating marriage, of course, must respect the constitutional rights of persons, see, e.g., Loving v. Virginia, 388 U.S. 1, 87 S. Ct. 1817, 18 L. Ed. 2d 1010 (1967); but, subject to those guarantees, "regulation of domestic relations" is "an area that has long been regarded as a virtually exclusive province of the States." Sosna v. Iowa, 419 U.S. 393, 404, 95 S. Ct. 553, 42 L. Ed. 2d 532 (1975).

The recognition of civil marriages is central to state domestic relations law applicable to its residents and citizens. See Williams v. North Carolina, 317 U.S. 287, 298, 63 S. Ct. 207, 87 L. Ed. 279 (1942) ("Each state as a sovereign has a rightful and legitimate concern in the marital status of persons domiciled within its borders"). The definition of marriage is the foundation of the State's broader authority to regulate the subject of domestic relations with respect to the "[p]rotection of offspring, property interests, and the enforcement of marital responsibilities." Ibid. . . .

Against this background DOMA rejects the long-established precept that the incidents, benefits, and obligations of marriage are uniform for all married couples within each State, though they may vary, subject to constitutional guarantees, from one State to the next. . . .

The Federal Government uses this state-defined class . . . to impose restrictions and disabilities. That result requires this Court now to address whether the resulting injury and indignity is a deprivation of an essential part of the liberty protected by the Fifth Amendment. What the State of New York treats as alike the federal law deems unlike by a law designed to injure the same class the State seeks to protect. . . .

By doing so it violates basic due process and equal protection principles applicable to the Federal Government. See U.S.Const., Amdt. 5; Bolling v. Sharpe, 347 U.S. 497, 74 S. Ct. 693, 98 L. Ed. 884 (1954). The Constitution's guarantee of equality "must at the very least mean that a bare congressional desire to harm a politically unpopular group cannot" justify disparate treatment of that group. Department of Agriculture v. Moreno, 413 U.S. 528, 534–535, 93 S. Ct. 2821, 37 L. Ed. 2d 782 (1973). In determining whether a law is motived by an improper animus or purpose, " '[d]iscriminations of an unusual character' " especially require careful consideration. Supra, at 2692, 186 L. Ed. 2d, at 826 (quoting Romer, supra, at 633, 116 S. Ct. 1620, 134 L. Ed. 2d 855). DOMA cannot survive under these principles. The responsibility of the States for the regulation of domestic relations is an important indicator of the substantial societal impact the State's classifications have in the daily lives and customs of its people. DOMA's unusual deviation from the usual tradition of recognizing and accepting state definitions of marriage here operates to deprive same-sex couples of the benefits and responsibilities that come with the federal recognition of their marriages. This is strong evidence of a law having the purpose and effect of disapproval of that class. The avowed purpose and practical effect of the law here in question are to impose a disadvantage, a separate status, and so a stigma upon all who enter into same-sex marriages made lawful by the unquestioned authority of the States.

The history of DOMA's enactment and its own text demonstrate that interference with the equal dignity of same-sex marriages, a dignity conferred by the States in the exercise of their sovereign power, was more than an incidental effect of the federal statute. It was its essence. . . .

The Act's demonstrated purpose is to ensure that if any State decides to recognize same-sex marriages, those unions will be treated as second-class marriages for purposes of federal law. This raises a most serious question under the Constitution's Fifth Amendment.

DOMA's operation in practice confirms this purpose. When New York adopted a law to permit same-sex marriage, it sought to eliminate inequality; but DOMA frustrates that objective through a system-wide enactment with no identified connection to any particular area of federal law. DOMA writes inequality into the entire United States Code. The particular case at hand concerns the estate tax, but DOMA is more than a simple determination of what should or should not be allowed as an estate tax refund. Among the over 1,000 statutes and numerous federal regulations that DOMA controls are laws pertaining to Social Security, housing, taxes, criminal sanctions, copyright, and veterans' benefits. . . .

By its great reach, DOMA touches many aspects of married and family life, from the mundane to the profound. It prevents same-sex married couples from obtaining government healthcare benefits they would otherwise receive. . . .

DOMA also brings financial harm to children of same-sex couples. It raises the cost of health care for families by taxing health benefits provided by employers to their workers' same-sex spouses. See 26 U.S.C. § 106; Treas. Reg. § 1.106–1, 26 CFR § 1.106–1 (2012); IRS Private Letter Ruling 9850011 (Sept. 10, 1998). And it denies or reduces benefits allowed to families upon the loss of a spouse and parent, benefits that are an integral part of family security. . . .

The liberty protected by the Fifth Amendment's Due Process Clause contains within it the prohibition against denying to any person the equal protection of the laws. See Bolling, 347 U.S., at 499–500, 74 S. Ct. 693, 98 L. Ed. 884; Adarand Constructors, Inc. v. Peña, 515 U.S. 200, 217–218, 115 S. Ct. 2097, 132 L. Ed. 2d 158 (1995). While the Fifth Amendment itself withdraws from Government the power to degrade or demean in the way this law does, the equal protection guarantee of the Fourteenth Amendment makes that Fifth Amendment right all the more specific and all the better understood and preserved. . . .

The federal statute is invalid, for no legitimate purpose overcomes the purpose and effect to disparage and to injure those whom the State, by its marriage laws, sought to protect in personhood and dignity. By seeking to displace this protection and treating those persons as living in marriages less respected than others, the federal statute is in violation of the Fifth Amendment. This opinion and its holding are confined to those lawful marriages.

The judgment of the Court of Appeals for the Second Circuit is affirmed.

NOTES

1.   The *Windsor* decision elicited heated dissents written and joined variously by Justices Roberts, Scalia, Thomas and Alito. All but Alito objected vigorously to the Court's having agreed to hear the case in the absence of a "live controversy" between the parties, the U.S. already having agreed to accept the District Court's characterization of DOMA as unconstitutional. But the dissenters also disagreed with the Court's holding on the merits, contending that: "Interests in uniformity and stability amply

justified Congress's decision to retain the definition of marriage that, at that point, had been adopted by every State in our Nation, and every nation in the world."

2. *A Constitutional right to same-sex marriage?* The same day it handed down its decision in *Windsor,* the Court, in Hollingsorth v. Perry, 133 S.Ct. 2653 (2013), sidestepped on jurisdictional grounds the next question on observers' minds: Whether it is constitutional for states to limit marriage to opposite-sex couples. The *Windsor* majority, as well as Justice Roberts, took care to caution that no implication was intended to be drawn from *Windsor* about this issue; but in his dissent Justice Scalia expressed concern that was only a "pretense that today's prohibition of laws excluding same-sex marriage is confined to the Federal Government (leaving the second, state-law shoe to be dropped later, maybe next Term)." Since *Windsor* a series of lower courts have found it unconstitutional for states not to extend marriage rights to same-sex couples. (See Campaign for Southern Equality v. Bryant, 2014 U.S. Dist. LEXIS 165913 (N.D. Miss. 2014), at n. 1, for an exhaustive listing of decisions as of the end of November, 2014.) But several courts, including the Court of Appeals for the Sixth Circuit, DeBoer v. Snyder, 2014 WL 5748990 (6th Cir. 2014), have held to the contrary. As of this writing, the final word is being awaited from the Supreme Court, which granted *certiorari* in the *DeBoer* case.

3. *Implications for benefit plans.* As the Court noted, over 1,000 federal statutes are affected by the definition of "spouse," among which are included quite a few employee benefits rules. These include the REAct rules on spousal protection (See Chapter 7), for example, and the tax-exempt status of health insurance benefits—which extend to spouses but not to non-spouses. *Windsor* ushered in an era of uncertainty for plan sponsors in administering these provisions. For a comprehensive discussion of employee benefits questions that arise in the wake of *Windsor,* see Teresa S. Renaker, Julie Wilensky, and Nina Wasow, "Overview of U.S. v. Windsor and its Effect on Employee Benefits," Bloomberg BNA Benefits Practice Resource Center, Benefit Practitioners' Strategy Guide, July 2014 (version available at http://www.americanbar.org/content/dam/aba/events/labor_law/am/2014/9a_post-doma.authcheckdam.pdf).

a. *Immediate implications*: Two months after the *Windsor* decision, the IRS issued Revenue Ruling 2013–7, 2013–38 Int. Rev. Bull 201. This Ruling announced the IRS's position that for all federal tax purposes (including the rules governing qualified retirement plans and tax-exempt health benefits) "spouse" would be given the meaning applied by the "state of celebration" of the marriage—meaning that if a same-sex couple were married in New York, for example, they would be treated as spouses for federal tax purposes no matter where they live. Thus, in a state like Texas, which does not recognize same-sex marriages, a plan sponsor must nonetheless treat as a spouse, for purposes among other things of the qualified joint and survivor annuity rules, the same-sex spouse of an employee who was married in a state that recognizes such marriages. Same-sex spouses who participate in a group health insurance plan are also entitled, for example, to receive those benefits on a federally tax-exempt basis—again, no matter where they live.

At the same time, the Revenue Ruling made clear these tax consequences extend only to married couples—not to other categories recognized by some states, such as "registered domestic partners" or "civil union partners."

b. *Longer-term implications.* Meanwhile, as discussed above, it remains unclear whether it is constitutional for a state *not* to extend marriage rights to same-sex couples. Some states not only do not authorize such marriages, but specifically prohibit them. Plan sponsors in those jurisdictions are left, at this writing, in something of a quandary—it not being clear whether and in what contexts their plans: (i) must, (ii) might, or (iii) must not, extend benefits to same-sex couples, and in general how their plans should define, or interpret, the word "spouse" for benefit plan purposes.

E. OTHER EMPLOYMENT LAWS THAT AFFECT PLANS

1. USERRA

The Persian Gulf conflict of 1991–92 gave rise to the first situation in many years in which large numbers of armed force reserve and National Guard personnel were called up to active service. Many of these soldiers had full-time careers, fulfilling their Guard or reserve duties on weekends and/or vacations. The conflict required their absence from these careers for extended periods. To make sure reservists and Guard members did not suffer adverse employment consequences from their activation, Congress in 1994 enacted USERRA, which generally prohibits discriminating against employees on the basis of military service. 38 U.S.C. §§ 4301 et seq.

In addition to the requirement that a returning service member be offered his or her job back (with seniority) upon return from active service, USERRA contains a number of specific employee benefit-related items. These include: The opportunity to purchase continued, COBRA-like medical coverage during active service; immediate participation upon return in employee benefit plans with service credit for the period of absence; and the right to missed employer contributions (and an extended opportunity for making up missed employee contributions) to defined contribution retirement plans. As discussed in Section B above, the FMLA was also recently amended to provide expanded leave of absence opportunities for family members of active duty military personnel.

2. STATE WAGE AND HOUR LAWS

A completely separate topic that might be said to fall under the heading of "employment law" is that of state wage and hour laws. Most states have laws and enforcement agencies intended to ensure that employers pay their workers any wages owed them. Because these laws are aimed at cash compensation instead of benefits, they are not generally preempted by ERISA. The laws can be implicated, however, by benefit plans such as vacation and severance policies that provide for replacing employees' wages.

By way of example, Michigan has a set of provisions under the title "Wages and Fringe Benefits" at MCLA §§ 408.471 et seq. Section 408.473 states that "An employer shall pay fringe benefits to or on behalf of an employee in accordance with the terms set forth in the written contract or written policy." "Fringe benefits" is defined to include things like holiday, sickness and vacation pay, as well as bonuses. As noted earlier, in Chapter 3, these sorts of benefits often are not "employee benefit plans" subject to ERISA; instead they are mere "payroll practices." Hence this state law is not preempted; hence a Michigan employer's failure to pay accrued sick or vacation pay is a violation of state statute, invoking the enforcement authority of the Michigan Department of Labor and Economic Growth and subjecting the employer to potential (misdemeanor) criminal liability. Michigan's law is typical of that of other states.

PART 5

EMPLOYER-SPONSORED HEALTH PLANS

CHAPTER 19

HEALTH PLANS AND HEALTH CARE COVERAGE

Analysis

Introduction

Health insurance plans are now a major subject of U.S. employee benefits law, having gone from being an afterthought at the time of ERISA's enactment to being a focus of one of the most far-reaching and heavily scrutinized recent pieces of federal legislation, the Affordable Care Act of 2010 ("ACA"). We begin this chapter with some context about the significance of employer-sponsored health plans in current American life; trace their regulation from ERISA forward, including state efforts to regulate such plans, in the face of ERISA's preemption clause; and summarize the ACA. At the end of the chapter we discuss several topics of special interest, including retiree medical plans and health savings accounts, a recently popular type of defined contribution employer medical plan.

A. HEALTH CARE COSTS AND COVERAGE

1. *Cost growth.* Health care costs mushroomed in economic significance during the last half-century. Expenditures for health care in the United States in 1960 were $27 billion, which constituted 5.1 percent of gross domestic product (GDP). In 2002, the figure had grown nearly sixty-fold to $1.5 trillion, or 14.9 percent of GDP. Health care spending grew 3.7 percent in 2012, reaching $2.8 trillion or $8,915 per person. Health spending accounted for 17.2 percent of GDP. See Centers for Medicare & Medicaid Services, National Health Care Expenditures: Historical Overview, available at www.cms.gov/Research-Statistics-Data-and-Systems/Statistics-Trends-and-Reports/NationalHealthExpendData/ NationalHealthAccountsHistorical.html. The Milliman actuarial firm estimated in 2005 that the average family of four with an employer-sponsored health care plan spent more than $12,200 per year on medical expenses, of which the plan covered 83 percent. "Average Family Medical Costs Will Exceed $12,200 This Year," Wall St. J., May 26, 2005, at D2. By 2014, the total cost had risen to $ 23,200, 58 percent of which was paid by the employer. Furthermore, "increasing proportions of costs have been shifted to employees. Since 2007, when the economic recession began, the average cost to employers has increased 52%—an average of 6% per year—while the expenses borne by the family, through payroll deductions and out-of-pocket costs, have grown at an even faster rate, 73% (average of 8% per year)." 2014 Milliman Medical Index, available at http://www. milliman.com/uploadedFiles/insight/Periodicals/mmi/pdfs/2014-mmi.pdf.

2. *Employer-provided plans.* Most private health insurance is provided through an employer sponsored plan. In 2012, 58.5 percent of the nonelderly population had employment-based health benefits, down from 68.4 percent in 2000 and 62.2 percent in 2007. Paul Fronstin, Sources of Health Insurance and Characteristics of the Uninsured: Analysis of the March 2013 Current Population Survey, EBRI Issue Brief, Sept. 2013. The percentage of non-elderly individuals without health insurance coverage increased from 15.6 percent in 2000 to 17.7 percent in 2012. Id.

Between 1999 and 2014, the average annual cost of family health insurance coverage increased from $5,791 to $16,834: the average employer payment increased from $4,247 to $12,011 and the average employee payment from $1,543 to $4,823. Kaiser Family Foundation, 2014 Employer Health Benefits Survey, Summary of Findings, www.kff. org. "Fifty-five percent of firms offer health benefits to their workers, statistically unchanged from 57% last year and 61% in 2012. The likelihood of offering health benefits differs significantly by size of firm, with only 44% of employers with 3 to 9 workers offering coverage. . . ." Id. at 9. According to a 2014 survey, "Whether they have health insurance through an employer or buy it on their own, Americans are paying more out-of-pocket for health care now than they did in the past decade. A Commonwealth Fund survey in the fall of 2014 asked consumers about these costs. More than one of five 19-to-64-year-old adults who were insured all year spent 5 percent or more of their income on out-of-pocket costs, not including premiums, and 13 percent spent 10 percent or more. Adults with low incomes had the highest rates of steep out-of-pocket costs. About three of five privately insured adults with low incomes and half of those with moderate incomes reported that their deductibles are difficult to afford. Two of five adults with private insurance who had high deductibles relative to their income said they had delayed needed care because of the deductible." The Commonwealth Fund, Too High a Price: Out-of-Pocket Health Care Costs in the United States, http://www.commonwealthfund.org/publications/issue-briefs/2014/nov/out-of-pocket-health-care-costs.

Employers have responded to the pressures of increasing health care costs in many ways. Adaptations include increasing the amount of participant copayments, encouraging or requiring the use of health maintenance organizations (HMOs), preferred provider organizations (PPOs) or other managed care organizations (MCOs), and adopting a high-deductible health plan with a savings option, either a health reimbursement account or a health savings account. "PPO plans remain the most common plan type, enrolling 58% of covered workers in 2014. Twenty percent of covered workers are enrolled in a high-deductible plan with a savings options (HDHP/SO), 13% in an HMO, 8% in a POS plan, and less than 1% in a conventional (also known as an indemnity plan) (Exhibit E). Enrollment in HDHP/SOs increased significantly between 2009 and 2011, from 8% to 17% of covered workers, but has plateaued since then (Exhibit E). In 2014, twenty-seven percent of firms offering health benefits offer a high-deductible health plan with a health reimbursement arrangement (HDHP/HRA) or a health savings account (HSA) qualified HDHP." Kaiser Family Foundation, supra, at 6. Difficult questions have arisen regarding the application of ERISA's fiduciary and preemption rules to HMOs and MCOs: see Chapters 12 and 17 and sections D and I of this chapter.

The patterns of health coverage resemble those for pension coverage described in Chapter 1, supra. Large employers are much more likely to offer health benefits than small employers. Better paid employees are more likely to have coverage than low earners. Health insurance for a family of four is now more expensive than the $14,500 a full-time (2,000 hours) minimum-wage worker earns in a year. Managerial and manufacturing employees have higher rates of coverage than blue collar and service sector workers. Fronstin, supra. Unionization remains a powerful predictor of health care coverage. Paul Fronstin, Union Status and Health Care Coverage of Workers: The Impact of the Recession, EBRI Notes, July 2011.

A notable difference between the patterns of coverage in pension plans and health plans is that pension plans cover (that is, provide retirement income to) only the participant and his or her spouse, whereas health care plans typically provide, as an extra-cost option, coverage for the participant's dependents (primarily, children) and an increasing number also cover unmarried partners.

Large employers traditionally provided health coverage not only for active workers and their families, but also for former workers and their dependents. This so-called retiree health coverage has given rise to special problems, discussed later in this chapter.

3. *Tax subsidy*. Employer provided health care escapes federal and state income and employment taxes. Internal Revenue Code Sections 105 and 106. The estimated 5 year income tax expenditure for health plan coverage (the exclusion of employer contributions for health plan coverage and the exclusion of payments for coverage of the self-employed) is almost $ 1.2 trillion. Office of Management and Budget, Analytical Perspectives, Budget of the U.S. Government, Fiscal Year 2015, Table 14–1.

4. *Critiques of employer-centric health insurance provision.* Following is an extract from a prominent critique of health care finance in the United States, written in 1989. It encapsulates some of the central problems identified with the private health insurance system in the years prior to the Affordable Care Act.

[The] present system of financing health care in the United States is unfair. It provides most people—those who are regularly employed by a medium-sized or large employer—with coverage either at no cost or at prices subsidized by the employer and the tax system. But the system denies the opportunity of coverage to millions of others for no good reason—to seasonal and part-time employees, self-employed persons, widows, divorcees, early retirees, the unemployed, and others whose employers choose not to provide health care coverage. Not all uninsured people are poor or unemployed. In fact, nearly two thirds of them are members of families with incomes above the poverty level; more than two thirds of uninsured adults belong to the labor force. Viewed another way, when the uninsured are seriously ill (and most expenses are for seriously ill patients), taxpayers, insured persons, or both end up paying for most of their care. Voluntarily or involuntarily, some people are taking a free ride. Those who can do so ought to contribute their fair share to their coverage and be insured. . . .

In recent years, efforts by employers and the government to contain costs have [placed hospitals] under increased financial pressure to develop strategies to avoid caring for those who cannot pay—even to the point of closing their emergency rooms. Many who cannot pay turn to public providers of last resort, such as county hospitals. But these institutions are also under increasing financial pressure as public finances are strained and the numbers of the uninsured increase.

The present system is wasteful in many respects. . . . The association between jobs and health insurance complicates and interferes with job mobility, because most people must change health plans when they change jobs. The presence of large numbers of uninsured persons imposes large costs on providers when they perform determinations of eligibility and coverage. The uninsured obtain much of their primary care in the outpatient departments and emergency rooms of public hospitals, instead of in the much less costly setting of a primary care physician's office. The deferment of care for conditions such as hypertension and diabetes adds to health risks and can cause much more expensive emergencies later. The lack of prenatal care can lead to very costly premature delivery and the birth of children with handicaps. The unavailability of insurance imposes heavy penalties on the uninsured: the postponement or denial of treatment, causing avoidable sickness and suffering, and the depletion of personal savings.

For all these reasons, our present system of health care does not reflect American values. We cherish efficiency and fairness, but we have a system that is neither efficient nor fair. Very few Americans believe that other Americans should be deprived of needed care or subjected to extreme financial hardship because of an inability to pay. There is widespread public outrage when a hospital turns away a delivering mother or an injured person for this reason. Congress has passed laws to punish hospitals that do this. But we have failed as a society to create institutions that assure all persons of the opportunity to obtain needed care, when they need it and without an excessive financial burden.

Alain Enthoven & Richard Kronick, A Consumer-Choice Health Plan for the 1990s, 320 New England J. of Medicine 29, 30 (1989).

B. ERISA COVERAGE OF HEALTH AND WELFARE PLANS

1. NONPENSION PLANS

ERISA's fiduciary rules, certain of its reporting and disclosure requirements, and much of its enforcement system (Title I, Parts 1, 4, and 5) apply not only to pension plans, but also to "employee welfare benefit plans." See ERISA § 3(1) (definition, reproduced in section B.2 below). Welfare benefit plans are maintained for employees either by an employer or by a union (or jointly). Included are plans providing health care benefits; benefits upon accident, death, or disability; unemployment benefits; vacation benefits; training programs; and a variety of others. There are major differences between pension plans and these nonpension plans. A pension plan envisions a decades-long program of saving for retirement and dissaving during retirement; the potential for forfeitures and for underfunding—practices that ERISA was meant to restrict— arise on account of the long-term character of a pension plan. The typical single-employer welfare benefit plan, by contrast, is handled on the sponsor's books on a current or pay-as-you-go basis. Thus, the drafters of ERISA carefully avoided extending the vesting and funding rules to welfare benefit plans.

It will be seen repeatedly in this chapter that Congress' decision to lump both pension and nonpension plans under ERISA has created considerable difficulty. ERISA regulates the content of pension plans in considerable detail, but provides almost no such regulation of welfare benefit plans. Nevertheless, ERISA's broad preemption provision applies to both types of plan, and most preemption litigation involves welfare plans rather than pension plans. Bear in mind the question of whether Congress made a misjudgment in extending ERISA to nonpension plans.

What light does the legislative history throw on the rationale for subjecting such disparate plans to a common scheme of regulation in the areas of reporting and disclosure, fiduciary responsibility, enforcement and remedies, and preemption?

2.   WHY REGULATE NONPENSION PLANS?

ERISA is centered on pension plans, a preoccupation reflected in the very title of the Act, which addresses "retirement income security." The statute is widely called the "pension reform law." The decision to include nonpension plans within ERISA has given rise to major difficulties, especially in regard to judicial review of benefit denials (discussed in Chapter 15) and preemption of state law (discussed in Chapter 17). Accordingly, it is important to ask why the drafters determined to reach beyond pension plans. First, we begin with a look at just how ERISA covers welfare benefit plans.

1.   *Structure of the statute.* ERISA § 3(1) defines the term "employee welfare benefit plan" to include any "plan, fund, or program" within its subsections (A) or (B). Subsection (A) enumerates "medical, surgical, or hospital care or benefits, or benefits in the event of sickness, accident, disability, death or unemployment, or vacation benefits, apprenticeship or other training programs, or day care centers, scholarship funds, or prepaid legal services." Subsection (B) incorporates by reference benefits identified in § 302(c) of the Taft-Hartley Act of 1947, 29 U.S.C. § 186(c). Section 302(c)(5)(A) of the Taft-Hartley Act, which is reproduced and discussed in Chapter 15, enumerates most of the ERISA § 3(1)(A) benefits. Taft-Hartley § 302(c)(6) enumerates "vacation, holiday, severance or similar benefits. . . ."

ERISA § 4(a) provides, with some exclusions not presently important, that Title I applies to "any employee benefit plan." Section 3(3) defines "employee benefit plan" to include both pension and welfare benefit plans. Consequently, the provisions of ERISA will pertain to welfare benefit plans except as excluded. The main exclusions, which are cross-referenced in § 4(a), are §§ 201 and 301. Section 201 excludes welfare benefit plans from ERISA's vesting rules and related participation rules. Section 301 excludes welfare benefit plans from the funding rules. Title IV, ERISA's plan termination insurance system, also excludes welfare benefit plans; the insurance system affects defined benefit pension plans only.

The result of this statutory latticework is that the only portions of ERISA as originally enacted that applied to welfare benefit plans were three parts of Title I: the reporting and disclosure requirements of Part 1, the fiduciary rules of Part 4, and the enforcement and remedial measures of Part 5. Title I of ERISA was subsequently amended to add Parts 6 and 7, which regulate various aspects of health care plans. These parts of ERISA apply exclusively to such welfare benefit plans.

2.   *ERISA's exclusions: vesting, funding, termination insurance.* Pension plans are prototypically arrangements of long duration. Benefits accrue across decades of employment and are distributed across further decades of retirement. Welfare benefit plans, by contrast, provide services or other benefits on a "current account" or "pay as you go" basis.

With the important exception of retiree health care, which is discussed below, welfare benefit plans do not ordinarily entail long-term promises. The covered employee either uses or declines the child care, health care, job training, life insurance, or whatever, but these entitlements do not cumulate over time. Unlike pension benefits, welfare benefit entitlements are too short-term in character to have attracted much in the way of long-term service conditions. Thus, vesting protections have not been thought necessary.

Likewise, the framers of ERISA saw no need to impose funding requirements for transitory benefits. Funding rules guard against default by the plan sponsor in the conduct of its long-term saving program for distantly payable benefits. By contrast, in the parlance of accounting, the sponsor of a welfare benefit plan "expenses" the plan's costs on a current basis as they arise; the sponsor carries the plan on a "pay-as-you-go" basis.

ERISA's funding rules also function derivatively to protect the Pension Benefit Guaranty Corporation (PBGC). PBGC operates the plan termination insurance system of ERISA's Title IV, which insures against the consequences of sponsor default on pension promises. Title IV does not apply to welfare benefit plans.

3. *Rationale for inclusion.* Perhaps more difficult to understand than the exclusion of welfare benefit plans from ERISA's vesting, funding, and termination insurance requirements is Congress' decision to subject welfare benefit plans to ERISA at all. Why regulate under a common scheme such fundamentally different things as a long-duration pension plan and a short-duration welfare benefit plan?

The legislative history provides a straightforward explanation for ERISA's entanglement of pension and welfare benefit plans. The reporting-and-disclosure, fiduciary, and enforcement measures that ERISA imposes upon both pension and welfare benefit plans were directed at abuses that affected both types of plans. The animating concern behind these parts of ERISA was to prevent the looting, self-dealing, and other forms of corruption that had been discovered in union-dominated multiemployer plans. (See Michael Gordon's account, extracted in chapter 3.) Moreover, before ERISA forced the separation of the two types of plan, it was common for one multiemployer plan to offer both pension and nonpension benefits. See, e.g., UMWA Health & Retirement Funds v. Robinson, 455 U.S. 562, 563 (1982) (collectively bargained plan established in 1950 provided both pension and health benefits, until separated in 1974 to comply with ERISA).

From the standpoint of the victim, it does not much matter whether money is stolen from your pension plan or from your health or accident insurance plan. Thus, in the movement to interpose fiduciary restraints against self-dealing and other mismanagement in multiemployer plans, the drafters of ERISA chose (in Title I, Part 4) to impose a common scheme of fiduciary regulation on both pension plans and welfare benefit plans. The reporting rules (Title I, Part 1) that were also made applicable to welfare benefit plans reinforce the fiduciary law through disclosure (and through the deterrence that the threat of disclosure is meant to promote). Likewise, ERISA's remedial provisions (Title I, Part 5) were extended to welfare benefit plans, in order to facilitate enforcement of the substantive fiduciary standards.

Assuming that the drafters were on sound policy grounds in applying ERISA fiduciary law and its ancillary disclosure and enforcement provisions to some welfare benefit plans, was it a mistake to include all such plans? If the problem was multiemployer plans, why should the statute have applied to single-employer plans, in which the plan sponsor's incentives and powers under corporate law to prevent waste and thievery were so much stronger?

4.   *Preemption.* In hindsight, the decision to lump pension and welfare benefit plans in a single regulatory endeavor has revealed two major flaws. First, as discussed in Section G below, so-called retiree health plans (plans that promise health care for retired workers) do not fit easily where the statute puts them, on the welfare benefit side of the pension/welfare benefit line.

The other great sore point has been the application of ERISA's immensely broad preemption clause to welfare benefit plans. Section 514 effectively federalizes the law of welfare benefit plans, except in a few preserves, notably under the insurance savings clause. Yet ERISA supplies standards for these plans only in the spheres of fiduciary responsibility, reporting and disclosure and the specific group health plan requirements later enacted as Parts 6 and 7 of Title I. As a result, federal courts have displaced state courts in areas in which state law was often adequate, sometimes denying all remedy, or else intruding patchy federal common law in place of comprehensive state law. *Most preemption litigation concerns welfare benefit plans.* There is little reason to think that Congress understood how ERISA preemption would magnify the decision Congress made to impose federal fiduciary standards to prevent looting and other abuse of these non-pension plans. (The legislative history of ERISA's preemption provision is discussed in Chapter 17)

5.   *Amending welfare benefit plans.* As noted above, ERISA Part 1, Title II, regulating vesting and benefit accrual, including the anti-reduction rule of § 204, applies only to pension plans, not to welfare benefit plans. See ERISA § 201(1). Accordingly, as the Supreme Court has remarked, the plan sponsor is "generally free under ERISA, for any reason at any time, to adopt, modify, or terminate welfare plans." Curtiss-Wright Corp. v. Schoonejongen, 514 U.S. 73, 78 (1995).

The celebrated *McGann* case, reproduced next, shows the participant in a health care plan, who was dying of AIDS, struggling to resist a plan amendment that stripped him of his coverage.

3. MCGANN V. H & H MUSIC CO.

946 F.2d 401 (5th Cir.1991), cert. denied, 506 U.S. 981 (1992).

■ GARWOOD, CIRCUIT JUDGE. Plaintiff-appellant John McGann (McGann) filed this suit under section 510 of [ERISA] against defendants-appellees H & H Music Company (H & H Music), Brook Mays Music Company (Brook Mays) and General American Life Insurance Company (General American) (collectively defendants) claiming that they discriminated against McGann, an employee of H & H Music, by reducing benefits available to H & H Music's group medical plan beneficiaries for treatment for acquired immune deficiency syndrome (AIDS) and related illnesses. The district court granted defendants' motion for summary judgment on the ground that an employer has an absolute right to alter the terms of medical coverage available to plan beneficiaries. 742 F.Supp. 392. We affirm. . . .

McGann, an employee of H & H Music, discovered that he was afflicted with AIDS in December 1987. Soon thereafter, McGann submitted his first claims for reimbursement under H & H Music's group medical plan, provided through Brook Mays, the plan administrator, and issued by General American, the plan insurer, and informed his employer that he had AIDS. McGann met with officials of H & H Music in March 1988, at which time they discussed McGann's illness. Before the change in the terms of the plan, it provided for lifetime medical benefits of up to $1,000,000 to all employees.

In July 1988, H & H Music informed its employees that, effective August 1, 1988, changes would be made in their medical coverage. These changes included, but were not limited to, limitation of benefits payable for AIDS-related claims to a lifetime maximum of $5,000. No limitation was placed on any other catastrophic illness. H & H Music became self-insured under the new plan and General American became the plan's administrator. By January 1990, McGann had exhausted the $5,000 limit on coverage for his illness.

In August 1989, McGann sued H & H Music, Brook Mays and General American under section 510 of ERISA, which provides, in part, as follows:

"It shall be unlawful for any person to discharge, fine, suspend, expel, discipline, or discriminate against a participant or beneficiary for exercising any right to which he is entitled under the provisions of an employee benefit plan, . . . or for the purpose of interfering with the attainment of any right to which such participant may become entitled under the plan. . . ."

McGann claimed that defendants discriminated against him in violation of both prohibitions of section 510. He claimed that the provision limiting coverage for AIDS-related expenses was directed specifically at him in retaliation for exercising his rights under the medical plan and for the purpose of interfering with his attainment of a right to which he may become entitled under the plan.

Defendants, conceding the factual allegations of McGann's complaint, moved for summary judgment. These factual allegations include no assertion that the reduction of AIDS benefits was intended to deny benefits to McGann for any reason which would not be applicable to other beneficiaries who might then or thereafter have AIDS, but rather that the reduction was prompted by the knowledge of McGann's illness, and that McGann was the only beneficiary then known to have AIDS.[4] On June 26, 1990, the district court granted defendants' motion on the

---

[4] We assume, for purposes of this appeal that the defendants' knowledge of McGann's illness was a motivating factor in their decision to reduce coverage for AIDS-related expenses, that this knowledge was obtained either through McGann's filing of claims or his meetings with defendants, and that McGann was the only plan beneficiary then known to have AIDS.

ground that they had an absolute right to alter the terms of the plan, regardless of their intent in making the alterations. The district court also held that even if the issue of discriminatory motive were relevant, summary judgment would still be proper because the defendants' motive was to ensure the future existence of the plan and not specifically to retaliate against McGann or to interfere with his exercise of future rights under the plan. . . .

McGann contends that defendants violated both clauses of section 510 by discriminating against him for two purposes: (1) "for exercising any right to which [the beneficiary] is entitled," and (2) "for the purpose of interfering with the attainment of any right to which such participant may become entitled." . . .

At trial, McGann would bear the burden of proving the existence of defendants' specific discriminatory intent as an essential element of either of his claims. *Dister v. Continental Group, Inc.*, 859 F.2d 1108, 1111 (2d Cir.1988) (section 510 claimant must prove specific intent to engage in activity prohibited by section 510); *Gavalik v. Continental Can Co.*, 812 F.2d 834, 851 (3d Cir.1987) (claimant must prove specific intent to violate ERISA). Thus, in order to survive summary judgment McGann must make a showing sufficient to establish that a genuine issue exists as to defendants' specific intent to retaliate against McGann for filing claims for AIDS-related treatment or to interfere with McGann's attainment of any right to which he may have become entitled.

Although we assume there was a connection between the benefits reduction and either McGann's filing of claims or his revelations about his illness, there is nothing in the record to suggest that defendants' motivation was other than as they asserted, namely to avoid the expense of paying for AIDS treatment (if not, indeed, also for other treatment), no more for McGann than for any other present or future plan beneficiary who might suffer from AIDS. McGann concedes that the reduction in AIDS benefits will apply equally to all employees filing AIDS-related claims and that the effect of the reduction will not necessarily be felt only by him. He fails to allege that the coverage reduction was otherwise specifically intended to deny him particularly medical coverage except "in effect." He does not challenge defendants' assertion that their purpose in reducing AIDS benefits was to reduce costs.

Furthermore, McGann has failed to adduce evidence of the existence of "any right to which [he] may become entitled under the plan." The right referred to in the second clause of section 510 is not simply any right to which an employee may conceivably become entitled, but rather any right to which an employee may become entitled pursuant to an existing, enforceable obligation assumed by the employer. "Congress viewed [section 510] as a crucial part of ERISA because, without it, employers would be able to circumvent the provision of *promised* benefits." *Ingersoll-Rand Co. v. McClendon*, 498 U.S. 133, 143 (1990) (emphasis added).

McGann's allegations show no *promised* benefit, for there is nothing to indicate that defendants ever promised that the $1,000,000 coverage limit was permanent. The H & H Music plan expressly provides: "Termination or Amendment of Plan: The Plan Sponsor may terminate or amend the Plan at any time or terminate any benefit under the Plan at any time." There is no allegation or evidence that any oral or written representations were made to McGann that the $1,000,000 coverage limit would never be lowered. Defendants broke no promise to McGann. The continued availability of the $1,000,000 limit was not a right to which McGann may have become entitled for the purposes of section 510. To adopt McGann's contrary construction of this portion of section 510 would mean that an employer could not effectively reserve the right to amend a medical plan to reduce benefits respecting subsequently incurred medical expenses, as H & H Music did here, because such an amendment would obviously have as a purpose preventing participants from attaining the right to such future benefits as they otherwise might do under the existing plan absent the amendment. But this is plainly not the law, and ERISA does not require such "vesting" of the right to a continued level of the same medical benefits once those are ever included in a welfare plan.

McGann appears to contend that the reduction in AIDS benefits alone supports an inference of specific intent to retaliate against him or to interfere with his future exercise of rights under the plan. McGann characterizes as evidence of an individualized intent to discriminate the fact that AIDS was the only catastrophic illness to which the $5,000 limit was applied and the fact that McGann was the only employee known to have AIDS. He contends that if defendants reduced AIDS coverage because they learned of McGann's illness through his exercising of his rights under the plan by filing claims, the coverage reduction therefore could be "retaliation" for McGann's filing of the claims.[6] Under McGann's theory, any reduction in employee benefits would be impermissibly discriminatory if motivated by a desire to avoid the anticipated costs of continuing to provide coverage for a particular beneficiary. McGann would find an implied promise not to discriminate for this purpose; it is the breaking of this promise that McGann appears to contend constitutes interference with a future entitlement. . . .

The Supreme Court has observed in dictum: "ERISA does not mandate that employers provide any particular benefits, and does not itself proscribe discrimination in the provision of employee benefits." *Shaw v. Delta Air Lines*, Inc., 463 U.S. 85 (1983). To interpret "discrimination" broadly to include defendants' conduct would clearly conflict with Congress's intent that employers remain free to create, modify and terminate the terms and conditions of employee benefits plans without governmental interference. . . .

As persuasively explained by the Second Circuit, the policy of allowing employers freedom to amend or eliminate employee benefits is particularly compelling with respect to medical plans:

> "With regard to an employer's right to change medical plans, Congress evidenced its recognition of the need for flexibility in rejecting the automatic vesting of welfare plans. Automatic vesting was rejected because the costs of such plans are subject to fluctuating and unpredictable variables. Actuarial decisions

---

[6] We assume that discovery of McGann's condition—and realization of the attendant, long-term costs of caring for McGann—did in fact prompt defendants to reconsider the $1,000,000 limit with respect to AIDS-related expenses and to reduce the limit for future such expenses to $5,000.

concerning fixed annuities are based on fairly stable data, and vesting is appropriate. In contrast, medical insurance must take account of inflation, changes in medical practice and technology, and increases in the costs of treatment independent of inflation. These unstable variables prevent accurate predictions of future needs and costs." *Moore v. Metropolitan Life Ins. Co.*, 856 F.2d 488, 492 (2d Cir.1988) (*Metropolitan Life*).

In *Metropolitan Life*, the court rejected an ERISA claim by retirees that their employer could not change the level of their medical benefits without their consent. The court stated that limiting an employer's right to change medical plans increased the risk of "decreas[ing] protection for future employees and retirees." . . .

McGann's claim cannot be reconciled with the well-settled principle that Congress did not intend that ERISA circumscribe employers' control over the content of benefits plans they offered to their employees. McGann interprets section 510 to prevent an employer from reducing or eliminating coverage for a particular illness in response to the escalating costs of covering an employee suffering from that illness. Such an interpretation would, in effect, change the terms of H & H Music's plan. Instead of making the $1,000,000 limit available for medical expenses on an as-incurred basis only as long as the limit remained in effect, the policy would make the limit *permanently* available for all medical expenses as they might thereafter be incurred because of a single event, such as the contracting of AIDS. Under McGann's theory, defendants would be effectively proscribed from reducing coverage for AIDS once McGann had contracted that illness and filed claims for AIDS-related expenses. If a federal court could prevent an employer from reducing an employee's coverage limits for AIDS treatment once that employee contracted AIDS, the boundaries of judicial involvement in the creation, alteration or termination of ERISA plans would be sorely tested. . . .

ERISA does not broadly prevent an employer from "discriminating" in the creation, alteration or termination of employee benefits plans; thus, evidence of such intentional discrimination cannot alone sustain a claim under section 510. That section does not prohibit welfare plan discrimination between or among categories of diseases. Section 510 does not mandate that if some, or most, or virtually all catastrophic illnesses are covered, AIDS (or any other particular catastrophic illness) must be among them. It does not prohibit an employer from electing not to cover or continue to cover AIDS, while covering or continuing to cover other catastrophic illnesses, even though the employer's decision in this respect may stem from some "prejudice" against AIDS or its victims generally. The same, of course, is true of any other disease and its victims. That sort of "discrimination" is simply not addressed by section 510. Under section 510, the asserted discrimination is illegal only if it is motivated by a desire to retaliate against an employee or to deprive an employee of an existing right to which he may become entitled. The district court's decision to grant summary judgment to defendants therefore was proper. Its judgment is accordingly AFFIRMED.

NOTES

1. *Plan Amendment as Discrimination.* The decision in *McGann*, and the Supreme Court's denial of certiorari, were widely followed not only in the employee benefits literature, but also in the general press. E.g., Employers Winning Right to Cut Back Medical Insurance, New York Times, Mar. 29, 1992, at A1; Supreme Court Refuses to Hear Appeal of Benefit Cuts for Workers with AIDS, Wall St. J., Nov. 10, 1992, at A4. McGann died of AIDS during the pendency of the litigation. The certiorari proceedings in the Supreme Court were conducted by his executor on behalf of his estate, sub nom. Greenberg v. H & H Music Co. The Eleventh Circuit in Owens v. Storehouse, Inc., 984 F.2d 394 (11th Cir.1993), followed *McGann*, concluding that ERISA § 510 did not prevent the employer from amending its health care plan to impose a $25,000 lifetime benefit cap for AIDS-related claims.

2. *Questioning the exclusion of welfare benefit plans from ERISA's vesting and anti-reduction protections.* In ERISA § 201(1) Congress decided not to extend vesting and anti-reduction protection to nonpension benefits. Is the litigation strategy in *McGann* effectively an attempt to overturn Congress's policy judgment, by transforming ERISA § 510 into a vesting rule for nonpension benefits? Was Congress wise to exclude nonpension benefits from the vesting and anti-reduction protections of ERISA §§ 203–204?

The opinion in *McGann* gives a standard justification for employer autonomy in plan design: Since employers are not required to offer health care or other employee benefit plans, employers should be free to revise existing plans at will. Is that argument effectively a recycled version of the "gratuity theory" of pensions, the now-discredited approach to pension rights discussed supra in Chapters 1 and 4? Doesn't the argument for employer autonomy in *McGann* apply with equal force to pension benefits, which Congress has withdrawn from employer autonomy by means of the vesting and anti-reduction rules? Or is there some fundamental difference between welfare benefit plans and pension plans that justifies the different treatment in ERISA?

3. *Distinguish preexisting conditions?* The modification in the health care coverage in *McGann* was applied to what is called, in the argot of health care finance, a preexisting condition. The disease had materialized before the employer instituted the change in insurance coverage. The employer's decision to revise its health care coverage severely restricted coverage for a worker already afflicted with AIDS. Even if the court is correct that the plan and ERISA authorize the employer to alter the terms of the health care coverage that the employer offers as an employee benefit, might it be argued that the employer's power to make such alterations ought not to extend to coverage for preexisting conditions? Why?

In Wheeler v. Dynamic Engineering, Inc., 850 F.Supp. 459, 468 (E.D.Va.1994), the court held "that an employer's amendment to its health plan cannot be applied retroactively to deny [coverage]." The court purported to distinguish *McGann* as a "discrimination case" under ERISA § 510, in which "[t]he question of whether coverage had been amended after a course of treatment had commenced was addressed in a more cursory fashion."

The Health Insurance Portability and Accountability Act of 1996 amended ERISA effective in 1997 to add new ERISA § 701, imposing some restrictions on the ability of health care plans to exclude coverage for preexisting conditions in job change circumstances. Had this measure been in effect at the time of *McGann*, would the case have been decided differently? The Patient Protection and Affordable Care Act of 2010 bans preexisting condition exclusions and premium increases based on health status, starting in 2014 (although the prohibition of the use of preexisting condition exclusions for children is effective for plan years beginning after September 22, 2010). PHSA § 2704.

4. *Need for flexibility.* Plan sponsors alter health plans incessantly, adjusting benefit levels and copay amounts (i.e., deductibles) in response to cost experience and other factors. In recent years, for example, there has been extensive revision of benefits for mental health and for substance abuse programs in response to large increases in cost and in usage. In an amicus brief on behalf of the employer in the certiorari proceedings in *McGann*, the Solicitor General observed that health care plans routinely limit coverage for mental illness, and that neither the DoL nor any court had ever questioned this form of discrimination. 19 BNA Pension Rptr. 2061 (1992). Congress has since amended ERISA to restrict autonomy of plan design regarding mental health benefits. ERISA § 712.

5. *Preemption.* ERISA preemption, even when unmentioned, lurks in the background of many benefit denial cases, a theme emphasized in Chapter 15. So, too, in *McGann*: If ERISA preemption had not federalized the case, the plaintiff could have brought claims under state contract and insurance law. The *New York Times* article, supra, discussing *McGann* and *Owens v. Storehouse, Inc.*, supra, observed that if the plaintiffs in those cases "had bought their coverage from an insurance company, state laws in both Georgia and Texas would have required that the original AIDS coverage be continued." New York Times, Mar. 29, 1992, supra, at A1. See generally Note, AIDS and ERISA Preemption: The Double Threat, 41 Duke L.J. 1115 (1992).

6. *ERISA § 510.* ERISA's antidiscrimination measure, § 510, has been studied previously in Chapter 4, where its connection to ERISA's anti-forfeiture policy for pension benefits was emphasized. We saw that in *Gavalik/McLendon*, the prototypical § 510 case, the sponsor's conduct in terminating participants for the purpose of preventing their pension rights from vesting was found to violate § 510. By contrast, in *McGann* the participant was claiming that the employer's exercise of its power to amend the plan violated § 510. As in *McGann*, such claims rarely succeed, because of the scope of the sponsor's autonomy over setting benefit levels, especially in welfare benefit plans to which the anti-reduction rule does not apply. See also McGath v. Auto-Body North Shore, Inc., 7 F.3d 665 (7th Cir.1993). Does it follow that because the employer retains the power to amend a pension plan, the employer can use that power for the express purpose of defeating pension eligibility for a particular employee? In both *McGann* and *McGath*, the courts reasoned that because the amendments in question would apply equally to other participants identically situated, the amendments did not discriminate against the particular participant, even though the circumstances of the particular participants had motivated the plan amendments. Should the standard of review be more searching when a plan amendment foreseeably affects an ascertained individual?

See also Haberern v. Kaupp Vascular Surgeons Ltd. Defined Benefit Plan & Trust Agreement, 24 F.3d 1491, 1502–04 (3d Cir.1994), cert. denied,

513 U.S. 1149 (1995), emphasizing the employer's management discretion, and following *McGath* with approval.

For a case sustaining the applicability of § 510 to a plan amendment, see Stephen Allen Lynn, P.C. Employee Profit Sharing Plan and Trust v. Stephen Allen Lynn, 25 F.3d 280 (5th Cir.1994) (amending pension plan in order to preclude spouse's enforcement of a qualified domestic relations order held actionable under § 510).

In Coomer v. Bethesda Hospital Inc., 370 F.3d 499, 509 (6th Cir.2004) the employer amended a pension plan to allow a terminating employee to take a lump sum distribution (LSD) (to help him pay for medical school expenses), but refused to allow other employees to take LSDs, some of whom sued. The court dismissed the claim, saying "that unequal treatment in the design of the plan does not give right to an action under ERISA § 510." Accord Hanifen v. Ball Corp., 2005 WL 1712004 (S.D. Ohio 2005) (no § 510 violation where plan gratuitously increased benefits for one group of employees but not another).

7.   *Americans with Disabilities Act.* As discussed in Chapter 18, the Americans with Disabilities Act (ADA), which became effective in July 1992, prohibits discrimination "against a qualified individual with a disability because of the disability in regard [to] employee compensation [and] other terms, conditions, and privileges of employment." 42 U.S.C. § 12112(a).

Had the ADA been in effect at the time of the employer conduct that was challenged in *McGann*, would the ADA have altered the outcome? On its precise facts, does *McGann* survive the ADA?

C. POST-ERISA FEDERAL REGULATION

As illustrated by the material above, in ERISA Congress put in place a statute that not only—as with retirement plans—does not mandate any form of employer-provided health insurance, but also—unlike retirement plans—does not restrict an employer from terminating or amending health insurance benefits. More or less coincident with the statute's adoption, medical costs began what would become a precipitous increase, in the face of which many employers began to find continued provision of such benefits uneconomic. By 2005, according to the Census Bureau, approximately 16% of the American population was not covered by health insurance of any kind. The uninsured group numbered some 47 million individuals, of whom over eight million were children under the age of 18. U.S. Census Bureau, Historical Health Insurance Table HI–7. Health Insurance Coverage Status and Type of Coverage by Age: 1987 to 2005, available at http://www.census.gov/hhes/www/hlthins/data/historical/org hihistt7.html.

These developments increased the pressure for federal and—as will be seen in the next section—state action to increase the rate of health insurance coverage. In the decades leading up to enactment of the ACA in 2010, Congress took several more incremental steps toward this end. These start with so-called "COBRA continuation coverage" requirements, as described below.

1. COBRA: CONTINUATION OF HEALTH BENEFITS

Title X of the Consolidated Omnibus Budget Reconciliation Act of 1985 (COBRA) added a new Part 6 to ERISA Title I, requiring that the sponsor of a group health plan make available continuing coverage following an event that might otherwise result in loss of coverage. COBRA does not require an employer to offer health coverage, but COBRA does require an employer that does offer coverage to continue it in prescribed circumstances. Employers of fewer than 20 employees are exempted. ERISA § 601(b). Many states have "mini-COBRA" statutes that cover smaller employers.

Section 603 prescribes the "qualifying events" that would otherwise result in loss of coverage of a "qualifying beneficiary." The plan sponsor must make available continuing coverage (1) for the spouse of the covered employee when the covered employee dies or divorces the spouse; (2) for the covered employee who is terminated, other than for "gross misconduct"; (3) for a dependent child who ceases to be dependent; and in a few other cases. ERISA § 603.

The duration of required coverage varies, up to 36 months. Thus, the purpose is to provide coverage for a transition period.

COBRA does not create a new class of covered employees or require increased benefits. COBRA does, however, significantly increase the obligations of an employer who provides group health benefits, by requiring the employer to continue to provide coverage at group rates for the various statutorily-qualified beneficiaries.

1. *Main provisions.* Section 601(b) provides that the statute's scheme of continuation rights applies to the health plans of employers who employed more than "20 employees on a typical business day during the preceding calendar year." Under section 601(a), the plan sponsor of each group health plan must give "each qualified beneficiary who would lose coverage under the plan as a result of a qualifying event" the right to elect continuation coverage. The continuation coverage requirement applies only to health benefits under group health plans—generally medical, dental, vision, medical expense reimbursement, and similar benefits—but not to accident, life, or disability benefits. Continuation coverage must be made available to the covered employee and to that employee's spouse or dependent child who was a beneficiary under the plan before the qualifying event.

Section 602(1) requires that the coverage provided to the employee to whom the qualifying event has occurred be identical to the coverage provided to a similarly situated beneficiary under the plan. Under § 602(2), the period of transitional coverage is either 18, 29 or 36 months depending on the type of qualifying event. Section 602(4) mandates that COBRA continuation coverage may not be conditioned on evidence of insurability, meaning that health conditions existing at the time of the qualifying event cannot be the basis for exclusions from coverage.

COBRA covers health care plans only, and courts have resisted efforts to twist the language to extend COBRA rights to disability plans. Austell v. Raymond James & Assocs., Inc., 120 F.3d 32 (4th Cir.1997).

2. *Costs and charges.* Section 602(3) provides that the plan may require a covered person to pay a premium for the continuation coverage, in an amount not to "exceed 102 percent of the applicable premium" for active employees.

Despite this measure of seeming cost recovery, COBRA coverage has proved to be costly to employers. "The average cost for COBRA continuation coverage in plan year 1991 was $1.93 per $1.00 of claims for active employees." Employers' COBRA Costs, EBRI Notes 1 (Nov. 1992). The reason COBRA coverage has been so costly is that COBRA invites adverse selection. Persons entitled to COBRA coverage who are young and healthy can buy other insurance cheaply, and such people are also the most likely to be quickly reemployed with health coverage from the new employer. Thus, the former employer "is stuck with providing COBRA coverage to the high-risk qualified beneficiaries. The result is that the individuals who purchase COBRA coverage tend to use more medical services than active employees." 2 ERISA Litigation Reporter 7 (Oct. 1993).

3. *Notice rules.* Section 606 requires the group health plan to provide a "written notice to each covered employee and spouse of the employee" regarding his or her COBRA rights at the commencement of coverage under the plan and when a qualifying event occurs. This section also requires the covered employee or qualified beneficiary to notify the administrator when a qualifying event occurs. Section 605(1) requires that qualified beneficiaries be given at least 60 days after the qualifying event or the date of the § 606 notice to make the COBRA health care continuation election. It has been held that notice to the employee does not satisfy the spouse's right to notice of his or her COBRA rights. McDowell v. Krawchison, 125 F.3d 954 (6th Cir.1997).

Suppose the employee claims that he or she never received notice of his or her COBRA rights? In Truesdale v. Pacific Holding Co./Hay Adams Division, 778 F.Supp. 77 (D.D.C.1991), the court said that the employer's mailing of the COBRA notice to the employee's last known address indicated on her employment application and on an employee data card created a presumption of good-faith compliance with the statutory notice requirement. (Notice the resemblance to the so-called mailbox rule of contract law, that the acceptance is presumed effective upon mailing, even if not received.) The court in *Truesdale* found that evidence that the address used was imperfect did not overcome the presumption, since the employer had sent other important documents to the address, which had been received.

In Degruise v. Sprint Corp., 279 F.3d 333 (5th Cir.2002), the employer sent the COBRA notice by certified mail to the employee, but the post office mishandled it and returned it to the employer marked "undelivered." Even though the employer knew that the notice had not been received, the court held that the employer's good faith effort at compliance sufficed. Should ERISA fiduciary law, especially the duty to inform plan participants discussed in Chapter 13 be read to require an employer in such a case to make further efforts to locate and notify the participant?

In Scott v. Suncoast Beverage Sales, Ltd., 295 F.3d 1223 (11th Cir.2002), the employer, Suncoast, routinely used a third party service provider to send out COBRA notices. Suncoast notified that provider to send a COBRA notice to Scott. Scott claimed not to have received it. There was no evidence bearing directly on whether the provider had sent the notice. Suncoast contended that it had acted in the requisite good faith. Does that defense suffice?

Does a mistaken COBRA notice bind the employer? In National Companies Health Benefit Plan v. St. Joseph's Hospital, 929 F.2d 1558 (11th Cir.1991), a former employee elected COBRA coverage that was offered in error, and to which he was not entitled under COBRA. His wife gave birth to twins with medical complications requiring costly medical care, and the employer attempted to deny the medical coverage. The Eleventh Circuit held that the former employee had detrimentally relied upon the employer's representation of continued coverage by not electing to purchase alternative coverage available to him through his wife's employer, and thus that his employer could not disaffirm the mistakenly provided COBRA coverage.

As a remedial matter, in the event that the plan administrator fails to give the required notice, a court may treat the employee or qualified beneficiary as having made the COBRA election. Swint v. Protective Life Insurance Co., 779 F.Supp. 532 (S.D.Ala.1991). Accordingly, the employer can be liable for the medical bills that the lapsed insurance would have covered. Smith v. Rogers Galvanizing Co., 128 F.3d 1380 (10th Cir.1997).

The tension between plan terms and the description in a summary plan description (SPD), discussed in Chapter 13, also arises in connection with the SPD's description of COBRA terms. The courts protect reliance upon the SPD. Fallo v. Piccadilly Cafeterias, Inc., 141 F.3d 580, 584 (5th Cir.1998) ("where the requirements of the SPD are more lenient than those contained in the Plan, the SPD is controlling").

4. *Delay in electing coverage.* Courts have suspended the 60-day COBRA period for electing continuation coverage in circumstances in which the qualified person is incompetent to make the election. See, e.g., Branch v. G. Bernd Co., 955 F.2d 1574 (11th Cir.1992) (election period held tolled from date of incapacitation until the date that a guardian was empowered to make the election); Sirkin v. Phillips Colleges, Inc., 779 F.Supp. 751 (D.N.J.1991) (incompetent entitled to reinstate coverage by paying amount due within reasonable time after guardian was appointed to act for her).

5. *Gross misconduct.* COBRA's principal qualifying event is the termination of employment for reasons other than the employee's "gross misconduct." ERISA § 603(2). In Burke v. American Stores Employee Benefit Plan, 818 F.Supp. 1131 (N.D.Ill.1993), the court followed Illinois law for determining eligibility for unemployment benefits if an employee is discharged for misconduct. The court held that theft of coupons for free turkeys constituted "gross misconduct" and justified denial of COBRA benefits. Theft is an easy case. Contrast Avina v. Texas Pig Stands, Inc., 1991 WL 458848 (W.D.Tex.1991), in which the court defined "gross misconduct" to include "substantial deviation from the high standards and obligations of a managerial employee that would indicate that said employee cannot be entrusted with his management duties without

danger to the employer." The court found that cash handling irregularities qualified as "gross misconduct."

Suppose the employer turns out to be mistaken in thinking the employee to have engaged in acts of gross misconduct? In Kariotis v. Navistar Int'l Transp. Corp., 131 F.3d 672 (7th Cir.1997), the employer had a private investigator surreptitiously videotape the behavior of an employee who was dismissed for suspected malingering. The employee's physician, whom the employer did not consult before terminating the employee, insisted that the employee was indeed disabled. The Seventh Circuit held that the employer's honest belief protected it from liability under ADA, ADEA, and ERISA § 510, but not under COBRA. "While antidiscrimination statutes compel us to discern an employer's intentions, COBRA does not. It is a welfare benefit statute, not a wrongful discharge statute." Id. at 679.

An employee was dismissed for violating a company rule against breaching confidentiality regarding another employee. The employer deemed the behavior to be gross misconduct. The employee sued for COBRA benefits. What result? See Paris v. F. Korbel & Bros., 751 F.Supp. 834 (N.D.Cal.1990).

6. *Dual coverage.* Section 602(2)(D) provides that the qualified beneficiary loses COBRA coverage if he or she becomes covered under another plan. The Supreme Court dealt with a dual coverage case in Geissal v. Moore Medical Corp., 524 U.S. 74 (1998). The Court read ERISA § 602(2)(D)(i) to support a distinction between an employee who gains coverage under another plan after making his COBRA election, and an employee whose coverage under the other plan (typically, as in *Geissal*, under a spouse's plan with the spouse's employer) existed at the time he made his COBRA election. For background, see Paul M. Hamburger, *Geissal v. Moore Medical Corp.*—A Case of Textual Orientation, 7 ERISA Litigation Reporter 9 (Jun. 1998); Sarah R. Cole, Continuation Coverage Under COBRA: A Study in Statutory Interpretation, 22 J. Legislation 195 (1996).

2. OTHER FEDERAL ENACTMENTS

As has been emphasized, health care plans are voluntary, in the sense that employers are not required to offer such plans, and many employers, especially smaller employers, do not. However, in the 1980s Congress began to regulate the contents of health care plans by insisting that, if offered, the plans must provide certain benefits. (COBRA benefits described just above exemplify such mandated features.)

Following the defeat of the Clinton Administration's national health insurance proposals in 1994, Congress enacted a number of additional special-purpose health benefit mandates, which are collected in Part 7 of ERISA Title I. These include the Health Insurance Portability and Accountability Act of 1996, codified as ERISA §§ 701–703, restricting the scope of preexisting condition exclusions; the Newborns' and Mothers' Health Protection Act of 1996, codified as § 711, directed at so-called drive-by deliveries, requiring plan coverage for a minimum of 48 hours of hospital care for mother and infant; the Mental Health Parity Act of 1996, expanded in 2008 and codified as ERISA § 712, forbidding a health plan to apply limits on mental health care different from the plan's limits on other care; the Women's Health and Cancer Rights Act of 1998, codified as ERISA § 713, requiring coverage of post-mastectomy reconstructive surgery; and the Genetic Information Nondiscrimination Act of 2008, codified in ERISA § 702.

The following statutes, in addition to COBRA, affect health plans:

1. *The 1993 QMCSO addition.* The Omnibus Budget Reconciliation Act of 1993 (OBRA '93) amended ERISA Title I, Part 6, to add new ERISA § 609, which requires health plans to comply with any court-ordered "Qualified Medical Child Support Order" (QMCSO). "A QMCSO is a child support order, judgment or decree (including a court-approved marital settlement agreement) that creates or recognizes the right of a child to receive benefits from a parent's group health [plan]. A QMCSO has been dubbed by some as a 'Kiddie-QDRO' because its relationship to a health plan is similar to a Qualified Domestic relations Order's (QDRO) relationship to an employer-sponsored retirement plan." Janet M. Hill, Group Health Plans: New Requirements Under OBRA '93, Probate & Property 17 (Jul.–Aug. 1994). (The QDRO rules are discussed in Chapter 7)

The QMCSO provisions of new ERISA § 609 were placed with the COBRA rules in Title I, Part 6, presumably because § 609 deals with health care, but the QMCSO provisions differ fundamentally from the COBRA rules. The COBRA rules require only transitional continuation of benefits, whereas the QMCSO rules mandate plan recognition of state court decrees requiring long term plan eligibility for children of a dissolving family.

The QMCSO will usually be a decree of a state domestic relations court, designating the child as an "alternate recipient" of the health plan's benefits. The QMCSO effectively inserts the alternate recipient as a plan participant, and it may not require the plan to provide any benefit that the plan does not otherwise provide. See generally William F. Brown, What the Heck Is a QMSCO and How Do You Get One?, 22 J. Pension Planning & Compliance 48 (1996). For one of the few reported QMCSO cases, see O'Neil v. Wal-Mart Corp., 502 F.Supp.2d 318 (N.D.N.Y.2007) (holding that a stepchild is a valid "alternate recipient" so long as the stepchild is a dependent child).

2. *Uniformed Services Employment and Reemployment Rights Act of 1994* (mentioned in Chapter 18) provides expanded employee benefit protections for individuals who return from service in the armed forces.

3. *Health Insurance Portability and Accountability Act of 1996 (HIPAA).* HIPAA added ERISA Title I, Part 7, and amended ERISA Title I, Part 6, to impose certain portability requirements upon employer-provided and other health insurance. The legislation limits the application of preexisting condition exclusions to individuals who change jobs.

4. *Mental Health Parity Act of 1996 (MHPA).* Codified as ERISA § 712, the MHPA requires health plans to offer the same annual and lifetime dollar limits for mental health coverage that pertain to medical and surgical health benefits. The law does not apply to benefits for substance abuse or chemical dependency and contains exemptions for

small employers and for any health plan or coverage if application of the parity provisions would result in an increase in cost of at least one percent.

5.   *Defense of Marriage Act of 1996 (DOMA)*. For purposes of federal law, DOMA defined "marriage" as "a legal union between one man and one woman as husband and wife"; it defined "spouse" as "a person of the opposite sex who is a husband or a wife." After DOMA, rights that were contingent upon marriage or spousal status were unavailable to same-sex domestic partners unless the plan instrument provided otherwise. On June 26, 2013, the Supreme Court, in a 5–4 decision, held that the above provision of DOMA is unconstitutional as a deprivation of the equal liberty of persons protected by the Fifth Amendment. U.S. v. Windsor, 133 S.Ct. 2675 2013. See Chapter 18 for further discussion.

6.   *Newborns' and Mothers' Health Protection Act of 1996*. The Act, codified as ERISA § 711, was directed at health plan cost containment measures that had resulted in short-term hospital stays for childbirth ("drive-by deliveries"). The Act requires plans to cover at least 48 hours of hospitalization for mothers and newborns after conventional deliveries and at least 96 hours of hospitalization following caesarean sections.

7.   *Women's Health and Cancer Rights Act of 1998*. The Act, codified as ERISA § 713, requires health plans to cover post-mastectomy reconstructive surgery.

8.   *Medicare Prescription Drug, Improvement, and Modernization Act of 2003* created health savings accounts.

9.   *Genetic Information Nondiscrimination Act of 2008*: Title I of GINA prohibits group health plans and health insurance issuers from discriminating, on the basis of genetic information, in eligibility, premiums, and contributions. Title II prohibits employers from discriminating on the basis of genetic information in employment decisions and from acquiring genetic information except in limited circumstances (*e.g.*, wellness programs that meet certain criteria). Genetic information includes information about genetic tests of an employee and the employee's family members, and also the family medical history. "Family members" is broadly defined. These rules have a significant impact on wellness programs.

10.   *Mental Health Parity and Addiction Equity Act of 2008* (MHPAEA) expanded the protections under MHPA and requires that financial requirements (co-pays, deductibles) and treatment limitations (such as visit limits) applicable to mental health and substance use disorder (MH/SUD) benefits are no more restrictive than the predominant requirements or limitations applied to substantially all medical or surgical benefits. The Act does not require plans to provide MH/SUD benefits.

11.   *American Recovery and Reinvestment Act of 2009* (the Act) provides premium assistance for COBRA benefits and COBRA-type benefits required under state law. The Act expands HIPAA privacy requirements to employees of covered entities (health care providers that conduct certain electronic transactions, health care clearinghouses, and health plans) and to individual or corporate persons that perform any function or activity involving the use or disclosure of protected health

information (PHI) on behalf of a covered entity ("business associates"). The Health Information Technology for Economic and Clinical Health Act (HITECH), enacted as part of the Act, significantly increases penalties for noncompliance with the HIPAA privacy requirements.

12. *Children's Health Insurance Program Reauthorization Act of 2009* extends the Children's Health Insurance Program (CHIP), allows states to subsidize premiums for employer-provided group health coverage for eligible children and families, and amends ERISA to provide special enrollment rights, new notice and disclosure obligations, and penalties for non-compliance.

D. POST-ERISA STATE REGULATION: PREEMPTION REVISITED

Not only the federal government but also some of the states sought, in the years after ERISA, to take steps to improve access to health insurance by mandating types of medical coverage or expanding the scope of health benefit plans or rights. These state efforts have, however, often run head-on into the broad preemption clause of ERISA Section 514, which we first encountered above in Chapter 17. The following materials illustrate the interplay that has arisen between state efforts to regulate or expand health insurance coverage and judicial interpretation of ERISA's preemption clause. In this context the insurance "savings clause" of Section 514, as well as the "deemer clause," both introduced in Chapter 17 and discussed in the next case, have played particularly important roles.

1. METROPOLITAN LIFE INS. CO. V. MASSACHUSETTS

471 U.S. 724 (1985).

■ JUSTICE BLACKMUN delivered the opinion of the Court.

A Massachusetts statute requires that specified minimum mental healthcare benefits be provided a Massachusetts resident who is insured under a general insurance policy, an accident or sickness insurance policy, or an employee healthcare plan that covers hospital and surgical expenses. The [question] before us in these cases is whether the state statute, as applied to insurance policies purchased by employee healthcare plans regulated by the federal Employee Retirement Income Security Act of 1974, is preempted by that Act. . . .

General health insurance typically is sold as group insurance to an employer or other group. Group insurance presently is subject to extensive state regulation, including regulation of the carrier, regulation of the sale and advertising of the insurance, and regulation of the content of the contracts. Mandated-benefit laws, that require an insurer to provide a certain kind of benefit to cover a specified illness or procedure whenever someone purchases a certain kind of insurance, are a subclass of such content regulation.

While mandated-benefit statutes are a relatively recent phenomenon, statutes regulating the substantive terms of insurance contracts have become commonplace in all 50 States over the last 30 years. Perhaps the most familiar are those regulating the content of automobile insurance policies.

The substantive terms of group-health insurance contracts, in particular, also have been extensively regulated by the States. . . .

Mandated-benefit statutes, then, are only one variety of a matrix of state laws that regulate the substantive content of health-insurance policies to further state health policy. Massachusetts Gen.Laws Ann., ch. 175, § 47B is typical of mandated-benefit laws currently in place in the majority of States. With respect to a Massachusetts resident, it requires any general health-insurance policy that provides hospital and surgical coverage, or any benefit plan that has such coverage, to provide as well a certain minimum of mental-health protection. . . .

Section 47B was designed to address problems encountered in treating mental illness in Massachusetts. The Commonwealth determined that its working people needed to be protected against the high cost of treatment for such illness. It also believed that, without insurance, mentally ill workers were often institutionalized in large state mental hospitals, and that mandatory insurance would lead to a higher incidence of more effective treatment in private community mental-health centers.

In addition, the Commonwealth concluded that the voluntary insurance market was not adequately providing mental-health coverage, because of "adverse selection" in mental-health insurance: good insurance risks were not purchasing coverage, and this drove up the price of coverage for those who otherwise might purchase mental-health insurance. The legislature believed that the public interest required that it correct the insurance market in the Commonwealth by mandating minimum-coverage levels, effectively forcing the good-risk individuals to become part of the risk pool, and enabling insurers to price the insurance at an average market rather than a market retracted due to adverse selection. . . .

[Appellant] Metropolitan [argues] that ERISA preempts Massachusetts' mandated-benefit law insofar as § 47B restricts the kinds of insurance policies that benefit plans may purchase.

While § 514(a) of ERISA broadly preempts state laws that relate to an employee-benefit plan, that preemption is substantially qualified by an "insurance saving clause," § 514(b)(2)(A), which broadly states that, with one exception, nothing in ERISA "shall be construed to exempt or relieve any person from any law of any State which regulates insurance, banking, or securities." The specified exception to the saving clause is found in § 514(b)(2)(B), the so-called "deemer clause," which states that no employee-benefit plan, with certain exceptions not relevant here, "shall be deemed to be an insurance company or other insurer, bank, trust company, or investment company or to be engaged in the business of insurance or banking for purposes of any law of any State purporting to regulate insurance companies, insurance contracts, banks, trust companies, or investment companies." Massachusetts argues that its mandated-benefit law, as applied to insurance companies that sell insurance to benefit plans, is a "law which regulates insurance," and therefore is saved from the effect of the general preemption clause of ERISA. . . .

Appellants are [insurers] who are located in New York and Connecticut respectively and who issue group-health policies providing hospital and surgical coverage to plans, or to employers or unions that employ or represent employees residing in Massachusetts. Under the terms of § 47B, both appellants are required to provide minimal mental-health benefits in policies issued to cover Commonwealth residents.

In 1979, the Attorney General of Massachusetts brought suit in Massachusetts Superior Court for declaratory and injunctive relief to enforce § 47B. The Commonwealth asserted that since January 1, 1976, the effective date of § 47B, the insurers had issued policies to group policyholders situated outside Massachusetts that provided for hospital and surgical coverage for certain residents of the Commonwealth. It further asserted that those policies failed to provide Massachusetts-resident beneficiaries the mental-health coverage mandated by § 47B, and that the insurers intended to issue more such policies, believing themselves not bound by § 47B for policies issued outside the Commonwealth. In their answer, the insurers admitted these allegations. . . .

The Superior Court issued a preliminary injunction requiring the insurers to provide the coverage mandated by § 47B. After trial, a different judge issued a permanent injunction to the same [effect]. [The] Supreme Judicial Court of Massachusetts granted the insurers' application for direct appellate review and affirmed the judgment of the Superior Court. . . .

The narrow statutory ERISA question presented is whether § 47B is a law "which regulates insurance" within the meaning of § 514(b)(2)(A), and so would not be preempted by § 514(a). . . .

The insurers nonetheless argue that § 47B is in reality a health law that merely operates on insurance contracts to accomplish its end, and that it is not the kind of traditional insurance law intended to be saved by § 514(b)(2)(A). We find this argument unpersuasive.

Initially, nothing in § 514(b)(2)(A), or in the "deemer clause" which modifies it, purports to distinguish between traditional and innovative insurance laws. The presumption is against preemption, and we are not inclined to read limitations into federal statutes in order to enlarge their preemptive scope. Further, there is no indication in the legislative history that Congress had such a distinction in mind.

Appellants assert that state laws that directly regulate the insurer, and laws that regulate such matters as the way in which insurance may be sold, are traditional laws subject to the clause, while laws that regulate the substantive terms of insurance contracts are recent innovations more properly seen as health laws rather than as insurance laws, which § 514(b)(2)(A) does not save. This distinction reads the saving clause out of ERISA entirely, because laws that regulate only the insurer, or the way in which it may sell insurance, do not "relate to" benefit plans in the first instance. Because they would not be preempted by § 514(a), they do not need to be "saved" by § 514(b)(2)(A). There is no indication that Congress could have intended the saving clause to operate only to guard against too expansive readings of the general preemption clause that might have included laws wholly unrelated to plans. Appellants' construction, in our view, violates the plain meaning of the statutory language and renders redundant both the saving clause it is construing, as well as the deemer clause which it precedes, and accordingly has little to recommend it.

Moreover, it is both historically and conceptually inaccurate to assert that mandated-benefit laws are not traditional insurance laws. As we have indicated, state laws regulating the substantive terms of insurance contracts were commonplace well before the mid-70's, when Congress considered ERISA. The case law concerning the meaning of the phrase "business of insurance" in the McCarran-Ferguson Act, also strongly supports the conclusion that regulation regarding the substantive terms of insurance contracts falls squarely within the saving clause as laws "which regulate insurance."

Cases interpreting the scope of the McCarran-Ferguson Act have identified three criteria relevant to determining whether a particular practice falls within that Act's reference to the "business of insurance": "*first,* whether the practice has the effect of transferring or spreading a policyholder's risk; *second,* whether the practice is an integral part of the policy relationship between the insurer and the insured; and *third,* whether the practice is limited to entities within the insurance industry." Application of these principles suggests that mandated-benefit laws are state regulation of the "business of insurance."

Section 47B obviously regulates the spreading of risk: as we have indicated, it was intended to effectuate the legislative judgment that the risk of mental-health care should be shared. It is also evident that mandated-benefit laws directly regulate an integral part of the relationship between the insurer and the policyholder by limiting the type of insurance that an insurer may sell to the policyholder. Finally, the third criterion is present here, for mandated-benefit statutes impose requirements only on insurers, with the intent of affecting the relationship between the insurer and the policyholder. Section 47B, then, is the very kind of regulation that this Court has identified as a law that relates to the regulation of the business of insurance as defined in the McCarran-Ferguson Act. . . .

In short, the plain language of the saving clause, its relationship to the other ERISA preemption provisions, and the traditional understanding of insurance regulation, all lead us to the conclusion that mandated-benefit laws such as § 47B are saved from preemption by the operation of the saving clause.

Nothing in the legislative history of ERISA suggests a different result. There is no discussion in that history of the relationship between the general preemption clause and the saving clause, and indeed very little discussion of the saving clause at all. In the early versions of ERISA, the general preemption clause preempted only those state laws dealing with subjects regulated by ERISA . . .

We therefore decline to impose any limitation on the saving clause beyond those Congress imposed in the clause itself and in the "deemer clause" which modifies it. If a state law "regulates insurance," as mandated-benefit laws do, it is not preempted. Nothing in the language, structure, or legislative history of the Act supports a more narrow reading of the clause, whether it be the Supreme Judicial Court's attempt to save only state regulations unrelated to the substantive provisions of ERISA, or the insurers' more speculative attempt to read the saving clause out of the statute.

We are aware that our decision results in a distinction between insured and uninsured plans, leaving the former open to indirect regulation while the latter are not. By so doing we merely give life to a distinction created by Congress in the "deemer clause," a distinction Congress is aware of and one it has chosen not to alter. We also are aware that appellants' construction of the statute would eliminate some of the disuniformities currently facing national plans that enter into local markets to purchase insurance. Such disuniformities, however, are the inevitable result of the congressional decision to "save" local insurance regulation. Arguments as to the wisdom of these policy choices must be directed at Congress. . . .

We hold that Massachusetts' mandated-benefit law is a "law which regulates insurance" and so is not preempted by ERISA as it applies to insurance contracts purchased for plans subject to ERISA.

2. THE INSURANCE EXCEPTION

1. *The purpose behind the insurance exception.* The insurance savings clause is meant to reconcile ERISA with the policy of the McCarran-Ferguson Act of 1945, 15 U.S.C. §§ 1011–1015, which remits insurance regulation to the states. But in excepting insurance from ERISA preemption, Congress undermined the otherwise fundamental policy of ERISA, to achieve uniform federal regulation for employee benefit plans. Why should ERISA forbid that interference with the calculation of pension benefits that New Jersey attempted in *Alessi,* while allowing Massachusetts to interfere with the terms of health plans as in *Metropolitan Life*? If ERISA is wise to promote national uniformity in plan design and administration, can the insurance exception be defended? Regarding tensions inherent in the present system, see Jonathan R. Macey & Geoffrey P. Miller, The McCarran-Ferguson Act of 1945: Reconceiving the Federal Role of Insurance Regulation, 68 N.Y.U.L. Rev. 13 (1993).

The insurance industry sought and defends the McCarran-Ferguson Act, preferring state to federal regulation. The suggestion is sometimes made that the industry is better able to get its way in state legislatures and state regulatory commissions than if it faced SEC-type regulation at the federal level. Notice, however, that in *Metropolitan Life* it was the insurance companies who were seeking to escape the insurance exception and to preempt state law.

The Supreme Court gives a respectful account of the purposes of § 47B of the Massachusetts statute. In interest-group terms, whom do you suppose was really behind § 47B?

2. *Mandated provider laws: health or insurance?* The Supreme Court in *Metropolitan Life* found "unpersuasive" the insurers' argument that § 47B was better characterized as a "health" law than an "insurance"

law. The insurers urged that the insurance savings clause be limited to "state laws that directly regulate the insurer, and laws that regulate such matters as the way in which insurance may be [sold]." 471 U.S. at 741. The Court found linguistic grounds for dismissing this distinction. Consider, however, whether as a matter of policy such a distinction might have helped reconcile the conflicting interests in minimizing state interference in plan design and administration while preserving traditional spheres of state regulatory authority over the insurance industry.

3. *The deemer clause and self-insured plans.* Fox and Schaffer, excerpted in Section A.2 of Chapter 17, "call the result of [ERISA § 514] 'semi-preemption' because the statute has been read to mean that the states can regulate employer-provided health insurance if the employer buys it from an insurance company but not if the employer self-insures." Fox & Schaffer, supra, at 48. When the employer self-insures, the plan is outside the insurance savings clause and state regulation is preempted. The deemer clause, ERISA § 514(b)(2)(B), reinforces this result. As a matter of federal policy, can it be desirable to encourage employers to self-insure?

One reason to self-insure is that it may simply be cheaper to bear a risk than to pay an insurer to bear it. But ERISA has created a powerful additional incentive. By self-insuring, an employer can avoid having to pay for the whole range of benefits mandated by state law for insured plans. The Supreme Court made clear in *Metropolitan Life* that self-insured plans could not be required to provide the benefits mandated by the Massachusetts statute.

For large employers, the risks of self-insurance may be minimal, but for small employers self-insurance is extremely risky. One employee's catastrophic illness could bankrupt the firm. One common solution for such employers is to purchase so-called "stop-loss" insurance, which insures the employer against the event of costs exceeding a specified threshold. So far the circuits have been unanimous in holding that self-funded plans that purchase stop-loss insurance remain self-funded for ERISA purposes and are therefore not subject to state regulation. See, e.g., Bill Gray Enterprises, Inc. Employee Health and Welfare Plan v. Gourley, 248 F.3d 206 (3d Cir.2001) ($40,000 threshold); Lincoln Mutual Casualty Co. v. Lectron Products, Inc., 970 F.2d 206 (6th Cir.1992)($75,000 threshold); Thompson v. Talquin Building Products Co., 928 F.2d 649 (4th Cir.1991)($25,000 threshold). See also Administrative Co. of Wal-Mart Associates Health & Welfare Plan v. Willard, 302 F.Supp.2d 1267 (D.Kan.2004), aff'd, 393 F.3d 1119 (10th Cir.2004) (citing with approval cases finding the stop-loss insurance does not change the self-funded status of a plan). Maryland tried to circumvent these holdings by establishing a minimum attachment point ($10,000 per beneficiary) for stop-loss insurance and deeming stop-loss insurance policies with lower attachment points to be health insurance and therefore subject to Maryland's mandatory benefit laws. By directly regulating only the stop-loss insurance policy and not the plan, Maryland had hoped to avoid preemption. But in American Medical Security, Inc. v. Bartlett, 111 F.3d 358, 363 (4th Cir.1997), the Fourth Circuit nevertheless held the Maryland regulations preempted by ERISA.

Because "their purpose and effect are directed at self-funded [plans]," the regulations ran afoul of the deemer clause.

Would the result be different if the stop-loss policy insured claims in excess of $100 per employee? $1? The reasoning of the Third Circuit in *Bill Gray Enterprises* would suggest not:

> Merely by purchasing stop-loss insurance and at the same time retaining financial responsibility for plan participants' coverage, self-funded plans may not rely on the assets of an insurance company in the event of insolvency. It follows that reimbursement and subrogation rights are vital to ensuring the financial stability of self-funded plans. Consistent with other courts of appeals, therefore, we hold that when an ERISA plan purchases stop-loss insurance but does not otherwise delegate its financial responsibilities to another third party insurer, it remains an uninsured self-funded welfare plan for ERISA preemption purposes. Because stop-loss insurance is designed to protect self-funded employee benefit plans, rather than individual participants, plans purchasing stop-loss insurance are not deemed "insured" under ERISA.

248 F.3d at 214.

In Technical Release 2014–01, Guidance on State Regulation of Stop-Loss Insurance, November 6, 2014, DoL noted that "The National Association of Insurance Commissioners (NAIC) subsequently adopted a model law that prohibits the sale of stop-loss insurance with a specific annual attachment point below $20,000. For groups of 50 or fewer, the aggregate annual attachment point must be at least the greater of (i) $4,000 times the number of group members, (ii) 120% of expected claims, or (iii) $20,000. For groups of 51 or more, the model law prohibited an annual aggregate attachment point that was lower than 110% of expected claims." DoL concluded that "States may regulate insurance policies issued to plans or plan sponsors, including stop-loss insurance policies, if the law regulates the insurance company and the business of insurance. Insurance regulation of group health insurance clearly limits insurance policy choices available to third parties, including employee benefit plans. Insurance regulation of stop-loss insurance can have a similar consequence without ERISA preempting the insurance regulation. Thus, a State law that prohibits insurers from issuing stop-loss contracts with attachment points below specified levels would not, in the Department's view, be preempted by ERISA. Thus far, about ten States have enacted laws using the same approach as the NAIC model. The Department is not aware of any challenges to such laws based on ERISA preemption."

4. *The movement away from the McCarran-Ferguson factors.* In *Metropolitan Life,* the Supreme Court applied the three criteria developed under the McCarran-Ferguson Act in determining whether Massachusetts' mandated benefit law was a law regulating insurance. The criteria are "*first,* whether the practice has the effect of transferring or spreading a policyholder's risk; *second,* whether the practice is an integral part of the policy relationship between the insurer and the insured; and *third,* whether the practice is limited to entities within the insurance industry." 471 U.S. at 743.

The Supreme Court first signaled a move away from the McCarran-Ferguson factors in its 1999 decision in Unum Life Insurance Co. of America v. Ward, 526 U.S. 358 (1999). *Ward* involved the question whether ERISA preempts California's notice-prejudice rule, under which an insurer cannot avoid liability when insured persons submit claims outside the time limit set in the insurance policy in the absence of a showing that the insurer was prejudiced by the delay. After determining that California's law appears to regulate insurance "as a matter of common sense," the Court turned to the McCarran-Ferguson factors. It began its analysis by rejecting Unum's claim that an insurance regulation must satisfy all three McCarran-Ferguson factors to be a law regulating insurance.

> Our precedent is more supple than Unum conceives it to be. We have indicated that the McCarran-Ferguson factors are 'considerations [to be] weighed' in determining whether a state law regulates insurance, [and] that, '[n]one of these criteria is necessarily determinative in itself.' [*Metropolitan Life*] asked first whether the law there in question 'fit a common-sense understanding of insurance regulation,' and then looked to the McCarran-Ferguson factors as checking points or 'guideposts, not separate essential elements . . . that must each be satisfied' to save the State's law.

Id. at 373–74. The Court found that California's notice-prejudice rule satisfied the second and third elements of McCarran-Ferguson, since it was an integral part of the relationship between the insurer and the insured and was limited to entities in the insurance industry. Accordingly, the Court did not have to engage with the lower court's determination that the statute did not have the effect of transferring or spreading a policyholder's risk.

A year later, the Supreme Court had another occasion to address the question of what constitutes regulating insurance under ERISA § 514(b)(2)(A). In Rush Prudential HMO v. Moran, 536 U.S. 355 (2002), the Court addressed whether ERISA preempted the independent review provision of Illinois' Health Maintenance Organization Act, which gave recipients of health coverage from such organizations the right to independent medical review of benefit denials. Although the Court invoked the McCarran-Ferguson factors to determine whether the independent review provision was a law regulating insurance, it again observed that "the factors are guideposts, a state law is not required to satisfy all three McCarran-Ferguson criteria to survive preemption." Id. at 373. Because the state law satisfied the second and third criteria, the Court said it need not determine whether the mandated independent review had the effect of transferring or spreading a policyholder's risk in order to conclude that the law regulated insurance.

5.   *Miller.* A year after *Rush*, the Court completed its movement away from the *McCarran-Ferguson* factors as the test for whether a law regulates insurance in Kentucky Association of Health Plans v. Miller, 538 U.S. 329 (2003).

Kentucky law provides that "[a] health insurer shall not discriminate against any provider who is located within the geographic coverage area of the health benefit plan and who is willing to meet the terms and conditions for participation established by the health insurer, including the Kentucky state Medicaid program and Medicaid partnerships." Ky.Rev.Stat. Ann. § 04.17A 270 (West 2001). Moreover, any "health benefit plan that includes chiropractic benefits shall . . . [p]ermit any licensed chiropractor who agrees to abide by the terms, conditions, reimbursement rates, and standards of quality of the health benefit plan to serve as a participating primary chiropractic provider to any person covered by the plan." § 304.17A171(2). The Supreme Court granted certiorari to decide whether ERISA preempts either, or both, of these "Any Willing Provider" (AWP) statutes.

Petitioners included several HMOs and a Kentucky-based association of HMOs. In order to control the quality and cost of healthcare delivery, these HMOs had contracted with selected doctors, hospitals, and other healthcare providers to create exclusive "provider networks." Providers in such networks agreed to render healthcare services to the HMOs' subscribers at discounted rates and to comply with other contractual requirements. In return, they received the benefit of patient volume higher than that achieved by non-network providers who lacked access to petitioners' subscribers.

Kentucky's AWP statutes impaired petitioners' ability to limit the number of providers with access to their networks, and thus their ability to use the assurance of high patient volume as the *quid pro quo* for the discounted rates that network membership entails. Petitioners believed that AWP laws would frustrate their efforts at cost and quality control, and would ultimately deny consumers the benefit of their cost-reducing arrangements with providers.

In April 1997, petitioners filed suit against the Commissioner of Kentucky's Department of Insurance, in the United States District Court for the Eastern District of Kentucky, asserting that ERISA preempts Kentucky's AWP laws. [The] District Court concluded that although both AWP statutes "relate to" employee benefit plans under [ERISA § 514(a)], each law "regulates insurance" and is therefore saved from preemption by [ERISA § 514(b)(2)(A)]. In affirming the District Court, the Sixth Circuit also concluded that the AWP laws "regulat[e] insurance" and fell within ERISA's savings clause. The Supreme Court affirmed, in a decision by Justice Scalia.

Petitioners claimed that Kentucky's statutes were not "specifically directed toward" insurers because they regulated not only the insurance industry but also doctors who seek to form and maintain limited provider networks with HMOs. . . .

The Court stated that "regulations "directed toward" certain entities will almost always disable other entities from doing, with the regulated entities, what the regulations forbid; this does not suffice to place such regulation outside the scope of ERISA's savings clause."

Petitioners also claimed that the AWP laws did not regulate insurers with respect to an insurance practice because, they did not control the actual terms of insurance policies. Rather, they focused upon the relationship between an insurer and *third-party providers*—which in petitioners' view does not constitute an "insurance practice."

The Court emphasized "that conditions on the right to engage in the business of insurance must also substantially affect the risk pooling arrangement between the insurer and the insured to be covered by ERISA's savings clause. . . . By expanding the number of providers from whom an insured may receive health services, AWP laws alter the scope of permissible bargains between insurers and insureds in a manner similar to the mandated-benefit laws we upheld in *Metropolitan Life*, the notice prejudice rule we sustained in *[Ward]*, and the independent-review provisions we approved in *Rush Prudential*. No longer may Kentucky insureds seek insurance from a closed network of healthcare providers in exchange for a lower premium. The AWP prohibition substantially affects the type of risk pooling arrangements that insurers may offer."

The Court concluded: "Today we make a clean break from the McCarran-Ferguson factors and hold that for a state law to be deemed a "law . . . which regulates insurance" under § 514(b)(2)(A), it must satisfy two requirements. First, the state law must be specifically directed toward entities engaged in insurance. See *Pilot Life*, *[Ward]*, *Rush Prudential*. Second, as explained above, the state law must substantially affect the risk pooling arrangement between the insurer and the insured. Kentucky's law satisfies each of these requirements."

3. DETERMINING WHETHER A LAW REGULATES INSURANCE POST-*MILLER*

1. *The Court's "clean break."* According to the Court in *Miller*, a state law regulates insurance if (1) it is specifically directed toward entities engaged in insurance, and (2) substantially affects the risk pooling arrangements between the insurer and the insured. While the *Miller* framework is simpler than the abandoned McCarran-Ferguson test, is it an improvement? Interestingly, under the new test, affecting the risk pooling arrangement is now central; recall that the McCarran-Ferguson factor that went to shifting risk was the one that the Court ignored both in *Rush* and in *Ward*.

2. *Bad faith claims.* A variety of state law cause of action that has generated considerable case law is that of bad faith claim processing, which was at issue in one of the earliest Supreme Court decisions. Pilot Life Ins. Co. v. Dedeaux, 481 U.S. 41 (1987). Pilot Life administered a disability benefit plan for Dedeaux's employer. Following an injury, Dedeaux applied for benefits under the plan. Pilot Life paid benefits for two years, then terminated and reinstated benefits several times over the next three years as it reviewed the evidence in the case. Dedeaux sued Pilot Life in a diversity action, alleging Mississippi state law grounds, including "tortious breach of contract," also described as "the Mississippi law of bad faith." He sought both compensatory damages for emotional distress and punitive damages. The Mississippi cause of action was not preempted, he argued, because it "regulates insurance" within the meaning of ERISA's insurance savings clause. The Supreme Court unanimously rejected the argument and held the claim preempted. "Even though the Mississippi Supreme Court [has] identified its law of bad faith with the insurance industry, the roots of this law are firmly planted in the general principles of Mississippi tort and contract law." Id. at 50. Applying the McCarran-Ferguson formulation set forth in *Metropolitan*

Life, the court in *Pilot Life* found that the Mississippi common law of bad faith exhibited neither of the first two McCarran-Ferguson criteria and met the third only tenuously if at all. Id. at 50–51.

Notwithstanding *Pilot Life,* some lower courts have concluded that a bad faith claim should not be preempted because it is a law regulating insurance. See, e.g., Stone v. Disability Management Services, 288 F.Supp.2d 684 (M.D.Pa.2003); Rosenbaum v. Unum Life Ins. Co., 2002 WL 1769899, 28 EBC (BNA) 2022 (E.D.Pa.2002) (unreported), *reconsideration denied,* 2002 WL 1769899, 31 EBC (BNA) 1541 (E.D.Pa.2003) (unreported). However, in the wake of *Miller,* the trend among courts is to find that the bad faith claim is not saved from ERISA preemption as a law regulating insurance, because it does not affect the risk pooling arrangement between the insurer and the insured. See, e.g., Barber v. Unum Life Ins. Co., 383 F.3d 134 (3d Cir.2004); Allison v. Unum Life Ins. Co., 381 F.3d 1015 (10th Cir.2004).

3. *Any willing provider statutes.* Health maintenance organizations (HMOs), often in the form of preferred provider organizations (PPOs), have become increasingly important health care providers. To control costs, HMOs usually limit in some fashion the participants' range of choice of health care providers (doctors, pharmacists, etc.) Pressured by excluded would-be providers, many states have adopted statutes like Kentucky's to compel HMOs to include additional providers. Prior to the Supreme Court's decision in *Miller,* lower courts had disagreed about whether ERISA preempted these "any willing provider" statutes. Compare Stuart Circle Hospital Corp. v. Aetna Health Management, 995 F.2d 500 (4th Cir.1993), cert. denied, 510 U.S. 1003 (1993) (saved as law regulating insurance) with CIGNA Healthplan of Louisiana v. State of Louisiana, 82 F.3d 642 (5th Cir.1996) (preempted because statute is not a law regulating insurance). *Miller* puts the disagreement to rest by holding that any willing provider statutes both are specifically directed toward entities engaged in insurance and substantially affect the risk pooling arrangement between the insurer and the insured. Nonetheless, two lower court decisions post-*Miller* have suggested that it is still necessary to examine whether the particular remedies provided under an Any Willing Provider statute conflict with ERISA's remedial scheme. See Prudential Insurance Co. of America v. National Park Medical Center, 413 F.3d 897 (8th Cir.2005); Quality Infusion Care, Inc. v. Unicare Health Plans of Texas, 2007 WL 760368 (S.D.Tex.2007). The issue of conflict with ERISA's remedial scheme is discussed further in Chapter 17.E supra.

As noted earlier in this chapter, the legislative history of ERISA's preemption provision is sparse, but Senator Williams, one of the Senate sponsors of ERISA, stated that "this language would preempt states from imposing on prepaid legal service plans a requirement of [open] rather than [closed] panels." Fox & Schaffer, supra. Is *Miller* consistent with the legislative history?

4. *State antisubrogation laws.* Many plans have subrogation clauses pursuant to which a participant agrees to reimburse the plan for benefits paid if the member recovers on a claim in a liability action against a third party. The tort bar is hostile to subrogation clauses and sometimes succeeds in obtaining state legislation restricting or

forbidding enforcement of such clauses. As mentioned in Chapter 17, in FMC Corp. v. Holliday, 498 U.S. 52 (1990), the Supreme Court addressed the question whether § 514 of ERISA preempted a Pennsylvania law precluding employee welfare benefit plans from exercising subrogation rights on a participant's tort recovery. The Court held that Pennsylvania's antisubrogation law "related to" an employee benefit plan and that ERISA's insurance savings clause protected it from preemption. Regarding the latter holding, the Court said that the statute "directly controls the terms of insurance contracts by invalidating subrogation provisions that they contain." Id. at 60. Nonetheless, the application of the statute to the plan at issue in *Holliday* was preempted, because the plan was self-funded. By virtue of the deemer clause, "self-funded ERISA plans are exempt from state regulation insofar as that regulation 'relates to' the plans. State laws directed toward the plans are preempted because they relate to an employee benefit plan but are not 'saved' because they do not regulate insurance. State laws that directly regulate insurance are 'saved' but do not reach self-funded employee benefit plans because the plans may not be deemed to be insurance companies, other insurers, or engaged in the business of insurance for purposes of such state laws." Id. at 61.

In the wake of *Miller*, courts continue to find that state laws dealing with subrogation are laws regulating insurance. In Singh v. Prudential Health Care Plan, 335 F.3d 278 (4th Cir.2003), cert. denied, 540 U.S. 1073 (2003), the Fourth Circuit addressed the question whether ERISA preempted provisions of the Maryland HMO Act that Maryland courts had read to prohibit HMOs from "pursu[ing] its members for restitution, reimbursement, or subrogation after the members have received damages from a third-party tortfeasor." *Id.* at 281. The court held that the Maryland HMO Act's prohibition against subrogation substantially affected risk pooling within the meaning of *Miller*. The court opined that it is difficult to "imagine an antisubrogation law [as] anything other than an insurance regulation, as it addresses who pays in a given set of circumstances and is therefore directed at spreading policyholder risk." Id. at 286. However, in Levine v. United Healthcare Corp., 402 F.3d 156 (3d Cir.2005), the Third Circuit held that because New Jersey's antisubrogation statute was not aimed solely at the insurance industry, the statute was not saved as a law regulating insurance and was thus preempted. The court observed that "New Jersey did not define [its statute] as an 'antisubrogation law,' nor did New Jersey place this statute among the statutes regulating insurance. Rather, the statute is entitled, 'Personal injury or wrongful death actions; benefits from sources other than joint tortfeasor; disclosure; deduction from plaintiff's award,' and is included in the portion of New Jersey's statutes dealing with civil actions. The plain language of the statute reveals that this statute is not limited to regulating either health insurance or liability insurance providers." *Id.* at 165.

5.   *Content conflict and the savings clause.* In Unum Life Insurance Co. of America v. Ward, 526 U.S. 358 (1999), discussed supra, the Court implied that § 514(b)(2)(A) of ERISA would not save a state insurance law from preemption if the law conflicted with a substantive provision of ERISA. The Court in *Ward* was persuaded that California's notice-prejudice rule did not present such a conflict, because the state law

merely provided a relevant rule of decision for a § 502(a) suit. In Rush Prudential HMO v. Moran, 536 U.S. 355 (2002), the Court reaffirmed the idea that a state insurance law would nonetheless be preempted if it conflicted with ERISA's remedial scheme. Although the Court ultimately found that the independent review provision at issue in the case did not create an alternative enforcement scheme, it gave substantial attention to the question. In Aetna Health Inc. v. Davila, 542 U.S. 200 (2004), reproduced infra, the Court reiterated that "[u]nder ordinary principles of conflict preemption, even a state law that can arguably be characterized as 'regulating insurance' will be preempted if it provides a separate vehicle to assert a claim for benefits outside of, or in addition to, ERISA's remedial scheme."

4. DAMAGE CLAIMS AGAINST HMOS AND INSURERS: *DAVILA*

Much of the controversy in recent years regarding ERISA preemption has arisen from court decisions preempting state causes of action against insurers and HMOs for wrongfully delaying or denying healthcare benefits. Without a state remedy, participants and beneficiaries are left with no effective remedy, because, as we saw in Chapter 16, ERISA's remedies are quite limited; punitive damages and damages for consequential injury are not permitted.

Many of the state law claims that have been brought against HMOs and insurers have involved state common law claims. Moreover, a number of states have passed their own statutes imposing duties and restrictions on managed care organizations. The Supreme Court addressed the effect of ERISA § 514 on such statutes in Aetna Health Inc. v. Davila, 542 U.S. 200 (2004).

The decision attempts to resolve some of the confusion resulting from prior Supreme Court decisions concerning which claims against managed care entities are preempted.

In *Davila*, two individuals sued their respective HMOs for alleged failures to exercise ordinary care in the handling of coverage decisions, in violation of a duty imposed by the Texas Health Care Liability Act (THCLA), Tex. Civ. Prac. & Rem. Code Ann. interlocking §§ 88.001–88.003 (2004 Supp. Pamphlet). The Court granted certiorari to decide whether the individuals' causes of action were completely pre-empted by ERISA. The Court held that the causes of action were completely pre-empted and hence removable from state to federal court.

I

The respondents both suffered injuries allegedly arising from the petitioners' decisions not to provide coverage for certain treatment and services recommended by respondents' treating physicians: in one case, Vioxx to remedy arthritis pain, and an extended hospital stay in the other. Respondents brought separate suits in Texas state court. Petitioners removed the cases to Federal District Courts, arguing that respondents' causes of action were therefore completely pre-empted by, ERISA § 502(a). The respective District Courts agreed, and declined to remand the cases to state court.

Both respondents appealed the refusals to remand to state court.

The Court stated that "any state-law cause of action that duplicates, supplements, or supplants the ERISA civil enforcement remedy conflicts with the clear congressional intent to make the ERISA remedy exclusive and is therefore pre-empted." and that

"The pre-emptive force of ERISA § 502(a) is still stronger." Citing *Metropolitan Life Ins. Co. v. Taylor*, 481 U.S. 58, 65–66 (1987), the Court stated that "the ERISA civil enforcement mechanism is one of those provisions with such "extraordinary pre-emptive power" that it "converts an ordinary state common law complaint into one stating a federal claim for purposes of the well-pleaded complaint rule." *Metropolitan Life*, 481 U.S., at 65–66. Hence, "causes of action within the scope of the civil enforcement provisions of § 502(a) [are] removable to federal court." Id., at 66."

According to the Court, "respondents complain only about denials of coverage promised under the terms of ERISA-regulated employee benefit plans. Upon the denial of benefits, respondents could have paid for the treatment themselves and then sought reimbursement through a § 502(a)(1)(B) action, or sought a preliminary injunction."

The respondents contended that the duty of ordinary care under the Texas law was an independent legal duty.

The Court disagreed. "The duties imposed by the THCLA in the context of these cases, however, do not arise independently of ERISA or the plan terms . . . if a managed care entity correctly concluded that, under the terms of the relevant plan, a particular treatment was not covered, the managed care entity's denial of coverage would not be a proximate cause of any injuries arising from the denial. Rather, the failure of the plan itself to cover the requested treatment would be the proximate cause. More significantly, the THCLA clearly states that "[t]he standards in Subsections (a) and (b) create no obligation on the part of the health insurance carrier, health maintenance organization, or other managed care entity to provide to an insured or enrollee treatment which is not covered by the health care plan of the entity." § 88.002(d). Hence, a managed care entity could not be subject to liability under the THCLA if it denied coverage for any treatment not covered by the health care plan that it was administering."

The Court concluded that "Petitioners' potential liability under the THCLA in these cases, then, derives entirely from the particular rights and obligations established by the benefit plans. [Hence,] respondents bring suit only to rectify a wrongful denial of benefits promised under ERISA-regulated plans, and do not attempt to remedy any violation of a legal duty independent of ERISA. We hold that respondents' state causes of action fall "within the scope of" ERISA § 502(a)(1)(B) and are therefore completely pre-empted by ERISA § 502 and removable to federal district court."

In explaining its reversal of the Court of Appeals, the Court clarified its holding in Rush Prudential: "Nowhere in *Rush Prudential* did we suggest that the pre-emptive force of ERISA § 502(a) is limited to the situation in which a state cause of action precisely duplicates a cause of action under ERISA § 502(a). Nor would it be consistent with our precedent to conclude that only strictly duplicative state causes of action are pre-empted. [Congress'] intent to make the ERISA civil enforcement mechanism exclusive would be undermined if state causes of action that supplement the ERISA § 502(a) remedies were permitted, even if the elements of the state cause of action did not precisely duplicate the elements of an ERISA claim."

Respondents also argued that the Texas law was a law that regulates insurance, and hence that ERISA § 514(b)(2)(A) saved their causes of action from pre-emption (and thereby from complete pre-emption). The Court disagreed: "Under ordinary principles of conflict pre-emption, then, even a state law that can arguably be characterized as "regulating insurance" will be pre-empted if it provides a separate vehicle to assert a claim for benefits outside of, or in addition to, ERISA's remedial scheme."

Finally, the Court dismissed the respondents' argument that, under *Pegram,* causes of action such as respondents' do not "relate to [an] employee benefit plan," and hence are not pre-empted.

Justice Ginsburg and Justice Breyer wrote a concurring opinion,

"The Court today holds that the claims respondents asserted under Texas law are totally preempted by § 502(a). That decision is consistent with our governing case law on ERISA's preemptive scope. I therefore join the Court's opinion. But, with greater enthusiasm, as indicated by my dissenting opinion in *Great-West Life & Annuity Ins. Co. v. Knudson,* 534 U.S. 204 (2002), I also join "the rising judicial chorus urging that Congress and [this] Court revisit what is an unjust and increasingly tangled ERISA regime." *DiFelice v. AETNA U. S. Healthcare,* 346 F.3d 442, 453 (CA3 2003) (Becker, J., concurring).

Because the Court has coupled an encompassing interpretation of ERISA's preemptive force with a cramped construction of the "equitable relief" allowable under § 502(a)(3), a "regulatory vacuum" exists: "[V]irtually all state law remedies are preempted but very few federal substitutes are provided." *Id.*, at 456. . . .

As the array of lower court cases and opinions documents, . . . fresh consideration of the availability of consequential damages under § 502(a)(3) is plainly in order."

NOTES

1. *Vioxx.* The plaintiff's grievance in *Davila* was that his ERISA-covered HMO had refused to supply him with the drug Vioxx for his arthritis pain. He subsequently suffered complications from a substitute drug. Some months after the decision in *Davila*, the manufacturer of Vioxx removed it from the market after studies indicated that the risk of cardiovascular side effects from Vioxx was too severe. See News Release, "Merck Announces Voluntary Worldwide Withdrawal of Vioxx," Sept. 20, 2004. Thousands of tort suits have since been brought against the manufacturer, alleging injury and death from the drug.

2. *Malpractice vs. wrongful claims denial.* In addressing the question whether ERISA preempts claims against managed care organizations, courts have typically drawn a distinction between claims that challenge the quality of care and claims that challenge the denial of benefits under a plan,

preempting the latter but not the former. Commonly cited as an example of a case preempting what was essentially a denial of benefits is Corcoran v. United Healthcare, Inc., 965 F.2d 1321 (5th Cir.1992). *Corcoran* involved a plaintiff who was covered under her employer's ERISA-governed health plan. She had a difficult pregnancy. Her doctor recommended hospitalization for constant monitoring as she neared term. United Healthcare, the plan's utilization review service provider, disagreed, and authorized instead ten hours per day of home nursing care. During the fourteen-hour stretch that the nurse was not on duty, Mrs. Corcoran's fetus went into distress and died. She and her husband sued United Healthcare (and the health plan) for wrongful death and consequential damages. The defendants removed to federal district court, which held the claims preempted, reasoning that "[b]ut for the ERISA plan, the defendants would have played no role in Mrs. Corcoran's pregnancy." The Fifth Circuit agreed. Because the plaintiff was "attempting to recover for a tort allegedly committed in the course of handling a benefit determination," the lawsuit was preempted under *Pilot Life*. Id. at 1332.

Similarly, in Bast v. Prudential Insurance Co., 150 F.3d 1003 (9th Cir.1998), Prudential, serving as administrator and stop-loss insurer of a self-funded plan, initially denied coverage for an autologous bone marrow transplant procedure recommended by Bast's physician for treatment of her breast cancer. Five months later Prudential reversed its decision and decided that Bast would be covered for the procedure, but by then the cancer had spread to such an extent that she was no longer eligible for the procedure. After her death, Bast's husband and minor son sued Prudential for breach of contract, loss of consortium, loss of income, emotional distress, breach of duty of good faith and fair dealing, violation of the Washington Consumer Protection Act and the Washington Insurance Code, and ERISA. The Ninth Circuit, citing *Pilot Life*, held that all of the state law causes of action were preempted and also held that the punitive and compensatory damages sought were not available remedies under ERISA. The court noted that Bast "could have sought an injunction to compel Prudential to authorize the ABMT procedure when Prudential first denied coverage." Id. at 1010 n.1.

By contrast, in Dukes v. U.S. Healthcare, Inc., 57 F.3d 350 (3d Cir.1995), the Third Circuit addressed claims brought by representatives of two ERISA plan beneficiaries against an HMO for medical negligence. One plaintiff argued that the HMO was negligent in failing to order a blood test that would have diagnosed the condition that led to the beneficiary's death. A second plaintiff alleged that the HMO doctor ignored symptoms of preclampsia during the third trimester of a plan beneficiary's pregnancy, leading to the delivery of a stillborn baby. The Third Circuit found that neither plaintiff was complaining about a failure to provide benefits. Rather, both plaintiffs "complain about the low quality of the medical treatment that they actually received and argue that the U.S. Healthcare HMO should be held liable under agency and negligence principles." *Id.* at 357. Thus, neither claim was preempted.

The Supreme Court's decision in Pegram v. Herdrich, 530 U.S. 211 (2000) adopted the distinction between claims regarding quality of care (malpractice) and those alleging denial of benefits. Although *Pegram* involved a claim of breach of fiduciary duty, *Pegram* signaled the Court's view that medical malpractice actions against HMOs and other medical providers who were not ERISA fiduciaries were not preempted. Indeed, shortly after its decision in *Pegram*, the Court let stand the Third Circuit's decision in In re U.S. Healthcare, Inc., 193 F.3d 151 (3d Cir. 1999), cert. denied, 530 U.S. 1242 (2000), which upheld a state negligence claim against an HMO. Accord Pryzbowski v. U.S. Healthcare, 245 F.3d 266 (3d Cir.2001) (negligence claims against physician not preempted).

In the wake of *Pegram*, courts continue to treat as preempted claims challenging the administration of benefits, including decisions made by utilization review case managers that do not involve treatment decisions. E.g., Marks v. Watters, 322 F.3d 316 (4th Cir.2003) (claim by estate of mental health patient who committed suicide against plan administrator and utilization review case manager preempted); Haynes v. Prudential Health Care, 313 F.3d 330 (5th Cir.2002) (claim regarding HMO's decision that insured's physician was not primary care physician preempted; decision was administrative and not treatment decision). Not everyone thinks that the divide drawn by the Court is sound. See Patricia Mullen Ochmann, Managed Care Organizations Manage to Escape Liability: Why Issues of Quantity vs. Quality Lead to ERISA's Inequitable Preemption of Claims, 34 Akron L. Rev. 571 (2001). Nonetheless, when it is clear that a plaintiff's claim is properly characterized as a denial of benefits rather than a treatment decision, the claim is preempted. E.g. Lind v. Aetna Health, Inc., 466 F.3d 1195 (10th Cir.2006).

The Supreme Court's discussion in *Pegram* of the relationship between ERISA and state malpractice law implies that a mixed treatment and eligibility decision, at least when made by the treating physician, is an appropriate subject of a state-law malpractice claim. The question that results is where to draw the line between an eligibility decision (governed by ERISA) and a mixed treatment and eligibility decision (governed by state law). For example, on which side of the line was the decision in *Corcoran*?

In Klassy v. Physicians Plus Insurance Co., 371 F.3d 952 (7th Cir.2004), a married couple who were practicing Jehovah's Witnesses sought approval for a bloodless hip surgery for the wife, because their religion forbade blood transfusions. The HMO refused to authorize the surgery by the only known surgeon who could perform such a procedure, because the surgeon was not a plan physician. Rather than undergo the approved standard surgery in violation of their religious beliefs, the participants paid for the bloodless procedure and then sued, alleging medical malpractice for failure to authorize the alternative procedure. The Seventh Circuit rejected the patient's claim that the HMO's decision was a treatment or a mixed treatment and eligibility decision. "[T]here is no dispute as to the appropriate *medical* treatment; rather, the Klassys seek alternative treatment based on their religious beliefs. Although we are sensitive to the Klassys' sincerely held religious beliefs, the sole question facing Dr. Johnson was one of eligibility and whether a bloodless surgery performed by an out-of-network physician was covered by the Plan. Therefore, [because] the sole issue was one of eligibility, [the] claim is preempted by ERISA." *Id*. at 956. Do you agree?

3. *Davila's contribution to the analysis of mixed treatment and eligibility decisions*. In *Davila* the Court addressed a question not answered by *Pegram*: Does ERISA preempt a mixed treatment and eligibility decision that is made by someone other than the treating physician? Consider the

pre-and post-*Davila* decisions in *Cicio v. Does*, 321 F.3d 83 (2d Cir.2003), cert. granted, judgment vacated by Vytra Healthcare v. Cicio, 542 U.S. 933 (2004), on remand, 385 F.3d 156 (2d Cir.2004). In *Cicio*, plaintiff brought a state law malpractice claim based on a benefit review decision by an HMO to deny one form of treatment as experimental and to approve a different form of treatment. Although the Second Circuit suggested that "at first blush" the decision concerns a benefit determination, it concluded based on its analysis of *Pegram* that the decision "must be treated as a mixed decision because it allegedly involved both an exercise of medical judgment and an element of contract interpretation." 321 F.3d at 102. The court concluded that such a mixed decision was not preempted by ERISA, saying that no distinction should be drawn between decisions made by treating physicians and by utilization review agents.

When the 2003 decision in *Cicio* was remanded in light of *Davila*, the Second Circuit admitted that *Davila* "fatally undermine[d]" its reasoning. Since "[n]either of the [Cicio] defendants were actually providing medical care" to the plaintiff, *Davila* dictated a finding that the plaintiff's claim was preempted. 385 F.3d at 157. Similarly, the Eleventh Circuit reconsidered its earlier decision in litigation involving CIGNA Healthcare of Florida. See Land v. CIGNA Healthcare of Florida, 339 F.3d 1286 (11th Cir.2003), cert. granted and judgment vacated by CIGNA HealthCare of Florida v. Land, 542 U.S. 933 (2004) (Land I) (determining based on *Pegram* that state malpractice claim was based on a mixed eligibility and treatment decision and not preempted); Land v. CIGNA Healthcare of Florida, 381 F.3d 1274 (11th Cir.2004) (Land II) (reconsidering Land I on the basis of *Davila* and determining that plaintiff's cause of action was one for denial of benefits under ERISA and was thus preempted).

It has been argued that *Davila* "gives priority to organizational form at the expense of a functional analysis of the nature of decision-making in the managed care context." Theodore R. Ruger, The Supreme Court Federalizes Managed Care Liability, 32 J. L. Med. & Ethics 528, 529 (2004). Ruger writes:

> *Pegram* held that a "mixed" treatment/eligibility decision made by a treating physician was not a fiduciary act, and so was not preempted by ERISA, and so was amenable to state malpractice lawsuits. *Aetna* holds the reverse, and grounds the distinction in the placement of the decision within the managed care organization's hierarchy. Mixed treatment and coverage decisions made by treating physicians are not fiduciary acts, but similar decisions made by plan administrators—which the Court acknowledged are "infused with medical judgments"—are treated quite differently in *Aetna*, despite the functional similarities of the decisions themselves. Like the physician's decision in *Pegram*, the coverage decisions plan administrators make (say to authorize one drug and not another, or to extend or limit a hospital stay) are "mixed" decisions about eligibility and treatment efficacy, and are often made in the shadow of occasionally crosscutting incentives to provide quality care on the one hand, and to contain costs on the other. *Aetna* and *Pegram* stand together to mean that the same substantive decision about patient care might be subject to different liability rules based on the identity of the decision-maker.

By grounding its decision on the characteristics of the decision-maker rather than the decision itself, the court missed another opportunity to more substantively discuss the rich array of competing values and considerations that inhere in any decision to ration medical care.

Is there any justification for the distinction that the Supreme Court made in *Davila*? If cost control is essential to maintaining employer-provided health plans, would viable cost control be feasible if plan coverage decisions were subject to state malpractice claims, including compensatory and punitive damages?

4.   *Vicarious liability.* Just as state malpractice claims against doctors are not preempted, courts have held that ERISA does not preempt claims against HMOs or similar organizations for vicarious liability based on the negligence of their participating physicians in providing medical care. For example, in Pacificare of Oklahoma v. Burrage, 59 F.3d 151 (10th Cir.1995), the patient was admitted to the hospital suffering from abdominal pain and a huge hematoma in her lower abdominal wall. After being seen by a physician, the patient was discharged, even though she was actively bleeding. That night, the patient bled to death. Her daughter filed suit against the doctor, the hospital, and the HMO, claiming that the doctor was the "ostensible agent" of the HMO. The Tenth Circuit ruled that "[j]ust as ERISA does not preempt the malpractice claim against the doctor, it should not preempt the vicarious liability claim against the HMO if the HMO has held out the doctor as its agent." Id. at 155.

By contrast, vicarious liability claims have been preempted in cases in which the plaintiff seeks to hold an HMO or similar organization vicariously liable for plan benefit determinations. See, e.g., Pryzbowski v. U.S. Healthcare, 245 F.3d 266 (3d Cir.2001) (preempting vicarious liability claim based on alleged negligence of HMO in hiring, training, and supervising employees who approve benefits).

5.   *A need for preemption reform.* The tort bar has long resented ERISA preemption. The rise in managed care and the corresponding complaints associated with MCO decisionmaking has led to increased criticism of ERISA's preemptive effect. As Justice Ginsburg's concurrence in *Davila* suggests, many federal judges believe legislative action is necessary. In DiFelice v. Aetna U.S. Healthcare, 346 F.3d 442 (3d Cir.2003), cited by Justice Ginsburg, Judge Becker of the Third Circuit wrote that "the current situation is plainly untenable," and urged Congress to revisit "what is an unjust and increasingly tangled ERISA regime." Id. at 453, 467. Judge Becker expressed particular concern about ERISA's preemptive effect on laws regulating welfare benefit plans, believing it "unlikely that Congress intentionally created this so-called 'regulatory vacuum,' in which it displaced state-law regulation of welfare benefit plans while providing no federal substitute." Id. at 467.

Although bills have been proposed at various times to limit the scope of ERISA preemption, excluding certain claims against managed care entities, no legislation has been adopted. Is the better approach one that would expand the causes of actions and remedies available under ERISA or one that would limit the scope of preemption? Does the former avoid the risk that plans could be subject to conflicting state regulation?

5. MANDATED EMPLOYER HEALTH EXPENSES

The failure of many employers to provide health insurance for their employees has led to a large number of uninsured Americans. During the run-up to ACA, discussed next, a number of states and localities enacted laws designed to increase coverage of their workers employed in their states. Two circuits have had occasion to consider the preemptive effects of such laws.

The Maryland Fair Share Care Fund Act, enacted in 2006, required employers with 10,000 or more Maryland employees to either spend 8% of their total payroll on their employees' health insurance costs or to pay to the state of Maryland the amount of the shortfall between that 8% amount and the amounts they actually spend. Although only peripherally relevant to the court's analysis, the statute was worded such that the only employer in the state to which the statute applied was Wal-Mart. In Retail Industry Leaders Association v. Fielder, 475 F.3d 180 (4th Cir.2007), the Fourth Circuit held that the statute was preempted by ERISA. The court rejected the state's argument that its legislation imposed only the sort of mandates upheld in *Travelers* and *Dillingham*, that is, laws that create economic incentives affecting employers' choices without effectively dictating their choices. Instead, the court viewed Maryland's statutory scheme as creating the type of direct regulation of an employer's structuring of its employee benefits akin to the schemes preempted in *Shaw* and *Egelhoff*.

The Fourth Circuit did not view the "choices given in the Fair Share Act, on which the Secretary relies to argue that the Act is not a mandate on employers" as providing meaningful alternatives to allow employers to comply with the statute without affecting its ERISA plans. First, while there are various ways an employer can provide for health care for its employees, "the undeniable fact is that the vast majority of any employer's healthcare spending occurs through ERISA plans. Thus the primary subject of the Fair Share Act are ERISA plans, and any attempt to comply with the Act would have a direct effect on the employer's ERISA plans." Second, the court did not view the employer's option to pay the State rather than altering its healthcare spending as creating a meaningful option. Since there are only narrow conditions under which it would be rational for an employer to select that option, "the overwhelming effect of the Act is to mandate spending increases" through employer plans. Thus, because the statute "leaves employers no reasonable choices except to change how they structure their employee benefit plans," the Fourth Circuit held it to be preempted by ERISA. 475 F.3d at 196–97. A vigorous dissent in *Fielder* rejected the notion that the statute carried any mandate. Id. at 201–03.

In 2006, the city of San Francisco enacted an ordinance mandating that employers of a certain size who do business within the city of San Francisco make "required health care expenditures to or on behalf of" their employees. S.F. Admin. Code § 14.3(a). Such expenditures could be made in a number of ways, including through an ERISA plan, by paying such funds to the city to be used to provide its employees with medical care, or otherwise making such funds available to provide medical care to employees. If an employer chose to pay funds to the city, such funds would be used to provide uninsured San Francisco residents (including eligible uninsured employees of the employer) with benefits under the Health Access Program established by the city under the ordinance and to establish or maintain health care reimbursement accounts for an employer's covered employees, whether or not they were San Francisco residents.

In Golden Gate Restaurant Association vs. City and County of San Francisco, 546 F.3d 639 (9th Cir.2008), the Ninth Circuit held that the San Francisco ordinance was not preempted by ERISA. The court began its analysis with two observations, noting first that the ordinance "does not require employers to establish their own ERISA plans or to make any changes to existing ERISA plans," and second that the ordinance "is not concerned with the nature of the health care benefits an employer provides its employees," only the dollar amount of the payments an employer makes to provide such benefits. Id. at 646–47.

Unlike the Fourth Circuit, the Ninth Circuit held that the regulation at issue here was not only "in stark contrast" to the laws held preempted in *Shaw* and *Egelhoff*, but exerted an influence "even less direct than the influence in *Travelers*." The ordinance does not require an employer to adopt an ERISA plan or provide any specific benefits under an ERISA plan; it does not bind administrators to any particular choice of rules for determining eligibility or entitlement to benefits; and it imposes no administrative or financial burden on plan administrators. Id. at 656–57.

The Ninth Circuit, while noting that it was neither adopting nor rejecting the analysis of the Fourth Circuit in *Fielder*, believed there to be a significant difference between the Maryland statute and the San Francisco ordinance. Whereas the Fourth Circuit found that the only rational choice for employers was to structure their ERISA plans to meet the state's minimum spending threshold, the Ninth Circuit believed that "the City-payment option offers San Francisco employers a realistic alternative to creating or altering ERISA plans." Id. At 660. Because the ordinance provided tangible benefits to employees of an employer who elected to pay the City, it offered employers a meaningful alternative and thus could not be characterized as a mandate.

How much of a "rational choice" is necessary to decide that a state/local scheme does not mandate that employers adopt a particular benefit structure? The majority in *Fielder* relied, in part, on Wal-Mart's assertions that it would increase benefits under its ERISA plans rather than pay the fee into the state. How much weight, if any, should the employer's assertions carry in the court's analysis?

E. THE AFFORDABLE CARE ACT

1. INTRODUCTION

The big problem with an employment-based coverage system is that many people (approximately 50 million, in the United States, as of 2010) are not covered. You're not covered under such a system, for a start, unless you or someone in your immediate family has a job. Even if a family member does have a job, his or her employer may not provide health insurance, especially if the employer is small. Prior to 2010, whether to provide health insurance was left entirely to the employer, although several measures, such as the COBRA continuation coverage rights and limits on pre-existing condition exclusions described above, had been adopted to limit gaps in employer-provided coverage.

President Obama signed the Patient Protection and Affordable Care Act, Pub. L. 111–148 (ACA), on March 23, 2010, and the Health Care and Education Reconciliation Act, Pub. L. 111–152 (HCERA) on March 30, 2010 (ACA and HCERA are sometimes referred to collectively as the "Act" or ACA). The ACA dramatically changed the health insurance plan landscape, with a series of legal incentives and sanctions intended to encourage employers to provide group health insurance, as well as a system of insurance exchanges intended to make it easier to purchase individual insurance in situations where employer-based coverage is unavailable. As discussed below, the Supreme Court upheld the constitutionality of the ACA in 2012, but a critical interpretive issue remains pending decision by the Court as of this writing.

2. THE GENERAL APPROACH

In the multi-year run-up to the ACA, a number of alternatives were advocated for addressing the problem of covering uninsured Americans. One was the so-called "single-payer" approach adopted in many other countries, where the government would have become responsible for health insurance—an approach that would have effectively ended the role of U.S. employers as a provider of health insurance. This idea was rejected, however, in favor of a system that is, by contrast, at least intended actually to reinforce the centrality of employer-provided plans.

The overall approach of PPACA is three-fold:

- First, solve the adverse selection problem (which previously made individual policies largely infeasible), whereby health insurance is disproportionately purchased by less healthy individuals, by effectively requiring everyone to secure coverage, one way or another.

- Second, create insurance "exchanges" to facilitate the purchase of individual insurance policies by anyone not covered by an employer plan, and subsidize (up to 100%) the cost of that purchase for lower-income Americans.

- Third, encourage the widest possible adoption of employer-sponsored plans, through a system of incentives for providing such coverage and penalties for failing to provide it.

These aims were to be accomplished by a series of provisions that successively took effect during the period generally between 2010 and 2015, and which are described below. Under ACA, large U.S. employers (those with 50 or more employees) are generally faced with a choice: Provide their employees with group health insurance that meets specified minimum requirements; or, alternatively, potentially pay what is effectively a penalty for failing to provide that insurance.

3. CHALLENGES TO THE ACA

The law continues to be very controversial. Challenges to the Act have taken four main forms: a challenge to the constitutionality of the Act's individual mandate; a challenge to the constitutionality of the Act's contraceptive mandate; a challenge to the availability of premium subsidies in the federally-run exchanges; and repeated attempts to repeal the entire Act.

In June, 2012, a sharply divided United States Supreme Court held, to the surprise of many, that the Act is constitutional. The most controversial provision, the individual mandate, was upheld as a valid exercise of the taxing power, although the Court rejected the Government's argument that the statute was a valid exercise of Congress' commerce power. National Federation of Independent Business et al v. Sebelius, 132 S. Ct. 2566 (June 28, 2012). The Court did strike down one important part of the Act, which would have required the States to accept a substantial expansion of Medicaid. As a result, the majority of States have not expanded their Medicaid programs pursuant to the Act.

The Religious Freedom Restoration Act of 1993 (RFRA) prohibits the Federal Government from substantially burdening a person's exercise of religion, even if the burden results from a rule of general applicability, unless the Government demonstrates that application of the burden to the person is in furtherance of a compelling governmental interest, and is the least restrictive means of furthering that compelling governmental interest. Regulations promulgated by HHS under the ACA require employer group health plans to furnish "preventive care and screenings" for women without "any cost sharing requirements". Nonexempt employers are generally required to provide coverage for the 20 contraceptive methods approved by the Food and Drug Administration. In Burwell v. Hobby Lobby Stores, Inc., 134 S. Ct. 2751 (2014), the Supreme Court held by a 5–4 majority, and over strong dissents, that, as applied to closely held corporations, the regulations violate RFRA.

On the legislative side, the House of Representatives has approved, on many separate occasions, legislation to repeal the Act. In voting for repeal, Republicans have essentially ignored a Congressional Budget Office (CBO) analysis finding that repeal would increase the federal budget deficit by a total of $145 billion from 2012 to 2019, and by $230 billion from 2012 to 2021. Letter from Douglas W. Elmendorf, Director, Congressional Budget Office, to Hon. John Boehner, Speaker of the House (Jan. 6, 2011), available at http://www.cbo.gov/doc.cfm?index =12040. The CBO also said that the repeal bill "would increase federal deficits in the decade after 2019 by an amount that is in a broad range around one-half percent of GDP" and that repealing the law would result in about 32 million fewer nonelderly Americans having health insurance in 2019, leaving a total of about 54 million nonelderly people uninsured. Republicans said that the CBO analysis is flawed because it includes only six years of benefits under the law, and does not include the cost to fix Medicare's physician payment system.

In the wake of the 2012 Supreme Court decision Republicans again stated their intention to repeal the Act. It is unlikely that they will do so.

However, they probably will continue to try, through the appropriations process, to stifle implementation of the Act. States with Republican governors have declined to establish exchanges to facilitate the individual purchase of insurance. (See "The Exchanges" below.) Following their success in the 2014 midterm elections, Republicans have said that they will chip away at the law piece by piece. See, e.g., Republicans Plan to Chip Away at ACA by Redefining Work Hours, Pension & Benefits Reporter (BNA), Nov. 17, 2014.

The "single most important outstanding legal issue" under the ACA as of this writing is "whether the federally facilitated insurance exchanges that serve two thirds of the states can grant premium tax credits to individuals purchasing health insurance plans." Timothy S. Jost, Subsidies and the Survival of the ACA- Divided Decisions on Premium Tax Credits. N. Eng. J. Med. Sept. 4, 2014 at 890. On November 7, 2014, the Supreme Court granted certiorari in King v. Burwell, 2014 U.S. LEXIS 7428 (2014), to decide the following question: "whether the IRS may promulgate regulations to extend tax-credit subsidies to coverage purchased through Exchanges established by the federal government under section 1321 of the Patient Protection and Affordable Care Act." Earlier in 2014, the Fourth Circuit had unanimously upheld the regulations, King v. Burwell, 759 F.3d 358 (4th Cir. 2014). The D.C. Circuit had held 2–1 that the regulations were invalid. Halbig v. Burwell, 758 F.3d 390 (D.C. Cir. 2014), but that decision was later vacated and a rehearing, en banc, granted. 2014 U.S. App. LEXIS 17099 (D.C. Cir. Sept. 4, 2014).

4. THE ACA'S EFFECTS ON EMPLOYER PLANS

The Act amends part A of Title XXVII of the Public Health Service Act (PHSA), relating to group health plans and health insurance issuers in the group and individual markets. PPACA adds section 715 to ERISA and section 9815 to the Internal Revenue Code, to make these provisions of the PHSA applicable to group health plans, and health insurance issuers providing coverage in connection with group health plans, as if those provisions were included in ERISA and the Code. The PHSA sections incorporated by this reference are sections 2701 through 2728.

The Act imposes penalties on larger employers (50 or more employees) that fail to offer adequate or affordable health benefits to their employees, but these penalties equal only a small fraction of the cost to employers of providing health benefits. Nevertheless, most surveys suggest that few employers will cease offering health benefits to their employees. [See, e.g., Employer Reaction to PPACA Ruling Mixed, Many To Continue Coverage, Survey Finds, 39 Pens. & Benefits Rep. (BNA) 1282, July 3, 2012; 2012 Deloitte Survey of U.S. Employers: Opinions about the U.S. Health Care System and Plans for Employee Health Benefits, www2.deloitte.com/content/dam/Deloitte/us/Documents/life-sciences-health-care/us-lshc-employee-survey-101614.pdf]. For many employers, the apparent cost savings of paying the penalties in lieu of providing coverage are outweighed by other considerations, such as the ability to attract and retain talented employees. A 2012 report by a health policy research firm found that employers that drop their group health insurance plans and accept the penalties under the Act would experience no immediate or long-term cost advantages. [Truven Health Analytics, Modeling the Impact of "Pay or Play" Strategies on Employer Health Costs, http://media.benefits pro.com/benefitspro/article/2012/07/09/PayPlay_Truven_WP_July2012_ 217015.pdf] According to one 2014 survey, "only 1 percent of plan sponsors are planning to eliminate health benefits in 2015. However, while most workers will not see major changes to their benefits next year, they are likely to see a continuation of changes that employers have been making for a number of years." What to Expect During Open-Enrollment Season: Findings from the SHRM/EBRI 2014 Health Benefits Survey, EBRI Notes, Dec. 2014, www.ebri.org.

As Buck Consultants noted, "There are generally three possible health care strategies that employers should consider for 2014 and later:

☐ Drop employer-sponsored health care coverage

☐ Drop employer-sponsored health care coverage and subsidize Exchange coverage

☐ Continue employer-sponsored health care coverage.

The approach an employer takes could vary for different segments of its workforce or business operations, depending on the flexibility allowed in final regulations. Any adopted strategy needs to reflect the employer's overall benefit philosophy and maintain its ability to attract and retain a productive workforce." [Buck Consultants, What the Supreme Court's Health Care Ruling Means for Employers, For Your Information, Volume 35, Issue 44, July 11, 2012]

Some provisions of the Act, such as coverage of adult children, are unlikely to be repealed, because they are very popular.

Because of the Act's length and complexity, this Chapter will only include a brief description of those provisions which are most important to employers.

5.   SUMMARY OF THE MAJOR PROVISIONS OF THE ACA

a.   Grandfathered plans: Under § 1251 of ACA, as modified by § 10103 of ACA and § 2301 of HCERA, certain plans or coverage existing on the date of enactment ("grandfathered plans") are subject only to certain provisions of the new law, as long as they retain grandfathered status. Grandfathered plans remain subject to many provisions of the Act. Also, a plan can lose grandfathered status in several ways. [See 45 CFR § 147.140] An employer seeking to rely on the grandfathered plan exception should review its plans carefully to make sure that grandfathered status has not been lost. Employers seeking to rely on grandfathered status must provide special notices to plan participants, maintain records dating back to March 23, 2010, documenting the plan terms, and make those records available for examination. The following major requirements are affected by grandfathering:

• Coverage of employees' adult children up to age 26 (for plans that allow coverage of dependents): limited exception for grandfathered plans until January 1, 2014.

• First-dollar coverage of preventive care services (grandfathered plans excepted).

- Patient protection provisions (e.g., choice of primary care provider, coverage of out-of-network emergency services) (grandfathered plans excepted).

- Prohibition on lifetime limits and restrictions on annual limits for essential health benefits (grandfathered plans excepted from some restrictions).

- Enhanced requirements for claims and appeals, including the addition of external review, the treatment of eligibility decisions as subject to claims and appeals and external review in many instances, and inclusion of notices of availability of non-English language services and documents depending on the country to which the claim or appeal information is sent (grandfathered plans excepted).

- Preventive care for women (grandfathered plans excepted).

Employers with non-grandfathered plans must now be able to demonstrate to DoL that their plans were amended to comply with reforms applicable to such plans. Employers must also produce copies of notices required to be furnished to participants, including copies of the required participant notices communicating a plan's grandfathered status.

b.　Employers must report the value of health benefits on W-2 forms. [I.R.C. § 6051(a) (14)] The Service has issued interim guidance in Notice 2012–9 [2012–1 C.B. 315], which amends and supersedes the guidance provided in Notice 2011–28. [2011–1 C.B. 656] As Notice 2012–9 points out, "This reporting to employees is for their information only. The reporting is intended to inform them of the cost of their health care coverage, and does not cause excludable employer-provided health care coverage to become taxable."

c.　Summary of benefits and coverage: Plan sponsors must provide to employees a uniform summary of benefits and coverage, during the open enrollment period. Participants and beneficiaries who enroll other than through an open enrollment period (e.g., new hires), must receive an SBC on the first day of the next plan year. [See 77 Fed. Reg. 8668 and 8706 (Feb. 14, 2012)]

d.　Flexible spending accounts: Employers must amend health plan documents by December 31, 2014, regardless of the plan year, retroactive to the beginning of the 2013 plan year, to include a $ 2,500 indexed annual cap on employee contributions to health flexible spending accounts. [I.R.C. § 125(i)].

e.　Rebates: Insurance companies must have a medical loss ratio (MLR) of at least 85 percent in the large group market (50 plus employees) and 80 percent in the individual and small group market. The MLR is (1) the amount spent on medical care and health care quality improvement, rather than on administrative costs, divided by (2) the total premiums paid. If the MLR is below this threshold, the insurer must provide a rebate to the customer. The MLR is intended to make the insurance marketplace more transparent and make it easier for consumers to purchase plans that provide better value for their money.

Under the previous rule, some rebates in the group market would have been subject to tax. The final rule directs issuers to provide rebates to the group policyholder (usually the employer) through lower premiums or in other ways that are not taxable. The process will vary by plan type. Policyholders must ensure that the rebate is used for the benefit of subscribers. The final rule also requires that issuers provide notice of rebates to enrollees and the group policyholder. All enrollees must be given information about the MLR and its purpose, the MLR standard, the issuer's MLR, and the rebate provided.

Self-insured, stop-loss, dental, and vision plans are all exempt from MLR rule. Employers must establish procedures to handle rebates under the MLR rules. [See the DHHS final rule, 77 Fed. Reg. 28790, May 16, 2012] Plan sponsors must determine whether rebates are plan assets and ensure that they are used consistently with applicable fiduciary responsibilities. [See DOL Technical Release 2011–04]

f.   Coverage through exchanges: The Act aims to create a competitive private health insurance market through insurance exchanges. The exchanges are designed to serve as marketplaces where consumers can choose among insurance plans whose costs and benefits are easy to compare. The Center for Consumer Information and Insurance Oversight (CCIIO) has issued rules outlining a framework that enables States to build exchanges. Exchanges offer a choice of different health plans, certifying plans that participate and providing information to help consumers better understand their options. "Beginning in 2014, Exchanges will serve primarily individuals buying insurance on their own and small businesses with up to 100 employees, though states can choose to include larger employers in the future. States are expected to establish Exchanges—which can be a government agency or a non-profit organization—with the federal government stepping in if a state does not set them up. States can create multiple Exchanges, so long as only one serves each geographic area, and can work together to form regional Exchanges. The federal government will offer technical assistance to help states set up Exchanges." [Kaiser Health Reform Source, http://health reform.kff.org/faq/what-is-a-health-insurance-exchange.aspx]

Employers were required to provide a written notice to employees about the availability of coverage through exchanges, and how such exchanges can be accessed, by March 1, 2013. New employees must be given notice at the time of hire. [Act § 1512] A 2012 report by the Employee Benefit Research Institute found that employer interest in providing health coverage to employees through exchanges may increase as a way to control health care costs. [EBRI Issue Brief No. 373, July, 2012, www.ebri.org.] In 2014, there were 17 state-based exchanges, 7 partnership exchanges and 27 federally facilitated exchanges. [http://kff. org/health-reform/state-indicator/health-insurance-exchanges/] Federal officials and federal contractors set up and run the exchange in any state that is unable or unwilling to do so." [Robert Pear, Most Governors Refuse to Set Up Health Exchanges, New York Times, Dec. 14, 2012]

g.   Contraceptives. Non-grandfathered plans must offer contraceptive drugs and devices on a first-dollar basis, with no participant cost-sharing. An exception is available for religious employers. This requirement is highly controversial, and is the subject of numerous lawsuits, on behalf of both religiously-affiliated entities that do not meet the definition of "religious employer" and of private employers with religious convictions against artificial contraception. See the discussion above of the Supreme Court's decision in the *Hobby Lobby* case.

    h.   Claims and appeals. The Act introduced new rules that apply only to non-grandfathered plans. The rules specify how the plan must handle an appeal ("internal review"). If the plan still denies payment after considering the appeal, the law allows the participant to have an independent review organization decide whether to uphold or overturn the plan's decision ("external review"). [Appealing Health Plan Decisions, http://www.healthcare.gov/law/features/rights/appealing-decisions/index. html; see also Interim Final Rule, 75 Fed. Reg. 43330 (2010), as amended by 76 Fed. Reg. 37208 (2011); DOL Technical Releases 2010–02, 2011–01 and 2011–02].

    i.   Preventive health services. Non-grandfathered group health plans must provide recommended preventive health services without cost-sharing and must adjust the services covered in accordance with changes to recommended preventive services guidelines.

    j.   Automatic enrollment: Employers with more than 200 full-time employees must provide automatic health plan enrollment for employees. [Fair Labor Standards Act § 18A, added by Act § 1511] This requirement has been delayed until the DOL issues guidance. [DOL Technical Release 2012–01] As comments have noted, automatic health plan enrollment is far more challenging than automatic 401(k) plan enrollment because of the variety of plans and types of coverage (e.g., single versus family) offered by larger employers.

    k.   Wellness incentives. Group health plans may increase permitted wellness incentives from 20 percent to 30 percent, 50 percent for programs to reduce tobacco use. 79 Fed. Reg. 8544. On November 20, 2012, DHHS, DOL and Treasury issued proposed rules [77 Fed. Reg. 70620], which apply to both grandfathered and non-grandfathered group plans. Under the proposed rules, a wellness program must offer alternatives for employees whose health conditions make it "unreasonably difficult" or for whom "it is medically inadvisable" to meet the specified health-related standard, and discounts or other rewards must be available to workers annually. The regulations were finalized in May, 2013 [78 Fed. Reg. 33,158]. To the surprise and indignation of many practitioners, the Equal Employment Opportunity Commission has sued three employers (Orion Energy Systems, Flambeau and Honeywell) in 2014, alleging that their wellness programs violate the Americans with Disabilities Act and the Genetic Information Nondiscrimination Act. Many consider that the EEOC's actions are in direct conflict with the ACA. See, e.g., Tom Starner, EEOC Throws a Wellness Curve, Human Resource Executive Online, Nov. 17, 2014; Alden J. Bianchi, EEOC v. Honeywell and the Future of Wellness Programs, Dec. 1, 2014, www. employmentmattersblog.com.

    l.   Penalties will be imposed on large employers (50 or more full-time employees, including full-time equivalent employees) that do not provide health benefits to full-time employees, or provide health benefits that are not affordable, or do not provide minimum value. [Code

§§ 4980H, 5000A] In determining the number of employees, the controlled group rules of Code §§ 414(b), (c), (m) and (o) (which generally relate to qualified retirement plans) apply.

Generally, an employee is full-time if he or she works an average of 30 or more hours per week. IRS Notice 2012–58 [2012–2 C.B. 436] provides employers with safe harbor methods for determining whether an employee is a full-time employee. [See also Notice 2011–36, 2011–1 C.B 792, Notice 2011–73, 2011–2 IC.B. 474, and Notice 2012–17, 2012–1 C.B. 430]

In February 2014, IRS issued final regulations providing further guidance. [79 Fed. Reg. 8544] The regulations affect only employers that meet the definition of "applicable large employer." Generally, liability for a penalty under Code § 4980H may arise because, with respect to a full-time employee who has been certified to the employer as having received an applicable premium tax credit or cost-sharing reduction, the employer's coverage is unaffordable within the meaning of Code § 36B (c) (2) (C) (i) or does not provide minimum value within the meaning of Code § 36B (c) (2) (C) (ii).

The rules provide that health benefits are "affordable" if the employee portion of the self-only premium for the employer's lowest cost coverage that provides minimum value does not exceed 9.5 percent of the employee's household income.

Under § 36B (c) (2) (C) (ii), a plan fails to provide minimum value if the plan's share of the total allowed costs of benefits provided under the plan is less than 60 percent of those costs. Act § 1302 (d) (2) (C) sets forth the rules for calculating the percentage of total allowed costs of benefits provided under a group health plan or health insurance plan.

A large employer that fails to offer health coverage to its full-time employees and their dependents may be subject to a nondeductible penalty if any full-time employee enrolls for coverage through an exchange and qualifies for the premium tax credit or reduced cost-sharing. The maximum annual penalty is $2,000 multiplied by the number of full-time employees in excess of 30.

Large employers that offer health coverage to their full-time employees and their dependents will potentially be subject to a second nondeductible penalty if at least one full-time employee enrolls in exchange coverage and qualifies for a premium tax credit or reduced cost-sharing because the employer coverage fails to provide minimum value or the provided coverage is unaffordable. The maximum annual penalty is $3,000 for each full-time employee who enrolls in exchange coverage and qualifies for the premium tax credit or reduced cost-sharing, subject to the maximum penalty that could be imposed if no coverage had been offered. Neither of the penalties applies when a retiree or part-time employee enrolls in exchange coverage and qualifies for the premium tax credit or reduced cost-sharing.

Under the Act, individuals eligible for Medicaid are not eligible for premium tax credits or cost sharing subsidies and thus the employer penalties do not apply with respect to such employees. If a state does not adopt expanded Medicaid eligibility, employees with income between 100 percent and 140 percent of the federal poverty level in that state could enroll in an exchange plan and receive a premium tax credit or cost-sharing subsidy, thus potentially subjecting the employer to a penalty. "Employers will also need to track Medicaid eligibility requirements by state, as the standards and qualified income levels could vary by state. Employers should monitor those states in which they have a significant workforce to determine whether they have decided to expand Medicaid eligibility." [Buck Consultants, supra]

Notice 2013–45, 2013–2 C.B. 116, issued on July 9, 2013, provides as transition relief that no employer shared responsibility payment applies for 2014. [Questions and Answers on Employer Shared Responsibility Provisions Under the Affordable Care Act, Q–29, http://www.irs.gov/uac/Newsroom/Questions-and-Answers-on-Employer-Shared-Responsibility-Provisions-Under-the-Affordable-Care-Act] The shared responsibility provisions are effective for 2015 but there is 2015 transition relief. [Id., Qs 30–39]

m. Waiting periods. The Act includes a prohibition against waiting periods in excess of 90 days. Notice 2012–59 [2012–2 C.B. 443 (issued by DoL, DHHS and Treasury)] provides guidance on the prohibition.

n. Transitional Reinsurance Program premiums. In March, 2014, DHHS released regulations regarding the annual contributions that are required to be paid to HHS from employer-sponsored group health plans (insured or self-insured) to finance state transitional reinsurance programs. The reinsurance programs are intended to help stabilize premiums for coverage in the individual market during the first three years the state health insurance exchanges are operational (2014 through 2016). The final regulations establish the program's fee for 2015 at $44 per covered life. The previously-established fee for 2014 is $63 per covered life.

o. The new Medicare taxes. The IRS has issued final regulations concerning the additional Medicare tax imposed on the wages or earned income of individual taxpayers. [78 Fed. Reg. 71,468] The additional tax is 0.9 percent of wages (self-employment income) over $200,000 ($250,000 for married taxpayers filing jointly, $125,000 for a married employee filing a separate return), increasing the employee-paid Medicare tax on this income from 1.45 percent to 2.35 percent. An employer must withhold the tax from wages it pays to an employee in excess of $200,000 in a calendar year, regardless of the individual's filing status or wages paid by another employer. The IRS also issued regulations implementing the net investment income tax, which is 3.8 percent of net investment income for high income individuals, estates, and trusts. [78 Fed. Reg.72394).]

p. Fees for the Patient-Centered Outcomes Research Trust Fund. IRS has issued final regulations [77 Fed. Reg. 72721] that implement and provide guidance on the fees imposed by the Act on issuers of certain health insurance policies and plan sponsors of certain self-insured health plans to fund the Trust Fund. [Code §§ 4375 and 4376] The fee is $2 ($1 for years ending before October 1, 2013) multiplied by the average number of covered lives. The DOL has indicated that these fees (unlike the reinsurance contributions) generally are not permissible plan expenses under ERISA, since they are imposed on the plan sponsor and not the plan.

q. **Pre-existing conditions exclusions.** Group health plans cannot impose exclusions on coverage for pre-existing conditions. [See 75 Fed. Reg. 37188]

r. **Dollar limits.** Under the Act, a plan may no longer put lifetime limits on the amount of "essential health benefits" (EHBs) provided by the plan. Also, a plan generally may not impose an annual limit on the amount of EHBs. [ACA § 2711] The prohibitions do not (1) apply to specific treatment limits, like "number of visits" limits, (2) limit the ability of a plan sponsor to exclude all benefits for a specific disease or condition (though such an exclusion may be limited by other state or federal laws), or (3) restrict the plan sponsor's ability to impose limits on nonessential health benefits. [45 CFR § 147.126]

s. **Certification of "Minimum Essential Coverage."** Employers that sponsor self-insured health plans must provide certification to DHHS regarding whether their health plans provide minimum essential coverage.

t. **Essential Health Benefits**. The Act requires that all policies sold on the individual market and to small groups (inside or outside the exchanges): (1) cover the ten categories of EHBs; (2) meet annual cost-sharing limits when covering EHBs; and (3) meet actuarial value limits for EHB coverage.

The law does not require large or self-funded plans either to cover all ten EHBs, or adhere to cost-sharing rules when covering EHBs. However, for large or self-funded employers, EHBs bear on other reform mandates, such as lifetime limits. For example, if a self-funded plan does cover any EHBs, it may not impose limits on them. The rule issued by DHHS, DoL, and Treasury in February, 2013, affirms that states can choose the exact package of benefits that insurers must provide. [78 Fed. Reg. 12834]

u. **Premium pricing.** The final rule issued in February, 2013, allows insurers to vary their rates based on age, tobacco use, family size, and where a person lives. [78 Fed. Reg. 13406] An insurer may not charge higher premiums for sick people or based on gender. Insurers may charge tobacco users 50 percent more than non-users, with an exemption for those who participate in smoking cessation programs. The Act limits premiums for older people to three times what younger people are charged. The rule prohibits premium rate variation for individuals under age 21, and allows insurers to charge slightly more annually until a person reaches age 64. Above age 64, all enrollees would pay the same rate.

v. **Plan actuarial value.** Actuarial value is defined as the percentage paid by a health plan of the total allowed costs of benefits. Differences in the levels of coverage reflect variations in cost-sharing, not differences in the underlying benefits. [See Kaiser Family Foundation. What the Actuarial Values in the Affordable Care Act Mean, April, 2011] "Total allowed benefit costs" is defined as the anticipated covered medical spending for EHB coverage paid by a health plan for a standard population, based on the health plan's cost sharing rules. The actuarial level of coverage must be 60 percent for a bronze plan, 70 percent for a silver plan, 80 percent for a gold plan and 90 percent for a platinum plan. The rule includes an AV calculator for health plans. Variations in AV of plus or minus two percent are *de minimis*. [78 Fed. Reg. 12834] The percentage a plan pays for an individual enrollee will generally be different from the actuarial value, depending on the services actually used by that person.

Insurance sold to individuals and small businesses must, unless the plan is grandfathered, be at one of the 4 actuarial value levels. Plans must also cap the maximum out of pocket costs for enrollees, based on the out of pocket limits for high-deductible health plans that can be paired with a health savings account. Most people will be required to have insurance that is at least at the bronze level, or pay a penalty. The Act allows insurers to sell a lower actuarial value catastrophic plan in the non-group market, to individuals who (1) are under age 30 or (2) would otherwise be exempt from the individual mandate because available coverage is unaffordable or enrollment in available coverage would be a hardship.

w.　Limits on deductibles and out-of-pocket maximums. Non-grandfathered plans may not impose an annual deductible of more than $2,000 for an individual and $4,000 for any other coverage tier. In addition, they are prohibited from having out-of-pocket maximums that exceed the limits imposed on high deductible health plans that are compatible with health savings accounts. [ACA § 1302(c)] DoL has informally indicated that the limits apply to all non-grandfathered group health plans, including self-insured plans.

x.　No discrimination against providers acting within the scope of their licenses. Non-grandfathered plans are prohibited from discriminating against health care providers acting within the scope of their licenses when providing services covered by the plan.

y.　Longer-term issues. The following provisions are not yet fully effective under the ACA:

i.　<u>The Cadillac tax</u>: A 40 percent excise tax (the "Cadillac tax") takes effect in 2018 for inflation-adjusted health coverage costs exceeding $10,200 for single coverage and $27,500 for family coverage, subject to certain adjustments [Act § 9001]. The thresholds increase at CPI + 1% in 2018 and 2019, and CPI only thereafter. As a result, more and more plans will be subject to the tax if, as is almost certain in the short term, health care inflation exceeds the general rate of inflation. The tax will be imposed on the insurer, or on the plan sponsor if the plan is self-insured. Liability for the tax is based on the total cost of benefits, not what the employer pays, so shifting costs to employees does not help.

ii.　<u>Nondiscrimination rules applicable to all employer health plans</u>: [Public Health Service Act (PHSA) § 2716; I.R.C. §§ 9815(a), 105(h)] Since 1980, self-insured health plans been subject to Code § 105(h), which prohibits discrimination in eligibility or benefits in favor of "highly compensated individuals." If a self-insured plan fails to meet the nondiscrimination requirements, the highly compensated individuals are taxed on some or all of their benefits. The Affordable Care Act extends these nondiscrimination rules to insured health plans. A grandfathered plan is not subject to the new rules.

Under a discriminatory *self-insured* plan, discrimination results in additional income taxation to the highly compensated individuals. A discriminatory *insured* plan may be subject to suit under ERISA, and the plan sponsor may be liable for a penalty of $100 multiplied by the number of individuals discriminated against and the number of days the plan does not comply. I.R.C. § 4980D(b)(1).

In Notice 2010–63 [2010–2 C.B. 420], the IRS requested public comments on guidance needed regarding § 2716. Treasury, the Service, DOL and the Department of Health and Human Services (DHHS) determined that compliance with § 2716 should not be required until a regulation or other administrative guidance of general applicability has been issued. "In order to provide insured group health plan sponsors time to implement any changes required as a result of the regulations or other guidance, the Departments anticipate that the guidance will not apply until plan years beginning a specified period after issuance. Before the beginning of those plan years, an insured group health plan sponsor will not be required to file IRS Form 8928 with respect to excise taxes resulting from the incorporation of PHS Act § 2716 into § 9815 of the Code." [Notice 2010–63; see also Notice 2011–1, 2011–1 C.B. 259, containing a further request for comments]. It is not clear when such guidance will be issued, but it does not appear to be an immediate priority.

Although enacted in 1978, § 105(h) has not been enforced consistently. In 1986, Congress enacted the notorious Code § 89, which attempted to apply uniform nondiscrimination rules to health and welfare plans. Because of its complexity, § 89 was repealed before going into effect. Time will tell whether the new provision will fare any better.

Many of the same policy issues raised by the tax subsidy for retirement plans are raised by the tax-free treatment of other employee benefits. For example, if the goal is to encourage health benefits for nonhighly compensated employees, making the benefits tax-free, even if they are subject to nondiscrimination tests, may be a costly and ineffective device for achieving the goal. How would you evaluate a proposal to require employers to provide a certain level of health coverage?

F. HEALTH SAVINGS ACCOUNTS

So prevalent has the defined contribution concept become that it has begun to spill over from pension plans to welfare benefit plans, in the form of the health savings account (HSA). The Medicare Prescription Drug, Improvement, and Modernization Act of 2003 authorized HSAs. HSAs allow eligible individuals and families to contribute money into savings accounts to be used for the payment of qualified medical expenses.

An individual can contribute to an HSA if he or she is covered by a high-deductible health plan (with an annual deductible of at least $1,000 for individual coverage and $2,000 for family coverage) and is not eligible for Medicare. These minimum deductibles are indexed and are $1,300 and $2,600, respectively, for 2015. Rev. Proc 2014–30, 2014–1 C.B. 1009. For 2015, annual HSA contributions are generally limited to $3,350 for an individual and $6,650 for a family, subject to cost of living adjustments after 2015, with additional contributions (for 2015, $1,000 for single or family coverage) permitted for older employees. Subject to these limits, the contributions made to an HSA are tax deductible. Contributions made in excess of these limits are subject to an excise tax of 6%. Earnings on contributions accumulate tax free. Additionally, no tax is paid on HSA distributions, so long as they are used to pay qualified medical expenses (that is, amounts paid for medical care for the individual and any of the individual's dependents that are not covered by insurance or otherwise reimbursable). Distributions not used to pay for qualified medical expenses are included in gross income and subject to a 20% penalty tax (10% for distributions made before 2011). Upon death the HSA may be transferred to the participant's spouse tax-free. A more detailed consideration of the tax treatment of HSAs can be found in Louis A. Mezzullo, Health Savings Accounts—What You Need to Know, 30 ACTEC Journal 30 (2004).

Employers have shown a strong interest in HSAs. According to one 2014 survey, twenty percent of covered workers are enrolled in a high-deductible plan with a savings option (HDHP/SO). Enrollment in HDHP/SOs increased significantly between 2009 and 2011, from 8% to 17% of covered workers, but has plateaued since then. In 2014, twenty-seven percent of firms offering health benefits offered a high-deductible health plan with a health reimbursement arrangement (HDHP/HRA) or a health savings account (HSA) qualified HDHP. Kaiser Family Foundation, 2014 Employer Health Benefits Survey, Summary of Findings, at 6.

What explains the strong interest in HSAs among employers?

Is the application of the defined contribution concept to health care a positive step? Some would say yes, arguing that HSAs will encourage participants "to become more astute health care consumers." Paul Fronstin & Sara R. Collins. Early Experience with High-Deductible and Consumer-Driven Health Plans: Findings from the EBRI/Commonwealth Fund Consumerism in Health Care Survey. Employee Benefit Research Institute Research Brief No. 288 (December 2005), at 4, available at http://www.ebri.org/publications/ib/index.cfm?fa=ibDisp& content_id=3606.

The suggestion is that HSAs will cause participants to become more informed and make more responsible decisions about health care expenditures. Critics are less enthusiastic, arguing that "no matter how much you dress up these plans in the rhetoric of 'consumer empowerment,' cost shifting—in the form of higher deductibles, co-insurance, office visit fees, and benefit exclusions—is inherent to their design." EBRI, Retirement Income Security: A Look at Social Security, Employment-Based Retirement Plans, and Health Savings Accounts, Aug. 2005, at 7.

When an employer facilitates the establishment of HSAs by its employees, does it create a plan subject to ERISA? In April 2004, the DoL issued a field assistance bulletin suggesting that employer contributions to an HSA would not be viewed as a "plan" under ERISA if "the establishment of the HSA is completely voluntary on the part of the employees and the employer does not: (i) limit the ability of eligible individuals to move their funds to another HSA beyond restrictions imposed by the Code; (ii) impose conditions on utilization of HSA funds beyond those permitted under the Code; (iii) make or influence the investment decisions with respect to funds contributed to an HSA; (iv) represent that the HSAs are an employee welfare benefit plan established or maintained by the employer; or (v) receive any payment or compensation in connection with an HSA." Department of Labor, Health Savings Accounts, Field Assistance Bulletin 2004–1 (Apr. 7, 2004).

G. RETIREE HEALTH PLANS

1. RETIREE MEDICAL PLANS: SUMMARY AND CONTEXT

Some employer-provided health care plans provide varying types of coverage not only for active participants (and their dependents) but also for former workers (and their dependents). A plan that covers retirees is commonly called a retiree health plan, even though what is usually meant is not that the plan covers only retirees, but that retirees are included in a plan that covers active participants.

Most health care for retired persons is provided under the federal Medicare program for persons 65 and over. Retiree health plans provide primary coverage for persons who retire before age 65, and supplementary coverage for non-Medicare-reimbursed expenses for persons over 65.

1. *Trends.* Retiree health coverage began in the 1940s and 1950s as what has been called a "throw-away benefit," inexpensive to provide and therefore easily granted. (The phrase is that of Diana J. Scott, who managed the Financial Accounting Standards Board project to revise FASB Standard No. 106, discussed below.) Life expectancies were shorter, health care was less extensive and far less expensive.

"The skyrocketing cost of providing postretirement medical coverage is traceable to several factors. First, and most obvious, the cost of medical care has risen rapidly in recent years. Second, the ratio of retired employees to active employees has increased steadily for virtually all employers, particularly those in older industries and industries that reduced their active work forces in the 1980s. Third, the trend toward earlier retirement has increased the proportion of retired workers not covered by Medicare in many plans. Finally, changes in Medicare coverage have shifted the burden of retiree medical costs to corporate plans." Stephen R. Miller, Michael S. Melbinger & Nicholas Giampietro, Postretirement Medical Benefits Plans: An Analysis of Funding and Termination Issues, 12 J. Pension Planning & Compliance 193, 193–94 (1986).

By 1986 it was reported that "the post-retirement health care liability for the 'Fortune 500' industrials considerably exceeds their total assets." Bruce D. Pingree, Current Issues in Termination and Modification of Welfare Plans, 14 Tax Management Compensation Planning J. 311, 312 (1986). A 2014 report found that the Fortune 1000 companies reported an estimated $285 billion in retiree medical obligations in 2013. 67 percent of the companies with a liability had no assets set aside for that purpose. The report notes that "volatility of the discount rate makes the obligation variable and unpredictable" and "longer life expectancies could increase the projected obligation." Towers Watson, Fortune 1000 Companies Have a $285 Billion Liability for Retiree Medical, Nov. 2014, www.towerswatson.com. As the magnitude of the retiree health liability came to be perceived, and the cost of providing retiree health continued to increase, many employers ceased to offer retiree health coverage to new participants and attempted to reduce or terminate it for present participants and retirees. The legal constraints on amending such plans are discussed below.

By 1999, only "about one-third of large employers and less than 10 percent of small employers" offered retiree health coverage. GAO, Retiree Health Insurance: Gaps in Coverage and Availability, GAO–02–178T, Nov. 1 2001, at 1. EBRI data indicate that the percentage of private sector workers employed by a firm offering retiree health insurance declined from 29 percent in 1997 to 18 percent in 2010. Paul Fronstin and Nevin Adama, Retiree Health Benefits: Trends in Access and Coverage, 1997 to 2010, EBRI Issue Brief No. 377, Oct. 2012 [hereafter cited as Fronstin and Adams]. "In 2009, among employers with 200 or more workers that offered health coverage to active workers, 29 percent also offered health benefits to retirees, down from 35 percent in 2000 and 66 percent in 1988." Alliance for Health Reform, www.allhealth.org, citing Kaiser Family Foundation and Health Research and Educational Trust, 2009 Employer Health Benefits Survey.

Out of pocket medical expenses have a major effect on the financial security of the elderly, and on their retirement decisions: "The results show that the premium costs associated with retirement before age 65 and expected out-of-pocket health care costs after 65 substantially delay retirement. . . . Despite Medicare and various types of supplemental coverage, in 2004 Americans age 65 and older spent about three times as much on out-of-pocket health care costs as nonelderly adults. Median out-of-pocket health care spending as a share of income totaled 14 percent for adults age 65 to 74 in 2003 and 22 percent for those age 85 and older. These figures are likely to increase in the future as health care costs rise, despite the 2006 introduction of Medicare Part D, which lowered out-of-pocket prescription drug costs for older adults. Premiums for Medicare Parts B and D will rise with total Medicare spending, because premiums are set to cover 25 percent of program costs. The Medicare Trustees (2007) project that real monthly Part D premiums will increase by about 70 percent by 2016, to about $46 in 2007 dollars. A typical older married couple could devote about 35 percent of its after-tax income to health care in 2030. Medicare reforms could further exacerbate the financial burden of health care costs for older Americans. . . . Several previous studies have found that access to employer-sponsored retiree health benefits is an important predictor of retirement. Access to government health benefits, such as those provided to veterans, also appears to encourage early retirement." Do Out-Of-Pocket Health Care Costs Delay Retirement? Richard W. Johnson, Rudolph G. Penner, and Desmond Toohey, Center for Retirement Research at Boston College, CRR WP 2008–4, February 2008.

For local and state government employees, however, the percentages and the trends are quite different. "Among state employers, the percentage offering retiree health benefits increased between 1997 and 2003. In 2003, 94.9 percent were providing health coverage to early retirees and 88.6 percent were providing health coverage to Medicare-eligible retirees (Figure 4). However, recently, the percentage of state-government employers offering retiree health benefits has fallen. By 2010, 70 percent were offering health coverage to early retirees and 63.2 percent were offering it to Medicare-eligible retirees. Similarly, there has been a recent decline in the percentage of local-government employers offering retiree health benefits. Between 2006 and 2010, the percentage of local governments with 10,000 or more workers that offered health coverage to early retirees fell from 95.1 percent to 77.6 percent, and the percentage offering it to Medicare eligible retirees fell from 86.2 percent to 67.3 percent (Figure 5)." Fronstin and Adams, supra, at 8.

What accounts for the difference in the patterns of retiree health coverage between private and public sector employers?

The Governmental Accounting Standards Board (GASB) has issued new accounting rules for state and local government employers, discussed in paragraph 4, infra.

Is the tax subsidy for employer-provided health care, which extends to retiree health coverage, justified? An official of the American Association of Retired Persons observed to a New York Times reporter that those retirees who have employer-provided health coverage tend to be "the best off. It seems like a funny way to spend your tax money." Costly Accounting Change Planned, N.Y. Times, Sept. 15, 1988, at 29, 34.

2.   *Is a retiree health plan really a pension plan?* Is the architecture of ERISA sound as regards retiree health plans? Does such a plan belong where the statute places it, in the category of welfare benefit plan, or might it better be thought of as a pension plan?

A plan that provides health benefits across the period of a worker's retirement functions as a type of pension plan, which pays in specie rather than in dollars. If the plan did not supply medical services, the retiree would have to spend pension dollars to buy medical services. Because retiree health plans and pension plans are in this sense substitutes, would it not seem sensible to treat them alike for regulatory purposes?

Because a retiree health plan resembles a pension plan in function, it differs importantly from the garden variety welfare benefit plan. Welfare benefit plans, it will be recalled, are excused from ERISA's funding and vesting rules on the view that they are current-account plans. For other welfare benefit plans, the sponsor's obligation accrues and is discharged on a current basis. Retiree health plans, by contrast, entail obligations for the care of the retiree (and dependents) that can stretch out across decades. As both the value and the duration of the retiree health promise increase, the decision to exempt retiree health plans from funding and vesting standards comparable to those for pension plans becomes more questionable.

Despite the similarities between retiree health plans and pension plans, any effort to treat retiree health plans like pension plans meets with serious difficulties.

(a) *What is the benefit, and what will it cost?* Pensions are paid in cash, according to accrual formulas that result in dollars-and-cents precision. But what, exactly, is the level of health care to which a plan participant will be entitled twenty years from now? "Unlike cash benefits, [future] health insurance costs also depend on the long-term rate of health-care cost inflation, changes in the delivery of health care, and changes in medical technology." EBRI, Employer-Paid Retiree Health Insurance, EBRI Issue Brief 10 (Oct. 1985).

Could you draft a plan that spells out the benefit level with accuracy for health care that is to be delivered well into the twenty-first century? The largest variable may be political: How generous will Congress and the states be across the decades in funding Medicare and other public programs? Can you predict the future of these programs, and what coordination-of-benefits rules they will follow for persons having private health insurance?

(b) *Multiple employers.* Since the typical worker serves several employers, should the cost of post-employment health care be borne only by the last employer? Should an effort be made to vest employees in health care benefits with each employer for whom the employee renders substantial service, as is now the policy with ERISA's vesting of pension benefits? A retiree who vests under several pension plans can cash checks from all of them. But "the possibility of vesting in more than one retiree health insurance plan represents a practical problem in coordinating benefits from multiple plans, as well as Medicare, and constitutes an additional source of uncertainty in forecasting plan costs." EBRI, Issue Brief 10 (Oct. 1985). (ERISA's requirements for the vesting of pension benefits are discussed in Chapter 4).

(c) *Dependent care.* "[S]urvivorship rights under a retiree health plan cannot be factored into the benefit payout in the same way a pension plan can reduce annual benefits when retirees elect joint and survivor benefits. As a result, survivors' benefits can add significantly to net plan costs and make forecasting those costs even more uncertain." EBRI, Issue Brief 10 (Oct. 1985). (ERISA's requirements for spousal benefits are discussed in Chapter 5).

The suggestion has been made that the way to avoid these coordination-of-benefits problems is for federal policy to encourage the provision of retiree health care through defined contribution accounts, such as the HSA accounts discussed above. Each worker might have such a portable "medical IRA," to which contributions would be made across his or her working career. The account would then be used to purchase health insurance or health care when the worker retired.

As with any defined contribution plan, investment risk would incide on the employee. In addition, the employee would bear the burden of inflation in health care costs. For some persons, especially those with marginal employment histories, there would not be enough money in the account to buy adequate retirement health care or health insurance. For other persons, the account might be in surplus.

For reasons such as these, retiree health plans continue to be regulated as welfare benefit plans, despite the awkwardness of fitting them with other such plans.

3.   *FASB 106: Accrual Accounting for Retiree Health.* Into the 1990s the generally applicable accounting standards allowed employers to expense retiree health costs on a "current" or pay as you go basis. After years of deliberation, the Financial Accounting Standards Board in 1990 issued its Standard No. 106, "Employers' Accounting for Postretirement Benefits Other than Pensions," known as FASB 106, effective in 1992.

FASB 106 requires that companies account for retiree health benefits on an accrual basis. Companies must accrue liabilities for future health care expenditures on their financial statements, and they must amortize the present value of expected future retiree health obligations.

"The premise [behind FASB 106] is two-fold. First, these benefits are a form of deferred compensation and should be accounted for during the period in which the services are rendered. Second, some would suggest that they present a significant liability and that financial statements are misleading if an estimate is omitted." Carol A. Noer, Accounting for Postretirement Health Care Benefits: The Implementation and Ramifications of FAS 106, 20 Tax Management Compensation Planning J. 87, 88 (1992).

FASB 106 resulted in huge one-time charges as companies booked the liabilities for retrospective conversion to FASB 106 standards. IBM's FASB 106 writeoff was $2.3 billion, GE's was $1.8 billion, AT & T's $6.6 billion. The Big Three automakers booked $33.2 billion in charges: $20.8 billion for GM, $7.5 billion for Ford, $4.7 billion for Chrysler. The change eliminated three fourths of the net worth of GM. Pensions & Investments, May 3, 1993, at 9; Wall St. J., Apr. 22, 1993, at A3; Wall St. J., Feb. 8, 1993, at A3; Pensions & Investments, Sept. 30, 1991, at 3.

The General Accounting Office estimated the aggregate FASB 106 liability for private employers in 1993 at $412 billion. "A 1993 survey of 322 businesses conducted by [the consulting firm of] Towers Perrin showed a reduction in annual pretax profits of 4.6 percent and an increase in payroll costs of 3 percent annually as a result of [FASB 106 requirements]." EBRI Issue Brief 25 (Jun. 1994).

Is FASB 106 worthwhile? Alain Enthoven has been quoted as saying "that fussing with the accounting and legal issues surrounding retiree health benefits is akin to rearranging the deck chairs on the Titanic." EBRI, Employee Benefits Notes 4 (Nov. 1988). Is he right?

The pressure from FASB to recognize retiree health liabilities presages new concern with funding mechanisms. At present the tax code lacks a structure comparable to the qualified plan funding system that allows contributions and earnings of pension funds to be tax deferred. For discussion of the alternatives, including IRC § 401(h) and 501(c)(9) mechanisms, see Chapter 10. Lack of funding of retiree health benefits has been one of the major issues in the recent financial travails of the U.S. automakers. General Motors Corp. replaced its traditional health care plan for salaried retirees under age 65 with a consumer-driven health plan, effective January 1, 2010. GM had already eliminated health coverage for Medicare-eligible salaried retirees. GM also stopped providing retiree health coverage to UAW members effective January 1, 2010. Instead, it contributes to a 501(c)(9) trust controlled by the union. Jerry Geisel, GM replacing traditional health plan for some retirees, Oct. 21, 2009, www.businessinsurance.com/article/20091021/NEWS/9102 19990.

4. *GASB 45: Accrual Accounting for Governmental Employers.*

In 2004 and 2005, the Governmental Accounting Standards Board (GASB) released three final statements including GASB Statement No. 45, which, similarly to FAS 106, requires governmental employers to recognize the cost of post-retirement benefits other than pensions (OPEB) on an accrual basis rather than a pay-as-you go basis. Employers must also report a liability on their balance sheets for the amount of any expense that has not been funded. Also, as under the FASB rules, implicit rate subsidies must be recognized as OPEB.

As Credit Suisse pointed out in a 2007 report: "The old rules made it very easy for most state and local governments to promise their employees OPEB benefits in retirement, as doing so had no effect on their balance sheets, and the costs were only reflected in the budget and on the income statement when the benefits were paid to retirees (many years later, long after the politicians that had made these promises left office). In fact, most didn't even bother to measure the promises they made." Credit Suisse, You Dropped a Bomb on Me, GASB, Mar. 22, 2007, available at http://online.wsj.com/public/resources/documents/Dropped B.pdf. A Cato Institute report found the average unfunded OPEB liability to be $135,000 per worker, and extrapolated this to a total national unfunded liability of $1.4 trillion. Cato Institute Bulletin, Unfunded State and Local Health Costs: $1.4 Trillion, Oct., 2006, available at http://object.cato.org/sites/cato.org/files/pubs/pdf/tbb_0925-40.pdf. Credit Suisse estimated "over $1.5 trillion in unfunded OPEB liabilities. . . . To put that into perspective, the size of the municipal bond market at the end of 2006 was $2.4 trillion and the OPEB plans of the companies in the S & P 500 were 'only' $326 billion underfunded at the end of 2005 . . . In the aggregate, we found the OPEB underfunding of the 50 states was about 34% of their $1.6 trillion in assets, while it was 32% of the $284 billion in total assets for the 25 largest cities." Credit Suisse, supra.

Because it is not a governmental agency, GASB has no power to mandate compliance with its standards. However, most government entities issue reports that comply with GASB's standards. Some are required to do so by state or local statute, while others comply with GASB in order to maintain good credit ratings in the municipal bond market. In addition, the Code of Professional Conduct of the American Institute of Certified Public Accountants (AICPA) requires auditors to note any departures from GASB when they express an opinion on financial reports that are presented in conformity with GAAP. As such, governments are usually expected to prepare financial statements in accordance with these standards.

Although the new rules are now in effect, it appears that many governmental employers have done little or nothing to bring themselves into compliance. "So what are most governments doing? Unfortunately, for many the answer is 'nothing.' Paralysis has set in, as the absence of sufficient funding leaves many budget offices declining to set up a properly funded OPEB trust. Many public officials have simply put their heads in the sand and decided to wait out the recession before looking seriously at their OPEB problems." Girard Miller, The OPEB Acid-test: Paralysis must yield to analysis—soon, May 7, 2009, www.governing.com/column/opeb-acid-test.

Most of the states are in poor financial condition, so it is not surprising that there is intense focus on the level of benefits under, and funded status of, public employee plans. Many of the allegations are highly partisan, but the respected Pew Center on the States reported in *February, 2010* that there was a $1 trillion gap at the end of fiscal year 2008 between the $2.35 trillion states had set aside to pay for employees' retirement and retiree health benefits and the $3.35 trillion cost of those promises. [The Trillion Dollar Gap: Underfunded State Retirement Systems and the Road to Reform, http://www.pewcenteronthestates.org/report_detail.aspx?id=56695] New accounting rules approved by the Governmental Accounting Standards Board (GASB) in June, 2012 (GASB 67 and 68) are likely to put additional pressure on governmental pension sponsors.

The bankruptcy filings by Detroit and several California cities have recently focused attention on underfunded public sector plans. See, generally, David Pratt, The Detroit Bankruptcy and Its Implications for Public Employee Retirement Plans, 21 J of Pension Benefits No. 2 at 3 (2014); Amy Monahan, Understanding the Legal Limits on Public Pension Reform, American Enterprise Institute (2013); Christine S. Chung, Government Budgets As The Hunger Games: The Brutal Competition For State and Local Government Resources Given Municipal Securities Debt, Pension and OPEB Obligations, And Taxpayer Needs, 33 Review of Banking and Financial Law 663 (2014); Christine S. Chung, Zombieland/the Detroit Bankruptcy: Why Debts Associated with Pensions, Benefits, and Municipal Securities Never Die . . . and How They Are Killing Cities Like Detroit, 41 Fordham Urban Law Journal 771 (2014).

2. AMENDING RETIREE HEALTH PLANS

M&G Polymers USA, LLC v. Tackett

574 U.S. ___, 135 S.Ct. 926 (2015).

■ JUSTICE THOMAS delivered the opinion of the Court.

This case arises out of a disagreement between a group of retired employees and their former employer about the meaning of certain expired collective-bargaining agreements. The retirees (and their former union) claim that these agreements created a right to lifetime contribution-free health care benefits for retirees, their surviving spouses, and their dependents. The employer, for its part, claims that those provisions terminated when the agreements expired. The United States Court of Appeals for the Sixth Circuit sided with the retirees, relying on its conclusion in *International Union, United Auto, Aerospace, & Agricultural Implement Workers of Am.* v. *Yard-Man, Inc.*, 716 F. 2d 1476, 1479 (1983), that retiree health care benefits are unlikely to be left up to future negotiations. We granted certiorari and now conclude that such reasoning is incompatible with ordinary principles of contract law. . . .

Respondents Hobert Freel Tackett, Woodrow K. Pyles, and Harlan B. Conley worked at (and retired from) the Point Pleasant Polyester Plant in Apple Grove, West Virginia (hereinafter referred to as the Plant). During their employment, respondent United Steel, Paper and Forestry, Rubber, Manufacturing, Energy, Allied Industrial and Service Workers International Union, AFL-CIO-CLC, or its predecessor unions (hereinafter referred to as the Union), represented them in collective bargaining. . . . Petitioner M&G Polymers USA, LLC, is the current owner of the Plant.

When M&G purchased the Plant in 2000, it entered a master collective-bargaining agreement and a Pension, Insurance, and Service Award Agreement (P & I agreement) with the Union, generally similar to agreements the Union had negotiated with M&G's predecessor. The P & I agreement provided for retiree health care benefits as follows:

> "Employees who retire on or after January 1, 1996 and who are eligible for and receiving a monthly pension under the 1993 Pension Plan . . . whose full years of attained age and full years of attained continuous service . . . at the time of retirement equals 95 or more points will receive a full Company contribution towards the cost of [health care] benefits described in this Exhibit B–1. . . ."

Exhibit B–1, which described the health care benefits at issue, opened with the following durational clause: "Effective January 1, 1998, and for the duration of this Agreement thereafter, the Employer will provide the following program of hospital benefits, hospital-medical benefits, surgical benefits and prescription drug benefits for eligible employees and their dependents. . . ." The P & I agreement provided for renegotiation of its terms in three years.

In December 2006, M&G announced that it would begin requiring retirees to contribute to the cost of their healthcare benefits. Respondent retirees, on behalf of themselves and others similarly situated, sued M&G and related entities, alleging that the decision to require these contributions breached both the collective-bargaining agreement and the P & I agreement, in violation of § 301 of the Labor Management Relations Act, 1947 (LMRA) and § 502(a)(1)(B) of [ERISA]. Specifically, the retirees alleged that M&G had promised to provide lifetime contribution-free health care benefits for them, their surviving spouses, and their dependents. They pointed to the language in the 2000 P & I agreement providing that employees with a certain level of seniority "will receive a full Company contribution towards the cost of [healthcare] benefits described in . . . Exhibit B–1." The retirees alleged that, with this promise, M&G had created a vested right to such benefits that continued beyond the expiration of the 2000 P & I agreement.

The District Court dismissed the complaint for failure to state a claim. It concluded that the cited language unambiguously did not create a vested right to retiree benefits.

The Court of Appeals reversed based on the reasoning of its earlier decision in *Yard-Man*. *Yard-Man* involved a similar claim that an employer had breached a collective-bargaining agreement when it terminated retiree benefits. Although the court found the text of the provision in that case ambiguous, it relied on the "context" of labor negotiations to resolve that ambiguity in favor of the retirees' interpretation. Specifically, the court inferred that parties to collective bargaining would intend retiree benefits to vest for life because such benefits are "not mandatory" or required to be included in collective-bargaining agreements, are "typically understood as a form of delayed compensation or reward for past services," and are keyed to the acquisition of retirement status. The court concluded that these inferences "outweigh[ed] any contrary implications [about the termination of retiree benefits] derived from" general termination clauses.

Applying the *Yard-Man* inferences on review of the District Court's dismissal of the action, the Court of Appeals concluded that the retirees had stated a plausible claim. "Keeping in mind the context of the labor-management negotiations identified in *Yard-Man*," the court found "it unlikely that [the Union] would agree to language that ensures its members a 'full Company contribution,' if the company could unilaterally change the level of contribution." . . . And it discerned an intent to vest lifetime contribution-free health care benefits from provisions tying eligibility for health care benefits to eligibility for pension benefits.

On remand, the District Court conducted a bench trial and ruled in favor of the retirees. It declined to revisit the question whether the P & I agreement created a vested right to retiree benefits, concluding that the Court of Appeals had definitively resolved that issue. It then issued a permanent injunction ordering M&G to reinstate contribution-free health care benefits. . . .

The Court of Appeals affirmed. . . .

This case is about the interpretation of collective-bargaining agreements that define rights to welfare benefits plans. The LMRA grants federal courts jurisdiction to resolve disputes between employers and labor unions about collective-bargaining agreements. When collective-bargaining agreements create pension or welfare benefits plans, those plans are subject to rules established in ERISA. ERISA defines pension plans as plans, funds, or programs that "provid[e] retirement income to employees" or that "resul[t] in a deferral of income." It defines welfare benefits plans as plans, funds, or programs established or maintained to provide participants with additional benefits, such as life insurance and disability coverage.

ERISA treats these two types of plans differently. Although ERISA imposes elaborate minimum funding and vesting standards for pension plans, it explicitly exempts welfare benefits plans from those rules. Welfare benefits plans must be "established and maintained pursuant to a written instrument," but "[e]mployers or other plan sponsors are generally free under ERISA, for any reason at any time, to adopt, modify, or terminate welfare plans," *Curtiss-Wright Corp.* v. *Schoonejongen*, 514 U. S. 73, 78 (1995). As we have previously recognized, "[E]mployers have large leeway to design disability and other welfare plans as they see fit." *Black & Decker Disability Plan* v. *Nord*, 538 U. S. 822, 833 (2003). And, we have observed, the rule that contractual "provisions ordinarily should be enforced as written is especially appropriate when enforcing an ERISA [welfare benefits] plan." *Heimeshoff* v. *Hartford Life & Accident Ins. Co.*, 571 U. S. ___ (2013) (slip op., at 7). That is because the "focus on the written terms of the plan is the linchpin of a system that is not so complex that administrative costs, or litigation expenses, unduly discourage employers from offering [welfare benefits] plans in the first place."

We interpret collective-bargaining agreements, including those establishing ERISA plans, according to ordinary principles of contract law, at least when those principles are not inconsistent with federal labor policy. . . .

In this case, the Court of Appeals applied the *Yard-Man* inferences to conclude that, in the absence of extrinsic evidence to the contrary, the provisions of the contract indicated an intent to vest retirees with lifetime benefits. As we now explain, those inferences conflict with ordinary principles of contract law. . . .

The Court of Appeals has long insisted that its *Yard-Man* inferences are drawn from ordinary contract law. In *Yard-Man* itself, the court purported to apply "traditional rules for contractual interpretation." The court first concluded that the provision governing retiree insurance benefits—which stated only that the employer "will provide" such benefits—was ambiguous as to the duration of those benefits. To resolve that ambiguity, it looked to other provisions of the agreement. The agreement included provisions for terminating active employees' insurance benefits in the case of layoffs and for terminating benefits for a retiree's spouse and dependents in case of the retiree's death before the expiration of the collective-bargaining agreement, but no provision specifically addressed the duration of retiree health care benefits. From the existence of these termination provisions and the absence of a termination provision specifically addressing retiree benefits, the court inferred an intent to vest those retiree benefits for life.

The court then purported to apply the rule that contracts should be interpreted to avoid illusory promises. It noted that the retiree insurance provisions "contain[ed] a promise that the company will pay an early retiree's insurance upon such retiree reaching age 65 but that the retiree must bear the cost of company insurance until that time." Employees could retire at age 55, but the agreement containing this promise applied only for a 3-year term. Thus, retirees between the ages of 55 and 62 would not turn 65 and become eligible for the company contribution before the 3-year agreement expired. In light of this fact, the court reasoned that the promise would be "completely illusory for many early retirees under age 62" if the retiree benefits terminated when the contract expired.

Finally, the court turned to "the context" of labor negotiations. It observed that "[b]enefits for retirees are . . . not mandatory subjects of collective bargaining" and that "employees are presumably aware that the union owes no obligation to bargain for continued benefits for retirees." Based on these observations, the court concluded that "it is unlikely that such benefits . . . would be left to the contingencies of future negotiations." It also asserted that "retiree benefits are in a sense 'status' benefits which, as such, carry with them an inference that they continue so long as the prerequisite status is maintained."

Although the contract included a general durational clause—meaning that the contract itself would expire at a set time—the court concluded that these contextual clues "outweigh[ed] any contrary implications derived from a routine duration clause."

Two years after *Yard-Man*, the court took this analysis even further. In a dispute between retirees and a steel company over retiree health insurance benefits, it construed the language "will continue to provide at its expense, supplemental medicare and major medical benefits for Pensioners aged 65 and over" to "*unambiguously* confe[r]" lifetime benefits. *Policy* v. *Powell Pressed Steel Co.*, 770 F. 2d 609, 615 (CA6 1985) (emphasis added). . . . The court refused to give any weight to provisions that supported a contrary construction—namely, one establishing a fund to pay pension, but not welfare, benefits, and another providing for the continuation of pension, but not welfare, benefits after the agreement expired. According to the court, a contrary interpretation "would render the Company's promise [of benefits for retirees aged 65 and over] in substantial part nugatory and illusory" to retirees who were 62 or younger when the 3-year agreement was signed. And it faulted the District Court for failing "to give effect" to *Yard-Man*'s admonition "that retiree benefits normally . . . are interminable." The Court of Appeals has continued to extend the reasoning of *Yard-Man*. Relying on *Yard-Man*'s statement that context considerations outweigh the effect of a general termination clause, it has concluded that, " '[a]bsent specific durational language referring to retiree benefits themselves,' a general durational clause *says nothing* about the vesting of retiree benefits." *Noe* v. *PolyOne Corp.*, 520 F. 3d 548, 555 (CA6 2008) (emphasis added). It has also held that a provision that "ties eligibility for retirement-health benefits to eligibility for a pension . . . [leaves] little room for debate that retirees' health benefits ves[t] upon retirement." Commenting on these extensions of *Yard-Man*, the court has acknowledged that "there is a reasonable argument to be made that, while th[e] court has repeatedly cautioned that *Yard-Man* does not create a presumption of vesting, [it] ha[s] gone on to apply just such a presumption." *Cole* v. *ArvinMeritor, Inc.*, 549 F. 3d 1064, 1074 (CA6 2008).

We disagree with the Court of Appeals' assessment that the inferences applied in *Yard-Man* and its progeny represent ordinary principles of contract law.

As an initial matter, *Yard-Man* violates ordinary contract principles by placing a thumb on the scale in favor of vested retiree benefits in all collective-bargaining agreements. That rule has no basis in ordinary principles of contract law. And it distorts the attempt "to ascertain the intention of *the parties*." 11 Williston § 30:2, at 18 (emphasis added). *Yard-Man*'s assessment of likely behavior in collective bargaining is too speculative and too far removed from the context of any particular contract to be useful in discerning the parties' intention.

And the Court of Appeals derived its assessment of likely behavior not from record evidence, but instead from its own suppositions about the intentions of employees, unions, and employers negotiating retiree benefits. . . . Although a court may look to known customs or usages in a particular industry to determine the meaning of a contract, the parties must prove those customs or usages using affirmative evidentiary support in a given case. 12 Williston § 34:3. *Yard-Man* relied on no record evidence indicating that employers and unions in that industry customarily vest retiree benefits. Worse, the Court of Appeals has taken the inferences in *Yard-Man* and applied them indiscriminately across industries. . . .

Because the Court of Appeals did not ground its *Yard-Man* inferences in any record evidence, it is unsurprising that the inferences rest on a shaky factual foundation. . . . *Yard-Man* also relied on the premise that retiree benefits are a form of deferred compensation, but that characterization is contrary to Congress' determination otherwise. In ERISA, Congress specifically defined plans that "resul[t] in a deferral of income by employees" as pension plans, and plans that offer medical benefits as welfare plans. Thus, retiree health care benefits are not a form of deferred compensation.

Further compounding this error, the Court of Appeals has refused to apply general durational clauses to provisions governing retiree benefits. Having inferred that parties would not leave retiree benefits to the contingencies of future negotiations, and that retiree benefits generally last as long as the recipient remains a retiree, the court in *Yard-Man* explicitly concluded that these inferences "outweigh[ed] any contrary implications derived from a routine duration clause terminating the agreement generally." The court's subsequent decisions went even further, requiring a contract to include a specific durational clause for retiree health care benefits to prevent vesting. These decisions distort the text of the agreement and conflict with the principle of contract law that the written agreement is presumed to encompass the whole agreement of the parties.

Perhaps tugged by these inferences, the Court of Appeals misapplied other traditional principles of contract law, including the illusory promises doctrine. That doctrine instructs courts to avoid constructions of contracts that would render promises illusory because such promises cannot serve as consideration for a contract. See 3 Williston § 7:7 (4th ed. 2008). But the Court of Appeals construed provisions that admittedly benefited some class of retirees as "illusory" merely because they did not equally benefit *all* retirees. That interpretation is a contradiction in terms—a promise that is "partly" illusory is by definition not illusory. If it benefits some class of retirees, then it may serve as consideration for the union's promises. And the court's interpretation is particularly inappropriate in the context of collective-bargaining agreements, which are negotiated on behalf of a broad category of individuals and consequently will often include provisions inapplicable to some category of employees.

The Court of Appeals also failed even to consider the traditional principle that courts should not construe ambiguous writings to create lifetime promises. See 3 A. Corbin, Corbin on Contracts § 553, p. 216 (1960). . . .

Similarly, the Court of Appeals failed to consider the traditional principle that "contractual obligations will cease, in the ordinary course, upon termination of the bargaining agreement." *Litton Financial Printing Div., Litton Business Systems, Inc.* v. *NLRB*, 501 U. S. 190, 207 (1991). . . .

We reject the *Yard-Man* inferences as inconsistent with ordinary principles of contract law. But because "[t]his Court is one of final review, not of first view," the Court of Appeals should be the first to review the agreements at issue under the correct legal principles. We vacate the judgment of the Court of Appeals and remand the case for that court to apply ordinary principles of contract law in the first instance.

■ JUSTICE GINSBURG, with whom JUSTICE BREYER, JUSTICE SOTOMAYOR, and JUSTICE KAGAN join, concurring.

Today's decision rightly holds that courts must apply ordinary contract principles, shorn of presumptions, to determine whether retiree health-care benefits survive the expiration of a collective-bargaining agreement. Under the "cardinal principle" of contract interpretation, "the intention of the parties, to be gathered from the whole instrument, must prevail." 11 Williston § 30:2, p. 27. To determine what the contracting parties intended, a court must examine the entire agreement in light of relevant industry-specific "customs, practices, usages, and terminology." *Id.*, § 30:4, at 55–58. . . .

Contrary to M&G's assertion, no rule requires "clear and express" language in order to show that parties intended health-care benefits to vest. "[C]onstraints upon the employer after the expiration date of a collective-bargaining agreement," we have observed, may be derived from the agreement's "explicit terms," but they "may arise as well from . . . implied terms of the expired agreement." *Litton Financial Printing Div., Litton Business Systems, Inc.* v. *NLRB*, 501 U. S. 190, 203, 207 (1991).

On remand, the Court of Appeals should examine the entire agreement to determine whether the parties intended retiree health-care benefits to vest. Because the retirees have a vested, lifetime right to a monthly pension, a provision stating that retirees "will receive" health-care benefits if they are "receiving a monthly pension" is relevant to this examination. So is a "survivor benefits" clause instructing that if a retiree dies, her surviving spouse will "continue to receive [the retiree's health-care] benefits . . . until death or remarriage." If, after considering all relevant contractual language in light of industry practices, the Court of Appeals concludes that the contract is ambiguous, it may turn to extrinsic evidence—for example, the parties' bargaining history. The Court of Appeals, however, must conduct the foregoing inspection without *Yard-Man*'s "thumb on the scale in favor of vested retiree benefits."

Because I understand the Court's opinion to be consistent with these basic rules of contract interpretation, I join it.

3. THE RETIREE HEALTH PLAN LITIGATION

1. *CBA and plan.* Most of the retiree health plans that have resulted in litigation about the sponsor's right to amend or terminate have been collectively bargained. Breach of a collective bargaining agreement (CBA) is actionable under § 301 of the Labor Management Relations Act (LMRA), 29 U.S.C. § 185. It is common for plaintiffs to invoke both ERISA and LMRA grounds in these cases.

The question of whether benefits outlive the CBA that creates them can arise with respect to pension plans as well, e.g., United Steelworkers of America v. North Bend Terminal Co., 752 F.2d 256 (6th Cir.1985). However, ERISA's vesting and anti-reduction rules limit the scope of the parties' freedom to contract for reduction or forfeiture of pension benefits.

2. *Construction. Tackett* exemplifies the recurrent situation in retiree health cases. The contract or plan is silent or ambiguous on the question of whether the employer retains the right to modify or cancel retiree health benefits, and the court approaches the task as one of contract construction. Where there is a CBA, only infrequently does the court treat the plan in litigation as unambiguous. E.g., United Steelworkers of America v. Connors Steel Co., 855 F.2d 1499 (11th Cir.1988) (CBA unambiguously obligated the employer to continue the plan beyond the life of the agreement and for the lives of retired employees). See also Dewhurst v. Century Aluminum Co., 649 F.3d 287 (4th Cir. 2011) (CBA unambiguously provided that benefits were to remain in effect only for the duration of the CBA, and nothing in the CBA inferred an intent to continue benefits beyond its expiration date).

When a plan is collectively bargained, both management and the union participate in drafting plan terms. In non-CBA plans, by contrast, the employees are less likely to have input into the drafting. Should the maxim, "construe strictly against the drafter," apply to construction questions arising only in non-CBA cases?

The starting point in any construction case is the language of the instrument and its surrounding circumstances. In the context of a collectively bargained plan, the relevant instrument is the CBA. In nonunion plans, the relevant instrument is the SPD.

3. Yard-Man *and the Sixth Circuit's approach to implied vesting: "status" benefits.* As recounted by Justice Thomas, during the thirty-year period leading to the decision in *Tackett* the Sixth Circuit (home to some of the largest unionized employers in the country) had, starting with *Yard-Man*, staked out a position increasingly divergent from those of the rest of the Courts of Appeals concerning the vested status of collectively bargained retiree medical benefits. *Yard-Man* had in particular become influential in the mid-1980s for its suggestion that "retiree benefits are in a sense 'status' benefits" that may not be freely terminable regardless of what the plan permits. As further recounted by Justice Thomas, the Sixth Circuit had proceeded, in a series of decisions over the ensuing years, to come close to holding that collectively bargained retiree medical benefits would be deemed vested for life barring express language to the contrary in the relevant collective bargaining agreement. In *Tackett* the Supreme Court unanimously reversed this position.

The Court's opinion, above, relied heavily on black-letter contract interpretation rules, such as that interpretation of an ambiguous contract must rest in part on "customs or usages in a *particular industry*," and faulted the Sixth Circuit for applying its contractual inference "indiscriminately across industries." Is the ambiguity at issue in these cases connected with any terms whose meaning is industry-specific? Is it inherently plausible that the collective bargaining negotiators, in any industry, intended that the post-retirement benefits for which they were negotiating could be terminated at the end of the next (typically three-year) contract term?

4. *Should retiree health benefits vest?* Recall the now disparaged "gratuity" theory of pensions, discussed supra in Chapters 1 and 4. Does the employer's power unilaterally to alter or to terminate a retiree health plan resemble the gratuity theory of pensions? The gratuity theory was overcome in the movement to make private pension promises nonforfeitable. Should Congress see a parallel and extend the vesting rules to retiree health plans? To other welfare benefit plans? Arguments for vesting-like protections are mustered in Joan Vogel, Until Death Do Us Part: Vesting of Retiree Insurance, 9 Industrial Relations L.J. 183 (1987).

5. *Evidentiary issues.* In Eardman v. Bethlehem Steel Corp. Employee Welfare Benefit Plans, 607 F.Supp. 196 (W.D.N.Y.1984), there was evidence that the company routinely conducted "exit interviews" when employees retired, and that company representatives repeatedly stated at these occasions that retirees' health benefits could not be changed. Does such evidence bear materially on what the parties to the CBA or to the plan intended? See Comment, Rethinking *Yard-Man:* A Return to Fundamental Contract Principles in Retiree Benefits Litigation, 37 Emory L.J. 1033, 1073 (1988), discussing *Eardman* and similar cases and arguing that such facts fit more easily under the heading of estoppel than contract interpretation. "Courts must be careful, however, not to enforce promises on which no reasonable person would rely." Id.

In Moore v. Metropolitan Life Ins. Co., 856 F.2d 488 (2d Cir.1988), there was evidence that the employer's informational programs and filmstrips about benefits for employees did not mention the employer's power to amend or terminate retiree health benefits, although the plan and the summary plan description (SPD) did. Which prevails? When the plan contains a restriction but the SPD does not, which prevails? The case law on conflicts between the plan and the SPD is discussed in Chapter 13.

6. *Active and retired workers.* Under the Sixth Circuit's (now-overturned) construction in *Yard-Man,* the contract intended for the retirees to have nonterminable rights, but for the active workers' rights to be terminable. Does it seem likely that retirees should have been intended to fare better than active workers? Would you expect to find such a pattern in health care plans in which the issue of terminability was foreseen and was addressed unambiguously?

An argument for special solicitude for retirees appears in the district court opinion in Musto v. American General Corp., 615 F.Supp. 1483 (M.D.Tenn.1985), rev'd in part, 861 F.2d 897 (6th Cir.1988). "Once an employee has rendered his years of service to the employer, his 'sweat equity,' and has taken retirement, the employee furnishes little to the employer that generates revenue; hence, the employer may perceive little risk in reducing the level of benefits previously promised. [To] permit the enforcement of termination/modification clauses without a showing of good cause has the effect of reducing the status of hard earned welfare plan benefits to mere gratuities." Id. at 1496–97. Is the court correct in asserting that an employer has no incentive to avoid treating retirees opportunistically?

7. *Bankruptcy.* Even if the employer's liability for retiree health benefits is quite unambiguous under the contract or plan, the employees may not receive any benefits if the employer is insolvent and unable to pay what was promised.

It will be recalled that pension promises were similarly at risk in the days before ERISA—the plan participant bore the risk of the sponsor's default. ERISA's funding requirements and plan termination insurance scheme effectively shifted most of that risk away from participants. The sponsor's general creditors may not reach the assets of the separate pension trust fund, nor will underfunding defeat the pension claims. It has been seen (in Chapter 6) that if on account of underfunding or other causes the assets in the trust fund are inadequate to pay promised benefits, the Pension Benefit Guaranty Corporation (PBGC) will make up the shortfall (up to the amount of a generous ceiling).

The question of what happens to retiree health benefits in the event of the sponsor's default became a cause célebre in 1986 in the LTV bankruptcy. LTV filed a Bankruptcy Code Chapter 11 petition and immediately terminated the health and life insurance benefits of approximately 78,000 retirees. LTV's position was that the Bankruptcy Code required this step, because the retirees were creditors like any others, whose rights would have to abide the bankruptcy proceedings. Litigation and congressional hearings followed. LTV requested and received bankruptcy court permission to restore the benefits temporarily. Stopgap legislation was enacted requiring companies undergoing Chapter 11 reorganization to pay all retiree medical and life insurance benefits. P.L. 99–591, P.L. 99–656, P.L. 100–41, P.L. 100–99; Senate Report No. 100–119, reprinted in U.S.Cong. & Admin.News Leg.Hist. 683 (1988).

Subsequently, Congress enacted a permanent modification of the Bankruptcy Code, the Retiree Benefits Bankruptcy Protection Act of 1988, P.L. 100–334. It added Section 1114 to the Bankruptcy Code, which requires companies filing under Chapter 11 to continue paying retiree health and life insurance benefits unless the court orders a modification. The court may enter such an order if it finds that "such modification is necessary to permit the reorganization of the debtor and assures that all creditors, the debtor, and all of the affected parties are treated fairly and equitably, and is clearly favored by the balance of the [equities]." Bankruptcy Code § 1114(g)(3). A bankruptcy court's finding that a modification is "necessary" is likely to be accorded significant weight. E.g., In re Ormet Corp., 355 B.R. 37 (S.D.Ohio 2006) (upholding bankruptcy court's finding that modification was necessary; findings were not clearly erroneous).

In tossing this standardless grant of discretion to the court, Congress was tracking the solution devised in Bankruptcy Code § 1113, for situations in which a company in Chapter 11 reorganization undertakes to reject an ordinary CBA. Is the analogy between an ordinary CBA and a retiree health plan sound? The CBA structures future employment relationships; but the retiree health claim is a matured obligation, hence a debt resembling the debtor's other obligations.

In *In re Doskocil Cos.*, 130 B.R. 870 (Bankr.D.Kan.1991) a company undergoing a Chapter 11 reorganization was allowed to modify health and life insurance benefits of salaried retirees without complying with the Bankruptcy Code § 1114 procedures because the company had reserved the right to modify the benefits before entering bankruptcy. A company cannot avoid the procedural protection provided by Bankruptcy Code § 1114 by terminating employees on the verge of retirement. In re General DataComm Industries, Inc., 407 F.3d 616 (3d Cir.2005).

In *In re Visteon*, 612 F.3d 210 (3rd Cir. 2010), the Third Circuit broke with the view expressed in cases like *Doskocil*, holding that a bankrupt employer cannot unilaterally terminate non-vested retiree benefits while in bankruptcy, even if it retained the contractual right to do so outside of bankruptcy. Based on the plain language of § 1114 and its legislative history, the court agreed with the union's claim that "Congress intended to restrict a debtor's ability to modify or terminate, except through the § 1114 process, *any* retiree benefits during a Chapter 11 bankruptcy proceeding, regardless of whether the debtor could terminate those benefits outside of bankruptcy." Id. at 212. In reaching its holding, the court relied heavily on an article written by one of us: Susan Stabile, Protecting Retiree Medical Benefits in Bankruptcy: The Scope of Section 1114 of the Bankruptcy Code, 14 Cardozo L. Rev. 1911, 1932 (1993).

The Retiree Benefits Bankruptcy Protection Act pertains only to Chapter 11 reorganizations, not to Chapter 7 liquidations. Is Chapter 11 a sensible place to protect retiree health benefits? Most firms that file for Chapter 11 bankruptcy do not survive, nor do firms that file for Chapter 7 liquidation, nor do firms that dissolve outside of bankruptcy. Why protect retiree health rights during Chapter 11 reorganization, that is, when the firm stays in business, but not when the firm goes out of business?

Retiree claims to health benefits in bankruptcy are typically settled as part of the bankruptcy negotiations. Three methods are commonly used. First, the reorganized employer can continue to provide benefits, although not necessarily at the same level as before the bankruptcy. Second, the retirees are sometimes given cash payments. This has the drawback of being taxable income and wages subject to FICA taxes, but retirees are often happy to receive a lump sum. Third, and probably the most common arrangement, the company makes payments into an IRC § 501(c)(9) trust, i.e., a voluntary employees' beneficiary association (VEBA), and the retirees essentially run their own health benefit program. The IRS has consistently been willing to characterize these VEBAs as maintained pursuant to a collectively bargained plan, even if the retirees were not union members, because the VEBAs result from arm's length negotiating between the committee representing the retirees and the debtor. See, e.g., Private Letter Ruling 9050023 (Dec. 14, 1990). This characterization allows the income generated by the assets of the VEBA to be exempt from the unrelated business income tax that would otherwise be applicable if the VEBA were not collectively bargained. See IRC §§ 419A & 512(a)(3)(E). The taxation of VEBAs is discussed in Chapter 10.

8. *ERISA fiduciary law.* Most retiree health litigation takes the form of an action for benefits due under the alleged plan. In some cases, however, the plaintiffs may seek remedy for breach of fiduciary duty. For example, in Jones v. American General Life & Accident Ins. Co., 370 F.3d

1065 (11th Cir.2004), the court dismissed the retiree plaintiffs' claim that contract language caused the health benefits to vest, but sustained the actionability of a claim that the employer in its capacity as plan fiduciary engaged in a "systematic pattern of misrepresentation" in violation of ERISA's fiduciary duty of disclosure that induced the plaintiffs to rely upon the continuity of the benefits. 370 F.3d at 1071. However, not all courts welcome such claims. In Frahm v. Equitable Life Assur. Soc., 137 F.3d 955, 961 (7th Cir.1998), Judge Easterbrook said that "a person cannot rely on an oral statement, when he has in hand written materials disclosing the truth."

It has been seen in Chapter 13 that in certain circumstances the courts have imposed fiduciary duties to disclose information about forthcoming changes in plan terms. The attempt is sometimes made to link retiree health cases to these developments in fiduciary law. The Sixth Circuit in *Sprague* rejected such an argument, saying "GM did not act as a fiduciary in deciding to change" the terms of the plan. 133 F.3d at 404, citing Lockheed Corp. v. Spink, 517 U.S. 882 (1996). The Sixth Circuit went on to discuss Varity Corp. v. Howe, 516 U.S. 489 (1996), reproduced in Chapter 12. The Sixth Circuit read *Varity* to indicate that GM may have acted in a fiduciary capacity when it explained its retirement program to retirees, but the court found as a matter of law that GM breached no fiduciary duty in its oral representations. The court saw "a world of difference between the employer's deliberate misleading of employees in *Varity Corp.* and GM's failure to begin every communication to plan participants with a caveat."

9. *Literature.* Retiree health benefits have been the subject of substantial commentary. See Richard L. Kaplan, Nicholas J. Powers & Jordan Zucker, Retirees at Risk: The Precarious Promise of Post-Employment Health Benefits, 9 Yale J. Health Policy, Law & Ethics 287 (2009); William T. Payne & Pamina Ewing, Union-Negotiated Lifetime Retiree Health Benefits: Promise or Illusion, 9 Marquette Elder's Advisor 319 (2008); David A. Pratt, The Past, Present and Future of Retiree Health Benefits, 3 J. Health & Biomedical L. 103 (2007); Norma M. Sharara & Christopher E. Condeluci, Cutting Back or Terminating Your Retiree Medical Benefits Program? A Cook-Book of How to Avoid Potential Liability, 30 Tax Management Compensation Planning J. 87 (2002); Catherine L. Fisk, *Lochner* Redux: The Renaissance of Laissez-Faire Contract in the Federal Common Law of Employee Benefits, 56 Ohio State L.J. 153 (1995); Wilber H. Boies & Nancy G. Ross, The Struggle over Retiree Medical Benefits, 19 Employee Relations L.J. 169 (1993–94).

H. CLAIM DENIALS UNDER HEALTH PLANS

Four types of welfare plans feature centrally in the benefit denial case law: occupational disability plans, severance pay plans, health care plans, and plans that insure against accidental death and injury. See generally Peter A. Myers, Discretionary Language, Conflicts of Interest, and Standard of Review for ERISA Disability Plans, 28 Seattle L. Rev. 925 (2005). Disability plan issues have been extensively discussed in chapter 15, in connection with the Unum/Provident scandal.

Health care is the largest American industry, and most health care for the nonelderly is delivered through ERISA-covered employee benefit plans. Although relatively few benefit denials under health care plans become contentious, the sheer magnitude of the health care enterprise has resulted in extensive litigation. Among the recurrent issues in cases contesting health benefit denials:

1. *Preexisting conditions.* Until recently, health plans commonly excluded coverage for so-called preexisting conditions, that is, for medical problems that arose before the start of the participant's coverage under the particular plan. See, e.g., Bullwinkel v. New England Mutual Life Ins. Co., 18 F.3d 429 (7th Cir.1994); Pitcher v. Principal Mutual Life Ins. Co., 93 F.3d 407 (7th Cir.1996). Provisions of the Health Insurance Portability and Accountability Act of 1996 (HIPAA), codified as ERISA § 701, restricted the exclusion of preexisting conditions in two ways. Section 701(a)(1) imposes a six-month look-back rule, which allows such exclusions only for conditions diagnosed or treated "within the 6-month period ending on the enrollment date" that the employee joins the plan. Earlier treatment may not be the subject of a preexisting condition exclusion. Section 701(a)(2) imposes a twelve-month look-forward rule, forbidding such an exclusion from extending for more than 12 (or in certain cases, 18) months beyond the enrollment date.

The Patient Protection and Affordable Care Act of 2010 bans preexisting condition exclusions and premium increases based on health status, starting in 2014. PHSA § 2704.

2. *Experimental treatment.* Health plans commonly contain exclusions for experimental, cosmetic, and optional procedures, variously defined. The question whether some procedure fits these definitions has often been litigated. E.g., Mayeaux v. Louisiana Health Service & Indemnity Co., 376 F.3d 420 (5th Cir.2004); Exbom v. Central States, Southeast and Southwest Areas Health and Welfare Fund, 900 F.2d 1138 (7th Cir.1990).

"[The] archetypal experimental treatment lawsuit has been one in which a gravely-ill patient petitions the court for an order directing his or her insurance company to authorize certain [newer] procedures [that] the patient's treating physician recommends [as] the best opportunity to sustain the patient's health and life. [The] insurance company refuses to pre-authorize [the requested procedures on the ground] that the procedures constitute experimental treatments excluded from coverage." Natalie L. Regoli, Insurance Roulette: The Experimental Treatment Exclusion and Desperate Patients, 22 Quinnipiac L. Rev. 697 (2004).

A treatment for breast cancer called high dose chemotherapy with autologous bone marrow transplanting has been the subject of much health plan litigation. Compare Holder v. Prudential Ins. Co., 951 F.2d 89 (5th Cir.1992) (held experimental), and Farley v. Benefit Trust Life Ins. Co., 979 F.2d 653 (8th Cir.1992) (accord), with Fuja v. Benefit Trust Life Ins. Co., 809 F.Supp. 1333 (N.D.Ill.1992) (not experimental), and Adams v. Blue Cross/Blue Shield of Maryland, 757 F.Supp. 661 (D.Md.1991) (accord). Some policies expressly exclude the procedure. A related treatment, autologous blood stem cell transplant, figures in Zervos v. Verizon New York, 277 F.3d 635 (2d Cir.2002). Cases are collected in Annot., Propriety of Denial of Medical or Hospital Benefits for Investigative, Educational, or Experimental Medical Procedures Pursuant to Exclusion Contained in ERISA-Governed Health Plan, 122 A.L.R. Fed. 1 (1994 & Supp.2009). One article contends that variations in insurance company determinations of whether the treatment is or is not experimental are hard to correlate with plan language or patient condition. W. Peters & M. Rogers, Variation in Approval by Insurance Companies of Coverage for Autologous Bone Marrow Transplantation for Breast Cancer, 330 New England J. Medicine 473 (1994).

Literature: Judith C. Brostron, The Conflict of Interest Standard in ERISA Cases: Can It Be Avoided in the Denial of High Dose Chemotherapy Treatment for Breast Cancer?, 3 DePaul J. Health Care L. 1 (1999); Donald W. Light, Life, Death and the Insurance Companies, 330 New England J. Medicine 498 (1994); Richard S. Saver, Reimbursing New Technologies: Why Are the Courts Judging Experimental Medicine?, 44 Stanford L. Rev. 1095 (1992). Case law is collected in Annot., Judicial Review of Denial of Health Care Benefits under Employee Benefit Plan Governed by [ERISA]—Post Firestone Cases, 128 A.L.R. Fed. 1 (1995 & Supp.2009).

Is infertility an "illness" under a health plan? See Egert v. Connecticut General Life Ins. Co., 900 F.2d 1032 (7th Cir.1990), holding infertility not an illness, with the result that the cost of an in vitro fertilization procedure was excluded from coverage. Accord, Thomas v. Truck Drivers and Helpers Local No. 355, Health & Welfare Fund, 771 F.Supp. 714 (D.Md.1991) (male infertility not an illness, hence corrective surgery excluded from coverage).

3. *Custodial care.* Many plans attempt to distinguish covered "medical" or "health" care from excluded "custodial" or "rehabilitative" care. Such determinations are reviewed under the A&C standard when the plan so provides, otherwise under *Firestone's* de novo standard. Compare Dvorak v. Metropolitan Life Ins. Co., 965 F.2d 606 (8th Cir.1992) and Adelson v. GTE Corp., 790 F.Supp. 1265 (D.Md.1992) (not custodial), with DeVille Nursing Service, Inc. v. Metropolitan Life Ins. Co., 789 F.Supp. 213 (W.D.La.1992) (custodial care). Regarding rehabilitative care, see Anderson v. Blue Cross/Blue Shield of Alabama, 907 F.2d 1072 (11th Cir.1990) (services were within plan exclusion for primarily "rehabilitative services"); accord, Vasseur v. Halliburton Co., 950 F.2d 1002 (5th Cir.1992).

4. *Provisional relief.* ERISA cases concerning the denial of health plan benefits commonly arise in the circumstance in which treatment has already been given, and the issue is whether the plan will pay for it. If the plan successfully refuses, the burden falls on the patient who has private means, otherwise on the health care providers or the public reimbursement mechanisms. Occasionally, however, the question of entitlement to plan health benefits arises in advance of treatment, at what is sometimes called the preclearance stage. In these situations, the provider commonly denies the participant the requested care if the plan administrator does not approve the treatment.

Because of the dire consequences of denying health coverage, courts will order a preliminary injunction to prevent denial of benefits on a showing that the participant is likely to prevail on the merits. E.g., Leonhardt v. Holden Business Forms Co., 828 F.Supp. 657

(D.Minn.1993) (autologous bone marrow transplant); Wilson v. Group Hospitalization and Medical Services, Inc., 15 E.B.C. 1446 (D.D.C.1992) (same).

5.   *Amendments to plans*. As discussed in Section B of this chapter, ERISA's lack of vesting of welfare benefits means that employers are free to make changes to their medical plans, and they frequently reserve the right to do so in their plan documents. Nonetheless, participants aggrieved by changes to their plans do try to challenge plan amendments. E.g., Saltzman v. Independence Blue Cross, 384 Fed. Appx. 107 (3d Cir. June 10, 2010), holding that participants had no claim for relief based on plan's reclassification of Plavix in a way that resulted in a higher co-payment for the drug. The Third Circuit held that participants had no vested right as to the amount of the copayment and that the decision to re-categorize Plavix was an exercise of discretion that did not conflict with the terms of the plan.

6.   *Claims and appeals*. The Patient Protection and Affordable Care Act of 2010 requires covered individuals to have access to an effective internal and external appeals process. PHSA § 2719. This is generally effective for plan years beginning after September 22, 2010. The new regulations supplement the existing DoL regulations governing claims and appeals procedures for ERISA plans.

The internal claims and appeals rules are applicable to both insured plans and their insurers: if either the insurer or the plan complies, then the obligations of both are satisfied. For external review, only the insurer of an insured plan is responsible, provided that the insurer is subject to state external review procedures satisfying the minimum standards imposed by the regulations. Self-insured ERISA plans must comply with the internal claims and appeals procedures and with federal external review procedures to be detailed in future guidance.

Neither grandfathered plans nor "excepted benefits" are required to comply with PHSA § 2719 or the regulations. Excepted benefits are those excepted from HIPAA's portability rules and include most health FSAs, some HRAs, limited scope dental and vision plans, and certain others. For a complete list of excepted benefits, see 26 C.F.R. § 54.9831–1. Excepted benefits sponsored by ERISA employers are not subject to the new rules, but generally remain subject to the existing DoL regulations.

The new regulations impose six new obligations in addition to the existing ERISA claims procedures: (1) a broader definition of "adverse benefit determination", to include a rescission of coverage; (2) a requirement that urgent care claims be decided as soon as possible, but generally no later than 24 hours following receipt (previously 72 hours); (3) additional criteria to ensure that a claimant receives a full and fair review, including a requirement that a plan provide to the claimant, free of charge, any new or additional evidence considered or generated in connection with the claim, as well as an explanation of the rationale underlying the determination, *before* providing notice of the final adverse benefit determination; (4) a requirement that all claims determinations and appeals must be designed to ensure impartiality and independence with respect to the persons making the decisions; (5) new notice standards; and (6) a requirement of strict adherence, in the absence of which there will be a deemed exhaustion of internal claims and appeals procedures, regardless of whether (1) the plan substantially complied with the requirements or (2) any error is "de minimis." Non-compliance with the new claims procedures could enable a claimant to seek external review or immediate judicial review of the benefit denial. Claims are deemed denied on review without the exercise of discretion by an appropriate fiduciary, which could cause the plan to lose deference to its claim determination and lead a court to apply the de novo standard on judicial review.

The plan or issuer must provide continued coverage pending the outcome of any appeal. As under the current regulations, advance notice and an opportunity for an advance review must be provided before benefits for an ongoing course of treatment are reduced or terminated.

If a claimant's appeal is denied, he or she is entitled to a review of that determination through an external review process. The regulations set forth rules determining whether a state or federal external review applies, except that self-insured plans are generally not subject to state external review processes and generally will be required to comply with the federal external review process.

I. FIDUCIARY STATUS OF MEDICAL PROVIDERS

The applicability of ERISA fiduciary law to welfare benefit plans that provide health care benefits has become an area of considerable difficulty, uncertainty, and controversy.

The initial understanding was that the administrator of an ERISA health care plan was a fiduciary, but that health care service providers such as physicians and hospitals were not. See William E. Mattingly, Employer Liability for a Medical Plan, 16 Tax Management Compensation Planning J. 159 (1989).

The growth of managed care health services, which place in the hands of physicians and other health care personnel considerable discretion about whether to make care available, put pressure on this line between ERISA plan administrator and medical service provider. In particular, the question arose whether to characterize as ERISA fiduciaries decisionmakers in health maintenance organizations (HMOs) and other such managed care organizations (MCOs), including physicians and other gatekeepers.

In litigation settings these cases have arisen most prominently in circumstances in which an employee (or a deceased employee's successor) claims that the financial incentives for cost containment in the employer-provided HMO or MCO induced the physician or other provider to withhold appropriate care, in violation of ERISA's fiduciary's duties of loyalty and prudence, § 404(a)(1)(A)–(B). The question reached the Supreme Court on certiorari from the Seventh Circuit, which had held the HMO in question and an affiliate to be "plan fiduciaries due to their discretionary authority in deciding disputed claims." Herdrich v. Pegram, 154 F.3d 362, 370 (7th Cir.1998), petition for rehearing denied, 170 F.3d 683 (7th Cir.1999).

In a notable dissent from the denial of rehearing, Judge Easterbrook cautioned "that the panel has condemned HMO and managed-care systems on medical grounds, and used its view of good medical practice as the basis of a conclusion that the HMO structure violates ERISA." 170 F.3d at 684. He criticized the panel's application of ERISA's definition of "fiduciary" in § 3(21)(A):

> [T]he panel emphasized sub-(iii) [of the ERISA § 3(21) definition of "fiduciary"], concluding that [the HMO] has "discretionary authority or discretionary responsibility in the administration of such plan." Discretionary authority is obvious; but does [the HMO] exercise discretion "in the administration of [the] plan", or only in the provision of medical services? [A] surgeon exercises a great deal of discretion when deciding how (if at all) to perform an operation, but the fact that an ERISA welfare benefit plan pays for the medical procedure does not make the surgeon a "fiduciary" of the patient and convert all medical-malpractice claims to federal common law under ERISA in the process. What is true at the level of a medical professional is true at the level of a medical practice group such as [the HMO in this case]. Unless the group exercises, not discretion in the abstract, but discretion "in the administration of [the] plan," it is not a fiduciary under ERISA.

The Supreme Court, in the unanimous opinion discussed below, undertook to resolve the question whether treatment decisions made by an HMO, acting through its physician employees, are fiduciary acts within the meaning of ERISA. The Court held, in a unanimous decision authored by Justice Souter, that they are not. Pegram v. Herdrich, 530 U.S. 211 (2000).

1. PEGRAM V. HERDRICH

530 U.S. 211 (2000).

■ JUSTICE SOUTER delivered the opinion of the Court. . . .

I

The plaintiff sued her physician and the HMO in state court for medical malpractice, and she later added two counts charging state law fraud claims. The defendants responded that ERISA preempted the new counts, and removed the case to federal court, where they sought summary judgment on the fraud counts. The District Court granted their motion as to one count but granted the plaintiff leave to amend the one remaining. This she did by alleging that provision of medical services under the terms of the HMO organization, rewarding its physician owners for limiting medical care, entailed an inherent or anticipatory breach of an ERISA fiduciary duty, since these terms created an incentive to make decisions in the physicians' self-interest, rather than the exclusive interests of plan participants.

Herdrich sought relief under ERISA § 409(a) which provides liability for breach of ERISA fiduciary duties.

When the defendant HMO moved to dismiss the ERISA count for failure to state a claim upon which relief could be granted, the District Court granted the motion. The original malpractice counts were then tried to a jury, and Herdrich prevailed on both, receiving $35,000 in compensation for her injury. She then appealed the dismissal of the ERISA claim to the Court of Appeals for the Seventh Circuit, which reversed. The court held that the HMO was acting as a fiduciary when its physicians made the challenged decisions and that her allegations were sufficient to state a claim. . . .

"Since inducement to ration care goes to the very point of any HMO scheme, and rationing necessarily raises some risks while reducing others (ruptured appendixes are more likely; unnecessary appendectomies are less so), any legal principle purporting to draw a line between good and bad HMOs would embody, in effect, a judgment about socially acceptable medical risk. A valid conclusion of this sort would, however, necessarily turn on facts to which courts would probably not have ready access: correlations between malpractice rates and various HMO models, similar correlations involving fee-for-service models, and so on. And, of course, assuming such material could be obtained by courts in litigation like this, any standard defining the unacceptably risky HMO structure (and consequent vulnerability to claims like Herdrich's) would depend on a judgment about the appropriate level of expenditure for health care in light of the associated malpractice risk. But such complicated factfinding and such a debatable social judgment are not wisely required of courts unless for some reason resort cannot be had to the legislative process, with its preferable forum for comprehensive investigations and judgments of social value, such as optimum treatment levels and health care expenditure.

We think, then, that courts are not in a position to derive a sound legal principle to differentiate an HMO like Carle from other HMOs. For that reason, we proceed on the assumption that the decisions listed in Herdrich's complaint cannot be subject to a claim that they violate fiduciary standards unless all such decisions by all HMOs acting through their owner or employee physicians are to be judged by the same standards and subject to the same claims. . . .

Beyond the threshold statement of responsibility, however, the analogy between ERISA fiduciary and common law trustee becomes problematic. This is so because the trustee at common law characteristically wears only his fiduciary hat when he takes action to affect a beneficiary, whereas the trustee under ERISA may wear different hats.

Speaking of the traditional trustee, Professor Scott's treatise admonishes that the trustee "is not permitted to place himself in a position where it would be for his own benefit to violate his duty to the beneficiaries." 2A Scott, § 170, at 311. Under ERISA, however, a fiduciary may have financial interests adverse to beneficiaries. Employers, for example, can be ERISA fiduciaries and still take actions to the disadvantage of employee beneficiaries, when they act as employers (*e.g.*, firing a beneficiary for reasons unrelated to the ERISA plan), or even as plan sponsors (*e.g.*, modifying the terms of a plan as allowed by ERISA to provide less generous benefits). Nor is there any apparent reason in the ERISA provisions to conclude, as Herdrich argues, that this tension is permissible only for the employer or plan sponsor, to the exclusion of persons who provide services to an ERISA plan.

ERISA does require, however, that the fiduciary with two hats wear only one at a time, and wear the fiduciary hat when making fiduciary decisions. See *Hughes Aircraft Co. v. Jacobson*, 525 U.S. 432, 443–444 (1999); *Varity Corp. v. Howe*, 516 U.S. 489, 497 (1996). Thus, the statute does not describe fiduciaries simply as administrators of the plan, or managers or advisers. Instead it defines an administrator, for example, as a fiduciary only "to the extent" that he acts in such a capacity in relation to a plan. [ERISA § 3(21)(A)]. In every case charging breach of ERISA fiduciary duty, then, the threshold question is not whether the actions of some person employed to provide services under a plan adversely affected a plan beneficiary's interest, but whether that person was acting as a fiduciary (that is, was performing a fiduciary function) when taking the action subject to complaint. . . .

E

The pleadings must also be parsed very carefully to understand what acts by physician owners acting on Carle's behalf are alleged to be fiduciary in nature. It will help to keep two sorts of arguably administrative acts in mind. What we will call pure "eligibility decisions" turn on the plan's coverage of a particular condition or medical procedure for its treatment. "Treatment decisions," by contrast, are choices about how to go about diagnosing and treating a patient's condition: given a patient's constellation of symptoms, what is the appropriate medical response?

These decisions are often practically inextricable from one another, as amici on both sides agree. . . . The kinds of decisions mentioned in Herdrich's ERISA count and claimed to be fiduciary in character are just such mixed eligibility and treatment decisions: physicians' conclusions about when to use diagnostic tests; about seeking consultations and making referrals to physicians and facilities other than Carle's; about proper standards of care, the experimental character of a proposed course of treatment, the reasonableness of a certain treatment, and the emergency character of a medical condition. . . .

III

A

Based on our understanding of the matters just discussed, we think Congress did not intend Carle or any other HMO to be treated as a fiduciary to the extent that it makes mixed eligibility decisions acting through its physicians.

First, we need to ask how this fiduciary standard would affect HMOs if it applied as Herdrich claims it should be applied, not directed against any particular mixed decision that injured a patient, but against HMOs that make mixed decisions in the course of providing medical care for profit. Recovery would be warranted simply upon showing that the profit incentive to ration care would generally affect mixed decisions, in derogation of the fiduciary standard to act solely in the interest of the patient without possibility of conflict. . . . It is enough to recognize that the Judiciary has no warrant to precipitate the upheaval that would follow a refusal to dismiss Herdrich's ERISA claim. The fact is that for over 27 years the Congress of the United States has promoted the formation of HMO practices. . . . If Congress wishes to restrict its approval of HMO practice to certain preferred forms, it may choose to do so. But the Federal Judiciary would be acting contrary to the congressional policy of allowing HMO organizations if it were to entertain an ERISA fiduciary claim portending wholesale attacks on existing HMOs solely because of their structure, untethered to claims of concrete harm. . . .

The fiduciary is, of course, obliged to act exclusively in the interest of the beneficiary, but this translates into no rule readily applicable to HMO decisions or those of any other variety of medical practice. While the incentive of the HMO physician is to give treatment sparingly, imposing a fiduciary obligation upon him would not lead to a simple default rule, say, that whenever it is reasonably possible to disagree about treatment options, the physician should treat aggressively. . . . Nor would it be possible to translate fiduciary duty into a standard that would allow recovery from an HMO whenever a mixed decision influenced by the HMO's financial incentive resulted in a bad outcome for the patient. It would be so easy to allege, and to find, an economic influence when sparing care did not lead to a well patient, that any such standard in practice would allow a factfinder to convert an HMO into a guarantor of recovery.

These difficulties may have led the Court of Appeals to try to confine the fiduciary breach to cases where "the sole purpose" of delaying or withholding treatment was to increase the physician's financial reward. But this attempt to confine mixed decision claims to their most egregious examples entails erroneous corruption of fiduciary obligation and would simply lead to further difficulties that we think fatal. While a mixed decision made solely to benefit the HMO or its physician would violate a fiduciary duty, the fiduciary standard condemns far more than that, in its requirement of "an eye single" toward beneficiaries' interests, *Donovan v. Bierwirth*, 680 F.2d 263, 271 (C.A.2 1982). But whether under the Court of Appeals's rule or a straight standard of undivided loyalty, the defense of any HMO would be that its physician did not act out of financial interest but for good medical reasons, the plausibility of which would require reference to standards of reasonable and customary medical practice in like circumstances. That, of course, is the traditional standard of the common law. See W. Keeton, D. Dobbs, R. Keeton, & D. Owens, Prosser and Keeton on Law of Torts § 32, pp. 188–189 (5th ed.1984). Thus, for all practical purposes, every claim of fiduciary breach by an HMO physician making a mixed decision would boil down to a malpractice claim, and the fiduciary standard would be nothing but the malpractice standard traditionally applied in actions against physicians.

What would be the value to the plan participant of having this kind of ERISA fiduciary action? It would simply apply the law already available in state courts and federal diversity actions today, and the formulaic addition of an allegation of financial incentive would do nothing but bring the same claim into a federal court under federal-question jurisdiction. It is true that in States that do not allow malpractice actions against HMOs the fiduciary claim would offer a plaintiff a further defendant to be sued for direct liability, and in some cases the HMO might have a deeper pocket than the physician. But we have seen enough to know that ERISA was not enacted out of concern that physicians were too poor to be sued, or in order to federalize malpractice litigation in the name of fiduciary duty for any other reason. It is difficult, in fact, to find any advantage to participants across the board, except that allowing them to bring malpractice actions in the guise of federal fiduciary breach claims against HMOs would make them eligible for awards of attorney's fees if they won. See [ERISA § 502(g)(1)]. But, again, we can be fairly sure that Congress did not create fiduciary obligations out of concern that state plaintiffs were not suing often enough, or were paying too much in legal fees.

The mischief of Herdrich's position would, indeed, go further than mere replication of state malpractice actions with HMO defendants. For not only would an HMO be liable as a fiduciary in the first instance for its own breach of fiduciary duty committed through the acts of its physician employee, but the physician employee would also be subject to liability as a fiduciary on the same basic analysis that would charge the HMO. . . .

We hold that mixed eligibility decisions by HMO physicians are not fiduciary decisions under ERISA. Herdrich's ERISA count fails to state an ERISA claim, and the judgment of the Court of Appeals is reversed.

2. SHIELDING HMOS

1. *What Pegram decided. Pegram* rejects a line of reasoning that runs roughly as follows: The HMO exercised "discretionary authority" over the allocation of plan benefits within the meaning of ERISA § 3(21)(A). Accordingly, the HMO and its physician agent, Pegram, owed Herdrich the duty to exercise this discretionary authority pursuant to ERISA's fiduciary duty of loyalty, that is, "solely in the interests of the participants and beneficiaries" and "for the exclusive purpose [of] providing benefits" to them. ERISA § 404(a)(1)(A). The HMO's incentive structure, however, encouraged Pegram to prefer her own financial interest under over Herdrich's interest in timely care, contrary to ERISA's fiduciary duties of loyalty and prudence.

The Supreme Court rejected this claim, by finding that the HMO (and hence its agent, Pegram) were not acting as ERISA fiduciaries. *Pegram* covers a lot of turf, and accordingly, it's a good idea to be clear about what the Supreme Court actually decided:

(a) *Distinguish the ERISA plan from the HMO.* The Seventh Circuit in *Pegram* showed some confusion on the question of whether the HMO was the plan. The Supreme Court opinion (in § II.F) cleared it up. "The HMO is not the ERISA plan," said the Court. "[W]hen employers contract with an HMO to provide benefits to employees subject to ERISA, the provisions of documents that set up the HMO are not, as such, an ERISA [plan]." This view of the matter was strongly argued to the Court in the Solicitor General's amicus brief, 1999 WL 1067499.

(b) *Plan design not fiduciary.* The Court reiterated its support of the plan design distinction, previously voiced in Lockheed Corp. v. Spink, 517 U.S. 882, 887 (1996), and elsewhere, saying (in § II.E): "The specific payout detail of the plan was, of course, a feature that the employer as plan sponsor was free to adopt without breach of any fiduciary duty under ERISA, since an employer's decisions about the content of a plan are not themselves fiduciary acts." Does it follow that an employer is privileged as a matter of plan design to offer a health care plan that subjects the participant to the hazards of conflict of interest intrinsic to HMO structure?

(c) *Service provider is not necessarily a fiduciary.* An HMO, like any other service provider to an ERISA plan, does not become an ERISA fiduciary unless it assumes fiduciary functions. However, "although [an HMO] is not an ERISA fiduciary merely because it administers or exercises discretionary authority over its own HMO business, it may still be a fiduciary if it administers the plan." (§ II.D).

(d) *Was the HMO engaged in plan administration?* The issue in the case thus became whether the HMO and its agent, Pegram, could be rightly characterized as ERISA fiduciaries on the ground that they were making coverage and benefit determinations. Because such determinations are the core fiduciary work of health plan administration, these activities were alleged to entail the exercise of "discretionary authority" under ERISA § 3(21)(A).

(e) *Categorizing HMO health care decisionmaking as mixing eligibility and treatment.* To resolve that question, the key passage in *Pegram* (§ II.F) contrasts pure "eligibility decisions" about coverage, from nonfiduciary "treatment decisions," that is, from diagnosis and medical response. Because as a practical matter medical care decisions in an HMO commonly entail both, "eligibility decisions cannot be untangled from physicians' judgments about reasonable medical treatment. . . ." The Court thus concluded (in § IV) that such "mixed eligibility decisions by HMO physicians are not fiduciary decisions under ERISA."

Why does it follow that because fiduciary-type eligibility decisions and nonfiduciary-type treatment decisions "cannot be untangled," the mixture becomes nonfiduciary rather than fiduciary? Why should the nonfiduciary prevail over the fiduciary in a situation in which both are present?

For a thoughtful discussion of the Court's opinion, see Note, *Pegram v. Herdrich*: The Supreme Court Wades in and out of HMO Controversy, 8 ERISA Litigation Rptr. (Aug. 2000), at 3. For critiques of the Court's refusal to treat the HMO as an ERISA fiduciary, see E. Haavi Morreim, Another ERISA Twist: The Mysterious Case of *Pegram* and the Missing Fiduciary, 63 U. Pittsburgh L. Rev. 235 (2002); Michael T. Cahill & Peter D. Jacobson, *Pegram*'s Regress: A Missed Chance for Sensible Judicial Review of Managed Care Decisions, 27 American J. L., Medicine & Ethics 421 (2001). Post-*Pegram* case law is reviewed in Jayne E. Zanglein, Lawrence A. Frolik & Susan J. Stabile, ERISA Litigation 720–25 (4th ed.2011).

2. *Questioning the appropriateness of fiduciary analysis.* The Court's opinion in *Pegram* (§ III.A) "doubt[s] that Congress would ever have thought of a mixed eligibility decision as fiduciary in nature," because in trust law "fiduciary duties characteristically attach to decisions about managing assets and distributing property to beneficiaries. [The] common law trustee's most defining concern historically has been the payment of money in the interest of the beneficiary." The court contrasted "[m]ixed eligibility decisions by an

HMO acting through its physicians" as having "only a limited resemblance to the usual business of traditional trustees."

Do these differences from routine trust administration bear on the question of whether ERISA's duty of loyalty might appropriately forbid a self-interested decisionmaker such as Dr. Pegram from denying timely medical care under an ERISA plan? Recall the Court's language four years earlier in *Varity*, reproduced supra in this chapter, "that trust law does not tell the entire story. After all, ERISA's standards and procedural protections partly reflect a congressional determination that the common law of trusts did not offer completely satisfactory protection." 516 U.S. at 497.

3. *Subordinating the actual injury.* A striking peculiarity of *Pegram* is the abstractness of the issue that was ultimately framed for the Supreme Court. The lawsuit began with the grievance that Pegram, operating under the perverse incentives of the HMO's compensation system, injured Herdrich by denying her timely remedy for her appendicitis. By the time the case got to the Supreme Court, the allegations of the complaint had so bleached out these compelling facts that the Court (in § II.E) found Herdrich's claim of "fiduciary [breach] difficult to understand. [Herdrich] does not point to a particular act [as] a breach. She does not complain about Pegram's actions, and at oral argument her counsel confirmed that the ERISA count could have been brought, and would have been no different, if Herdrich had never had a sick day in her life."

Recall, however, that in the federal district court, after Herdrich's ERISA fiduciary claims were dismissed on the pleadings, the court retained jurisdiction and tried her state malpractice claims to a jury, which awarded her $35,000.

4. *Interaction with ERISA remedy law.* ERISA's contorted remedy law may also have influenced the way in which Herdrich's complaint was drafted. It has been seen in Chapter 16 that the Supreme Court has interpreted ERISA § 502(a)(1)–(3) largely to preclude relief for consequential injury, such as the bodily impairment, pain, and suffering that Herdrich suffered. Instead, said the Court (§ III.B) Herdrich sought "the return of profit from the pockets of [the] HMO's owners, with the money to be given to the plan for the benefit of the participants. See [ERISA § 409(a)] (return of all profits is an appropriate ERISA remedy)."

5. *Safeguarding the HMO form.* A recurrent theme in *Pegram* is the Court's concern not to be responsible for undermining the viability of the HMO system of delivering medical care.

(a) The opinion downplays (in § II.A) the conflict of interest inherent in an HMO structure that rewards physicians for undertreating, observing that there are perverse incentives in fee-for-service medicine as well.

(b) The Court then says (§ II.B) that "the legislative process" is a better place to decide the acceptability of HMOs.

(c) The Court contends (in § III.B) that Herdrich's suit presages "nothing less than elimination" of HMO medical care, in tension with legislation enacted in 1973 to encourage HMOs. Accordingly, the Court reasons, it would be "acting contrary to the congressional policy of allowing HMO organizations [to] entertain an ERISA fiduciary claim portending wholesale attacks on existing HMOs solely because of their structure. . . ."

Why should the 1973 legislation, which did not deal with questions of fiduciary law, be taken to resolve what ERISA, the later-enacted of the two statutes, meant to achieve in its fiduciary law?

6. *Measuring HMO performance.* In refusing to engage with the merits of HMO medicine, the court left unexplored a strong body of empirical evidence indicating that HMOs deliver superior medical outcomes in the aggregate. "In general, the literature [consistently] shows that costs are lower in managed-care systems, with quality equal to or better than that in fee-for-service care." Donald M. Berwick, Quality of Health Care: Part 5: Payment by Capitation and the Quality of Care, 335 New England J. Medicine 1227, 1228 (1996) (citing studies).

As regards the medical event in *Pegram*, an episode of appendicitis and rupture, "[t]he evidence suggests that Herdrich was less likely to suffer a rupture from treatment at an HMO than she would have been in a fee-for-service system. A study of almost 100,000 hospitalizations of patients aged 18–64 with acute appendicitis, in California during 1984–1989, found a rupture rate of 29.3 percent for fee-for-service patients, and 25.8 percent for managed care patients." Richard A. Ippolito, Freedom to Contract in Medical Care: HMOs, ERISA, and *Pegram v. Herdrich*, 9 Supreme Court Economic Rev. 1, 33 (2001).

Should the Court have dealt with the empirical evidence about HMO medicine in an opinion that was so centered on not impairing the HMO form of organization?

7. *Federalism implications; preemption.* The balance of federal/state interests in the legal regulation of medicine was a theme lurking in the background to *Pegram*.

(a) *Malpractice.* Medical malpractice, like most tort law, is mainly state law. Recall that *Pegram* began as a malpractice action in the Illinois state court. The defendant HMO removed the case to federal court when the ERISA issues emerged. A jury awarded the plaintiff $35,000 in damages on the malpractice claims. Judge Easterbrook, dissenting from the Seventh Circuit's refusal to rehear in *Pegram*, cautioned that "mak[ing] the surgeon a 'fiduciary' [would] convert [medical] malpractice claims" into ERISA actions. 170 F.3d at 685. The Supreme Court endorsed this concern (in § III.C), fearing that "every claim of fiduciary breach by an HMO physician making a mixed decision would boil down to a malpractice claim, and the fiduciary standard would be nothing but the malpractice standard traditionally applied in actions against physicians." Transforming torts into breaches of ERISA fiduciary law would federalize much of medical malpractice law, which the Supreme Court wanted to leave in the state court systems.

Furthermore, the Court said, federalizing medical malpractice as ERISA fiduciary law would probably have the effect of suppressing state malpractice law against medical defendants who had become ERISA fiduciaries, under ERISA's preemption provision, § 514(a). The Court doubted that such cases could survive preemption, even under the more tolerant approach to state law announced in New York State Conference of Blue Cross & Blue Shield Plans v. Travelers Ins. Co., 514 U.S. 645 (1995), reproduced in Chapter 17.

By implication, therefore, *Pegram* signalled strongly the Court's view that medical malpractice actions against HMOs and other medical providers who were not ERISA fiduciaries were not preempted. This branch of the opinion in *Pegram* attracted attention in the literature, see Phyllis C. Borzi, *Pegram v. Herdrich*: A Victory for HMOs or the Beginning of the End for ERISA Preemption?, 1 Yale J. Health Policy, L., & Ethics 161 (2001); Thomas R. McLean, Managed Care Liability for Breach of Fiduciary Duty after *Pegram v. Herdrich*: The End of ERISA Preemption for State Law Liability for Medical Care Decision Making, 53 Florida L. Rev. 1 (2001); Edward A. Zelinsky, *Pegram* and Preemption, 88 Tax Notes 1053 (2000).

(b) *Benefit determinations*. The Supreme Court returned to the preemption aspects of *Pegram* in Aetna Health Inc. v. Davila, 542 U.S. 200 (2004), discussed in this chapter; for commentary see Theodore W. Ruger, The Supreme Court Federalizes Managed Care Liability, 32 J. L. Medicine & Ethics 528 (2004); William G. Schiffbauer, Unmixing Mixed Decisions: *Davila* Parses *Pegram* to Clarify Medical Necessity, 31 BNA Pension & Benefits Rptr. 1645 (2004).

Davila underscored that HMO determinations about benefit entitlement apart from the physician's mixed eligibility/treatment decision in *Pegram* can be fiduciary under ERISA, hence preempting state regulation. "Classifying any entity with discretionary authority over benefits determinations as anything but a plan fiduciary [would] conflict with ERISA's statutory and regulatory scheme." 542 U.S. at 220. Indeed, this view had been signalled in a footnote in *Pegram*, in which the Court said that the HMO in that case could be an ERISA "fiduciary insofar as [the HMO] has discretionary authority to administer the plan, and so is obligated to disclose characteristics of the plan and of those who provide services to the plan, if that information affects beneficiaries' material interests." 530 U.S. at 227 n.8. Lower courts have held, however, that HMOs do not have a fiduciary duty to disclose physician incentives to HMO plan members. Horvath v. Keystone Health Plan East, Inc., 333 F.3d 450 (3d Cir.2003); Ehlmann v. Kaiser Foundation Health Plan of Texas, 198 F.3d 552 (5th Cir.2000).

8. *PBM litigation*. Under many health care plans, the plan contracts with a third-party entity called a pharmacy benefits manager (PBM) to supply prescription medicines and related administrative services to plan members. The PBM negotiates further supply contracts on behalf of the plan with drug manufacturers and retail pharmacy chains and by mail order. Regarding the industry, see Barbara Martinez, Selling Generic Drugs by Mail Turns into Lucrative Business, Wall St. J., May 9, 2006, at 1. In a series of lawsuits decided in the 2000s, the theory was asserted that, despite contrary recitals in the plan/PBM contract, the PBM was an ERISA plan fiduciary, whose compensation arrangements with manufacturers and others violated ERISA's loyalty and prohibited transactions rules. The PBMs defended that they were arms-length service providers to ERISA plans, not ERISA plan fiduciaries, and hence that their contracts with suppliers were not subject to ERISA fiduciary law. The courts have in general agreed with

the PBMs. See, e.g., Chicago District Council of Carpenters Welfare Fund v. Caremark, Inc., 474 F.3d 463 (7th Cir.2007); Mulder v. PCS Health Systems, Inc., 432 F.Supp.2d 450 (D.N.J.2006).

INDEX

References are to Pages